D1062869

WITHDRAWN
University of
Illinois Library
at Urbana-Champaign

The City Builders
Property Development in New York and London, 1980–2000
Second Edition, Revised

Susan S. Fainstein

 University Press of Kansas

© 1994, 2001 by the University Press of Kansas

All rights reserved

Originally published by Blackwell, Oxford, UK, and Cambridge, MA.

Published by the University Press of Kansas (Lawrence, Kansas 66049), which was organized by the Kansas Board of Regents and is operated and funded by Emporia State University, Fort Hays State University, Kansas State University, Pittsburg State University, the University of Kansas, and Wichita State University

Library of Congress Cataloging-in-Publication Data

Fainstein, Susan S.
  The city builders: property development in New York and London, 1980–2000 / Susan S. Fainstein.— 2nd ed., rev.
     p. cm.—(Studies in government and public policy)
Originally published: Oxford, UK ; Cambridge, Mass. : Blackwell, 1994.
Includes bibliographical references and index.
  ISBN 0-7006-1132-0 (cloth : alk. paper)—ISBN 0-7006-1133-9 (pbk.
  : alk. paper)
  1. Urban renewal—England—London.   2. Urban renewal—New York
(State)—New York.   3. Real estate development—England—London.   4.
Real estate development—New York (State)—New York.   5. Urban
policy—England—London.   6. Urban policy—New York (State)—New York.
I. Title. II. Series.
  HT178.G72 L56365 2001
  307.76'09421—dc21
                              2001026015

British Library Cataloguing in Publication Data is available.

Printed in the United States of America

10 9 8 7 6 5 4 3 2 1

The paper used in this publication meets the minimum requirements of the American National Standard for Permanence of Paper for Printed Library Materials Z39.48-1984.

307.7609421
F149c
2001

City Planning
DEC 2 1 2001

WITHDRAWN
University of
Illinois Library
at Urbana-Champaign

Contents

List of Illustrations and Tables   vii

List of Abbreviations   ix

Preface   xi

1. Economic Restructuring and Redevelopment   1

2. The Development Industry and Urban Redevelopment   27

3. Markets, Decision-Makers, and the Real-Estate Cycle   64

4. Policy and Politics   79

5. Economic Development Planning Strategies   98

6. Public-Private Partnerships in Action: King's Cross and Times Square   118

7. Creating New Centers: Spitalfields and Downtown Brooklyn   138

8. Creating a New Address I: Battery Park City   160

9. Creating a New Address II: Docklands   175

10. Real-Estate Development: Why Is It Special and What Is Its Impact?   197

11. Development Policy for the Inner City   219

Appendix: Population and Economy of London and New York   231

Notes   235

Bibliography   277

Index   301

Illustrations and Tables

ILLUSTRATIONS

Figure 2.1. Greater London   40
Figure 2.2. Broadgate center courtyard   49
Figure 2.3. The reconstructed Globe Theater   53
Figure 2.4. The Tate Gallery of Modern Art   54
Figure 2.5. The New York Metro Area   56
Figure 6.1. Times Square recent and expected additions, 2000   132
Figure 7.1. Spitalfields   139
Figure 7.2. Spitalfields Market, with a view of Hawksmoor's Christ Church   142
Figure 7.3. MetroTech Center   149
Figure 7.4. A scale model of MetroTech Center   151
Figure 8.1. The World Financial Center   167
Figure 8.2. The Winter Garden at the World Financial Center   168
Figure 8.3. Gov. Nelson A. Rockefeller Park at Battery Park City   172
Figure 9.1. Docklands Light Rail   179
Figure 9.2. Docklands old council housing   180
Figure 9.3. Docklands Transport   184
Figure 9.4. Canary Wharf Towers   186

Figure 6.1 was supplied by the 42nd Street Redevelopment Corporation, Figure 7.4 by the Forest City Ratner Companies, and Figure 9.4 by the Canary Wharf Group. The remaining photographs were taken by the author.

TABLES

Table 2.1. Office Market: Comparable Cities   37
Table 2.2. Office Stock and Net Additions, 1981–1990   38
Table 2.3. Average Office Rents and Vacancy Rates   43
Table A.1. Greater London Population, 1931–1998   231
Table A.2. New York City Population, 1940–2000   232
Table A.3. London Employment by Industry, 1961–1997   232
Table A.4. New York City Employment by Industry, 1960–1998   233

Abbreviations

ACSP	Association of Collegiate Schools of Planning
AESOP	Association of European Schools of Planning
ALA	Association of London Authorities
AMC	American Multi-Cinemas
ATURA	Atlantic Terminal Urban Renewal Association
BID	business improvement district
BPCA	Battery Park City Authority
BR	British Rail
CBD	central business district
CDBG	community development block grant
CDC	community development corporation
CEO	chief executive officer
CSFB	Credit Suisse First Boston
DCC	Docklands Consultative Committee
DETR	Department of the Environment, Transport and the Regions
DJC	Docklands Joint Committee
DLMA	Downtown Lower Manhattan Association
DoE	Department of the Environment
EDC	Economic Development Corporation
ELP	East London Partnership
ESDC	Empire State Development Corporation
FAR	floor area ratio
FBS	financial and business services
FCB	Financial Control Board
FHA	Federal Housing Administration
GDP	gross domestic product
GLA	Greater London Authority

GLC	Greater London Council
GLE	Greater London Enterprise
GLEB	Greater London Enterprise Board
HDA	Housing and Development Administration
HDC	housing development corporation
HHC	Health and Hospitals Corporation
HPD	Housing Preservation and Development
HRB	Housing and Redevelopment Board
ICIB	Industrial and Commercial Incentives Board
ICIP	Industrial and Commercial Incentives Program
KXT	King's Cross Team
LDA	London Development Authority
LDDC	London Docklands Development Corporation
LEntA	London Enterprise Agency Ltd.
LISC	Local Initiatives Support Corporation
LPAC	London Planning Advisory Committee
LRC	London Regeneration Consortium
MAC	Municipal Assistance Corporation
O & Y	Olympia & York Developments Ltd.
OSDC	Office of the State Deputy Comptroller (for New York City)
PATH	Port Authority Trans-Hudson
PDC	Public Development Corporation
PILOT	payments in lieu of taxes
PLA	Port of London Authority
REBNY	Real Estate Board of New York
RFP	request for proposals
RLCDG	Railway Lands Community Development Group
RPA	Regional Plan Association
S&Ls	savings and loans
SCDG	Spitalfields Community Development Group
SDG	Spitalfields Development Group
SIAC	Securities Industry Automation Corporation
SRB	Single Regeneration Budget
UDAG	Urban Development Action Grant
UDC	Urban Development Corporation
ULURP	Uniform Land Use Review Process
WFC	World Financial Center

Preface

When I completed the first edition of this book, the property markets in London and New York had sunk deep into recession. With typical social-scientific foresight, I assumed that present conditions would prevail for a substantial amount of time. Even though I knew that real estate would follow its usual cyclical pattern and once again revive, I did not expect the upturn to come nearly as quickly as it did, nor that it would be so particularly powerful in New York and London. At that time, before the Internet revolution and the 1990s stock market boom fueled by high tech, the prospects for strong economic recovery within the two cities looked rather bleak. Now, in retrospect, I can see that these two cities, with their repositories of creative talent and their global centrality, were well-poised to exploit the trends of the century's final decade.

One consequence of the rapid turnaround in the property sectors of the two cities was the equally precipitous obsolescence of the first edition of *The City Builders*. Thus, the principal purpose of this new version is to update the case studies and argument in the light of ensuing events. In general, I have discovered that the character of the property market changed significantly, as it became much more driven by demand rather than by the availability of financial capital. I also found that the behavior of government and developers within the two cities, which had strongly converged during the '80s, began to differ again. Government in London became more committed to planning and more inclusive, while New York continued, and even intensified, its earlier reliance on subsidizing private developers while regulating them little. The property industry itself responded to earlier events and changed its way of doing business. Financial institutions and developers, traumatized by their losses during the recession of the early '90s, simply did not allow themselves the speculative fling on which they had embarked ten years before. Therefore, my analysis of strategies of development had to take this new cautiousness into account. As a consequence, while the arguments I had made earlier did not change dramatically, they did need to be modified.

I conceived the first edition of this book at a time when the property industry was rapidly transforming the character of metropolitan areas in the United States and the United Kingdom. Not only were annual construction rates at their highest points since the boom years of the early 1970s, but new development was creating a strikingly different urban form from that of the preceding era. No longer were we seeing a thinning of the core and a simple decentralization of urban functions to suburbia. Rather, new construction was producing reconcentration in urban centers and intensifying development within clusters on the periphery. Although planners had long urged denser development, the scattered islands of intense use (surrounded by ever-increasing sprawl in the U.S. case) did not result from planners' conceptions of desirable spatial patterns. Even when the restructured metropolis incorporated planning principles in isolated developments, its overall fragmentation contravened them. Instead, it represented the confluence of an explosion of speculative building for profit and a surging demand for space within a context of local incentives to growth and national policy antagonistic to regulation.

Nowhere within the Western world had development proceeded at so strong a pace and produced such a visible effect on the environment as in the London and New York metropolitan areas in the 1980s. In these two cities not only was a proliferation of new large office buildings replacing smaller structures within the old cores, but enormous, highly visible mixed-use projects were springing up on vacant or derelict land. Two of these—Docklands in London and Battery Park City in New York—came to symbolize the economic and social transformation of the 1980s. Built for financial and advanced-services firms, they possessed an opulence that asserted the dominance those two industries and their employees had assumed over the metropolitan economy.

My purpose was to investigate the economic, political, technological, and cultural factors that caused developers to make the decisions that were shaping the physical form of these two cities. It was my belief that the contemporary urban built environment did not represent an uncomplicated response to demand but rather that developers both molded demand and responded to public-sector initiatives and regulations. While the locational choices of firms that ultimately occupied new structures had been much studied, the strategies of speculative developers were less well understood. Given the long lead time and resource mobilization involved in major construction efforts, developers could not respond immediately to an existing market. Instead, they based their calculations on the availability of financing, governmental incentives, community acquiescence, and anticipated demand. I was interested in discovering the criteria underlying their predictions.

During the course of my research, however, the developmental juggernaut that had begun rolling during the early 1980s on both sides of the Atlantic abruptly halted. It reasserted itself, but, as indicated above, more cautiously, in the middle

1990s. Moreover, even as I write, that upturn begins to appear fragile. It may be that property markets in the two cities are yet about to begin another plunge, although if they do, it will occur in a context of less overbuilding than previously. At any rate, the great volatility of the industry underlies my concern with the causes of its cyclical behavior and with its impact on urban economic stability. By 1987 it had become apparent that both London and New York would have surpluses of commercial and luxury residential space in the 1990s. Yet developers were continuing to propose and gain financing for projects seemingly doomed to stand empty upon completion, making inevitable the sharp downturn that did indeed mark the early '90s. *Why?* Then, how did they respond to later revival? These issues led me to question further the underlying logic of property development and to inquire into its similarities to, and differences from, other forms of commodity production.

Ultimately, the purpose of my inquiry—applicable in times of both expansion and contraction within property markets—became an understanding of the factors influencing the dynamic of real-estate development and, in turn, the influence of that dynamic on the prosperity and attractiveness of urban areas. I sought to explore this dynamic by investigating the reasoning and strategies adopted by key actors in property development, the struggles that occurred among them, the extent to which various participants got their way, and the impact that development had on urban life. In focusing on London and New York, I both examined property development in the places where the stakes were biggest and addressed subsidiary questions concerning the effect of world-city status on urban form and locational patterns.

The stimulus to this book came from numerous sources. Like most scholars, I selected topics based on personal predilections. I have always preferred the excitement of living in a city to pastoral meditation, and my lifelong commitment to studying central cities reflects this bias, as did my choice, fifteen years ago, to abandon suburban residence for a loft in the heart of Manhattan. Since my first trip to London nearly forty years ago, I have appreciated the civilized values and greater provision for working-class people incorporated in that metropolis. My desire to see those virtues adopted in American cities had led me many years earlier to embark on comparative research.

As noted above, this volume contains a thorough revision of the first edition. I have brought all the main case studies up to the present and have introduced material on projects begun during the '90s. I have incorporated recent literature into the theoretical discussion and have revised my argument concerning property cycles. Although I have not rewritten every sentence, many have been changed, and I have added considerable new material. The questions that I listed in the first chapter of the previous edition remain the same; the answers I give, however, are somewhat different.

I am grateful to the Lincoln Institute of Land Policy for supporting the additional research conducted during 1999–2000. I especially wish to express my gratitude to Greg Clark and Deborah Newlands of Greater London Enterprise (GLE) for their assistance in providing volumes of information and introducing me to other helpful people. Other Londoners who provided me with advice and information include Bob Colenutt, Chris Hamnett, Michael Edwards, Michael Keith, Michael Hebbert, Sir Peter Hall, Roger Taylor, and Andy Thornley. In New York, thanks go to Bryna Sanger, who kindly facilitated my meeting with important people in the industry. Thanks as well to my editor at the University Press of Kansas, Fred Woodward, who encouraged me to carry out this revision and has been helpful in every way. Finally, I am appreciative of the fine research and editorial assistance provided by Deike Peters, David Gladstone, Louis Gladstone, and Gregory Godfrey.

Many people cheerfully submitted to interviews, a number for the second time, even when they suspected that my conclusions were likely to be critical of their point of view. I was extremely impressed by the graciousness, articulateness, and cogent analyses of many of the individuals within the real-estate industry and the public sector to whom I talked. I feel rather embarrassed at finding fault with them and hope they find it in their hearts to forgive me.

I have had the extraordinary benefit over the years of extended conversations with a circle of urbanists, whose ideas and idealism have affected me greatly and are woven into the arguments of this book. As well as some of the people already mentioned, these include Janet Abu-Lughod, Robert Beauregard, Manuel Castells, Lily Hoffman, Michael Harloe, Dennis Judd, John Logan, Enzo Mingione, John Mollenkopf, David Perry, Edmond Preteceille, Saskia Sassen, Richard Sennett, and Michael Peter Smith. Finally, I wish to express special appreciation to three people whose assistance to my original research endeavor was extraordinary. Sydney Sporle so greatly facilitated my work in London that I cannot imagine how I would have proceeded without his intellectual and logistical help. My editor at Blackwell, Simon Prosser, worked diligently on the manuscript in the tradition of editors of old, when book publishers were concerned with the content as well as the marketability of books. He was constantly interested in and sustaining of my endeavor. Norman Fainstein read and commented on each chapter in each of its iterations.

Support for the research in the first edition was provided by the Rutgers University Research Council; the Rutgers University President's Council on International Programs; the Rutgers University Center for the Critical Analysis of Contemporary Culture; and the Social Science Research Council. My graduate research assistants at Rutgers ably performed a number of boring but important chores, and I thank Susana Fried, Grant Saff, Lissa LaManna, and Denise Nickel for their contributions. Michael Siegel prepared the maps.

This book is a revision of the first edition published by Blackwell Publishers (Oxford, U.K. 1994). The original edition contained parts of revised versions of work that I have published elsewhere. Articles and book chapters on which I have drawn are listed below, and I am grateful to the publishers for permission to use them: "The Second New York Fiscal Crisis," *International Journal of Urban and Regional Regional Research* 16 (March 1992): 129–37; "Promoting Economic Development: Urban Planning in the United States and the United Kingdom," *Journal of the American Planning Association* 57 (Winter 1991): 22–33; "Rejoinder to: Questions of Abstraction in Studies in the New Urban Politics," *Journal of Urban Affairs* 13 (1991): 281–87; "Politics and State Policy in Economic Restructuring," in *Divided Cities: London and New York in the Contemporary World,* ed. Susan S. Fainstein, Ian Gordon, and Michael Harloe (Oxford, UK, and Cambridge, MA.: Blackwell, 1992), 203–35 (Ken Young, coauthor); "Economics, Politics, and Development Policy: The Convergence of New York and London," *International Journal of Urban and Regional Research* 14, no. 4 (December 1990): 553–75; "Economic Restructuring and the Politics of Land Use Planning in New York City," *Journal of the American Planning Association* 53 (Spring 1987): 237–48 (Norman I. Fainstein, coauthor); "The Politics of Criteria: Planning for the Redevelopment of Times Square," in *Confronting Values in Policy Analysis,* ed. Frank Fischer and John Forester (Newbury Park, CA: Sage Publications, 1987), 232–47; "The Redevelopment of Forty-Second Street," *City Almanac* 18 (Fall 1985): 2–12; and "Government Programs for Commercial Redevelopment in Poor Neighborhoods: The Cases of Spitalfields in East London and Downtown Brooklyn, New York," *Environment and Planning A* 26 (1994): 3–22.

1

Economic Restructuring
and Redevelopment

Our image of a city consists not only of people but also of buildings—the homes, offices, and factories in which residents and workers live and produce. This built environment structures social relations, causing commonalities of gender, sexual orientation, race, ethnicity, and class to assume spatial identities. Social groups, in turn, imprint themselves physically on the urban structure through the formation of communities, competition for territory, and segregation—in other words, through clustering, erecting boundaries, and establishing distance. Urban physical form also constrains and stimulates economic activity. The built environment etches the division in time and distance between home and work and generates the milieu in which productive enterprises relate to each other. As a source of wealth through the real-estate industry, a cost of doing business, and an asset and expense for households, physical structures are a critical element in the urban economy.

The distinction between the use of real estate for human activity and its market role is often summarized as the difference between use and exchange values.[1] Frequent tension between the two functions has provoked the community resistance to redevelopment and highway programs and the endemic antagonism between neighborhood groups and development agencies which have marked urban politics in the United States and the United Kingdom in recent years. The immense stakes involved have meant that decisions of real-estate developers and the outcomes of struggles over the uses of urban land have become crucial factors in determining the future character of the urban economy.

For policy-makers, encouragement of real-estate development seems to offer a way of dealing with otherwise intractable economic and social problems. Governments have promoted physical change with the expectations that better-looking cities are also better cities, that excluding poor people from central locations will eliminate the causes of "blight" rather than moving it elsewhere, and

1

that property development equals economic development. The quandary for local political officials is that they must depend on the private sector to finance most economic growth, and they have only very limited tools for attracting expansion to their jurisdictions. Their heavy reliance on the property sector partly results from their greater ability to influence it than other industries. How much government programs for urban redevelopment actually do stimulate business is, however, an open issue.[2]

This inquiry is intended both to respond to theoretical questions concerning the building of cities and to address important policy issues for community groups and local governments. Within the academic literature, the economic and political forces that shape real-estate development and its social consequences are the subject of considerable debate. Does real-estate development simply respond to speculative gambles by individuals out to make fast profits, or is it an answer to genuine social needs? Does the type of development that occurred during the final decades of the twentieth century in London and New York inevitably generate "two cities"—one for the rich and one for the poor? Do the subsidies that governments direct toward the property sector represent a sellout by politicians and planners to capitalists or a method by which the public can, with a small investment, gain employment and public amenities as externalities of development schemes? Progrowth coalitions, consisting of business groups and public officials, have expressed confidence in the efficacy of public-private partnerships as engines of economic expansion. Neighborhood groups have frequently, although not always, opposed large-scale redevelopment, because they have feared its environmental effects and its tendency to displace low-income residents and small businesses. Other critics, tracing back to the economist Henry George, have asserted that the profits from development were created by the whole community and have been illegitimately appropriated by property owners. Generally, leftist scholars have supported the pessimistic view on the causes and results of development, while conservatives have celebrated its entrepreneurial base and transforming consequences.

A major aim of this study has been to discover the conditions under which the speculative property-development sector invests in a place and the role of the public sector in providing those conditions. Evaluation of the impacts of publicly supported physical development is more difficult, since there are many confounding variables, but it is a further goal.

PHYSICAL DEVELOPMENT AND THE CONTEST OVER URBAN SPACE

Since the mid-1970s American and British local governments in their policies toward property development have aimed more at stimulating economically productive activities than at enhancing the quality of life for residents. To achieve their objectives, they have promoted the construction of commercial space over housing and public facilities. Even though many of the new skyscrapers, festive malls, and downtown atriums produced by commercial developers have arguably created more attractive cities, the provision of amenities has been only a secondary purpose of redevelopment efforts.

Economic development strategies have typically involved subsidies and regulatory relief to development firms, as well as to businesses that could be expected to engage in long-term productive activity.[3] Indeed, in both London and New York, stimulation of commercial property development was the most important growth strategy of the latter part of the century. Yet, for most of this period business expansion was not hampered by a shortage of office space. Public incentives for construction were not a response to a bottleneck that was stifling investment. Instead, the authorities hoped that, by loosening regulations, supplying land and infrastructure, and offering subsidies, they would cause developers to offer higher quality, cheaper space. They intended that the lowered costs would draw leading businesses to these dense central areas. Evidently, policy-makers believed that an increase in the supply of privately owned, competitively priced, first-class space would create its own demand. Moreover, despite their proclaimed belief in market principles, they seemingly did not consider that tax subsidies would be reflected in rising land costs, even though landowners could charge more for the same parcel if final costs were brought down by tax abatement.

Two reports written during the 1980s, *London: World City* and *New York Ascendant,* written at the behest of governments in London and New York, embody the strategic considerations that guided policy-makers in the ensuing decades.[4] The documents are typical of a number of such efforts in Britain and the United States, which attempted to chart a course that would capitalize on service-sector advantages in the face of a continuing decline of manufacturing. Like most of these plans, they were intended as guides to action and were not officially adopted as legally binding policies. Nevertheless, they represent a reasonable summary of the attitudes of public officials and private-sector leaders toward the likely prospects for economic growth.

The writers of the reports perceive the principal advantages of London and New York to be their world-city statuses. They defend the governmental policies of the '80s and justify what they regard as the only practical course for attaining economic prosperity within their high-cost environments. In explaining their emphasis on a few industries, they point out that despite out-migration of manufacturing and wholesaling enterprises, these two financial capitals had increased their prominence as centers for investment markets, banking, and business services. In their discussion of growth strategies, the reports' authors call for heightened targeting of these core-service businesses by lowering their operating costs. The London report stresses transport and expanding the central business district. As well as identifying these ways in which government can assist the sector, the report of the New York commission endorses offering loans and tax subsidies to attract business to less expensive locations within the city.

Analyses of the Development Industry

Although government agencies play an important role in affecting the physical environment, the main progenitor of changes in physical form within London and New York is the private real-estate development industry.[5] Examination of real-estate investment decisions reveals the ways in which urban redevelopment is channeled at the same time by broad political and economic imperatives and by the industry's own specific modus operandi. An analysis of its operations shows how economic and social forces create its opportunities and hazards and, in turn, how its strategies etch themselves into the set of possibilities that exist for economic and social interaction.

To a greater extent than I initially anticipated when starting this research, I found that not just economic and political pressures but personality and gender factors affect the development industry. Development continues to be a highly entrepreneurial industry, and particular enterprises strongly reflect the aspirations of the men who run them. Although women now constitute a significant proportion of real-estate brokers, men continue to dominate the major development firms. As I have studied the large projects that have changed the faces of London and New York, I have been struck by the extent to which they have been driven by individual male egos that find self-expression in building tall buildings and imprinting their personae on the landscape.

Despite its key economic role and political influence, the development industry has only recently become the focus of serious political-economic analysis. For almost a decade David Harvey was virtually alone in examining real-estate development from a broad theoretical perspective.[6] More recently, especially in the United Kingdom, social scientists have begun to subject the property industry to extensive empirical and theoretical investigation.[7] American interest in this subject has also picked up, and several works examining the history, dynamics, and impacts of real-estate investment have recently appeared.[8] The bulk of scholarship, however, remains within the domain of academic programs that train real-estate practitioners. As would be expected in such a context, the emphasis is on how to do it rather than causes and social impacts. Within the United States a considerable popular literature on real-estate development tends toward hagiography of developer-heroes rather than critical analysis. In a typical example, Douglas Frantz extols "the men who shaped and built Rincon Center [a project in San Francisco], the dreamers who seek riches and immortality by launching great buildings onto today's urban landscapes."[9]

Urban redevelopment has received far more scholarly attention than has the real-estate sector alone. Studies of redevelopment, however, have largely focused on governmental rather than private decision making. Although they have investigated the influence of private developers on public policy, they have taken the motives and responses of property investors as givens rather than inquiring into their sources. This book attempts to address that omission, while taking as its starting point the scenario that the redevelopment literature has fairly consistently chronicled and that is recounted below. For in most British cities during the Thatcher period and in most American cities throughout the history of urban redevelopment, there is a typical story.[10] The research reported in this book is directed at filling in the gaps in this story, not at contradicting it.

THE TYPICAL REDEVELOPMENT SCENARIO

The story goes as follows: In the past thirty years almost all of the major metropolitan areas of the developed world have been affected by changes in the national and international economic system, such that they have either attracted a surge of capital and well-to-do people or suffered from disinvestment and population withdrawal.[11] In both advancing and declining cities, growth has been a contested issue, and groups have mobilized to affect population and capital flows, to either limit or attract development. Within the United States, business groups, usually in concert with political leaders, have promoted growth and tried to impose their objectives within the context of elite coalitions, of which Pittsburgh's Allegheny Conference is the prototype.[12] Urban movements, driven by equity, preservationist, and environmental concerns, have opposed subsidized downtown redevelopment and unregulated profit-driven expansion. They have also, although less frequently, promoted alternative plans for neighborhood redevelopment. The outcomes of these contests have varied. Regardless, however, of whether the result has been growth or decline, or greater or less equity, deal making on a project-by-project basis rather than comprehensive planning has been the main vehicle for determining the uses of space.

Overall, business interests have dominated the negotiations among government, community, and the private sector on the content of redevelopment.[13] They have been supported by elite and middle-class consumers seeking downtown "improvements" and attractive, centrally located housing. Neighborhood and lower-income groups have received some gains in some places from redevelopment. Generally, however, the urban poor, ethnic communities, and small businesses have suffered increased economic and locational marginalization as a consequence. Central business district (CBD) expansion has increased property values in areas of low-income occupancy, forcing out residents, raising their living expenses, and breaking up communities. The emphasis on office-based employment within most large redevelopment schemes has reinforced the decline of manufacturing jobs and contributed to the employment difficulties of unskilled workers. More recent strategies toward creating entertainment districts have produced somewhat more ambiguous results in terms of employment. While businesses have received direct subsidies, taxpayers at large have borne the costs and received benefits only as they have trickled down.

U.S./U.K. Redevelopment Experiences

British and American experiences differed before the 1980s and, at the beginning of the new century, are diverging again. Until Margaret Thatcher's election in 1979, redevelopment in Britain conformed less closely to the logic of private capital than it did in the United States.[14] The intimate relationship between local elected officials and real-estate interests that is a hallmark of U.S. local government, wherein developers are the largest contributors to municipal political campaigns, did not (and still does not) exist in Britain. British local authorities restricted private development and built millions of units of council (i.e., public) housing. In contrast, "slum clearance" was a major component of the American urban renewal program, resulting in the demolition but not the replacement of tens of thousands of units of poor people's housing. Furthermore, land taking for highway building produced an even greater loss of units.

In Britain, social housing (i.e., publicly owned or subsidized housing at below-market prices) was placed throughout metropolitan areas, minimizing gross ethnic and income segregation. American public housing, while much more limited in scope, was available only to the poorest residents and was usually located in low-income areas.[15] Urban renewal efforts, often derisively labeled "Negro removal" programs by their opponents, targeted ghetto areas that were near to business centers or to more affluent residential districts. Their intent was either to extend the more prosperous area or to cordon it off from the threat of lower-class invasion. Their effect was to displace nonwhite residents into more isolated, homogeneously minority territories.

As in the United States, British local authorities raised revenues through taxation on business and residential property ("rates"). Unlike their American equivalents, however, British local governments that could not meet the service demands on them through internal sources received a compensating central-government grant. They therefore did not need to attract business and high-income residents to maintain themselves and could afford to be more attuned to the negative environmental and social impacts of growth.

During the periods when the Labour Party controlled the British central government, it enacted measures to limit the gain that private developers could achieve through enhanced property values resulting from attaining planning permission on a piece of land. Under the Community Land Act of 1975, adopted during the third postwar Labour government, local authorities were granted the power to acquire land needed for development at a price below market value.[16] Developers would then lease the land from the local authority at market rents. The difference in value would constitute a development tax on landowners of about 70 percent. The purpose was to ensure that the community as a whole would recoup most of the development value of land. Local authorities largely failed to implement the scheme, and the Conservatives dismantled it; nevertheless, while in existence it acted as a deterrent to speculative increases in land prices.[17]

Despite these differences, the British and American cases during the twenty years preceding the ascendance of Conservative government in the United Kingdom did not wholly diverge. Under the American urban renewal program, public authorities had tried to attract developers by putting roads, sewers, and amenities into land that municipalities had acquired for redevelopment. Similar efforts began early in London's outer boroughs. Thus, for example, in Croydon, where 6.5 million square feet of office space was constructed in the 1960s, the council made a major effort to reduce the costs of development through providing basic infrastructure.[18]

As in the United States, a major surge of speculative commercial construction occurred in the United Kingdom in the early 1970s. The British expansion began when the Conservative central government increased credit as a means to stimulate the economy. While its action was not specifically directed at the property sector, it set off an intense building boom.[19] Despite the government's commitment to decentralizing population and economic activity out of London, much of the new construction arose in the core, and the Cities of London and Westminster,[20] which made up the commercial center of the metropolis, increasingly took on the look of Manhattan.[21] Parallel to the experience in a number of U.S. cities, office growth in the center of London led to gentrification of adjacent areas, while government subsidies to owner occupancy hastened the transformation of private rental into owner-occupied units.[22] In spite of the greater control on development in Britain, its 1970s boom ended like its American counterpart's in a wave of defaults and bankruptcies.

In the latter part of the 1970s, as had been the case in the United States for a much longer time, commercial redevelopment became a specific tool of British urban policy. Thus, the Labour government, in its growing economic desperation, encouraged commercial expansion into low-income areas next to the City of London (i.e., the financial district) well before the Thatcher regime took office and contrary to its avowed commitment to preserving working-class jobs and expanding the supply of affordable housing.[23]

During the 1980s, development policies in the two countries converged.[24] The British Urban Development Corporations (UDCs), modeled after similar American ventures, insulated development projects from public input.[25] Governed by independent boards and reporting only to the central government, they acted as the planning authorities for redevelopment areas. The consequence was the removal of decision-making powers from the local councils. The UDCs were oriented toward stimulating the private market rather than comprehensive planning.[26] In another case of transatlantic cross-fertilization, the majority of American states, although not the federal government, adopted the British innovation of the enterprise zone. Put in place early in the Thatcher regime, enterprise zones were designated geographic areas where firms were rewarded for investments with a variety of tax incentives, regulatory relief, and access to financing.[27]

In general, the dominant objective in both countries was to use public powers to assist the private sector with a minimum of regulatory intervention. Earlier emphases in redevelopment programs on the provision of housing, public amenities, and targeted benefits to low-income people were downplayed, as aggregate economic growth—measured by the amount of private investment "leveraged"—became the criterion of program success.

The sponsors of the regeneration programs of the '80s claimed that they had achieved a remarkable reversal in the trajectory of inner-city decline. Numerous studies, however, have characterized this growth as extremely uneven in its impacts, primarily benefiting highly skilled professionals and managers and offering very little for workers displaced from manufacturing industries except low-paid service-sector jobs. Moreover, as economic restructuring and contraction of social benefits produced a broadening income gap, growing social inequality expressed itself spatially in the increasing residential segregation of rich and poor, black and white. Rapid development also produced undesirable environmental effects. While the gleaming new projects upgraded the seedy appearance of many old core areas and brought middle-class consumers back to previously abandoned centers, their bulk and density often overwhelmed their surroundings, stifled diversity, and, in the crowded centers of London and New York, overloaded transportation and pedestrian facilities.[28]

The economic downturn of the early '90s eased pressures on inner-city land and thus for a while stemmed the negative environmental impacts of the extravagant ventures of the previous years. It also caused at least a temporary halt to gentrification, but it did not produce a turnaround in either the widening gap between rich and poor or the governmental pursuit of private investment through subsidies to businesses. By the year 2000, economic recession was a dim memory, and demand for space surged once again, producing transformative influences on urban form, inflating real-estate prices, and sparking intense competition for well-located space. In New York, reactions to this renewed real-estate boom by the public sector did not involve the sponsorship of megaprojects, as had been the case in the '80s; instead, the city's development strategy relied almost wholly on subsidies to developers and the occupants of their buildings. In London the opposite strategy was adopted, as tax subsidies were phased out and huge projects were begun. So far neither city is showing evidence of the speculative overbuilding that characterized the 1980s. London, however, has now turned toward strategic planning, while New York, except for an effort to revise the zoning code, displays little interest in planning at all.

THEORETICAL CONTROVERSIES

Most analyses of urban redevelopment have been built around case studies of individual cities. The more ambitious of these works develop theories concerning the crucial determinants of urban change.[29] Understanding urban redevelopment, however, was not the central issue for the first case studies that dealt with this subject. Rather, it simply constituted an arena in which to study the question of urban power structures. Thus, Robert Dahl's *Who Governs?*[30] and a number of subsequent reanalyses of New Haven, Connecticut, examined decision making in that city's urban renewal program but did not scrutinize the outcomes of redevelopment.[31] Nevertheless, Dahl and his associates, Nelson Polsby and Raymond Wolfinger, generally assumed that redevelopment was a widely beneficial goal, as the title of Wolfinger's book *The Politics of Progress*[32] implies.[33] Critics of their work, however, attacked it for overlooking the costs of redevelopment programs to poor and minority groups.[34]

For the decade of the 1960s, the power-structure debate dominated American discourse on urban politics. Within this discourse the question of race was hardly mentioned. But by mid-decade racial issues, urban social movements, and antipoverty efforts turned the urban arena into a battlefield. As a result, the scope of discussion widened considerably beyond Dahl's initial formulation. Bachrach and Baratz, in their critique of the pluralists, argued that in order to understand power, one must ask who benefits as well as who governs.[35] As their thesis began to prevail, analyses of decision making shifted to examinations of the effects of public policy, and the benign assumptions concerning the progressive qualities of urban renewal were dropped.[36] Thus, doubtless to Dahl's surprise, *Who Governs?* stimulated a body of research that ultimately connected redevelopment policy with the social and economic roots and impacts of decision making and formed the basis for much of the later writing on urban political economy, as will be discussed below. Although these studies conflicted on whether redevelopment coalitions could actually claim credit for economic growth, they generally agreed on the regressive distributional consequences of almost all central-city redevelopment programs.[37]

Urban politics emerged more slowly as a field of study in the United Kingdom than it did in the United States. The much weaker position of British local government, as well as the lesser prominence of urban social movements there, had much to do with this relative obscurity. Studies of redevelopment were carried out for a variety of purposes rather than, as in the United States, to contribute to the evolving debate on community power. A number of works stressed planning, housing, and redevelopment for their own sake, reflecting the much stronger British planning tradition. Unlike the Americans, British investigators spent little time debating whether seeming consensus on redevelopment programs had been manipulated, since the conflicting programs of the Labour and Conservative Parties made dissension obvious. Rather, they concerned themselves more with the functions of planning for capital accumulation and legitimation. British authors were less inclined from the start to examine public decision making in isolation from its broader economic and social context, and they therefore scrutinized the relationship between economic transformation, class structure, and urban form earlier than did their American counterparts.[38]

EXPLANATIONS OF REDEVELOPMENT POLICY

Explanations for the redevelopment story as summarized above fit into liberal and structuralist frameworks, with an overlapping third category designated regime theory.[39] At the risk of injustice to the range of works within the types described, the next sections provide a brief overview of the principal arguments.

Liberal Theories

Liberal analyses stress the importance of choice in producing redevelopment scenarios. They can be divided according to their stress on economic or political factors in shaping redevelopment activities. Conventional economically oriented studies identify regularities in the urban growth process and generally trace the changing fortunes of cities to the effects of economic competition, suburbanization, and technological change on the attractiveness of places.[40] The response of city officials to urban decline, according to this depiction, results from the need to compensate for competitive disadvantage by offering incentives to industry. This viewpoint is not incompatible with structuralist analysis but rather, within that framework, represents a superficial explanation, since it does not account for the forces underlying the ceaseless competition among places, the contradictions that such competition creates, the necessary relationship between uneven development and profit, the dependence of the democratic state on capital, and the power exerted by business to bias the outcomes of the process. In other words, it accepts uncritically the workings of the global capitalist system.

Another, more political, strand of liberal thought separates economic and political power and stresses the role of political decisions. Dahl and Polsby, writing before the resurgence of Marxist thought in the 1970s, were more concerned with contesting the single-elite model than with confronting structuralism.[41] Implicit in their focus on local decision making, however, was a rejection of economic determinism. They regarded the local decision-making stratum as comprising multiple elites that specialized in different issue areas. Redevelopment was only one of these areas and was not of great salience to most people. The key decision-making role belonged to public officials, who were checked by popular sentiment as expressed through elections. Savitch provides an updated version of pluralist thought.[42] While incorporating state theory into his model and thus somewhat parting company with his predecessors, he explicitly repudiates neo-Marxist arguments, contending that the most power is held by elected officials, who "can pursue an autonomous path and exercise great discretion."[43] Similarly, Swanstrom, concerned that the political economy viewpoint excludes the hope of progressive political action, contests what he regards as its fatalism.[44] The numerous critiques of pluralism in the power structure debate focused on its failure to comprehend the systemic privileging of business and to examine the distribution of benefits.

The more radical writers within the liberal tradition consider redevelopment a more central issue than do the pluralists and regard politics as the confrontation between elite and community rather than the jockeying of constrained elites acting within the confines of popular consensus. This group differs from the structuralists, however, in identifying progrowth coalitions rather than ineluctable economic pressures as the reason why business elites are favored within the redevelopment process.[45] This argument allows for greater local variation and the overcoming of dominant coalitions by countermobilization through both protest movements and voting. It stresses voluntarism in the formation of political groupings rather than the economic logic that structuralists see as causing people to join urban social movements.

The Left liberals, however, fail to demonstrate that redevelopment programs ever favor nonelite groups over the long term. Such a finding would be necessary in order fully to contradict structuralist analyses. Their argument that business groups do not get their way automatically but must organize themselves and follow conscious political strategies indicates indeterminacy in the urban system. But they do not show that outcomes can routinely favor majorities of the population, that lower-income groups typically participate in dominant coalitions, or that the democratic capitalist system offers much potential for sustained incorporation of nonelite interests in urban decision making. They create a straw person by caricaturing the Marxist argument as depicting absolute domination by business and by the logic of capital rather than only claiming the privileged position of capital and the dependence of government and the working population on the investment decisions of capitalists.

Structuralist Theory

I use the term "structuralist" to refer to theories giving primacy to economic relations in determining social actions. Although such theories are rooted in Marxist thought, their more recent manifestations break with Marxist determinism and economic reductionism to such an extent as to make the label "Marxist" misleading.

Contemporary structuralist explanations refer to the logic of capital operating in an era of global economic restructuring and extreme social and spatial inequality. Within this tradition, however, analyses vary as to whether they stress production or collective consumption in their analysis of the built environment.

Functions of redevelopment. Many observers, liberal and structuralist alike, have noted the correlation between urbanization and economic growth. Employers need proximity to labor pools, and producers require access to suppliers and to markets. Economic actors therefore cluster around each other or near to transportation nodes and telecommunications facilities so as to overcome the friction of distance. The structuralist twist on this recognition of the advantages of agglomeration displays two aspects: first, that the form of agglomeration is in tune with the interests of capitalists rather than the preferences of workers or consumers; and second, that any particular agglomeration is unstable because it embodies underlying contradictions. In the words of David Harvey:

> Capital flow presupposes tight temporal and spatial coordinations in the midst of increasing separation and fragmentation. It is impossible to imagine such a material process without the production of some kind of urbanization as a "rational landscape" within which the accumulation of capital can proceed. Capital accumulation and the production of urbanization go hand in hand.
>
> This perspective deserves modification on two counts. Profit depends upon realizing the surplus value created in production within a certain time. The turnover time of capital . . . is a very important magnitude. . . . Competition produces strong pressures to accelerate turnover time. The same pressure has a spatial manifestation. Since movement across space takes time and money, competition forces capitalism toward the elimination of spatial barriers and "the annihilation of space by time." Building a capacity for increased efficiency of coordination in space and time is one of the hallmarks of capitalist urbanization. Considerations derived from a study of the circulation of capital dictate, then, that the urban matrix and the "rational landscape" for accumulation be subject to continuous transformations. In this sense also, capital accumulation, technological innovation and capitalist urbanization have to go together.[46]

In this view, economic expansion requires the constant demolition of the fixed investment in buildings and infrastructure that supported the previous round of economic transactions. Government-sponsored redevelopment, according to the model set by Haussmann in nineteenth-century Paris and emulated by Robert Moses in twentieth-century New York, provides a vehicle for "continuous transformations." Since, however, the city remains the realm of collective consumption, capitalist efforts to reconstitute it are perennially contested by communities of residents and by those businesses that still benefit from the older spatial arrangements. Urban politics arises from this contested terrain.[47]

Castells, in his early work, traced urban social movements to the inequalities arising in the workplace and contended that urban political conflict represented a displacement of conflict from the realm of production into consumption.[48] His approach and that of others who examined the heightened importance of local state services[49] rooted the activities of the local state in various of the contradictions arising from the capitalist mode of production. Urban redevelopment efforts, as well as being required to improve production, were needed in order to reproduce the labor force through the provision of housing and other services. The functionalism underlying this argument contrasts sharply with the voluntarism embodied in liberal pluralist thought.

For the purposes of my discussion, there are four important points deriving from the structuralist position presented thus far:

1. The local state necessarily becomes involved in the capitalist demand for a more efficient urban landscape, since capitalists cannot carry out the task of redevelopment on their own.
2. Redevelopment policy is an arena for class- and community-based conflict in which resident groups confront capital indirectly through the local state.
3. State actors, in pursuing their own aims of maintaining revenues and power, depend on private capital investment to reproduce and expand the urban environment, resulting in a bias toward capital.[50]
4. The redevelopment process itself requires specialists in property development. They, however, have a collective interest in the profitability of the buildings they finance and construct rather than the operations that go on within them, and this interest can put them at odds with other capitalists. Moreover, the particular structure of their industry, as detailed in Chapters 2 and 3, leads them to take speculative risks that differentiate them from other producers and generate an added element of instability in the urban system.

Rent theory. A subset of structuralist studies concentrates on the Marxian theory of value and the theory of rent derived from it, in an effort to connect land use and development to production more generally.[51] While a theory of rent has also been developed within conventional economics, it does not play a central role in analyses of urban redevelopment.

Neo-Marxist arguments concerning rent bear directly on the character of the investment market in real estate and the strategies of the actors within it. The return that investors on property receive is divided between the earnings from (1) greater output or lower costs of production enabled by physical improvements on land; and (2) rent. Rent, in orthodox Marxist analysis, refers to the amount extracted from surplus value that is transferred to the owner of a property simply as a consequence of his or her holding a legal right of possession. As such, it involves a mere transfer rather than an addition to value or a lowering of production costs. The concept has a moralizing flavor since it refers to an income that neither derives from production, as does the return to capital investment in machinery, nor flows from labor.

The significance of rent to the question of urban redevelopment relates to the impact of public subsidies on economic growth and the benefits from it. If the subsidies simply become capitalized as returns to landowners—that is, as rent—rather than lowering the costs of production and offering an incentive to economic expansion, they constitute a transfer to a fraction of capital.[52] Furthermore, if rents increase as a consequence of the behavior of the collectivity—that is, if they result from factors external to the property—but are privately appropriated, then the landlord realizes an unearned increment, having contributed nothing him/herself. The identification of this unearned increment was the basis of the economics of Henry George, who argued for confiscatory taxation of this gain.

Regime Theory

Regime theory straddles the boundary between the liberal and structuralist formulations. The original liberal concern with decision making gave rise to this broader approach to the study of redevelopment, which takes into account dominant ideology, agenda setting, access networks, and latent power.[53] Clarence Stone delineates its applicability to Atlanta:

> [The business] elite controls resources of the kind and in the amount able to enhance the regime's capacity to govern. Minus these business-supplied resources, governing in Atlanta . . . would consist of little more than the provision of routine services. In Atlanta, then, the very capacity for strong governance is dependent on active business collaboration. . . . The position of Atlanta's business elite in the affairs of the community is *not* that of a passive partner in a courtship conducted by public officials. The elite has collective aims that it is mobilized to pursue.[54]

Regime theory, like neopluralist theory, accepts individual choice as the basis for political action: "The use of the selective incentives concepts as the core of the explanation of regime origins and reproduction means that, as an explanatory framework, regime theory is grounded in the methodology of rational choice theory. Within the regime perspective, the political process is understood . . . in terms of decision making in the face of patterns of costs and benefits in which means-end rationality is deployed to provide the greatest returns to self-interested individuals."[55] For Stone, public officials behave as they do because they are acting in their individual rational self-interest. He breaks with pluralism, however, in minimizing the importance of elections in affecting public policy and in questioning how preferences are formed. Whereas pluralists assume that public support for urban renewal programs reflects the interests of the populace, regime theorists point to the role of the governing regime in shaping those preferences.[56] As Stone puts it, "Those with more resources . . . have a superior opportunity to rally support to the cause they favor. . . . Resources need not be material. . . . However, material resources are especially useful."[57]

Regime theory, in its discussion of the social bases of conflict and cooperation in redevelopment, more easily accommodates racial differentiation and ideological forces than do most structuralist critiques. It detects structural biases within the political economic system of capitalism that channel the redevelopment process, but, more than the clearly Marxian analyses, it accepts the importance of political and ideological factors. Its weaknesses are that its formulation applies principally to the United States and that its focus on political analysis avoids explicit theoretical linkages with economic structures.[58] In other words, while regime theory recognizes the importance of economic structure, it does not incorporate the forces creating that structure into its argument.

INTERESTS AND THEIR INTERPRETATION

My own approach largely embraces the tenets of regime theory, but it also attempts to unravel the economic factors that lead to particular political-ideological construction of material interest by social groups. Balbus defines the Marxian concept of interest as follows: "Individuals whose life-chances are similarly *affected* by similar objective social conditions are said to have a *common interest* whether they perceive any such interest or not."[59] But even if, in the case of property developers, individuals perceive a common interest, ideology and uncertainty affect their view of how that interest can best be served. In turn, different interpretations of their interest by powerful groups make possible different social outcomes.

My formulation differs from arguments like that of Kevin Cox,[60] who takes a more fixed view of interest formation. In asserting that the class interest of locally dependent capitalists drives urban redevelopment, he assumes that local dependence is a wholly obvious characteristic. Yet, as the following illustration shows, its definition is malleable and varies according to the particular strategies that individual actors adopt. For example, the managers of a downtown department store may invest heavily in branches and disinvest or close the main store; they may participate in a downtown growth coalition, renovate their original store, move upmarket, and endow a foundation that supports affordable housing; or they may, as employees of a multilocational retail conglomerate, transfer to another subsidiary in a completely different part of the country and take no interest in the redevelopment program of their original location. In this instance, even though the alternatives are all premised on economic interest alone, they reflect different readings of a situation and indicate how the circumstance of local dependency results from perception and activity. Moreover, each choice can alter the "objective situation" in which the actors find themselves, as well as the fate of downtown redevelopment.

In other words, perceived interest is neither an automatic response to economic position nor a wholly voluntaristic option among possible stances. It rather represents a structured position derived from the interaction between economic, communal, and ideological forces at a particular historical moment.[61] The tools used in this book for detecting the economic factors driving interest formation come primarily from structuralist thought. I do not assume, however, that economic factors produce only one possible interpretation of interest or that economic situation (as opposed to community, race, and gender) is the only "objective social interest" to be maximized. Instead, the formation of interest is the subject of exploration, particularly as nongovernmental (business and community) redevelopment actors construct their viewpoints.

Because the definition of interest contains such an important interpretative element, factors that shape consciousness are of particular importance in affecting human action. Value traditions, ideology, and personality are therefore underlying causes of urban development. They cannot simply be reduced to the social relations of production, because their origins, even if economically based, may be traced back to earlier historical periods or be the products of social fragments rather than the totality of relations in a society.[62] Moreover, group identifications may be at odds with economic interests—and not simply as a result of manipulation by privileged elites.

What Matters?

The chief difference between the liberal and structuralist explanations of the urban redevelopment process is the insistence in the former on the importance of power and decision making and in the latter on economic logic and class domination in explaining the course of events.[63] For pluralist liberals, power is not a simple manifestation of economic ascendancy but requires choosing to expend resources. These resources extend beyond money to organization, political support, and conviction. Marxists trace all forms of power to the relations of production and regard the strategic choices of actors as the consequence of their economic position; more flexible structuralists identify large areas of relative autonomy in social institutions and identify race and gender as separable determinants. For the regime theorists, who represent something of a synthesis of the two outlooks, control of capital outweighs other sources of power, but the development process cannot be understood simply through examining a "logic" of capitalism, since that logic is itself fabricated through human activity, including resistance by other groups to capitalist aims.[64]

Can Local Officials Produce Growth with Equity?

In the study of urban redevelopment, the recognition that localities are embedded within a global economic system whose overall contours do not respond to local initiatives has caused a debate over the efficacy of local action. Urban redevelopment efforts have taken place within the larger framework of the hypermobility of capital and intensified national and international economic competition. These factors have seemingly and inexorably caused the decline of manufacturing and the flight of employment from older cities. Within this context, social scientists have questioned whether, regardless of who controls the local regime, local actors can affect their economies and carry out redistributional policies.[65]

The feverish attempts by governments around the world to attract business challenge the view of economic determinists that market forces will by themselves allocate economic functions to their optimum locations. Interestingly, this belief in the power of the market is held not just by conservative economists but also by progressive critics of government subsidies to business.[66] Both argue that businesses do not choose a location because governmental incentives are available but rather because of factors such as the price of labor or the presence of clients, which immediately affect production costs or marketing effectiveness. Accordingly, businesses do not pick their locations because of governmentally proffered concessions but rather simply take advantage of them to enhance their profits at the expense of taxpayers.[67]

Paul Peterson, in his influential book, *City Limits,* considers that local governments can affect the economic situation of their jurisdictions even though they cannot directly improve the welfare of their poorer citizens.[68] He explicitly repudiates the possibility of redistributive actions by local governments, contending that they must pursue growth and cannot enact redistributional policies without sacrificing their competitive positions. For Peterson, if municipal officials attempt to assist poor people, thereby scaring away businesses through increasing their tax burden, they will have nothing to redistribute.

In response, Sanders and Stone[69] maintain that political conflict determines who wins and who loses from the redevelopment process; while they do not explicitly stipulate an alternative path to redevelopment, they imply that it can be achieved through community-based rather than downtown expansion. In other words, local politics matters in determining both the geographic targets of redevelopment programs and who benefits from them. According to this school of thought, urban policy-makers do not have to submit to the logic of capitalism; if they do so, it is because of political pressure rather than economic necessity.[70]

Is the Issue Resolvable?

There are several ways to address the issue of local autonomy. Differences between American and European cities and variation among cities that had similar economic bases thirty years ago imply that political factors influence the capability of cities to fit into new economic niches.[71] Within the United States, where local governments have a much greater say over levels of welfare spending than in the United Kingdom, economically comparable cities spend different amounts of money on poor people, indicating that the extent to which cities engage in redistribution is not simply determined by competition among localities. At the same time, the downward pressure on social welfare expenses that has characterized all of the advanced capitalist countries since the mid-1970s points to serious restrictions on local deviationism.[72]

Definitive conclusions based on observation are, however, impossible: For every example of local activity resulting in regeneration or redistribution, there is a counterexample of seemingly insurmountable external forces. My own position is that incentives to investors do make a difference and that growth can be combined with greater equity than has typically been the outcome of redevelopment programs. But perhaps the farthest one can go in addressing the issue is to identify areas of indeterminacy that can be seized locally within the overall capitalist economic structure—that is, to identify courses of action that can produce lesser or greater growth, more or less progressive social policies, without expecting either an inevitable economic trajectory resulting from market position or socialism in one city deriving from effective political action. The research and policy problem then becomes to recognize those decisional points, rather than to inquire whether localities matter in general. The subject of investigation therefore switches to the strategies followed by local actors, the factors influencing their choices, and how and under what circumstances these strategies affect what happens. My intention is to raise these issues within London and New York in relation to the striking transformations that have occurred in their built environments in the last 25 years.

Space

A number of urban geographers have been assertive in contending that space matters.[73] For them, spatial relations are part of society's underlying structure. Regardless of whether economy or politics has primacy in affecting the location of social groups and economic enterprises, the configuring of space that contributes to and ensues from locational decisions remains crucial in affecting human relations.

Within this intellectual framework, part of the explanation for the marked acceleration of real-estate development in global cities during the 1980s and latter part of the 1990s hinges on the spatial causes and effects of the heightened role of financial capital and business services within the world economic system. As production sites and financial markets have become increasingly dispersed throughout the world, financial firms and investment advisers respond to the need for global coordination and trading.[74] In turn, core areas become crucial for the deal making in which the expanding financial industry engages.[75] By offering a venue for face-to-face encounters among the numerous parties to high-level negotiations, central areas that had lost their former value as manufacturing, rail, or port facilities find a renewed role based on the clustering of business services.[76] Space at different scales thus enters into the process at two points: The compact area of the urban core allows the structuring of deals; and the distant spaces of the world economy require integration through financial coordination so that raw materials, labor, and capital in various locations can be brought together in a production function.

It is actually difficult to find anyone who explicitly denies that spatial relationships are important, and thus the "debate" over space is somewhat one-sided. Rather, geographers accuse others of ignoring them,[77] resulting in what Edward Soja terms a "hidden history of spatialization."[78] Fundamental to the argument of Soja and other geographers is the contention that uneven spatial development is basic to the dynamics of capitalist investment.[79] As this thesis applies narrowly to urban redevelopment, it explains why redevelopment of core areas can be extremely profitable. The underlying reasoning is that central-city land occupied by low-income residents, marginal businesses, or derelict facilities sells for a value much lower than its potential price. If, however, the land is transformed through demolition or rehabilitation of existing structures and conversion of ownership and occupancy, it becomes suitable for highly remunerative development.[80] For gentrification of residential areas, buildings that were broken up into small flats are reconfigured into larger units and their initial occupants displaced; for commercial construction, small holdings are usually consolidated into large tracts allowing unified ownership and management. The huge gains available to investors derive from the previously undervalued nature of the property—without uneven development, such speculative advantages could not be achieved.

What Matters When?

In the controversies over what matters, there are two opposing tendencies: One is to overly polarize the issue so that only structure or only agency, only economics or only politics, only space or only history becomes the determinant of outcomes; the other is to say that everything matters. The intellectual framework used in this book privileges the economic and spatial structures in the sense that they, more than other structures, restrict choice in regard to strategies intended to further economic well-being. Everything may matter, but not equally. Nevertheless, uncertainty over the strategies adopted by other actors, the contradictions between individual and social rationality, the power of ideology in shaping human constructions of rational behavior, and the force of noneconomic motivation—all of these factors make the consequences of particular actions indeterminate. And, of course, the aggregate of individual actions constantly both reproduces and transforms the economic and spatial structure. The investigator's task becomes to figure out not what matters in general, but what matters when, for what results.

According to this approach, developers, politicians, and local activists are important within a restricted range of variation, and the character of the urban regime is a key element in determining the differences in redevelopment efforts among cities. Even if the primum mobile of service-led growth is the world economy, the unfolding of the process involves initiatives and responses within particular places.[81] The strategies and actions that produce urban redevelopment within the spaces of London and New York comprise my subject matter.

LONDON AND NEW YORK

Why study London and New York? First, London and New York—with Tokyo—are the preeminent global cities, performing a vital function of command and control within the contemporary world system.[82] The contributions of property developers to the situations of global cities have so far been little explored, apart from investigations of the financial industry.[83] Development firms, however, differ from purely financial institutions in their physicality and greater volatility. Their connection to globalization and overall economic stability, as well as their symbiotic relationship to the financial institutions that dominate the economies of global cities, require further inquiry.

Second, London and New York are ideal sites for the exploration of property-led redevelopment because the impact of the real-estate industry within them during the past two decades has been so uniquely large. Both cities were the locations of several mammoth projects as well as a range of lesser enterprises. Moreover, real-estate activity in the two cities generated some of the greatest fortunes made during a period of rampant money making and became symbolic of the spirit of the era.

The reversal of economic decline in London and New York in the 1980s was based in considerable part on a property boom. The erection of such flashy projects as Trump Tower in Manhattan and Broadgate in London symbolized the creation of new wealth and seemingly testified to growing general prosperity. And, indeed, the flurry of new construction coincided with a major expansion in employment, income, and tax revenues.[84] On both sides of the Atlantic, policies promoting physical redevelopment through public-private partnerships were heralded as the key to economic success.

The real-estate crash of the '90s, accompanied by sharp economic contraction, called this model into question. Not only did empty office buildings and apartment houses act as a direct drag on economic activity, but the heavy commitment made by financial institutions to the real-estate industry threatened the soundness of major banks. The real-estate slump affected cities throughout the United States and the United Kingdom but was particularly significant in New York and London, where the world's major developers were located and where financial institutions both financed and consumed large amounts of space. Once the recession ended, however, the availability of cheap, vacant space facilitated the surprisingly quick business expansion at the century's end and bolstered the competitive position of the two cities. This outcome raises an important question, discussed in Chapter 10, of the effect of property cycles on the urban economy.

LOCAL CONDITIONS AND NATIONAL CONTEXTS

London and New York also make a particularly useful comparison because their striking similarities simplify efforts at understanding the influence of national differences. The economic histories of the two metropolises have proceeded so synchronously as to highlight the roots of social, institutional, and policy dissimilarities in politics and culture. Both cities developed as great ports; both act as centers of international trade—and the requirements for financing that trade caused them both to become the locations of the world's most important financial markets. Each has been the financial capital of the dominant global economic power, and each faces increased competition from other world centers. Although the United Kingdom's international economic position has declined, London has retained its place as a financial capital. In both cities manufacturing employment diminished by about three-quarters between 1960 and the end of the century, while office employment increased (although far more dramatically in New York).[85]

Growth in employment stimulated an expansion of office space, including major government-sponsored development schemes, and pressure on conveniently located housing.[86] The two cities each have inner-city concentrations of poverty and are surrounded by affluent suburban rings. In both, manufacturing jobs have moved out of easy access for the inner-city poor.

The two cities, however, have strikingly different political institutions. New York is governed by a mayor and council; governmental departments report to the mayor's office. London is divided into 33 localities, each headed by a council larger than the one that governs all of New York. The borough councils are organized in a fashion similar to Parliament, with the leader of the majority party acting as the head of an executive committee, each of whose members has responsibility for a particular governmental function. New York's government has considerable autonomy from higher levels of government, although its charter and its revenue-raising measures must be approved by the government of the State of New York. London's local authorities are strictly subordinate to the central government, which can overrule any local action, and there is no regional authority comparable to an American state government to which they are responsible. Although Londoners elected their first mayor in May 2000, the powers of his office are quite limited compared with those of the mayor of New York—the national government continues to exercise strong control over local action, and the borough councils maintain jurisdiction over most services. The mayor's chief responsibility is strategic planning, but his powers in this respect are subject to review.

The systems of local government in the United Kingdom and the United States became less alike during the 1980s, when the Thatcher government eliminated general-purpose metropolitan authorities in Britain's largest conurbations. One could argue that the result simply reproduced the American situation, in which regions consist of numerous uncoordinated municipalities. Nowhere in the United States, however, do agglomerations exist on the scale and density of London's core area without an overarching general-purpose government. In addition, the move by the central government to exert ever-greater fiscal and policy control over local government restricted home rule to an extent unimaginable in the United States. Before the demise of the Greater London Council (GLC), which had jurisdiction over all of London within the surrounding Green Belt for purposes of planning, environmental controls, and transportation, London's government had considerable leeway. The GLC was able to pursue a course strikingly at variance with national policy, for example, by sharply reducing public transit fares and by engaging in economic planning. Afterwards, however, the possibility of significant deviation became totally blocked.

The advent of a new national Labour government in 1997, and its decision to institute an elected mayor and council for London, represented a reversal of the trend toward ever-greater centralization. It remains to be seen, however, what actual power these new entities will possess. Ken Livingstone, the former Labour leader of the GLC, won the first mayoral election in May 2000, confounding Prime

Minister Tony Blair, who did not regard "Red Ken" as representing "New Labour."
Since most of the mayor's statutory authority depends on central government
acquiescence, and since the individual boroughs will retain their roles as local
governments, London's new political officials will not have anything like the
influence of the mayor and city council of New York.[87] The London borough
councils are much more powerful than New York's community boards, providing an important mechanism for the expression of community-based interests.
London is organized by competing political parties with articulated programs. New
York is virtually a one-party city, despite the election of a Republican mayor,
Rudolph Giuliani, in 1993. The council is overwhelmingly Democratic, the city's
charter limits the mayor to two four-year terms, and there is no likely Republican
successor. The Democratic Party, however, has no machinery for enforcing a
program and, in reality, has no program to impose; essentially, public officials act
independently of party control.

Nationally, there are quite dissimilar policy frameworks, although these differences lessened considerably during the 1980s as Conservative governments in
the United Kingdom dramatically reduced the state's role in planning and social
welfare.[88] Throughout most of the twentieth century the British state took a much
stronger role than the U.S. government did in promoting and regulating development. It constructed new towns, built council housing, and prohibited private investment in improvements on land unless the developer received specific planning
permission. In the United States the government engaged in very little direct construction activity, preferring to offer incentives to the private sector; although it
did build public housing, the total amount produced was minuscule compared with
what was achieved in the United Kingdom.[89] The U.S. government also did much
less than the British public sector to provide social service and recreational facilities. Victorious "New Labour" has committed itself to limiting the role of the state
in the United Kingdom; thus, Labour's ascendance to power has not brought with
it an enlargement of social welfare activity. It has, however, encouraged the resurrection of land-use and transportation planning, and it is in this area that differences between the two countries have sharpened once again.

The British party system also continues to diverge from the American one in
being far more programmatic. Under Thatcher the Conservative Party had become
even more centralized; the extent to which Blair's policies of devolution will
change the character of the Labour Party is as yet unclear. Great Britain now has
a three-party system (more, if the regional parties in Scotland, Wales, and Northern Ireland are counted); at the city level, there is not the single-party dominance
that characterizes most big American municipalities and has shaped New York
politics during the postwar years. The elimination of the metropolitan level of
government meant that no one party had control throughout London; rather, party
control varied among the 33 local councils. In 1991 Conservatives and Labour
each held a majority in 16, with one council controlled by the Liberal Democrats.
In 2000 there was a Labour mayor who had run as an independent, and the bor-

ough councils split 18 Labour, 4 Conservative, 3 Liberal, 1 Independent, and 7 with no overall control.[90]

Despite these important differences, London and New York increasingly share some political and social characteristics. Government agencies in each city have actively pursued private investment and have met strong opposition from neighborhood and preservationist forces. Borough councils in London and community boards in New York are comparable forums in which planning issues are first debated. In both cities ethnic divisions exacerbate conflict over turf. Both cities have systems of rent regulation, although London differs from New York in having a majority of owner occupants. During the last two decades of the century, each operated in a national context of conservative, market-oriented ideological ascendancy but had strong internal political forces demanding continued state intervention within a significant tradition of state-sponsored social service and housing provision. Indeed, New York has been the most "European" of American cities in the historical activism of its government.

The two cities have also both experienced important changes in the relations between men and women, which have expressed themselves in economic transformation, new family structures, and changed consciousness. These in turn have both affected and been affected by the uses of space, as women have sought access to work, better housing, and assistance in their parenting roles. The increased participation of women in the labor force and the strains they have felt as a consequence of the "double burden" of home and work have expanded their need for convenient job locations, better transportation systems, and day care. Their heightened political activism has intensified the community rebellion against systems of housing, land use, and transportation that do not take their needs into account.

During the 1980s and for much of the '90s the governing regimes of the two cities followed similar redevelopment strategies with similar results. Restructuring of the urban environment took place under comparable economic pressures and in the name of similar conservative ideologies. Economic factors did not determine these ideologies; the power of ideological formulations, however, reinforced the restructuring process within the cities' economic and spatial systems. The increasing integration of the world economy heightened the importance of these two global cities, as the worldwide investment opportunities of their dominant financial industries increased. At the same time, globalization threatened their status through the challenge of increased competition from other aspirants for their economic niche.

METHODOLOGY

I carried out the investigation for the first edition of this book sporadically over seven years, although mainly between 1989 and 1992. In 1999–2000 I revisited the sites of the original investigation and conducted a new, less extensive set of interviews. Data are drawn from interviews; statistical material published by governmental, academic, and business sources; property company reports; publications of community groups; and academic studies. In the initial round, I conducted about 100 in-depth interviews with developers, officers of financial institutions, public and private-sector planners, chartered surveyors, politicians, community leaders, and knowledgeable observers in the two cities. In 1999–2000 I carried out 30 additional interviews, some with people I had spoken to before but most with individuals who had assumed the roles of my previous sample during the intervening years.[91] Respondents were selected by a reputational method, in which I relied on informants to supply me with the names of others who could be helpful to my endeavor. I chose respondents either because they were prominent actors in the redevelopment arena or because they were particularly well informed. Generalizations were made when the comments of several independent informants were in agreement. In many respects, my technique more closely resembled investigative journalism than standard social science. I have repeated the views of informants when they seemed to me insightful rather than because they represented a statistical average. Since I guaranteed anonymity to the people I interviewed, I do not usually quote them by name.

All comparative research runs into difficulties in the matching up of comparable units and data. Methods for record keeping and calculation are never uniform from country to country. The problem is exacerbated when the unit of analysis is a city, where jurisdictional lines do not coincide with physical or economic borders. Descriptive statistics for cities often derive from estimates using very small samples. Sometimes statistics do not exist at all for the comparable area and it is necessary to construct them from data on other territorial units. London and New York present especially perplexing situations, because London for much of the period between 1980 and 2000 did not have an official boundary, while New York City merely forms the core of an area that sprawls over three states. For reasons of practicality, the analysis in this book is largely restricted to London within the Green Belt (the territory of the terminated GLC and of the new mayoral administration) and New York City. For both places the labor market area extends much farther than the political jurisdiction; the cores under discussion here, however, comprise most of the spaces that have been subject to redevelopment, which is the focus of my study.

KEY ISSUES

The main objects of my inquiry are the local economic, political, social, and environmental contributions to and consequences of property-led redevelopment.[92] I ask the question: What is the logic of urban redevelopment, and what are its consequences? The assumption, however, is that this logic is not abstract but constructed, containing inductive as well as deductive elements.

I focus on the aims and effects of redevelopment policy and on the real-estate industry as an economic sector. Policy-makers and scholars seem to believe that property development is a simple response to economic opportunity—that there is an obvious determining capitalist logic to which it conforms. According to this reasoning, if there is a demand for office or residential space, then developers will come along and fill it, and if governmental programs let developers build more and larger projects, then they will make more money. My premise instead is that the development industry constructs and perceives opportunity through the beliefs and actions of its leaders operating under conditions of uncertainty. Real-estate developers participate in a dynamic process in which they sell themselves to governments, financial institutions, and renters; combat their opponents; and estimate their competitors' intentions. They do not merely react to an objective situation but operate within a subjective environment partly of their own creation. Often they build projects with little chance of success and press for governmental policies that may not be in the best long-term interests of their industry. Because personal rewards are not wholly tied to the ultimate profitability of projects, individuals within both government and the industry often succumb to wishful thinking in pushing for ever more, ever larger development.

One of my main purposes is to outline the broad characteristics of the real-estate industry and of real-estate markets within London and New York. I examine the relationships among politicians, community groups, and developers; I investigate, as well, interactions among advisers, financiers, and developers within the property industries of the two cities. Several key questions structure my inquiry:

1. What is the relationship between economic restructuring and the conditions of real-estate development? In what ways is redevelopment both a functional response to and a causal agent of restructuring?
2. What contradictions are incorporated in urban redevelopment policy? On what basis do real-estate developers select their projects? What are the causes and consequences of property cycles in capitalist development?
3. How is the real-estate industry affected by government programs? How does it influence political regimes? What explains the redevelopment policy of the local public sector? What are the roles of planners and the functions of urban planning?
4. What are the similarities and differences in redevelopment activities in London and New York, two cities with similar economic bases but quite different institutional traditions?
5. What are the special characteristics of real estate as an economic sector? Does it contribute to real urban economic growth or only to growth in fictitious capital, where fictitious capital refers to increases in the paper value of assets because of anticipated future gains? (Is fictitious capital a useful concept?)[93]
6. By what criteria should we evaluate the redevelopment process? Who wins and who loses in it and under what conditions?

7. How can redevelopment be incorporated into a realistic, progressive policy for economic growth?

The inquiry conforms to a "realist" methodology in which the point is not to delineate a general process that occurs at all times in all places. Rather, the objective is to understand the mix of general and specific factors that create the London and New York of this moment in time. Although a few cities displaying similar characteristics will share similar outcomes, other cities will be different precisely because of the existence of London and New York. To put this another way, we have to understand the processes creating London and New York in order to find out why other cities take on other functions. There is no single model of the late-twentieth-century metropolis, but rather there is a network of places, with some monopolizing particular, specialized niches. Because the financial capitals of the United Kingdom and the United States are in London and New York, other cities differ from them even though they are affected by them. New York and London are special cases, but their atypicality makes them worth studying, not because they present a model of all other cities but because they exemplify a certain, and especially influential, class of city.

2

The Development Industry and Urban Redevelopment

The development industry is in some ways the basic industry of New York City.

Linda Davidoff[1]

Some day a sociologist in the business faculty of one of the great universities will take it into his [sic] *head to study the development of the commercial property business in the 1980s. When he does, he's in for a shock.*

He will find that, over a 10 year period, everything changed.

The Hillier Parker Magazine[2]

The 1980s marked an extraordinary surge in property development in London and New York, followed by an equally precipitous drop at the end of the decade. A new boom gathered force in the mid-1990s and continued through 2000. The two property booms closely tracked spurts in the economies of the two cities, largely attributable to growth in finance and business service sectors throughout the twenty years, but also to expansion in media and tourism, especially in the latter part. Although in many respects the '90s represented a continuation of previous trends, that decade, as we shall see, had some elements that differentiated it from the earlier period.

As the '80s boom hit its peak, high-ranking public officials were celebrating an "urban renaissance," embodied in the grand new building complexes of London and New York. At the same time, writers, academics, and community-based critics were condemning the pretensions and social impacts of the recently constructed projects. In his widely read book, *Bonfire of the Vanities,* Tom Wolfe describes the scene on the trading floor of a New York City investment firm. His words capture both the physical setting of the great financial markets within these world cities and the social ambience they engendered:

It was a vast space, perhaps sixty by eighty feet. . . . It was an oppressive space with a ferocious glare, writhing silhouettes, and the roar. The glare came from a wall of plate glass that faced south, looking out over New York Harbor, the Statue of Liberty, Staten Island, and the Brooklyn and New Jersey shores. The writhing silhouettes were the arms and torsos of young men, few of them older than forty. They had their suit jackets off. They were moving about in an agitated manner and sweating early in the morning and shouting, which created the roar. It was the sound of well-educated young white men baying for money.[3]

The real-estate investment market, while not quartered on a few trading floors like the stock and bond exchanges, formed a very significant part of the 1980s speculative milieu chronicled by Wolfe. It uniquely combined the visible, physical endeavor of constructing the environment in which that activity took place. Property development belonged to the '80s financial boom as cause, effect, and symbol. Profits on large projects, huge tax benefits from real-estate syndication in the United States,[4] and trading margins from mortgage securitization formed the basis for vast fortunes. As their wealth and visibility made them prominent actors in the cultural and social scene, the names of developers like Donald Trump, William Zeckendorf, Jr., and Mortimer Zuckerman in New York, or Stuart Lipton, Godfrey Bradman, and Trevor Osborne in London became widely publicized. Financial institutions that underwrote the property market likewise prospered. For example, the mortgage department of Salomon Brothers, headed by Lewis Ranieri, had made the bond-trading firm into the most profitable business on Wall Street.

> The wonderfully spontaneous mortgage department [of Salomon] was the place to be if your philosophy of life was: Ready, fire, aim. The payoff to the swashbuckling raiders, by the standards of the time, was shockingly large. In 1982 . . . Lewie Ranieri's mortgage department made $150 million. . . . Although there are no official numbers, it was widely accepted at Salomon that Ranieri's traders made $200 million in 1983, $175 million in 1984, and $275 million in 1985.[5]

The burgeoning space needs of the expanding financial institutions, the businesses that provided them with services, and their suddenly wealthy employees produced a great surge in demand that was in part refueled by the office requirements of the development industry itself, its financial backers, and its service providers. The steeply climbing curve of returns from real-estate investment prompted a stream of new development proposals, which justified their costs with prognoses of ever-increasing earnings. The shiny skyscrapers housing the boisterous trading floors of the fabulously profitable investment banks; the high-rise condominiums and converted lofts affording havens for the young urban professionals; the renovated mansions and penthouses sheltering their bosses; and the glamorous marble-clad shopping malls, festive marketplaces, deluxe hotels, and opulent restaurants catering to their consumption whims constituted the symbolic setting for the excesses of the period.

In a keynote address to an international conference of planners, David Harvey declared that the two forces destroying New York City were drugs and the real-estate development industry.[6] Although Harvey's wholly negative assessment of developers might provoke disagreement, few would dispute that speculative property investment did indeed transform the functions and appearance of New York and London during the '80s; nor would they disagree that while the public purse helped finance physical change, private entrepreneurs using borrowed money were in charge. Since developers saw little profit in building factories or working-class housing, they confined their activities to producing offices and luxury residential units. The consequence of their development strategies was an economic and spatial restructuring of London and New York that was dramatically uneven in its components.

Simultaneous investment and disinvestment created not just the juxtaposition of rich and poor, made obvious by the ubiquitous homeless within even the most affluent neighborhoods, but also sent whole communities on opposite trajectories.[7] The growing numbers of relatively and absolutely impoverished city residents, displaced from factory jobs as a consequence of economic restructuring, dislodged from their homes by gentrification and financial catastrophe, or deinstitutionalized and suffering from disabilities, provided the counterpoint to good fortune. The symbolism of these contrasts was interpreted by the left as revealing the mordant injustice of privately led economic development programs and by the right as a moral lesson demonstrating the differential in rewards to the deserving and undeserving, the entrepreneurs and the wastrels.

For most of the '80s the constant fanfare trumpeting new development projects and the army of building cranes punctuating the London and New York skylines did appear to herald progress, whatever its imperfections. The visibility and hopefulness of new construction tended to override the caveats of critics. Community representatives who railed against the overwhelming effects of large projects on their neighborhoods were derided for standing in the way of progress. Despite soaring office vacancy rates in other American cities as the '80s progressed, New York developers continued to propose ever-larger projects. And in London, memories of the property-market collapse of the mid-1970s faded, as banks ratcheted up their real-estate investments.

In 1980 it was by no means obvious that London and New York would witness such accelerated growth.[8] Employment and population had been declining in both cities; existing levels of development made land acquisition difficult and expensive; very high occupancy costs discouraged prospective commercial tenants; while planning restrictions combined with community opposition to create formidable obstacles to developers' ambitions. Then, abruptly, the economic trajectories of London and New York reversed, as increased world trade, global financial deals, and expanding national markets for their producers' services complexes caused economic transactions within them to multiply exponentially during the decade.

The 1987 stock market crash, however, heralded another turn in the fortunes of the two cities. In 1989 the property market, which had lagged the decline of equity markets, also collapsed and for a five-year period manifested soaring vacancy rates, plummeting prices, and developer bankruptcies. The enormous increase in office space resulting from the speculative investments of the '80s ran into declining demand. But again, as the national economies of the two nations recovered from the steep but short recession that started the decade, the economies of the two cities revived also. The cheap, vacant space proved an advantage, as growing firms found that they could expand without hindrance. Moreover, developers and financial institutions proved more cautious than in the past, with the result that new development did not race ahead of demand. In fact, by the beginning of the new century the slack had been absorbed, rents were rising far faster than the overall rate of inflation, and firms were having trouble acquiring sufficient space for their needs. Much of the development that did occur involved the conversion of vacant or underutilized warehouse and industrial space into offices and condominiums rather than new construction. Consequently, the face of the two cities changed relatively little; rather, the physical transformation achieved during the 1980s solidified.

This chapter examines, first, the heightened importance of global cities within the world economy during the latter part of the twentieth century. Second, it describes changes in the production of, and demand for, space. Finally, it analyzes the effect of economic change and government policy on the physical development of London and New York. The following chapter investigates the causes and consequences of cyclicity in real-estate markets and the similarities and differences in the property development cycle that occurred in London and New York between 1980 and 2000.

THE INCREASED IMPORTANCE OF GLOBAL CITIES

New York and London, along with Tokyo, are the preeminent global cities, as defined by their influence on world financial markets. Recent work emphasizes that these cities are not unique in being heavily involved in global flows of capital, that international transactions do not comprise the largest share of their economic base, and that other cities have more rapidly growing financial and business services (FBS) sectors.[9] Nevertheless, in the sheer magnitude of their FBS sectors, the number of foreign firms doing business within them, and their cultural and social connections with the rest of the world, London and New York can claim to be in a different league from other cities. An investigation of the driving forces behind real-estate investment in recent decades uncovers the dominant role played by those economic sectors most closely tied to the global economy in stimulating development. Especially during the '80s the FBS sectors were key; in the '90s, although the two economies became somewhat more diverse, FBS—especially the securities industry—continued to play a major role.[10]

Initial analyses of the rising importance of global cities[11] generally offered three reasons for the phenomenon: (1) the greater size and velocity of world capital flows; (2) the increased need for centralized command-and-control posts in a decentralized world economy; and (3) the extensive technical infrastructure needed by the FBS industries. These arguments were based on observations of growth driven by FBS in the '80s. Later, renewed expansion of these cities was dependent also on the surprising rapid growth of media-related, informational, and cultural enterprises. In New York particularly, the '90s saw an eruption of Internet and telecommunications firms, which were nowhere evident when the first edition of this book was written.

World Capital Flows

Several factors produced the explosion in the FBS sectors that fueled the economies of both London and New York in the boom years at the end of the century and spurred their physical redevelopment. The internationalization of investment and the growth of international trade had greatly heightened the importance of the financial industry and financial markets. The restructuring of companies, the rapid expansion of mergers and acquisitions, and the restless search by corporations for low-cost production sites and marketing advantages accelerated the volatility of capital and thereby enlarged the role of firms that specialized in managing flows of capital. According to Sassen, transactions increasingly took place between firms located in financial centers rather than within the large American banks.[12] In other words, while the management of manufacturing and retail industries became more and more integrated *within* large corporations, ever-greater financial flows were increasingly controlled through joint ventures, deals, and trades involving numerous actors. During the '90s the soaring stock market, growth in venture capital and other niche investment firms, and expansion of the NASDAQ exchange in New York further enlarged the financial sector, more than compensating for contraction in the traditional banking sector resulting from downsizing and mergers.

The debt crisis that began in the 1970s had cut off third-world outlets for investment at the same time as financial institutions continued to acquire massive amounts of capital from pension and mutual funds. Moreover, this capital was increasingly either lent directly to borrowers by investors, who purchased interest-bearing bonds, or used to purchase equity in firms. Thus, instead of savings flowing into commercial banks and then being lent by these banks to firms seeking to grow, funds circumvented the traditional banking system (a process known as "disintermediation"). This shift greatly increased the activity level and profits of investment bankers, who were the underwriters and traders of these instruments, and investment banking firms accordingly added personnel and operational space.

A host of other financial "products" was invented, including "swaps"[13]—exchanges of debt holdings among institutions; junk bonds—high-yield notes that were rated below investment grade;[14] and index futures—agreements to purchase a group of stocks at a preestablished price at a later date. Globalization of investment and production increased the possibility of loss through currency devaluation or sudden, unforeseen market shifts, stimulating the development of new financial instruments as hedges against risk. The securitization of debt (initially mortgages and third-world debt, then consumer debt, including student loans) meant that banking institutions could "bundle"—that is, aggregate—their loans to businesses and individuals, then convert them to attain liquidity through selling their loans for an amount based on the present value of their expected returns.

The development of markets for all of these novel financial products magnified the number of instruments traded within what had become an increasingly closed and volatile system of circulation of capital among the most developed countries. In the meantime, takeovers and leveraged buyouts fueled the volume of new debt issues. Once-conservative investment institutions, ranging from university endowments to major insurance companies, sought the high rates of return offered by speculative financial instruments and became far more dynamic players in the hyperactive financial world.[15]

Deregulation of the financial industry combined with the various product innovations and huge increases in capital flows to heighten the frenetic trading activity and deal making that characterized the financial world of the two cities. In the United States the Reagan and Bush administrations' distaste for enforcing antitrust laws allowed the mergers and acquisitions and leveraged buyouts to involve more and more companies and greater and greater sums of money, along with ever-larger phalanxes of legal and financial advisers. Despite wide publicity surrounding its prosecution of Microsoft for violating antitrust laws, the Clinton administration was no more zealous in blocking the giant buyouts and vast mergers that transpired during the '90s, especially in banking and media. The relaxation of the barriers that had existed between different types of financial institutions, such as investment, savings, and commercial banks,[16] further stimulated growth within the financial service industries.

Changes in the world financial system during the last quarter-century were direct causes of London's spatial restructuring, especially within the "square mile" constituting the City. Response to foreign competition led to the weakening of restrictions on London's financial firms, culminating in the "Big Bang" of 1986. At the same time as fixed commissions on all domestic securities transactions were eliminated (a move that had taken place in the United States a decade earlier), membership on the stock exchange was opened to foreign institutions for the first time. Not only did these changes directly result in greater business activity, but they attracted numerous foreign firms, which mainly sought space in the vicinity of the City of London. As described by Michael Pryke, "The City was to become the hub not of a culturally familiar, slow-paced, empire-oriented regime of trade finance but of a new fast-moving capitalism in which the City itself was to become equally international."[17] Many of the newcomers, however, ultimately found that the increase in financial activity did not meet their anticipations.

As corporate debt shifted from bank loans to direct borrowing, the major banks lost their previous dominance of financial transactions. Nonetheless, from the early 1970s onward, branches of foreign banks increased in number within both London and New York and continued to expand throughout the rest of the century.[18] The growing volume of international trade, the greater presence of foreign subsidiaries in all economic sectors, the increasing numbers of executives from abroad in connection with this internationalized economic activity, and the end of fixed exchange rates all contributed to the demand for retail and commercial banking services. Growth in the real-estate industry itself stimulated bank expansion, since almost all construction loans emanated from the banking sector. Moreover, as large international banks like Barclay's and Citibank increasingly took on functions similar to those of investment banks by acting as financiers for corporate mergers and acquisitions, they too got caught up in the cycle of speculative growth within the corporate investment arena.[19]

Agglomeration Effects

Transactions in the various securities took place mainly on trading floors within individual firms rather than through the exchanges. Nevertheless, the major investment banks and the headquarters of commercial banks felt it necessary to cluster close to the old markets. Because there is a very high level of interaction both among financial firms and between the financial sector and the concerns that provide it with legal, public relations, management consulting, and other services, this group of enterprises is led to settle only in those locations where an agglomeration of financial and advanced-services firms already exist.[20] Accountants, lawyers, tax consultants, and other advisers to the deal-makers also highly valued proximity to the investment bankers, since their presence at meetings of the various parties to a deal was frequently required. Large suburban firms have continued to rely on Manhattan for most of their service needs despite some gradual decentralization.[21] Thus, even firms headquartered outside the London and New York central business districts (CBDs) apparently found it more convenient to obtain business services within the supermarket of their dense advanced-services agglomerations rather than closer to home.[22]

Proximity was crucially important for the participants in a major deal. For example, the account in *Barbarians at the Gate* of the marathon negotiations in the buyout of RJR Nabisco shows that numerous investors, as well as virtually every significant law firm and investment bank in the country, took part.[23] Although Nabisco's headquarters was in Atlanta, Georgia, and its subsidiaries were scattered around the world, the action, which involved hundreds of corporate officers, investment bankers, lawyers, and financial advisers, took place in New York. On numerous occasions discussions lasted until dawn, and the presence of principals would suddenly be required at extremely odd hours. One cannot imagine where else but in Manhattan it would have been possible to assemble all the participants. Only the common location within a major financial center of the financial and legal firms involved permitted the necessary transactions.

As well as responding to the burgeoning demand for space to house the rapidly growing FBS sectors and their workforce, property development activity was fueled by the ready supply of funds flowing into the real-estate industry. Property investment became interchangeable with other kinds of debt and equity commitment. Previously, because of its low liquidity and unique characteristics, property investment had been the province of a limited group of financial institutions and knowledgeable individuals. Now, however, greater opportunities for real-estate investment syndication, in which limited partners did not take an active role but received an income stream and could sell their interests in a project fairly easily, eliminated any reason but rate of return to prefer one type of investment over another. The prospect of high speculative gains attracted many to the property market. Moreover, the favorable tax treatment that real estate received in both the United Kingdom and the United States, although especially the latter, often tipped the balance of investment decisions toward it, thereby increasing the flow of capital into the development industry.

Decentralization of Production

In her discussion of the causes of global city formation, Sassen emphasizes the effect of the dispersal of manufacturing and of such routine business-service functions as claims processing or monitoring of inventories.[24] Her argument is that spatial decentralization within the large corporation makes necessary the elaboration of sophisticated managerial functions to maintain control over the disparate parts. These managerial-control functions, she asserts, are physically concentrated: "The spatial dispersion of economic activity has brought about an expansion in central functions and in the growing stratum of specialized firms servicing such functions."[25] Only a few cities offer a pool of sophisticated personnel, technological capabilities, and consultant services sufficient to enable the direction of such complicated organizations. Thus, the concentration of economic control within a small number of corporations makes necessary the existence of geographic centers to manage a dispersed production and marketing system.

Sassen's analysis is partly correct: The specialized firms that provide services to the management of multinational corporations continued to be concentrated, as shown in the Schwartz studies cited above. Sassen does not, however, convincingly demonstrate that the "central functions" occur in global cities, and she in fact modifies her argument in later work. There she considers that only certain kinds of headquarters need to locate in major cities. These are of firms in highly competitive and innovative activities, firms with highly internationalized businesses, or firms that constitute part of the producers' services complex.[26] The out-migration of the corporate headquarters of manufacturing, transportation, and retail firms from New York indicates that no necessary connection exists between central management functions and geographic location.[27] The number of Fortune 500 manufacturing and mining enterprises headquartered in New York was more than halved between 1965 and 1976; it dropped by an additional 43 percent, from 84 to 48 firms, or to less than 10 percent of the 500 biggest industrial firms, in the next twelve years, even while the size and number of big financial firms headquartered in New York were expanding.[28] In 1999, 45 of the largest firms, including financial and media firms, had headquarters in New York City, and an additional 20 were located in its suburbs.[29]

In contrast with their U.S. counterparts, British industrial headquarters remained clustered in London, where in 1990 they still comprised more than half of such offices in the country.[30] The commanding status of London stemmed primarily from a combination of cultural factors and the political hegemony of the capital within a highly centralized state, rather than from purely economic causes.[31] In other words, other factors besides economic efficiency impelled British corporations to establish their headquarters in London. And even in the United Kingdom, London's importance for internal control of large manufacturing corporations was diminishing.

Large multinational corporations depend on networks of suppliers and distributors that are geographically dispersed, and their own offices, plants, and laboratories likewise span the globe. Thus, location of corporate headquarters in a global city does not bring them into proximity with the essential components of their operations. Moreover, these firms can easily purchase accounting, advertising, and legal services without being physically close to the providers. In short, while restructuring has increased the power of a small number of corporations over the worldwide production of goods and services, the headquarters of these firms have not flocked to the global cities. Intensification of work within the headquarters still there, however, probably did add to the number of jobs and transactions taking place within London and New York. Moreover, many firms located outside these cities retain an agent or office within them, thereby further adding to economic activity.[32]

Technological Factors

A number of contemporary theorists have stressed the importance of information, rather than natural resources or physical capital, to economic development. In the words of Manuel Castells,[33] contemporary capitalism is defined by the "informational mode of development." The impact of telecommunications and computer technology on the locational choices of firms cuts two ways. Even though new technologies foster decentralization by reducing the need for physical proximity among participants in a production process, they free those units that find advantages in city-center locations to seek out core areas, rather than staying with the routine processing sections of the enterprise. Thus, headquarters can remain in London and New York after routine operations have departed, and firms headquartered elsewhere can maintain a presence within them.

Within the "space of flows," as Castells characterizes the new world economy, certain places stand out because they have the labor pools and technological structures to support the computer and telecommunications systems necessary for the management of the global economy. The enormous expansion in financial and advanced business services depended on the development of a technology adequate to handle the soaring volume of transactions. And, in a circular process, only relatively few centers had sufficient activity to support the necessary infrastructure.[34]

Nevertheless, according to a study by Coopers & Lybrand Deloitte, London and New York did not have an absolute advantage in these technologies.[35] At least six other office centers (New Jersey, Chicago, Los Angeles, Paris, Tokyo, and Singapore) all offered a sufficient technological base, and the number is rapidly increasing. The requirements for modern firms relying on information retrieval and processing include a heavily backed-up communications grid and a pool of technical personnel to operate and repair equipment. Modern office structures with building managers who continuously upgrade the information and telecommunications systems are also necessities.[36] In 1980 many old buildings were not sufficiently adaptable for renovation to accommodate the demand for large trading floors and adequate space for cables and outlets. Business leaders and public officials in many cities, however, were aware of these needs and increasingly invested in their provision. The rapid installation of fiber-optics systems linking most large office centers further reduced the edge of London and New York. By the end of the century, even all second-tier cities offered linkages to broadband fiber-optic cables. In addition, within the two global cities the high level of traffic congestion and histories of insufficient investment in transport (a non-high-tech but equally significant part of the infrastructure) meant that both failed to provide easy physical access to their business districts. Thus, while the technological infrastructure of London and New York has been a necessary underpinning of their global-city status, it does not guarantee their future dominance.

In summary, then, London and New York used their preeminence as the world's leading locations for securities and money markets to capture, in absolute terms, substantial growth in the financial and advanced-services industries during the last two decades of the twentieth century. At the same time, their relative position was declining in relation to competing cities (for New York, in the rest of the United States, and for London, in Europe). They already possessed the critical mass of resources needed to direct the financial flows that energized the world economy, but they also needed to provide appropriate space for expansion. The requirement was provision of offices that met the technological demands of the computer age and construction of luxury residential and high-end consumption facilities to cater to the needs of the leaders of the expanding industries. Although other cities competed vigorously to attract office-based industries, even the appeal of much lower operating costs elsewhere did not shake loose many of the firms anchored in London and New York. Their competitive edge, however, was threatened, and one of the factors driving policy was fear that rivals could offer superior, less expensive space.

THE 1980s BOOM

Comparisons with other cities manifest the preeminence of London and New York as office-based service centers (Table 2.1). Worldwide, only Tokyo and Paris were in the same league as measured by office space; within Britain and the United States their status was supreme.

In terms of capital value, central London in 1990 contained an estimated 60 percent of the United Kingdom's entire office stock.[37] While New York's share of the national total was considerably less, it still approximated a dominating 21 percent.[38] Los Angeles, even after a major expansion in the 1980s and despite its overall economic and demographic competitiveness, had less than one-third the office space of New York. Chicago, the nearest challenger, possessed less than half. The area closest to Manhattan in the size of its office stock is its own metropolitan periphery within New Jersey, southern Connecticut, and Westchester County; these adjacent locales contained 209 million square feet of space in 1990.[39] Although other European and American cities added larger amounts of space in percentage terms at the peak of the development boom in the late '80s, none equaled the increment to London and New York in absolute numbers (Table 2.1).[40]

Table 2.1. Office Market: Comparable Cities

City	Sq. ft. of office stock, 1990 (millions)*	Sq. ft. added, 1985–90 (millions)
New York	243.0	35.0
Tokyo	189.0	n.a.
Paris	171.7	6.3
London	154.7	26.0
Chicago	103.0	18.2
Frankfurt	82.8	8.6
Los Angeles	75.0	20.0

*Different sources disagree on the magnitude of these figures. Richard Ellis (1991) estimates the stock of Paris at 185 million square feet, of Frankfurt at 85.6 million square feet, and of Tokyo at 163.7 million square feet. A comparable set of figures is not available for 2000, but, given the relatively small amount of new office construction that occurred during the 1990s, this table gives a fairly good picture of the relative size of the office sector among the cities listed.
Source: Byrne and Shulman (1991).

Table 2.2 shows the magnitude of the office development surge during the '80s. In both cities, but particularly in London, most new investment was in commercial rather than residential property.[41] London added nearly 30 percent to its office supply and New York more than 20 percent, almost all in redeveloped areas rather than on green-field (i.e., undeveloped) sites. This redevelopment took place either within the already developed CBDs or within nearby areas occupied by residences and small businesses. Some of it required the demolition of occupied structures, but the largest projects were placed on vacant land generated by the abandonment of obsolete transportation, manufacturing, wholesale market, and port facilities or created by landfill.[42]

Residential redevelopment expanded as well during the 1980s and again during the '90s, although in neither city did it rival earlier peaks. When measured by the value of new orders obtained by contractors, annual private house-building activity within Greater London increased sixfold between 1980 and 1987, with a net gain of 110,000 dwelling units during the period.[43] Within inner London the great bulk of the additions to the housing stock was attributable either to conversions, primarily within the inner London boroughs of Camden, Kensington, and Westminster, or to new construction on derelict land in the Docklands.[44]

In New York City between 1981 and 1987 there was a net gain of about 50,000 housing units, the first time in a quarter of a century that the housing stock grew continuously for six consecutive years.[45] Another 155,000 units were added be-

Table 2.2. Office Stock and Net Additions, 1981–1990

	London[a]	New York[b]
(1) Office stock, 1990 (millions of sq. ft.)	154.7[c]	243.0
(2) Net addition, 1981–1990 (millions of sq. ft.)	44.7	53.0
(3) (2) as percentage of (1)	29	22
(4) (1) as percentage of metropolitan area stock	61	54

[a] Central London and Docklands only.
[b] Manhattan only.
[c] Richard Ellis gives the figure of 152 million square feet for central London, not including Docklands. As of July 1990 an additional 2.7 million square feet had been completed in Docklands with an additional 6.9 million square feet under construction (Meuwissen, Daniels, and Bobe, 1991).

Other sources give larger numbers for both central London and Manhattan.

Estimates of office stock vary according to whether they include government-owned and -occupied offices, how the measure of net as opposed to gross space is calculated, whether buildings that were converted from other uses or are mixed-use structures are included, and, in the case of London, where the boundaries of central London are drawn.
Sources: Byrne and Shulman (1991); Byrne and Kostin (1990); Real Estate Board of New York, unpublished data, 1991; Jones Lang Wootton Consulting and Research (1987); Richard Ellis (1991); Coopers & Lybrand Deloitte (1991).

tween 1987 and 1996,[46] many of these attributable to the reclamation of abandoned housing under the Mayor's Ten-Year Housing Program.[47] Between 1981 and 1987, 33,000 units were added to the city's housing stock as a consequence of either conversions from nonresidential to residential use or conversions within the residential sector;[48] there were 7,000 more conversions between 1993 and 1996.[49] Almost all of these conversions took place in the gentrifying neighborhoods of Manhattan and Brooklyn. Moreover, the great bulk of new residential construction occurred in Manhattan on previously utilized land.[50]

London

By the end of the '80s London was witnessing the largest office-building boom in its history. During the mid-1970s a rise in interest rates had meant that property companies were no longer able to meet their obligations based on current earnings; their shaky financial situation, following on a decade of speculative growth, had threatened many banks and required intervention by the Bank of England.[51] A decade afterward, however, surplus space had been absorbed, and the anticipated advent of the Big Bang and, later, of European integration provoked high expectations of exploding demand and the seeming assurance of ever-higher rates of return. The ensuing boom signaled the reentry of banks into large-scale property lending after the secondary bank crisis of the 1970s, although insurance companies and pension funds remained wary of risking their assets on the property market.[52] A small number of development companies was behind most of the new speculative enterprises,[53] and much of the financing came from Japanese banks.

The initiative for promoting redevelopment activity in London did not come from a local-growth coalition of business leaders and governmental officials, as had been the case in many American cities.[54] Rather, the urgings of the national government, which incorporated Margaret Thatcher's views that private investors operating in a free market would create local economic growth, opened up London's once highly regulated property development arena for speculative ventures. According to Harding, the shift in local government priorities from an emphasis on social welfare to economic boosterism "was forced through from the national level."[55]

After the Thatcher government took office in 1979, it introduced a series of measures intended to spur private economic activity and diminish local-authority activism. In 1982 the capital gains tax was indexed to the rate of inflation, greatly increasing the potential profitability of property ownership; reduction of corporation taxes further encouraged activity by property companies. The Bank of England relaxed its requirement that primary banks be located within the square mile around its building on Threadneedle Street, thereby opening up additional territory for office space to house banking operations.[56] The government's establishment of the London Docklands Development Corporation (LDDC) and of an

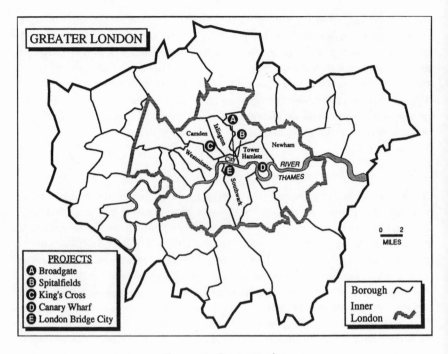

Figure 2.1. Greater London

enterprise zone in the Isle of Dogs portion of Docklands attracted a massive influx of capital to that partially abandoned area.[57] In addition, the central government put considerable pressure on local authorities to relax planning regulations,
sell property, and enter into joint ventures with the private sector. Through a series of circulars, legislation, and decisions by the Secretary of State for the Environment, it pressed local authorities to grant planning permission more readily. It
capped (i.e., put a ceiling on) local-authority expenditure, forcing localities to look
to the private sector for benefits that had previously been publicly financed. Centrally imposed limits on their revenue-raising capacity caused local authorities to
regard sales of publicly owned land to property developers as a potential revenue
source; central-government interdictions on land banking also stimulated localities to put land in the hands of developers.

    Each of the 33 local authorities that made up Greater London set its own de-
velopment policy. Until the abolition of the Greater London Council (GLC) in
1986, London's boroughs nominally conformed to the Greater London Development Plan, which the GLC approved in 1969. This plan gave high priority to construction of council housing and stimulation of manufacturing employment. Lack
of support for the plan by the Conservative central government, however, weak-

ened its mandate well before its actual abrogation.[58] Once the GLC was abolished, its plan had no status, and the Secretary of State for the Environment had the task of providing "strategic planning guidance" to the local authorities, each of which was required to formulate a development plan that would "facilitate development while protecting the local environment."[59] During the '80s developers avoided building in jurisdictions whose councils made life difficult for them.[60] Even though the British tax system stopped rewarding local authorities that attracted business enterprises when Parliament established a national business tax, few authorities could afford to ignore the benefits of new investment in terms of increased employment and services.[61] Therefore, they became increasingly competitive with one another, and even the more recalcitrant borough councils eventually assumed a prodevelopment posture. By the end of the '90s all local authorities had become willing partners in development schemes. At the same time, the renewed importance of London-wide strategic planning and the termination of special status for the Docklands meant that competition among the boroughs had lessened (in contrast to the New York metropolitan region, where the battle between New York and New Jersey for office occupants had, if anything, intensified).

Much of the new office construction went up on land that had been in the possession of public bodies, which they released initially as a consequence of the Thatcher government's promptings. Local authorities had originally acquired large holdings in anticipation of building housing or other public facilities on them. Other governmental corporations—for example, British Rail and the Port of London Authority—found themselves owning tracts on which the previous uses had become obsolete. Such vacant or derelict property became the sites for major construction projects.

The freeing up of developable sites, especially around London's numerous railroad stations, along with demands from potential tenants for more modern buildings, spurred many schemes. Developers, accustomed to the formidable barriers to planning permission that had long restricted new construction within London, responded quickly to their new opportunities. As one of Britain's most prominent speculative developers declared when asked about his siting criteria: "Projects went wherever people would let them."[62] Another head of a very large company commented: "Planning had been archaic, disorganized, unpredictable, fraught with pitfalls. You spent your time bargaining like a lunatic. It could take 20 years to get permission." The unaccustomed compliance of local authorities loosed a flood. At the same time, changes in technology had made the low ceilings and small floor areas of most existing office buildings obsolete. Potential tenants had begun to indicate a preference for high-quality space over a central location, which until then had been the sine qua non of site selection.[63] This shift, combined with the early successes of fringe-area projects like Broadgate, which was located on the edge of the City of London, made feasible the development of property formerly considered unsuitable for offices.

THE PROPERTY BUST

The downfall of the property markets in London and New York trailed the October 1987 stock market crash by about two years. Once in motion, however, the loss in value of property was both swift and steep. The failure of most observers to predict the end of the boom magnified its abruptness. Experienced property-market analysts had shown a remarkable lack of prescience concerning the future of the market. In a book written earlier but whose publication coincided with the free fall in property values, members of a London property consultancy began their chapter on prospects for the property industry by commenting: "1987 and 1988 have marked a clear turning point for the property industry. In our view, these years represent the final emergence of property from the long backwash of two major recessions in the last fifteen years."[64] While noting some potential instability, they went on to say: "Property companies, indeed, might stand as a model of the Thatcherite economy: a freer market, a rash of new enterprises growing rapidly on the back of readily available loan and equity finance—and a crop of new property millionaires to provide an example to the rest of us."[65] Similarly, Jones Lang Wootton Consulting and Research, on the eve of the property recession, claimed that its 1987 study of office demand "has provided yet further evidence of the strength of the Central London Office Market."[66]

On the other side of the Atlantic, analysts expressed only slightly less optimism. In a report about the New York economy written the year after the stock market plummeted, the Port Authority's research arm showed some caution but nevertheless prophesied: "We would expect that some proposed projects will be postponed or canceled. This is a moderating picture: the Manhattan real estate market is not generally considered to be overbuilt and will remain one of the strongest ones in the U.S."[67]

The lagged effect of continued investor confidence in 1988 and 1989 meant that millions of square feet of new space were becoming available just when demand was dropping precipitously. Figures depicting average rents and vacancy rates indicate the steepness of the decline in real-estate values that ensued just after the boom peaked in 1989. Table 2.3 records the sudden downward movement of the office market;[68] steep as the drop shown is, however, rental figures are misleadingly high, as they show rents paid by primary tenants who may have sublet their space at a loss.[69] In many cases, the values of buildings fell considerably below the amount of principal outstanding on their mortgages.

The collapse in real-estate values quickly rippled through the entire financial sector; in turn, troubles in financial institutions holding large real-estate investments aggravated the property situation as their own needs for office accommodation shrank. According to the *Economist,* in the first five months of 1990 the shares of half of the property companies listed on the London stock market lost more than one-quarter of their market value;[70] for more than 25 percent of the 80

Table 2.3. Average Office Rents and Vacancy Rates

London (in pounds per net buildable sq. ft.)					
City— Average rent	Vacancy rate (%)	West End— Average rent	Vacancy rate (%)	Docklands— Average rent	Vacancy rate
1986	30	3.5	25	4.0	15	n.a.
1988	55	4.0	50	3.0	25	n.a.
1990	50	15.0	55	7.0	24	n.a.
1991	44	17.1	52	10.0	24	n.a.
1998	52	6.0	55	n.a.	n.a.	n.a.
1999	52	5.0	60		33*	2.5

New York–Manhattan (in dollars per net buildable sq. ft.)					
Average rent	Vacancy rate (%)	Average rent	Vacancy rate (%)	Downtown average rent	Vacancy rate (%)
	Midtown					
1980	22.9	2.1			13.3	5.1
1982	40.1	4.1			28.0	2.1
1984	39.6	5.4			31.3	6.4
1986	41.0	8.9			31.5	11.6
1988	41.2	10.7			35.3	12.6
1990	39.2	14.5			31.6	17.6
	Midtown North		*Midtown South*			
1996	37.0	10.5	23.0	14.0	25.2	21.0
1998	47.0	8.5	30.0	8.0	31.0	12.0
1999 (Dec.)	51.3	6.8	34.0	5.1	34.3	9.9
	Midtown					
2000 (Aug.)	61.0	4.9			42.0	5.0

Note: Figures are drawn from a variety of sources and are approximate. The sources are not wholly consistent with each other.
*Canary Wharf's rents are about £37 per square foot, while rents in other Docklands areas are about £28 per square foot.
Sources: Byrne and Kostin (1990); *Economist,* May 5, 1990; *Walls* (1991); *Financial Times,* April 30, 1992; information supplied by Real Estate Board of New York, 1992; GVA Grimley (2000); Insignia Richard Ellis (2000); GVA Grimley (1999); GVA Williams (1999); *New York Times,* September 19, 2000.

such firms listed, debt exceeded equity, and interest payments were more than twice their rent receipts.[71]

The weakness in the property market, resulting in nonperforming loans, undermined the asset base of major banks. In the years 1987–1990 banks had increased their property lending in Britain from £10 billion to £34 billion, or about 8 percent of total loans. However, since approximately 40 percent of these loans came from overseas banks, the British banking system suffered less than the American one from the consequences of falling property values. Moreover, foreign, especially Japanese, involvement was greater than that of British lenders in London's more risky ventures, as British banks restricted their participation mainly to less speculative endeavors.[72]

In New York the real-estate exposure of two of its largest banks, Chemical and Manufacturers Hanover, led them to a merger in 1991, which itself resulted in a major contraction of their space requirements and a consequent further weakening of the market.[73] Chemical Bank vacated its 800,000 square foot headquarters building on Park Avenue and its 1.2 million square foot data-processing facility downtown; the two banks were also to give up an additional 750,000 square feet of office space elsewhere in the city, and 70 to 80 branches were to be closed.[74]

As the real-estate crisis worsened, major developers found themselves in increasing difficulty. In New York the icon of the '80s, Donald Trump, underwent a complicated workout of his monumental indebtedness, estimated at more than a billion dollars.[75] Although Trump did not formally declare bankruptcy, he essentially turned over control of his assets to his creditors.[76] Similarly, in London Godfrey Bradman of Rosehaugh PLC, another celebrity developer whose rise had also symbolized the seeming triumphs of the times, defaulted on his loans. Bradman was forced to give up his leadership of the firm, which had a net indebtedness of £310 million.[77] Most serious of all was the crumbling of the empire of Olympia & York Developments Ltd. (O & Y), the world's largest development firm. Creator of Battery Park City in New York and Canary Wharf in London,[78] it was New York City's biggest office property owner (controlling nearly 22 million square feet)[79] as well as a major force in central London.[80] O & Y owed more than $18 billion, exceeding the indebtedness of most third-world nations.[81] Its tangle of debts created a symbiosis between the markets of the two cities, as it used its older New York buildings as collateral to finance its equity contribution to London's Canary Wharf.

Like the other developers in trouble, O & Y could not refinance its loans, as investors cut off lending to the property sector. Since all construction loans are short-term and intended to be refinanced through long-term mortgages when construction is finished, withdrawal of mortgage money from the market destroyed the viability of developers whose buildings were approaching completion. Firms like O & Y, which had issued short-term bonds backed by occupied buildings as collateral so as to finance further growth, were in the especially unenviable situation of needing to either pay off or roll over the bonds on a quarterly or even monthly basis.

The real-estate slump was not restricted to commercial development; in fact, residential properties had felt the downturn in the market before offices had. Even though serious housing shortages at low and moderate price levels persisted in both London and New York, the shock of the 1987 stock market crash set off a crisis in the luxury market. Thousands of new units in Docklands, intended for the rising stars of the City of London, and multitudes of new dwellings in Manhattan, created in time to beat the elimination of the 421a tax subsidy, flooded a shrinking market.

In New York the problem for developers of co-ops and condominiums was exacerbated by the 1986 federal Tax Reform Act, which eliminated passive losses for individual real-estate investors, thereby converting paper losses into real ones. Because the size of the tax loss, which was derived from a depreciation formula, was based on the value of the property rather than the individual investor's actual contribution, over the years its worth in taxes forgone by the government greatly exceeded the investor's stake. Once the tax advantages were lost, investors could no longer sustain underutilized structures, and a theoretical oversupply became real.[82] Since thousands of apartments had been purchased for tax purposes,[83] the termination of these tax advantages dealt a heavy blow to the upper end of the market.

Continued demand for *affordable* housing, on the other hand, had not elicited increased production by the public sector in either London or New York, and activity by nonprofit entities only somewhat compensated for governmental withdrawal. In Greater London, local authorities' production of dwellings shrank from more than 16,000 units in 1980 to 1,260 in 1987, rising only slightly to 1,818 in 1990, while nonprofit housing associations produced approximately the same number of units as local authorities in 1990.[84] In New York by the early 1990s most housing construction involved publicly subsidized affordable housing built by community nonprofit housing development corporations. The cuts in the city's capital budget resulting from the newest fiscal crisis, however, translated into serious reductions in support for these groups.[85] Plans for 1992 involved ending all major housing production programs, including new housing for moderate- to middle-income households and major rehabilitation of vacant buildings, thus limiting activity to moderate rehabilitation of occupied buildings.[86]

At the same time, the general economic recession that marked the end of the decade in Britain and the United States dampened retail sales. Consequently, vacancies glutted the market for retail space, and in New York returns on store rentals plummeted. Developers, who had based their optimistic revenue forecasts for mixed-use, office-retail, and residential-retail buildings on the very high earnings projected for street-level stores, failed to realize their rosy predictions. In London retail rents moved down only slightly, despite the rising level of vacancies. In Manhattan, however, the last three years of the '80s saw rents in prime Upper East Side areas slipping from a range of $150–$300 per square foot to $90–$225 per square foot.[87] The silver lining on the retail side, which kept the vacancy level from reaching the same proportions as in offices, was the continuing demand for space at some price. Whereas office use was simply contracting, many prospective retailers, previously frozen out of the market, stood ready to take advantage of bargains. Consequently, after Manhattan retail vacancies shot up by about 75 percent between 1988 and 1990, they began to decline in 1991.[88] Although the return from many of these establishments was insufficient to cover the owners' carrying costs, it was in no one's interest to let the property remain vacant. Thus, in Manhattan the fall in retail rents stimulated a minor resurgence in marginal

service establishments, such as coffeehouses and bookstores, that had been driven
out in the '80s; X-rated video outlets, odd-lot retailers, and suburban chain stores
also moved in to fill the gap.

REVIVAL

Improvement of the U.K. national economy gradually stimulated recovery in
London's property market. The city's economic output declined between mid-1989
and the start of 1991 to a negative 6 percent annual rate and did not reach positive
growth until the end of 1992. By 1994, however, London's gross domestic product was rising at an estimated rate of nearly 6 percent, and it continued near this
level for the next several years.[89] Total employment peaked in 1988 at 3.5 million, fell by almost half a million in the next five years, then slightly exceeded the
1988 level one decade later.[90] During most of the '90s office expansion involved
the take-up of existing space; at the same time, much obsolete office and warehouse property was converted to residential and leisure uses.[91] New office construction sank in value by 1993 to slightly more than one-fifth of its 1989 peak
and only increased slightly by the end of 1998 to about 40 percent of its 1989
level.[92] As a consequence of conversions and relatively little growth in supply,
rent levels recovered strongly from their low point in the mid-1990s, achieving a
growth rate of nearly 7 percent in 1999.[93] In contrast to office construction, building
of new residential structures climbed sharply upward, surpassing the 1988 peak
in 1997.[94]

Favorable economic conditions in the '90s did not produce the wild speculative ventures of the earlier period within real-estate markets. Whereas the '80s
boom in office construction was driven by the availability of capital, growth of
supply in the '90s proceeded in response to demand, as lenders scrutinized projects
more carefully and demanded that tenant commitments be in place before a building could go up. Banks and insurance companies had become leery of committing funds to property ventures, requiring developers to put substantial amounts
of their own funds into their projects and demanding equity stakes in the property
for themselves. Both new construction and conversions incorporated the specifications of office occupants. By contrast, the residential market was more speculative.
Very high earnings in the financial industry and the general professionalization of
employment heightened the demand for luxury accommodation.[95] Despite substantial new construction and residential conversion, vacancy rates remained low.

In the '90s London's policy-makers changed their approach toward planning
and regeneration. Government programs for decayed areas now required participants to form development partnerships involving participation by business, government, and community representatives. Initially, the City Challenge program,
sponsored by the Conservative government, then its later and still-continuing offspring, the Single Regeneration Budget (SRB), required collaboration among dif-

ferent elements to put together proposals for the development of target areas. The concept of partnerships spread beyond collaboration on specific projects, and a number of ongoing coalitions involving multiple local authorities, business groups, and nongovernmental organizations sprang up. These partnerships conducted research, worked out strategies, and generally changed the character of the development process, making it less competitive and more likely to create positive externalities. The increased potential for community betterment through planning gain (i.e., developer-provided benefits in exchange for planning permission)[96] made communities that had previously opposed large-scale development more compliant. Although somewhat comparable to America's local-growth coalitions, these partnerships have been less dominated by narrowly construed business interests. Along with the input of the London Planning Advisory Committee (LPAC), a body made up of the 33 boroughs, and the Government Office for London, they also increased the amount of coordination among the boroughs.

Even though efforts toward a coordinated development policy gained momentum as the years passed, London's 33 local authorities still adopted different stances toward development during much of the two decades between the ascendance of the Thatcher government in Westminster and the election of a London mayor. It is, therefore, useful when chronicling the development history of that period to discuss some parts of the metropolis separately.

The City of London[97]

Nowhere did governmental efforts to instigate local development activity have a greater effect than in the City, where more than 16.5 million square feet of office space was constructed between 1985 and 1990.[98] Until 1983, concerns with historic preservation and the obduracy of the various guilds and titled families holding ancient freehold rights had blocked much potential development within the square mile.[99] Since the City did not harbor the antagonism to business evident in the Labour-dominated boroughs, however, once the economic benefits of restricting growth ended, attitudes toward physical change easily became more flexible, and the commitment to tradition weakened.

For a long period, financial firms that already possessed space adjacent to the Bank of England benefited from their monopoly position and had no motivation to favor expansionary policies. Financial deregulation and competition changed the stakes. Competitive office development in the nearby Docklands threatened the interests represented within the Corporation of the City of London.[100] If the City refused to accommodate expansion when deregulation was prompting accelerated financial-sector activity, firms already located there risked losing their locational advantage as the center of gravity shifted eastward. On the other hand, landowning interests within the Corporation, as well as the Corporation itself, which owned 20 percent of the land in its jurisdiction, stood to make considerable money through more intensive development of their holdings. Moreover, when the central government introduced a uniform national business tax, to be distributed to localities on a formula basis, it gave to the City of London alone the right to keep 15 percent of the business rate collected within its boundaries. Thus, increasing local commercial property values would greatly enhance the City's revenue position.

Once the Corporation decided to reverse the previous conservationist direction, the City's administrative officers embarked on an active promotional effort. The planning director solicited advice from firms concerning their space needs and encouraged developers to seek planning permission for buildings to accommodate them.[101] In addition, he identified new developable land, including space over highways and railroad tracks. In the process, the local development plan was modified to raise floor area ratios ("plot ratios") sufficiently to permit an average 25 percent expansion in the size of buildings. While the local authority relaxed regulations and made discreet contacts with developers and potential tenants, it did not engage in an elaborate sales effort on the LDDC model[102] nor deal making in the frenzied New York City mode. Only in the case of the European Bank for Reconstruction and Development, which had been contemplating a site in the Docklands, was there an outright effort at enticing it to take a City location. An influential member of the governing body claimed that "it would be beneath us" to set up such an operation. Rather, he said, that "we create an atmosphere." He did note that the Lord Mayor possessed a trust fund allowing him to entertain foreign visitors, adding that "we like to meet people and mix, but we do it in a private way."

Initially, either because of this subtle form of public relations or simply in response to availability of new, first-class space, tenants rushed to let the additions to the City's office stock. The new space that came on the market in the City between 1981 and mid-1987 boasted almost 100 percent occupancy by the time of the October stock-market crash, 57 percent of it by banking and finance enterprises.[103] By far the largest single project adding to the stock during the latter part of the decade was the Broadgate, a joint venture between the privately owned development firms of Stanhope and Rosehaugh and the publicly owned British Rail. Costing more than £2 billion by 1991, this still ongoing enterprise transformed derelict railroad yards adjacent to Liverpool Street Station into a mixed-use retail and office complex. Its siting in the City "fringe," adjacent to the low-income East London commercial and residential borough of Tower Hamlets, represented a distinctive break with tradition. As the development's first fourteen buildings reached completion, initial success in attracting stellar tenants, even after the 1987 jolt to financial markets, seemed to augur unlimited possibilities for those developers willing to invest in the most technologically advanced, luxuriously appointed projects.

The story changed radically by 1990, then reversed itself again later in the decade. As a result of sustained contraction in the financial industry and simultaneous continued large-scale speculative construction, the City considerably ex-

Figure 2.2. Broadgate center courtyard

ceeded the rest of central London in the amount of commercial space left unoccupied during the recession. Like downtown Manhattan, however, it recovered rapidly by century's end. As the surplus space was absorbed, the vacancy rate plunged to 5 percent, while rents climbed to £52 per square foot on average (Table 2.3) and considerably above that for prime sites.

New construction only began to pick up once more in 1996, when work commenced on more than two million square feet of office space; by 1998 construction was proceeding at the rate of more than five million square feet a year.[104] Initially, the developers of new space were continental companies building for their own use. After a period of hesitancy caused by the Asian financial crisis, the pace of activity picked up again by the end of 1999. According to the Corporation of London's chief planner, the character of redevelopment in the '90s differed substantially from the previous decade: "In the 1980s the big personalities were developers. From 1995 on you don't see big developers any more. The big personalities are in business, and property is responding to business. . . . This made for a more stable environment."[105] Companies preferred to have structures custom-built to their requirements rather than moving into existing space, even if this caused a delay in their move.

The Corporation of London, which earlier had worked on attracting companies, had become less concerned with competition from the Docklands and saw its role as facilitator for businesses already committed to coming. In particular, its planners tried to assist firms in getting permission for buildings with large floor areas despite the constraints presented by the congestion and historic importance of the area. It also was working much more closely with neighboring boroughs. It was in part responding to pressure from the central government for partnership arrangements, but also it saw advantages to development in the fringe areas along its borders. The Corporation was keen to maintain itself as the primary central business district of London, and expansion could only occur through activity crossing into adjacent boroughs, with the City remaining as the heart of the district. Considerable conversion of office into residential space made the need for new territory even more exigent.[106]

Westminster

As home to the royal family, Parliament, government departments, and prestigious private firms, as well as London's most exclusive residences and hotels, Westminster has always constituted an extremely attractive location for office development. Unlike in the City, however, office uses had to compete with residential, hotel, and retail functions for space.[107] Resembling Manhattan's East Side in its array of different land uses,[108] Westminster likewise possessed residents who often found themselves at odds with developers and commercial occupants. A lengthy battle in the 1970s over the redevelopment of London's old wholesale food market in Covent Garden, located in the heart of Westminster by the theater district, mobilized numerous conservation groups and residents. The ultimate resolution of the original controversy was preservation of the old market buildings as a festive mall and the listing (i.e., protection as historic structures) of numerous surrounding buildings. The conflict left a legacy of mistrust, which was reactivated during the 1980s in a dispute over the intention of the Royal Opera House to erect an office building so as to finance renovation of its premises from the proceeds. The recession mooted this controversy, since the market for the office space had disappeared, and the opera house renovation eventually came to fruition in 1999, financed by proceeds from the National Lottery.

Covent Garden's renewal stimulated the subsequent transformation of the entire surrounding area to trendy retail and entertainment uses, featuring fashionable shops alongside cafés, restaurants, and bookstores. Changes within the market area came along with a general tendency toward the boutiquing of Westminster's commercial sector and an increased orientation toward tourism rather than services for residents. Like South Street Seaport, its counterpart project in New York, the rehabilitated Convent Garden satisfied those historic preservationists whose aims were limited to the conservation of architecture, demonstrated that property developers could prosper equally from renovation and new construction, and continued to provoke disdain from community organizations representing low-income groups and preservationists devoted to authenticity.

Whereas in the City of London the governing body relaxed its planning controls, Westminster's council, despite its Conservative majority and close ties to the Thatcher government, moved in the opposite direction. Intensified development threatened the substantial public amenities of the area,[109] and rising land prices squeezed out residents.[110] Increasingly, the council came to regard its mandate as protection of its residents rather than promoting business expansion,[111] especially once it became apparent that, under the uniform business tax, ratepayers would gain no advantage from commercial growth. The Westminster council refused to allow rezoning of residential property for commercial uses, and it insisted that the development of Paddington Basin, spurred by the construction of a rail link between Paddington Station and Heathrow Airport at the end of the '90s, be primarily residential. The Westminster council, unlike the Corporation of London, served only a residential constituency that had little economic interest in further development. Consequently, it subjected development proposals to ever-stricter examination, and its planning staff was committed to extracting as much planning gain as possible from development schemes. Between 1990 and 1999 the residential population of the borough increased by 25 percent, from 175,000 to 220,000.

The slower pace of office construction in Westminster than in the City left it with higher rents and a lower vacancy rate during the recession, and office owners enjoyed soaring property prices at the end of the '90s. Moreover, the character of commercial uses changed, as businesses seeking larger floor areas moved eastward, while entertainment and leisure functions took over vacated space. As well as boasting a notable number of tourism attractions, ranging from West End theaters to Westminster Abbey, the borough also contains most of London's major hotels. The council has sought to dampen hotel construction, but toward the end of the century it began to give permission for construction of small hotels.

Labour-Controlled Boroughs

Despite the preference of developers for operating within congenial Tory boroughs, several large projects and many smaller ones were planned or built during the 1980s in the inner-London Labour-controlled boroughs of Southwark, Camden, and Islington. The redevelopment of the Surrey Docks, south of the Thames in Southwark, was largely completed by 1989 and represented the first major crossing of the river by upscale development. The most important project there, London Bridge City, was owned by the Bank of Kuwait. Containing one million square feet of an office and retail complex on land adjacent to London Bridge Station, it is one tube stop away from the City and is the terminus of rail lines to the wealthy commuter areas surrounding the metropolitan area (the "home counties"). This complex succeeded in attracting the routine operations ("back offices") of many foreign and domestic banks, including Citicorp, the Banque Arabe et International, and Lloyds. Another million square feet was built nearby to accommodate the *Daily*

Mail, which had joined many of London's other newspapers in deserting Fleet Street in the City for the more spacious Docklands. Furthermore, by mid-1988, when the housing market had begun to crash, 5,000 units of housing, of which almost 90 percent was intended for owner occupation, were either completed or under construction in the Surrey Docks area.[112]

Intense community resistance within this working-class borough had little effect on these projects. The new developments were initially unrelated to their surroundings, the park and shops were not used by local people, and relatively few of the new jobs were taken by local residents. Since 80 percent of the housing was sold to outsiders, the population composition of the borough began to change. The council, which at the start of the decade consisted of traditional Labour politicians, was initially extremely unsympathetic to the community-based radicalism that fought the projects. As a result, it reflexively dismissed the proposals put forth by community organizations that were seeking alternative modes of development.[113] Interestingly, the old trade union–based Labour organization from which this council sprang did not feel threatened by the functional conversion that new development would bring. Rather, the councillors believed that office construction would revitalize the borough's economy and that the sons and daughters of working-class residents would find jobs in the white-collar enterprises quartered in the new structures.[114]

The expulsion of the old Labour leadership, however, did not change the course of development. At mid-decade, the previously excluded radicals gained control of the party machine, but planning powers over the area now belonged to the LDDC, and its strategy of market-driven property investment prevailed over council antagonism. Eventually, the council's new political leadership succumbed to the pressures emanating from the central government, and five years after its ascendance the borough was actively seeking planning deals with private developers, including the trading of land for concessions of housing, amenities, and job-training schemes.

A new planning and development director, hired during the '90s, became an adept proponent of commercial development. His reign coincided with the conversion of the previously seedy waterfront into an entertainment and leisure center.[115] The reconstruction of Shakespeare's Globe Theater and its adjacent exhibit space, previously opposed by the council, became a magnet for visitors. The Coin Street development, put together by an oppositional community coalition, as well as housing craft shops and low-income dwellings, contained one of London's most stylish restaurants. The renovated Butler's Wharf became a restaurant, gallery, and retail center. The new Tate Gallery of Modern Art occupied the structure of a huge old power station, opening with great fanfare in the spring of 2000. Various other museums, art galleries, and restored properties appeared, among them the Clink Prison Museum and the London Dungeon, which features "torture, execution, and the story of Jack the Ripper."[116] All of the various attractions were linked by an attractive landscaped walkway along the river. According to the

Figure 2.3. The reconstructed Globe Theater

development director, no one had formulated a master plan for Bankside; rather, the council acted opportunistically: "If we can use culture to attract the kind of development we want, we'll do it."[117]

Still, the Bankside only extended one block south of the river, and much of Southwark remained mired in poverty. The development director commented: "We aren't concerned over gentrification. We must overcome concentrated poverty. We want a balanced, mixed community." The Southwark Council intended to achieve this goal through increasing densities. Plans particularly centered on Elephant and Castle, a commercial and residential area, heavily populated by ethnic minorities, that the Government Office for London had identified as a strategic development node. In spring 2000, 21 development consortia were bidding to be designated as the developers of more than one million square feet of commercial space and 8,400 housing units. The strategy was to use market-rate units to subsidize the replacement of the existing 4,200 units of affordable housing. In addition, the national Single Regeneration Budget was providing £25 million for infrastructure and job placement programs. Since the council owned much of the land and had jurisdiction over giving planning permission for the rest, it could control the character of development.

In the borough of Camden, experienced community groups mounted strong resistance to the initiatives of developers during the '80s.[118] Nevertheless, British Rail saw another opportunity to exploit its landholdings proximate to a major sta-

Figure 2.4. The Tate Gallery of Modern Art

tion at King's Cross, and developers immediately showed strong interest in the project.[119] Ultimately, the council, feeling that it had no alternative course, agreed to negotiate with the developers. Similarly, in Islington the Labour local authority became active in negotiations with developers, despite considerable community dissent. Although gentrification of this borough (the home of Prime Minister Tony Blair) had proceeded rapidly throughout the '80s, large-scale developer interest only occurred toward the decade's end. In both Camden and Islington the real-estate slump of the '90s temporarily halted implementation of the proposed efforts. Thus, while the Labour-controlled boroughs did acquiesce in the strategy of property-led regeneration, by the time they did so, development opportunities had temporarily passed. As a consequence, except in the sections under LDDC control, these boroughs received relatively little property investment until the property market gained steam again in the latter part of the '90s. By then the borough councils, as in Southwark, had changed their views on development, seeing it as a chance to make a deal rather than a threat to their interests. Thus, three of the largest projects planned for the new century were in Southwark (Elephant and Castle), King's Cross, and Greenwich (Greenwich Peninsula).[120]

New York

The last quarter of the twentieth century saw New York riding an economic roller coaster. After the city suffered huge job losses and virtual governmental bankruptcy in the mid-1970s, an unexpected economic recovery began in 1977. The city's decline in the preceding years had been sharper than London's; likewise, its revival was more dramatic.[121] By 1981 office construction skyrocketed, rivaling, although never equaling, the pace of the early 1970s. During the 1990s recession, office construction halted altogether, and during the late '90s it revived only slowly, as lenders were reluctant to engage in the speculative financing of the earlier decade. Redevelopment in the '90s largely took the form of rehabilitation and conversion rather than new development. According to *Crain's New York Business,* upgrades of older office properties and conversions of industrial space added 15 million square feet of prime office space in two years (1998–1999), comprising an investment of $3 billion. This compared to an average annual rate of new construction of 6.9 million square feet during the peak years (1987–1989) of the '80s boom.[122] In particular, Manhattan's far West Side, south of 42nd Street, became a coveted location for telecommunications and Internet-related firms.[123] It profited from numerous fiberoptic cable linkages and proximity to the main cable, exceptionally large spaces, heavy weight–bearing floors, and huge elevators in old factory buildings. The area also became the home of scores of art galleries, driven out of SoHo by boutiques and rising prices and attracted by cheap, disused industrial space.

Downtown Manhattan prospered in the '90s as well. Having suffered from the highest vacancy rates in the city during the downturn, it became the focus of development policy. Business interests in the area formed the Downtown Alliance, a business improvement district (BID) and effective lobbying group. Because policy-makers were pessimistic that the surplus of office space, particularly Class B space, would soon, if ever, be absorbed, the city sponsored a program of tax incentives to promote the conversion of office buildings into residences in this previously all-commercial area. As described in *New York* magazine, "Preserva-

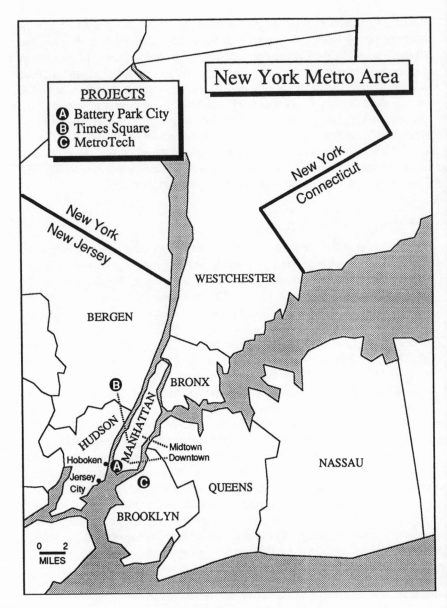

Figure 2.5. The New York Metro Area

tionists, good-government types, techies—and the free market—are working to-gether to do nothing less than turn this skyscraper national park into a 24-hour urban 'village' that breaks down the geographic and psychic space between com-merce, recreation, and daily life. The working model of Tomorrowland Wall Street is a hot-wired urban hive—dense, frenetic, whirring with synergies, a critical mass of art, industry, and communications."[124]

The city also offered incentives for upgrading the technical infrastructure of buildings to attract "new economy" firms in communications, media, and the Internet to the area. Primarily as a result of extraordinary growth in these sectors, downtown succeeded beyond anyone's imaginings in again becoming a desirable office location. In fact, the demand for offices became so great that developers shelved plans for residential conversions to pursue the more lucrative commer-cial office market. Thus, New York's "Silicon Alley" consists of Chelsea, once a factory district; Midtown South, formerly a secondary office area; and downtown, previously devoted wholly to the financial industry.

Even though the city's economy was in the midst of a period of extraordi-nary expansion, only one new major office project was under construction outside of Times Square. On the site of the old Coliseum, the city's former convention center, the Related Companies, headed by Stephen Ross, was building Columbus Centre, a very large, mixed-use complex. During the '80s, the Triborough Bridge and Tunnel Authority, which owned New York's Coliseum, insisted on ac-cepting the highest bid for its land, which had resulted in a building plan that aroused fierce objections to its size. Delays in accepting the plan caused by community objections got the project caught in the real-estate slump. The original developer, Mortimer Zuckerman, was awarded the right to develop the site in 1985 but for-feited it in 1994. Finally, in 2000, two years after he had been awarded control of the site, Ross received a $1.3 billion construction loan from the General Motors Acceptance Corporation. The project, reduced to a still massive 2.1 million square feet, was to house the headquarters of AOL–Time Warner, an auditorium for Jazz at Lincoln Center, a five-star Mandarin Oriental hotel, 225 luxury condominiums, and several floors of upmarket retail space.[125] It incorporated two characteristic aspects of turn-of-the-century real-estate financing. First, rather than relying on traditional bank lending for his construction loan, the developer borrowed from a nonbank lender. Second, his struggle to obtain financing only succeeded once he had anchor tenants in place.

Business groups. The role of business interests in promoting downtown was un-usual. Perhaps because of the global scope of their interests, New York's busi-ness leaders have not worked as vigorously as those in other American cities to frame an agenda for their metropolis.[126] Even the business press has noted the reluctance of corporate heads to become involved with city issues: "They view themselves as running worldwide enterprises that just happen to be located in New York. . . . It's almost provincial to be concerned and involved in what happens

here; that kind of local focus is for the quaint burghers out in Chicago and Atlanta."[127] New York's elite is philanthropically active, ornamenting the boards of
the city's numerous cultural institutions and contributing generously to them. A
number of upper-class good-government groups, some dating back to the start of
the twentieth century, reliably testify at hearings concerning major land use proposals. Yet, New York, like London, has had no powerful business-led growth
coalition to formulate a citywide planning strategy. The Real Estate Board of New
York takes positions on particular issues of concern to the industry—e.g., property and rent taxes, revisions to the zoning code. The Regional Plan Association,
a nonprofit good-government group, has proposed a development plan for the New
York region with little effectiveness. The New York City Partnership, an alliance
of chief executive officers, sponsors affordable housing and holds occasional forums but largely plays a low-key role.

During the 1975 fiscal crisis, New York's business elite strongly promoted
its conservative response to the budgetary shortfall;[128] after that, while it has lobbied extensively against taxes and has supported public-sector redevelopment
initiatives and transit improvements, it has not participated actively in redevelopment planning. Rather, particular elements of business—especially developers and
securities firms—influenced politicians directly through heavy contributions to
political campaigns.[129] The approach of these political influentials was not to press
for comprehensive solutions to New York's problems but to seek specific benefits such as tax abatements and zoning variances.

Public programs. Spending on major capital projects had virtually halted during
the years following the fiscal crisis and private-sector recession of the mid-1970s.[130]
After 1981, however, increased local revenues arising from the city's economic
revival combined with state and federal subsidies for economic development to
launch a number of major development projects. Chief among these were South
Street Seaport, Battery Park City, the Javits Convention Center, and the Times
Square Marriott and Grand Hyatt hotels, all located in midtown or downtown
Manhattan. The city paid for supporting infrastructure and granted tax subsidies;
it also used federal Urban Development Action Grants (UDAGs) to subsidize the
Seaport, developer Donald J. Trump's Grand Hyatt—his first major enterprise,
which adjoined Grand Central Station—and the massive Marriott, located in the
heart of Times Square. The Urban Development Corporation (UDC), later renamed
the Empire State Development Corporation (ESDC), a semi-independent agency
of the State of New York with the mission of promoting economic development,
was revived from bankruptcy by the infusion of new state funds. It managed the
construction of the convention center and the planning and infrastructure for
Battery Park City. The corporation's legal powers, exercised through separately
incorporated subsidiaries for each project (the Convention Center Development
Corporation, the Battery Park City Authority, the Times Square Redevelopment

Corporation), freed it from oversight requirements that affected city-sponsored efforts: It did not need to go through the normal process of community consultation for project approval; it did not have to request a variance[131] if it did not conform to the zoning law; and the city's governing bodies had no authority over it.

Tax subsidies. Besides participating in those major projects where public authorities took the initiative, private developers took advantage of tax-subsidy programs for new construction. Since under New York law all local revenue measures must be enacted by the state government, these programs were products of state legislative action; nevertheless, they applied to local property levies rather than state tax liabilities. The Industrial and Commercial Incentives Board (ICIB), which administered a tax incentive program for businesses, participated in office-building, hotel, and retail projects, initially almost all in Manhattan. Although the initial purpose of the ICIB had been to revive New York's manufacturing base, it quickly turned into a real-estate development program, and the construction of new speculative office buildings became equated with economic growth in the views of the program's sponsors. Two tax-subsidy programs for residential development—421a for new construction and J-51 for rehabilitation[132]—were also heavily used to assist luxury housing in Manhattan. On the East Side, always New York's wealthiest district, publicly subsidized projects included Donald Trump's Grand Hyatt hotel and his famous Trump Tower luxury retail and condominium residence, as well as the AT&T (now Sony) Building, designed by Philip Johnson as a postmodern statement, and across from it, the IBM building. In 1981 and 1982 alone, twelve office buildings, comprising more than 7 million net square feet, were completed on Manhattan's already very densely developed midtown East Side. Although restrictions were eventually placed on the tax incentive programs to direct them to less affluent parts of the city, before these limits were imposed late in the '80s, almost every building intended for wealthy business or residential occupants made use of such subsidies. (They were later restored for downtown Manhattan.)

The strategy of targeting firms facing lease expirations or seeking new or additional space and offering them tax breaks has continued through the administrations of Edward Koch, David Dinkins, and Rudolph Giuliani. Tax deals have gone to very wealthy firms in the most desirable parts of Manhattan, based on the argument that high rents and operating costs would otherwise drive them out of the city. Thus, for example, the investment firm Bear Stearns got a $75 million exemption from sales taxes; part of the break was tied to the creation of new jobs.[133] The city also gave additional tax relief to firms that had already received large tax benefits either directly or as part of a package of incentives for the buildings they occupied.[134] Within five years the Giuliani administration had granted more than $2 billion in tax breaks and other subsidies to more than four dozen of the city's biggest corporations.[135] Unlike the planning gain deals in London, besides stipulations for job retention and creation, the enforcement of which is dubious, there were no requirements for public benefits, and one clear detrimental effect was the shifting of the tax burden to small and medium-sized companies.

In the '90s downtown Manhattan received the benefit of the new subsidy programs discussed above as well as even greater subsidies for specific projects, justified as measures to keep businesses from fleeing the city. Currently pending is a deal that would cost the city and state about $1 billion to "retain" the New York Stock Exchange in lower Manhattan in response to its threat of moving to New Jersey. The Exchange claimed that it needed additional space for an enlarged trading floor, although recently, as the Exchange has contemplated moving to an entirely electronic trading system, the need for that floor has been questioned.[136] As of this writing, it is not clear whether the deal will actually be consummated, but it is illustrative of the kinds of special packages of benefits that the public sector has been putting together for particular firms.

Media responses. The New York press has largely acted as a reliable booster of real-estate investment. The failure of the mainstream media to offer a general assessment of the city's redevelopment priorities has meant that conflicts over particular schemes took the form of local skirmishes rather than contributing to a citywide debate over appropriate economic strategies. Although the architecture critics of the *Times* frequently found fault with particular buildings for their bulk and occasionally delivered broadsides against the city's failure to formulate coherent strategies for expansion,[137] the media largely did not question the basic equation of real-estate development with economic growth.[138] In particular, Donald Trump, New York's best-known (although by no means biggest) developer, adeptly used the media to promote his glamorous skyscrapers[139] and, by inference, the whole ambiance of Upper East Side luxury that surrounded them. Trump was not only man but metaphor. *New York* magazine,[140] in the preface to an excerpt from his autobiography, declared that "Donald Trump is one of the most remarkable figures of the roaring eighties—a true creature of the age. More than a New York real-estate developer and deal-maker, Trump has become the personification of hustle and chutzpa." *Newsweek,* which featured him on its cover, marveled:

> Donald John Trump—real estate developer, casino operator, corporate raider, and perhaps future politician—is a symbol of an era. He is the man with the Midas fist. For better or worse, in the 1980s it is OK to be fiercely ambitious, staggeringly rich and utterly at ease in bragging about it. . . . For the new rich, says a New York real-estate broker, the name [Trump on a building] is synonymous with "status."[141]

Although Trump faltered during the recession, he managed to avert bankruptcy and by 2000 was building both his long-delayed West Side apartment complex and, on the East Side, to the horror of its neighbors, the world's tallest residential building.

Intensity of development. New York, unlike London between 1986 and 2000, possessed a unified, centralized city government and a department of city planning; it nevertheless never produced a citywide development plan. Development proceeded project by project as developers assembled a site, raised financing, and exploited available subsidies. If they did not require zoning variances or seek zoning bonuses,[142] they did not need planning permission at all and could build as of right. The zoning code already offered a floor area ratio (FAR) of 12:1 (i.e., twelve square feet of floor space for every square foot of the total site) on most lots that were zoned for office use. It granted bonuses to developers who provided public amenities like plazas or subway station improvements; typically such awards raised the FAR to 15:1, three times the level of London. Developers could also purchase the air rights[143] from adjacent buildings, pyramiding these allowances on top of their bonuses, thus building even higher.[144]

The city government has largely refrained from developing plans that would specify its priorities as to kinds of structures, preferred locations, or desired amount of space. When influential civic groups, led by the Municipal Art Society, protested about overbuilding on the East Side, the City Planning Commission responded with a report recommending restrictions on East Side development and more permissive zoning on the Midtown West Side so as "to move development westward."[145] By the following year, however, when the proposal was implemented, hardly a buildable site remained on the East Side that was not already in process of development. Under the stimulation of this "new midtown zoning," which raised the allowable floor area ratio on the West Side from 15:1 to 18:1, many millions more square feet of office space were constructed even without the prospect of tax abatement. This was intended as a temporary inducement that would exist for only six years. Consequently, developers hastened to beat the deadline, constructing eight buildings, comprising 4.5 million square feet of space, in the last year of the program.[146]

New residential construction, almost all for the luxury market until 1987,[147] continued unabated wherever potential sites were not protected by historic-district status. Extremely strong demand for residential space in the heart of the city allowed developers to obtain extraordinarily high returns on their investments. Nevertheless, the city continued to provide tax benefits for luxury residential development under the 421a program until 1986. When the city government finally decided to end subsidies for buildings in central Manhattan, developers rushed to put foundations in the ground so as to take advantage of the tax benefits before they disappeared.[148]

The high level of development activity during the boom years of the '80s markedly changed the appearance of Manhattan.[149] The midtown and downtown office cores expanded and became much more dense. A number of large apartment buildings replaced low-rise structures on the Upper West Side and filled in the gaps remaining in the West Side Urban Renewal Program dating from the 1960s. Battery Park City, to the west of Wall Street, and Tribeca, an old industrial area just north of the financial district, gained thousands of housing units, producing a residential community in a part of New York that had been devoted wholly to business for well over a century. Huge new residential structures lined the East Side between the East River and Third Avenue. Almost all of the new construction in Manhattan required the demolition of existing buildings. In contrast, the development spurt of the century's end, relying much more heavily on conversions and rehabilitation, had a less obvious effect on the city's appearance.

The spin-off effects of both Manhattan booms were mainly felt across the Hudson River in New Jersey, where by 1989 a number of new, large commercial and residential projects lined the waterfront. At the beginning of the new century, millions more square feet were on the drawing boards to house back offices of, among others, Goldman Sachs, Chase Bank, Paine Webber, American Express, and Merrill Lynch.[150] Although New York City's boroughs felt some residential pressure, their business districts remained mostly untouched by office construction. Only one major project, MetroTech in downtown Brooklyn, represented a serious attempt to decentralize office functions to New York City's boroughs.[151] Undertaken during the Koch administration, this precedent seemingly did not impress the Giuliani administration, which launched no major projects except for baseball stadiums outside Manhattan.

A proposal to build a large-scale development at Hunters Point in Queens (Queens West), directly across the East River from Midtown Manhattan, hung fire for a decade, because of lack of developer interest.[152] Eventually, a single residential building arose on the site, and three more were under construction in 2000. Hoped-for commercial projects, however, remained unfulfilled in 2000, because of either the reluctance of businesses to move to Queens or governmental unwillingness to provide a sufficient level of subsidy.[153] The city does have a number of incentive programs to induce businesses to move to the boroughs. Critics of the administration, however, believe that site clearance and infrastructure investment are necessary prerequisites to establishing locations in the boroughs as major office centers. According to the developer who has been most active in the boroughs, creation of commercial centers there requires the city to do land assembly, not simply provide incentives to firms.[154]

ECONOMIC AND REAL-ESTATE CYCLES

The business cycles of the last quarter of the twentieth century affected London and New York very strongly. Tied as they were to global financial markets, they had little to buffer them from either the manic investment climate of the boom periods or the depressive withdrawal of capital during the declines. Thus, during the '80s they reached an apogee of wealth creation, physically reflected in the erection of huge new structures. Then, suddenly, a few years after the cave-in of financial markets in October 1987, the construction boom foundered, and the enthusiastic portrayal of a prosperous future for London and New York as global cities faded along with it. The newspaper business pages presented a staccato of defaults and bankruptcies where formerly they had published the press releases of the deal-makers. The cranes disappeared, and in their stead empty office buildings and vacant flats eerily recalled previous optimism. As the job gains of the decade vanished, little else remained to mark the flush times besides the millions of square feet of space that had been created. Both London and New York suffered disproportionately from the recessions affecting their countries. Worst of all, the very industries that during the '80s had been the object of their economic strategies, the source of their growth, and the symbol of their accomplishments lost the most employment. In London, jobs in the financial and business services sectors fell by 90,000 between 1990 and 1992, wiping out all of the FBS employment gains of the preceding five years.[155] During 1989–1991, New York sustained comparable losses, as FBS employment dropped by 91,000, returning the city's job level to the lowest figure since 1983.[156]

Revival came quickly in London, more slowly in New York, although neither regained all of the jobs it had lost until the end of the decade. During the '90s, for the most part, economic and construction activity followed trend lines established in the '80s: Core strengths continued to be in finance and business services; construction focused on office and luxury residential sectors. There were, however, some differences. Tourism and media contributed strongly to economic growth. Particularly in New York, the "new economy" businesses associated with information technology exploded, while motion picture production became the fastest-growing sector as measured by percentage increase.[157] In the words of one real estate adviser: "Nobody dreamed of them [the technology companies] in 1990. We never anticipated [entertainment and media] companies like Bertelsmann, Disney, Viacom. The nature of retailing has changed. Retail and entertainment are much more closely allied." Construction had become much less speculative. The amount of new office space added was relatively small compared to the '80s, although as noted earlier, conversion of industrial space or upgrading of existing offices meant that much more was added than would have been obvious to an observer looking at the skyline.

The next chapter examines the causes and consequences of real-estate boom and bust and probes the effect of governmental policy on these swings.

3

Markets, Decision-Makers, and the Real-Estate Cycle

Swings in property markets can be understood in various ways. Real estate has always conformed to highly cyclical trends, and a number of theoretical analyses seek to explain this trait.[1] My discussion attempts to identify the factors underlying the ups and downs of the market that occurred in London and New York in the 1978–2000 period.

In general, we can describe a typical property cycle. During periods of economic expansion the demand for space will shoot up, but since the supply of space is relatively inelastic in the short run, rents and property values will increase very rapidly. The result is that those people who anticipated the surge in demand will enjoy soaring profits. At this point, others notice the condition of insufficient supply and start a multitude of projects. Overproduction of space occurs when investors expect increases in the value of buildings to outpace the growth of other investments. Usually, however, supply quickly exceeds demand, and if, as happened in the late '80s, the overall economy contracts, causing the demand for space to shrink, a surplus quickly appears. Values then sink as rapidly as they rose. Owners seek desperately to attract or keep tenants through offering lower rents, rent-free months, custom fixturing, etc. Developers find themselves with vacant or half-filled buildings and either cannot count on a cash flow to service the debt on their construction loans or cannot refinance their loans with long-term mortgages on the completed building. Financial institutions are no longer willing to invest in property, and foreclosures depress the price of real estate even further, as lenders seek to dispose of the property they have acquired.

After such a contraction, new construction comes to a stop, meaning that if businesses begin to expand again or desire quarters that conform to different standards—for example, multiple access points to broadband fiber-optic cable—the previously generated surplus is absorbed. Because financial institutions are still reluctant to invest in property, developers do not have new buildings ready to go up, and demand once more begins to outrun supply. Returns to property again escalate rapidly, and the cycle begins anew.

WHY DID IT HAPPEN?

In London and New York the property market has been particularly dependent on financial and business services (FBS) as principal users of office space and on employees in those sectors as purchasers of expensive residential accommodation. The highly cyclical nature of FBS industries has made real-estate markets in the two cities especially volatile. The boom of the '80s and collapse of the early '90s could be directly traced to the behavior of FBS and the close link between growth in finance and growth in business services dependent on the financial industry (e.g., accountants, law firms, management consultants). The situation in the later part of the '90s was more complex. Although the increases in property values of this period were certainly driven in part by the extraordinary rise in the stock market, employment in financial services did not grow nearly as rapidly as did earnings in the sector. Demand for space came from a variety of sources, including business services such as advertising and architecture that instead of being closely connected to finance were directed at other industries, especially telecommunications, information technology, entertainment, and leisure. Thus, the expansion of those industries and the sectors serving them accounted for most of the absorption of space during the end of the century. At the same time, banks and other financial institutions had become much more cautious about property investment, meaning that seven years into the boom the demand for space was outpacing supply by an increasing margin, resulting in skyrocketing commercial rents.[2] Whether or not this balance will continue, and whether the greater diversity of users will result in more stability, cannot be foretold. The remainder of this chapter looks more closely at the conditions of oversupply and shortage.

Oversupply

The standard explanation for overproduction of real estate is that projects take so long to come to fruition that investors cannot easily foresee the market at the time of completion. Just as farmers must plant their fields long before they can know the market for their crops, developers cannot easily adjust their inventory to current demand. In this respect, real-estate investment is by definition speculative.

The structure of the industry also contributes to its strong cyclical tendencies. Like the agricultural sector, and for many of the same reasons, the property industry tends to overproduce. While the real-estate industry is less competitive than agribusiness, no small group of firms dominates the market sufficiently to control overall supply;[3] thus, even when developers anticipate oversupply, they cannot put a cap on the total amount built. Developers have sought to reduce risk by preleasing buildings prior to construction, and often financial institutions will not lend without an assurance of an anchor tenant.[4] During the '80s lenders were extraordinarily willing to lend for speculative buildings; in the '90s they refused to do so. In London, Olympia & York, as we shall see in Chapter 9, through buying into other development firms, was following a deliberate although ultimately unsuccessful policy of seeking to control the market.

By 1987 it was becoming fairly obvious that already planned projects in London and New York could meet all likely demand. Moreover, prospective investors in these two cities could look to numerous other locations, especially in the U.S. Sun Belt, for examples of vastly overbuilt office markets. As early as 1986, *Fortune* magazine had called the period "the worst times for real estate," noting that more than a fifth of U.S. office space was empty despite the generally expanding economy.[5] In places like Denver, Miami, and Dallas, the vacancy rate throughout the '80s had hovered at above 18 percent, bearing witness to the enthusiasm of builders who had responded to earlier service-industry expansion by constructing millions of square feet of space in excess of demand.[6] A little prudence would have identified the same factors at work in London and New York as well. Nevertheless, developers continued to dream up ever-bigger projects; banks increased their lending; property analysts persisted in advising their clients to continue investing in real estate; and governmental authorities kept on turning to property-led development as the remedy for fiscal and employment shortfalls.

The Pressure to Build

When I asked leading developers, officers of lending institutions, property consultants, and public officials why project commitments had continued in the face of mounting evidence of their fragility, they responded fairly unanimously that there had been a herd instinct at work. ("They're all like sheep, these fund managers," snapped one company director.) The CEO of one of Britain's largest firms, who claimed to have started selling off property steadily since 1986 and thus to be relatively undamaged by the slump, declared: "It came from stupidity. Most people in the business have a pretty impoverished level of intellectual capacity. Most lenders are uneducated, not well trained." In virtually the same words a partner in a famous investment firm remarked: "Banks have a herd mentality. They didn't learn the lessons of 1974. They are not run by the very intelligent." Another London CEO proclaimed: "The market is not driven by experience or technology but by emotion."

Americans in the industry came to similar conclusions. In the words of one observer who had held a number of high-level public- and private-sector positions, "Financial institutions had a lot of money. They never learn." A consultant stated: "Real estate was where everyone wanted to be. There was a tremendous bias toward real estate. In the seventies a momentum began to be built up. In the eighties it exploded. The projections were all rosy. People were unwilling to see when saturation would occur. And there was optimism that 'my project was best' along with an explosion of available cash." Many observers echoed the explanation that individual developers managed to persuade themselves—and investors—that their project would work even if others would not. Another popular interpretation of rash commitments was the "greater fool" theory; under this hypothesis it was always possible to rid oneself of a poorly performing property.[7]

Knowledgeable analysts agreed that the availability of financing drove the market, that developers would build as long as someone was willing to provide the necessary funds.[8] In the words of one developer: "There is a belief that bankers finance what builders build. In fact, the opposite is true. Money is the sine qua non. If you have money, you will build." Because developers during the '80s needed to put so little of their own equity into a project, they had little motivation for caution. As another developer commented, "Every property man loves to build. They forget the risk. They're not using their own money. It's lovely building with other people's money." Even if developers foresaw problems, they could avoid personal jeopardy—most development firms received nonrecourse financing, in which the loan's collateral was the building and the builder was not further liable in case of default.[9] Developers were also encouraged by political leaders who expected new development to generate employment and tax revenue.

Moreover, without a stream of new projects, developers could not keep their organizations going and their own salaries paid. One developer compared his operation to a movie production, wherein he was the impresario who brought together the cast of architects, contractors, lawyers, accountants, financial consultants, investors, construction workers, and others who created and financed a building project. Although the core staff employed by the development firm itself was small, any reduction of its size made future productions difficult and undermined the personal relations that undergirded this type of entrepreneurial organization.

Bankers seemingly had stronger incentives than did developers to scrutinize risks. But as another CEO remarked: "Banks competed to get deals rather than doing an overall assessment." One investment banker saw himself in virtually the same position as a developer: "Investment bankers are just intermediaries. They will underwrite if there are buyers [of the bonds]." Commercial banks appeared to be in a different position from investment institutions, since they bore direct responsibility for the loan and therefore presumably had reason to be more careful (although even they could pass off some of their risk through syndication and, eventually, through securitization).[10] They, however, lacked other outlets for loans and, in addition, received payments for services connected with the granting of funds. The vice-president of a leading American pension fund that invested heavily in property mused: "Commercial banks have been the largest source of money for property. They are driven by the desire for fees. They saw very high returns at the time relative to other lines of business."

The director of a very big, quite conservative property investment company in the United Kingdom reflected on the pressures that had operated on him in the '80s: "I'm on a public company treadmill. All these analysts are sniping at you all the time." Because his company's assets were not fully leveraged, his firm was a tempting takeover target, and he had been forced to devote considerable energy to defeating such a maneuver. Although in 1991 he could pride himself on the stability of his firm, he remained defensive about the obloquy he had sustained during expansionary years: "They accused us of being too dozy." In the hyperactive, deal-making world of 1980s finance, an accusation of sleepiness seemed the most embarrassing insult of all.

In fact, the pressure to make deals did not simply arise out of faddism or the spirit of a go-go age. While the long-term interests of firms might depend on wise investing practices, the immediate rewards for individuals seeking bonuses, promotions, and rising equity depended on increasing the firm's business. For publicly held enterprises, stock prices depended on growth. Within the banks and other investment institutions, which for much of the '80s were paying out high interest rates to investors and depositors, there was a desperate search for highly remunerative outlets.[11] Past successful experience with using real estate as a hedge against inflation further bolstered the view among investors that property represented a wise investment choice.

Undersupply

In both the 1980s and the 1990s sharp increases in property prices came when particular industrial sectors suddenly began a period of unanticipated growth. In the '80s these were finance and associated business services; in the '90s they were various sectors of the "new economy" based on information technology, along with tourism and leisure. In neither case, if one read the prognostications of economic analysts at the beginning of these two decades, could one find any indication that this growth was expected. In 1980 there had been continued concern over decentralization of jobs to the urban periphery or abroad. No one foresaw that increasing globalization would heighten the importance of the business districts of cities that were financial centers. At the beginning of the '90s information technology was expected to enable further decentralization, and no one prophesied the Internet revolution. If they had, they certainly would not have imagined that it would call on the talents of graphic artists, advertising agencies, and media figures, already located within the centers of London and New York, to provide it with content. Unexpected also was the renewed strength of cultural industries, including the New York and London theaters, as well as the movement of themed entertainment out of exurban parks into the hearts of these two cities. These new or renewed clusters of activity became the forces for heightened economic dynamism and consequent need for new kinds of buildings and transformation of land uses. The fact of these failures of foresight perhaps explains why property interests are often averse to relying on research and analysis as the basis for their decision making.

Advice and Research

Real-estate developers and property investors need two types of information when contemplating an enterprise: First, what the likely overall market situation is when the development is completed; and second, what type of project on which site is most likely to produce the greatest return. In my investigation of the industry I sought to discover the sources of such information and its effect on investment decisions.

As in any other large industry, property-investment and development firms use both in-house staff and outside consultants for advice and research. The training of people who fill these roles differs between London and New York. Within the United Kingdom the profession of chartered surveyor encompasses a group of individuals who, through a combination of formal education and apprenticeship, study all aspects of property, from construction techniques to financing methods to valuation. A number of the officers of major development firms have such training, as do many planning officers of local authorities; in addition, firms of chartered surveyors offer consulting services to both the public and private sectors.[12] In the United States no comparable professional category exists, and its functions are divided among planners, lawyers, real-estate brokers, and business-school graduates. Consequently, in the United States strategic analyses tend to be more fragmented and impressionistic. Although the similar conditions of the London and New York property markets during the '90s recession apparently belied the advantages of the expertise provided by chartered surveyors, the fact that large speculative risks were taken by only a small number of bankers and developers in London might support the hypothesis that adequate analysis was available to those who sought it.

Few development firms in either city boasted in-house research units; those that did primarily investigated consumer satisfaction with their earlier developments and sought to identify amenities that would help sell future projects. Heads of development firms on both sides of the Atlantic indicated that they had little faith in the utility of formal research endeavors. The CEO of a very large London firm commented: "We've got various marketing research advisers. They do research. But they get it [the market] wrong." The chairman of a major firm that was teetering on the edge of bankruptcy in 1991 asserted during earlier, better times: "We don't do a lot of research. We know the market. A feel for the market is the most important thing." The head of a huge British property corporation declared: "We don't have a real research department. The research is in my head. I talk to people in the [financial] markets every day. . . . We have a sort of circle." A leading New York developer similarly declared: "Most developers sense intuitively where there is an opportunity. They don't rely on economic studies. . . .

As a practical matter you are guessing ahead—so the past does not tell you what you need to know." Another New York CEO likewise dismissed the usefulness of research results: "It's today's wisdom extrapolated into the future." One of the few women in the development business observed: "You smell things, touch them."

By the end of the '90s, opinions on the usefulness of research diverged somewhat between the two cities. One London developer commented: "There are good people in research now. In the 1980s the statistics were no good. Now the quality of information is okay." A principal in one of the leading property consultancies remarked: "Nearly everything we're doing now [i.e., that is happening in London] is planning led and research led." A director of English Partnerships, the government-backed, semi-independent regeneration agency for London, stated: "Previously too much of the speculative boom was based on unrealistic figures and projections. Now we interrogate figures very carefully." A major developer said that he used consultants for research, which focused on the particular site in which he was interested. The managing director of the Canary Wharf Company declared: "I do a lot of research all the time. Canary Wharf has been researched to death. Research is about understanding the broad marketplace. We need to understand our clients' needs. The concentration here is such that you can afford to do it. We try to analyze sectors in broad terms to respond to clients' needs."

Recent views on the use and value of research varied in New York. One developer claimed: "The real-estate business is the last great domain of the entrepreneur. Each site is sui generis. Research won't help. It's serendipity." A consultant thought that research was used more and that it "had made the industry more conservative"—not necessarily for the better. His firm provided advice to developers on how to identify technology tenants and what physical improvements and financial measures were needed to attract them. A leading planner asserted that "real-estate guys don't have any analytic capacity."

Despite at least some greater reliance on research and analysis, intuition and connections remain fundamental to the way the industry operates. Several developers indicated that they relied on tips and chance encounters when identifying a site on which to build. According to one New York developer: "I picked one site by seeing a sign on a building. I knew the area was good, so I followed it up. I get calls from brokers all the time—some of them pay off. Lawyers make significant introductions." A real-estate lawyer upheld this commentary: "If you're in this business you get phone calls—from brokers, friends, clients, others who are just knowledgeable, hoping for a brokerage fee. They will call me [i.e., a lawyer] instead of a client because they know that this way a number of clients are potential buyers. At this stage you're not an attorney, you're just a facilitator."

Even in financial institutions, personal relationships underlie judgments concerning developments that officers are willing to back. A director of the pension fund with the largest real-estate holdings in the United States, who managed its New York City portfolio, indicated that her investment decisions depended fundamentally on who the developer was: "We build up great familiarity with the major players. Our investments are almost always with developers with whom we have experience. We must trust the developer, share his philosophy. We do not work with a large staff, and therefore we must depend on the developer's decision making." A managing partner in a British investment firm stated that "we would get involved in a real-estate deal because we believe in the man first, the market second, and the location third." The vice-president for real-estate finance of a major bank asserted: "We only do deals with people we know and trust."

Developers mainly seek advice when they have very specific questions. They turn to trade organizations like the British Property Federation and the Real Estate Board of New York (REBNY) for information on tax law, landlord-tenant legislation, and building regulations. They consult planners and attorneys for assistance on planning permission and zoning matters once they have identified a site that they wish to develop. Their research is primarily directed at the likely prospects for the individual property that they are developing; the assumption is that present overall trends will continue, and the forces shaping the broad contours of the market are not usually the subject of investigation. Only retail developers do much market research, but their focus is mainly on demographic projections rather than on the likely actions of their competitors—that is, they predict changes in demand, not supply.

Institutional investors usually rely much more on market data when making their decisions than do developers.[13] Various financial advisory firms provide regular market updates to their clients. According to the managing director of such a firm: "Within London, financial institutions that looked carefully at the market used the [1980s] boom to unload properties. The people who built the buildings were speculators, not users of research, not long-term thinkers. Most of the money came from nontraditional sources, especially Japanese banks." In New York it is more difficult to make such a clear-cut distinction between the types of institutions that relied on research to guide them to withdraw from the market before it peaked and those that were willing to finance speculative real-estate development. Many major U.S. domestic banks and insurance companies made substantial real-estate commitments just before the 1989 crash; greater caution was a function of individual management rather than being associated with general categories of firms.

Even if developers and investors had relied less on their intuition and more on professional advice, they probably would not have acted much differently during the '80s. As one chartered surveyor admitted wryly: "It was not to the advantage of consultants to tell everyone to pull back when the future was beginning to worsen." Among the lawyers, chartered surveyors, brokers, and other advisers to the property industry, there were virtually no disadvantages to promoting further construction projects. Large consultancy fees depended on a commitment being made; the only penalty for bad advice was loss of reputation—and since everyone was encouraging property investment, it was unlikely that any firm would be singled out for culpability.

Interestingly, however, attitudes were quite different during the more recent boom. Everyone interviewed in both London and New York agreed that lenders were examining deals very closely, requiring a much greater equity commitment (in the neighborhood of 25 percent) from developers, and demanding a share in the equity for themselves. Banks and insurance companies had reduced their real-estate portfolios, while a number of nontraditional lenders, including investment banks and lending subsidiaries of financial holding companies, had taken up the slack. In general, less was being lent, and the risk was more widely spread than previously. Memories of the last downturn had not faded, and investors in real estate, as compared to those seeking to make their fortunes through buying initial public offerings on the stock market, seemed downright conservative.

The Role of Government

During the '80s, not only did governing bodies in both London and New York forgo their earlier predilection to regulate growth, but they instead devoted themselves to reinforcing expansionary tendencies (see Chapter 4). The various specific benefits given to developers, including the provision of infrastructure, low-priced land, grants, loans, and regulatory and local tax relief, further induced activity. Combined with encouragement of private-market strategies for economic growth at the level of the national government and biases in favor of real-estate investment in the tax codes of both countries, these local efforts had the effect of loosening the remaining constraints on supply.

In Britain, where the Treasury resists the use of tax incentives, governmental encouragement of real-estate development during the '80s mostly arose from the relaxation of restraints. At the end of that decade the government had identified a limited number of sites for development, and it was using infrastructure construction and site aggregation to leverage private investment. Some British developers came to lament the lack of an overall planning authority for London, as reflected in their support for the establishment of the Greater London Authority. They felt that the industry would have benefited from more coordinated and limited development during the preceding decade. The chairman of a firm that was then among the most active in London remarked: "It is socially and economically harmful to be overbuilt. . . . I am [now] urging for restraint through planning. It has been too easy to get permission. All you have to do is buy them [the local authorities] with planning gain. Market-led development has turned out not to be as great as we expected. Without tension between restraint and entrepreneurship, there is no balance."

In contrast, no New York real-estate leader whom I interviewed wished to see governmental constraint..When the head of one firm, who had formerly directed a city agency, was asked whether the city would have been better off if it had restricted development, he responded typically: "Why should government worry about oversupply? Government shouldn't protect the market." Nevertheless, New York developers, somewhat surreptitiously, attempted to restrict the amount of development by funding environmental groups that were opposing projects of other developers. Thus, community opponents of 42nd Street redevelopment had substantial sums at their disposal, provided by unidentified sources, and the developer Seymour Durst, a property owner in the Times Square area, openly supported attempts at blocking the development of four large office towers there (eventually his firm, by then with his son as head, became one of the designated developers). Donald Trump, in an effort to prevent construction of a competing building across Fifth Avenue from Trump Tower, paid the $50,000 legal fee of an attorney representing the Municipal Art Society, a civic group fighting the project.[14]

During the 1980s government officials in both London and New York rejected the view that it was their role to guide the market. One London borough council leader commented: "I always find it extraordinary that developers, who are proponents of the free market system, should want planning. No one forces developers to overbuild." A councillor in the City of London remarked: "There had not been overbuilding. More availability is good from the tenant's point of view. The choice of whether to build is one of the owner, not the planner—planning permission does not mandate construction. Planners should not predict the marketplace; they are not qualified to make the judgment."

A New York development agency head, interviewed in 1991, asked: "Did we overbuild or did we just lose an awful lot of jobs? Today's surplus is the result of decisions made four or five years ago." He argued that "government could not have accurately predicted the current situation." Interestingly, in San Francisco, public officials and business interests fiercely resisted a citizens' ballot initiative to restrict office development to under a million square feet a year. Restrictions, however, were adopted, and vacancy rates, as a consequence of the controls on new construction, dropped from 18 percent in 1986 to 12 percent in 1991 depite the recession.[15] Evidently, governmental controls have the potential to stabilize the industry despite itself.

LONDON AND NEW YORK COMPARED

London and New York followed similar trajectories during the last quarter of the twentieth century in respect to the amount and type of property investment. During the 1980s and the first part of the 1990s they also resembled each other in the character of both public and private decision making. By the end of the '90s, however, they began to diverge, as governmental intervention to guide the development process became increasingly significant in London but not in New York. Although the changed emphasis of government decision making was more evident once a Labour government took power, the tendencies toward greater directiveness had begun earlier.

Some reasons for differences in attitudes among developers in the two cities come from the types of firms they lead. London's property firms are mainly publicly held, and heads of firms usually proceed up through the ranks as in other business organizations. In New York, on the other hand, many major firms are not only privately held but are run by groups of relatives: The Lefraks, the Roses, the Rudins, the Tishmans, the Dursts, and the Trumps are among New York's leading real-estate families with firms bearing their names. In a number of cases, the present CEO is the son or grandson of the founder. The culture of New York's firms tends to be more personalistic than that of their London counterparts, and relations with governmental officials are closer.

In the New York property world, the clubbiness of the City of London, where relationships are often based on implicit understandings rather than formal rules, is replaced by an equally informal but more explicit quid pro quo. Favoritism is not a product of club memberships and old school ties. Instead, developers contribute heavily to political compaigns and expect consideration in return.[16] Construction unions and contractors are notoriously crooked and politically influential; developers routinely pay the costs associated with inflated labor charges and kickbacks. In the words of one insider:

> The political system in . . . [New York] City and State is thoroughly corrupt and psychologically geared to a time when corporations had to be in the city. The system was devised to divide up action that was assumed to be there. In the '80s the money was there again for a little while. But the political system increases the costs of doing business, and businesses no longer have to stay. There is a significant massive indirect tax levied by a corrupt political system.

In contrast, even the most virulent critics of London's property firms do not believe that personal payoffs significantly warp the dealings between government and development interests. The CEO of a British firm with assets of £2 billion commented that his firm would no longer work in New York because of the level of corruption there. He did not believe that maintaining close contact with politicians would be useful in London and claimed that he did not contribute to political campaigns.

During the '80s London firms borrowed to cover virtually all development costs and usually built without commitments from tenants. Although on the face of it their operations appeared more speculative than those of their New York counterparts, office developers in London in fact have operated within a more predictable market. Although the system eventually broke down because of weak demand, office tenants typically held 25-year leases, which were subject to five-year, upward-only rent reviews performed by firms of chartered surveyors. The owner and the tenant each had a surveyor who represented their interests; if they could not reach agreement, an arbitrator made the final decision. Since relatively few leases expired in a single year, this system assured that during downturns in the market most tenants could not easily search out bargains; for those whose leases still had many years to run, buying out their leases was a very expensive proposition. In New York the plunge in the market allowed many large tenants to assiduously pursue deals with their landlords, effectively pushing the average price down much more quickly than in London (see Table 2.3).

During the '90s, as the market heated up and several years passed without substantial additions to the supply of space, landlords in both cities ceased offering deals to new tenants, and rents ultimately reached and surpassed their previous levels. Formerly undesirable areas became attractive to business, either because they were cheaper or because they presented space well adapted to their needs. This was especially true in New York, where "new economy" firms could find prestige in industrial structures, implying that they were on the leading edge, rather than a stodgy midtown address.

London's tenants have fewer alternatives than New York's, as no other city within the United Kingdom seriously competes with London for financial and advanced-services firms. Whereas in the United States a central-city location does not carry particular prestige, within the United Kingdom considerable prejudice remains against locations outside central London.[17] While this situation is changing as the southeast of England becomes increasingly polynodal, for the medium term traditional preferences remain a significant factor in maintaining London's strength as against the rest of Great Britain. In contrast, New York's preeminence is threatened not only by other major U.S. financial centers, like Los Angeles and Chicago, but also by its own periphery. Within its suburbs a number of locations like Princeton, New Jersey, and Stamford, Connecticut, carry as much cachet as Manhattan, if not more. Moreover, Jersey City, directly across the Hudson River from downtown Manhattan, has developed a dense, high-rise central business district that, while located in another state, is essentially an extension of New York City that offers lower operating costs. In the future, competition from continental Europe may challenge London's preeminence, but Paris, Frankfurt, and Brussels are unlikely either to dislodge London from its dominant position in financial markets or to overcome the advantages of English-speaking service firms within the world market more generally.

Relative to all other cities except Tokyo, London has exceptionally high occupancy costs.[18] These result from several factors, including the leasing arrangements described above, its long history of strict planning controls, and the monopolistic position of landowners. While this situation protects owners of occupied buildings and lenders to them, it injures London's competitive position within the world and generally inflates prices within the metropolis. In simple terms, it benefits the property industry relative to all other British industries.

THE CONSEQUENCES OF THE PROPERTY CYCLE

Despite market differences, developers in both London and New York made similar types of calculations during the real-estate booms. The large office or multiuse structure was the principal investment object of the '80s; conversions of existing structures to residential or office uses accounted for a considerable amount of space provided in the '90s. In both cities during the '80s property analysts stressed the need of financial firms for large trading floors that could not be accommodated in older buildings. The total number of firms requiring such facilities, however, was quite small, and the downturn in securities markets caused them to reduce their staffs and contract their demand for space. Moreover, even within firms with large staffs of traders, the technological necessity for keeping them within shouting distance of each other has never been wholly clear and is diminishing with the development of advanced computer networks.[19] Although securities firms and investment banks expanded again during the bull market of the '90s, other financial industry sectors, including banking and insurance, consolidated operations, moved back offices to peripheral locations, and became absorbed through mergers and acquisitions. The growth of online trading means that brokerage firms will reduce their space needs. Thus, reliance on the financial industry to absorb large amounts of space may diminish in both New York and London.

Whereas residential market structures used to be very different in London and New York, they have become more alike during the last 25 years. Public-sector housing production in Britain has dwindled to a near halt, although housing associations continued to build a limited amount of subsidized housing. In a striking turnaround, New York's commitment to publicly subsidized affordable housing considerably exceeded London's for a part of this period, as a result of the Koch administration's ten-year housing plan. Under Giuliani, however, the commitment to production of housing for low-income people diminished substantially. Private developers in both cities built almost exclusively for the luxury market in condominium or cooperative forms of ownership. Demand for their product fluctuated with the general economy; during the recession it was almost nonexistent, but in the prosperous parts of the '80s and '90s prices spiraled upward far ahead of the overall rate of inflation, reaching dizzying levels by century's end.

During the '80s in both cities the main governmental strategy for urban regeneration was encouragement of property development. In London this was achieved primarily through relaxation of planning regulation but also, within the jurisdiction of the London Docklands Development Corporation, through investment in infrastructure, land sales at low prices, and tax abatement. In New York during this period tax concessions were the principal means for stimulating development, but, as is described in the case studies in this book, other methods were employed as well. In the '90s the United Kingdom terminated its urban development corporations and enterprise zones, thereby ending many of the special advantages given to property developers. At the same time, the various agencies entrusted with planning for London began to develop more strategic forms of guidance. They sought to limit large-scale development to certain locations, to restrict peripheral shopping malls, to ensure that developers provided community benefits in exchange for the mandate to build, and to provide employment and other social programs alongside new development. In the year 2000 many of these projects were still in gestation, but they clearly represented a change in approach. London businesses, which participated in the numerous partnerships established to promote development, did not seem to regard the tying of property development to social aims as inimical to their interests. In contrast, in New York during the '90s development continued to be opportunistic, heavily reliant on tax subsidies, unrelated to social programs—except in the federal Harlem/South Bronx Empowerment Zone—and restricted primarily to Manhattan.

The property-led strategy for economic development has meant that public resources that might have been used elsewhere became embedded in real estate. Governmental stimulation of large-scale commercial development incurs major public cost: It involves heavy public staffing expenses; it often relies on the sale of publicly owned land at below-market prices; it requires considerable expenditure on infrastructure; it crowds out alternative uses of land and contributes to gentrification; it causes a focus on the central business district at the expense of neighborhood development; and its impact on the quality of the urban environment has been at best mixed. If the true purpose of this investment was to attract firms, and therefore employment, through lowering occupancy costs, then the alternatives to subsidizing construction would have been to invest directly in those enterprises—by providing training for their labor forces, by offering loans and grants for equipment and start-up costs, or by taking an equity interest. In reality, public subsidy represented a taxpayer investment in a leading industry—the property industry itself; ironically, the failure of the public sector to moderate expansion during the '80s destabilized the property sector. In the boom of the late 1990s, the problem of oversupply did not become evident, primarily because of the caution shown by investors, lenders, and developers.

Defenders of expansionary policies argue that empty office buildings do no harm, that the new buildings will eventually be filled while the old ones deserve abandonment, and that by bringing down prices, vacancies will encourage economic growth. The performance of the London and New York property sectors, and economies more generally, after the early '90s crash seems to have justified this position. The existence of large amounts of relatively inexpensive space permitted companies to start up or expand without encountering bottlenecks. It allowed businesses associated with new media and the information economy to grow up in these big, dense metropolises rather than being driven to suburban fringes. This was not, however, an inevitable result of the property overhang. If a new wave of innovation had not come along exactly at the propitious moment, much of this space would have remained empty. And, especially in New York, overreliance on a single industry—finance—was replaced by heavy dependence on fragile "dot.com" firms, many of which were to have only short life spans.

Initially, public intervention was intended to prevent inflation in land prices from making property unaffordable to businesses and residents. Rather than moderating price increases, however, it first inflamed speculation that produced leaps in land values greatly exceeding the average rise in living costs; eventually, it contributed to the oversupply that caused rapid and damaging devaluation and a corresponding reduction in the value of the public's investment.[20] Even if the price of property in 2000 were the same as would have prevailed if, instead of alternating boom and bust, there had been moderate yearly price increases, the social consequences were quite different. Moderately profitable businesses of all sorts lost their premises, causing the breakup of established patterns of patronage; business and residential communities dissolved and could not be reconstituted. The bargains made available eventually contributed to the viability of diverse business districts and mixed residential neighborhoods, as lower-cost uses moved into formerly unaffordable venues. Such gains, though, came at the cost of great disruption in the lives and fortunes of lenders and developers, who had bet on ever-rising prices and found that their assets had lost most of their value. Then, on the upswings the costs were borne by those who were driven out by soaring prices and displacement. These consequences of creative destruction, according to Schumpeter, are the inevitable price of capitalist growth; the question remains whether moderation of the cycle would necessarily diminish creativity. If not, there is a strong argument for restraining destruction.

In the first edition of this book, I stated that we did not know yet whether London and New York were in the process of continuing the descent that preceded the '80s or were simply in a routine cyclical trough from which renewed demand would lift them. With the advantage of hindsight, I can now declare that the availability of low-priced space contributed to 1990s growth, although it was not the prime cause. Nevertheless, for lenders and developers who had bet on ever-rising prices, certain lessons are apparent from the experience of the '90s: Promoting real-estate development is not identical with fostering stable economic growth, and the opposition by the industry to regulation is not even in its own long-term interest.

4
Policy and Politics

London and New York have quite different political structures, resulting in important dissimilarities in local autonomy, political expression, and planning. London is the national capital; it is directly subordinate to the central government; a programmatic, nationally controlled, multiparty system structures its mode of political representation. Between 1986 and 2000 its municipal government was wholly decentralized to 33 local authorities, and even after the introduction of the Greater London Authority, most municipal functions remain vested in the borough governments. In contrast, New York is neither its nation's capital nor even that of its own state; it has powers of home rule; its politics is dominated by a single, locally based party; and it possesses a centralized, general-purpose government.

Despite these differences, the policy histories of London and New York passed through a similar, although not precisely synchronous, set of stages in the postwar years. During the 1950s and 1960s, reconstruction of war-damaged property and large-scale housing programs transformed the appearance of London. The public sector bore direct responsibility for building many of the new housing estates itself. It also played a strongly interventionist role in shaping private development, both in limiting developable sites and in specifying desirable types of projects. Simultaneously, New York—under the leadership of Robert Moses,[1] an appointed official who during his 44-year career controlled its parks, urban renewal, public housing, and highway programs—underwent major physical changes, as expressways and massive low- and middle-income housing projects remade the city. In London nothing was built to compare with the enormous highway system that Moses imposed on New York; on the other hand, invest-

Parts of this chapter are drawn from a work that I coauthored with Ken Young (Fainstein and Young, 1992). I wish to acknowledge his contribution to some sections of the writing.

ment in public transit continued there, with both the modernization and extension of Underground and commuter rail lines.

For much of the postwar period New York City government invested heavily
in infrastructure, housing, and welfare institutions, including public hospitals, social service centers, and recreational facilities. As well as using federal subventions,
it had access to substantial funding from the State of New York for its construction
programs. A series of liberal mayors, strongly supported by trade-union organizations, led the city until the late 1970s.[2] John Lindsay, elected first as a Republican
then as an Independent, held office for eight years during the politically turbulent
period starting in the late 1960s. His regime's policies, which shifted emphasis
from the concerns of the white working class to those of the black and Hispanic
poor, stimulated a realignment of political forces and set the stage for the divisions that defined New York during the following decades. Although the Lindsay
administration's economic strategies encouraged continued investment in the
Manhattan central business district, it used federal funds to target the poorest areas
of the city for housing and community development programs. Lindsay did not
take the strong ideological positions of London's Labour leadership, but he did
incorporate minorities into his regime and raise the level of social spending.
Lindsay's administration was supplanted by the caretaker government of Abraham
Beame, whose lackluster response to the 1975 fiscal crisis quickly brought his
mayoralty into disrepute. In 1978 Edward I. Koch replaced Beame as mayor and
committed himself to restoring economic prosperity.

During the 1970s the British Labour government mounted an inner-city strategy modeled on the War on Poverty and Model Cities programs that had begun
and ended earlier in New York.[3] Under the leadership of Ken Livingstone, the
Greater London Council (GLC) of the 1980s sought to fuse an industry-based
economic development strategy with political radicalism.[4] Although comparable
to the Lindsay regime of the previous decade in New York, the GLC went much
further in seeking to combine elaborate social-service programs with community
participation and economic revitalization strategies built on a "bottom-up" rather
than a "trickle-down" approach. To this end, it established the Greater London
Enterprise Board (GLEB) as its principal instrument.[5] In the Docklands it sought
to foster manufacturing, in contrast to the later emphasis of the London Docklands
Development Corporation (LDDC) on office construction.[6] Labour-dominated
borough councils similarly stressed small-scale development and continued provision of social housing. GLC activism, however, stimulated the wrath of the
Thatcher government, which brought about the GLC's abolition in 1986, thereby
bringing both its own directly administered programs and its support for Labour
boroughs to a halt.

After the sharp economic downturns that both cities experienced in the mid-
1970s, their governing regimes actively promoted growth in economic activity
and employment. Their dedication to social amelioration and community participation over the same time span was less certain. During the 1980s New York's

mayoral administration and the British ministry with responsibility for London displayed strikingly similar social philosophies.[7] As well as defining governmental planning and regulation as inimical to economic vitality, these regimes used real-estate development (in contrast to job training or infrastructure investment) as their primary strategy for stimulating expansion. They identified global-city status as the hallmark of their economic advantage and fostered those forms of development—especially first-class office space and luxury housing—which responded to the needs of the upper echelons of the financial and advanced-services industries participating in world economic coordination.

The two regimes also resembled each other in confronting conflicting political agendas at subordinate levels of government and in operating within a region fragmented by numerous uncoordinated governing bodies. New York, however, in addition to lacking London's dominating position within the national economy and governmental system, faced serious challenges even within its own region. Its economic primacy extended only to finance and advanced services, and its political influence within both the state and national governments was weak. Adjacent municipalities on the New Jersey waterfront and in suburban Westchester (New York) and Fairfield (Connecticut) Counties competed to capture the generators of growth and to exclude those populations and facilities that imposed financial, social, or environmental costs without commensurate benefits.[8]

INSTITUTIONAL STRUCTURES

Differences in the governance of London and New York stem fundamentally from national differences between the United States and the United Kingdom. In the United States a federalist, presidential system creates checks and balances that prevent any branch of government from dominating the others. Cabinet government in the United Kingdom can produce much more sudden reversals in policy than occur in the United States, where divided government provides a considerable flywheel effect. The abrupt change that Margaret Thatcher's electoral triumph produced in British policy, making it much more market-driven, reflects this institutional difference. After Thatcher's 1990 ouster from office, the government's policies became more moderate under the stewardship of her Tory successor, John Major. They shifted again after the 1997 Labour victory, but not nearly to the extent that occurred during the earlier Conservative takeover.

In the United States, home rule (i.e., the devolution of authority to municipalities by state governments) has traditionally strengthened local representation and made it easier than in the United Kingdom for urban regimes to adopt policies opposed by the national party in power.[9] The nonprogrammatic nature of political parties and territorial divisions within metropolitan areas, however, prevent the adoption of broadly redistributive strategies at the local level. In contrast, centralized parliamentary government has consistently limited the autonomy of local government within the United Kingdom.[10] The principles of cabinet rule and party control make national-party programs dominant both through the mechanism of parliamentary supremacy and, for the national opposition parties, through the party machinery. Final responsibility for local planning rests with the cabinet minister who heads the Department of the Environment, Transport and the Regions (DETR), which, with added functions, replaced the Department of the Environment (DoE). The power of the central government to curtail the level of local taxation and expenditure further constrains local authorities.

Local Governance

London. The fourteen-year absence of a municipal administration to govern the urban core area put London sharply at variance with New York. Even when the Greater London Council (GLC), established in 1965 as a metropolitan government, reigned over both central London[11] and the outer boroughs, it did not possess as much authority as the government of New York City had, and its successor, the Great London Authority (GLA), has even less. The central government could always overrule the GLC's decisions, and the borough authorities retained control of most housing provision, land-use planning, and housekeeping functions like street cleaning and fire fighting. The leader of the GLC did not have the dominant position in framing the city's agenda possessed by the mayor of New York; the new mayor of London, the same Ken Livingstone who headed the GLC, has only limited powers. During the interregnum period, overall executive authority shifted to the DoE (and ultimately the Prime Minister), but the DoE's London office never devised a policy for the city comparable in scope or detail to the program of a New York mayor. Nor, of course, was it specifically responsible to London's electorate. Under the Government Office for London during the final years of the twentieth century, there was a move toward greater agenda setting, but a strong citywide program still awaited formulation in the year 2000.

Responsibility for day-to-day government in London rests with 33 elected local authorities.[12] Although relatively weak compared with local governing bodies in the rest of the United Kingdom, they have far more power than New York's subsidiary jurisdictions (boroughs and community planning districts) have. Organized like the national Parliament, local councils are run by the majority party with an executive group consisting of a leader and chairs of the various functional areas for which the council is responsible (e.g., education, housing, social services, finance, planning, and transportation). Councillors are elected by ward; the number of councillors for each borough varies but in all cases exceeds the 51 that constitute the membership of New York's newly enlarged city council, which has jurisdiction over the entire city. Under London's governmental system, not only does a representative body operate at a level far closer to the neighborhood than in New York, but the location of administrative offices in every borough allows its citizens to conduct their transactions with government much closer to home than their New York counterparts can do. As well as dispensing a full range of municipal services, local authorities were until recently the principal suppliers of shelter for low- and moderate-income households.

Local authorities raise substantial funds themselves. For most of London's history, rates (i.e., property taxes on households and businesses) along with miscellaneous fees, rents, and property sales were their principal sources of revenue. In 1990 rates were supplanted by the community charge or "poll tax," which required each adult householder within a locality to contribute the same amount, regardless of income or property holdings. In 1993 a new form of local taxation called the "council tax" reintroduced a levy based on values of residential property. In addition, a grant from the central government supplements local-government revenues, with the amount received by each local authority varying according to its resources and level of need.[13] The partial equalization resulting from the central-government grant means that local authorities do not need to engage in the intense competition for tax base that afflicts American municipalities. The termination of the locally paid business rate in 1990 and its replacement by a uniform national business tax that is redistributed to local authorities removed all incentives to attract business simply for its revenue-enhancing potential.

New York. New York City, like most other large American metropolises, has its governing powers divided between a mayor, who possesses executive authority, and a council with legislative powers.[14] The council is elected by district, and the mayor is chosen at large. Until 1990, however, New York also possessed a unique body called the Board of Estimate. With final authority over all land use and contract matters, it wielded extraordinary influence over the city's affairs and caused the council to play a relatively minor role.[15] After the elimination of the Board of Estimate, the council assumed its powers. Although the 1990 City Charter revision improved its staffing, the council continued to lack a sufficiently unified organizational structure to enable it to wield coherent authority.

The borough presidents, who formerly exercised legislative power when sitting on the Board of Estimate, also hold some executive power within their own boroughs; there is not, however, a corresponding borough legislative body. The establishment in 1977 of 59 community boards allows for some decentralization within the city government, but far less than is the case for the London boroughs.[16] Community board members, who are appointed by the borough presidents and the city council members from their districts, exercise advisory power over land use and capital budget matters but have no executive authority.

New York, like all American cities, must depend primarily on tax revenues generated within its own boundaries; federal aid to New York City has comprised only about 10 to 12 percent of its total revenue for the last decade.[17] The tristate division of the New York region, moreover, allows the creation of tax differentials much greater than those that typify other U.S. metropolitan areas.[18] The city government, which cannot share in the tax base of its suburban ring, must forever strive to keep revenue-generating people and industries within its borders in order to stay fiscally solvent. Even if, from a regional standpoint, economic rationality justifies moving manufacturing, back-office, and warehouse facilities outside the city limits, New York's fiscal situation forces its government to oppose such moves.

Planning

London. Patrick Abercrombie's plan for postwar London, updated by the Greater London Development Plan of 1968, set forth the principles of green-belt preservation, peripheral manufacturing, and population deconcentration, thereby providing a framework for development that had no New York counterpart.[19] Planning officials emphasized clustered development around town centers and a sharp demarcation between city and country; regulation was much stricter than in New York; and the preservation of the green belt around London constituted a cardinal principle. Preservationist concerns played a much greater role in limiting and directing development in London than in the New York region throughout the 1980s.[20] London still has many more restrictions on the right to build than New York has, and each local authority within the region produces development plans to guide growth within its jurisdiction.[21]

Until the 1970s British public policy aimed at decentralizing population and economic activity out of London.[22] The policy of deconcentration, however, was eventually reversed, as London began to lose industry along with population at an unanticipated rate, causing a weakening of the city's economy. With the encouragement of the Labour government of the mid-1970s, central London's planners began seeking to retain population and industry in the city, and throughout the '80s planners in London increasingly shared the same economic goals as their New York counterparts.

During the Thatcher years, the Prime Minister's emphasis on using the market to allocate investment resulted in a notable relaxation of planning controls, although Great Britain still continued to regulate development far more than the United States.[23] The end of the GLC meant the elimination of any authoritative planning body for the London region as a whole and the fulfillment of the Thatcher government's planning philosophy, which was expressed as follows: "London's future depends on the initiative and energy of the private sector and individual citizens and effective co-operation between the public and private sectors, not on the imposition of a master plan. The role of the land use planning process is to facilitate development while protecting the local environment."[24]

In the absence of a planning authority for the metropolis, the London Planning Advisory Committee (LPAC) was installed to give planning advice concerning London to the central government. Consisting of a small staff that reported to a joint committee of 33 members drawn from all London's boroughs, LPAC had to achieve a consensus among Conservative and Labour constituencies for its recommendations.[25] LPAC's *Strategic Planning Advice* reflected a surprising degree of agreement,[26] and its recommendations went sufficiently beyond total nonintervention to irritate the DoE's London office during the Thatcher period. At that time, the combination of central-government antagonism and local-authority resistance meant that it could achieve little. When asked about the effect of central-government control of strategic planning for London, a local-authority planning director responded: "LPAC is toothless. They don't even know what's going on any more. DoE studies are crap. They propose a recipe for disaster in land use planning and transport. The borough associations [of which there are two, one of Conservative and one of Labour authorities] can be unified—they are now on traffic and transport. But central government doesn't listen to local government."[27]

Although the DoE was responsible for planning the metropolitan region, it did not interpret its mission as the aggressive coordination of local initiatives or the preparation of a detailed comprehensive plan. It acted primarily as an appeals body, frequently overturning lower-level decisions that had denied planning permission to developers. Borough councils became more and more inhibited from blocking development proposals for fear of having to defend their decisions on appeal to the Secretary of State for the Environment and, if they lost, being required to pay the developer's costs as well as their own. In addition, the Secretary of State had the power to "call in" a proposal if he so chose, thereby removing it from the jurisdiction of the local authority even without an appeal. Thus, while avoiding a formative role for itself in shaping the region, the central government also limited planning by local authorities.

After Margaret Thatcher left office, the various bodies entrusted with planning functions increasingly engaged in formulating development strategies, and support for planning grew. LPAC became more effective in influencing policymakers as the tide turned. Nonetheless, its advice remained just that—and neither the boroughs nor the central government needed to heed it unless they so desired. With the establishment of the GLA, LPAC was dissolved as a joint committee of the boroughs and became its strategic-planning arm. The hope was that economic and spatial planning would be integrated under the new system and that policy planning documents would be implemented more easily.

Planning proposals for the regeneration of areas in decline become meaningful when capital begins to flow into new construction. It was only at the end of the property recession in the late '90s that the desire of policy-makers to see revitalization began to achieve fruition. Three major infrastructure initiatives, however, were implemented during the '90s, and they proved instrumental in fostering private investment once developers were again looking for opportunities. These were an express train linking Heathrow Airport to London's Paddington Station, the extension of the Jubilee tube line into East London, and the construction of the Channel Tunnel. The Heathrow rail link stimulated planning for a major multiuse development around Paddington Basin, of which the first stage was under way at the turn of the twenty-first century. The second allowed the resumption of development in Docklands and sparked new initiatives in the borough of Southwark.

The third was responsible for new development in Stratford and would eventually stimulate investment around King's Cross, as these were the intended terminuses of a new high-speed link between London and the English Channel. Although King's Cross was officially designated as the train's ultimate destination, financing was only committed in 2001. Altercation over the site consumed years and produced great uncertainty for all of the enterprises that would be affected by the decision. So far the government has not committed itself to an overall strategic transportation plan for the region; this effort, which aims to integrate transportation, land use, and economic development planning for the area, will be the most important responsibility given to the new London Development Authority (LDA), which was established in 2000.

New York. The New York City Planning Commission and the Economic Development Corporation (EDC), often in conjunction with the New York State Empire State Development Corporation, are the city's main planning organs. Outside the five boroughs, few institutional mechanisms provide a framework for regional planning or the resolution of territorial inequities. The Metropolitan Transportation Authority plans and operates public transit in suburban New York State as well as the city, but its purview does not extend to either Connecticut or New Jersey.

The Port Authority of New York and New Jersey has responsibilities on both sides of the Hudson. Although its mandate is limited to transportation and some development activities, it does have the financial resources to implement its plans itself. It operates autonomously, however, and gives first priority to maintaining the fiscal soundness of its investments. The principal democratic check on its operations is the requirement that the minutes of its board meetings (and therefore any decisions it might take) be approved by the governors of New York and New Jersey. This provision resulted in a nearly two-year stalemate between 1998 and 2000, as the two governors feuded and refused to approve any actions by the authority.[28] Its capabilities have been further thwarted by the antagonism of New York's Mayor Giuliani, who has accused it of favoring New Jersey and has called for removing LaGuardia and Kennedy airports from its jurisdiction. Its own increasingly ossified bureaucracy and weak leadership have also hampered its assuming a more significant role in recent times. Its reluctance to participate in construction of transit links to the airports resulted in New York's lagging far behind other major cities in this respect. Only after considerable pressure and the levy of a surcharge on plane tickets did it finally agree to construct these connections, which are scheduled to open during the first five years of the new century.

Despite their proximity,[29] New Jersey and New York City not only do not coordinate their activities but engage in active competition with each other. A 1991 pledge by the governments of New York City and State and New Jersey not to raid each other for business investment quickly broke down. In retaliation for New Jersey's subsidies to firms leaving New York City for New Jersey locations, Vincent Tese, New York State's director of economic development, vowed: "We will be targeting New Jersey firms that for whatever reason are looking to change locations. . . . Then New Jersey will wind up spending money keeping firms they've got, and it's not going to be a pleasant situation for them."[30]

Overall, peripheral expansion has continued unchecked. The most egregious example is rapid commercial growth along the Jersey side of the Hudson River—the principal recipient of overspill development from the Manhattan business district during the boom periods of the '80s and '90s. Each of the numerous municipalities that line the Jersey waterfront has virtually total responsibility for construction within its borders.[31] Millions of square feet of offices sprang up in the narrow band between the river and the Palisades behind it; altogether northern New Jersey offers nearly 120 million square feet of space, almost all of it comprising modern structures capable of meeting the needs of computer-reliant firms. During 2000, Chase Manhattan Bank, Goldman Sachs, and John Wiley Publishers all announced plans for construction of major facilities on the Jersey side of the Hudson, amounting to millions of additional square feet of space in Hoboken and Jersey City. Despite serious problems of transportation access from the suburban hinterland on the New Jersey side, each riverfront locality continues to accept further development, in part to increase tax revenues, but also because of the pervasive influence of real-estate interests within municipal governing bodies. The proximity to Manhattan and lower costs offered by New Jersey comprise the principal justification for the generous assistance offered by New York City's government to firms threatening to leave its jurisdiction. And, indeed, the absolute absence of any regional policy for targeting office development leaves the city constantly vulnerable to raids on its economic base by its neighbors.

POLITICS AND IDEOLOGY

Although New York in the 1970s surpassed other U.S. cities in its commitment to social welfare policies, London still presented a model of greater state intervention. By the mid-1980s, however, there was a remarkable convergence between the two cities in both the content of public policy and its justification. In an article written at that time, Norman Fainstein and I attributed the government's more interventionist and redistributional role in London than in New York to three factors within the British sociopolitical system: (1) the political capacity of the state to establish a sphere of autonomy for itself; (2) the influence of business leaders who construed their interests collectively and held a paternalistic vision of their role in society; and (3) the political capacity of subordinate groups to influence state policy in their own interests.[32] The two cities continued to differ on the first of these three dimensions throughout the '80s. But the state autonomy that formerly allowed British bureaucratic personnel to take the initiative in augmenting universalistic welfare programs permitted the Thatcher regime to reverse direction more abruptly than could a government under greater constraint.

Differences along the latter two dimensions narrowed during the Thatcher period.[33] Under pressure from competition abroad, responding to ideological trans- formation at home, and changing in composition because of displacement within their ranks, British business leaders increasingly emulated the individualistic, entrepreneurial style of their American counterparts. In both countries conserva- tive national regimes reinforced the position of those business groups that sup- ported their electoral successes; in turn, business managers as a group responded to the ideological currents emanating from the governing regimes and moved in a more conservative direction. At the same time, the working class became in- creasingly stressed and fragmented by the consequences of economic and spatial restructuring, amid increasing income inequality, massive commercial develop- ment, and gentrification.[34] The increased assertiveness of management in the workplace and the lack of sympathy of the national government to community- based demands for housing and social-service programs contributed to the accel- erating weakness of subordinate classes. Neither the major opposition parties nor community-based movements were able to develop an effective counterprogram that impressed electoral majorities as containing a strategy for economic growth as well as social equity.[35] During the '90s the ascendance of a Democratic admin- istration in Washington, the ouster of Prime Minister Thatcher in Britain, and the eventual election of a Labour government in 1997 weakened but did not destroy the earlier pressures toward reliance on the market to guide development.

Indeed, the Blair government continued the Conservative program of priva- tization of public services and reliance on the private sector to finance regenera- tion schemes: "Blair made it very clear that the Labour Party would continue to support the business community and that the imperatives of the market would be paramount in the new government's thinking. The need to compete internation- ally was seen as an important influence on government. . . . In this respect, there appears to be strong continuity with the ideology of Thatcherism."[36] An im- portant difference, however, was greater government involvement in the pro- cess of deciding the location and nature of investments. This was achieved through the identification of sites for extensive regeneration projects and the use of a competitive-bidding process for selection of developers for them. Criteria for judg- ing bids were to include environmental sustainability and social benefit as well as purely economic contributions.

Nevertheless, while national currents thus fundamentally affected politics in the two cities, local conflicts and events also played a role, to which I now turn.

London

Despite the influence of the central government on London, local interests con- tinued to affect its fate during the Thatcher-Major era. Labour control of about half the boroughs meant that opponents of Conservative policies could shape local-authority agendas and use them as bases of resistance to the initiatives of developers. Whereas white male trade-union leaders had previously dominated the Labour councils, by the time the Thatcher government came into power their composition had changed considerably. Throughout the 1970s intense political struggles went on within the Labour Party between liberal-left, largely home-owning university graduates and still-dominant right-wing manual workers. At the start of the '80s the former group had largely triumphed, although the closed regimes of the eastern London boroughs continued to distribute patronage to their supporters and to exclude middle-class constituents for half a decade longer. Based on tiny ward organizations and self-selection for office, these local political machines were finally forced to yield power when the challengers took over the ward parties and expelled sitting councillors from their candidacies.[37] The new activists focused on different kinds of issues from their predecessors and were, on the whole, less favorable to development proposals.

Ethnicity and gender. Blacks and feminists also successfully challenged the white male dominance of Labour strongholds in east and south London. However, even though Asians and Afro-Caribbeans increasingly achieved representation on councils in boroughs with large minority populations, and women also gained additional council seats, class still defined the major fissures in London society and politics. Whites remained the majority group in every borough; although immigration into London continued, its scale was dwarfed by the influx of immigrants to New York.[38] Hence, the racial-ethnic competition for jobs and living space that underlies New York's politics displays itself only weakly in London. Moreover, there is no history within London of urban redevelopment programs' having been widely used as a method of racial relocation (as happened in the 1950s and '60s in New York, where they left a significant residue of mistrust). While the Bengali community regards expansion of office uses on the eastern fringe of the City of London as a threat to its continued residence there, development politics is not usually construed in racial-ethnic terms, as often occurs in New York.

Fiscal issues. London, like New York, has suffered from fiscal stress in the last two decades, although less as a result of local conditions. Even Labour, when it controlled the central government in the 1970s, sought to deal with national budget deficits by reducing grants to local governments; under Margaret Thatcher this necessity became a principle;[39] and the present Labour government continues to practice fiscal stringency.[40] Consequently, the London local authorities— like most other municipal governments throughout the United Kingdom—have confronted social deterioration with diminished revenues and reduced staffs.

British tax policy has not permitted local governments to offer tax breaks to firms threatening to depart from their environs.[41] Thus, London has mainly avoided New York's controversies over tax giveaways to the rich. The one exception to this policy lay in the tax incentives provided within the Isle of Dogs enterprise zone in the Docklands, where all entering firms received a five-year tax holiday.

This system, however, differed from New York's in that every investor received the same deal, preventing the development authority from entering into bidding wars. Docklands developers also benefited from cheap land sales offered by the LDDC. Political opponents of Docklands development seized on these advantages given to business interests while investment was simultaneously withdrawn from social housing, contending that these policies demonstrated class bias. The London enterprise zone no longer exists, while New York City continues to offer ever-larger tax benefits to property developers and business firms.

Ideological constraints. The conflict over the abolition of the GLC had importance beyond its immediate implications for planning and administration. Under Ken Livingstone the GLC had become a significant political force in opposition to Thatcherism; its commitment to low transit fares, manufacturing investment, social housing, and "fringe" cultural institutions brought upon it the wrath of the Conservative central government. During the six-year period from 1978 to 1984 its expenditures increased in real terms by 65 percent.[42] Its abolition took place in 1986 under the rubric of administrative efficiency, despite a referendum showing support for its continuation by an overwhelming majority of Londoners. Its elimination was widely and correctly interpreted as an attack on municipal radicalism and local autonomy.[43]

Conservative success in terminating the GLC subdued opponents of the central government's free-market ideology, undermining the institutional and ideological support that had previously legitimated redistributional policies.[44] With GLC support gone, local authorities opposing the central government's market-led policies lost access to resources that had assisted them in steering a more independent course. A further consequence was to produce a kind of local political paralysis: The ease with which the Conservatives simply wiped out a whole level of government inhibited local-government activism, as it seemed to show that deviation from central-government policy would have little chance of success.

By the end of the 1980s local-authority politicians and officers who had once opposed central-government policies had largely given up. Although they lacked enthusiasm for market-led development, they acquiesced in its inevitability. One planning director of a Labour-controlled borough formerly viewed as "difficult" by developers described the situation succinctly: "We have embraced the new realism. I have no enthusiasm but little choice." Bob Colenutt, a Docklands activist and longtime critic of "the property machine," observed to me that the Tories were divided between those who favored more planning and community service and those who would "let the market do its business and get the public sector out of the whole thing." But, he went on, "All are ideologically pleased that they have smashed Labour, destroyed local authorities, and [in their terms] regenerated the inner city. Many senior Labour politicians would admit they have no real alternatives. They are critical but they have no other agenda."

After Labour regained power, local authorities did not return to their earlier oppositional stances. According to the development director of Southwark, "The [Labour-dominated] council was totally committed to [commercial] development. Previously it had been totally opposed. . . . If nothing happens, there is no money for housing improvement." Bob Colenutt, now a local-authority official, observed in 2000 that "the action groups of the '70s and '80s demanding affordable housing, etc., are much quieter. . . . There is controversy over environmental issues but not equity. . . . Has anything really changed? Regeneration is [still] primarily property led. There is no public-sector alternative program to private-sector leadership. . . . Social goals depend on the success of private market initiatives." The Labour leader of the Tower Hamlets council considered that opposition to development schemes collapsed when lobbyists obtained an affordable-housing requirement connected to private, market-rate residential investment:[45] "The left position is now contingent on obtaining development. They need to do deals." A somewhat cynical scholar and activist commented: "It's hard to say what Labour is doing. They make all these same speeches about public-private partnerships—same as the Tories. Identical."

Partnerships among local authorities (including with each other), communities, and business are, in fact, the principal vehicles for large development schemes. Originating in the City Challenge program, they provide the required framework for bids to obtain Single Regeneration Budget (SRB) funds (see Chapter 5). The basic concept is that public money should leverage a substantially greater sum of private investment. Ironically, the roots of this concept lie in the American Urban Development Action Grant (UDAG) program, begun by President Carter and terminated during the Reagan presidency. In contrast, New York's main access to federal funds for redevelopment is through the formula-based community development block grant (CDBG).[46] London's local authorities in the meantime are constantly competing for central-government funds, and the requirement for collaboration with business and communities in the writing of proposals has given birth to the various ongoing partnership arrangements. The ultimate result has been the movement toward a much more consensual development politics, arguably more productive than before but also involving the cooptation of working-class leadership.

A recent manifestation of the impulse toward partnership is the amalgamation of the former Greater London Enterprise Board (GLEB), later renamed Greater London Enterprise (GLE), with the London Enterprise Agency Ltd. (LEntA), an agency supported by eleven of the country's largest firms[47] and the Corporation of London to form New LEntA. The purpose of this entity, which would be a subsidiary of GLE, was to "fight poverty, unemployment and dereliction in London by promoting enterprise, investment, and regeneration."[48] GLEB began as a socialist project sponsored by the GLC to create publicly owned industry. After the Tories killed off its parent body, it continued as an enterprise wholly owned by the London boroughs. As such, it managed the assets it possessed and reinvested them, seeking to support small- and medium-sized businesses in deprived areas. It engaged in direct lending and also acted as an intermediary between financial institutions and borrowers; in addition, it directly owned and operated property so as to provide affordable small-business accommodation;[49] and it made various services (e.g., design, financial consulting, etc.) available to organizations seeking to promote economic development and affordable housing.

New York

The Democratic Party has dominated postwar electoral politics within New York City.[50] It is, however, divided into "reform" and "regular" wings, with the regulars devoting themselves almost entirely to the allocation of nominations and patronage. Whereas in the 1960s the Reform Democrats had strong, liberal policy positions, their influence and ideology have waned during the ensuing decades. In general, the party system exists primarily for the purpose of contesting elections rather than for exercising programmatic control, and it has therefore largely failed as a vehicle for representing neighborhood or minority interests.[51] It is not possible to describe a party program on economic development for the simple reason that there is none. Hence, in contrasting New York and London, one cannot compare Democrats with Labourites or Republicans with Conservatives on either this dimension or the evolution of ideologically based internal party divisions.

During the real-estate booms, district-based representatives, including both state legislators and city councillors, frequently played ombudsman roles in city affairs and lobbied for neighborhood concerns. Lacking formal responsibility for land-use decisions, however, the most such officials could do in this crucial arena was to put pressure on elected officials with executive power.[52] These policymakers usually responded to more highly organized and wealthier constituencies and almost uniformly supported large development projects. The dominant role played by the Board of Estimate in the governance of a city of over 7 million people made it extremely difficult for community-based representatives to build their reputations and attain sufficient financing to seek higher office.

Ethnic divisions. Mobilization by low-income minority groups in the late '60s strained the alliance between New York's working-class communities, labor organizations, and progressive, elite civic associations that had previously sustained governmental activism. As the city's population became increasingly nonwhite, its extensive array of social services failed to adapt sufficiently to the demands of their new clients and began to suffer crises of financing and legitimacy. In part because its urban-renewal program had eliminated pockets of black population scattered throughout Manhattan, and also because "white flight" had emptied many formerly middle-class neighborhoods in the boroughs, the city became increasingly segregated. Demands by racial and ethnic minorities for school desegregation, the ending of job discrimination, and improved services met resistance from the predominantly white city bureaucracy. The various subsidized housing programs foundered over the racial issue, as white voters refused to support programs that they saw as primarily benefiting minorities.

By 1968 minority groups had switched from demanding the desegregation of housing and schools to pressing for community power in areas where population composition was homogeneously black and Hispanic. During the crisis over community control of schools, which pitted black parents against white principals and teachers and resulted in that year's three-month-long teachers' strike, lines were drawn that were never subsequently erased.[53] In particular, the public service unions, which had formerly joined forces with their clientele to press for the enlargement of social programs, now regarded their vociferous clients as hostile and vice versa. The unions continued to make demands for salary and pension improvements, but the ostensible beneficiaries of their activities no longer saw themselves as gaining from budget increases for salaried city workers.

Fiscal distress. New York's fiscal crisis of 1975 marked the demise of a governing regime incorporating labor and minority interests. As with the abrogation of the GLC, the resolution of the fiscal crisis proved a traumatic event in the political history of New York. The immediate cause of the city's 1975 revenue shortfall was the refusal of banks to refinance New York's short-term debt once the city lost its approval by the principal investment bond-rating firms. Unlike the nation, New York still had not recovered from the recession at the beginning of the '70s; as a consequence, its revenues were falling, but its financial commitments went on rising. The city government increasingly borrowed to fund current expenditures, backing its bonds with mythical or previously committed anticipated revenues. Once the banks refused to continue lending, New York City had no alternative source of financing by which to meet its obligations.

Essentially, the fiscal crisis resulted from the effort to sustain a strongly interventionist public sector within a situation of economic contraction without greater support from the national and state governments. Interventionism comprised both large subsidies to capital, in the form of infrastructure investment to support new development, and major guarantees of social welfare. The costs of government were further expanded by relatively high total compensation for municipal employees.[54] With no new revenues and inexorable pressures to spend, the crisis could not be averted.

The two years after the 1975 crisis marked an interregnum in New York's political life. Negotiations to provide new capital and keep the city from formally declaring bankruptcy caused the New York State government to create a number of business-dominated bodies to oversee future spending. Control of public policy shifted from the office of Mayor Abraham Beame to these new agencies—the Municipal Assistance Corporation (MAC), the Financial Control Board (FCB), and the Office of the State Deputy Comptroller (OSDC) for New York City.[55] The semi-autonomous MAC had been guaranteed a revenue stream against which to borrow and was entrusted with the job of restoring the city's credit. The FCB, which was an agency of New York State, oversaw and had veto power over the city's financial plan, while the deputy comptroller acted as its staff, auditor, and research component. Businessmen chaired the MAC board and the FCB, which consisted of public officials and business and civic leaders; the MAC board had one African-American member, while the FCB included no members of minority groups.

The criterion these boards used for evaluating city policies was their effect on the balance sheet. Even after the 1977 election of Mayor Edward I. Koch and the subsequent return to a more assertive city government, these agencies strongly influenced the city's budgetary priorities in a fiscally conservative direction. Under their direction, the city cut thousands of municipal jobs, drastically curtailed services, halted all major capital programs ranging from school to subway building, froze civil-service salaries and public-assistance levels, introduced tuition fees in the City University, and deferred routine infrastructure maintenance. The municipal unions, whose strikes and strike threats had enabled them to wring billions of dollars of concessions from the Wagner and Lindsay administrations, grudgingly agreed to purchase the MAC bonds that no one else showed much interest in buying. Their leadership began to meet regularly with bank executives to work out mutually acceptable strategies for city expenditures.

During the bleak years following New York's near bankruptcy, almost the only investment activity that took place within the city involved the renovation and conversion of existing residential and factory buildings into middle- and upper-income homes. These projects took advantage of tax-subsidy programs that substantially reduced costs to new occupants and resulted in the gentrification of parts of Manhattan and Brooklyn where working-class people had inhabited architecturally appealing buildings.[56] The single major effort to provide low-income housing consisted of the in rem program, which used federal CDBG funds for maintenance and rehabilitation of buildings seized for tax delinquency. At the same time, large numbers of units dropped out of the housing stock as a consequence of landlord abandonment, condemnation, and fire.

Ideological transformation. Koch's electoral victory signaled the empowerment of a regime with little practical or symbolic commitment to low-income minorities and which, once prosperity returned in the mid-1980s, continued to emphasize economic development rather than social welfare activities.[57] The mayor summed up his attitude as follows: "I speak out for the middle class. You know why? Because they pay taxes; they provide jobs for the poor people."[58]

The period 1975–1980 was one in which New York City appeared hostage to financial institutions and economic forces well beyond its control.[59] It was also a time in which, contrary to many predictions, retrenchment led low-income groups to moderate their claims rather than threaten the legitimacy of the government. Even before the conservative tide swept over the U.S. national government after the Reagan election of 1980, New York City's regime expressed its determination to control governmental extravagance, which was interpreted as providing for the poor rather than offering incentives for investors and services for the middle class. Whereas in the late 1960s and early 1970s groups rooted in New York's poor neighborhoods mobilized strongly in favor of programs to improve their communities and brought protesters out into the streets when they opposed a program, the post–fiscal crisis policy switch met with acquiescence.

After the economy began to turn around in the early 1980s, the resolution of the fiscal crisis through the creation of new institutions to ensure solvency on terms set by business provided the context for the development politics of the next two decades. Ideologically, these new institutions—combined with widespread popular belief attributing fiscal demise to the squandering of resources on the undeserving (and predominantly black and Hispanic) poor—undermined the city government's traditional role in assuaging the frictions between classes and ethnic groups through patronage and welfare provision.[60] The achievement of economic growth and fiscal solvency was substituted for service provision as the test of governmental legitimacy.

The establishment of a group of institutions to guide New York City's fiscal policy constituted a parallel event to the elimination of the GLC and the parceling out of its functions to higher and lower levels of government. They were rooted in different causes and took on contrasting institutional forms. Their effects, however, were similar: They weakened the power of local elected officials; they delegitimized redistributional local policies; and they strengthened the ideological onslaught in favor of market-led economic development programs. The variance that had previously existed in both cities between national and local policy directions, wherein the municipal regime followed a more radical course, was consequently substantially reduced.

Whereas the ideological currents in London shifted before the 1997 change in national governments, the commitment to economic development with no special focus on low-income people continued in New York. The four-year mayoralty of David Dinkins, an African American elected in 1989, marked a brief interruption in which the interests of minority populations gained greater attention. Since, however, the context of the entire Dinkins administration was economic recession and consequent contraction of the city budget, intentions of enhancing social programs could not bear fruit. Moreover, the Dinkins administration did not break with the precedents of offering tax benefits to firms threatening to leave New York.

Rudolph Giuliani, a Republican, won the mayoral election in 1993 and proceeded to play to his electoral base of white middle- and working-class constituents. Except for Staten Island,[61] where he owed substantial political debts, he largely ignored the situation of the other boroughs, focusing on Manhattan, which already housed the greatest concentration of wealth in the country. His principal emphasis was on lowering the crime rate and the perception that New York was too dangerous a place in which to do business. Whether as a consequence of his policing policies or not, the crime rate did fall dramatically during his administration, and the perception of a cleaner, safer city did contribute to economic stability and the expansion of tourism. He did not concern himself particularly with affordable housing, and the city's earlier commitment to increasing the housing supply for low-income people dwindled substantially. The administration, however, was attempting to rid itself of the in rem housing stock it had acquired through tax foreclosure, often by selling it to the highest bidder and thereby removing it from the low-income stock. At the same time, the economic boom that coincided with his mayoralty caused enormous pressure on the housing market, as gentrification, which had halted during the early '90s, came back with a vengeance.[62] Although community development corporations (CDCs) continued to construct and rehabilitate housing for poor people, rising land prices in all parts of the city seriously inhibited their activities. The combination of economic expansion, stratospheric rewards to upper-echelon workers in the securities and legal services industries, and the spawning of Internet millionaires made the rich richer than ever.[63] At the same time, absolute incomes of the bottom two deciles of the population fell by 19 percent between 1989 and 1997, and the income of the middle quintile declined by 8 percent.[64]

In contrast to London, which during the late '90s entered a period of consensus building, in New York resentments against the administration among minority citizens festered. The kinds of partnerships and increased community participation in planning that were becoming institutionalized in Britain were largely absent in New York. Nevertheless, by 2000, when because of terms limits the end of the Giuliani administration was in sight, opposition to the mayor was muted.[65] Community groups were mainly trying to stall until they found an administration more to their liking. Business interests were doing too well to find fault with the mayor and, unlike their London counterparts, showed little interest in strategic planning for the city. Despite a substantial budget surplus, little effort was going into improving the city's increasingly challenged transportation system, and even though businesses were inconvenienced by it, they put little pressure on the government.

Thus, whereas the policy-making contexts of New York and London converged during the '80s, they moved farther apart in the next decade. These differences point to the importance of ideology and governing regime (at the national as much as the local level) in affecting urban programs. Whether or not the ultimate outcomes—as measured by quality-of-life and equity indicators—would turn out to be vastly different remains to be seen. London's projects were mainly still in the planning stage, the American stock markets had plunged, and New York was on the brink of new elections at the time of this writing. If economic expansion continued, London's various flagship projects would move toward completion. In New York at this moment, a number of redevelopment projects were being proposed, but except for minor-league sports stadiums and some redevelopment on Staten Island, few had obtained commitments despite a large budget surplus. Both cities suffered from extraordinarily inflated housing prices and lacked major, publicly sponsored programs to build affordable housing. Requirements that market-rate builders provide low-income housing in London and incentives rewarding them for doing so in New York were unlikely to make a substantial difference in supply. Consequently, the extent to which the bottom quartile of the population in either city would benefit greatly from their prosperity was far less than certain.

5

Economic Development
Planning Strategies

For much of this century, urban planning in both London and New York concentrated on controlling and improving the physical environment. Planners engaged primarily in determining land uses and proposing public investments in infrastructure, amenities, and housing. To be sure, infrastructure planners have always sought to improve economic function, and inner-city redevelopment planning has throughout the postwar period aimed at eliciting private investment. The premise of these types of planning, however, was essentially physically determinist—planners assumed that changes in the physical environment would yield an economic response. Holding a supply-oriented view of urban space, planners expected that private investors would avail themselves of adequately serviced, centrally located land without further incentives.

Until the 1970s, urban planning's justification lay in comprehensiveness, an orientation to the long term, protection of the environment, and attention to the needs of all social groups. Numerous critics have argued that these goals were never achieved, that planning always primarily benefited business interests, and that economic advantage has perennially constituted the real objective of city planning.[1] Nevertheless, even if the unspoken goal of planning has always been private economic gain, both the rhetoric surrounding its attainment and the modus operandi of planners have changed. Moreover, the earlier construction of urban problems as defined by poverty and inner-city decline has been reconstituted in terms of competitiveness and fiscal solvency.

The Discourse of Planning

The discourse in which planners in London and New York interpret the world and communicate their intentions shifted during the 1980s from long-term concerns with environmental quality to an emphasis on short-term accomplishments.

Much of planning theory during the 1960s and 1970s had focused on the specification of the rational model, by which planners generated a possible range of actions to reach previously designated goals.[2] Only shortly after this effort to portray a universal approach to planning had triumphed in the theoretical literature, however, a quite different but broadly generalizable planning mode was emerging in practice. Modeled on the methods of the corporation rather than the laboratory, this planning strategy deviated considerably from the formulaic norm of the rational model. Rather than framing and testing an exhaustive and abstractly constructed set of alternatives, planners concerned with maintaining neighborhoods or bringing new investment into the central business district aimed at discerning targets of opportunity. Instead of picturing an end state and elaborating means to arrive at it, they established narrow goals and grabbed for that mixture of devices that would permit at least some forward progress.[3]

Even planners who worked for government or nonprofit groups and did focus on distributional effects became absorbed into the discourse of business negotiations and a single-minded concentration on the deal at hand.[4] Their goals, which centered on employment for unskilled or displaced workers, low-cost housing, and neighborhood economic development, likewise were met piecemeal through the funding of individual projects. Without national government support for comprehensive neighborhood programs, which were briefly attempted under the Model Cities program in the United States and the Community Development Project in the United Kingdom, community-based planners had few choices but to seek support in whatever quarter they could find it.

Whereas the vocabularies of architecture and the law once permeated their discussions, planners now spoke in the same language as investment bankers, property brokers, and budget analysts.[5] The old arguments for planning had been comprehensiveness and reducing negative externalities—that is, preventing development from harming the environment around it.[6] The new claims were competitiveness and efficiency. The debate over the utility of the rational model became meaningless when planners spent their time negotiating with private investors rather than devising plans. Whereas planning was previously seen by both its supporters and its right-wing critics as antithetical to markets, it was now directed at achieving marketability of its product: urban space.[7] (By this term I mean not just territory but the set of development rights and financial capabilities associated with a piece of land.)

Many planners continued to work at traditional planning functions like zoning or transportation. The new discourse of planning affected them relatively little. For an increasing number of planners, however, the focus changed dramatically, regardless of the particular scheme to which they devoted their time. Projects on which planners worked varied from the grand scale of megadevelopments like Battery Park City and Canary Wharf to the small scope of shopping-strip revitalization or Neighborhood Housing Services. The *style* of local economic development planning behavior, however, varied less than the types of projects. At different scales, regardless of whether the project was an office development, a high-tech manufacturing center, or a low-income housing cooperative, planners performed a mediating function, bringing together private investors and public sponsors, interceding between utility companies and energy-using businesses, dealing with outraged members of the public, and cajoling developers for exactions or planning gain. Negotiation rather than plan making has become the planner's most important activity. The director of planning of London's City of Westminster remarked to me that nothing in his training as a planner fortified him for his role as a deal negotiator: "Education won't prepare you for the experience of having a megamillion-pound individual sitting across from you who will break your legs!"

The resulting landscape reflected the piecemeal, accomodationist mode in which planning was carried out during the '80s in both cities and throughout the '90s in New York. Most office projects and upper-income condominiums, which once would have formed part of a larger development program, were single-site efforts uncoordinated with their surroundings, contributing to the postmodern vista of checkerboard development, unmatching architecture, uncontrolled congestion, and sharp juxtaposition of rich and poor. Low-income housing, unlike the large public-housing complexes of yesteryear, was now almost always placed opportunistically, wherever a site could be found or a private developer enticed. In both London and New York, planners depended on private developers to build mixed-income projects in which market-rate units subsidized the much smaller percentage of low-income ones. In New York, planning was interstitial rather than comprehensive throughout the final quarter of the twentieth century. Within London the comprehensive model, absent during the '80s, began to reassert itself during the '90s, although its realization awaited the institutionalization of the London Development Authority.

In an important critique, David Harvey depicts planning as the coordination of the interests of business.[8] He accurately portrays the activities of most economic development planners in London and New York. Nevertheless, his analysis fails to explain why the scope of planners was limited to facilitating specific projects rather than extended comprehensively to the relationships of projects to each other and to the housing and transit systems. While certain business groups, especially property developers, used local government to advance their positions, business elites largely did not attempt to deploy governmental power more broadly to plan for their long-term interests in an efficient urban system.[9]

The independent deal making associated with each project and the efforts by individual developers and separate communities to gain the most advantage for themselves reinforced the fragmentation already created by the local governmental system. Within Harvey's terminology, the particular interests of individual capitalists triumphed over their combined interest in strategic management. This outcome resulted not just from democratic and institutional factors. To understand the constraints on comprehensive planning, one must examine the role played by community groups and politicians and understand the location of planning agencies within the governmental structure.

The democratic contradiction. While under the influence of business interests, planning is also subject to what Foglesong calls the democratic contradiction: Governments depend on capital for their resources, but they remain accountable to electorates.[10] Institutional devices for popular representation and legal challenge are insufficient to give voters a determinative role in development planning, but they do offer them channels sufficient for considerable veto power.

Citizens in London and New York have few avenues for taking planning initiatives, but a variety of requirements for public hearings—and, in New York, considerable opportunity for litigation—allow them to delay and sometimes block projects completely. In London, local authorities demanded project modifications and community benefits. Likewise, the New York community boards provided a forum for critics and a location for trading concessions between developers and neighborhood groups. While New York State legislators had no official role in development approvals, they too provided a route for opposing projects or negotiating changes. Most major development proposals therefore involved a good deal of bargaining among the parties.

In New York, landmarks and environmental legislation present the grounds for lawsuits, even though the basis on which they are brought often has little to do with the real objections to a project. Thus, for example, plans for Westway, a federally funded expressway along the Hudson River in Manhattan, foundered when a judge ruled that the road would threaten the spawning grounds for striped bass. The contest over the highway actually revolved around the desire of public officials and developers to create acres of developable property on landfill above and next to the road and the intense opposition by West Siders to increased density, traffic, and the effects of ten years of construction. These broader considerations, however, did not constitute a basis in law for blocking the road, while endangering a species did. When the development is entirely a private-sector project, builders can proceed as of right if their scheme fits within the zoning code, and efforts to block it must find a basis in environmental law rather than simply unsuitability. Thus, for example, opponents of a privately owned waste-transfer station in the Bronx brought suit demanding preparation of a formal environmental impact statement.[11] Their purpose was to delay implementation until a time when a more sympathetic city administration might be in power.[12] In another case, residents seeking to stop a large development scheme on Manhattan's Upper East Side, where Consolidated Edison was closing a generating plant, sued to prevent the utility from enlarging a different facility that was to replace the power produced by the decommissioned plant.[13]

The role of politicians. The orientation of local elected officials in both London and New York has shifted away from a focus on government-sponsored programs

to concern with benefits generated by the private sector. In both cities the influence of local politicians increased in relation to department and agency heads who
previously had an expanding flow of funds coming from the national government
at their disposal. In London during the 1980s a number of Conservative councillors switched their emphasis from environmental quality and service delivery to
attracting business enterprises. In particular, the chairs of planning in the Cities
of London and Westminster took the lead in overcoming opposition to large commercial projects within their jurisdictions. Thus, Michael Cassidy, the City of
London planning chair during the '80s, declared to me that his purpose was to
preserve the City as a financial center when its dominance was threatened by
Docklands development. He considered that the corporation previously had maintained a "curious attitude" in which councillors did not concern themselves with
attracting desirable businesses. He took pride in having been instrumental in changing the City's stance toward development and streamlining its process for appli-
cations for planning permission. Similarly, David Weeks, the planning chair of
Westminster, while somewhat worried about the possibility of overdevelopment,
described to me his efforts to overcome community opposition to projects he
thought desirable. He recounted his assistance to the Royal Opera House, which
needed planning permission to build an office building adjacent to its Covent
Garden site so as to fund expansion: "I had to push it through. It required being
rough and aggressive."[14]

By the end of the '90s the Tory-led Westminster council, which even during
the earlier boom had reservations about further commercial growth, had become
less interested in office development. Councillors, under pressure from their
constituents, would not allow rezoning from residential to commercial and had
become restrictive on the construction of hotels. In Paddington Basin, despite
proposals involving hotels and offices, initial construction was residential. The
council was asking for a £50 million contribution from the developers to be used
for local infrastructure. According to the developer, his firm was committed to
community payments and to building affordable housing. He commented: "The
change in the [national] government has had an effect. The Government Office
for London has created a different agenda—the emphasis is not just on the environment but on the social needs of the local community." He noted that he had
worked with the community in securing a £13.5 million grant from the Single
Regeneration Budget, to be used for job training.[15]

On the other side of the political fence, Labour councillors interested themselves in improving retail districts and—without much success—attracting light
manufacturing to their areas. Eventually, they saw financial deals with developers as the only path to community improvement. One Labour council leader, who
had previously held a high position in the GLC and who called himself a "participatory socialist," indicated that he tried to hire "entrepreneurial" officers to head
departments. He described with pride one deal by which a developer built a park
over an old gravel pit in return for the right to develop an office, and another under

which the council collected a percentage of the rents from a shopping mall built on the site of the old town hall. He differed from the Conservative councillors to whom I spoke, however, in being highly committed to community participation in formulating development schemes.

Many Labour councillors and officers that I interviewed regarded the situation at the start of the new century as an improvement. As one put it, "The leaders are more inclusive. It is practice, not just rhetoric." At the same time, they expressed ambivalence: "But has anything really changed? Regeneration is still primarily property led. There is no [public-sector] alternative to private-sector leadership. . . . The market is no longer seen as the enemy. Social goals depend on the success of private-market initiatives." The leader of Tower Hamlets council, a scholar familiar with the urban politics literature, mused: "The growth machine literature is now more applicable to the U.K. because of the enlarged role of private business [in public decision making]. At the same time the terms are changing. . . . [Developers] are involved with social programs—it's a sort of corporatist local government."[16]

In New York, where the previous generation of politicians prided themselves on the size of the grants they could obtain from Washington, the current group expended its energy on making the city attractive to business. Like the Labour councillors in London, New York's more progressive politicians emphasized assistance to manufacturing, nonprofit organizations, and small businesses rather than large corporations, but they also affirmed the system of providing private-sector incentives. Thus, for example, Ruth Messinger, former borough president of Manhattan and losing Democratic candidate for mayor in 1997, supported the granting of subsidies to the commodities exchanges for construction of a building in downtown Manhattan and sponsored a study to recommend assistance intended to keep the diamond industry in Manhattan. In an interview, she indicated to me that "there are ways out of oversubsidizing developers, but we must give subsidies. We have to assume that the New Jersey threat [to New York] is real."

The situation of planning agencies. The present operating style of planning agencies reflects both the expectations of politicians that they will act as negotiating agents and the institutional framework that inhibits comprehensiveness. Because the development process did not take place under the aegis of a powerful metropolitan planning body in either city, the very structure of government caused both geographical and functional fragmentation. The division of London into boroughs, and of New York into much larger boroughs and somewhat smaller community planning districts, meant that each development proposal followed a different path to approval and had to be framed in relation to localized situations. How much this will change in London once the London Development Authority (LDA) becomes established is not yet clear.

In each city the allocation of primary responsibility for infrastructure and facilities planning to a variety of agencies (roads, public transit, ports, parks, education, etc.) with distinct lines of authority means that Herculean efforts are required to coordinate their intentions. Since, in addition, these agencies report to different levels of government or are semi-autonomous, the problem is exacerbated. In the United Kingdom the Secretary of State for the Environment formerly and of the Environment, Tranport and the Regions now theoretically has the power to impose unity on the various levels. During the Thatcher period he was ideologically opposed to exercising it; more recently, with the establishment of the Government Office for London, the department has achieved greater coordination. In particular, it has identified a number of sites on the periphery of inner London as priority locations for major development. The office's most recent *Strategic Planning Guidance* for London was fairly detailed compared to earlier versions. Nevertheless, an overall development plan that charts the future of transport and its impact on land use awaits the LDA.

In New York no elected official has authority over all the agencies that plan the city, much less the region. New York did once have a much more unified planning and development apparatus than most American cities; both the creation and the breakdown of this apparatus incorporated specifically local factors. For decades planning and development in New York City had proceeded in accordance with Robert Moses's set of priorities. When Moses's hegemony finally crumbled in the early1960s, the reaction was to give primary responsibility for both commercial and residential planning to agencies under mayoral control. Although Moses's transportation functions were devolved to a regional agency, the city's Housing and Redevelopment Board (HRB) and Department of City Planning took charge of development planning. Later Mayor John Lindsay merged the HRB with other housing agencies to form a single "superagency," the Housing and Development Administration (HDA), with the object of creating a coherent program that would integrate preservation and redevelopment efforts. Mayoral policy insisted that priority for neighborhood and housing improvement be given to those areas that were the neediest. In its (last) 1969 master plan, the City Planning Commission presented a general strategy of promoting incentives for office development in Manhattan and residential improvements in the boroughs. By the late 1970s, however, the Department of Housing Preservation and Development (HPD—the remodeled HDA) had few federal funds at its disposal and, because of the fiscal crisis, no city capital budget; it exercised its reduced authority mainly in the realm of housing rehabilitation and no longer played an important role in guiding development. The Department of City Planning virtually gave up any pretense of overall land-use planning and devoted itself mainly to studies of specific zoning changes and project impacts. In the meantime, the economic development agencies became the lead players in devising redevelopment strategies.

In 2000 the City Planning Department did produce a new draft zoning ordinance that would impose new height limits, restrict transfer of development rights, establish a design review panel, and simplify zoning formulas. This quite moderate proposal, which nowhere approximated a master plan but simply aimed at improving the quality of the built environment, provoked the wrath of the building industry as well as the opposition of nonprofit organizations that could no longer benefit as much from selling their development rights. At the same time, many neighborhood groups felt that it did not go nearly far enough. As of June 2000 the future of the proposal remained in doubt.[17] Press commentary pointed to the power of the developer lobby with the city's politicians as key to the ordinance's future: "The real estate industry is a major source of contributions to political campaigns, and political observers believe that neither Mayor Rudy Giuliani nor the City Council would back a zoning revision strongly opposed by the industry."[18] This situation contrasts strikingly with London, where such blatant political intervention by property interests does not happen.

PUBLIC-PRIVATE PARTNERSHIPS

The common interest of both government and developers in maximizing the potential of a site enables public-private partnerships to flourish. Most of these arrangements involve joint public-private participation in major commercial projects. Partnerships do exist as well, however, to assist low-income individuals and neighborhood businesses. Within London the partnership structures now all include neighborhood representatives. In New York, in the Harlem/South Bronx Empowerment Zone, the partnership arrangement resembles the British model. In the rest of the city, however, resident interests have little input into development decision making, and, except for housing developers who must make 20 percent of their units available to low-income people if they receive a city subsidy, few deals incorporate benefits for low-income people.

The revised relationship between the public and private sectors that began to characterize planning during the mid-1970s had its roots in those changes in global relations that transformed urban economies and increased interurban competition. As investment, financial management, communications, and information-providing activities burgeoned and manufacturing shrank, pressures for reconfiguration of the existing built environment grew and became the basis on which the governing regimes of London and New York built their growth strategies. Within an extraordinarily fluid space economy, land development offered private investors opportunities for enormous profit; facilitating such development gave planners leverage over the private sector at the same time as nationally provided resources that formerly supported regeneration programs were withdrawn. Governmental agencies had largely abdicated their earlier direct role in urban regeneration, whereby they acquired and serviced land and built public facilities.[19] But government could use its tax and borrowing authority to lower development costs and thereby make projects more attractive to the investors on which the development industry depended without incurring the high front-end expenditures entailed by the previous approach. Moreover, the large scale of the most profitable projects meant that almost none qualified for governmental approval without the relaxation of regulations, nor could they be developed without the provision of infrastructure. This need for governmental intervention created the opening for bargaining, in which public officials traded governmental approval or capital spending for private contributions to housing or public facilities.

The trading of public and private benefits, implemented through planning gain and exactions, together with the melding of public and private powers into development corporations, constituted the principal vehicles by which the urban redevelopment process proceeded in London and New York during the 1980s. These arrangements took a variety of forms, including, among others, the trading of planning permission in return for the construction of affordable housing; the collaboration of public agencies with community organizations in low-income neighborhoods to form local development corporations; and the granting of tax holidays to private investors within enterprise zones in the hope of employment expansion. During the '90s, the United Kingdom closed down its urban development corporations and enterprise zones, while New York continued along the previous path of using public corporations exempted from normal zoning and oversight requirements and of granting tax and regulatory relief. Its newest redevelopment projects—for example, the Coliseum at Columbus Circle—involved few requirements that the developer provide public benefits.[20]

PLANNING GAIN AND EXACTIONS

Public officials in London and New York have expanded the concept of exactions beyond its original meaning. Initially, developers were called upon to satisfy infrastructure needs created by their undertakings (e.g., streets and sewers) or to provide compensation (impact fees) for the negative effects of a project.[21] More recently, however, planners have made developers contribute to off-site improvements, including affordable housing and day care centers, as a condition for approval of their proposals. Developers anxious to get their projects moving will frequently offer a range of concessions in order to elicit cooperation from planners; planners who can no longer look to higher levels of government for substantial capital assistance see negotiations with developers as their principal opportunity for obtaining community benefits.[22] The package of public permissions and developer obligations becomes incorporated into a development agreement.

Because British local authorities have great discretion in the granting of planning permission, London local-authority planners occupy a potentially dominating position in the quest for planning gain. One planning director described a typical deal in which, in return for being allowed to build offices on a two-acre publicly owned site, a developer agreed to build 50 industrial units and a hostel for the homeless, as well as contributing to improvements in the local tube station. Within the Spitalfields Market development area the development consortium donated twelve acres to a community land trust so as to elicit cooperation from neighborhood groups (see Chapter 7). The Thatcher government sought to prevent local authorities from negotiating with developers to obtain community benefits not directly related to project impacts.[23] However, whereas the Conservatives regarded such bargaining as extortion, the present Labour government encourages it.

In New York, even though developers do not need to seek planning permission if their project conforms to existing zoning, most are willing to engage in bargaining that permits them to build a bigger project than would be permissible under the zoning statute. Other deals are made in order to gain public subsidies. For example, developer William Zeckendorf, Jr., built hundreds of units of affordable housing in return for permission to construct two large developments over neighborhood objections. In an unusual bargaining arrangement that occurred before the project entered the public approval process,[24] Donald Trump negotiated with West Side community groups concerning the configuration and contents of his huge proposed project on old railroad yards. The developer agreed to donate land to the city for a rerouted West Side Highway, to build a park, and to construct affordable housing; in return, the civic organizations acceded to the scale and density of the plan for this long-contested site.[25]

In addition to negotiated exchanges, developers in New York can tap into a set of regularized rewards to which they are entitled if they undertake certain actions viewed as providing community benefits. Thus, they receive tax benefits for working outside Manhattan under the Industrial and Commercial Incentives Program (ICIP); they can obtain the right to build additional space if they construct specified public amenities under the zoning bonus system; and, under the "80-20" housing program, residential developers receive various subsidies and regulatory relief if 20 percent of their units are affordable housing.

URBAN DEVELOPMENT CORPORATIONS AND OTHER PUBLIC-PRIVATE ORGANIZATIONS

While development agreements represent ad hoc relationships between the public and private sectors, the urban development corporation (UDC) is a formal vehicle through which government entices private developers to participate in fulfilling its economic development objectives. UDCs retain many of the governmental powers of their participating public agencies while not being subject to the normal requirements on the public sector, such as holding open public meetings, filing extensive reports of their activities, providing avenues for community participation, and conforming to civil-service rules. While ultimately responsible to public elected officials, UDCs operate much like private firms, employing the entrepreneurial styles and professional image-building techniques more customary in the corporate than in the governmental world.[26]

British Approaches

The beginnings of a new approach to redevelopment in Great Britain appeared in the Labour government's Inner Urban Areas Act of 1978, which gave urban partnerships (comprising central government, certain local authorities, private business, and local voluntary organizations) powers to encourage industrial and commercial development.[27] Under this program, as well as providing site improvements and supporting infrastructure, local authorities could offer loans and grants to private firms. After the Conservative triumph of 1979 made Margaret Thatcher Prime Minister, stimulation of private-sector investment became much more important than previously, and UDCs became the centerpiece of urban policy. The central government designated and financed UDCs, which were directly accountable to it but not to the local planning authorities in the areas in which they operated.[28] Although British UDCs resembled New York's development corporations in many respects, they differed in that the American entities had considerable autonomy from all levels of government and no connection at all with the national government. The British UDCs were given limited life spans, and all have now completed their terms.

The London Docklands Development Corporation. The London Docklands Development Corporation (LDDC) was established by Parliament in 1981 as the planning and development agency for 8.5 miles of territory in East London and was the most prominent partnership agency in London throughout the 1980s (a more detailed analysis of it appears in Chapter 9). It encompassed within its jurisdiction parts of the boroughs of Tower Hamlets, Newham, and Southwark, superseding their planning authority in the area along the Thames. Throughout the 1970s these three local authorities (along with the adjacent borough of Greenwich) had sought to implement an overall planning strategy for Docklands that emphasized industrial and social-housing uses. When the Conservative government took power in 1979, however, although progress had been made in infrastructure preparation and the demolition of derelict structures, little new investment had been attracted.[29]

The LDDC obtained title to much of the vacant land in the redevelopment area and sold it cheaply to private developers. Public contributions consisted of an enormous infrastructure program, overall planning and management, tax breaks within the enterprise zone that had been established on the Isle of Dogs, and a sales and public-relations effort. Except for infrastructure planning, most of the energy of LDDC personnel went into selling the location to potential investors, and they mounted an extremely sophisticated and elaborate public-relations and sales effort to do so.

The intended scope of Docklands redevelopment was vast and included within it a variety of separate projects. Proposals for the area included offices, housing, schools, retailing, recreational space, a sports arena, an exhibition hall, and some manufacturing and warehousing.[30] The largest office complex, Canary Wharf, located within the Isle of Dogs Enterprise Zone, was to be developed by Olympia & York (O & Y) on an order of magnitude even greater than O & Y's World Financial Center within New York's Battery Park City; ultimately, the venture was to encompass 12.5 million square feet of commercial space (see Chapters 8 and 9).

During the peak of London's property development boom, the LDDC was wildly successful in attracting private investment; in the first eight months of 1988 alone, £4.4 billion ($7.5 billion) of private money had been committed.[31] Only shortly thereafter, however, the future of O & Y's Canary Wharf investment had become doubtful, and many other Docklands projects were in serious trouble or even bankruptcy.

The LDDC was heavily attacked for its emphasis on roads at the expense of transit, its encouragement of development in such an inaccessible area, its causing a bias in the entire transportation investment program of the United Kingdom toward the Docklands, and its neglect of the area's original residents.[32] Its focus on office development meant that few new jobs would match the skills of existing residents, although it should be noted that while the service industries moving into the office complexes offered little employment for displaced dockers, they did provide clerical and retail jobs for local women. Its residential strategy of selling land to for-profit housing developers meant that most local residents could not afford the new units. Furthermore, the UDC mechanism, under the control of a board appointed by the central government, excluded residents from the planning process.[33] Bob Colenutt, director of the Docklands Consultative Committee (DCC), commented to me: "Power in Docklands lies outside the people we represent. It's with the big developers, the LDDC. The local authorities have very little power, and where they do, they don't use it."

During the late '80s, however, the LDDC did begin to emphasize job training and social programs to benefit longtime occupants, and by 1997 the LDDC had spent £110 million on social and community development, about half of which was for education and training.[34] During the 1990s property slump, when land values fell, nonprofit developers took over a number of the housing ventures;[35] in addition, the LDDC contributed to improving the quality of 8,000 existing social housing units.[36] By the time of its termination, the LDDC had been responsible for a net increase of 23,000 jobs and substantial additions to the public transport and road systems.[37] Responding to the rhetoric of partnership, the LDDC in its later years became more open to community consultation. Whereas a poll conducted in 1988 showed that 61 percent of Docklands residents thought that the LDDC did not take account of local voices, the number expressing that sentiment dropped to 34 percent in 1996.[38]

City Challenge and the Single Regeneration Budget. The City Challenge program marked the first large-scale institutionalization of the partnership concept, in which government funds would leverage private monies within a deprived area.

Places would bid to be named recipients of City Challenge funds in a national competition; the bids would be put together collaboratively by all sectors of the community and would lay out the regeneration strategy. Later, the same principle underlay the Single Regeneration Budget (SRB), which consolidated a variety of central government–sponsored regeneration efforts into a single program.[39] Like the American Community Development Block Grant (CDBG) program, the SRB was intended to give communities considerable leeway in designing their approach to regeneration. But, whereas CDBG money is distributed on a formula basis to all localities, local authorities had to compete for City Challenge and SRB funds. The need to demonstrate cooperation among the parties to the bid undercut the hostility that formerly existed between impoverished community residents and business leaders. It also caused business elites, who had formerly held aloof from local politics, to become involved in their localities.

City Challenge was the stimulus for a major regeneration effort adjacent to the City of London. In response to a request for proposals, the Tower Hamlets council applied for a City Challenge grant for Bethnal Green, one of its neighborhoods. It received the grant in 1992 for a community-oriented effort at achieving redevelopment under the auspices of a public-private partnership (see Chapter 7). Here, while large developers were still regarded as the main source of development capital, greater provision was made for community participation in planning for the area; program goals included housing construction and the provision of business premises for the original occupants; and the East London Partnership, which acted as the coordinating agency, did not have the special powers of the LDDC.

City Challenge, while much more responsive to local communities than the UDC approach, still broke with traditional local decision making that occurred within the regular governmental structure. The government contribution was intended to leverage private-sector commitments, and community organizations were supposed to assist small-scale entrepreneurship. Thus, the grant program was aimed at encouraging activity by the kinds of elite corporate entities and community development groups long active in American inner cities but not yet very visible within the United Kingdom. Because, historically, local authorities had both taken the initiative and provided the funding for community-based economic and housing activity, these kinds of intermediate organizations had been rare in London, although community advocacy associations were plentiful. Eight years later, further stimulated by the successor SRB program, partnerships had multiplied and had become part of every regeneration effort.

Housing associations. Housing associations are the closest British equivalent to American housing development corporations. They have a long history in London, stretching back to the philanthropic and church-based organizations that sponsored improved housing for slum-dwellers in the nineteenth century. While a subset of these associations are neighborhood-based cooperatives, the great majority are run by boards drawn from outside the communities in which they operate. Although they typically function as charities rather than community organizations, they have transcended their religious roots, having become large, professionally run associations. Most are simply landlords, but many of them also develop housing, and under the Conservative government they displaced local councils as the builders of social housing. Beginning in the mid-1990s local authorities began transferring the housing estates under their control to housing associations; as a consequence, some of the housing associations now manage massive numbers of units.[40] The Blair government continued the policy of relying on these extragovernmental institutions for implementation of its housing programs.

The central government's Housing Corporation is the principal financial underwriter of housing-association construction and has become the main conduit of central-government funds into low-income housing construction. British tax law does not provide special incentives for corporations to invest in low-income housing, and therefore there is no comparable source of funding to that provided by the Low Income Housing Tax Credit in the United States (see below). Housing associations increasingly also raise money in the private credit market, but with some difficulty. Britain has no equivalent to the American Community Reinvestment Act, which requires banks to invest in their service areas, and the government usually does not offer loan guarantees to defray risks to private lenders. Although many housing associations specialize in building housing for special populations (e.g., the handicapped or single people), others have been active with particular communities, especially within the East End, or have addressed the problems of immigrant populations and the homeless. Throughout the '80s they produced an average of about 1,500 housing units per year in Greater London, equaling or exceeding public production in 1985–1989.[41]

As resources available to local authorities for council-housing production evaporated, they have come increasingly to rely on the housing associations to take up the slack. Although many housing associations are highly professional, experienced, and flexible, the limited funds at their disposal keep them from greatly enlarging the pool of housing available to low- and moderate-income households. They stepped up their production considerably in the mid-'90s to nearly 8,000 units per year, but then curtailed their production by more than 60 percent as the decade drew to a close.[42] Meanwhile, the sale of council housing to tenants under the Conservative "Right to Buy" program had resulted in a large reduction in the number of units affordable by low-income households. Thus, construction of affordable housing increasingly became the responsibility of private developers building large mixed-occupancy schemes, who were required to apportion a fraction of their units to low-income households.

U.S. Approaches

Public-private cooperation has always formed the touchstone for U.S. urban redevelopment policy. Local government never played the major role of British local authorities in housing provision and industrial development. Elite, business-dominated groups like Pittsburgh's Allegheny Conference, Boston's "Vault," and San Francisco's SPUR had long acted as quasi-official planning agencies for their municipalities. A series of federal housing and development programs, beginning with the Housing and Urban Renewal Act of 1949, have relied primarily on private developers to rebuild blighted areas by using public subsidies to stimulate private investment. During the 1970s, however, a discernible shift took place in the character of U.S. programs, as the federal government reduced its financial support and withdrew from its oversight role.

The contraction in federal subsidies forced localities to turn to the private sector for start-up funds for major projects. In 1974 Congress terminated the Urban Renewal and Model Cities programs and substituted CDBG, which, as well as reducing the amount of subsidy received by big cities, switched the emphasis from large-scale redevelopment efforts requiring comprehensive planning to individual projects and housing rehabilitation.[43] Urban Development Action Grants (UDAGs), introduced in 1977, made federal support for a project contingent on the leveraging of private funds, with local governments acting as intermediaries. Although the Reagan administration eventually terminated this program, it set a precedent for future activities under local auspices (and was imitated by the British government, which uses this model for its SRB grants). Local governments became increasingly entrepreneurial in attempting to stimulate private investment, actively promoting their available sites and hawking a range of subsidies, training programs, and expedited procedures designed to facilitate business operations.[44] The break with the past lay not in the priority given to private-sector desires but in the heightened level of local-government initiative in enticing private-sector involvement and the requirement that the private sector commit to a project before it is launched.

The Economic Development Corporation. In New York an array of development corporations provided the structure through which the city worked with private firms to foster physical development. The Public Development Corporation (PDC), renamed the Economic Development Corporation (EDC) in 1991, acted as the lead agency in collaboration with the private sector.[45] Established as a quasi-independent local development corporation with a board of prominent business people, the PDC played an entrepreneurial role in spurring construction during the '80s. Unlike the LDDC, it did not have a limited geographical jurisdiction; rather, its boundaries were coextensive with the city's. When New York real-estate investment was at its peak, the PDC was active in every borough; during 1987 it was involved with 200 projects, worth $13 billion.[46] As reconstituted, the EDC's responsibilities included the development, marketing, selling, and managing of city-owned land; funding of commercial, industrial, and waterfront projects, including markets and some transport facilities; working to retain private businesses in the city; and obtaining loans and financial assistance for devel-

opers. The EDC, like its predecessor agency, acted primarily as a financial intermediary, putting together packages of land improvements, tax abatements, and
funding for specific development sites.[47] In 2000 it began a program to promote
the location of new-technology firms in the boroughs and Harlem, and it has been
involved in stimulating biomedical-related enterprises. It has not, however, sought
to tie jobs to neighborhood development. The Department of City Planning, which
technically has responsibility for land-use planning, largely deferred to the PDC/
EDC's definition of the city's development strategy.[48]

For its larger projects, the PDC/EDC worked together with New York State's
Urban Development Corporation (UDC), now the Empire State Development
Corporation. The two agencies spun off separate development corporations to
operate particular projects, including the construction and operation of the Javits
Convention Center and the 42nd Street Redevelopment Project (see Chapter 6).
In addition, the Battery Park City Authority (BPCA), which planned and developed a large mixed-used project on landfill adjacent to Wall Street, was a semi-
autonomous UDC subsidiary (see Chapter 8). Originally established to develop
housing for low- and moderate-income groups, the UDC shed its housing mandate and was reborn as an economic development agency. Within New York City
it retained its original power to override local zoning and citizen participation
requirements.[49] Its involvement in development projects, therefore, permitted a
streamlined process of regulatory approvals.

Community development corporations. Nonprofit community (housing and
commercial) and industrial development corporations have become increasingly
important nongovernmental actors outside the Manhattan business district.[50] Once
incorporated, Community Development Corporations (CDCs) are free to seek financing from public and private lenders and grantors. Sources of funding are quite
varied, including state and local governments, religious organizations, private
philanthropists, and constituent businesses and housing groups. Two national
groups—the Local Initiatives Support Corporation (LISC) and the Enterprise
Foundation—funnel money to CDCs, primarily in support of housing construction and rehabilitation, but also for business development in low-income neighborhoods. Most of these funds come from monies provided under the Low Income
Housing Tax Credit program, whereby corporations receive tax credits in return
for their investments.[51] Between 1987 and 2000 LISC invested $840 million in
around 50 CDCs in New York, resulting in about 9,000 units of low-income housing.[52] Furthermore, a number of banks have set up autonomous development corporations that lend money in low-income neighborhoods. These corporations,
which are expected to make a profit, generally participate only in projects in which
some part of the costs is subsidized.

Except for renovation work on some of its own properties, the city has relied
on nonprofit development corporations to implement its affordable housing program. Housing development corporations (HDCs) have built or rehabilitated many

thousands of units of housing throughout New York; typically an HDC will mix grants, loans, and revenues from several sources in any single project. The Brooklyn Ecumenical Council, for example, consisting of 25 churches throughout Brooklyn, sponsors an HDC. This organization in 1990 had 1,800 units of in rem housing[53] committed to it by the city, which it was rehabilitating using funding from LISC, the Roman Catholic Archdiocese, and the city. By renting some of the units at market rates, it was able to use proceeds from the more expensive dwellings to cross-subsidize those for low-income households. Although HDCs resemble British housing associations in their nonprofit status and freedom to choose their projects, they differ in their funding sources, their community base, and their more entrepreneurial organization.

Housing programs. During the 1970s a tide of housing abandonment and neglect swept over New York City. In the '80s, economic recovery stimulated waves of gentrification. Both processes exacerbated the always difficult housing situation of low-income households. New York historically had been a national leader in using government funds and tax credits to subsidize housing construction. These programs, however, largely lapsed by the beginning of the '80s, as federal money for public housing dried up and the state's Mitchell-Lama program for moderate-income housing ended.

For most of his time in office Mayor Koch had no program to address the city's low-income housing crisis. During the 1980s the shortage of all but luxury housing in New York City became increasingly acute.[54] Indicators of the crisis were rapidly growing homelessness, a vacancy rate below 2.5 percent overall and below 1 percent in low-income housing in 1987, and soaring housing costs.[55] Despite the salience of the problem and rising political pressure from middle-class constituents as well as advocates for the poor, the Koch administration directed most of its attention to attracting private commercial development. Only in 1988 did the mayor specify the housing program he had announced in 1986. He proposed to use city funds directly to finance construction and rehabilitation of low-income units on city-owned property, as well as to assist private developers willing to construct additional affordable units for low- and middle-income households.

The published "plan" made few specific promises and was not really a plan. It did not indicate the city's exact intentions in regard to, for example, the rehabilitation of residential neighborhoods in the South Bronx or the housing of Manhattan's homeless. In sharp distinction to typical redevelopment plans, it contained no maps and named no projects. Rather, as stated in its introduction: "The Plan does not designate specific projects or allocate funds to specific neighborhoods. However, it does provide a general outline as to the kinds of programs which will operate over the next ten years and the proportion of the total funding which will be devoted to these programs."[56] It did, however, commit the city to building and rehabilitating a great deal of housing. Essentially, it freed the hands of the implementing agencies to pursue individual projects as they saw fit, to whatever extent community support would allow.

Mayor Koch tilted the implementation of the program toward assistance to moderate- and middle-income projects; under his successor, David Dinkins, it shifted more toward housing low-income and homeless people but still retained a middle-class component. The initial commitment to new construction for middle-income households generated considerable controversy. Between 1981 and 1991, the nonprofit Housing Partnership received public subsidy for the construction of more than 5,000 units for owner occupants.[57] Many community advocates castigated the Partnership for its top-down planning style and its targeting of the relatively affluent. Its suburban-looking, one- and two-family detached homes combined a 20 percent city and state contribution with market-level loans from commercial banks. Defenders contended that the program retained a middle-class population in the inner city that would otherwise have moved to the suburbs; that 85 percent of the buyers were minorities; and that three-quarters either lived or worked in the neighborhoods where they invested.[58] Ultimately, the city responded to political pressure, and as of 1998, low-income households, including the formerly homeless, accounted for two-thirds of the units committed for renovation or construction.[59]

The fiscal crisis, resulting from the recession of the early 1990s, caused major cutbacks in the entire New York City housing program. In 1989 (an election year) construction or rehabilitation of more than 26,000 dwellings was begun with city assistance, representing a public expenditure of $738 million.[60] Expenditures dropped and then picked up again during the Dinkins administration but declined steadily under the Giuliani mayoralty despite the city's improved fiscal situation. The number of units receiving assistance from the city's budget declined to an annual rate of about 6,000, or about a quarter of the peak level. The drop is attributable both to administration policies and to the exhaustion of the in rem housing supply, which had formed the bulk of the units rehabilitated.[61]

In the decade 1989–1999 New York spent more on its housing programs than all other major U.S. cities combined, almost all from its own revenue sources. Within the South Bronx, for many years internationally famous for its bombed-out appearance and stratospheric crime rate, the program could take credit for the area's resurrection.[62] Once the favorite spot for politicians and foreign visitors to observe the forces of decay, the Bronx became the symbol of redemption. Schwartz's analysis of the effectiveness of the program, however, concludes on an ambiguous note:

> New York City's housing policy is at a critical juncture. In the 13 years since its inception, the plan has produced and rehabilitated more than 150,000 units of housing and in so doing has helped transform and stabilize many communities. Yet housing problems remain severe. In 1996, nearly one-quarter of

the city's households confronted a severe housing affordability problem (spent at least 50 percent of their income on rent) or lived in physically deficient housing. However, the city is unlikely to continue down the path [of supplying housing] it has followed since 1986.[63]

CONVERGENCE AND DIVERGENCE

During periods of both growth and recession, the governing regimes of London and New York similarly relied on private-market actors to expand their economies and provide public facilities. Although the systems of local government in the United Kingdom and the United States had become less alike during the 1980s, the actions of public officials determining local initiatives increasingly resembled each other. Using the tools of development agreements, development corporations, regulatory relief, tax subsidies, advertising, public relations, and financial packaging, officials stressed the economic development function of government to the detriment of social welfare and planning.

During the '90s the two approaches gradually began to diverge again. To understand the reasons for this evolution, we must look not to institutional correspondences but to economic forces as they were filtered through ideologically and politically driven interpretations of appropriate response. Prime Minister Margaret Thatcher, in the name of freeing up the market and stimulating an enterprise culture, reduced redistributive governmental programs and forced the borough councils to make land available for private developers. Her Conservative successor, John Major, moderated the ideological edge of his party's program and sponsored partnership programs that encompassed social as well as economic considerations. The Blair government, with its attempt to find a "Third Way" and its desire to dampen the conflictual character of British politics, has striven for consensus by involving businesses and communities in its programs and has fostered regeneration schemes with a more strongly redistributive character. At the same time, it has not reverted to the heavy government involvement of the pre-Thatcher era.

In New York, Mayor Edward Koch, without precisely emulating the laissez-faire mentality of the Republican national government in power at that time, cozened developers in the name of the increasingly embattled middle class. His successor, David Dinkins, despite a more inclusionary rhetoric, had little leeway to redirect policy at a time of severe economic distress. At the national level, those proposing greater state intervention in the economy and higher levels of redistribution failed to persuade the voting public that they had a formula for economic expansion. The consequence was a significant reduction in federal aid to cities. The electoral success of a more sympathetic national administration in 1992 had little effect on funding for urban programs. Cities did not attract much attention from the "New Democrats" of the Clinton administration, and a conservative

Congress, with a Republican majority for most of Clinton's two terms of office, gave him few opportunities to provide urban assistance. In striking contrast to Britain, whatever American cities were going to accomplish in terms of redevelopment they were going to do on their own. The 1991 triumph in New York of a conservative mayor, who regarded public safety as his most important economic development program, precluded any significant effort toward economic improvement of poor neighborhoods beyond what trickled down from overall growth. Mayor Giuliani's fierce defense of aggressive police tactics, his exclusion of people of color from significant positions in his administration, and his refusal to develop ties with political leaders of low-income groups resulted in serious antagonism between the government and many of New York's citizens. Whereas London's politics was becoming increasingly harmonious, the opposite was occurring in New York.

In both London and New York during the '80s and '90s, the national failures of the left kept local advocates for the poor to relatively narrow issues and a primarily negative stance. They had few alternatives but to work within the confines of the deal-based system of public-private negotiation. Despite changes of government, programs continued to rely on private-sector initiatives. The election of a Democratic administration in Washington and a Labour government in Britain moderated but did not fundamentally change the ideological climate. Only the growth of a strong ideological counterforce would be likely to cause a shift in direction in either place.

6

Public-Private Partnerships in Action: King's Cross and Times Square

The negotiated quality of urban redevelopment schemes means that the dynamics of each one is different. The next three chapters examine four major redevelopment programs in London and New York to reveal the complex interplay of forces that operate in particular situations. My aims are (1) to trace the source of each initiative; (2) to find out what resources the different participants had at their disposal; (3) to identify their objectives; (4) to assess their costs and benefits; and (5) to understand the values involved in reactions to them. All six of the projects discussed here are ongoing more than 20 years after their inception, and only two—downtown Brooklyn and Battery Park City—are almost complete. In the first edition of this book I stated that evaluations of their likely outcomes were necessarily tentative. As it turned out, my expectations concerning two of the cases—Times Square and London Docklands—were far off the mark. Now it is possible to speak with more assurance about them. Two London development schemes—King's Cross and Spitalfields—have progressed little in the last eight years, and their ultimate resolution remains unknown.

The six cases selected for closer scrutiny constitute three sets of similar pairs. This chapter focuses on two proposals for massive land-use changes on centrally located tracts still in active commercial use when attempts at their redevelopment had begun: King's Cross in London and Times Square in New York.[1] Planning for both commenced at the beginning of the 1980s real-estate boom; they each became bogged down in controversy and financial difficulties. By the end of the '90s, Times Square had become the epicenter of New York's late-century burst of development, while King's Cross still languished. The developments, as originally proposed, exemplified the type of massive office project that has mobilized community resistance in a number of cities.[2] In later plans they changed character substantially. Even so, the two undertakings, in both earlier and later manifestations, had several common characteristics: They involved the reuse of commercial areas by different types of enterprises that would cater to new kinds of customers; they required a major restructuring of land uses and the relocation or closure of existing business premises; and they were likely to cause changes in the composition of the working and residential populations in the project areas and their surroundings. The environmental effects of these huge projects, as well as fears by residents of adjacent neighborhoods that rising property values would lead to their displacement, fueled antagonism to the schemes. The real-estate bust of the early '90s forced reconsideration of both projects, resulting in endeavors more appropriate for their contexts. Times Square, while an overwhelming success in relationship to its economic development objectives, is massive in its impacts and highly controversial as regards its effect on the quality of the urban environment. King's Cross now appears as if it will be an incremental effort rather than a wholesale transformation.

KING'S CROSS

The original attempt to redevelop the railroad lands surrounding the King's Cross and Saint Pancras stations began in the mid-1970s. The local authority of Camden wished to stimulate economic activity on the 134-acre site,[3] which contained derelict railroad sidings, loading depots, and storage facilities, as well as a number of "listed" (landmarked) structures, including the two railroad stations and several gas-storage tanks. Located in north-central London, adjacent to a busy shopping area, the large tract lay close to the location of the new national library and was surrounded by residential areas housing people of moderate means.

During the mid-1980s the Camden council produced a strategy document calling for a comprehensive approach to the whole site rather than piecemeal improvements. It expressly limited further office development, calling instead for a mixed development including manufacturing, retail, housing, and recreational uses at relatively low densities. At the time of the first major development proposal in 1987, a number of small businesses with short-term leases were operating on the site. While some were prosperous, all required inexpensive premises to maintain their profitability.

Two major landowners, the still publicly owned British Rail (BR) and the privatized National Freight Consortium, controlled most of the land. British Rail, which until the 1980s showed little interest in developing its landholdings, had become suddenly alert to the capital-producing potential of its property in the vicinity of London's stations. Pressures from the government on the remaining publicly owned firms in Britain to become self-financing had much to do with this heightened awareness. BR had especially great financial needs at King's Cross, because it confronted the expected expense of building a new concourse for the terminus of the Channel Tunnel train and decking over its tracks.[4]

BR operated within the confines of the Thatcherite interpretation of the appropriate role of a government agency within an enterprise culture. In the words of Michael Edwards, a scholar who had assisted the King's Cross opponents:

> British Rail . . . is an instance of an essentially 80s phenomenon: a state agency increasingly deprived of state funding but still prohibited from raising money on the private markets, under increasingly strong imperatives to make profits from each and every one of its assets. Such agencies . . . tended to adopt private sector accountancy practices, basing their investment and operating decisions on short-run financial criteria.[5]

Although BR had the capacity to act as a strategic planning body for London through its control of so much centrally located land, its public ownership did not inhibit it from behaving exactly like a speculative private landowner, gambling on an ever-increasing market for its properties.[6]

BR held a competition to select the developer for King's Cross. By requiring that the winning proposal achieve the highest possible financial return on its land, it ensured that the developer would opt for intensive commercial use. Nevertheless, bidders had to guess what types of development would be acceptable, as the request for proposals (tender offer) and the borough's planning brief were vague. BR awarded the development contract to the London Regeneration Consortium (LRC), a partnership between National Freight and Rosehaugh Stanhope Developments, the developer of the successful Broadgate project at London's Liverpool Street Station.[7] The LRC's proposal was accepted by British Rail without any input from the community. When the development consortium later fleshed out its concept and presented its master plan to the Camden council, that body faced a fait accompli, since the consortium could not significantly change the plan and meet its obligations to BR.[8]

The Camden council nonetheless demanded community consultation before it would review the application for planning permission, and its planning office prepared a community planning brief stipulating its criteria for plan approval. While not specifying the scale and nature of the commercial component, the brief did lay out in general terms the council's requirements for housing, employment, shopping, recreation, design, environmental protection, transport, and traffic.[9] The council had concluded that its only hope of obtaining much-needed housing was by tapping into private-sector funds as part of a development agreement and was willing to make concessions on office construction in return. The council further felt compelled to show flexibility toward the developers, since if it failed to negotiate an agreement, the Secretary of State for the Environment would probably overrule it on either a call-in or appeal. Councillors also thought that they had averted the creation of a rumored urban development corporation (UDC) for the area only by persuading the central government that they would be "reasonable." A UDC would have removed all control from the local authority.

The Proposal

The initial LRC planning application called for 6.9 million square feet of office space; subsequently, this was reduced first to 6.5 million, then to 5.9 million, and finally to 5.25 million square feet.[10] The Camden planning director remarked that in the past "office construction on this scale was unthinkable." Now the best outcome he could envision was a modest reduction in size and the achievement of planning gain, by which the consortium would promise public benefits in return for planning permission. His aim was to get LRC to commit itself to 1,800 units of low-cost housing, a worker training scheme, a variety of community facilities, and a trust arrangement for their upkeep.

An umbrella organization for local community groups, the Railway Lands Community Development Group (RLCDG), formed to express opinions on the plan and received some funding from the borough council. It strongly opposed the size of the office component. A number of community groups testified in public hearings against the proposed "office city"; BR, however, refused to attend the hearing on the grounds that "it was legally inadvisable given that they were simultaneously presenting evidence on the Channel Tunnel Terminal to the House of Commons Select Committee."[11] Camden officials professed bewilderment at this reasoning; the council's report on the hearing indicated that the absence of BR "was widely deplored."[12]

A technical advisory group based at the Bartlett School of University College London worked with the RLCDG on a critique of the LRC proposal and the preparation of an alternative plan.[13] Its funding came initially from the councils of Camden and Islington and the London Strategic Policy Committee, a short-lived successor body of the Greater London Council (GLC), and later from a local developer/businessman, Martin Clarke, who sought to rebuild the area according to a different strategy.[14] The advisory group disputed the amount of office space necessary to produce an acceptable rate of return to the developer.

The Bartlett group also examined the employment impact of the scheme.[15] They pointed out that the site housed at least 87 firms, with 1,500 employees, not all of whom were actually working on the site. Warehousing, retailing, and wholesaling accounted for the majority of businesses.[16] Although very few of these firms planned to move unless forced to do so, practically none would be able to afford premises on the redeveloped site. The majority anticipated losses in the event that they had to leave their present location, especially if they could not remain in the vicinity. Existing employment was overwhelmingly of white males, working predominantly for small firms in nonunionized, low-wage jobs. The proposed development, while increasing the workforce in the area, would reduce its proportion of local residents and replace low-skilled with high-skilled jobs.

The Bartlett group's discussion of employment concluded by raising some crucial issues, which apply also to the Times Square case discussed below:

Is it correct to perceive sites like the King's Cross Railway Lands, as the developers do, as derelict and degraded property which unquestionably needs "renewal"? Or do such locations in fact play an essential part in the inner city economy by providing cheap premises for activities ranging from theatre scenery storage to cheap hostels, on which the inner city economy and society depend?

To what extent should a local authority be seeking to protect businesses displaced by redevelopment such as those on the Railway Lands? . . . Much of the employment provided by these firms is of a character and quality which makes only limited contribution to certain important local government policy objectives. As well as [raising] . . . issues about gender and ethnic distribution and workplace relations and conditions . . . few of the firms . . . contributed to any formal training provision. On the other hand we know that, in inner London generally, underprivileged groups have had lower chances of getting jobs in newly-generated firms than of retaining employment in established firms which survive.[17]

The RLCDG devised four alternative plans to the one presented by LRC.[18] The consultants worked out the first of these plans (the King's Cross Team [KXT] plan) in meetings with community groups; the other three resulted from an outreach effort to involve disadvantaged elements of the community that had not participated in the meetings. All four greatly reduced the scale and density of the project as well as changing the proportions to be devoted to different uses.

Later Developments

Although the original timetable released by the borough of Camden scheduled a final council decision for March 1990, only in August 1992 did it agree to a revised proposal when the LRC agreed to further reduce the size of the office scheme.[19] By that time, however, the development consortium behind the project had begun to fall apart. Godfrey Bradman, the principal developer, had been forced out of the chairmanship of Rosehaugh; the company was in serious financial straits and eventually collapsed.[20] Its partnership with Stanhope, which had worked well in the creation of Broadgate, had undergone strains, and talks aimed at merger between the two firms had foundered. Stanhope, in the meanwhile, was entangled in the financial problems of Olympia & York.[21] Even were these firms in better condition, the state of the 1992 property market in London prevented any starts on large-scale office construction.

The Camden council also lacked motivation to expedite the development, since the softness of the office market undermined hopes that planning gain could provide a reliable source of funding for public amenities. Since planning gain depended on a sufficient difference between debt service and rent roll to allow the developer a profit and the locality its payoff, fulfillment of the promises to

Camden would have required BR to lower its profit expectations. Despite its public-sector ownership, BR refused to do so, thereby forcing the proportions of the project to exceed a size acceptable to the community and making any start on the project impossible until the market could again absorb a large amount of office space.[22]

Only in 1996 did Parliament finally decide the route by which the high-speed railroad from the Channel would reach Saint Pancras Station via East London.[23] Construction, however, involved miles of very expensive tunneling, and it took five years to obtain the necessary financial commitments from Railtrack, the now privatized British Rail, the goverment, and private investors. The consequence was that even with the revival of London's property market, investment in the part of the King's Cross area affected by the railroad was stymied by uncertainty over whether it would actually arrive. Small-scale private investment, however, was flowing into the rest of the district for upgraded retailing, luxury housing, rehabilitation of listed buildings, and small hotel development. The new activity was sufficiently incremental that it was not resulting in serious displacement of existing small businesses.[24] As currently envisioned, rather than hosting a large office complex, the quarter will specialize in arts and entertainment and small-scale office uses.[25]

The King's Cross Partnership, an organization encompassing business, community, government, and housing association representatives, was receiving Single Regeneration Budget (SRB) funds to develop housing, environmental improvements, job training, and social service programs. The partnership's executive director commented that the earlier model of regeneration had been overly physical, while the present model emphasized people.[26] Her organization and its vision of the future King's Cross represented the current trend in London's regeneration schemes: involvement by multiple interests in planning; mixed-use development; the combining of social and physical programming; and reliance on private-sector finance. Previous animosities had ebbed away. The question remained, however, whether all this good feeling would present tangible results.

TIMES SQUARE

Times Square is one of the world's most famous locales. Centrally located in Midtown Manhattan, illuminated at night by kinetic megasigns, locus of the nation's most televised New Year's Eve celebration, it offers 24-hour-a-day activity. Stretching five blocks north from the intersections of 42nd Street with Broadway and Seventh Avenue, it is the center of New York's theater industry, including associated enterprises like restaurants, set designers, theatrical booking agents, ticket agencies, dance studios, and costume rental establishments. Alongside this array of socially acceptable entertainment activities until recently stood an extensive agglomeration of sex-related industries that gave Times Square its unsavory reputation. Pornography shops and X-rated cinemas acted as magnets for loiterers, drug dealers, street hustlers, and prostitutes, causing the area, despite its crowds of theater-goers, tourists, and commuters, to display an intimidating aspect and register a high crime rate.

A low-rise, low-rent district, Times Square in the '80s had a number of virtues despite its blatant problems. Before the construction flurry at the decade's end, its scale made it one of the few areas in Manhattan where afternoon sunlight reached both sides of the street simultaneously. Many of the theater support services, as well as other respectable but marginally profitable businesses, relied for their continued operation on the inexpensive rents available on upper floors of nondescript structures scattered throughout the district. Obsolete construction and marginal uses, however, brought down real-estate valuations. As a result, the city received only a tiny proportion of the tax revenues potentially available from a location served by almost all major subway lines and close to the Port Authority bus terminal, the hub for commuter traffic from New Jersey.

Just to the west of Times Square lies the Clinton neighborhood, once known as Hell's Kitchen. It is the last low-income area in central Manhattan. The five-story tenements that line its streets have felt the pressure of gentrification, as landlords have forced out their tenants, often brutally, and converted their buildings into condominiums. Formerly the home of generations of longshoremen working on the nearby, now-defunct Hudson River docks, it houses people from a dazzling variety of ethnic backgrounds. Many of its residents work as laborers within the theater industry or as maids, porters, waiters, and kitchen help in the hotels and restaurants clustered around Times Square. The community contains several active Roman Catholic parishes and a parochial school; the churches, which once responded to the spiritual needs of largely Irish and Italian congregations, currently provide places of worship for Filipinos, Latin Americans, Dominicans, and other Caribbean islanders.

The original impetus for the redevelopment of Times Square came from Clinton residents, theater and restaurant owners, and community leaders, especially clergy, who were dismayed by the sleaziness of the district. During the 1970s the western portion of 42nd Street had been upgraded through the construction of two large residential towers[27] and the rehabilitation of a strip of storefronts, together with a former airline terminal building, into off-Broadway theaters, performance studios, and restaurants.[28] The replacement of prostitution and marginal business uses on these blocks by a lively, upscale entertainment scene seemed to show that physical improvements could also produce social transformation.

At the same time, a group of upper-class civic organizations, led by the Municipal Art Society, was becoming increasingly concerned with the impact of new office development on Manhattan's East Side. Home to New York's wealthiest residential community and most exclusive stores, the East Side had many leaders with easy access to decision-makers. The logical reaction was to "move development westward."[29] The City Planning Commission responded by producing the "new midtown zoning," which limited further development on the East Side and encouraged construction to the west by raising the allowable building size there. While much publicity proclaimed the harm that additional buildings could inflict on the East Side, neither the civic organizations nor the City Planning Commission paid great attention to the impact of higher densities on the West Side, which was simply assumed to be vastly underutilized. Moreover, the West Side was now seen as a potential magnet for those firms that were threatening to flee to New Jersey or beyond. Times Square's seedy character was believed to discourage development for blocks around its central location. But if it were massively redeveloped, it could make the entire west midtown area more desirable as an office location. Within the planners' mental maps, Times Square was shifting from being the entertainment core of Manhattan to becoming primarily an office and wholesaling district.

The Proposal

Throughout the years various developers and design groups had presented proposals for redevelopment of the 42nd Street heart of the Times Square area. None attracted serious backing, however.[30] In 1981 the city government distributed a request for development proposals that conformed to the new office-center vision and called on developers to follow a set of architectural guidelines. Devised by the firm of Cooper-Eckstut, which had created the much-praised design for Battery Park City, the specifications for Times Square emphasized a lively streetscape, to be achieved through building setbacks, glass street walls, and large neon signs. Even though the guidelines allowed for building heights up to 56 stories, at first they did not stimulate any protest.

The city government, in conjunction with the New York State Urban Development Corporation (UDC), selected a group of developers for the project, each with responsibility for a different component. Park Tower Realty, headed by George Klein, won the competition to develop the office section, the largest portion of the enterprise. The most immediately striking characteristic of the proposed development was its massive scale. The existing structures on the four corners straddling Times Square at 42nd Street would be replaced by four huge edifices, designed by Philip Johnson and John Burgee, totaling more than 4 million square feet of space. The heights of the buildings were to be 29, 37, 49, and 56 stories. Their appearance was somber compared to the existing architecture of the area, and they did not conform to the design criteria set forth in the Cooper-Eckstut guidelines. Generally, the aesthetics of the buildings signified the seriousness of the business activity planned for their extensive interior spaces rather than the frenetic entertainment industry that had historically dominated the area. In addition, the UDC's plan included a 2.4 million square foot wholesale market on a corner of Eighth Avenue opposite the Port Authority Bus Terminal and a 550-

room hotel facing it. It called for renovation of nine theaters on 42nd Street between Seventh and Eighth Avenues and elaborate rehabilitation of the busy Times Square subway station. Untouched, however, would be New York's largest "adult entertainment" emporium, which lay directly across the street from the site.[31]

The size of the office buildings and wholesale market greatly exceeded what was allowable under the city's zoning regulation. As at King's Cross, supporters justified the project's bulk on the grounds that only very large buildings would produce enough revenue to pay for land acquisition and the funding of community benefits. In both cases, the public body choosing among the competing bidders used financial return rather than design as its criterion. Also similar to King's Cross, the Times Square developers believed that they could obtain financing only if they were able to promise rent levels well below those in more prestigious locations; therefore, more space had to be provided to produce overall revenues comparable to other areas.[32]

Responsibility for coordinating the scheme rested with a public-private partnership, the 42nd Street Redevelopment Corporation, comprising two public agencies and the private developers. On the governmental side, both the UDC and the city's Public Development Corporation (PDC, later to become the Economic Development Corporation, EDC) carried out planning, staffing, and implementation functions, using the UDC's powers of eminent domain (compulsory purchase) and authority to override local zoning. On the private side, the participating developers, in addition to bearing the construction costs of their buildings, would contribute to theater and subway improvements[33] and would pay for the UDC's land acquisition costs up to a specified level. The city's Board of Estimate approved the project in October 1984. In the ensuing years a series of lawsuits and other setbacks delayed its implementation, and over the course of time all of the original private-sector participants except the office developer and theater owners dropped out. In 1992, when the UDC began to vacate the site, the office buildings did not have any tenant commitments, while the theaters lacked adequate funding for renovations and operations.

In the meanwhile, the Department of City Planning began to respond to concerns that transformation of the area was destroying the elements that nurtured the entertainment industry. Stimulated by the permissive new midtown zoning, thirteen buildings were either under construction or planned around Times Square by 1988. All overshadowed what had been the area's tallest structure by at least seven stories; seven of them exceeded forty stories.[34] Hoping to overcome the deadening effect of these new towers as well as of the large buildings proposed for the 42nd Street project, the city planners drafted a sign ordinance for the entire vicinity. This required all structures to provide for huge exterior signs, on the model of Piccadilly Circus in London or the Shinjuku district in Tokyo.[35] Initially resisted by developers and building owners. this requirement turned out to be immensely profitable, contributing an estimated $100 to $125 million a year to the city's economy.[36]

In another, less superficial, effort to maintain the character of the area as an entertainment district, the Department of City Planning also obtained city council approval for a change in the zoning, so that all buildings in the Times Square district had to devote 5 percent of their floor space to entertainment-related functions.[37] Office developers generally resented being forced to cater to entertainment uses at all and pressed for the most inclusive definition possible. In response to developers' concerns, permissible uses, which included rehearsal halls, wigmakers' premises, and lighting designers' studios, were extended to include record stores and movie theaters. Because the latter type of high-volume establishment generates greater rent-paying capability, it drives out the more modest activities upon which the theater industry depends and will inevitably dominate the designated "entertainment-related" spaces. Many in the industry remained skeptical that the space reserved for theater support services would, in fact, keep them in Manhattan.

In 1989, responding to attacks on the appearance of the office towers,[38] the firm of John Burgee[39] redesigned them so that they reflected "the neon and honky-tonk atmosphere" of the existing district.[40] The new design incorporated setbacks, cutouts, asymmetrical grids, angled roofs, reflective surfaces in blue and green glass, and built-in multicolored neon signs.[41] The changes, however, did little to assuage the alarm of the critics:

> The good news is that these buildings try to be entertaining; they represent a serious attempt to evolve a viable new esthetic out of Times Square's tradition of lights and signs. . . . The bad news is that this is all cosmetics. For the problem with the original design was never just the way it looked, bad as that was; it was the fact that the towers were too big and too bulky, and threatened to put what little is left of Times Square and the theater district into shadow.[42]

Despite the assertions of the project's planners that the only alternative to massive redevelopment was no development at all, the stretch of 42nd Street west of the project site indicated the potential for a more moderate procedure. Here the modest effort, described earlier, which produced a row of theaters and restaurants along with a low-income residential project, had greatly ameliorated the environment without a drastic reconfiguration of uses. A similar strategy addressed to the project blocks would combine rehabilitation and new construction. Under such an approach, eminent domain, by forcing out the most undesirable uses, could allow the rehabilitation of existing structures if their owners resisted upgrading. Mainly, the city could have bettered the area simply through working with the property holders from whom they seized the site. It could have used tax abatement to assist the owners of the movie theaters, who claimed that they were willing to fix up their properties using their own capital without the contributions of office developers. Spot demolition would have created the opportunity for some new construction. The block closest to the existing subsidized apartment complex could have been used for a mixed residential-commercial structure, containing both market-rate and subsidized housing units. But, although such an approach could produce redevelopment without enormous disruption, it would not create the kinds of huge public and private revenues promised—although not immediately delivered—by the chosen approach.

Financing

The bank that was the original financial backer of the office component, Manufacturers Hanover Trust, withdrew from its commitment. The Prudential Insurance Company, which became an equity partner and ultimately the owner of the office sites, then agreed to provide the financing, obtaining a $150 million letter of credit from Morgan Guaranty Trust.[43] Initially Klein's firm, Park Tower, reached a preleasing agreement with a large law firm; when it withdrew, Chemical Bank[44] signed on as an anchor tenant but then also backed out. Trammell Crow, who had been selected as the developer of the wholesale market, also quit the project, as did the developer of the hotel.

While acquisition of the land and existing structures depended on the use of the UDC's power of eminent domain, purchase costs up to $150 million were to be borne by the developers. Of this amount, Park Tower was originally responsible for $88 million; its commitment was increased further in subsequent negotiations and eventually assumed by Prudential.[45] The remaining land purchases were covered by the city out of funds borrowed from Prudential at an interest rate above the prime rate and returned to it through forgiveness of later payments in lieu of taxes (PILOT) that it would otherwise owe the city once the buildings were occupied. Thus, the city was assuming land costs above a set amount and moreover would be paying the developer above-market-rate interest on its initial outlay.[46]

The public sector therefore incurred few of the front-end costs of the project. It did, however, provide an ongoing subsidy to the developers through a tax abatement. The size of this abatement was estimated at about $650 million over 15 years.[47] Property tax revenues in the project area in 1982 were just $5.1 million. If the land costs did not greatly exceed the developer's contribution and if the buildings produced anything close to the predicted rate of return, the city through the PILOT would still receive considerably more revenue from the area, even under the abatement, than had previously been the case. Further financial benefits to the city included participation in rent collections from the tenants of the various structures. Title to the land and structures, which were to be leased for 99 years, would remain with the UDC. After 15 years, however, the lessees could purchase the properties; for the office buildings, the buyout price was specified at only 45 percent of the average annual net rent roll.

Responses to the Plan

The New York City Board of Estimate, before approving the proposals, sponsored hearings on the draft environmental impact statement and then on the final plans. Many who testified complained of the haste with which the scheme was being pressed—and certainly the subsequent eight years of delay in starting the project retrospectively raise serious questions concerning the justification for hurry. Even its supporters objected to the incomplete information on which judgments had to be based and to the size of the office towers. A group of eleven design-oriented civic groups, which had formed an association called the President's Council, expressed concerns over bulk, density, and vitality. Its membership ultimately split over whether to accept the large buildings as the price of progress. Residents of the Clinton neighborhood, located directly to the west of Times Square, mobilized against the project, contending that it would force up property values and accelerate the gentrification of their neighborhood. Community Board 4, whose constituency included Clinton, opposed the plan; Board 5, which represented the Times Square area itself and contained a number of members drawn from the business and real-estate industries, issued a catalogue of objections but did not take a firm stand. Some Clinton groups, including the Ninth Avenue Business Association and the pastor of a major Roman Catholic church, endorsed the proposal. Representatives of the clothing industry, located to the south of the project site, expressed fears that rents in the garment district would be forced up as office uses encroached on its territory. Although theater owners and managers supported the plan, others in the industry opposed it, fearing that entertainment uses would lose their critical mass in the area.

Politicians split on the issue, with those at higher levels, including Gov. Mario Cuomo, Sen. Daniel Patrick Moynihan, Mayor Edward Koch, and former mayors Abraham Beame and Robert Wagner, strongly praising the scheme. These notables even turned up to testify at the hearings, making frequent reference to the bright lights, dancing feet, and glamour that once characterized Times Square and arguing that only a tremendous redevelopment effort could restore its former glory. They did not address the problematic relationship of an office complex to this nostalgic vision. In contrast, the city council members and state assembly representatives from the area resisted the project.

The planning agencies sponsoring the venture asserted that they had consulted extensively with community groups during the years preceding Board of Estimate approval. Their communications, however, were predominantly one-way, and only the urgency of obtaining final political approval created any flexibility. Just before the decisive Board of Estimate vote, state and city negotiators began to engage in frenzied discussions with Clinton neighborhood representatives. The key intermediaries in translating outside pressure into concessions were the elected officials rather than the planners, who until this point had remained obdurately committed to the plan. The principal concession granted was the allocation of

$25 million from the regular state and city budgets to the Clinton neighborhood, to be used over the next five years for low-income housing and community development purposes. Clinton representatives failed to achieve their objective of obtaining the money from the private developers rather than public revenues. They had wanted to set a linkage precedent whereby developers would be obligated to compensate communities for project impacts. This failure proved fortunate for Clinton, since ultimately the developers managed to obtain relief from even the minimal obligation for subway refurbishment that they had assumed.

Unlike the King's Cross community, residents and businesses in the Times Square area did not receive public funding for support of a project area committee to advise on the plan (as was once required in the United States under federal urban renewal legislation).[48] State Senator Franz Leichter remained the project's fiercest opponent, persistently lobbying against it and publicizing what he regarded as its misguided intentions.[49] A group of developers with investments in surrounding areas bankrolled sporadic efforts at devising an alternative plan and exposing the negative financial impacts of this one.[50] The construction of numerous buildings in the vicinity without comparable subsidies led opponents to argue that financial assistance for the 42nd Street project was unnecessary and caused it to compete unfairly with the new structures.[51] Project sponsors responded that it was only the promise of their undertaking that created the vision of the area as an office center; without it, the other structures would not have been built.

Outcomes

Each year after the project's approval, the sponsoring agencies declared with much fanfare that work was about to begin. Lawsuits, however, kept the UDC from acquiring the site until 1990, and then negotiations with existing tenants caused further postponements. In 1992 the UDC finally evicted the occupants, but by then the enthusiasm of Prudential and Park Tower for proceeding with the project had lapsed. The empty office buildings and theaters on 42nd Street gave a ghost-town aspect to the area. Having passed into government ownership, the sites ceased to generate any real-estate taxes.[52] Relocation of 240 businesses resulted in hardships for many of the companies involved, especially the smaller firms.[53] One of the 42nd Street buildings housed the studios of 21 artists: "Many of the [evicted] artists . . . see a paradox in being evicted by public officials who claim to support the arts and have used better-known artists to sanitize Times Square. . . . The artists in the building said they watched [the erection of art exhibits in the area] with a sense of dread as the art improved the street. They knew they were seeing a harbinger of their own evictions."[54] Action movie fans lamented the absence of their favorite theaters: " 'They're looking to move in a new class of people here,' said Wayne Williams, a hospital worker from . . . Brooklyn. 'They want to get rid of the poor folks. Who's going to pay $22 to see Shakespeare? I want to pay $5 to see two karate movies.' "[55]

Despite its considerable investment in land taking and relocation of occupants, adding up eventually to more than $400 million, the Prudential Insurance Company decided in the summer of 1992 that it would not proceed with the office project. The UDC sought to hold it to its word but finally acquiesced to a compromise in which Prudential and Park Tower agreed to reserve their right to build offices on the site.[56] Until they considered the time ripe for new construction, they would invest about $20 million in refurbishment of the existing buildings for retail, restaurant, and entertainment uses. They were exempted from the earlier requirement that they contribute to subway station improvements, and half their required contribution to theater renovation would be reimbursed to them. Tax benefits were increased, although the city and the UDC would continue to participate in rental profits. The benefits from abatement of real-estate taxes could go up to as much as $1.5 billion over the 20-year abatement period if the real-estate market took off.[57]

By default, the moderate renovation of the area, in which no one was initially interested, became the interim development plan for Times Square. It permitted a market-driven process to determine what kinds of companies would choose to locate in Times Square. Despite the weakness of the city's economy at that time and the insecurity of the leases, which permitted the developers to exercise eviction rights when they chose, initial response to the new scheme was very strong. Numerous retail, restaurant, and entertainment tenants immediately sought space on 42nd Street.[58] The process was aided by the formation of the Times Square Business Improvement District (BID). Funded by a self-imposed tax on local businesses, the BID took charge of street cleaning, marketing, and public safety. Its high-powered leadership took an active role in promoting the area and attracting businesses that would add to its vitality. It was instrumental in changing the image of Times Square.

In the meantime, a harbinger of Times Square's future direction came when Bertelsmann AG, the giant German media conglomerate, purchased a one-million-square-foot tower on Broadway a few blocks to the north of 42nd Street. This building was one of several empty structures built under the liberalized zoning code that prompted a wave of construction at the end of the '80s. Bertelsmann bought the building for less than half of its construction cost from a consortium of Japanese and American banks that had financed the building and received it when the developer failed. On the ground-floor level it rented space to what purports to be the world's largest music store, which has created a carnival ambiance reminiscent of a theme park pavilion. Along with its bargain price, Bertelsmann gained a variety of tax subsidies from the city and in return agreed to finance street improvements and provide below-market-rate space for foreign firms moving to New York.[59] In the ensuing years a number of other media companies, including Reuters, MTV, Viacom, and ABC, followed Bertelsmann into Times Square.

Still, despite the gradual move of various enterprises into the area north of 42nd Street, that street, which had been the focus of the redevelopment effort and

1 4 Times Square: Conde Nast, Skadden Arps Slate Meagher & Flom, NASDAQ Visitors Center, ESPN Zone
2 E-Walk: Loews Cineplex, Broadway City, Chevy's Fresh Mex, other retail (fall 1999)
3 Westin New York: 860 room hotel designed by Arquitectonica (spring 2002)
4 Forest City Ratner: Madame Tussaud's Wax Museum, AMC 26-screen theater, HMV Records, Just For Feet, Ruby's Diner, other retail (end 1999)
5 Doubletree/Forest City Ratner 460 room hotel
6 3 Times Square: Reuters' US headquarters, retail (2001)
7 5 Times Square: Ernst & Young's 1 million square foot headquarters, developed by Boston Properties (2002)
8 The New 42 building: The Duke theater, rehearsal and office space (early 2000)
9 Selwyn Theater: renovated by Roundabout Theatre Co. (fall 1999)
10 One Times Square: Warner Brothers Store
11 2-story Irish pub and offices
12 Second Stage Theater and retail
13 World Wrestling Federation restaurant and retail
14 Times Square Studios
15 St. Andrews Scottish bar and restaurant
16 The Premier hotel
17 New hotel
18 Times Square BID Sanitation headquarters
19 Times Square Visitors Center
20 Teatro Grill
21 Planet Hollywood hotel

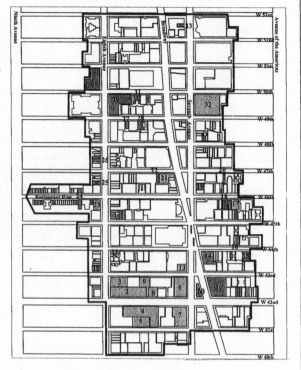

22 Local restaurant
23 70-unit supportive housing project with restaurant and retail
24 Dorsay restaurant
25 Kevin St. James bar and restaurant
26 New York Apple Tours ticket center and Burger King
27 The Garrick Bistro
28 The Time hotel with Palladin restaurant
29 The Gershwin: 35-story rental building with Palm restaurant and A&P market

30 Longacre House: 26-story residential building with Rite Aid and Blockbuster Video
31 Zona Grille
32 Rockefeller West: 33-story Morgan Stanley Dean Witter Plaza
33 CVB Visitors Center

Source: Times Square BID

Figure 6.1. Times Square recent and expected additions, 2000

the recipient of half a billion dollars of investment, remained only partially occupied. All prospects changed, however, when the Disney organization, having achieved great financial success with its Broadway production of *Beauty and the Beast,* indicated interest in the landmark New Amsterdam Theater. The theater, which the city acquired in 1982 and which at that time was in good repair, had been allowed to deteriorate and, because of a leaky roof, would cost at least $50 million to restore.[60] Disney's attention spurred the notice of others, including Madame Tussaud's; American Multi-Cinemas (AMC), which built a 25-screen multiplex; and MTV, which developed a production facility.[61] Renovation of the theater was eventually undertaken by the Disney Corporation with considerable help from the city. 42nd Street once again became a center for mass entertainment.

Disney was a reluctant suitor, demanding many enticements from the city before it was willing to anchor the development. Besides asking for major financial concessions, Disney declared it would not commit itself to the street unless two other major entertainment firms did likewise. At the eleventh hour, just before the company's deadline, the city did come up with two other bids, and the long-awaited rejuvenation of 42nd Street began. In addition to the costly restoration of the street's most ornate theater, which became the home of the immensely successful *Lion King,* Disney constructed an adjacent megastore; Warner Brothers built a similar enterprise across the street; several more theaters underwent renovation; another movie complex went up; and two big new hotels anchored the western end of the block between Seventh and Eighth Avenues.

With the New York economy finally revived, Prudential, which had become the sole owner of the office sites, decided to sell them rather than developing them itself. As of 2000, one was in operation, a second nearing completion, and the other two just begun. The scale of the buildings remained as in the original plan, although the architecture was much more playful, and the buildings no longer formed a uniform ensemble. The Condé Nast Publishing Company committed itself as the anchor tenant for one of the buildings, reinforcing the image of Times Square as a media center.[62] It shares the building, which opened in 1999, with Skadden Arps Slate Meagher & Flom, the city's largest law firm. Reuters, the British news service, took the office site across the street. It forged an equity partnership with the developer, William Rudin, and designed the building for use both as headquarters of its American news operations and as the location of the trading floor for its online stock venture. Reflecting both the time it took for the Times Square scheme to come to fruition and the character of New York's real-estate companies, Rudin commented: "My father was involved in [the] effort to redevelop Times Square 25 years ago."[63]

The new Times Square is perhaps unique in its diversity of commercial uses. The original plans for the office buildings envisioned them as single-use structures of sufficient sobriety to overcome Times Square's raffish image. No one imagined that a prestigious law firm would willingly share a building with the ESPN Zone, a themed sports bar and restaurant that occupied the ground floor of the Condé Nast Building, or that the publisher of the *New Yorker* would counte-nance a megasign on its building.[64] Surprisingly, Times Square attracted not only media and publishing headquarters but also major financial firms. Thus, Morgan Stanley/Dean Witter occupied two buildings, one of which was adorned with "zip-per" signs flashing the latest stock market figures. An industry breakdown of Times Square commercial leaseholders found that finance and law had the largest shares, closely followed by fashion, entertainment, and banking. In terms of employment, business services headed the list, followed by retail trade, banking and finance, and entertainment services. In addition, 28 hotels, containing one-fifth of the city's hotel rooms, were in the area in 1999, and several more were scheduled to open the following year.[65]

The synergy created by the relationship between the production and the con-sumption of entertainment has heightened the district's attraction to tourists and suburbanites, who constitute more than two-thirds of the pedestrians in the area.[66] Thus,

> the production and marketing needs of the entertainment industry result in a remaking of the global city as a tourist mecca on a previously undreamed-of scale. Whereas the production sites of other industries are rarely magnets for visitors (except when retrofitted as historic or tourist sites), the actual fabri-cation of the entertainment product—and the themed stores and restaurants that give the visitor a vicarious feeling of participation in the creative pro-cess—become major attractions in themselves. Further, urban culture becomes an exotic object of tourism increasingly mediated through the entertainment industry. This outcome undercuts old distinctions between sites of produc-tion and sites of consumption.[67]

A visitor to Times Square encounters vast crowds and sensory overload. If economic expansion, visual excitement, and popularity are the criteria for suc-cessful redevelopment, then Times Square is a winner. Yet many have attacked the redone Times Square for its fakery, for sanitizing or Disneyfying an area that was formerly genuinely diverse and that now only provides a simulacrum of di-versity, a safe adventure. In the words of one thoughtful critic:

> In the final analysis, it is possible to criticize the redevelopment of Forty-second Street with regard to its implications for a democratic public space. In an effort to create a place marketable to mainstream tourists and corporate tenants, a coalition of public and private elites imposed a Disney model of controlled, themed public space on an area of remarkable, if unsettling, di-versity. In so doing, they sacrificed the provocative, raw energy produced by the friction of different social groups in close interaction for the stultifying hum of a smoothly functioning machine for commercial consumption. In this way, public and private elites arguably destroyed the essence of Times Square as a contested public space.[68]

Without a doubt, Times Square is both safer[69] and more expensive than it was 20 years ago. As noted above, its economic composition is much more diverse than previously. In addition, more people visit it than ever, and the proportion that is poor and minority has almost certainly diminished in relative terms, but it is not clear that it has declined absolutely in number. A survey of daytime pedestrians on a summer day in 1998 identified 58 percent as white, 21 percent as African American, and 11 percent as Hispanic; 31 percent had incomes below $30,000. These figures indicate that the area has certainly not become completely gentrified, even though the study reported that the average pedestrian was young, single, middle class, and college educated.[70] Should we say that a place is less diverse or less democratic because it now attracts the middle mass where previously poor people of color were perceived to dominate? Are visitors better off with real risk than with ersatz adventure? Marshall Berman, a somewhat ambivalent observer of the new Times Square, queries:

> So should we worry? . . . The scale, incandescence, and symbolic power of Times Square make everything here more urgent and intense. Long-standing rage against Disney is part of the deal. This is based partly on an accurate view . . . but also on prejudices of our own: prejudices of many intellectuals against mass culture, prejudices of seltzer against orange juice, of ethnic easterners against middle America, of New York against the world. I'm not exactly saying these prejudices are wrong: I'll fight for most of them, but they could stand some critical scrutiny.[71]

Times Square is a product of big capital in alliance with government. A different development scheme might have proved more sympathetic to the aspirations of nearby residents and less transformative of the city's fabric. In the first edition of this book, written at a time when the project appeared to have failed, I wrote that less ambitious development and the use of regular capital budget funds for public improvements, while not as immediately lucrative, would in the long run be cheaper and contribute more to the quality of life of those who lived and worked in the area. The choice to proceed with the office-center strategy resulted from acceptance of the growth criterion untinctured by a commitment to equity and human scale in design and also unconstrained by caution over the likely demand for space. As it turned out, the less ambitious strategy, constituted in the interim plan, acted as the launching pad for the four enormous office buildings. Given Times Square's central location and the demand for space at the turn of the new century, its redevelopment acquired a certain inevitability.

My critique of the city's policy does not rest on the destruction of public space, which seems to me not nearly as serious as the detractors allege. Times Square remains a place of mass entertainment, and even though the cheap movies may have departed, one can stand on the street and watch television shows being made, visit the Virgin music megastore without buying anything, purchase half-price theater tickets, and play video games in immense arcades. That the great majority of people on the streets are tourists and suburbanites should not in itself be construed negatively.[72] Rather, I fault city policy for the enormous tax giveaways involved, its failure to get much in return from the developers, and its relaxed interpretation of the zoning ordinance to allow the construction of oversized structures in an already extraordinarily congested area.[73]

LESSONS

Initiation of both projects began within the public sector. Pressures from the public side (BR in the King's Cross case and the City of New York for Times Square) forced the developers to design a complex that would produce the maximum return. With manufacturing regarded as a vestige of the past, public officials and developers insisted that only offices for financial and advanced-services firms could nurture economic expansion; they were extremely unwilling to entertain other possibilities. The King's Cross consortium, even when confronting a market that would not support its planned development for many years, still refused to examine the alternative plans presented by the Railroad Lands Community Development Group. The Camden council, caught in the middle, acquiesced to the developers' viewpoint so that it could have access to the resources offered by planning gain. In the Times Square area, the development partnership initially ignored the obvious strategy of an improved entertainment and retail district. Despite its reluctance, however, it eventually yielded to market pressures and endorsed the concept of its opponents.

In both cases, the ironic outcome of the early '90s recession was to force acceptance of a more varied and appropriate concept for development. Although little has come to fruition in King's Cross so far, when redevelopment does finally occur, its scale will be more modest than originally conceived, and its orientation will be toward tourism, entertainment, and small business. In Times Square, promotion of an entertainment district ended up making the area safe for the kinds of financial and service firms that the planners had sought at the start. The outcome resembles that in Soho earlier, where popular opposition to demolition for a highway allowed the unplanned growth of an arts-oriented district that ultimately succumbed to the infusion of capital in the form of high-end retailing and upper-income habitation. It turns out that the popularity of spontaneously generated spaces makes them quite as receptive to investment by major capitalist enterprises as planned megadevelopments are.

Although members of the affected communities never were able to shape the planning process to their will, they did succeed in delaying the projects until the market had collapsed. In King's Cross, where the failure to achieve early planning permission meant that existing occupants were not evicted, no drastic, disruptive change in the status quo occurred. Businesses located there, however, had to operate under great uncertainty, which continued after the slump as a result of the government's vacillation over a financial commitment to the Channel Tunnel railroad station. In Times Square many small businesses and ancillary enterprises to the theater industry were driven out, and 42nd Street itself, as well as several of the new office buildings to the north of it, was vacant for a number of years.[74]

Both the King's Cross and Times Square schemes point to the strongly speculative element in wholesale redevelopment. By forcing the development teams to propose very large projects, the public sector increased the risk element. The opportunity costs of this strategy are quite high—its all-or-nothing approach can, with a downturn in the market, produce nothing. In both cases, the obduracy of the original development consortia in adhering to their aspirations for a megacomplex of offices doomed their projects, not because of direct community antagonism but because their business assumptions were faulty. Times Square's rebound eventually more than fulfilled the city's aspirations, but, except for the theater owners, none of the original developers profited from it.

Initial planning for the projects did not take into account the particular character of the surrounding neighborhoods. The types of jobs anticipated were not appropriate for existing workers, and the kinds of businesses were not outgrowths of commercial enterprises already there. Although large, centrally located tracts like these should be planned to serve the city as a whole, such planning need not be blind to existing strengths nor wholly ignore the particularities of locale. The early '90s slump in the office market seemingly saved King's Cross and Times Square from disaster as it provided the breathing space to allow for more gradual development.

7

Creating New Centers: Spitalfields and Downtown Brooklyn

Spitalfields and downtown Brooklyn were areas considered peripheral to their cities' central business districts, although on the basis more of psychological than of physical distance. Each contained underused old commercial sites surrounded by very poor neighborhoods with predominantly minority populations. Plans for their redevelopment involved an array of government subsidies; in both locations private developers committed sums for the betterment of the area. Although the developments proposed for these two locations involved land use changes that threatened existing residents and businesses, they also promised employment and other economic benefits in parts of the city otherwise offering scant opportunity. Consequently, governmentally sponsored redevelopment initiatives found greater favor with the local community than was the case at King's Cross and Times Square. Many community activists saw the potential for gaining commitments to their enterprises from the project's public and private sponsors.

SPITALFIELDS

From an upper-floor window of the Broadgate office complex, home to many of the world's leading financial and advanced-services firms, one can survey the sprawling structure that once held the Spitalfields produce market. For more than 300 years its merchants purveyed fruits and vegetables to the greengrocers and restaurants of central London.[1] In the year 2000 the market was the temporary location of a hodgepodge of vendors, restaurants, and athletic facilities, while it awaited transmutation into a multiuse office-retail-residential complex. Additional sites along Brick Lane, further to the east, were also targets for redevelopment. As in King's Cross, the character of the expected redevelopment had changed over the preceding fifteen years, with the goal of building yet another giant office com-

138

plex receding. Instead, as in King's Cross, change was coming incrementally and on a lesser scale. The Spitalfields area constitutes a ward within the "neighborhood" of Bethnal Green, which itself is part of the borough of Tower Hamlets. The boundary between the City of London and Bethnal Green runs through the market site. Yet, while only a block separated the financial traders in Broadgate from the produce traders of the market, they existed in separate worlds, marked by vast divergences in both land uses and population. Even today clothing manufacturing ("the rag trade") and leather-working remain the principal industries of the Spitalfields area. Commercial outlets located on Brick Lane are mostly downmarket "Indian" (actually Bengali) restaurants and groceries, sari shops, and workingmen's pubs. Buildings are low-rise, and many of the shops have domiciles above them. Unlike the City of London, where few people live, the area is densely populated, and the dominant form of tenancy is council housing and private-rental tenements.[2]

In the centuries since the inception of textile manufacturing by Huguenot silk weavers, this part of East London has been the first stop for waves of immigrants entering England. After the Huguenots, Irish and Jewish groups settled the area; Bangladeshis now make up a majority of the population, with the remainder con-

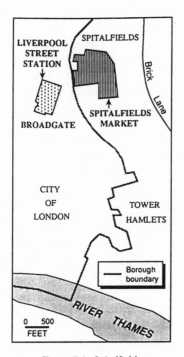

Figure 7.1. Spitalfields

sisting of a diversity of nationalities.[3] The newcomers have lived under squalid conditions in extreme poverty:

> Despite the repeated pattern of successive migrations of peoples from rural areas to the same bad housing and the same jobs, the different groups of migrants share little else. They have found themselves in Spitalfields for many reasons, and have expected a multitude of different things from their stay. The Jews were fleeing pogroms, their previous existence was unstable, they had nowhere to return to. They came in desperation. Bangladeshis came from settled rural communities whose basic patterns were unbroken even by the British empire. They came in hope; they never expected to settle here.[4]

The plight of Spitalfields' inhabitants did not improve despite their proximity to the economic frenzy a stone's throw away in the City. In a 1986 ranking of London wards derived from four indicators of deprivation, Spitalfields ranked the most deprived; only one ward exceeded it in unemployment, and none even approached it in levels of overcrowding.[5] The growth of financial services employment in adjacent areas, however, had produced demographic change in other parts of its borough of Tower Hamlets. High-end residential development, spurred by the London Docklands Development Corporation, filled the Thameside wards with newcomers who worked as professionals, managers, or white-collar support personnel in the City. At the same time, the children of the old, white working class increasingly moved out to more suburban locales. Nevertheless, even with this boost to the upper end of the Tower Hamlets population, a 1998 ranking placed it as the sixth most deprived local authority in the United Kingdom. Current ward-level data are not available, but this fact indicates that the poorer sections of the borough remained extremely disadvantaged. And, although "ethnic color" and landmark buildings did attract a fair number of visitors, the area largely remained insulated from the cosmopolitan metropolis around it.

The majority of the borough council saw large-scale development as a chance for planning gain and local economic improvement. According to a councillor who opposed the various development initiatives:

> In a community like this, people don't know where to go. People are out of school, they don't have any sign of employment. This is an underclass community. It is easily manipulated by the wealthy. The developers came and gave them hope, they used the leaders to manipulate the local community. The larger community will lose from development in Spitalfields. But the leaders were bought out, and the community is divided.

Community and Business Groups

A long history of community activism had produced a number of Bengali advocacy groups in Bethnal Green.[6] They were rooted in two main struggles: the effort to obtain decent living accommodations for Bengali families and the need to protect the Bengali community from racialist attacks, particularly prevalent in the late 1970s. These groups had succeeded in establishing a housing cooperative, attracting several housing associations into the area, and making the neighborhood fairly secure.

At the start of the '80s, community organizations feared a repetition of the wholesale conversion and exclusion of local viewpoints that they perceived as taking place in the Docklands.[7] In 1981 the London Docklands Development Corporation (LDDC) had taken over planning authority for the portion of Tower Hamlets alongside the Thames. The proposed restructuring of the western portion of Spitalfields for office uses threatened to reproduce the Docklands scenario there. The developers in the meantime, anticipating fierce opposition and lacking the protection of the LDDC, attempted to assuage local antagonisms through an expressed willingness to negotiate and through contributions to local betterment.

Business firms had become unusually active in sponsoring local programs within East London. Typically, British business leaders had not involved themselves in community activities; as developers' interest in this area grew, however, they began working through an association called the East London Partnership (ELP). The ELP was originally chaired by Sir Alan Shepherd, head of the Grand Metropolitan conglomerate, which owned the Truman's Brewery within Spitalfields—one of the proposed development sites. An offspring of the national organization Business in the Community,[8] the ELP counted in its membership the head officers of 45 large and medium-sized companies operating within the three East London boroughs of Hackney, Tower Hamlets, and Newham. As well as acting as a lobby on transit issues,[9] it provided small grants and technical assistance to community groups, including Bengali women's organizations, within East London.

The Market Site

As the City fringe began to fill up with office buildings and smart service establishments, the vegetable hawkers and the motor traffic that they attracted became more and more at odds with their surroundings. At the same time, some of the historic structures surrounding the market were gaining appeal as residential locations. The psychological barrier that had separated the City of London from Tower Hamlets became breachable. The Corporation of the City of London, which owned the Spitalfields market, issued a tender document for the 11-acre site in 1987; the winning bidder would commit itself to relocating the market traders in return for a long-term lease that would permit it to develop the site for office and retail uses.

A consortium consisting of three major property developers, calling itself the Spitalfields Development Group (SDG),[10] successfully proposed a multiuse, predominantly office scheme for the market buildings and their vicinity. As a first step, it spent £40 million to move the market to Hackney. This required an act of

Figure 7.2. Spitalfields Market, with a view of Hawksmoor's Christ Church

Parliament to revoke the royal charter that had established the market in the 1600s; in the more than two years that it took to achieve parliamentary assent, antagonism to the proposal built up and a "Save Spitalfields" campaign germinated. Criticism came from two sources: middle- and upper-class conservationists concerned with the project's impact on the historically significant environment, and community advocates who feared the socially and economically destabilizing effect of office and modern retail establishments on the Bengali community.

The SDG was close to receiving planning permission from the Tower Hamlets council in 1990 when the plan was called in by the Secretary of State for the Environment for examination of its influence on the historic setting. The Secretary of State, who had the power to remove development decisions from the jurisdiction of the local authority, was responding to pressure from the conservationists within English Heritage and the Royal Fine Arts Commission rather than from the resident community.

By the time the market relocation actually took place in 1991, the effect of the Big Bang on the office market turned out to be less than anticipated, and the SDG indicated its willingness to reduce the floor areas first proposed. After discussions with the Department of the Environment (DoE), the developers agreed to redesign their project and hired a U.S. architect, Ben Thompson, with a British firm acting as local agent. Thompson had become famous for his design of Faneuil

Hall Marketplace in Boston—the first major festive retail mall developed on a historic market site. His modifications to the plan overcame conservationists' objections, but Labour politicians continued to fault the scheme for its alleged insensitivity to local residents.

Planning permission was still in abeyance at the time of the market relocation in 1991. Outline consent was finally granted in 1992 by the Tower Hamlets local authority and the Corporation of London, but as of March 1993 the DoE was still considering the proposal. The plan, as approved by Tower Hamlets, called for 1.1 million square feet of offices (including a 16-story modern glass tower, designed by Sir Norman Foster, the principal architect of the King's Cross plan, "to be a gateway into the Spitalfields site"),[11] together with 68,000 square feet of shops and 165 flats.[12] Governmental participation in the various Spitalfields projects did not involve the kinds of financial subventions New York City provided for developers. Public-sector incentives were of two kinds: (1) The City of London offered the developers a large, central site at a low initial cost and tied future payments to returns on the property; and (2) Tower Hamlets relaxed density standards to increase the developer's profit potential.

The SDG negotiated its planning gain package with the Tower Hamlets council. The Spitalfields Community Development Group (SCDG, described below) did not participate in these discussions; to the extent that local residents were represented, it was through the affected neighborhood councils.[13] In addition to assuming the costs of market relocation, the SDG committed itself to a development agreement whereby the 127 houses on the market site would be deeded to local housing associations. It also assented to the payment of a £5 million contribution to a charitable trust (the Spitalfields Development Trust) and to a pledge of £150,000 per year for job training.

Labour politicians in Tower Hamlets nevertheless continued to oppose the development on the grounds that it would result in secondary residential displacement and would drive out unskilled jobs. The developers—in a familiar refrain—contended that only a massive development could provide enough return to support debt service, the land rent, and the planning gain package. Whereas community representatives felt that the council had succumbed to a Faustian bargain, an officer of the SDG commented to me in 1991: "If we were asked to sign up today, we wouldn't." He expressed gratitude for the delays that had held up final planning permission, given the absence of financing and the glut of office space that prevailed at that time.

In the years since then, various initiatives have occurred within the market and its immediate vicinity. A housing developer put up a number of residences across from the market buildings that included both upmarket, owner-occupied units and affordable housing. The Spitalfields Development Group sold part of the site to the London Futures Market, but it failed to realize its expectations and was bought out by the City of London Corporation. The SDG's loss totaled about £150 million in 2000, although it still retained the right to develop part of the site.

In the meantime, in an extremely unusual precedent, the SDG brought in an entrepreneur, Eric Reynolds, to develop the venue for interim uses. He filled the market hall with stalls for craftspersons to vend their wares; courts for handball and other sports; ethnic food stands; bars; and hip restaurants. Decor was minimal, and, once the space was vacated, as was expected during the year 2000, the tenants were invited to move their premises to the Bishopsgate Goods Yard (see below).[14] Despite the rather minimal investment and informality that characterized the interim market uses, the enterprise created about 1,000 jobs, almost two-thirds of which went to local residents.[15]

The SDG only received final, detailed planning permission for its scheme for the part of the market it still owned in mid-July 2000. Likely occupiers would be legal and financial firms. The other part of the market, now owned by another developer, was still in limbo, but the intention was to refurbish it for retail and restaurant use.

Brick Lane

Brick Lane constitutes the heart of the Spitalfields community. For much of the twentieth century, the establishments of kosher butchers and Jewish tailors lined the street. With the arrival of the Bengalis, the ownership of the local clothing manufacturers changed, and the cuisine purveyed along the street became that of the Indian subcontinent. When the SDG's initial plans for a redeveloped market, only three blocks to the east of Brick Lane, were announced, the Bengali community saw a threat to its meager economic base. Two large parcels of land comprising 27 acres on Brick Lane—the Truman's Brewery and the above-mentioned Bishopsgate Goods Yard—became identified as development sites. The Truman's Brewery, like the market, was a centuries-old institution; its owner, Grand Metropolitan, a large conglomerate with interests in land development as well as food and leisure activities, shut down brewing operations as it prepared a development plan for the area. The vacant Bishopsgate railroad yard had earlier also been envisioned as the location for a large office development. British Rail saw the disused goods yard as yet another opportunity to transform its property holdings into negotiable assets.

Community groups that had unsuccessfully contested the government's plans for Docklands and had opposed redevelopment of the market turned their attention to Brick Lane. In response to the perceived threats and opportunities of large-scale commercial development there, most of these groups came together under the umbrella of the Spitalfields Community Development Group (SCDG). The SCDG, rather than simply opposing development, argued that the two Brick Lane sites should be addressed within an integrated plan for the whole area. In return for community acceptance of office uses on the two sites, it asked that part of the land should be placed in trust for the community's own uses. The SCDG envisioned a "Banglatown" shopping center, which would both serve the community and draw a broader market of consumers seeking ethnic food and crafts. It also called for a training strategy and for social housing to be built before office construction.

In 1989, using funds provided by the central government's Spitalfields Task Force and by Business in the Community, the SCDG published a detailed community plan.[16] The following year, with the backing of the Bethnal Green Neighborhood Council, it achieved an agreement with Grand Metropolitan in which twelve acres would be donated to a community trust. The SCDG had three principal concerns: (1) The projects should generate retail opportunities for Bengalis; (2) garment manufacturers, especially leather-goods makers, who were regarded as the only local manufacturers with much market potential, would have access to capital; and (3) project sponsors would make a serious effort at implementing employment training schemes. To ensure that the agreement would be implemented, the SCDG demanded ongoing participation in the planning and execution of Brick Lane development, not simply a one-time planning gain agreement.

When the regeneration projects for the brewery and the goods yards were stymied by the property slump of the early '90s, the hopes of the SCDG also foundered, tied as they were to contributions from the developers that had not materialized. During the later part of the decade, however, pressure on land increased, as office buildings immediately adjacent to the Broadgate—including a huge structure built for the Dutch bank ABN AMRO—began to encroach on land that had formerly been considered part of the East End. Increased demand for housing by upper-income individuals wishing to live near their jobs in the City also pushed up prices within Spitalfields. Because few of the local small businesses owned their own premises, rising property values were likely to drive them out.[17]

In the absence of major development initiatives, small-scale enterprises began to transform the area. The Truman's Brewery became a thriving center for cultural industries, housing about 200 businesses involved in the arts, fashion, music, and design industries. In fact, the area had suddenly become chic:

> [Brick Lane] is part of a larger area of which, it is often said . . . that there are more artists per acre than anywhere else in Europe. . . . Yet there is room for more, and more have arrived, particularly around the huge Truman Brewery, now a nest of workshops, studios and shops. Last September the brewery celebrated its new identity with an event called Designers' Block, and 8,000 came in a day. . . . The eclectic style of the neighbourhood . . . knowingly combines the cool and the designed with the uncool and the undesigned. It is contrived, without wishing to seem too controlled.[18]

The owners, though, had never determined the long-term fate of the venue and had merely settled on these occupants as an interim measure. The lively atmosphere created by this concentration of cultural industries made the area more attractive to large property users, and it was still possible that the brewery would eventually be used for back offices of financial firms. Similarly, the Bishopsgate

Goods Yard, which had lain empty throughout the '90s and was now receiving the sports facilities that had left the Spitalfields Market, was attracting new attention. Owned by Railtrack, the privatized successor to British Rail, its nine acres had the potential to accommodate some very large structures. Its attractiveness was further enhanced by the likely announcement of a new tube line to run across the northern section of the site.[19]

Thus, in Spitalfields, as in Times Square, interim uses oriented toward leisure, entertainment, and cultural production changed the image of the area. It became one more in the list of places that were made safe for capital by uses proposed by opponents of large-scale developments. The precedents of Coin Street in London, Soho and Times Square in New York, and numerous other locales show that moderate investment and changed perceptions can provide a context that ensures the viability of later, more intense investment. The result is doubly ironic. On the one hand, the development coalitions that thought they had to bulldoze communities in order to transform them have been proved wrong; on the other, the defenders of community and diversity, while getting their way in the short run, seem only to produce a situation where they lose their dominance in the longer term.

City Challenge

Although the new wave of property investment might eventually produce some of the hoped-for planning gain that was committed in the original development plans, so far funding of the area's social programs has depended on government assistance. In July 1991, the Bethnal Green district, of which Spitalfields formed a part, was awarded a City Challenge grant for a program of social and physical regeneration (see Chapter 5). City Challenge was an effort spearheaded by Michael Heseltine upon his reappointment as Secretary of State for the Environment.[20] It removed money from various local aid programs in a process known as "top-slicing" and targeted it to needy places, where it would be used for coordinated programs operated by public-private partnerships. According to the Tower Hamlets CEO, the winning of the grant (11 were chosen out of 21 bidders) had largely resulted from a visit by Heseltine to Tower Hamlets. He urged the council to bid for the grant because he was intrigued by its abortive experiment, under Liberal Democratic dominance, with governmental decentralization.

The City Challenge grant provided £7.5 million per year for five years. Responsibility for running the program rested with a nonprofit community organization comparable to an American community development corporation.[21] Its board contained representatives from all the governmental and nongovernmental groups with interests in the area, including the property developers, the council, the ELP, the SCDG, and the housing associations. The emphasis of the program was on job training for construction, office, and child care jobs; English language study; support for local small-business development through grants and technical assistance; and council housing renovation and new construction sponsored by housing associations. It was hoped that the relatively small government grant would act as a catalyst for private contributions. But obtaining private funding depended on implementation of the schemes for the development sites. The bankruptcy of Olympia and York (O & Y) in the summer of 1992 squelched these expectations (see Chapter 9). O & Y had been the major investor within East London; it was an active force within the East London Partnership; the financial positions of other developers were entangled with its affairs; and its vast Canary Wharf complex had been envisioned as the anchor for development to the east of the City. Without resource commitments from developers, City Challenge became one more underfunded inner-city program.

The government replaced support from City Challenge with funding from the Single Regeneration Budget (SRB) for a program called Cityside. Launched in 1997, it involved a grant of £11.4 million over five years. Cityside's main aims were to link local workers and businesses with corporations in the City of London; to contribute to the development and diversification of the local economy; and to make the area more attractive to visitors. Another SRB program, which applied to several other boroughs as well as Tower Hamlets, focused on skill development for the unemployed, environmental improvements, and cultural development. Funding from it, however, was small.

In contrast to earlier regeneration schemes, planning for Spitalfields did not limit itself to physical redevelopment—the City Challenge and SRB grants required the integration of physical and social planning, as well as participation by both business and community representatives. The framers of the City Challenge proposal explicitly dealt with programs to improve residents' language skills, job qualifications, and housing. Cityside focused on local small business and job placement. But, as in Times Square and King's Cross, if the neighborhood were to receive large sums as spin-offs from property development, the projects had to be sufficiently remunerative—and therefore sufficiently large—to create a financial surplus. Projects of this scope, however, would inevitably end up changing the character of the area.

The juxtaposition of the poorest ward in London, populated predominantly by people of color, with the City of London financial district in a period when finance was growing in power and employment presented a perhaps insoluble dilemma. The possibility of even moderate redistribution of the wealth generated in the City to its downtrodden neighbors gave them access to resources lacking by low-income communities on the urban periphery. But any upgrading of a neighborhood so conveniently located was bound to encourage gentrification. Only strong government intervention could really stop this process. But the dependence on the private sector for project funding precluded this level of interference with the market.

DOWNTOWN BROOKLYN

Brooklyn's downtown stood as the business center of an independent municipality until New York's consolidation in 1898. From the start, however, the "city of homes and churches," as Brooklyn was labeled, lived in the shadow of Manhattan; the nearness of "the city," originally accessible by ferry and then by auto and subway, reduced downtown Brooklyn to the status of a secondary service node.[22] Once middle-class customers left the borough for the suburbs, all that remained to sustain the downtown core were government offices, one last major department store, a large but struggling group of small retailers, and the Brooklyn Academy of Music.[23] Earlier urban renewal efforts had caused the demolition of a number of buildings, but no replacements ever reached the construction stage.[24] In the mid-1980s several single-room-occupancy hotels housed the homeless; destitute men hung out in the refuse-strewn vacant lots; prostitution and the drug trade flourished. The only skyscraper was the 34-story Williamsburgh Savings Bank building constructed in 1929, the year before the Great Depression signaled the end of commercial real-estate development in central Brooklyn for the next sixty years.

While depopulation and disinvestment shaped the circumstances of downtown Brooklyn throughout the forty years after World War II, nearby neighborhoods fared better. Brooklyn Heights, directly facing the Manhattan skyline across the East River and isolated from the rest of Brooklyn by topographic boundaries, had maintained itself as an elite white residential area throughout the period. The adjacent Cadman Plaza urban renewal scheme, which produced a shopping center and a complex of high-rise, modernist middle-income residential buildings, further insulated the Heights. Other districts (Park Slope, Cobble Hill, Fort Greene), in which an exodus of the original affluent inhabitants had left a large stock of handsome brownstone houses, became the targets of gentrification. The black population of Bedford-Stuyvesant and Fort Greene expanded, and their large public housing projects sheltered an increasingly impoverished population; nevertheless, parts of these neighborhoods were upgraded by middle-income, mainly black, homeowners, and the hub of African-American culture moved from Harlem to central Brooklyn.[25] Brooklyn also became the destination for a highly diverse flow of Caribbean immigrants—estimated between 1983 and 1986 alone to include 16,000 Jamaicans, 15,000 Haitians, 12,000 Guyanese, 2,500 Granadans, 3,000 Barbadians, and 4,000 Trinidadians.[26] They provided a willing low-wage labor force, and their economic ambitions stimulated the growth of small business within the borough.

A number of factors came together by the end of the 1980s to stimulate the various initiatives aimed at reconstructing downtown Brooklyn. Primary was the felt need by the New York City government to compete with New Jersey in attracting the back offices of major companies. Only in the boroughs was land sufficiently cheap to allow competitively low rental prices. Shifting development interest to Brooklyn would both create a less expensive business core that could vie with out-of-state locations and deflect criticism that the mayor's office cared only about Manhattan.[27] Moreover, it would respond to the urgings of the Regional Plan Association (RPA), an influential private body, which had envisioned downtown Brooklyn's elaborate transit infrastructure as creating the potential for a "third node of the Manhattan business district."

In tandem with the government's desire to see office development in the borough, private developers had begun searching more broadly for developable locations as Manhattan's construction boom absorbed the remaining parcels within its central business district. Two large Brooklyn sites presented themselves. One, adjacent to Polytechnic University, a private engineering school located on the edge of downtown, was being promoted by that institution as an ideal site, offering a potential synergy between the university's technical capacity and the needs of high-tech industry. Called MetroTech, this project opened for occupancy in 1990. The second, Atlantic Terminal, appeared the best prospect for commercial growth, as it was located above the largest confluence of subway and train lines in New York.[28] It opened in 1996.

MetroTech

In 1984 Polytechnic University announced expansion plans and issued a request for proposals (RFP) to develop its surrounding area; the university's board envisioned the construction of a high-tech center, a sort of Silicon Valley East. Al-

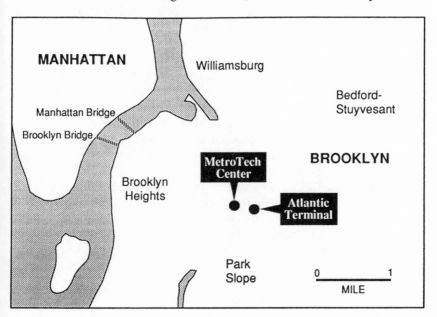

Figure 7.3. MetroTech Center

though the sixteen-acre site had years earlier been designated as an urban renewal area, it still housed about 100 families, 60 small businesses, and five governmental agencies. Bruce Ratner, a former New York City commissioner of consumer affairs, felt that the location had potential. He had recently entered into a joint venture arrangement with Forest City Enterprises,[29] a Cleveland, Ohio, development firm[30] run by members of his family, and he persuaded his partner to join with him in responding to Polytechnic's RFP.

Forest City Enterprises is a publicly held firm that originally specialized in secondary markets. Its officers described it as an institutional rather than a speculative developer—that is, it projected future earnings on the basis of present market conditions rather than assuming that increases in returns on its investments would exceed the rate of inflation. Although its shares dropped nearly two-thirds in value between 1989 and 1992, it remained solvent by avoiding heavy leveraging; according to its founder, it had "almost no cross-collateralized mortgages or corporate guarantees . . . no second mortgages or recourse on our mortgages."[31] Forest City tried to identify areas where it would not face competition, and it did not seek construction financing until the building was at least half preleased. While superficially the sorts of places it selected appeared to offer weak prospects, they presented cost advantages, and public subsidies were available to further reduce risk.[32] During the '90s it continued its practice of investing in peripheral locations, but it also increasingly participated in large, centrally located projects that attracted other developers, especially if they involved governmental subsidy.

Polytechnic's RFP corresponded exactly with Forest City Enterprises' strategic criteria of the time: No other developer was sufficiently interested in the area even to make a bid, and substantial governmental assistance could be obtained. According to one of the development company's officers, "Forest City Ratner realized that financial services were the high-tech firms of New York. They were big computer users. They could be advantaged by proximity to Polytechnic." The original vision of research laboratories and software outfits became transformed into yet another corporate office scheme, although somewhat disguised by the rubric of "high-tech." The development firm formulated a concept for a 4.2 million square foot office project in which it would pursue the computer processing operations of the financial industry.

Many of Forest City Ratner's staff members had worked in city government, and they knew how to use public benefits to bring total occupancy costs for tenants down to New Jersey levels. As a Forest City executive described the process: "Unless you worked in the public sector, understanding it is not easy. We were able to structure subsidies by setting up a 'pro forma' showing costs in Brooklyn versus New Jersey and then identifying the gap and filling it in rather than just throwing money away."

The Public Development Corporation (PDC) (later to become the Economic Development Corporation) acted as the lead city agency on the project. At the behest of Polytechnic University and the development firm, it condemned the land, demolished the existing structures, and relocated the residents and businesses. In return, the city government was to receive a ground rent. Forest City Ratner put in about 10 percent of the private equity investment itself and obtained the rest of its financing from Japanese banks. Even though it adhered to its policy of not building until there were committed tenants, it still had considerable difficulty gaining a long-term mortgage, as financial institutions continued to regard Brooklyn as a risky proposition.

Under the city's Industrial and Commercial Incentives Program (ICIP) all firms moving into MetroTech benefited from a pass-through of property tax reductions for 22 years; a twelve-year exemption from the commercial occupancy

Figure 7.4. A scale model of MetroTech Center

tax; and a $500 per employee credit on the city's business profits tax for twelve years. Brooklyn Union Gas, a private utility, took advantage of the incentives and committed itself to vacating its old headquarters and moving to the nearby site; an $8 million federal Urban Development Action Grant (UDAG) supplemented the developer's investment in its building. The Securities Industry Automation Corporation (SIAC), a nonprofit provider of computer services to the stock exchanges, became the first tenant of the new MetroTech complex to move from Manhattan. In addition to the standard ICIP incentives, it received a $6 million federal UDAG, a $10 million equity investment from the city's Municipal Assistance Corporation (MAC), and a $5.5 million construction grant from the city's capital budget. Because New York's extremely high utility charges penalized heavy computer users, it was necessary to provide cheap electrical power. The company therefore received a substantial discount from the privately owned Consolidated Edison electrical utility, which in turn got a city tax subsidy for its largesse.[33]

The next enterprise that left Manhattan for Brooklyn did even better. The Chase Manhattan Bank in 1988 indicated that it was seriously interested in moving its data processing operations with their 5,000-person workforce to Jersey City. In exchange for reconsidering and committing itself to MetroTech, it obtained more than $100 million above the as-of-right incentives. Altogether the value of tax relief, site improvements, and electricity discounts amounted to $235 million,[34] and part of the tax abatement was granted to Chase's headquarters in Manhattan. In defending the arrangement against criticism of its munificence, Gov. Mario Cuomo rationalized: "Nobody held us up. This is a tremendous deal." The vice-president of the Regional Plan Association (RPA) commended the city: "It is appropriate and a very practical approach to give away the store to get the first firms in."[35] Chase bought a full-page advertisement in the *New York Times,* in which to express its gratitude for the efforts of Governor Cuomo and Mayor Koch in making Brooklyn attractive to it;[36] according to the ad, however, "what tipped the scale in favor of New York was the simple fact that for nearly 200 years New York has been our home."[37]

The financial concern Bear Stearns, the next company to win a special package of benefits for coming to MetroTech, did not justify its move in such sentimental terms:

> "The only way we could go to Brooklyn—because we figured that Brooklyn and Jersey City were roughly equal—was if the city would do more," Mr. Lang [its managing director] said. . . . As Mr. Lang told it, his message was: "We need relief at 245 Park [its headquarters in midtown Manhattan] or the MetroTech deal won't work. You're killing us with the real-estate taxes."[38]

The estimated value of the discretionary benefits given Bear Stearns on top of the ICIP package was $17 million, including the provision of lower-cost New York Power Authority electricity to the Manhattan building. Other reasons presented for its choice of Brooklyn were the speed with which the Dinkins administration put together the subsidy program; the fact that space in the Brooklyn Union Gas building was immediately available; and the knowledge that 57 percent of its 1,500 employees lived in Brooklyn, Queens, and Staten Island and would have difficulty commuting to New Jersey.[39]

Both the Chase and Bear Stearns deals involved tax benefits to structures in the Manhattan CBD occupied by other sections of the target firms. Therefore, although ICIP subsidies had been deliberately removed from Manhattan some years earlier, the outcome of directing discretionary benefits to Brooklyn was, in effect, to provide assistance in Manhattan. This breaching of the intent of the ICIP restrictions began under Mayor Koch and continued under Mayor Dinkins.

The subsidy program had succeeded in bringing enterprises to Brooklyn that otherwise would have avoided it. MetroTech, which included a three-acre outdoor commons, added a clear amenity to the decayed downtown. The complex, constructed according to a master plan created by the New York firm of Haines Lundberg Waehler, opened out onto the regular street grid, and it did not present the walled-off visage that characterizes most new development in areas perceived as dangerous. Different architects designed each building, with Skidmore, Owings & Merrill, the best-known of the participating firms, responsible for the largest amount of space. Although the architecture of the various buildings was undistinguished, it was not overbearing, and local people seemed to use and enjoy the greenery and special events provided in the commons. Intensive policing by both the New York Police Department and a private security force combined with a greatly increased amount of foot traffic to cause the felony crime rate to drop by 23 percent between 1989 and 1991.[40]

MetroTech unquestionably revitalized the area. The development strategy produced a project more than 95 percent occupied, and surrounding retail and service businesses began to feel multiplier effects,[41] but they also were confronted by sharply rising rents, and local owners saw the arrival of competition from well-capitalized chains.[42] Forest City Ratner purchased the Albee Mall, a faltering nearby shopping center, with the aim of improving its appearance and merchandise. The MetroTech business improvement district (BID), funded by the businesses within the project and its vicinity, provided sanitation and security; programmed special events; and worked with community groups, merchants, and local high schools on public events and beautification projects. Receipts from the sales tax on construction purchases were set aside to fund an employment training council, and part of an office building was established as a business incubator, wherein fledgling businesses would pay low rents and receive technical and administrative services. Thus, the economic benefits of the project were spread to some degree around the surrounding area.

In the spring of 1992 black groups formed the African-American Coalition for Economic Development over the issue of jobs at MetroTech. It contended that the heavily subsidized office complex did not create employment for Brooklyn's black population. Officials at Forest City disputed this claim, arguing that 10 percent yearly turnover in clerical jobs within the complex assured hiring of neighborhood people. Hard data are not currently available on the employment effects of the project.

Atlantic Terminal

Spurred on by its success at MetroTech, Forest City Ratner apparently decided that with contributions from government, it could transform all of downtown Brooklyn. Except for one hotel and office complex across the street from MetroTech,[43] the firm assumed the responsibility for developing every potential commercial location in the area. Most significantly, it entered into a partnership with Rose Associates to develop the city-owned Atlantic Terminal urban renewal area, a site that had been awaiting construction activity since 1968. In 1985 Mayor Koch, with the usual publicity barrage, had announced a $255 million project to include 600,000 square feet of office space, a movie theater, 400 middle-income condominium housing units, a 45,000 square foot regional supermarket, and a shopping center.[44] The city had pledged $18.3 million of its own money toward construction as well as the usual tax benefits. The mayor also promised that the city's Health and Hospitals Corporation (HHC) would become the anchor tenant for the office component.

The city invested $16.2 million in demolition and site improvements. However, Rose Associates, the designated developer, with long experience in the New York market as a major builder of both office and residential structures, had always followed a conservative investment strategy. After the HHC, under cost pressures and heavily criticized for extravagance, withdrew from the project, Rose apparently lost interest in moving forward. Despite Atlantic Terminal's excellent transit access, Rose found the Brooklyn location too risky. Forest City Ratner's experience, however, raised confidence in the area, and in 1991 the two firms announced their joint venture.[45] With little hope of finding office tenants, the partnership made the shopping center and the very large supermarket, now planned at more than 50,000 square feet, its first priority.[46]

A coalition of local groups, the Atlantic Terminal Urban Renewal Association (ATURA), had formed at the time of the original 1986 project announcement to oppose the development plan. Members were particularly concerned over the possibility of secondary displacement (i.e., that development would cause surrounding areas to become unaffordable to present occupants, forcing them out) and were disturbed that on-site housing would be for middle-income owners only.[47] They recalled that years earlier, when housing on the partially vacant site had been torn down, residents had been promised replacement units. ATURA proposed a mix of affordable housing units, a much smaller supermarket to serve only the local community, and small-scale retail and office development; it lacked the resources, however, to formulate a full-blown alternative plan. With the assistance of pro bono public-interest law firms, it brought three lawsuits related to the project's physical and social impacts and won one, resulting in the judge's ordering a study of its impacts on racial groups.

ATURA considered that the regional supermarket concept would bring unendurable car and truck traffic into the already heavily congested and polluted area and would negatively affect tenants of an adjacent low-income housing complex. Its stance on the supermarket and housing, however, was not shared by all elements within the neighborhood. The community board saw a need for the supermarket as well as economic opportunities in the shopping center that it would anchor, and it thought that middle-income condo owners would help stabilize the neighborhood. It therefore enthusiastically supported the project. ATURA accused the board of being a rubber stamp and faulted it for not even demanding anything in return for its approval.

As in Spitalfields, the community split according to whether or not factions saw potential advantages to themselves if the development proceeded. The housing issue was particularly divisive, since even low-income residents feared that provision of permanent housing for the homeless would worsen the social environment. Although the main criticisms of the development were based on concerns of residents for their living conditions, the African-American Coalition for Economic Development expressed its intention of monitoring Atlantic Terminal's employment outcomes. Like ATURA, its interests kept it from favoring office uses, but it was not clear that it and ATURA would be in agreement on issues of scale. As at Times Square, the demise of requirements for regular citizen participation by project-area residents produced a situation where solicitation of community opinion depended on informal arrangements and on the willingness of elected representatives to act as advocates.

In 1992 the borough president's office set up an Atlantic Terminal advisory committee incorporating a variety of city officials and community representatives but heavily weighted toward project supporters. There were indications that city funds would be used to change the income mix of the housing, reflecting the greater concern of the Dinkins administration than its predecessor for assisting low-income people. Modifications to the parking plan lessened adverse neighborhood effects. The office component vanished from the discussion. The development team feared that plan modifications, which had been introduced in response to the changed real-estate market, might force it to undergo the land use review process again. It therefore showed responsiveness to community concerns in the hope that its spirit of cooperation would dissuade neighborhood groups from pressing the issue of formal reconsideration.

The real-estate slump of the '90s had a less dampening effect on the Brooklyn projects than on Manhattan development for two principal reasons. First, the city offered extremely high levels of subsidy to the area, including the commitment of some of its own agencies as tenants and assumption of site-acquisition costs. Although its tax subsidies at Times Square were commensurately great, it could not justify filling that site with city offices. Rental costs would have been unacceptably high; the location was quite distant from the civic center clustered around City Hall; and the justification for building office towers on 42nd Street would have been wholly undercut.

Second, Forest City Ratner—the dominant private-sector actor in downtown Brooklyn—proved exceptionally canny in exploiting the attributes of its location. Companies like Brooklyn Union Gas had to stay in Brooklyn, and no one else was bidding for them. MetroTech's placement in Brooklyn's governmental core attracted further governmental activity to the area. Bruce Ratner's experience in city government taught him how to use the public sector to his great benefit, through both personal connections and program understanding. He took advantage of New Jersey's attraction to New York financial firms by getting the city to heap ever more subsidy on his development, and he had the backing of Brooklyn politicians who had long complained about favoritism to Manhattan.

Like Mayor Koch before him, Mayor Dinkins felt compelled to respond to every notice by a major firm that it was considering a move to New Jersey with a counteroffer. And indeed, if Manhattan was not a viable alternative for the firms that settled in Brooklyn, and if their move to New Jersey would result in heavy, long-term job loss for Queens and Brooklyn residents, encouragement of a critical mass of new construction in the latter might have been necessary for continued economic viability. If MetroTech and Atlantic Terminal sustain a local multiplier effect, and if pressures for employment of minority community residents prevail, the city's massive involvement in promoting Brooklyn will have important benefits for its citizens. Additionally, an environmental argument can be made for developing a business center with excellent public transit connections outside Manhattan's congested core. Unfortunately, though, Brooklyn's roadway situation and the backups within it caused by difficulties of automotive access to the island of Manhattan mean that growth there has serious negative environmental consequences of its own.

Whether or not New York City should incur heavy costs to entice businesses out of Manhattan to the boroughs remains controversial. A widely publicized study by New York University's Urban Research Center argued that the city should play to its strengths and continue to emphasize its Manhattan core.[48] By mid-1992, however, in addition to taxes foregone, the city had spent $166 million in capital improvements in downtown Brooklyn; in that year its Brooklyn expenditures amounted to nearly three-quarters of its capital budget for economic development.[49] Forest City Ratner, for its part, had invested just $300 million, only somewhat more than twice as much as the city, yet the city had no equity participation in the project.[50] Certainly, it is hard to rationalize this extraordinary amount of public subsidy at the same time that the government was sustaining a budget crisis.

Brooklyn had indeed been established as the third node of the city's business district, but not without considerable cost. When, in the early '90s, recession was causing the citywide tax base to contract, the government was giving away more tax breaks, forcing small businesses to shoulder an increased proportion of the tax burden. Meanwhile, larger concerns took advantage of the various tax subsidy programs, and every firm could see the logic of indicating its interest in New Jersey. MetroTech contributed to density and congestion in an area already subject to very high levels of motor vehicle traffic and consequent air pollution; Atlantic Terminal promised to add to these problems. The extent to which the economic development incorporated in MetroTech benefited the citizens of Brooklyn remained problematic. Even though the companies within MetroTech had pledged commitments to job training and the placement of Brooklyn residents within their workforces, "the residents' biggest concern . . . is that downtown Brooklyn will become an isolated bubble, shut off from the rest of the borough."[51]

By the end of the century, downtown Brooklyn had stabilized. Forest City Ratner was planning on constructing the final building in its complex, which it was seeking to have rezoned to accommodate a one million square foot building, twice the size originally planned. Employment in the area stood at about 90,000, and all of downtown Brooklyn's six million square feet of quality commercial space had been leased.[52] The owner of the Renaissance Plaza hotel-office center was considering expanding his property. But Brooklyn leaders had expressed concern that "the borough has not been able to capitalize on MetroTech's success to turn its downtown into a magnet for other businesses."[53]

THE DYNAMICS OF DEVELOPMENT

Initiatives for the four redevelopment efforts described in this and the preceding chapter were fashioned by a variety of sources including private developers, community groups, and nonprofit organizations as well as government. Except in Brick Lane, developers' interest was provoked by a governmental request for proposals. All four enterprises aimed at the creation of new commercial nodes in unfashionable locations, and all required considerable public investment. Despite their differing origins, each bore a striking resemblance to the others in incorporating plans for very large office complexes that were subsequently rethought during the real-estate slump of the '90s.

The developments all threatened to overwhelm surrounding communities and provoked resistance over their physical environmental impacts and potential displacement effects on businesses and households. The various projects involved the retention of prestigious internationally known architectural firms. Except in Brooklyn, they designed complexes at odds with their surroundings, determined to make a statement and demonstrate that the redeveloped areas had a radically different character from what preceded them. Moreover, designation of the areas as renewal sites, and land clearance preliminary to redevelopment, had the immediate effect of dampening economic activity as the long delays and uncertainty inhibited current occupants and potential investors from improving the properties. Both Times Square and Spitalfields, however, presented exceptional remedies to this common problem. The decision to develop interim uses invigorated the areas and created a context propitious for more intense development.

All four cases involved conflicts of values as between local and citywide objectives, public-good and market criteria, and equity versus growth. Redevelopment of established areas necessarily has differential impacts on present occupants, with only a minority able to capitalize on the transformed uses. The commercial development embodied in the projects was touted as containing growth potential for these two world cities. With manufacturing regarded as a vestige of the past, public officials and developers contended that only offices for financial and advanced-services firms could nurture expanding enterprises. Even if their predictions were correct concerning the type of industry that would flourish in the future, however, the nature of office-centered growth seriously limited the extent to which the poor and working-class populations of inner London and New York would benefit from business expansion. While the jobs created or retained would provide few career opportunities for poorly educated citizens, the public investment involved in their creation increased the tax burden on these same citizens and on small businesses.

Planning agreements required compensation of residents for the costs to them—housing and employment programs in King's Cross, Spitalfields, and Brooklyn; a community development fund for the Clinton neighborhood next to Times Square; construction of public amenities in all four places. Some community opponents were assuaged by these side payments, while others considered them to be inadequate but their only realistic option. In both Spitalfields and Times Square not all of them materialized, as they were dependent on the development going forward as originally planned. In Spitalfields and King's Cross the size of future development and associated community benefits remains unclear; in Times Square the developers were freed of their obligation to contribute to the rebuilding of the subway station and had their already small contribution to theater reconstruction reduced.

Besides the uncertainty involved in such reliance on the private sector, bargaining between the community and private investors fails to offer the potential advantages of comprehensive planning in creating a satisfactory overall environment. It does, however, fit well within a liberal-economics paradigm of trade-offs. At the end of the century, London—although still heavily reliant on the vehicle of planning gain—had moved away from the narrow project focus that prevailed during the Thatcher years. There was a return to planning and an effort to use the SRB as a vehicle to integrate social with physical planning in deprived areas. In contrast, New York City's government under Mayor Rudolph Giuliani had, except in Staten Island, largely withdrawn from promoting new large-scale development in peripheral locations and thus engaged neither in planning nor in the trading of benefits. The only exception was within the Harlem/South Bronx Empowerment Zone, which resembled the various London projects in its provision of social funding and partnership arrangements.

In both London and New York the projects had governmental sponsors, but the willingness of government to offer direct subsidy to the developer was far greater in New York. Neither of the two British projects was to receive any tax relief. Except in enterprise zones, British law did not allow tax subsidies, although the Labour goverment is currently proposing to change that stance. In Spitalfields, the use of City Challenge and SRB funds to encourage private-sector activity was indirect—public capital expenditure did not directly support the private components of the developments. Thus, although all the projects as originally planned tilted toward growth over equity in their value orientation, governmental expenditures in London were used for public purposes.

In three of the four locations, the effect of the property recession of the '90s was to cause a rethinking of the projects. In King's Cross and Spitalfields the result was a scaling down of ambition and a greater emphasis on community participation and neighborhood benefits. In Times Square it was a revived recognition of the importance of the area as an entertainment district, with the surprising result that entertainment uses attracted the very kind of office development that had originally been desired. All three areas ended up with a greater diversity of land uses than the initial office schemes had embodied. Of the four, only MetroTech ended up fulfilling the original plan. This was the consequence of much greater direct investment by the public sector in the enterprise, allowing it to weather the recession despite coming on the market at a very unpropitious time. It also stemmed from the caution of the development company, which by not borrowing so heavily and by preleasing its properties, avoided the risks incurred in the other cases.

8

Creating a New Address I:
Battery Park City

In the spring of 1992 observers of the real-estate market were beginning to detect signs that the slump had bottomed out. Then a new tremor shook the market as the vast empire of Olympia & York (O & Y) began to founder. O & Y owned more New York commercial property than any other landlord; its Canary Wharf project was the largest development in Europe; it possessed substantial interests in other property firms; and a number of major banks held big stakes in its debt. Its inability to refinance its short-term notes and meet its interest obligations threatened the stability of the entire property market. Moreover, O & Y was not just a huge developer; it also represented the cream of the industry. Its previous enormous profitability, the scope of its projects, its responsiveness in working with government, its innovative building techniques, and the commitment of its owners, the Reichmann family, to high-quality construction and public amenities supposedly demonstrated the synergistic potential of public-private partnerships to rebuild cities.

O & Y had transformed a landfill next to New York's financial center into the most prestigious corporate address in Manhattan. Although retrospectively the World Financial Center in Battery Park City appeared to have numerous competitive advantages, the project had been on the brink of failure before the Reichmanns made their investment. Their achievement in New York made them seem invincible. When they stepped in to create an even more mammoth complex on London's Isle of Dogs, the British government, which had seen an earlier investor group withdraw, thought it had found salvation. But whereas the World Financial Center had hit the crest of the property wave, Canary Wharf was destined to plumb the trough. The overall state of the market conjoined with specific attributes of the Docklands situation to produce a failure with all the inevitability of Greek tragedy. The very qualities of the Reichmann family that had produced their previous triumphs seemed inexorably to beget their devastation.

Then, in yet another reversal of fate, the economic boom that began in both countries in the mid-1990s resulted in the gradual absorption of the vacant office space in London and New York. Although the firm Olympia & York no longer existed, Paul Reichmann, who had led the earlier enterprise, reentered the scene as a principal in the reconstituted Canary Wharf Company. Canary Wharf, which only a few years earlier seemed doomed to become a mere secondary office location, filled up with major companies, and its management embarked on expansion.

This chapter tells the story of the rise of Olympia & York and examines the broader development scheme of Battery Park City in New York, of which O & Y's project formed the most important part. The following chapter recounts the history of development in London's Docklands, the role played there by Olympia & York, and the rise, fall, and resurrection of Canary Wharf. As in earlier chapters, my aim is to capture the dynamics of the development process, including the interplay between individual personality, economic opportunity, and governmental intervention. In the instance of the Reichmanns' developments, personality played an especially significant role. The impact of O & Y in New York and London was, for a while, so immense that it shaped general expectations concerning the future and character of the property market. Its daring and triumph in "creating a new address," as Paul Reichmann termed its achievement, made the strategy of property-led regeneration appear brilliant. Its demise raised important questions concerning governmental policies for fostering development. The ultimate outcome showed the unpredictability of property markets.

THE RISE OF OLYMPIA & YORK

Paul, Albert, and Ralph Reichmann, the heads of O & Y, were among the six children of Samuel and Renée Reichmann.[1] The parents spent their youth in Hungary; they then settled in Vienna, where Samuel Reichmann established a highly successful egg wholesaling business. As the Nazis moved into Austria, they fled with their young children first to Paris, then to Madrid, and finally to Tangier. Samuel Reichmann managed to escape with some capital, and in Tangier he set up a small banking operation, specializing in currency exchange. The Reichmanns, and Renée in particular, devoted themselves to assisting Jews escape from occupied Europe. Renée Reichmann was personally responsible for saving hundreds, perhaps thousands, of lives; she even made an extraordinarily daring rescue mission to Hungary in 1942.[2] She established relations with the major relief organizations and devised an elaborate system for sending food and clothing to concentration camp inmates; ingeniously, she worked at getting them large quantities of chocolate, apparently so that they could use the candy as currency.

After the war, the Reichmanns remained in Tangier, where Samuel Reichmann's business prospered. Their home was a center for displaced persons, and their reputation for piety and charity grew as they assisted camp survivors in starting new lives. Eventually, the family decided to leave Tangier, and the sons, now grown, searched for an appropriate new location. As extremely Orthodox Jews, the Reichmanns could reside only in a community that would support their way of life. Ultimately, they picked Canada, reportedly rejecting the United States because they were repelled by McCarthyism. They moved there in 1955, with some family members settling in Montreal and others in Toronto.

The brothers, educated in yeshivas and constrained by their Orthodox Judaism from pursuing a professional or technical education, started a building supply company, Olympia Tile and Wall, in the late 1950s. The company benefited from a rapidly increasing demand for lavish bathrooms. It entered the development business when it acted as its own general contractor to build a new warehouse.

The shift to property development began in earnest in 1965, when Albert and Paul Reichmann, who had formed a firm called York Developments, purchased land next to Toronto's Don Valley Parkway for $25 million from failing New York developer William Zeckendorf. They subdivided it and paid for the entire parcel by selling off the lots that they did not develop. In 1969 the family incorporated as Olympia & York Developments Ltd. and, while continuing to operate the tile company, rapidly expanded their development enterprises within this privately held company.

Paul Reichmann, who was the chief real-estate strategist for the family concern, foresaw the potential profits in government-sponsored central-city redevelopment. He became involved in the planning process for downtown Toronto's enormous retail and office complexes, and O & Y began work on the enormous First Canadian Place in 1974. At the time it was built, the 3.5 million square foot size of the development was unprecedented in Canada, and skeptics doubted that it could ever be filled. The project proved immensely profitable, however, and it acted as the basis for financing later ventures. In fact, in 1988 O & Y managed to sell $400 million in bonds secured by the leases on the building without even pledging any part of the complex as collateral.

In building First Canadian Place, the brothers experimented successfully with financing and construction techniques that they later used in their other projects. Thus, they assumed the risk of borrowing short-term at variable rates, enabling them to take advantage of falling long-term rates when they became available. They also pioneered in the use of new construction methods and office design. Among their innovations was a computerized system of winches, turntables, and elevators, including one that could accommodate loaded trucks, to carry materials to preassigned floors and thus reduce construction time. They increased their market appeal by building structures with jagged corners that allowed them to double the number of corner offices and thereby command higher rents.[3]

In 1990, before the rapid devaluation of its assets that ensued shortly thereafter, the estimated value of O & Y's real-estate holdings was $24 billion.[4] The meteoric rise in the Reichmann family's fortunes resulted from strategic low-priced acquisitions and ingenious use of financial instruments. At the depth of the New York City fiscal crisis and economic recession in 1977, it had entered the New York market, buying the properties of Uris Brothers, another bankrupt New York firm; it paid $50 million in cash and took over mortgages worth $288 million on the eight buildings.[5] A decade after their purchase, the buildings were valued at ten times the original price, and the Reichmanns had become billionaires.

The astute use of new financial instruments was another source of the family's increase in wealth. O & Y was the first real-estate firm to use commercial paper, issuing its own short-term notes; its reputation for success made it one of the few development companies able to raise financing on this basis. The firm also increased its operating capital through employing elaborate currency hedges and debt swaps, a practice that considerably increased its flexibility but also made its financial situation extraordinarily complex.

O & Y functioned with a lean organization and was staffed by officers widely known for their breadth and capability. A number of its high-ranking employees came out of public-sector jobs, where they had gained extensive experience in negotiating agreements with developers, learning in the process what kinds of deals could be had from government. Michael Dennis, Toronto's former housing commissioner, led the Canary Wharf enterprise from the position of executive vice-president. In 1990 the family hired John Zuccotti, former chair of the New York City Planning Commission and later deputy mayor, as president of its U.S. subsidiary. An extremely well connected "fixer" within New York's governmental system, he was the first outsider to act as CEO of one of the family's wholly owned companies. Meyer Frucher, previously the president of the Battery Park City Authority, took on the job of executive vice-president of the U.S. company.

The Reichmann brothers represented an unusual combination of conservatism and recklessness. Despite their great wealth, they continued to live modestly in the upper-middle-class Toronto suburb of North York, within walking distance of their synagogue. Although famous for their philanthropic spending, especially but not exclusively on Jewish charities, their personal consumption habits were abstemious. They strictly observed *kashruth,* following the detailed set of rules governing Orthodox Jewish life, and totally closed down all business within the firm on Jewish holidays and the Sabbath. Unlike many of the flamboyant developer-heroes of the 1980s, they were extremely secretive, refusing to grant interviews or expose their family lives to public view. One journalist described them as "so colorless that they are colorful."[6] Their reputation for trustworthiness in a business not known for its ethics allowed them to consummate deals with a handshake and to obtain noncollateralized loans from usually wary bankers.

At the same time, they were avid speculators. Paul Reichmann's credo was that "the right time to go into any field is when the market's perception is that the time is wrong."[7] For more than two decades his contrarian tactics worked, giving O & Y the assets, the confidence, and the reputation to embark on ever-greater gambles. The firm's mettle was in its willingness to risk its own funds on its ventures and in its modus operandi of buying out the unexpired leases of prestigious tenants to entice them to move into its properties.

The riskiest gambit of all, however, was taking on projects of prodigious size in places off the beaten track. In the words of an admiring *Business Week* article:

> Perhaps the most distinctive Reichmann trademark is the brothers' willing- ness to take huge gambles that only pay off way down the line. That's what endears them to governments. In massive public-private partnerships like the World Financial Center, they put up the financing, the government provides cheap land, and together they create whole new urban centers.[8]

O & Y's greatest triumph, the World Financial Center in New York's Bat- tery Park City, and its fatal failure, Canary Wharf in London's Docklands, em- body the methods that brought the family first to its heights and then to a precarious position. We turn now to the story of the World Financial Center. This project demonstrated the firm's capacity to hedge its bets through using its enormous resources to assure tenantry of its buildings. It did so by constructing a project large and luxurious enough to constitute a whole new business center and by offering sufficient incentives to attract tenants with time remaining on their exist- ing leases.

BATTERY PARK CITY

At the southern tip of Manhattan lies a small green space now called Battery Park, created on landfill in the early nineteenth century.[9] It gained its name from a gun emplacement, the West Battery, which was situated there, overlooking New York Harbor, to guard the city against naval attack. Once its military function ended, the fortification served as an entertainment arena named Castle Clinton and became a reception center for immigrants, later the location of the municipal aquarium, and, finally, a picturesque ruin. At midcentury Robert Moses, New York's highway construction czar, sought to run a ramp to his proposed Brooklyn- Battery Bridge through the park; after his plans were defeated, he still tried to destroy the historic structure. Blocked by conservationists from completely de- molishing it, he left only its wall. In the postwar years Battery Park and its sur- roundings provided the only public waterfront access in downtown Manhattan. Directly to the north lay the towers of Wall Street; rotting piers and unused ma- rine facilities lined the adjacent waterfront to the northwest.

During the 1960s David Rockefeller, head of Chase Manhattan Bank, led a drive by the Downtown Lower Manhattan Association (DLMA) to retain the Wall Street area as a financial center in a period when business was increasingly mov- ing to midtown. Part of the DLMA's strategy was to have the Port Authority con- struct a world trade center on a site facing the Hudson River, a few blocks north of Battery Park. Rockefeller's ambitions for the area were supported by his brother

Nelson, the governor of New York State, who shepherded a bill through the state legislature allowing the Port Authority of New York and New Jersey to embark on this venture.[10] Excavation for the giant complex, harbinger of later mega-developments, produced a great amount of debris, which could be cheaply removed if dumped in the Hudson River directly off-site. The action would create a large stretch of vacant city-owned territory in one of the world's most densely built areas. The city's Department of Marine and Aviation, which had already proposed filling in the space around its obsolete docking facilities in the vicinity, welcomed the landfill proposal.[11]

The Plan

There was considerable debate among officials of the city, the state, the Port Authority, and the DLMA as to what should be built on the new land, with many advocating the use of part of the site for subsidized housing. In 1968 state legislation set up the Battery Park City Authority (BPCA) with responsibility for financing and construction on the 92-acre site. The 1969 joint state-city "master development plan" for the tract envisioned a modernist new town, composed of superblocks constructed on platforms elevating it above its surroundings. A consortium of architects had worked on the plan, but the dominant force was Gov. Nelson Rockefeller's favorite firm, Harrison & Abramovitz, progenitors of Lincoln Center for the Performing Arts and the Albany State Mall.[12] The following year the BPCA entered into a master lease with the city, which stipulated a housing mix in which each building would contain an equal number of low-, middle-, and upper-income units. The housing agreement was later discarded. Only one development was ever constructed according to the original physical plan: Gateway Plaza, a 1,712-unit middle-income rental building, was begun in 1980, its ground breaking delayed for years by problems in obtaining Federal Housing Administration mortgage insurance. The *New Yorker* architectural critic Brendan Gill characterizes the slab-style, high-rise complex as having "a grim, gray penitentiary look."[13]

To finance the demolition of the old piers, complete the landfill, and build infrastructure, the BPCA issued $200 million in "moral obligation" revenue bonds in 1972. Under this now-abandoned form of financing, the state recognized an obligation to back the bonds but was not legally required to do so, thereby exempting them from the normal procedure of voter approval by referendum.[14] The landfill was not completed until 1976, by which time the city was in the throes of fiscal crisis, the office market was glutted with unused space, and federal and state housing subsidy programs had largely vanished. New Yorkers began to use the vacant tract as an informal recreation area, and it became the location for exhibits of giant environmental sculptures. City officials started to fear a "people's park" where protesters would demand that the landfill be permanently maintained as public open space.

Hugh Carey, who had become governor of New York State in 1975, sought to restart the stalled project. Not until 1979, however, did he gain control of its three-member board of directors. In that year the board named Richard Kahan,[15] then the head of the state's Urban Development Corporation (UDC), to lead the BPCA. Under a memorandum of understanding with the city, the UDC condemned the site and took possession of it for a dollar. Through this act the BPCA essentially became a subsidiary of the UDC and therefore exempt from the city's planning regulations and public review procedures.[16] In exchange for giving up its ownership rights, New York City was to receive all future profits and tax equivalents.

When Kahan took over, the BPCA needed immediate approval from the state legislature to refinance its bonds, or the project would have gone into semipermanent suspension. Kahan, who disliked the master plan he had inherited and moreover thought that its all-or-nothing approach to construction inhibited developer interest, commissioned the firm of Alexander Cooper and Stanton Eckstut to design a new plan in time to forestall legislative termination. "According to the [architects'] report, among the internal reasons for the project's failure were the master plan's 'excessively rigid large-scale development format,' which had prevented gradual development of the site; and unduly complicated controls over every detail of the project."[17] The commitment to a residential income mix vanished from the prospectus.

The new plan, which provided for staged residential development spreading out from the project's nexus with the World Trade Center, attracted highly favorable comment. It freed designers from the detailed review processes of the earlier scheme, established a street-level grid, and called for architectural styles in harmony with New York's traditional commercial and residential neighborhoods:

> The physical character of the Cooper/Eckstut site plan was as much a rediscovery of New York's history of incremental private development of small land parcels as it was a romantic invocation of its most livable neighborhoods. . . . The reasons for [the] . . . enthusiastic response [to the plan] are not hard to understand. The Cooper/Eckstut plan draws on familiar New York neighborhood images and assembles them in a street and block pattern which extend (as view corridors) the Lower Manhattan streets to the waterfront.[18]

What Was Built

In July 1980 the BPCA invited development proposals for the commercial area, where financial pressures made rapid construction extremely desirable. It selected O & Y from among eleven serious bidders as the developer of a billion-dollar, 6.3 million square foot group of structures to be called the World Financial Center (WFC). As well as promising to complete the work in five years—much more quickly than any of its competitors offered—the Reichmanns undertook to put up

Figure 8.1. The World Financial Center

$50 million of Olympia & York's money to guarantee the BPCA's bond payments for 25 years.[19]

O & Y held a design competition and chose the firm of Cesar Pelli & Associates, which created a cluster of four 34- to 51-story towers featuring 40,000 square foot floors. The office complex, which opened in 1985 and was completed in 1988, attracted Merrill Lynch, American Express, Dow Jones, and Oppenheimer & Company as its anchor tenants. To bring in these prestigious firms and "create an address," O & Y took over a number of their existing tenures, thereby becoming New York City's largest landlord. Much of the space it acquired in this way needed considerable investment if it was to retain first-class office uses.

While the WFC buildings, which flanked a 3.5-acre public waterfront plaza, were in a mainly modernist style, their setbacks and masonry bases evoked Manhattan's classic skyscrapers: "Pelli devised an artful transition from a heavy masonry base with small windows, through a series of setbacks that became progressively lighter and glassier, culminating in top stories of sheer glass crowned by illuminated spires in geometric shape."[20] Everything visible was built to the highest luxury standard, while the office facilities incorporated the latest technological advances.

In the midst of the office buildings, O & Y installed a Winter Garden, a 120-foot-high vaulted atrium sheltering sixteen tall palm trees and entered by a grand marble staircase from the skyway that connects the complex to the World Trade

Figure 8.2. The Winter Garden at the World Financial Center

Center.[21] The Winter Garden forms the gateway to a shopping mall with expensive stores specializing in leather goods, stylish men's and women's clothing, designer chocolates, art books, and handmade Italian paper. O & Y was at first reluctant to develop much retail space in the project, feeling that downtown does not draw shoppers. When it finally did agree to do so, it restricted rentals to the most luxurious of establishments. The firm's first instincts appear to have been correct. Although data are not available on the success of the stores, casual observation of the quietude of the shopping area indicates that they are not doing well, although as the area's population increases, business will likely improve. Most of the restaurants around the Winter Garden and adjacent indoor courtyard, which operate as open-air cafés on the outdoor plaza in the summer, do, however, seem to be flourishing, and the public events produced in the Winter Garden are considerable draws.

A waterfront walkway runs the 1.2-mile length of Battery Park City. Its midsection, lined with benches and decorative lampposts, reminds the stroller of the Brooklyn Heights esplanade. The parks on its south section are exceptional examples of landscape architecture. The first, with its wild rushes and tumbling rocks, suggests the eighteenth-century shoreline; another features an elaborate flower garden. In a rare effort to solicit citizen participation, the BPCA invited residents of the new apartments and of the adjoining Tribeca neighborhood to advise on the design of the northern park. Their input caused a greater emphasis on active recreation, and the park offers basketball courts and a vast, extremely elaborate, and imaginative playground. Residents and passersby can enjoy stunning views of the harbor, Ellis Island, the Statue of Liberty, and the New Jersey shore. Battery Park City has made the waterfront accessible as never before and has given New Yorkers a uniquely spectacular open space.[22]

The residential section of the project is expected eventually to include up to 14,000 housing units, all at market rate. A main street forms an interior spine for the apartment groupings; service stores line its edges. In 1992 about a third of the housing units had been finished; the great majority were luxury condominiums, and the rest were expensive rentals.[23] Commissioned by the multiplicity of developers offered sites, different architects designed the mostly high-rise apartment buildings. In employing a variety of building materials and heights, they followed the Cooper-Eckstut design guidelines, which aimed at reproducing the feel of New York's old residential sections. None of the apartment buildings makes a major architectural statement, but they do produce pleasant neighborhood settings. Unfortunately for the developers, the effort to imitate traditional styles with facades along the street line produced one of the typical drawbacks of standard building design—many units lacked views and consequently were initially difficult to sell.

During the 1990s real estate slump, construction at Battery Park City went into a hiatus except for public facilities. Construction of a new Stuyvesant High School was completed in 1992 at a cost of nearly $200 million. One of the city's five competitive-entrance academic secondary schools, its students battle fiercely to gain admission. Its presence is unlikely to present any of the social problems that often afflict the environs of other New York City educational institutions. In 1994 work began on the Museum of Jewish Heritage and two of the parks. The BPCA itself decided to act as developer for a mixed-income building consisting of larger units for families. In addition to apartments to rent for up to $6,000 a month (the 1999 market rate), almost a quarter of the units were reserved for middle-income families.

The end of the slump, in 1995, marked the beginning of further private market activity. The New York Mercantile Exchange, another Forest City Ratner project, began construction with substantial city subsidy. By 1999 ten of the remaining undeveloped parcels were either in the active planning stage or involved in new construction. These included a high-end assisted-living building for the elderly and four "80-20" buildings, where 20 percent of the units would be made available to those earning 50 percent or less of the New York City median income. A family of four with income between $19,000 and $25,000 would qualify for a two-bedroom apartment at $525 a month, in contrast to the market rate of over $4,000. A hotel and entertainment complex, developed by the ubiquitous Forest City Ratner Companies, opened in 2000 with 463 rooms and a 4,000-seat multiplex cinema. Another hotel, scheduled to open in 2001, was to form the base of an apartment tower, which would also house the Skyscraper Museum, an independent nonprofit institution that had previously lacked a permanent home.[24]

Financial Arrangements

The public role in Battery Park City consisted of the $200 million landfill investment from the original bond issue; additional infrastructure investment;[25] installations, upkeep, and services for the public spaces; provision of the BPCA staff; and a set of tax incentives to the developers. The World Financial Center received 150 percent of the normal tax subsidies granted under the Industrial and Commercial Incentives Program (ICIP) in determining its payment in lieu of taxes (PILOT). The residential portion was given a ten-year tax abatement under the 421a program for everything that was built before 1992. Later market-rate residential development did not receive abatements, but the buildings constructed under the 80-20 program obtain both abatements and below-market-rate finance.

The BPCA continues to own the land and rents it to the developers on a lease that runs without a purchase option until 2069. It receives ground lease payments, the PILOT, and a civic facilities payment to cover upkeep expenditures on the common spaces. These revenues are aggregated to pay the debt on the various bond issues, maintenance of public spaces, the BPCA's rent for its headquarters within the World Financial Center, and staff salaries. In 1991 the authority had 62 people on its payroll, up from 55 during the peak building period of the mid-1980s; according to the *New York Observer*, a number of these new hires were "well-connected political operatives."[26] The staff then stabilized at about this level.

After its expenditures are netted out, the authority passes along the remainder to the city. By 1991 the BPCA had contributed close to $90 million to the general fund; in that year, however, payments dropped to roughly $18 million from about $28 million in the preceding two years. In 1999 the Authority estimated that it would turn over $44 million to the city, after operating expenses of $21 million and debt service of $65 million.[27] In addition, its projected revenues supported the issuance of $400 million in bonds to pay for affordable housing elsewhere in the city (see below). Once the debt on the project is retired, all profits, originally estimated at $10 billion, will go to New York City.[28]

Assessment

The physical aspects of Battery Park City have mostly won rave reviews from professional critics and the public. The *Times* architectural critic termed it "close to a miracle" when the first buildings opened.[29] Later he commented: "There has been nothing like Battery Park City in New York or anywhere else in our time—a 92-acre complex of housing and office buildings in which parks, waterfront promenades, streets and public art rank as important as the buildings themselves. . . . The result is a place, not a project."[30]

Dissenters, however, dispute the mainstream consensus on the total aesthetic and social success of Battery Park City. Detractors of its physical manifestation cite its Disneyesque quality. It is too flawless, too luxurious, too unreal. Its very splendor makes it vulnerable to Michael Sorkin's general attack on recent planned urban developments:

> This new realm is a city of simulations, television city, the city as theme park. This is nowhere more visible than in its architecture, in buildings that rely for their authority on images drawn from history, from a spuriously appropriated past that substitutes for a more exigent and examined present. . . . Today, the profession of urban design is almost wholly preoccupied with reproduction, with the creation of urbane disguises. . . . [T]his elaborate apparatus is at pains to assert its ties to the kind of city life it is in the process of obliterating.
>
> Here is urban renewal with a sinister twist, an architecture of deception which, in its happy-face familiarity, constantly distances itself from the most fundamental realities. The architecture of this city is almost purely semiotic, playing the game of grafted signification, theme-park building. Whether it represents generic historicity or generic modernity, such design is based in the same calculus as advertising, the idea of pure imageability, oblivious to the real needs and traditions of those who inhabit it.[31]

Battery Park City is the antithesis of the naturally developing, heterogeneous urban district prescribed by Jane Jacobs, but it incorporates many of her lessons nevertheless.[32] It is dense and has multiple uses, short blocks, buildings along the street line, and small accessible parks. Its single management permits the creation of an artificial diversity, with carefully selected tenants and idealized versions of the city of memory.[33] It lacks the spontaneous contrasts of the real early-twentieth-century metropolis, and social commentators fault its exclusionism, contending that even its gorgeous open spaces inhibit public access:

> How public *is* public space, when it has been embedded in a context that raises such formidable social barriers that the masses of ordinary working people (not to mention those out of work) would feel uncomfortable entering it? How many poor families may be expected to cross the raised bridge into that citadel of wealth, the World Financial Center, and wander through the privileged enclaves of South End Avenue and Rector Place before reaching their permitted perch along the waterfront?[34]

Wall Street's white-collar proletariat uses the parks during weekdays, and on weekends an ethnically diverse group uses the playgrounds and basketball courts. Still, Battery Park City otherwise remains mainly a recreation zone for the relatively well-to-do.[35] The interiors of the World Financial Center are in the standard style of corporate opulence, and entry to the upper floors is restricted to those with reasons to be there. Despite the vaunted efforts of the planners to attach the site to the city's street grid, the bulky structures of the World Trade Center and an eight-lane highway separate Battery Park City from the rest of the financial dis-

Figure 8.3. Gov. Nelson A. Rockefeller Park at Battery Park City

trict. Employees can easily enter their workplace from the PATH train, subway, or parking garage without ever setting foot on the ground, although the attractiveness of the outdoor area may tempt them out.

Yet the ambition of the Battery Park City planners to make it part of New York does not wholly fall short. Brendan Gill did not speak only for himself when he expressed "a tentative, infinitesimal tremor of hope . . . [that] Battery Park City might have succeeded in weaving itself into the fabric of the city . . . [as] a symbol of the enduring vitality of the city."[36] Large numbers of people do visit the area, and it is an oversimplification to dismiss the enjoyment it affords them as a sham or to decide that they are only the undeserving privileged classes.[37] The luxuriousness of Battery Park City's edifices symbolizes the reality that it shelters—the World Financial Center *is* the capital of capital, not a mere simulacrum. The parks and promenades do have genuine roots in New York's natural environment, and they are hospitable to a variety of uses and users once the psychological barrier to entering them is crossed.[38] Leftist urban critics like to put down sanitized environments, but gritty is not necessarily preferable to pretty. There are few New Yorkers of any social stratum who do not welcome the occasional opportunity to visit a park open to the sea and unsullied by detritus; Battery Park City satisfies a genuine human need. It hints at being a cliché, at evidencing a sameness with other large developments even as it seeks distinction. Simultaneously, however, its unique natural setting and the genuine creativity of its design team cause it to rise above easy criticisms of its genesis and function. As a physical space it has power and gives pleasure.

Sponsors justified the initial exclusion of low-income people from the project's residences and the granting of large subsidies for luxury apartments and opulent office towers by the project's support of affordable housing elsewhere in the city.[39] Under 1986 state legislation, the BPCA issued $400 million of revenue bonds for low-income housing, and it committed itself to contribute another $600 million toward the city's housing program by the year 2000.[40] By 1992, however, it had placed further bond issues on hold, and so far, despite additional profitable construction in the late '90s, it has not raised additional money for housing.[41] The postponement was originally explained as a response to the turbulent state of the real-estate market and the fear that O & Y's difficulties would deter investors from buying the bonds. At that time, a Battery Park City official indicated to me that the halt was only temporary. The choice to continue to use the growing revenue surplus entirely to contribute to the city's general fund rather than as backing for housing bonds reflects the much lower priority given to housing programs by the Giuliani administration than was true of its predecessors.

When it did use its revenues for housing production elsewhere, the authority essentially acted as a device whereby the city did off-budget borrowing for housing construction. The effect would be the same if the city rather than the BPCA issued the housing bonds, and the BPCA, which accordingly would not have had to meet debt service on those bonds, turned over the resulting augmented revenues as part of its payment to the city. Borrowing through the authority, however, shrank the apparent size of the city's budget, ensured that the funds were allocated to housing, isolated the revenue stream that supported it, and provided a more advantageous interest rate than the city would get using general obligation bonds.

Battery Park City, then, is a carefully coordinated total environment, with substantial financial benefits disseminated to the general population. Its principal private developer went beyond meeting its contractual obligations and provided the public with significant amenities. The authority also used its funds to make the city more appealing. Nevertheless, except in some of its park planning, it has involved no public participation whatsoever.[42] Its commercial and residential structures are reserved for the wealthiest corporations and families in the United States, although any well-behaved individual can use its public facilities on a daily basis.

In terms of the indicators of private-sector funds leveraged and jobs kept in the city, Battery Park City was an economic success. The question is always raised whether the funds and jobs would have been there regardless; given the centrifugal forces that constantly operate on New York, the answer is probably no. Moreover, thanks to its location on landfill next to the financial district, it did not displace anyone either economically or spatially. The city did receive something meaningful in exchange for its largesse. If the project is to be faulted, it must be on the grounds of opportunity costs. The public sector could hypothetically have borrowed the funds it put into capital expenditures for Battery Park City for some other, more socially beneficial purpose. The taxes foregone might have been directed toward another, more productive endeavor that would have produced more jobs for the neediest and less spatial segregation. Within the constraints of New York's political and economic situation, however, it is hard to imagine an alternative strategy for the site that would have resulted in a more desirable outcome or that in the absence of any development there, commensurate resources would have been mobilized for a more socially beneficial cause.

9

Creating a New Address II: Docklands

The name "Docklands" applies to that part of East London which borders the Thames. The East End has always been home to London's poorest inhabitants. Until the 1960s it also offered jobs to its residents—on the docks, in port-related activities, and in manufacturing. With the advent of containerization, however, the docks became obsolete. At the same time, the area's industrial structure was becoming increasingly antiquated, and its resident population was shrinking. Poor motor-transport connections led industries to either move or close up rather than reinvest in the area; the trend of industrial disinvestment was hastened when the docks finally closed between 1967 and 1981.[1] This chapter chronicles the transformation of Docklands from a port and manufacturing area to a smart location for offices and luxury flats.

REDEVELOPMENT STRATEGIES

In the decades following World War II, public authorities constructed large social-housing estates, mainly in the inner areas, with the number of units growing from 30,000 to 125,000. This redevelopment, however, did not relieve the physical congestion of those sections that remained populated, nor did it reverse decay where industry and trading activities had once flourished. Instead, population became concentrated in bleak, institutional enclaves, while the extensive tracts of abandoned industrial and docking facilities appeared increasingly gloomy and forbidding.[2] Peter Marris[3] has succinctly captured the situation at the beginning of the 1980s:

> From the outset, London's docks had been haphazardly laid out, quickly outdated, and mutually frustrating in their competition. They kept in busi-

ness partly because the Port of London, however inefficient, was the capital of an empire; but even more because whenever their commercial survival was threatened, they relentlessly drove down the price of labour. The merging of the dock companies into a public authority at the beginning of this century did not fundamentally change this balance of militancy and vulnerability. When the dockers at last gained security after the Second World War, their way of life and the communities they had made, with all their pride of craft, and practical radicalism, grimness and history, were already facing drastic transformation. The old docks, trapped by the congested city which had grown up around them were not adaptable to the intensive mechanization which would keep them profitable.

The Port of London Authority (PLA), which had built a modern container port downriver at Tilbury in the 1960s, was severely criticized by Docklands community leaders and the Greater London Council (GLC) for its failure to maintain the London docks as a going concern. In a 1985 report the GLC contended that the upstream docks in the East End, while unsuitable for long-distance containerized cargo, retained usefulness for intra-European trade and should be reopened.[4] Even with investment for that purpose, however, their economic value would have remained limited. The end of London's central role within world trading patterns, combined with technological change, meant that at best their employment potential was very small.

At any rate, the PLA, like the Port Authority of New York and New Jersey, began to see its inner-area facilities as more valuable for real-estate development than for transport and began exploiting its property holdings as financial resources to fuel its port modernization enterprises elsewhere. The GLC had already set a precedent when, during the early 1970s, St. Katharine's Docks, a short walk from the Tower of London, became the location of a mixed-use project of flats, offices, a hotel, and a marina, indicating the possibilities for adaptive reuse. Although architecturally conventional, the complex afforded attractive views of the water, and the area around the yacht basin allowed office workers and hotel guests to take their leisure in surroundings isolated from, but close to, the bustle of the City. On the south side of the Thames in Southwark, the closing of Hays Wharf and the zoning of the surrounding area for office construction generated a rapid rise in property values, reinforcing the cost pressures that were pushing manufacturing firms out of the area.[5] While the mid-1970s property slump caused a hiatus in the implementation of the plans for the south side, the area's trajectory from industrial to office use was not reversed. Other than the maritime industries, the main employers in the river wards had been printing, food and drink processing, engineering, and metals fabrication, mostly operating in relatively small establishments. They lacked sufficient capital and potential profitability to upgrade their premises. At the same time, mechanization and rationalization reduced the maritime labor force from 23,000 in 1969 to only 12,000 four years later and to 7,000 in 1979.[6]

With the closing of the docks, ancillary warehouse and transport facilities, and industrial plants, increasing amounts of land lay unused. During the 1970s the Conservative central government established a study team to assess the area's development potential. Its presentation of planning alternatives mainly stressed the commercial potential of the riverfront acres, the largest available area of inner-city land in western Europe, and was received with hostility by local community leaders.[7] When a national Labour government gained power in 1974, it threw out the report and set up a strategic-planning authority for the area, the Docklands Joint Committee (DJC). The DJC included representatives from the central government, the GLC, and the local authorities, as well as the Port of London Authority and the trade unions; the associated Docklands Forum solicited citizens' opinions. The DJC produced a comprehensive plan that stressed preservation of manufacturing, council housing production, and social programs for current residents.

The plan, however, lacked powerful backing, and the difficulty in funding it doomed it to oblivion. The election in 1977 of a Tory GLC that was antagonistic to the East London local authorities had an immediate blocking effect on implementation of the plan. Beyond that, the very large expenditures required to make the Docklands usable, the fiscal weakness of all levels of government, and the unattractiveness to private capital of the DJC plan meant that Docklands regeneration would require a major change of strategy. A substantial regeneration program required either much larger amounts of government investment than could be imagined within the political and economic context of the time or a plan that offered far greater incentives to the private sector.

The London Docklands Development Corporation

After the Conservatives returned to power nationally in 1979, they sought a new approach to reviving the area, and in 1981 they established the London Docklands Development Corporation (LDDC).[8] The administrative jurisdiction of the LDDC, which covered 8.5 square miles (5,500 acres), encompassed the riverside portions of three boroughs—Tower Hamlets, Newham, and Southwark[9]—where it became the official planning authority. It worked closely with the London office of the Department of the Environment (DoE) and involved cabinet members in decision making on its bigger deals. It diverged from its New York counterpart, the Battery Park City Authority, by giving developers much more latitude in project selection and design. Its style was entrepreneurial, and its staff, which peaked at 470 in 1990, focused on implementation rather than planning.[10] As one of its executives declared to me, "There was never any grand master plan. Reg Ward [the first CEO] just wanted to make things happen."

The LDDC's principal aim was to promote growth in Greater London; improvement of the lives of those residing in the riverside localities was at best a subsidiary goal. Its consultation with local authorities was perfunctory, and it established no formal mechanisms for citizen participation. Instead of viewing the territory under its planning control as embedded within the Docklands boroughs, the LDDC pictured the riverbank as a new vibrant core for the whole metropolis. Its ambition was to attract the immense sums of private investment capable of transforming this vision into reality. Since its main asset was land rather than financial capital, it focused on turning over that asset to property developers rather than on an alternative development approach that would target operating firms. In other words, it was capable only of being a land development agency, not a development bank.

The LDDC took possession of most of the land within its jurisdiction owned by either the boroughs or the GLC; in addition, it purchased Port Authority holdings within the development area and acquired additional, privately owned parcels through compulsory purchase.[11] It was responsible for preparing the land it owned for development, then disposing of it to a suitable developer. Site preparation was often a costly process, since it involved clearing structures, cleaning up environmental hazards, and filling areas under water. At first the LDDC barely broke even on its land sales; on the Isle of Dogs its initial offerings sold for about £80,000 per acre. But by 1986 the price had shot up to £250,000 per acre, and some parcels even sold for £3 million per acre at the height of the speculative boom.[12] In 1988 the LDDC was receiving £165 million from a central-government grant and £63 million from property sales; by 1991 income from property sales had shrunk to £27 million, while the grant had leaped to £315 million, constituting more than a third of the government's total expenditures on urban development in the country.[13]

The poor transport connections of the area, where formerly workers had walked to their jobs and cargo was waterborne, meant that development for office uses required a massive transportation building program. The LDDC's initial transit investment consisted of the construction of a light railway subject to frequent breakdowns; as a result of efforts to curtail expenses, it opened with a terminus not directly accessible from the main underground system and with quite limited carrying capacity.[14] Rebuilding it to a higher standard cost about £500 million, and, because of the problems posed by working on an operating system, it proved far more difficult than if the work had been done originally. Even with the improvements, the railway did not have sufficient capacity to meet anticipated demand. Consequently, London Transport planned to extend the Jubilee tube line to the east. In addition, both the LDDC and the Department of Transport undertook a group of very expensive road-building projects, while a private company opened an airport by the Thames in 1987 and intended to enlarge it. Although the LDDC identified the airport as an important catalyst for development and a generator of jobs, the GLC had opposed it on the grounds that the employment claims would not materialize and that it would contribute to air and noise pollution.[15] At first the GLC's claim appeared valid, as for quite some time the airport was little used; by the end of the century, however, it had become an important terminal for intra-European travel and begun to show a profit.

Figure 9.1. Docklands Light Rail

Residential Development

Between 1981 and 1998, about 24,000 housing units were completed within the Docklands development area. Approximately three-quarters of them were for owner occupation at market rates, causing the percentage of owner occupants within the development area to increase from about 5 to nearly 40 percent. About 6,400 units were newly constructed social housing; in addition, LDDC funding supported renovation of nearly 8,000 existing units owned by either local authorities or housing associations.[16] By 1998 the area's population had jumped from 39,000 to 84,000, with a predicted end state of 115,000.[17] Although some of the new units were in rehabilitated warehouses, the great majority occupied newly constructed buildings. Except for the nautical themes of their names, the residential complexes made little architectural reference to the communities they colonized—nor, for that matter, to central London. Thus, for example, the Brunswick Quay, Surrey Quays, and Blyth's Wharf developments resembled suburban blocks of low-rise flats elsewhere in the southeast, although at higher levels of density.

The residential strategy meant that ultimately the population would be dominated by inhabitants with sharply different values, political affiliations, and incomes from the former occupants.[18] Nevertheless, the Docklands retained close to 40,000 of its original inhabitants, many displaced from their industrial and port employment, mostly living in more than 13,000 council and housing association units.[19] As a consequence, even with its infusion of new owner-occupied housing, the area remained economically mixed, with sharp juxtapositions of well-to-do and poor.[20] Because the area had previously been so homogeneously working class, the contrast between old and new residents was especially noticeable.[21] Janet Foster quotes one of the new residents of the Isle of Dogs, who comments on the impact of middle-class newcomers:

> Normally even in places like Clapham or Hackney or wherever there's always been a cross section of people and here it was all working class, all dockers, all that sort of thing, there wasn't, you know, the middle class. . . . They were all the same . . . that's why there's the problem. Not because people have come in but because they were all the same before.[22]

After the stock market's Black Monday of October 1987, financial industry expansion triggered by the Big Bang reversed itself, and the housing market in Docklands stagnated; by 1989 the entire London private residential sector had collapsed, and a number of developers ran into severe financial trouble. Virtually all plans for additional market-rate construction were shelved the next year; several developments were halted while only partially complete; and the number of new housing units finished fell far below the LDDC's predictions.[23] Moreover, steeply rising interest rates meant that developers had to offer substantial inducements, including mortgage subsidies, to attract any buyers. By 1992 residential construction activity in the Docklands was limited to housing-association projects

Figure 9.2. Docklands old council housing

and council-estate renovation, and LDDC land sales to for-profit housing developers had ended. As in most of the case studies described in this book, the property bust had a silver lining, both because it prompted the dedication of more housing to the affordable housing pool[24] and because it dampened housing turnover: "Ironically, the long recession following the collapse of house prices actually generated a degree of stability and forced newcomers who had not initially planned to be on the Island [i.e., the Isle of Dogs] for any length of time to stay. Some, much to their surprise . . . found they liked the area and wanted to remain."[25]

The market in Docklands recovered along with the rest of the London housing market. The completion of road connections, extension and upgrading of the Docklands Light Railway, and the 1999 completion of the Jubilee tube line into Docklands greatly increased accessibility, integrating the area with the rest of Greater London. By 2000, vacant residential buildings were a dim memory, and new structures were rising to accommodate growing demand. Reflecting the changed composition of the population, but perhaps also showing some change of heart among earlier residents, polls showed that the rating of the LDDC's performance by local people had improved substantially. In 1988 only 32 percent thought that the LDDC took account of the views of local people, while 61 percent thought they did not; by 1996, 49 percent said they did, while 34 percent thought they did not.[26] By 1997, 68 percent of local residents thought the LDDC had done a good job.[27]

CANARY WHARF

After its great success in developing the World Financial Center (WFC) in New York, Olympia & York (O&Y) enjoyed a reputation as the world's largest and best-managed property development firm. Its owners, the Reichmann brothers, had become immensely wealthy and had begun to extend their economic power far beyond their base in property. While still in the process of constructing and tenanting the WFC, they started seeking other outlets for their fortune besides high-stakes real-estate activities, to diversify their holdings. They invested especially heavily in natural-resources firms, reportedly on the expectation that the balance sheets of such enterprises would run counter to the real-estate cycle. The seemingly cautious strategy of diversification, however, was undercut by the specialization in natural resources—another notoriously speculative area—which in the late 1980s proved to move in tandem with the real-estate market. And, although O & Y had previously avoided excessive indebtedness by self-financing much of its real-estate operation, it borrowed heavily for its new acquisitions.

Other investments also proved destabilizing. A takeover bid for the distiller Hiram Walker resulted in a publicly ignominious defeat. A large investment in Robert Campeau's real-estate and retailing company came to naught as well.[28] A further effort at hedging likewise produced the opposite result. To protect its real-estate projects, O & Y bought substantial interests in competing property-development firms in Canada, the United States, and England. The effect of these investments, along with accepting real estate as collateral for a loan granted to Campeau, was to increase the firm's vulnerability to the 1990s downturn in the property market.[29]

The chief cause of the Reichmanns' downfall, however, lay at the core of their principal business in property development. Overconfident from their triumph in creating a prestigious new office center on a Manhattan landfill, they tried to re-peat their earlier feat in London's Docklands. In England, however, they had the misfortune to bring their property onto the market when it was tumbling into the bottom of a cycle. Moreover, they had as their partner a government that turned its back on them when they were unable to cover their obligations; a site further from the existing financial center than the one in New York; and a local market of office users that was less willing to discard its traditional locational preferences. As a consequence, O & Y's endeavor to build an office complex more than twice as big as the World Financial Center at Canary Wharf on the Isle of Dogs brought down its British and Canadian branches and temporarily produced the world's largest ghost town on the bank of the Thames.

As part of its effort to stimulate private investment, the Conservative gov-ernment had designated 482 acres of the Isle of Dogs as an enterprise zone. Origi-nally a peninsula formed by a curve in the Thames about 2.5 miles east of the City of London, it was cut off from the adjacent land mass by a canal in the nine-teenth century. In 1802 it had become the site of the West India Docks. As the docks expanded, a warehouse was built on the land between the canal and the main dock. Called Canary Wharf, it was used to store cargoes of bananas and sugar cane from the West Indies and fruits from the Canary Islands—ultimately, it gave its name to the vast twentieth-century complex built on its site. By 1900, it was handling most of London's fruit and vegetable imports from South Africa and New Zealand. As late as the mid-1960s, about 20,000 men still worked at the West India Docks; by 1981, however, the docks were closed.[30]

The enterprise zone classification freed firms within the zone's boundaries from conforming to most planning regulations and from paying business rates (i.e., property taxes), as well as allowing them to deduct 100 percent of their capital expenditure on industrial and commercial construction from their corporate in-come taxes.[31] Qualification for benefits under the enterprise zone ended in 1992, ten years after its inception, and this provision meant that developers hastened to begin construction before the tax subsidies lapsed. The enterprise zone deadline had the same effect as the scheduled termination of New York's special midtown zoning: Developers rushed to construct buildings in the absence of any obvious demand for space, to obtain the benefits before they disappeared. Although en-deavors begun in the enterprise zone after 1992 did not qualify for tax advantages, allowances under it could be taken until 2002 for projects begun before the dead-line. It was estimated that as a result of low land prices and enterprise zone incentives, net costs of development in the zone would be half as much as in central London, and occupancy costs just 59 percent.[32]

Initially, the LDDC expected that relatively small office and industrial firms would take advantage of the enterprise zone benefits. But as the boom of the '80s heated up, office developers began to bid on space wherever they could find it. In 1985 a consortium headed by an American developer, G. Ware Travelstead of First Boston Real Estate, proposed to build an 8.8 million square foot office development for financial and advanced-services firms at Canary Wharf.[33] In return for its commitment to the development and its willingness to underwrite a proportion of the costs of upgrading the Docklands Light Railway, the consortium received a promise from the LDDC that it would continue the Docklands Light Railway westward, connecting it directly with the Bank Underground station. The Travelstead agreement also required the LDDC to provide infrastructure, primarily roads, initially estimated to cost £250 million; the key to the roads plan was the Limehouse Link, which would traverse the Isle of Dogs, making the project area accessible at both its east and west ends. The road required extensive tunneling and the relocation of 558 families.[34] The resulting costs made it the most expensive road per mile ever built in the United Kingdom, and eventually the LDDC's road investment vastly exceeded the originally estimated amounts.[35]

In mid-1987 the Travelstead consortium withdrew from the negotiations, and, to the great relief of the government, Olympia & York stepped in. It committed itself to develop at least 4.6 million square feet of floor space by 1992 and an additional 7 million square feet thereafter, pay £8.2 million for the LDDC land, and contribute £150 million toward the extension and upgrading of the Docklands Light Railway.[36] To entice the Texaco Corporation into the complex, it advanced plans for construction of an additional 925,000 square foot building, resulting in the production of more than 5 million square feet in 1991–1992. Later, in its effort to persuade the government to route the proposed extension of the Jubilee tube line through Canary Wharf and to expedite its authorization, O & Y pledged £400 million to that project. Although the DoE, which participated directly in the negotiations, raised the question of receiving a share in the profits from the development, along the Battery Park City model, "both the Department and the LDDC considered that to do so might jeopardize the whole development."[37]

Design

Imitating the design precepts that guided Battery Park City, Paul Reichmann called for a plan that would give the illusion of natural growth. A number of architects, including Cesar Pelli, I. M. Pei, and Skidmore, Owings & Merrill, designed individual structures, thereby simulating the diversity of an evolving city. As in Battery Park City, their walls feature setbacks and varieties of facing material. The edifices surrounding Westferry Circus, the roundabout terminating the complex at the western end, mime the great squares of central London. Only the central

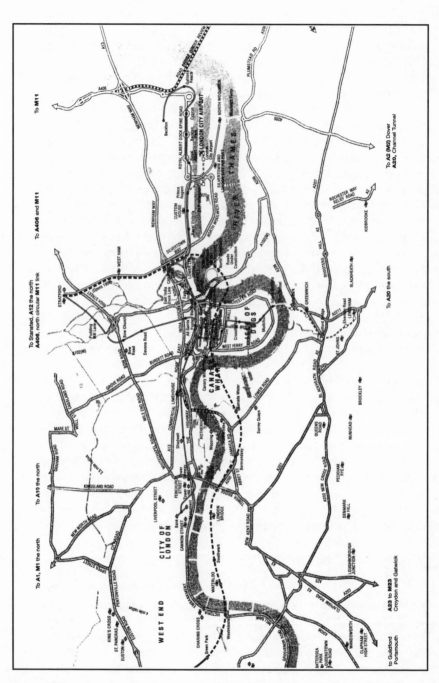

Figure 9.3. Docklands Transport (dotted line shows route of Jubilee extension)

tower, at 48 stories the tallest building in Britain, makes a deliberate break with the rest of London. In order to have buildings open directly onto the street, deep excavations were dug to accommodate underground parking garages. Canary Wharf also resembles Battery Park City in having much of its land (more than one-third) dedicated to open space, visible fixtures of the highest quality, and buildings equipped with advanced communications technologies.

Community Benefits

O & Y committed itself to hire 500 local construction workers as part of its agreement with the LDDC. It also financed the running of a construction training college, established a £2 million trust fund for local schools and colleges,[38] and contributed £70 million to the extension of the Docklands Light Railway. When the riverbus, which offered boat service between the Docklands and Charing Cross Pier in central London, ran into financial difficulty, O & Y took it over and made up the shortfall. As in Battery Park City, the Reichmanns spared no expense in providing a high level of public amenity, manifested here in an elaborate plaza centered on a monumental fountain and full-grown trees imported from Germany.

Inducements

O & Y used a variety of extremely expensive devices to lure companies out of central London. It repeated its New York practice of attracting tenants by buying out their existing leases. Costly as this practice had been in New York, it was even more so in London, where leases were much longer and rents much higher. To get the *Daily Telegraph,* already located on the Isle of Dogs, to move into Canary Wharf, the Reichmanns purchased the newspaper's South Quay building at £20 million above book value.[39] O & Y also offered fitting-out subsidies aggregating to £200 million and rent concessions rumored to include rent-free periods up to five years.[40]

THE DOWNFALL OF OLYMPIA & YORK

The first real evidence that Olympia & York was in difficulty came in September 1990, when the Reichmann family attempted but failed to sell a 20 percent share in its U.S. property holdings.[41] Although the move marked the first time that the company had sought outside investors in its real-estate portfolio, its officers denied that the offering and a subsequent refinancing of Canary Wharf obligations indicated a liquidity problem. Many observers, however, wondered whether the Reichmanns' assets were sufficient to withstand the real-estate troubles afflicting the urban centers in which the firm operated.[42] Between 1990 and 1992 the family desperately strove to shore up its empire by investing $500 million of its own

Figure 9.4. Canary Wharf Towers, including computer-generated images of Citigroup and HSBC towers, under construction in 2000.

money, putting individual assets up for sale in order to achieve liquidity.[43] It sold some of its nonproperty holdings at prices well below its original investment, but by 1990 the transatlantic real-estate market was dead, and it could not find purchasers willing to pay an amount exceeding the debt on any piece of property.

Even as oversupply was causing the values of its properties around the world to plummet, O & Y was continuing to invest billions in Canary Wharf, the future of which looked less and less assured. In a 1990 advertisement in the *Sunday Times,* Paul Reichmann had asserted that Canary Wharf represented less of a risk than the World Financial Center did, claiming: "Doing one building there would be risky; doing nearly a dozen is not. On a scale of one to 10, if you say the risk with Battery Park was nine, here it would be one."[44]

Despite the optimistic predictions and all the various incentives to occupants, 53 percent of the office space nearing completion remained unlet in the summer of 1992.[45] Little of the retail space had been rented either, and without a critical mass of office workers, there was small likelihood that it would be. The *Telegraph* turned out to be the only major British tenant O & Y succeeded in attracting. The other large committed tenants, in addition to Credit Suisse First Boston (CSFB), were all American firms—Morgan Stanley, Bear Stearns, and Texaco.[46] The absence of a prestigious British financial or service firm meant that the Reichmanns had failed in creating an address. One developer quoted in the *Independent* argued that it was O & Y's inability to understand the mystique of the City of London for British companies that was at the root of its miscalculation: "What did Paul Reichmann do wrong? North Americans have no sense of place, or of history. He didn't realize that British people and businesses are tied by invisible threads to places: to the Bank of England or just to a set of streets, some shops, a restaurant."[47] Although these threads eventually loosened, they initially placed O & Y at a serious disadvantage in its competition with property owners within the City of London, especially once the office glut there eroded the previous cost differential between the City and the Docklands.

The Final Months

A concatenation of events began in February 1992, which led irresistibly to the collapse of Olympia & York. The first of these was a downgrading of the company's commercial paper by a Canadian bond-rating service, which estimated that the value of O & Y's listed investments (i.e., investments in publicly held companies) had fallen by more than 40 percent, from C$6.6 billion to C$3.9 billion, in the preceding two years.[48] The firm had typically borrowed on notes that matured every thirty to ninety days and would roll them over when they came due. Now it could no longer refinance its short-term debt through selling directly to investors, nor could it find bankers willing to take up the slack. After the downgrade by the rating agency, the company began buying up about $400 million of its own commercial paper.[49] On March 22, 1992, O & Y admitted that it was sustaining a "liquidity crisis" and called a meeting of its creditors to restructure about $12 billion of its debt. The next week the firm failed to make the first installment on its £400 million contribution toward the Jubilee Line extension.[50]

In the following months O & Y missed a series of bond and mortgage payments on instruments secured by a tower in the World Financial Center, the Aetna Center in Toronto, and First Canadian Place. In response to its increasingly fran-

tic effort to stave off bankruptcy and to prepare Canary Wharf for tenants scheduled to arrive during the summer, it obtained two short-term bank loans adding
up to $58 million. On May 14 the Canadian parent company and some of its sub-
sidiaries filed for bankruptcy protection in Canada, and some of the subsidiaries
filed for Chapter 11 protection in the United States as well. The Canadian bankruptcy court restricted the firm's ability to shift money from its Canadian properties to other projects, including Canary Wharf. By the end of the year, lenders had
begun to take possession of the firm's Canadian holdings.

The U.K. government indicated that it was considering moving the headquarters of the DoE to Canary Wharf. When the government continued to procrasti-
nate, however, the banks decided that they could wait no longer to take action.[51]
Eventually, the headquarters of the London Underground did move to Canary
Wharf, but it was too late for O & Y.[52] On May 27 the effort to save Canary Wharf
from bankruptcy failed, as eleven banks with about £550 million in loans to the
project refused to provide new funds to fund the Jubilee Line obligation and to
keep construction going beyond the end of the month. At that time O & Y had put
£1.4 billion in the project and the banks another £1.2 billion; it was estimated that
an additional £600 million was required to finish construction of the first phase.[53]

The banks all had to absorb very substantial losses, but, in *Business Week*'s
words, "the sheer number of its [O & Y's] banks . . . has spared any single lender
from a life threatening exposure."[54] Many banks had already written off parts of
their loans to the company and had put the rest in the nonperforming category.
Thus, their situation was not changed by the bankruptcy declarations. In 1993
American banks were divesting themselves of the property they had taken over
through default, resulting in a substantial loss in the value of their assets but much
greater liquidity. They were saved by a dramatic fall in interest rates, which made
their performing loans much more profitable, and by the general revival of the
U.S. economy. British banks had avoided the heavy property exposure of their
U.S. and Japanese counterparts; the latter were suffering the most from the events
in London, along with the repercussions of the puncturing of the Japanese "bubble
economy."

Canary Wharf was placed under the administration of three partners in the
accounting firm Ernst & Young by a U.K. bankruptcy court. Under British law,
administrators run a bankrupt company and present the court with a plan determining the company's ultimate fate. In contrast to Chapter 11 bankruptcy in the
United States, where the firm's management remains in control of the organization and presents a restructuring plan that avoids liquidation of the firm, British
bankruptcy procedures favor creditors.[55]

In the meantime, the transport and infrastructure requirements of converting
the Isle of Dogs into an office center consumed more and more of the LDDC's
resources. Despite a great increase in the size of its government grant, the LDDC
ran into growing financial difficulties. In 1990 its chief executive, Michael Honey,
abruptly resigned from his post.[56] By mid-1991 the new CEO, Eric Sorensen, a

DoE civil servant, announced plans to cut its 456-member staff by 40 percent over the next two years.[57]

Why Did It Happen?

The causes of the world's largest real-estate failure range from the specific to the general. They include the financial situation of O & Y; personal characteristics of the Reichmanns; and the state of the international commercial property market.

Financial obstacles to salvaging O & Y. The Reichmanns' hopes that they could get agreement from their creditors on a restructuring plan that would pump necessary additional funds into their projects were unrealizable for several reasons. First, the loss in value of their properties caused by the real-estate slump meant that their liabilities exceeded their assets.[58] Consequently, they no longer had unencumbered property to use as collateral against additional loans. Bankers would only be willing to acquire equity in the properties if they believed that the shares were going to increase in value, but expectations for market recovery were low. Second, there were significant differences in the status of the various lender banks in their claims on O & Y's assets and revenues. Banks that had lent £500 million for Canary Wharf in the 1990 refinancing had their loans secured by O & Y's assets; later lenders took shares in Canary Wharf companies as security, causing them to rank behind the former group in their claims on the parent company. Additional loans would only worsen the situation of the latter group. Third, the Reichmanns had been seeking to redeem their short-term paper, amounting to C$800 million, thus putting all the banks, which numbered about 100, behind the commercial paper holders.[59]

Personal characteristics and international property markets. The basis of the Reichmanns' wealth was a very high tolerance of risk. In staking their fortune on Canary Wharf, they apparently felt that they had a sufficient cushion to endure a market downturn. Indeed, in 1988 they were reported to have net assets of C$11 billion and borrowings of less than C$2 billion.[60] But the internationalization of real-estate investment meant that contrary to their expectations, markets in different cities tended to move together, so that their multiple investments did not counterbalance one another. The downturn was both longer and deeper than they predicted, and it occurred when their non-real-estate investments were going sour as well.

Many commentators have wondered why the Reichmanns took so many chances when their taste for consumption was quite limited and their fortune established. Speculations recounted by John Lichfield provide some insight into the interaction between personal characteristics and public events.[61] He quotes a Reichmann business associate as believing that "their heads were turned" by

Margaret Thatcher's personally urging them to seize the opportunity to demonstrate the vigor of capitalism in the once socialist-dominated Docklands. Lichfield repeats an explanation from a Toronto Jewish scholar:

> After the war years, many Jewish families wanted to build a safe, secure base from which they would never have to run again. The Reichmanns appear to me driven to go beyond that, to create a base so wealthy that they could practise their own interpretation of the law without the kind of compromises—such as social contact with gentiles and non-orthodox Jews—which were forced on them in exile. And beyond that to raise the funds to begin to recreate, in scholarship at least, the shattered, enclosed world of their orthodox communities in Europe.[62]

Finally, Lichfield recapitulates the observations of Peter Forster, the author of a book on the Reichmanns:

> The key to everything is the psychology of Paul Reichmann. He is a deal junkie. Deal-making is what he lives and breathes for, the obsessive need to go on making bigger and better deals. And the need to encompass it all in his head, with no proper management structure. With most businessmen, money is not the driving force. . . . His motivation is really the game itself, to do things bigger and better, to work out ever more intricate and imaginative deals.[63]

The Recovery of Canary Wharf

Only three years later, the tide had turned along the Thames, and Canary Wharf once again appeared to be an attractive investment. Paul Reichmann led a group of investors bidding to buy Canary Wharf back from the banks at a fraction of its cost of construction. According to the *Economist,* the losses he and his family incurred on all their holdings added up to $10 billion.[64] Nevertheless, he was able to leverage their remaining $100 million sufficiently to acquire an estimated 10 percent interest in the new company.[65] The Canary Wharf Group, as the new firm was called, obtained loans sufficient to allow it to honor its commitment toward building the tube line and subsequently became a publicly listed company on the London Stock Exchange. The *New York Times* opined that "a rebound in the British economy and the London property market from the deeply depressed levels of a few years ago seems to be proving that his [Reichmann's] original strategy in building the complex was not so far off, except in its timing."[66] A lavish marketing campaign had succeeded in producing a positive image for the area, and it attracted several new, prestigious occupants, including the investment arm of Barclay's Bank. This move marked the acceptability of the address to British firms.

The attractions of Canary Wharf were its lower rents (in 1995 about 60 percent of those in the City), the existence of planning permissions that allowed immediate construction tailored to the needs of the occupying firms, the capacity to build very large floor areas, and the high quality and technological sophistication of the structures. The hiatus in new construction within London had meant that vacant space was being absorbed, while conversions of office to residential and hotel accommodation had caused a substantial number of buildings to be removed from the office market. Thus, by the mid-1990s, Canary Wharf was competing in a situation of growing demand and diminished supply. As the project filled up, it began to lose the forbidding, abandoned quality that had characterized it at the time of bankruptcy and instead acquired a certain amount of glamour. It achieved nearly 80 percent occupancy in 1995, and planning had begun for additional buildings.

By the beginning of the new century, Canary Wharf was once again the scene of major construction activity. Now, however, unlike at the time of the project's launch, most buildings were purpose-built for committed tenants, and the infrastructure connecting the Wharf with the rest of London was in place. In particular, the extension of the Jubilee tube line and the construction of the Limehouse Link, Britain's most expensive road, had turned the area into an easy commute for most Londoners. Occupancy was at 98 percent of the existing 4.5 million square feet of office and retail space. More than 3.5 million square feet of additional space was under construction, including two 44-story towers, one designed by Norman Foster and the other by Cesar Pelli, for the major banking companies HSBC and Citigroup. A complex developed by another firm, in which the Canary Wharf Group held an interest, opened in 1999 with a Four Seasons hotel and 322 residential units.[67] According to a consultant's report, by 2006 the company would have added 8.9 million square feet. At that time they expected the rents at Canary Wharf to be about 15 percent lower than rents for space in the City, as compared to 31 percent lower in January 2000.[68]

Thus, as was the story at Times Square, the economic boom of the late '90s and its impact on property markets caused a seemingly doomed project to revive and prosper. The banks that had lent money to O & Y lost billions of dollars, as did the Reichmann family, when much of the asset value of O & Y's property holdings simply vanished during the recession.[69] Otherwise, however, the bankruptcy of the world's largest real-estate firm had only a short-term impact. In the long run, London has a third business district and has improved its competitive position in the European system of cities.[70] Within the terms of the LDDC's mandate,[71] Canary Wharf can now be seen as a total success in relation to the goal of reviving the economy of the Isle of Dogs, even if the path toward its triumph was less direct and more time-consuming than had been foreseen. The more debatable aspects of the complex, and of the larger Docklands scheme more generally, are whether more planning would have improved the development process, whether there should have been more citizen and local-authority involvement in policy making, and whether local residents benefited appropriately from the revival of East London.

IMPACTS OF DOCKLANDS REDEVELOPMENT

When the Thatcher government set up the LDDC, it intended to give as much leeway to the market as possible. Thus, even though the subsidies incorporated in the enterprise zone and the operations of the LDDC amounted to major governmental intervention, private investors determined the types of structures to be built and their location.[72] The government also wished to see the private sector contribute substantial financial support to the construction of necessary infrastructure. This precluded the government's putting the infrastructure in place before developers began their work.

The Docklands development scheme aimed at achieving the outcome of earlier British new-town investment—the creation of a whole new urban center. The use of a development corporation as the government's instrument replicated the new-town organizational structure.[73] But instead of using public money for the bulk of up-front capital expenditures, the Conservatives relied on the private sector to put in most of the financing and to provide major public benefits besides. It did so out of a pragmatic desire to avoid large expenditures and an ideological commitment to private enterprise. The predictable consequence was that Docklands replicated the fate of the U.S. new-town experience, wherein developers foundered because they could not meet their loan obligations before their projects had attained a positive revenue flow.[74] Given the size of initial investment, the length of time from project inception to conclusion, the cyclical nature of the property market, and the inability of private developers to refinance their debt when lending institutions lose confidence in the market, only under the most fortuitous circumstances could any developer carry out such a project. Olympia & York was the world's richest development firm; its failure indicates the limits on turning to the private sector for achieving public ends.

The Conservative government did eventually invest heavily in infrastructure for Docklands, and O & Y's successor company did finally contribute to financing the tube line. It would, however, have been more realistic for the government to have begun and paid for the construction at the start of development and received the project's contribution after occupancy. The absence of adequate transportation infrastructure initially limited the project's appeal to both investors and tenants. Many comments have been made about Londoners' aversion to moving outside the core and the significance of the much greater distance between Canary Wharf and the City than between Wall Street and the World Financial Center in Battery Park City. With good road and rail connections, however, the friction of distance would have been outweighed by the attractions of the new surroundings, as later proved the case.

The other strategy that the government could have adopted at the outset would have emulated Paris's La Défense in its policy mechanisms as well as its physical form. This project, which is comparable to the commercial core of Docklands, represented a very different, far more regulated approach to eliciting private-sector investment. A public corporation quickly put in the necessary infrastructure, including rail transport, at the start. As the 19 million square feet of office space within the complex went up, the government first restricted then almost halted permissions to construct commercial buildings within central Paris.[75] When financial crisis hit during the mid-1970s, the cabinet pumped in additional public revenues as well as giving tax advantages to firms settling in La Défense.[76] Thus, while the French used private-sector resources to create a whole new section of Paris, they did not rely on the market to regulate the flow of those resources.

In contrast, the British government remained obdurate in its endorsement of market mechanisms. It refused to restrain the Corporation of the City of London in its competition with Docklands, thereby ensuring the oversupply of London office space that made it impossible for Docklands developers to fill their buildings. It would not release O & Y from its transport commitments, and it was willing to move civil servants into Canary Wharf only if rentals did not exceed the lowest going rate for comparable space.[77]

Prime Minister John Major declared that the government would not bail out Canary Wharf: "The future of the development must be a matter for the administrator and for the banks, and not necessarily for the Government."[78] Yet the LDDC and the whole Docklands approach was a creation of the U.K. central government; its latter-day puritanism about letting the market do its work contradicted the project's state-based origin. If the government initially had been content simply to await private initiatives, at most there would have been a gradual development of Docklands, moving slowly outward from the boundary with the City.

In the end, one could argue that the results were the same as if the government had been more consistently supportive. The roads and transit connections got built, and the commercial sites prospered. The private sector took the losses commensurate with its risks; whether the public gained or lost as a result is a difficult issue to resolve. On the one hand, the wave of bankruptcies that swept the property sector reinforced the overall recession affecting the London economy. On the other, total public expenditure of £3.9 billion induced £8.7 billion of private investment by March 1998, with another several billion pounds expected to materialize within the next decade.[79]

The structure of the LDDC insulated decisions over location and type of facility constructed from the political arena. Although Docklands development evoked considerable protest and hostility in general, specific investment decisions remained outside public scrutiny, which would not have been the case if developers had had to seek planning permission from local authorities. A more democratic process would probably have produced a different type of commercial development, one less single-mindedly devoted to financial and business services. Such a trajectory would have been more responsive to the specific needs of the host boroughs but less contributory to the economic development of Greater London.

More planning, if it had aimed at tying physical to social programs, would have connected education and training efforts within the Docklands boroughs more closely to the projects going up. In the LDDC's first years, its focus was exclusively physical. Later, in response to widespread criticism, the LDDC did begin to emphasize social regeneration as a significant part of its mission.[80] Both politicians and business leaders began to recognize that special efforts were required if the physical improvement of an area was to benefit its residents. Contemporary British urban policy under the Single Regeneration Budget explicitly requires such program integration. The official evaluation of the LDDC notes that the corporation had spent £110 million on social and community development, representing about 7 percent of net expenditure. It concludes that "most of the population will have benefited from this activity," but it makes no effort to explicate these benefits.[81] In an analysis of the labor-market effects of Docklands development, Church and Frost indicate that there are insufficient data to allow an estimate of the access to jobs of original Docklands residents.[82] The in-migration of many middle-class residents to the new, owner-occupied housing estates, combined with the move of earlier residents out of social housing complexes into owner occupation, means that future censuses of the area will be unable to determine the employment impacts on original residents.

According to LDDC figures, unemployment in the development area basically tracked the rate for Greater London as a whole.[83] In 1998 the number of jobs in the development area had increased from about 27,000 to 80,000, but only 23,000 of the gain represented net additions to total employment rather than transferred positions.[84] There was little to indicate that the low-income, unemployed residents of the Docklands boroughs realized direct employment and income benefits from the huge investments placed in their vicinity. Possibly the most important effect was the link to employment in the rest of London provided by the tube extension, which, even if it was intended primarily to bring workers out to Docklands, also transported Docklands residents to the rest of the metropolis.

In relation to housing development, rather surprisingly given the LDDC's initial aversion to social housing, the local community has obtained measurable gains from LDDC investment. Social housing in the urban development area was estimated to be 40 percent higher than would have been the case in the absence of the LDDC.[85] At the same time, the number of houses available for owner occupation increased by nearly 16,000 units, resulting in a tenure mix of 37.6 percent owner-occupied in 1997 (compared to 5.3 percent in 1981) and 49.1 percent social housing (compared to 82.8 percent in 1981). In Mark Kleinman's words, Docklands "has become more like a 'normal' housing market, more in line with the rest of London, in terms of housing tenure and housing mix."[86] The final mix was the consequence of developer initiatives, deals in which affordable housing was created along with market-rate units, and the substitution of social for market-rate housing during the property recession. At the start of the development period, the local authorities showed no interest in developing housing for owner occupation, and most of the housing developed exceeded the means of existing residents. Nevertheless, those of their children who were upwardly mobile were able to stay in their old neighborhoods as a consequence of the LDDC's housing program.

Democracy

From the outset, the two sides of the Docklands debate were clearly differentiated. The position of the Conservative government and its supporters was that Docklands could be an engine of growth, propelling London into a dominant position in twenty-first-century Europe. They frequently mentioned the French success in creating a business center on the Parisian periphery at La Défense and cited central London's restrictions on growth, congestion, and obsolescent office stock as reasons to plan a new development designed from the start to fulfill contemporary needs. The past failures of Labour governments in promoting alternative, smaller-scale strategies of growth were taken to indicate that only private capital, leveraged by strategic public-sector contributions, could succeed in moving Docklands from wasteland to viability. Opponents of converting the Docklands into a financial and advanced-services headquarters maintained that current residents would receive few housing and employment benefits; that these would only be incidental to the main goal of stimulating private property investment; and that the amount of public financing required to make the project feasible represented a perverse tax on the rest of British society, which would be deprived of adequate governmental support for other community development efforts.

Bob Colenutt, the former director of the Docklands Consultative Committee, was the leading spokesman for those promoting an alternative development path. He rejected the Tory conception of Docklands as a new business and residential center for London. Colenutt suggested instead a gradualist strategy toward regeneration that would give priority to assuaging inner-city deprivation.[87] He proposed, among other things, (1) emphasizing job training and technical assistance to business rather than property development; (2) developing comprehensive strategic plans rather than stimulating "flagship" developments to act as magnets for growth; and (3) increasing local accountability and democracy. His approach was less flashy and, ironically, much more conservative than the Conservatives' tactics. It would not have attracted large sums of capital, and, despite his call for a stronger regional planning approach, it would probably have sacrificed the potential of Docklands as a strategic resource for Greater London as a whole. Colenutt did not espouse a parochialism that would limit the benefits of Docklands development simply to its low-income residents, as did the earlier DJC plan. But neither did he indicate what would attract business to the area. The great merit of his approach lay in its direct confrontation of the sources of social and economic inequality; its deficiency was in the weakness of its stimulus to growth.

Present strategies of London continue to rely heavily on "flagship projects." The UDC format, however, is a thing of the past. Both planning and public participation are requirements in the new developments; local authorities constitute the institutional arbiter for investment; and social programs are built in from the start. Reflecting the Blair government's "Third Way," these projects attempt both growth and redistribution. The sharp disagreements over planning objectives characteristic of the early '80s have disappeared. Instead, a strategy of consensus-building consonant with the prescriptions of planning theory for communicative or collaborative planning prevails.[88] Whether underlying conflicts of interest in a city with growing inequality can, in fact, be resolved in this fashion remains to be seen.

10

Real-Estate Development: Why Is It Special and What Is Its Impact?

Urban redevelopment has attracted the scrutiny of scholars and community activists since the inception of large government programs to rebuild cities after the Second World War. Initial interest centered on the governmental decision-making process, the role of the state, and community conflict. Although many studies identified the influence of business leaders on decisions and outcomes, there was little investigation of the factors affecting the actions of speculative developers. Their great prominence during the real-estate boom of the 1980s, their contribution to economic retreat at the beginning of the '90s, and their diminished role at the end of that decade have formed the central theme of this book. The conclusion of Chapter 1 lists six questions that make up the framework of my inquiry. The first four—the relationship between economic restructuring and real-estate development, the contradictions within the process of development that produce oversupply, the relationship between governmental activity and property development, and the similarities and differences between London and New York—have already been considered in earlier chapters. This chapter addresses the fifth and sixth questions: the special characteristics of real estate as an economic sector, and the impacts of redevelopment.

THE NATURE OF THE REAL-ESTATE SECTOR

Real-estate development shares characteristics with many other sectors of production in both its impacts and its operations; its uniqueness lies in the way it combines attributes usually belonging to quite dissimilar industries. Like manufacturers, property developers produce a tangible product. At the same time, the development industry resembles the entertainment business more than heavy manufacturing in having a profound cultural influence, in the singularity of each

197

item produced, and in the process by which the elements of a project are combined. As in entertainment, production away from the firm's headquarters is ad hoc; unlike most other multinational corporations, big development companies do not set up permanent facilities around the world, but, rather, like film-production companies, they use temporary field offices for specific projects. Yet, despite resemblances to film or television production, the industry is also similar to agriculture in its cyclical structure, its susceptibility to market glut, and its close relation with government. Although government does not directly control levels of production as in agriculture, the development industry depends heavily on public-sector decisions concerning investment in infrastructure, tax policy, and regulation of construction.

Organization of Production

Major development firms typically differ from big industrial corporations in not producing on a mass scale. The fluctuating nature of the property market and the fact that most purchases of space are from secondhand stock have meant that the industry, except for large housing subdivision builders, could never count on a market sufficient to justify mass production. In the United States and the United Kingdom, development firms also have not adopted the same organizational structures as major industrial producers have—they have not integrated most phases of the production process within their enterprises,[1] and they usually do not operate on a global or even a national scale.[2]

Developers usually contract for most services with third parties rather than relying on internal provision. This strategy allows them simply to withdraw from activity during slumps, as they have little overhead to maintain.[3] By providing development firms with other sources of income, like brokerage, management, and architectural fees, vertical integration could reduce their costs during peak periods and offer them protection against cash-flow problems during downturns in the development cycle. Few firms, however, have tried to adopt this model.[4] Olympia & York did move toward vertical integration during the 1980s real-estate boom by issuing its own notes and retaining property for its own management operation. It also operated in a number of countries. As it turned out, both self-financing and working in unfamiliar locales contributed heavily to its undoing.

Ironically, construction used to be contrasted with integrated, mass-produced, capital-goods and consumer-durables manufacturing to demonstrate its backwardness. Now, however, the "hollow corporation" that relies on subcontractors, "just-in-time" methods, and temporary staff has been touted as the leading edge of the restructured global economy. In the era of flexible organization of enterprises and short production runs, the development industry begins to look as if all along it had occupied the vanguard rather than the rear.

Property Markets

The property development industry has a paradoxical situation with regard to market position:[5] It is simultaneously monopolistic and highly competitive. Although any structure monopolizes its site, and property owners can achieve monopoly pricing within districts, no developer or small group of developers can control overall supply in a metropolitan area.[6] Ease of entry into the market and the potential of previously undeveloped districts to compete with developed areas destabilizes market domination. Unlike farmers, whom the government compensates for accepting constraints on production, developers do not receive benefits when they are not developing; consequently, they have strongly resisted governmentally imposed restrictions on supply, even though without such restrictions it becomes impossible to maintain high prices. The situation whereby a small group of owners can monopolize a niche but not a whole market contributes to the cyclical behavior of property markets. A competing node must reach a critical mass before it threatens an established area, but once it does, it affects the entire price structure. Thus, suburban office complexes only began to threaten the dominance of urban central business districts (CBDs) once they reached a critical mass and took on the characteristics of edge cities. At that point, however, they became competitive and forced property owners in the CBD to either lower their prices or offer superior quality.

The 1980s witnessed a move toward dominance of the London and New York inner-city new-construction markets by a small number of big firms. Subsequent hard times, however, either drove them into default or caused them to withdraw from active production of space until the market's revival in the late 1990s. In New York, commercial landlords on the midtown East Side commanded very high rents as a result of limitations on the supply of space in a uniquely prestigious area. Renovation of older buildings in adjacent areas by small-scale developers and massive new development in other parts of Manhattan and in New Jersey, however, created "new addresses," leading office-renters to vacate large amounts of space on the East Side as they took advantage of lower prices elsewhere. The pressure on building owners burdened with so much empty space meant that they could not sustain the old rent level even after developers had stopped adding newly constructed space to the area. Thus, the value of their initial monopoly position dropped substantially. In the case of Canary Wharf, its supply of cheaper, high-quality space caused the City of London to respond by encouraging new production, thereby pushing down the price of office rentals within the City. Once the vacant space was finally absorbed by the end of the '90s, rents returned to and eventually even exceeded their previous peak. The price differential between the old and new centers, however, diminished.

The most anomalous aspect of the pricing of real estate derives from the dual role of a building in functioning within both factor and consumption markets. In other industries, ownership of the product is distinct from ownership of the company or rights to future increases in the value of its production. A building, however, is both part of capital stock and a commodity. It is as if the cost of cars to the consumer fluctuated with the shares of General Motors, or as if purchases of bread reflected the price of grain futures. (The price of these goods does, of course, to some degree reflect anticipation of future scarcity and resale possibilities, but the connection is far less strong than in real-estate markets since the amount of product available can be much more easily controlled.) The dual character of property as commodity and vehicle for capital accumulation explains why investors will risk funds on a property where production costs exceed capitalized revenues calculated on the basis of present value.

The general rule that a firm should produce until marginal cost equals marginal revenue is difficult to apply in the property industry since expectations about marginal revenue are extremely subjective. Although calculating marginal revenue in all industries requires an estimate of a future price, in no other industry is such a prediction so uncertain, so subject to the externalities of the actions of others, and carried out over such a long time span. The price of a commercial property in ten years depends on the amount of space that others build; desirability of the area in which it is located (which is itself very subjective and can be perturbed by unanticipated events); the changeable technical needs of the occupant (e.g., for "smart buildings," large trading floors, or private offices with windows); governmental decisions concerning infrastructure, taxation, interest rates, and regulation; and expansion and contraction of the industry for which the building is designed.

During the 1980s financial institutions were willing to lend money to developers using optimistic estimates of the future value of the building rather than a simple ratio of the immediately anticipated rent roll to capital inputs. Consequently, far more space was built than could be justified, based on immediate returns. As shown in Chapter 3, it was this flow of capital into the property industry rather than demand that stimulated the huge amount of new construction at the end of the decade. After the crash of the early '90s, lenders virtually ceased to support speculative development. Thus, by the end of the decade, despite demand that reduced vacancy rates to extraordinarily low levels, little new supply of office stock was coming onto the market.

The Contribution of Property to Value

Two much-discussed arguments of David Harvey bear on the issue of the consequences of property investment;[7] both signify that gains from property are particularly ill gotten. First, in his theory of switched investment, Harvey argues that investment moves into the secondary circuit of capital, to which the built environment belongs, when there is overaccumulation in the primary circuit.[8] Harvey's implication is that such switching dampens productive investment, and his use of the term "circuit" indicates that once capital moves into this realm it will stay there.

Yet, as syndication and securitization make property debt increasingly negotiable, the distinction between circuits fades. There is, moreover, little evidence that the behavior of property counters movements in other parts of the economy, as would be the case if the switching argument were valid.[9] When times are generally tough, property suffers likewise. The lag in the property cycle as compared to the goods-production cycle largely results from the long lead time involved in real-estate development projects.[10]

During the 1970s in the United States there was a major shift of funds into property. This phenomenon is more convincingly regarded as the result of using property as a hedge against inflation and of tax advantages allocated to this sector than as a consequence of overaccumulation in the primary circuit. In addition, the tendency of banks, particularly those of Japan and the oil-producing countries, to overinvest in property grew partly out of the move by industrial companies toward disintermediation; the refusal of companies with large capital needs to turn to banks meant that the banks lacked outlets for their funds. The absence of investment opportunities for banks in the primary sector did not necessarily reflect overaccumulation in that sector.

Harvey develops his second argument concerning the effects of investment in property in his discussion of "fictitious capital" (defined as debt instruments).[11] He uses the term "insanity" to describe "a society in which investment in appropriation (rents, government debts, etc.) appears just as important as investment in production."[12] According to both these arguments, the property sector absorbs rather than generates value—value is only created through "real" production (including the actual building of a structure but not some of the other costs associated with it, such as sales taxes and interest).[13]

The classical (Ricardian) definition of land rent, which assumes a completely inelastic supply of land, likewise implies that the property sector is essentially parasitic. According to this reasoning, property attains its value from the way it is used by its occupant rather than from any activity of the owner.[14] Speculative transactions appear to support this point. Thus, the spiraling price of an undeveloped piece of land that keeps changing hands on the expectation of future use illustrates the unearned quality of real-estate gains, as does a huge increase in the rent for an unchanged storefront at the expiration of a lease.

Despite such instances of wholly unproductive investment in property, real-estate development can create value beyond the cost of its production. If agglomeration and access do transform territory into location; if restructured space increases business efficiency; if subdivision of land or reuse of empty warehouses creates a residential neighborhood where none previously existed; if the regulations that limit construction in a given district do actually produce a more attractive environment—then increases in land value resulting from development are genuine. The value of a tennis racket is dependent on a court, of a bedroom on a bed, of a steel mill on raw materials (and vice versa)—virtually all values exist in combinations and are increased or lowered, based on the context in which they are used. Physicality does not make a process real, nor does the intangibility of factors like agglomeration make them unreal. It is the concatenation of externalities from development that creates place, which as a whole may have a value greater than a simple summation of the costs of producing it.[15] The claim that such gains are socially created does not overturn this assertion—the question of who deserves to receive the gain is analytically separable from the issue of whether it exists. Value anticipated from development is not fictitious.

Factors Causing Government Involvement

The inherently social nature of the production of place has underlain the historically high level of government involvement in the property sector. First, because ownership of property is a set of rights rather than physical possession, government has always regulated "private" property. How property rights are defined, bought, and sold is defined by law and adjudicated through courts. Second, property development has an immediate neighborhood effect, and the aggregate of development projects has important impacts on the economic future and quality of life of an entire settlement. The use and disposal of property almost necessarily involves more parties than simply the nominal buyer and seller. Third, the obligation of government to provide public goods means that even in the most market-driven societies, governments themselves have major landholdings and do some land banking. Governments act as property developers when carrying out public functions ranging from assuring the water supply to constructing parks to building infrastructure. How they perform these functions significantly affects growth and the distribution of benefits within their jurisdictions.

Together public and private property development contributes significantly to the creation of place. Place has within it the elements of territory, of location, and of community.[16] Place is a critical component of human welfare for several reasons: (1) It provides a basis for human affiliation; (2) it is the setting for economic development and consumption; (3) it is the locus of political representation; and (4) it is the arena in which public policy acts on people. Given the crucial functions of place, it is not surprising that its constitution is among the most contested of policy issues.

HOW SHOULD WE EVALUATE THE PLACES THAT THE CITY BUILDERS HAVE MADE?

Practitioners of both city planning and urban sociology long held as a basic tenet that urban form shapes social life. Throughout much of this century, planners, whose roots lay in the design professions, believed that well-ordered cities would make people lead better lives. During the same period urban sociologists, claiming a scientific basis for their hypotheses, were arguing that environmental factors explained human behavior—Lewis Wirth, in his famous essay on urbanism that epitomized this approach, identified the size, density, and heterogeneity of a settlement as the determining elements of social relations within it.[17]

Subsequently, however, leftist scholars disputed that place had independent effects, claiming that planners and sociologists had mistakenly confounded the results of a class-divided industrial society with the consequences of urban form and spatial clustering.[18] These later theorists argued instead that urbanism was a mediating factor based on the socioeconomic relations of modern industrial capitalism. In its Marxist version, this analysis regarded space as shaped by the dominant class using spatial divisions to its advantage and by subordinate classes, which on occasion were able to mobilize from a territorial base to contest their situation.[19] More conservative thinkers did not share the Marxists' starting point in the economic structure. Nevertheless, they also increasingly saw physical form as an outcome instead of a cause of human activity, differing from the Marxists in tracing the qualities of places to popular preferences and technological imperatives rather than to the logic of capitalism.[20]

Most recently, urbanists, usually from a left perspective, have placed a renewed emphasis on urban design and spatial configuration, although without explicitly reviving the design or environmental reductionism of their planning and sociological forebears.[21] In line with contemporary poststructuralist thought, they have largely avoided identifying the form of the city as a direct cause of social behavior; rather, they have read from the physical contours of cities the meaning of urban life. Their analyses stress the symbolic importance of design; chart the way in which it expresses relations of domination and subordination, oppression and resistance; and examine the interaction between environmental factors and human consciousness.[22] In particular, recent writings on the city have explored the inclusionary and exclusionary aspects of urban spatial formations, as part of a broad concern by their authors with the politics of diversity and a normative commitment to the acceptance of difference.[23] Whereas their Marxist predecessors had evaluated the material costs and benefits flowing from the creation and use of urban space, today's cultural critics have scrutinized the late capitalist city with "the conscience of the eye."[24]

The evolving literature on the meaning of spatial configurations provides one set of concerns through which we can assess the development history of London and New York between 1978 and 2000. It also allows us to describe the culture of urban development and to understand how different social groups shape and respond to the new urban form. Nevertheless, I find serious problems in the arguments of this contemporary group of urbanists, which stem from their simultaneous embrace of the related but also contradictory values of diversity, authenticity, and democracy. In the remainder of this chapter, in which I present my evaluation of redevelopment in London and New York, I distill the main elements of this recent critique of contemporary redevelopment practice drawn from a number of recent works, either generally on the making of the contemporary city or more specifically on London and New York. For simplicity's sake, I label this body of analysis "poststructuralist." My presentation of the poststructuralist analysis attempts to offer a fair summary of the main arguments, but the reader should keep in mind that I am not fully in agreement with them. Afterward, I specify what I see as the weaknesses of the approach and set forth some correctives that assist in overcoming these difficulties. Finally, I discuss additional ways of understanding and evaluating urban redevelopment, based on a more materialist analysis.

The Poststructuralist Critique

The "public-private partnerships" that have controlled the planning and implementation of redevelopment in American and British cities express themselves in the lineaments of the cities that they build. Within these partnerships the private sector usually dominates the relationship through its command over investment choices; moreover, despite their hybrid status, the partnerships typically adhere to a market-led, closed-to-the-public style that is a hallmark of a private business. Whether the recent British partnerships, which involve more prominent roles for government officials and affected communities, result in substantially lessened private dominance remains to be seen as projects move toward implementation. In the past, in pursuing their aims of economic expansion, public-private partnerships imprinted the built environment with their attributes of privatism, competition, and commodification of relationships.[25] According to poststructuralist analysis, the resulting environment is hostile to authentic human expression and represses subordinate groups.

To ensure the safe pursuit of profit within the reconstructed city, designers intentionally set projects off from their surroundings so as to create defensible space: "Faced with the fact of social hostility in the city, the planner's impulse in the real world is to seal off conflicting or dissonant sides, to build internal walls rather than permeable borders."[26] A number of measures ensure that only certain people can gain access to the new constructions that define the urban landscape: isolation of projects behind highways, raised plazas, or actual walls; direct connections to parking garages and transit, obviating the need to use city streets; segregation of uses; extensive deployment of security measures; private ownership of outdoor parks and indoor courtyards, allowing the banning of unsavory individuals and political speech; high prices for renting attractive quarters and for buying goods sold within the new stores; and stylistic markers that make lower-class people feel out of place. The unrelatedness of one project to the next further diminishes the public realm. In the words of the architect Moshe Safdie:

> The legibility of the city depends on the public domain as the connective framework between individual buildings. This is exemplified in the agora and the markets of the past, but it does not exist today. We are unable to connect buildings as part of the urban experience. The Galeria in Houston,

the grand space of Philip Johnson's IDS building in Minneapolis, the great spaces created by Portman are an attempt to respond to our desire for public places worthy of the kind of urban life that we want. But, by definition, built as individual pieces, they are introverted and, hence, they are private and not connectable.[27]

The resulting urban form is paradoxically neither coherent nor diverse. Physical incoherence, instead of fostering pluralism, produces segmentation[28]—separation rather than juxtaposition. The adjectives typically used to depict the contemporary city are "divided," "fragmented," and "fractured." Although the residences of the rich and poor were rarely in close proximity throughout the history of the industrial city, the commercial core previously retained a social heterogeneity, springing from its use by all strata of the population. The construction of fortified spaces within the city, however, allows the commuting businessperson and the resident gentry to experience urbanity without confronting "the other." In Richard Sennett's words: "Battery Park City . . . is planned according to current enlightened wisdom about mixed uses and the virtues of diversity. Within this model of community, however, one has the sense . . . 'of an illustration of life' rather than life itself."[29]

Even projects like Covent Garden and South Street Seaport, which were modeled on the busy marketplaces of earlier times, produce only a simulacrum of urbanism—an "analogous city."[30] In commenting ironically on the influence of Jane Jacobs, whose *Death and Life of Great American Cities* had espoused diversity as the prime urban value, Trevor Boddy contends:

Sadly, the cornerstones of Jacobsian urbanism—picturesque ethnic shops piled high with imported goods, mustachioed hot-dog vendors in front of improvised streetcorner fountains, urban life considered as one enormous national-day festival—are cruelly mimicked in every Rouse market [i.e., urban shopping districts developed by the Rouse Corporation, which specializes in festive marketplaces] and historic district on the [American] continent. Contemporary developers have found it eminently easy to furnish such obvious symbols of urbanism, while at the same time eliminating the racial, ethnic, and class diversity that interested Jacobs in the first place.[31]

To the poststructuralist critics the glory of cities lies in their capacity to bring together strangers, allowing people to move beyond the "familiar enclaves" of families and social networks "to the more open public of politics, commerce, and festival, where strangers meet and interact."[32] The diminution of this capacity reinforces the hegemony of the white males who designed the modern city and whose economic and political power it incorporates.[33] In turn, the city symbolizes gendered power; popular response to its message reaffirms acquiescence to hierarchy and repressive norms of appropriate behavior. According to Elizabeth Wilson, the modern city and its postmodern successor signify the triumph of the "masculine approach" of "intervention and mastery" over feminine "appreciation and immersion."[34] In his discussion of the City of London, Michael Pryke comments that the value system of the English public school combined with a style of British masculinity to create there a gendered territory of "upper class patriarchy."[35] He argues that the introduction of information technology into these gendered confines produced "a spatial demonstration of predominantly male corporate power structures," as men staked out their positions on the trading floors of the financial firms while women assumed the jobs deskilled by computerization.[36]

The claim that diversity is excluded while its illusion is created underlies the further accusation that unlike the streets and markets of old, these new development projects lack authenticity:

> Places like Battery Park City, Times Square, and South Street Seaport are sustained . . . by the expansion of historical tourism, the desire to "just look" at the replicated and revalued artifacts and architecture of another time. Yet to historicize is to estrange, to make different, so that a gap continually widens between then and now, *between an authentic and simulated experience.*[37]

Even the Prince of Wales joined the attack on the failure of the modern cityscape to conform to an authentic historical tradition, and his intervention helped to block several of the megaprojects that would have rent the fabric of central London.[38] As on Main Street in Disney World—the apogee of simulated historicism—the purpose of presenting the past in the architectural references of the postmodern office structures and festive marketplaces is to induce consumption.[39] The granite-clad facades, classical pediments, and restored warehouses persuade corporate officers to pay high rents for symbols of prestige or lead tourists to buy the unneeded commodities so fetchingly displayed. Rather than situating the visitor in historical continuity with a real past, these imitative projects project him or her into a fantasy world wherein an ostensibly meaningful existence can be purchased off the rack.

In New York's Battery Park City, a residential community designed to evoke traditional neighborhoods springs up on a site that was only recently under water. In London's Canary Wharf, streets lined with august buildings seemingly built long ago suddenly appear on land formerly covered with warehouses and shipping cranes. In Covent Garden and the Fulton Street Fishmarket, T-shirt vendors and fashionable cafés take over the same structures occupied by the wholesale purveyors and raucous taverns of yesteryear. Whether the projects contain new structures built to resemble old ones or genuinely old buildings with new functions, their sameness, their artificiality, and their omnipresent security forces all seem to validate the poststructuralist perspective. The impulse for the critique derives from laudable commitments to democracy and egalitarianism and a vision of a city to which all people have an equal right and where everyone has freedom of expression. The perspective, however, even though it is rooted in a political and social analysis of space, suffers from weaknesses of political and social perception. It is to these weaknesses that this discussion now turns.

Inadequacies of Poststructuralist Analysis

Certain of the flaws in poststructuralist urban analysis are not fundamental to its critique. Its crucial theses are its attack on exclusionism and its identification of the urban core as expressing the dominance of a ruling group or power bloc. Many of its proponents, however, base their argument on two assumptions, which they fail to justify: (1) that the city once nurtured diversity more than it does now, and (2) that a desirable city would be more authentic than the one currently being created. These two assumptions are not, however, essential, and a modified version of the main contentions about exclusionism and power can be retained without believing in a golden past and the virtue of authenticity. My discussion first explains the problems with the two assumptions, continues by examining the deficiencies of the exclusionism and domination arguments, and then attempts to salvage them.

A golden age of greater diversity? Many of the poststructuralists quoted above assume that a golden age—or at least a better time—once existed, when cities did harbor the daily interaction of diverse people and urban form expressed an authentic relationship with the forces of production and reproduction. Two obvious facts, however, undermine the nostalgic recollection of a past when urban space fostered greater tolerance of difference.[40] First, in both London and New York people deemed unacceptable by the larger society were kept out of those parts of the city where the upper classes congregated. The enforcement of vagrancy laws and the general lack of restraint on police discretion meant that the least attractive elements of society were simply contained in particular parts of town. The Bowery in New York and Limehouse in London were not necessarily the preferred location of their down-and-out denizens. These individuals did not, however, dare to intrude into upper-class areas for fear of physical assault or incarceration at the hands of the law. In addition, the confinement of the mentally ill removed them from the city streets. It was the ubiquitous presence of the homeless, substance abusers, and the mentally ill in even the best parts of Manhattan and central London that stimulated the reactive construction of secure spaces.[41] Whether in sum the variety of people in central places is greater or less now than formerly is unclear. The inward-turning characteristics of the atrium hotels like New York's Marriott Marquis, the glitzy atmosphere of Covent Garden and South Street Seaport, and the isolation of megaprojects like Battery Park and London Bridge Cities do separate the users of these facilities from the rest of the population. Nonetheless, at least superficially, the range of types to be seen within the festive markets seems to exceed the spectrum of those who patronized the downtown department stores of my youth.[42] And even with the existence of "glass ceilings" for women and minorities, the corporations that populate the new office buildings are considerably more heterogeneous now than earlier in the century.

Second, in New York the exclusion of people of color from commercial spaces and housing was a fact of life and not illegal until midcentury. Even though patches of African-American habitation existed throughout Manhattan until their extirpation by urban renewal after World War II, the existence of these islands did not mean that their occupants mixed with other social groups. Moreover, until the Second World War the great majority of the African-American population did not abide in northern cities but lived in the South, where it was subject to extreme legal segregation. Thus, the mechanisms that currently keep most of the now much larger populations of people of color out of certain spaces in central New York, however outrageous they may be, still are not as exclusionary as previous modes.[43]

A more authentic form? The dismissal of contemporary redevelopment projects as inauthentic implies that authenticity once reigned. While putting off momentarily a discussion of the broader meaning of the term, we can temporarily accept a limited definition of authenticity in design as either historical accuracy or lack of artifice (form following function). As part of the discussion of whether there was once a golden age of the city, we can then consider if current design is less meticulous in representing the past or a less natural outcome of the economy and daily lives of the population than the constructions of earlier generations.

With this question in mind, the censure of Battery Park City, Canary Wharf, South Street Seaport, and Covent Garden for their artificiality and historical inaccuracies seems on the face of it odd. The Western urban tradition since the Renaissance has always sustained the false front and the faulty imitation of times past. Those most urbane and praised of seventeenth-century urban squares—Madrid's Plaza Mayor and Paris's Place de Vosges—achieve their uniformity from the placement of identical facades on a hodgepodge of buildings. London's beloved Nash terraces, built in the early nineteenth century, employ columns and porticoes in imaginative imitation of Athenian architecture. New York's Metropolitan Museum of Art is basically hackneyed Roman Revival. If one can identify any characteristic style of major structures in the Western city since the Renaissance, it is bastardized historical re-creation.

Authenticity defined and evaluated. The second unsubstantiated assumption of the poststructuralist interpretation is the exaltation of the value of authenticity itself and the implied definition of it that underlies the attacks on new projects as inauthentic. Although the critical literature is replete with accusations of fakery, the nature of authentic late-twentieth-century design is rarely specified. For example, Michael Sorkin, the former architecture critic for the *Village Voice,* New York's leading alternative newspaper, excoriates Disneyland for its unreality: "The simulation's referent is ever elsewhere; the 'authenticity' of the substitution always depends on the knowledge, however faded, of some absent genuine."[44] But what is the "absent genuine" in a nation whose main industries produce intangibles and whose economic stability depends on stimulating ever-higher levels of consumption? Sorkin goes on to assert that the "Disney-zone" is a meretricious fake:

> Disney invokes an urbanism without producing a city. Rather, it produces a kind of aura-stripped hypercity, a city with billions of citizens (all who would consume) but no residents. Physicalized yet conceptual, it's the utopia of transience, a place where everyone is just passing through. This is its message for the city, to be a place everywhere and nowhere, assembled only through constant motion.[45]

Sorkin's prose interestingly echoes Manuel Castells's description of the effect of information technology on society more generally: We are seeing "the emergence of a *space of flows* which dominates the historically constructed space of places, as the logic of dominant organizations detaches itself from the social constraints of cultural identities and local societies through the powerful medium of information technologies."[46] If Castells is right, then Disney World is an *authentic* reflection of underlying economic and social processes, however little we may like them. It *is* the genuine, while the absent Main Streets and Hollywood studios have, in fact, disappeared, as their economic functions have withered or are performed through other means.

Much of the poststructuralist literature rests on an unformulated premise that what is genuine comprises either the production and transportation of goods (e.g., craft workshops, steel mills, and working ports) or the housing of production workers (e.g., cottages and tenements). Spectacles and pageants are authentic if they are produced by their participants rather than fabricated to manipulate them. The subtext, based on Marxist concepts of alienation and commodity fetishism, is that virtue lies in material production and that producing for one's own consumption is better than purchasing mass-produced goods and services—activity is always preferable to passivity (in this code of ethics, buying and using finished goods is not an active pastime).[47] Such a moral stance is increasingly at odds with the reality of an economy organized around corporate power, information flows, the manufacture of financial products, mass tourism, and the consumption of services. If we are going to criticize the new urban landscape for its significations, authenticity is not the appropriate value to apply, since deconstruction of the urban environment reveals a reasonably accurate portrayal of the social forces underlying it. Indeed, form is following function.

A deeper critique must instead show that this landscape fails to satisfy important human needs. But to do so puts the critic on the thorny ground of explicating what activities afford genuine as opposed to false satisfaction.[48] The effort to show that theme parks and shopping malls do not afford real pleasure is a reprise of old Marxist claims concerning false consciousness, and it founders on the same shoals of circular argumentation—only acceptance of identical premises concerning values and evidence can lead to the same evaluation of phenomena as genuine or false.[49] Indeed, the popularity of some of the new shopping areas, mixed-use projects, and cultural centers seems to drive the cultural critics into paroxysms of annoyance as they attempt to show that people *ought* to be continually exposed to the realities of life at the lower depths.[50] Thus, a commentator on the Olympia & York projects in London and New York declares: "Both Canary Wharf [in Docklands] and WFC [the World Financial Center at Battery Park City] are spectacular diversions that draw a veil over the realities of deepening social polarization, ghettoization, informalization and burgeoning homelessness which characterize London and New York."[51]

Such analyses place too much blame for social evil on middle-class escapism, in the limited sense of people's preference for looking at a pleasing environment.[52] A negative evaluation of Canary Wharf and Battery Park City depends on whether a feasible better option exists.[53] The alternative for Docklands development proposed by Labour in the 1970s remained unfulfilled because it rested on an obsolete vision of a manufacturing-based economy. Canary Wharf achieved its present success because it provided the type of space needed by expanding firms. Battery Park City was built on a vacant tract of land adjacent to extremely expensive, very intensively used real estate, making it logical to extend the same use pattern. Unlike the predecessor plan for the site, it managed to attract investors' interest, and it represents a far higher quality of development than the earlier plan. Although some of the undertakings I have described—especially the initial schemes for King's Cross and Times Square—were located in places where better practical alternatives were possible, Covent Garden and Battery Park City have arguably made good use of their sites and need not be condemned just because they are pretty or because they cater to the middle class. The cultural critics are frequently in the same uncomfortable position as their modernist predecessors. They justify their ideas in the name of democracy but speak for an intellectual elite, which seems to be as unanimous in its distaste for the new projects as the popular media are concerted in their praise.

The evaluation of authenticity depends heavily on the taste of the observer, and references to a previous golden age when urban life conformed more closely to the model of tolerant diversity are unconvincing. The aspects of the poststructuralist critique based on the assumptions of contemporary inauthenticity and recollections of a better past fail to persuade. Nevertheless, the core of the poststructuralist argument still remains an important starting point from which to assess the impacts of real-estate development in London and New York. The most important concern of poststructuralists is with the relationship between spatial configuration, social diversity, and power in a context where social groups are differentiated by class and culture. This facet of their argument, however, also raises problems, which stem from the tension between majoritarian democracy and respect for difference, especially when identity is defined through membership in an ascriptive group.

Democracy, Diversity, and Cultural Identity

The value that poststructuralists place on diversity arises from a vision of democracy in a multicultural, stratified society. Their attack on architectural repetition and spatial segregation asserts that these modes of spatial development neither respond to democratic preferences nor offer subordinate groups a place in which they can both express themselves and interact peacefully with each other. The weakness of their argument is that if democracy is defined as majoritarianism,[54] most people do not seem to desire diversity. Thus, even though support for recognition of difference arises from a democratic impulse which maintains that people are different but equal and therefore entitled to equal privileges and respect, institutionalized democracy tends to suppress difference. Numerous theoretical and practical attempts have been made to devise a method of combining democracy with difference in the face of majorities demanding conformity, but the underlying contradiction between commitment to majority rule and recognition of the rights and dissonant interests of others remains.[55]

In a comment on my discussion contained in the first edition of this book, Alexander Reichl argues: "We should not drop our concerns about democracy and authenticity in urban life. It is still possible to defend these ideas as valid (and interrelated) principles for judging urban development. . . . Nor would we hesitate to challenge majority opinion on this issue as something sacred and immutable. . . . Public attitudes about segregation are learned responses shaped by biased public policies."[56] He goes on to describe "the ideal authentic public space [as] . . . one where the physical environment supports a diversity of uses and users, thus creating an area for genuine, or relatively unrestricted, social interaction. . . . Where a dictatorial planning power spends seemingly unlimited amounts of money to reshape an area, healthy diversity is precluded. A necessary, if not sufficient condition for authentic places, then, is the absence of overriding control imposed from above on the physical form and its contents."[57]

Although I would not dispute that "an area for genuine, or relatively unrestricted, social interaction" does represent an ideal public space, I am less convinced that it is "authentic." Nor am I persuaded that "the absence of overriding control" would ensure its realization. Like Jane Jacobs, to whom he refers with admiration, Reichl implies that spontaneously produced places will produce a vitality lacking in planned areas. Yet, in the absence of top-down planning the only alternative possibilities are either the market or grassroots participation. The former, if wholly unregulated by zoning, does tend to produce mixed uses, but it rarely if ever produces socially diverse populations. Nor will grassroots participation typically create such a result unless the participants are already a diverse group. Even then, within community organizations single-interest groups, especially homeowners, frequently take over the process. The ideal that Reichl presents is certainly one to be pursued, but it is an elusive one, most easily achieved when the affected groups are heterogeneous but not extremely divided. The best available example in modern Western countries is Amsterdam, where tolerance for diversity is a hallmark, based on a tradition of reconciling differences within a context of cosmopolitanism and considerable economic equality.[58] In other words, a fairly egalitarian social structure underlies spatial heterogeneity. In places with more hierarchical societies, use of space will reflect rather than transform social structure.

An article by David Harvey presents the conflict over access to Tompkins Square Park in New York as paradigmatic of contests over the control of space.[59] Parties to the dispute were the homeless who squatted in the park; motorcycle gangs who raucously convened there; gentrifiers who lived in adjacent buildings; land speculators whose property would appreciate in value if the gentrifiers succeeded in routing the squatters and motorcyclists; anarchist supporters of the homeless who campaigned vociferously and unpleasantly against gentrification; working-class neighborhood residents, many of them immigrants, who disliked the noise, drugs, hostility, and threats to personal safety emanating from the park but also opposed gentrification; and the city government, which eventually used the police to force the occupants out of the park.

The issues raised are classic ones in political theory bearing on the rights of minorities. Opponents of the city's eviction action contend that the government was acting on behalf of real-estate interests, not of the neighborhood (in this interpretation gentrifiers are not considered part of the neighborhood). While that may be the case, it is also true that most residents of the area, including working-class people and longtime occupants, preferred to have the park available for peaceful recreation rather than as a sanctuary for social outcasts. Harvey, to his credit, does not romanticize either the self-proclaimed revolutionaries in the drama or the benefits of the park as a site for cultural mixing.[60] Instead, he remarks: "To hold all the divergent politics of need and desire together within some coherent frame may be a laudable aim, but in practice far too many of the interests are mutually exclusive to allow their mutual accommodation."[61] At this point in the unfolding of his argument, Harvey arrives at the same juncture that he reaches midway in his book *The Culture of Post-Modernity*[62] after he has identified the set of conflicting social interests based on culture and gender that make up the condition of postmodernity. As in the book, he escapes the implications of his thesis regarding mutually exclusive interests by reducing the production of invidious difference to capitalism. Thus, while he does not confuse all social antagonism with class conflict, he dissolves intractable divisions—differences that pit one group irreconcilably against another—by tracing them back to "the material basis for the production of difference"—that is, the capitalist mode of production.[63]

Harvey's logic leads to the old Marxist dream of a society in which group oppression would disappear along with private ownership of the means of production.[64] Harvey's apparent adherence to this vision seems surprising, given the extent to which it has been discredited by attacks from theorists of racial and gender oppression. Since, however, he does not expect imminent socialist revolution, the point is moot. Rather than discussing system transformation, he endorses planning and public policy under the present economic system that would empower "the oppressed" and give them "the ability to engage in self-expression."[65] The implication is that we always know who is the oppressor and who the oppressed, that the claims of the oppressed should always prevail even if they injure other groups, and that it is possible to attain these ends through democratic procedures.

Harvey's aim of restoring materialist analysis to the discussion of urban form is praiseworthy. Materialist analysis, however, should not simply mean rooting all social phenomena in the organization of production. Material interests also rest in rights to real property, not just instruments of production.[66] Privileged positions in relation to both property and consumption (status positions, in Weberian terms) are far more broadly distributed throughout the population than is ownership of the means of production. Furthermore, as Sharon Zukin correctly points out, the organization of consumption is as important as production in determining relations in space.[67] Consequently, a materialist analysis must recognize that a large proportion of the population chooses to exclude others, based on rational calculation and genuine preference. The ineluctable conclusion is that many public policy choices will pit those groups that Harvey designates as oppressed against popular majorities acting on their real interests. And even if the widespread home ownership that underpins middle-class exclusionism is a product of capitalist efforts at legitimation, the interests deriving from it remain real.

There is no easy resolution of the issue of exclusion.[68] The desire of people to live with others sharing similar outlooks and modes of behavior is understandable. Indeed, the poststructuralists are generally willing to grant that right to subordinate groups if they choose to separate themselves, but not to ruling groups.[69] This is not an illogical stance, since subordinate groups are not usually denying others a material benefit (e.g., better schools, access to jobs) in making this choice. Nevertheless, the exclusionism practiced by nonelite groups complicates the problem by undercutting the principle of social integration. In addition, the wish to live in personal safety is obviously legitimate, as Harvey acknowledges,[70] and is most easily obtained through the creation of boundaries. Giving up exclusivity may require real sacrifice of important communal and material values by ordinary people.

In an insightful essay, the political scientist Alan Wolfe contends that the erection of boundaries may be a defensible endeavor necessary for the maintenance of community, even while it is also discriminatory and harmful to those excluded.[71] He concludes by maintaining that there can be no universal moral principle on the subject, that judgments must be issued case by case. With Wolfe's caution in mind, along with the recognition that we must honor democratic process as well as democratic outcomes, we can examine the overall redevelopment strategy followed in London and New York, as well as the particular projects that were erected and their efforts.

WHAT KIND OF PLACE HAVE THE CITY BUILDERS MADE?

London and New York remained the leading centers for financial transactions and associated services during the last quarter of the twentieth century, a fact that was expressed symbolically and materially in their landscapes. The speculative nature of the development process in the 1980s led to the inevitable crash, as too much investment went into expensive real estate for which there was a limited market. At the same time, not all the strategies were wrong-headed, nor were all the projects ill-conceived, and the economic revival of the last part of the '90s made good use of the vacant space left over from the previous expansion. Growing office employment, new technical requirements for information-based industries, and shrinking manufacturing sectors had dictated revision of land uses. Competition among places for growth industries and the prior specializations of London and New York in finance and business services meant that a strategy catering to those industries made sense. Nevertheless, expansion of commercial space and a high-end service strategy did not necessitate the neglect of manufacturing industry, the failure to address the housing needs of low-income people, and government's abdicating to financial institutions and developers the responsibility for decision making concerning developmental priorities.

Redevelopment took the form of islands of glittering structures in the midst of decayed public facilities and deterioration in living conditions for the poor. The symbolic statements made by the new, completed projects were irritating—not because their internal environments were obnoxious in themselves but because of the contrast between them and the remainder of the city, especially in New York. The lead public institutions in implementing the development projects of the '80s—the London Docklands Development Corporation, the London office of the U.K. Department of the Environment, the Battery Park City Authority, the New York City Public Development Corporation—operated in insulation from democratic inputs. By focusing on the construction of first-class office space, luxury housing, and tourist attractions and shortchanging the affordable housing, small-business, and community-based industry sectors, they encouraged developers to engrave onto the landscape the image of two cities—one for the rich and one for the poor. Private financial institutions were an equally important stimulant to the enterprises undertaken by property developers, and they encouraged the same types of developments as did the public agencies. Developers, because these sorts of projects had the greatest potential for profit, obviously wanted to build them and sold them to the government and financiers. While in London the tilt toward the growth coalition abated during the '90s, it has continued in New York.

Two types of developers operated during the 1980s boom: conservative builders, who predicted their returns based on rent rolls and did not build without tenant commitments; and speculators, who not only optimistically forecast fully rented buildings even without preleasing, but based their financial projections on expectations of major appreciation in the value of the structures. The speculative developers both played the most active role in lobbying government to rely on property as the basis for economic growth and caused the overbuilding that produced the crash at the end of the decade. The main difference between the '80s and the late '90s was that all commercial developers became conservative, partly because of their earlier experiences but mainly because financial institutions would no longer lend for speculative office projects. Forest City Ratner, developer of MetroTech in Brooklyn, represented something of an anomaly during the '80s. Although, like developers in the first category, it worked only when tenants already had signed up—and it reinforced the security of its investments by requiring substantial governmental subsidy—it ventured into untried areas where other developers would not go. Ironically, it had much more difficulty obtaining financing than did the highly speculative developers who operated in the most prestigious and already most expensive parts of the city. Its most recent major projects have been in locations that are no longer deemed risky (Times Square and Battery Park City), but it still seeks locations belonging to government-sponsored schemes.

In the aftermath of the 1980s boom, it became clear to both investors and governmental bodies that long-term profitability and growth were injured by the failure to rein in the speculators. Even though economic development was the justification for the pattern of investment that had occurred, no one was responsible for calculating aggregate growth targets. Public officials frequently assert that such projections are outside their realm of responsibility and that it is up to private business to foresee demand and shape supply accordingly. Since public funds and deregulation underpinned redevelopment activity, however, the refusal of government to play such a role presented an irresponsible squandering of public resources. The unwillingness to plan comprehensively meant that too much space for the same kind of use was built on too large a scale, while there was insufficient production of needed housing, public services, and, during the '80s, infrastructure (especially, in New York, efficient transit to the airports, and, in London, access to Docklands). Making financial and business services the centerpiece of each city's development strategy was not in itself a mistake; the error lay in emphasizing these sectors virtually to the exclusion of all else and relying too much on real estate as the method of encouraging them. Highly uneven outcomes were foreordained by an economic development strategy that did not stress job training and placement and did not involve aggressive efforts to identify industries with the potential to generate employment.

Developing Docklands as an office center was not wrong. The availability of a huge tract of mainly vacant land in the heart of the London metropolitan area represented an enormous asset, and one that rightfully should have been developed for the benefit of all Londoners, not just the small number of nearby residents. It was the government's initial refusal to bolster the enterprise with major social and educational programs, to limit competitive commercial development elsewhere, and to construct infrastructure in advance of development that created the debacle of Olympia and York's bankruptcy. The area's later success, once the necessary infrastructure was in place and the London economy had recovered, demonstrated that the type of space constructed filled a need. The favorable opinion of Docklands development given by the majority of Docklands residents to the Cambridge Research Associates evaluation also supports a positive view of the ultimate outcome, if not of the process by which it arrived.

Some of the other projects whose histories I have chronicled were better conceived. Plans for Spitalfields, developed under City Challenge and extended through the Single Regeneration Budget, combined economic and social programming, thereby representing a more sensible approach to area redevelopment than initially occurred in Docklands. The amount of funds committed by the government, however, has been small and may well prove inadequate to support the goals of the plan. Downtown Brooklyn embodies a successful strategy to create a new business district, although the level of public subsidy—through supplying infrastructure, providing tax benefits, and renting space—justifies a greater public share of the profits than was obtained. Battery Park City, despite its luxurious appearance, offers broad benefits. Ongoing governmental ownership of the land has produced significant public revenues for general purposes, for low-income housing, and for the creation of desperately needed green space on the site, which is legally as open to the public as Central Park.

The major schemes, except for New York's 42nd Street Redevelopment Project, can be justified by the same rationale as new towns were. If development nodes are to be established in out-of-the-way locations, substantial front-end investment is necessary to create a critical mass. The periphery of the City of London (site of the Broadgate development), Docklands, the King's Cross railyards, the Battery Park landfill, and downtown Brooklyn all offered prime, vacant, or underutilized territory for large-scale development. The size of structures and types of uses to be placed on them were controversial public policy issues, but there is no prima facie argument against investing substantially in their comprehensive development. The original justification for urban renewal programs—that only through coordinated development of large tracts can central cities maintain their primacy as business sections—holds true. Evaluation of their outcomes requires an examination of who benefits from them and what their environmental effects are. If, in their newness, they have a sanitized quality that contravenes cultural urbanity, we can hope that over time they will become more interesting.

The goal of urban diversity does not need to be met by developing each site for mixed-use, mixed-income, multicultural purposes. The provision of buffers between groups with, in Harvey's words, "interests [that] are mutually exclusive" makes some sense. When he was mayor, David Dinkins liked to refer to the fabric of New York as a "gorgeous mosaic"; in a mosaic, there is proximity but also separation. Creating spaces that many people enjoy, even if they do not faithfully reproduce the past, and even if they make some people feel like outcasts, is not in itself so terrible. If we wish to prevent the upper class from invading working-class neighborhoods or wholly isolating itself in suburban enclaves, then we ought not to forbid the creation of housing and offices for the elite in central places, if this can be accomplished without causing displacement.

London and New York have not channeled pedestrians into skyways and tunnels, as have Minneapolis and Toronto.[72] Their streets continue to teem with people of seemingly infinite variety, and their neighborhoods mainly abut one another rather than being separated by highways or tracts of wasteland. Successful popular opposition to highway construction and mobilization against some of the most egregious attempts to homogenize the environment have been important in maintaining overall diversity. Community participation, however, has not been sufficiently institutionalized to allow the public to influence the citywide allocation of investment or to formulate plans for neighborhood improvements.

The lack of "strong democracy" and heavy reliance on market determinations has meant that political elites and property development interests have mapped the extant city.[73] Christine Boyer describes the situation well:

Public expenditures are written off in the rhetoric of economic vitality as market incentives that have helped private enterprise to reinvest in the city. This privatization of public discourse parallels the privatization of public space. Both bypass, by denial and suppressed linkages, the source of social inequality and conflict. The politics of spatial restructuring are antipolitical in the sense that there is no overall public agenda or city plan and no forum for debate by those affected. Instead of constructing restructuring as a public issue, the spectacle of global capitalism and the power of multinational corporations capture our imaginations, even as they condition our everyday lives and bypass political accountability.[74]

Within the realm of policy making, exclusion has indeed happened. Nevertheless, greater inclusion of the public in developmental decision making would probably not produce the kind of urban environment the poststructuralists seek. Although more resources would find their way outside the central business districts, residents with a vested interest in upgrading the character of their area—including tenants of council housing and rent-regulated structures, as well as both resident and absentee property owners—would try to restrict nonconforming uses and screen out needy persons who threatened their security or lifestyles. Moreover, more democratic decision making would almost certainly favor the interests of moderate- and middle-income people in the allocation of housing funds, rather than giving priority to the homeless.[75]

An overall evaluation of the redevelopment process in London and New York and the role of developers within it yields similar broad generalizations to those made about other cities:[76] Public-private partnerships were unequal; the process resulted in the construction of spectacular projects that changed the appearance and functioning of the cities but left other areas untouched or deteriorated; and overreliance on property development as an economic growth strategy left unpursued other strategies that would develop worker skills and directly spur job creation and placement. My final chapter proposes a more effective mode of incorporating property redevelopment into a general policy for economic improvement.

11

Development Policy for the Inner City

Four intertwined aspects of inner-city real-estate development define the crux of the policy debate: (1) government's use of land development as an instrument for stimulating economic growth; (2) the exclusion of the public from decisions about property; (3) the impact of public and private development activity on the environment; and (4) the influence of public and private development activity on social equity. The fourth issue has two facets: the direct impacts of projects on different social groupings, and the extent to which the public receives the benefits of socially created gain in the value of property.

ECONOMIC GROWTH

One of the themes of this book has been the overreliance of government on the property industry as the vehicle for growth policy. In the short run, during the peaks of the real-estate cycle, the economic effects of property-led development were mixed. Deregulation and assistance to developers did not guarantee that benefits would be translated into increased employment. Moreover, while demand was robust, nothing forced developers to reduce prices to occupants, even when development costs had been lowered by governmental action. It appears that when prices were very high during the 1980s, government subsidy and regulatory relief had an inflationary effect, much of it being capitalized into land values rather than bringing down the cost of doing business. By the end of the 1990s rent levels were exceeding earlier peaks. In London tax relief no longer existed, except in the Isle of Dogs for sites that had obtained exemptions when the enterprise zone was still operative. In New York, however, higher rents were used as justification for ever-larger tax subsidies at a time when the vacancy rate had dropped to virtually nonexistent. Given the paucity of new supply of space, the principal effect of the subsidies was to push land values even higher.

We would like to know if firms were attracted to inner London and New York City because of the various public incentives to development. Unfortunately, there is no clear-cut answer to this question. New York and, to a lesser extent, London did face competitive incentive programs from other cities and their own suburban peripheries which compelled them to offer similar advantages. Part of the attraction of London and New York, however, is an amorphous quality that indicated that they were the right places to be. Perhaps governmental programs contributed to that perception, although it is likely more a result of cultural stimuli than public policy. Moreover, many firms in finance and related industries had to have offices in these global centers, regardless of comparative cost, and developers would have responded to this demand even without publicly provided incentives.

What makes the question genuinely imponderable is the agglomerative nature of urban development. Other attractions outweigh cost disadvantages in locational decision making when a critical mass of skilled workers, market opportunities, supportive alliances, and prestige exists in a place.[1] Would London and New York have had such a critical mass without government prompting? At the beginning of the '80s both cities were viewed as being in serious decline. They overcame this judgment, but to disentangle the role of policy in achieving this result is nearly impossible. Certainly, some credit should go to governmental efforts. The policy issue is how such efforts can be improved.

Economic Planning

Public redevelopment programs and assistance to the private sector can form part of a sensible program for long-term economic growth. They need, however, to be within the context of economic planning. A good economic plan for a city would set levels of desired space for each market sector and each part of the city, with subsidies and regulatory relief geared to these objectives. The aim of policy should not simply be to create more space but rather to ensure that there is enough space to support industry without glutting the market. Such a strategy, in addition to contributing to stable economic growth, would, by maintaining price levels in a sector, make more funds available to government by increasing the property tax base. If government could also participate in development profit in return for its assistance, it would have a further source of revenue.

Economic planning has always been largely anathema in the United States. In the United Kingdom, the Tory government was similarly hostile, but the present Labour government is more sympathetic to at least moderate efforts at economic forecasting and plan formulation.[2] Without unduly interfering with the market, government can identify sectors it will assist and only provide that assistance if businesses within the sector conform to the government's strategy. Such planning would only represent intelligent supervision of governmental expenditure without precluding the private sector from taking risks if it was willing to forgo government help.[3] Whatever errors of forecasting might be made, they could not be worse than offering subsidies and exemptions from planning regulations indiscriminately. The assistance provided developers in London by the London Docklands Development Corporation (LDDC) and the Docklands enterprise zone and in New York by a plethora of incentive programs already constituted market intervention. What they lacked were controls to ensure that the public would gain from these efforts.

Strategies

The governments of both London and New York, in the period under consideration, not only did relatively little to encourage growth in economic sectors unimportant to large property developers but allowed important industries to be injured as a result of high rents. Rather than seeking ways to encourage economic diversity within the central areas, they let speculative office buildings drive out all other uses. Thus, for example, even though many studies have identified the arts as extremely significant components of the economies of New York and London,[4] arts groups were forced out of centrally located space because they could not afford it. Such was also the fate of numerous small businesses and nonprofit organizations. While the New York City government was actively bringing down the occupancy costs of Chase Manhattan Bank and Morgan Stanley, it ignored the situation of drama groups, bookstores, artists' workshops, galleries, acting studios, coffeehouses, and rehearsal halls, which were going bankrupt or losing their leases. In London, within the West End and the City, developers were encouraged to redevelop the peripheral areas that housed "marginal" businesses. It was somehow assumed that such businesses did not have an economic future rather than regarding them as essential components of the complex fabric of the city and the possible progenitors of future expansion.

In the speculative frenzy of the 1980s, developers projected future returns on a linear extrapolation of escalating rents and were therefore willing to pay extremely high prices for land acquisition. They thereby incurred indebtedness which could only be covered through gargantuan buildings and a wholly unrealistic rental structure that was destined to destroy their market as occupancy costs forced tenants out of business. The tragedy for the city as a whole was the destruction of industries ranging from light manufacturing to theater production, which could not easily be restored once cheap space again became available after the boom. During the less speculative upturn at the end of the century, displacement still proceeded at a rapid pace. Shortages of Class A office space encouraged expanding firms to take over buildings previously used by less profitable ventures. In New York the printing and garment industries were particularly affected. In London, in addition to conversions of warehouse and manufacturing space to offices, expensive residences displaced both industrial and office space.

In the conventional theory of land markets, no harm results from constant competition for space and awarding it to the highest bidder. The phenomenon of high rents chasing high profits, however, produces great instability, particularly among retailers, entertainment purveyors, and restaurateurs, as eventually they must raise their prices beyond the reach of their customers in order to pay their rent. The doctrine of "highest and best use" justifies planning that pushes low-return businesses to the periphery and reserves the center for the most remunerative. Theoretically, new nodes of experimental theater can be produced in outlying areas like Lambeth or Brooklyn; craft workshops can move to peripheral locations like Hounslow or Queens. Unfortunately, communities of specialists are not usually portable, and a critical mass may never be reassembled, or at least not within the same metropolitan area. Furthermore, for those industries that require proximity to high-income consumers, the distance between Mayfair and Hounslow, the Upper East Side and Queens, is insurmountable.[5]

Good economic policy would aim to stabilize those sectors that harbor innovation or give the city a unique competitive advantage. London and New York have traditionally been magnets for talented people. In addition, they afford markets for highly specialized businesses that cannot survive elsewhere. Although the gross revenues of such enterprises may not allow them to bid for expensive locations, they create a milieu that gives these cities their special attraction. Policies to encourage economic diversity would reinforce the functions of creativity and specialized activity. Inexpensive refurbishment of older buildings to serve as incubators for a variety of for-profit and nonprofit businesses can assist in fostering originality and maintaining complexity. Very moderate commercial rent control, limiting rent increases to, say, 40 percent upon renewal of a lease and less thereafter, can keep the short-term greed of landlords from driving potentially long-term tenants out of business through rent rises in multiples of the original amount.

Greater emphasis on assisting the nonprofit sector presents another strategy for ensuring stable growth. Within both London and New York an enormous array of nonprofit organizations, ranging from charitable trusts to hospitals to trade groups, provide large numbers of jobs and are much more insulated from global economic competition than multinational corporations. Public-sector investment in appropriate space for such entities can contribute considerably more to steady overall economic growth than high public expenditure to attract front-office facilities of corporations subject to mergers. Outside the central areas, greater financial and technical support for local enterprises would diminish the need to seek ways of attracting outside investors. In New York, community economic development corporations (CDCs) offer a framework for such assistance, which would be much larger if reliable funding sources existed. Secure financing for CDCs would release their staffs from devoting the greater part of their time to raising money rather than operating programs. In London, where the CDC vehicle does not exist, cooperatives offer a similar opportunity.

I part company with many of my progressive colleagues by endorsing large-scale planned development of business centers on vacant or underutilized peripheral sites. The old central business districts of London and New York are overcrowded and distant from populations living in outer areas. Intensifying uses within them is environmentally and socially destructive. Consequently, I think that Canary Wharf and MetroTech, located on largely vacant land in working-class districts close enough to the old centers to attract business, justified government promotion. MetroTech, albeit expensive, succeeded in stimulating the economic development of Brooklyn; its deficiencies lie in the failure of government to ensure that it be connected with job training and placement programs and that the public sector receive more financial return from its sizable input. Canary Wharf, despite its problematic beginning, became a substantial success and allowed firms that otherwise could not have found a place to locate within London to find a home. According to one London financial analyst: "It's the only place in London that you can build premium office space on big sites. There is nowhere in the City that you can build more than a million square feet and have it delivered in three years."[6] More consistent governmental support for the project from its outset might have spared it the trauma of bankruptcy and nearly a decade of losses. In return for pledging this kind of support, the government could have retained rights to the site and obtained ground rent of the sort that the Battery Park City Authority receives in New York.

Improved Public-Private Partnerships

There are four conceivable sources of risk capital for economic regeneration: the private, for-profit sector; the state; employee savings and benefit funds; and the nonprofit sector. Each has advantages and disadvantages. To attract private capital to territories not regarded as inherently profitable by capitalist managers, state officials feel compelled to offer incentives, with all of the likely negative consequences discussed in this book. Direct state participation in quasi-governmental corporations can save failing industries and permits greater public control of the outcomes than state subsidy of purely private entities does. (The effect of Amtrak, the U.S. passenger railroad corporation that connects a number of old U.S. central cities and whose revival has spun off an important employment and retailing multiplier, is a good example of revitalization through the use of this kind of instrument.) Such corporations, though, when they are profitable and capitalized on a large scale, tend to behave little differently from private firms and will also seek least-cost locations.[7] In contrast, firms run directly by the state will be less profit-oriented and, theoretically at least, susceptible to democratic control. They tend, however, to avoid risks, invest insufficiently, and avoid cost-reduction measures.

Critics of business-dominated arrangements who recognize the necessity of tapping into private capital need to devise innovative versions of the public-private partnership. This requires a recognition of the importance of management and entrepreneurship and coming to terms with the multinational corporation. The reality that giant multinational, service-producing corporations dominate economic transactions means that progressive policy-makers must find ways of tapping into their economic power rather than dismissing them on moral grounds. Public-private partnerships under these conditions are inevitable; what needs to be done is to ensure that the public component is more controlling and shares more in the proceeds.[8]

Public-private partnerships can involve the participation of small firms. Public assistance to consulting, computer, high-tech, restaurant franchise, nursing home, home health care, and similar enterprises, as well as small-scale manufacturing, could generate a stable small-business sector to occupy inner-city sites. Such arrangements, however, will raise equity problems. If small businesses are to thrive, they will involve internal hierarchies with returns to managers sufficient to induce competent, experienced individuals to assume those roles. Managers will require discretion in rewarding workers' performance. Under such an approach, social equalization, if it is to occur, would come through redistribution within the tax and welfare system rather than the firm. In other words, even a progressive policy toward inner-city redevelopment will generate serious inequalities in the rewards to labor if it is to stimulate growth.

Eisinger especially emphasizes the expanding public role in identifying product niches for local industry, promoting product development, training workers for firms in expanding areas, and marketing local outputs.[9] The typical version of these endeavors, as in the public-private partnership and the venture capital funds, allows public assumption of the risk and private appropriation of the profit. A better model would be the hotel and convention bureaus of many municipalities, where a tax on receipts supports their marketing efforts. Eisinger notes that some states participate in royalties from inventions resulting from state participation in product innovation. As a general rule, the more public bodies receive a revenue stream keyed to the profits derived from public investment, the better the community can protect itself from the continual undercutting of the public fisc caused by antitax pressures.

Under the Single Regeneration Budget (SRB) the U.K. government has attempted to foster more inclusive partnership arrangements than typically operate in the United States. Every bid for SRB money involves partnerships between business, government, and affected communities. A national, government-sponsored body, English Partnerships, reports to the Department of the Environment, Transport and the Regions (DETR); it implements various SRB expenditures on behalf of the government by investing in areas targeted for regeneration. It thus purchases and oversees the development of land, mediates among stakeholders, and encourages the formation of local partnerships. According to one of its senior executives, "In the '80s there was much more ad hoc development. Now it is much more strategic. . . . Successful developers have to come up with partnership schemes.

Earlier developments failed because they didn't have enough participation. . . . The present planning process takes account of local authorities, local communities." He noted that the partnership approach led to different kinds of projects than had prevailed during the '80s: "Historically property-led schemes did not affect the bottom strata. We now encourage the use of local labor. This is a condition on every planning application—builders must present a policy. And SRB money is linked to training schemes in all the new developments." Unlike Greater London Enterprise, which is unconnected with the government and must be self-financing, English Partnerships does not have to worry about making money on its schemes. Nevertheless, when it gives a grant, it does maintain an equity stake in the project and has clawback provisions to insure a return on any eventual profit.

Numerous local institutions have sprung up in response to these government initiatives and continue on a permanent basis. For example, the King's Cross Partnership was founded in 1995 and consists of representatives of business, the community, government, and housing associations. As well as having put together an SRB bid, it continues to market the area to businesses and potential residents. In combination with other organizations, it runs programs for housing, the environment, job training, community development, and health. Similar coalitions exist throughout London. The rhetoric of these partnerships is inclusive, and bids they put together do combine physical and social programs. Whether the level of social investment is adequate remains an issue.

In New York there is much less public participation in large-scale redevelopment schemes. At the neighborhood level, where such activities are sponsored by community development corporations (CDCs), local small business has representation on CDC boards, and residents may also be involved. There are, however, no requirements connected with the city's redevelopment programs to seek wide input, and federal involvement is minimal. By far the largest city expenditures to promote redevelopment are the various tax forgiveness schemes; no community input is solicited for these, and they simply constitute deals between the city and the business involved.

Recently New York has instituted a "plug and go" scheme whereby it provides marketing money to information technology firms that agree to locate within the outer boroughs or in Harlem. The program shows signs of being successful in attaining its aim of spreading employment to areas outside Manhattan. Like the tax abatement programs, however, it does not involve local participation in decision making. Even without this program, the pressure on land in Manhattan would have forced firms to look further for space. There is considerable concern in the areas zoned for industrial and commercial use within the outer boroughs that these new high-tech firms will inflate rents beyond the means of existing businesses and will not employ local workers. There is no institutionalized forum in which these problems can be addressed.

ht226   THE CITY BUILDERS

PRIVATE DECISION-MAKING AND PUBLIC OVERSIGHT

Developers who work within central business districts are generally inclined to think that they are dangerously overregulated—although London's property entrepreneurs, having experienced the effect of deregulation, had second thoughts and have become much more accepting of planning. To the extent that regulation does exist, it is usually tied to environmental rather than economic effects. Government scrutiny of the financial viability of development enterprises is restricted to evaluating bids for particular sites in response to a government's request for proposals. The high externalities of developmental decisions, however, mean that the consequences of developers' decisions are widely felt. Therefore, as discussed above, economic planning measures are needed.

Greater direct governmental intervention, however, would exacerbate tensions that already exist over questions of representation in planning decisions. The rise of urban development corporations in both London and New York responded to the purported inefficiencies of elected governmental bodies in determining priorities and implementing economic development strategies. These corporations excluded direct community input in their deliberations; in addition, some—like the LDDC and the New York State Empire State Development Corporation (formerly the Urban Development Corporation)—could make land-use decisions without seeking approval from the elected bodies of the territories where they worked. The staff members and boards of these organizations believe that they do their best to represent the interests of the public. They view protesting community groups as narrowly favoring their own interests and unable to conceptualize or sacrifice for programs that would benefit the whole city. The community groups, on the other hand, justifiably feel that they bear the costs of improvements while others realize the gain, that wealthy citizens are rarely asked to give up their privileges for the common good, and that their intimate knowledge of their neighborhoods is disregarded.

I remember attending a meeting between the staff of New York's 42nd Street Development Corporation and the "Midtown Citizens Committee," a community group consisting predominantly of major business executives and other notables in the area.[10] The event took place in the penthouse boardroom of the New York Telephone Company. The concerns of the Clinton neighborhood, which was vehemently opposing the development corporation's plans, seemed as remote to the assembled persons as the pedestrians 42 stories below. To them the working-class populace of Clinton appeared only obstructionist, and their own desire to turn Times Square into a high-rise office district seemed forward-looking and public-spirited. Many of those attending the meeting did not stand to gain personally from the project. None of them, however, was capable of the act of empathy required to put themselves in the place of the vociferous neighborhood residents, who, unlike these suave, well-dressed "citizens," tended to be rude, scruffy, and suspicious of newcomers to the area.

It is an extremely difficult task to devise an appropriate system for land use and economic development planning that takes metropolitan area–wide considerations into account, operates efficiently and effectively, involves citizens in reviewing development proposals without succumbing to the "not-in-my-backyard" syndrome ("NIMBYism"), and responds to initiatives emanating from urban neighborhoods. Because planning must cope with genuine conflicts of interest, trade-offs between long- and short-term considerations, and considerable uncertainty over the results of any project, no process will produce a fully satisfactory result. Nevertheless, the creation of a strategic planning framework, as is currently undergoing formulation in London, can allow inputs at various levels.

The past failures of planners, as evidenced in highway programs, urban renewal, and modernist council estates, make recommendations for more planning suspect. Mine are made on the optimistic assumption that planners can learn from their mistakes, that in fact they were learning at the time the urban renewal program was terminated in the United States and council house-building virtually ended in Britain. Planners had learned to recognize the costs of destroying social communities and developing out-of-scale projects; they had increasingly incorporated citizen participation, housing rehabilitation, and the coordination of housing and social services into these programs in the years before their surcease. There is, therefore, reason to hope that a revival of planning could produce a more sensitive process. Most important, without such an effort urban populations will remain hostage to "private" decisions shielded from democratic scrutiny despite their public significance.

Environmental Decisions

Environmental protection and improvement have been the traditional concerns of public planning. During the 1980s, restrictions on building heights, bulk, and transit impacts were jettisoned in order to encourage development. In New York, planners discovered that they could use zoning bonuses to gain concessions from developers without pecuniary costs to the city. The Corporation of the City of London, threatened by competition from Docklands, threw out environmental restrictions so that developers would continue to build there. Even though systematic extension of the central business district into derelict riverfront sites, with simultaneous restrictions on development elsewhere, represents a superior land-use strategy to intensification of development in already overbuilt areas, the London governing powers abjured such a strategy. This approach would have denied autonomy to the City of London local authority—in conflict with the goal of devolving planning from the metropolitan level—and it would have contravened the avowed intention of the government to overcome obstacles to development. In the actual case, Britain got centralized decision making for Docklands and local jurisdiction for the City of London; this inconsistency produced the worst of all possible worlds, with simultaneous massive development in both places. Although the surplus space was absorbed by the century's end, the roller-coaster ride of boom and bust produced many losers in the interim. Besides financial institutions and property developers themselves, these included the small retail businesses that had hopefully transplanted themselves to the new developments and languished for lack of trade. They also encompassed the employees of all of the businesses dependent on the property sector that laid off workers in response to falling revenues.

Social Equity

Social equity demands a balanced redevelopment policy that addresses the distributional effects of economic development and provides for consumption as well as investment needs. As most studies of redevelopment show, policy aimed at growth had little regard for social impacts. Better policy requires the coordination of economic and social programs, including the integration of employment and redevelopment programs; linking of housing and office construction; much higher and more consistent levels of subsidy for affordable housing; opportunities for small business in publicly assisted commercial developments; measures to ensure that any corporation that received public-sector benefits be prevented from cashing in and then decamping; and clawback provisions requiring that public investment receive a return from profitable enterprises that it stimulated.

The flaw of the usual progressive critique of redevelopment, with which I am otherwise generally sympathetic, is that it focuses on provisions for consumption (housing, parks, day care centers, etc.) and does not offer a formula for growth. So far the left has not discovered an effective method for stimulating substantial investment in declining areas that differs significantly from the business subsidy approach of the Right, except that it would direct more assistance toward manufacturing. The task is to formulate a strategy that is as activist as and less destructive than the modus operandi of typical urban growth coalitions. Social democrats need to do what is necessary to foster incentives and reward entrepreneurship. Without a program for growth, progressives have little chance of achieving or retaining political power. Criticisms of the depredations caused by unregulated capital or prescriptions for cooperative industry are insufficient. Most people will accept growing inequality in preference to stagnation or absolute decline in the standard of living. English Partnerships and GLE are moves in the right direction. Such organizations, however, are always susceptible to business domination if the private sector is providing the bulk of the funding and if market success is the determining criterion of survival.

Advocates for the poor need to be mindful of the political opposition to extremely redistributional programs. In New York, supporters of the homeless insist that their clients should receive absolute preference for subsidized housing. Consequently, they sacrifice the political backing of the middle class and working poor. Moreover, by totally dissociating any criterion of worthiness from eligibility for public benefits, they contravene the deeply held beliefs of most people. Distinctions between the deserving and undeserving poor are indeed invidious. But refusal to recognize that low-wage workers may have as strong a claim to housing assistance as do jobless substance abusers is not clearly the morally superior position. If equality is the only value one seeks to maximize, and if one sees all bad behavior as socially caused, then a purely redistributional policy is consistent. Acceptance of democratic norms that require yielding to majority views, however, as well as a desire to reward individual effort, leads to a more balanced policy that reserves a substantial portion of aid for people who are in want but are not the poorest. To say that everyone who needs it should receive assistance evades the issue of how to set priorities when resources are insufficient to fulfill that goal.

To speak of the tasks for progressive local forces without noting their national context is to dodge a central issue. Cities are limited in their autonomy not only by general economic forces but also by the national political system of which they form a part. Ideological, institutional, and fiscal factors constrain their ability to operate in political isolation from the rest of the nation. Within the United States in the Reagan-Bush years and in the United Kingdom during the Thatcher-Major period, progressive local regimes had to swim against the ideological current. They had difficulty maintaining a broad base of support when the national propaganda attack pictured them as "loony" or unrealistic. More recently, liberal national regimes in the United States and the United Kingdom were more supportive of local advocates for the poor. Blair's "Third Way" purported to locate a path between market and dependence on government—the partnership approach is its embodiment. Similarly, Clinton administration programs aimed at developing community capacity, and the federal empowerment zones directed federal funds to areas outside the central business district. Both national regimes, however, sought to produce inner-city betterment without a substantial increase in government funding.

In contrast, planning and social welfare expenditures still retain much greater legitimacy in the northern European states, and national regimes are less inclined to glorify the free market. In those countries localities have greater capabilities for managing development. Thus, for example, the Dutch state supports 90 percent of local government expenditures, promulgates a national structure plan within which localities do their own planning, and pays sufficiently high levels of income and housing support that no one is extremely poor and the rich are not as rich as elsewhere. The result is that the Amsterdam municipal government constantly presses, with considerable success, for class integration within neighborhoods, prevents encroachment on residential properties by offices, and ensures an active and varied cultural scene.[11]

London and New York, having emerged from the recession of the '90s, remain the dominant economic centers of the world. Good redevelopment policy means nurturing the special attributes of these diverse places so that creativity is not overwhelmed by overspecialization in finance and business services and cultural commodification. It requires recognizing the potential contribution for growth of other sectors in the economy. It further means that first priority be given to the welfare of the mass of citizens and that policy be assessed in terms of its direct effects on the comfort and employment prospects of popular majorities, with particular attention given to its impact on those most directly affected. There is no simple formula for providing growth with equity or efficient yet participatory planning. These, nevertheless, must be the overriding ambitions for policy-makers and the guiding propositions for their efforts at urban redevelopment.

Appendix: Population and Economy of London and New York

Table A.1. Greater London Population, 1931–1998 (in thousands)

		Percentage born in New Commonwealth* & Pakistan	Percentage non-white
1931	8,110		
1951	8,197		
1961	7,992		
1971	7,452	13	
1981	6,696	18	
1991	6,680		20
1998	6,989		25

*Includes the Caribbean, India, Pakistan, Bangladesh, Cyprus, Gibraltar, Malta, and the Far East.
Sources: Great Britain, Annual Abstract of Statistics (London: HMSO, 1987), table 2.8; UK, 1991 Census of Population, Great Britain, Labour Force Survey (London: ONS, 1998).

Table A.2. New York City Population, 1940–2000 (in thousands)

	1940	1950	1960	1970	1980	1990	2000
New York City	7,455	7,892	7,782	7,895	7,072	7,323	8,008
Percentage white[a]	94	90	85	n.a.	61	52	45
Manhattan	1,890	1,960	1,698	1,539	1,428	1,456	1,537
Percentage white	83	79	74	n.a.	59	59	54
Brooklyn	2,698	2,738	2,627	2,602	2,231	2,301	2,465
Percentage white	95	92	85	n.a.	56	47	41
Bronx	1,395	1,451	1,425	1,472	1,169	1,173	1,333
Percentage white	98	93	88	n.a.	47	36	30
Queens	1,298	1,551	1,810	1,986	1,891	1,911	2,229
Percentage white	97	96	91	n.a.	71	58	44
Staten Island	174	192	222	295	352	371	444
Percentage white	98	96	95	n.a.	89	85	78

[a] Individuals of Hispanic origin are included in both white and non-white categories depending on how they identified themselves. The city contained 21 percent of Hispanic origin in 1980, 24 percent in 1990, and 27 percent in 2000. Percentage white is not supplied for the year 1970 because the treatment of those of Hispanic origin in that year differed from the rest of the series. Groups not included in the "white population" are blacks, native Americans, Asian/Pacific Islanders, and "others."
Sources: L. C. Rosenwaike, *Population History of New York City* (Syracuse: Syracuse University Press, 1972); pp. 121, 133, 136, 141, 197; U.S. Bureau of the Census, State and Metropolitan Area Data Book 1986, p. 202, table A; Port Authority of New York and New Jersey, *Demographic Trends in the NY-NJ Metropolitan Region;* U.S. Bureau of the Census, Census 2000, www.census.gov.

Table A.3. London Employment by Industry, 1961–1997 (in thousands)

	1961	1981	1991	% of total 1991 employment	1997	% of total 1997 employment
Manufacturing, mining, energy, and agriculture	1,468	690	399	12	292	8
Construction	281	165	118	4	110	3
Transportation, utilities, wholesale distribution	740	663	954	29	280	8
Retail trade	506	300	n.a.		547	16
Finance and business services	462	593			1,066	31
FIRE			283	9		
Business services			451	14		
Other services	384	265	1,049[a]	32	433	13
Government (health, education, welfare, public administration)	606	890	n.a.		730	17
Total Employment	4,447	3,566	3,354[b]		3,458	

[a] Includes figures for retail trade and government for 1991.
[b] It is estimated that employment in London fell by 251,000 between its December 1988 peak and June 1991 (LPAC, Errata for LPAC 1991 annual review).
Sources: Derived from Nick Buck, Ian Gordon, and Ken Young, *The London Employment Problem* (Oxford: Clarendon Press, 1986), tables 4.1, 4.2; LPAC, *Strategic Trends & Policy, 1991 Annual Review* (London: LPAC, 1991); Amer K. Hirmis, "Labour market and industry structure: Greater London," (London: LPAC, 1991); Great Britain, Annual Employment Survey (London: 1997).

Table A.4. New York City Employment by Industry, 1960–1998 (in thousands)

	1960	1970	1980	1990	% of total 1990 employment	1998	% of total 1998 employment
Manufacturing	949	768	497	346	9.6	262	7.4
Construction	125	110	77	110	3.1	101	2.9
Transportation and utilities	318	323	257	222	6.2	207	5.9
Wholesale and retail trade	745	736	613	614	17.1	588	16.7
Finance, insurance, and real estate	386	460	448	512	14.1	484	13.7
Services[a]	607	785	894	1184	32.9	1,326	37.6
Government	408	563	516	607	16.9	556	15.8
Total Employment	3,538	3,745	3,302	3,595		3,524	

[a]1998 figures are for "Services & misc."
Sources: Temporary Commission on City Finances, The Effect of Taxation on Manufacturing in New York City, December 1976, table 1; Real Estate Board of New York, Fact book 1983, October 1982, table 56; U.S. Bureau of Labor Statistics, Employment and Earnings, 37 (December 1990); The Port Authority of New York and New Jersey, Regional Economy: Review and Outlook for the New York–New Jersey Metropolitan Region, August 1999.

Notes

1. ECONOMIC RESTRUCTURING AND REDEVELOPMENT

1. Logan and Molotch (1987).

2. Turok (1992).

3. While other industries have received subsidies through loans, grants, tax relief, and job training, the sums involved overall have been considerably less than those directed at real-estate development.

4. London Planning Advisory Committee (1991); Commission on the Year 2000 (1987). LPAC was composed of members of the 33 borough councils; at the time this report was written, it was mandated to give advice to the Government Office for London, located in what was—before its reorganization into the Department of Environment, Transport and the Regions—the U.K. Department of the Environment. See Simmie (1994) for a discussion of the LPAC report. The Commission on the Year 2000 was a specially appointed group of notables brought together by Mayor Edward I. Koch.

5. I use the terms real estate and property development interchangeably, although the former term is exclusively an American usage.

6. See Harvey (1973). See also Lamarche (1976) and Massey and Catalano (1978). An important contribution to the discussion in the early 1980s was contained in a number of pieces in Dear and Scott (1981), especially those by Shoukry Roweis and Allen Scott, Chris Pickvance, and Martin Boddy.

7. See especially Balchin et al. (1988); Healey et al. (1992); Healey and Nabarro (1990); Healey and Barrett (1990); Ball et al. (1985); Hamnett and Randolph (1988); Corbridge et al. (1994); Simmie (1994); and Hall (1996, 1998).

Much of the reason for greater activity in Britain than in the United States is the existence of chartered surveying as an academic and professional field in the United Kingdom and its absence in the United States. Training of chartered surveyors involves study of all aspects of the property industry, including public policy; in its inclusiveness and more academic orientation it differs substantially from the training of real-estate professionals in the United States.

Serious work on property development is also under way in Australia and New Zealand. See Berry and Huxley (1992); Low and Moser (1990); Searle and Bounds (1999); and Moricz and Murphy (1997). In Finland, Anne Haila (inter alia, 1988, 1991, 1999) has also written extensively on the subject. On Japan, see Dehesh and Pugh (1999).

8. See, inter alia, Downs (1985); Feagin and Parker (1990); Frieden and Sagalyn (1990); Weiss (1989); Logan (1992); and Smith and DeFilippis (1999).

9. Frantz (1991), p. 3. Shachtman (1991) comments that "these men and their peers [New York City's developers] . . . shared a love of soaring buildings that was more than an appreciation of their worth as pieces of property" (p. 7).

10. Exceptions are the "progressive" cities, where political leadership elected by leftist or antideveloper constituencies has sought to channel development away from typical trickle-down programs oriented toward central business districts into neighborhood endeavors and to extract large public benefits from for-profit developers. See Clavel (1986) for a study of five such progressive cities; Krumholz and Forester (1990) for an examination of the Cleveland experience; Squires et al. (1987) on Chicago under Mayor Harold Washington; Conroy (1990) on Burlington, Vermont; Lawless (1990) on the changing tactics of Labour authorities in Sheffield; Goss (1988), who chronicles the experience of the London Labour borough of Southwark; and Brindley, Rydin, and Stoker (1996), who examine "popular planning" within a London borough and "public-investment planning" in Glasgow. Of the various progressive cities described in the literature, only a minority have managed to maintain a consistent posture over the course of several elected administrations.

11. Among the many works on urban redevelopment that support this story are Fainstein et al. (1986); Stone (1976, 1989); Imbroscio (1997); Saunders (1979); and Brindley, Rydin, and Stoker (1996).

12. Organized in 1943 under the leadership of Richard King Mellon, head of Pittsburgh's leading bank, the Allegheny Conference drew up the plans for the transformation of Pittsburgh from a manufacturing to a service city. The public sector's role was primarily the reactive one of implementing the Allegheny Conference's strategies. The partnership between private and public sectors was institutionalized within the city's Urban Redevelopment Authority. See Sbragia (1990).

13. Jonas and Wilson (1999); Molotch (1980); Mollenkopf (1978).

14. Rydin (1998); Fainstein and Fainstein (1978).

15. Harloe et al. (1992); Harloe (1995).

16. The first two postwar Labour governments sought to nationalize all undeveloped land.

17. See Balchin et al. (1988), chapter 9.

18. See Saunders (1979).

19. Ambrose (1986), pp. 98–103.

20. Greater London contains 33 local authorities (i.e., municipal governments). Thirty-one of them are called boroughs; two (Westminster and London, which compose the central business district) are called cities. The City of London contains the financial district and frequently is referred to simply as "the City."

21. Pickvance (1981).

22. Hamnett and Randolph (1988); Badcock (1984), pp. 162–68.

23. Forman (1989).

24. A number of studies are explicitly comparative and reach something of a con-

sensus concerning the similarities in the impact of global economic restructuring on U.K. and U.S. cities and on the direction of urban policy in the two countries during the 1980s. See Parkinson et al. (1988); Barnekov, Boyle, and Rich (1989); Savitch (1988); A. King (1990); Sassen (1991); S. Fainstein et al. (1992); and Zukin (1992).

25. Rydin (1998).

26. See Imrie and Thomas (1999).

27. Green (1991).

28. Among the many studies that reach the conclusions summarized in this paragraph, see Parkinson and Judd (1988); Squires (1989); and Logan and Swanstrom (1990b) on growth strategies and their economic and social impacts; see Ambrose (1986); Sennett (1990); and Sorkin (1992b) on impacts on diversity and the environment.

29. See Cox (1991), who doubts the theoretical coherence of the empirical literature.

30. Dahl (1961).

31. See Wolfinger (1974); Domhoff (1978); Polsby (1963); Bachrach and Baratz (1962); and Yates (1973, 1977) for discussions of New Haven in relation to the power-structure debate.

32. Wolfinger (1974).

33. Paul Peterson's (1981) controversial argument that economic development programs enjoy consensual support goes over Dahl's and Wolfinger's New Haven findings once again, ignoring all of the subsequent studies that undermine that conclusion.

34. See Fainstein and Fainstein (1986a).

35. Bachrach and Baratz (1962).

36. See, for example, Stone (1976).

37. The literature on American urban redevelopment is enormous. See especially Altshuler (1965); Beauregard (1989); Caro (1974); Cummings (1988); S. Fainstein et al. (1986); Friedland (1983); Judd and Parkinson (1990); Logan and Swanstrom (1990b); Mollenkopf (1983); Parkinson et al. (1988); Rosenthal (1980); M. Smith and Feagin (1987); Squires (1989); Stone (1976, 1989); Stone and Sanders (1987); Swanstrom (1985); and Wilson (1966).

38. Early important works on British planning, housing, and development activities include Foley (1972); Pahl (1975); Young and Willmott (1957); and Marriott (1967).

Peter Hall's (1963, 1973, 1989) immensely influential works on urban growth and change were more directed to influencing policy-makers and thus less critical of observed trends than were those within the structuralist tradition. But even he criticizes "conservationist planning" for protecting the upper-class way of life while crowding the working class into "a more sanitary version of the labourer's cottage of a century ago" (Hall et al., 1973, p. 628). These, however, are not, according to Hall, the "true victims" of the planning system; the biggest losers are the poor, occupying private rental housing in the central city, who cannot gain entry into either the suburban owner-occupier market or the public housing sector.

Additional British studies of redevelopment include Simmie (1974, 1981); Saunders (1979); Marris (1987); Brindley, Rydin, and Stoker (1989); and Goss (1988).

39. See Judge, Stoker, and Wolman (1995).

40. See, for example, Sternlieb and Hughes (1975); and P. Peterson (1981).

41. Dahl (1961); Polsby (1963).

42. Savitch (1988).

43. Ibid., p. 7.

44. Swanstrom (1993).

45. Mollenkopf (1978); Molotch (1980); M. Smith (1988); and Harding (1995).

46. Harvey (1985a), p. 190.

47. The attacks on Harvey's formulation that pepper the literature (see, e.g., Saunders, 1986, chapter 7; and M. Smith, 1988) accuse him of regarding the results of urban political controversies as predetermined to favor capital rather than subject to contingency and the intervention of human agency. In fact, while Harvey lapses into mechanistic language in his more abstract theorizing, he more than anyone has looked historically at the agency through which redevelopment has occurred (see the long chapter on Paris in Harvey, 1985b).

48. Castells (1977).

49. See Preteceille (1981).

50. David Imbroscio (1997) traces current (American) regime formation to "the 'external economic dependence' and 'internal resource dependence' of city public officials. The first refers to the need for city officials to attract and retain mobile economic investment; the second, the need for those officials to garner extrastate resources from the local community in order to govern their cities effectively" (p. xv).

51. See Haila (1991) for a summary of the various theories and for a discussion of the economic functions of land markets and the return to investment in land and property.

52. Harvey (1985c) is more generally concerned with the functions of rent in allocating land uses and coordinating the flow of capital into the built environment. These functions and the impacts of different types of rent need not concern us here.

53. Elkin (1987), discussing the meaning of a business-dominated regime, comments: "The heart of the entrepreneurial political economy was the business elite's ability to create and maintain a political system in which those who held elected and appointed office did not have to be told what to do" (p. 68). Norman Fainstein and I (1986b) use the term "directive" to describe those urban regimes that planned large-scale redevelopment with little opposition and consequently made few concessions to nonelite interests.

54. Stone (1989), p. 234. Italics in original.

55. Painter (1997), p. 133.

56. See Stoker (1995).

57. Stone (1993), p. 11.

58. Lauria (1997); Harding (1994).

59. Balbus (1971), p. 167. Italics in original.

60. See Cox (1991); and my response, S. Fainstein (1991a).

61. In later work Cox comes closer to this position. See Cox (1997).

62. See Beauregard and Haila (2000).

63. There is, of course, a marked difference in vocabulary: "economic development" versus "capital accumulation"; "businesspeople" versus "capital"; "rate of return," "profit," or "earnings" versus "surplus value"; "recession" versus "crisis of accumulation."

64. Stone (1993) states that regime theory "recognizes the enormous political importance of privately controlled investment, but does so without going so far as to embrace a position of economic determinism. . . . Regime analysts explore the middle ground between, on the one side, pluralists, with their assumption that the economy is just one of several discrete spheres of activity, and, on the other side, structuralists, who see the mode

of production as pervading and dominating all other spheres of activity, including politics" (p. 2).

65. See Cooke (1989); Harloe, Pickvance, and Urry (1990); N. Smith (1987); M. P. Smith (1988); and S. Fainstein (1990a).

66. See Swanstrom (1988).

67. Fisher and Peters (1998); *New England Economic Review* (1999). Nestor Rodriguez and Joe Feagin (1986), whose thesis is rooted in a left critique of governmental action, come to a contrary conclusion regarding the efficacy of local action. They investigated the factors historically causing cities to occupy specialized positions in the world economic system. They deny that the capture of a niche results from the logic of the invisible hand—that is, it is not simply a product of automatic response to market forces. They argue instead that the existence of specialized economic centers is rooted in the political actions of business leaders, who force their ambitions on local government, which acts as an agent of their interests both in directly providing them with assistance and in lobbying higher levels of government. Thus, which one of a limited group of competitors for a particular slot—e.g., financial center, oil service industry capital—prevails depends on the activities of local business and governmental elites.

68. P. Peterson (1981).

69. Sanders and Stone (1987).

70. Logan and Swanstrom (1990a).

71. See M. P. Smith (1988), chapter 1.

72. Gourevitch (1986).

73. Not surprisingly, political scientists affirm the salience of politics, while geographers insist on the importance of space.

74. Castells (1989) also strongly emphasizes the coordinating function of financial capital in overcoming the friction of distance in his discussion of New York City.

75. Sassen (1991, 1994).

76. The concept of agglomeration advantages, originally developed in the nineteenth century by Alfred Marshall, has taken on renewed importance in recent research by economic geographers and economic development strategists. In particular, the work of Michael Porter has been central, and his article on the competitive advantage of inner cities has been extremely influential (Porter, 1995). The specialization of the central business districts of London and New York in financial and business services, as Amin and Thrift (1992) argue, can be analyzed as a case of industrial clustering. Likewise, the enhanced importance of areas within central cities as entertainment districts results from similar processes.

77. The ambiguity of the antecedent to "them" here is deliberate. One suspects that the concern is not just over omissions in regard to spatial determinants but also to the isolation of the discipline from other social sciences.

78. Soja (1989), p. 47.

79. See N. Smith (1984).

80. N. Smith (1979) coined the term "rent gap" to describe this potential as it applies to the gentrification of housing.

81. Massey (1995).

82. See Friedmann and Wolff (1982) and Friedmann (1986) for presentation of the "global city hypothesis." For research on global cities, see Savitch (1988); A. King (1990);

Sassen (1991, 1994); Fujita (1991); Mollenkopf and Castells (1991); S. Fainstein, Gordon, and Harloe (1992); Sudjic (1992b); and Knox and Taylor (1995).

83. Saskia Sassen (1991) is the most searching in her inquiry into the root causes of global city status, but she fails to differentiate the behavior of the real-estate industry from that of financial and business services.

84. See Appendix for employment data on the two cities.

85. See Appendix.

86. S. Fainstein (1990b).

87. As of this writing, elections for the council had not been held.

88. Thornley (1999); S. Fainstein and Young (1992).

89. Buck and N. Fainstein (1992).

90. Information supplied by Andy Thornley.

91. I carried out almost all of the interviews personally, but a small number of the New York ones were conducted by a research assistant.

92. Patsy Healey and Susan Barrett (1990) support a similar approach: "The critical task for the analyst seeking to understand the processes of production of the built environment is an examination of how such *external pressures are reflected in and affected by the way individual agents determine their strategies and conduct their relationships as they deal with specific projects and issues, and as they consider their future stream of activities*" (p. 90). Italics in original.

93. Harvey (1982) provides an extensive discussion of "fictitious capital." While real property is a significant component of fictitious capital, the term includes all values based on anticipated revenues and thus is not specifically spatial. Its management requires evaluation of investment opportunities, structuring of deals, and allocation of capital.

2. THE DEVELOPMENT INDUSTRY AND URBAN REDEVELOPMENT

1. Linda Davidoff was executive director of the Parks Council, a civic group active in New York City. The quotation appears in "Senator Ohrenstein Reports to Manhattan," a 1992 newsletter to his constituents from state senator Manfred Ohrenstein.

2. No date (1990?), p. 17. This glossy, expensively produced magazine is published by one of Britain's largest and most internationalized firms of charted surveyors.

3. T. Wolfe (1987), p. 57.

4. The 1981 Tax Act shortened the period for computing depreciation on real-estate investments to 15 years from a range between 22 and 40 years, thereby stimulating an explosion in real-estate syndication operations. Passive investors in a real-estate project could deduct huge paper losses from their taxes on the basis of a relatively small investment in the project; therefore, they invested in real estate (i.e., became part of a syndicate developing or owning a property) not because of its potential profits but because of its effect on their tax return. The syndicators received large fees, the investors gained major tax benefits, and the developers did not have to promise a positive rate of return in order to attract funds (Downs, 1985, chapter 6).

5. The spectacular profits achieved by Ranieri did not involve direct investment in new construction but rather the provision of a facility by which the deregulated savings and loan industry could acquire liquid capital through unloading disastrous real-estate loans

and simultaneously purchase mortgage bonds underwritten by Salomon, representing the nonperforming loans of other thrift institutions. Since the federal government guaranteed the mortgages and also insured depositors, it bore the final cost of the wave of real-estate and banking defaults that eventually swept over the country at the end of the 1980s. (See Lewis, 1989, chapter 6.) The sums listed seem less grandiose by the standards of the late '90s, when speculation in Internet firms created even greater fortunes. For their time, however, they were extraordinary.

6. Keynote address to the joint conference of the American Collegiate Schools of Planning (ACSP) and the Association of European Schools of Planning (AESOP), Oxford, U.K., July 1991.

7. Mollenkopf and Castells (1991).

8. See Buck and N. Fainstein (1992).

9. Logan (2000); A. Markusen and Gwiasda (1994).

10. Bram and Orr (1999); McCall (1998).

11. See Sassen (1991); Leyshon, Thrift, and Daniels (1987); Thrift, Leyshon, and Daniels (1987); Thrift and Leyshon (1990); Pryke (1991); Castells (1989, chapter 6); Beauregard (1991); and Healey, 1990.

12. Sassen (1991), p. 19. Castells (1989), like Sassen, devotes most of his discussion of the New York economy to an analysis of capital markets. See also Buck, Drennan, and Newton (1992).

13. Leyshon, Thrift, and Daniels (1987) define a swap as "the exchange of debt obligations between two counter-parties which is designed to take advantage of differing interest rates or currency opportunities that each can obtain" (p. 19). Thrift, Leyshon, and Daniels (1987) characterize the swap market as the most important new market and credit it with bringing about an increasingly integrated world financial system.

14. While there had always been high-yield bonds, it was Michael Milken, of the investment banking firm Drexel Burnham Lambert, who gave them the sobriquet "junk" and transformed what had been a minuscule sector of the financial markets into what became their largest and most profitable sector during the height of the boom. See Bruck (1989). Ultimately, Milken was convicted of securities fraud.

15. In the United States, for commercial banks and savings and loans (S&Ls) that were paying interest rates to depositors higher than the returns they were receiving from mortgages, and for insurance companies that were forced to lend money against life insurance policies at rates lower than the price of new funds to them, solvency depended on finding highly profitable investments. Mortgage securitization allowed banks to liquefy their old loans at a discount to their face value and invest the funds released in potentially more remunerative offerings. S&Ls, which had been freed from restrictions limiting their investments to home mortgages, were most affected by mortgage securitization and used their sudden liquidity to become most involved with high-risk instruments. They were particularly impelled to do so because of the asset loss resulting from the write-downs on their mortgage loans, although the pain of this loss was partially compensated for by a tax break allowing them to offset their losses against any taxes paid over the previous ten years (Lewis, 1989, pp. 103–4). The subsequent collapse of the junk-bond and real-estate markets produced the ensuing wave of bank and S&L failures.

16. In the United Kingdom, building societies are roughly equivalent to U.S. savings banks (also called thrift institutions), and the major commercial banks are referred to as clearing banks.

17. Pryke (1991), p. 210.

18. Between 1977 and 1986 the number of employees of foreign banks and security houses in London more than doubled, from 24,294 to 53,833 (Thrift, Leyshon, and Daniels, 1987, table 5); in New York City foreign bank employment alone (excluding securities houses) grew by 25 percent, from 125,000 to 149,000 between 1979 and 1988, expanding from 15 to 24 percent of all bank employment (Byrne and Shulman, 1991, figure 4). In 1990 there were 450 foreign banks in London and 479 in 2000 (GLE, 2000, p. 26); in 1990 there were 392 in New York; the number had grown to 450 by 1993 (PANYNJ, 1991, figure 20; 1994, p. 4).

19. Sassen (1991), p. 78–83.

20. See Amin and Thrift (1992).

21. Schwartz (1992, 1994).

22. The study found that of the suburban-based Fortune 1,000 industrial companies for which data were available, all use Manhattan-based investment bankers, 89 percent use Manhattan-based law firms and commercial banks, 59 percent use Manhattan-based auditors, and 43 percent use Manhattan-based actuarial consultants (Schwartz, 1992, p. 15).

23. Burrough and Helyar (1990).

24. Sassen (1991).

25. Ibid., p. 19. Castells (1989, p. 343), who acknowledges the influence of Sassen's work on his own, likewise attributes spatial concentration to the functional need for control over dispersed production networks: "What explains this striking paradox of the increasing concentration of global flows of information, controlling global flows of capital, in a few congested blocks of one particular city? Several elements seem to be at work. The first is the concentration there of high-level directional corporate activity in the U.S. economy."

26. Sassen (1994), p. 67.

27. See Schwartz (1992).

28. Buck, Drennan, and Newton (1992), p. 99.

29. My own calculation.

30. Buck, Drennan, and Newton (1992), p. 99.

31. See Pryke (1991); Harloe and S. Fainstein (1992).

32. Bruck (1989) tells the story of the move of the headquarters of Triangle Industries, an industrial firm in New Brunswick, New Jersey, into Manhattan. Although seemingly contradictory to my argument, it actually illustrates it. The move was not occasioned by the needs of the firm's tiny wire manufacturing operation but by the personal desires of its owner, who, using junk bonds arranged by Drexel Burnham, transformed it into a shell for the purposes of taking over the National Can Corporation. National Can itself remained in Chicago, and Triangle's wire-manufacturing enterprise ultimately folded. Thus, while Triangle Industries was nominally a manufacturing firm when it moved into Manhattan, in fact it was really a financial holding company.

33. Castells (1989), p. 10.

34. Castells (1985); Moss (1986); and Sassen (1991).

35. Coopers & Lybrand Deloitte (1991a).

36. Daniels and Bobe (1990).

37. Walls (1991), p. 1.

38. Byrne and Shulman (1991), p.13.

39. Ibid. Other things being equal, real-estate investors prefer to put their resources into already large markets because of the greater possiblity they offer for selling assets and thus for providing liquidity (Dijkstra, 1991). Between 1985 and 2000 Jersey City added 10 million square feet of office space, and an equal amount was being planned for the next five years. Rents in Class A space in New Jersey in 2000 were $32–35 per square foot, as compared to Manhattan's $40–$60 per square foot (Traster, 2000, p. 61).

40. Figures available for Tokyo are so extremely discrepant that I have not shown any estimate.

41. U.K. DoE (1991); PANYNJ (1991). While most investment was in office space, there was considerable hotel construction, especially in Manhattan, where the number of rooms in major hotels increased by 32 percent, from 45,000 in 1980 to 57,301 in 1990 (REBNY, 1987, p. 10). In both London and New York much of the office development was for mixed use, involving retailing on the ground floor.

42. The construction of Battery Park City in New York on landfill adjacent to Wall Street technically constitutes new development rather than redevelopment. Its absolutely central location, however, implies that even though there had been no preexisting use, it involved a restructuring of the core.

43. See U.K. DoE (1991), tables 1.3 and 9.1. In terms of contribution to the value of new housing construction, the public sector constituted about one-third over the 1980–87 period. While public exceeded private investment in 1980, the private share steadily increased and was 3.7 times the public's in 1987 (ibid., table 1.3).

44. Hamnett and Randolph (1988); Harloe, Marcuse, and Smith (1992).

45. Stegman (1988), pp.199–200. London's net gain in units exceeded New York's because of a much lower rate of demolition and abandonment, not because of greater new construction.

46. Lee (1999), table 4.1.

47. See Chapter 5.

48. Stegman (1988), table 9.1.

49. Lee (1999), table 4.2. Data on conversions are not available for the period 1987–1992.

50. REBNY (1985, 1990).

51. Smyth (1985), chapter 7; Ambrose and Colenutt (1975).

52. Morley et al. (1989), chapter 1.

53. In an interview, Rupert Nabarro, managing director of the Investment Property Databank, estimated that 50 percent of the property developed in the 1980s boom years had been produced by five development companies: Olympia & York, Speyhawk, Stanhope, Greycoat, and Rosehaugh.

54. Mollenkopf (1983).

55. Harding (1994), p. 374.

56. Pryke (1991).

57. See Chapter 9.

58. Thornley (1991); Ambrose (1986).

59. U.K. DoE (1989), p. 5.

60. The developers I interviewed indicated that they bypassed boroughs (usually Labour-led but also Tory environmentalist) which they regarded as uncooperative.

61. Before the introduction of the uniform business rate in 1990, local authorities lacking business ratepayers received a compensating central government grant. Once

the uniform rate was in place, no locality could increase its revenues through attracting business.

62. Where published sources are not cited, material is drawn from interviews I conducted.

63. Daniels and Bobe (1990).

64. Key, Espinet, and Wright (1990), p. 17.

65. Ibid. (1990), p. 40.

66. Jones Lang Wootton (1987), p. 3.

67. PANYNJ (1988), p. 6.

68. In New York, assessed values declined by 8.6 percent in fiscal year 1992 from the previous year (New York State OSDC, 1991, p. 12).

69. AT&T sublet its Upper East Side world headquarters to Sony at a reported price of $20 per square foot, barely more than half the ostensible average rent for the area (*Barron's*, 1991, p. 10). It was also reported that the Bank of Nova Scotia sublet some of its downtown space to a financial firm for $12 a square foot after a one-year rent-free period (*Crain's New York Business*, 1992). Rental figures also fail to reflect the deals—for example, free provision of fixtures, buyouts of current leases, etc.—that most developers had to offer to attract tenants.

70. During the 1974 U.K. property crash, when prices dropped by 40 percent, the vacancy rate was only 11 percent (*Economist*, 1990, p. 82).

71. Comparable statistical information is not available for New York, where development firms are privately held and thus not subject to the disclosure requirements of public corporations.

72. Byrne and Kostin (1990).

73. S. Fainstein (1992). In 1991 these two banks together held $4.1 billion in outstanding real-estate loans, $1 billion in foreclosed property, and $6.7 billion in foreclosed and problem loans. In even more serious trouble was Citicorp, New York's largest bank, which held $7 billion in outstanding loans, $2 billion in foreclosed property, and $14 billion in foreclosed and problem loans (*Barron's*, 1991). These loans, of course, were not restricted to New York City.

74. *Crain's New York Business* (1991a). In addition to its direct effects on jobs and the use of space within the restructured banking organization, the merger caused the downsizing of a number of firms that provided services to its two predecessors, since now only one supplier would be required.

75. Barrett (1992).

76. More than 60 banks, many of them foreign, had participated in syndicates underwriting the Trump properties. Peter Kalikow, another of New York's best-known speculative developers, sought bankruptcy protection in mid-1991. His more than $1 billion in debts was owed primarily to New York banks. He also owed the city more than $1 million in real-estate taxes (*New York Times*, 1991).

77. *Financial Times* (1991).

78. See Chapter 9.

79. To induce tenants to move into its two large new developments, O & Y bought out their existing leases. Consequently, in addition to owning a number of older buildings in the two cities, it held the leasehold of many more blocs of space.

80. Complicating depiction of its London holdings was its participation in the equity of other large development firms, including Stanhope, of which it owned 20 percent.

81. Of 66 third-world debtors, at the peak of the third-world debt crisis in 1987, the bank debt of only four (Argentina, Brazil, Mexico, and Venezuela) exceeded $18 billion (U.S. Bureau of the Census, 1991, table 1486).

82. Feagin and Parker (1990), p. 84.

83. The tax benefits were such that investors could rent out apartments at a price less than their carrying charges yet make a profit as a consequence of their tax situation. They achieved this because they could claim the rapid depreciation of the entire cost of the unit as a deduction on their personal income tax, even while they had borrowed most of this cost.

84. U.K. DoE (1991), table 6.4. Housing associations receive a subsidy from the central government's Housing Corporation, but they operate autonomously and are responsible to private boards.

85. The city had initially planned to spend $1.34 billion between 1992 and 1996 on subsidies for affordable housing; a reduction of nearly 38 percent ($510 million) was proposed (*New York Times, * 1992f).

86. *New York Times* (1992a).

87. REBNY (1987, 1990).

88. *Crain's New York Business* (1991b). In the office sector, despite continuing contraction, lower rents did succeed in forestalling moves to the suburbs that had previously been contemplated by Manhattan firms (*Crain's New York Business, * 1992).

89. GVA Grimley (1998), p. 1.

90. GLE (2000a), table 3.

91. Between 1993 and 1998 an estimated 9.2 million square feet of office space was converted to residential or hotel use, and a further 5.1 million square feet was planned (London Property Research, 1999, p. 23).

92. GVA Grimley (1999), p. 1.

93. GVA Grimley (2000), p. 2.

94. GVA Grimley (1999), p. 1.

95. Hamnett (1994).

96. The stipulations concerning developer contributions are known as Section 106 agreements. The equivalent term for planning gain in the United States is exactions.

97. Because of the differing policies of the various local authorities, the discussion of London that follows includes separate depictions of parts of central London as well as an analysis of the whole.

98. Byrne and Kostin (1990).

99. In 1981, 22 conservation areas, affecting 28 percent of the land area in the City, were designated.

100. The City is governed by a Corporation, consisting of 159 common councilmen and 26 aldermen. Unlike the borough councils, whose members are selected only by residents, members of the Corporation of the City of London are chosen by business firms as well as the small resident population. Approximately 14,000 voters, the majority of whom are not residents, elected the members of the Corporation. Changes in the electoral system have recently been instituted, but not only has the principle of allowing businesses to vote been maintained, but businesses formerly excluded have now received suffrage rights.

101. Until the 1980s the City did not have a planning officer but only an architect, who concerned himself with design approvals.

102. See Chapter 9.

103. Jones Lang Wootton (1987), figures 14 and 17.

104. Corporation of the City of London (1999).

105. Interview, January 11, 2000.

106. Between 1993 and 1998 more than half a million net square feet of office space had been converted into hotels and residences within the City, and an additional 735,000 square feet was planned (London Property Research, 1999).

107. In 1985–1989 Westminster added somewhat over 4 million square feet of office space, or about 25 percent of the City's total (Byrne and Kostin, 1990).

108. Although the East Side cannot lay claim to residents as illustrious as the Queen and the Prime Minister or buildings as exalted as Westminster Abbey and Buckingham Palace, it does contain the United Nations and its associated embassies, as well as the city's most desirable residential addresses.

109. In 1990 Westminster contained 12,000 listed (i.e., protected) buildings.

110. In addition to commercial pressures on the housing stock, demand for short-term leases by business visitors inflated prices beyond the reach of prospective permanent residents.

111. Westminster (1988).

112. Information supplied by LDDC, January 1989.

113. Goss (1988), p. 92.

114. Ibid., p. 101.

115. P. Newman and Smith (2000).

116. Southwark Council (n.d.).

117. Interview, January 6, 2000.

118. Edwards (1992). Peter Hall chronicles the controversy over the siting of Britain's new National Library within Camden. He comments on the original plan, which involved extensive demolition within the Bloomsbury section of the borough: "Few decisions can ever have excited such instant obloquy from the British establishment" (Hall, 1980, p. 177). Somewhat similar to New York's West Side in social composition, home to several colleges of the University of London and numerous cultural institutions, Camden housed many highly articulate citizens who, as on the West Side, made common cause with working-class neighbors on development issues.

119. See the detailed discussion of the King's Cross project in Chapter 6.

120. Greenwich Peninsula was the site, in 2000, of the Millennium Dome, intended to be London's showpiece for that year's celebrations. Instead, it turned out to be a planning disaster, failing to even come close to its predicted number of visitors and being a widespread object of derision in the media. See Thornley (2000).

121. Buck, Drennan, and Newton (1992).

122. Aron (2000), p. 50.

123. Holusha (1999); Rothstein (1998).

124. Williams (1996), p. 35.

125. Croghan (2000a), p. 3; Dunlap (1998).

126. Nicholas Lemann has observed that, even in cities formerly characterized by strong business leadership, the effect of large corporate ownership has been to cut the ties between local capitalists and their cities throughout the United States: "One associates the toppling of [local] establishments with busts, as in the case of the Great Depression. . . .

But today it is the boom that is toppling them, by buying and trading the institutions they formerly controlled" (Lemann, 2000, p. 44).

127. *Crain's New York Business* (1992), p. 11.

128. In the second fiscal crisis that began in 1989, business leaders, with the exception of Felix Rohaytn, partner in Lazard Frères and head of the Municipal Assistance Corporation, largely withdrew from a prominent role. It was alleged that the reason for their previous assiduousness and more recent passivity is that whereas in the mid-1970s New York banks had invested heavily in New York's bonds, this time they had ensured that they would not be seriously at risk. See Fainstein (1992).

129. See Sleeper (1987); Newfield and DuBrul (1981); and Barrett (1992).

130. See Fainstein and Fainstein (1988).

131. A zoning variance refers to permission exempting a developer from a regulation contained in the zoning code. The zoning code specifies the type of use (e.g., office, manufacturing, etc.) to which a parcel of land may be put; the height, bulk, and density of the structure; its relationship to the street; the presence of curb cuts, etc.

132. The numbers refer to sections of the governing statute.

133. Bagli (1997a).

134. Bagli (1997b, 1999a).

135. Bagli (1999b).

136. Bagli (2000c); Sandler and Ip (2000); Kolbert (2000).

137. The *Times* itself was pursuing a tax deal for its proposed new home on Eighth Avenue.

138. A lengthy piece by Jason Epstein (1992) in the influential *New York Review of Books* made the city's failure to support manufacturing and its heavy support of real-estate growth the cornerstone of its argument concerning the reason for the perceived deterioration of New York. Written in 1992, however, within the context of a completely dead real-estate market, it represented a rather belated response.

139. Barrett (1992) characterizes a Sunday *New York Times Magazine* profile of Trump as "fawning" (p. 311).

140. *New York* (1987), p. 50.

141. *Newsweek* (1987), p. 52.

142. A zoning bonus refers to permission to exceed the space limits contained in the zoning law.

143. Air rights existed when a building did not take full advantage of the "envelope" allowed it in the zoning ordinance. Essentially, a building owner who did not use up the entire envelope could sell the unused portion to the developer of an adjacent site in the form of rights to that amount of space.

144. A study of a sample of buildings that received bonus floor area in exchange for the provision of amenities estimated that the market value of the benefits received by the developers was $108 million, while the cost of the amenities they provided was about $5 million (New York State OSDC, 1988, p. MS-3).

145. NYCPC (1981).

146. Information supplied by the Real Estate Board of New York.

147. In 1986 Mayor Koch introduced the Ten-Year Housing Plan, aimed at producing, preserving, and rehabilitating 252,000 affordable housing units between 1987 and 1996. See Chapter 5.

148. More than 12,000 units of expensive housing, more than twice the previous year's amount, were started in 1985, the last year of the program. REBNY (1990).

149. Between 1985 and 1990, 5.4 million square feet went up on the midtown East Side, 7.8 million on the midtown West Side, and 17.7 million downtown. Information supplied by the Real Estate Board of New York.

150. Lentz (2000a).

151. See Chapter 7. Even people who live in the Bronx, Brooklyn, Queens, and Staten Island refer to Manhattan as "the city" and their own location as "the boroughs." In London the usual distinction is between central London, comprising the area formerly within the jurisdiction of the London County Council, and "the outer boroughs." Most of the outer boroughs more closely resemble New York's suburban area rather than its boroughs. The area beyond the London Green Belt is called "the outer metropolitan area"; it roughly corresponds with New York's peripheral suburban area.

152. Fainstein and Fainstein (1987).

153. Trager (2000).

154. Ratner (2000).

155. SERPLAN (1992), p. 3.

156. PANYNJ (1992), pp. 6–8.

157. Jobs in motion pictures jumped by more than 24,000 between 1992 and 1998, representing a compound annual growth rate of 13.2 percent. Next largest, in percentage terms, was business services, which grew by 75,200 jobs, or a compounded rate of 5.1 percent from a much bigger base. PANYNJ (1999), Exhibit 13.

3. MARKETS, DECISION-MAKERS, AND THE REAL-ESTATE CYCLE

1. See, for example, Lichtenberger (1991), who presents an institutionalist analysis; Mills (1980), J. R. Markusen and Scheffman (1978), and Sweeney (1977), who examine market determinants using econometric modeling techniques; and Weiss (1991), who looks into the political influence and objectives of the industry at various points in the cycle.

2. Bagli (2000b).

3. The real-estate literature emphasizes the ease of entry into the industry and pictures it as a highly competitive arena. While this depiction is partly accurate, it really does not apply to large-scale projects for which access to major amounts of credit is essential. Only a handful of firms are capable of raising hundreds of millions of dollars for a project.

4. As the case of 7 World Trade Center in New York indicates, such assurances do not necessarily hold. This nearly 2 million square foot building had been intended to house Drexel Burnham Lambert; that firm, however, had declared bankruptcy by the time the building was completed and did not occupy it. It finally became the home of Salomon Smith Barney.

5. Taylor (1986), p. 29.

6. In 1986, Manhattan had the lowest vacancy rate of any major U.S. office market, being one of only three cities with rates below 10 percent. Fourteen of the 21 major office markets had vacancy rates exceeding 14 percent; Denver, with the highest, had a rate of 26 percent (REBNY, 1987, p. 8).

7. Barrett (1992) notes that Donald Trump always assumed he could unload his holdings on a greater fool.

8. Leitner (1994) also argues that property booms are a consequence of the supply of finance.

9. Many of Donald Trump's troubles arose because he pledged his personal credit on a number of his projects.

10. The establishment of a secondary market in home mortgages by Fannie Mae in the 1930s preceded by more than 60 years the use of tradable securities for office buildings. See Hu and Pennington-Cross (2000) on the importance of securitization.

11. Downs (1985), chapter 10.

12. See Leyshon, Thrift, and Daniels (1990).

13. See McNamara (1990).

14. Barrett (1992), p. 320.

15. REBNY (1987); Colliers International Property Consultants (1991).

16. See Newfield and Barrett (1988).

17. Pryke (1991); Meuwissen, Daniels, and Bobe (1991).

18. I have not displayed the different rates by city as I did in the first edition, since the sources I have consulted are extremely inconsistent. Recent currency fluctuations, particularly the rise in value of the dollar and the pound and the decline of the Euro, mean that translating rents into dollar equivalents is highly distorted and estimates vary considerably depending on the exchange rate chosen.

19. The fashion in office buildings has proved changeable. For a while demand switched to slimmer structures that offered many private offices with windows. Then, with the '90s stock market boom, the drive for large trading floors resurfaced. The rise of media and Internet firms led to yet different kinds of space needs, with industrial-style loft spaces favored.

20. I owe thanks to Patsy Healey for her clarification of this point to me.

4. POLICY AND POLITICS

1. Robert Moses held public office from 1924 to 1968. During that time he possessed a number of titles, none of which gives a full indication of his power. The most important was as head of the Triborough Bridge and Tunnel Authority. Lewis Mumford contended that "in the twentieth century, the influence of Robert Moses on the cities of America was greater than that of any other person" (quoted in Caro, 1974, p. 12).

2. See Buck and N. Fainstein (1992).

3. Lawless (1989).

4. Mackintosh and Wainwright (1987).

5. The evolution of this organization is discussed later in this chapter.

6. Marris (1987).

7. Barnekov, Boyle, and Rich (1989).

8. Danielson and Doig (1982).

9. A prime example of this capacity is New York City's system of rent regulation. Anathema to the national Republican administration, it nevertheless endured despite, under the Reagan presidency, efforts to cut off federal aid to cities that controlled private-sector

rents. These efforts never got very far, primarily because they would have constituted federal intervention in a local matter and thus strongly contravened federalist principles whereby cities are creatures of state rather than national government.

While federalism has enhanced the capacity of local regimes to enact policies different from those of the national government, it has typically protected private enclaves of power from national regulation and limited the development of the national welfare state (Robertson and Judd, 1989).

10. Loughlin, Gelfand, and Young (1985); Hambleton (1989).

11. This area was governed by the London County Council until the formation of the GLC.

12. Whereas in the United States the term "authority" refers to a nonelected body with the power to issue revenue bonds, in the United Kingdom it is used to denote both elected and nonelected bodies with governing powers.

13. Travers (1986).

14. New York City has a "strong mayor" system, meaning that the mayor has the power to hire and fire the heads of city departments. Although the city council is nominally coequal to the mayor, in reality it is a much weaker entity.

15. The Board of Estimate consisted of the mayor, with three votes; the city council president and controller, with two each; and the borough presidents, with one vote apiece. It was declared an unconstitutional violation of the principle of one person, one vote by the U.S. Supreme Court in 1989. The equal voting power possessed by the borough presidents had given the same representation to Brooklyn, with its 770,000 registered voters, as to Staten Island, with 170,000.

16. Marcuse (1987).

17. Citizens Budget Commission (various years).

18. Until 1990, New Jersey's income tax was considerably lower than New York State's, while Connecticut had no income tax at all. New York City has its own income tax, on top of the state's; residents of suburban municipalities typically pay no local income tax, although they must pay state income taxes. There is wide variation in property tax rates, licenses and users' fees, and nuisance and sales taxes among municipalities and among the states. In 1991 Connecticut introduced an income tax. Even so, residents and businesses in New York City still pay a higher proportion of their income and revenues in taxes than do similar groups outside the city.

19. Clawson and Hall (1973); Foley (1972).

20. The United States and New York State and City do have more elaborate regulations concerning the environmental impacts of all kinds of projects than does the United Kingdom, and unlike London, New York requires mitigation of negative environmental effects.

21. Each London local authority is required to produce a "unitary development plan." In contrast, New York's community boards have been empowered to develop local plans only since the 1990 Charter revision. The formulation of such plans is, however, optional, and only some boards actually do so.

22. Buck, Gordon, and Young (1986), chapter 2.

23. See Rydin (1998).

24. U.K. DoE (1989), p. 5.

25. During the late 1980s borough control was equally divided between the two parties, with the single Liberal Democratic borough of Tower Hamlets holding the balance.

26. LPAC (1988, 1994, 1996).

27. Unless otherwise indicated, quotations are drawn from my interviews. This interview took place in 1989.

28. Smothers (2000).

29. To reach Hoboken or Jersey City, two of the municipalities on the Hudson waterfront, requires only a four-minute ride from the World Trade Center in downtown Manhattan via the Port Authority–owned PATH train.

30. Prokesch (1992a).

31. New Jersey has two important state planning endeavors that guide new development: the Meadowlands Authority and the state land-use plan. The Meadowlands Authority wields planning powers over a swampy area a few miles west of Manhattan, which had remained partially undeveloped for much of the century; the area under its control includes parts of a number of communities. It has succeeded in promoting large-scale commercial and residential development as well as a major sports complex, despite friction with subordinate municipalities. Governmental units within its boundaries share the tax revenues from new development.

The state land-use plan seeks to channel growth within certain municipalities while restricting development elsewhere. While protecting rural parts of the state, it does not limit development within the already dense cities that lie between the Palisades, a rocky ridge to the east of the Meadowlands, and Manhattan.

32. Fainstein and Fainstein (1978), pp. 139–42.

33. Jenkins (1988).

34. Rees and Lambert (1985); Buck, Gordon, and Young. (1986); Townsend (1987).

35. Krieger (1986).

36. Thornley (1999), p. 187.

37. Goss (1988).

38. In 1981 approximately 18 percent of the population of Greater London was born in the New Commonwealth and Pakistan; the proportion of people of color in the population did not increase considerably in the following decade, as a result of the United Kingdom's strict immigration laws. In contrast, 39 percent of New York City's population was classified as nonwhite in 1980, the proportion increased to 48 percent in 1990, and to 55 percent in 2000. Groups not included by the census in the "white" population are blacks, Native Americans, Asian/Pacific Islanders, and "others" (see Appendix).

39. Glassberg (1981); Parkinson (1987), pp. 2–7; Pickvance (1988).

40. HM Treasury (2000); *Economist* (2000).

41. At the time the community charge was established as the principal form of local taxation, the Conservative government exempted businesses from local taxation and instead set up a national business tax, effective in 1991, that would go directly to the national treasury, then be dispersed to local authorities on a formula basis. Local authorities that had previously benefited from the presence of industry within their boundaries were held harmless by this policy—that is, the amount they received under the previous system could not be diminished—and thus the policy did not sacrifice the future revenue streams of the affected boroughs. The tax had the effect of reducing incentives among jurisdictions to compete for industry.

42. Smallwood (1984), p. 4.

43. Mackintosh and Wainwright (1987); O'Leary (1987).

44. D. King (1989).

45. Under Section 106, any new residential development exceeding 20 units must contain provision for social housing.

46. The Harlem/South Bronx Empowerment Zone is the result of a similar contest to those called for by the SRB; empowerment zones, however, are a limited program, and so far, no city has more than one of them.

47. Core members were Marks & Spencer, HSBC, BT, United Biscuits, Sainsbury's, John Laing, Cadbury, Schweppes, Corporation of London, Diageo, Lloyds TSB, Unilever, the Post Office, and Whitbread. LEntA's aim was to "exemplify how the coporate sector can take a lead in tackling social and economic exclusion" (GLE, 2000b).

48. GLE (2000b).

49. Its director, Greg Clark, claims that GLE in 2000 was the single largest landlord for small businesses in London, owning 2 percent of the market.

50. John Lindsay's victory as a liberal Republican in 1969 marked the last time a Republican won the mayoralty until the election of Rudolph Giuliani in 1993. The city council is overwhelmingly Democratic.

51. Mollenkopf (1988).

52. Until the elimination of the Board of Estimate, its members were the final arbiters of all development decisions. A study by State Senator Franz Leichter's office showed that campaign contributions to Board of Estimate members in 1984 and 1985 came predominantly from real-estate interests and financial institutions. Of the total $8.5 million raised, 16 large contributors were responsible for half; of that amount, real-estate interests accounted for $3 million, while $1.2 million came from financial institutions. Much of this money was donated while the contributors had major items before the Board of Estimate (Mollenkopf, 1992, p. 95). The transfer of decision-making authority from the Board of Estimate to the city council has not cut into the ability of developers to obtain approval for their plans in the face of community opposition. Thus, in 1993 the council voted to approve Donald Trump's application for his huge Riverside South development on Manhattan's Upper West Side and also assented to a plan to build a garbage-burning incinerator in Brooklyn (Dunlap, 1993).

53. Fainstein and Fainstein (1974).

54. McCormick, O'Cleireacain, and Dickson (1980), after comparing twelve large cities, concluded that New York City paid neither the most nor the least, although in examining seven job categories they found New York's employees predominantly within the upper half.

55. Shefter (1985); Morris (1980).

56. Sternlieb, Roistacher, and Hughes (1976); Zukin (1982); Tobier (1979); and Hudson (1987).

57. Mollenkopf (1992).

58. Koch (1984), p. 221.

59. Tabb (1982); Alcaly and Mermelstein (1976).

60. Interpretations of the1975 fiscal crisis have been heavily contested. Radical critics blamed the city's plight on overspending for capital accumulation and the rapacity of banks and political insiders. They argued that the crisis was deliberately provoked so as to discipline the city's government (see Tabb, 1982; Marcuse, 1981).

Liberal defenders pointed to obligations like higher education, public hospitals, and welfare borne by the city government for which higher levels of government took responsibility elsewhere. They contended that the crisis would not have happened if New York State had shouldered its appropriate burden (Morris, 1980). Within the electoral arena, however, the interpretation of excessive attention to the poor at the expense of the middle class prevailed with the election and successive reelections of Edward Koch.

61. Staten Island had been the home of Fresh Kills, the city's last remaining landfill. The mayor promised to close it in 2001 despite the absence of a viable alternative. He also invested $71 million in a minor league baseball stadium and associated development. In return for a modest rent, the team would pay no money for construction and receive the majority of revenues for any events booked into the stadium when the team was not playing (Bagli, 2000a).

62. Lambert (2000).

63. Income of the top quintile grew by 29 percent between 1989 and 1997 (Fiscal Policy Institute, 1999), and the number of households showing more than a million dollars a year in income nearly doubled between 1994 and 1997 (*New York Times,* 2000).

64. Fiscal Policy Institute (1999), table 1.2.

65. His term was to end in December 2001.

5. ECONOMIC DEVELOPMENT PLANNING STRATEGIES

1. The many criticisms along this line include, inter alia, the arguments of Altshuler (1965) that the planner's limited knowledge makes special insight into the public interest and comprehensiveness impossible; of Gans (1968) that planning expressed the interests of the upper classes; and of Harvey (1978) and Foglesong (1986) that it is primarily oriented toward capital accumulation and, on the occasions when it is concerned with equity, toward legitimation.

2. See Dror (1968); Faludi (1986, 1987).

3. The depiction here refers to those planners participating in what Beauregard (1990) calls the city-building process.

4. Teitz (1989).

5. Boyer (1983).

6. Klosterman (1985).

7. Levy (1990).

8. Harvey (1978).

9. Fainstein and Fainstein (1985).

10. Foglesong (1986).

11. Stewart (2000).

12. Although the transfer station was to be a private facility, it had been proposed in response to Mayor Giuliani's promise to close the Fresh Kills landfill and his intention of relying on shipping residential waste out of the city. The Organization of Waterfront Neighborhoods, which opposed the siting of transfer stations exclusively in low-income neighborhoods already heavily affected by waste-transfer stations for commercial refuse, were demanding an alternative plan (Bautista, 2000). Because newly instituted term limits meant that the mayor's tenure in office had to end in 2001, delaying tactics would ensure consideration by a new administration. In fact, Giuliani capitulated to the opposition and eventually backed off from his original plan.

13. Kahan (2000).

14. Eventually this plan was defeated.

15. Interviews with Nick Roberts of Chelsfield (January 11, 2000) and Harvey Marshall of the Westminister council (January 10, 2000).

16. Interview with Michael Keith, January 13, 2000.

17. Dunlap (2000).

18. Lentz (2000b), p. 4; see also Dunlap (2000).

19. Canary Wharf and Battery Park City are unusual among recent projects in the extent of the government role in supplying land, infrastructure, and facilities. The additional advantages that government gave developers through tax forgiveness meant that these projects exceeded earlier renewal/regeneration programs in the amount of governmental largesse. They have also, however, required a larger private contribution for public purposes than had characterized earlier projects.

20. Columbus Centre is the largest development project begun in the new century (see Chapter 2). The one proviso imposed by the city was that it include theater space to accommodate Jazz at Lincoln Center (Dunlap, 1998).

21. Alterman and Kayden (1988).

22. In a theoretical discussion of the incidence of exactions, Dick Netzer (1988) concludes that they "are far from perfect substitutes for the ideal ways of privatizing the financing of the private goods aspects of urban public services that cannot be entirely removed from the public sector: Explicit marginal cost-based user charges would be better. But exactions, when properly structured, can be a reasonably good second-best solution" (p. 49).

23. Rosslyn Research Limited (1990).

24. New York's Uniform Land Use Review Process (ULURP) sets forth a series of hurdles through which a project must pass before ultimately receiving city council approval.

25. Bagli (1991). As initially proposed in the mid-'80s, Trump's plans for what was then called Trump City included a regional mall, a 150-story tower, and a line of 60-story buildings blocking views of the riverfront; together these structures would encompass 14 million square feet. The new proposal reduced the project size to 8.3 million square feet as well as providing the various contributions called for by the community groups. Although a number of community organizations agreed to the project, others remained opposed and viewed the acquiescences as sellouts.

26. See Lassar (1990); Squires (1989).

27. Rees and Lambert (1985).

28. Parkinson and Evans (1990).

29. Marris (1987); Brindley, Rydin, and Stoker (1989).

30. LDDC (1988a).

31. *Guardian* (1988).

32. See ALA and DCC (1991); and DCC (1988). The ALA was the association of borough councils under Labour leadership, and the DCC was an advisory body to the Docklands boroughs; it was funded by the affected local authorities and no longer exists.

33. Lawless (1987); Church (1988a, b).

34. U.K. DETR (1998a), p. 7.

35. Sampson (1998), p. 149.

36. U.K. DETR (1998a), p. 7.

37. Rhodes and Tyler (1998).

38. Brownill, Razzaque, and Kochan (1998), pp. 58–59.

39. The SRB was introduced in April 1994. It combined 20 previously separate programs (U.K. DETR, 1998b, p. 2).

40. The Peabody Trust, for example, in 2000 managed 17,000 units, and some managed more than 40,000 (interview with Dickson Robinson, director, Peabody Trust, January 12, 2000).

41. U.K. DoE (1991), table 6.5.

42. In 1987, 2,578 units of social housing were constructed by housing associations and local authorities in about equal number. By 1992 almost no more council housing was being built, but housing associations were responsible for the building of nearly 4,000 units. In the peak year of 1994, housing associations constructed 7,779 units, and local authorities put up 488. By 1999, however, total social housing constructed amounted to only 2,885 units, all of it built by housing associations (information supplied by U.K. DETR, July 1, 2000).

43. S. Fainstein et al. (1986), chapter 1. New York used most of its CDBG for rehabilitation of city-owned, tax-foreclosed housing. In contrast, it had used urban renewal money for massive rebuilding of large areas of the city, mainly in Manhattan.

44. Eisinger (1988).

45. Fainstein, Fainstein, and Schwartz (1989).

46. *New York Observer* (1988).

47. Lin (1991). The change from PDC to EDC mainly involved consolidation of the city's old Department of Ports and Trade into the new agency.

48. In 1992 the City Planning Commission released a comprehensive plan for waterfront development (Dunlap, 1992a). A product of a new commission under the directorship of a Dinkins appointee drawn from academe, the document represented the first serious attempt by the agency to chart the course of development in two decades. It had no binding power, however, and development of the waterfront has proceeded only slowly and piecemeal.

49. It lost these powers in the rest of New York State, where its initial efforts to build housing for low-income people in suburban areas stimulated massive, politically potent resistance.

50. Any community group may incorporate itself simply by filing a form with the U.S. Internal Revenue Service and paying a small fee. It then becomes a "501(C) (3)" organization, so named after the section of the Internal Revenue Code designating its tax status. For housing development corporations, such filing usually occurs at the initiative of a community group that wants to develop housing or qualify for a public program; for business development organizations, it often occurs when the city government or a foundation is seeking an entity to manage services in a neighborhood and sets up a geographically based corporate structure with a local board to receive funds. There is not a precisely equivalent category within the United Kingdom. Community enterprises and cooperatives carry out similar functions, but there are far fewer of them than CDCs in the United States, and they do not possess a special status under the tax code.

51. LISC and the Enterprise Foundation rely partly on philanthropic contributions for their financing, but most of their funds are drawn from the tax credit program. LISC

was founded in 1979 by the Ford Foundation. It provides funds in the form of loans, grants, recoverable grants, guarantees, lines of credit, and equity investments (information supplied by P. Jefferson Armistead, vice-president, LISC, May 4, 1992).

52. Information supplied by P. Jefferson Armistead, February 20, 2000.

53. In rem housing is acquired by the city government through tax foreclosure.

54. Fainstein and Fainstein (1987).

55. Stegman (1988), pp. 45, 47.

56. New York City DHPD (1989), p. 1.

57. Typically these houses contain a rental unit, which assists the owner in meeting his or her mortgage obligation.

58. Mittlebach (1991).

59. Schwartz (1999), p. 845.

60. Lambert (1991).

61. Schwartz (1999).

62. Van Ryzin and Genn (1999), pp. 800–802.

63. Schwartz (1999), p. 865.

6. KING'S CROSS AND TIMES SQUARE

1. Unless otherwise indicated, information on the cases and quotations come from interviews I conducted between 1989 and 1992 and in 1999–2000.

2. See Squires (1989) for discussions of American cases and Brindley, Rydin, and Stoker (1996) for British examples.

3. Different documents describe the site as anywhere from 125 to 150 acres, depending on whether or not they include railroad uses.

4. The government eventually decided on terminals at Stratford and King's Cross. At the time that planning for King's Cross began, the government had not yet made its final routing decision on the connecting line to the tunnel.

5. Edwards (1992).

6. Although not all of its plans came to fruition, BR proposed developments around all the major stations. At the same time as it was working on its King's Cross enterprise, it was also participating in a large-scale proposal for the Paddington Station area in Westminster. As discussed in Chapter 2, Broadgate adjacent to Liverpool Street Station already represented the largest redevelopment project in London outside of Docklands, and London Bridge Station formed the core of another large redevelopment area.

7. Rosehaugh Stanhope was itself a partnership of two firms. Rosehaugh was headed by Godfrey Bradman, characterized by the *Financial Times* (1991) as "once the highest flying property developer on the stock market"; Stanhope's chair was Stuart Lipton, one of the most respected developers in Britain. Thirty-three percent of the ownership of Stanhope and 8 percent of Rosehaugh were in the portfolio of Olympia & York (*Observer,* 1992).

8. Edwards (1992).

9. Camden (1988).

10. Camden (1989a, b); *Camden Citizen* (1990); *Financial Times* (1992).

11. Camden (1989c).

12. Ibid.

13. The critique is contained in King's Cross RLCDG (1989); see UCL Bartlett School (1990) for the alternative plan.

14. Communication from Michael Edwards, June 1, 1992.

15. UCL Bartlett School (1990), chapter 3.

16. Some of the firms classified as manufacturing actually had different functions as their principal activity. Important groups of firms included construction and construction supplies; haulage and distribution; vehicle repair and hire; theater suppliers; hotels and cafés; and nonprofit organizations.

17. UCL Bartlett School (1990), p. 37.

18. Parkes, Mouawad, and Scott (1991).

19. *Financial Times* (1992).

20. Bradman is currently one of the principals in the development of Paddington Basin.

21. See Chapter 9.

22. In New York the insistence by the Triborough Bridge and Tunnel Authority, which owned New York's old convention center, the Coliseum, on accepting the highest bid for its land also resulted in a building plan that aroused fierce objections to its size (see Chapter 2).

23. Saint Pancras and King's Cross Stations sit side by side.

24. Interview with Michael Edwards, January 10, 2000.

25. English Partnerships (1999).

26. Interview with Joan Toovey, January 12, 2000.

27. The two towers had received public subsidies and had been intended for middle-income owner occupancy. The location, however, deterred middle-class purchasers, and the city was desperate to fill the building. It ultimately received Section 8, low-income housing commitments from the federal government to subsidize rentals. Because, however, the structures were envisioned as a vehicle to raise the social class of the neighborhood, the city did not wish them to be occupied by the typical impoverished recipients of public subsidies. It, therefore, restricted occupancy of most of the units to households with members in the performing arts, thereby ensuring a tenant body that had a middle-class lifestyle if not a middle-class income. From the city's point of view, the ploy worked extremely well as the buildings filled up rapidly and sustain a long waiting list. Since they were originally built to high standards, the carrying costs of the structures are substantial and the subsidy per apartment extremely large; the subsidy, however, is borne by the federal government, not New York City.

28. This strip is being upgraded once again, as the original buildings are being slated for demolition and replacement. The uses, however, will remain the same (see below).

29. See Chapter 2.

30. These proposals all featured entertainment uses. Among the failed ideas were a 15-story Ferris wheel to provide the centerpiece of an indoor amusement park and a "car-o-rama" featuring automobiles rotating on a moving belt behind a high glass facade.

31. Show World, as this multilevel enterprise is called, contains a large store selling pornography and sex equipment and theaters devoted to X-rated films and live sex acts. Although reduced in size, it was still in business in 2000.

32. When, finally, two of the office buildings went up at the turn of the new century, they were able to command premium rents, reflecting the new stylishness of Times Square. The subsidies, however, were not reduced and thus seemingly represented a grant to the landlord.

33. The contribution to the subway station was to be $90 million; $14 million, with an inflation adjustment, was to go toward renovation of the nine theaters.

34. Dunlap (1988).

35. Interestingly, while the playfulness of the new signs seems to arise from a postmodernist architectural orientation, the effect of fitting the signs on the buildings was to force them into a modernist mold: "It's much easier to graft exterior lighting and commercial signs onto a modern form than a classically inspired one. Can you do classical pediments and column capitals in neon?" (Goldberger, 1990).

36. Times Square BID (1999).

37. Stasio (1989).

38. The *New York Times,* whose editorial offices are located in the Times Square area, has generally supported the project, which promised to enhance the value of its real estate and the atmosphere of its surroundings. Its architectural critic, however, although normally a fan of Philip Johnson's work, joined in the vitriolic assessment of the project's architectural merits: "The project's design, never any great shakes to start with, has come to seem a truly depressing prospect as the years have gone on, making this surely one of the only major works of architecture to look utterly out of date before it was even started" (Goldberger, 1989a).

39. Philip Johnson had by then retired, but he continued to act as a consultant to Burgee.

40. The stress on honky-tonk contrasts with the traditional modern architect's commitment to purity of design. If one evaluates this impulse charitably, one sees in it a reflection of the insights of Robert Venturi, Denise Scott-Brown, and Steven Izenour's *Learning from Las Vegas,* which famously declared that "BILLBOARDS ARE ALMOST ALL RIGHT" (1977, p. 6). One can also regard it as just the latest faddism on the design front. Comments by the architects could uphold both interpretations: "Asked why the original plans . . . had not reflected the character of Times Square, Mr. Burgee and Mr. Johnson said trends in architecture as well as public opinion have changed. . . . 'A big revolution in architecture happened in those six years,' Mr. Johnson said. 'We wanted to make a unified impression; we were going to make a great new Times Square, like Rockefeller Center. Now, besides the popular reaction—let's have more lights and people—inside the architecture profession we changed from classicism, like the A.T.&T. Building and copying the 1920's, to something we call the new modern'" (Goldberger, 1989b).

41. Chira (1989).

42. Goldberger (1989b).

43. Prudential, which either wholly owns or participates in a number of large projects throughout the United States, differs from most insurance companies in pursuing an active role as a developer (P. Grant, 1989). Among its holdings were the Embarcadero Center in San Francisco, Century Plaza Towers in Los Angeles, Town Center outside Detroit, and the Prudential Center in Boston.

44. Manufacturers Hanover and Chemical Bank later merged; then both were acquired by Chase.

45. New York City PDC (n.d.); Stuckey (1988).

46. Hoff (1989).

47. Mollenkopf (1985).

48. In Manhattan's West Side Urban Renewal Area, to the north of Clinton, the project area committee had played an important role in monitoring and changing the renewal plan throughout the 1960s and into the 1970s.

The termination of the federal urban renewal program in 1974 abrogated its citizen participation requirements, which had been built up over the years in response to protests over its neighborhood impacts. The CDBG program, which replaced urban renewal in the 1974 act, had only a vague mandate for citizen input. Under Republican administrations the federal government withdrew from oversight of local CDBG expenditures. The program, at any rate, has shrunk in size to inconsequentiality. Because CDBG funds are so limited, central business district redevelopment is rarely conducted using federal subsidies and thus need not comply with federal regulations.

49. Project supporters accused Leichter of fronting for competing developers who had contributed to his campaigns. He responded that the politicians favoring the project had accepted far larger contributions from George Klein, the designated 42nd Street developer at that time.

50. Including potential interest costs that the city would have to pay if it was forced to borrow from the developer to meet land costs, Leichter calculated that the total public subsidy could equal $1.5 billion. While this might be an overestimate, the city will incur substantial interest payments on its borrowing to support land acquisition, causing its overall subsidy to include considerably more than simply foregone taxes and infrastructure investment.

51. These buildings did receive the benefits of the more permissive zoning regulations under the special midtown zoning and of a standard ICIB tax abatement for new commercial construction.

52. Douglas Durst, the eventual developer of the Condé Nast building, who for years opposed the Times Square project, was quoted as saying: "They've turned 42nd Street into a desolate area, decreased the value of surrounding property and eliminated about $3 million in tax revenues. They've managed to completely louse things up" (*Crain's New York Business,* 1992).

53. P. Grant (1990).

54. McKinley (1994).

55. The 42nd Street theaters catered to specialized tastes. A *New York Times* reporter interviewed former viewers after the auditoriums were shuttered: Fans "wish they could still watch a one-armed kung fu master. They are angry at the demise of the world's finest concentration of movie theaters devoted to zombies, nymphomaniacs, aliens, chainsaws, surfers, martial artists, cannibals and, of course, women in prison. . . . The government redevelopers insist they will put cheap entertainment—perhaps even action movies—back in some theaters, but the promises have not appeased serious students of The Deuce's [i.e., 42nd Street's] movies. These are the kind of film critics who classify works into such subgenres as beasts-on-the-loose, stalk-and-slash, sword-and-sandal, and bimbos-behind-bars" (Tierney, 1991).

56. Dunlap (1992b).

57. Municipal Art Society (1994).

58. Martin (1993).

59. Bagli (1992).

60. Neuwirth (1990).

61. Pulley (1995).

62. The developer of the building was Douglas Durst, who, along with his father, Seymour, had lobbied vigorously against the renewal plan. Prudential reached a settlement with George Klein, the developer originally designated (Croghan, 2000b). He sub-

sequently returned to the scene as part of a consortium headed by Boston Properties'
Mortimer Zuckerman that successfully bid for the two remaining office sites on the south
side of the street. (Zuckerman had been the original developer of the Coliseum site but
gave up control in 1994 (see Chapter 2). The consortium paid $330 million for the land
(Leonard, 1998).

63. Holusha (1998).

64. The architectural critics of the *New York Times* have praised the requirement that
buildings have large signs and allocate part of their structures to entertainment uses. For
example, Herbert Muschamp (1998) commented: "It [Times Square] is well on its way to
becoming the media center of the world. . . . With the retail and entertainment center also
taking shape here, the area should become the globe's liveliest meeting ground for the producers and consumers of popular culture. And the new buildings, bedecked with signs, will
express that social mix in visual form." Yet the *Times*, which is itself planning a new building on the site originally designated as a wholesale mart (Eighth Avenue across from the
Port Authority Bus Station), has indicated that it would prefer not to meet the requirements
for signs and entertainment uses (Bagli, 1999c). Reportedly, the *Times*, which has frowned
on tax giveaways, is asking the city for a substantial tax break and other incentives (Bagli,
1999c). Interestingly, the *Times* reporter who covered this story was unable to get any confirmation from the newspaper itself and relied on leads from government officials.

65. Times Square BID (1999).

66. Ibid., p. 18.

67. Sassen and Roost (1999), pp. 153–54.

68. Reichl (1999), p. 179.

69. Overall crime dropped 57 percent between 1993 and 1999, and robberies fell by
78 percent (Times Square BID, 1999, p. 28).

70. Ibid., p. 18.

71. Berman (1997), p. 82.

72. See Martinotti (1999).

73. Brendan Sexton, at that time president of the Municipal Art Society, remarked:
"The office towers only became possible after entertainment pulled Times Square out of
the muck. We'll now get two big, blunt office towers on two scrawny sites [on the south
side of 42nd Street]. Given the level of public subsidies, New Yorkers should get some
fabulous buildings, not just two towers like any others in Manhattan" (quoted in Bagli,
1998). Sexton later became head of the Times Square BID.

74. A project on the far western part of 42nd Street, where a group of off- and off-
off-Broadway theaters occupied renovated tenement buildings, will replace the theaters
with new homes and supply an additional, larger theater within a new apartment building.
It will also replace some of the rehearsal spaces forced out of Times Square. The earlier
renovation during the mid-1970s had marked the beginning of the reclamation of 42nd
Street (Feiden, 1999).

7. SPITALFIELDS AND DOWNTOWN BROOKLYN

1. The actual market structures were of much more recent construction, with the
main building having been erected in the 1880s and the western part in the 1920s. Nevertheless, the frontage buildings of the older section are listed.

2. The area's population dropped for many years, but the effects of World War II bombing and the demolition of slum dwellings meant that there were still very high levels of crowding within the remaining housing units.

3. Population estimates for Spitalfields ward were 6,654 in 1981, of which 37 percent were born in Bangladesh, and 8,821 in 1989, with 80 percent from Bangladesh (Community Development Group, 1989, p.18). The larger Spitalfields area has a population of approximately 20,000, of which the Bangladeshi community forms about half (Bramidge, 1998, p. 4).

4. Forman (1989), p. 6.

5. Townsend (1987), appendix 4. The other two indicators that composed the index were home ownership and car ownership.

6. Forman (1989).

7. See Church (1988a).

8. Similar to the New York City Partnership, Business in the Community consists of managing directors and CEOs of large firms. The Prince of Wales was its president.

9. Its primary effort was to press for the routing of the channel tunnel train to Stratford in the east.

10. The SDG consisted of (1) Balfour Beatty Limited, a construction and development firm that was a wholly owned subsidiary of BICC PLC, a large holding company; (2) County and District Properties Limited, a wholly owned subsidiary of Costain Group, an international natural resources, construction, and property development company; and (3) London and Edinburgh Trust PLC, one of the United Kingdom's largest property developers, which subsequent to the original bid was taken over by a Swedish insurance company. Until the 1980s Swedish firms could not invest in property outside their country. Once able to do so, they sought control of established firms with knowledge of local conditions.

11. The rendering of the Foster tower shows a building wholly out of character with the market and also in sharp contrast to Broadgate's more traditional masonry facade.

12. Houlder (1992).

13. In 1986, in an experiment in governmental decentralization, the Tower Hamlets borough council, which had recently passed from Labour to Liberal Democratic control, divided the borough into seven districts, each with a partisan, elected council responsible for service delivery within its boundaries. The council had been dominated by a traditional, male, blue-collar Labour leadership that had been unresponsive to community input both from leftists among the incoming professionals and from the immigrant community: "By the mid-1970s a group largely made up of elderly white men, with a record in organized labour, was representing a borough where one person in four was from an ethnic minority, one in five was unemployed and most of the industry had gone elsewhere or closed down" (Forman, 1989, p. 39). Once Labour, now taken over by a coalition of younger, more progressive members, won the next local election, it disbanded the neighborhood councils.

14. Interview with Eric Reynolds, April 1, 1999.

15. Segal Quince Wicksteed Ltd. (1996). The development of the market for interim uses received assistance from Bethnal Green City Challenge, discussed later in the chapter.

16. Community Development Group (1989).

17. Bramidge (1998).

18. Moore (1999). This quotation comes from an article that appeared in the entertainment, food, and fashion magazine of the daily newspaper, the *Evening Standard.*

19. Information supplied by Andrew Bramidge, July 18, 2000.

20. Michael Heseltine was Margaret Thatcher's original Secretary of State for the Environment. He briefly returned to the position after Thatcher was defeated.

21. Parliamentary legislation was required to establish this form of community corporation.

22. Glueck and Gardner (1991).

23. BAM, as this venerable institution is familiarly known, houses a major opera house and two theaters. It specializes in avant-garde works and has a devoted following. Despite some exceptional successes, however, it typically has difficulty in attracting audiences from Manhattan, who tend to regard Brooklyn as the end of the earth.

24. Willensky (1986).

25. Arguably, Harlem regained its ascendancy at the end of the next decade.

26. Stollman (1989), p. 12.

27. This consideration prevailed during the Koch mayoralty. It did not cause the Giuliani administration to attempt similar office-oriented redevelopment projects in the boroughs.

28. All of the subway lines passing through Brooklyn and the Long Island Railroad have stops here.

29. Forest City Ratner is an affiliate of Cleveland-based Forest City Enterprises, the largest publicly traded development corporation in the United States. In 2000 it was worth more than $3.6 billion and owned, developed, and managed property throughout the United States. Its holdings included 41 retail centers, 114 apartment complexes, 24 office buildings, and 9 hotels (Forest City Enterprises, 2000).

30. The joint venture had just constructed the first high-rise office building to go up in Brooklyn in nearly 40 years, a purpose-built structure for the investment firm of Morgan Stanley, outside downtown on the edge of Brooklyn Heights. Brooklyn Heights inhabitants had vehemently opposed the building, which required a zoning change, contending that it intruded undesirable commercial uses into their quiet residential neighborhood. The city had endowed the structure with a generous package of subsidies.

31. Rudnitsky (1992), p. 48.

32. An indicator of Forest City's unusual niche is that it was the largest single recipient of federal UDAGs within the United States.

33. Forest City Ratner (1992); Dunlap (1991).

34. Lueck (1988).

35. Ibid.

36. *New York Times* (1988).

37. In 2000, however, Chase announced that it was moving 1,900 workers to a new building in Jersey City (Lentz, 2000a).

38. Dunlap (1991).

39. Ibid.

40. Myers (1992).

41. Retkwa (1992).

42. Vizard (1992).

43. This long-stalled project, called Renaissance Plaza, was rescued by the Dinkins administration when it signed a 20-year lease to move the Brooklyn district attorney's office out of six locations into its untenanted office tower (Mitchell, 1992). The complex included a Marriott hotel, the first hotel to be built in Brooklyn in 50 years. The city took

360,000 square feet at an initial rent of $19 a square foot. The rent level was typical for Class A office space in peripheral areas at that time, but the city did not receive the rent bonuses and free fixturing that characterized virtually all private-sector rental deals in the early '90s. The complex also benefited from ICIP tax incentives, and, of course, the public-sector occupants would be permanently exempt from sales and commercial occupancy taxes. Until the city's commitment, the developer, Muss Development Company, a Queens-based firm, had not been able to get financing.

44. Two plans had preceded this one. In 1969 Mayor John Lindsay had presented a $500 million plan to build office buildings, department stores, and apartment houses there. Then in 1975 a large portion of the site had been designated as a new campus for Baruch College, a unit of the City University. Both plans, however, were abandoned.

45. Breznick (1991).

46. Initially, the developers had proposed a publicly funded sports arena. Impassioned community opposition, as well as doubts about utilization, caused this enterprise to join the list of abandoned proposals for the spot.

47. The houses would each have rental units attached, thereby assisting the owner in covering his or her carrying costs. The rental suites would be at market rate.

48. O'Neill and Moss (1991).

49. Myers (1992).

50. Rudnitsky (1992).

51. Myers (1992).

52. Croghan (2000c), p. 13.

53. Lentz (2000c), p. 36.

8. BATTERY PARK CITY

1. The history of the Reichmann family presented here is drawn from *U.S. News & World Report* (1988); *Maclean's* (1988a, b); Lever (1988a, b); *Business Week* (1990); Hylton (1990a); and a long article by Elaine Dewar (1987) in *Toronto Life* magazine. The latter essay chronicled the family's flight from Austria to Tangier to escape the Nazis and the subsequent building of their fortune. While it specifically recounted only positive—in fact, sometimes heroic—deeds by the parents, it nevertheless nastily implied, without any supporting evidence, that still unrevealed secrets sullied the family's extraordinary reputation for probity.

The Reichmanns brought a libel suit against the author, the magazine, and the *Globe and Mail,* Toronto's leading newspaper, which had editorialized against the suit. The article's factual narrative appeared generally correct; it was its innuendoes that made it potentially libelous. Ultimately, the case was settled out of court, when the family agreed to accept a contribution to charity and an apology by the author.

2. Dewar (1987) quotes an interview she conducted with Edward Reichmann, one of the brothers: "Late in 1941 and in 1942 there were all kinds of rumors from Europe about a crackdown in Czechoslovakia and the situation of Jews there. . . .By then the war was in full swing. Mother decided to travel to Hungary. . . . She went to France, Italy, then Yugoslavia and into Hungary. Neither my father nor her friends could dissuade her. From Tangier, it was not clear that she could help in Europe. But it turned out she saved thousands. . . . She had a letter saying that she was a representative of the Spanish Red Cross" (p. 132).

3. Lichfield (1992).

4. Hylton (1990b). In 1992 the company's North American property portfolio consisted of almost 40 million square feet of mainly office space: 54 percent in New York City, 17 percent in Toronto, 10 percent in Calgary, 5 percent in Ottawa, and the balance scattered among smaller cities (Hylton, 1992a).

5. Shachtman (1991), p. 290. When O & Y purchased the buildings, they were in the possession of National Kinney, a former parking-lot corporation that the late Stephen Ross renamed Warner Communications and used as his base ultimately to gain control of Time Warner Communications, one of the largest corporate buyouts in history. At the time the Reichmanns bought them, the properties were losing money. Among them was 55 Water Street, the world's largest commercial office building. During the mid-1980s this building became a very stylish address for some of New York's most active investment banking firms, including Lehman Brothers, Bear Stearns, and L. F. Rothschild. In 1986 the building had a 99 percent occupancy rate, and O & Y raised a $548 million Eurobond loan on it (Dizard, 1992).

6. *Maclean's* (1988a), p. 48.

7. *U.S. News and World Report* (1988), p. 38.

8. *Business Week* (1990), p. 33.

9. Principal sources for the discussion of Battery Park City are Ponte (1982); Lopate (1989); Gill (1990); Sclar and Schuman (1991); Battery Park City Authority (1992); Dunlap (1999); the Battery Park City Web site, www.batteryparkcity.org/index.htm; and interviews with BPCA officials.

10. The State of New Jersey, whose agreement also had to be obtained for the Port Authority to proceed with the project, acceded to this investment in exchange for the Port Authority's assumption of the Hudson and Manhattan tubes, a bankrupt rail system connecting New Jersey with Manhattan.

11. The city owned all the land under water between the riverbank and the pier heads.

12. Harrison & Abramovitz specialized in high modernism with an overlay of glitz. Their post-Corbusian large structures, isolated from each other on superblocks, embodied the style that was a particular butt of Jane Jacobs's criticism of urban renewal programs. Jacobs (1961) characterized these programs as producing "luxury housing projects that mitigate their inanity, or try to, with a vapid vulgarity. Cultural centers that are unable to support a good bookstore. Civic centers that are avoided by everyone but bums, who have fewer choices of loitering place than others. . . . Promenades that go from no place to nowhere and have no promenaders. . . . This is not the rebuilding of cities. This is the sacking of cities" (p. 4).

13. Gill (1990), p. 103. The developer was the Lefrak Organization, and the architects were Harrison & Abramovitz.

14. Moral obligation bonds were invented by John Mitchell, when he was a New York bond attorney. He later gained notoriety as Richard Nixon's attorney general during the Watergate scandal.

15. Richard Kahan's career was intertwined with many of the major public-private partnerships in New York City, on both sides of the public-private divide. Just out of Columbia Law School, he joined the UDC staff and then served as vice-president of the Lefrak Organization, one of the nation's largest development firms. He then returned to the UDC and while still in his early thirties served simultaneously as head of the UDC,

the BPCA, and the Convention Center Development Corporation, which was then constructing the Javits Center. After leaving his public-sector posts, he joined another large development firm, Tishman Speyer, as a partner. Then he, along with sociologist Richard Sennett, became head of the Urban Assembly, a group aimed at improving third-world cities; at the same time, he served as director of Riverside South, a consortium of community groups working with Donald Trump on a plan for his West Side Rail Yards. In 2000 he was heading a group seeking to get athletic facilities built for New York City schools, many of which lacked any playing fields.

16. Battery Park City, the 42nd Street Redevelopment Corporation, and the Convention Center Development Corporation all took advantage of the UDC's special powers.

17. Gill (1990), p. 102.

18. Sclar and Schuman (1991), p. 17.

19. Shachtman (1991), pp. 317–18.

20. Ponte (1982), p. 14.

21. While the plaza and the Winter Garden were both open to the public, they were built and held by O & Y.

22. The 1979 master plan allocated 30 percent of the land to public open space, not including streets.

23. In 1986 apartments generally sold for about $350 a square foot or rented for $25 a square foot a year (*New York Times,* 1986). After the real-estate slump, prices fell, and developers had difficulty in disposing of new units. Two builders auctioned off units in 1991, averaging $267 per square foot. In 2000 apartments were selling for as much as $756 per square foot, or $660,000 for a small two-bedroom apartment with good views and in the $400s for one-bedroom units. Rentals for spacious two-bedroom units with two baths were advertised at more than $7,000 per month, while a one-bedroom apartment was going for $3,288. Most of the original apartments were studios or one-bedrooms. Later buildings contained more family-sized units, and a number of occupants of the smaller units bought adjacent apartments to combine them.

24. Dunlap (1999); BPCA (2000).

25. By and large, the authority has received nothing but praise for the lavishness of its investments in public art and landscape architecture. In one instance of unfavorable publicity, however, David Emil, who succeeded Meyer Frucher as president of the authority, was criticized for ordering design changes in the third footbridge connecting Battery Park City to the rest of Manhattan. This bridge, which is attached to Stuyvesant High School, was originally to have cost $4 million. The redesigned structure cost twice as much. In defending his decision, Emil remarked: "This will be an enchanting, beautiful bridge. . . . Bridges have inherent in them a sort of magical imagery, and for whatever reasons the bridges to the south don't capture that. This bridge will" (Golway, 1991).

26. Ibid.

27. Dunlap (1999).

28. I. Peterson (1988).

29. Goldberger (1986).

30. Goldberger (1988).

31. Sorkin (1992a), pp. xii–xiii.

32. Jacobs (1961).

33. See Boyer (1983).

34. Lopate (1989), p. 24; italics in original.

35. The absence of the homeless, who inhabit Battery Park and the nearby Staten Island Ferry Terminal in large and visible number, from Battery Park City raises questions of how genuinely open to the public it is. BPCA officials, however, claim that the outdoor spaces are not treated differently from the rest of New York. While there is a small unarmed security patrol in addition to normal New York City Police Department coverage, it does not devote itself to keeping out unwanted sojourners. And, in my own frequent visits to the site, while I have rarely seen anyone who looked particularly disreputable, neither have I seen anyone harassed. The opinion of those I have interviewed on the subject is that physical and psychological barriers keep out such people.

36. Gill (1990), p. 105. Brendan Gill was the *New Yorker* magazine's architectural critic and had been chairman of both the Landmarks Conservancy and the Municipal Art Society, civic groups concerned with protecting and improving New York's architectural heritage.

37. I know of no survey of users of Battery Park City's public areas. Casual observation reveals them as predominantly white middle class but, depending on the time of day and week, with a considerable admixture of working-class people of varying ethnicity. On summer weekends, the strollers and café patrons are New Yorkers who pursue the sun in a city park rather than retiring to their home "in the country."

38. Gordon (1997).

39. Gill (1990) quotes Meyer Frucher, Richard Kahan's successor as president of the BPCA: "When Governor Cuomo asked me to become president of Battery Park City Authority he said to me, 'Give it a soul. Without a soul the beauty will be superficial.' This was a difficult challenge, but one that I think we have met in essentially two ways: through the Housing New York Program and by making Battery Park City a destination for all New Yorkers" (p. 103).

40. Schmalz (1987).

41. From the initial issue, $150 million supported construction of 1,850 substantially rehabilitated apartments in Harlem and the South Bronx, to be provided to a mix of families, with homeless constituting 30 percent; low income, 45 percent; and moderate income, 25 percent (Oser, 1987).

42. Given the population that resides within Battery Park City, the lack of participation may well produce a more egalitarian result than would occur if residents could direct the authority's policies. The recent decisions to have mixed-income housing and to connect the parks at the southern and northern ends of the complex to the rest of the city, thereby reducing isolation, met with opposition from residents. Some residents have objected to paying fees added on to their rents that support parks maintenance, on the grounds that the parks are used so heavily by the general public.

9. DOCKLANDS

1. Between 1951 and 1981 manufacturing jobs in inner southeast London dropped by 68 percent, from 148,000 to 47,000 (Buck, Gordon, and Young, 1986, pp. 6–7).

2. Ibid., p. 7.

3. Marris (1987), pp. 60–61.

4. GLC (1985).

5. The name of Hays Wharf lives on as the Hays Galleria within the London Bridge City complex, which opened in 1988 (see Chapter 2) (Ambrose and Colenutt, 1975, chapter 4).

6. There had been 52,000 registered dockers in 1920 (Marris 1987, p. 61; Brindley, Rydin, and Stoker, 1989, p. 98).

7. Church (1988a); Brindley, Rydin, and Stoker (1989).

8. See Chapter 5. The original legislation did not fix the life span of the new agency, but in 1991 the government indicated its intention to terminate the country's ten urban development corporations by 1996.

9. The DJC also included parts of Greenwich and Lewisham in its planning.

10. Cambridge Policy Consultants (1998), p. 10; Brindley, Rydin, and Stoker (1989).

11. In its first ten years of operation the corporation acquired 2,109 acres of land and water through vesting and purchase. After allowing for 401 acres of water and 483 acres for roads, railway, or environmental purposes, 1,225 acres remained for development. Land disposals to March 31, 1991, amounted to 661 acres, leaving 564 acres awaiting reclamation, being reclaimed, or awaiting development (LDDC, 1991, p. 171).

12. Buchan (1990).

13. LDDC (1991); Fazey (1991).

14. Pessimism over the size of future demand inhibited the government from investing in heavy transport.

15. GLC (1985).

16. Cambridge Policy Consultants (1998), pp. 19–20; Kleinman (1999).

17. Rhodes and Tyler (1998), table 1.

18. A. Smith (1989).

19. LDDC (1988a, 1992).

20. Brownill (1991). The *New York Times* described the extreme contrasts involved: "The wall, a brick sentinel that shields one world from another, stands as a symbol of sweeping change and resultant bitter divisions in London's once-derelict dock area. On one side of the wall, affluent newcomers occupy a stylish private housing development. On the other, a bleak public housing complex, with laundry hanging from balconies with peeling ceilings, is home to the working class and poor. 'The developers built that wall so those people wouldn't have to look at this,' Steve Amor, chairman of the local tenants' association, said as he climbed the stairs to his cramped apartment" (Rule, 1988).

21. Recent data on the number of initial residents who purchased new private housing are not available. The Cambridge Research Associates study (1998, p. 21) indicates that as of March 1988, 45 percent of the new homes constructed on LDDC-owned land were sold to residents already living in one of the three Docklands boroughs.

22. Foster (1999), p. 176. Foster's excellent, detailed ethnographic study of the effect of redevelopment on the inhabitants of the Isle of Dogs captures the complex relationships and ambivalent feelings among the old residents and new arrivals.

23. The LDDC expected the number of units to double between 1988 and 1990, from 12,000 to 24,000, but only slightly more than 15,000 were actually completed by then (LDDC, 1988b, 1992).

24. Sampson (1998), p. 149. According to Kleinman (1999), "To some extent, LDDC's financial involvement with social housing, both new build and refurbishment, came about as a result of the collapse in the property market. LDDC were supporting several mixed tenure development ideas in which planning gain would lever in subsidy

from private developers to allow some social housing on neighbouring sites. However, when the rent fell, LDDC were left with no private sector partner, and so agreed to provide direct grant" (pp. 16–17).

25. Foster (1999), p. 308.

26. Brownill, Razzaque, and Kochan (1998), p. 59.

27. D. Stevenson (1998), p. 31.

28. Robert Campeau, a Canadian entrepreneur specializing in leveraged buyouts, spent exorbitantly on the acquisition of the Allied and Federated department store chains in the United States. Only a few years after his lionization as the king of retailing, his entire debt edifice crashed when the revenues from the stores, diminished by weakened consumption after the 1987 stock market collapse, fell far below the amount necessary to service his huge debt. Olympia & York initially rushed to his assistance with an emergency $250 million loan, then refused to bail him out further. In 1990 Campeau was forced to seek Chapter 11 bankruptcy protection in the United States, devaluing the Reichmanns' equity share.

29. The *New York Times* (Hylton, 1990a) showed the company's holdings in 1990 as follows: Olympia & York Developments Ltd. wholly owned three subsidiaries—the U.S. and London real-estate companies and Olympia & York Enterprises. The last of these was the holding company for its other equity interests. According to the *Times* (which is not entirely in agreement with other sources on percentages), O & Y Enterprises owned the following percentages in publicly owned companies: 82 percent of Abitibi-Price; 74 percent of Gulf Canada Resources Ltd.; 36 percent of Trizec; 33 percent of Stanhope Properties, the British developer; 25 percent of Landmark Land Co.; 19 percent of Santa Fe Pacific; 14 percent of Trilon Financial Corp.; 10.5 percent of Campeau; and 8.2 percent of Rosehaugh PLC, another British development concern. In addition, it owned 89 percent of GW Utilities, another holding company that in turn owned 82 percent of Consumers' Gas Co., 41 percent of Interhome Energy, an oil and pipeline company, and 10 percent of Allied Lyons, the parent company of Hiram Walker.

30. Fathers (1992).

31. Morley et al. (1989), p. 133.

32. Buchan (1990).

33. The consortium also comprised two U.S.-based merchant banks, Credit Suisse First Boston (CSFB, parent company of First Boston Real Estate) and Morgan Stanley. The origin of the consortium's interest in Canary Wharf lay in the inability of the two financial firms to locate suitable office space in central London during the mid-1990s (Daniels and Bobe, 1991).

34. LDDC (1991), p. 12.

35. Road investment by the LDDC totaled £248 million in FY 1990–91 and was projected to total more than £650 million for the subsequent three-year period (LDDC, 1991). Highways to be built by the U.K. Department of Transport, which would connect Docklands to the national road system, were estimated in 1987 to cost another £348 million (National Audit Office, 1988, p. 14).

36. Ibid., p. 19.

37. Ibid.

38. Buchan (1990).

39. Ibid.

40. Rodgers and Nisse (1992); *Economist* (1991a). After the project went into bankruptcy administration, the administrators feared that the liabilities incurred in the inducements to tenants surpassed the benefits of occupancy and calculated that the enterprise's balance sheet would improve if the committed tenants were persuaded not to come. Nevertheless, O & Y and CSFB, which owned one of the Canary Wharf buildings, opposed American Express's application to withdraw from its lease. In July 1992 the question of whether American Express could withdraw was under judicial consideration. The firm had argued that O & Y had defaulted on its lease obligations when it ceased paying contractors to complete work on the structure (Simon, 1992a), and ultimately it did not move. Committed tenants feared that bankruptcy would free the project's sponsors from the obligation to assume their old leases, leaving them with empty, possibly unlettable space on their hands on which they would have to continue paying high rents.

41. Hylton (1990b; 1992b).

42. Prokesch (1990).

43. Hylton (1992a).

44. Quoted in Sullivan et al. (1992).

45. Some companies had already moved in during the preceding year; in May 1992 the buildings were 11 percent occupied. The larger committed tenants were scheduled to arrive during the summer.

46. CSFB and Morgan Stanley were part of the original Canary Wharf consortium and remained as backers of the project, each agreeing to take an equity position in its own building. Morgan Stanley's agreement with O & Y, however, required the developer to purchase its building upon completion if it so demanded. O & Y resisted the exercise of this option and lost in court.

47. Buchan (1990), p. 5.

48. Simon (1992b).

49. Hylton (1992c).

50. From March through June 1992 the tribulations of O & Y received virtually daily coverage in the business press and weeklies in both the United States and the United Kingdom. For a chronology of the events recapitulated here, see the *New York Times* (1992b).

51. Peston (1992).

52. At the time they moved in, they received a bargain rent of £12 per square foot. When their rent review was to occur in 2000, it was expected that the amount would more than double (Mortished, 1999).

53. Sullivan, Parker-Jervis, and Shamoon (1992).

54. *Business Week* (1992).

55. Prokesch (1992b).

56. *Economist* (1990), p. 71.

57. Houlder (1991a).

58. The value of O & Y's assets at the time of filing was the subject of considerable discussion. An estimate published in *Barron's* put the shortfall at between $6 billion and $10 billion (Isaac, 1992).

59. Peston and Simon (1992a). Different sources gave different figures for the number of banks involved, ranging from 91 to more than 100. Major lenders, as listed in the *New York Times,* included large Japanese banks—Tokai Bank Ltd. ($250 million), Fuji ($100 million), Dai-Ichi Kangyo ($180 million), and other Japanese institutions (at least

$250 million). Other bank lenders were the Hong Kong and Shanghai Banking Corporation (750 million); Canadian Imperial Bank of Commerce ($713 million); Royal Bank of Canada ($647 million); Commerzbank International of Frankfurt ($287.5 million); Credit Lyonnais ($262 million); Citibank ($480 million); Barclay's ($315 million); and Lloyds ($100 million) (*New York Times,* 1992c; Parker-Jervis, 1992). *Barron's* (1992) gives much larger figures for some of these banks. For example, it shows Credit Lyonnais as being owed $1.25 billion and Citibank more than $1 billion; these numbers seem much too high. The *Observer* (Sullivan, 1992) showed Citibank as holding $380 million in loans to O & Y. In addition to the bank loans, it was estimated that O & Y had about fifteen outstanding bond issues backed by mortgages on specific buildings, although some were also backed by shares in its energy and forestry companies (Hylton, 1992d).

60. Peston and Simon (1992b). This indebtedness figure seems too low in view of their earlier acquisitions of natural-resource companies.

61. Lichfield (1992).

62. Quoted in Lichfield (1992).

63. Ibid.

64. *Economist* (1997), p. 67.

65. The *Economist* (ibid.) placed Paul Reichmann's share at 5 percent; however, other sources, including an officer of the Canary Wharf Company, have given the 10 percent figure.

66. Stevenson (1995).

67. Canary Wharf (1999?).

68. Morgan Stanley Dean Witter (1999).

69. In 1999, the property was appraised at approximately £2 million.

70. In particular, Frankfurt, which unlike London operates inside the Euro zone, was seen as a major threat to London's preeminence as the home of finance. "Frankfurt 2000" was a ten-year plan to construct more than 60 million square feet of office space in that metropolis (Browne, 1999). The Corporation of the City of London, which had earlier regarded Docklands as a serious rival, increasingly began to see it as an ally in its battle against continental European cities.

71. The LDDC ceased operations in March 1998. Like all of the British UDCs, it was set up with a time limit for its activities. There are now neither enterprise zones nor UDCs remaining in the United Kingdom.

72. Imrie and Thomas (1999).

73. Potter (1988).

74. At the same time that Britain was building government-sponsored new towns, the United States was offering shallow subsidies to private developers, who were supposed to install the basic infrastructure themselves and construct a critical mass of structures. Almost all of the U.S. ventures failed entirely or required financial restructuring.

75. In 1995, 24.3 million square feet of commercial and industrial space had been constructed within the Docklands (LDDC, 1995, p. 3).

76. Savitch (1988), chapter 5.

77. The government's behavior in relation to the financial problems of the Channel Tunnel was similar.

78. Quoted in Nisse (1992).

79. Rhodes and Tyler (1998), p. 32. The meaning of the private-sector amount is somewhat clouded by the fact that it was substantially devalued during the recession,

and the appraised value of property has not yet reached the amount that was invested in it.

80. Brownill, Razzaque, and Kochan (1998).

81. Cambridge Policy Consultants, p. 29.

82. Church and Frost (1998), pp. 84–85.

83. LDDC (1995), p. 6.

84. Rhodes and Tyler (1998), pp. 32–33.

85. Cambridge Policy Consultants (1998), p. 21.

86. Kleinman (1999), p. 24.

87. Colenutt (1990).

88. See S. Fainstein (2000); and Healey (1997).

10. REAL-ESTATE DEVELOPMENT

1. Bacow (1990) indicates that the integrated firm is more common on the European continent.

2. See Logan (1992) for a discussion of the trend toward global firms in the 1980s and its breakdown in the subsequent slump.

3. Bacow (1990), p. 5.

4. Ibid.

5. Balchin, Kieve, and Bull (1988, p. 15) list a number of factors that make the property market inefficient and always in disequilibrium. These include the uniqueness of each site and building, illiquidity, the legal rights of property interests, the influence of conservationists, and the slowness of response to changes in demand.

6. See Harvey (1985c). At times firms have managed to obtain monopoly prices because of the scarcity resulting from governmental restrictions on construction; these restrictions, however, were ostensibly aimed at environmental protection, not price support.

7. Harvey (1981). See the discussion in Haila (1991).

8. Harvey (1981).

9. Beauregard (1991).

10. Leitner (1994).

11. Harvey (1982), pp. 266–70.

12. Ibid., p. 269.

13. Harvey (1982) comments: "Indeed, since money capitalists absorb rather than generate surplus value, we may well wonder why capitalism tolerates such seeming parasites" (p. 261).

14. Ball (1983, p. 146) distinguishes between rent and development profit, the latter being a consequence of development activity rather than land price. The distinction, however, is impossible to apply when urban land is in question, since land price does not exist independently of the value generated by agglomeration.

15. My argument, as should be obvious, does not rely on the labor theory of value. Rather, I see value as arising more generally out of social relationships and accept the classical economist's view of the intersection of supply and demand as denoting the value of a commodity at a given time. This acceptance, however, does not imply that I regard the shape of the supply-and-demand curves as a legitimate outcome of a fair distribution of income or of choices freely made. Nor does it mean that total value equals the aggre-

gate of the individual values of commodities produced. The value of a pair of shoes versus the sum of the value of two left shoes is a mundane example of why simple aggregates fail to indicate the value of an ensemble.

Marxism has two separate concepts of value, neither one of which is satisfactory. In the first, the labor theory of value purports to explain exchange values. The observed discrepancies between the aggregated cost of average labor time in a product and the price of the product, however, force believers in the labor theory of value into endless contortions of epicyclic dimensions to retain its applicability (the distinction between productive and unproductive labor further muddles the issue). In the second, exchange values are contrasted to use values, but there is no theorized relationship between use value and labor value, except that in a communist society they would be identical.

16. See Agnew (1987), p. 28.

17. Wirth (1938).

18. See Gans (1968) for analyses of the class biases of planners and their assumptions concerning the impact of physical form; see Castells (1977, chapter 5) for a critique of Wirth and the ecological approach to urban sociology.

19. See Saunders (1986) for a summary and critique of the Marxist arguments.

20. See, e.g., Bish (1971).

21. Much of this work traces back to Henri Lefebvre's (1991; original French edition, 1974) arguments, which, while rooting space in the mode of production, imbued it also with transcendent power: "'Change life!' 'Change society!' These precepts mean nothing without the production of an appropriate space. . . . new social relationships call for a new space, and vice versa" (p. 59). Lefebvre divides his analysis of space into three parts: (1) spatial practice, referring to the way in which space is used; (2) representations of space, alluding to the design of spatial forms; and (3) representational spaces, embodying the symbolic meaning of space (p. 33).

22. An article by R. J. King (1988) contends that "urban design is . . . concerned with *the purposive production of urban meaning* (the 'urban symbolic'), to be seen as a subset of the broader *production and reproduction (both purposive and otherwise) of urban meaning*" (p. 445). Italics in original.

23. See, inter alia, Sennett (1990); Gottdiener (1985); Sorkin (1992b); I. M. Young (1990); Harvey (1992); Soja (1989, 1996, 2000); M. Davis (1990); Zukin (1991, 1995); Judd (1995); Boyer (1995); and Lash and Urry (1994).

24. Sennett (1990).

25. Many observers have commented on the private character of the American city throughout its history (see Warner, 1968, for the best-known such analysis). Thus, the recent crescendo of opprobrium is only a matter of degree.

26. Sennett (1990), p. 201.

27. Safdie (1987), p. 153.

28. Interestingly this analysis recapitulates Dahl's depiction of pluralism in *Who Governs?*, where his picture of multiple elites depended on each operating in their own sphere. Dahl viewed the resulting dispersion as a cause of celebration, as it provided multiple spheres of power. The poststructuralists are less willing to regard those issue arenas shunned by economic dominants as domains of power.

29. Sennett (1990), p. 193.

30. Boddy (1992).

31. Ibid., p. 126n.

32. I. M. Young (1990), p. 237.

33. Marcuse and van Kempen (2000) argue that while "cities have always shown fucntional, cultural and status divisions, . . . the differentiation between areas has grown and lines between the areas have hardened, sometimes literally in the form of walls that function to protect the rich from the poor. . . . Walls, literal or symbolic, prevent people from seeing, meeting and hearing each other; at the extremes they insulate and they exclude" (p. 250).

34. Wilson (1991), p. 25.

35. Pryke (1991), p. 202.

36. Ibid., p. 212.

37. Boyer (1992), p. 199; italics added.

38. Few of the poststructualists, of course, would accept the Prince's image of a mythologized traditional England as appropriate, either.

39. R. Robertson (1990, p. 54) distinguishes between contemporary nostalgia, which he sees as intimately bound up in consumerism, and the "willful synthetic" nostalgia of the late nineteenth and early twentieth centuries, which was intended to stimulate nationalist loyalties.

40. The poststructuralist rejection of nostalgia embodied in architectural reference does not preclude the critics' own nostalgia for a time when architecture was not used for manipulative purposes.

41. Oscar Newman's (1972) pioneering work on defensible space initially appeared to be a more humane method of offering protection than the cruder devices of forcible removal or legalized violence. Present interpretations see defensible space as only a subtler form of cruelty.

42. I know of no survey research that indicates the mix of people using the new retail centers, nor, if such exists, are there data that would allow us to compare it with earlier counterparts.

43. Suburban exclusion is much more extreme than what exists in the central areas. To the extent that suburbanization has meant a great increase in the absolute physical distance between different population groups and decreased the likelihood that they will ever cross paths at all, the argument that greater diversity once existed deserves credence. For people who actually enter the urban core, however, their likelihood of contact with someone very different from themselves has not clearly decreased.

44. Sorkin (1992c), p. 216.

45. Ibid., p. 231.

46. Castells (1989), p. 6; italics in original.

47. Marx's concept of unproductive labor and David Harvey's use of the term "fictitious capital" are similar negations of activities that do not produce sweat.

48. Dennis Judd, who criticizes the exclusionary aspects of shopping malls and mixed-use megaprojects but does not go so far as to issue a blanket condemnation of all their aspects (see Judd, 1995), commented to me that the writings on festive marketplaces and Disneyland display an unfortunate tendency to sneer at people for having fun.

49. Conventional economists avoid such arguments altogether by asserting that interpersonal comparisons of utility are impossible.

50. Gans (1988, p. x), without wholly endorsing the tastes and prejudices of middle America, reacts strongly against the cultural elite that would dismiss the middle strata as

"right-wing racists, greedy materialists, or uncultured 'Joe Sixpacks.'" Many of the cultural critics seem to reject anyone who actually likes the targets of their opprobrium as manipulated or narrow-minded.

51. Crilley (1993), p. 143.

52. Within the United States, and to some extent the United Kingdom, the ability of middle-class people to escape the tax burden of supporting service-dependent populations by fleeing to the suburbs does, however, contribute substantially to the problems mentioned.

53. Paul Knox (1993, p. 258 and note 1), who edited the book in which the quotation from Crilley concerning "spectacular diversions" appears and who is otherwise generally sympathetic to poststructuralist insights, remarks in exasperation concerning David Harvey's negative assessment of Baltimore's Inner Harbor development: "Harvey does not say what alternative uses for a decaying industrial landscape he might propose." Knox notes that he was led to his observation concerning the Inner Harbor by the enthusiasm of a black Baltimore cab driver over the business that the development had generated for him.

54. According to Tocqueville (1957), "The very essence of democratic government consists in the absolute sovereignty of the majority" (p. 264).

55. The classic theoretical treatment is Rousseau's distinction between the general will and the will of all, wherein the general will represents the social good. The general will desires what everyone would want if each person understood his or her long-term interests, while the will of all embodies the self-serving, narrow interests of individuals. The practical solution incorporated in the United States Constitution and other similar founding documents invests rights in minorities that cannot be contravened by majorities.

56. Reichl (1999), p. 176.

57. Ibid., p. 177.

58. S. Fainstein (1997, 1999).

59. Harvey (1992).

60. Harvey's description of the situation builds on the work of Neil Smith (1992), which, more than Harvey's analysis, identifies the squatters as the good guys and the neighborhood residents who long for peace and quiet as the bad guys.

61. Harvey (1992), p. 591. A socialist academic of my acquaintance, who lives near the park, admitted to me that while he strongly opposed the police action, he had found life pleasanter since its occurrence.

62. Harvey (1989).

63. Harvey (1992), p. 596.

64. Political theorists are much more inclined than other social philosophers to regard conflicting interests as inherent in social life and to seek ways of managing conflict. Marxists and other social constructionists view conflicting interests as created by elites protecting their privileges; their aim is to dissipate hierarchy and thereby extirpate conflict.

65. Harvey (1992), pp. 599–600.

66. See J. E. Davis (1991, chapter 5), who sees neighborhoods as divided into four property interest groups: property capitalists, owner occupants, tenants, and the homeless.

67. Zukin (1991).

68. Contemplation of this issue caused me to list my own inclusions and exclusions and recognize their inconsistencies. I endorse women's colleges but not men's clubs. I think that public funds should subsidize highbrow public radio even though its listeners are a small elite group. I support racial integration in schools but not necessarily class mixing, at least in practice—I moved my family from a white lower-middle-class school district, where my children got regularly beaten up, to a racially integrated, but much more homogeneously upper-middle-class district. I attended an elite private university (as did many of the critics of Battery Park City), and while I have many ambivalences about that institution, I do not regret going there. I live in an extremely crowded, mixed-use section of Manhattan, but my favorite vacation resorts are far less diversely populated than Disney World, although mainly a consequence of taste and inaccessibility rather than control by their owners. Although I am identifiably Jewish, I intensely dislike the particularism of American Jewish groups and strongly reject their "chosen people" outlook. I favor a multicultural curriculum but feel that such an approach should criticize subordinate as well as dominant groups.

69. See, e.g., Marcuse and van Kempen (2000), who distinguish between enclaves and ghettos. The analysis, however, fails to examine whether or not individuals who belong to ascriptive groups necessarily wish to identify themselves fully with their group. Thus, for example, Iris Marion Young (1990) falls into the trap of subsuming the individual in the group and assuming that the standpoint politics of group leaders represents the genuine desire of members.

70. Harvey (1992), p. 600.

71. A. Wolfe (1992).

72. Boddy (1992).

73. Barber (1984).

74. Boyer (1995), p. 107.

75. See Bennett (1998).

76. See Chapter 1, note 11.

11. DEVELOPMENT POLICY FOR THE INNER CITY

1. Amin and Thrift (1995).

2. It is inconceivable that any private business would make capital expenditures without specifying output targets and calculating in advance the impacts of increasing production.

3. The Labour-sponsored GLEB did do economic planning and provides something of a model. As reconstituted in the present GLE, it focuses on developing London's entrepreneurial, small-business sector.

4. See, for example, O'Neill and Moss (1991); and Coopers & Lybrand Deloitte (1991b).

5. For a discussion of the importance of place and the effects of disaggregation, see S. Fainstein and Markusen (1993).

6. Bloomberg.com.uk, September 20, 2000 (www.bloomberg.com/uk/bus_news3).

7. Rueschemeyer and Evans (1985), pp. 57–59.

8. Robert Beauregard (1989) discusses the importance of the state playing a role in requiring preferential hiring agreements for residents when it participates in development.

His analysis is restricted to construction hiring, but the principle can be extended to operating firms.

9. Eisinger (1988).

10. Its members included the president of the Shubert Organization, New York's largest theater owner; Celeste Holm, the actress; and Vincent Sardi, the owner of the famous restaurant bearing his name.

11. S. Fainstein (1997).

Bibliography

Advisory Commission on Intergovernmental Relations. 1987. *Significant Features of Fiscal Federalism.* Washington, DC: ACIR.

Agnew, John. 1987. *Place and Politics.* Winchester, MA: Allen & Unwin.

Alcaly, R. E., and David Mermelstein, eds. 1976. *The Fiscal Crisis of American Cities.* New York: Vintage.

Alterman, Rachelle, and Jerold S. Kayden. 1988. Developer provisions of public benefits: Toward a consensus vocabulary. In *Private Supply of Public Services,* edited by Rachelle Alterman. New York: New York University Press.

Altshuler, Alan A. 1965. *The City Planning Process.* Ithaca, NY: Cornell University Press.

Ambrose, Peter. 1986. *Whatever Happened to Planning?* London: Methuen.

Ambrose, Peter, and Bob Colenutt. 1975. *The Property Machine.* Harmondsworth, Middlesex, UK: Penguin.

Amin, Ash, and Nigel Thrift. 1995. Globalisation, institutional "thickness," and the local economy. In *Managing Cities: The New Urban Context,* edited by Patsy Healey et al. Chichester, UK: John Wiley.

———. 1992. Neo-Marshallian nodes in global networks. *International Journal of Urban and Regional Research* 16 (December): 571–87.

Aron, Laurie Joan. 2000. The untold story: Yes, Virginia, there *is* new top-flight office space: Vast square footage added in bets that have paid off—so far. *Crain's New York Business,* April 17, pp. 31, 50.

Association of London Authorities (ALA) and Docklands Consultative Committee (DCC). 1991. *10 Years of Docklands: How the Cake Was Cut.* London: ALA and DCC, June.

Bachrach, Peter, and Morton S. Baratz. 1962. Two faces of power. *American Political Science Review* 56 (December): 947–52.

Bacow, Lawrence S. 1990. Foreign investment, vertical integration, and the structure of the U.S. real estate industry. *Real Estate Issues* 15 (Fall/Winter): 1–8.

Badcock, Blair. 1984. *Unfairly Structured Cities.* Oxford: Blackwell.

Bagli, Charles V. 2000a. At least one Yankee team gets its wish. *New York Times,* February 9.

————. 2000b. Office shortage imperils growth in New York City. *New York Times,* September 19.

————. 2000c. Doubts rise on new site for big board. *New York Times,* June 6.

————. 1999a. CBS granted more tax cuts to stay put. *New York Times,* January 29.

————. 1999b. Office tower said to get tax breaks. *New York Times,* June 6.

————. 1999c. Times is said to consider a new tower. *New York Times,* October 14.

————. 1998. Fierce bidding expected as Prudential sells 2 development sites in Times Sq. *New York Times,* March 8.

————. 1997a. Pledge to stay in city wins Bear Stearns a tax break. *New York Times,* August 28.

————. 1997b. Companies get second helping of tax breaks. *New York Times,* October 17.

————. 1992. City continues to blink in real estate dealings. *New York Observer,* March 9.

————. 1991. Old foes make strange bedfellows on Trump's long-fought project. *New York Observer,* April 22.

Balbus, Isaac. 1971. The concept of interest in pluralist and marxian analysis. *Politics and Society* 1 (February): 151–78.

Balchin, Paul N., Jeffrey L. Kieve, and Gregory H. Bull. 1988. *Urban Land Economics and Public Policy.* 4th ed. London: Macmillan.

Ball, Michael. 1983. *Housing Policy and Economic Power.* London: Methuen.

Ball, Michael, V. Bentivegna, M. Edwards, and M. Folin. 1985. *Land Rent, Housing, and Urban Planning.* London: Croom Helm.

Barber, Benjamin R. 1984. *Strong Democracy.* Berkeley: University of California Press.

Barnekov, Timothy, Robin Boyle, and Daniel Rich. 1989. *Privatism and Urban Policy in Britain and the United States.* Oxford: Oxford University Press.

Barrett, Wayne. 1992. *Trump.* New York: HarperCollins.

Barron's. 1992. May 18.

————. 1991. July 22.

Battery Park City Authority (BPCA). 2000. *Time Line.* New York: BPCA.

————. 1992. *Battery Park City Fact Sheet.* New York: BPCA.

Bautista, Eddie. 2000. Lecture at ICAS Citizenship Seminar. Urban Planning: Critiques and New Approaches. New York University, April 7.

Beauregard, Robert A. 1991. Capital restructuring and the new built environment of global cities: New York and Los Angeles. *International Journal of Urban and Regional Research* 15, no. 1: 90–105.

————. 1990. Bringing the city back in. *Journal of the American Planning Association* 56 (Spring): 210–15.

————, ed. 1989. *Atop the Urban Hierarchy.* Totowa, NJ: Rowman & Littlefield.

Beauregard, Robert A., and Anne Haila. 2000. The unavoidable continuities of the city. In *Globalizing Cities,* edited by Peter Marcuse and Ronald van Kempen. Oxford: Blackwell.

Bennett, Larry. 1998. Do we really wish to live in a communitarian city? Communitarian thinking and the redevelopment of Chicago's Cabrini-Green public housing complex. *Journal of Urban Affairs* 20, no. 2: 99–116.

Berman, Marshall. 1997. Signs of the times. *Dissent* 44, no. 4 (Fall): 76–83.

Berry, Mike. 1990. Economic restructuring and the transformation of urban space: The view from Australia. Paper presented to the World Congress of the International Sociological Association. Madrid, Spain, July.

Berry, M., and M. Huxley. 1992. Big build: Property capital, the state, and urban change in Australia. *International Journal of Urban and Regional Research* 16, no. 1: 35–59.

Bish, Robert L. 1971. *The Public Economy of Metropolitan Areas.* Chicago: Markham.

Boddy, Trevor. 1992. Underground and overhead: Building the analogous city. In *Variations on a Theme Park,* edited by Michael Sorkin. New York: Hill and Wang.

Boyer, M. Christine. 1995. The great frame-up: Fantastic appearances in contemporary spatial politics. In *Spatial Practices,* edited by Helen Liggett and David C. Perry. Thousand Oaks, CA: Sage.

———. 1992. Cities for sale: Merchandising history at South Street Seaport. In *Variations on a Theme Park,* edited by Michael Sorkin. New York: Hill and Wang.

———. 1983. *Dreaming the Rational City.* Cambridge, MA: MIT Press.

Bram, Jason, and James Orr. 1999. Can New York City bank on Wall Street? Federal Reserve Bank of New York. *Current Issues in Economics and Finance* 3, no. 11 (July): 1–5.

Bramidge, Andrew. 1998. Developing a sustainable middle ground between property-led regeneration and small-scale community initiatives. Master's thesis, University of Westminster, UK.

Branson, Noreen. 1979. *Poplarism, 1919–1925.* London: Lawrence and Wishart.

Breznick, Alan. 1991. Forest City will join big Brooklyn project. *New York Times,* February 18.

Brilliant, Eleanor. 1975. *The Urban Development Corporation.* Lexington, MA: D. C. Heath.

Brindley, Tim, Yvonne Rydin, and Gerry Stoker. 1996. *Remaking Planning.* 2d ed. London: Routledge.

———. 1989. *Remaking Planning.* London: Unwin Hyman.

Browne, Anthony. 1999. The market left out in the cold. *Observer* (London), March 21.

Brownill, Sue. 1991. London Docklands: Social or physical regeneration? The need for a reassessment of regeneration dichotomies. Paper presented at the joint meeting of the Association Collegiate Schools of Planning and the Association of European Schools of Planning, Oxford, UK, July.

Brownill, Sue, Konnie Razzaque, and Ben Kochan. 1998. From exclusion to partnership? The LDDC and community consultation and participation. *Rising East: The Journal of East London Studies* 2, no. 2: 42–72.

Bruck, Connie. 1989. *The Predators' Ball.* New York: Penguin.

Buchan, James. 1990. A high-risk business. *Sunday Review—The Independent on Sunday.* December 16, pp. 2–5.

Buck, Nick, Matthew Drennan, and Kenneth Newton. 1992. Dynamics of the metropolitan economy. In *Divided Cities,* edited by Susan S. Fainstein, Ian Gordon, and Michael Harloe. Oxford: Blackwell.

Buck, Nick, and Norman Fainstein. 1992. A comparative history, 1880–1973. In *Divided Cities,* edited by Susan S. Fainstein, Ian Gordon, and Michael Harloe. Oxford: Blackwell.

Buck, Nick, Ian R. Gordon, and Ken Young. 1986. *The London Employment Problem.* Oxford: Oxford University Press.

Burrough, Bryan, and John Helyar. 1990. *Barbarians at the Gate: The Fall of RJR Nabisco.* New York: Harper & Row.

Business Week. 1992. Can O & Y escape? Maybe it's not too big to fail. June 1.

————. 1990. Inside the Reichmann empire: Why their gambles usually pay off. January 29.

Butterworth, R. 1966. Islington Borough Council: Some characteristics of single-party rule. *Politics* (Australasia) 1.

Byrne, Therese E., and David J. Kostin. 1990. *London Office Market II: Breaking the Code.* Salomon Brothers Bond Market Research—Real Estate, August.

Byrne, Therese E., and David Shulman. 1991. *Manhattan Office Market II: Beyond the Bear Market.* Salomon Brothers Bond Market Research—Real Estate, June.

Cambridge Research Associates. 1998. *Regenerating London Docklands.* Report to the UK Department of Environment, Transport and the Regions. London: DETR.

Camden, London Borough of. 1989a. *King's Cross Development Proposals: Progress Report on the Planning Application: Main Report,* September 19.

————. 1989b. King's Cross development proposals. The new scheme: Have they got it right? Photocopied flyer.

————. 1989c. King's Cross development proposals. A development benefitting the community or an "office city"? Report back cover. September.

————. 1988. *The King's Cross Railway Lands: A Community Planning Brief.* June.

Camden Citizen. 1990. King's Cross development: The new proposals. Supplement 1.

Canary Wharf, London. N.d. (1999?). *Fact File.* London: Canary Wharf Group.

Caro, Robert. 1974. *The Power Broker: Robert Moses and the Fall of New York.* New York: Knopf.

Castells, Manuel. 1989. *The Informational City.* Oxford: Blackwell.

————. 1985. High technology, economic restructuring, and the urban-regional process in the United States. In *High Technology, Space, and Society,* edited by Manuel Castells. Beverly Hills, CA: Sage.

————. 1977. *The Urban Question.* Cambridge, MA: MIT Press.

Chira, Susan. 1989. New designs for Times Square try to reflect neon atmosphere. *New York Times,* August 31.

Church, Andrew. 1988a. Demand-led planning, the inner-city crisis, and the labour market: London Docklands evaluated. In *Revitalising the Waterfront,* edited by B. S. Hoyle, D. A. Pinder, and M. S. Husain. London: Belhaven Press.

————. 1988b. Urban regeneration in London Docklands: A five-year policy review. *Environment and Planning C: Government and Policy* 6: 187–208.

Church, Andrew, and Martin Frost. 1998. Trickle down or trickle out: Job creation and work-travel impacts of Docklands regeneration. *Rising East: The Journal of East London Studies* 2, no. 2: 73–103.

Citizens Budget Commission. Various years. *Five-Year Pocket Summary of New York City and New York State Finances.* New York: Citizens Budget Commission.

Clavel, Pierre. 1986. *The Progressive City.* New Brunswick, NJ: Rutgers University Press.

Clawson, Marion, and Peter Hall. 1973. *Planning and Urban Growth: An Anglo-American Comparison.* Baltimore: Johns Hopkins University Press.

Colenutt, Bob. 1990. Urban development corporations—The Docklands experiment. Summary. Paper presented at Conference on Economic Regeneration. Chicago, September.

Colliers International Property Consultants. 1991. *Colliers International Worldwide 1991 Office Survey.* July 29.

Commission on the Year 2000. 1987. *New York Ascendant.* New York: Commission on the Year 2000.

Community Development Group (Spitalfields). 1989. *Planning Our Future.* London: Community Development Group.

Conroy, W. J. 1990. *Challenging the Boundaries of Reform: Socialism in Burlington.* Philadelphia: Temple University Press.

Cooke, Philip, ed. 1989. *Localities.* London: Unwin Hyman.

Coopers & Lybrand Deloitte. 1991a. Wealth creation in world cities. Annex to London Planning Advisory Committee (LPAC), *London: A World City Moving into the 21st Century.* London: LPAC.

———. 1991b. *London, World City.* Consultants Stage II Report. London: LPAC.

Corbridge, Stuart, Ron Martin, and Nigel Thrift. 1994. *Money, Power, and Space.* Oxford: Blackwell.

Corporation of London. 1999. Development info. Department of Planning, Corporation of London.

Cox, Kevin. 1997. Governance, urban regime analysis, and the politics of local economic development. In *Reconstructing Urban Regime Theory,* edited by Mickey Lauria. Thousand Oaks, CA: Sage.

———. 1991. Questions of abstraction in studies in the new urban politics. *Journal of Urban Affairs* 13, no. 3: 267–80.

Crain, Rance. 1992. By keeping city's lid on, Dinkins revives '93 hopes. *Crain's New York Business,* May 11.

Crain's New York Business. 1992. March 23.

———. 1991a. July 22.

———. 1991b. October 21.

Crilley, Darrel. 1993. Megastructures and urban change: Aesthetics, ideology, and design. In *The Restless Urban Landscape,* edited by Paul L. Knox. Englewood Cliffs, NJ: Prentice-Hall.

Croghan, Lore. 2000a. Related secures Coliseum loan. *Crain's New York Business,* May 29, p. 3.

———. 2000b. Douglas Durst productions give Times Square a new beginning. *Crain's New York Business,* May 15, p. 26.

———. 2000c. Topping off MetroTech complex. *Crain's New York Business,* January 10, p. 13.

Cross, Malcolm, and Roger Waldinger. 1992. Migrants, minorities, and the ethnic division of labor. In *Divided Cities,* edited by Susan S. Fainstein, Ian Gordon, and Michael Harloe. Oxford: Blackwell.

Cummings, Scott, ed. 1988. *Business Elites and Urban Development.* Albany, NY: SUNY Press.

Cushman, John H. 1992. House approves tax bill with $14.4 billion in breaks. *New York Times,* July 3.

Dahl, Robert. 1961. *Who Governs?* New Haven: Yale University Press.

Daniels, P. W., and J. M. Bobe. 1991. High rise and high risks: Office development on Canary Wharf. SIRC Working Paper no. 7. Portsmouth Polytechnic. May.

———. 1990. Information technology and the renaissance of the City of London office building. SIRC Working Paper no. 3. Portsmouth Polytechnic. December.

Danielson, M., and J. Doig. 1982. *New York: The Politics of Urban Regional Development.* Berkeley: University of California Press.

Davis, John Emmeus. 1991. *Contested Ground.* Ithaca, NY: Cornell University Press.

Davis, Mike. 1990. *City of Quartz.* London: Verso.

Dear, Michael, and Allen J. Scott, eds. 1981. *Urbanization and Urban Planning in Capitalist Society.* London: Methuen.

Dehesh, Alireza, and Cedric Pugh. 1999. The internationalization of post-1980 property cycles and the Japanese "bubble" economy, 1986–96. *International Journal of Urban and Regional Research* 23, no. 1 (March): 147–64.

Dewar, Elaine. 1987. The mysterious Reichmanns: The untold story. *Toronto Life,* November, pp. 61–186.

Dijkstra, Fer. 1991. Address given at the annual meeting of the Institute of British Geographers. January.

Dizard, John. 1992. Boom to tomb at 55 Water St. as prestigious leases expire. *New York Observer,* April 13.

Docklands Consultative Committee (DCC). 1988. *Urban Development Corporations: Six Years in London's Docklands.* London: DCC, February.

Domhoff, William. 1978. *Who Really Rules?* Santa Monica, CA: Goodyear.

Downs, Anthony. 1985. *The Revolution in Real Estate Finance.* Washington, DC: Brookings Institution.

Drennan, Matthew. 1988. Local economy and local revenues. In *Setting Municipal Priorities, 1988,* edited by Charles Brecher and Raymond D. Horton. New York: New York University Press.

Dror, Yehezkel. 1968. *Public Policy Reexamined.* San Francisco: Chandler.

Dunlap, David W. 2000. Battle lines drawn on new zoning plan. *New York Times,* Section 11, June 4.

———. 1999. Filling in the blanks at Battery Park City. *New York Times,* Section 11, February 7.

———. 1998. At Columbus Circle, a circuitous path to Columbus Centre. *New York Times,* Section 11, September 6.

———. 1993. Council's land-use procedures emerging. *New York Times,* Section 10, January 3.

———. 1992a. Charting the future of the waterfront. *New York Times,* Section 10, November 15.

———. 1992b. New Times Sq. Plan: Light! Signs! Dancing! Hold the offices. *New York Times,* August 20.

———. 1991. How developers and city hall retain big tenants. *New York Times,* June 16.

———. 1988. From dust of demolition, a new Times Square rises. *New York Times,* July 6.

Economist. 2000. February 12.

———. 1997. May 24.

———. 1992. March 28.

———. 1991a. June 22.

———. 1991b. October 20.

———. 1990. May 12.

Edwards, Michael. 1992. A microcosm: Redevelopment proposals at King's Cross. In *The Crisis of London,* edited by Andy Thornley. London: Routledge.

Eisinger, Peter K. 1988. *The Rise of the Entrepreneurial State.* Madison: University of
Wisconsin Press.

Elkin, Stephen L. 1987. *City and Regime in the American Republic.* Chicago: University
of Chicago Press.

English Partnerships. 1999. King's Cross Railway Lands (Position statement, July 1999).
Typed copy.

Epstein, Jason. 1992. The tragical history of New York. *New York Review of Books,*
April 9, pp. 45–52.

Fainstein, Norman I., and Susan S. Fainstein. 1988. Governing regimes and the political
economy of development in New York City, 1946–1984. In *Power, Culture, and
Place,* edited by John Hull Mollenkopf. New York: Russell Sage Foundation.

———. 1978. National policy and urban development. *Social Problems* 26 (December):
125–46.

Fainstein, Susan S. 2000. New directions in planning theory. *Urban Affairs Review* 35,
no. 4 (March): 451–78.

———. 1999. Can we make the cities we want? In *The Urban Moment,* edited by Sophie
Body-Gendrot and Robert Beauregard. Thousand Oaks, CA: Sage.

———. 1997. The egalitarian city: The restructuring of Amsterdam. *International Planning Studies* 2, no. 3: 295–314.

———. 1992. The second New York fiscal crisis. *International Journal of Urban and
Regional Research* (March): 129–37.

———. 1991a. Rejoinder to: Questions of abstraction in studies in the new urban politics. *Journal of Urban Affairs* 13, no. 3: 281–87.

———. 1991b. Promoting economic development: Urban planning in the United States
and the United Kingdom. *Journal of the American Planning Association* 57 (Winter): 22–33.

———. 1990a. The changing world economy and urban restructuring. In *Leadership and
Urban Regeneration,* edited by D. Judd and M. Parkinson. Newbury Park, CA: Sage.

———. 1990b. Economics, politics, and development policy: The convergence of New
York and London. *International Journal of Urban and Regional Research* 14, no. 4:
553–75.

Fainstein, Susan S., and Norman I. Fainstein. 1994. *Urban Political Movements.* Englewood
Cliffs, NJ: Prentice-Hall.

———. 1987. Economic restructuring and the politics of land use planning in New York
City. *Journal of the American Planning Association* 53 (Spring): 237–48.

———. 1986a. New Haven: The limits of the local state. In Susan S. Fainstein et al.,
Restructuring the City. Rev. ed. New York: Longman.

———. 1986b. Regime strategies, communal resistance, and economic forces. In Susan
S. Fainstein et al., *Restructuring the City.* Rev. ed. New York: Longman.

———. 1985. Is state planning necessary for capital? *International Journal of Urban and
Regional Research* 9, no. 4 (December): 485–507.

Fainstein, Susan S., Norman I. Fainstein, Richard Child Hill, Dennis Judd, and Michael
Peter Smith. 1986. *Restructuring the City.* Rev. ed. New York: Longman.

Fainstein, Susan S., Norman I. Fainstein, and Alex Schwartz. 1989. Economic shifts and
land-use in the global city: New York, 1940–87. In *Atop the Urban Hierarchy,* edited by Robert Beauregard. Totowa, NJ: Rowman and Littlefield.

Fainstein, Susan S., Ian Gordon, and Michael Harloe, eds. 1992. *Divided Cities.* Oxford: Blackwell.

Fainstein, Susan S., and Michael Harloe. 1992. Introduction to *Divided Cities,* edited by Susan S. Fainstein, Ian Gordon, and Michael Harloe. Oxford: Blackwell.

Fainstein, Susan S., and Ann R. Markusen. 1993. Urban policy: Bridging the social and economic development gap. *University of North Carolina Law Review* 71 (June): 1463–86.

Fainstein, Susan S., and Ken Young. 1992. Politics and state policy in economic restructuring. In *Divided Cities,* edited by Susan S. Fainstein, Ian Gordon, and Michael Harloe. Oxford: Blackwell.

Faludi, Andreas. 1987. *A Decision-Centered View of Environmental Planning.* New York: Pergamon.

———. 1986. *Critical Rationalism and Planning Methodology.* London: Pion.

Fathers, Michael. 1992. What went wrong with what went up. *Independent on Sunday,* May 17.

Fazey, Ian Hamilton. 1991. Urban development bodies plan their own extinction. *Financial Times,* February 21.

Feagin, Joe R., and Robert Parker. 1990. *Rebuilding American Cities: The Urban Real Estate Game.* 2d ed. Englewood Cliffs, NJ: Prentice-Hall.

Feiden, Douglas. 1999. Theater Row mounts a major revival. *Daily News,* May 6.

Financial Times. 1992. August 1–2.

———. 1991. December 7–8.

Fiscal Policy Institute. 1999. *The State of Working New York: The Illusion of Prosperity: New York in the New Economy.* New York: Fiscal Policy Institute.

Fisher, Peter S., and Alan H. Peters. 1998. *Industrial Incentives.* Kalamazoo, MI: Upjohn.

Foglesong, Richard E. 1986. *Planning the Capitalist City.* Princeton, NJ: Princeton University Press.

Foley, Donald L. 1972. *Governing the London Region.* Berkeley: University of California Press.

Forest City Enterprises. 2000. The New York Times Company selects Forest City Ratner Companies as real estate developer. Press release, February 18.

Forest City Ratner Companies. 1992. MetroTech Center Fact Sheet. February.

Forman, Charlie. 1989. *Spitalfields: A Battle for Land.* London: Hilary Shipman.

Foster, Janet. 1999. *Docklands: Cultures in Conflict, Worlds in Collision.* London: UCL Press.

Frantz, Douglas. 1991. *From the Ground Up.* New York: Henry Holt.

Frieden, Bernard J., and Lynne B. Sagalyn. 1990. *Downtown, Inc.* Cambridge, MA: MIT Press.

Friedland, Roger. 1983. *Power and Crisis in the City.* New York: Schocken.

Friedmann, John. 1986. The world city hypothesis. *Development and Change* 17: 69–83.

Friedmann, John, and G. Wolff. 1982. World city formation: An agenda for research and action. *International Journal of Urban and Regional Research* 6, no. 3: 69–83.

Fujita, Kuniko. 1991. A world city and flexible specialization: Restructuring of the Tokyo metropolis. *International Journal of Urban and Regional Research* 15, no. 2: 269–84.

Gans, Herbert J. 1988. *Middle American Individualism.* New York: Oxford University Press.

―――. 1968. *People and Plans.* New York: Basic Books.

Gill, Brendan. 1990. The sky line: Battery Park City. *New Yorker,* August 20, pp. 99–106.

Glassberg, A. 1981. Representation and urban community. London: Macmillan.

Glueck, Grace, and Paul Gardner. 1991. *Brooklyn: People and Places, Past and Present.* New York: Harry N. Abrams.

Goldberger, Paul. 1990. A huge architecture show in Times Square. *New York Times,* September 9.

―――. 1989a. Times Square: Lurching toward a terrible mistake? *New York Times,* February 19.

―――. 1989b. New Times Square design: Merely token changes. *New York Times,* September 1.

―――. 1988. Public space gets a new cachet in New York. *New York Times,* May 22.

―――. 1986. Battery Park City is a triumph of urban design. *New York Times,* August 31.

Golway, Terry. 1991. Battery Park City's Emil is assailed as a meddler. *New York Observer,* August 5–12.

Gordon, David L. A. 1997. *Battery Park City: Politics and Planning on the New York Waterfront.* Amsterdam: Gordon and Breach.

Gordon, Ian. 1996. The London economy: Performance & prospects. In *Four World Cities: A Comparative Study of London, Paris, New York, and Tokyo,* edited by Llewelyn Davies. London: University College London, Comedia.

Goss, S. 1988. *Local Labour and Local Government.* Edinburgh: Edinburgh University Press.

Gottdiener, M. 1985. *The Social Production of Urban Space.* Austin: University of Texas Press.

Gourevitch, Peter. 1986. *The Politics of Hard Times.* Ithaca, NY: Cornell University Press.

Grant, James. 1992. The Olympia ordeal: It won't end soon. *New York Times,* Section 3, May 24.

Grant, Peter. 1990. Tenants see tricks, no treats, with shift. *Crain's New York Business,* October 22.

―――. 1989. Why Prudential needs Times Square. *Crain's New York Business,* September 4.

Greater London Council. 1985. *London Industrial Strategy: The Docks.* London: GLC.

Greater London Enterprise. 2000a. The financial services sector. Draft document. London: GLE.

―――. 2000b. Alliance of big business and London boroughs to help capital's disadvantaged. Press release, June 14.

Green, Roy E., ed. 1991. *Enterprise Zones.* Newbury Park, CA: Sage.

Guardian. 1988. August 24.

GVA Grimley. 2000. Economic and property market review: Research. First quarter. London: GVA Grimley, International Property Advisers.

―――. 1999. Central London office commentary. Second quarter. London: GVA Grimley, International Property Advisers.

―――. 1998. Central London office commentary. Autumn. London: GVA Grimley, International Property Advisers.

GVA Williams. 1999. *The Williams Report.* London: GVA Williams.

Haila, Anne. 1999. Why is Shanghai building a giant speculative property bubble? *International Journal of Urban and Regional Research* 23, no. 3 (September): 583–88.

————. 1991. Four types of investment in land and property. *International Journal of Urban and Regional Research* 15, no. 3 (September): 343–65.

————. 1988. Land as a financial asset: The theory of urban rent as a mirror of economic transformation. *Antipode* 20, no. 2: 79–100.

Hall, Peter. 1998. *Cities and Civilization.* New York: Pantheon.

————. 1996. *Cities of Tomorrow.* Updated edition. Oxford: Blackwell.

————. 1989. *London 2001.* London: Unwin Hyman.

————. 1980. *Great Planning Disasters.* Berkeley: University of California Press.

————. 1963. *London 2000.* London: Faber and Faber.

Hall, Peter, Harry Gracey, Roy Drewett, and Ray Thomas. 1973. *The Containment of Urban England.* London: Allen & Unwin.

Hambleton, Robin. 1989. Urban government under Thatcher and Reagan. *Urban Affairs Quarterly* 24: 359–88.

Hamnett, Chris. 1994. Social polarisation in global cities: Theory and evidence. *Urban Studies* 31, no. 3: 401–24.

Hamnett, Chris, and Bill Randolph. 1988. *Cities, Housing, & Profits.* London: Hutchinson.

Harding, Alan. 1995. Elite theory and growth machines. In *Theories of Urban Politics,* edited by David Judge, Gerry Stoker, and Harold Wolman. London: Sage.

————. 1994. Urban regimes and growth machines: Toward a cross-national research agenda. *Urban Affairs Quarterly* 29, no. 3 (March): 356–82.

————. 1990. Property interests and urban growth coalitions in the U.K.: A brief encounter? Working Paper no. 12, Centre for Urban Studies, University of Liverpool, March.

Harloe, Michael. 1995. *The People's Home.* Oxford: Blackwell.

Harloe, Michael, and Susan S. Fainstein. 1992. Conclusion: The divided cities. In *Divided Cities,* edited by Susan S. Fainstein, Ian Gordon, and Michael Harloe. Oxford: Blackwell.

Harloe, Michael, Peter Marcuse, and Neil Smith. 1992. Housing for people, housing for profits. In *Divided Cities,* edited by Susan S. Fainstein, Ian Gordon, and Michael Harloe. Oxford: Blackwell.

Harloe, Michael, Chris Pickvance, and John Urry, eds. 1990. *Place, Policy, and Politics: Do Localities Matter?* London: Unwin Hyman.

Harvey, David. 1992. Social justice, postmodernism, and the city. *International Journal of Urban and Regional Research* 16 (December): 588–601.

————. 1989. *The Condition of Post-Modernity.* Oxford: Blackwell.

————. 1985a. *The Urbanization of Capital.* Baltimore: Johns Hopkins University Press.

————. 1985b. *Consciousness and the Urban Experience.* Baltimore: Johns Hopkins University Press.

————. 1985c. Class-monopoly rent, finance capital, and the urban revolution. In *The Urbanization of Capital,* edited by David Harvey. Baltimore: Johns Hopkins University Press.

————. 1982. *The Limits to Capital.* Chicago: University of Chicago Press.

————. 1981. The urban process under capitalism: A framework for analysis. In *Urbanization and Urban Planning in Capitalist Society,* edited by Michael Dear and Allen J. Scott. London: Methuen.

————. 1978. Planning the ideology of planning. In *Planning Theory in the 1980s,* edited by Robert Burchell and George Sternlieb. New Brunswick, NJ: Rutgers University Center for Urban Policy Research.

———. 1973. *Social Justice and the City.* Baltimore: Johns Hopkins University Press.

Healey, Patsy. 1997. *Collaborative Planning.* Houndmills, Basingstoke, Hampshire, UK: Macmillan.

———. 1990. Understanding land and property development processes: Some key issues. In *Land and Property Development in a Changing Context,* edited by Patsy Healey and Rupert Nabarro. Aldershot, Hants, UK: Gower.

Healey, Patsy, and Susan M. Barrett. 1990. Structure and agency in land and property development processes: Some ideas for research, *Urban Studies* 27, no. 1: 89–104.

Healey, Patsy, Simin Davoudi, Solmaz Tavsanoglu, Mo O'Toole, and David Usher. 1992. *Rebuilding the City: Property-Led Urban Regeneration.* London: E & FN Spon.

Healey, Patsy, and Rupert Nabarro, eds. 1990. *Land and Property Development in a Changing Context.* Aldershot, Hants, UK: Gower.

Hoff, Jeffrey. 1989. Who should pay to transform Times Square? *Barron's,* September 25.

Holusha, John, 1999. Bites and bytes at an old cookie factory. *New York Times,* Section 11, December 5.

———. 1998. A corporate headquarters next to Bugs and Mickey. *New York Times,* Section 11, September 6.

Houlder, Vanessa. 1992. Two projects in the City come nearer to fruition. *Financial Times,* Weekend, March 28/29.

———. 1991a. Docklands body to cut 40% of staff. *Financial Times,* April 30.

———. 1991b. Rosehaugh losses grow to £226.6m after provisions. *Financial Times,* Weekend, December 7/8.

Houlder, Vanessa, Michael Smith, Roland Rudd, and Ivo Dawnay. 1992. Hanson believes Canary Wharf project is worth £600m at most. *Financial Times,* June 2.

Hu, Dapeng, and Anthony Pennington-Cross. 2000. *The Evolution of Real Estate in the Economy.* Institute Report no. 00-02. Washington, DC: Research Institute for Housing America, June.

Hudson, James R. 1987. *The Unanticipated City.* Amherst: University of Massachusetts Press.

Hylton, Richard D. 1992a. Olympia to disclose lost value. *New York Times,* July 1.

———. 1992b. $240 million demand on developer. *New York Times,* January 16.

———. 1992c. Slumping real estate leaves giant reeling. *New York Times,* March 24.

———. 1992d. Banks fear losses as builder reels. *New York Times,* March 30.

———. 1990a. Olympia & York selling stake in U.S. holdings. *New York Times,* September 20.

———. 1990b. Reshaping a real estate dynasty. *New York Times,* November 28.

Imbroscio, David L. 1997. *Reconstructing City Politics.* Thousand Oaks, CA: Sage.

Imrie, Rob, and Huw Thomas. 1999. Assessing urban policy and the Urban Development Corporations. In *British Urban Policy,* edited by Rob Imrie and Huw Thomas. London: Sage.

Insignia Richard Ellis. 2000. *London Office Market Bulletin.* London: Insignia Richard Ellis.

Isaac, Paul J. 1992. Just the beginning. *Barron's,* May 18.

Jacobs, Jane. 1961. *The Death and Life of Great American Cities.* New York: Vintage.

Jenkins, Peter. 1988. *Mrs. Thatcher's Revolution.* Cambridge, MA: Harvard University Press.

Jonas, Andrew E. G., and David Wilson. 1999. *The Urban Growth Machine: Critical Perspectives Two Decades Later.* Albany: SUNY Press.

Jones Lang Wootton Consulting and Research. 1987. *The Central London Office Market,* June.

Judd, Dennis R. 1995. The rise of the new walled cities. In *Spatial Practices,* edited by Helen Liggett and David C. Perry. Thousand Oaks, CA: Sage.

Judd, Dennis R., and Michael Parkinson, eds. 1990. *Leadership and Urban Regeneration.* Newbury Park, CA: Sage.

Judge, David, Gerry Stoker, and Harold Wolman, eds. 1995. *Theories of Urban Politics.* London: Sage.

Kahan, Richard. 2000. Lecture at ICAS Citizenship Seminar. Urban Planning: Critiques and New Approaches. New York University, April 7.

Key, Tony, Marc Espinet, and Carol Wright. 1990. Prospects for the property industry: An overview. In *Land and Property Development in a Changing Context,* edited by Patsy Healey and Rupert Nabarro. Aldershot, Hants, UK: Gower.

King, Anthony D. 1990. *Global Cities.* London: Routledge.

King, Desmond S. 1989. Political centralization and state interests in Britain: The 1986 abolition of the GLC and MCCs. *Comparative Political Studies* 21 (January): 467–94.

King, R. J. 1988. Urban design in capitalist society. *Environment and Planning D: Society and Space* 6: 445–74.

King's Cross Railway Lands Community Development Group (RLCDG). 1989. *The King's Cross Development—People or Profit?* London: King's Cross RLCDG, July.

Kleinman, Mark. 1999: A more normal housing market? The housing role of the London Docklands Development Corporation, 1981–1998. LSE London Discussion Paper, May.

Klosterman, Richard. 1985. Arguments for and against Planning. *Town Planning Review* 56, no. 1: 5–20.

Knox, Paul L. 1993. The postmodern urban matrix. In *The Restless Urban Landscape.* Englewood Cliffs, NJ: Prentice-Hall.

Knox, Paul L., and Peter J. Taylor, eds. 1995. *World Cities in a World System.* Cambridge, UK: Cambridge University Press.

Koch, Edward I. 1984. *Mayor.* New York: Simon and Schuster.

Kolbert, Elizabeth. 2000. The last floor show. *New Yorker,* March 20, pp. 84–93.

Krieger, Joel. 1986. *Reagan, Thatcher, and the Politics of Decline.* New York: Oxford University Press.

Krumholz, Norman, and John Forester. 1990. *Making Equity Planning Work.* Philadelphia: Temple University Press.

Labaton, Stephen. 2000. Oligopoly. *New York Times,* Section 4, June 11.

Lamarche, Francois. 1976. Property development and the economic foundations of the urban question. In *Urban Sociology,* edited by Chris Pickvance. New York: St. Martin's.

Lambert, Bruce. 2000. Housing crisis confounds a prosperous city. *New York Times,* Metro Section, July 9.

———. 1991. The way cleared for long-delayed housing. *New York Times,* Section 10, April 14.

Lash, Scott, and John Urry. 1994. *Economies of Signs & Space*. Thousand Oaks, CA: Sage.

Lassar, Terry Jill, ed. 1990. *City Deal Making*. Washington, DC: Urban Land Institute.

Lauria, Mickey. 1997. Introduction to *Reconstructing Urban Regime Theory*. Thousand Oaks, CA: Sage.

Lawless, Paul. 1990. Regeneration in Sheffield: From radical intervention to partnership. In *Leadership and Urban Regeneration*, edited by Dennis Judd and Michael Parkinson. Newbury Park, CA: Sage.

———. 1989. *Britain's Inner Cities*. 2d ed. London: Paul Chapman.

———. 1987. Urban development. In *Reshaping Local Government*, edited by Michael Parkinson. New Brunswick, NJ: Transaction Books.

Lee, Moon Wha. 1999. *Housing New York City, 1996*. New York: New York City Department of Housing Preservation and Development.

Lefebvre, Henri. 1991. *The Production of Space*. Translated by Donald Nicholson-Smith. Cambridge, MA: Blackwell.

Leitner, H. 1994. Capital markets, the development industry, and urban office market dynamics: Rethinking building cycles. *Environment and Planning A* 26: 779–802.

Lemann, Nicholas. 2000. No man's town. *New Yorker*, June 5, pp. 42–48.

Lentz, Philip. 2000a. Boroughs get D in Class A space. *Crain's New York Business*, June 12, pp. 3, 62.

———. 2000b. Rezoning divides city hall. *Crain's New York Business*, May 15, p. 4.

———. 2000c. Ignored Brooklyn gets down to business. *Crain's New York Business*, February 14, p. 3.

Leonard, Devin. 1998. Zuckerman ends up with surprise space in Times Square deal. *New York Observer*, April 20.

Lever, Lawrence. 1988a. Canary Wharf saviour sings Britain's praise: Born again Anglophile of Docklands. *Financial Times*, May 9.

———. 1988b. Reichmanns aim for Stanhope. *Financial Times*, May 11.

Levy, John M. 1990. What local economic developers actually do: Location quotients versus press releases. *Journal of the American Planning Association* 56 (Spring): 153–60.

Lewis, Michael. 1989. *Liar's Poker*. New York: Penguin.

Leyshon, Andrew, Nigel Thrift, and Peter Daniels. 1990. The operational development and spatial expansion of large commercial property firms. In *Land and Property Development in a Changing Context*, edited by Patsy Healey and Rupert Nabarro. Aldershot, Hants, UK: Gower.

———. 1987. The urban and regional consequences of the restructuring of world financial markets: The case of the City of London. Working Papers on Producer Services no. 4, University of Bristol and Service Industries Research Centre, Portsmouth Polytechnic. July.

Lichfield, John. 1992. Downfall of a towering ambition. *Independent on Sunday*. May 17.

Lichtenberger, Elisabeth. 1991. Product cycle theory and city development. *Acta Geographica Lovaniensia* 31: 88–94.

Lin, Paul. 1991. The super-agency. *City Limits* 16 (November): 8–10.

Logan, John R. 2000. Still a global city: The racial and ethnic segmentation of New York. In *Globalizing Cities*, edited by Peter Marcuse and Ronald van Kempen. Oxford: Blackwell.

————. 1992. Cycles and trends in the globalization of real estate. In *The Restless Urban Landscape,* edited by Paul L. Knox. Englewood Cliffs, NJ: Prentice-Hall.

Logan, John R., and Harvey Molotch. 1987. *Urban Fortunes.* Berkeley: University of California Press.

Logan, John R., and Todd Swanstrom. 1990a. Urban restructuring: A critical view. In *Beyond the City Limits,* edited by John R. Logan and Todd Swanstrom. Philadelphia: Temple University Press.

————, eds. 1990b. *Beyond the City Limits.* Philadelphia: Temple University Press.

London Docklands Development Corporation (LDDC). 1995. *LDDC: Key Facts and Figures.* London: LDDC.

————. 1992. *LDDC Key Facts and Figures to the 31st March 1992.* London: LDDC, April.

————. 1991. *Annual Report & Financial Statements for the Year Ended 31 March 1991.* London: LDDC.

————. 1988a. *London Docklands Development Corporation.* London: LDDC. Ref: 134A.1, March.

————. 1988b. *London Docklands* (promotional brochure). London: LDDC.

London Planning Advisory Committee (LPAC). 1996. *Strategic Planning Advice.* London: LPAC.

————. 1994. *Strategic Planning Advice.* London: LPAC.

————. 1991. *London: A World City Moving into the 21st Century.* London: LPAC.

————. 1988. *Strategic Planning Advice for London: Policies for the 1990s.* London: LPAC.

London Property Research. 1999. *London Office Policy Review.* London: London Property Research.

Lopate, Phillip. 1989. The planner's dilemma. *7 Days,* February 15.

Loughlin, M., M. D. Gelfand, and K. Young, eds. 1985. *Half a Century of Municipal Decline, 1935–1985.* London: Allen and Unwin.

Low, N. P., and S. T. Moser. 1990. Markets as political structures: The case of Melbourne's central city property boom. Paper presented at the World Congress of Sociology, Madrid, July.

Lueck, Thomas J. 1988. New York gives a bank a break; the return is uncertain. *New York Times,* November 13.

Mackintosh, Maureen, and Hilary Wainwright. 1987. *A Taste of Power: The Politics of Local Economics.* London: Verso.

Maclean's. 1988a. June 27, pp. 46–48.

————. 1988b. October 24, pp. 41–50.

Marcuse, Peter. 1987. Neighborhood policy and the distribution of power: New York City's community boards. *Policy Studies Journal* 16: 277–89.

————. 1981. The targeted crisis: On the ideology of the urban fiscal crisis and its uses. *International Journal of Urban and Regional Research* 5: 330–55.

Marcuse, Peter, and Ronald van Kempen. 2000. Conclusion: A changed spatial order. In *Globalizing Cities.* Oxford: Blackwell.

Markusen, Ann, and Vicky Gwiasda. 1994. Multipolarity and the layering of functions in world cities: New York City's struggle to stay on top. *International Journal of Urban and Regional Research* 18 (June): 167–93.

Markusen, J. R., and D. T. Scheffman. 1978. The timing of residential land development: A general equilibrium approach. *Journal of Urban Economics* 5 (October): 411–24.

Marriott, Oliver. 1967. *The Property Boom.* London: Hamish Hamilton.

Marris, Peter. 1987. *Meaning and Action.* London: Routledge & Kegan Paul.

Martin, Douglas. 1993. 42d Street project remains on track. *New York Times,* January 25.

Martinotti, Guido. 1999. A city for whom? Transients and public life in the second-generation metropolis. In *The Urban Moment,* edited by Sophie Body-Gendrot and Robert Beauregard. Thousand Oaks, CA: Sage.

Massey, Doreen. 1995. *Spatial Divisions of Labor.* 2d ed. New York: Routledge.

Massey, Doreen, and A. Catalano. 1978. *Capital and Land.* London: Edward Arnold.

McCall, Carl. 1998. New York City's economic and fiscal dependence on Wall Street. Report 5-99, New York State Office of the State Deputy Comptroller for the City of New York. August 13.

McCormick, M., C. O'Cleireacain, and E. Dickson. 1980. Compensation of municipal workers in large cities: A New York City perspective. *City Almanac* 15: 1–9, 16–20.

McKinley, James C., Jr. 1994. For artists, there's no art in a wrecking ball. *New York Times,* December 20.

McNamara, Paul. 1990. The changing role of research in investment decision making. In *Land and Property Development in a Changing Context,* edited by Patsy Healey and Rupert Nabarro. Aldershot, Hants, UK: Gower.

Meuwissen, J., P. W. Daniels, and J. M. Bobe. 1991. The demand for office space in the City of London and the Isle of Dogs: Complement or competition? SIRC Working Paper no. 9. Service Industries Research Centre, Portsmouth Polytechnic. October.

Mills, David E. 1980. Market power and land development timing. *Land Economics* 56 (February): 10–20.

Mitchell, Alison. 1992. Brooklyn office project gets long-term tenant. *New York Times,* February 26.

Mittlebach, Margaret. 1991. Suburbs in the city. *City Limits* 16 (May): 12–16.

Mollenkopf, John Hull. 1992. *A Phoenix in the Ashes: The Rise and Fall of the Koch Coalition in New York City Politics.* Princeton, NJ: Princeton University Press.

———. 1988. The place of politics and the politics of place. In *Power, Culture, and Place.* New York: Russell Sage Foundation.

———. 1985. The 42nd Street Development Project and the public interest. *City Almanac* 18 (Summer): 12–15.

———. 1983. *The Contested City.* Princeton, NJ: Princeton University Press.

———. 1978. The postwar politics of urban development. In *Marxism and the Metropolis,* edited by William K. Tabb and Larry Sawers. New York: Oxford University Press.

Mollenkopf, John Hull, and Manuel Castells, eds. 1991. *Dual City.* New York: Russell Sage.

Molotch, Harvey. 1980. The city as a growth machine: Toward a political economy of place. *American Journal of Sociology* 82 (September): 309–32.

Moore, Rowan. 1999. Stars in the east. *ES Magazine,* March 30, pp. 12–16.

Morgan Stanley Dean Witter. 1999. *Canary Wharf Group: Towering above the Property Sector.* London: Canary Wharf Group.

Moricz, Zoltan, and Laurence Murphy. 1997. Space traders: Reregulation, property companies, and Auckland's office market, 1975–94. *International Journal of Urban and Regional Research* 21, no. 2 (June): 165–79.

Morley, Stuart, Chris Marsh, Angus McIntosh, and Haris Martinos. 1989. *Industrial and Business Space Development.* London: E & FN Spon.

Morris, Charles R. 1980. *The Cost of Good Intentions.* New York: Norton.

Mortished, Carl. 1999. Airborne Canary leaves ruins of the tower in its wake. *Times* (London), February 3.

Moss, Mitchell L. 1986. Telecommunications and the future of cities. *Land Development Studies* 3: 33–44.

Municipal Art Society of New York. 1994. 42nd Street Development Project, description and status. Press release. November.

Muschamp, Herbert. 1998. Lending architectural order and grace to chaotic Times Square. *New York Times,* March 8.

Myers, Steven Lee. 1992. The prime of "Wall Street East." *New York Times,* May 15.

National Audit Office. 1988. *Department of the Environment: Urban Development Corporations.* Report by the Comptroller and Auditor General. London: HMSO.

Netzer, Dick. 1988. Exactions in the public finance context. In *Private Supply of Public Services,* edited by Rachelle Alterman. New York: New York University Press.

Neuwirth, Robert. 1990. New Amsterdam Theater falling down? *Village Voice,* October 2.

New England Economic Review (Federal Reserve Bank of Boston). 1999. March/April.

Newman, Peter, and Ian Smith. 2000. Cultural production, place, and politics on the South Bank of the Thames. *International Journal of Urban and Regional Research* 24, no. 1 (March): 9–24.

New York. 1987. November 16.

New York City Department of Housing Preservation and Development (DHPD). 1989. *Ten-Year Housing Plan, Fiscal Years 1989–1998.* New York: DHPD.

New York City Planning Commission (NYCPC). 1981. *Midtown Development.* New York: Department of City Planning. June.

New York City Public Development Corporation (PDC). N.d. (1984?). *Forty-second Street Development Project Fact Sheet.* New York: PDC.

New York Observer. 1988. February 15.

New York State Office of the State Deputy Comptroller (OSDC) for the City of New York. 1991. *Review of the Financial Plan of the City of New York, Fiscal Years 1992 through 1995.* Report 4-92. June 17.

———. 1988. *New York City Planning Commission Granting Special Permits for Bonus Floor Area.* Report A-23-88. September 15.

New York Times. 2000. June 12.

———. 1992a. April 5.

———. 1992b. May 29.

———. 1992c. June 4.

———. 1992d. March 30.

———. 1992e. November 18.

———. 1992f. March 24.

———. 1991. August 21.

———. 1990. Section 4, March 18.

———. 1988. November 10.

———. 1986. March 23.

Newfield, Jack, and Wayne Barrett. 1988. *City for Sale.* New York: Harper & Row.

Newfield, Jack, and Paul DuBrul. 1981. *The Permanent Government*. New York: Pilgrim Press.

Newman, Oscar. 1972. *Defensible Space*. New York: Macmillan.

Newsweek. 1987. September 28.

Nisse, Jason. 1992. Docklands tube link derailed. *Independent*, May 29.

Observer (London). 1992. May 17.

O'Leary, Brendan. 1987. Why was the GLC abolished? *International Journal of Urban and Regional Research* 11, no. 2: 193–217.

O'Neill, Hugh, and Mitchell L. Moss. 1991. *Reinventing New York*. New York: Urban Research Center, Robert F. Wagner Graduate School of Public Service, New York University.

Oser, Alan S. 1988. Lease gives impetus to Brooklyn project. *New York Times*, April 3.

———. 1987. "Public housing" in abandoned buildings. *New York Times*, October 4.

Pahl, R. E. 1975. *Whose City?* 2d ed. Harmondsworth, Middlesex, UK: Penguin.

Painter, Joe. 1997. Regulation, regime, and practice in urban politics. In *Reconstructing Urban Regime Theory*, edited by Mickey Lauria. Thousand Oaks, CA: Sage.

Parker-Jervis, George. 1992. Olympia & York drop dead days. *Observer* (London), April 19.

Parkes, Michael, Daniel C. Mouawad, and Michael J. Scott. 1991. King's Cross Railwaylands: Towards a people's plan. Draft. June.

Parkinson, Michael, ed. 1987. *Reshaping Local Government*. New Brunswick, NJ: Transaction.

Parkinson, Michael, and Richard Evans. 1990. Urban development corporations. In *Local Responses to Economic Development*, edited by Michael Campbell. Paris: Cassell.

Parkinson, Michael, Bernard Foley, and Dennis Judd, eds. 1988. *Regenerating the Cities: The UK Crisis and the US Experience*. Manchester, UK: Manchester University Press.

Parkinson, Michael, and Dennis Judd. 1988. Urban revitalisation in America and the UK— The politics of uneven development. In *Regenerating the Cities: The UK Crisis and the US Experience*, edited by Michael Parkinson et al. Manchester, UK: Manchester University Press.

Peston, Robert. 1992. O & Y's Canary Wharf in administration. *Financial Times*, May 28.

Peston, Robert, and Bernard Simon. 1992a. Banks cautious on O & Y debt plan. *Financial Times*, April 14.

———. 1992b. A victim of hubris falls at Canary Wharf. *Financial Times*, April 13.

Peterson, Iver. 1988. Battery Park City: A new phase begins. *New York Times*, June 19.

Peterson, Paul. 1981. *City Limits*. Chicago: University of Chicago Press.

Pickvance, Chris. 1988. The failure of control and the success of structural reform: An interpretation of recent attempts to restructure local government in Britain. Paper presented at the International Sociological Association RC 21 Conference on Trends and Challenges of Urban Restructuring. Rio de Janeiro, Brazil, September.

———. 1981. Policies as chameleons: An interpretation of regional policy and office policy in Britain. In *Urbanization and Urban Planning in Capitalist Society*, edited by Michael Dear and Allen J. Scott. London: Methuen.

Polsby, Nelson. 1963. *Community Power and Political Theory*. New Haven: Yale University Press.

Ponte, Robert. 1982. Building Battery Park City. *Urban Design International* 3 (March/April): 10–15.

Port Authority of New York and New Jersey (PANYNJ). 1999. *Regional Economy: Review and Outlook for the New York–New Jersey Metropolitan Region.* New York: PANYNJ. August.

Port Authority of New York and New Jersey (PANYNJ). 1994. *Regional Economy: Review 1993, Outlook 1994 for the New York–New Jersey Metropolitan Region.* New York: PANYNJ. March.

———. 1992. *Regional Economy: Review 1991, Outlook 1992 for the New York–New Jersey Metropolitan Region.* New York: PANYNJ. March.

———. 1991. *Regional Economy: Review 1990, Outlook 1991 for the New York–New Jersey Metropolitan Region.* New York: PANYNJ. March.

———. 1988. *Regional Economy: Review 1987, Outlook 1988 for the New York–New Jersey Metropolitan Region.* New York: PANYNJ. March.

Porter, Michael E. 1995. The competitive advantage of the inner city. *Harvard Business Review* (May–June): 55–71.

Potter, Stephen. 1988. Inheritors of the new town legacy? *Town & Country Planning* (November): 296–301.

Preteceille, Edmond. 1981. Collective consumption, the state, and the crisis of capitalist society. In *City, Class and Capital,* edited by Michael Harloe and Elizabeth Lebas. London: Edward Arnold.

Prokesch, Steven. 1992a. New Jersey and New York collide in new competition to lure jobs. *New York Times,* December 1.

———. 1992b. 3 named to administer Olympia London Project. *New York Times,* May 29.

———. 1990. London betting on itself and on Canary Wharf. *New York Times,* November 13.

Pryke, Michael. 1991. An international city going "global": Spatial change in the City of London. *Environment and Planning D: Society and Space* 9: 197–222.

Pulley, Brett. 1995. A mix of glamour and hardball won Disney a piece of 42nd Street. *New York Times,* July 29.

Ratner, Bruce. 2000. Talk given at *Crain's* Mid-Year Economic Forecast Forum. June 20.

Real Estate Board of New York (REBNY). 1990. *Real Estate Reporter.* Fall.

———. 1987. *Manhattan Market Profile.* March.

———. 1985. *Fact Book, 1985.* March.

Rees, Gareth, and John Lambert. 1985. *Cities in Crisis.* London: Edward Arnold.

Reichl, Alexander J. 1999. *Reconstructing Times Square.* Lawrence: University Press of Kansas.

Retkwa, Rosalyn. 1992. MetroTech a boon for Brooklyn environs. *Crain's New York Business,* April 20.

Rhodes, John, and Peter Tyler. 1998. Evaluating the LDDC: Regenerating London's Docklands. *Rising East: The Journal of East London Studies* 2, no. 2: 32–41.

Richard Ellis. 1991. The impact of the existing built form on the potential for change and growth in world cities. Annex to London Planning Advisory Committee (LPAC), *London: A World City Moving into the 21st Century.* London: LPAC.

Robertson, David B., and Dennis R. Judd. 1989. *The Development of American Public Policy.* Glenview, IL: Scott, Foresman.

Robertson, Roland. 1990. After nostalgia? Wilful nostalgia and the phases of globaliza-
tion. In *Theories of Modernity and Postmodernity,* edited by Bryan S. Turner. Lon-
don: Sage.
Rodgers, Peter, and Jason Nisse. 1992. Canary Wharf may spurn tenants. *Independent.*
May 29.
Rodriguez, Nestor P., and Joe R. Feagin. 1986. Urban specialization in the world-system:
An investigation of historical cases. *Urban Affairs Quarterly* 22 (December): 187–220.
Rosenthal, Donald B., ed. 1980. *Urban Revitalization.* Beverly Hills, CA: Sage.
Rosslyn Research Limited. 1990. *Planning Gain.* Summary presentation for KPMG Peat
Marwick Management Consultants, August.
Rothstein, Mervyn. 1998. Refurbished behemoth is filling up in Chelsea. *New York Times,*
Section B, July 15.
Rudnitsky, Howard. 1992. Survivor. *Forbes,* June 8, p. 48.
Rueschemeyer, Dietrich, and Peter B. Evans. 1985. The state and economic transforma-
tion: Toward an analysis of the conditions underlying effective intervention. In *Bring-
ing the State Back In,* edited by Peter B. Evans, Dietrich Rueschemeyer, and Theda
Skocpol. Cambridge, UK: Cambridge University Press.
Rule, Sheila. 1988. At new Docklands, a tale of 2 cities. *New York Times,* October 15.
Rydin, Yvonne. 1998. *Urban and Environmental Planning in the UK.* London: Macmillan.
Safdie, Moshe. 1987. Collective significance. In *The Public Face of Architecture,* edited
by Nathan Glazer and Mark Lilla. New York: Free Press.
Sampson, Alice. 1998. The lessons of Winsor Park: Creating a new community: The role
of the LDDC. *Rising East: The Journal of East London Studies* 2, no. 2: 142–59.
Sanders, Heywood T., and Clarence N. Stone. 1987. Developmental politics reconsidered.
Urban Affairs Quarterly 22 (June): 521–39.
Sandler, Linda, and Greg Ip. 2000. Taking stock of big board's pricey "big box." *Wall
Street Journal,* March 15.
Sassen, Saskia. 1994. *Cities in a World Economy.* Thousand Oaks, CA: Pine Forge.
———. 1991. *The Global City.* Princeton, NJ: Princeton University Press.
Sassen, Saskia, and Frank Roost. 1999. The city: Strategic site for the global entertain-
ment industry. In *The Tourist City,* edited by Dennis R. Judd and Susan S. Fainstein.
New Haven: Yale University Press.
Saunders, Peter. 1986. *Social Theory and the Urban Question.* 2d ed. New York: Holmes
& Meier.
———. 1979. *Urban Politics.* Harmondsworth, Middlesex, UK: Penguin.
Savitch, H. V. 1988. *Post-Industrial Cities.* Princeton, NJ: Princeton University Press.
Sbragia, Alberta. 1990. Pittsburgh's "third way": The nonprofit sector as a key to urban
regeneration. In *Leadership and Urban Regeneration,* edited by Dennis Judd and
Michael Parkinson. Newbury Park, CA: Sage.
Schmalz, Jeffrey. 1987. New York City reaches agreement on housing. *New York Times,*
December 27.
Schwartz, Alex. 1999. New York City and subsidized housing: Impacts and lessons of
the city's $5 billion capital budget housing plan. *Housing Policy Debate* 10,
no. 4: 839–78.
———. 1994. Cities and suburbs as corporate service providers. Final Report to the Economic Development Administration Technical Assistance and Research Division.
CUPR Policy Report no. 13. New Brunswick, NJ: Rutgers University.

————. 1992. The geography of corporate services: A case study of the New York urban region. *Urban Geography* 13, no. 1: 1–24.

Sclar, Elliott, and Tony Schuman. 1991. The impact of ideology on American town planning: From the Garden City to Battery Park City. Unpublished paper.

Searle, Glen, and Michael Bounds. 1999. State powers, state land, and competition for global entertainment: The case of Sydney. *International Journal of Urban and Regional Research* 23, no. 1 (March): 165–72.

Segal Quince Wicksteed Ltd. 1996. Employment benefits of Spitalfields market: A report to Bethnal Green City Challenge. October.

Sennett, Richard. 1990. *The Conscience of the Eye.* New York: Knopf.

SERPLAN. 1992. The South East Region of England in Europe Post-1992. Draft Policy Statement from the Economic Strategy Group. November.

Shachtman, Tom. 1991. *Skyscraper Dreams.* Boston: Little, Brown.

Shefter, M. 1985. *Political Crisis, Fiscal Crisis.* New York: Basic Books.

Simmie, James. 1994. *Planning London.* London: UCL Press.

————. 1981. *Power, Property, and Corporatism.* London: Macmillan.

————. 1974. *Citizens in Conflict.* London: Hutchinson.

Simon, Bernard. 1992a. Reprieve for Canary Wharf after Toronto court ruling. *Financial Times,* July 1.

————. 1992b. Olympia & York ratings lowered. *Financial Times,* February 25.

Sleeper, Jim. 1987. Boom & bust with Ed Koch. *Dissent,* Special issue, In Search of New York. Fall.

Smallwood, Frank. 1984. The demise of metropolitan government? London and the metropolitan county councils. Paper presented at the annual meeting of the American Political Science Association, Washington, DC, September.

Smith, Adrian. 1989. Gentrification and the spatial constitution of the state: The restructuring of London's Docklands. *Antipode* 21, no. 3: 232–60.

Smith, Michael Peter. 1988. *City, State, and Market.* Oxford: Blackwell.

Smith, Michael Peter, and Joe R. Feagin. 1987. *The Capitalist City.* Oxford: Blackwell.

Smith, Neil. 1992. New city, new frontier: The Lower East Side as wild, wild west. In *Variations on a Theme Park,* edited by Michael Sorkin. New York: Hill and Wang.

————. 1987. Dangers of the empirical turn: Some comments on the CURS initiative. *Antipode* 19: 59–68.

————. 1984. *Uneven Development.* Oxford: Blackwell.

————. 1979. Toward a theory of gentrification: A back to the city movement by capital not people. *Journal of the American Planning Association* 45 (October): 538–48.

Smith, Neil, and James DeFilippis. 1999. The reassertion of economics: 1990s gentrification in the Lower East Side. *International Journal of Urban and Regional Research* 23, no. 4 (December): 638–53.

Smothers, Ronald. 2000. Governors end Port Authority rift that blocked billions in projects. *New York Times,* June 2.

Smyth, Hedley. 1985. *Property Companies and the Construction Industry in Britain.* Cambridge, UK: Cambridge University Press.

Soja, Edward W. 2000. *Postmetropolis.* Oxford: Blackwell.

————. 1996. *Thirdspace.* Oxford: Blackwell.

————. 1989. *Postmodern Geographies.* London: Verso.

———. 1980. The socio-spatial dialectic. *Annals of the Association of American Geographers* 70: 207–25.

Sorkin, Michael. 1992a. Introduction to *Variations on a Theme Park*. New York: Hill and Wang.

———, ed. 1992b. *Variations on a Theme Park*. New York: Hill and Wang.

———. 1992c. See you in Disneyland. In *Variations on a Theme Park*. New York: Hill and Wang.

Southwark Council. N.d. *Southwark Riverside London: A Guide to Attractions from Bankside to Butler's Wharf*. London: Southwark Council Tourism Unit.

Squires, Gregory, ed. 1989. *Unequal Partnerships*. New Brunswick, NJ: Rutgers University Press.

Squires, Gregory, Larry Bennett, Kathleen McCourt, and Philip Nyden. 1987. *Chicago: Race, Class, and the Response to Urban Decline*. Philadelphia: Temple University Press.

Stasio, Marilyn. 1989. Now playing on Broadway, the big squeeze. *New York Times*, July 9.

Stegman, Michael. 1988. *Housing and Vacancy Report, New York City, 1987*. New York: New York City Department of Housing Preservation and Development.

Sternlieb, George, and James W. Hughes. 1975. *Post-Industrial America: Metropolitan Decline & Inter-Regional Job Shifts*. New Brunswick, NJ: Center for Urban Policy Research, Rutgers University.

Sternlieb, George, Elizabeth Roistacher, and James Hughes. 1976. *Tax Subsidies and Housing Investment*. New Brunswick, NJ: Center for Urban Policy Research, Rutgers University.

Stevenson, Drew. 1998. Setting the scene: Assessing the impact of the LDDC. *Rising East: The Journal of East London Studies* 2, no. 2: 19–31.

Stevenson, Richard W. 1995. From debacle to desirable: Canary Wharf is no longer the outcast of London. *New York Times*, July 18.

Stewart, Barbara. 2000. Bronx loudly opposes waste station plan. *New York Times*, March 9.

Stoker, Gerry. 1995. Regime theory and urban politics. In *Theories of Urban Politics*, edited by David Judge, Gerry Stoker, and Harold Wolman. Thousand Oaks, CA: Sage.

Stollman, Rita. 1989. Borough's residences in revival. *Crain's New York Business*, July 10.

Stone, Clarence N. 1993. Urban regimes and the capacity to govern: A political economy approach. *Journal of Urban Affairs* 15, no. 1: 1–28.

———. 1989. *Regime Politics*. Lawrence: University Press of Kansas.

———. 1976. *Economic Growth and Neighborhood Discontent*. Chapel Hill, NC: University of North Carolina Press.

Stone, Clarence N., and Heywood Sanders, eds. 1987. *The Politics of Urban Development*. Lawrence: University Press of Kansas.

Stuckey, James P. 1988. Letter to the editor. *New York Newsday*, December 7.

Sudjic, Deyan. 1992a. Towering ambition. *Guardian*, April 17.

———. 1992b. *100 Mile City*. London: Andre Deutsch.

Sullivan, Lorana. 1992. O & Y's leaning tower of debt. *Observer* (London), May 17.

Sullivan, Lorana, George Parker-Jervis, and Stella Shamoon. 1992. Nightmare in Docklands. *Independent*, May 31.

Swanstrom, Todd. 1993. Beyond economism: Urban political economy and the postmodern challenge. *Journal of Urban Affairs* 15, no. 1: 55–78.

⸻. 1988. The effect of state and local taxes on investment: A bibliography. *Public Administration Series: Bibliography.* Monticello, IL: Vance Bibliographies.

⸻. 1987. The limits of strategic planning for cities. *Journal of Urban Affairs* 9, no. 2: 139–57.

⸻. 1985. *The Crisis of Growth Politics.* Philadelphia: Temple University Press.

Sweeney, James L. 1977. Economics of depletable resources: Market forces and intertemporal bias. *Review of Economic Studies* 44 (February): 125–41.

Tabb, William K. 1982. *The Long Default.* New York: Monthly Review Press.

Taylor, Alex. 1986. Smart moves for hard times. *Fortune,* December 8, pp. 28–30.

Teitz, Michael B. 1989. Neighborhood economics: Local communities and regional markets. *Economic Development Quarterly* 3: 111–22.

Thornley, Andy. 2000. Dome alone: London's millennium project and the strategic planning deficit. *International Journal of Urban and Regional Research* 24: 689–99.

⸻. 1999. Is Thatcherism dead? The impact of political ideology on British planning. *Journal of Planning Education and Research* 19, no. 2: 183–92.

⸻. 1991. *Urban Planning under Thatcherism.* London: Routledge.

Thrift, Nigel, and Andrew Leyshon. 1990. In the wake of money: The City of London and the accumulation of value. Working Papers on Producer Services no. 4. University of Bristol and Service Industries Research Centre, Portsmouth Polytechnic, July.

Thrift, Nigel, Andrew Leyshon, and Peter Daniels. 1987. "Sexy greedy": The new international financial system, the City of London, and the South East of England. Working Papers on Producer Services no. 8. University of Bristol and Service Industries Research Centre, Portsmouth Polytechnic, October.

Tierney, John. 1991. Era ends as Times Square drops slashers for Shakespeare. *New York Times,* January 14.

Time. 1992. April 6.

Times Square Business Improvement District (BID). 1999. Annual Report. www.times squarebid.org

Tobier, Emanuel. 1979. Gentrification: The Manhattan story. *New York Affairs* 5: 13–25.

Tocqueville, Alexis de. 1957 (orig. pub. c. 1848). *Democracy in America.* New York: Vintage.

Townsend, Peter. 1987. *Poverty and Labour in London.* London: Low Pay Unit.

Trager, Cara S. 2000. Vying to build "next MetroTech Center," but in Queens. *Crain's New York Business,* January 17, pp. 47, 67.

Traster, Tina. 2000. Converted NJ warehouse spurs tide of transplants. *Crain's New York Business,* April 17, pp. 61–62.

Travers, Tony. 1986. *The Politics of Local Government Finance.* London: Allen & Unwin.

Turok, I. 1992. Property-led urban regeneration: Panacea or placebo? *Environment and Planning A* 24: 361–79.

U.S. News & World Report. 1988. March 14, pp. 37–39.

U.K. Department of the Environment (DoE). 1991. *Housing and Construction Statistics, 1980–1990: Great Britain.* London: HMSO.

⸻. 1989. *Planning Guidance for London.* July.

U.K. Department of the Environment, Transport and the Regions (DETR). 1998a. *Regeneration Research Summary: Regenerating London Docklands,* no. 16. London: DETR. www.regeneration.detr.gov.uk/rs/01698/index.htm

⸻. 1998b. *Regeneration Research Summary: Evaluation of the Single Regeneration*

Budget Challenge Fund, no. 19. London: DETR. www.regeneration.detr.gov.uk/rs/ 01998/index.htm

U.K. HM Treasury. 2000. *Budget: March 2000.* www.hm-treasury.gov.uk/budget2000/ leaflet.html

University College London (UCL), Bartlett School. 1990. *King's Cross Second Report.* London: UCL, Bartlett School.

U.S. Bureau of the Census. 1991. *Statistical Abstract of the United States.* Washington, DC: U.S. Government Printing Office.

Van Ryzin, Gregg G., and Andrew Genn. 1999. Neighborhood change and the City of New York's ten-year housing plan. *Housing Policy Debate* 10, no. 4: 799–838.

Venturi, Robert, Denise Scott Brown, and Steven Izenour. 1977. *Learning from Las Vegas.* Rev. ed. Cambridge, MA: MIT Press.

Vizard, Mary McAleer. 1992. Planning strategies for a new retail environment. *New York Times,* June 14.

Walls, Christopher. 1991. *The Central London Office Market, Interest Rates and Property Shares.* London: Salomon Brothers UK Equity Research—Property, April 22.

Warner, Sam Bass, Jr. 1968. *The Private City.* Philadelphia: University of Pennsylvania Press.

Weiss, Marc A. 1991. The politics of real estate cycles. *Business and Economic History,* Second Series, vol. 20: 127–35.

———. 1989. Real estate history: An overview and research agenda. *Business History Review* 63 (Summer): 241–82.

Westminster, City of. 1988. *District Plan.* London: City of Westminster.

Wheaton, William. 1987. Cyclic behavior of the national office market. *Journal of the Real Estate and Urban Economics Association* 14, no. 4: 281–99.

Willensky, Elliot. 1986. *When Brooklyn Was the World.* New York: Harmony Books.

Williams, Alex. 1996. Wall Street wonderland. *New York,* November 4, pp. 33–39.

Wilson, Elizabeth. 1991. *The Sphinx in the City.* London: Virago Press.

Wilson, James Q., ed. 1966. *Urban Renewal.* Cambridge, MA: MIT Press.

Wirth, Lewis. 1938. Urbanism as a way of life. *American Journal of Sociology* 44 (July): 1–24.

Wolfe, Alan. 1992. Democracy versus sociology: Boundaries and their political consequences. In *Cultivating Differences,* edited by Michele Lamont and Marcel Fournier. Chicago: University of Chicago Press.

Wolfe, Tom. 1987. *Bonfire of the Vanities.* New York: Farrar, Straus, Giroux.

Wolfinger, Raymond. 1974. *The Politics of Progress.* Englewood Cliffs, NJ: Prentice-Hall.

Yates, Douglas. 1977. *The Ungovernable City.* Cambridge, MA: MIT Press.

———. 1973. *Neighborhood Democracy.* Lexington, MA: Lexington Books.

Young, Iris Marion. 1990. *Justice and the Politics of Difference.* Princeton, NJ: Princeton University Press.

Young, Michael Dunlop, and Peter Willmott. 1957. *Family and Kinship in East London.* London: Routledge.

Zukin, Sharon. 1995. *The Cultures of Cities.* Oxford: Blackwell.

———. 1992. The city as a landscape of power: London and New York as global financial capitals. In *Global Finance & Urban Living,* edited by Leslie Budd and Sam Whimster. London: Routledge.

———. 1991. *Landscapes of Power.* Berkeley: University of California Press.

———. 1982. *Loft Living.* Baltimore: Johns Hopkins University Press.

Index

Abercrombie, Patrick, 84
Agglomeration, effects in New York and
    London, 33–34
Allegheny Conference, Pittsburgh, 5, 112
Atlantic Terminal, Brooklyn
    potential effect of completed, 157
    urban renewal area, 154
Atlantic Terminal Urban Renewal
    Association (ATURA), 154–55
Authorities, local
    fiscal constraints throughout the United
        Kingdom, 89
    in London, 82–83, 88–89
    partnerships among London's, 91
    planning permission discretion of, 106
    role in King's Cross planning, 119–23

Bachrach, Peter, 9
Balbus, Isaac, 15
Baratz, Morton S., 9
Battery Park, 164
Battery Park City
    assessment of, 171–74
    benefits of, 216
    economic success of, 174
    new Stuyvesant High School, 169–70
    New York Mercantile Exchange in,
        170
    public sector role in, 170

quality of development of, 210
residential section, 169, 206
symbolism of, xii
waterfront walkway, 169
World Financial Center in, 166–70
Battery Park City Authority (BPCA), 113
    as developer, 170
    initial actions (1960s, 1970s), 165–66
    ownership of land and revenues, 170–
        71, 233
    plan for World Financial Center, 166–
        67
Beame, Abraham, 80
Bertelsmann AG, 131
Bethnal Green, City Challenge grant for,
    146–47
Blair, Tony, 22
Blair, Tony, government of
    privatization of public services by, 88
    "Third Way," 116, 196, 229
Board of Estimate, New York City
    authority of, 83
    dominance of, 92
    Times Square–related hearings, 129
Boddy, Trevor, 205
Boroughs, London
    minorities and women gain
        representation in, 89
    municipal functions of, 79

Boroughs, New York City
  activities of Economic Development
    Corporation, 113–14
  activities of Public Development
    corporation in, 112
  councillors elected from, 82–83
  incentive programs for businesses, 62
Boyer, Christine, 217
Bradman, Godfrey, 44
British Property Federation, 71
Broadgate project, London, 48–49, 120,
  138–39
Brooklyn
  African-American Coalition for
    Economic Development, 153–55
  Atlantic Terminal, 149
  Brooklyn Heights and Cadman Plaza,
    148
  MetroTech project, 149–54
  plans for downtown redevelopment,
    138
  as third node of New York's business
    district, 156
  urban renewal, 148
Bush, George, administration of, 32
Business cycles, 62–63
Business groups
  active in Spitalfields redevelopment,
    140–41
  in promoting downtown New York
    City, 55, 57–58
  use of tax-subsidy programs, 59
  See also Financial and business
    services (FBS) sectors
Business improvement districts (BIDs)
  of MetroTech in Brooklyn, 153
  New York's Downtown Alliance, 55, 57
Butler's Wharf renovation, 52

Canary Wharf, 109
  architectural design, 183, 185
  justification for, 223
  original use of, 182
  proposed development of, 183
  recovery of, 190–91
  research for, 70
  success of, 210, 223

Canary Wharf Group, 190–91
Capital
  risk capital for economic regeneration,
    223
  world flows of, 31–33
Carey, Hugh, 166
Cassidy, Michael, 102
Castells, Manuel, 12, 35–36, 209
Central business districts (CBDs)
  overcrowded old, 233
  property values with expansion of, 5
  threats to dominance of, 199
Channel Tunnel train terminal, 119, 121,
  123
Cities, global
  formation of, 34
  importance of, 30–37
  office space in, 37–39
City Challenge program, United Kingdom
  grant to Bethnal Green district,
    146–47
  London, 91, 109–10
  provisions for program in grant to,
    146–47
  required development partnerships, 46–
    47
City council, New York City
  councillors for each borough, 82
  election of, 83
City Planning Commission, New York
  City
  master plan (1969), 104
  midtown zoning rules, 125
Clink Prison Museum, 52
Clinton, Bill, administration of
  inner-city policy of, 229
  mergers during, 32
  urban assistance policy of, 116–17
Clinton neighborhood, New York City,
  124, 129–30, 226
Coin Street development, 52
Colenutt, Bob, 90–91, 109, 195
Columbus Circle, New York City
  Coliseum at Columbus Circle, 106
  Columbus Centre complex, New York
    City, 57
Community boards, New York City, 83

Community Development Block Grant
(CDBG)
focus of, 112
local distribution of, 110
as New York City's access to federal
funds, 91
Community development corporations
(CDCs)
housing projects in New York City
(1990s), 96, 113
potential assistance to nonprofits, 222
Community Development Project, United
Kingdom, 99
Community groups
active in Spitalfields redevelopment,
140–41, 144–46
activities related to Atlantic Terminal
project, 154–57
Community Land Act (1975), United
Kingdom, 6
Community Reinvestment Act (CRA),
United States, 111
Condé Nast Publishing Company, 133
Corporation of London, development
strategy of, 47–50
Covent Garden
good use of site, 210
renewal project, 50
Cox, Kevin, 15

Dahl, Robert, 9, 10
Decentralization, influenced by
technology, 35–37
Democratic contradiction, 101
Dennis, Michael, 163
Department of the Environment (DoE),
United Kingdom, 82, 85, 104
Department of the Environment,
Transport and the Regions (DETR),
United Kingdom, 82, 104
Developers
bargaining in exchange for project
approval, 106–7
concessions for Times Square
redevelopment, 127
differences between New York and
London, 74

information required by, 69–72
negotiated exchanges of, 106–7
in Spitalfields redevelopment, 141–44
See also Forest City Ratner
Development corporations
formation in London and New York,
106
See also Housing development
corporations (HDCs); Urban
development corporations (UDCs)
Development projects, New York City
intensity of, 61–62
lack of citywide plan for, 61
Dinkins, David, 95, 115–16, 216
Docklands development area
aim of, 192
airport, 178
assessment of, 192–95
Docklands Light Railway, 181, 183
housing development, 179, 194–95
Isle of Dogs enterprise zone, 40, 89–
90, 108–9, 182–83
Jubilee tube line into, 85, 181, 191
labor market opportunities in, 194
Limehouse Link, 181, 191
office center development in, 215–16
office development (1980s), 47
population growth, 179–80
symbolism of, xii
Downtown Lower Manhattan Association
(DLMA)
plan for Wall Street area (1960s), 55,
57, 164–65
Durst, Seymour, 73

East London Partnership (ELP), 141
Economic development
in postwar London, 80
property-led strategy for, 75–78
Economic Development Corporation
(EDC), New York City, 86, 112–13
Edwards, Michael, 120
Eisinger, Peter K., 224
Empire State Development Corporation
(ESDC), 58–59, 113
English Partnerships, 70, 224–25
Enterprise Foundation, United States, 113

Enterprise zones
  British and American, 7
  in London's Isle of Dogs, 40, 89–90,
    108–9, 182–83, 219
  New York City, 90
European Bank for Reconstruction and
    Development (EBRD), 48

Financial and business services (FBS)
    sectors
  cyclical nature of, 65
  expansion of, 36–37
  factors influencing growth of, 31–32
  in global cities, 30–31
  New York City and London, 30–32
Financial Control Board (FCB), New
    York City, 93–95
Fiscal policy
  after 1975 financial crisis in New York
    City, 93–94
  for London, 89–90
  in New York City (1980s), 95
Forest City Ratner
  in Atlantic Terminal redevelopment,
    154, 156–57
  in Brooklyn MetroTech project, 150–
    51, 215
  construction of New York Mercantile
    Exchange, 170
Forster, Peter, 190
42nd Street Redevelopment Corporation,
    73, 126, 216
Foster, Janet, 180
Foster, Norman, 143
Frucher, Meyer, 163

Gentrification
  in London, 7
  in New York City (1980s), 114
  in parts of Manhattan and Brooklyn,
    94, 148
George, Henry, 13
Gill, Brendan, 173
Giuliani, Rudolph, 22, 86, 95–96
Giuliani, Rudolph, administration of
  low-income housing production under,
    76

tax breaks and subsidies granted by,
    59–60
Globe Theater reconstruction, 52–53
Government
  incentives to firms locating in
    MetroTech, 150–53, 159
  resources used for property-led
    development, 75–78
  role in Atlantic Terminal project, 154–
    57
  role in Battery Park City project, 164–
    66, 170–74
  role in property development, 202
  See also Authorities, local;
    Government, local; specific
    agencies
Government, local
  issue of autonomy of, 17–18
  promotion of commercial space
    construction, 2–3
  in United States and United Kingdom,
    21
Government, New York City, postwar
    investment in infrastructure, 79–80
Government, United Kingdom
  centralization under Conservatives, 22
  City Challenge program, 46
  commercial expansion policy of, 7
  credit policy of Conservative, 7
  development in boroughs controlled
    by, 51–55
  devolution plans of, 22
  Inner Urban Areas Act, 108
  investment in Docklands infrastructure,
    192
  land-use policy of, 116
  LDDC formed by, 192
  local councils in London, 82–83
  London postwar reconstruction, 79
  participation in City Challenge
    program, 146–47, 159
  participation in Spitalfields
    redevelopment, 143–44, 159
  partnership programs of, 116
  planning policy for London, 84–85
  reversal of social welfare policy,
    87–88

role in Canary Wharf project, 182–83, 188–90
role in Docklands development, 177–81, 192–95
role of UDCs under, 108
Single Regeneration Budget, 46–47
tax incentives of, 39–41
See also Authorities, local; Blair, Tony, government of
Government, United States
federal grants for urban redevelopment, 152
Housing and Urban Renewal Act, 112
Local Initiatives Support Corporation, 113
Low Income Housing Tax Credit program, 113
Tax Reform Act (1986), 45
Urban Development Action Grants, 58, 91, 112, 152
Greater London Authority (GLA)
replaces LPAC, 85
succeeds GLC, 82
Greater London Council (GLC)
abolition (1986), 21, 40–41, 80, 90
approves Greater London Development Plan (1969), 40–41
development strategy (1980s), 80–81
Greater London Enterprise Board (GLEB), 80, 91
Greater London Development Plan, 40–41, 84
Greater London Enterprise (GLE), New LEntA as subsidiary of, 91
Greater London Enterprise Board (GLEB), 80, 91

Harlem/South Bronx Empowerment Zone, partnership and social funding in, 105, 158
Harvey, David, 12, 29, 100, 200–201, 212–13, 216
Heseltine, Michael, 146
Housing, United Kingdom
housing associations, 110–11
public, 6
Housing, United States, public, 6

Housing and Development Administration (HDA), New York City, 104
Housing and Redevelopment Board (HRB), New York City, 104
Housing and Urban Renewal Act (1949), United States, 112
Housing Corporation, United Kingdom, 111
Housing development corporations (HDCs), New York City, 113–14
Housing Preservation and Development (HPD), New York City, 104
Housing programs, New York City
effect of fiscal crisis (1975), 115
Housing Partnership, 115
low- and middle-income, 114–15
spending for, 115–16
subsidized, 93
Hunters Point proposal, 62

Industrial and Commercial Incentives Board (ICIB), 107
subsidies to Brooklyn MtroTech project, 151–53
subsidies to World Financial Center, 170
tax incentive program administered by, 59
Information, needed by developers and property investors, 69–72
Inner Urban Areas Act (1978), United Kingdom, 108
Interest
Marxian concept of, 15
perceived, 15
Isle of Dogs enterprise zone, 40, 89–90, 108–9, 182–83. *See also* Canary Wharf

Kahan, Richard, 166
King's Cross Partnership, 225
King's Cross redevelopment
allowance for gradual, 137
alternative plans for, 121–22, 136
lessons from, 136–37
Koch, Edward I., 80, 94, 114–16

Koch, Edward I., administration of
  emphasis on economic development,
    94
  housing plan, 76
  housing program of (1988), 114–15

La Défense, Paris, 192–93, 195
Land use
  decisions of some urban development
    corporations for, 226
  devising a system for, 227
  interest of business groups in New
    York City, 55, 57–58
  in King's Cross and Times Square
    projects, 119–22
  in post–World War II London, 175–77
  value resulting from development of,
    201–2
Lichfield, John, 189–90
Lindsay, John, 104, 80
Livingstone, Ken, 21–22, 80, 82, 90
Local Initiatives Support Corporation
    (LISC), United States, 113
London
  compared with New York City, 20–23
  council tax, 83
  government by local council, 82–83
  governance compared to New York
    City, 81–87
  Greater London Development Plan, 40
  housing associations in, 110–11
  local authorities of, 79, 82–83
  local borough authorities' view of
    development, 47
  office-building boom (1980s), 39–41
  oversupply of office space, 42–46
  plan for postwar, 84–86
  planning agencies, 103–4
  political structure of, 79
  property investment compared to New
    York City, 73–75
  See also Greater London Authority
    (GLA); Greater London Council
    (GLC)
London Bridge City, 51
London Development Authority (LDA),
    86, 103–4

London Docklands Development
  Corporation (LDDC), 39–41,
    80, 108–9
  administrative jurisdiction of, 177
  financial problems of, 188
  funding for housing renovation, 179
  land acquisition and site development
    by, 178
  official evaluation of, 194
  principal aim, 177–78
  residential development resulting from,
    140
  road investment, 183
  role in Canary Wharf project, 188–89
  transit investment of, 178
London Planning Advisory Committee
    (LPAC), 47, 84–85
London Planning Advisory Council
    (LPAC), 84–85
London Regeneration Consortium (LRC)
  criticism of King's Cross proposal,
    121–22
  proposal for King's Cross, 12–21
Low Income Housing Tax Credit
    program, United States, 113

Major, John, 81, 116, 193
Manhattan
  Downtown Alliance, 55, 57, 164–65
  public programs, 58–59
  tax subsidized property development,
    77
  See also New York City
Marris, Peter, 175–76
Mayor, of London
  election of, 47
  powers of, 21–22
Mayor, of New York City
  election of, 83
  influence of, 22
Messinger, Ruth, 103
Metropolitan Transit Authority (MTA),
    New York City, 86
MetroTech project, Brooklyn
  effect of completed, 153–54, 157, 159,
    223
  incentives for firms moving to, 150–53

justification for, 62, 223
public and private funding for, 150–53
Model Cities program, United States, 99
Moses, Robert, 12, 79, 104, 164
Municipal Assistance Corporation
    (MAC), New York City
  equity investments of, 152
  formation of, 93–95

New Amsterdam Theater, 133
New Jersey
  commercial and residential projects
    (1980s), 62
  commercial growth along Hudson
    River, 87
  competition with New York City, 86–
    87, 148, 156
New London Enterprise Agency Ltd., 91
New York City
  Board of Estimate, 83
  City Charter (1990), 83
  City Planning Department, 104–5
  compared with London, 20–23
  fiscal crisis (1975), 93–95
  governance compared to London, 81–
    87
  government of, 79
  governing powers of mayor and city
    council, 83
  Harlem/South Bronx Empowerment
    Zone, 77, 105, 158
  jurisdiction of city council, 82–83
  legislative power of city council, 83
  new housing (1980s), 61–62
  oversupply of office space, 42–46
  planning agencies, 104
  political structure of, 79
  postwar investment in infrastructure,
    79–81
  property investment (1975–2000), 73–
    75
  property investment compared to
    London, 73–75
  Regional Plan Association (RPA), 58
  revision of City Charter (1990), 83
  subsidies to Housing Partnership
    (1981–91), 115

  tax revenues of, 83–84
  See also Manhattan
New York City Partnership, 58
New York City Planning Commission, 86
New York State
  Department of Marine and Aviation,
    165
  Empire State Development Corporation
    of, 58, 86
  Office of State Deputy Controller for
    New York City, 93–94
  post–fiscal crisis oversight of New
    York City, 93–95
New York Stock Exchange, 60
New York University, Urban Research
    Center, 156
NIMBYism (not-in-my-backyard), 227
Non-profit organizations, urban, 222

Olympia & York (O&Y)
  creation and development of, 162–63
  development of Canary Wharf, 181,
    183, 185
  development of World Financial
    Center, 166–70
  downfall of, 185–89
  rise of, 161–64
Olympia & York Developments Ltd., 44

Paddington Basin development, 85
Partnerships, public-private, in London
    and New York City, 105–16
Payment in lieu of taxes (PILOT), 128
Peterson, Paul, 17
Place
  characteristics of, 202
  elements contributing to creation of, 202
Polsby, Nelson, 9, 10
Port Authority of New York and New
    Jersey, 86
Port of London Authority (PLA), 176
Property
  commercial development of, 3
  government incentives in Britain to
    develop, 76–77
  incentives in United Kingdom for
    commercial, 7

Property *(continued)*
  tax subsidies in New York City related
    to development, 77
  See also Land use
Property market
  cycles and volatility in, xi, 62–65, 75–
    78, 198–201
  effect of boom (1990s), 191
  effect of FBS cycles on, 65
  increased values (1990s), 65
  oversupply of real estate, 65–66
  post-1987 decline, 42–46
  pressure to build, 66–68
  pricing real estate in, 199–200
  real-estate value in London and New
    York (1989), 42–44
  recovery (1990s), 46–49
  research and information sources for,
    69–72
  undersupply of real estate, 68–69
  See also Real-estate industry
Property market, London
  demand for space (1990s), 65
  dependence on financial and business
    services, 65
Property market, New York City
  demand for space (1990s), 65
  dependence on financial and business
    services, 65
  intervention in planning in, 104–5
Property rights, 202
Pryke, Michael, 32–33, 206
Public Development Corporation (PDC),
    New York City, 126
  in Brooklyn MetroTech project, 150–
    51
Public-private partnerships
  King's Cross Partnership, 225
  London and New York City, 105–6
  under U.K. Single Regeneration
    Budget, 224–25

Railway Lands Community Development
    Group (RLCDG), 121–22, 136
Ratner, Bruce, 150, 156
Reagan, Ronald, administration of, 32
Real Estate Board of New York, 58, 71

Real-estate development, government role
    in, 72–73
Real-estate industry
  characteristics of development in, 197–
    98
  cycles of, 65
  effect of economic downturn (1980s,
    1990s), 42–49
  expression of male egos in, 4
  information required by property
    investment firms, 69–72
  organization of production by firms in,
    198
  as vehicle to stimulate economic
    growth, 219
  volatility of, xiii
  See also Developers
Redevelopment
  current proposed projects in New York
    City, 96–97
  effect of (1970s, 1980s), 8
  experience in United States and United
    Kingdom, 6–8
  groups marginalized by, 5, 29
  public investment to create commercial
    nodes, 157–59
  regime theory to explain, 14
  structuralist explanation of, 11–12
  typical scenario of urban, 5–8
  See also Times Square redevelopment;
    Urban redevelopment
Redevelopment policy
  feature of good, 229–30
  liberal theory of, 10–11
  plans and incentives in New York City,
    55, 57
  regime theory, 14
  structuralist theory, 11–13
Regime theory, 14
Regional Plan Association (RPA)
  development plan for New York City,
    58
  vision for downtown Brooklyn, 149
Reichl, Alexander, 211
Reichmann family, 160–64, 181–82, 185–
    91
Rent, in urban development, 13

Residential development
  Dinkins administration housing
    program, 115
  and Docklands development, 179–81,
    191, 194–95
  public housing in United Kingdom and
    United States, 6
  redevelopment in New York City and
    London, 38–39, 61–62
  social housing in Docklands project,
    194
  See also Gentrification
Reuters news service, 133
Rockefeller, David, 164
Rockefeller, Nelson, 165
Ross, Stephen, 57
Rudin, William, 133

Safdie, Moshe, 204–5
Sanders, Heywood T., 17
Sassen, Saskia, 34–35
Savitch, H. V., 10
Schwartz, Alex, 115–16
Segregation
  in New York City (1960s), 92–93
  as result of urban redevelopment, 8
Sennett, Richard, 205
Shepherd, Alan, 141
Single Regeneration Budget (SRB), 91,
    102, 110
  Cityside program, 147
  funding for Bankside development, 53
  funding to King's Cross Partnership,
    123
  public-private partnerships under, 224–
    25
  required collaboration for development,
    46–47
  urban policy under, 194
Skadden Arps Slate Meagher & Flom, 133
Social welfare policy
  during Koch administration, 94–95
  London, 87
  New York, 87
  See also Residential development
Soja, Edward, 18
Sorkin, Michael, 171, 208–9

Space
  debate about, 18–19
  spatial restructuring in London, 32–33
Spitalfields
  actions of community and business
    groups, 140–41
  Brick Lane area, 138–40, 144–46
  as City Challenge development, 216
  as focus for redevelopment, 138–40
  market relocation, 141–42
  Spitalfields Community Development
    Group (SCDG), 143
  Spitalfields Development Group
    (SDG), 141–44
  Spitalfields Market development, 106–
    7
  See also Bethnal Green
Stone, Clarence, 14, 17
Structuralist theory
  contemporary, 11–12
  redevelopment functions, 11–13
  rent theory, 13
Subsidies
  to Battery Park City project, 170–74
  in Brooklyn MetroTech project, 150–
    53
  for Isle of Dogs enterprise zone, 89–90
  to New York developers (1990s), 8
  offered for Atlantic Terminal project,
    155–57
  tax-subsidy in New York, 59–60, 77
  for Times Square project, 128
  of UDAGs, 58
  for urban commercial development, 3
Surrey Docks
  housing construction, 52
  redevelopment, 51
Swanstrom, Todd, 10

Tate Gallery of Modern Art, 52, 54
Tax Reform Act (1986), United States, 45
Tese, Vincent, 86–87
Thatcher, Margaret, 81, 84, 87–88, 108,
    116, 192
Thompson, Ben, 142–43
Times Square Business Improvement
    District, 131

Times Square redevelopment
  allowance for gradual, 137
  impetus for, 123–25
  interim development plan, 131
  lessons from, 136–37
  market-driven process for, 133–36
  public and private sector financing for,
    128
  responses to plan, 129–30
Transportation
  in Canary Wharf project, 183, 185,
    190–91
  in Docklands development, 178, 181,
    194
  initiatives in London to improve, 85–86
  role in New York planning, 86–87
Travelstead, G. Ware, 183
Trump, Donald, 44, 58, 60, 73, 107

UDAGs. See Urban Development Action
  Grants
United Kingdom. See Government,
  United Kingdom
Urban Development Action Grants
  (UDAGs), United States
  in Brooklyn MetroTech project, 152
  post-1981 subsidies in New York City,
    58
  program, 91, 112
Urban Development Corporation (UDC),
  New York State, 113
  acquisition of Times Square
    redevelopment sites, 130–31
  plan for Times Square redevelopment,
    125–26

Urban development corporations (UDCs)
  British public-private organizations,
    107–11
  function of, 107
  private market role in United Kingdom,
    7, 108
  rise in New York City and London,
    226
  urban policy during Tory regime, 108
  U.S. public-private organizations, 111–
    16
Urban redevelopment, 7
  by development corporations (1980s),
    106
  evaluation of projects in London and
    New York City, 214–18
  materialist analysis of, 212–13
  need for social equity in, 228–30
  poststructuralist critique, 204–10
  public-private partnerships of, 204
Weeks, David, 102
Westminster, London, 50–51
Wilson, Elizabeth, 205–6
With, Lewis, 203
Wolfe, Alan, 213
Wolfinger, Raymond, 9
World Financial Center (WFC)
  developed by Olympia & York, 166–70
  Winter Garden of, 167–69
World Trade Center, 167, 169

Zeckendorf, William, Jr., 107
Zuccotti, John, 163
Zuckerman, Mortimer, 57
Zukin, Sharon, 213

4075
. . (

This book is a product of the Modern Chinese History Project carried on by the Far Eastern and Russian Institute of the University of Washington. Members of the group represent various disciplines in the social sciences and humanities. The work of the project is of a cooperative nature with each member assisting the others through critical discussion and the contribution of ideas and material. The responsibility for each study rests with the author.

The Taiping Ideology

ITS SOURCES, INTERPRETATIONS, AND INFLUENCES

By

VINCENT Y. C. SHIH

UNIVERSITY OF WASHINGTON PRESS
Seattle and London

Copyright © 1967 by the University of Washington Press
Library of Congress Catalog Card Number 66-19571
All rights reserved

MOUNT UNION COLLEGE
LIBRARY

951.03
S555t

147034

PRINTED IN JAPAN
BY GENERAL PRINTING CO., LTD., YOKOHAMA

Preface

In substance this study was completed in 1954. Since then Jen (Chien) Yu-wen has brought out his monumental works on Taiping institutions and history. I regret that I have not been able to give them the treatment they deserve, although on the basis of some of his papers published earlier which are now included in these works I have revised my views about his interpretation of the *T'ai-p'ing t'ien-kuo*. In mainland China we find also a few papers on the nature of the Taiping Rebellion. But the whole chorus of voices is still harping on the orthodox Communist view, drowning out any occasional feeble but discordant note. I have not found it necessary to change any of my views about the Communist interpretation.

In the process of writing this monograph, I have received generous help from my colleagues of the Modern Chinese History Colloquium at the University of Washington in the form of friendly criticisms, and I wish especially to thank George Taylor, Director of the Far Eastern and Russian Institute, Franz Michael, Chairman of the Modern Chinese History Colloquium, Chung-li Chang, Kung-chuan Hsiao, and Hellmut Wilhelm. If I have not on all occasions followed their advice, I have always considered their suggestions seriously. It is indeed a refreshing experience to be exposed to views and disciplines other than one's own. For this broadening of my scope I feel deeply grateful. It is safe to assume that this work would not be what it is if I had to work in isolation without the benefit of constant discussions with a group of scholars who had nothing but the scholarly interests at heart. Not any less do I owe gratitude to Miss Gladys Greenwood and her assistants for their untiring effort to bring the book into its present form. While grateful for the help my colleagues have given me, I alone am responsible for the final result.

University of Washington
August 12, 1963

VINCENT Y. C. SHIH

Contents

Preface v
Introduction ix
PART ONE: EXPOSITION OF THE TAIPING IDEOLOGY 1
Chapter I: Religion 3
Chapter II: Moral Views 31
Chapter III: Social Ideals and Social Structure 45
Chapter IV: The Economic Aspect 81
Chapter V: Political and Military Aspects 85
Chapter VI: The Development of the Taiping Ideology . . . 105
PART TWO: SOURCES AND INTERPRETATIONS OF THE
           TAIPING IDEOLOGY 141
Chapter VII: Christianity 147
Chapter VIII: The Classics and Confucianism 165
Chapter IX: Buddhism, Taoism, and Mohism 273
Chapter X: Other Sources of the Taiping Ideology 285
Chapter XI: Some Rebel Ideologies Prior to the Taipings . . . 329
PART THREE: INTERPRETATIONS OF THE *T'ai-p'ing t'ien-kuo* . . . 391
Chapter XII: Nineteenth-Century Interpretations 395
Chapter XIII: Twentieth-Century Interpretations 427
Chapter XIV: A Transcendent Interpretation 469
Reign Periods of the Ch'ing Dynasty 499
Abbreviations 501
Bibliography 503
Index 527

Introduction

An analytical study of an ideology is believed to be a key to the understanding of the society in which it takes form. This belief is based on the assumptions that ideas are functions of the persons who express them[1] and that "the shape that ideas take is relative to the culture and era in which they develop and are used."[2] On the other hand we are also aware that "there are internal standards of validity in ideas themselves."[3] It is precisely this study of the intrinsic validity of ideas themselves (or categories of the understanding, according to philosophers) that distinguishes philosophy from ideology, the latter being a system or systems of ideas always conceived in conjunction with social, economic, political, and other objective conditions. However inadequate this view of the sociology of knowledge may be in reference to ideas which have intrinsic

[1] Karl Mannheim, *Ideology and Utopia: An Introduction to the Sociology of Knowledge* (New York, 1936), p. 50.

[2] Max Lerner, *Ideas Are Weapons* (New York, 1939), p. 8. See also Max Scheler's *Die Probleme der Geschichtsphilosophie* (Leipzig, 1923), p. 48, where he takes the position that all knowledge is determined by the social conditions out of which it arises; and Emile Durkheim's *The Elementary Forms of the Religious Life*, translated by Joseph Ward Swain (New York, 1926), in which Durkheim holds that "they [referring to categories of understanding without which no thinking is possible] are born in religion and of religion; they are a product of religious thought" (p. 9). Hence Durkheim's general conclusion: these categories are social in character.

[3] Max Lerner, *loc. cit.* Philosophers since the time of Aristotle have been trying to map out intellectual life in terms of fundamental categories of the understanding. Even Max Scheler also seeks to escape the sociologistic implication of his position that the social factors which condition knowledge also determine the validity of that knowledge by the metaphysical device of constructing two separate realms of existence: value essences and concrete existential facts. See his "Erkenntnis und Arbeit" in his *Die Wissensformen und die Gesellschaft* (Leipzig, 1926), p. 347.

validity, ideas which are components of an ideology do reflect the reality in which they emerge and so should be treated in conjunction with objective conditions. But it does not follow that ideas are the effects, and conditions the cause. The first cause or causes of history are forever beyond our understanding. All we can do in studying historical developments and movements is to take a convenient point in history and start to analyze the course of events from then on. We shall then find that there are times when ideas, while reflecting the conditions of the time, also influence the course of events and the action of men; and men's action is after all the chief factor in determining the nature of their society. Whatever our view of ideas in relation to concrete conditions, ideas do furnish us with valuable primary data with which to study our society—both the existing society and the society the ideology is meant to create.

On the basis of this understanding of ideas, the approach and purpose of our study of the ideology of the *T'ai-p'ing t'ien-kuo* can be simply stated. We seek to know what kind of movement the *T'ai-p'ing t'ien-kuo* was and what kind of society it sought to replace, and for what reason. To do this obviously requires a careful analysis of the social, political, and economic conditions at the time it took its rise as well as an analysis of its ideology—its sources, its functions, its development, its interpretations. In the process of finding the unique characteristics that distinguish the Taiping ideology from previous rebel ideologies, I have found a more or less uniform pattern in all rebellions: the recurring conditions prior to the emergence of rebellions, the nature and components of rebel ideologies, and the reasons for success or failure. These similarities show that rebel ideologies tend to have a tradition of their own, a tradition which on closer scrutiny turns out to be part and parcel of the main current of the orthodox ideology.

As ideas reflect the reality in which they emerge, so the Taiping ideology reflected China in the middle of the nineteenth century and the periods immediately preceding. China was then rudely shaken out of her complacent belief that she was the center of the world, culturally or otherwise. The empire, beset with troubles of all kinds, was well on its way to decline. The process of decline had started some time earlier. Just as in the past the seeds of decline had been sown during periods of prosperity and strength (during the reign of Emperor Wu, 140–87 B. C., in the Han and during the T'ien-pao reign, A. D. 742–56, in the T'ang), so in the Ch'ing it was during the unprecedented period of peace

and prosperity of the Ch'ien-lung reign, 1736–95, that the dynasty began to show signs of weakening. During the periods immediately before Hsien-feng, 1851–61, hardly a year went by without some riots, uprising, revolts, and a variety of natural and man-made calamities. Government corruption, which was already evident during the Ch'ien-lung reign, as attested by the case of Huo Shen, continued to be a major factor affecting the quality and efficiency of both the central and local government. The economic life of the people was fast approaching its lowest ebb. The frustration of unsuccessful candidates in the imperial examinations added to the general malcontent of the people and supplied them with rebel leadership. The fact that the ruling regime was a non-Chinese dynasty provided the rebels with a rallying ideal: to oust the barbarians and return China to the Chinese. All these political, economic, social, and ethnic factors are external to the ideology, but they bring into bold relief the motives of the rebellion. In Chapter XIV, "A Transcendent Interpretation," these factors and their relation to the Taiping ideology are discussed.

The Taiping ideology itself is taken up in Part One, where, for the sake of narrative, I have treated it under five topics: religious, moral, social, economic, and political and military. The final section is devoted to a discussion of the development of the ideology both as a whole and as it was held by individual leaders.

All ideas have histories of their own, and the Taipings obviously did not originate all their ideas. So the next step in our study of the Taiping ideology is to ferret out all the possible sources from which the Taiping ideas may have been derived. This leads me to cover most of the cultural aspects of China as well as Christian and some other minor religious influences of the West. This lengthy analytical work is given in Part Two.

I can well imagine that my presentation of the material in Parts One and Two may raise in the mind of the reader the question: Was there no unity in the Taiping ideology? The author has successfully anatomized a living ideology into bits of information, correct perhaps, but cold, rigid, and soulless, like a corpse on a dissecting table, devoid of the moving spirit that once inspired hope and enthusiasm in the minds of thousands and then millions of people, and created an *esprit de corps* that saw them through all adversities and enabled them to establish a new dynasty at Nanking in a matter of three years. The Taiping ideology must be more than the mere parts that have been so neatly presented in array. Unfortunately, this difficulty is inherent in any form of discursive

presentation. An ideology when systematically presented must necessarily lose some of its emotional appeal, because its force lies in its persuasiveness and seldom in its logical validity; its aim is efficacy in action rather than logical coherence. Certainly there is unity in the Taiping ideology; but this unity is practical rather than logical. When a group of people are bound together by common aims and purposes, these aims and purposes breathe into their thought life a kind of practical unity. The unity of the Taiping movement was derived from the movement itself. Because of the enthusiasm and passion with which the ideology was embraced, the ideology in turn intensified the unity of the movement. The unity of the ideology was the unity of the movement, and the unity of the movement was the unity its own ideology helped to create.

The necessity of emphasizing this practical unity of the Taiping ideology also shows up more clearly its lack of a logical unity. It is not a logically consistent system. There are layers of conceptual schemes that can be detected in it, piled one on top of another, of which some are logically irreconcilable. This nondescript nature and the inner contradictions can largely be explained by the fact that neither the hold of ideas on the human mind nor their acceptance is a completely conscious and rational affair. The exigencies of the situations demanded quick action, and the Taipings adopted whatever ideas seemed to serve their immediate practical purposes.

With all its logical deficiencies, we must envisage the Taiping ideology as a complete whole. What bound the nondescript ideology into a concrete whole was the religious element which had figured importantly in all previous rebel ideologies. This religiously based organic quality of the Taiping ideology is most clearly indicated in many of their documents. For example, "The Land System of the Heavenly Dynasty" (T'ien-ch'ao t'ien-mou chih-tu), the most important of all Taiping documents, first mentions political and military titles and then deals with economic equality, together with a land system and common sharing of goods, based on the concept that the family of God is one. Next the Sabbath is mentioned, when men and women attend Sunday services in their segregated quarters. Then follows the judiciary procedure, in which military officers perform the duties of a judge; the system of reward and punishment, promotion and demotion; and the military organization. Finally, the document is brought to a close on a religious note. The reader is made to feel that all these problems are

organically related and woven around the central core of the Taipings' religious life.

Another example of this organic and practical unity is found in the first two articles in the "Ten Camping Regulations" in the "Taiping Rules and Regulations" (T'ai-p'ing t'iao-kuei). Although the regulations concern discipline, these two articles do not deal with military matters but with religious ones, such as obeying the heavenly orders, memorizing the Heavenly Commandments, and attending the morning and evening services. Apparently the religious discipline is also the military discipline, and their identification in the regulations shows that the Taipings made no distinction between them. The life of the Taipings, like that of the Hebrews, was dominated by religion; for both, all judgments were divine judgments and all duties divine commandments. There is not the slightest doubt that the religious element in the Taiping ideology was the fundamental unifying force of the Taiping movement.

There was a historical justification for this religious emphasis at that particular moment. The Taipings were consciously or unconsciously looking for something that would replace the traditional ideology, which had been in effect for so long that the people were blinded by its indoctrination to the gross injustice that had been done them by the ruling clique under the cloak of moral training. They were seeking some positive outlook that would enable them to break the hold of the orthodox ideology upon the minds of the people so that they could see straight for themselves without having their judgments warped by the official views. Just at this moment came Christianity, which must have seemed to the Taipings a God-sent gift to lift them out of the morass into which the traditional attitude of fatalism had sunk them. We shall see that this Christian element not only served as the unifying force of the Taiping movement but also distinguished it from all previous rebellions which also had some form of religious element.

As the Taiping movement developed, some changes took place in the minds of the leaders, and other changes in the ideology were brought in by new figures in the administration. The changes in the different editions of the Taiping documents show a gradual moving away from the traditional pattern to one that seems increasingly confused and nondescript. Hung's final religious outlook was an extreme fanaticism, attributable to the diseased brain of a deranged man. At the same time, the ideology as represented by the Kan Wang had become increasingly

traditional on the one hand and surprisingly modern on the other. Recommendations for both the reintroduction of Confucianism into the Taiping ideology and the modernization of China were made during the Kan Wang's stewardship after 1859. The former recommendation, while reflecting his own educational background, seems to have been due to the Kan Wang's awareness of the importance of recapturing the support of the gentry; his reform proposals seem to have grown out of his intimate contact with Western missionaries, who must have been the inspiration of his effort.

The ideology was not accepted by all and was not taken in the same spirit throughout the period of rebellion. At the beginning of the campaign, it was taken seriously by almost all segments of the Taiping army. As time went on, the edge of their enthusiasm seems to have dulled. The ideology was perhaps effective at points within the reach of central control, but its force became increasingly weakened in proportion to the region's distance from the seat of the central government. To many of the leaders who joined the movement later, the Taiping religion and commandments became a matter of routine, not the living ideas that had at first fired the hearts of the original followers. The Chung Wang's confession speaks eloquently of the cold and formal air accorded to the Taiping religion. His criticism is all the more significant if we remember how the Chung Wang was praised by Western writers as the paragon of Taiping religious virtue. The reason seems to be that the Taipings, with the exception of a few devout followers, were not profoundly affected by the Christian ideas which Hung and other leaders sought to instill in their minds. Even their early enthusiasm may have been due to their relief at escaping their previous political and economic frustrations.

Questions concerning the nature and significance of the Taiping movement are given in Part Three, where various interpretations of the movement since the time of the Taipings are put forward. Here I shall discuss briefly what I believe the Taiping movement to be and what its significance is.

Many scholars have described the Taiping society and ideology as revolutionary. This is a view which does not appear accurate if one accepts the definition of "revolution" given in Chapter XI. There it is stated that for a movement to be called revolutionary, not only must violence be the means for bringing about change, but the leaders must show a desire to make changes in the nature of the society they wish to supplant; one of these changes is a reshuffling of the classes in that

society. In the case of the Taipings there does not seem to have been such an indication; the leaders merely wished to take over the reins of government and showed no real revolutionary spirit—no wish to introduce fundamental changes into their society, whether in the form of government or in the fundamental pattern of their mental outlook. There were certain ideas borrowed from Christianity and the West which held a genuine possibility of bringing about a real revolution. But this possibility was nullified when, because of years of indoctrination in the traditional outlook, the Taipings were unable to perceive Christian ideas except through the colored glasses of traditional concepts. Indeed, the elements of Christianity they accepted seem to have been only those that they could anchor to Chinese concepts.

Many scholars consider the Taiping concepts of social and economic equality and the Kan Wang's reform program revolutionary. It is questionable, however, whether their newness in itself can be considered revolutionary. Whether the concept of equality and cultural elements such as railroads, steamships, postal service, and newspapers can be considered revolutionary has to be determined by their effects. If they succeeded in producing a change in the mental attitude of the people, if they succeeded in bringing about a new pattern of behavior, then they may be considered revolutionary. Despite all the official proclamations of the Taipings, the spirit of equality was absent from their society; neither was there a pattern of behavior indicating revolutionary advance. The Taiping ideology contains some revolutionary elements, but as a whole it falls within the main currents of China's tradition.

The nature of Taiping Christianity has also been a constant subject of debate. I for one do not believe that there is any point in calling it either true or distorted Christianity, for true Christianity can be defined only in a strictly circumscribed context. Although Taiping Christianity is not free from the coloring of the native religious and traditional ideas, the Taiping publications seem as orthodox as one can find anywhere, if we can depend on the view of Dr. Medhurst, who translated and examined the early publications of the Taiping documents. I agree with most missionaries that, untutored and without spiritual instructors, the Taipings' unenlightened minds must have understood many of the scriptural texts in terms of their own background. This complication accounts for their unfailing attempt to anchor these new ideas to the native tradition. This religious perversion, however, cannot be construed

to be a conscious effort; hence, it would be wrong to follow some of the Western scholars who dub Hung an impostor.

Similarly, it would be wrong to call the Taiping religious views a political camouflage in spite of the political use to which they were put. There seems to be no *a priori* reason to doubt the sincerity of their initial religious endeavors. Some of the early missionaries thought that their movement was originally a religious one but that it was forced to become a political campaign by the government persecution. The truth seems to be that the Taiping movement was both a religious war and a political rebellion. Religion gave the Taipings a crusader's zest, and politics gave them a practical direction. They called their Manchu enemy "imps" or "devils" *(yao)*, terms which definitely connote a religious attitude; and their ideal was a combination of the religious element of the kingdom of heaven and the political element of worldly peace.

Was the Taiping movement a peasant revolution and the war a peasant war? My answer is a decided no, and this for a number of reasons. First, the leaders do not seem to have identified themselves in their ideology with the peasant, although they knew full well the propaganda value of an issue such as a peasant war. They may have been genuinely sincere in their pronouncement or genuinely sympathetic with the peasants, but their ambition was elsewhere. True they had formulated a land system, and the continuation of war may have kept them from putting it into effect; their actual practice in land administration, however, showed no enthusiasm for bettering the lot of the peasants. They did not attempt to do away with the landlords and give the land to the tillers, and at times even sided with the landlords much as the Ch'ing regime had done before.[4]

Second, there was no evidence of peasant consciousness being reflected in the minds of the Taiping followers (assuming that a peasant war presupposes a peasant group with a distinct consciousness of themselves as a specific group). At the time of joining, Taiping followers cast

---

[4] Wu Yen-nan in his "A Tentative Discussion of the Taiping Land System" (Shih-lun T'ai-p'ing t'ien-kuo ti t'u-ti chih-tu) says that the Taipings even helped the landlords collect their rent, much as the Ch'ing regime had done before. The article appeared in *Li-shih yen-chiu*, No. 2 (1958). Another article in the same issue confirms this view and concludes: "Their method in dealing with land problems is: recognize the landlord's obligation to pay tax to the *T'ai-p'ing t'ien-kuo* and at the same time offer protection and support to the landlords in their effort to collect rent from their tenants." Lung Sheng-yün, "The Application of the Taiping Land System during the Last Years of the T'ai-p'ing t'ien-kuo" (T'ai-p'ing t'ien-kuo hou-ch'i t'u-ti chih-tu shih-shih wen-t'i), pp. 35–54.

aside with unbounded joy their role as peasants and had nothing but pity for those who had to stay behind to farm. "The Land System of the Heavenly Dynasty" reflects this outlook very well when it decrees that those who violate the Heavenly Commandments are to be demoted to peasants.

On the basis of these reasons, it is obvious that it is wrong to dub the Taiping movement a peasant war. If the Taiping rebellion was neither a peasant war nor a revolution, it would be doubly objectionable to call it a peasant revolution, as the Chinese Communists would like us to believe it was. All we can say about the Taiping movement is that it was a rebellion with some characteristics of its own which distinguished it from all previous rebellions.

On the surface the Taipings were like any other group of rebels who were dissatisfied with their circumstances and had the desire to improve their situation. Here we may enumerate all the classic causes of any rebellion (Chapter XI). But we must add to them what is specific to the Taiping movement: the new international situation, economic changes due to foreign trade with the accompanying collapse of the village economy, and the introduction of Christian ideas. These are some of the factors that made the Taiping movement more significant than the previous rebellions. This movement affords us a vantage point for viewing China in transition, going through the throes of adapting herself to the modern world. All the defects of later Chinese intellectual attempts to modernize China in an effort to respond to the West, particularly in the fields of ideas and institutions, science and technology, seem to have been ominously indicated in the Taiping rebellion. Although they did not distort Western philosophy and religion in the same way that Hung and his group distorted Christianity, the ignorance of later Chinese leaders was just as profound. The Kan Wang's reform program shows the same confusion as the programs of those who tried to adopt technology without making a fundamental change in attitude and who looked upon technology as if it were science itself.

Why the Taiping movement occurred at the moment it did will probably forever remain an enigma, but on the basis of our study we may make a few conjectures. The government was inept and corrupt. The whole empire was overrun with confusion and chaos. The people were suffering from poverty. The government had just suffered humiliating defeats, with all its military weakness completely exposed. There were natural calamities throughout the land. But these conditions alone

would not necessarily have led to rebellion. They could have caused a few sporadic uprisings here and there such as had occurred throughout Chinese history, but they would not have initiated a rebellion with a program, an ideology, and a far-reaching purpose and aim. Such a rebellion required imagination and strong leadership. Hung, in addition to his magnetic personality, offered both, and Yang strengthened the leadership. But these leaders would still have found it difficult to persuade people long indoctrinated in the official ideology to join them had there not been the happy coincidence of the coming of Christianity, the catalytic influence of a new ideology. In the fatherhood of God and the brotherhood of man the Taipings had a theoretical basis for demanding equality, although they had only the vaguest idea of what equality really meant. Without this new ideology, it would have been nearly impossible to break the hold that orthodoxy had on the mind of the people. Any one of these factors alone might not have had very great force; but taken together they constitute a strong reason for the movement to have happened when it did. Social, political, and economic conditions persisted while ideas changed; hence the upheaval. Why all these factors converged at a particular time remains a mystery.

As enigmatic as the problem of the causes for the rise of the movement is that of the causes for its failure. The Communist claim that the movement failed because of the lack of proletarian leadership can be dismissed without a hearing. The man who led the Chinese Communists to power can hardly be described as a proletarian. Often mentioned also as reasons for the downfall of the Taipings are their bad strategy in not marching on Peking but settling down in Nanking and the internal strife among the kings. Both were undoubtedly responsible for the Taipings' missing the opportunity to gain a sweeping victory and caused confusion within the movement, which eventually sapped the vitality of the regime. But supposing they had adopted the right strategy, and had remained a united fighting force long enough to establish a new dynasty, would they have lasted long? I doubt it. It is one thing to fan the emotions of a group of people into flame and to take advantage of the initial enthusiasm to start a movement. But it is quite another to keep the spirit high and maintain the same discipline when settling down to rule. Much of the enthusiasm that comes from expectation of adventure dies down. Instead of adventure, one is confronted with the routine discharge of duty. Furthermore, the psychology of a spoils system may work havoc among the followers, or, more often, among the

leaders themselves. Some people forever feel that they are short-changed, regardless of the magnitude of their reward. To be able to ride over these storms successfully, leaders are needed whose far-reaching purposes and aims are practical; these leaders must be sincere in their attempts to realize their aims. In my study of the Chinese rebel ideologies, I have shown that the degrees of success the leaders of the different rebellions received seem to vary in direct proportion to their effort and sincerity in carrying out the ideas they have proclaimed. Both Huang Ch'ao and Li Tzu-ch'eng took the capital, and for a short while were proclaimed emperor. But how long did either last? I believe that the same fate was awaiting the Taipings had they taken Peking. Their internal strife, too, was only symptomatic of deeper ills that were plaguing their minds: their inadequate grasp of the situation, which made them propagandists instead of reformers, their lack of real understanding of the living issues of their time as shown in their suicidal struggle for power, their lack of true convictions in spite of the noisiness of their ideology, and their want of sincerity in their attempts to carry out even their meager ideas. Their lack of concern about their own land system is a case in point. Had they taken certain of their ideas more seriously and tried to carry them out more sincerely, I would like to believe that they could have adopted a better strategy and would not have fallen upon one another so viciously. As it was, the Taipings, though vastly different from any rebel group before, finally succumbed to their own shortcomings and became another relic in the history of Chinese rebellions.

PART ONE
Exposition of the Taiping Ideology

Chapter I

Religion

Taiping society was permeated by a religious atmosphere. A clear understanding of their religious beliefs and practices and their attitude toward other religions is a key to the understanding of the Taipings' mental outlook. The Taipings' complex religious beliefs were based upon: a hierarchy of God, Jesus, the T'ien Wang (Heavenly King), and the Tung Wang (Eastern King); in addition they believed in the existence of the devil and his followers and in heaven and hell.

The central conception of the Taiping religion was God. One of the many Chinese terms used by them for God was *T'ien*, meaning "Heaven." *T'ien* and God coincided in the minds of the Taipings in many respects, but they were not completely identical. While *T'ien* was used to represent God as a deity, it also seems to have had a wider application: since *T'ien* can be used as an adjective but "God" cannot, it was employed in a further sense to mean a pervasive force permeating all important phases of life in the Taiping society.[1] With this distinction, we shall henceforth speak of the two as equivalent terms. The other names for God were *Ti* (the Supreme Ruler), *Shang-ti* (the Supreme Ruler on High), *Huang Shang-ti* (Sovereign Supreme Ruler on High), *Huang-t'ien Shang-ti* (Sovereign Heaven, Supreme Ruler on High), and finally *T'ien-chu* (Heavenly Lord) and *Shang-chu* (Lord on High). All

---

[1] The pervasive nature of Heaven can be seen by the manner in which the Taipings characterized things important to them: God was called *T'ien-fu* (Heavenly Father); Jesus, *T'ien Hsiung* (Heavenly Brother); Hung himself, *T'ien Wang* (Heavenly King); the state, *t'ien-kuo* (heavenly kingdom); the dynasty, *t'ien-ch'ao* (heavenly dynasty); the capital, *t'ien-ching* (heavenly capital); the soldiers, *t'ien-ping* (heavenly soldiers) and *t'ien-chiang* (heavenly generals); the Commandments, *T'ien-t'iao* (Heavenly Commandments); and their way of life or highest principle, *t'ien tao* (the heavenly way).

these terms were used as exact translations of "God," with no appreciable difference.[2] God alone might be called *Ti* or *Huang Shang-ti;* no mortal could assume these honorific titles. According to the Taipings, the reason Hui-tsung and Ch'in-tsung of the Sung dynasty met defeat was that they disrespectfully changed the title of God to *Hao-t'ien chin-ch'üeh yü-huang shang-ti* (Jade August God Within the Golden Gates in the Vast Heaven).[3] All the emperors *(ti)* in Chinese history were, in the minds of the Taipings, pretenders.

God was said to be the only true spirit *(shen)*. He existed before heaven and earth, for heaven and earth together with the myriads of things were created by him; and this act of creation necessarily made God the only God.[4] The story of the creation appears in many of the Taiping publications. The most complete, of course, is the one given in the Book of Genesis, reproduced by the Taipings. But here is the story in their own words, from the "Taiping Songs on World Salvation" (T'ai-p'ing chiu-shih-ko):

I, the chief of staff, in searching into the time before the world was formed, have found that there appeared to be a chaos, wherein nothing existed. It was through the heavenly grace of our Heavenly Father, the Lord on High, Huang Shang-ti, who manifested his power to create heaven and earth, the mountains and rivers, and men and all things, that *ch'ien* [the male principle, heaven] and *k'un* [the female principle, earth] were established, the sun and moon were born and the constellations fixed. What is bright is day, and what is dark is night. The day and the night ceaselessly follow one another in a circle for all eternity, making life on earth an endless process. The earth with the fullness of the ten thousand things[5] exists for the benefit of human life. The heavenly grace of our Heavenly Father, the Lord on High, Huang Shang-ti, is indeed very deep and very difficult to repay. Since man has been given the fortune to be born into the world, he should [worship God] in the spirit of sincerity and reverence. In six days the Heavenly Father created heaven and earth, the mountains and rivers, and man and all things. On the seventh day the work was done, and this seventh day is the Heavenly Father's holy day; therefore, our Heavenly Father ordered it to be the Sabbath day, and appointed it as the day for worship, as an eternal reminder to the people that true happiness is be-

[2] The difference in conception is not simply a matter of terminology but part of the larger problem of whether or not the teachings of the Taipings can be considered true Christianity. This problem will be taken up in a later chapter.

[3] "T'ai-p'ing chao-shu," in Hsiao I-shan (compiler), *T'ai-p'ing t'ien-kuo ts'ung-shu*, hereafter cited Hsiao, *Ts'ung-shu*, ts'e 1, p. 12b.

[4] *Ibid.*

[5] "Ten thousand things" is a phrase used to include all things in the world.

stowed upon them through the grace of our Heavenly Father, that they should forever remember the Heavenly Father's great kindness. Since heaven and earth and the myriad of things were made by the Heavenly Father, it is apparent that the Heavenly Father is the only true spirit, the most honorable, and without rival.[6]

God was considered to have a more intimate relation to man than merely that of a creator. He was the father of all mankind, and like an earthly father he was vitally concerned with the affairs of his children. He gave birth to them, sustained them, and protected them. "Proclamation on the Origin of Principles for the Awakening of the Age" (Yüan-tao chüeh-shih chao) expresses the Taipings' continuing dependence on God the father:

> It seems to me [Hung Hsiu-ch'üan] that though the people of the world are many, they are all created by God and born of God. Not only are they born of God, they also depend on him for growth, and for their clothing and food. Huang Shang-ti is the Great Father, common to all people on earth. Death, life, calamity, and happiness are all in his hands. All our clothing, food, and the tools we use were created by him.... If, at the time of creation, God had created only heaven and not the earth, where would you stand, and would you have farms to till?... If, after creating heaven and earth, God had not created mulberry trees, hemp, grain, wheat, pulse, grass, plants, water, fire, gold, iron, and so forth, or created fish and shrimp in the water, flying birds in the air, animals both wild in the mountains and domesticated at home, would you have anything to wear, to eat, or to use?... Though all these things have been created through God's grace, if for a year God did not let the sun come out to shine on you people on earth, or let rain fall to give you moisture, or thunder to subdue the devils for you, or wind to scatter away your melancholy, would you have any harvests, or any peace?... If, out of anger, Huang Shang-ti should one day cut short your spiritual breath and life, would you be able to talk with your mouth, see with your eyes, hear with your ears, hold with your hands, walk with your feet, or make plans with your minds? Surely you would not. Let me ask again, is it possible, even for a moment, for the whole world not to receive grace from God? Certainly not. From this it will be seen... that Huang Shang-ti is unmistakably present to give men protection.[7]

The concept of the fatherhood of God was derived through the relationship of man's soul to God. God was, specifically, the father of man's soul, which he caused to enter the womb of a woman and be born

---

[6] Hsiao, *Ts'ung-shu, ts'e* 4, p. 1a-b.

[7] "T'ai-p'ing chao-shu," in Hsiao, *Ts'ung-shu, ts'e* 1, pp. 9b–11a.

with a mortal body.[8] Thus the Heavenly Father was also called *yün fu* or *yün yeh* (the father of the soul).

Since God was the father of all, he was not to be worshiped only by the emperor, but was naturally considered an object of universal worship. The Taipings believed that all people, whether noble or humble, should worship him as the only true spirit.

In one of the proclamations against the Manchus, there is a passage which seems to suggest that in the minds of the Taipings the "world" created by God was simply China.

> China is a spiritual continent, and the barbarians are devils. The reason China is called a spiritual continent is because our Heavenly Father, the Huang Shang-ti, is the true spirit who made heaven and earth and the mountains and rivers; therefore, in former times China was designated the spiritual continent.[9]

In another decree Hung Hsiu-ch'üan made the following statement:

> Father had ordained the Heavenly Kingdom to be in China; since China [*Chung-hua*] was originally the home of the Heavenly Kingdom, it is therefore also the name of Father [*Yeh-ho-hua* (Jehovah), the character used for *hua* being the same as that in *Chung-hua*]. Before Father descended to the earth, China belonged to Father, and yet the barbarian devils stole into Father's Heavenly Kingdom. This is the reason Father decreed that I should come to destroy them.[10]

There was also a vague pantheism in the Taiping religion, in which God was thought to be revealed in the phenomena of nature.

> Warmth is conferred by the sun, and moisture by the rain; thunder is symbolic of movement, and the wind a sign of dissemination. All these ex-

---

[8] "Pan-hsing chao-shu," in Ch'eng Yen-sheng (compiler), *T'ai-p'ing t'ien-kuo shih-liao*, 1st Series, hereafter cited Ch'eng, *Shih-liao*, I, 8a, contains the statement: "Your body of flesh is born of your parents of flesh; but your soul is born of God." Robert J. Forrest, in "The Christianity of Hung Tsiu Tsuen: A Review of Taeping Books," *Journal of the Royal Asiatic Society, North China Branch*, New Series No. 4 (Dec., 1867), pp. 201–2, quotes this comment by Hung on I Cor. 1:4: "Every one born first receives the soul, and afterwards the body of flesh. The Lord of souls creates a soul and then sends it into the mother to get a body put to it. The body is begotten of the mother but the soul is of the Lord of souls."

[9] "Pan-hsing chao-shu," in Ch'eng, *Shih-liao*, I, 4b.

[10] "T'ien Wang chao-chih" No. 2, in Hsiao I-shan (compiler), *T'ai-p'ing t'ien-kuo chao-yü*, hereafter cited Hsiao, *Chao-yü*, plate 2.

press the profound mystery of the nature of God. Those who repay the grace of T'ien will receive glory.[11]

And again,

Raising our heads we see in t'ien [heaven in a physical sense] the sun and the moon and the constellations, the thunder, the rain, and the wind and the clouds, and all these are the miracles of God. Looking down on earth, we see the mountains, rivers, and marshes, together with the birds in the air, the fish in the water, and the animals and plants, which are all the creations of God. These things are obvious and easy to see and know. It is for this reason that God is called the true spirit.[12]

God was conceived to be omnipotent, omniscient, and omnipresent; because of these attributes, God was considered the ground and reason for all that was good and valuable. The Taipings attributed a success in battle, the capture of a city, even the happy event of the birth of a son, to the power of God. His intelligence, a phase of his omniscience, was conceived to be infallible; this divine intelligence was called "the Eye of Heaven," and was described as being so bright that nothing escaped it.[13]

Since God was all-powerful and all-knowing, it would have been natural for the Taipings to expect easy victories and an assured livelihood. It is understandable, therefore, that the Taiping leaders found it necessary to explain the difficulties they encountered. The Taiping leaders had two explanations for this apparent contradiction. First, they viewed difficult circumstances as God's instrument for the training of his children; it was only through such training that ordinary metal could become gold. In the last analysis, responsibility rested with the individual himself. Hamberg quotes Hung, who almost rose to a lofty philosophical height in his understanding of sorrow and tribulation and of the real meaning of riches and prosperity when he said: "They think that the idols assist them in attaining such happiness, or that heaven is favouring them; and they do not know that heaven often bestows riches and prosperity even upon the wicked, but that the holy ones are perfected by much sorrow and tribulation."[14] Their second explanation was

[11] "T'ai-p'ing chao-shu," in Hsiao, *Ts'ung-shu, ts'e* 1, p. 2a.
[12] *Ibid.*, p. 9b.
[13] See "T'ien-fu shih" No. 164, in Hsiao, *Ts'ung-shu, ts'e* 7.
[14] Theodore Hamberg, *The Visions of Hung-Siu-tshuen, and Origin of the Kwang-si Insurrection*, p. 44.

that sometimes the will of God was inscrutable, as in the Taipings' failure to take Kuei-lin and Ch'ang-sha, which finally proved to the advantage of the Taipings. "From this we know that God is working behind the scenes, though it may not be easy for men to see."[15]

God was also believed to possess a moral nature. Since the Taipings conceived of the world as having been created by God, it was logical for them to think of God as a moral principle pervading the world. By virtue of the omnipresence of God, the world becomes, to a certain degree, a moral order itself. The Taipings' pantheistic conception of God, hinted at above, seems to have been definitely established in their view of the moral nature of the world. This line of thought will be taken up again in later sections dealing with moral precepts and rewards and punishments.

To the Taipings, the will or decree of Heaven seemed very important. Since God was conceived to be omnipotent, his power was thought to be identical with his will; therefore, all things owed their being and welfare to the will of God. God's will, or the way of Heaven, was conceived to be inexorable, completely just, and free from selfishness. What God decreed, no man could change; the law of Heaven could not be altered. The application of this conception was all-inclusive, from life and death to the appointment of the Son of Heaven.[16] The concept of the decree of Heaven dominated the minds of the Taipings, and it is to be found everywhere in their publications. For example, all proclamations are prefaced with the phrase, "Truly decreed by T'ien."

Turning our attention to their other ideas about God, we find that the Taipings' conception of the deity was very anthropomorphic. This fact dismayed most missionaries who followed the Taiping movement. The physical appearance of God is described in two Taiping documents in nearly identical terms. In the "Taiping Heavenly Chronicle" (T'ai-p'ing t'ien-jih) there is the following passage: "The Heavenly Father, the Lord on High, the Sovereign God, wore a hat with a high brim, and was dressed in a black dragon robe, with a golden beard that flowed from about his mouth down to his belly. Tall, husky, and well built, he sat solemnly on his throne with his costume neatly arranged, his two

---

[15] "T'ien-ch'ing tao-li shu," in Hsiao, Ts'ung-shu, ts'e 5, p. 13a.

[16] See Lo Yung and Shen Tsu-chi (compilers), T'ai-p'ing t'ien-kuo shih-wen ch'ao, hereafter cited Lo and Shen, Shih-wen ch'ao, I, 47–48, for reference to the idea of the will of Heaven in the I Wang's reply to Tseng Kuo-fan's request for his surrender.

hands on his lap."[17] In the "Gospel Jointly Witnessed and Heard by the Imperial Eldest and Second Eldest Brothers" (Wang-chang-tz'u-hsiung ch'ing-mu ch'ing-erh kung-cheng fu-yin-shu) there is this description: "The Father has a tall and husky physique. He wears a black dragon robe, and has a golden beard that flows down to his navel."[18]

This was God as Hung Hsiu-ch'üan saw him in his vision. Hung also related that God taught him how to dress and how to hold an erect sitting posture, with head high, chest out, the hands on the lap, and the feet placed with the toes pointing outward to form a *pa* (the Chinese character for "eight").[19] Thus, in the eyes of the Taiping leaders the physical appearance of God was similar to the traditional picture of a man of importance. To make the object of worship more tangible, God was represented by statues. The T'ien Wang was said to have owned an image of God cast in gold, which was later stolen from him.[20]

In addition, God had a family life that paralleled family life on earth:

Sometimes the Heavenly Father... urged him repeatedly, and the lord [referring to Hung and not to Jesus or God] was compelled to descend. He would descend several layers of heaven, and then go back again, thus incurring the anger of the Heavenly Father.... The lord then told his wife, "You must first go home with our son and live with the Father and Mother, the Elder Brother and sister-in-law, and the younger sisters. Let me go down to the world to attend to the affairs of our Father; when I have completed my errand, I shall ascend again to heaven and enjoy comfort and happiness with you here."[21]

Such a God can be expected to have emotions. In sending Jesus down to save the world, God was said to feel the same pain of separation that a worldly parent might experience. He was also ambitious for his children: "The T'ien Wang deeply desires those in this world who are misled and troubled by the devils to wake up immediately and turn away from the wrong course, so that they may strive to satisfy the ambition of our Father and give glory to our Elder Brother."[22]

---

[17] *I-ching*, No. 13 (Sept. 5, 1936), p. 5. Also in Hsiang Ta *et al.* (compilers), *T'ai-p'ing t'ien-kuo*, II, 632–33.

[18] "Fu-yin ching lu," in Hsiao, *Ts'ung-shu, ts'e* 8, p. 7b.

[19] *I-ching*, No. 13 (Sept. 5, 1936), p. 6. Also in Hsiang, *T'ai-p'ing t'ien-kuo*, II, 634.

[20] Ling Shan-ch'ing (ed.), *T'ai-p'ing t'ien-kuo yeh-shih*, hereafter cited Ling, *Yeh-shih*, 20:44. This report is in apparent contradiction to the iconoclasm of the Taipings.

[21] *I-ching*, No. 14 (Sept. 20, 1936), p. 23. Also in Hsiang, *T'ai-p'ing t'ien-kuo*, II, 641.

[22] "T'ien-ch'ing tao-li shu," in Hsiao, *Ts'ung-shu, ts'e* 5, p. 26b.

Although God was kind and compassionate, he could also be jealous. He demanded absolute devotion from his worshipers and punished Confucius for making his name greater than that of God. "The Heavenly Father is compassionate and has pity on the misery of men; he deeply hopes that the people on this earth will be freed from all hardships. If he sees one man suffering, the Heavenly Father feels deep sadness in his heart."[23]

The purpose of "the true *tao* of the heavenly nature" was to save people from suffering: "The end of the true *tao* of the heavenly nature lies in salvation from suffering. A kindly heart is necessary in order to be free from eternal pain. If you save people from suffering when you see them in pain, T'ien will save you from suffering when you are in pain."[24]

Divine visitations are recorded in many of the Taiping publications. The most dramatic are given in two documents, both called "The Book of Declarations of the Divine Will Made During the Heavenly Father's Descent to Earth" (T'ien-fu hsia-fan chao-shu). In the first of these, God came down in the person of the Tung Wang, Yang Hsiu-ch'ing, to prove the guilt of Chou Hsi-neng, who was accused of attempting to betray the Taipings to the government forces. In the other, God, again in the person of the Tung Wang, severely chastised the T'ien Wang, and even threatened him with flogging. Only the Tung Wang was used as God's "medium," and after the death of the Tung Wang no further visitations from God are recorded. Hsiao Ch'ao-kuei, the Hsi Wang, was the instrument for the visitations of Jesus.[25]

In "The Taiping Heavenly Chronicle" and Hung's commentary on the Bible, God was represented as having a wife, from whose womb came Jesus, the T'ien Wang, and the Tung Wang. Because of this the T'ien Wang and the Tung Wang enjoyed a peculiarly privileged position. They were not the children of the Heavenly Father in the usual sense of the word. No other mortals were said to have come from the womb of the Heavenly Mother.

Thus we learn that God has a wife and three sons: Jesus, the Heavenly Eldest Brother (*T'ien Hsiung*); the T'ien Wang, the second eldest brother; and the Tung Wang. The names of both Jesus and the T'ien Wang were given the honorific prefix of *T'ien*.

---

[23] "T'ien-fu shih" No. 315, in Hsiao, *Ts'ung-shu, ts'e* 7.
[24] "T'ien-fu shih" No. 314, in Hsiao, *Ts'ung-shu, ts'e* 7.
[25] Kuo T'ing-i, *T'ai-p'ing t'ien-kuo shih-shih jih-chih*, hereafter cited Kuo, *Jih-chih*, I, 65–66, 119, 128.

When the people of the world turned away from God and started to worship idols and devils, the symbol of which was the serpent, God reluctantly sent his eldest son Jesus down to redeem them from their sins. His mission is recorded in many Taiping publications, but the following, found in "The Book on the Principles of the Heavenly Nature" (T'ien-ch'ing tao-li shu), is perhaps the most complete:

> When the Huang-Lao [a Taoist sect] was introduced during the Ch'in dynasty and Buddhism was accepted by the Han, the temptation of the devil in the minds of the people became greater every day. Everybody forgot the Heavenly Father's grace and kindness and absurdly attributed the Heavenly Father's merits to the devil. Therefore, when the Heavenly Father viewed these things from on high and saw that the people on earth either followed the devil or transformed themselves into devils, and assumed all sorts of outlandish forms, no longer appearing like human beings, he again became angry. Should he destroy them all? He did not have the heart to do so. Should he let them go? It would not be right to do so. At that moment, our Heavenly Elder Brother, Jesus, the Heir Apparent, bravely came forward to take up the task, willing to give his own life to redeem the people of the world from their sins. The Heavenly Father, the Lord on High, Huang Shang-ti, his pity for the world and his love for the people being very deep, sent without regret his Heir Apparent to be born in Judah to redeem us from our sins, to propagate the true doctrine, and to tell the people of the date of redemption. As a result, he was falsely accused and condemned to death on the cross in order that all people might be cleansed of their sins through his precious blood, and that the grace of the Heavenly Father in sacrificing him for the sake of the people might be fully demonstrated. What sufferings our Heavenly Elder Brother had to go through to fulfill his mission to save the world! He came back to life three days after his death to preach the gospel to his disciples. Forty days later he returned to heaven. On the point of his ascension he told his disciples to go forth to foreign lands to preach the gospel to all peoples, so that the believers would return to heaven, while the unbelievers would be punished. The true doctrine has come down to us without being destroyed because of the preaching of our Heavenly Brother. But for the meritorious act of the Heavenly Eldest Brother in sacrificing himself for us, how could we brothers and sisters enjoy our present happiness?[26]

In the minds of the Taipings, Jesus shared the authority of God in respect to everything on earth and was as much concerned as God with the welfare of the faithful. The people of the world (China), however, remained idol-worshipers even after Jesus' incarnation and ascension.

[26] Hsiao, Ts'ung-shu, ts'e 5, pp. 6b–7b.

Things became intolerable when the world created by God (China) was occupied by the Manchus, who were considered serpent-demons. The Taipings offered no explanation as to why God created the serpent, or why the evil of the Manchus existed in China. They would probably have explained it as a necessary evil inflicted by God as a means of perfecting his people. However necessary it may have been, it was evil nonetheless. So the stage was set for a new mission to save the world from evil, and Hung believed he was appointed to carry out that mission. This mission, Hung thought, was revealed in the Book of Matthew 27:38–40, where the number three (symbolized by Christ and the two thieves on the cross, and by the three days between the crucifixion and the resurrection) was taken to stand for the character *hung* 洪, written with three dots at the left side. This was the character used in Hung Hsiu-ch'üan's surname. Hung believed that this was a prophecy that he was to become the Lord and rebuild the Temple.[27] Notwithstanding Hung's unorthodox notions about the significance of the number three, the Taipings accepted the Christian Trinity of God, Jesus, and the Holy Ghost.

The divine nature of the T'ien Wang and his position as the "truly appointed Son of Heaven" were announced as postulates. Statements to this effect are to be found everywhere in the Taiping documents. There are, however, two works, the "Taiping Heavenly Chronicle" and the "Gospel Jointly Witnessed and Heard by the Imperial Eldest and Second Eldest Brothers," which reveal with especial clarity the beliefs of Hung Hsiu-ch'üan and the Taiping leaders who accepted his story. A brief sketch of Hung's story of his visit in heaven, based on these documents, is given below.

In the year 1837, Hung Hsiu-ch'üan fell ill and went into a prolonged trance. He later claimed that during this time he went to heaven in a sedan chair, accompanied by many angels, and was received at the gate of heaven by many beautiful girls. Soon he arrived in paradise, a place of dazzling splendor, peopled with dignitaries in dragon gowns and peaked hats. He was then ordered to submit to having his abdomen cut open and his internal organs replaced with new ones. Then the Heavenly Mother, who called him "my son," led him to a river where he was

---

[27] Forrest, in "The Christianity of Hung Tsiu Tsuen," *Journal of the Royal Asiatic Society, North China Branch*, N.S. No. 4 (Dec., 1867), p. 201, says that Hung believed Christ's words on the cross, "Eli, Eli, lama sabacthani," were a secret indication that Hung was to be the Lord and rebuild the Temple.

bathed and purified. Afterward he was presented to the Heavenly Father, whose physical appearance has been described above. After haranguing the people for their ingratitude and pointing out to Hung the evil deeds of the devils on earth, the Heavenly Father said that the devils were to be found not only on earth but also in the thirty-three heavens, including the highest heaven. The Heavenly Father traced the evil work of the devils to the teachings of Confucius, and reprimanded him for it. Confucius tried to escape with the devil leader (Yen-lo), only to be brought back, whereupon he was bound and soundly flogged. God then gave Hung Hsiu-ch'üan a seal of authority and a devil-killing sword, and ordered him to drive the devils out of heaven. With the help of the angels, he began to drive them down out of the thirty-three levels of heaven, and a hard battle ensued. Since Hung had God and Jesus to back him up and the magical power of the seal to protect him, the guile of the devil leader, who was capable of eighteen different transformations, was of no avail. For some reason God allowed Yen-lo to escape, but the rest of the demons were successfully driven down out of the successive levels of heaven, and finally down into the lowest level of hell. The Heavenly Mother and all the younger sisters brought Hung candies and fruit, and the Heavenly Father conferred upon him the title, "Taiping Heavenly King, Sovereign Ch'üan of the Great Way" *(T'ai-p'ing T'ien Wang ta-tao chün-wang Ch'üan)*. The last seven characters of the title were ordered by God to be hung on the door of Hung's room.

When Hung Hsiu-ch'üan recovered from his trance, his mother discovered the seven characters on his door. He told his father and brothers that, by the decree of T'ien, he was the truly appointed Son of Heaven, sent to kill the evildoers and to save the upright. He told his sister, who came to see him, that he was the *T'ai-p'ing t'ien-tzu* (the Son of Heaven of Great Peace). When his father reprimanded him for saying such things, Hung said that he was not his son, and therefore, how dared he scold him?

Before his vision Hung had acquired a pamphlet on the Christian religion entitled "Ch'üan-shih liang-yen" (Good Words to Admonish the Age), by Liang A-fa, but Hung was said to have given it only a superficial reading at the time. Several years after his vision, when he came to study the pamphlet more thoroughly, he definitely identified his "Heavenly Father" with the Christian God described in it.

The mission of Hung Hsiu-ch'üan is not clearly expressed in the two documents from which this story was taken. The religious mission is

unmistakable, but it was only in later proclamations that his political mission was made known.

Robert J. Forrest, British acting consul at Ningpo during this time, quotes a revealing passage from Hung's commentary on the Bible:

> The Elder Brother, myself, and the Tung Wang, before the heavens and earth, were by the favour of the Heavenly Father, born from the womb of his original wife, the Heavenly Mother. Afterwards the Father sent the Elder Brother to be a redemption for sin, and to enter into Mary to be incarnate. This is why the Elder Brother said—"Before Abraham was I am!" When I was in heaven at the time of Abraham I have some recollection of knowing that the father was about to send the elder brother to be born of the seed of Abraham. I therefore went down and blessed and saved Abraham. At that time too, I knew that the Father was going to send me to rule the world, therefore I had a desire to show myself below as Lord: afterwards when I received the Father's commands to enter my mother's womb and descend into the world, I knew that the imp Yenlo (Abbadon) would raise a disturbance, so I besought the father that no harm should arise through him. Afterwards the father commanded me from heaven to be born from the womb of another mother from heaven so that I might be incarnate. I remember that I entered into the womb of this mother, and that the father gave a sign, namely clothing her with the sun to make manifest that which she had conceived was the Son. I knew that the serpent devil Yenlo also knew that in the womb of this mother was I. Shangti especially sent me into the world to exterminate this serpent. Therefore was it that he wished to devour me and usurp God's heritage; but God is omnipotent and the son born to him could not be injured by the serpent. Behold I testify the truth of myself. In former times Melchisedec was I, and after the Elder Brother had ascended, the child born of the sunclad woman was myself also: now the Father and Elder Brother have come down and brought me to be the lord especially to exterminate this serpent. Lo! the serpents and beasts are slain and the empire enjoys Great Peace. It is fulfilled. Respect this![28]

Thus, as the appointed Son of Heaven, Hung's mission was to exterminate the devils, to regain the paradise lost to the people who had been misled by the devils, to rule the world when the devils had been driven out, and to propagate the true *tao* of T'ien. The seal of authority used by God in creating the world, which he later gave to Hung, and the devil-killing sword were the symbols of Hung's authority.

As the symbol for God was *T'ien*, heaven, so the symbol for Hung was

---

[28] *Ibid.*, p. 203.

jih, the sun. *Jih*, the traditional symbol of a monarch,[29] represented his source of power; *T'ien* was the all-pervading providence and *jih*, its concrete expression. Some of the Taiping documents, for example the calendars, have depicted on their flyleaves two dragons and two phoenixes paying homage to the sun. Since Hung was the representative of T'ien, his way was the way of T'ien. "The Heavenly Father said, 'I sent your lord down to earth to be the T'ien Wang (Heavenly King). His words are heavenly decrees, and you should all obey him.' "[30] In one of the "Poems by the Heavenly Father" (T'ien-fu shih) it is said, "To follow T'ien and to follow wang [the king] is to follow the way of T'ien; to follow oneself is to take the wrong way, which leads to hell."[31]

The T'ien Wang's principal assistant was the Tung Wang, Yang Hsiu-ch'ing. Yang was also said to have been born from the womb of the "original" wife of God (the term "original wife" suggests that in the event of her death, God might take a second wife). He claimed to be the savior of the people, delivering them from pestilence and plague, and to be the voice of the true *tao* of T'ien. It was his duty to teach the people not to worship false spirits and not to follow the way of the devils, but to forsake wickedness for righteousness, and the false for the true. The wind was chosen as the symbol for the Tung Wang, designating him as a sort of consoler or comforter of the people. Each member of the religious hierarchy—God, Jesus, the T'ien Wang, and finally the Tung Wang—shared in the divine power and glory.

The choice of natural phenomena as signs and symbols for Hung, Yang, and the other kings seems to suggest that the Taiping leaders believed themselves to be rulers not merely of the human world but also of the natural world.[32] By virtue of their heavenly ties, that is, Hung's and Yang's relationship to God, the Taiping rulers considered nature to be part of their domain. Nature, in the minds of the Chinese, was synonymous with T'ien and was always thought of as something divine, the object of worship. Because of this, the Taiping leaders also considered

[29] Mencius, speaking of the singularity of the monarch of the world (China), compares his position to that of the sun in heaven by quoting Confucius: "Heaven has not two suns; and the people have not two kings." *Meng-tzu yin-te*, 35/5A/4.

[30] "T'ien-ming chao-chih shu," in Ch'eng, *Shih-liao*, I, 2a.

[31] Poem No. 271, in Hsiao, *Ts'ung-shu, ts'e* 7.

[32] In addition to the symbol for the Tung (East) Wang, which was the wind, the symbol for the Hsi (West) Wang was the clouds; for the Nan (South) Wang, rain; for the Pei (North) Wang, thunder; and for the I (Assistant) Wang, lightning. Some of the wangs were named after natural phenomena, e.g., the Yen (Frost) Wang and the Yü (Dew) Wang.

themselves rulers of the spiritual world. We have seen how Hung identified his way with the way of God. If God was the Lord of the universe,
Hung, his second son, the sun of the universe, together with his entourage, could assume authority to rule the universe without appearing to be
a pretender.

The Taipings also believed in the existence of devils, the leader of
which was the serpent, created by God.

> The devils are the enemy of God, and also my enemy, and the enemy of
> you and the people of the ten thousand nations in the whole world as well.
> Who are the devils? They are the idols you worship. What are these idols?
> They are the followers and demonic soldiers of the serpent devil, the red-
> eyed Yen-lo. And who is this serpent devil, the red-eyed Yen-lo? He is none
> other than the serpent the Sovereign God created when he created the
> world. Once he has transformed himself into the devil, he has the power
> to transform himself into seventeen or eighteen shapes. The dragon devil
> in the Eastern Sea is also this serpent devil. He is the leader of all the devils,
> and his work is to seduce and capture the souls of men and throw them
> down into the eighteen layers of hell.[33]

The devil leader and his followers are most vividly described in
Hung's story of his encounter with them during his visit to heaven.
However, he did not believe the devils to have any power to answer
men's entreaties, although they were able to tempt and mislead men
into the way of wickedness, that is, the worship of idols. The impunity
with which the Taipings destroyed religious images wherever they went
was "proof" that the devils were helpless in the hands of God-worshipers,
whose God was the only true spirit and was alone capable of answering
the prayers of men.

These devils roamed all over the world spreading their evil influence
and worked their way into the heavens as well. In the "Taiping Heavenly Chronicle," God told Hung that "not only in the world are there
devils, there are even devils up here in the thirty-three heavens."[34]

A description of heaven and hell is given in one of the "Poems by the
Heavenly Father," which reads:

> There is no sickness in heaven, but there is in hell;
> There is no misery in heaven, but there is in hell;
> There is no hunger in heaven, but there is in hell;

[33] "Pan-hsing chao-shu," in Ch'eng, *Shih-liao*, I, 8b.
[34] "T'ai-p'ing t'ien-jih," in Hsiang, *T'ai-p'ing t'ien-kuo*, II, 634.

And there is no ugliness in heaven, but there is in hell.[35]

This is a negative description of heaven and hell. We also have a positive picture:

Now that the edict of Sovereign God has been proclaimed, those who repent before Sovereign God, who renounce the worship of wicked spirits and indulgence in wicked deeds, and determine not to violate the heavenly precepts, will be permitted to ascend to heaven, where they will enjoy happiness for one thousand and ten thousand years, where there will be boundless freedom and life without concern, and eternal glory. ... [As for those who do not] they will be condemned to suffer for a thousand and ten thousand years in hell, where there will be endless misery, suffering, and pain.[36]

Heaven was conceived of in the most materialistic terms, as a definite place where God and his family, including the Heavenly Mother, Jesus and his wife, and numerous sisters and angels, dwelt. At times the Taipings identified paradise with the heavenly capital (Nanking), as the ultimate of God's will in the creation of the world. Those who worshiped God with awe, reverence, and sincerity would go to heaven, which meant either the heavenly capital in this life or heaven in the next, while those who lived counter to the way of Heaven would be condemned to hell. The Taipings' conception of heaven and hell seems to have had both a spiritual and temporal aspect. Both terms were vague, representing reward and punishment either here on earth or in the next world.

The Taipings believed that when they died they would all go to heaven. For them, dying was synonymous with ascending to heaven, and this was probably the reason why they forbade mourning on the occasion of death. Nevertheless, the Tung Wang is reported to have lost his eyesight from crying over the death of his son.[37]

Since God was the creator and the Father, the Lord on High, to whom men and things owed their being, men were duty bound to worship and believe in him. But worship and belief without awe, reverence, and sincerity were considered sacrilegious and hypocritical. Therefore these

[35] "T'ien-fu shih" No. 277, in Hsiao, *Ts'ung-shu, ts'e* 7.

[36] Preface to "T'ien-t'iao-shu," in Hsiao, *Ts'ung-shu, ts'e* 1, p. 1a.

[37] Hsieh Chieh-ho, *Chin-ling kuei-chia chi-shih lüeh*, in Hsieh Hsing-yao (compiler), *T'ai-p'ing t'ien-kuo ts'ung-shu shih-san chung*, hereafter cited Hsieh, *Ts'ung-shu, chi* 2, pp. 3a, 4a.

became the most important religious virtues of the Taipings. "Heaven's grace is boundless...and to repay its grace one must revere Heaven."[38]

Reverence for Heaven, however, had to be expressed concretely through the performance of religious duties. There were also certain ethical responsibilities to be fulfilled, for to the Taipings, religion and ethics were one.

The religious duties were outlined in the "Ten Heavenly Commandments," and the first duty of a member of the Taiping community was to observe these Commandments reverently and truthfully. The following precepts were promulgated as laws and explained in "The Book of Heavenly Commandments" (T'ien-t'iao-shu):

1. Thou shalt honor and worship the Sovereign God on High.
2. Thou shalt not worship false gods.
3. Thou shalt not take the name of the Sovereign God on High in vain.
4. On the seventh day, the day of worship, thou shalt praise the Sovereign God on High for his grace and virtue.
5. Thou shalt be filially pious to thy parents.
6. Thou shalt not kill or injure.
7. Thou shalt not commit adultery or be licentious.
8. Thou shalt not steal or plunder.
9. Thou shalt not utter falsehoods.
10. Thou shalt not conceive a covetous desire.[39]

"The Book of Heavenly Commandments" also included practical religious duties, such as prayer, the singing of praises, the offering of sacrifices, and the reading of the scriptures.[40] Prayers were offered many times a day and on numerous special occasions: at morning and evening worship, on birthdays, on the day a child was one month old, at weddings, and at meals. The purpose of prayer was to ask for protection against the temptation of the devils, to give thanks for the Heavenly Father's grace, to confess sins, and to show repentance. To receive the forgiveness of God, the Taipings believed that after prayer one must bathe one's face, take a bath, or immerse oneself in a river. Hamberg gives the following account of Taiping religious practices:

[38] "T'ai-p'ing chiu-shih-ko," in Hsiao, *Ts'ung-shu*, *ts'e* 4, p. 7a.

[39] Hsiao, *Ts'ung-shu*, *ts'e* 1, pp. 6b–8a.

[40] Hsieh Chieh-ho, *op. cit.*, p. 7a, reported that "on the seventh day of the first moon, which was the Taiping New Year's Day, it snowed heavily. Before dawn the sounds of singing and praise shook heaven and earth."

At the commencement, Siu tsheun had only vague notions concerning the true manner of religious service. When he had taken away his own idols, he placed the written name of God in their stead, and even used incense-sticks and gold paper as a part of the service. But in a few months he found that this was wrong, and abolished it. His step-mother declared, however, that it was a great pity that he had taken away the name of God from the wall, for during that time they had been able to add a few fields to their estate, which she considered as a special blessing and sign of divine favour. When the congregation in Kwang-si assembled together for religious worship, males and females had their seats separated from each other. It was customary to praise God by the singing of a hymn. An address was delivered either upon the mercy of God, or the merits of Christ, and the people were exhorted to repent of their sins, to abstain from idolatry, and to serve God with sincerity of heart. When any professed to believe in the doctrine, and expressed their desire to be admitted members of the congregation, the rite of baptism was performed in the following manner, without reference to any longer or shorter term of preparation or previous instruction. Two burning lamps and three cups of tea were placed upon a table, probably to suit the sensual apprehension of the Chinese. A written confession of sins, containing the names of the different candidates for baptism, was repeated by them, and afterwards burnt, whereby the presenting of the same to God was to be expressed. The question was then asked, if they promised, "Not to worship evil spirits, not to practise evil things, but to keep the heavenly commandments." After this confession, they knelt down, and from a large basin of clear water, a cupful was poured over the head of every one with the words, "Purification from all former sins, putting off the old, and regeneration,". . . Upon rising again, they used to drink of the tea, and generally each one washed his chest and region of the heart with water to signify the inner cleansing of their hearts. It was also customary to perform private ablutions in the rivers, accompanied by confession of sins and prayer for forgiveness. Those who had been baptized now received the different forms of prayer to be used morning and evening, or before their meals. Most of these forms of prayer are now printed at Nanking in the Book of Religious Precepts. . . with some alterations or additions. Upon the celebration of festivals, as for instance at a marriage, a burial, or at the New Year, animals were offered in sacrifice, and afterwards consumed by those present. ([Hambergs' note] It is to be hoped that these and other rites inconsistent with the pure Christian worship of God, and which Hung-Siu-tshuen introduced or connived at, either from misunderstanding the truth, or to comply with long established customs of the Chinese, which he found it difficult at once to abolish, may gradually be corrected.)

When they engaged in prayer, they used to kneel down all in one direction towards the open side of the house from which the light entered, and closing their eyes, one spoke the prayer in the name of the whole assembly. [41]

[41] *The Visions of Hung-Siu-tshuen*, pp. 35–36.

Regulations concerning religious worship were strictly enforced whenever possible. On one occasion Hung Jen-ta, the T'ien Wang's brother, arrived late for worship, and it was discovered that his tardiness was due to the fact that he had been smoking opium. Yang Hsiu-ch'ing ordered that he be executed for this act of sacrilege and lack of reverence. Through the T'ien Wang's personal intervention, however, he was released with only a flogging.

Religious observance was mandatory among the troops. Wherever they went they built platforms from which the officers preached the Taiping doctrine. Sir George Bonham, the British envoy, reported the following: "There is a somewhat strange peculiarity distinguishing these insurgents. The accounts received from Mr. Meadows describe them as Puritanical and even fanatic. The whole army pray regularly before meals."[42]

Regardless of whether the Taipings were sincere in their worship, there is no doubt that there was a great deal of religious activity. In September, 1853, when Shih Feng-k'uei fell back and retreated to T'ien-chia-cheng, Lo Ta-kang wrote to him, "Victory and defeat are commonplace to a soldier. I hope that you will explain the principles of the heavenly nature to the rank and file, and teach them that with perseverance God's protection will be ours."[43] The preaching seems to have been quite effective. T'ang Cheng-ts'ai, who became commander of the Taiping navy, was said to have enlisted for no other reason than that he had heard some of the preaching, which dwelt on reform and salvation, and was greatly moved.[44] A Western newspaperman (presumably from the *North China Herald*) went to inspect the residence of the Chung Wang, Li Hsiu-ch'eng, after the fall of the Taipings and commented upon the "earnestness of the Taiping officers' belief in their religion." He said that at the rear of the residence there was a large room, on the door of which hung a sign (made by Taiping troops) which read, *T'ien-fu t'ang* (the hall of the Heavenly Father). On the walls inside were pictures of Christ being condemned by Pilate and carrying the cross to the place of crucifixion.[45]

The practice of prayer seems to have been common among the Taiping

[42] Bonham to the Earl of Clarendon, No. 4, in *Papers Respecting the Civil War in China, Parliamentary Papers*, 1852–53, Vol. LXIX.

[43] Chang Te-chien (editor and compiler), *Tse-ch'ing hui-tsuan, ts'e* 5, *chüan* 8.

[44] Ling, *Yeh-shih*, 13:27.

[45] *Ibid.*, 20:50.

troops, especially for the souls of persons killed in battle. When Ch'in Jih-kang perished in the fire that razed the palace of the Tung Wang, the T'ien Wang was so saddened that he dismissed the court and prayed. It was also reported that when Shih Hsiang-chen was killed by a stray bullet while pursuing the government troops of Tso Tsung-t'ang, the entire officialdom in Nanking prayed for him; he was mourned for several days. On another occasion, at the news of Tseng T'ien-yang's death during the defense of Yüeh-chou, the whole army mourned and prayed. When Chi Wen-yüan was killed by an arrow in battle, Lin Feng-hsiang and Li K'ai-fang mourned him and prayed for him together.[46]

Although death was thought of as "ascending to heaven," it was an occasion on which the Taipings realized their helplessness and the necessity of appealing for divine help. But this was not the only occasion upon which they felt such need. We have records which indicate that praying was a regular practice in the Taiping army. For example, when Li Shih-hsien retreated to Hua-yüan, Tso Tsung-t'ang attacked the place with flaming arrows and set the camp on fire. Shih-hsien fell on his knees and prayed, and suddenly rain began to pour down and the fire was extinguished. He then ordered the soldiers to shout at the tops of their voices, "Heaven helps the Taiping army and gives them success."[47] On another occasion, when the fall of Soochow was imminent, T'an Shao-kuang gathered all his officers together for a conference. After a meal together they prayed, and only then did they file into the hall for the conference.[48]

The Taipings also sacrificed to the Heavenly Father. It was proclaimed that "on every Sunday all officers of the world should, each according to his rank and function, with pious sincerity, sacrifice to God with meat and food, and worship him and praise him, and explain the Holy Scriptures [to the people]. Those who dare to neglect this will be demoted to the status of peasants."[49] The meat used for sacrifice was often dog meat,[50] but other kinds of meat were also used. The Reverend

[46] *Ibid.*, 15:9.

[47] *Ibid.*, 13:22.

[48] *Ibid.*, 19:7. Shao-kuang was assassinated by traitors during the conference and the city was turned over to the Ch'ing army under Li Hung-chang. The traitors who surrendered were executed by Li, and this incident precipitated the bad relationship between Li and General Gordon.

[49] "T'ien-ch'ao t'ien-mou chih-tu," in Hsiao, *Ts'ung-shu, ts'e* 4, pp. 3a, 8a.

[50] Ling, *Yeh-shih*, 20:34.

W. H. Medhurst, speaking of an occasion when the Heavenly Father reportedly spoke to the faithful through the medium of the Tung Wang, made the following observation: "After the examination was concluded, and the Father had returned to heaven, the whole army rejoiced together at the goodness of God, and proceeded to kill pigs and oxen, and offer them up in thanksgiving to the Father of all. . . . It is evident from this that the insurgents are neither Jews nor Mohammedans, or they would not offer unclean animals to God."[51] Sacrifices were also offered at the birth of a child, when a child was one month old, at weddings, and on other occasions for thanksgiving.

All religious precepts and duties were promulgated as laws, and their violation was punishable by law. Hung gave specific orders to this effect to the Tung Wang:

> By his royal edict, the T'ien Wang proclaims that the father of souls created the ten thousand things in six days, so that today we may be able to destroy the devils. The rotation of the earth is the sign of a new land, and the movement of heaven is the symbol of the establishment of an eternal dynasty.
>
> By his royal edict the T'ien Wang proclaims that you, brother Ch'ing [referring to Yang Hsiu-ch'ing], be informed that edicts and decrees be promulgated to tell the rank and file that they should obey orders and observe the heavenly precepts, which teach that in all the world there is only one *Huang-ti* [traditional title for the emperor] and that he is none other than the Heavenly Father, the Lord on High, the Sovereign God. Should anyone other than the Heavenly Father, the Lord on High, the Sovereign God, take the title *Huang-ti*, he shall be punished according to the law of heaven, which means death. The Elder Brother Jesus is the only Heavenly Brother. Should anyone other than Jesus assume the name of "Heavenly Brother," he shall be punished according to the law of heaven, which means death. From now on, after this clear proclamation to the whole world, if there are any more violaters, there shall be no excuse for them. Respect this.[52]

But religious discipline cannot be maintained by laws alone. We find that religious observance varied according to the officers in charge. There was even one report of the soldiers cursing the T'ien Wang and the Tung Wang when they were supposed to be saying their prayers.[53]

[51] Medhurst, "General Views of the Chinese Insurgents," Inclosure 10 in No. 6, in *Papers Respecting the Civil War in China, Parliamentary Papers*, 1852–53, Vol. LXIX.

[52] Chang, *Tse-ch'ing*, ts'e 4, *chüan* 7.

[53] Chang, *Tse-ch'ing*, "Li-pai," ts'e 5, *chüan* 9.

The extensive preaching of the Taipings was not always limited to religious purposes. Even before the outbreak of the rebellion, at the time of the *Shang-ti hui* ("God Society," an abbreviation for "God-Worshipers Society"), preaching was apparently an effective method of recruiting members for the Society. For instance there is the story of how Ch'in Jih-kang was enlisted. To escape punishment for the murder of his superior he had changed his name and become a servant to a land-owner. He became dissatisfied, however, and complained: "With the whole world in turmoil," he said, "how can a man like me lie low among the fields for long!" His employer, a member of the *Shang-ti hui*, then told him about Hung and his preaching, and as a result, Ch'in joined the society. Hung Hsiu-ch'üan was apparently very successful in recruiting new members for the society. According to a contemporary report, preaching also served as a means of soliciting funds for the Taiping treasury and occasionally as a means of calling the people together.[54]

In introducing a new religious ideology into Chinese society, the Taipings attempted to break away from the traditional pattern of Chinese life. This attempt was evident in their attacks on idolatry, superstition, Confucianism, Taoism, and Buddhism.

Idol-worshiping was the first object of attack because the Taipings considered it counter to the Heavenly Commandments and the will of God.

> When the Sovereign God descended to Mount Sinai, he wrote the Ten Heavenly Commandments with his own hand on a stone tablet and gave them to Moses. He told Moses with his own lips that he was the Lord on High, the Sovereign God, and that the people on earth should never set up any idols, on earth or in heaven, for the purpose of worship. To worship idols is to disobey the will of God, and yet the people said the various idols were made to help the Sovereign God to protect men. How thoroughly the devils have deceived them and confused their minds![55]

Neither was God to be represented by an image. In his comment on Joseph Edkins' essay in Chinese, "Shang-ti yu-hsing wei yü, wu-hsing nai shih lun" (That God Is Corporeal Is Allegorical, and That God Is Incorporeal Is True), Hung wrote a poem of ten seven-character lines. The first four lines read:

[54] Hsieh Chieh-ho, *Chin-ling kuei-chia chi-shih lüeh*, in Hsieh, *Ts'ung-shu, chi* 2, pp. 1a, 10a.

[55] "T'ai-p'ing chao-shu," in Hsiao, *Ts'ung-shu, ts'e* 1, p. 10a–b.

> What God hates most is idols;
> The people of the world are forbidden to view the person of God.
> Jesus and I are both God's own children;
> We see God because we are in his lap.[56]

Wherever they went the Taipings destroyed temples and monasteries. One of Hung Hsiu-ch'üan's iconoclastic adventures is narrated in the "Taiping Heavenly Chronicle":

> When he arrived at the Kan Temple, he hit the idol [of Kan-yao] with a large bamboo stick and berated him, "Do you not know that I am the truly appointed Son of Heaven? In the year of *t'ien-yu* [the year *ting-yu*, 1837, according to the traditional Chinese calendar], I ascended to heaven. My Heavenly Father, the Lord on High, the Sovereign God, ordered me to fight and, with the help of the angels, to drive you out. There was not one of you devils at that time who was not subdued. Do you still recognize me? If you do, it would be well for you to get down to hell as fast as possible.[57]

On another occasion Hung was told by the inhabitants of a district in Kwangsi about a certain temple in which there were images of a man and a woman that were said to be wonderfully responsive to prayers.

> The lord asked, "Were they husband and wife?" "No," answered the natives, "they sang to each other in these mountains and had illicit relations. And after they died a tale was circulated to the effect that they had achieved the *tao* [equivalent to enlightenment in Buddhism]. So they [the local people] made statues of them and began to worship them." Then the lord said, "Is this true? How very stupid are the people of the world. This couple lived in adultery and are certain to have been destroyed by Heaven, and yet the people say they attained the state of *tao*. Attained the state of what *tao*, may I ask?" From this he began to realize that it was due to the evil influence of such demonic examples that the men and women of Kwangsi were so licentious in their lives that their conduct could not even be compared with that of beasts.[58]

The attack on idolatry was strengthened by the reasoning that the worship of idols was not efficacious. In "The Book on the Principles of the Heavenly Nature" it is said:

---

[56] Hsiao, *Chao-yü*, p. 27.

[57] "T'ai-p'ing t'ien-jih," in *I-ching*, No. 16 (Oct. 20, 1936), pp. 20–21. Also in Hsiang, *T'ai-p'ing t'ien-kuo*, II, 648.

[58] "T'ai-p'ing t'ien-jih," in *I-ching*, No. 16 (Oct. 20, 1936), p. 17. Also in Hsiang, *T'ai-p'ing t'ien-kuo*, II, 644.

May I ask my brothers who formerly worshiped only the devils a question? The reason for worshiping idols is to get protection from the devils. Has anyone ever received protection from the devils? Take this as an example. In time of drought, everyone worships and prays to the devils for rain. None seem to know that everything is due to the power of the Heavenly Father. If the Heavenly Father decrees drought, there shall be drought; and if he decrees rain, there shall be rain. Should the Heavenly Father choose not to grant rain, then even though all the devils in the world are supplicated, there will still be drought.... There is a proverb that says, "Bean-curd is only water and Yen-lo is only a ghost." From this, one will see that the devils are not efficacious and cannot protect us. If they cannot give us rain when we pray for it, what is the use of worshiping them?[59]

Hung's battle against the devils while he was in heaven was then cited as proof that they had all been conquered by him.

In another Taiping publication the vanity of idol worship was condemned thus:

Alas! You see clearly before you the most revered and noblest true spirit, the Heavenly Father of all, whom you should worship day and night. And yet you do not worship him, but find it necessary to worship devils and ghosts, whose special work is to seduce and capture the souls of men. It is indeed foolish. You see clearly before you the most intelligent and enlightening true spirit, the Heavenly Father of all, who would give what you pray for and be yours when you seek him, who would open the door for you when you knock, and who should be worshiped day and night by all. And yet you do not worship him but find it necessary to worship insentient idols made of wood, stone, mud, and paper—stupid things which have mouths but are unable to speak, noses but are unable to smell, ears but are unable to hear, hands but are unable to hold, and feet but are unable to walk.[60]

Hung argued further that since man is the most intelligent of the ten thousand things and existed before idols, which were made by man, the idols could not be expected to provide protection. Hung deplored the fact that men made overtures to the devils and invited them to confuse and deceive their minds.

Some "idols" were statues of historical figures who, because of their achievements and contributions to society during life, became objects of the people's veneration and worship. The Taipings considered this

[59] "T'ien-ch'ing tao-li shu," in Hsiao, *Ts'ung-shu*, *ts'e* 5, pp. 8a–9a.

[60] "T'ai-p'ing chao-shu," in Hsiao, *Ts'ung-shu*, *ts'e* 1, p. 11b.

practice extremely foolish: "Some of the idols made by men may have
been men of virtue. But they have long since gone to heaven; how then
could they be here amongst men enjoying their worship?"[61]

In discussing the Taiping attack on Buddhism and Taoism, it must be
understood that the Buddhism and Taoism referred to here are the
popular forms, and we are concerned mainly with their patterns of
worship. The Taipings were not interested in the philosophical aspects
of these religions; they looked upon them merely as two sects of idol-
worshipers. After describing the grace of God and the ingratitude of
men in turning away from God to worship idols, Hung laid the blame
on various emperors and other historical figures, such as Shao-hao,
Chiu-li, San-miao, Han-wen, Han-wu, Han-hsüan, Han-huan, Han-
ming, Liang-wu, T'ang-hsien, Sung-hui, for leading the people astray
by contributing to heretical beliefs in Taoist immortals and the Buddha.[62]

> Strange people are the Buddhists and Taoists, who, deceived by the
> devils themselves, lead others like the blind leading the blind. They fool
> people with things unknowable in order to satisfy their own selfish ends,
> and persuade people to sacrifice and pour libations to the dead in order
> to fatten their own purses. As their minds are occupied by the devil, they
> put forth numerous perverse doctrines to deceive and destroy the people
> of the world. For example, at the time of the Ch'in, these heretics said there
> were three spiritual mountains in the Eastern Sea. Ch'in Cheng then sent
> men out to sea in search of them, and thus originated the fantastic theory
> of later times about the immortals.[63]

Their attack on Buddhism was largely directed against the belief in
Yen-lo as the prince of Hades, who held in his hands the fate of a man's
life and its span.

> Recently some strange monks have been saying false things about Yen-lo
> yao [the devil Yen-lo]. There is also the strange book *Yü-li chi* circulating
> in the world, and there are bookworms in the world who are often deceived
> by the false doctrine in the book. The fate of life and death indeed is not
> a trivial thing. Since it is not a trivial matter [that Yen-lo is said to control
> the fate of life and death], it should have been discussed in books in China
> and in foreign countries throughout the ages, to be proclaimed to posterity.
> However, after a careful search into the matter we find that that which has
> been discussed in books both in China and in foreign countries throughout

[61] *Ibid.*, p. 13a.
[62] *Ibid.*, p. 12a–b.
[63] *Ibid.*, pp. 7b–8a.

the ages, to be proclaimed to posterity, has been found to be merely such things as "born of Heaven," "descended by the decree of Heaven," or "the Sovereign God gives birth to man and protects him." There is never anything said about Yen-lo yao.... But the bookworms of the world do not believe the classics which have been in circulation from time immemorial down to the present, far and near, yet they do believe the unwarranted and eccentric writings of these odd persons. Are they not being greatly deceived?[64]

Thus the Taipings considered both Buddhism and Taoism to be false doctrines.

There is reason to believe that the Taipings took the order condemning Buddhism seriously. In the *T'ai-p'ing t'ien-kuo yeh-shih (Unofficial History of the Taiping Heavenly Kingdom)* it is reported:

> When Shao-kuang [the Mu Wang, surnamed T'an] was in charge of the defense of Soochow, his troops captured a scholar.... Shao-kuang clapped him on the back and felt that he was cold, so he gave him his own coat. The scholar was a believer in Buddhism, and at night when there was no one around, he would worship the stars. Shao-kuang happened to see this and warned him that idolatry was prohibited in his camp; it was lucky that it was Shao-kuang who saw him at worship, for he would not do anything to harm him. However, there was a dark-complexioned, husky fellow [or fellows] in the camp who was tough and ruthless, and if he had seen it, the scholar would certainly have had his head cut off.[65]

This account also suggests that spies were placed in the Taiping camps with the specific duty of detecting and stamping out idolatry.

Other manifestations of popular superstitions that were singled out for attack included geomancy, divination, witchcraft, and soothsaying, all of which were connected in one way or another with Buddhism or Taoism. One of the aims of introducing the "Taiping New Calendar" was to do away with all forms of superstition contained in the old calendar, which advised people to select auspicious dates and to avoid inauspicious ones for various activities.

> All the heretical theories and wicked examples given in the traditional almanacs are falsehoods of devils for the deception of men, and these have been omitted because the years, months, and days have all been set by the Heavenly Father, and every year is a lucky year, every month a lucky

[64] *Ibid.*, pp. 8b–9a.
[65] Ling, *Yeh-shih*, 13:27 note.

month, and every day an auspicious day. There is no reason for choosing among them.[66]

A story is told in the *T'ai-p'ing t'ien-kuo yeh-shih* about Ho Ch'ao-yüan, one of the original members of the Kwangsi group. Before he joined the Taipings, he was practicing medicine by means of charms. But when he became physician to the Taiping army, Yang Hsiu-ch'ing and Shih Ta-k'ai called his art demonic and forbade him to make use of his magical charms in healing.[67]

The Taipings attacked Confucianism mainly on religious grounds. They were opposed to the Confucian practice of ancestor worship. A contemporary observer reported that the Taipings prohibited the people from worshiping their ancestors, and that those who disobeyed were considered to be devils.[68] A local gazetteer of Tz'u-ch'i *hsien*, Chekiang, recorded the following: "Today is the first day of the twelfth year of *T'ai-p'ing t'ien-kuo* [January 12, 1862], and Shen Chen, the civil governor, and Chou Shen-jung, the military governor, have ordered the people by proclamation to change their styles of dress and caps, and have prohibited them from worshiping their ancestors."[69]

The tablets of Confucius and his disciples, placed in schools and Confucian temples, were apparently also considered idols, for the first thing Hung did after identifying the "old man" in his dream with the Heavenly Father in Liang A-fa's pamphlet, "Good Words to Admonish the Age," was to destroy the tablet of Confucius in his school.[70] As soon as a convert to Hung's religious society was baptized, the convert discarded his Confucian tablet. And wherever the Taipings went, they destroyed not only Buddhist and Taoist temples, but Confucian temples as well. Tseng Kuo-fan, in his "Proclamation" against the Taipings, said:

> When Li Tzu-ch'eng reached Ch'ü-fou, he did not molest the temple of the Sage; when Chang Hsien-chung came to Tzu-tung, he sacrificed to Wen Ch'ang.[71] But the Yüeh [Kwangsi] rebels set the school at Liu-chou

---

[66] "T'ai-p'ing t'ien-kuo kuei-hao san-nien hsin-li," in Hsiao, *Ts'ung-shu, ts'e* 3, p. 2a.

[67] Ling, *Yeh-shih*, 17:4.

[68] Hsieh Chieh-ho, "Chin-ling kuei-chia cho-t'an," quoted by Hsieh Hsing-yao in *T'ai-p'ing t'ien-kuo ti she-hui cheng-chih ssu-hsiang*, p. 25.

[69] *Tz'u-hsi hsien-chih*, 55:28, quoted by Kuo in *Jih-chih*, II, 857.

[70] Kuo, *Jih-chih*, I, 31–32.

[71] Wen Ch'ang is the god of literature. According to the *Ming-shih*, 50:18a–b, after Chang Ya-tzu died in battle, a temple was erected in his honor. Later he became the patron god of schools.

on fire, destroyed the tablet of the Sage [Confucius], and scattered the tablets of the ten other sages, and the tablets along the two porches, on the ground in confusion. After that the first thing they did was to destroy the temples. Even the temples of ministers of great loyalty and righteousness, such as Kuan-ti and Yüeh-wang, were molested and trampled upon. As to the Buddhist and Taoist temples and altars of the city god, none of them escaped fire and no statues escaped destruction.[72]

It is apparent that the Taipings considered the Confucian temples no different from any other kind: they were simply more places for idol worship.

[72] *Tseng Wen-cheng kung ch'üan-chi,* "Wen-chi," 3:2a.

Chapter II

Moral Views

Nearly all of the Taiping publications are moral exhortations, and we shall try in this section to disentangle the various moral precepts and principles upon which they are based. Their interpretation, however, will be left to a later chapter.

As mentioned in Chapter I, the Taipings thought of religion and ethics as a single entity. This is especially evident in the concepts of *chen-tao* (the true doctrine) and *t'ien-tao* (the heavenly doctrine). The term *tao* literally means "the way," although at times it can best be translated as "doctrine" or "principles." In one of the Taiping publications it is said, "The great origin of the doctrine is in heaven."[1] This statement, together with the title of "The Book on the Principles of the Heavenly Nature" (T'ien-ch'ing tao-li shu), suggests that to the Taipings the doctrine was religious in nature. In "The Book of Heavenly Commandments" (T'ien-t'iao-shu) the true doctrine of Heaven is described as being different from the way (or principles) of the world as it is "able to save the souls of men and provides the means for them to enjoy happiness without end."[2] In "The Book on the Principles of the Heavenly Nature" the true doctrine is said to be identical with the ethical doctrines of the ancients; this statement is supported by quotation after quotation from various classics. This seems to suggest that the Taipings at times put the golden age in the remote past. In the preface to "The Book on the Principles of the Heavenly Nature" we find such remarks as: "The way of the world is every day declining, and the

[1] "T'ai-p'ing chao-shu," in Hsiao I-shan (compiler), *T'ai-p'ing t'ien-kuo ts'ung-shu*, *ts'e* 1, p. 1a.

[2] Hsiao, *Ts'ung-shu*, *ts'e* 1, p. 6a.

minds of the people go farther and farther from what is ancient; indeed, the light of the true doctrine has long been hidden."[3] And in the "Proclamation on the Origin of Principles for the Awakening of the Age" (Yüan-tao chüeh-shih chao), there is this passage on the nature of the true doctrine: "As to the *tao* [doctrine], there is a true one. In general all doctrines that may be applied to the present but cannot be applied to the ancient, or that may be applied to the near but cannot be applied to the far, are false, wicked, and trivial."[4] It is clear that by "true doctrine" the Taipings meant both their religious and moral teachings.

Before entering into any discussion of moral concepts, it is important to understand the Taiping conception of man. In "The Proclamation on the Origin of Principles for the Awakening of the Age," it is said: "Within the boundaries of heaven and earth man is noblest of all; and among the ten thousand things man is the most intelligent."[5] Belief in man's nobility and intelligence was based upon the idea that he was created by God, who was his Heavenly Father. This "intelligence" was very vaguely conceived. When the Taipings spoke of man as the "most intelligent" of all, it seems that they implied an intellectual element; but in other references there seems to have been more of a stress on moral nature: "Who is the master of the self? It is the intelligent mind which God confers on us. When the mind is upright, it will be the true master of the body, and the organs will naturally obey its orders."[6] The mind which God bestowed on man was conceived of as originally good; its corruption occurred later. Concerning the worship of anything other than God, it was said: "Not only is this of no benefit, it can be of great harm; for great will be one's sins if the original mind is allowed to become overshadowed. If the original mind is not lost, one will naturally know that the breath of life depends on Heaven."[7] The mind must return to its original purity and be made upright before one can attain salvation. One of the "Poems by the Heavenly Father" (T'ien-fu shih) reads:

---

[3] "T'ien-ch'ing tao-li shu," in Hsiao, *Ts'ung-shu, ts'e* 5, pp. 1a, 5b.

[4] "T'ai-p'ing chao-shu," in Hsiao, *Ts'ung-shu, ts'e* 1, p. 7b.

[5] *Ibid.*, p. 12b.

[6] "Yu-hsüeh-shih," in Hsiao, *Ts'ung-shu, ts'e* 4, pp. 11b–12a. This moralistic conception of the mind is a Confucian tradition.

[7] "T'ai-p'ing chao-shu," in Hsiao, *Ts'ung-shu, ts'e* 1, p. 1b.

Your sins will not be light if you keep your mind wicked;
But if you keep your mind upright you will gain life eternal.
Keep your mind directed diligently toward heaven and you will be
given great happiness.
Act in accordance with your original mind forever.[8]

The notions of *cheng* (correctness or uprightness) and *pu-cheng* (wicked-ness) run through all the moral ideas of the Taipings, and their moral precepts may be divided according to these two general categories. In the "Ode on the Hundred Correct Things" (Pai-cheng-ko), certain historical occurrences are listed to prove the superiority of uprightness over wickedness.[9] The idea of "uprightness" is expressed thus in the "Taiping Songs on World Salvation" (T'ai-p'ing chiu-shih-ko): "The heavenly way is correct and upright, hampered neither by partisanship nor by prejudice."[10] According to this, *cheng* means the principles of uprightness and absolute impartiality. That which is wicked *(pu-cheng)* is described in the "Proclamation on the Origin of the Principles of World Salvation" (Yüan-tao chiu-shih chao) as being adultery, lack of filial piety, murder, theft and robbery, witchcraft, and gambling.

In the "Ode on the Hundred Correct Things," there are two defini-tions of *cheng:* "Uprightness is what distinguishes man from the beasts," and "Uprightness is the original nature of man."[9] Thus man's original nature is good, and, as we have seen above, it also has the characteristic of intelligence. If a man preserves his original nature, his conduct will naturally be right; if he loses it, he loses his soul as well. This original nature is a sort of innate moral sense, or conscience. The "upright man" *(cheng-jen)* with a "true mind" *(chen-hsin)* so frequently mentioned in the "The Perfect Auspicious Poems" (Shih-ch'üan ta-chi shih) may then be considered "a man with a true moral sense, or conscience." This con-science is man's essential characteristic, setting him apart from the beasts.

If human nature is originally good, the less we interfere with its workings the better. In one of the "Poems by the Heavenly Father" there is the line: "Those whose minds are pure shall see the Father and the Mother."[11] In the "Proclamation on the Origin of the Principles of World Salvation," it is said: "Heroes who have the ambition to become

---

[8] No. 276, in Hsiao, *Ts'ung-shu, ts'e* 7.
[9] See "Pai-cheng-ko" in the Appendix to Hsiao, *Ts'ung-shu, ts'e* 1, pp. 2a–3a.
[10] Hsiao, *Ts'ung-shu, ts'e* 4, p. 9b.
[11] "T'ien-fu shih" No. 95, in Hsiao, *Ts'ung-shu, ts'e* 7.

completely selfless are urged to return to the original primitiveness and truth."[12] In the verse "On Managing the Ears" in the "Ode for Youth" (Yu-hsüeh-shih), there is the line, "To all the sounds of the ten thousand things, I listen with an inward calm."[13] Owing to the Christian emphasis on spiritual values, "Give up the worldly life" became an exhortation often repeated to the followers. It was natural, therefore, that they should eulogize the spirit of humility and generosity toward their fellow men preached by Jesus.

The moral precepts of a society are illustrated in its social relationships. The prescribed Taiping social relationships are presented in the little book of verses called "Ode for Youth." The book first takes up man's relationship to God and Jesus, characterized by reverence *(ching)*. Next, filial piety is considered, defining the attitude of a son in his relationship to his parents. Then other relationships are described, based upon the general concept of filial piety: the way of being a sovereign, a minister, a member of a family, a father, mother, son, daughter-in-law, elder brother, younger brother, elder sister, younger sister, husband, wife, elder brother's wife, younger brother's wife, and the way of being a man, a woman, and a relative through marriage. There is no doubt that the Confucian idea of the "rectification of names" was in the mind of the writer of this pamphlet. In the "Gospel Jointly Witnessed and Heard by the Imperial Eldest and Second Eldest Brothers" (Wang-chang-tz'u-hsiung ch'ing-mu ch'ing-erh kung-cheng fu-yin-shu), there is the following strongly Confucian passage:

> At times the T'ien Wang says, from the "Edict of Foresight," that the princes do not act like princes, the ministers do not act like ministers, fathers do not act like fathers, sons do not act like sons, husbands do not act like husbands, and wives do not act like wives. Efforts must be made so that princes will be princes, ministers will be ministers, fathers will be fathers, sons will be sons, husbands will be husbands, and wives will be wives. Respect this.[14]

These relationships were said to be heavenly relationships[15]—again, religion and ethics were considered as one.

There were examples, however, of official position being considered

[12] "T'ai-p'ing chao-shu," in Hsiao, *Ts'ung-shu, ts'e* 1, p. 2b.
[13] Hsiao, *Ts'ung-shu, ts'e* 4, p. 12b.
[14] "Fu-yin ching lu," in Hsiao, *Ts'ung-shu, ts'e* 8, p. 7b.
[15] See "T'ien-fu shih" No. 302, in Hsiao, *Ts'ung-shu, ts'e* 7.

more important than natural relationships. For example, Wei Yüan-chieh, the father of the Pei Wang, Wei Ch'ang-hui, fell in line with the rest of the courtiers in paying respect to Ch'ang-hui, and sometimes even knelt down before him as required by the court etiquette.[16] Chang Te-chien gives the following reason for this practice: "The rebels call their fathers 'flesh fathers,' and consider themselves born of the Heavenly Father; therefore they receive homage from their own fathers with calm."[17]

Ching is considered perhaps the most important of the moral precepts of the Taipings. Reverence for God and Jesus is conceived of as both religious and moral. When God and Jesus are considered as objects of worship, reverence is a religious precept; but when God is thought of as the Father and Jesus as the Elder Brother, such reverence becomes a moral precept involving filial piety, which in turn cannot be divorced from loyalty. To express an attitude of *ching*, the Taipings obeyed the decrees of Heaven and the orders of the T'ien Wang. They stressed that to revere the T'ien Wang was also to revere God: "To repay the Heavenly Father's grace, everyone must be good, and everyone must train himself to be upright, and try his best to attend to his parents, to be loyal, and to repay the goodness of his lord [referring to Hung]; for only thus can he act in accordance with the mind of Heaven and attain heavenly happiness."[18]

In one of the "Poems by the Heavenly Father" there are the following lines:

> If one reveres Heaven, one is certain to revere the lord [Hung];
> For to revere the lord is the only way to revere Heaven.
> As Heaven gave birth to the lord,
> Reverence for Heaven and reverence for the lord are closely
> related.[19]

Though *ching* (reverence), *hsiao* (filial piety), and *chung* (loyalty) were all merged into a sort of moral compound, loyalty took precedence over the other two. "There are five human relationships, of which filial piety and brotherly love rank first. Once the family is ordered, one will be able to contribute to the state. So [in filial piety and brotherly love]

---

[16] Chang Te-chien (editor and compiler), *Tse-ch'ing hui-tsuan*, *ts'e* 1, *chüan* 2.
[17] *Ibid.*
[18] "T'ai-p'ing chiu-shih-ko," in Hsiao, *Ts'ung-shu*, *ts'e* 4, p. 3a–b.
[19] "T'ien-fu shih" No. 318, in Hsiao, *Ts'ung-shu*, *ts'e* 7.

there is also loyalty."[20] Filial piety was considered only a preliminary step to loyalty, which came first and last in the moral life:

> We owe our birth to our parents, but we depend on the lord for the fulfillment of our lives. The grace of the lord is most great, and nothing can compare with it. In making our utmost effort to fulfill the duty of loyalty, we cannot even give thought to our parents. We should know only our lord, and forget about ourselves. We should exert our energies to the utmost, and choose righteousness and sacrifice our lives.[21]

Thus, when it became impossible to fulfill one's duty both to one's parents and to the lord, it was imperative for one to choose loyalty to the lord. "We know only the state; it is impossible to be both loyal and filial."[22]

When filial piety came into conflict with either reverence for the Heavenly Commandments or duty to the state, it had to give way again.

> Ch'ao-kuei [the Hsi Wang, Hsiao Ch'ao-kuei] was by nature brutal, but he was a firm believer in [Taiping] religion. When the Taiping army was on its way to Hunan from Yung-an, his father sent for his wife and slept with her. This was a violation of the Taiping Heavenly Commandments, and Ch'ao-kuei had his father and mother publicly accused and then executed, as a warning to others. Then he made the following announcement: "Parents who violate the Heavenly Commandments are not parents."[23]

To the Taipings, loyalty was manifested only through courage or bravery. Although the virtue of loyalty belongs to a private order, it had an important public function, as Taiping society was mainly a military society.

To encourage faithful observance of the moral precepts, the principle of *li* was employed as the regulator of social conduct. According to this idea, the high was distinguished from the low, and each was assigned his appropriate place in society. When properly taught, *li* works more effectively than laws. Yen Hui, a disciple of Confucius, is cited by the Taipings as the model of good conduct because he would not look at,

[20] "T'ai-p'ing chiu-shih-ko," in Hsiao, *Ts'ung-shu, ts'e* 4, p. 9a.
[21] *Ibid.*, p. 7b.
[22] *Ibid.*, p. 10b.
[23] Ling Shan-ch'ing (ed.), *T'ai-p'ing t'ien-kuo yeh-shih*, 12:12. The Taipings interpreted "Thou shalt not commit adultery" as an injunction against any contact between sexes. For an explanation of the Taipings' segregation of sexes, see Chapter III.

listen to, speak about, or do what was contrary to *li*.[24] The Taipings were also aware of the function of *li* as stated in the classics, where *li* is considered a requisite for social harmony. According to "The Book on the Principles of the Heavenly Nature," "We have to understand that the function of *li* is harmony."[25] It was through the observance of proper distinctions that different elements in a society were believed to be brought together in harmony. These distinctions were most concretely expressed in the "Taiping Social Decorum" (T'ai-p'ing li-chih), which gives a system of addresses proper to all ranks of dignitaries.

The Taipings also stressed a few private virtues, which of course had their public aspects as well. First among these was sympathetic love. The line "Love others as yourself" occurs repeatedly in their publications. One of the "Poems by the Heavenly Father" describes the function of this virtue:

> If you go to the rescue of others in danger,
> Heaven will help you when you are in danger.
> Look at the calamity and misery of others as if it were your own;
> Look at the hunger and cold of others as if it were your own.
> To live for others is to live for God;
> Never pretend you do not know this truth
> And let your opportunity slip by.[26]

Because the whole world is but one family and all men are brothers, it is in accordance with the nature of this society that men should rid themselves of all selfish thoughts. The Taipings put the state before the family and public interests before private ones. The spirit of magnanimity was considered characteristic of a great man, and the lack of it a sign of smallness.

Next to sympathy for others, the Taipings extolled the virtue of having a sense of responsibility for one's own destiny. In the "Ode for Youth," it is stated: "Whether one is to be noble or mean is a matter dependent entirely on one's own efforts: hence each should do his best to strengthen himself."[27] The same thought is abundantly expressed in the "Poems by the Heavenly Father," for example:

[24] "T'ai-p'ing chao-shu," in Hsiao, *Ts'ung-shu*, *ts'e* 1, Postscript, p. 1b. Also in Hsiang Ta *et al.* (compilers), *T'ai-p'ing t'ien-kuo*, I, 88.

[25] "T'ien-ch'ing tao-li shu," in Hsiao, *Ts'ung-shu*, *ts'e* 5, p. 30b.

[26] "T'ien-fu shih" No. 105, in Hsiao, *Ts'ung-shu*, *ts'e* 7.

[27] "Yu-hsüeh-shih," in Hsiao, *Ts'ung-shu*, *ts'e* 4, p. 14a.

> The same man may be noble and yet mean;
> If he acts according to the doctrine he will be noble,
> And if he acts contrary to the doctrine he will be mean.
> The same man may be a man or a devil;
> If he has a good heart he will be a man,
> And if he has wicked heart he will be a devil.[28]

The choice between nobility and meanness lies with the individual, for it is his own responsibility if he chooses to act contrary to the will of Heaven.

The Taipings also valued perseverance, the virtue of which was based on a number of observations. First, there was the notion that true gold is unafraid of fire, and that the more it is subjected to fire, the better in quality it becomes.[29] For the same reason, the virtue of a man truly loyal to his prince was said to shine even more brightly under adverse circumstances. Another incentive for perseverance was the belief that present adversity leads to future bliss. The will of Heaven was invoked as the basis for submitting to discipline and accepting trials. Perseverance was necessary to the morale of the Taipings. Mencius' words and the Tung Wang's early poverty and illness were cited as evidence that Heaven instilled discipline in those whom it wished to build up for great things.[30] Even the difficulties encountered by the Taipings, such as enemy assaults and shortages of food and gunpowder, were looked upon as tests provided by God. Therefore, "Let us persevere and be patient" became the persistent cry.

The Taipings must have been aware of the fallibility of man's nature. The idea of repentance was stressed over and over again in their writings. In "The Book of Heavenly Commandments," the rules for repentance are listed with the prayers appropriate to the occasion. A number of the "Poems by the Heavenly Father" are on this theme; the following are two examples:

> The true way [tao] of Heaven lies in knowing our mistakes;
> If we do not know our mistakes we will become devils.
> One who wishes to ascend to heaven must immediately find out his
>   mistakes.
> When one knows one's mistakes and knows how to repent,
> One will be ready to see the Father and Elder Brother.[31]

[28] "T'ien-fu shih" No. 405, in Hsiao, *Ts'ung-shu, ts'e* 7.
[29] "T'ien-fu shih" No. 100, in Hsiao, *Ts'ung-shu, ts'e* 7.
[30] "T'ien-ch'ing tao-li shu," in Hsiao, *Ts'ung-shu, ts'e* 5, pp. 15a, 10b–11b.
[31] "T'ien-fu shih" No. 319, in Hsiao, *Ts'ung-shu, ts'e* 7.

The way of Heaven lies in one's knowledge of one's mistakes.
When one has mistakes, why not acknowledge them?
If one knows one's mistakes and acknowledges them,
The mistakes will no longer be mistakes;
But if he does not know them or does not acknowledge them,
He will be doubly wrong.[32]

In any interpretation of Taiping society and ideology it is necessary to examine the moral beliefs of the rebels. The Taiping belief in the moral nature of the world stemmed from the idea that God, who was of moral character, was omnipotent and omniscient. Thus, as a corollary, the world was believed to be morally determined. The "Ode on the Hundred Correct Things" contains the following lines:

If one is not upright, calamity will fall upon him as the result of
    his accumulated evil deeds;
If one is upright, happiness will be his due as the result of his
    accumulated good deeds.
If the nobles are not upright, one day they will become oppressed;
If the rich are not upright, one day they will be swallowed up by
    others.[33]

This moral causality was thought to be a law of Heaven, inexorable in nature. Those who lived in accordance with the laws of Heaven would be preserved, and those who lived contrary to them would be destroyed, for it was the way of Heaven to bring blessings to the good and calamities to the evil. "The house which accumulates good deeds will have happiness in abundance; but the house which accumulates evil deeds will have more than its share of calamities."[34] The "Ode for Youth" says: "Parents who have been filial, have filial children. This sort of recompense is truly wonderful."[35]

The Taipings also believed in fatalism. In an explanation of why it is not upright to gamble, it was said:

There may be various ways of seeking things, but whether one will get them is determined by fate. Don't demoralize yourself. What is allotted

---

[32] "T'ien-fu shih" No. 461, in Hsiao, *Ts'ung-shu, ts'e* 7.
[33] "Pai-cheng-ko," in "T'ai-p'ing chao-shu," in Ch'eng Yen-sheng (compiler), *T'ai-p'ing t'ien-kuo shih-liao,* 1st Series, II, 4b.
[34] *Ibid.,* II, 4a.
[35] "Yu-hsüeh-shih," in Hsiao, *Ts'ung-shu, ts'e* 4, p. 3b.

to you by fate will be yours without gambling; but what fate has not decreed will not be yours whether or not you gamble for it. In the last analysis, whether one will be poor or rich is determined by Heaven. I shall follow my own inclinations and live in freedom. Confucius and Yen Hui enjoyed a life of happiness, though they lived on simple foods and water. High in spirit, they understood fate and were content and happy in poverty.[36]

The following quotations also illustrate this point:

Death, birth [or life], calamity, and sickness are all determined by Heaven.[37]

Wealth and honor are in the hands of Heaven, and death and life are matters of fate.[38]

The ten thousand things are all determined by Heaven: who will say that we may do as we please?[39]

To the Taipings, everything was determined in this life. In the "Poems by the Heavenly Father," we read:

Whether one is to be a man or a ghost is determined in this life;
Whether one is to be of the noblest or the lowliest is determined in this life;
Whether one will ascend to heaven or fall into hell is determined in this life;
Whether one will have eternal bliss or eternal misery is also determined in this life.[40]

From belief in fatalism, it is only one step to a feeling of contentment and resignation. As the Taipings expressed it, "Wealth and honor are like floating clouds, not worth our concern."[41] In "The Book of Heavenly Commandments," the followers were urged to be "contented in poverty" and to be satisfied with their own lot in life.[42]

Though they thought that in important things all was predetermined,

---

[36] "Yüan-tao chiu-shih ko," in "T'ai-p'ing chao-shu," in Ch'eng, *Shih-liao*, II, 3a. The last two lines are omitted in the revised edition, contained in Hsiao, *Ts'ung-shu, ts'e* 1.

[37] "T'ai-p'ing chao-shu," in Ch'eng, *Shih-liao*, II, 3a.

[38] *Ibid.*, II, 3b.

[39] "Hsing-shih wen," in Hsiao, *Ts'ung-shu, ts'e* 8, p. 8a.

[40] "T'ien-fu shih" No. 450, in Hsiao, *Ts'ung-shu, ts'e* 7.

[41] "Yüan-tao chiu-shih ko," in "T'ai-p'ing chao-shu," in Ch'eng, *Shih-liao*, II, 2b.

[42] "T'ien-t'iao-shu," in Hsiao, *Ts'ung-shu, ts'e* 1, p. 8a.

the Taipings seemed to believe that individual industry might bring
results. "Small wealth is the fruit of industry, but great wealth is a
matter of fate. Since times of old, it has been a man's duty to exert
himself."[43] Apparently the Taipings were unaware that they were
inconsistent in believing in moral causality, fatalism, and individual
industry simultaneously.

In a discussion of the moral views of the Taipings their attitude
toward Confucianism should also be considered. Although the Taipings
were opposed to Confucianism as a form of worship, they seem to have
had little of a positive nature to say against it. It was simply an arbitrary
condemnation, and they never attempted to point out which Confucian
teachings were false, or why. The attack was directed mainly against the
Confucian classics. In the "Taiping Heavenly Chronicle" (T'ai-p'ing
t'ien-jih), there is this passage:

> They traced the devil's evil work to the mistakes Confucius perpetuated
> in the books he used to teach people.... The Heavenly Father...said to
> the lord [Hung], "...These are the books left behind by Confucius, and
> also the books you read when you were in the world. There are many mis-
> takes in these books, and even you have been spoiled by studying them."
> Then the Heavenly Father reprimanded Confucius, saying "Why did you
> instruct people in such a way as to confuse them so that they do not even
> recognize me, and your name has become greater than mine?" At first
> Confucius still wanted to argue with God, but later he became silent, hav-
> ing nothing to say. The Heavenly Elder Brother Jesus Christ also repri-
> manded Confucius, saying, "You wrote such books for instructing the peo-
> ple! Even my own younger brother was spoiled by reading them." Then
> all the angels began to chastise him.... Seeing that everyone in the high
> heaven pronounced him guilty, Confucius stealthily crept off and tried
> to go down into the world, thinking of escaping with the devil leader. But
> the Heavenly Father sent the lord and the angels chasing after Confucius,
> and had him bound and dragged before Him. God was very angry and told
> the angels to flog him. Confucius appealed to Jesus for mercy. The more
> he was flogged the more he asked for mercy. Thereupon the Heavenly
> Father...allowed him to stay in heaven to enjoy happiness, thinking of
> his past merits, which balanced up his sins. But he was prohibited from
> going back down to earth.[44]

In an extra examination granted on the occasion of the birthday of

[43] "Yüan-tao chiu-shih ko," in "T'ai-p'ing chao-shu," in Ch'eng, *Shih-liao*, II, 3b.
[44] *I-ching*, No. 13 (Sept. 5, 1936), p. 7. Also in Hsiang, *T'ai-p'ing t'ien-kuo*, II, 635–
36.

Hung Hsiu-ch'üan at the beginning of the *T'ai-p'ing t'ien-kuo*, Ho Cheng-ch'üan was made the chief examiner. Hung sent him an imperial decree, which said:

> The selection of officials through examinations is beset with dangers, and it has never pleased me. Now at the beginning of the establishment of the state, there are a hundred things to be done. Apparently the only way to cope with the situation is to select as many men of learning as possible to do the job. This is the reason for taking the occasion of my birthday to give this examination as a temporary measure. However, the *Analects* [of Confucius] and *Mencius* should most certainly not be used, because of the fact that the doctrines contained in them are contrary to our sacred teachings. Do you have any good way to handle this situation?
>
> "I have an excellent idea," answered Cheng-ch'üan. "The Heavenly Commandments and the precious teachings are really sacred decrees, and should be learned by all. In this examination, we may pick our topics from these, to give the scholars of later times an incentive to learn them even without persuasion. With this stone two birds will be killed at once."
>
> The T'ien Wang was extremely pleased by this.[45]

From what we have seen, it is not surprising to find the Taipings attempting to revise the Confucian classics. In the third year of the *T'ai-'ping t'ien-kuo*, Tseng Chou-yang, Lu Hsien-pa, and Tseng Shui-yüan were ordered to revise the six classics and rewrite the "Trimetrical Classic" (San-tzu-ching). In the same year the Bureau of Sacred Books was established.[46] It is a matter of regret that with the exception of the "Trimetrical Classic," none of the revised books have come down to us.

In the early years of the *T'ai-p'ing t'ien-kuo* the T'ien Wang's attitude toward the Confucian scholars was one of disgust and loathing, like that of Kao-tsu, first ruler of the Han dynasty:

> In the seventh moon of the second year of the *T'ai-p'ing t'ien-kuo*, a corps general in Wang-chiang hsien, Anhwei province, recommended a scholar from that *hsien* by the name of Lung Feng-lien as a man of great ability in the art of government. Lung and his father came to Chiang-ning [Nanking] and sent in a petition tens of thousands of words long, comparing him [the T'ien Wang] to King Wu of the Chou dynasty and Kao-tsu of the Han. The T'ien Wang paid no attention to him, but wrote the following comment: "King Wu of the Chou and Kao-tsu of the Han are my predecessors. Did you know that?" Lung did not understand him.... He was never appointed to office.[47]

[45] Ling, *Yeh-shih*, 17:1.
[46] *Ibid.*, 17:1, 3.
[47] *Ibid.*, 20:48–49.

The Taipings strictly enforced the proscription of the Confucian classics and the works of the philosophers. Even the son of the T'ien Wang was not allowed to read them. In the "Young Monarch's Confession" (Yu-chu yüan-kung), he said, "The T'ien Wang...did not allow me to study the ancient books, which were called evil. But I secretly read over thirty books."[48] The Confucian classics and the works of many non-Confucian philosophers suffered destruction by fire, as well as revision, mutilation, and proscription. In the collection of essays entitled "Treatises on Affixing the Imperial Seal on Proclamations and Books for Publication" (Chao-shu kai-hsi pan-hsing lun), published in the Taiping third year (1853), there is one written by Huang Tsai-hsing, which contains the following passage:

> At present the books on the true doctrine are three in number, namely "The Sacred Book of the Old Testament" (Chiu i-chao sheng-shu), "The Sacred Book of the New Testament" (Hsin i-chao sheng-shu), "The Book of Heavenly Decrees and Proclamations" (T'ien-ming chao-chih shu). All works by Confucius, Mencius, and the philosophers of the hundred schools should be committed to the flames.[49]

There is no doubt that this suggestion was carried out. Many records describing conditions in Kiangnan immediately after the Taiping Rebellion have come down to us. One account says:

> In the various cities along the river [Yangtze] there are a number of book collectors, including Yeh Yün-su of Han-yang, Yüan Wen-ta of Yang-chow, Ch'in Tun-fu, and Ch'eng Mu-t'ang. Their houses were formerly filled with tens of thousands of scrolls, like exhibits of jade and pearls. But when the Taiping army went through the cities they committed them to the flames, using them to smoke away mosquitoes or to make tea; sometimes they even used these books to wrap up their horses' hoofs, or as toilet paper. What a misfortune to literature, a misfortune even greater than that which it met with in the Ch'in fire.[50]

Hsieh Hsing-yao wrote: "At the time of the provincial examination [referring to the time immediately after the suppression of the rebellion],

---

[48] "Yu-chu yüan-kung," in Hsieh Hsing-yao (compiler), *T'ai-p'ing t'ien-kuo ts'ung-shu shih-san chung, chi* 2, p. 6a.

[49] Hsiao, *Ts'ung-shu, ts'e* 4, p. 11a.

[50] Wu-hsi yeh-sou, "Man-fen hui-pien," quoted by Hsieh Hsing-yao [Wu Chih] in his "T'ai-p'ing hua," *I-ching*, No. 3 (April 5, 1936), p. 24.

it was impossible for the scholars to buy the Four Books or Five Classics, for the Taiping army had pronounced them heretical and burned them."[51]

However, Hung often mentioned the *Book of Poetry* and the *Book of History* in favorable terms. He said that during his visit to heaven many of the younger sisters studied these books with him, which made him so happy that he did not want to leave heaven and go back to earth. And God often told him that he should study more of the *Book of Poetry* and *Book of History* so that he might have something to go on in the future. But he would still have to descend to earth.[52] In the preface to "Imperial Regulations Governing Scholarly Ranks" (Ch'in-ting shih-chieh t'iao-li), published in 1861, it was said, "Books by Confucius and Mencius need not be discarded entirely," but the public would have to wait for the revised editions.[53] This would suggest that the Confucian classics were not used and were not in circulation before their revised versions were published. However, the Taipings' attitude toward the classics changed later owing to the influence of the Kan Wang, Hung Jen-kan.

---

[51] Hsieh, "T'ai-p'ing hua," *I-ching*, No. 3, p. 26.
[52] "T'ai-p'ing t'ien-jih," in *I-ching*, No. 14 (Sept. 20, 1936), p. 23. Also in Hsiang, *T'ai-p'ing t'ien-kuo*, II, 641.
[53] Hsiao, *Ts'ung-shu*, ts'e 9, pp. 13a, 32b–33a.

Chapter III

Social Ideals and Social Structure

The Taiping social ideals were based upon the idea of the brother-hood of men. This idea may have been conceived as a corollary of the religious tenet that God is the universal Father and all men are his children. Social equality is thus theoretically implied, but how far the Taiping ideals of brotherhood and equality were realized can only be ascertained by considering the structure of the Taiping society.

Taiping society was a sort of fraternity, whose members were not merely sworn into a brotherhood but were considered real brothers on the theological ground that God was the Father of them all. Yang Hsiu-ch'ing, the Tung Wang, and Hsiao Ch'ao-kuei, the Hsi Wang, said in one of their proclamations:

> Your bodies were born of your parents, but your souls were born of God. God is our true Father, and is your true Father too. He is even the true Father of all peoples of the ten thousand countries of the whole world. This is why the ancient proverb says, "The world is a family and all [men] with-in the four seas are brothers."[1]

In another proclamation they said:

> The world is one family and all the people in the world are brothers. Why? With regard to man's fleshly body, each has his own parents and a definite family name, and it seems that each is clearly separated from the other. However, the ten thousand family names were derived from one name; and the one name came from one ancestor. Thus their origins need

[1] "Pan-hsing chao-shu," in Ch'eng Yen-sheng (compiler), *T'ai-p'ing t'ien-kuo shih-liao*, 1st Series, I, 8a.

not be considered different. With regard to man's soul, the soul was born of and emanated from Huang Shang-ti through his great power and virtue. This is what is meant by "One is diversified into many and many are gathered up into one."[2]

In the "Proclamation on the Origin of the Principles of World Salvation" (Yüan-tao chiu-shih chao) we find:

> Under heaven all are brothers,
> Their souls all come from heaven;
> In the eyes of God they are all his sons,
> What a pity that men should destroy one another.[3]

From the concept of the fatherhood of God and the brotherhood of man the Taiping ideal of social equality evolved. In a previous section, we discussed the Taiping contention that all men had an equal right to worship God against the traditional view that only the Son of Heaven, or emperor, was so privileged. Since the people were all children of God, it was self-evident to the Taipings that this privilege belonged to each of them.

The principle of equality is most clearly expressed in the Taipings' elimination of discrimination in their government examinations against those traditionally considered as "mean people," or outcasts—for example, prostitutes, actors and actresses, underlings, and yamen runners. *Tse-ch'ing hui-tsuan*, a book containing intelligence reports on the rebels, says: "Any persons, whether commoners, members of the gentry, scholars, prostitutes, actors or actresses, underlings or yamen runners, who have passed the examinations will be [granted the title of] *chuang-yüan* or *han-lin*." The same report says: "There is no definite quota in the local examinations, and no restrictions are imposed from consideration of family background."[4]

Hung himself was reported to have said in a letter to the President of the United States:

[2] "T'ai-p'ing chao-shu," in Hsiao I-shan (compiler), *T'ai-p'ing t'ien-kuo ts'ung-shu, ts'e* 1, p. 7a–b. Thomas T. Meadows, reporting his conversations with the Pei Wang and I Wang, said: "He stated that as children and worshippers of one God we were all brethren." "Report of Conversations between Mr. Interpreter Meadows and the Insurgent Chiefs at Nanking and Chin Keang," Inclosure 1 in No. 6, in *Papers Respecting the Civil War in China, Parliamentary Papers*, 1852–53, Vol. LXIX.

[3] "T'ai-p'ing chao-shu," in Hsiao, *Ts'ung-shu, ts'e* 1, p. 3a.

[4] Chang Te-chien (editor and compiler), *Tse-ch'ing hui-tsuan, ts'e* 2, *chüan* 3, "Wei k'o-mu."

I have heard that your country emphasizes the importance of the people, that in everything they are considered equal, that freedom is your fundamental principle, and that there are no obstacles in the association of men and women. In these things, I am greatly delighted to find that your principles agree completely with those upon which we have based the establishment of our dynasty.[5]

The Taipings gave serious consideration to the principle of equality of the sexes. Women enjoyed equal rights in the distribution of land. "The Land System of the Heavenly Dynasty" (T'ien-ch'ao t'ien-mou chih-tu) stipulates: "Land is to be distributed according to the number of persons [in a family], irrespective of sex."[6] The same document also says: "Men and women shall receive land on reaching the age of sixteen."[7]

In a society based on the concept that all men are brothers, it was natural that there should evolve specific duties for each to perform and measures by which each would if necessary receive the care and attention of the state. In "The Land System of the Heavenly Dynasty" the responsibilities and obligations of all members of the society are defined, and it is indicated that those in need of state assistance are to be provided for: "As to the widowed and orphaned, and the crippled and sick, they shall be exempted from military service and supported by the state."[8] Although the state was to care for the unfortunate, "The Book on the Principles of the Heavenly Nature" (T'ien-ch'ing tao-li shu) stated that each individual had some measure of responsibility toward the other members of the society.

Since we were all born of the same father of souls, why should there be any distinction between you and me or between others and ourselves? When there are clothes, let us wear them together; when there is food, let us enjoy it together. Whenever calamity or sickness befalls anyone, we should get a doctor to attend him and minister to his needs by making medicine for him. As for orphans, either boys or girls, or anyone who has passed the prime of life and is weak and debilitated, let us be all the more careful in attending to their needs, let us bathe them and help them change their clothes. Only thus will it be possible not to lose sight of the ideal of sharing happiness and woe, of sharing the burden of illness and disease.

[5] Ling Shan-ch'ing (ed.), T'ai-p'ing t'ien-kuo yeh-shih, 20:2.
[6] Hsiao, Ts'ung-shu, ts'e 4, p. 1b.
[7] Ibid., p. 2a.
[8] Ibid., p. 8a.

Giving security to the aged and love to the young stems from the Tung Wang's understanding of our Heavenly Father's love for the living and from the magnanimity of the T'ien Wang, who looks upon all as his own brothers.[9]

This sense of social responsibility led to the development of a concept referred to as the capacity of the heart, or the spirit of magnanimity. This theme is developed in the "Proclamation on the Origin of Principles for the Enlightenment of the Age" (Yüan-tao hsing-shih chao) in the "Taiping Imperial Declaration" (T'ai-p'ing chao-shu), beginning with these words:

> When [one's] happiness is great, his capacity must be great; when his capacity is great, he must be a great man. When [one's] happiness is small, his capacity must be small; when his capacity is small, he must be a small man. Therefore, T'ai Shan is able to achieve its height by never refusing to take in a little soil; the rivers and seas are able to achieve their depth by never refusing to receive a small flow of water; and God is able to enlarge his virtue by giving birth to the multitude. All these achievements are the result of capacity.[10]

The document continues with an explanation of the origin of likes and dislikes, of how they arise through narrow-mindedness, and how this results in mutual hatred between nations, provinces, prefectures, districts, villages, streets, and even families. When the capacity of the heart is small, even love is petty, growing out of selfishness. The best medicine for ills of this sort is the knowledge that the world is one, and God is the Father of all men and women, who are real brothers and sisters. Only through this knowledge can we rid ourselves of selfishness.

"Proclamation on the Origin of Principles for the Enlightenment of the Age" depicts ta-t'ung shih-chieh (a world of Great Harmony), a world where the strong do not take advantage of the weak, nor the many molest the few, nor the clever cheat the foolish, nor the brave impose indignities upon the timid. A passage from the Li-chi, one of the Confucian classics, is quoted to illustrate this ideal:

> Confucius said, "When the great principle prevails, the world will belong to the public. The virtuous and the able will be selected [to rule], [in the spirit of] winning the confidence [of the people] and cultivating har-

[9] Hsiao, Ts'ung-shu, ts'e 5, p. 28a–b.
[10] Hsiao, Ts'ung-shu, ts'e 1, p. 5b.

mony [with their neighbors]. Therefore, the people will not love merely their own parents and their own sons. The aged will have a place to complete their natural span of life, the able-bodied a specific function to perform; the young will have their elders to look up to, and the widowed, orphaned, and the crippled and sick will have means of support. The men will have their part to play, and the women a home in which to settle down. Goods will not be wasted, but neither will they be accumulated for selfish purposes; energy will not be kept unused within oneself, but neither will it be employed for the benefit of oneself. For this reason, the way to wickedness will be closed; there will be no robbers, thieves, or rebels, and the outer gates will not need to be shut. This is *ta-t'ung* (The Great Harmony)."[11]

This social ideal of the Taipings was also the basis of their economic regulations, which will be discussed in the next chapter.

As has been pointed out above, the extent to which the Taipings practiced their ideals of brotherhood and social equality can only be ascertained by reference to their social structure; thus, a complete picture of the Taiping society should be presented before any fair judgment is attempted.

The Taiping society was composed of people from different levels of Chinese society. Among the first to join were members of various secret societies, especially of the *T'ien-ti hui* (the Heaven and Earth Society) and the *San-ho hui* (the Three Together Society); "volunteers" who were dismissed after the war with Great Britain;[12] charcoal workers;[13] Hakkas and "Meaon-tsze" (southern barbarians) from "Kwa-chow" (Huan Chou?);[14] miners;[15] and river porters. But the greatest number of followers came from the peasantry, and many of these peasants were Hakkas.[16]

This conglomeration of people from different walks of life was at first vaguely pictured by the Taiping leaders as a single group having no class distinctions.

[11] Hsiao, *Ts'ung-shu, ts'e* 1, "Postscript," p. 3a–b. See also *Li-chi chu-shu, chüan* 21, "Li-yün," p. 3a–b.

[12] Chang, *Tse-ch'ing, ts'e* 1, *chüan* 1.

[13] Ling, *Yeh-shih*, 12:13; also Lo Erh-kang, *T'ai-p'ing t'ien-kuo shih-kang*, p. 48.

[14] "Report of Conversations between Mr. Interpreter Meadows and the Insurgent Chiefs at Nanking and Chin Keang," Inclosure 1 in No. 6, in *Papers Respecting the Civil War in China, Parliamentary Papers*, 1852–53, Vol. LXIX. See also Kuo T'ing-i, *T'ai-p'ing t'ien-kuo shih-shih jih-chih*, I, 96.

[15] *Hsün-chou fu-chih*, quoted in Jen [Chien] Yu-wen, *T'ai-p'ing t'ien-kuo Kwangsi ch'i-i chi*, p. 193.

[16] Lo, *op. cit.*, p. 47; Jen, *op. cit.*, pp. 192–93.

Speaking separately, the world is composed of ten thousand countries; but speaking from the standpoint of unity, there is only one family. The Huang Shang-ti is the universal Father of all in the world; he governs and regulates [all nations], including China which is near us and all foreign nations which are far from us. He gives birth to, sustains, and protects all nations, including all the foreign nations which are far from us and China which is near us. All men in the world are brothers, and all women are sisters. How can it be right for us to entertain selfish distinctions between this and that, how can it be right for us to entertain the idea of mutual annihilation?[17]

However, as soon as the Taiping organization took shape, social stratification began. The first act of the Taiping organization was to proclaim the establishment of a new dynasty, making Hung Hsiu-ch'üan the supreme ruler. Below Hung the titles of *wang* (king) and *hou* (marquis) were created and made hereditary; they were conferred upon those members who had formed the original nucleus of the Taiping group. These ranks were further divided into different grades, each with a specific social status. Below this central clique were the military officers and administrative corps, headed by Yang Hsiu-ch'ing, the Tung Wang, who was chief assistant to Hung in both military and administrative affairs. The soldiers formed the last of the organized elements of the society and were also considered part of the elite, as distinguished from the masses of people. The masses provided economic support for the rebellion and were the source from which the Taipings drew their soldiery. The people found in the areas the Taipings occupied were vaguely described in terms of the traditional classifications of *shih*, *nung*, *kung*, and *shang* (scholars, farmers, artisans, and merchants). The attitude of the Taipings toward the peasantry is revealed by the regulation in "The Land System of the Heavenly Dynasty," declaring that officers would be demoted to peasant status for any offense. This attitude was also expressed by early recruits to the Taiping army. Entire families often sold their property and joined the movement. When asked why he had joined the Taipings a volunteer usually replied: "I am going to be a prefect or a general, no longer a rustic farmer like you." And a woman usually answered: "I am going to be a lady, no longer a rustic woman like you."[18]

Artisans were grouped according to occupation into different camps. Members of these camps were considered part of the Taiping army, for

[17] "T'ai-p'ing chao-shu," in Hsiao, *Ts'ung-shu*, *ts'e* 1, p. 6b.
[18] *Hsün-chou fu-chih*, 21:30a.

all were connected in one way or another with the military life of the society.[19] The masons' camps were composed of coal-diggers whose function it was to destroy the walls of enemy cities by tunneling under the walls and igniting explosives; the water camps, whose members were originally intended to build bridges, gradually developed into a navy. There were also carpenters' camps, goldsmiths' camps, weavers' camps, shoemaking camps, and embroidery camps.

This classification led to social distinctions; the minds of the people in the areas occupied by the Taipings were prepared for the distinctions through religious and moral indoctrination. The Taipings attempted to maintain these distinctions in various ways.

Social status was closely related to official rank, according to *Tse-ch'ing hui-tsuan*:

> The title of *wang* is the highest rank, followed in order by *hou, ch'eng-hsiang* [chancellor], *chien-tien* [senior secretary], *chih-hui* [commander], and *chiang-chün* [general]—these describe in general the officials in the court or the central government. In the army, *tsung-chih* [corps commandant] ranks first, followed by *chien-chün* [corps superintendent], *chün-shuai* [corps general], *shih-shuai* [colonel], *lü-shuai* [captain], and lowest of all, *tsu-chang* [lieutenant, also known as *pei-chang*] and *liang-ssu-ma* [sergeant].[20]

Officials of the same rank, however, differed in status according to that of the wang under whom they served. Officials serving under the T'ien Wang were higher in status than those serving under any of the other wangs, and those serving under the Tung Wang were next highest in status. In addition, the importance of a position or office was often determined by the person who occupied it, as shown by the fact that the seals of high-ranking officers were engraved with both the official rank and the personal name of the owner. Ranks were often created for particular persons and left vacant when these persons died or were promoted. The Taipings, in their quest for personal glory, seem to have been blind to the rare opportunity for creating a new social system.

The principle of rectification of names was also employed by the Taipings. By "rectification of names" they apparently meant exactly what Confucius meant when he used the term, for in the "Gospel Jointly Witnessed and Heard by the Imperial Eldest and Second Eldest

[19] Chang, *Tse-ch'ing, ts'e* 3, *chüan* 4, "T'u-ying."
[20] *Ibid., ts'e* 2, *chüan* 3, "Wei p'ing-chi ch'üan-hsüan."

Brothers" (Wang-chang-tz'u-hsiung ch'ing-mu ch'ing-erh kung-cheng fu-yin-shu), Hung was reported to have decreed:

> The princes do not act like princes, the ministers do not act like ministers, fathers do not act like fathers, sons do not act like sons, husbands do not act like husbands, and wives do not act like wives. Efforts must be made so that princes will be princes, ministers will be ministers, fathers will be fathers, sons will be sons, husbands will be husbands, and wives will be wives.[21]

In the "Ode for Youth" (Yu-hsüeh-shih) the scope was broadened to include the entire family, describing the functions and obligations of each member. The Son of Heaven was described as the absolute ruler of the whole world and the source of authority in granting pardons or in ordering executions. It was considered necessary for the ruler to be upright and enlightened in order to inspire ministers to do their duty; ministers were encouraged to look to great ministers of the past for models. In a family, a general atmosphere of love and harmony was expected to prevail. A father was characterized by dignity and strictness, setting an example for his children. A mother's great asset was impartiality; she was expected to be loving and patient in rearing her children, and a good example for her daughters-in-law. A son was to lead his wife in a life of good discipline, and his duty was to obey his parents. There were particular virtues defining the pattern of conduct appropriate to each member of the family or society.

In keeping with the social distinctions, a system of addresses was devised and promulgated as law, under the title of the "Taiping Social Decorum" (T'ai-p'ing li-chih), indicating the manner in which persons of different social classes were to address one another. For example, the T'ien Wang's first son was to be addressed Yu-chu wan-sui (ten thousand years to the young master); his first daughter, T'ien-chang-chin (the first gold of heaven); the Tung Wang's first son, Tung-ssu-chün ch'ien-sui (one thousand years to the heir of the Tung Wang); and his first daughter, Tung-chang-chin (the first gold of the Tung Wang). Soldiers were required to learn these addresses and use them,[22] although in reality the system was not rigidly followed.[23]

Social distinctions were also expressed through sumptuary laws. For

[21] "Fu-yin ching lu," in Hsiao, Ts'ung-shu, ts'e 8, p. 7b.
[22] "T'ai-p'ing t'iao-kuei," in Hsiao, Ts'ung-shu, ts'e 2, p. 2a.
[23] Chang, Tse-ch'ing, ts'e 4, chüan 6, "Wei ch'eng-hu."

example, salary was expressed in quantity of meat. A wang was entitled to ten pounds of meat, and others received smaller amounts according to their rank. Authority and rank were also shown by insignia; kinds of palaces, carriages, and chairs; colors and materials used for flags, uniforms, dresses, and caps; and the entourage and paraphernalia used for official visits. To emphasize social superiority, people were warned to keep at a distance when an official of importance was expected to pass.[24] Persons of a lower rank were forbidden to use any insignia or marks which properly belonged to a higher rank. Using paraphernalia reserved for a higher rank was condemned as usurping the rights of a higher rank, thus offending the established social principles, and was punishable by law.[25]

On the main gate of Hung Hsiu-ch'üan's palace two dragons and two phoenixes were painted; the palaces of the Tung Wang and the Hsi Wang had only one dragon and one phoenix; the other wangs and the *hou* had one dragon and one tiger. (The palaces of the wangs were called *fu*, and those of the *hou, ya.*) Chancellors had an elephant on the main gate of their palaces; senior secretaries through commanders and corps commandants, a deer; corps superintendents and corps generals, a leopard standing on clouds; and colonels through sergeants, a leopard standing on the ridge of a hill.[26]

The size of the seals and the material they were made of indicated the ranks of officials. The seals of all wangs were cast in gold. The T'ien Wang's seal was eight inches square; the Tung Wang's and Hsi Wang's were 6.6 inches by 3.3 inches; and those of the remaining wangs decreased by .2 inch in length and .1 inch in width according to rank. The seals of the *hou* were .4 inch shorter and .2 inch narrower than that of the lowest-ranking wang. The seal of a chancellor was 5 inches by 2.5 inches; the seals decreased in size for each lower rank through sergeant by .25 inch in length and half the width. The seals of the *hou* and *cheng-ch'eng-hsiang* (the first chancellor) were made of silver, and those of the lower-ranking officials of wood.[27]

After the Taipings occupied Nanking, they created offices for the supervision of ritual paraphernalia such as carriages and chairs. Distinction in rank was shown by the color and number of insignia on

[24] Ling, *Yeh-shih*, 18:4.
[25] "T'ai-p'ing t'iao-kuei," in Hsiao, *Ts'ung-shu, ts'e* 2, p. 3a.
[26] Chang, *Tse-ch'ing, ts'e* 4, *chüan* 6.
[27] *Ibid.*

each carriage and chair. Sedan chairs belonging to wangs were covered with yellow silk embroidered with dragons and clouds; those belonging to *hou*, chancellors, senior secretaries, and commanders were covered with red silk, embroidered with dragons and phoenixes in clouds, the distinguishing mark being the number of dragons and phoenixes. The sedan chairs of generals, corps commandants, and corps superintendents were green; those of corps generals, colonels, and captains were blue; and those of lieutenants and sergeants were black. The T'ien Wang had sixty-four carriers, the Tung Wang forty-eight, and the number decreased according to rank down to sergeants, who had only four.

The caps and coats of all wangs were yellow. Hung's coat was embroidered with nine dragons, Yang's with eight, those of the other wangs with four, and those of the *hou* down to the commanders with only two. Hung's cap was embroidered with a pair of dragons and a pair of phoenixes, and those of the other members of the Taiping hierarchy were also decorated in a prescribed manner. Officials could be distinguished by the number of dragons embroidered on their boots. Hung's boots were embroidered with nine dragons, Yang's with seven, Wei's with five, and those of Shih Ta-k'ai, Ch'in Jih-kang, and Hu I-huang with three. All the wangs used yellow, the *hou* down to the commanders used red, and the generals on down used black.[28]

Only persons above the rank of senior secretary were allowed to wear gold ornaments; those below that rank were allowed only silver bracelets and rings. Those using silver were allowed only a certain number of ounces, depending upon their rank. Those below the rank of corps general were not allowed more than five ounces and below captain, not more than four.[29] The size of the banners and the color with which they were trimmed was another way of indicating rank.[30] In addition, the

---

[28] *Ibid.*

[29] *Ibid.*

[30] *Ibid., ts'e* 3, *chüan* 5. The banners of all officials were yellow; those of the wangs down to commanders were of silk. The banners of the wangs and those officials above and including the rank of senior secretary were decorated with red characters, and those of commanders with black characters. The Tung Wang had a green border on his banner; the Hsi Wang, a white border; the Nan Wang, red; the Pei Wang, black; the I Wang, blue; the Yen Wang and the Yü Wang through the commanders, pink. The banners of the Tung Wang and Hsi Wang were 9 feet, 5 inches; those of the Nan Wang and Pei Wang, 9 feet; I Wang, 8 feet 5 inches; Yen Wang and Yü Wang, 8 feet; *hou* and chancellors, 7 feet 5 inches; senior secretaries, 7 feet; commanders, 6 feet 5 inches. The size of the banners for the remaining officials through sergeants decreased according to rank alternately by 5 and 7 inches.

uniforms worn by soldiers under the command of the various wangs differed in color to indicate the status of the wang.[31]

Court ceremony was one more means of maintaining distinctions. At first ceremony was very simple. When paying court to the T'ien Wang, the Taipings simply knelt before him. Officers and officials of the same rank met on equal terms without any ceremony at all; when two of unequal rank met, the higher-ranking officer would sit and the other would first kneel and then get up and sit beside his superior. After the Taipings settled down in Nanking, however, Hung and Yang seldom appeared in public, Hung only on the most important occasions. The rules of propriety and decorum for the audiences of the T'ien Wang then became especially complicated, and each of the other wangs received his subordinates according to a specially prescribed ceremony.

Rank distinction was also indicated by the terms employed by an official in his proclamations and correspondence. Even his envelopes were of a specific form. The proclamations of the T'ien Wang were called *chao* or *chao-chih* (decree), the Tung Wang's were called *kao-yü* (command), the Pei Wang's *chieh-yü* (commandment), the I Wang's *hsün-yü* (instruction), and the Yen and Yü Wang's *hui-yü* (counsel). The kind of paper used varied according to rank. All wangs used yellow paper and envelopes, and all *hou* used red paper and envelopes. The insignia on the envelopes also differed accordingly.[32]

In correspondence, a definite system of terms evolved. Petitions addressed to the T'ien Wang were termed *pen-chang* (memorials); those to the Tung Wang, *ping-tsou* (memorials); those to the Pei and I Wang, *ping-pao* (reports); and those to the Yen and Yü Wang, *ping-shen* (reports). All petitions addressed to the *hou* and others lower in rank were called *ching-ping* (reports).[33]

There seem to have been some regulations as to the number of wives and concubines each Taiping official was allowed to have. It is reported in *Chin-ling kuei-chia chi-shih lüeh* that each wang had a definite quota:

[31] *Ibid.*, *ts'e* 4, *chüan* 7. The yellow vests which all soldiers wore were trimmed according to the importance of the wang under whom they served. Those of the T'ien Wang's soldiers had no trim; those of the Tung Wang's soldiers were trimmed with green; the Hsi Wang, white; the Nan Wang, red; the Pei Wang, black; the I Wang, blue.

[32] *Ibid.*

[33] *Ibid.*

the T'ien Wang and Tung Wang were each entitled to six women, the Pei Wang to two, and the I Wang to one.[34]

There also seem to have been some regulations concerning funeral ceremonies: in *T'ai-p'ing t'ien-kuo yeh-shih* it is stated, "Ch'ao-kuei was later buried according to a wang's ceremony outside the South Gate when the T'ien Wang attacked Ch'ang-sha."[35]

Another means of maintaining social distance and inspiring awe was the practice of name and word taboos. The Taipings listed a number of words that were to be applied only to God, including *sheng* (sage), *shang* (above), *huang* (sovereign), and *ti* (supreme ruler). *Wang* was reserved for the use of Hung, Yang, and the others to whom the title had been given. Even those who had previously assumed the title of *wang* were not allowed to retain it. In their titles the "dog" radical 犭 was placed to the left of *wang* 王, thus creating a new meaning for the symbol 狂.[36]

The personal names of the wangs were held sacred and became taboo for the people. If anyone had the same character in his name as a wang, it had to be changed before he could join the Taiping army. A few are listed below:[37]

Original Name	Names of Titles of Kings Violated	Changed Name
Meng Te-t'ien 天	T'ien Wang	Meng Te-en
Li Chün-ch'ang 昌	Wei Ch'ang-hui	Li Chün-liang
Li K'ai 開 -fang	Shih Ta-k'ai	Li Lai-fang
Lu Hsien-ta 達	Shih Ta-k'ai	Lu Hsien-pa
Huang I-yün 雲	Feng Yün-shan	Huang I-yün 芸
Huang T'ien 天 -shen	T'ien Wang	Huang Tsai-hsing
Tseng T'ien 天 -yang	T'ien Wang	Tseng T'ien 添 -yang

Some of the changes did not affect the sound of the names because of the numerous homophones in the Chinese language. Many characters

---

[34] Hsieh Chieh-ho, *Chin-ling kuei-chia chi-shih lüeh*, in Hsieh Hsing-yao (compiler), *T'ai-p'ing t'ien-kuo ts'ung-shu shih-san chung*, chi 2, p. 6b. Later, when the separate women's quarters were dissolved, extra women were allotted to persons lower in rank, such as chancellors and relatives of the wangs. In 1861 the T'ien Wang decreed that the Tung Wang and the Hsi Wang (referring to the children of the Tung Wang and Hsi Wang) were to have eleven each; the other wangs, six; high-ranking officers, three; and low-ranking officers, one. See Kuo, *Jih-chih*, II, 748.

[35] Ling, *Yeh-shih*, 12:12.

[36] Chang, *Tse-ch'ing*, ts'e 5, chüan 8.

[37] *Ibid.*, ts'e 1, chüan 2.

were thus dropped from common use because they were connected with taboo names or had something to do with God.

The following table lists a number of taboo characters and their substitutes. All were homophones in the dialect spoken by the Taipings with the exception of number 2 and number 23, which are synonyms only. Numbers 3, 4, and 13 are also synonyms or words closely related in a particular sense. The pronunciations given below are in the Mandarin dialect, and therefore differ slightly from that of the Taipings.[38]

Original Characters	Names or Titles Violated	Substitutes
1. Yeh 爺	Yeh-ho-hua (Jehovah)	Ya 牙
2. Ho 火	Yeh-ho-hua	Ho 夥 or Yen 炎
3. Hua 華	Yeh-ho-hua	Hua 花
4. Hsiu 秀	Yang Hsiu-ch'ing (Tung Wang)	Hsiu 繡
5. Ch'üan 全	Hung Hsiu-ch'üan	Ch'üan 泉
6. Ch'ing 清	Yang Hsiu-ch'ing	Ching 菁
7. Ch'ao 朝	Hsiao Ch'ao-kuei (Hsi Wang)	Ch'ao 潮
8. Kuei 貴	Hsiao Ch'ao-kuei	Kuei 桂
9. Yün 雲	Feng Yün-shan (Nan Wang)	Yün 芸
10. Shan 山	Feng Yün-shan	Shan 珊
11. Cheng 正	Wei Cheng (Pei Wang)	Cheng 政
12. Ch'ang 昌	Wei Ch'ang-hui (Pei Wang)	Ts'ang 瑲
13. Hui 輝	Wei Ch'ang-hui	Hui 暉
14. Ta 達	Shih Ta-k'ai (I Wang)	T'a 闥
15. K'ai 開	Shih Ta-k'ai	Chieh 偕
16. Huang 皇	Huang Shang-ti (name for God)	Huang 黃
17. Shang 上	Huang Shang-ti	Shang 尚
18. Ti 帝	Huang Shang-ti	Ti 諦
19. T'ien 天	T'ien (Heaven)	T'ien 添
20. Wang 王	Wang (king)	K'uang, Wang, or Huang 狂, 汪, 黃
21. Sheng 聖	Sheng (sage, applicable only to God)	Sheng 勝
22. Shen 神	Chen-shen (true Spirit)	Ch'en 辰
23. Lao 老	Lao (venerable, applicable only to God)	K'ao 考

[38] *Ibid.*, *ts'e* 5, *chüan* 8. In southern dialects, 王 and 黃 are both pronounced the same and 神 and 辰 are both pronounced the same.

In Taiping writings distinctions were also indicated by elevation in spacing. The degree of honor and respect due to each was expressed by the number of spaces that the title was elevated. "God" or *T'ien* was elevated four spaces, "Jesus" three, *T'ien Wang* two, and *Tung Wang* one.

The Taipings established a principle of conferring the greatest honors upon those who had joined the campaign early. The *Tse-ch'ing hui-tsuan* reported:

1. All who fought in breaking the siege of Yung-an had conferred upon them the two-character title *kung-hsiung* [meritorious], irrespective of their official rank.
2. All who participated in the celebration of Hung's birthday at Chint'ien had conferred upon them the five-character title *kung-hsiung chia i-teng* [one rank higher than meritorious], irrespective of their official rank.
3. All those who fought the battle of San-ch'a-ho had conferred upon them the five-character title *p'ing-hu chia i-teng* [one rank higher than pacifier of devils], irrespective of their official rank.
4. Those who fought both in breaking the siege of Yung-an and in the San-ch'a-ho battle had conferred upon them the seven-character title *kunghsiung p'ing-hu chia i-teng* [one rank higher than meritorious and pacifier of devils].
5. Those who took part in the Chin-t'ien founding celebration and also fought in the San-ch'a-ho battle had conferred upon them the seven-character title *kung-hsiung p'ing-hu chia erh-teng* [two ranks higher than meritorious and pacifier of devils].
6. Those who participated in the Chin-t'ien celebration, fought in the San-ch'a-ho battle and had the further distinction of having taken a city, and had received *chia i-teng* [one rank higher], had conferred on them the five-character title *kung-hsiung chia san-teng* [three ranks higher than meritorious].[39]

Some of the distinctions between the old and the new members of the society were legalized, as can be seen from the regulations described above, but others were not. Most of them were taken for granted by all members even without any institutional basis. The Taipings tried to set a line of demarcation between the old and the new members at the outset of the campaign. It was reported in the *T'ai-p'ing t'ien-kuo yeh-shih* that the Taiping army had agreed that "the sage soldiers" (the old members who joined the army in Kwangsi) were to be considered highest in status, and that those who joined later would not be promoted

[39] *Ibid., ts'e* 2, *chüan* 3.

beyond the ranks of colonel and captain even though they showed great merit. This practice was discontinued when the Taipings reached Wuch'ang because there was a vast number of new soldiers.[40] Such unequal treatment as was evidenced in the following intelligence report led to a great deal of discontent among the followers.

> In marching, the rebels applied very strict discipline. Anyone who fell out of formation was executed to prevent desertion. If during the march a person wanted to take time out to relieve himself, he had to ask two or three persons near him to wait for him; then they would return to their positions in an orderly manner. Should anyone leave the ranks alone, the commanding rebel might cut off his head to serve as an example to the rest. For this reason there were many who would rather let their water and night-soil have their free course than to drop out of formation. However, it was all different with the long-haired old rebels. They were allowed to ride in chairs and stay in the houses of the people.[41]

In battle the new members always bore the brunt of the attack. The old members, appearing to be in front, would actually retreat to the rear, leaving the new members to do the heavy fighting. These new recruits, believing that the old members had already gone ahead, would fight courageously in their encounter; even when they were defeated, the old members would be safe.[42]

It was naturally difficult to put the old members under discipline. In his confession Huang Wen-ying, the Chao Wang, reported the following case:

> When I arrived at Nanking, I tried to persuade a comrade from Kwangtung, who had taken away by force a horse belonging to a comrade from Liang-hu, to return it to the latter, but he stabbed me with a spear. I brought it up with the Kan Wang, but he could not do a thing about it.[43]

Among the old members, there was a distinction between those from Kwangtung and those from Kwangsi. *Tse-ch'ing hui-tsuan* said that Lo Ta-kang was brave, tactful, and astute and enjoyed great popularity with the rebels. But he never was promoted to the position of a wang or a *hou* merely because he was not from Kwangsi.[44] He was very unhappy about this and once said:

[40] Ling, *Yeh-shih*, 13:23.
[41] Chang, *Tse-ch'ing*, *ts'e* 3, *chüan* 4.
[42] *Ibid.*, *ts'e* 3, *chüan* 5.
[43] Hsieh, *Ts'ung-shu*, *chi* 2, "Chao-wang k'ou-kung," p. 7b.
[44] Chang, *Tse-ch'ing*, *ts'e* 1, *chüan* 2.

I joined the army at the same time as Ch'in Jih-kang and Hu I-huang, and my achievement is in no way inferior to theirs; they were both made wangs simply because they came from Kwangsi, but because I came from Kwangtung, I cannot even get to be a *hou*. Can you imagine anything more unfair than this? It looks as if the T'ien Wang himself has forgotten that he also came from Hua-hsien.[45]

In spite of the social distinctions among the Taipings it would be unfair to say that they had no notions of equality. An anecdote in the *Yeh-shih* will illustrate this point:

When the Taiping troops took up quarters in the residences of wealthy people, they usually broke the red sandalwood tables to pieces and used them for firewood. When questioned why they did it, they would say: "These are the things the wealthy people take great pride in showing to people, so we destroyed them in order to destroy the class distinction between the rich and the poor." On another occasion the Taiping troops got into a lady's boudoir, where they found a large quantity of bright pearls, which they ground to powder and swallowed with boiled water. They said: "If we handed them over to the officers above, it might lead them to luxury and abandonment. If we kept them for ourselves, it might be the cause of our downfall [referring apparently to the regulation that no soldier was allowed to keep private movable property]. But if we swallow the unlucky things we might receive the approval of the Heavenly Father."[46]

There seems to have been an honest desire on the part of the rank and file to do away with discriminatory distinctions.

Another element of change in the social structure introduced by the Taipings concerned the position of women. In theory, Taiping women were equal to men, and to a certain extent this was true. They were allowed to fight in the army, take examinations, and take office in the government, and they enjoyed certain privileges.

Tse-ch'ing hui-tsuan stated that the rebels had women troops, most of whom were relatives of the wangs and had been brought up in caves in Yao and Chuang. They wore turbans wrapped around their heads, climbed the cliffs barefooted, and were much more courageous than men. They actually took part in battles and often inflicted great damage on the government troops.[47] According to another observer, the author of *Fa-i ch'u-chi*, most Taiping women did not bind their feet. They fought

[45] Ling, *Yeh-shih*, 15:3.
[46] *Ibid.*, 20:51.
[47] Chang, *Tse-ch'ing*, *ts'e* 2, *chüan* 3.

for the chance to go to paradise (to die) and were more fierce than men.[48] Among the poems written on the top of Tu-hsiu-feng in Kwangsi there was one with lines describing the participation of women and children in a battle:

> Midst the troops were women surging forward
>   east and west,
> War cries were mixed with the voices of children,
>   heard near and far.[49]

The *Yeh-shih* contains stories about a number of Taiping women warriors, among whom were the T'ien Wang's wife, one of his concubines, his sister Hsüan-chiao, and two other women named Yang Erh-ku and Hsiao San-niang.

The T'ien Wang's wife was from a family named Lai of Chia-ying-chou in Kwangtung. Her father was a scholar. His study of the late Ming period inspired him to revive the Ming dynasty. At that time many ambitious loyalists in Liang-yüeh [Kwangtung and Kwangsi] had associated themselves with secret societies and found refuge in lowly occupations. Lai befriended these people and gave them financial help whenever needed. When the T'ien Wang was in financial straits, his wife sold her jewelry to help him, and her father also helped.... In the breaking of the siege of Yung-an, his wife, sword in hand, led the women on horseback into the battle to help the menfolk defeat the Ch'ing forces.[50]

A woman whose family name was Hsiao was one of the T'ien Wang's concubines and a cousin of Hsiao Ch'ao-kuei. She was a great acrobat and very clever on horseback. [It was a great sight to see] a beauty so charmingly clad galloping as if she were flying. Women from Kwangsi are usually strong. They formed an army and contributed a great deal to the success in breaking the siege of Yung-an.[51]

When the revolution broke out in Chin-t'ien, all members of the God Worshipers' Society joined with their families, so that there were many women with the army. Hsüan-chiao [the T'ien Wang's sister] organized them into army corps and made herself the commander. Every time Ch'ao-kuei went to battle, Hsüan-chiao would lead the "big-footed" women clad in gorgeous clothes to his help. They were good at using firearms and were

[48] Ming-hsin tao-jen, *Fa-i ch'u-chi*, in *I-ching*, No. 17 (Nov. 5, 1936), p. 27.
[49] Hsieh, *Ts'ung-shu, chi* 3, "T'ai-p'ing shih-shih," p. 11b.
[50] Ling, *Yeh-shih*, "Pen-chi, hou-chi," 1:16.
[51] *Ibid.*, 1:17.

dead shots. The morale of the Ch'ing army was often broken by their presence. In the battle of Ch'ang-sha, Ch'ao-kuei was killed. Hsüan-chiao, while wearing mourning, assumed command of the troops and kept them from dispersing. When the great army arrived, she gave the command to [Yang] Hsiu-ch'ing and went to live with the T'ien Wang.[52]

Yang Erh-ku was Yang Fu-ch'ing's younger sister. She possessed great courage and a power of decision not to be found even among men. Her husband, Chiang Te-sheng, served under Yang Fu-ch'ing as a commander and was also very brave. They went into battle together, Erh-ku wearing a yellow headdress and a red skirt, plunging dauntlessly into the thickest of the battle. She was also skillful at throwing knives from horseback and never missed one throw in a hundred. Those struck by her knives were invariably killed. The knives were seven inches long and the sharpest that there were. She always carried a bag of them into battle and called herself the "divine knife-thrower."[53]

In the Taiping army there was a woman by the name of Hsiao San-niang, known as the "woman commander." Some said that she was Ch'ao-kuei's younger sister. She was at least twenty, tall and long-armed, a great general on horseback. She could shoot an arrow with either hand. When the Taiping army captured Chen-chiang, she led several hundred women soldiers and climbed the city wall, braver and fiercer than the men. All who met them fell back. The T'ien Wang's sister, Hsüan-chiao, could ride and take part in battle like San-niang, but she could only give orders to the troops and could not actually fight in battles.[54]

Chang Pin-yüan, in a letter to Hsiang Yung, made the suggestion, "When the city falls, all the Kwangsi women should be put to death and no mercy should be shown them, because these women are all brave and fierce and have acted as soldiers in defending the city."[55] And in another letter he said, "Yesterday Hsia-kuan, chancellor of the rebels, sent a command ordering the women rebels out to fight."[56]

Women were also allowed to compete in Taiping civil examinations. The *Yeh-shih* gives the following account:

After the *T'ai-p'ing t'ien-kuo* opened the civil examinations, they also gave examinations for women. Hung Hsüan-chiao was appointed the chief ex-

[52] *Ibid.*, 18:1.
[53] *Ibid.*, 20:45.
[54] *Ibid.*, 20:21.
[55] Quoted by Lo Erh-kang in "Nü-ying k'ao," *Hsien-tai shih-hsüeh*, No. 1 (Jan., 1933), p. 77.
[56] Quoted in *ibid.*

aminer, assisted by Chang Wan-ju and Wang Tsu-chen, the former from Anhwei and the latter from Hupeh. The subject was a chapter [from the *Analects*] which contains the line, "Only the women and small people are difficult to teach." More than two hundred women came to take the examination. Fu Shan-hsiang, daughter of Fu Huai of Chin-ling, came out first; her essay, in which she refuted the idea of "difficult to teach" by bringing in as evidence all the great women in history who had contributed to the success of their husbands, met with great approval from the T'ien Wang. She was then dressed in an embroidered gown, crowned with laurel, and sent parading behind the band along the streets for three days. All women called her *nü chuang-yüan* [woman number one]. The second place went to Miss Chung and the third to Miss Lin.[57]

The right to take examinations and the right to take office in the government were closely connected. The *Yeh-shih* states: "In the second year of Taiping, their army took Nanking. All the women in the city were confined to women's quarters, which were organized into army corps. They were examined so that the talented could be selected for office."[58]

Fu Shan-hsiang, who took first place in the state examinations, was one of the most notable Taiping women officials. She was made *chung-t'uan t'uan-shuai* (an officer commanding twenty thousand women) by the Tung Wang, and was also given the privilege of reporting directly to the Tung Wang.[59]

Ch'en Hui-yen in his *Wu-ch'ang chi-shih* said: "Women also occupied official positions similar to the men. Sometimes they also went out to fight wearing red silk headdresses and grass sandals, and they were quite brave."[60] *Tse-ch'ing hui-tsuan* gives a detailed description of the positions occupied by women officials both in the army and in the government. Very often they were actually concubines of the leaders under whom they served.[61]

---

[57] Ling, *Yeh-shih*, 8:5.
[58] *Ibid.*, 18:2. "The second year" is apparently a mistake.
[59] *Ibid.*
[60] Quoted in Lo, "Nü-ying k'ao," *Hsien-tai shih-hsüeh*, No. 1 (Jan., 1933), p. 77.
[61]   *Women Court Officials*
                           First rank
Women chiefs of staff (4): 女軍師
  Woman left minister and first chief of staff 女左輔正軍師
  Woman right minister and second chief of staff 女右輔又正軍師
  Woman front guide and first deputy chief of staff 女前導副軍師
  Woman rear protector and second deputy chief of staff 女後護副軍師

Second rank

Chancelloresses (12): 女丞相
  Chancelloress of the Heaven Department 女天官正丞相
  Deputy chancelloress of the Heaven Department 女天官副丞相
  Chancelloress of the Earth Department 女地官正丞相
  Deputy chancelloress of the Earth Department 女地官副丞相
  Chancelloress of the Spring Department 女春官正丞相
  Deputy chancelloress of the Spring Department 女春官副丞相
  Chancelloress of the Summer Department 女夏官正丞相
  Deputy chancelloress of the Summer Department 女夏官副丞相
  Chancelloress of the Autumn Department 女秋官正丞相
  Deputy chancelloress of the Autumn Department 女秋官副丞相
  Chancelloress of the Winter Department 女冬官正丞相
  Deputy chancelloress of the Winter Department 女冬官副丞相
Honorary chancelloress (no definite number) 女恩賞丞相

Third rank

Women senior secretaries (36) 女檢點
Honorary woman senior secretary (no definite number) 女恩賞檢點
Lady keeper of the inner gate of the T'ien Wang's inner palace 天朝女內掌門
Lady-in-waiting of the Tung Wang's palace 東殿女內貴使
Lady-in-waiting of the Hsi Wang's palace 西殿女內貴使

Fourth rank

Women commanders (72) 女指揮
Women commanders of the embroidery camp (240) 女繡錦指揮
Honorary woman commander 女恩賞指揮
Lady keeper of the inner gate of the Tung Wang's inner palace 東殿女內掌門
Lady keeper of the inner gate of the Hsi Wang's inner palace 西殿女內掌門
Lady-in-waiting of the Nan Wang's palace 南殿女內貴使
Lady-in-waiting of the Pei Wang's palace 北殿女內貴使

Fifth rank

Women generals (40) 女將軍
Women generals of the embroidery camp (200) 女繡錦將軍
Honorary woman general 女恩賞將軍
Lady keeper of the inner gate of the Nan Wang's inner palace 南殿女內掌門
Lady keeper of the inner gate of the Pei Wang's inner palace 北殿女內掌門
Lady-in-waiting of the I Wang's palace 翼殿女內貴使

Sixth rank

Women corps commandants of the embroidery camp (120) 女繡錦總制
Lady keeper of the inner gate of the I Wang's inner palace 翼殿女內掌門
Lady-in-waiting of the Yen Wang's palace 燕殿女內貴使

Seventh rank

Women corps superintendents of the embroidery camp 女繡錦監軍
(Chang, *Tse-ch'ing*, *ts'e* 2, *chüan* 3, "Wei-nü kuan." See also *ts'e* 2, *chüan* 3, "Wei-kuan piao" and "Wei-ch'ao nei-kuan.")

Women Field Officers 軍中女官

The women's army corps consisted of the following officers:

First rank

Women corps commandants (40) 女總制

Second rank

Women corps superintendents (40) 女監軍

The new status of women did not mean merely that they enjoyed privileges, for they were assigned to work ordinarily given to men. Hsieh Chieh-ho, in *Chin-ling kuei-chia chi-shih lüeh*, says: "When the great camp of the Eastern Gate was formed, the rebels were afraid and sent out twenty thousand women every day to dig ditches."[62] Hsieh also reports, "The wheat outside the Eastern Gate had already ripened and had stood for a long time unharvested; they [the rebels] therefore sent women out to harvest it."[63] Naturally the Taipings were sharply criticized for employing women in work to which they were unaccustomed. Wang Shih-to, in his *I-ping jih-chi*, explains the matter:

> The rebels came originally from the mountainous regions, and their womenfolk were used to farming, weaving, dyeing, and so forth. They did not realize that the women of Chin-ling were not used to doing work like this. Thinking that whatever they [their women] could do the others could do too, they ordered them [the women of Chin-ling] to do their own share of the work in carrying rice, pounding grain, felling bamboo, digging ditches, carrying bricks, harvesting wheat and grain, carrying salt and water, and other such work. Since their bound feet made working hard for these [Chin-ling] women, they were ordered to loosen the bindings on their feet. They [the Taipings] did not realize that their feet would not grow again once they had been bound. For this reason, the Taipings were called ruthless. However, only the Kiangsu women suffered from this; the women from Anhwei took it as a matter of course and did not feel strange about it.[64]

Thus, in some cases women in the Taiping society were the equals of men, enjoying the same privileges and contributing toward the group life a fair share of work.

Another unique feature of Taiping society was the segregation of sexes. As mentioned previously, the Taipings considered adultery to be

---

Third rank
Women corps generals (40) 女軍師
(each women's army included 2,500 soldiers)
Fourth rank
Women lieutenants (1,000, each in charge of 100 women soldiers) 女卒長
Fifth rank
Women sergeants (4,000, each in charge of 25 women soldiers) 營長即兩司馬
(Chang, *Tse-ch'ing, ts'e* 6, *chüan* 11. See also *ts'e* 2, *chüan* 3, "Wei-chün chung-kuan.")

[62] Hsieh, *Ts'ung-shu, chi* 2, p. 4b.
[63] *Ibid.* See also pp. 3b and 4a, where women were reported to be carrying salt and bricks and to be digging ditches.
[64] *Wang Hui-weng i-ping jih-chi*, 3:3b.

the greatest offense. The seventh commandment in "The Book of Heavenly Commandments" (T'ien-t'iao-shu) says: "Thou shalt not commit adultery." And the note adds:

> All men in the world are brothers and all women in the world are sisters. With regard to the children in paradise [Nanking], men must go to the men's camps and women to the women's camps. They must not intermingle. Men or women who commit adultery are "turning into devils." The greatest violation against the Heavenly Commandments is casting evil eyes and having a lustful heart.[65]

"The Proclamation on the Origin of the Principles of World Salvation" says: "Adultery is the greatest of all *pu-cheng* [evil deeds], for T'ien hates most that men should turn into devils."[66] The poem attached to the seventh heavenly commandment says: "Adultery is the greatest of all sins, and nothing is more pitiable than being transformed into a devil."[65] One of the "Poems by the Heavenly Father" (T'ien-fu shih) reads: "No sin is unpardonable except the violation of the seventh commandment, for this is a sin of the most dreadful sort."[67] The Taipings laid emphasis on this at the very outset of their campaign at Yung-an. On the twenty-seventh day of the first moon, 1852, the T'ien Wang gave the following edict:

> By the edict of the T'ien Wang: "The male and the female troops and officers in the whole army should obey the Heavenly Commandments. These are my special instructions to brother Ch'ing [Yang Hsiu-ch'ing, the Tung Wang], brother-in-law Kuei [Hsiao Ch'ao-kuei, the Hsi Wang], brother Shan [Feng Yün-shan], brother Cheng [Wei Cheng, the Pei Wang], brother Ta [Shih Ta-k'ai], and all the commanders in the various army corps that they should from time to time make close inspections for the purpose of discovering any violations of the seventh heavenly commandment. Should there be any violaters of this commandment, they should be executed immediately after their crime is discovered, and there should be no pardon. Let no soldier or officer try to protect the criminals, for in doing so they are sure to offend the Heavenly Father, the Huang Shang-ti, and incur his righteous indignation. Let everybody be aware of this. Respect this."[68]

[65] Hsiao, *Ts'ung-shu, ts'e* 1, p. 7b.
[66] "T'ai-p'ing chao-shu," in Hsiao, *Ts'ung-shu, ts'e* 1, p. 2a.
[67] No. 465, in Hsiao, *Ts'ung-shu, ts'e* 7.
[68] "T'ien-ming chao-chih shu," in Hsiang Ta *et al.* (compilers), *T'ai-p'ing t'ien-kuo*, I, 68.

In this the Taipings may have been prompted by a consideration of the effect of family burdens on the efficiency of the fighting force. In the *Yeh-shih* Ling Shan-ch'ing writes: "At first the T'ien Wang, afraid that the officers and soldiers might be burdened by their families, prohibited men and women from living together. Thus the women's quarters or camps were instituted. Women were given food daily and taught handicrafts."[69]

Whatever their reason, the Taipings at the very beginning of the uprising established separate quarters for men and women. The fifth of the "Ten Important Regulations for the Stationary Camp," in "Taiping Rules and Regulations" (T'ai-p'ing t'iao-kuei), is: "Observe the separation between the men's and women's camps."[70] Tu Wen-lan in his *P'ing-ting Yüeh-fei chi-lüeh* records the following:

> The rebels were very strict in the segregation of the sexes. The men cap- tured during a campaign were quartered in the men's camps under the supervision of the corps general; the captured women were quartered in separate camps in the rear, under the control of the women from Kwangsi. The control was greatly tightened when they [the Taipings] arrived at Nanking, much more strict than when they were on the march. Occasion- ally some men made their way into the women's quarters by stealth, but the quarters were daily investigated and numbered and were strictly super- vised in the name of the chief of the quarters. Every month their register was presented to the Imperial Decree Bureau for inspection. Thus, even the old rebels from Kwangsi dared not disturb the order. Many girls from great families were thus able to keep their character.[71]

Even husbands and wives were forbidden to live together. Lu Hsien- pa was reported to have lost his office and Ch'en Tsung-yang his head for violating this regulation.[72] In the early days Hsiao Ch'ao-kuei even had his parents tried and executed for the same violation. In the men's camps, the segregation rules were laid down with the same strictness. It is said that those who hired women to come to the camp to wash or to mend clothes were to be executed.[73]

The women's camps were later dissolved; among the various ex- planations offered as reasons for their dissolution, the *Yeh-shih* gives two,

[69] Ling, *Yeh-shih*, 18:1.
[70] Hsiao, *Ts'ung-shu*, ts'e 2, p. 1b.
[71] *P'ing-ting Yüeh-fei chi-lüeh*, Appendix II, p. 8b.
[72] Chang, *Tse-ch'ing*, ts'e 1, chüan 2, "Wei chen-kuo-hou Lu Hsien-pa." For Ch'en Tsung-yang, see Chang, *Tse-ch'ing*, ts'e 6, chüan 12.
[73] *Ibid.*, ts'e 4, chüan 7, "Wei-kao shih."

the shortage of food and jealousy of Hsüan-chiao (Hung's sister) over Fu Shan-hsiang (the Tung Wang's favorite), which resulted in the Tung Wang's decision to have the camps dissolved.[74] Of another opinion, Huang Chün-tsai says in *Chin-hu ch'i-mo*:

> When the rebels occupied Nanking, they established women's quarters under the supervision of the Kwangsi women; not even husbands and wives or mothers and sons could see each other. When they ran short of food, they sent the paler ones out to cut and gather in the grain—as a matter of fact, they were deliberately giving them a chance to escape. This went on for a month, when the rebels again gave orders that the women should be given away in marriage, and officials were appointed to take charge of the arrangements. Men and women above fifteen were ordered to report to the office. The number of women a man was to receive was determined by his rank; the highest-ranking men received more than ten women, and the number decreased as the rank lowered. They were allowed to sleep together only at the end of the month, however, and during the remaining days they were not to violate the precept against adultery. The marriage order proved to be a mess. In many cases old men were wedded to young girls and old women were coupled up with young men, causing a great deal of heartbreak. When the order was proclaimed, many of the women committed suicide by hanging themselves, jumping into wells, cutting their own throats, or taking poison. In trying to get a list of their names, my friend Yü Shu-chih counted more than nine hundred women who died thus.[75]

Tu Wen-lan's account gives a still different reason for the dissolution of the women's quarters:

> From Chin-t'ien to Chin-ling, [the rebels] kept the men and women strictly apart; even husbands and wives were to be executed for violating the heavenly commandment if they were found sleeping together. They were afraid that if their soldiers were concerned about their families they would not give their all in battle, so they established the women's quarters which followed the army in order to keep a hold on them. These were indeed good tactics. In the first month of the fifth year of Hsien-feng [1855], Tseng Shui-yüan, *t'ien-kuan ch'eng-hsiang*, (chancellor of the Heaven Department) lost his position because of his delay in reaching Wu-hu. His younger brother, resenting the action and regretting [having joined himself], fled. The chief rebel was angry, and thinking that Shui-yüan was behind his brother's scheme, had him executed. He then made inquiries among his confidants as to why even the old members were deserting like

[74] Ling, *Yeh-shih*, 18:1–2 and 20:5.
[75] Huang, *Chin-hu ch'i-mo*, "Chin-hu tun-mo," 2:6a–b.

the new members. The answer was that the leaders had promised the rebels at Yung-an that when they got to Nanking it would be like ascending to paradise, where husbands and wives would be allowed to reunite. Now [that they were in Nanking] they were still denied the privilege of having their family with them, and it was feared that from now on the number of deserters would increase. The chief rebel then sent out an order allowing men and women to get married. Official matchmakers were appointed to take charge of the arrangements. Both men and women between fifteen and fifty were to report to the office to get matched. Men of the rank of chancellor were given more than ten women in marriage, relations of the wangs were given eight, and the rest were given a decreasing number according to their rank. Those who had no rank were also given one woman. The method of assigning was by lot drawn by the official matchmakers. As a result, some old men obtained young wives, and some boys obtained old wives; but once they were allotted there was no change. Women of good character committed suicide by the thousands. Thus the women's quarters were emptied.[76]

Wang T'ao in his *Wen-yu yü-t'an* gives a similar account and identifies the chief rebel leader as the Tung Wang.[77] Thus the segregation of the sexes came to an end in 1855, affecting members from the rank of chancellor down. The wangs already had unlimited license. When Hsiao Ch'ao-kuei was first made a wang, he took Lo Chi-lung's younger sister as his concubine because of her beauty.[78] While the Taiping army was in Hupeh, hundreds of thousands of women were captured, and the beautiful ones were taken into the palaces as concubines.[79] The T'ien Wang himself set an example in collecting concubines when he reached Nanking. Scholars of Nanking and Yang-chou wrote poems recording what took place when the Taipings took over Nanking. According to one: "Beautiful as flowers were these three thousand heartbroken girls; a hundred and eighty of them are weeping in the mud into which they have fallen."[80] Neither did the generals who went out to fight give heed to the regulation. Ch'en Ping-wen ordered his subordinates to select women from among the people for concubines when he took Hangchow.

According to Augustus Lindley, better known as Lin-le, who had had "four years' military service and social intercourse with the Ti-pings,"[81]

---

[76] Tu, *P'ing-ting Yüeh-fei chi-lüeh*, Appendix III, p. 9a–b.
[77] Wang, *Wen-yu yü-t'an*, 8:10a.
[78] Ling, *Yeh-shih*, 15:14.
[79] Chang, *Tse-ch'ing*, ts'e 2, chüan 3.
[80] Ling, *Yeh-shih*, 20:18–19.
[81] Lin-le [Lindley], *Ti-ping Tien-Kwoh: The History of the Ti-ping Revolution*, I, vii,

"a plebian Ti-ping is allowed but one wife, and to her he must be regularly married by one of the ministers."[82] Wei and Shih issued a proclamation prohibiting plural marriages among the people.[83] And according to "The Land System of the Heavenly Dynasty," marriage was not to be contracted simply on the basis of wealth.[84] As to those who held official rank, the number of wives was determined by their rank. According to the Yu Wang (Hung's son), the T'ien Wang had eighty-eight wives, and when the Yu Wang was nine years old he was given four wives.[85]

The right to marry must have been given to the people at a later time. According to the date on the certificate of his commission, Lin-le could not have been with the Taipings earlier than 1859. At the beginning of the regime, only those above the rank of chancellor were allowed to marry. Ku Shen reports:

> The boy guide again took me to visit various places.... We saw groups of women roaming the streets. They were all beautifully dressed and made up, but some seemed to be very happy and others depressed and worried. The boy said, "These are all the wives of the 'Long Hairs.'..."I asked, "May all the 'Long Hairs' marry?" The boy said, "Only those above the rank of chancellor may have wives, and they must first petition the T'ien Wang; those below that rank cannot have wives."[86]

Even those who were already married were separated and were allowed to reunite only when the women's quarters had been abolished. Wang T'ao reports in his *Wen-yu yü-t'an:*

> ...The rebel Tung [the Tung Wang] said, "You are certainly ignorant of the deep intention of the Heavenly Father. The longer you wait, the more wives you will have. But since you will not wait, those with a high rank will be allowed only a little more than ten women, and the lower your rank the fewer you will get. Then won't you still be dissatisfied?" At that moment the rebel Tung feigned that the Heavenly Father had descended upon him; then he said that the Heavenly Father had graciously granted them the right to marry. Two official matchmakers were appointed, one man and one woman. All rebels who had accumulated merit to the rank

[82] *Ibid.*, I, 301.
[83] Chang, *Tse-ch'ing, ts'e* 4, *chüan* 7, "Wei kao-shih," says: "It is a matter of course that there be one husband to one wife."
[84] "T'ien-ch'ao t'ien-mou chih-tu," in Hsiao, *Ts'ung-shu, ts'e* 4, p. 3a.
[85] Hsieh, *Ts'ung-shu, chi* 2, p. 6a.
[86] Ku, *Hu-hsüeh sheng-huan chi*, in Hsiang, *T'ai-p'ing t'ien-kuo*, VI, 736.

of chancellor were to be allotted ten or more women, relations of the wangs were to have eight, and those without rank were allowed to reunite with their wives if they had been married before.[87]

The polygamy practiced by the leaders was also a form of social distinction, as we have noted before, but this did not silence their critics who accused them of being licentious. Chang Te-chien, in his *Tse-ch'ing hui-tsuan*, makes the following comment:

> The wangs collected about them numerous wives and concubines, and yet deprived their subordinates of the source of human relationship. They falsely promised them that when peace prevailed they would be granted the right to marry.... Those who had accumulated great merit would be allowed to have concubines.... Violaters of the Heavenly Commandments were often pardoned if they had been valuable to the rebels, but they were punished by having their marriages delayed for three years after everybody else had been given the right to marry; and they were not allowed to have any extra wives.... By granting them the right to have wives the riffraff would fight to the very last in order to have their desires satisfied.[88]

Women officials were often in reality concubines of the wangs. Chang Te-chien records the following report by refugees from Nanking:

> According to the refugees from Nanking, the T'ien Wang has one wife, who is called the queen; the other wangs also have one wife, each of whom is titled lady [*wang-niang*]. The chief rebel selected forty concubines at Wu-ch'ang, one hundred and eight on arriving at Nanking, and has increased the number steadily to close to two hundred. But several thousand women officials are in fact also his concubines. The concubines of the wangs are titled *fu wang-niang* [deputy lady] and number between thirty and forty. But all lady keepers of the palace inner gates are also their concubines.[89]

And we are told that Meng Te-an, *ch'un-kuan cheng ch'eng-hsiang* (chancellor of the Spring Department), was commissioned to find beautiful girls and obtain them for the wangs as concubines.[90] Even generals in the field were entrusted to capture women. The *Yeh-shih* says: "When Feng-hsiang left Tseng Li-ch'ang to defend Yang-chou, he brought

[87] *Wen-yu yü-t'an*, 8:10a.
[88] Chang, *Tse-ch'ing, ts'e* 6, *chüan* 12.
[89] *Ibid.*
[90] *Ibid., ts'e* 1, *chüan* 2.

with him all the wealth and women he had collected there to *T'ien-ching* [Nanking].''[91]

Thus, the attitude of the Taipings toward women was not very consistent. In theory they looked upon women as the equals of men, but in fact the treatment of women differed according to circumstance. The women from Kwangsi were treated as equals of the men to a great extent, but the women from other places were not. In respect to the ownership of land, civil examinations, vocation, and the right to hold office, women were given equal opportunity, subject only to the condition that Taiping plans were carried out; if these plans were not carried out, their men fared no better. This did not apply to the small elite group, whose habit of misusing women, whether concubines, successful candidates in the civil examinations, or women officials and officers, seems to have made mockery of the whole idea of the equality of the sexes.[92] The very use of women as a reward for courageous fighting and the denial of the right to have a wife as punishment for misdemeanors reveal the attitude of the Taiping leaders.

In addition the Taipings extolled the traditional three forms of obedience. The "Ode for Youth" in the sections entitled "The Way of a Husband" (Fu-tao) and "The Way of a Wife" (Ch'i-tao) says:

> The way of a husband is based on the quality of firmness, and his love for his wife should be measured. Should he hear the roar of a lioness of Ho-tung [termagant], he should not be afraid and confused. The way of a wife is based on three forms of obedience, and she should never disobey her husband. Should a hen desire to herald the arrival of the morning, it is one sure way of making the home miserable.[93]

One of the "Poems by the Heavenly Father" reads:

> For goodness sake, a hen must not try to crow;
> It is provided by Heaven that a hen's crowing will be followed by execution.[94]

To the Taipings a woman's place was with the family, and she was not to

[91] Ling, *Yeh-shih*, 15:5.

[92] "T'ien-fu hsia-fan chao-shu (II)," in Hsiang, *T'ai-p'ing t'ien-kuo*, Vol. I, where the T'ien Wang was reprimanded by the "Heavenly Father" in the person of the Tung Wang for kicking pregnant concubines in his harem. See especially p. 51.

[93] "Yu-hsüeh-shih," in Hsiao, *Ts'ung-shu*, *ts'e* 4, p. 9a–b.

[94] "T'ien-fu shih" No. 457, in Hsiao, *Ts'ung-shu*, *ts'e* 7.

meddle in the affairs of her husband. Another of the "Poems by the Heavenly Father" reads:

> Women in the rear palaces should not try to leave;
> If they should try to leave it would be like hens trying to crow.
> The duty of the palace women is to attend to the needs of their husbands;
> And it is arranged by Heaven that they are not to learn of the affairs outside.[95]

The "Ode for Youth" contains a poem similar in tone:

> The way of a woman is to cherish chastity, and never approach a man;
> If she maintains her proper position within [the family], all happiness will be hers.[96]

It goes without saying that the T'ien Wang kept a jealous eye on his harem, and many of the Heavenly Father's poems were inspired by Hung's desire to keep his concubines from being untrue to him.

> Once you are well tried, you will be honored forever;
> And for ten thousand years you will occupy the position of royal wives.
> Once you are misdirected to the wrong way, you will forever be humble;
> And for ten thousand years you will be forbidden to see the T'ien Wang.[97]

> If you are well taught in the way, when you become royal wives,
> Your names will be known throughout the ten thousand nations of the world.
> And gold houses of gold bricks will be your dwellings;
> Forever majestic as the consorts of the T'ien Wang.[98]

> If you are pious in mind, pious in words, pious in head and face,
> In hand, in body, with clothing bright;
> If you are pious in these six ways and bright in this one,
> You will be majestic and happy ten thousand years.[99]

[95] "T'ien-fu shih" No. 458, in Hsiao, *Ts'ung-shu, ts'e* 7.
[96] "Yu-hsüeh-shih," in Hsiao, *Ts'ung-shu, ts'e* 4, p. 11a.
[97] "T'ien-fu shih" No. 25, in Hsiao, *Ts'ung-shu, ts'e* 7.
[98] "T'ien-fu shih" No. 26, in Hsiao, *Ts'ung-shu, ts'e* 7.
[99] "T'ien-fu shih" No. 27, in Hsiao, *Ts'ung-shu, ts'e* 7.

In their attempt to make constructive social reforms, the Taipings first found it necessary to break old practices that had persisted. They made an all-out attack on superstitions, which were among the most powerful forces shaping the behavior pattern of the people. Their revision of the Four Books and adoption of a new calendar were designed to free the people from superstitious beliefs and practices.

According to Wang Shih-to, the parts of the Four Books and Five Classics that were deleted by the Taipings were those concerned with sacrifices and the worship of spirits and gods. In his *I-ping jih-chi* he says:

> The rebels, in revising the Four Books and Five Classics, have deleted [all passages] on worshiping and sacrificing to spirits and gods, and [those] on rituals [for happy occasions]. This is indeed an action of great merit which is comparable to that of the sages, and we should not discard the rebels' words simply because they are rebels. In times to come there may be some who will consider their words valuable.[100]

One of the aims in adopting a new calendar was to do away with superstitions concerning auspicious or inauspicious years, months, days, and hours. Hung Jen-kan, in answer to a hypothetical question as to why the new calendar of the heavenly kingdom gave no list of auspicious and inauspicious days to guide the people in their choice for the execution of their important affairs, said:

> The calendar was originally based on the endless movement of the natural course of events. But people of later periods began to vie with each other in their subjective knowledge and artificiality, and created the system of "heavenly stems" and "earthly branches" and the ideas of "giving birth to" and "conquering [the five elements]." Then they designated certain days and hours to be either auspicious or inauspicious and went so far as to use these as a basis for astrological observations. This resulted in many divergent opinions, leading far astray from the path of truth....The course of Heaven is firm and steady and remains eternally constant.... True, there are discrepancies observable at present that were not apparent in former times; but this is the result of the slow accumulation of infinitesimal inaccuracies which were not great enough to be evident to the people of old but have now accumulated to the point where they are observable. These inaccuracies cannot be attributed to the movements of Heaven. The course of Heaven is complicated, and the intelligence of men is limited. When we measure heavenly phenomena by means of instruments, we cannot be certain we are penetrating the truth. Furthermore, the calendar has

[100] *Wang Hui-weng i-ping jih-chi*, 2:10b.

been revised more than once, and the inaccuracies have become greater. . . .

Those who divided the days and hours into *huang-tao* [the yellow way] and *hei-tao* [the black way], initiating the practice of rushing toward lucky days and hours and avoiding unlucky ones, actually propagated a falsehood in making a distinction between heavenly grace and heavenly condemnation. Why did they not realize that the years, months, days, and hours are all designated by our Heavenly Father, so that every day is a good day and every hour is a good hour, and no day or hour differs from any other day or hour? Therefore the *Book of Changes* says, "Princely men, lucky; mean men, unlucky; and repentant and hard-working, lucky; aimless, unlucky." The apparent lesson is: it will be lucky if one chooses to be a princely man and does good deeds, but it will be unlucky if one chooses to be a mean man and does evil. The divination and selection of days and months have nothing to do with the coming of calamity or happiness.[101]

Historically, the art of divination began with Kuo P'u of the Chin dynasty. He made people believe that he had received *Ch'ing-nang ching* [The Green Bag Classic] which enabled him to tell auspicious or inauspicious [times and places for] burials and to give people directions for avoiding calamity and attaining happiness. Yang Sung-yün of the T'ang dynasty continued in this mistake and aggravated it. So all those who practice the art of astrology today are disciples of these two men. But Kuo P'u never enjoyed the happiness of wealth and honor; on the contrary, he suffered the misfortune of having his whole clan wiped out. And Sung-yün throughout his life remained poverty-stricken and shiftless, without a place to rest his body. If the originators did not know how to escape calamity and win happiness, how can those who have inherited their teachings be able to teach others how to escape calamity and acquire happiness?[102]

Now our heavenly dynasty has a new heaven and new earth, with new suns [days] and new moons [months]; therefore a new calendar has been adopted to show new influences at work. For this reason the wrong teachings and superstitions of the past have been treated and explained in detail so that people may be shown their mistakes and know the great enlightenment of the heavenly kingdom's new calendar. . . . From now on farming will be timely and the four seasons will be correct, and the movements of the heavenly course will continue endlessly and eternally; and all people both within and without China will enjoy happiness under the bright heaven and the glorious sun [referring to the heavenly kingdom]. All the abstruse and occult customs and outrageous teachings of old will disappear of themselves. Will it not be wonderful![103]

[101] "Ying-chieh kuei-chen," in Hsiao, *Ts'ung-shu, ts'e* 10, pp. 35a–36b.
[102] *Ibid.*, p. 37a–b.
[103] *Ibid.*, pp. 38b–39a.

Apart from superstition, there were many other social customs the Taipings wanted to break. Prostitution, foot-binding, wine-drinking, and opium- or tobacco-smoking were prohibited. These prohibitions were either announced as proclamations or issued as regulations.

The *Tse-ch'ing hui-tsuan* says: "Those who smoke opium or tobacco, drink wine, loot, or rape will be executed."[104] These rules were stated elsewhere in the same book:

> All who gather to drink and confer privately on military matters, once discovered, will be executed.
>
> Those who smoke opium will be executed.
>
> *   *   *   *   *
>
> The punishment for those who smoke yellow tobacco is a hundred lashes and a week in the cangue for the first offense, a thousand lashes and three weeks in the cangue for the second offense, and execution for the third offense.
>
> *   *   *   *   *
>
> At court [Nanking] or in the army, all brothers who gamble will be executed.[105]

"The Ode on the Origin of the Principle of the Salvation of the World" (Yüan-tao chiu-shih ko) in the "Taiping Imperial Declaration" contains the following lines:

> Just think of Chieh and Chou, who presided over the empire,
> And included the hills and rivers within their iron rule;
>   yet they perished through wine.[106]

In the later edition of the same work under the title "The Proclamation on the Origin of the Principles of World Salvation" (Yüan-tao chiu-shih chao), the following lines were substituted:

> Wine is what the Heavenly Father our God hates most;
> Never be misled by demons who would cause your destruction.[107]

A warning against opium-smoking is found in these lines from the same document:

104 Chang, *Tse-ch'ing, ts'e* 5, *chüan* 8.
105 *Ibid.*
106 "T'ai-p'ing chao-shu," in Hsiang, *T'ai-p'ing t'ien-kuo*, I, 90.
107 "T'ai-p'ing chao-shu," in Hsiao, *Ts'ung-shu, ts'e* 1, p. 5a.

As for those who would bring about their own downfall, the easiest way to become crazed is to smoke opium [foreign tobacco]. How many heroes there are who have hurt themselves by smoking opium.[108]

Tse-ch'ing hui-tsuan reports the following concerning the prohibition of foot-binding:

The women rebels are all country women from the mountainous regions of Kwangsi; they walk barefooted and are not a bit weaker than the men. When the rebels reached Nanking, all women were prohibited from practicing foot-binding. Violaters were to be executed. Those whose feet were already bound were unable to walk when they were suddenly ordered to unbind them.[109]

The prohibition against prostitution is also given in the *Tse-ch'ing hui-tsuan, chüan* 7, under the title, "The Rebels' Proclamations." Here Wei and Shih warned the people to turn away from old "degenerate customs" and return to the right principle *(cheng tao)*. One of the commands reads:

Prostitution should by all means be prohibited. Men have the men's quarters to go to and women have the women's quarters; men should learn to be scholars, farmers, artisans, and merchants; and women should learn tailoring and the management of a home. It is a matter of course that a man should be matched with a woman. Should any persons indulge in immoral conduct, or should any officers, soldiers, or common people secretly go to sleep in houses of prostitution and violate the regulation [they shall be punished]. Those who run houses of prostitution shall be summarily executed along with their entire families; and their neighbors who arrest them and hand them over to the government shall be rewarded, while those who connive to let them go shall be punished. Those who know the regulation but intentionally violate this shall be executed.[110]

The Taiping efforts to create a popularized style of writing should not be passed over without a word. All Taiping documents were written in a style condemned as vulgar by the scholars, but it was just this popular flavor that the Taipings wanted to have associated with their writings. Their theory was fully propounded by the Kan Wang in the following proclamation:

[108] *Ibid.*
[109] Chang, *Tse-ch'ing, ts'e* 6, *chüan* 12. See also *ts'e* 2, *chüan* 3.
[110] *Ibid., ts'e* 4, *chüan* 7, "Wei-wen kao."

A proclamation of the entire court, for all the officials within and without and all secretarial clerks and scholars to know:

Whereas the written word is to record facts, superficial language must be eradicated; words are more noble when spoken from the heart and artful words have always been prohibited. The Heavenly Father and the Heavenly Eldest Brother, greatly displaying the heavenly favor, have personally ordered our true sacred sovereign, the T'ien Wang, to come down into the mortal world to govern, to promote the correct way, to preserve the true, to eliminate the deceptive, and to wipe out degenerate customs. As a result, our true sacred sovereign has previously issued an edict ordering the revision and editing of all old documents and books not in conformity with the heavenly nature. Even the Six Classics have all been corrected by the imperial brush. It was not that our true sacred sovereign minded hard work, but he feared that these books might seduce men's minds and disturb the true way. Therefore he could not but speedily eliminate the false and abide by the true, and discard the superficial and preserve the substantial, so that people would all know that empty words are worthless, while true principles always exist in men's minds. Moreover, during the present founding period of the state, all memorials and public notices have special political significance; hence they should be all the more simple and clear and should never contain to the slightest degree words which are inciting or agitating, or which would set people against each other, thereby deliberately causing surprise or fear among the people. In addition, in the preparation of memorials, such demon-like expressions as "dragon virtue," "dragon countenance," "hundred spirits gather to offer support," and "the spirits of land and grain [the dynasty] and the imperial clan temple" must not be used. As for such meaningless phrases used on birthday occasions as "a crane's age" and "a turtle's longevity," "born of the mountain summit," and "the good fortune of three lives," these are even more absurd and besides are fantastic. The reason for the appearance of such expressions is that men of letters, in their youthful arrogance, like to indulge in brave talk or, because of their pride in their achievements, wish to boast of their learning. Some even indulge in fancy writing; hence, in one sentence there may be two different tones indicating both praise and disapproval, and on one matter there may be two different views, making it difficult to distinguish between right and wrong. If one reads without understanding, the consequences may be serious. Thus it is apparent that the use of superficial expressions is not only unprofitable but even harmful. I, the chief of staff, and the others, in our recent audience, were verbally instructed by our true sacred sovereign first of all to acknowledge the grace of Heaven, the sovereign, and the Tung Wang and Hsi Wang; and second, to state matters factually indicating the year, month, day, place, person, and all other evidence. Each word must be true, not a single expression should be beautified, and not so much as half a word superficial and false. Only sincere and respectful ideas are necessary; classical allusions need not be employed. Therefore, I have revised the *tzu-tien*

[dictionary of classical allusions] into the *tzu-i* [dictionary of literal meaning].

I, the chief of staff, and the others, having memorialized at court that we have accepted these instructions, will most respectfully comply. Hence a proclamation is hereby promulgated with the expectation that, in the entire court, the officials within and without and all secretarial clerks and scholars shall one and all know this. Hereafter, all memorials and reports, as well as other correspondence and notes, shall be precise and clear, enabling the people at one glance to understand them. For only in this way can they accord with the heavenly nature and conform to the true way. Under no circumstances shall anyone be permitted to continue the old practices of employing specious superficialities and thus fail to appreciate the sincerity of the vigorous admonitions of this chief of staff and the others. Special proclamation is hereby made. All must tremblingly comply.[111]

---

[111] "Ch'in-ting chün-tz'u shih-lu," in Hsiang, *T'ai-p'ing t'ien-kuo*, II, 616–17.

Chapter IV

The Economic Aspect

Taiping thinking in the economic field is expressed in a document entitled "The Land System of the Heavenly Dynasty" (T'ien-ch'ao t'ien-mou chih-tu). This is perhaps the most important document published by the Taipings, for in it are found ideas concerning nearly all aspects of the Taiping society, including economic ideals, land regulations, and the principle of common sharing. "The Land System of the Heavenly Dynasty" states:

> All lands in the empire must be cultivated by all the people in the empire as a common concern. If there is a deficiency of land in one place, the people must be removed to another; and if there is a deficiency of land in another place, the people must be removed to this place. The yields of all the land in the empire, whether the crops are good or bad, should be universally circulated. If there is a famine at one place, the [surplus food] of the place yielding good crops must be transported to relieve the famine-stricken place, and vice versa. The purpose is to enable all the people in the empire to enjoy together the abundant happiness provided by the Heavenly Father, Lord on High, and Sovereign God. If there is land, it shall be shared by all to till; if there is any food, clothing, or money, these shall be shared by all. In this way all places will share the abundance equally and all will be equally well fed and clothed.[1]

This is the ideal society of the Taipings, a world of Great Harmony—expressed in economic terms, a commonwealth in the sense of commonweal. The economic and social ideals were really one. The Kan Wang in "The Book on the Principles of the Heavenly Nature" (T'ien-ch'ing tao-li shu) says:

[1] Hsiao I-shan (compiler), T'ai-p'ing t'ien-kuo ts'ung-shu, ts'e 4, pp. 1b-2a.

We should know that the ten thousand names came originally from one name, and all members of that name came from one ancestor: their source is the same. Since the Heavenly Father gave birth to us and brought us up, we have assumed the same physique though with different bodies, and breathed the same breath though occupying different positions. This is what is meant by "All within the four seas are brothers." Through the great bounty of Heaven we are brothers and sisters of the same family. Since we were all born of the same father of souls, why should there be any distinction between you and me or between others and ourselves? When there are clothes, let us wear them together; when there is food, let us enjoy it together.[2]

We can readily see that in a society like this the people would have a sense of economic security, a condition necessary to the realization of the "Heavenly Kingdom of Peace."

In order to bring about this state the Taipings devised a system of land regulations and collective ownership of goods through state control. In discussing land regulations, we shall let the Taipings speak for themselves.

All land is to be divided into nine grades; every mou of land which during two seasons produces 1,200 pounds of grain shall be ranked as a superior field of the first class; every mou of land that produces 1,100 pounds, as a superior field of the second class; and every mou that produces 1,000 pounds, as a superior field of the third class. Every mou that produces 900 pounds shall be considered a middling field of the first class; every mou that produces 800 pounds, a middling field of the second class; and every mou that produces 700 pounds, a middling field of the third class. Every mou that produces 600 pounds shall be considered an inferior field of the first class; every mou that produces 500 pounds, an inferior field of the second class; and every mou that produces 400 pounds, an inferior field of the third class. A first-class superior field shall be considered equal to 1.1 mou of a second-class superior field, and to 1.2 mou of a third-class superior field; also to 1.35 mou of a first-class middling field, to 1.5 of a second-class middling field, and to 1.75 of a third-class middling field; further, to 2 mou of a first-class inferior field, to 2.4 mou of a second-class inferior field, and to 3 mou of a third-class inferior field.[3]

*   *   *   *   *

The division of the land must be according to the number of persons in a household, whether male or female; if they are numerous, then the amount of land must be increased, and if few, diminished; these shall also

[2] Hsiao, *Ts'ung-shu, ts'e* 5, pp. 27b-28a.
[3] "T'ien-ch'ao t'ien-mou chih-tu," in Hsiao, *Ts'ung-shu, ts'e* 4, p. la-b.

be arranged in such a way that the nine grades of land shall be proportionately divided.[4]

* * * * *

For every person, whether male or female, of 16 years and upward a certain portion of land must be allotted; for every person 15 years of age and under, half that quantity. Thus for those above 16 years of age, a mou of first-class superior land, and for those under that age half a mou; if the land is of the third-class inferior kind, three mou are to be allotted to those above 16, and one and a half mou to those under 15.[5]

The Taipings also stressed secondary occupations for the peasants:

Throughout the empire the mulberry tree is to be planted close to every wall, so that the women may engage in rearing silk worms, spinning silk, and making garments. Every family throughout the empire should take care to have five hens and two sows, which must not be allowed to miss their proper season for procreation.[6]

Thus the Taipings evolved a system of land distribution that was intended to give everyone in the empire a measure of economic justice.

In an attempt to establish the principle of common sharing, the Taipings passed a law declaring that all things were to be shared among their members. We have noted that the crops were to be shared by all people in the empire. *Tse-ch'ing hui-tsuan* quotes from a proclamation: "All the rice and grain of the peasants and all the capital of the merchants in the empire belong to the Heavenly Father; therefore they should all be turned over to the sacred treasury. The adults each will receive one *shih* a year and the children, each five *tou* for food."[7]

This system of sharing through the establishment of sacred treasuries was started early in the campaign. In 1851 it had already been decreed that no precious things were to be kept as private property but should be handed over to the sacred treasury. And again in 1852 the same regulation was proclaimed.[8] In "The Land System of the Heavenly Dynasty" we read: "If all people in the empire do not receive things as their private property and everything is turned over to the Lord on High,

---

[4] *Ibid.*, p. 1b.

[5] *Ibid.*, p. 2a.

[6] *Ibid.*, p. 2a-b.

[7] Chang Te-chien (editor and compiler), *Tse-ch'ing hui-tsuan*, ts'e 5, chüan 10, "K'o-p'ai."

[8] *Ibid.*, ts'e 5, *chüan* 9, "Wei-shu nei t'ien-ming chao-chih shu."

then the Lord will have enough to distribute universally and every place will receive equal shares and everyone will be well fed and clothed."[9]

However, only state control of movable property was effected through the sacred treasuries. There seems to have been no administrative organ to take care of the land distribution.

"The Land System of the Heavenly Dynasty" says:

> But the sergeant must keep an account of the money and grain in a book, which he must present to the superintendent of money and grain, as well as to the accountants for receipts and disbursements.
>
> In every circle of five and twenty families there must be a public treasury and a church, where the sergeant must reside. And whenever the happy events of marriage or birth occur within the said circle, all expenses are to be defrayed by the public treasury. But a limit must be observed, and not a single cash be used beyond what is necessary.[10]

State control was apparently based on the idea that everything belonged to God. And the T'ien Wang, being the chief representative of God and the concrete symbol of the state, was naturally the rightful disposer of all things. Tseng Kuo-fan had this in mind when he said of the Taiping government: "The peasants cannot have their own land to till and to pay tax on, for all land belongs to the T'ien Wang. The merchants cannot trade and make money, for they say all commodities belong to the T'ien Wang."[11]

---

[9] "T'ien-ch'ao t'ien-mou chih-tu," in Hsiao, *Ts'ung-shu, ts'e* 4, p. 2b.

[10] *Ibid.* See also Chang, *Tse-ch'ing, ts'e* 5, *chüan* 10, "Ts'ang-k'u," for an eyewitness account of the Taiping treasuries.

[11] Tseng Kuo-fan, *Tseng Wen-cheng kung ch'üan-chi*, "Wen-chi," 3:16.

Chapter V

Political and Military Aspects

The Taiping society was a military organization and its political activities were in the main directed toward certain military objectives. The same may also be said of the other aspects of the society, but its political and military aspects are so closely associated that it seems convenient to discuss them together.

The political ideal of the Taipings is revealed by the title they adopted for their kingdom—*T'ai-p'ing* (Peace). As we have seen in Chapter IV, the economic measures advocated by the Taipings were meant to ensure peace in the empire. And the attempt to overthrow the Manchus was merely a concrete expression of this determined desire to give peace to the Chinese, who had suffered miserably under the Manchus. "Yün-shan proposed to Hsiu-ch'üan that the government of the barbarians had put the land of China in confusion, and the Chinese people had long been longing for peace. The kingdom should thus be called *T'ai-p'ing t'ien-kuo* (Heavenly Kingdom of Great Peace)."[1] In a proclamation Hung Hsiu-ch'üan said, "The Heavenly Father, God, is the Heavenly Father of Peace at all times and in all places under heaven: the Eldest Brother is the Heavenly Brother of Peace at all times and in all places under heaven; and I am the Son of Heaven of Peace *(T'ai-p'ing t'ien-tzu)*."[2] And indeed the social and economic ideals were merely this political ideal translated into specific proposals.

Toward the last years of the dynasty, however, Hung's religious sentiment increased to such a degree that he proposed a new title for the

---

[1] Ling Shan-ch'ing (ed.), *T'ai-p'ing t'ien-kuo yeh-shih*, 12:14.

[2] "T'ai-p'ing t'ien-kuo hsin-yu shih-i-nien hsin-li," in Hsiao I-shan (compiler), *T'ai-p'ing t'ien-kuo ts'ung-shu, ts'e* 3, p. la-b

dynasty. In 1861, in one of his edicts, dated the twenty-sixth of the first month, he ordered that the title *T'ai-p'ing t'ien-kuo* be changed to *Shang-ti t'ien-kuo* (the Heavenly Kingdom of God).[3] But there is no evidence that this proposal was carried into effect.

To achieve the ideal of peace, the Taipings set up as their immediate aims the overthrow of the Manchus and the establishment of a new dynasty. These same aims had been religiously expressed as the extermination of the devil and his followers, the realization of the kingdom of God on earth.

In "Taiping Songs of World Salvation" (T'ai-p'ing chiu-shih-ko) we read:

> Our Heavenly Father's love for the people of the world was so deep that ...he again [after Jesus] sent our lord the Heavenly King [the T'ien Wang] to come on earth as the truly appointed lord to exterminate the devils, awaken the world, and give peace to the ten thousand nations, so that everyone might share the true happiness.[4]

And the *Yeh-shih* says: "Fortunately our Heavenly Father has not forsaken the Chinese and has appointed the T'ien Wang, who has had his initial success in Chin-ling (Nanking) in eliminating the Manchus."[5] And again: "God became angry and appointed the T'ien Wang to exterminate the northern barbarians and re-create the spiritual continent [China]."[6]

The same source reported that a Taiping general named Feng, in response to the note of the consuls of various countries, wrote: "God has appointed the T'ien Wang to be the lord of China, with the mission to attack the sinful and save the people."[7]

It seems that Hung's hatred for the Manchus, combined with his ambition, determined in part the course of his career. His ambition may be seen in a poem quoted by Hamberg:

> With the three-foot sword in our hand,
> Do we quiet the sea and the land.

[3] Robert J. Forrest, "The Christianity of Hung Tsiu Tsuen: A Review of Taeping Books," *Journal of the Royal Asiatic Society, North China Branch*, New Series No. 4 (Dec., 1867), p. 199.

[4] Hsiao, *Ts'ung-shu, ts'e* 4, p. 2a.

[5] Ling, *Yeh-shih*, 20:2.

[6] *Ibid.*, 20:3.

[7] *Ibid.*, 20:4.

> Surrounded by ocean, all forming one clan,
> Dwells man in harmonious union.
> We seize all the Demons, and shut them up
> In the cords of the earth,
> We gather the traitors, and let them fall
> In the heavenly net.
> All the four parts of the world
> Depend on the sovereign pole.
> The sun, the moon, and the stars
> Join in in the chorus of triumph.
> The tigers roar, the dragon sings,
> The world is full of light.
> When over all great peace prevails,
> O! what a state of bliss.[8]

The translation is excellent and accurate, but there are two points which need to be clarified. First, "All the four parts of the world" referred to *tung* (east), *nan* (south), *hsi* (west), and *pei* (north), and these apparently were employed in determining the titles of the four kings—Tung, Nan, Hsi, and Pei. Another point is that in the last line of the original poem (the second to the last in the translation), the idea of grand unification of the world, so strongly expressed in the original, is missed in the translation.

Hamberg also mentions Hung's hatred for the Manchus, quoting Hung as follows: "God has divided the kingdoms of the world, and made the Ocean to be a boundary for them, just as a father divides his estates among his sons; every one of whom ought to reverence the will of his father, and quietly manage his own property. Why should now these Manchoos forcibly enter China, and rob their brothers of their estate?"[9] To recover this estate, the Manchus would have to be driven out.

Hamberg reported how Hung's aim differed from that of the Triad Society. While the Triad Society wanted to overthrow the Manchus for the purpose of restoring the Ming, Hung wanted to establish a new dynasty. Hamberg quotes Hung's assertion of his aims:

> Though I never entered the Triad Society, I have often heard it said that their object is to subvert the Tsing and restore the Ming dynasty. Such an expression was very proper in the time of Khang-hi, when this society

---

[8] Theodore Hamberg, *The Visions of Hung-Siu-tshuen, and Origin of the Kwang-si Insurrection*, p. 24.

[9] *Ibid.*, p. 29.

was at first formed, but now after the lapse of two hundred years, we may
still speak of subverting the Tsing, but we cannot properly speak of restoring the Ming. At all events, when our native mountains and rivers are
recovered, a new dynasty must be established. How could we at present
arouse the energies of men by speaking of restoring the Ming dynasty?[10]

That the Taipings did not aim at restoring the Ming dynasty can be
seen from their attitude toward the Ming emperor. In quoting Ku Yen-
wu on the titles of examination degrees, Hung Jen-kan changed "Emperor T'ai-tsu of the Ming" 明太祖 to "Duke T'ai of the Ming" 明太侯,[11]
just as he changed "Emperor Hsüan-tsung of the T'ang" to "Duke
Hsüan of the T'ang," and "Emperor Kao-tsung of the T'ang" to "Duke
Kao of the T'ang."

The publication of a new calendar followed the practice of past
dynasty-makers in starting anew the reckoning of year, month, and day,
thus by implication doing away with all those evils responsible for the
downfall of the previous dynasty. The new dynasty was conceived as the
Ch'in dynasty was conceived. It was a grand unification of all the people
and territory in the world and a dynasty that would last forever. We
find these ideas expressed in Hung's proclamation written in 1859 as a
preface to a new edition of the Taiping calendar. The proclamation
began with the line: "The Heavenly Father and Lord on High and the
Heaven of Peace [*T'ai-p'ing t'ien*], and the Heavenly Kingdom of Peace
[*T'ai-p'ing t'ien-kuo*] of ten thousand and ten thousand years." It continued with these words.

> Now through the grace of Father and Eldest Brother they came down
> to earth and brought me along to be the lord, establishing the heavenly
> kingdom, the heavenly capital, the heavenly hall [*t'ien-t'ang*, paradise] and
> heavenly calendar, to be carried on forever and ever. [The dynasty, and
> so forth] will be handed down from the first year of Hsin-k'ai [1851]
> through one thousand, ten thousand, and tens of ten thousand years, with-
> out end.

And again:

> As a matter of fact, the heavenly kingdom, the heavenly capital, the
> heavenly court, and the heavenly hall are those over which the Father and
> the Eldest Brother brought me down to be the lord, uniting all elements

[10] *Ibid.*, pp. 55-56.
[11] "Ch'in-ting shih-chieh t'iao-li," in Hsiao, *Ts'ung-shu*, *ts'e* 9, p. 6a.

whether up in heaven, down beneath the earth, or in the human world to be one grand dynasty at all times and in all places.[12]

Thus it was not merely a new dynasty for China; it was a dynasty which was to unify the whole universe. This attitude was clearly expressed to those in the British mission who sought an audience with the leaders of the *T'ai-p'ing t'ien-kuo* in 1853. They were given to understand that "Whereas God the Heavenly Father has sent our Sovereign down on earth, as the true Sovereign of all nations in the world, all people in the world who wish to appear at his Court must yield obedience to the rules of ceremony."[13] Thomas T. Meadows, the interpreter for the British, also reported his conversation with the Pei Wang and I Wang in the following words:

> In reply to my inquiries respecting the Tae-ping Wang, the Prince of Peace, the Northern Prince explained in writing that he was the "True Lord" or Sovereign; that "The Lord of China is the Lord of the whole world; he is the second Son of God, and all people in the whole world must obey and follow him." As I read this without remark, he said, looking at me interrogatively, "The True Lord is not merely the Lord of China; he is not only our Lord, he is your Lord also."[14]

The British were apparently annoyed by this attitude, for we have also the following record: "As this [referring to a mandate of the Taipings to the British] stated that the Lord of China had been sent down into the world as the true "Lord of all Nations". . . it was returned by the bearers, with an unequivocal message, fitted to disabuse the senders of their notions of universal supremacy."[15]

This desire for universal supremacy is manifest in the arrangement of the imperial harem. Shen Mao-liang in his *Chiang-nan ch'un-meng-an pi-chi* (Memoirs Written in the Study of Spring Dream) has the following report:

[12] "T'ai-p'ing t'ien-kuo hsin-yu shih-i-nien hsin-li," Preface, in Hsiao, *Ts'ung-shu, ts'e* 3, pp. 1a, 1b, 2a.

[13] "Document Delivered by Two Insurgent Chiefs to Sir George Bonham: A Mandate," Inclosure 2 in No. 6, in *Papers Respecting the Civil War in China, Parliamentary Papers*, 1852-53, Vol. LXIX.

[14] "Report of Conversations between Mr. Interpreter Meadows and the Insurgent Chiefs at Nanking and Chin Keang," Inclosure 1 in No. 6, in *Papers Respecting the Civil War in China, Parliamentary Papers*, 1852–53, Vol. LXIX.

[15] *Ibid.*

In the Taiping palace [harem], with the exception of the chamber of the queen, all other chambers were named after the provinces, and the concubines were also housed in accordance to their native provinces. The most ridiculous thing was the assigning of four chambers called *yang-tung-hsi* and *pien-nan-pei* (chambers for eastern foreign girls and western foreign girls, chambers for southern border girls and northern border girls) to foreign girls, and the ordering of Hou Yü-k'uan and others to have strange costumes made and dress people in those costumes to appear before [the T'ien Wang], saying "Keluto, your servant from a tributary state beyond the western ocean, Heimolaita, your servant from a tributary state beyond the eastern ocean, Chichiyujen, your servant of a tributary state beyond the southern seas, and Hahaimuha, your servant from a tributary state beyond the northern barbarian borders, each of us presents eleven barbarian women as tributes." This was done to give the appearance of granting audience to foreign tributary states. After the ceremony, numerous gifts were showered upon these envoys. There was also a decree to the effect that "Now that the four foreign nations have come to pay their homage, the ten thousand directions are unified. As their tributes the nations from the east and south brought strong girls and the nations from the west and the north brought beautiful women. Unification under the Heaven of peace is indeed heavenly happiness truly worthy of being proud of."[16]

This new dynasty was a real thing to Hung Hsiu-ch'üan. Commenting on the Bible, he "upbraids people for saying the kingdom of heaven is in heaven when Jesus said it was coming quickly, and behold it is now come!"[17]

And commenting on Revelations 3:12–13 ("Him that overcometh will I make a pillar in the temple of my God,...") Hung remarked:

Now that the Eldest Brother has descended, the celestial dynasty has a temple of the true God, the Heavenly Father, Shang-ti, and a temple of the Elder Brother Christ, engraved with the names of God and Christ. The kingdom of God the Father and the new Jerusalem which came down from heaven are fulfilled in the present celestial capital [*t'ien-ching*, heavenly capital referring to Nanking]. Respect this![18]

And further on:

Now the Heavenly Father Shang-ti and the Elder Brother Christ have

[16] *Chiang-nan ch'un-meng-an pi-chi*, in Hsiang Ta *et al.* (compilers), *T'ai-p'ing t'ien-kuo*, IV, 442.

[17] Forrest, "The Christianity of Hung Tsiu Tsuen," *Journal of the Royal Asiatic Society, North China Branch*, N. S. No. 4 (Dec., 1867), p. 200.

[18] *Ibid.*, p. 202.

come down and taken myself and the son (Hung's son) to be lords. All countries have already submitted to God and Christ who have me rule for all generations. It is fulfilled. Respect this![19]

And again:

What John saw was the celestial hall in heaven above. Heaven above and earth are alike. The new Jerusalem is the present Nanking [t'ien-kuo in a literal sense]. God and Christ have descended to make us lords and open the lower celestial hall, so the heavenly hall of God is among men.[20]

That the heavenly kingdom was actually realized on earth with Hung as ruler was a belief common to all Taiping leaders. This is evident in their memorials to Hung. Yang Hsiu-ch'ing in a memorial starts with the following line, which is not accidental: "Our Heavenly Father, Sovereign God, and Lord on High has sent my lord the second eldest brother down on earth to be the true lord of the ten thousand nations."[21] And Wei Ch'ang-hui, the Pei Wang, prefaced his verbal report to Hung with: "Our second eldest brother is the true lord of the ten thousand nations under heaven, and his wealth is coextensive with the four seas."[22] It was a common practice for the Taipings to begin their documents with the following line: "Our Heavenly Father and our Heavenly Brother, with heavenly grace, have specially sent the T'ien Wang, the true lord, down to rule the world."[23]

The idea that Hung was the king of kings and the lord of lords was also manifested in the pattern adopted for the flyleaves of most Taiping publications. For example, on the flyleaf of "Calendar by Imperial Sanction, the Third Year" (T'ai-p'ing t'ien-kuo kuei-hao san-nien hsin-li), a new calendar published in 1853, there were two phoenixes and two dragons oriented toward the sun. Since the sun was the symbol of Hung, the whole pattern represented the idea of paying homage to him as the head of the Taiping dynasty.

Hung, however, was in fact merely a symbol or figurehead; the administrative and military power was concentrated in the hands of

[19] Ibid., p. 203.
[20] Ibid., p. 204.
[21] Chang Te-chien (editor and compiler), Tse-ch'ing hui-tsuan, ts'e 4, chüan 7, "Wei pen-chang shih."
[22] "T'ien-fu hsia-fan chao-shu," in Ch'eng Yen-sheng (compiler), T'ai-p'ing t'ien-kuo shih-liao, 1st Series, II, 23a.
[23] Chang, Tse-ch'ing, ts'e 4, chüan 7.

Yang Hsiu-ch'ing. Chang Te-chien repeatedly stressed this point. In *chüan* 6 of *Tse-ch'ing hui-tsuan* under "Wei ch'ao-i" (Court Etiquette of the Rebel Dynasty) he said, "All military affairs await rebel Yang's decision." That this was not mere guesswork is borne out by a statement in "The Book on the Principles of the Heavenly Nature" (T'ien-ch'ing tao-li shu), which was first published in 1854, one year after Chang compiled his book: "The Tung Wang is the chief administrator in charge of heavenly kingdom military affairs: he enforces military discipline in the name of heavenly law and corrects the hearts of men in conformity to heavenly taboos."[24]

Hung's only function was to attach his seal to whatever Yang had decided upon,[25] and Hung never put his seal on anything which had not borne first the seal of Yang.[26] Not only was Hung made a figurehead; all Yang's subordinates were mere puppets.[27] Such concentration of power in the hands of Yang, together with his arrogance and ambition, explains his eventual downfall and assassination.

There is no question that the Taipings felt they were justified in establishing a new dynasty. In contrast to *yao-ping* (devils' troop) they referred to themselves as *t'ien-ping* and *t'ien-chiang* (heavenly troops, heavenly generals).[28] Sometimes they also used the term *sheng-ping* (sage troop, "sage" being a term applicable only to God, hence an equivalent of *T'ien*).[29] In both cases, the principle of legitimacy employed is very clear. In the "Proclamation on the Origin of the Principle of World Salvation" (Yüan-tao chiu-shih chao) they questioned the wisdom of acting like Huang Ch'ao and Li Ch'uang,[30] and Chang Te-chien records the following couplet:

> Observe the teachings of Father of heaven and do not follow the
>   example of Huang Ch'ao and Li Ch'uang;

[24] *Ibid.*, *ts'e* 4, *chüan* 6; "T'ien-ch'ing tao-li shu," in Hsiao, *Ts'ung-shu*, *ts'e* 5, pp. 17b-18a.

[25] Chang, *Tse-ch'ing*, *ts'e* 2, *chüan* 3.

[26] *Ibid.*, *ts'e* 1, *chüan* 1.

[27] *Ibid.*, *ts'e* 2, *chüan* 3.

[28] Lo Erh-kang, *Chung Wang Li Hsiu-ch'eng tzu-chuan yüan-kao ch'ien-cheng*, p. 162.

[29] "Hsing-chün tsung-yao," in Hsiao, *Ts'ung-shu*, *ts'e* 6.

[30] "T'ai-p'ing chao-shu," in Hsiao, *Ts'ung-shu*, *ts'e* 1, p. 3a. Huang Ch'ao and Li Ch'uang, two ruthless rebels at the end of the Ming dynasty, are here singled out as examples of "not *cheng*." For details about these rebels, see Chapter XI.

Lead the troops under the office of earth and be Lu Su and Ts'ao
  Pin.[31]

The very fact that Huang Ch'ao and Li Ch'uang were singled out to
exemplify the lack of *cheng*[32] indicates that the Taiping leaders did not
consider themselves rebels. Their dynasty was the legitimate one, and
their ideas were the orthodox beliefs. They did not have to refer to
Chinese history to substantiate their claim, as had many previous rebel
leaders. They simply asserted that God had made Hung the lord, and
he was to be accepted as such by all.

The Taipings had a variety of means for maintaining political control.
The most general and effective were religious indoctrination and moral
inculcation. We have discussed the religious and moral principles and
precepts which they tried to impart to the minds of the members of their
society and the people at large. Here we shall merely mention a few
cases where their purpose for teaching these principles is evident.

There was an attempt to induce the people to identify themselves
with the T'ien Wang: "Wishes for the king are wishes for oneself."[33]
The precepts of reverence for heaven and loyalty to the T'ien Wang
were constant themes for exhortation.[34] Only through these could one
hope to attain a state of happiness.

One portion of disobedience to Heaven will be met by one
  portion of weeping,
And one portion of reverence will be met by one portion of
  happiness;
Ten portions [complete] of disobedience to Heaven will be met by
  ten portions of weeping,
And ten portions of reverence will be met by ten portions of
  happiness.[35]

Another poem begins with the line: "One portion of obedience to the
decree of [T'ien Wang] will be met by one portion of happiness." The
reasoning is clear. Reverence for Heaven leads to happiness and dis-

---

[31]   Chang, *Tse-ch'ing, ts'e* 5, *chüan* 8. Lu Su was a general in the state of Wu during
the Three Kingdoms period, famous for his sense of justice and his love of learning.
Ts'ao Pin, who assisted the first emperor of the Sung dynasty in his conquest of the
empire, was famed for his integrity and sympathy for people.

[32]   See note 30.

[33]   "T'ien-fu shih" No. 283, in Hsiao, *Ts'ung-shu, ts'e* 7.

[34]   See Chapters I and II on the Taipings' religion and moral views.

[35]   "T'ien-fu shih" No. 278, in Hsiao, *Ts'ung-shu, ts'e*7.

obedience leads to disaster. The last line of this ode, "Reverence for Heaven and reverence for the lord are related," follows logically.[36] To repay the Heavenly Father's grace each one must train himself to be good and to be upright, for it is only thus that one will be able to bring himself into harmony with the mind of Heaven and to attain the state of heavenly bliss.[37] In the moral sphere, the regulative principle of social conduct *(li)* is used very effectively in conjunction with the exhortation to observe social distinctions. This code of ethics, when properly administered, is indeed more effective than laws and regulations.

Religious practices were also used for political purposes. A passage in *Tse-ch'ing hui-tsuan* brings out the political function of some of the religious practices:

Oftentimes, when the rebels are engaged in the so-called "expounding of principles," they are carrying out other purposes. Whenever they punish a person, they always expound principles. Whenever they capture persons, they always expound principles. Whenever troops are dispatched in a hurry and instructions are given extemporaneously, they always expound principles. Whenever they select females to be the rebel imperial concubines, they always expound principles. Whenever they drive their followers to perform extremely toilsome and difficult tasks, they always expound principles. Whenever the number of soldiers who desert increases daily, they always expound principles. Whenever they intend to search and loot, they always expound principles. Whenever they force people to contribute, they always expound principles. As a whole, when the rebels expound principles, they merely assemble the people and deliver an order [to them]. As the purpose for expounding principles changes, the content of the orders naturally differs.[38]

Such religious activity not only produced results among the members of the Taiping society; it was impressive to the enemy as well. *Tse-ch'ing hui-tsuan* has the following report: "Through the practice of a heretic belief the rebels not only disarm the alertness of our commanding generals but break the morale of our troops as well. Furthermore, they are able to persuade the people who are forced to join their ranks to embrace the belief and not to revolt against them."[39]

In *Tse-ch'ing hui-tsuan* we find a list of rules and regulations, many of which are religious and moral in character; this recalls that the Taipings

[36] "T'ien-fu shih" No. 318, in Hsiao, *Ts'ung-shu, ts'e* 7.
[37] "T'ai-p'ing chiu-shih-ko," in Hsiao, *Ts'ung-shu, ts'e* 4, p. 3a-b.
[38] Chang, *Tse-ch'ing, ts'e* 5, *chüan* 9, "Chiang tao-li."
[39] *Ibid., ts'e* 3, *chüan* 5.

promulgated their moral and religious precepts as laws.[40] To them there was little difference between what was legal and what was moral and religious. It is especially interesting that while the leaders taught a kind of moral causality, ensuring automatic salvation to those who abided by their precepts and laws, they also spoke of the idea of *chun* (to permit), whereby the law-abiding people might go up to the heavenly hall *(t'ien-t'ang)* by permission of the leaders: "From now on all who will repent before Sovereign God, who resolve not to worship idols and not to do evil acts, and who will not violate the heavenly precepts, will be *permitted* to go up to the heavenly hall to enjoy happiness for the thousand and ten thousand and ten thousand years."[41] And those who did the contrary would be punished by being sent to hell. Apparently salvation or condemnation was not inherent in the acts themselves; in other words, the principle of moral causality did not hold in this case, and salvation had to rest ultimately with the decision of the leaders.

Many of the measures adopted by the Taipings were actually devised for political or military control. Separate camps for men and women were initiated to build up the efficiency of the society as a fighting machine, and they were done away with for the same reason. A similar reason underlay the prohibition against keeping personal belongings. In this connection the *Tse-ch'ing hui-tsuan* made the following observation: "Most of the rebels joined [the Taiping army] by compulsion. The prohibition of private accumulation by the leaders is designed to prevent deserters. Therefore, the regulations are strictly enforced."[42]

We have seen that God was conceived to be omniscient, and that it was impossible for anything to escape his comprehensive surveillance. This conception, combined with the belief in divine visitations, was fully exploited. The publicity given to the case of Chou Hsi-neng's treachery, which was solved through the intervention of God when he came down to investigate in person through the medium of Yang Hsiu-ch'ing, shows how the Taipings made use of this idea in checking the loyalty of their followers.[43]

Divine visitations were also used by Yang Hsiu-ch'ing (Tung Wang) and Hsiao Ch'ao-kuei (Hsi Wang) to establish their leadership and to

[40] *Ibid.,* ts'e 5, *chüan* 9.

[41] "T'ien-t'iao-shu," in Hsiao, *Ts'ung-shu,* ts'e 1, p. 1a.

[42] Chang, *Tse-ch'ing,* ts'e 4, *chüan* 6.

[43] Omnipotence, omnipresence, and omniscience of God and the universal reach of the Sun (T'ien Wang) were cited to convince Chou Hsi-neng that it was futile to refuse confession. See "T'ien-fu hsia-fan chao-shu," in Ch'eng, *Shih-liao,* Vol. II.

instill confidence in the minds of the followers whenever there was a need for such action. At the beginning of the Taiping campaign when Feng Yün-shan was in prison and Hung Hsiu-ch'üan was away in Kwangtung their followers, lacking leadership, were on the point of losing heart and scattering. Yang Hsiu-ch'ing then established himself as leader and succeeded in winning the confidence of the followers through divine visitation.[44] In the subsequent struggle for power, this tactic was frequently used. In one case even the T'ien Wang was made a victim of the practice, and Yang, the impersonator, had him thoroughly reprimanded for his misdemeanor.[45] Through similar tactics, Yang had the Pei Wang flogged[46] and disgraced Hung Jen-fa, Hung Hsiu-ch'üan's elder brother.[47] *Tse-ch'ing hui-tsuan* made the following remark: "Of all the [rebels] Yang Hsiu-ch'ing was the most cunning and able. In order to deceive the people he secretly conferred with the rebels to feign that the Heavenly Father descended upon him."[48]

[44] "T'ien-ch'ing tao-li shu," in Hsiao, *Ts'ung-shu, ts'e* 5, pp. 9b-12a.

[45] "T'ien-fu hsia-fan chao-shu," in Ch'eng, *Shih-liao*, Vol. II.

[46] Chang, *Tse-ch'ing, ts'e* 1, *chüan* 1.

[47] *Ibid., ts'e* 1, *chüan* 2.

[48] *Ibid., ts'e* 1, *chüan* 1. Divine visitation seems to have been a general practice among the rebels, and it was later appropriated by Yang Hsiu-ch'ing for political control. Hamberg, in *The Visions of Hung-Siu-tshuen*, pages 45 to 46, reported that when Hung and Feng arrived in Kwangsi in 1849 they learned that "during their absence in Kwang tung, some very remarkable occurrences had taken place in the congregation of the God-worshippers, which had brought disorder and dissension among the brethren. It sometimes happened that while they were kneeling down engaged in prayer, the one or the other of those present was seized by a sudden fit, so that he fell down to the ground, and his whole body was covered with perspiration. In such a state of ecstasy, moved by the spirit, he uttered words of exhortation, reproof, prophecy, etc. Often the words were unintelligible, and generally delivered in rhythm. The brethren had noted down in a book the more remarkable of these sayings, and delivered them to the inspection of Hung-Siu-tshuen. The latter now judged the spirits according to the truth of the doctrine, and declared that the words of those moved were partly true and partly false. Thus confirming the already expressed opinion of Yang-Siu-tshin, that they were 'partly from God and partly from the devil.' The most remarkable of those whom Hung-Siu-tshuen acknowledged as true, were the words of Yang-Siu-tshin, and Siao-Chau-kwui. Yang was originally a very poor man, but he joined the congregation with much earnestness and sincerity. Whilst there, he suddenly for a period of two months lost his power of speech to the astonishment of the brethren, who considered this to be an evil omen; but afterwards he again recovered the use of his tongue, and more frequently than any other was subject to fits of ecstasy, when he spoke in the name of God the Father, and in a solemn and awe-inspiring manner reproved the sins of the others, often pointing out individuals, and exposing their evil actions. He also exhorted to virtue, and foretold future events, or commanded what they ought to do. His words generally made a deep impression upon

The spiritual power of the leaders is especially emphasized in "Gospel Jointly Witnessed and Heard by the Imperial Eldest and Second Eldest Brothers" (Wang-chang-tz'u-hsiung ch'ing-mu ch'ing-erh kung-cheng fu-yin-shu) and the "Taiping Heavenly Chronicle" (T'ai p'ing t'ien-jih), where Hung is represented as the subduer of the devil and his followers.

The use of spiritual power to enlist the loyalty of the members is admitted by no less an authority than the Kan Wang, Hung Jen-kan. He said:

> It is said in a T'ien Wang's decree that the true spirit is able to create mountains and rivers and seas. Let the imps come from any direction, many heavenly traps and earthly nets have been set up. You soldiers may quit worrying and make the rounds and stand close guard night and day and plan to make the night march. If Yüeh Fei was able to break an army 100,000 strong by a force of 500, what could there be in the imps and devils whose destruction has already been determined that we should feel concerned about?

Then he cited another decree of T'ien Wang:

> Our Heavenly Father has great ability. Try as the imps and devils [the Manchus] may in their plots and intrigues, all their ten thousand plans cannot withstand one plan made by Heaven. And our Heavenly Brother is one who is amply able to shoulder his responsibility. The moment the heavenly troops arrive, that is the moment when the imps and devils will perish. The imps and devils have nothing to depend on; if we brothers will work together in a concerted effort, the destruction of the devils is indeed a foregone conclusion.[49]

It would be untrue to say the Taipings relied entirely on the power of God and Jesus for their success. They seem to have realized that God helps those who help themselves. This attitude was illustrated by the emphasis on close guard and planning and concerted effort among members. There is also reason to believe that the divine power was

---

the assembly. Siau-Chau-kwui spoke in the name of Jesus, and his words were milder than those of Yang. One of the Wang clan had spoken against the doctrine of Jesus, and led many astray, but he was excluded from the congregation, and his words declared false, being spoken under the influence of a corrupt spirit."

[49] Both quotations are from "T'ien-ch'ing tao-li shu," in Hsiao, Ts'ung-shu, ts'e 5, p. 29a.

invoked only after all possible human effort had been made.[50] But the habit of falling back on religion in the face of the inevitable and the tendency to use it as a means of control are only too apparent.

Examinations played an important role in the development of Taiping society. State examinations had for centuries been used as a means to recruit government officials, and as a result they became the most effective means of shaping the minds of the people in accordance with the desire of the government. The Taiping leaders were not slow in recognizing the advantages of the system. *Tse-ch'ing hui-tsuan* reports:

> During a provincial examination in Hupeh, more than 800 passed the examination out of a scant number of 1,000. The reason is simple. First of all, the examiners lacked scholarship, and men similar in nature flocked together. Secondly, Rebel Hung made wide the way to officialdom so as to encourage the scholars, and the resulting large number of successful candidates was offered as an evidence that he had won the hearts of the scholars.
>
> And their conscious attempt at indoctrination is clear in view of the topics assigned to the candidates to write on. In a provincial examination given at Anhwei, the topic assigned was "Truly Appointed Son of Heaven and Generals Born in Happiness."
>
> Besides examination, the rebels have a system for selecting the virtuous. In a city, district, or territory under their military occupation, proclamations are posted on the walls of their residences and offices urging the virtuous [to join the rebels]. In brief the proclamation runs: "In regulating the affairs of the state and surveying the land [we are aiming for good government], and this government is to be achieved through building up an educational system. We learn when we are young and we practice what we learn when we grow up; if we have any talent we expect it to be used. [If this is the case at ordinary times,] how much more so at a time when the mandate of Heaven is new and men of talent are in abundance. The heavenly dynasty appoints officials entirely on the merit of virtue; the need for talents is very urgent. All who are versed in civil and military affairs have been collected at court, and no experts of any art are left unemployed. However, we fear that our selection and search may not be complete and universal. . . ."
>
> Their idea is to dangle the fine titles and petty profit in the face of the people as an encouragement for the brave and intelligent to come to join them.[51]

The effectiveness of this system in controlling the minds of the people

---

[50] Chang, *Tse-ch'ing, ts'e* 4, *chüan* 7.

[51] *Ibid., ts'e* 2, *chüan* 3.

is more than demonstrated in the essays written by the candidates who took part in the examinations given by the Taipings.[52]

Officially the Taipings did not have any secret service organization, but the leaders in dealing with one another did appear to have some kind of system by which their behavior and conduct was mutually checked and information was collected. It seems that there were not only spies in the enemy territory to collect military intelligence but also agents who spied on the conduct of the members of their own society. The Tung Wang, Yang Hsiu-ch'ing, was probably the chief intriguer. *Tse-ch'ing hui-tsuan* describes these activities in the following words:

> Hsiu-ch'ing had many confidential subordinates who were secretly sent out among the members to check on them. Any members whose talk and conduct proved suspicious or indicated that they would rebel in response to the attack of the government troops, and any members who violated the rebels' decrees or orders, Yang took note of secretly. Then all of a sudden he would proclaim that the Heavenly Father had descended upon him and pointed out what certain members had done and when they had done it. The case would be immediately solved.[53]

147034

This statement may be borne out by the case of Chou Hsi-neng and Yang's uncanny power in detecting the secret affairs of his colleagues and subordinates.

The case of Chou Hsi-neng is recorded in a decree made by the Heavenly Father. Chou was on the point of being recommended for reward because he had been successful in his mission to recruit men for the Taiping army, when the Heavenly Father reportedly paid a surprise visit to Yang, ordering the arrest of Chou and denouncing him for his treachery. When Chou insisted that he was not guilty, the Heavenly Father reported through Yang in great detail a secret conversation Chou and Huang Wen-an had carried on the previous night, and what had occurred in Chou's home, involving the conduct of his wife and his son. Because of the Heavenly Father's power to see all this, Chou finally pleaded guilty of conspiring with the government forces to betray the Taiping army. The effectiveness of this method can be seen in Chou's

---

[52] Ch'eng, *Shih-liao*, Vol. III; Hsiao, *Ts'ung-shu*, ts'e 4. Ch'eng gives two essay titles: "On the Establishment of the Heavenly Capital at Chin-ling," and "Relegate the Den of the Devils [*chui-li*] to the Position of Sinful Territory." Hsiao gives one essay title: "Publication of Royal Decrees Stamped with the Royal Seal."

[53] Chang, *Tse-ch'ing*, ts'e 1, *chüan* 1.

final repentant speech before his death. He cried at the top of his voice to the brethren: "Today it is truly Heaven who is in charge of all affairs. You should all be unreservedly loyal to the state for the grace you have received. You should never follow my step in this treason against Heaven."[54] And it is significant that during the examination whenever certain truths were wrung from the culprit, Yang, speaking as the Heavenly Father, would turn to those present, reminding them of the Heavenly Father's omniscience and warning them that it would not pay to conspire against the state.

This knowledge of other people's secrets was portrayed in another case of a divine visit in which Yang Hsiu-ch'ing almost succeeded in having the T'ien Wang flogged.[55] Here, in the name of the Heavenly Father, Yang reprimanded Hung for his strong temper in mistreating women officials, his neglect in the bringing up of his son the young lord,[56] and his ruthlessness in kicking royal concubines. In connection with the last point, Yang said, when he was out of his trance: ". . . Second Eldest Brother, you should teach them with a lenient heart and should not kick them with the tip of your boot. If you do . . . you may find that the *niang niang* (royal concubines) may be pregnant and you would act counter to the Heavenly Father's desire for life."[57]

Hung's harem was very jealously guarded, as is clear from many of the Heavenly Father's poems, but Yang did not seem to have any difficulty in gathering the kind of information he was most delighted to have. This would suggest that even the T'ien Wang was at the mercy of Yang's spies; if the T'ien Wang was subject to such spying, there is no reason to doubt that the others were. This spying must have been a strong weapon against defection. Chang Te-chien has the following rebel report:

> There was a certain corps commandant of the Embroidery Camp by the name of Wu Ch'ang-sung, who had received great grace from the heavenly [dynasty] and yet had not the gratitude to serve the state in return; he entered into a secret alliance with the devil in an effort to take the heavenly capital. Fortunately, thanks to our Heavenly Father, their conspiracy was secretly pointed out by him, thus manifesting his great power. As a result the devil troops were beaten back and many traitors who cut their hair and were in secret communication with the devils were arrested

[54] "T'ien-fu hsia-fan chao-shu," in Ch'eng, *Shih-liao*, I, 13a.
[55] Ch'eng, *Shih-liao*, II, 1–25.
[56] *Ibid.*, II, 9a.
[57] *Ibid.*, II, 21b.

and executed. Again there was the devil woman Lai Ta-mei, who dared plot treason by storing up gunpowder for the purpose of assassinating the T'ien Wang. Again thanks to the Heavenly Father this was revealed.[58]

There is no doubt that this spying combined with the idea of the divine power of God formed a powerful weapon for ensuring the loyalty of Taiping members.

To arouse the feelings of the Chinese against the Manchus, the Taipings also raised the ethnic issue as often as opportunity presented itself. The most complete statement of the Taiping stand on this issue is found in three proclamations issued in the names of Yang and Hsiao.[59]

The principal ideas expressed in these proclamations were based upon the belief that God was the creator and master of the whole world,[60] and that the world, which was China, was to be called a spiritual continent because it had been created by the true spirit. The Taipings felt that only the Chinese were to rule over China, and the proclamations expressed this concept of legitimacy through *shun-t'ien* (following the way of T'ien).[61] The Manchu rule was therefore considered usurpation, contrary to the way of T'ien. The Taipings here maintained that there was no doubt they would succeed in destroying the Manchus as those who followed the way of T'ien would live and those who acted against the way of T'ien would be destroyed. The Manchus, they stated, had committed crimes against the Chinese people. Besides usurping the rule, they forced the Chinese to wear queues and to adopt barbarian dress. They contaminated the Chinese race by taking as wives Chinese women whose descendants the Taipings thus considered barbarians, a disgrace to Chinese womanhood; they forced barbarian laws upon the Chinese, disregarding the systems which China originally possessed; they substituted for the Chinese language *chin-ch'iang* (capital accent, or Peking dialect), thus bringing the Chinese language to a state of confusion. In times of famine caused by drought or flood they provided no relief, and the people either died or were driven to the open roads with no mercy

[58] *Tse-ch'ing, ts'e* 4, *chüan* 7, "Wei kao-shih."

[59] "Pan-hsing chao-shu," in Ch'eng, *Shih-liao*, Vol. I. Also in Hsiang, *T'ai-p'ing t'ien-kuo*, I, 159–67.

[60] In the 1850 edition of "Pan-hsing chao-shu," China is said to belong to China; but in the 1852 edition, China is said to belong to God.

[61] The publication of the three essays referred to in note 52 seems to be an attempt to establish the legitimacy of the Taiping rule in the minds of the people at large and particularly in the minds of those who joined the Taipings after they occupied Nanking.

shown them. Furthermore, these proclamations accused the Manchus of employing corrupt officials who cheated the Chinese all over China. They tried to exterminate the brave and intelligent Chinese, with the intention of crushing their spirit of revolt by atrocities such as the laws that decreed the destruction of nine clans.

The proclamations also reminded those under the rule of the Manchus that the Chinese were civilized and the Manchus were no better than beasts, descended from a white fox and a red dog, and that it would be the height of disgrace for civilized Chinese to submit themselves to the rule of the beasts. Former patriots and loyalists, such as Wen T'ien-hsiang and Hsieh Fang-te of the Sung, who refused to submit to the Yüan rule, and Shih K'o-fa and Ch'ü Shih-ssu of the Ming, who refused to submit to the rule of the Ch'ing, were cited in an attempt to arouse patriotic feelings. The people were exhorted to join the Taiping army on a holy mission for God on high and to drive the Manchus, the devil barbarians, from the spiritual continent of China. The reigning emperor with a heavy price on his head, was referred to as "dog Tartar Hsien-feng." Finally, it is stated that those who would join the army were promised rewards and those who would pay no heed to the proclamations were promised punishment both in this life and hereafter.

These proclamations are couched in such stirring phrases that they could not have failed to arouse the feelings of the people against the Manchus.

Li Hsiu-ch'eng, in his letter to Chao Ching-hsien persuading him to change his allegiance, said: "Furthermore, the distinction between the Chinese and the Manchus is clear....Because you and I are both Chinese, I do not have the heart [to leave you to your fate]. Whether your answer is 'Yes' or 'No,' 'agreed [to my proposal]' or 'opposed' to it, I expect to receive it while still standing."[62] There is no doubt that the Taipings sincerely believed that they were working in the interest of the Chinese in this campaign against the Manchus.

Another means of control was reward and punishment, a method touching the very spring of conduct of the people. Theoretically the Taipings based their concept of reward and punishment on the principle of moral causality, a law as inexorable as the laws of nature. This principle in turn is based upon belief in the moral character of God. The idea that those who follow the way of T'ien will live and those who act

---

[62] Hsieh Hsing-yao, *T'ai-p'ing t'ien-kuo shih-shih lun-ts'ung*, pp. 180-81.

against it will be destroyed can thus be seen as a natural corollary of this principle of moral causality.

With all the inexorability of the way of T'ien, the leaders seem to have had in their hands the final authority in conferring either reward or punishment. This is evident from the conception of permission by which the people were granted the privilege of going to heaven or were punished by being sent to hell. Even if we construe the permission as coming from God, it is clear that reward and punishment were administered only through the leaders.

So the people were not allowed to await the consequences of their own conduct, as might be expected in view of the inflexible nature of the principle of moral causality. Means mostly physical in nature were used to induce them to follow orders and to keep them from being disobedient. Titles, fine houses, clothing, and food were offered as rewards,[63] and floggings were given as punishment.[64] Thus the Taipings do not seem to have had much faith in a principle of moral causality.

There is no direct statement concerning the military aspect of Taiping ideology. All documents dealing with the military aspects of the Taiping society are concerned with organization, over-all strategy, stratagems, tactics, and regulations.[65] It is true there are ideological elements in some of these documents, especially in the regulations, but they appear as commands to the soldiers more religious than military in nature. As this has been discussed previously, we shall try merely to formulate Taiping military ideology on the basis of statements which in themselves may not have been military in nature.

One of the nine documents collected under the title "The Elements of Military Tactics on Troop Operations" (Hsing-chün tsung-yao) is entitled "Regulations Concerning the Welfare of Soldiers." In it we find that a new conception of soldiers has evolved: "Officers should take the welfare of the soldiers to heart. . . . The soldiers of the camps must be carefully taken care of. We should remember that all of us are born of the same father of souls and we are like bone and flesh."[66] This statement is important in its complete refutation of the traditional popular idea concerning a soldier, which runs: "Good iron is not to be made into nail and a good son will not be a soldier." It is obvious that the Taiping idea

---

[63] Haiao, *Ts'ung-shu, ts'e* 4, p. 3b.
[64] "T'ien-fu shih" Nos. 482 and 483, in Hsiao, *Ts'ung-shu, ts'e* 7.
[65] "Hsing-chün tsung-yao," in Hsiao, *Ts'ung-shu, ts'e* 6.
[66] *Ibid.*, p. 24a-b.

was derived from the religious conception of God as the common father.

We have seen how the Taipings demoted military personnel to the level of peasants for violation of precepts or laws. Since the Taiping society was a military society, it seems plausible at least to conclude that they considered a soldier higher than a peasant in the social scale of their society. This supports the point that they had a new conception of the soldier (for according to the traditional way of thinking, soldiery and peasantry were considered one). However, Li Kung of the Ch'ing classified soldiery as a separate class. Instead of the traditional four classes of *shih* (scholar), *nung* (peasant), *kung* (artisan), and *shang* (merchant), he gives five: *shih, nung, chün* (soldier), *kung,* and *shang.*[67] One might say that it was the Taiping conception of the peasantry that had changed; but it was the new conception of Taiping soldiers in the minds of their leaders which in turn led to the new attitude toward the peasants.

All the religious and moral precepts may be said to express the character of a soldier who was a member of the Taiping society, a member of the elite as distinguished from common peasantry. A glance at the two documents concerning regulations to be enforced on camp life, both stationary and on the march, is sufficient to show this. And the Taiping idea that to die is to go to heaven was certainly intended to give the soldiers courage in facing all the dangers of battle. Loyalty and *cheng* were important factors in keeping the soldiers under control. Every moral and religious precept was thus interpreted as a means to build a strong army of dependable character.

The severe army regulations enforced discipline and provided material for propaganda. The strictness with which these regulations were enforced at the initial stage of their movement won for the Taipings not only many followers but the sympathy of foreigners who wished and believed that they would succeed in overthrowing the fast declining, corrupt Manchu government.

[67] Li Kung, *P'ing-shu ting,* in *Chi-fu ts'ung-shu, ts'e* 231, p. la-b.

Chapter VI

The Development of
the Taiping Ideology

In previous chapters the Taiping ideology has been treated as a whole on a two-dimensional plane without regard to its temporal development. We have viewed it as a static system, as if it were an unchanging thing, created *in toto* by a sort of fiat, and as if there were no differences of opinion among the leaders of the Taping society. In fact, we know that though there was general agreement among the leaders concerning their ideological system, not all of them emphasized the same aspect in the same way. Neither was the system static and devoid of changes. The writer attempts in this section, therefore, first to discuss the individual contributions to the Taiping ideology; and second, to trace the development of ideas in the minds of the leading figures who were responsible for the ideology in its final form.

INDIVIDUAL CONTRIBUTIONS

Hung Hsiu-ch'üan was undoubtedly the most important person in formulating the Taiping ideology. According to Hamberg the "Taiping Imperial Declaration" (T'ai-p'ing chao-shu) which includes "Proclamation on the Origin of the Principles of World Salvation" (Yüan-tao chiu-shih ko), "Proclamation on the Origin of Principles for the Enlightenment of the Age" (Yüan-tao hsing-shih hsün), and "Proclamation on the Origin of Principles for the Awakening of the Age" (Yüan-tao chüeh-shih hsün) with "An Ode on Correctness" (Pai-cheng ko) attached to the first, was written by Hung himself.[1] There is no

---

[1] Theodore Hamberg, in *The Visions of Hung-Siu-tshuen, and Origin of the Kwang-si Insurrection*, p. 29, says: "The two following years, 1845 and 1846, Siu-tshuen remained at home, and was teacher of a school as formerly. During this time he wrote several

doubt that Hung was responsible for the religious elements in the ideology, and that both Feng Yün-shan and Hung Jen-kan were influenced by him. Hamberg told the story of Hung's conversion in the following words:

> Siu-tshuen felt as if awaking from a long dream. He rejoiced to have found in reality a way to heaven, and sure hope of everlasting life and happiness. Learning from the book the necessity of being baptized, Siu-tshuen and Li now, according to the manner described in the books, and as far as they understood the rite, administered baptism to themselves. They prayed to God, and promised not to worship evil spirits, not to practise evil things, but to keep the heavenly commands; they then poured water upon their heads, saying, "Purification from all former sins, putting off the old, and regeneration." When this was done, they felt their hearts overflowing with joy, and Siu-tshuen composed the following ode upon repentance:

> > When our transgressions high as heaven rise,
> > How well to trust in Jesus' full atonement!
> > We follow not the Demons, we obey
> > The holy precepts, worshipping alone
> > One God, and thus we cultivate our hearts.
> > The heavenly glories open to our view,
> > And every being ought to seek thereafter.
> > I much deplore the miseries of Hell.
> > O turn ye to the fruits of true repentance!
> > Let not your hearts be led by worldly customs.[2]

Hung then converted Feng Yün-shan and Hung Jen-kan, and baptized them in a school where Feng taught.

However, in the *Tse-ch'ing hui-tsuan* (A Collected Intelligence Report on the Rebels), Feng Yün-shan is said to have been the religious leader. In the biography of Yün-shan we read, "Yün-shan...a believer of *T'ien-chu chiao* (Heavenly Lord religion, commonly taken to mean the Catholic religion), and Hung Hsiu-ch'üan, Yang Hsiu-ch'ing, and Hsiao Ch'ao-kuei were all members of his sect."[3] Although Chang's

---

essays, discourses, and odes upon religious subjects, *viz:* 'An Ode of the Hundred Correct Things,' 'An Essay on the Origin of Virtue for the awakening of the Age,' 'Further Exhortations for awakening of the Age,' 'Alter the corrupt and turn to the correct'; to all of which he, however, afterwards made considerable additions, and most of which are contained in the 'Imperial declaration of Thaip'hing,' afterwards printed in Nanking."

[2] *Ibid.*, pp. 19–20.

[3] Chang Te-chien (editor and compiler), *Tse-ch'ing hui-tsuan, ts'e* 1, *chüan* 1, biography of Feng Yün-shan.

account was based on information from reliable informants of the time,[4] it seems likely that Hamberg's account is the more accurate, since it was based on the spoken words of Hung Jen-kan, who had been with Hung Hsiu-ch'üan from the very beginning and whose memory was still fresh at the time the story was told (1852).

The conception of Hung as the God-appointed man was at first thoroughly religious in nature. Hamberg reports:

> "These books," said he, "are certainly sent purposely by heaven to me to confirm the truth of my former experiences; if I had received the books without having gone through the sickness, I should not have dared to believe in them, and on my own account to oppose the customs of the whole world; if I had merely been sick but not also received the books, I should have had no further evidence as to the truth of my visions, which might also have been considered as mere productions of a diseased imagination. ...I have received the immediate command from God in his presence; the will of Heaven rests with me. Although thereby I should meet with calamity, difficulties, and suffering, yet I am resolved to act. By disobeying the heavenly command, I would only rouse the anger of God; and are not these books the foundation of all the true doctrines contained in other books?"[5]

Hung's words sound like those of a religious enthusiast rather than an ambitious political figure, but the nature of this religion did not remain unchanged. For according to Hamberg, "Siu-tshuen and his friends, left wholly to themselves, of course made many mistakes as to the real meaning." Thus in the Scriptures wherever Hung found the word *ch'üan* 全, which obviously means no more than "whole," "all," or "complete," he would construe it as referring to himself. "Altogether righteous" was rendered "Tshuen is righteous, more to be desired than gold."[6] From here it seems a natural step for him to take the position of considering himself the "God-appointed" one to rule the world. This political motive appears clearly in a poem which he wrote at this time

---

[4] The informants are: Chu Chu-p'ei, a *chü-jen* from Kwangsi, in long service in the army of Kwangsi; Li Ch'ai (Chu Ch'ai according to the note), a *ling-sheng* from Chekiang, long connected with Kwangsi high officials and also in the service of the Taipings for a long time before he cut himself away from them; Fang Ching, a student from T'ung-ch'eng in Anhwei, a civilian adviser in the army of Kwangsi; and Lo Feng-ch'ih, a *ling-sheng* from Kwangsi, leader of local corps (*yung*) with a great deal of military merit.

[5] *The Visions of Hung-Siu-tshuen*, pp. 21–22.

[6] *Ibid.*, pp. 22–23.

and which we have cited in Chapter V, page 87. As the poem was written in the year 1843, it is understandable that Hung did not attack the Manchus openly, although the metaphor "demons" could be thus interpreted. This is also true of the three essays written in the years 1845 to 1846. The political aspect of his allusion was made clear only when the Taipings openly rebelled against the Manchus. When the three essays written at this early date were first printed in the year 1852, the original titles, *ko* (ode) and *hsün* (teachings), were retained; but when they were reprinted in the following year (1853), *chao* (imperial decrees) was substituted for *ko* and *hsün*.

The ethnic issue raised in Taiping propaganda was of prime importance in the mind of Hung; his hatred of the Manchus is made only too clear in another passage from Hamberg's book, quoted in Chapter V, page 87. This hatred of the Manchus for their aggression against the Chinese seems to have been the motive behind one of his three early essays (1845–46) entitled "Proclamation on the Origin of Principles for the Enlightenment of the Age" which, after the style of Motzu, deals with sympathy and capacity of mind or heart to extend love to others.

Hung may also be considered responsible for the development of the moral ideas of the Taipings, since he wrote the "Taiping Imperial Declaration." But Feng Yün-shan may have helped formulate the moral ideology through his constant contact with Hung. Both were unsuccessful candidates in the official examinations and had been employed as teachers, which means that they must have had a smattering of knowledge of Confucian and Neo-Confucian philosophy as found in the Four Books and the Five Classics and in Chu Hsi's commentaries on these works. All prospective candidates were required to know these texts by heart.

Feng Yün-shan's influence in the formulation of the Taiping ideology was certainly very great, though he was not the religious leader that Chang Te-chien had made him in his *Tse-ch'ing hui-tsuan*. He and Hung Jen-kan were the first two converted and baptized by Hung Hsiu-ch'üan. He and Hung wandered together among the wild tracts and desolate mountains of the "Miau-tsze," preaching their newly adopted faith to the people.[7] Feng was instrumental in organizing the first God-Worshipers' congregation in Kwangsi.[8]

We may surmise that Feng was the author of some of the Taiping

[7] *Ibid.*, p. 27.
[8] *Ibid.*, pp. 28, 34.

official publications, though we cannot be sure which of these came from his pen. According to *Tse-ch'ing hui-tsuan*, "All the religious precepts and military orders and regulations were formulated by Yün-shan and Lu Hsien-pa."[9] This may be an exaggeration, but it shows Feng's influence in the formulation of the ideology. Had he not died so early (June 10, 1852), he might have exerted a greater influence on the development of the ideology.

Yang Hsiu-ch'ing's part in the formation of the Taiping ideology is revealed by the documents published either in his name or in the names of Yang and Hsiao as joint authors. We may safely conclude that Hsiao did not have any original ideas but followed the lead of Yang and so made no individual contribution to the formation of ideology, though in some important documents his name appears with Yang's as joint author.

Most prominent in Yang Hsiu-ch'ing's contribution to the Taiping ideology is the subordination of everything else to the military, and eventually to the political, success of the Taiping army. In Hung's writing one does get the feeling that he is a sincere believer in religion, however far he departs from the true interpretation of the faith; but in the case of Yang, one finds an ulterior motive between the lines. Apart from this, Yang's religious and moral conceptions do not differ from those made known under the name of the T'ien Wang.

As for the ethnic issue, Yang used it in his stirring speeches (proclamations) intended to arouse the Chinese against the Manchus. He probably did not write the proclamations himself, for he was not known to be a writer like Hung or Feng; but it is reasonable to assume that the essays were written in accordance with his desires. Yang undoubtedly realized the political significance of ideology and made use of it to the fullest extent. Though he contributed no original ideas, he injected life into the ideology by making it practical.

Hung Jen-kan, the Kan Wang, was also an important figure; but his influence was restricted to the latter part of the *T'ai-p'ing t'ien-kuo*, for he did not reach Nanking until 1859. His contributions will be discussed in the next section on the later modification of Taiping ideology.

We find few differences of opinion among the Taiping leaders in religious beliefs and moral concepts. To be sure there were contradictions in the system, but not of the kind that would result from individual differences. These contradictions are indications of the naive attitude of

[9] Chang, *Tse-ch'ing*, *ts'e* 1, *chüan* 1, biography of Feng Yün-shan.

the formulators, who uncritically entertained ideas logically incompatible. The majority of the members of the Taiping society accepted the whole system unquestioningly.

LATER MODIFICATIONS

Later modification of the Taiping ideology was due mainly to the T'ien Wang and the Kan Wang. The T'ien Wang became more deeply withdrawn in religious thinking toward the end of the reign, and the Kan Wang tried to reintroduce traditional elements into Taiping society together with certain startlingly new Western ideas. Though the T'ien Wang gave his approval for the publication of the Kan Wang's writings, in which traditional elements were re-evaluated and qualified, his tendency was to shift farther away from the traditional elements. We shall deal with each separately.

Modifications by Hung Hsiu-ch'üan

The change in Hung's ideas can be traced by comparing different editions of Taiping documents, assuming that the corrections or deletions were made by order to Hung, or at least with his approval. Many of the documents went into a later edition without any changes of ideological significance. "The Book of Declarations of the Divine Will Made During the Heavenly Father's Descent to Earth (I)" (T'ien-fu hsia-fan chao-shu I) is available to us in two editions. One is in Ch'eng's *T'ai-p'ing t'ien-kuo shih-liao*, First Series (hereafter abbreviated *Shih-liao*), Volume I; and the other is in *T'ai-p'ing t'ien-kuo shih-wen ch'ao*, Vol. II (hereafter abbreviated *Shih-wen ch'ao*). The former was printed in 1852; the latter is apparently an earlier edition, though also printed in 1852. The only difference between the two editions is in wording: where we find "Hsiu-ch'üan" in the earlier edition, we find *chen*, a symbol used by the emperor to refer to himself, in the later one. The second edition was of such an early date that we do not expect any further development in the ideology except that certain ideas had taken on greater importance politically. "The Book of Declarations of the Divine Will Made During the Heavenly Father's Descent to Earth (II)" (T'ien-fu hsia-fan chao-shu II) was printed in 1853. As this is the only edition available, no comparison is possible.

There are also two editions of "Ode for Youth" (Yu-hsüeh-shih) available, one of 1852 in Hsiao I-shan, *T'ai-p'ing t'ien-kuo ts'ung-shu* (hereafter abbreviated *Ts'ung-shu*) and one of 1851 in *Shin-wen ch'ao*.

Medhurst's translation in the *North China Herald* (hereafter abbreviated *NCH*) No. 147, May 21, 1853, is based on the 1852 edition. There is practically no difference between the ideas expressed in the two editions. Only one classical allusion was allowed to remain in the new edition, and there are two other modifications, one of which seems purely verbal:

1851 edition (in *Shih-wen ch'ao*)	1852 edition (in Hsiao, *Ts'ung-shu*)
有知與無知 誰非上帝生	有割與無割 誰非上帝生
Whether sentient or not sentient, Who is not produced by God?	Whether circumcised or uncircumcised, Who is not produced by God?
一身誰管轄 上帝賦心靈	一身誰管轄 上帝賦通靈

For controlling the whole body,
God has given to man an
  intelligent mind.
	For controlling the whole body,
	God has given to man
	  penetrating intelligence.

The second seems to be a purely verbal change, while the first suggests a better acquaintence with the Old Testament, though not necessarily a greater understanding of it.

There are two English translations of the "Trimetrical Classic" (San-tzu-ching) available here, one by Medhurst, published in *NCH*, No. 147, May 21, 1853, and the other by the Reverend S. C. Malan, published in London in 1856. Comparing these translations with the only Chinese edition available here, we find that they were both made from the same edition. It contains a great many historical allusions, many of them similar to those found in "Proclamation on the Origin of the Principles of World Salvation," proof that it was written after the pattern set by Hung himself.[10] The *T'ai-p'ing t'ien-kuo yeh-shih* (hereafter abbreviated *Yeh-shih*) mentions that "in the third year of *T'ai-p'ing t'ien-kuo*, Tseng

---

[10] According to Wang Shih-to's *Wang Hui-weng i-ping jih-chi*, 3:32a, both "San-tzu-ching" and "Yu-hsüeh-shih" came from the pen of Feng Yün-shan. If so, not only his ideas but his style as well are similar to Hung's. Or we may assume the two to be collaborators in the writing of all important Taiping documents, suggesting that there were no essential ideological differences between them.

Chao-yang, Lu Hsien-pa, and Tseng Shui-yüan were ordered to revise the Six Classics and write the 'Trimetrical Classic.' "[11]

The "Thousand Character Decree" (Ch'ien-tzu chao) was first published in 1854 and revised in 1858. Since the later edition is the only one available, no comparison is possible. We encounter no classical allusions in this work; but even if there had been historical or classical allusions, it is safe to assume that they would have been deleted in an edition published at such a late date.

The edition of "The Book on the Principles of the Heavenly Nature" (T'ien-ch'ing tao-li shu) available in Hsiao's collection has the following statement at the end: "A revised edition made by order of (the T'ien Wang?) in the year 1859." On the flyleaf we find "newly printed in the year of 1854," indicating that the original edition appeared in that year.[12] In the revised edition, the corrections do not seem quite thorough. In the revised editions of other works, such expressions as "The *Book of History* says" and "Mencius says" have been changed to "the old proverb says"; but "The Book on the Principles of the Heavenly Nature" in its 1859 edition retains the older expressions. Many of these classical allusions are the same as those deleted in the later editions of other works. On page 27a, a reference is made to the fact that "members of a family are still not united," a statement that clearly belongs to the version published before the abolition of the separate quarters for women in 1855. When there are quotations from "Yüan-tao chiu-shih ko (chao)," both *ko* and *chao* are used. At any rate, we have no original edition for comparison. It seems that the revision was not only a case of careless thinking and editing, but also indicated that the change was not absolutely necessary from the standpoint of principles.

There are, in addition to the documents revised with only slight ideological changes, a few very important documents which have more than one edition and which were significantly changed in the later editions. A comparison of their different editions will give us a fairly clear idea of the changes that must have taken place in Hung's mind during the latter part of the 1850's. The points in which the two editions differ will be put in two columns as a basis for our conclusions.

The English text of the 1852 edition of these documents is based on Medhurst's translation. Wherever necessary that translation has been

---

[11] Ling Shan-ch'ing (ed.), *T'ai-p'ing t'ien-kuo yeh-shih*, 17:1–2.
[12] "T'ien-ch'ing tao-li shu," in Hsiao, *Ts'ung-shu, ts'e* 5.

altered in order to provide the reader with a more exact meaning of the passage quoted.

"Yüan-tao chiu-shih ko" or "chao"

1852 edition (in Ch'eng, *Shih-liao*)[13]	1859 edition (in Hsiao, *Ts'ung-shu*)
Title: 歌 *ko* meaning "ode"	Title: 詔 *chao* meaning "edict" or "proclamation"
道統根源惟一正 The source of the orthodox doctrine is one, the upright.	真道根源惟一正 The source of the true doctrine is one, the upright.
歷代同揆無先後 Successive generations, whether early or late, come to but one conclusion.	皇天上帝的親傳 Personally handed down by Sovereign God himself.
盤古以下至三代 From the time of P'an-ku down to the Three Dynasties.	上古中國同番國 In the ancient times both China and foreign countries.
其時狂（王）者皆崇上帝 諸 侯 士 庶 亦 皆 然 During that period the sovereign honored God; The lords, scholars and plebeians all did the same.	Omitted.
賢否俱循內則篇 Both the worthy and the unworthy followed the "Nei Tse" [A chapter on the principle of family relations in the *Li Chi*].	賢否俱宜侍養虔 Both the worthy and the unworthy should reverently take care of [parents].
淫人自淫同是怪 盍歌麟趾永根源 歪俗移人誰挺立 Those who degrade others or [degrade] themselves are fiends. Far better to sing of the	淫人自淫均斬首 不犯天法得超身 魔鬼害人誰挺立 People, whether degrading others or themselves, will be executed just the same.

[13] W. H. Medhurst's translation in *North China Herald*, hereafter cited *NCH*, No. 150, June 11, 1853.

footprints of the gentle deer, and to celebrate a virtuous posterity [a reference to Poem No. 11 in the *Book of Poetry*].

Depraved manners overturn men; who under such circumstances can stand?

Those who do not violate heavenly laws will transcend life [Buddhistic idea of freedom from transmigration].

Once deceived by the devil, who under such circumstances can stand?

顏回好學不貳過
非禮四勿勵精神

Yen Hui loved learning, and did not repeat his faults;

His four cautions against improprieties are fit to arouse the mind.

Omitted.

古人所以誨諄諄
自古君師無異任

These are the instructions which the ancients repeatedly inculcated.

From of old princes and teachers had no other duties.

予今苦口誨諄諄
天命君師無異任

Now I am trying repeatedly to inculcate these instructions.

By decree of Heaven, princes and teachers have no other duties.

歷山號泣天為動
鳥為耘只象為耕
尊為天子富四海
孝德感天夫豈輕

The dweller of Li-shan [Shun, one of the legendary emperors] lamented, and all nature was moved;

The birds aided him in weeding, and the elephants in ploughing his ground.

Though exalted to the rank of emperor, and rich in the possession of the four seas,

His filial piety was such as to move Heaven; how could it be viewed lightly!

Omitted.

蓼莪詩可讀

Read the ode on the luxuriant southernwood [a reference to poem No. 202 in the *Book of Poetry*].

孝順條當守

The precept of filial piety must be observed.

是以先代不嗜殺
德合天心天眼開
寵綏四方惟克相
故能一統受天培
夏禹泣罪文獻洛
天應人歸無可猜

Hence it was that in former days
   men delighted not in murder;
In virtuous feeling they agreed
   with Heaven, and Heaven
   regarded them.
In cherishing and tranquilizing
   the four quarters, they aided
   the Supreme;
Therefore they were able to
   superintend the whole, and
   enjoyed protection of Heaven.
Yü of the Hsia dynasty wept over
   offenders; and Wan surrendered
   the Loh country;
Hence Heaven accorded and men
   reverted to them without
   hesitation.

Omitted.

楊震昏夜尚難欺、
管寧割席回（因？）歆顧、
山谷孤踪志不修、
夷齊讓國甘餓死、
首陽山下姓名垂、
古來善正修天爵、
富貴浮雲未足奇。

Yang-chin, though in the dusk
   of evening, would not be
   deluded by a bribe.
Kwan-ning, seeing the tendency
   of Hen's regards, cut
   connection with him,
And solitarily roamed the hills
   and valleys, without changing
   his mind.
E and Tse, resigning the throne,
   willingly died of hunger,
And Show-yang hill handed down
   their names to posterity.

皇天上帝實難欺、
天生善正修天爵、
不義之財何足奇。

The Sovereign Heavenly God
   cannot be deluded.
Heaven gives birth to the
   good and the upright who
   cultivate heavenly honors.
Wealth which comes through
   illegal channels is not
   to be valued.

From of old the honest and good
   have cultivated virtuous
   principles;
Riches and honors are but
   fleeting clouds, not fit
   to be depended upon.

孔顏疏水簞瓢樂
知命安貧意氣楊

Confucius and Yen-tsze made
   themselves happy on the
   plainest fare;
They regarded the will of Heaven,
   were content with poverty,
   and enjoyed happiness.

Omitted.

人生在世三更夢
何思何慮復何望
小富由勤大富命
自古為人當自強

The life of man, in the present
   world, is like a midnight dream.
What is there for one to think
   of, to worry and to hope for?
Small wealth results from
   industriousness, and great
   wealth is a matter of fate
   [destiny].
In all ages men have exerted
   themselves to do their duty.

人生在世遵天法
何思何慮復何望
凡情脫盡天情顯
自古為人當自強

Men living in this present world
   should observe the heavenly laws.
What is there for one to think
   of, to worry and to hope for?
With the worldly desires
   eliminated the heavenly nature
   will be revealed.
In all ages men have exerted
   themselves to do their duty.

士農工商耐久長

Shih, nung, kung, and *shang*
   [the four classes of people—
   scholars, farmers, artisans, and
   merchants] all will long endure.

遵守天條耐久長

Those who observe heavenly
   precepts will long endure.

請觀桀紂君天下
鐵統江山為酒亡

Just think of Chieh and Chou,
   who presided over the empire,
And included the hills and
   rivers within their iron rule;
   yet they perished through wine.

天父上帝最惡酒
切莫鬼迷惹滅亡

Wine is what the Heavenly
   Father, our God, detests most;
   Never be misled by demons
   who would cause your
   destruction.

禹稷勤勞憂饑溺
當身而顯及後狂（王）
周文孔丘身能正
陟降靈魂在帝旁

Yü and Chi were diligent, and
    anxious to prevent famine and
    flood.
Hence the one became emperor
    and posterity of the other
    obtained rule.
Wen of the Chow dynasty and
    Confucius were correct in their
    own persons.
Hence their souls were permitted
    to go up and down in the
    presence of God.

Omitted.

"Pai-cheng ko"

In the 1852 edition (in Ch'eng, *Shih-liao*), this ode is attached to "Ode on the Origin of the Principles of World Salvation"; but in the 1859 edition it is completely expunged. The only reason for this seems to be Hung Hsiu-ch'üan's growing impatience with the traditional reference and allusions and his greater absorption in religious musings. For the content of this "Pai-cheng ko," or "An Ode on Correctness," which is Medhurst's translation,[14] see J. Milton Mackie's *Life of Tai-ping-wang, Chief of the Chinese Insurrection*, pp. 351–53.

"Yüan-tao hsing-shih hsün" or "chao"

1852 edition
(in Ch'eng, *Shih-liao*)[15]
Title: 訓 *hsün* meaning teaching

王者不却衆庶、故
能成其德。

...so also a monarch does not
    disregard the common people
    by means of whom he completes
    his royal estate.

1859 edition
(In Hsiao, *Ts'ung-shu*)
Title: 詔 *chao* meaning edict

上帝廣生衆民、故
能大其德。

God gave birth to all people,
    so he made his virtue great.

[14] *Ibid.*
[15] *Ibid.*

退想唐虞三代之世、有無
相恤、患難相救、夜不閉
戶、道不拾遺、男女別途
舉選上德、堯舜病博施
何分此土彼土、禹稷憂饑
溺、何分此民彼民、湯武
伐暴除殘、何分此国彼
國、孔孟殆車煩馬、何分
此邦彼邦。

Omitted.

If we carry our thoughts back to
distant ages, to the times of Yao and
Shun and the Three Dynasties, we
shall find that, in those days, men
who possessed anything cared for
those who possessed it not; that
they aided each other in calamity;
that at night no man closed his
doors, and no man picked up that
which was dropped on the road;
that men and women walked on
different paths; and that in
promoting men to office virtue was
chiefly regarded. Yao and Shun
regretted that they could not
sufficiently supply the wants of
men; what difference did they
make between this land and that
land? Yü and Chi were anxious
lest the country should be involved
in famine and flood; what difference
did they make between this people
and that people? T'ang and Wu
attacked the violent and banished
the oppressor; what difference did
they make between one kingdom
and another kingdom? Confucius
and Mencius wore out their
carriages and horses in going about
to offer moral advice to rulers;
what difference did they make
between one state and another
state?

是故孔丘曰、大道之行也、天下
為公、選賢與能、講信修睦、故
人不獨親其親、不獨子其子、使
老有所終、壯有所用、幼有所長、
鰥寡孤獨廢疾者皆有所養
男有分、女有歸、貨惡其棄於地
也、不必藏於巳、力惡其不出於身
也、不必為巳、是故奸邪謀閉而
不興、盜竊亂賊而不作、故外
戶而不閉、是謂大同、而今尚可
望哉、然而亂極則治、暗極
則光、天之道也。

Therefore Confucius said, "When the great principle prevails, the world belongs to the public. The virtuous and the able will be selected to rule, in the spirit of winning the confidence of the people and cultivating harmony with neighbors. Therefore, the people will not merely love their own parents and their own sons. The aged will have a place to complete their natural span of life; the able-bodied, a specific function to perform; the young, some elders to look up to; and the widowed, orphaned, and the crippled and sick, means of support. The male will have his part to play, the female a home to settle down in. Goods should not be thrown away to the ground, but they need not be accumulated for the sake of oneself; energy should not be kept unused within oneself, but it should not necessarily be employed for the benefit of oneself. For this reason, the way to wickedness is closed, and no robbers, thieves, or rebels will be found. And the outer gates need not be shut. This is *ta t'ung* [the Great Harmony]." But now how can such a state of society be hoped for? Nevertheless, when disorder comes to the worst, order

Omitted.

is elicited; when the darkness is
extreme, light is found to spring
up—this is the course [*tao*, way]
of heaven [translation mine].

在易同人於野則亨、量大
之謂也、同人於宗則吝、量
小之謂也。
In the *Book of Changes* under the
hexagram "t'ung jen," it is said
that *t'ung jen* [to be harmonious
with people] in the wide world is
auspicious, because it means great
capacity [of heart]; but *t'ung jen*
in the clan is niggardliness, because
it means little capacity of heart
[translation mine].

心好天人亦世人
When one's mind [heart] is good,
one will be considered a man even
though one might have been a
fortune teller[16] [translation mine].

Omitted.

心好異人亦族人
When one's mind [heart] is good,
he will be considered a member of
the same clan even though he
might have been a member of a
foreign tribe.

"Yüan-tao chüeh-shih hsün" or "chao"

1852 edition (in Ch'eng, *Shih-liao*)[17] Title: 訓 *hsün* meaning teaching	1859 edition (in Hsiao, *Ts'ung-shu*) Title: 詔 *chao* meaning edict
皆稟上帝一元之氣、以生以出。 They are all derived from the one original breath of God.	皆由皇上帝大能大德、以生以出。 They are all derived from the great power and virtue of Sovereign God.
孔伋曰、天命之謂性。詩曰、天 生蒸民、書曰、天降下民。昭 昭簡編、洵不爽也、此聖人 所以天下一家、時廑民吾 同胞之懷、而不忍一日忘天下。	Omitted.

[16] *T'ien-jen* 天人 means a fortune teller, whom the Taipings considered to be a
worker of the devil. Here the fortune teller is contrasted with a normal man, a man
living on earth. For *t'ien-jen* see *Shih-chi*, 127:6b.

[17] Medhurst's translation in *NCH*, No. 151, June 18, 1853.

K'ung Chi said, "That which Heaven's decree conferred upon man may be termed common nature." The *Book of Odes* says, "Heaven produced all classes of people." The *Book of History* says, "Heaven sent down the inhabitants of this lower world." The truth so luminously expressed in these documents is far from incorrect. This is why the sages considered all under heaven as one family, and constantly cherished the feeling that all people are our brethren, while they did not, for one moment, overlook the interests of the whole world.

經史論及此乎、曰無有、
番國聖經載及此乎、曰、
無有。

Is this matter dealt with in the classics or historical records of China? No. Is it dealt with in any of the sacred books of foreign countries? No.

前代論及此乎、曰無有、
番國舊遺新遺載及
此乎、曰無有。

Is this matter dealt with in former dynasties [generations] in China? No. Is it dealt with in the Old and the New Testaments? No.

怪人佛老之徒出自陷迷
途貪圖射利誑人以不可
知之事。

Then came the fortune tellers, Buddhists and Taoists, who, in self-delusions and greed, attempted to delude people in matters which are unknowable....

怪人佛老之徒出自中魔
計以瞽引瞽誑人以不可
知之事。

Then came the fortune tellers, Buddhists and Taoists, who, having been trapped by the devil, attempted to delude people in matters which are unknowable, in much the same way as a blind man would lead others who were also blind.

天人
"Heavenly men," or fortune tellers.

怪人
Men of perverse principles.

孟軻曰天油然作雲沛
然下雨則苗浡然興之
矣。

古語云天油然作雲沛
然下雨則苗浡然興之
矣

Mencius said, "Heaven abundantly collects the clouds, and causes the rain to descend in torrents; then the young rice plant suddenly shoots up."

An ancient proverb says, "Heaven abundantly collects the clouds and causes the rain to descend in torrents; then the young rice plant suddenly shoots up."

周詩云
The "Ode of the Chou" says...

古語云
An ancient proverb says...
[content of quotation same].

前聖
Former sages.

前代
Former dynasties.

無他好生惡死慕福
懼禍恆情也。
This arises from no other cause than their following out the common feelings of aspiring after longevity, and seeking to avoid death; also from their panting after good fortune, and dreading ill luck.

此無他顧眼前忽
長遠恆情也。
This arises from no other cause than their following out the common feelings of being concerned with the present and overlooking the distant.

總為皇上帝所化所生。
They are all transformation and production of God.

總為皇上帝所造所生
They are all creation and production of God.

君王
The ruling king.

君長
The ruling chief.

歷考中國史冊自盤古至三代
Investigating Chinese historical records from P'an-ku to the Three Dynasties...

歷考中國前代上古之世
Investigating the former dynasties [generations] of ancient China...

北朝周武廢佛道毀淫祠
唐狄仁傑奏焚淫祠一千
七百餘所韓愈諫迎佛骨
宋胡迪焚毀無數淫祠明
海瑞諫建醮之數人者不
可謂無特識矣第其所毀
所焚所諫僅曰淫祠曰佛
曰建醮則其所不毀不焚
不諫者仍在不知彼所毀
所焚所諫者固當毀當焚
當諫即彼所不毀不焚不

Omitted.

諫者又何獨非當毀當焚
當諫乎

Thus the emperor of Wu of the
northern Chou dynasty set aside
the religion of Buddha, and
demolished improper temples. At
the instigation of Ti Jen-chieh, the
emperor of the T'ang dynasty
burned upwards of 1,700 improper
temples. HanYü reproved the
emperor for going out to meet a
bone of Buddha. Hu Ti, during the
Sung dynasty, burned down an
innumerable quantity of improper
temples; and Hai Jui of the Ming
dynasty reprobated the performance
of idolatrous rites: these people
cannot be said to have been
lacking in discernment. But what
they destroyed, burned, and
memorialized against was limited
to improper temples, Buddha, and
idolatrous rites. What they did not
destroy, burn, or memorialize
against is still of unknown quantity.
True, what they destroyed, burned,
and memorialized against should
have been destroyed, burned, and
memorialized against; but so
should what they did not destroy,
burn, and memorialize against.

自秦漢至今一二千年
From Ch'in-Han up to the present
in the last 1,000 or 2,000 years.

近一二千年
In the last 1,000 or 2,000 years

雖世間之主稱王足矣豈
容一毫僭越於其間哉
The monarchs of this world may be
called kings, and that is all; but
they cannot be permitted to
assume a single atom beyond this.

Omitted.

生前……死後之人昇天堂
In this life...after death the soul
ascends to the heavenly hall...

在世……昇天
While in this world...ascension to
heaven...

"T'ien-t'iao-shu"

Earlier edition[18]   Later edition

君狂   君長
Ruling king.   Ruling chief.

曷不觀三代時商湯始為   Omitted.
諸侯皇上帝是祇周文為
西伯昭事皇上帝他二人
非是既為君狂方拜皇上
帝也信如君狂方拜得皇
上帝難道商湯周文都拜
得不是乎果商湯周文拜
得不是緣何皇上帝看顧
商湯命商湯由侯而狂作
式法方九圍皇上帝又看
顧周文命周文留身為西
伯三分天下有其二至其
子周武遂得天下乎

Why not have a look at the Three
Dynasties? During that time T'ang
of the Shang first became a *chu-hou*
or vassal lord and respected God;
when King Wen of the Chou was
hsi-po, he worshiped God. These
two worshiped God not only after
they had become the ruling king.
If it is true that only the ruling
king may worship God, then could
it be said that both Shang T'ang
and Chou Wen were wrong in
their worship of God? If Shang
T'ang and Chou Wen were wrong
in their worship, why then did God
look after Shang T'ang and elevate
him from a vassal lord to king to
be the model ruler of nine
domains? And again why did God
look after Chou Wen and decree
that he during his lifetime become
hsi-po, possessing two-thirds of the
territory under heaven, and that
his son Chou Wu take possession
of the world?

[18] Medhurst's translation in *NCH*, No. 146, May 14, 1853.

中國有鑑史可考自盤古至
三代君民皆敬拜皇上帝藉
使三代時君民不是敬拜皇上
帝緣何大學有詩云殷之未
喪師克配皇上帝孟子又有
書曰天降下民作之君作之
師惟其克相皇上帝寵綏四
方（孟子原文惟曰其助上帝
寵之四方）雖有惡人齋戒沐
浴則可以祀皇上帝詩經又
有惟此文狂小心翼翼昭事
上帝聿懷多福皇矣上帝臨
下有赫帝謂文狂予懷明德
皇上帝臨爾毋貳爾心湯降
不遲聖教日躋昭格遲昼皇
上帝是祇帝命式於九圍書
經文有予畏皇上帝不敢不
正皇上帝弗順祝降時喪敢
祇承皇上帝以遏亂略惟皇
上帝不常作善降之百祥作
不善降之百殃易經又有先
代（王）以作樂崇德殷薦之皇
上帝乎今據說是從番難道
周武敢祇承皇上帝周文昭
事皇上帝商湯皇上帝是祇
顓頊敬事皇上帝盡是從番乎。

We may inquire into the historical records of China. From P'an-ku to the Three Dynasties, both rulers and the people respected and worshiped God. If the rulers and the people during the time of the Three Dynasties did not respect or worship God, why then does the *Great Learning* contain: "The *Ode* says, 'Before the Yin lost the people [the confidence of the people] they were able to be in harmony with the Sovereign God.' " [*Book of Poetry*, No. 235, "Wen-wang."] In *Mencius* we again find: "The *Book of History* says, 'T'ien created the people below and gave them rulers and teachers. As these were able to assist the Sovereign God, they brought grace and peace to

上古之世君民一體
皆敬拜皇上帝

In the ancient times both rulers and people reverenced and worshiped the Sovereign God.

the four quarters.' [*Mencius,*
IB/3.] 'Though a man may be
wicked, yet if he adjusts his
thoughts, fasts, and bathes, he may
sacrifice to the Sovereign God on
High.'" [*Mencius,* IVB/25. In the
place of plain *Shang-ti* or "God"
the Taipings substituted *Huang
Shang-ti* or "Sovereign God on
High."] The *Ode* again says, "This
King Wen worshiped the Sovereign
God with great respect and
received great happiness." [*Book
of Poetry,* No. 236, "Ta-ming."]
"Great is God, who supervises the
world below with majestic anger."
[*Book of Poetry,* No. 241, "Huang-i."]
"God told King Wen, 'I go along
with the man of enlightened
virtue.'" ["Huang-i."] "God
watches you, do not harbor double
thought." [*Book of Poetry,* No. 236,
"Ta-ming."] "Up to the time of
T'ang there was no slackening [of
principles], so his saintliness and
respect grew with time: his bright
virtue lingered long, entertaining
awe [or reverence] for God; thus
God ordered him to be the model
[the ruler] of the nine domains."
[*Book of Poetry,* No. 304, "Ch'ang-
fa."] Again the *Book of History*
says, "I am in awe of Sovereign
God, therefore I dare not be
anything but upright." [*Book of
History,* "T'ang-shih."] "Sovereign
God does not allow this, so God
poured destruction upon him,
[meaning King Chou Hsin, the
last ruler of the Shang]." [*Book of
History,* "T'ai-shih."] "I respectfully
followed the will of Sovereign God
to stop the way to chaos." [*Book
of History,* "Wu-ch'eng."] "The
Sovereign God does not have a
one-track mind: to men of good

conduct he gives one hundred blessings, but to evil doers he causes one hundred misfortunes." [*Book of History*, "I-hsün."] And in the *Book of Changes* it is said, "Former dynasties [originally *wang* or "kings"] were presented before the Sovereign God for their achievement in creating music and emphasis on virtue." [*Book of Changes*, "Diagram Yü."] Now if to worship God is to follow the way of foreigners, then when King Wu of the Chou respectfully received order from Sovereign God, King Wen of the Chou manifestly worshiped the Sovereign God, T'ang of the Shang reverenced the Sovereign God, and Chuan Yü reverently worshiped the Sovereign God, were they all following the way of foreigners?

考中國番國鑑史當初
幾千年
On the examination of Chinese and foreign historical records during the first several thousand years...

當初皇上帝六日造
成天地山海口口口來
At the beginning when the Sovereign God created heaven and earth and mountains and rivers in six days...

到秦漢以下
Since the time of the Ch'in and Han.

近一二千年
In the last one or two thousand years.

孟軻云天道一而己矣……
Mencius said, "As to heavenly *tao*, there is only one...."
[*Mencius*, IIIA/1.]

Omitted.

切莫痴呆昧性真
Do not let stupidity darken your true nature.

切莫鬼迷昧性真
Do not let devils' deceitfulness darken your true nature.

The changes shown above were apparently made because the Tai-pings wanted to get clear of what was traditional and historical and bring their expressions more into accord with the new pattern of thought. When *tao-t'ung* 道統 is changed to *chen-tao* 真道, or *t'ien-jen* 天人 to *kuai-jen* 怪人, we can with a fair degree of accuracy reconstruct the thinking processes which resulted in the change. *Tao-t'ung* suggests an "orthodox principle," transmitted from master to disciples in a direct line; and in China the line seems fairly well established, starting from Yao, Shun, Yü, T'ang, Wen, Wu, and Chou Kung, down to Confucius and Mencius. After Mencius there was a brief break, and the line was picked up by Han Yü of the T'ang and continued down to the Neo-Confucians in the Sung. Hung, after thinking more about his new faith, came to see the incongruity of this kind of orthodox doctrine in his system. Hence the change to *chen-tao*, simply the "true doctrine." *T'ien-jen* originally meant a "fortune teller," and Hung did use it in that sense. But since T'ien was conceived to be identical with God, it became sacrilegious to use the term in this connection. Hence the change to *kuai-jen*, "a man of perverse principle."

Evidently Hung also tried hard to break away from the historical past. This explains why he expunged historical and classical references. Even in cases where the text remains, the source has been dropped. "The Odes of Chou" was changed to "ancient proverb," and "Mencius" in a similar case was changed to the same "ancient proverb." In both cases, however, the texts remain unchanged. This seems to indicate that Hung, though conscious of the necessity of getting clear of tradition, was not able to free himself completely from what had dominated him for so long.

During the last years of the *T'ai-p'ing t'ien-kuo*, Hung became almost a religious fanatic. This religious fanaticism is revealed in his edicts, five of which, all dated 1861, have been included in a collection by Hsiao I-shan of Taiping edicts and decrees, published by the National Peiping Research Institute in 1935.[19] These five edicts deal exclusively with religious or superstitious matters, without a word about the affairs of the state. The first edict dwells on the necessity of honoring God and Jesus and tells how Jesus and Hung alone knew God through actual contact, and finally how God and Jesus in heaven and Hung as the true sun together create peace everlasting. The second edict explains the reason

---

[19] Hsiao I-shan (compiler), *T'ai-p'ing t'ien-kuo chao-yü*, hereafter cited Hsiao, *Chao-yü*.

China was named *Chung-hua:* it was because "Father placed the heavenly kingdom in *Chung-hua* and China was originally the home of God, therefore *Chung-hua* contains the name of the father." Here the "name of the father" referred to is *hua*, one of the three characters making up the name of God—*Yeh-ho-hua*. The edict is followed by a riddle containing the name of Hung Hsiu-ch'üan, undoubtedly reminiscent of the practice of secret societies. Edicts three, four, and five follow the same vein, dwelling on superstitious matters interspersed with riddles which seem to have nothing to do with the affairs of the state, with the government in Nanking, or with the battles of the time.

This religious fanaticism of Hung is also revealed through his conduct during the final days of the regime. Government forces under Tseng were pressing, and Li Hsiu-ch'eng was pleading with Hung to leave Nanking. But Hung retorted:

> I came by the saintly order of God and Jesus to this world to be the only true lord of the ten thousand nations. What do I have to fear? You need memorialize me no more, and you are not needed to take care of the government. Whether you would leave the capital or stay in it is your own affair. My rivers and mountains are as strong as an iron bucket. If you do not want to assist me [in running the government], somebody else will. You said we have soldiers. But my heavenly troops number more than water. Why should I be afraid of Tseng devils? Since you are afraid of death, probably you will die....[20]

And again Li said of Hung, "To all memorials the T'ien Wang's answer was either a talk about heaven or about earth; not for a moment did he give his attention to the state affairs."[21] Li also made the comment that the T'ien Wang relied completely on Heaven and had no confidence in man.[22] According to Li, the year before this the T'ien Wang had even changed the name of the government, calling the state "Kingdom of the Heavenly Father, Heavenly Brother, and Heavenly King *(T'ien-fu, T'ien-hsiung, T'ien Wang chih-kuo),*" and placed the symbol "heaven" as a prefix to nearly all things belonging to the dynasty.[23] Most historians in China attribute the Taiping collapse, at least in part, to the T'ien Wang's mental state in the last days of his rule.

[20] "Li Hsiu-ch'eng yüan-kung," in Men-shih t'an-hu k'o [Han Wen-chü], *Chin-shih Chung-kuo mi-shih,* p. 186.

[21] *Ibid.,* p. 185.

[22] *Ibid.,* p. 186.

[23] *Ibid.,* p. 187.

This religious fanaticism could be detected as early as 1852, because in the revised edition of "Proclamations by Imperial Sanction" (Pan-hsing chao-shu) printed in 1852, two years after its first publication in 1850, we already find changes similar to those we have dealt with above. Though this work, containing three essays, was issued under the names of Yang and Hsiao, we may attribute the changes to the general religious trend prevailing at the time as a result of Hung's influence on his followers. The two editions of the three essays are compared below.

"Feng-t'ien ch'u-yao chiu-shih an-min yü"

1850 edition 詩文鈔本—德本[24]

貪蠅頭之微利
Coveting advantages as small as the heads of flies...

況查爾們壯丁多是三合
會黨盍思洪門歃血實
為同心同力以滅清未
聞結義拜盟而反北面
於仇敵者
Moreover you valiant men are many of you adherents of the Triad Society, and why do you not reflect that you have entered into the Hung Society by blood covenant to exert your united strength and talents in exterminating the Manchus? Whoever heard of men joining in a sworn brotherhood and then turning about and surrendering themselves to their foes?

1852 edition 程本—法本[25]

瞞高天之大德
Obliterating the great virtue of Heaven on high...

況爾四民人等原是中
國人民須知天生真主
亟宜同心同力以滅妖
孰料良心盡泯而反北
面於讐敵者也
Moreover you four classes of people are originally people of the Chinese empire and ought to know that Heaven has produced the true sovereign. You ought therefore to exert your united strength and talents in exterminating the fiends. But who would have thought you should have obliterated your conscience and turned about to surrender yourselves to the foes?

"Feng-t'ien t'ao-hu hsi pu ssu-fang yü"

1850 edition 詩文鈔本—德本

1852 edition 程本—法本

[24] The earlier edition of these three essays appears in Lo Yung and Shen Tsu-chi (compilers), *T'ai-p'ing t'ien-kuo shih-wen ch'ao*, Vol. I, pp. 31a–35b.

[25] The 1852 edition of the essays appears in Ch'eng Yen-sheng (compiler), *T'ai-p'ing t'ien-kuo shih-liao*, 1st Series, Vol. I.

惟天下者中國之天下非胡虜
之天下也衣食者中國之衣食
非胡虜之衣食也子女人民者
中國之子女人民非胡虜之子
女人民也慨自有明失敗滿州
乘釁混亂中國盜中國之天下
奪中國之天下奪中國之衣食
淫虐中國之子女人民……

We believe that the empire belongs
to the Chinese and not to the
Tartars; the food and raiment
found therein belong to the
Chinese and not to the Tartars;
the men and women are subjects
and children of the Chinese and
not of the Tartars. But alas! ever
since the Ming misgoverned, the
Manchus availed themselves of
the opportunity to throw China
into confusion and deprive the
Chinese of their empire; they also
robbed them of their food and
clothing, as well as oppressed and
ravished their sons and daughters.
. . .

惟天下者上帝之天下非
胡虜之天下也衣食者上
帝之衣食非胡虜之衣食
也子女人民者上帝之子
女人民非胡虜之子女人
民也慨自滿清肆毒混
亂中國……

We believe that the empire
belongs to God and not to the
Tartars; the food and raiment
belong to God and not to the
Tartars; the men and women are
subjects and children of God and
not of the Tartars. Ever since the
Manchus spread their ruthlessness
and threw China into confusion...

自滿洲流毒中國虐焰
燔蒼穹

Since the Manchus spread their
spiteful venom, the flame of
oppression has risen up to heaven.

妖胡虐焰燔蒼穹

Since the devil barbarians spread
their ruthless cruelties, the flame
of oppression has risen up to
heaven.

乘中國之無人盜據華夏
御座之設野妖升據朝堂
之上沐猴而冠……受其
凌辱聽其號令甚至文武
官員貪圖利祿

At a time when China was
destitute of heroes they seized upon
the government of *Hua-hsia*
(China); the wild devil thus
ascended the imperial throne, and
monkeys were capped in court;
while our Chinese...allowed

乘中國之無人盜據中夏
妖座之設野狐升據蛇窩
之內沐猴而冠……受其
凌辱聽其嚇詐甚至庸惡
陋劣貪圖蠅頭

At a time when China was
destitute of heroes they seized
upon the government of *Chung-
hsia* (China); the wild fox thus
ascended the devil throne, and
monkeys were capped in the
snake's nest while our Chinese...

themselves to be insulted by them and obeyed their orders; and what is worse, the civil and military officers, coveting the gains of office...

allowed themselves to be insulted by them and submitted themselves to their intimidating and blackmailing; and what is worse, the useless, the wicked, the mean, and the depraved, coveting the heads of flies [petty gains]...

蓋我中國之天下今既蒙
皇上帝開大恩命我主天
王治之
Since the Sovereign God has shown great grace in mandating T'ien Wang our lord to rule the Chinese empire ...

蓋皇上帝當初六日造
成之天下今既蒙皇上
帝開恩命我主天王治之
Since the Sovereign God has shown great grace in mandating T'ien Wang our lord to rule the empire that the Sovereign God created in six days at the beginning...

華夷有定名
There is a definite distinction between the names of *Hua* (Chinese) and *I* (non-Chinese).

夏夷有定名
There is a definite distinction between the names of *Hsia* (Chinese and *I* (non-Chinese).

"Chiu i-ch'ieh t'ien-sheng t'ien-yang yü"

1850 edition

1852 edition

戌申歲三月上帝降凡
主張……今既三年矣
Since the third month of the year *wu-shen* [1848] when God descended ...it has been three years.

戌申歲三月上帝降凡
作主……今既五年矣
Since the third month of the year *wu-shen* [1848] when God descended ...it has been five years.[26]

From the differences between the two editions of the three essays, the following points seem apparent. First of all the Taipings wanted to get completely clear of any relation to the Triad Society, and this desire seems to be the motive behind the omission of the reference to that society in the 1852 edition. However, the omission also shows that they must have had a great deal to do with that society before this date. Secondly, we find a growing emphasis on religion; thus what was thought of as belonging to China was later thought of as created by God.

[26] Medhurst's translation of "Pan-hsing chao-shu" appeared in the *NCH*, No. 152, June 25, 1853, pp. 186–87.

The change from *Chung-kuo* (Chinese) to *Shang-ti* (Supreme Ruler on High) in the first and fourth quotations from "Feng-t'ien t'ao-hu hsi pu ssu-fang yü" seems to be due to this emphasis. Further, the emphasis on religion is shown by substituting *Chung-hsia* 中夏 for *Hua-hsia* 華夏 and *Hsia-i* 夏夷 for *Hua-i* 華夷; *hua* is part of the name of God (耶和華 *Yeh-ho-hua*) and had to be tabooed. Thirdly, the Taipings were becoming more conscious of the political issue and stopped using any term that might remotely suggest that the Manchu rule was legitimate. This explains why terms like *yü-tso* (御座 imperial throne), *ch'ao-t'ang* (朝堂 court of audience), *hao-ling* (號令 orders), *wen-wu kuan-yüan* (文武官員 civil and military officers), and *li-lü* (利祿 gains of office) were given up for plain condemnatory terms like *yao-tso* (妖座 devil seat), *she-wo* (蛇窩 snake's den), *ho-cha* (嚇詐 intimidating and blackmailing), *yung-o lou-lüeh* (庸惡陋劣 the useless, the wicked, the mean, and depraved), and *ying-t'ou* (蠅頭 fly heads, referring to small profit). And finally, they did not want to refer to the native Ming dynasty as responsible for the confusion and chaos in China at the end of the Ming, but tried to shift the burden to the ruthless aggression of the Ch'ing.

Modifications by Hung Jen-kan

Hung Jen-kan, the Kan Wang, joined the Taipings in 1859. His effort was exerted in three directions: justifying Taiping institutions, recognizing the value of some of the Confucian classics, and emphasizing the necessity of introducing new ideas and systems which he had learned about during his contact with foreign missionaries in Hong Kong and Shanghai.[27] We shall discuss these points in order.

Hung Jen-kan justified many of the Taiping institutions in his "A Hero's Submission to Truth" (Ying-chieh kuei-chen) and "True Re-

[27] Li Hsiu-ch'eng, in his reply to Joseph Edkins and Griffith John, mentioned that Hung Jen-kan had traveled through various nations; and Ling, *Yeh-shih*, reports in three different places that Hung Jen-kan had been to England, North America, and Japan (14:4) and had been sent out as an envoy to the United States of America (20:1, 2). If we follow Hung Jen-kan's career, these travels seem impossible, though they are accepted by Lo and Shen, compilers of *Shih-wen ch'ao* (I, 28b). See Kuo T'ing-i, *T'ai-p'ing t'ien-kuo shih-shih jih-chih*, I, 178. The conjecture that Hung visited several countries is plausible, because Hung Jen-kan in his testimony makes the assertion [I] traveled all over the oceans seeking refuge." "Kan Wang Hung Jen-kan kung-tz'u," in Hsieh Hsing-yao (compiler), *T'ai-p'ing t'ien-kuo ts'ung-shu shih-san chung, chi* 2, p. 1a. However, this does not explain Li's statement, which was made in 1860 and could not have been influenced by Jen-kan's testimony. Kuo T'ing-i in *Jih-chih* I, 178, is emphatic that Jen-kan did not travel beyond the boundary of China.

cord of [Hung Jen-kan's] War Campaigns" (Chün-tz'u shih-lu), both works published in 1861. In the former, a hypothetical case was presented in which a Manchu government official had deserted his side to join the Taiping army. Through a series of questions asked by this person, Hung Jen-kan explains many of the practices and institutions of the Taiping society.

Apart from the usual argument of the superiority of Chinese over all barbarians,[28] Jen-kan gave an economic justification for the Taiping stand on the ethnic issue. It was enough disgrace for the 500,000,000 Chinese to be under the rule of a few million "Tartar dogs," but there was more to add to the burden of the Chinese. Every year tens of thousands of taels of silver taken from the Chinese had been spent on opium, and other millions had gone to pay for the cosmetics of the Manchus. The Chinese had been reduced to poverty by these extortions; was this not reason enough that the Chinese should rise and question the right of the eastern provinces to hold them in slavery?[29]

This ethnic issue was also raised in the "True Record of [Hung Jen-kan's] War Campaigns" and "Proclamations on the Extermination of Demons" (Chu-yao hsi-wen). In the latter, Hung Jen-kan tried to revitalize the distinction between Chinese and non-Chinese. Written immediately after the death of the Hsien-feng emperor, the proclamation appeared at a most opportune time for this fresh effort to enlist the co-operation of the Chinese. All the points raised in Yang and Hsiao's proclamation against the Manchus are also raised here, with the added plea to the Chinese to seize this rare opportunity to overthrow the Manchu government.[30] Discussing the title T'ien Wang (heavenly king), Jen-kan sought justification in Confucius' Ch'un-ch'iu, in which Confucius was concerned first of all with the rectification of names:

> In writing Ch'un-ch'iu Confucius' first concern was rectification of names. He used the term T'ien Wang with great emphasis to show that wang was related to Heaven, signifying a grand unification. No person in the past has dared to assume this honorable title of T'ien Wang because God reserved it for the truly sage lord.[31]

When asked why the sun had been taken as the symbol of the T'ien

[28] "Ying-chieh kuei-chen," in Hsiao, Ts'ung-shu, ts'e 10, p. 2a.
[29] Ibid., pp. 5b–6a.
[30] Hsiang Ta et al. (compilers), T'ai-p'ing t'ien-kuo, II, 622–23.
[31] "Ying-chieh kuei-chen," in Hsiao, Ts'ung-shu, ts'e 10, p. 8a–b.

Wang, Jen-kan replied: "The sun is the symbol of the prince; its brightness lights ten thousand directions. . . ." Then to prove his contention he went on to cite incidents from Hung Hsiu-ch'üan's dreams and hallucinations and the poems Hsiu-ch'üan composed during his trance.[32]

Jen-kan also discussed the titles of different ranks. All Taiping titles were preceded by the term *t'ien*, to show that all things belong to T'ien. And the reason for adopting the six ranks *i* 義, *an* 安, *fu* 福, *yen* 燕, *yü* 豫, and *hou* 侯 instead of the traditional five ranks of *kung* 公, *hou* 侯, *po* 伯, *tzu* 子, and *nan* 男 is that the latter are all terms applied to members of a family. To use them as official ranks is not only confusing but vulgar as well. As to the titles from the rank of *ch'eng-hsiang* (丞相 chancellor) down to that of *liang-ssu-ma* (司馬 sergeant), they sounded strange to the ears because the people were not used to them; but compared with the Tartar's *patulutiehmuerh* 巴圖魯帖木兒, they were certainly not strange at all. And neither were they lowly in comparison with the traditional ranks, because they represent functions ordained by Heaven, and what can be higher and nobler than the Heaven-ordained? With respect to examination degrees, Jen-kan changed *hsiu-ts'ai* (秀才 outstanding talent) to *hsiu-shih* (秀士 sprouting scholar), *pu-ling* (補廩 graduate with a stipend) to *chün-shih* (俊士 superior scholar), *pa-kung* (拔貢 eminent graduate) to *chieh-shih* (傑士 distinguished scholar), *chü-jen* (舉人 elevated scholar) to *yüeh-shih* (約士 principled scholar), *chin-shih* (進士 advanced scholar) to *ta-shih* (達士 comprehending scholar), and *han-lin* (翰林 accomplished scholar) to *kuo-shih* (國士 leading scholar).[33] The general reason given for such changes was that the names of the traditional examination degrees, being of ancient historical origin, no longer described the degrees accurately. *Hsiu-ts'ai*, for example, was adopted as an examination title in the T'ang dynasty when it was used to refer to "*kung chü-jen* (貢舉人 elected elevated scholars), who were characterized by extensive knowledge, great talent, sound scholarship, readiness to answer the call of duty, and worthiness of being considered *chün* (俊 superior) and *hsüan* (選 select)."[34] According to its original meaning, then, the title *hsiu-ts'ai* was used to refer to people of high accomplishment and could not be applied to people who had just won their first degree. To change it to *hsiu-shih* 秀士 was to bring the term closer to its denotation, for *hsiu-shih* means "scholars who have just begun to show

---

[32] *Ibid.*, pp. 10a–12b.
[33] "Ch'in-ting shih-chieh t'iao-li," in Hsiao, *Ts'ung-shu, ts'e* 9, pp. 10b–11a.
[34] "Ying-chieh kuei-chen," in Hsiao, *Ts'ung-shu, ts'e* 10, p. 16a–b.

signs of promise and may be compared to the first show of luxuriance of plants and trees."[35] Similar reasons are adduced to show the need to change other titles to bring about an accord between "name and fact."

Hung Jen-kan gave the matter of not shaving one's hair great significance from the biological, moral, and social points of view. The hair protects one's brain and thus gives one a clear head. As it is bestowed on one by God and formed in the womb of one's mother, it would be highly unfilial of one to shave what by God's decree has been grown. Finally, the racial issue was brought to bear on the point, for the hair-shaving was forced upon the Chinese by the Tartars when they usurped the throne of the Ming. To refuse to shave was thus an open declaration of the intention to take revenge for the wrong the Tartars had done the Chinese.[36]

Many other questions Jen-kan disposed of either by recourse to the usual religious and moral considerations or by rationalization. The subjects taken up include destruction of idols; exclusion of lucky and unlucky days in the new calendar; the elimination of the practice of fortune-telling; and the meaning of "new heaven, new earth, new world, and new people," implying clearly there is only one heaven, one earth, one world, and one people. In his justifications, Jen-kan drew upon Confucianism and Christianity with equal freedom. His recognition of the value of the Confucian classics is also expressed in the explanations he offered.

There is no doubt that the Kan Wang was thoroughly steeped in Confucianism. He said of himself in the "True Record of [Hung Jen-kan's] War Campaigns" that he was brought up in a family of Confucian scholars. Whether this is true or not, the fact is that he considered himself a Confucian. From his emphasis on *hsing* (nature) and *li* (principle) and on action rather than on the study of books, his philosophy may be said to be Neo-Confucian. His candid recognition of the value of Confucianism seems to have been a matter of course to him.[37] Even his denouncement of Buddhism as an expression of a selfish desire to escape the responsibility of life is Neo-Confucian.

The Kan Wang's recognition of the value of the Confucian classics is shown in the two prefaces of the "Imperial Regulations Governing Scholarly Ranks" *(Ch'in-ting shih-chieh t'iao-li)*. Though these were not

---

[35] "Ch'in-ting shih-chieh t'iao-li," in Hsiao, *Ts'ung-shu*, *ts'e* 9, p. 10b.

[36] "Ying-chieh kuei-chen," in Hsiao, *Ts'ung-shu*, *ts'e* 10, pp. 22a–24a.

[37] Hsiang, *T'ai-p'ing t'ien-kuo*, II, 600, 604, 607.

written by Jen-kan himself, they must have represented his line of thinking, since they are attached to this work. The second preface particularly
tries to summarize the main points of an essay which Jen-kan wrote
giving instructions to the *shih* (scholars) on the five essential qualities a
scholar was expected to possess. However, the Confucianism is mixed
with Christianity in a way which justifies the conclusion that he was
trying to Christianize Confucianism.

In the first preface, it is noted that the knowledge of strategy is recorded in the *Book of Poetry* and the *Book of History*.[38] But the main
emphasis of Confucianism is brought out in the five points outlined in
the second preface. In point one, virtue is exalted as the most fundamental quality of a scholar, who was rated at the head of the *ssu-min* (four
classes of people); his talent, though important, was but secondary.[39]
In point two, Christian love and the Confucian idea of inner cultivation
are treated together.[40] In point three, reference is made to Paul's
philosophy, "patience is born of disaster...";[41] but point three ends
with the distinctly Confucian idea that one should observe the limit of
propriety imposed by social distinction and resign oneself to one's lot or
fate.[42] Here Jen-kan suggests Mencius' statement that only a scholar is
able to have a singleness of purpose without economic security. The
fourth point concerns material for study, which includes the New and
Old Testaments, decrees and other Taiping documents, and also Confucius' and Mencius' works. A reference is here made to a previous edict
by the Heavenly Father to the effect that "Works of Confucius and
Mencius need not be completely discarded. There is also a great deal of
teaching which agrees with the heavenly principle and way. Since these
have been made definitive by the royal pen of the true lord, the scholars
will all profit by reading them."[43] What is to be noted is that even Hung
Hsiu-ch'üan had changed his idea about Confucian books. The fifth
point refers to students of military affairs, concluding with the idea that
one should transform or sublimate one's physical bravery with one's
moral courage.[44]

The Kan Wang preached Christian teachings before he joined his

---

[38] "Ch'in-ting shih-chieh t'iao-li," in Hsiao, *Ts'ung-shu, ts'e* 9, p. 8a–b.
[39] *Ibid.*, p. 10a.
[40] *Ibid.*, p. 11a.
[41] Rom. 5:3.
[42] "Ch'in-ting shih-chieh t'iao-li," in Hsiao, *Ts'ung-shu, ts'e* 9, pp. 11a–12b.
[43] *Ibid.*, pp. 12a–13a.
[44] *Ibid.*, pp. 13b–14a.

cousin in Nanking. We can be sure that he believed in all the Christian doctrines with an understanding of which Hung Hsiu-ch'üan was not capable. However, like Hsiu-ch'üan, he also combined Christianity with Confucianism, mixing his talk on Christianity with quotations from the classics.[45] And he identified the selfish desire of men, an element which occupied the minds of all neo-Confucianists, with sin.[46] Here again we find the failure of a Taiping leader to understand the meaning of original sin; for selfish desire, according to the Neo-Confucianists, is not original but the result of empirical contamination.

Hung Jen-kan had been in close association with the Western missionaries before he came to Nanking and had had ample opportunity to become enthusiastic about Western ideas. He worked out a program for the Taiping government to adopt, in which he showed his clear understanding of the West and his desire to bring China abreast of the West in the material aspect of civilization. This program is outlined in a work entitled "A New Political Essay as a Guide to Government" (Tzu-cheng hsin-p'ien). It contains considerably more than Western ideas, but we shall confine ourselves to these in the following passage.

Jen-kan as revealed in this essay was a man remarkable for many of his views of the world at the time. He described in brief sketches the different nations of the world, including Great Britain, the United States of America, Germany, Sweden, Lo (Norway?), Denmark, France, Turkey, Russia, Persia, Egypt, Siam, Japan, Malaya, Peru, Australia, Singapore, India, and Tibet. He attributed the success and prosperity of some of these nations to the belief in Christ and the weakness of others to their ignorance of the faith. He distinctly realized that in China an inner accord had to be achieved to prevent the "fisherman" from profiting from the struggle of the "bird and the clam." This brought him to the ideal of a grand unification of China.

What he advocated may be summarized as follows:

1. Local self-government. This is clear from the way he expressed admiraration of the American system of electing local officials in his description of the United States of America.
2. Respect for public opinion. He endorsed the publication of newspapers and the opinion box.
3. Protection of freedom and independence through use of the secret ballot.

[45] Hsiang, *T'ai-p'ing t'ien-kuo*, II, 614.
[46] *Ibid.*, II, 612.

4. Establishment of a monetary and banking system.
5. Development of the mining industry.
6. Encouragement of private invention through patent and monopoly.
7. An over-all plan for land and water communication and a postal system.
8. Establishment of government news agencies to keep the public informed of good and bad local government.
9. Elimination of corruption by improving finance offices and the tax system.
10. Improvement of the judiciary system. He pointed out that no family members should be held responsible when another member of the family has commited a crime.
11. Social reforms. These included prohibiting the selling of children into slavery and the drowning of children.[47]

From this program we can see that Jen-kan was remarkably modern in his outlook. In one case he even contradicted the official Taiping position with regard to the taboo of the name of God. He said:

The name of God need not be tabooed. The name of our Heavenly Father is the greatest, the most reverend, the noblest, the most benevolent, the most righteous, the ablest, the most intelligent, the sincerest, the most sufficient, the most glorious, and the most powerful. What is there in a name which can in any way bring harm to God? If what is said is about what is upright, or for the purpose of propagating the principle, even a thousand or ten thousand words would be considered as glorifying [God]. However, what is prohibited is merely the use of it [God's name] for wrong purposes or for swearing and other sacrilegious purposes. If the name is tabooed, then in a few hundred years no man will know the name of the Heavenly Father. Furthermore, *Yeh-ho-hua* is the transliteration of the three native sounds of Judah into three characters. Each of these three characters has its own meaning. Taken together they mean omniscient, omnipotent, omnipresent, natural and spontaneous, the most righteous, and the most loving. God is reality. He is reality from the consideration of [the existence of] heaven and earth and the ten thousand things and of the birth of Christ.[48]

Apart from these new ideas, Jen-kan shared the general Taiping ideology with the rest of the leaders. The only difference is that his trend of thought was much more dominated by the traditional Confucian pattern than that of the others, and he was more candid in acknowledging the value of the traditional in thought and behavior. We may con-

[47] *I-ching*, Nos. 17–19 (Nov. 5, Nov. 20, Dec. 5, 1936).
[48] *I-ching*, No. 17 (Nov. 5, 1936), p. 21.

sider him a Taiping theorist who tried not only to Christianize Confucianism but to Confucianize Christianity as well.

PART TWO

Sources and Interpretations of the Taiping Ideology

To trace the elements of the Taiping ideology to their respective sources and attempt to give them a reasonable interpretation is our task in Chapters VII through XI. At the outset we are confronted with a difficulty inherent in the nature of the terms which we must use to designate these sources. Terms such as "Confucianism," "Taoism," "Buddhism," "traditionalism," and "popular pattern of thought" are all vague, for any one of them may have a number of aspects indistinguishable without lengthy discussion. The term "Confucianism," for example, may mean the philosophy of Confucius, Mencius, Hsün-tzu, and a host of other thinkers both ancient and modern; or it may mean Han Confucianism, which is a conglomeration of the Confucian teachings of the pre-Han period and the philosophy of the *Yin-yang wu-hsing* school combined with a great deal of the superstition of the time;[1] or it may mean the Neo-Confucianism of the Sung, Yüan, and Ming dynasties, which is a synthesis of Confucianism, Taoism, and Buddhism.

Since the time of the Six Dynasties, Confucianism, Taoism, and Buddhism have not been clearly defined concepts. The scholars interpret Buddhism in terms of Taoism,[2] and interpret Confucian texts by reference to Taoist ideas.[3] Many Buddhists were first of all Taoist scholars,[4] and Buddhism and Taoism were never kept clearly apart.[5] In the minds

---

[1] See Ku Chieh-kang's *Han-tai hsüeh-shu shih-lüeh*. Tung Chung-shu's *Ch'un-ch'iu fan-lu* is a good example of Han Confucianism.

[2] This practice is technically known as *ko-i* 格義.

[3] See Vol. II, chap. 5 of Fung [Feng] Yu-lan, *A History of Chinese Philosophy*.

[4] Hui-yüan (A.D. 334–416) is one among many good examples.

[5] See *Hung-ming chi*, compiled by Seng-yü (A.D. 445–518).

of the people at large, the confusion is even greater. The merging of all these "isms" can be seen clearly in the short stories written during the Chin and T'ang times. Lu Hsün, in his *Chung-kuo hsiao-shuo shih-lüeh*, makes the following remark about a short story by Yen Chih-t'ui (531–91), entitled "Yüan-hun chi": "[Yüan-hun chi], in its allusions to classics and histories for evidence to prove the principle of retribution, already started the merging of Confucianism and Taoism."[6] With the passage of time the merging has steadily increased. So pronounced is this amalgamating trait of the Chinese mentality that Johnston, when visiting China, observed that in the minds of the people of China popular Buddhism, Taoism, and Confucianism were all mixed. As an example, he pointed to a Buddhist pilgrim guide, where advice tinged with various religious colors was given.[7]

Even the term "Christianity" is not without its share of difficulty. The controversy over the question, "Is Taiping religion Christianity?" seems to be due in part to the absence of a working definition of Christianity.

Despite these difficulties, the terms convey some general scope or field within which they are applicable, and practical exigency demands that they be used. At any rate, whenever any of the terms is used some specific point will be referred to, and this specific reference will help to prevent confusion.

The Taiping ideology was, as we shall see, not a simple set of ideas. It was a mixture of many elements from different sources. We shall try to point out the origin of the various aspects of the Taipings' beliefs. The source of a single Taiping concept is often complex. A term such as *T'ien*, for instance, originated in the classics; it had a different connotation in Christian writings. The Taipings included in the term shades of meaning derived from both the classics and Christianity. They added their own interpretation to the word, so that the Taiping concept of T'ien was neither classical nor Christian but included some characteristics related to each of its sources. The reader should bear in mind the multiple origin of much of the Taiping ideology rather than conclude that any term or idea derives solely from one source.

We shall discuss the sources of the Taiping ideology under the follow-

---

[6] *Chung-kuo hsiao-shuo shih-lüeh*, in *Lu Hsün san-shih-nien chi*, IX, 58.

[7] Reginald F. Johnston, *Buddhist China*, p. 152. Novels seem to have played an important role in effecting this merging. *Chin-p'ing-mei* of the Ming dynasty and *Hung-lou-meng* of the Ch'ing are good examples.

ing topics: Chapter VII, Christianity; Chapter VIII, the classics and Confucianism; Chapter IX, Buddhism, Taoism, and Mohism; Chapter X, novels, the secret society called *T'ien-ti hui*, the Hakkas, and trance; Chapter XI, rebel ideologies. Taiping borrowings from these sources will be dealt with in their verbal, conceptual, and factual aspects. In many cases the verbal identity is the only indication of any borrowing of ideas, because quotations are often given in isolated poems or sentences, making conceptual reconstruction by reference to the context virtually impossible. Whenever possible, we shall consider quotations in context so as to establish the conceptual content. However, the connections we attempt to establish between the ideology and its source always remain speculative. And this for the simple reason that it is never possible to apply a term or a phrase out of its context to a situation in a new context without altering the meaning of the term or phrase. This difficulty is multiplied because we who are making this study live in a totally different socio-historical situation from that of the people whose ideology we are studying. Without ruling out the possibility that there may occasionally be valid reason to infer borrowing of ideas from similarity in wording, we must repeat that any such conclusions are highly speculative.

Chapter VII

Christianity

Hung Hsiu-ch'üan's contact with Christianity has been described by many writers including the Reverend Theodore Hamberg, whose work *The Visions of Hung-Siu-tshuen, and Origin of the Kwang-si Insurrection* has been one of the most important sources of information on Hung's early life. I shall therefore merely indicate that contact without giving the details.

In 1836 Hung was given a pamphlet entitled "Ch'üan-shih liang-yen" (勸世良言 Good Words to Admonish the Age) while he was in Canton for his examination. The work did not make any impression on him at the time, but seven years later (1843) his cousin Li Ching-fang urged him to study the work carefully. He did so and was greatly moved because he found confirmation in this tract of nine *chüan* for a great many of the visions he had seen in his dream during an illness. Hung had suffered the illness in 1837 after failing to pass the examinations for the third time. There is no doubt that the work contains the most important passages from the Scriptures, for W. H. Medhurst said of it:

> The texts chosen by Afa...are all of them of the first order in point of moment....We could only wish that the subjects had been handled with more ability, and attended to with more care by the present leader of the insurrection. Certain it is, that had Hung read his book a little more carefully, he would not have fallen into many of those extravagancies and improprieties which have marked and sullied his career.[1]

In 1846 Hung came into personal contact with the missionary I. J.

[1] Medhurst, "Connection between Foreign Missions and the Kwang-se Insurrection," *North China Herald*, No. 161, August 27, 1853, p. 15.

Roberts, with whom he stayed for a month or so.[2] Although he was disappointed in his desire to be baptized, he was exposed to the influence of the Bible.[3]

Hung's limited understanding of the Bible has been suggested in the quotation from Medhurst given above, and Hamberg shared Medhurst's opinion.[4] Hung's enthusiasm for the Bible is evident from the fact that in the very first year of the Taiping heavenly kingdom, when the Taipings were busily engaged in fighting the government troops, they began their printing of the Bible.[5] A bureau was established for this purpose, and it stopped operating only when the heavenly capital was thrown into confusion by the scarcity of food.[6]

HUNG'S BORROWINGS FROM CHRISTIANITY

Hung borrowed specific religious terms from an earlier revised edition of Medhurst-Gützlaff's Bible[7] and also from Liang A-fa's "Ch'üan-shih liang-yen," based on Morrison's translation of the Bible.[8] In going over the rebels' Genesis, Medhurst found that the Taipings designated God by the term *Shang-chu Huang Shang-ti* (上主皇上帝 the Supreme Lord, the Great God) which is evidently taken from Gützlaff's translation in Genesis 2:4 and numerous other places. Medhurst suggested that the attempt was to express "the Lord God," *Shang-chu* standing for "the Lord" and *Huang Shang-ti* for "God." The term *Shang-ti* (上帝 God on High) employed by Gützlaff to indicate eminence was used by the rebels throughout their works. *Shin* (*shen* 神 spirit) used for "gods" when

[2] "A month or so" in the year 1846 is according to Theodore Hamberg, in *The Visions of Hung-Siu-tshuen, and Origin of the Kwang-si Insurrection*, pp. 30–31. According to "T'ai-p'ing t'ien-jih," in *I-ching*, No. 15 (Oct. 5, 1936), p. 18, Hung was with Roberts "for several months" in 1847.

[3] "T'ai-p'ing t'ien-jih," in *I-ching*, No. 15 (Oct. 5, 1936), p. 18.

[4] Hamberg, *op. cit.*, pp. 22–24. On p. 22, Hamberg said: "The books [referring to A-fa's 'Ch'üan-shih liang-yen'], contained many portions of the Holy Scriptures which, though translated certainly in a faithful manner, yet had so much of foreign idiom, and were so often without any introduction and comments, that Siu-tshuen and his friends, left wholly to themselves, of course made many mistakes as to the real meaning." And on p. 24, he said: "Being however left to their own judgment as to the meaning, they were unable to distinguish between heavenly and earthly, spiritual and material matters."

[5] Ling Shan-ch'ing (ed.), *T'ai-p'ing t'ien-kuo yeh-shih*, 16:2.

[6] *Ibid.*, 17:3.

[7] W. H. Medhurst, "Ceremonial Regulations of the T'hae-ping Dynasty," *NCH*, No. 155, June 16, 1853.

[8] Medhurst, "Connection between Foreign Missions and the Kwang-se Insurrection," *NCH*, Nos. 160 and 161, August 20 and 27, 1853.

the Almighty is not mentioned, was also adopted. Medhurst concluded that "they may be said to have made Gutzlaff's translation of Genesis their text book."[9] Eugene Boardman, in his *Christian Influence upon the Ideology of the Taiping Rebellion, 1851–1864,* also traces *Huang Shang-ti* (皇上帝 Majestic God on High) and *Shang-ti* (上帝 God on High) to the 1847 Medhurst-Gützlaff edition.[10]

These are not the only terms Hung used to express his idea of God. Besides *shen* (神 spirit), he also used *shen-yeh* (神爺 spiritual father) and *hun-yeh* (魂爺 father of the soul; Medhurst renders *hun-yeh* as "ghostly father," showing that he was not acquainted with Hung's doctrine that God was the father of the soul of men). *Shen* and *shen-yeh* were evidently taken from Liang A-fa's tracts, with some misunderstanding, as Medhurst has pointed out. In the first volume of Liang's work there is the term *Shen Yeh-ho-hua* 神耶和華, intended to be a Chinese rendering of "God Jehovah." Medhurst has shown that the rebels must have taken the first two characters to mean "spiritual father," implying that the rebels did not know that *Yeh* is part of the personal name of God.[11] However, it is certain that Hung knew that *Yeh-ho-hua* 耶和華 was a personal name of God and ordered that these characters should be tabooed.[12] Thus, when *yeh* is used alone to stand for God, it seems to be an abbreviation of *Yeh-ho-hua.*

The term *hun-yeh,* which Medhurst translated as "ghostly father" and Boardman renders "spiritual father,"[13] is an invention of Hung's own imagination. In the light of his doctrine that God is the father of man's soul, not only the term but the idea as well seem to be original with him. He was trying to establish the proposition that God is the universal father of all men and to reconcile this with the fact that each of us has a father of his own. Hung devised the doctrine of God as spiritual father to get himself out of this apparent difficulty.[14] We have noted Hung's

[9] Medhurst, "Ceremonial Regulations of the T'hae-ping Dynasty," *NCH,* No. 155, June 16, 1853.

[10] Eugene P. Boardman, *Christian Influence upon the Ideology of the Taiping Rebellion, 1851–1864,* hereafter cited Boardman, *Christian Influence,* p. 55.

[11] Medhurst, "Connection between Foreign Missions and the Kwang-se Insurrection," *NCH,* No. 161, August 27, 1853, p. 15.

[12] Hsiao I-shan (compiler), *T'ai-p'ing t'ien-kuo chao-yü,* plate 5.

[13] Boardman, *Christian Influence,* p. 70, where *shen-yeh* and *hun-yeh* are rendered "divine father" and "spiritual father" respectively.

[14] For Hung's argument in this connection, see the first page of his "Yüan-tao chüeh-shih chao," in "T'ai-p'ing chao-shu," in Hsiao I-shan (compiler), *T'ai-p'ing t'ien-kuo ts'ung-shu, ts'e* 1, p. 7. For possible biblical support on this point, see note 49 below.

use of *yeh* and suggested that it might be an abbreviation of *Yeh-ho-hua*. But since the term in Chinese means "father" and was so used by Hung,[15] it apparently had for Hung both connotations, especially since *Yeh-ho-hua* was both God and father of men.

T'ien-fu (天父 Heavenly Father) is definitely and exclusively a Biblical term borrowed by Hung. But we find another term which has a double sense: that of "father" and that of "emperor." The term is *fu-huang* (父皇 father emperor),[16] a term that occurs in popular novels.

In the Taiping Genesis surveyed by Medhurst, Hung followed Gützlaff in the use of *shen* to stand for spirits other than God. But Hung also used it either alone or together with *chen* (真 true) in the compound *chen-shen* (真神 true Spirit) to mean "God." *Shen* meaning "spirits" is found in *chüan* 3 of Liang A-fa's work; but its appearance there may also have been due to the influence of traditional Chinese attitudes, for the pattern of Liang's mind was fundamentally Chinese.

Another important religious concept is that of the devil. For this Hung also had a variety of terms. Boardman has made a list of Taiping terms for the devil and evil spirits, which includes: *mo-kuei* (魔鬼 the devil), *kuei* (鬼 a spirit), and *lao-she* (老蛇 snake). The Taipings also used *hsieh-shen* (邪神 evil spirit), *yao* (妖 imps), *yao-mo* (妖魔 impish devil), and *Yen-lo* (閻羅 Chinese ruler of the nether world).[17] Boardman here rightly maintains that of the several symbols used by the rebels to stand for the devil "only the last [referring to *lao-she*] can be considered because of its un-Chinese nature as an out-and-out borrowing."[18] To be sure, the term *hsieh-shen* occurs in the very first line of Liang A-fa's work, which runs: "Hsieh-shen pien wei she-mo" (邪神變為蛇魔 Evil spirits transform themselves into snake devils).[19] But Liang was a Chinese and like Hung could project his earlier background into the supposedly Christian religion. Medhurst tried to show that Liang was unidiomatic in his language because he had been taught by foreign missionaries; but more

---

[15] In Hsiao, *Chao-yü*, Hung used *yeh* in the following ways: *yeh-yeh*, a common way to refer to one's father or grandfather; *yeh-ko*, coupling up father and elder brother; and *yeh-ma*, coupling up father and mother.

[16] Hsiao, *Chao-yü*, plate 5.

[17] Boardman, *Christian Influence*, p. 81.

[18] *Ibid.*, p. 83.

[19] See Medhurst, "Connection between Foreign Missions and the Kwang-se Insurrection," *NCH*, No. 161, August 27, 1853, p. 15.

important is Liang's cultural background, which he was unable to discard.[20]

Closely connected with terms for the devil and spirits are terms for idols. Two terms are used in Taiping documents: *ou-hsiang* (偶像 idols) and *p'u-sha* (菩薩, an abbreviation of Buddhisatva). Boardman has pointed out that these terms were used in the 1847 Gützlaff translation of the Bible.[21] However, these terms are also found in Volume I, section 2 of Liang A-fa's work, where idolatry, especially that of China, is discussed. This verbal borrowing suggests that Hung's iconoclasm has Liang's work as its source.

The name of the dynasty that Hung and his group established was *T'ai-p'ing t'ien-kuo* (太平天國 the Heavenly Kingdom of Peace; or, more freely, the kingdom of heaven where peace prevails). There is no doubt that this was intended to serve as a political title, but an examination of the terms reveals that even here the Bible may have had its share of influence. In the New Testament *t'ai-p'ing* (peace) occurs more than once. Two examples follow:

> Luke 2:13–14. And suddenly there was with the angel a multitude of the heavenly host praising God, and saying, Glory to God in the highest, and on earth peace, good will toward men.
> Luke 19:38.... saying, Blessed be the King that cometh in the name of the Lord: peace in heaven, and glory in the highest.

On the first passage Hung made the following comment: "Today it is realized. Respect this."[22]

A most suggestive passage is found in Hebrews 7:1–2; in his comment on this passage Hung spoke of his own coming to the world to be its lord. The text runs:

> For this Melchisedec, king of Salem, priest of the most high God, who met Abraham returning from the slaughter of the kings, and blessed him;
> To whom also Abraham gave a tenth part of all; first being by intepretation King of righteousness, and after that also King of Salem, which is King of peace.

[20] For Medhurst's view on Liang's style, see his article "Connection between Foreign Missions and the Kwang-se Insurrection," *NCH*, Nos. 160 and 161, August 20 and 27, 1853.

[21] Boardman, *Christian Influence*, p. 66.

[22] For this and other references to Hung's comments on the Scriptures, see *Ch'in-t'ing ch'ien-i-chao sheng-shu* and *Ch'in-ting chiu-i-chao sheng-shu*, the Taipings' New and Old Testaments with commentaries, located in the British Museum.

In Hung's comment he identified himself with this Melchisedec, King of peace.

The "kingdom of heaven," the other half of the title, also occurs many times in the New Testament. Another form, which Hung in later years wanted to use instead of the original *T'ai-p'ing t'ien-kuo*, is the "kingdom of God."

> Matt. 5:3. Blessed are the poor in spirit: for their's is the kingdom of heaven.
> Matt. 4:17.... kingdom of heaven is at hand.
> Matt. 5:19–20. Whosoever therefore shall break one of these least commandments, and shall teach men so, he shall be called the least in the kingdom of heaven: but whosoever shall do and teach them, the same shall be called great in the kingdom of heaven.
> For I say unto you, that except your righteousness shall exceed the righteousness of the scribes and Pharisees, ye shall in no case enter into the kingdom of heaven.

Here Hung made the following comment:

> The kingdom of heaven includes both heaven and earth. In heaven there is the kingdom of heaven and on earth there is the kingdom of heaven. Whether up in heaven or down on earth, both are God the father's kingdom of heaven. No one should misunderstand this to mean only the kingdom of heaven in heaven. This is why the Eldest Brother [Jesus] says in his decree: "... the kingdom of heaven is at hand [Matt. 4:17]." For the kingdom of heaven is come on earth. Today our Heavenly Father and Heavenly Brother have descended to earth to establish the kingdom of heaven; this is it. Respect this.

G. H. Gilbert, in his article "Kingdom of God," explains that Jesus used "kingdom of heaven" in a sense similar to that which Hung tried to attach to it: "The usage of Jesus differs from that of the prophets, further, in that He speaks of a Kingdom of God as existing on both sides of the grave, or in two spheres, an earthly and a heavenly."[23]

Jesus' references to the kingdom of heaven occur throughout the gospels:

> Matt. 5:10. Blessed are they which are persecuted for righteousness' sake: for their's is the kingdom of heaven.

[23] James Hastings (ed.), *Encyclopaedia of Religion and Ethics* (13 vols; New York: Charles Scribner's Sons, 1951), VII, 736.

Matt. 7:21. Not every one that saith unto me, Lord, Lord, shall enter into the kingdom of heaven; but he that doeth the will of my Father which is in heaven.

Matt. 19:14. But Jesus said, Suffer little children, and forbid them not, to come unto me: for of such is the kingdom of heaven.

Matt. 6:33. But seek ye first the kingdom of God, and his righteousness . . .

Mark 4:26. And he said, So is the kingdom of God, as if a man should cast seed into the ground;

Luke 17:20–21. And when he was demanded of the Pharisees, when the kingdom of God should come, he answered them and said, The kingdom of God cometh not with observation:

Neither shall they say, Lo, here! or lo, there! for, behold, the kingdom of God is within you.

Hamberg made it clear that Hung became interested in the phrase *t'ien-kuo* at the time he was earnestly engaged in the study of Liang's work: Jen (Chien) Yu-wen, apparently basing his information on Hamberg, mentions that the phrase *t'ien-kuo chiang-lin* (天國降臨 the kingdom of heaven come) engaged Hung's attention.[24]

This brief survey of the biblical passages where *T'ai-p'ing* and *t'ien-kuo* occur shows that Hung and his group must have had these passages in mind when they made their choice of the title for their new dynasty.

The use of the term *t'ien* to mean a place, in phrases like *sheng-t'ien* (昇天 ascension into heaven) or *shang-t'ien* (上天 to go up to heaven), seems to have been borrowed from the Bible too. "Heaven" meaning a place occurs in the Lord's Prayer, which the Taipings certainly knew well; for many of the phrases in this prayer were adopted by them. In the prayer we read: "Our Father which art in heaven . . . Thy kingdom come. Thy will be done in earth, as it is in heaven."[25] The Chinese equivalent found in the Taiping document called "The Book of Heavenly Commandments" (T'ien-t'iao-shu) runs: "Heavenly Father, Sovereign Supreme Ruler on High, thy will be done on earth, as it is in heaven."[26] "Heaven" meaning a place also occurs in Mark 12:25: "For when they shall rise from the dead, they neither marry, nor are given in marriage; but are as the angels which are in heaven."

The use of *Ch'üan-wei-shih* (勸慰師 Comforter) as a title for Yang Hsiu-ch'ing indicates that the Taipings identified Yang with the Holy Ghost.

[24] Hamberg, *The Visions of Hung-Siu-tshuen*, p. 24; Jen [Chien] Yu-wen, *T'ai-p'ing-chün Kwangsi shou-i shih*, hereafter cited Jen, *Shou-i shih*, p. 101.

[25] Matt. 6:9–10.

[26] In Hsiao, *Ts'ung-shu*, *ts'e* 1, p. 3a.

John 14:16. And I will pray the Father, and he shall give you another Comforter, that he may abide with you forever;

John 14:26. But the Comforter, which is the Holy Ghost, whom the Father will send in my name, he shall teach you all things, and bring all things to your remembrance, whatsoever I have said unto you.

John 15:26. But when the Comforter is come, whom I will send unto you from the Father, even the Spirit of truth, which proceedeth from the Father, he shall testify of me:

John 16:7–8. Nevertheless I tell you the truth; It is expedient for you that I go away: for if I go not away, the Comforter will not come unto you; but if I depart, I will send him unto you.

And when he is come, he will reprove the world of sin, and of righteousness, and of judgment.

The Taiping idea of the Trinity is at variance with the biblical doctrine of the Trinity; the Taipings took Yang to be the Holy Ghost, although Hung also discussed the authentic Trinity of God, Jesus, and the Holy Ghost.

Such borrowing of terms does not, however, warrant deduction that there was any borrowing of ideas, and this for several reasons. First, a term need not have the same conceptual content when used in two different contexts, especially when these two contexts differ in points of culture, time, and space. Secondly, distortion of ideas is almost inevitable when the borrowing has to be effected through translation from one language to another. Translation at best is a form of interpretation, and allowance must be made for possible misinterpretation. The seriousness of this problem of distortion is clearly brought out by a controversy in the 1850's over the right Chinese term to use for the Hebrew term *Elohim* or the Greek *Theos*.[27] The problem is complicated by Hung Hsiuch'üan's basing his first understanding of Christianity on Liang A-fa's "Ch'üan-shih liang-yen," which in turn was based on a translation (Morrison and Milne's) of the Bible. Further distortion occurred because of the traditional patterns of thought in the minds of both Hung and Liang. For these reasons we are not surprised to find the Taipings first trying to take only that which was congenial to their way of thinking and to omit many essential points equally available to them, and secondly trying to fit much of what they took over to their own patterns of thought.

With respect to the concept of God, the Taipings borrowed from both the Old and the New Testament. Like the Hebrews, the Taipings

[27] *NCH*, 1853–1856, *passim.*

believed their God to be the creator of the world; a deity who shows mercy and forgiveness but is jealous and intolerant of idolatry; a God who belongs to all and has direct relation with men; a God of battles who intervenes personally at critical moments.[28]

Although the Taiping idea of a universal God may logically have excluded them from thinking of him also as a tribal deity and of themselves as the chosen ones, as the Hebrews had done, the Taipings did give some evidence that they also considered God their tribal God and themselves the chosen people. They identified the kingdom of heaven with China and called the Manchu rule a usurpation. They definitely believed that the Chinese should rule China, the kingdom of heaven, as a chosen people. Jen (Chien) Yu-wen also believes that to Hung the phrase "God's chosen people" meant China and Hung.[29]

The idea of a covenant seems to be present in the Taiping conception as it was in the Hebrew conception of God.[30] In the mind of the Hebrews, God was related to them by a contract, expressed in the term "testament." Concerning Genesis, chapter 9, Hung wrote the following poem:

> Father to make an eternal contract orders the rainbow to appear,
> Like a bow the rainbow presents its arc...

Hung was not unaware of the meaning of the term "testament" as used in the title of the Bible, although he chose i-chao (遺詔 royal will) in its stead. His long comment on I John, chapter 5, contains the statement: "Father knows that there is error in the New Testament."

The Taipings, like the Hebrews, believed that sacrifice becomes insignificant without goodness of heart. Hung commented on Matt. 9:13: "Our Eldest Brother decreed that he desires mercy. When he dispenses with sacrifice he really means that only those who have a good heart may sacrifice; for to have a good heart is to offer sacrifice to God. He did not decree that man should not sacrifice to God. Respect this."

But, as Boardman rightly remarks: "The concept of one supreme God

---

[28] See Boardman, *Christian Influence*, pp. 54–58.

[29] Jen, *Shou-i shih*, p. 101. Boardman, however, believes that the Taipings did not think of their God as a tribal God or of themselves as the chosen people. See Boardman, *Christian Influence*, pp. 56–57.

[30] Here again we differ from Boardman's view. See his *Christian Influence*, pp. 56–57.

was the important borrowing, for monotheism became the keystone of the whole ideological structure."[31]

The Taiping God is characterized, like the God of the New Testament, by fatherhood, universality, and the presence of a spiritual adjunct or emanation called the Holy Spirit. But Hung refused to believe in the divinity of Jesus.

It seems clear that the terms Hung chose to stand for God do not necessarily imply borrowing of concepts. When his idea of God is considered in its entirety, it is not what a Christian would believe. During his visit to Nanking in 1860, I imagine I. J. Roberts would have been far happier if he had been dealing with one who knew nothing about Christianity instead of with Hung. What made Hung's idea of God so un-Christian despite so many borrowings from the Bible were his underlying traditional patterns of thought, which we shall discuss in Chapter VIII.

The working of the native mind is more apparent in Hung's idea of the devil. Hung was certainly more concerned with the traditional Yen-lo than the Satan of the Bible. The serpent symbol is the only aspect of the Taiping devil which has the Bible as its sole source. The Bible is therefore merely an auxiliary and not an indispensable source of Hung's idea of the devil. The religious title *T'ai-p'ing t'ien-kuo* does not mean that Hung understood what "the kingdom of heaven" or its alternate, "the kingdom of God" meant, though it did give the Taipings a religious mission: to establish on earth the principle of heaven *(t'ien-tao)*. Boardman is perfectly right in maintaining that Hung was not aware of the unworldly nature of these phrases. Hung merely took the term *T'ai-p'ing t'ien-kuo* to mean the new dynasty he established; he was quite ignorant of its spiritual content.

The Taipings appropriated many stories from the Bible, including the stories of the creation, of Noah and the flood, and of the delivery from Egypt.

The ten *T'ien-t'iao* (天條 Heavenly Precepts) differ from the Ten Commandments in two respects: the first precept concerns only the worship of Huang Shang-ti (皇上帝 Sovereign Supreme Ruler on High), and reference to worship of gods other than God is given in the commentary on the second precept; and the second heavenly precept prohibits worshiping the perverse spirits instead of image-making.

[31] *Ibid.*, p. 59. Boardman believes that the Taiping conception of God did not reach such a stature as to make the good heart the condition for the acceptance of a sacrifice.

The Taiping account of the basic facts of the life of Christ is quite accurate, except that Jesus was made the first-born rather than the only begotten son of the Father. The teachings of Christ, however, were for the most part touched upon with little discussion of their deeper meaning. The idea of sin and its forgiveness, the thought, "Ask, and it shall be given you, seek and ye shall find, knock and it shall be opened unto you . . .,"[32] the fragmentary expressions from the Sermon on the Mount, and the idea of love all found their way into the Taiping documents. The theme of love is repeatedly expressed in the line: *ai-jen ju-chi* (愛人如己 love others as oneself),[33] which is the Chinese rendering of". . .love thy neighbour as thyself."[34] From the Beatitudes, we find mention of humility and purity of heart in Taiping writings. The Taiping idea of humility may not be the same as that expressed in the New Testament; it is more likely that it stems from the *Book of History* and the *Book of Changes*. But the Taipings used another phrase which definitely suggests a Christian origin of the idea of humility. In one of the "Poems by the Heavenly Father" (T'ien-fu shih) we have the following line: "Those who consider themselves high will drop low, so do not desire to be high."[35] Another poem is even more explicit: "Heavenly Eldest Brother Jesus said, 'Those who consider themselves high will drop low.' "[36]

Purity of heart, as expressed in one of the Beatitudes,[37] is mentioned in "Poems by the Heavenly Father." In poem No. 12, a line runs: "Heavenly Eldest Brother Jesus said, 'Blessed are the pure in heart.' "[38] This is the first part of the sixth beatitude. The idea is completed in poem No. 95, where a line runs: "The pure in heart shall have the bliss to see Father and Mother."[39] The addition of "Mother" was a Taiping invention, of course.

In the matter of Christian rites and doctrines, the Taipings adopted baptism, observance of the Sabbath, incarnation, atonement, and the doctrine of the Trinity, the last of which is mentioned but not explained.[40]

---

[32] Matt. 7:7.

[33] "T'ien-fu shih" Nos. 11, 104, 474, in Hsiao, *Ts'ung-shu, ts'e* 7; and "T'ai-p'ing chao-shu," in Hsiao, *Ts'ung-shu, ts'e* 1, pp. 5b–7a.

[34] Matt. 22:39.

[35] Poem No. 131, in Hsiao, *Ts'ung-shu, ts'e* 7.

[36] Poem No. 12, in Hsiao, *Ts'ung-shu, ts'e* 7.

[37] Matt. 5:8.

[38] "T'ien-fu shih" No. 12, in Hsiao, *Ts'ung-shu, ts'e* 7.

[39] "T'ien-fu shih" No. 95, in Hsiao, *Ts'ung-shu, ts'e* 7.

[40] Although the Taipings mention belief in the Trinity several times, they offer no clear, consistent explanation of what the Trinity is. We can conclude that they bor-

For a very good reason possession by demons, which is mentioned in the Bible, is ignored in the Taiping writings. To the Taipings it appeared that God and Jesus had taken over this function of possessing individuals and spoke through the mouths of certain people who experienced trances; and it would be highly improper that demons should have the same function. This phenomenon has again to do with the dual sense of the term *shen* (神 spirit), which the Taipings used to stand for both God and spirits.

In the conception of heaven and hell, Boardman points out that the early translators of the Christian Bible employed the same words for "heaven" and "to get to heaven" as the Taipings did. And *ti-yü* is the customary Biblical rendering for "hell."[41] But it is the New and not the Old Testament that served as a "generous source of example and imagery to the creators of a Chinese eschatology."[42]

In general, the Taipings had a tendency to put a strong emphasis on obedience to the letter of the rules. On Ephesians 2:15, Hung commented: "With respect to God's Ten Commandments, our Eldest Brother's edict did not mean that I should come to annul laws. Not a dot, not a word of the laws may be cancelled. Respect this."

BORROWINGS OUTSIDE THE RELIGIOUS SPHERE

Christian influence upon the Taiping ideology was not limited to the religious aspect. The choice of the title of the new dynasty may have been influenced by the passages from the Bible which we have cited. Biblical influence may also explain why a political entity had the religious mission of disseminating the heavenly principle. The adoption of the *sheng-k'u* (聖庫 sacred treasury system), which is not mentioned in the Bible, may be a case in which the Taipings borrowed the spirit rather than the letter of the Bible. When the Taipings left their home and marched north, it was necessary for their leaders to fire them with an enthusiasm which was expressed by Jesus in the following words: "If thou wilt be perfect, go and sell that thou hast, and give to the poor, and thou shalt have treasure in heaven: and come and follow me."[43] The leaders may have had the same expectation of devotion from their fol-

---

rowed the term "Trinity" from Christianity but that their concept of the Trinity was not Christian, although they may have thought that it was.

[41] Boardman, *Christian Influence*, p. 87.

[42] *Ibid.*, p. 85.

[43] Matt. 19:21.

lowers that Jesus had from his when he said, "But lay up for yourselves treasures in heaven, where neither moth nor rust doth corrupt, and where thieves do not break through nor steal: For where your treasure is, there will your heart be also."[44] Whether or not the idea was accepted by the followers, it served the Taipings well as a measure of control.

Another possible influence of Christianity upon Taiping ideology is the idea of brotherhood of men. The following biblical passages may have given Hung the idea of brotherhood.

> Matt. 5:23–24. Therefore if thou bring thy gift to the altar, and there rememberest that thy brother hath ought against thee;
> Leave there thy gift before the altar, and go thy way, first be reconciled to thy brother, and then come and offer thy gift.

What Jesus meant by "brother" is distinctly not a blood relation.

> Matt. 12:46–50. While he yet talked to the people, behold, his mother and his brethren stood without, desiring to speak with him.
> Then one said unto him, Behold, thy mother and thy brethren stand without, desiring to speak with thee.
> But he answered and said unto him that told him, Who is my mother? and who are my brethren?
> And he stretched forth his hand toward his disciples, and said, Behold my mother and my brethren!
> For whosoever shall do the will of my Father which is in heaven, the same is my brother, and sister, and mother.

The word "brother" was used similarly to refer not to people in blood relation but to people in general in Matthew 18:15, Romans 14:10 and 15, Revelation 1:9. And the term "brotherhood" occurs in I Peter 2:17, where Paul says: "Honour all men. Love the brotherhood. Fear God. Honour the king." A most interesting passage is found in John 1:12–13: "But as many as received him, to them gave he power to become the sons of God, even to them that believe on his name: Which were born, not of blood, nor of the will of the flesh, nor of the will of man, but of God." This, taken with the previous passages, particularly the one from Matthew 12, suggests a type of brotherhood to which the God-Worshipers Society might very well belong.

The source of the Taiping idea of brotherhood can definitely be traced to either the traditional Confucianism or the ideology of Chinese

---

[44] Matt. 6:20–21.

secret societies. But since the Bible was available to the Taipings and the passages we have cited suggest brotherhood, we may be excused in our speculation on the relationship between the Taiping idea of brotherhood and the Bible. It would be very interesting indeed if we could know what Tseng Kuo-fan would have said of Jesus' words concerning his mother and brethren, for it was exactly the practice of the Taipings to neglect their flesh-and-blood relation for the religious brotherhood that excited his ire. He condemned the statement: "T'ien (天 Heaven) alone can be called father, and all fathers of the people are brothers and all mothers sisters."[45]

In making their new calendar, the Taipings gave the year 366 days. Thus it would seem that they got their idea from "Yao-t'ien" in the *Book of History*, where we find the following statement: "A year consists of 366 days."[46] But according to Professor Tung Tso-pin the Taipings did not adopt the 366-day year from the *Book of History* but from the Western leap-year calendar of 1852.[47] For this reason, we must give credit to Christian missionaries for supplying the Taipings with the idea for their new calendar.

In explanation of the Taiping failure to assimilate into their doctrine some of the essential teachings of Christianity, Boardman suggests: "As a result largely of the character of the founder, the Taipings were not exposed to the more vital parts of the Christian ethic."[48] In Chapter VIII, we shall show Hung's "character" by describing his mental make-up, which not only helps to explain why he ignored certain Christian teachings but also explains his misunderstanding of those teachings that he did accept.

TAIPING MODIFICATION OF CHRISTIAN IDEAS

To understand to what extent the Taiping ideology could be called Christian or un-Christian, it is not enough simply to point out what the Taipings failed to adopt from Christianity that is essential to any Christian creed. It is more important to show that there is in what they did borrow a great deal which cannot be called Christian because of its modification and distortion.

---

[45] *Tseng Wen-cheng kung ch'üan-chi*, 3:1b.

[46] *Shang-shu chu-shu*, "Yao-t'ien," p. 10b.

[47] Tung Tso-pin, "T'ien-li fa-wei," in Lo Erh-kang, *T'ai-p'ing t'ien-kuo shih k'ao-cheng chi*, p. 99.

[48] Boardman, *Christian Influence*, p. 113.

The Taipings took their idea of God from Christianity; but this Christian idea received so many bizarre modifications that at the end of the process it was no longer like the Christian idea. In the hands of the Taipings, God acquired a human physique and a wife. The human physique may have some basis in the Old Testament, but the posture conferred on God is definitely a traditional Chinese posture that speaks of grace and dignity. The idea of God having a wife, who in Taiping terminology was called an "original wife" (implying that God might take a second one should the original wife die), seems to be the result of the Taipings' taking the fatherhood of God literally. They thought that Jesus, Hung, and Yang were born in the usual way a mortal was born, that is, through the womb of a woman; hence the necessity of a heavenly mother. This literal thinking was also responsible for the doctrine that God was the father of men's souls, for only thus could the Taipings resolve the apparent contradiction between the fatherhood of God and the fact that each person has his own parents.[49] These modifications are understandable when we remember that Hung's cultural background was vastly different from that out of which the Christian belief grew.

We have mentioned that Hung failed to recognize the divinity of Jesus. Through demoting Jesus the Taipings sought to elevate themselves. Jesus was not God, not even the only begotten son of God; he was merely one of the children of God, Hung and Yang being his blood and flesh brothers. In this way the "divine" origin of Hung and Yang was established; and this was sure to serve them well in the eyes of the people, who were used to the idea of supernatural intervention in human affairs.

The Taiping conception of apostles as angels is of a biblical origin. On I Corinthians 6:2 Hung gave the following comment: "And the apostles are also angels." This is akin to the popular belief that great men are gods in heaven or spirits of stars incarnate.

[49] This idea of God being the father of man's soul is not, however, without biblical support. The idea is given in Hung's comment on I Cor. 15. The text of I Cor. 15:44–46 says: "It is sown a natural body; it is raised a spiritual body. There is a natural body, and there is a spiritual body. And so it is written, the first man Adam was made a living soul; the last Adam was made a quickening spirit. Howbeit that was not first which is spiritual, but that which is natural; and afterward that which is spiritual." Hung comments: "In the birth of a man, there is first the soul and then the body. For the father of his soul first gives birth to his soul, and then his soul enters the womb of his mother to form his flesh body, and it is only then that his body appears. Respect this." It is interesting to note that Hung altered the order of the spiritual and the natural.

The Taipings also introduced many popular ideas into their religion and mixed them with the biblical references. One of these is the idea of rebirth. Concerning Revelation 12:1–2 Hung made the following comment: "The Eldest Brother, myself, and the Tung Wang, before the creation of heaven and earth, were born of the womb of the Heavenly Mother, our Father God's original wife; later our Eldest Brother for the sake of redemption entered into the womb of Mary and became the body of man."

Another traditional idea Hung introduced is *fu-ming* (符命 a physical sign of heavenly mandate, or prognostication). In his comment on both Genesis 14 and 15, Hung made this remark: "In his course of action, T'ien always gives prognostication." His comment on Hebrews, chapter 7 illustrates what he meant by prognostication:

> This Melchisedec is no other than I. Formerly when in heaven our Heavenly Mother gave birth to our Eldest Brother and us, I knew that Father would through the descendant of Abraham send our Eldest Brother down. I therefore comforted the troops and gave blessing to Abraham. For Abraham was a good man. Father's edict says: "Ho-wang [King Ho, Ho being part of one of the two characters forming Hung's personal name, the explanation of which is given in Hung's comment on Revelation 14:15] will be the lord to save men to be good." This is the prognostication [or sign or proof] of my present being born into this world to be its lord.

The physical sign of this prognostication or the heavenly mandate was in the form of a seal, a sword to kill the imps, and the seven characters *T'ien Wang ta-tao chün-wang Ch'üan* (天王大道君王全 heavenly king, the great principle, monarch Ch'üan).

The influence of Hung's cultural background is also revealed through his modification of the biblical text. This is done by introducing certain terms used traditionally for specific honorific consideration. For example, wherever Jesus referred to himself, the word *chen* (朕, first person pronoun used by an emperor alone) was used; and whenever God or Jesus made any statement, the word *chao* (詔 edict), *chih* (旨 edict), or *sheng-chih* (聖旨 holy edict) was used.

In many cases Hung interpreted biblical passages as if they were riddles. His comment on Matthew 24 runs:

> Our Eldest Brother was afraid to let out the secret, so he decreed in a riddle that I am the sun (太陽 *t'ai-yang*): but when I came down to become

man, I changed into darkness. My wife is the moon (太陰 *t'ai-ying*); but when she came down to become a woman, she no longer gave out light. Heavenly troops and heavenly generals are stars and constellations which came down to become men; but when they came down to earth, they fell from heaven to earth.

A similar comment may be found on Revelation 6:12, where *t'ai-yang* and *t'ai-ying* occur in the text. What concerns us here is the use of riddles, which is apparently the result of secret society influence. Another example is from Hung's comment on Matthew 27:36–40 where the text runs:

And sitting down they watched him there;
And set up over his head his accusation written, This Is Jesus the King of the Jews.
Then were there two thieves crucified with him, one on the right hand, and another on the left.
And they that passed by reviled him, wagging their heads,
And saying, Thou that destroyest the temple, and buildest it in three days, save thyself.

Hung commented:

Three dots [referring to the two thieves on the right and the left and Jesus in the middle] mean Hung [洪, the left radical is water which is popularly called *san-tien-shui* 氵 three dot water], and three days mean Hung-jih [洪日; Hung was his name and *jih* was his symbol]. The eldest brother decreed in a riddle that Hung-jih will be the lord, and will re-establish the fallen temple of God. Respect this.

We shall see that this use of riddles is a native practice and is especially characteristic of Chinese secret societies.

The Taiping belief that God took possession of and spoke through a particular person may have some biblical basis. Hung's comment on two Bible passages was, "God descended upon and lived in our Eldest Brother."[50] The statements in the New Testament that the Holy Ghost descended upon people may have suggested to Hung that God would take over the mind and body of a person in a trance. That the practice of trance was started by Yang is a strong indication, however, that it had popular superstitions as its source.

[50] Comments on Matt. 9:27–31 and Acts 2:22.

Many examples show the composite nature of the Taiping mind. In the Taiping writings we come across expressions like *ch'ien k'un ting yen* (乾坤定焉 the male and female principles were established), from the *Book of Changes*.[51] But this element is introduced in the midst of a description of the creation taken from the Bible. The Taipings often referred to the Heavenly Father's love of life.[52] This is an adaptation of a sentence from the *Book of Changes*, where the term *t'ien-ti* (天地 heaven and earth) has been replaced by *T'ien-fu* (Heavenly Father). The original sentence runs: "The great virtue of heaven and earth is called life." This gave place to a popular version, "Heaven on high has the virtue of love of life."[53]

It is easy to see that most of the modifications the Taipings introduced into the Christian part of their religious ideology resulted from the working of native patterns of thought to which they had been exposed long before they came into contact with Christianity. One would expect these would show up in their version of Christianity.

---

[51] "T'ai-p'ing chiu-shih-ko," in Hsiao, *Ts'ung-shu*, *ts'e* 4, p. 1a. *Chou-i yin-te*, 39/*hsi, shang*/1, says, "The principles of *ch'ien* and *k'un* are established"; 44/*hsi, shang*/12 says, "The principles of *ch'ien* and *k'un* fall in line"; 47/*hsi, hsia*/9 says, "Are not *ch'ien* and *k'un* the gates of changes?"

[52] "T'ien-ch'ing tao-li shu," in Hsiao, *Ts'ung-shu*, *ts'e* 5, p. 28a; "T'ai-p'ing chiu-shih-ko," in Hsiao, *Ts'ung-shu*, *ts'e* 4, p. 3a.

[53] *Chou-i yin-te*, 45/*hsi, hsia*/1. In these quotations the word *sheng* 生, which we have rendered "life," needs some explanation. It really means "production of life." So *hao-sheng* means "the love of production of life," implying a hatred of destruction of life. For the sake of simplicity, we rendered the phrase *hao-sheng chih hsin* or *hao-sheng chih i* "a love of life."

Chapter VIII

The Classics and Confucianism

In this chapter a detailed analysis of "traditionalism" and its influence on the Taiping ideology will be given. Before taking up the specific aspects of traditionalism, a brief statement concerning its presence in the Taiping ideology and some of the ways in which it was expressed may be useful.

Tradition is perpetuated in the titles of many Taiping publications. The Taiping document called the "Trimetrical Classic" (San-tzu-ching) took its title and style from a popular primer.[1] The "Ode for Youth" (Yu-hsüeh-shih) purportedly fulfilled the same function as another popular work called *Yu-hsüeh ku-shih ch'iung-lin*,[2] though they differed completely in content; and the "Thousand Character Edict" (Ch'ien-tzu chao) was, in title, style, and content, patterned after another popular primer, *Ch'ien-tzu-wen*, which was traditionally attributed to Chou Hsing-ssu of the Liang (A.D. 502–57). The fact that one of these Taiping books, "Ode for Youth," differs completely in content from its counterpart, the *Yu-hsüeh ku-shih ch'iung-lin* (a kind of phrase dictionary), suggests that the Taipings may have borrowed these titles because of their established power over the minds of the people. In this manner the new ideas of the Taipings could be put over with little resistance. In addition the Taipings were keenly aware of the force of traditionalism and were cautious enough to resort to it.

[1] The primer was attributed first to Wang Ying-lin 王應麟 of the Sung but later proved to be the work of Ou Shih-tzu 區適子 of the end of the Sung, with later additions by Ming and Ch'ing scholars.

[2] The meaning of the term *yu-hsüeh* is given in "Ch'ü-li" in the *Li-chi*, which says: "The time one reaches the tenth year of age is called *yu-hsüeh*." The commentary says: "The term means that one is able to learn only when one is young." *Li-chi yin-te*, 1/8.

Many phrases in the Taiping documents testify that traditionalism permeated the minds of the Taiping leaders. Hung used *yüan-tao* 原道, a term first found in the *Huai-nan-tzu* and later used by Han Yü of the T'ang,[3] as part of the titles of the three important works he wrote during 1845 and 1846. The very first line of the first of these three important works of Hung runs: "The great source of *Tao* (Truth) emanates from T'ien."[4] This line comes from Tung Chung-shu: "The great source of *Tao* emanates from T'ien; T'ien does not change, and neither does *Tao*. For this reason Yü succeeded to Shun, and Shun succeeded to Yao; each of these three sages received from his predecessor the same *Tao*, which they all embraced."[5] Hung Jen-kan later embodied in the title of "The Book on the Principles of the Heavenly Nature" (T'ien-ch'ing tao-li shu) the phrase *t'ien-ch'ing* (天情 heavenly emotions), which Hsün-tzu took pains to explain in a chapter entitled "T'ien-lun" (On Heaven).[6]

Taiping writings are full of phrases which betray the traditional bent of Taiping thought. They called their way *chen-tao* (真道 the true way) but then identified it with *ku-tao* (古道 the ancient way). In studying the development of the Taiping ideology, we have seen how hard and how unsuccessfully Hung tried to forget about the past. He may have omitted the reference to "Liao-o,"[7] but the idea of filial piety expressed in this poem remained intact. He may have substituted "the ancient saying goes" for "the 'Book of Chou' says" or "Mencius says," but the quotations are still there to show that no conceptual change has taken place. In one of their early proclamations of 1853, when they first occupied Nanking, the following phrase occurs: *ssu-wen sao-ti* (this truth has fallen

[3] The first chapter of *Huai-nan-tzu* is entitled "Yüan-tao-hsün" 原道訓, and Kao Yu 高誘 of the Later Han gives the following commentary: "*Yüan* means 'source': its source in *tao* and its root in truth, [it] envelops heaven and earth and courses through ten thousand things. This is the reason for entitling the chapter 'Yüan-tao.' " *Huai-nan-tzu*, 1:1. And Han Yü of the T'ang wrote his most important essay under the title "Yüan-tao." *Ch'ang-li hsien-sheng chi*, 11:95. *Huai-nan-tzu* is an eclectic work, but its main trend is Taoistic.

[4] "Yüan-tao chiu-shih ko," in Ch'eng Yen-sheng (compiler), *T'ai-p'ing t'ien-kuo shih-liao*, 1st Series, II, 1a.

[5] *Han-shu*, by Pan Ku, 56:18a.

[6] Hsün-tzu said: "Heavenly offices having been established, and heavenly functions having been formed, the body takes shape and the spirit is born: and this has innate in it love and hate, pleasure and anger, sadness and happiness. These are what we call *t'ien-ch'ing* [天情 heavenly emotions or reality]." *Hsün-tzu*, chi 1, ts'e 1, p. 206.

[7] *Mao-shih yin-te*, 48/202. This poem expresses the pathos of a filial son who is unable to render his last services to his parents.

to the ground).[8] The principal part of this phrase, *ssu-wen*, is found in the Confucian *Analects*:

> The Master was put in fear in K'wang. He said, "After the death of king Wăn, was not *ssu-wen* (the cause of truth) lodged here in me?
>
> "If Heaven had wished to let this cause of truth perish, then I, a future mortal, should not have got such a relation to that cause. While Heaven does not let the cause of truth perish, what can the people of K'wang do to me?"[9]

When *ssu-wen* is viewed in connection with other terms like *t'ien-tao* (heavenly principle or way)[10] or *tao-t'ung* (orthodox principle),[11] or when it is considered together with the "protector-of-faith" spirit expressed in one of the stirring proclamations issued against the Manchus for imposing alien ways of life upon the Chinese,[12] one conclusion becomes clear: the Taipings were thoroughly imbued with the traditional pattern of thought and could not avoid it. The zest and passion with which Yang and Hsiao defended Chinese laws and institutions in their proclamation are striking, and might even be worthy of a Tseng Kuo-fan.

In the "Taiping Heavenly Chronicle" (T'ai-p'ing t'ien-jih) Hung mentioned how he and the little heavenly sisters studied together *Shih* (the *Book of Poetry*) and *Shu* (the *Book of History*) and played musical instruments. He also said that God often told him he should study more of the *Shih* and *Shu* so that he might have something to go on in the future. The usefulness of the *Shih* and *Shu* was a popular traditional idea and may be traced as far back as Confucius himself. In the *Analects*, Confucius is reported to have told his son: "If one does not study *Shih*, one will not have anything to converse on.... If one does not study *Li* [the *Book of Rites*], one will not have anything to stand on."[13] In spite of all their hatred of the books of Confucius and Mencius, episodes like this slipped in amid the Taiping denouncements of Confucius. With all

[8] Hsiao I-shan (compiler), *T'ai-p'ing t'ien-kuo chao-yü*, plate 10.

[9] James Legge, *The Chinese Classics*, I, 217–18.

[10] "Yüan-tao chiu-shih ko," in Ch'eng, *Shih-liao*, II, 1a.

[11] *Ibid.* This term was implied in Confucius' and Tung's statements and was passionately developed by Han Yü and the Neo-Confucians of the Sung. In the 1859 edition, this term was replaced by *chen-tao* (真道 the true doctrine).

[12] "Pan-hsing chao-shu," in Ch'eng, *Shih-liao*, I, 4a–7b. See Chapter VI for a detailed analysis of this document.

[13] *Lun-yü yin-te*, 34/16/13.

Hung's effort to get rid of traditional "prejudices,"[14] he was hopelessly entangled in them. This entanglement in traditionalism is quite understandable considering that both Hung Hsiu-ch'üan and Feng Yün-shan, the leaders who were largely responsible for the Taiping ideology, were unsuccessful candidates in the examinations.

The attitude of the Taiping leaders toward Confucius was ambiguous. In the "Taiping Heavenly Chronicle," written in the year 1848 and edited and published by Hung Jen-kan in 1862, it is stated that after having been reprimanded by God Confucius was allowed "to stay in heaven to enjoy happiness" in consideration of his "past merit which balanced up his sins." The nature of his past merit is not mentioned. In an earlier work, "Proclamation on the Origin of the Principles of World Salvation," (Yüan-tao chiu-shih ko), an appendix called "An Ode on Correctness" (Pai-cheng ko), pictured Confucius as one of the model sages in the following words:

> Confucius rendered 3,000 disciples submissive to instructions,
> Because he, by correct doctrines, converted those who were
>   incorrect.[15]

Here Confucius was praised for exactly that for which he was reprimanded later. The *ko* or ode was allowed to appear in 1852 when the whole series was published but was completely expunged in the 1859 edition. This suggests that Hung had not been sure of the position of Confucius in his own system of ideology at the beginning of the Taiping movement. At any rate, Hung did not desert Confucius completely. At the very moment when complete condemnation of Confucius was expected, his "merit" was recognized.

Traditionalism affected all phases of the Taiping ideology in specific ways. I shall attempt to indicate and analyze the effects of classical and

[14] Theodore Hamberg reports in *The Visions of Hung-Siu-tshuen, and Origin of the Kwang-si Insurrection*, p. 23, that Hung read the following passage from Liang A-fa's "Good Words to Admonish the Age": "It is therefore highly desirable that the man (or men) of the great and glorious Middle Kingdom who sees these books should not vainly boast of his own country being the land of true principles of propriety and fine literature, but with a humble mind put aside his own *prejudices* [italics are mine], and the thought of from what country they are derived, and consider that the God of Heaven created us to be men, and every one who is a man ought to know the saving doctrines of the Holy Scriptures."

[15] Translation is by J. Milton Mackie, in *Life of Tai-ping-wang, Chief of the Chinese Insurrection*, p. 352.

Confucian traditions on the religious, moral, social, economic, and political philosophies of the Taipings.

RELIGIOUS BORROWINGS FROM TRADITIONAL SOURCES

Taiping Conception of T'ien

The most important religious concept which the Taipings adapted from the Confucian and classical sources was the concept of T'ien or Shang-ti or Huang Shang-ti.

The first question that suggests itself is: did the term *T'ien* and its alternates mean the same thing to the Taipings as their terms for the Christian God or Jehovah? Were these identical terms that brought the same psychological responses? The answer is yes. This identification is clear from the Taipings' use of *T'ien* or its alternates when they had in mind what they thought to be the Christian God. In the older edition of "The Book of Heavenly Commandments" (T'ien-t'iao-shu) they proclaimed God the universal father of men and thereby refuted the traditional idea that only an emperor had the right to make sacrifices to T'ien. Since God is the universal father of men, he should be worshiped by all and not by the emperor alone. The Taipings cited from the *Book of History*, the *Book of Poetry*, and the *Book of Changes* to show that T'ang of the Shang and King Wen of the Chou worshiped God when they were only *chu-hou* (諸侯 vassal lords) and the people of the Yin or any people, including the wicked ones who were willing to effect an internal change through fasting and cleansing, worshiped God.[16] The Taipings used these traditional references to show that the worship of God was not an innovation from foreign lands but an ancient practice indigenous to China. Here the identification of the object of Christian worship with the object of the emperor's sacrifice and other ancient sages' worship is conclusively proved. God had been universally worshiped in ancient times; but the Chinese had deviated from the right way, being misled by the devil, while the foreign countries of the West had followed the right way of worship.[17]

In the revised edition of "The Book of Heavenly Commandments" many of the classical quotations are deleted, but the emphasis on the

---

[16] Preface to the "revised" edition of "T'ien-t'iao-shu," in Hsiao, I-shan (compiler), *T'ai-p'ing t'ien-kuo ts'ung-shu*, ts'e 1, pp. 1a–4a. The word "revised" is put in quotes because what Hsiao considered as revised is really the original or earlier edition.

[17] *Ibid.*, pp. 3b–4a.

universal right to worship God as the ancients had done remains unchanged. A similar line of thought was developed later by Hung Jen-kan
in "The Book on the Principles of the Heavenly Nature." He said: "Just
think. In ancient times there was nothing but the true way, and everybody, whether emperor, minister, scholar, or commoner, worshiped
Huang Shang-ti."[18] Jen-kan went on to cite almost identical passages
from the classics to prove his point. He also attacked the emperor's
prerogative of T'ien worship: "Then the worldly wind [way of life]
declined daily. Furthermore, those who in all appearance were rulers
were so blind and absurd in their mind that they, with a perverted view
of their own dignity and importance, declared that all below the rank of
prime minister were not allowed to make sacrifices to T'ien."[19] There is
not the least doubt that in the minds of Taiping leaders the terms designating the Christian God had the same connotation as *T'ien* and its
alternates.

If to the Taiping leaders the term *T'ien* connotes the same thing as
"God," it is reasonable to assume that the original conception of T'ien
has certain characteristics which are shared by the Taiping Christian
conception of God. We need not assume that the Taipings used both
conceptions interchangeably on account of these common features, but
these features would certainly make the Taiping religious practice more
intelligible. A cursory survey of some of the classical and Confucian
literature reveals that many characteristics which the Taipings attributed to their Christian God are present in the traditional conception of
T'ien. One of these characteristics is the parenthood of T'ien (heaven)
and *ti* (earth). In the *Book of Poetry*, there is the following line: "O vast
and distant Heaven, whom we Father and Mother call, to thee I cry."[20]
And in the *Book of History*: "Heaven and earth are the father and mother
of the ten thousand things."[21] This idea has always been present in the
minds of Confucian philosophers. For instance, Tung Chung-shu of the
Han said: "The monarch who has received the mandate is given the
mandate by the will of T'ien; for this reason he is called *t'ien-tzu* (天子
the Son of Heaven), looks upon T'ien as his father, and serves T'ien
with filial piety."[22] And Chang Tsai of the Sung said: *"Ch'ien* (乾 Heav-

---

[18] "T'ien-ch'ing tao-li shu," in Hsiao, *Ts'ung-shu, ts'e* 5, p. 4a.
[19] *Ibid.*, p. 6a.
[20] *Mao-shih yin-te*, 47/198/1.
[21] *Shang-shu t'ung-chien*, 21/0031–0037.
[22] Tung Chung-shu, *Ch'un-ch'iu fan-lu*, "Shen-ch'a ming-hao," 10:1–4,

en) is my father and *k'un* (坤 earth) is my mother...the people are my brothers, and all things are my comrades."[23]

Later Hung Jen-kan, in "A Hero's Submission to Truth" (Ying-chieh kuei-chen), drew a parallel between the Christian belief that the souls and spiritual nature of the people of all nations are born of the Heavenly Father and implications of the same idea in statements found in the classics and Mencius. Jen-kan quoted such classical statements as *T'ien chiang hsia min* (Heaven having produced the people below),[24] *T'ien sheng cheng-min* (T'ien gave birth to the people), [25] and *wei huang shang-ti chiang chung yü hsia-min* (the Sovereign Supreme Ruler on High conferred benefits on the people below)[26] in drawing the parallel. It seems clear that this parenthood of T'ien or Huang Shang-ti was important to the Taiping leaders.

The parenthood of T'ien need not be taken literally; in the minds of the ancients it may have meant nothing more than the vague idea that things including men sprang up from nature as trees and plants sprang up from the earth, or the idea that T'ien in an unexplained way was the creator of all, or a force which permeates all. This seems to be what is connoted by many of the classical references: "T'ien gave birth to the people,"[27] "T'ien gave birth to me,"[28] "T'ien gave birth to the people who have desires,"[29] or quotations from *Mencius*.[30]

In the *Book of Changes* there is the line: "There was heaven and earth and then there grew up the ten thousand things." Though the relationship between heaven and earth and the ten thousand things here is a temporal sequence, it does not exclude the vague idea that one is the

---

[23] Chang Tsai, *Chang-tzu ch'üan-shu*, 1:3–4. For the identification of *ch'ien* 乾 and *t'ien* 天, see *Chou-i yin-te*, 51/*shuo*/9–10.

[24] *The Works of Mencius*, in Legge, *The Chinese Classics*, II, 156. *Meng-tzu yin-te*, 6/1B/3. According to Chao's commentary, this was quoted from a missing chapter of the *Book of History*. As a matter of fact, we do find in the extant version of the *Book of History* a line which differs in only one word: "*T'ien yu hsia-min* . . ." See *Shang-shu t'ung-chien*, 21/0180–0189. Mencius could have misquoted the line, but since he was such a great authority he was thought by the commentator to have quoted from a lost chapter.

[25] *Mao-shih yin-te*, 67/255/1 and 71/260/1.

[26] *Shang-shu t'ung-chien*, 12/0029–0037.

[27] *Mao-shih yin-te*, 67/255/1 and 71/260/1.

[28] *Ibid.*, 46/197/3.

[29] *Shang-shu t'ung-chien*, 11/0034–0039.

[30] *Meng-tzu yin-te*, 6/1B/3; 37/5A/7; 38/5B/1; 43/6A/6; and particularly 21/3A/5, where Mencius said: "Furthermore, T'ien, in giving birth to things . . . "

cause of the other.[31] Even in this vague sense, we may conceive of the traditional idea of T'ien as having some resemblance to the Taiping conception of God.

The Taipings also thought of T'ien as a sovereign. We have learned that the Taipings allowed God alone to be called *Ti*, implying that he alone was the real ruler. This idea of God[32] as a sovereign was not alien to the ancient Chinese. In *Tso-chuan*, *T'ien* is used to define *chün* (a sovereign)[33] and in Ku-liang's commentary *chün* is the successor of T'ien as the lord of the world.[34] Though in the first case *T'ien* is used to define *chün* rather than *chün* to define *T'ien*, the function of T'ien as a sovereign is clear.

In both Tso and Ku-liang there has been an attempt to identify the will of the ruler with that of T'ien. We know how the Taipings labored this point to obtain complete obedience from their subordinates.

There are many passages in classical sources where *T'ien* is used to imply a heavenly government in much the same way as the Taipings used the term. The classical sources contain such phrases as: "receiving from T'ien one hundred [kinds of] salary,"[35] or "Tien conferring upon you salary,"[36] or "receiving salary from T'ien."[37] In *Mencius* there is a tendency to use *T'ien* in another way, also implying a heavenly government. Mencius spoke of *t'ien-chüeh* (heavenly rank),[38] *t'ien-wei* (heavenly position) and *t'ien-chih* (heavenly office),[39] *t'ien-li* (heavenly clerk [official]),[40] or *t'ien-min* (heavenly subject).[41] This use of *T'ien* as an adjective is shared by the Taipings. In all these phrases it is apparent that T'ien was conceived of as a sovereign who appointed people to positions with rank, salary, and function.

In the classics, particularly in the *Book of History*, T'ien is often represented as the protector of the people. In the *Book of History* alone, the following passages occur: "T'ien above protect the people below";[42] "Sove-

---

[31] *Chou-i yin-te*, 53/Hsü/2.

[32] Having identified the Taiping usage of *T'ien* and "God," we shall hereafter use them as synonyms.

[33] *Ch'un-ch'iu ching-chuan yin-te*, 185/Hsüan 4/note.

[34] *Ibid.*, 205/Hsüan 15/Ku.

[35] *Mao-shih yin-te*, 35/166/2.

[36] *Ibid.*, 63/247/7.

[37] *Ibid.*, 64/249/1.

[38] *Meng-tzu yin-te*, 46/6A/16.

[39] *Ibid.*, 40/5B/3.

[40] *Ibid.*, 16/2B/8.

[41] *Ibid.*, 52/7A/19.

[42] *Shang-shu t'ung-chien*, 12/0142–0147.

reign T'ien protect the Shang";[43] "T'ien protect the people below."[44] Though there are many other passages dwelling on the same theme, these suffice to indicate that the ancients considered God a protector.

Intelligence was an attribute of T'ien. We have dwelt on the Taipings' conception of God's intelligence and may safely say that for them God was omniscient and infallible. The classics also abound in passages suggesting such a connotation. The *Book of History* contains many references to T'ien's intelligence: "T'ien's intelligence is revealed through our people's intelligence."[45] "T'ien observes his virtue."[46] "T'ien is intelligent."[47] "Shang-ti oversees the people."[48] In the *Analects*, Confucius spoke of the impossibility of cheating T'ien, an idea the Taipings exploited to the full.[49] Confucius also appealed to T'ien when he found man failed to recognize him. He said, "Perhaps T'ien will know me!"[50]

As we have seen, the Taipings thought of God as having emotions. He loves his sons and becomes angry when the people forsake him and take to the way of the devil. The Taipings thought of God as kind and compassionate but jealous. T'ien in the minds of the ancient Chinese exhibits the same emotions: Tien is said to be compassionate and to love the people.[51] T'ien so loves the people that he grants them their wishes.[52] The sovereign T'ien is often angry when the people are misruled.[53] This anger finds vent in the punishment of the wicked. Tung Chung-shu of the Han describes the emotional nature of T'ien in the following words: "Heaven has its own feelings of joy and anger and a mind which experiences sadness and pleasure, analogous to those of man."[54]

[43] *Ibid.*, 14/0265–0270.

[44] *Ibid.*, 21/0180–0183.

[45] *Ibid.*, 04/0299–0306.

[46] *Ibid.*, 14/0038–0041.

[47] *Ibid.*, 17/0293–0296.

[48] *Ibid.*, 47/0113–0116. A similar idea is found in the *Book of Poetry*: "T'ien oversees the world below," or "T'ien oversees the Chou." *Mao-shih yin-te*, 59/236/4 and 71/260/1.

[49] *Lun-yü yin-te*, 16/9/12.

[50] *Ibid.*, 29/14/35.

[51] *Shang-shu t'ung-chien*, 21/0397–0400; 32/0280–0286. See also *Ch'un-ch'iu ching-chuan yin-te*, 281/Hsiang 14/fu 3 (6).

[52] *Shang-shu t'ung-chien*, 21/0279–0290; *Ch'un-ch'iu ching-chuan yin-te*, 334/Hsiang 31/4 Tso and 339/Chao 1/2 Tso. In the last reference, the author is quoting from the "T'ai-shih" in the *Book of History*.

[53] *Shang-shu t'ung-chien*, 21/0108–0111.

[54] Tung Chung-shu, *Ch'un-ch'iu fan-lu t'ung-chien*, 12:2a, translated by Fung Yu-lan in *A Short History of Chinese Philosophy*, p. 194.

The Taipings, though they seldom mentioned the sources of their fatalism, drew heavily upon their traditional background. Reserving a complete discussion of the moral principle of fatalism for a later section, we shall here take up only the idea of T'ien as a fatalistic principle. In the classical and Confucian sources are lines which subsequently became stock phrases with the Chinese; the Taipings reiterated these expressions just as other Chinese people did to rationalize their behavior. The line the Taipings repeated most often is found in the *Analects*: "Death and life are matters of fate, and wealth and honor are in the hand of T'ien."[55] This coupling of T'ien and *ming* (命 fate), which the Taipings so often adopted, is also found in Mencius, who said: "In connection with the way of T'ien, sages [consider it] *ming*."[56] In conceiving of T'ien as a fatalistic principle, the Taipings made a transition from religion to philosophy.

The Taipings made full use of the traditionally accepted moral nature of God, though they did not always cite the classical sources which discussed this moral nature.[57] The Taipings spoke of the Heavenly Father's love of life as a modification of a line in the *Book of Changes*: "The great virtue of heaven and earth is called life."[58]

God's virtuous nature is revealed in other Taiping lines: "The way of T'ien is to bring calamity to evildoers and to give happiness to the good."[59] "But God is not constant: he causes one hundred good things to happen to those who do good, and a hundred misfortunes to descend upon those who do evil."[60] Hung Jen-kan did give the source of the idea in the second quotation as the *Book of History*;[61] but these expressions usually appeared without source, as would any expression in common use. The classics are filled with such expressions.

The few given here are from the *Book of History*:

[55] *Lun-yü yin-te*, 22/12/5.

[56] *Meng-tzu yin-te*, 57/7B/24.

[57] This failure to give sources need not be taken as an indication of the Taipings' attempt to avoid connection with the traditional pattern of thought, which in some cases they did try to do; for the idea or ideas have been so thoroughly absorbed into the fibre of the Chinese popular mind that nobody bothers to find out where they originated.

[58] *Chou-i yin-te*, 45/Hsi, *hsia*/1.

[59] "Yüan-tao chiu-shih ko," in Ch'eng, *Shih-liao*, II, 1a.

[60] "Ying-chieh kuei-chen," in Hsiao, *Ts'ung-shu*, *ts'e* 10, p. 34a.

[61] *Shang-shu t'ung-chien*, 13/0311–0328.

The way of Heaven is to bring calamity to evildoers and to give happiness to the good.[62]

T'ien has no relative; those who are reverent are its relatives. [T'ien gives no favors, only those who are reverent receive its favors.][63]

Ghosts and spirits do not accept sacrifice with constancy: they accept the sacrifice of those who are reverent. *T'ien-wei* [heavenly position] is difficult [to maintain]: virtue results in peace while wickedness results in chaos.[64]

Not that T'ien plays favoritism with our Shang; T'ien extends protection to the virtuous.[65]

Whether T'ien confers calamity or happiness depends on virtue.[66]

Sovereign T'ien has no relative: it assists the virtuous.[67]

Two more examples are quoted from the *Ch'un-ch'iu*:

T'ien protects those with enlightened virtue.[68]

Shu-sun said, "Perhaps T'ien enriches the evildoer, for Ch'ing-feng is rich again." Mu-tzu said, "The riches of the good are their reward; but the riches of evildoers are their misfortune. T'ien will cause misfortune to descend upon him [Ch'ing-feng]. When he has collected his clan together they will be wiped out."[69]

These examples provide some idea of the connection between the Taiping idea of the moral nature of T'ien and that found in the classical sources. To be sure the idea is somewhat indefinite, for we do not yet know the meaning ascribed to "good" and "evil," though we do know that T'ien is on the side of the good and against the evil.

The Taipings made use of the Christian Ten Commandments and called them *Shih-t'ien-t'iao* (Ten Heavenly Precepts or Commandments). The idea of heavenly commandments or taboos was present in ancient times.[70] This line occurs in the *Book of Changes*: "Then are seen *t'ien-tse*

---

[62] *Ibid.*, 12/0085–0090.

[63] *Ibid.*, 14/0439–0446.

[64] *Ibid.*, 14/0455–0473.

[65] *Ibid.*, 15/0100–0111.

[66] *Ibid.*, 15/0145–0151.

[67] *Ibid.*, 37/0138–0145.

[68] *Ch'un-ch'iu ching-chuan yin-te*, 182/Hsüan 3/5 Tso.

[69] *Ibid.*, 321–322/Hsiang 28/6 Tso. For detail, see the story told in *Tso-chuan*.

[70] *Shang-shu t'ung-chien*, 09/0049–0054: "The early kings were respectfully mindful of the *t'ien-chieh* [heavenly taboos]." *Ch'un-ch'iu ching-chuan yin-te*, 108/Hsi 15/11 Kung: "*T'ien chieh* [Heaven warns] him, therefore makes him great." *T'ien-chieh* in the first quotation is a noun phrase, but in the second quotation *t'ien chieh* forms a clause with *t'ien* as the subject and *chieh* as the predicate.

(heavenly precepts)."[71] And in *Tso-chuan* there is the phrase *t'ien-fa* (heavenly laws).[72] The Taipings did not quote any of these phrases exactly. There is a possibility, however remote, that the Taipings were conditioned through their early acquaintance with these classical phrases to accept the idea of heavenly precepts from Christianity.

The idea of *t'ien-ming* (天命 heavenly mandate), which the Taipings used so extensively, is deep-rooted in Chinese tradition and is immensely popular with the Chinese at large. It has been the justification for rulers in their attempt to maintain their power and also for rebellious forces in their struggle to wrest that power away. Both legitimacy and the right to revolt are based upon this concept of the heavenly mandate, which was so prevalent in ancient times that the pages of the classics contain many allusions to it. For example:

> *T'ien ming yu te* [Heaven confers its mandate upon the virtuous].[73]
> *Ch'ih t'ien chih ming* [Administer the mandate of Heaven].[74]
> *Yu ming tzu t'ien, ming tz'u Wen-wang* [There is a mandate from Heaven which is conferred upon King Wen].[75]
> *T'ien so ming yeh* [This mandate is conferred by Heaven].[76]

That the good shall supplant the evil is determined by the mandate of Heaven.[77] The mandate of Heaven was not thought to be given once and for all time, but rather as transferable, as was illustrated by the change of rule from Hsia to Shang, and from Shang to Chou. For example, T'ang of the Shang was thought to have received the mandate of Heaven to replace Hsia.[78] This idea of transferability of the mandate of Heaven is expressed repeatedly in the classics, especially in the *Book of History* and *Book of Poetry*.[79] It inspired, on the one hand, a desire to keep the mandate by living according to the way of T'ien; and it led, on the other

[71] *Chou-i yin-te*, 2/1/yen. And *Mao-shih yin-te*, 61/241/7, says, "following the principles of God."

[72] "To make an effort to observe *t'ien-fa* [the heavenly laws]," *Ch'un-ch'iu ching-chuan yin-te*. 422/Chao 26/7 Tso.

[73] *Shang-shu t'ung-chien*, 04/0275–0278.

[74] *Ibid.*, 05/0534–0537.

[75] *Mao-shih yin-te*, 59/236/6.

[76] *Ch'un-ch'iu ching-chuan yin-te*, 182/Hsüan 3/5 Tso.

[77] "That the good takes the place of the bad is a matter of heavenly mandate," (*Shan chih tai pu-shan t'ien-ming yeh*). *Ibid.*, 328/Hsiang 29/fu 8.

[78] "Heaven then conferred assistance and mandate on Ch'eng-t'ang to discontinue the mandate given to Hsia." *Shang-shu t'ung-chien*, 21/0416–0425.

[79] *Ibid.*, 43/0085–0092; 16/0073–0078; 36/0011–0020. *Mao-shih yin-te*, 58/235/5.

hand, to the idea that through a new mandate one may act for T'ien to punish the wicked and, perhaps, become the new Son of Heaven. In ancient times those in power concerned themselves with perpetuating the mandate, while those trying to acquire power claimed they were acting in behalf of T'ien.[80]

From the idea of the heavenly mandate evolved another idea: if one acts in accordance with the way of T'ien one will be preserved; if one acts contrary to the will of T'ien one will be destroyed. The idea of living in accordance with T'ien is found in the *Book of Changes*: "The revolution of T'ang and Wu was in accordance with T'ien and in response to men."[81] The coupling of this idea with its opposite, *i t'ien* (逆天 acting contrary to Heaven) is found in Mencius: *Shun t'ien che ts'un, i t'ien che wang* (Those who act in accordance with Heaven will be preserved, and those who act against Heaven will be destroyed.)[82]

How did the Taipings adapt the mandate of Heaven to their frame of thought? They constantly reiterated *Shun t'ien che ts'un, i t'ien che wang*, claiming that they were in accordance with T'ien and hence legitimate rulers. They condemned the Manchus as acting contrary to T'ien and maintained that they should therefore be destroyed. In their attempt to overthrow the Manchus, the Taipings considered themselves instruments of T'ien, enacting the law of Heaven.[83]

The Taipings demanded great reverence for God; a similar sentiment toward T'ien is found in the minds of the ancients, as a line from the *Book of History* illustrates: "Kung [King Ch'eng, referring to the Duke

---

[80] The following quotations from *Shang-shu t'ung-chien* express a desire to preserve the heavenly mandate: "Keep eternally the heavenly mandate," 11/0331–0334; "May Heaven perpetuate my mandate at this new capital," 16/0095–0103; "Let not the precious mandate which has been conferred by Heaven fall," 26/0154–0160; "May the king be virtuous in order to pray for Heaven to perpetuate the mandate," 32/0601–0609. For the idea of acting in behalf of Heaven, see *Shang-shu t'ung-chien* 22/0165–0173: "Now I, Fa, respectfully carry out T'ien's punishment"; and 34/0430–0435, "I thus openly carry out T'ien's punishment"; and 34/0525–0533; and 38/0756–0765.

[81] *Chou-i yin-te*, 30/49/T'uan. Other examples from the same source are 3/2/T'uan "Then act in accordance with T'ien"; and 28/45/T'uan, "to act in accordance with *t'ien-ming* [heavenly mandate]."

[82] *Meng-tzu yin-te*, 27/4A/7.

[83] In "T'ien-ch'ing tao-li shu," in Hsiao, *Ts'ung-shu*, ts'e 5, p. 25a, Kan Wang said, "Enact the law on the authority of T'ien." And Yang and Hsiao issued their joint proclamation against the Manchus in the name of T'ien, saying in "Pan-hsing chao-shu," in Ch'eng, *Shih-liao*, I, 1a, "Exterminate the devil on the authority of T'ien."

of Chou], it is not your idea to dare not to revere the goodness of T'ien."[84] Often this reverence was accompanied by awe or fear, since T'ien assumed a majestic air that inspired such feeling.[85] Reverence was also extended to *kuei* (ghosts) and *shen* (spirits). The *Li-chi* says: "Revere the ghosts and spirits."[86] And Confucius said: "Revere the ghosts and spirits but keep at a distance from them."[87]

T'ien was also thought of as the abode of the dead. The Taipings spoke often of *shang-t'ien* (上天 going up to heaven) or *chuan-t'ien* (轉天 being transferred to heaven) or *sheng-t'ien* (昇天 ascending to heaven), heaven being a place for the dead to go. Hung in his vision saw Confucius in heaven. This conception was not alien to the Chinese ancients, for the *Book of Poetry* says: "The three sovereigns are in heaven."[88] The Taiping conception of T'ien as discussed above is remarkably traditional; but it also has its non-Confucian aspect, which will be discussed in a later section.

Although the Taipings made religious sacrifice to T'ien a practice open to everyone instead of the privilege of the emperor alone, the Taipings' idea of sacrifice seems derived from traditionalism rather than from any foreign source. The use of grain and animals for sacrifice is an old Chinese tradition, dating as far back in Chinese history as one can trace. From the *Li-chi* we learn, for instance, that the sacrifices of *chiao* (郊, a sacrifice offered to T'ien) and *she* (社, a sacrifice offered to earth) are for the purpose of worshiping Shang-ti (the Supreme Ruler on High, or God).[89] The sacrifice to T'ien at *chiao* (also meaning beyond the city wall where the sacrificial ceremony takes place) expresses the highest reverence for God.[90] The bronzes are sacrificial vessels for the purpose of holding either food or wine. The term *hsi-sheng* 犧牲 used in sacrificial

---

[84] "*Kung pu-kan pu-ching t'ien chih-hsiu*," in *Shang-shu t'ung-chien*, 33/0089–0096. The phrase *ching-t'ien chih-hsiu* occurs again in a later passage, 33/0130–0133.

[85] "In respectful dignity, revere and fear the mandate of T'ien." *Ibid.*, 35/0082–0087. In the *Book of Poetry* we find phrases like these: *ching t'ien chih nu* (revere the anger of T'ien), and *wei t'ien chih wei* (fear the majestic air of T'ien). *Mao-shih yin-te*, 66/254/8 and 74/272. These phrases are quoted in *Ch'un-ch'iu ching-chuan yin-te*, 435/ Chao 32/5 Tso and 171/Wen 15/12 Tso. See also *Meng-tzu yin-te*, 5/1B/3.

[86] *Li-chi yin-te*, 1/42.

[87] *Lun-yü yin-te*, 11/6/22. *Li-chi* contains a similar idea: "Worship the ghosts and revere the spirits, but keep at a distance from them." *Li-chi yin-te*, 32/12–13.

[88] *Mao-shih yin-te*, 62/243/1. "The three sovereigns" refers to Ta Wang, Wang Chi, and Wen Wang.

[89] *Li-chi yin-te*, 31/13.

[90] *Ibid.*, 10/35.

worship refers to animal sacrifice, *hsi* meaning "pure white" and *sheng* meaning "bull," "ram," or "boar." And the term *tzu-sheng* 粢盛 indicates that grains were also used as sacrificial offerings. In the sacrifice to T'ien the bull was used,[91] and in the sacrifice to the earth and spirits of the grains all three animals—bull, ram, and boar—were used.[92] In all cases, only male animals were used for sacrifices.[93]

Taiping Understanding of Shen

The Taipings called their God the only true *shen* (神 spirit), a term which they probably took from Liang A-fa, but which also appears in the traditional writings.

In the classics, *shen* is often coupled with *T'ien*.[94] And in *Shuo-wen* under *shen*, Hsü Shen said: "*T'ien-shen* is that which leads forth the ten thousand things."[95] In the *Chou-li*, *t'ien-shen* is mentioned in connection with music and dances.[96]

What, then, did the term *t'ien-shen* mean to the ancients? In his commentary on the meaning of *t'ien-shen* in the *Chou-li*, Cheng Hsüan of the Han said: "By *t'ien-shen* is meant the five gods and the sun, the moon, and the stars."[97] Chia Kung-yen of the T'ang made a similar comment: "This *t'ien-shen* means also the sun, the moon, and the stars, but not the

[91] "In sacrificing to heaven, the bull is used." *Ibid.*, 11/1.

[92] "But in sacrificing to the earth and the spirits of the grains, *t'ai-lao* is used." *Ibid.*, 11/1. The same thing is given in another connection in *ibid.*, 5/34: "When the Son of Heaven sacrifices to the earth and the spirits of the grains, *t'ai-lao* is always used; and when vassal lords sacrifice to the earth and the spirits of the grains, *shao-lao* is always used." In the Kung-yang commentary on *Ch'un-ch'iu*, we find the terms *t'ai-lao* and *shao-lao* explained in the following words: "When bull, ram, and boar, the three *sheng*, are all complete, it is called *t'ai-lao*. . . . When there are only two *sheng*, the ram and the boar, but no bull, then it is called *shao-lao*." *Ku-liang chuan*, Duke Huan 8, *chüan* 5, p. 2b.

[93] *Li-chi* says: "The sacrificial animals used [must be] white and male," and "The sacrificial [white] animals used must not be female." *Li-chi yin-te*, 14/2 and 6/9.

[94] "*Wei tien shen-t'ien*" (in charge of the sacrifices to *shen-t'ien*), *Shang-shu t'ung-chien*, 38/0427–0430. In *Chou-li* we find *t'ien-shen* as the object of worship: "[The office of] *ta-tsung-po* is in charge of the ceremony of [worshiping] *t'ien-shen*," and "On the arrival of the winter solstice, sacrifice to *t'ien-shen*." *Chou-li yin-te* 5/10a and 6/57a. In connection with the worship and sacrifice to *t'ien-shen*, certain specific music is mentioned: *ibid.*, 6/2b and 6/4a–b.

[95] Tuan Yü-ts'ai, *Shuo-wen chieh-tzu chu*, in *Huang-ch'ing ching-chieh*, 641a:4b.

[96] *Chou-li* says: "Use *huang-chung* and *ta-lü* [both keys or modes of music] and *yün-men* [dance] to worship *t'ien-shen*," and "At the sixth change of the music, sacrifice to *t'ien-shen*." *Chou-li yin-te*, 6/2b and 6/4a.

[97] *Chou-li chu-shu*, 22:22b.

great *t'ien-shen.*"[98] And in another place, Cheng identified Shang-ti with *wu-ti* (the five gods).[99] Thus in the Han dynasty scholars thought the ancients identified Shang-ti with *t'ien-shen.* However, to say that *Shang-ti* or *t'ien-shen* meant only the five gods does not necessarily destroy the conception of *t'ien-shen* as the supreme God; for at the time Chia Kung-yen identified *t'ien-shen* with the sun, the moon, and the stars, he also affirmed the idea of a great *t'ien-shen* 大天神, the supreme heavenly deity.

It is believed that Hsü Shen implied the idea of a supreme deity in his statement that *t'ien-shen* was that which led forth the ten thousand things. For Hsü Hao of the Ch'ing wrote this note to the statement: "Heaven and earth give birth to the ten thousand things: there is a lord of these things, and it is called *shen.* . . . It is said in the chapter on "Hsiu-wen' in *Shuo-yüan* [a work by Liu Hsiang of the Han], '*Shen* is the source of heaven and earth, and the origin of the ten thousand things' "[100]

Apart from these quotations, *t'ien-shen* is in most cases coupled with *ti-ch'i* 地祇. In *Yü-p'ien* 玉篇, *ch'i* 祇 is defined as the *shen* of the earth. Even in Hsü Shen's *Shuo-wen*, the statement on *t'ien-shen* is followed by a statement on *ti-ch'i.*[101] In such cases it is more logical to think of *shen* in the plural sense, speaking of "spirits of heaven" instead of "the spirit of heaven." Thus the ancients spoke of *pai-shen* (百神, one hundred—or simply all—*shen*).[102]

In ancient times the spirits often descended upon people who were refined and devoted and capable of being equable, respectful, sincere and upright. Such men were called *hsi* (覡 sorcerers); and such women were called *wu* (巫 witches). It was these sorcerers and witches who assigned dwelling places to the spirits, determined their positions at the sacrifices, and arranged their order of precedence.[103] In the *Chou-li* there

[98] *Ibid.*, 32:17a.

[99] Commenting on "When there are great affairs in the state, sacrifices will be offered to Shang-ti and *ssu-wang*," Cheng said: "Shang-ti means *wu-ti.*" *Ibid.*, 18:20b.

[100] Ting Fu-pao, *Shuo-wen chieh-tzu ku-lin*, I, 40. The *Shuo-yüan* quotation is from *Shuo-yüan*, XIX, 1a.

[101] "*Ti-ch'i* is that which raises the ten thousand things." There are many other cases of such coupling, though it is not always expressed in the same way. In the *Analects* we find the expression: *shang-hsia shen-ch'i* (spirits and deities of heaven above and earth below). *Lun-yü yin-te*, 13/7/35. Identical expressions are found in the *Book of History*: see *Shang-shu t'ung-chien*, 12/0081–0084 and 14/0026–0029. *Shang* and *hsia* in these places mean "heaven" and "earth."

[102] *Mao-shih yin-te*, 65/252/3 and 75/273/1; *Li-chi yin-te*, 23/3; *Meng-tzu yin-te*, 36/5A/5.

[103] *Kuo-yü, chüan* 18, "Ch'u-yü," *hsia*, pp. 1–2. In spite of the distinction in gender made by *Kuo-yü* between *hsi* and *wu*, the latter term was used generically for both male and female. See *Chou-li yin-te*, 5:8a, where *nan-wu* (man witches) are mentioned.

was an office called *ssu-wu,* whose function was to take charge of the administration of *wu* affairs.[104] Those who made *wu* their profession were called *shen-shih* 神士.[105]

Thus the Taiping use of *shen* to characterize God has the sanction of Chinese classical tradition, and the Taiping practice of falling into trances may be traced to the ancient activities of the *hsi* and *wu.* The influence of traditionalism on Taiping ideology in this case may not be direct, for it may have come through other sources, such as Liang A-fa's tracts and popular beliefs and practice. But there is no denying that the influence was there.

The term *shen* was, of course, used in other senses than those discussed. For example, its use in connection with *kuei* (ghost) suggests that *shen* denoted also the spirit of the dead.[106] *Shen* was also used to describe the spirituality of a sage[107] and the mysterious nature of things.[108] Since this book is concerned only with the Taiping borrowings from tradition, these other aspects of *shen* have not been considered.

MORAL BORROWINGS FROM TRADITIONAL SOURCES

The Taipings borrowed many of their moral values from classical and Confucian sources. We shall consider together the verbal and conceptual relationships between the Taiping moral system and its classical and Confucian sources, realizing that verbal similarity does not necessarily prove conceptual connection.

Nature and Human Nature

The formal aspect of the moral nature of the world has been considered and its relationship to the classical and Confucian sources established. To give content to this formal idea is our present task.

In Chapter II we suggested that the Taipings believed that man is the most intelligent being of all things and that human nature is originally good. The verbal connection between classical references and Taiping

---

[104] *Chou-li chu-shu* (1926 revision), 6:39b.

[105] *Ibid.,* 5:10a. For explanation of *shen-shih* as those who practiced *wu,* see the commentary.

[106] *Li-chi yin-te,* 1/6; 1/24; 1/42; 9/2; 9/4; 9/18; and many others.

[107] *Meng-tzu yin-te,* 57/7B/25: "When the sage is beyond our knowledge, he is what is called a spirit-man." Translation is from Legge, *The Chinese Classics,* II, 490.

[108] *Chou-i yin-te,* 41/Hsi *hsiang*/5, says: "The unfathomable nature of the *yin* and *yang* is called *shen.*" And 50/Shou/5 says: "By *shen* is meant the discourse dealing with the mystery of the ten thousand things."

statements about man's intelligence is obvious. In the *Book of History* there is this line: "Man is the most intelligent [one] among the ten thousand things."[109] This statement differs very little in wording and not at all in meaning from the Taiping version of it: "Among the ten thousand things man is the most intelligent."[110]

In the Taiping discussion of the original nature of man, both Confucius and Mencius were referred to tacitly. In "The Book of Declarations of the Divine Will Made During the Heavenly Father's Descent to Earth" (T'ien-fu hsia-fan chao-shu), in speaking of the education of Hung's son, Yang said that though the "young lord" was born with *hsing pen shan* (性本善 original good nature) he should be taught and guided in time so that *hsing hsiang chin* (性相近 the state of equal goodness by nature) might not become *hsi hsiang yüan* (習相遠 the state of drifting apart through habits).[111] The phrases *hsing pen shan, hsing hsiang chin,* and *hsi hsiang yüan* were familiar to all who had even begun to learn to read and write, for they are the second, third, and fourth lines of a primer called *San-tzu-ching*.[112] The primer takes these lines from the *Analects*, where Confucius is reported to have said: "By nature men are nearly alike; by practice they get to be wide apart."[113]

Mencius makes direct mention of the original goodness of human nature and indirect mention of the preservation of this original good nature, which both Mencius and the Taipings called "mind." It is stated in the first part of "T'eng-wen-kung": "Mencius teaches that nature is good."[114] In the first part of "Chin-hsin" Mencius says: "Preserve the mind and nourish [develop] the nature."[115] "Nourish" means just what Yang meant by *chiao tao* (教導 to teach and guide). The Taipings exhorted the people to "Act in accordance with your original mind forever."[116] According to Mencius this original mind may be lost if people give up ideals for worldly gains. This, Mencius said, "is tantamount to losing one's original mind."[117]

---

[109] *Shang-shu t'ung-chien,* 21/0038–0043.

[110] "T'ai-p'ing chao-shu," in Hsiao, *Ts'ung-shu, ts'e* 1, p. 12b.

[111] Ch'eng, *Shih-liao,* II, 3b.

[112] The primer, written by Ou Shih-tzu of the end of the Sung, received later additions by Ming and Ch'ing scholars.

[113] *Lun-yü yin-te,* 35/17/2. We have used the translation in Legge, *The Chinese Classics,* I, 318.

[114] *Meng-tzu yin-te,* 18/3A/1.

[115] *Ibid.,* 50/7A/1.

[116] "T'ien-fu shih" No. 276, in Hsiao, *Ts'ung-shu, ts'e* 7.

[117] *Meng-tzu yin-te,* 45/6A/10.

The Taipings told their people: "...great will be one's sins when one lets his original mind be overshadowed. If one does not lose one's original mind one will naturally know that the breath of life depends on Heaven."[118] It takes no great imagination to see that the link between the Taiping idea of original mind and that of Mencius is not an accidental one.

The idea of original mind and the original goodness of human nature is probably the reason the Taipings did not and could not understand sin in the same way as Christians understand it. For the latter, it is sin which is original and not the goodness of human nature. This opposite conception of human nature explains why the Taipings failed to grasp the deeper meaning of repentance. For them, as indeed for all Chinese whose pattern of thought has been conditioned by traditionalism, the idea of original sin and repentance appears very strange. Repentance for them does not exist. When they say *hui-kuo* (悔過 regretting mistake) or *kai-kuo* (改過 correcting mistake), they are merely expressing an awareness of some specific misdeed or wrong behavior with a desire to avoid any similar mistake in the future.

Cheng and *Pu-cheng*

The Taipings exemplified the principle of *cheng* 正 in "An Ode on Correctness"[119] and the principle of *pu-cheng* 不正 in "Proclamation on the Origin of the Principles of World Salvation."

The term *cheng* is used in classical sources in very much the same sense as the Taipings used it, that is, in the sense of the principle of uprightness and absolute impartiality.[120] The *Book of Changes* says: " 'Great' means *cheng* [upright]: when one is *cheng* [upright] and great one may be able to see the real nature of heaven and earth."[121] This sense of the term *cheng* comes very close to what Mencius meant by *hao-jan chih ch'i* (浩然之氣 the great breath of life), which later found eloquent expression in the "Cheng-ch'i ko" of Wen Wen-shan of the Sung.[122] And it is significant that the Taipings did use the term *cheng-ch'i* (正氣 the upright breath). A poem supposedly written by Yang runs thus:

---

[118] "T'ai-p'ing chao-shu," in Hsiao, *Ts'ung-shu*, *ts'e* 1, p. 1b.
[119] "Yüan-tao chiu-shih ko, " in Ch'eng, *Shih-liao*, II, 4a–b.
[120] "T'ai-p'ing chiu-shih-ko," in Hsiao, *Ts'ung-shu*, *ts'e* 4, p. 9b.
[121] *Chou-i yin-te*, 21/34/t'uan.
[122] Wen T'ien-hsiang, *Wen Wen-shan ch'üan-chi*, p. 375.

It is fine that younger brothers and sisters have all become mature,
With complete filial piety and complete loyalty they [do their part]
   as loyal subjects:
Looking up, they are not ashamed to face Heaven, looking down
   they feel no qualms at facing men,
The balmy *cheng-ch'i* [which is theirs] fills heaven and earth.[123]

The term occurs again in another poem supposedly by Yang: "August and majestic, *cheng-ch'i* permeates heaven and earth."[124] In another poem *cheng-ch'i* is described as *hao-jan* (浩然 boundless): "The great boundless *cheng-ch'i* reaches the paradise [the hall in heaven]."[125] There is a metaphysical ring to the idea of *cheng-ch'i* as expressed here.

Another sense of *cheng* may be described as ethical. The term may have been used in connection with archery and then borrowed as a figure to illustrate the principle of living. In the *Li-chi* there is this line: "In archery we first demand that we stand straight [upright], and we loose [the arrow] after we have righted ourselves."[126] When this self-righting attitude has been transferred inward, it becomes a moral principle to make the mind—in a moral rather than an intellectual sense—upright. This idea is found in a chapter entitled "Ta-hsüeh" (The Great Learning) in the *Li-chi*.[127] In "An Ode on Correctness" the Taipings conceived of the principle of *cheng* as that which differentiates man from animal.[128] They added: "*Cheng* is the original nature of man." In this ethical sense there is a definite connection between the Taiping use of the term and its classical use.

A third sense in which the term is used is political, an application of the ethical principle in the sphere of politics. In "An Ode on Correctness" it is said:

If *pu-cheng* [one fails to be upright] oneself, the people will follow
   their desires;

---

[123] "T'ien-ch'ing tao-li shu," in Hsiao, *Ts'ung-shu*, *ts'e* 5, p. 41a.

[124] *Ibid.*, p. 45a.

[125] *Ibid.*, p. 49a. *Hao-jan cheng-ch'i* also occurs in another poem on page 49b.

[126] *Li-chi yin-te*, 46/11. *Meng-tzu yin-te*, 13/2A/7, says: "The archer straightens himself before he shoots."

[127] *Li-chi yin-te*, 42/1–2.

[128] "*Cheng* is what differentiates man from birds." "Yüan-tao chiu-shih ko," in Ch'eng, *Shih-liao*, II, 4a. "Birds" is an abbreviated expression for *ch'in-shou* (birds and beasts). To use a part as the whole, a figure of speech known as synecdoche, is a common practice in the Chinese literary world.

If *cheng* [one is upright] oneself, the people will follow what one orders:

If *pu-cheng* [one fails to be upright] oneself, relatives will rebel against one;

If *cheng* [one is upright] oneself, the whole world will place its confidence in one.[129]

It is obvious that the term *shen* (oneself) refers to the ruler. In the "Ode for Youth" under "Chün-tao" we read:

The power over life and death is in the hands of the Son of Heaven;
Ministers shall not disobey.
One man leads out in *cheng*,
Ten thousand countries will all be settled in peace;
The king alone takes power
And the wicked escape to the ninth spring.[130]

For this idea of *cheng* there are numerous references in the classical sources. For example in the *Analects*:

Cheng [government] is *cheng* [to be upright]: if you lead [in the spirit of] *cheng* [being upright], who would dare *pu-cheng* [not to be upright]?[131]

The Master said, "If [one is] upright oneself, [the way] will prevail without an order; if [one is] not upright oneself, [the people] will not follow [one] even with an order."[132]

If [one is] already upright oneself, there is nothing in assuming the responsibility of government; if one fails to be upright oneself, how is one to make others upright?[133]

In *Mencius* we have the following:

I, too, wish to make people's mind upright and exterminate heretic teachings.[134]

If our conduct does not meet with approval of the people, we should all find the reason [for this] in ourselves. If we are upright ourselves, the world will follow us.[135]

[129] *Ibid.*, p. 4a–b.
[130] "Yu-hsüeh-shih," in Hsiao, *Ts'ung-shu, ts'e* 4, pp. 4b–5a.
[131] *Lun-yü yin-te*, 24/12/17.
[132] *Ibid.*, 25/13/6.
[133] *Ibid.*, 25/13/13.
[134] *Meng-tzu yin-te*, 25/3B/9.
[135] *Ibid.*, 27/4A/4.

If the ruler is upright, no one will dare not to be. Once the ruler is upright, the whole country will be pacified.[136]

There are great men; these keep themselves upright and everything becomes upright.[137]

References to *cheng* in its political sense occur in the *Li-chi*:

Cheng [government] is *cheng* [to be upright].[138]

If the ruler is *cheng* [upright], then the people will obey government [orders].[139]

If [one is] not upright oneself and not truthful in words, then one's principle will lack unity and one's conduct will not conform to the norm.[140]

In *Hsün-tzu* it is stated: "If the ruler above is just and upright, it will be easy to straighten up those below."[141] This last statement is found in a chapter entitled "Cheng-lün" (正論 A Discourse on *Cheng*). There is no proof that the Taipings in formulating their idea of the principle of *cheng* were influenced by the title of this chapter, but there is reason to believe that there is at least a verbal link, between the two. First, the Taipings adopted the terms *chün-tao* (君道 the way of the ruler), *ch'en-tao* (臣道 the way of ministers), *chia-tao* (家道 the way of a family), *fu-tao* (父道 the way of a father), *mu-tao*, (母道 the way of a mother), *tzu-tao* (子道 the way of a son), etc.[142] Hsün-tzu in his book wrote one chapter on "Chün-tao," another on "Ch'en-tao," and still another on "Tzu-tao."[143] Secondly, the dictatorial slant of the Taipings fits in well with Hsün-tzu's theory that *sheng-wang* (聖王 the sage kings) should be the teachers and standard in matters of logical discourse and naming.[144] A similar idea is more strongly expressed in Hsün-tzu's chapter entitled "Cheng-ming" (正名 Rectification of Names):

Should a true King arise, he must certainly follow the ancient terms and

---

[136] *Ibid.*, 29/4A/21.

[137] *Ibid.*, 52/7A/19.

[138] *Li-chi yin-te*, 27/2.

[139] *Ibid.*

[140] *Ibid.*, 33/17.

[141] *Hsün-tzu*, 12:214.

[142] "Yu-hsüeh-shih," in Hsiao, *Ts'ung-shu, ts'e* 4.

[143] Mencius also used the terms *chün-tao* and *ch'en-tao*. He said: "If desiring to be a ruler, then live with utmost devotion the way of a ruler; if desiring to be a minister, then live with utmost devotion the way of a minister." *Meng-tzu yin-te*, 26/4A/2.

[144] *Hsün-tzu, chi* 1, *ts'e* 1, 12:228.

make new ones. . . . When the kings had regulated names, the names were fixed and actualities distinguished. Their principles were thus able to be carried out, and their will could be known. They thus carefully led the people to unity. Therefore, the making of unauthorized distinctions between words, and the making of new words, so as thus to confuse the correct nomenclature, cause the people to be in doubt, and bring much litigation, was called great wickedness. It was a crime like that of using false credentials or false measures.[145]

Professor Fung Yu-lan, after quoting this passage, says:

Hsün-tzu then concludes that the rise of all these fallacies is due to the fact that no sage-king exists. Were there to be such a sage-king, he would use his political authority to unify the minds of the people, and lead them to the true way of life in which there is no place or need for disputation and argument.[146]

This verbal connection between the ideas of Hsün-tzu and those of the Taipings does not prove their conceptual relationship. The Taipings gave no evidence of any understanding of terms like *chün-tao* and *ch'en-tao* as used by either Mencius or Hsün-tzu. Even if they did actually borrow the terms from Hsün-tzu, they do not seem to have borrowed the ideas. The possibility that the Taipings compared themselves to Hsün-tzu's sage kings is vague, lacking even strict verbal connection. I merely suggest a possible general borrowing.

The Taipings expressed an idea of *cheng* similar to that in the first *Hsün-tzu* quotation in the following words:

If the lord is *cheng* [upright], then the ministers will be straight. If the ruler is enlightened, then the ministers will of course be good.[147]

Even though verbally the Taiping statement is not completely identical with any of the statements quoted, there is no doubt about the conceptual relation between the Taiping idea of *cheng* and that found in the ancient sources. The principle of rectification of names as applied to the political field by the Confucians is another aspect of the *cheng* concept. The Taipings made full use of this aspect of the concept to strengthen

[145] *Ibid.*, p. 275.
[146] Fung Yu-lan, *A Short History of Chinese Philosophy*, p. 153. The translation of the passage from *Hsün-tzu* is Fung's (p. 152).
[147] "Yu-hsüeh-shih," in Hsiao, *Ts'ung-shu, ts'e* 4, p. 5a.

their system of social distinctions, the ultimate purpose of which was political control.

Principle of Li

Li is the moral principle that regulates social conduct by defining the groups that make up society and establishing correct relationships among them. The principle of li embodies the spirit of traditionalism; this is evident in the term li-chiao (禮教 the teaching of li). The ancients thought of li as the "principle of things";[148] and this principle is based in heaven.[149]

The Taipings did not make any general statements about li, but some of their quotations concerning the function of li and the casual yet intimate way they referred to it suggest that they were imbued with the traditional spirit of li. In addition one document was specifically called "Taiping Institution of Li" (T'ai-p'ing li-chih). In "The Book on the Principles of the Heavenly Nature" it is stated: "We should know that among the functions of li, [to achieve] harmony is of the highest value."[150] This statement is an exact quotation from the Analects,[151] and there is one line in the Li-chi where a similar thought is directly expressed: "Harmony and peace are the function of li."[152]

In the Taipings' "Ode for Youth" it is said: "The principle that governs the two hands is none other than respect, and [the hands should not do anything] contrary to li."[153] Again in "Proclamation on the Origin of the Principles of World Salvation": "Yen Hui loved learning and never made a mistake twice; and he had four taboos [against activity contrary to li] for the purpose of drilling his spirit."[154]

The quality of kung (恭 respect) is indeed related to li in the Li-chi.

Kung chin li (Respect is close to li).[155]
Dignity, reverence, kung, and compliance form the formula of li.[156]
Kung, frugality, dignity, and reverence are the teachings of li.[157]

---

[148] "By li 禮 is meant li 理 (the principle of things)." Li-chi yin-te, 28/4.
[149] "Li must have basis in heaven." Ibid., 9/2 and 9/32.
[150] "T'ien-ch'ing tao-li shu," in Hsiao, Ts'ung-shu, ts'e 5, p. 30b.
[151] Lun-yü yin-te, 2/1/12.
[152] Li-chi yin-te, 47/4.
[153] "Yu-hsüeh-shih," in Hsiao, Ts'ung-shu, ts'e 4, p. 13b.
[154] "Yüan-tao chiu-shih ko," in Ch'eng, Shih-liao, II, 1b.
[155] Li-chi yin-te, 32/9.
[156] Ibid., 19/4.
[157] Ibid., 26/1.

The *Analects* says *Kung chin yü li* (Respect is close to *li*).[158] The reference to Yen Hui is a paraphrase of two other lines found in the *Analects*.[159]

From these quotations it seems clear that the connection between the Taiping conception of *li* and the classical one is more than just verbal.

Moral Precepts and Private Virtues

Moral precepts define the attitude and behavior of one member or one group of society to another; that is, moral precepts indicate the patterns of various social relationships. The Taipings, following the traditional view, spoke of five human relationships[160] and called them heavenly relationships.[161] The special tracts the Taipings issued concerning these relationships for the instruction of their youth indicate that in the statement of relationships was expressed the fundamental pattern of Taiping morality. A survey of classical and Confucian texts reveals that the pattern of Taiping morality was deep-rooted in these texts, and from our own experience we realize that the same pattern of relationships characterizes popular Chinese thought even down to recent times. From what sources did this popular pattern originate?

The relation between brothers is called *t'ien-lun* (heavenly relation) in Ku-liang's commentary on *Ch'un-ch'iu*: *Hsiung ti, t'ien-lun yeh* (Elder brother and younger brother are heavenly relation [heavenly related]).[162] A later statement in the same source implies that the relations between ruler and minister and between father and son are heavenly relations. In other sources these are called great relations or human relations. In the *Analects* Tzu-lu lashed out at the recluse, saying: "Not to take office is to abandon the righteous way. The principle that distinguishes between elder and younger may not be abandoned. How could the principle that distinguishes between ruler and minister be abandoned? These recluses, desiring to keep themselves clean [aloof from politics], have introduced confusion into the great relations."[163]

[158] *Lun-yü yin-te*, 2/1/13.
[159] *Ibid.*, 10/6/3 and 22/12/1.
[160] "T'ai-p'ing chiu-shih-ko," in Hsiao, *Ts'ung-shu, ts'e* 4, p. 9a, says:
    There are five human relations,
    Among which filial piety and brotherly love rank first.
    Once the family is ordered, one will be able to contribute to the state.
    So in [filial piety and brotherly love] there is loyalty already.
[161] "T'ien-fu shih" No. 302, in Hsiao, *Ts'ung-shu, ts'e* 7.
[162] *Ch'un-ch'iu ching-chuan yin-te*, 1/Yin 1/Ku.
[163] *Lun-yü yin-te*, 38/18/7.

In the *Li-chi* the relation between ruler and minister,[164] and the relation between father and son are called *lun* (倫 relation, particularly human relation).[165]

Mencius defined human relations as that which distinguishes man from the beasts.[166] He said:

> With man there is this principle: when well-fed, warmly clothed and comfortably housed and yet without education, he would approach [the state of] the beasts. The sage was concerned with this so he appointed Hsieh 契 to be *ssu-t'u* [司徒 minister of education] to teach men human relations. Thus: between father and son there is love 親; between ruler and minister there is justice 義; between husband and wife there is distinction 別; between elder and the younger there is order 叙 (亦作序); and between friends there is faith 信.[167]

Mencius also refers specifically to the relations between father and son, ruler and minister,[168] and husband and wife[169] as the great relations of man.

The *Li-chi* lists a similar but not exactly identical list of qualities or attitudes: "A father is to be loving, a son filial; an elder brother fraternally kind, a younger brother fraternally obedient; a husband just, a wife obedient; elders kindly, young ones attentive to the elders; and the ruler benevolent, the ministers loyal: these ten are called the human principles."[170]

The list of relationships given in the *Li-chi* includes the relationship between brothers, whereas that given in *Mencius* has in its place the relationship between friends. Nor are the attitudes expressed identical. For the sake of clarity and for convenience in comparing, the differences are listed below:

Relationship of:	*Mencius*	*Li-chi*
Father to son	Love	Love
Son to father	Love	Filial piety

---

[164] "The principle distinguishing ruler from minister is *lun*." *Li-chi yin-te*, 10/5.

[165] *Ibid.*, 25/11; 25/14.

[166] "Human relations" means "social order," for *lun* means *teng ti* 等第; and *lun* may also mean a "universal principle," *lun-ch'ang* 倫常.

[167] *Meng-tzu yin-te*, 20/3A/4. See also 31/4B/19.

[168] *Ibid.*, 14/2B/2.

[169] *Ibid.*, 34/5A/2.

[170] *Li-chi yin-te*, 9/23.

Ruler to ministers	Justice	Benevolence
Ministers to ruler	Justice	Loyalty
Husband to wife	Distinction	Justice
Wife to husband	Distinction	Obedience
Elders to young ones	Order	Kindliness
Young ones to elders	Order	Attentiveness
Friend to friend	Faith	. . . . .
Elder to younger brother	. . . . .	Fraternal kindness
Younger to elder brother	. . . . .	Fraternal obedience

These apparently different views may be partially harmonized by giving different interpretations to the same term. For example, the word *i* 義 may mean "principle," as in the *Hsiao-ching*, where it is said: "Filial piety is the law of T'ien and the *i* [principle] of *ti*."[171] Similarly in the *Ch'un-ch'iu*: "*Li* is the eternal principle of heaven and the regulative principle of earth."[172] Further on, the *Ch'un-ch'iu* says: "*Li* is the *wei* [principle] of the above and the below, and the warp and woof of heaven and earth."[173] The term *wei* here is used in the same sense in which the term *i* is previously used. In this case *wei* may be applied to the ruler. It may mean what is proper, as in *Hsün-tzu*: "In matters of status 分 and what is proper 義, they shall be clearly marked." The commentary of this last statement reads: "By *i* is meant each gets his due."[174] In this case it may be applied to a husband.

I may also mean loyalty unto death, as in Yang Hsiung's *Fa-yen*: "How could it be called *i?*" The commentary here says: "By *i* is meant that ministers and sons die in loyalty to their ruler and father."[175] In this case *i* may be applied to a son in relation to his father or to a minister in relation to his monarch. Also we may speak of "the *i* [principle] governing the husband-wife relationship."[176] In *Hsiao-ching* the way of the father and the son are defined in terms of the *i* [principle] of the ruler and the minister.[177]

The enumeration in the Confucian classics of the specific qualities characterizing these different relations or attitudes of one party

---

[171] *Hsiao-ching, chüan* 3, chap. 7, p. 3b.
[172] *Ch'un-ch'iu ching-chuan yin-te*, Chao-kung/25/2 Tso.
[173] *Ibid.*
[174] *Hsün-tzu*, chi 1, *ts'e* 1, 11:194.
[175] *Fa-yen*, "Yüan-ch'ien," 11:34.
[176] *Li-chi yin-te*, 44/3.
[177] *Hsiao-ching, chüan* 5, chap. 9, p. 6a.

toward the other affords a good opportunity to compare these qualities or attitudes with those the Taipings set down in the "Ode for Youth" and other documents. In the "Ode for Youth" the Taipings emphasized the aspect of *yen* [嚴 strictness] in the father's relationship and reserved love for the mother.[178] A father's strictness and a mother's love are apparently features of the popular mind, for to the Chinese the father is supposed to remain aloof from and be strict with his children, while the mother is the proper vehicle for the expression of parental feelings and love. But since strictness should grow out of love for the children, there is really no conflict between the Taiping idea of the father's attitude and the traditional one.

In the *Hsiao-ching*, the same term *yen* is also used to mean respect for the father: "No conduct of man is greater than filial piety and no filial conduct is greater than *yen* [respect] for the father."[179] In the popular conception as well as in that of the Taipings, *yen* means strictness.

However, the Taipings did not neglect the aspect of love of parents for their children. In "Taiping Songs on World Salvation" (T'ai-p'ing chiu-shih-ko] occur the following lines:

> In taking care of their children, when do a father and a mother enjoy peace at heart? In feeding them and raising them they give their whole attention to everything they do for them. When the children begin to grow up, the parents are concerned with the many pitfalls they may fall into. They teach them with *li* and *i* and all day long try to protect them. There is indeed no limit in their love for their children, the love of a firm heart.[180]

The Taipings also recognized that a son received his body from his parents, in spite of their theory that all men are children of the Heavenly Father. They reminded all children of this fact.[181] This idea is in keeping with the ancient dictum given in the *Hsiao-ching* that one's body and hair and skin were received from one's parents: not to do harm to these parts of one's body is the first step in fulfilling the filial duty of a son.[182]

---

[178] The "Ode for Youth," under "Fu-tao," says: "If the main beams are straight, the lower part will be straight of itself; if [a father is] upright and strict, the way will be complete of itself. Give no cause for the heart of the children to complain, and there will be harmony filling the house." "Yu-hsüeh-shih," in Hsiao, *Ts'ung-shu, ts'e* 4, pp. 5b–6a.

[179] *Hsiao-ching, chüan* 5, chap. 9, p. 1a.

[180] Hsiao, *Ts'ung-shu, ts'e* 4, p. 7a–b.

[181] *Ibid.*

[182] *Hsiao-ching, chüan* 1, chap. 1, p. 3a.

The Taipings were in accord with the ancients not only in this first step of filial piety. They agreed also about the last step. In "Taiping Songs on World Salvation" they emphasized making a name for oneself in order to give honor to the names of one's parents.[183] A line in *Hsiao-ching*, abbreviated below, expresses the same idea: "To establish oneself and live according to the way, and to make one's name known to posterity so as to honor the names of one's parents, is the final step of filial piety."[184]

A son, according to the Taipings, has to treat his wife in a proper way, or has to be a model to his wife; and his duty to his parents is to obey them.[185]

As regards the relation between ruler and ministers, the Taiping idea that the ruler should be upright came close to the idea of justice expressed in *Mencius*. But the idea of benevolence as expressed in the *Li-chi* is not given any consideration. However, the duty of ministers to be loyal to their sovereign is a theme to which the Taipings returned again and again. Their idea that one should transform filial piety into loyalty[186] was a reverberation of what the *Hsiao-ching* had said: "The Master said, 'Princely men serve their parents in the spirit of filial piety; therefore [filial piety may be transformed into] loyalty and shifted to the sovereign.' "[187] This loyalty was so emphasized that to devote oneself to it one would have to forget one's parents and one's own body. One had to give up his very life to embrace the *i*.[188]

Of the husband the Taipings said: "The way of a husband is based on *kang* [剛 firmness, or the principle of the male as contrasted with *jou* (柔 pliancy, or the principle of the female)], and his love for his wife should follow a proper way."[189] And the way of a wife lies in *san-ts'ung* (三從

---

[183] "T'ai-p'ing chiu-shih-ko," in Hsiao, *Ts'ung-shu, ts'e* 4.

[184] *Hsiao-ching, chüan* 1, chap. 1, p. 3a.

[185] "Yu-hsüeh-shih," in Hsiao, *Ts'ung-shu, ts'e* 4, p. 6b. The expression *hsing yü kua ch'i* is from the second stanza of "Ssu-ch'i" in the *Book of Poetry. Mao-shih yin-te*, 60/240/ 2. Cheng's note says: "King Wen treated his wife with propriety and law." But *hsing* also means "principle" or "model," which sense seems to fit better with the passage in the *Book of Poetry*.

[186] "T'ai-p'ing chiu-shih-ko," in Hsiao, *Ts'ung-shu, ts'e* 4, p. 7b.

[187] *Hsiao-ching, chüan* 7, chap. 14, p. 2a. The note says: "To serve the sovereign with filial piety is to be loyal."

[188] "Having followed exhaustively the principle of loyalty, one would also overlook one's parents. One knows only of one's ruler, unmindful of one's own physical body. One would toil with all his might to embrace martyrdom, gladly giving up one's own life." "T'ai-p'ing chiu-shih-ko," in Hsiao, *Ts'ung-shu, ts'e* 4, p. 7b.

[189] "Yu-hsüeh-shih," in Hsiao, *Ts'ung-shu, ts'e* 4, p. 9a.

three forms of obedience) ; she is not supposed to disobey her husband.[190] This formulation of the attitudes of a husband and a wife toward each other conforms to the idea expressed in the *Li-chi:* the husband is supposed to be just and the wife obedient. Mencius' idea of characterizing the husband-wife relation by distinction was applied by the Taipings to the relation between man and woman in general. Of man they said: "The male principle consists of firmness and sternness or respectability, and the position of a male is outside the house; he should be above all suspicion." This suspicion refers particularly to an improper relationship between man and woman.[191] And of woman, they said: "The female principle consists in chastity, and a woman should not go near men. Secluded, calm, and dignified, she finds her place inside the house; living in this way, she will enjoy her auspicious luck."[192]

The husband-wife distinction of Mencius is here adapted to the inside-outside distinction. This latter type of distinction has the sanction of the *Li-chi.* In a chapter called "Nei-tse" (Rules Governing Conduct Inside the House), the following is given: "Men do not speak of the inside and woman do not speak of the outside. . . . Words of inside should not come out; words of outside should not go in."[193] The *Li-chi* also says: "That there is distinction between men and women is considered great in the way of man";[194] and "If there is no distinction between men and women, there will be confusion."[195] When distinction is applied to the man-woman relation, it carries with it not only the usual idea of distinction but the idea of segregation as well.

This designation of the position of man and woman is also found in the *Book of Changes:*

> Chia-jen [The Family or The Clan]: Women have their correct position inside, and men have their correct position outside. [The achievement of] the correct [position] of men and women is the great principle of heaven and earth. Among the family members there are respectful lords: these are the parents. When father is father, son son, elder brother elder brother, younger brother younger brother, husband husband and wife wife, the way of the family will be correct. Once the family is correct, the world is pacified.[196]

[190] *Ibid.,* p. 9b.
[191] *Ibid.,* p. 10b.
[192] *Ibid.,* p. 11a.
[193] *Li-chi yin-te,* 12/12. And in 12/41: "Women live within,"
[194] *Ibid.,* 15/11.
[195] *Ibid.,* 19/6.
[196] *Chou-i yin-te,* 23/37/*t'uan.*

According to the *Li-chi,* the distinction between men and women is a step toward the fulfillment of the husband-wife relationship: "There is first the distinction between men and women, and then there is the principle governing the husband-wife relationship."[197]

The quality of a wife is obedience, and here the Taipings agreed with the *Li-chi* and the popular concept.[198] The idea of *san-ts'ung* is found in the *I-li,* which says: "Women have the duty to perform three forms of obedience; they have no right to independence. Therefore, before marriage they obey their father; after marriage they obey their husband; and after the death of their husband, they obey their sons."[199]

The brother-brother relation is absent from Mencius' list and the friend-friend relation is absent from the *Li-chi* list, and in their place both lists have the elder-younger relation. I wish to suggest a possible reason for this. While three of the five relations (father-son, monarch-minister and husband-wife relations) imply a definite order of status and prestige, the other two relations (brother-brother and friend-friend relations) have no such implication. Since brothers and friends are considered to be on the same social plane and level, age is the only possible basis upon which any order can be established. It is possible that for this reason on one list the age relation takes the place of the brother-brother relation and on the other it takes the place of the friend-friend relation. In another place the *Li-chi* combined all the relationships with a new one to form *ch'i-chiao* (七教 seven teachings), consisting of "father-son, brother-brother, husband-wife, monarch-ministers, elder-younger, friend-friend, and guest-guest."[200] Therefore, in spite of the discrepancy between the two lists, we shall consider the remaining two relations of brother to brother and friend to friend. Such consideration is encouraged by the discovery that the Taipings included the elder-younger relation in their relation of younger brothers to elder brothers.

The Taipings described very briefly the way of brothers in "Ode for Youth":

Elder brothers should instruct and guide their younger brothers, thinking earnestly of the fact that they are born of the same womb. When their

[197] *Li-chi yin-te,* 44/3.

[198] As a matter of fact, the Taipings told their people to follow the principles laid down in "Nei-tse," in *Li-chi.* "Yüan-tao chiu-shih ko," in Lo Yung and Shen Tsu-chi (compilers), *T'ai-p'ing t'ien-kuo shih-wen chao,* I, 8a.

[199] *I-li yin-te,* 11/8b.

[200] *Li-chi yin-te,* 5/59.

younger brothers make mistakes, it is proper that they [elder brothers] with tolerant hearts forgive them [younger brothers]. Since the order of elder and younger is fixed by Heaven, respect should be the attitude younger brothers entertain in listening to their elder brothers.[201]

Here the Taipings expressed both the "order" Mencius assigned to the elder-younger relation and the "fraternal kindness" and "fraternal obedience" given in the *Li-chi*. But the Taipings reached further into the classical sources to illustrate the harmony between brothers, and at the same time they widened the scope of brotherhood to embrace all those who joined the Taiping organization at Tzu-ching-shan. The Taipings characterized the quality of the brother-brother relationship thus:

When somewhat grown-up, one should be versed in the way of a younger brother. He should serve his elder brother with respect, for this is what ought to be. When in the house they should love one another; when out of the house they should follow shoulder to shoulder. In the *Book of Poetry* there is a poem called "T'ang-ti" [the title should be "Ch'ang-ti"]. Let all brothers chant this piece of poetry. With devotion fulfill brotherly duties, and hold fast to the teachings of that poem. Though disharmony may reign within the walls, brothers should still defend themselves against insult from outside, and all the time depend on each other. Like hands and feet, we brothers should be determined to serve T'ien. And like flute and ocarina responding harmoniously to each other, our love should fill our hearts. The judas tree is flourishing luxuriantly [*tzu-ching*, referring to the brethren who joined up at Tzu-ching-shan], and we should make one comforter and sleep together.[202]

The Taipings here referred to two poems from the *Book of Poetry* and a story from *Hou-Han-shu*. "Ch'ang-ti," which describes brothers feasting together, contains the following lines: "None of the people at the present time may be compared to brothers";[203] and "Brothers may quarrel inside the walls; they will defend themselves against insult from outside."[204] The second poem, "Ho-jen-ssu," was supposedly written by a demoted official condemning another responsible for his downfall. "Ho-jen-ssu" dwells on the theme that since both officials are ministers of the king, they should be like brothers to each other, one playing the

---

201 "Yu-hsüeh-shih," in Hsiao, *Ts'ung-shu, ts'e* 4, pp. 7b–8a.
202 "T'ai-p'ing chiu-shih-ko," in Hsiao, *Ts'ung-shu, ts'e* 4, p. 9b.
203 *Mao-shih yin-te*, 34/164/1.
204 *Ibid.*, 34/164/4.

ocarina and the other the flute.[205] The story of two brothers who slept under the same cover is found in the *Hou-Han-shu*: "Chiang Kung, whose *tzu* was Po-huai, a native of Kuang-ch'i in P'eng-ch'eng, was from a great family, famous for generations. Kung and his two younger brothers, Chung-hai and Chi-chiang, were all known for their filial piety. Their love for each other was deeply rooted in their nature. They always slept together and got up together."[206] In *Yu-hsüeh ku-shih ch'iung-lin*, part of the same story is related: "Although each of them was married, they could not bear to be separated at night. So they made a large cover and slept together."[207]

The Taipings made no mention of the friend-friend relation. This seems logical, since they believed that all men are brothers and all women sisters, being children of one and the same Heavenly Father. Traditionally it has always been believed that friendship could deepen into brotherly love, as in the case of sworn brotherhood; and on the other hand, brotherly love is often couched in terms of friendship, as is evident from the phrase *yu-ai* 友愛, which literally stands for "friendly love" but definitely means "brotherly love." In the classics the term *yu* (友 friend) is the standard term for "brotherly love." *Tso-chuan*, paraphrasing the *Book of History*, says: "Father is not loving, son not filial, elder brother not *yu* ['friendly' or fraternal], and younger brother not respectful."[208] The *Book of History* also says: "The elder brother is both loving and *yu* ['friendly']."[209] In the *Analects* there is this line: "*Yu* [to be 'friendly'] among the elder and younger brothers."[210] Similar application of the term *yu* to mean brotherliness may also be found in the *Book of History* and the *Book of Poetry*.[211] The indiscriminate use of the term *yu* to mean both fraternal and friendly may be the reason Mencius did not mention the brother-brother relation and the *Li-chi* did not mention the friend-friend relation. The Taipings had their own reason for omitting the friend-friend relation, as suggested above.

[205] "The elder brother plays the ocarina; the younger one plays the flute." *Ibid.*, 47/199/7.

[206] *Hou-Han-shu*, by Fan Yeh, biography of Chiang Kung. The commentary says: "Brothers slept under the same coverlet, and did not go to their own rooms, in an effort to comfort the heart of their mother."

[207] *Yu-hsüeh ku-shih ch'iung-lin*, Vol. I, *chüan* 2, p. 10.

[208] *Ch'un-ch'iu ching-chuan yin-te*, 143/Hsi 33/8 Tso.

[209] *Ibid.*, 423/Chou 26/*fu* 5.

[210] *Lun-yü yin-te*, 3/2/21.

[211] *Shang-shu t'ung-chien*, 29/0533–0536 and 0579–0584; 41/0014–0018. *Mao-shih yin-te*, 61/241/3. See also Chu Hsi, *Shih chi-chuan*, 10:5b.

The discussion of the five relations has yielded a set of precepts governing these relations. With the close parallelism between the Taiping and classical precepts, it is safe to say that these classical materials are the main sources upon which the Taipings drew to formulate their own precepts.

How thoroughly the Taipings were imbued with traditional thought concerning relationships may be illustrated by the following incident. The Tung Wang, apparently annoyed by the T'ien Wang's neglect in bringing up the young lord and by his brutal treatment of court ladies and royal concubines, was in reality determined to wrest the power of control from the T'ien Wang and possibly had some design to obtain court ladies from the T'ien Wang's harem. In the name of the Heavenly Father he subjected the T'ien Wang to a merciless court scene in which he threatened to have him flogged. From the conversation between the Tung Wang and the T'ien Wang following the scene, it is easy to see how traditional thought influenced the thinking of the Taipings.[212]

Before the Tung Wang went to the T'ien Wang's court, the Tung Wang said, in connection with bringing up the young lord, that human nature is originally good and all men share equally in this original nature; but through environmental influence men drift apart. At the T'ien Wang's court, after touching briefly on the necessity of controlling the behavior of the young lord, the Tung Wang began to lecture the T'ien Wang on the lesson: "A monarch should use the ministers with propriety, and the ministers should serve their ruler with loyalty." This statement is from the *Analects*,[213] but the Tung Wang attributed it to a proverb which the Heavenly Father had corrected. The Tung Wang added that the shortcomings of the court ladies and the case of those who had been condemned to death should be carefully reviewed so that there would be no possibility of wrongly sentencing an innocent person to death.

In response, the T'ien Wang glorified the loving kindheartedness of the Heavenly Father and promised in the future to consult the Tung Wang before acting so that those who would come after the T'ien Wang as ruler could look to him as a model for their conduct and could follow his example in consulting their good ministers for advice. Then after a few bits of repartee aimed at mutual commendation, the Tung Wang

---

[212] The whole episode is recorded in "T'ien-fu hsia-fan chao-shu," in Ch'eng, *Shih-liao*, II, pp. 1b–25a.

[213] *Lun-yü yin-te*, 5/3/19.

said: "This is second eldest brother's enlightened virtue 明德, which is established after the eternal pattern and is truly beautiful." The Tung Wang then turned to the officials and told them to treat their subordinates with consideration.

Two days later the Tung Wang and others went to the T'ien Wang's court again to give him their sympathy for his punishment by the Heavenly Father. The Tung Wang thought it a minister's duty to give advice to the ruler when the minister believed that the ruler did not conduct himself properly. He quoted the *Analects*: "If loyal, how then can there be no instruction?"[214] The Tung Wang went on to say that he disapproved of the young lord's disregard for the value of things. He emphasized that material things (wealth) were not easily obtained and quoted a line from the *Analects* to prove his point: "Be frugal in the use of things and love the people."[215] But as usual the Tung Wang referred to the quotation as a proverb.

The Tung Wang brought up the manner in which the T'ien Wang treated the concubines in his harem. He began with the statement, "Kingly transformation begins in the boudoir," expressing unmistakably the idea that the man who maintains harmony and order in his own family will be equipped to establish the same harmony in his district and state: the beginning of harmony in the state is harmony in the boudoir. This idea is embodied in the preface of the first poem in the *Book of Poetry*:

> "Kuan-chü" [the first poem in the *Book of Poetry*, the theme of which is marriage] is...the beginning of *feng* [the first part of the *Book of Poetry*, containing lyrical poems of various localities], the aim of which is *feng* [to move] the world and which makes proper the husband-wife [relation]. Therefore it is used in the district as well as in the state. Folklore or lyric is [figuratively] wind and education. As wind it moves them [the people], and as education it transforms them....If so, then the transformation of "Kuan-chü" and "Lin-chih" [the eleventh poem of the *Book of Poetry*, whose theme is "goodness of offsprings"] is the kingly wind...."Chou-nan" and "Shao-nan" [the first two sections in the "Feng" part of the *Book of Poetry*] express the way to make the beginning correct or proper [for *cheng-shih* K'ung Yin-ta's "Cheng-i" gives the following explanation: first make correct one's family, and then reach forth to one's state. That is:

---

[214] *Ibid.*, 27/14/7.
[215] *Ibid.*, 1/1/5.

make correct what is the beginning] and are the foundation of kingly transformation.²¹⁶

Chu Hsi's *Shih chi-chuan* gives a similar idea; "[They are] called wind because they were transformed by the above and then gave forth these expressions." Then referring to some old theory Chu said: "The two Nan [referring to "Chou-nan" and "Shao-nan"] are *feng* proper; therefore they are used in the boudoir, in the district, and in the state to transform the world."²¹⁷ With this remark, the Tung Wang went on to strike home the lesson all Confucianists know so well: "Therefore to make clear one's enlightened virtue to the world, one has first to have his state well governed; to have one's state well governed, one has first to have his family well ordered."²¹⁸ Thus the Tung Wang wanted the T'ien Wang to observe the proper rule of governing the boudoir as the first step toward "making clear the enlightened virtue to the world," or in other words before becoming the Son of Heaven.

The T'ien Wang, after listening to the Tung Wang's frank remarks, praised the Tung Wang for his advice, and said that the advice was indeed important and served as a remedy in "bringing order to the family, giving [good] government to the state, and pacifying the world." Finally, the T'ien Wang praised the Tung Wang for being what the ancients called *ku-keng chih ch'en* (骨鯁之臣 outspoken minister); and the Tung Wang praised the T'ien Wang for being a monarch able to follow advice like the flow of water. Thus the episode ended harmoniously.

It is very interesting to note that the *cheng-ch'en* (爭臣 remonstrating minister) in a chapter entitled "Chien-cheng" 諫諍 in the *Hsiao-ching* exhibits the same spirit that the Tung Wang expressed when he said that it is the duty of a minister to give advice, admonishing his ruler when the ruler falls short of his duty.²¹⁹

In this section "moral precepts and private virtues" have been treated

²¹⁶ *Mao-shih chu-shu*, Part 1 of *chüan* 1, pp. 3b–18b. "Kuan-chü," "Lin-chih," "Chou-nan," and "Shao-nan" are titles of poems. *Feng* literally means "wind"; it has come to mean "influence" or "education," which moves people in a particular direction just as the wind moves blades of grass in a particular direction. *Feng* also means folk songs or folklore or "lyrics," all of which move or influence people. In the poem "Kuan-chü," the osprey is used to symbolize the eternal loyalty of husband and wife in marriage.

²¹⁷ Chu Hsi, *Shih chi-chuan*, 1:1a.

²¹⁸ This is, of course, a passage from "Ta-hsüeh" in the *Li-chi. Li-chi yin-te*, 42/1. The Tung Wang had previously used the phrase "enlightened virtue."

²¹⁹ *Hsiao-ching*, *chüan* 7, chap. 15, pp. 3b–4a.

together because to the ancient Chinese the distinction between the public order and the private order was not very clearly made. The ancient Chinese considered politics a continuation of ethics, much as Aristotle had done. However, there are some attitudes the Taipings entertained which can be properly considered personal and private. Here as elsewhere the Taipings were heavy borrowers from classical sources.

Most of these private virtues necessitate the training of moral character. Humility was mentioned in many of the Taiping documents. We believe that the Taiping concept of humility owed its origin more to Chinese classical literature than to the Bible. Comparing a few quotations from the classical sources with Taiping statements will indicate their similarity. The Taipings used the expression *shou-i i ch'ien* (受益以謙 receive increase because modest).[220] The *Book of History* says: "Fullness invites decrease; *ch'ien* [modesty] *shou-i* [receives increase]."[221] And the *Book of Changes* states: "The heavenly principle takes away from the full and adds to the *ch'ien* [humble or modest]" and "Ghosts and spirits bring calamity to the full and confer bliss upon the *ch'ien* [humble]."[222]

The Taipings made a general statement regarding the idea of vigilance: "If we are not respectful even in the most trivial manner, this will eventually be a spot on our virtuous character. Before the arrival of solid ice, we have to be careful in treading on the frost."[223] The first part of this quotation is from the *Book of History*[224] and the second part is a paraphrase of a statement in the *Analects*.[225]

The Taipings were firm believers in developing strong moral character through trial. For explanation they either referred to the will of the Heavenly Father or appealed to some classical source. Illness befell the Tung Wang at Chin-t'ien because the Heavenly Father wanted to try his devotion. At the time the Taipings first rose in rebellion they were short of food, also because the Heavenly Father wanted to test their loyalty by trying them.[226] The Heavenly Father did not exterminate the devils in the beginning because they served him as a means for training and strengthening the character of the Taipings.[227] At the same time the

[220] "T'ai-p'ing chiu-shih-ko," in Hsiao, *Ts'ung-shu, ts'e* 4, p. 10a.
[221] *Shang-shu t'ung-chien*, 3/3088–3093.
[222] *Chou-i yin-te*, 11/15/t'uan.
[223] "T'ai-p'ing chao-shu," in Hsiao, *Ts'ung-shu, ts'e* 1, p. 5a.
[224] *Shang-shu t'ung-chien*, 25/0196–0203.
[225] *Lun-yü yin-te*, 14/8/3. The line also occurs in the *Book of Changes*: *Chou-i yin-te*, 3/2/ch'u; 4/2/yen; 3/2/ch'u hsiang.
[226] "T'ien-ch'ing tao-li shu," in Hsiao, *Ts'ung-shu, ts'e* 5, pp. 11b–12a.
[227] *Ibid.*, p. 14b.

Taipings turned to Mencius for an explanation of why the Tung Wang was born poor and why he suffered such hardships:

> Let us take the case of the Tung Wang. The Tung Wang received personal command from the Heavenly Father to come to the world to be the left prime minister and the commander-in-chief, to save people from starvation and illness and save all younger brothers and sisters of the ten thousand countries in the world. It would be reasonable to expect that when he was born he should encounter no poverty or hardships. But none there is who is poorer than the Tung Wang and none there is who suffers more than the Tung Wang. He lived among the distant mountains, lost his father at five and lost his mother at nine. A forlorn orphan, he lived in utter misery. This is sufficient to prove that when the Heavenly Father wished to give great responsibility to the Tung Wang, appointing him to assist our true Lord, he first had to make his mind suffer, his tendon and bone labor, and his body starve. Thus in giving suffering to our Tung Wang, Heaven was really bringing him to the state of perfection.[228]

It is obvious that the language in this quotation comes directly from Mencius, with some very suggestive modifications.[229] Mencius' *T'ien* is replaced by *T'ien-fu* (天父 Heavenly Father) in the Taiping text, a substitution which supports the idea that to the Taipings the ancient T'ien was identical with their Heavenly Father.

The Taiping attitude toward wealth was completely traditional. In the "Proclamation on the Origin of the Principles of World Salvation" there is the statement: "A princely man when confronted with wealth would not accept it without principle."[230] This line comes from the first chapter of the *Li-chi*,[231] but the term *chün-tzu* (君子 superior man) is inserted by the Taipings to take the place of *hsien-che* (賢者 the worthies) implied in the *Li-chi*. At the same place in the "Proclamation on the Origin of the Principles of World Salvation" two more lines follow: "Heaven gives birth to the good and upright, who cultivate heavenly rank: what is so wonderful about wealth ill-gained?"[232] The idea of heavenly rank is found in Mencius: "The ancients cultivated their heavenly rank and the man-made rank followed."[233] And the idea of ill-gained wealth is from the *Analects*: "If ill-gained, both wealth and

---

[228] *Ibid.*, pp. 14b–15a.
[229] Compare *Meng-tzu yin-te*, 50/6B/15.
[230] "T'ai-p'ing chao-shu," in Hsiao, *Ts'ung-shu, ts'e* 1, p. 3b.
[231] *Li-chi yin-te*, 1/3.
[232] "T'ai-p'ing chao-shu," in Hsiao, *Ts'ung-shu, ts'e* 1, p. 3b.
[233] *Meng-tzu yin-te*, 46/6A/16.

honor would be floating clouds to me."[234] The Taipings drew the conclusion: "Whether poor or rich, it is determined by Heaven; for my part, I shall follow my own inclination in my excursion."[235] A parallel idea is found in the *Analects*, where the Master says: "If wealth could be sought, I would seek it even if I had to be a groom; but if it is not to be sought, I shall follow my own inclination."[236]

Beliefs in Fatalism and Moral Causality

A discussion of the Taipings' attitude toward wealth reveals their belief in fatalism. Time and again they expressed the idea that poverty and wealth are matters in the hand of Heaven. By examining a few such expressions we can determine to what extent the Taipings were traditionally conditioned in their thinking:

Wealth and honor, rank and fame are arranged and fixed by Heaven.[237]
Death, life, calamity, and illness are all determined by Heaven.[238]
Wealth and honor are matters in the hand of Heaven, and life and
  death are matters of fate.[239]
Since the time of old death and life have always been arranged and
  fixed by Heaven;
Where on earth can anyone become a man depending on himself
  alone?[240]

In "A Hero's Submission to Truth" the Kan Wang explained the attitude toward wealth in the following words: "Man's life is in the hand of Heaven; when Heaven orders man to live, man cannot but live; when Heaven wills man to die, man cannot but die. Thus we know life and death are matters of fate, and wealth and honor are matters in the hand of Heaven."[241]

The Taipings advocated an outlook on life based on acceptance and enjoyment of one's fate; adoption of such an outlook would alleviate one's sufferings and help make one's burdens more bearable. That outlook is couched in such phrases as *chih-ming* (知命 know your fate), *an-p'in*

---

[234] *Lun-yü yin-te*, 12/7/16.
[235] "T'ai-p'ing chao-shu," in Hsiao, *Ts'ung-shu, ts'e* 1, p. 4b.
[236] *Lun-yü yin-te*, 12/7/12.
[237] "T'ien-fu shang-ti yen-t'i huang-chao," in Hsiao, *Ts'ung-shu, ts'e* 1, p. 4a.
[238] "T'ai-p'ing chao-shu," in Hsiao, *Ts'ung-shu, ts'e* 1, p. 4a.
[239] *Ibid.*, p. 5a.
[240] "T'ien-fu shih" No. 5, in Hsiao, *Ts'ung-shu, ts'e* 7.
[241] "Ying-chieh kuei-chen," in Hsiao, *Ts'ung-shu, ts'e* 10, p. 44b.

(安貧 resign to your poverty), and *lo-t'ien* (樂天 enjoy your heavenly lot).

The earlier edition of the Taiping "Proclamation on the Origin of the Principles of World Salvation" says: "Confucius and Yen Hui enjoyed the simplest of food; and they knew their fate, were content with poverty, and enjoyed happiness."[242] This idea of enjoying one's fate is also retained in a later edition: "Enjoy your heavenly mandate [natural fate]. Why doubt it?"[243]

The whole idea of fatalism as expressed by the Taipings is thoroughly Confucian. The ideas of enjoying one's heavenly lot and knowing one's fate are first found in the *Book of Changes*.[244] The *Analects* says: "Death and life are matters of fate, and wealth and honor are matters in the hand of Heaven."[245] Confucius said he knew the heavenly mandate at fifty;[246] he also said, "The small man does not know the heavenly mandate,"[247] and "If ignorant of the heavenly mandate, one has nothing that may make one a princely man."[248] This idea of fate was given a universal application by Mencius: "All is a matter of fate: we should receive obediently what is correctly ascribed to us."[249] Mencius also said: "If there is a way to seek it, and yet the getting is a matter of fate, then seeking will not do any good to the getting. This seeking is for what is outside [for what does not depend on us]."[250]

The seemingly optimistic outlook on life is also Confucian. The Taipings wished their people to emulate the attitude of Confucius and Yen Hui, who were happy with their fate. The idea of natural contentment is clearly expressed in the *Book of Changes*: "He is happy with Heaven [what is natural] and knows his fate; therefore he is free from worry."[251]

This outlook on life has become one of the dominant features of the Chinese pattern of thought, as the following quotations will illustrate. Su Shih of the Sung, in a memorial he wrote for Chang Fang-p'ing, said: "Furthermore, I your servant [臣 *ch'en*] have heard that all who under-

---

[242] "Yüan-tao chiu-shih ko," in Lo and Shen, *Shih-wen ch'ao*, I, 11a.

[243] "T'ai-p'ing chao-shu," in Hsiao, *Ts'ung-shu*, ts'e 1, p. 3b. This line is also the last line in T'ao Yüan-ming's "Kuei-ch'ü-lai tz'u," a poem on homecoming after retirement, in T'ao, *Ching-chien hsien-sheng chi*, 5:11a.

[244] *Chou-i yin-te*, 40/hsi 1/4.

[245] *Lun-yü yin-te*, 22/12/5.

[246] *Ibid.*, 2/2/4.

[247] *Ibid.*, 34/16/8.

[248] *Ibid.*, 42/20/3.

[249] *Meng-tzu yin-te*, 50/7A/2.

[250] *Ibid.*, 51/7A/3.

[251] *Chou-i yin-te*, 40/hsi 1/4.

take great things must act in accordance with the will of Heaven. If one acts in the direction of Heaven, one must succeed; if one acts in the direction against Heaven, one must fail."[252] Yao Nai of the Ch'ing, in answering a letter from Yao Ch'un-mu asking for advice on a literary venture Ch'un-mu was about to take up, said:

I believe this [referring to the success of the literary venture] is a matter fixed by Heaven. For one to be born and become rich and honorable or to die with a name, to be a success or a failure, great or small, all is given by Heaven. Literary ventures [historical writings] are that by means of which one gains one's fame. Therefore, if Heaven desires that it should succeed, it will succeed; if Heaven desires that it should be transmitted, it will be transmitted. Otherwise, it will be obliterated. You may go ahead and take up the venture; and leave the rest to the will of Heaven.[253]

It is conceivable that Yao Nai doubted Yao Ch'un-mu's ability to carry out such a great venture and was politely warning him. Even so, the very fact that Yao Nai chose this particular form to express his doubt is significant.

The Taiping belief in fatalism should imply that the Taipings did not believe in individual purpose or freedom. This was not so. Their equally strong belief in personal effort, expressed in the form of moral causality, formed an important part of their ideology. Buddhism, through its principle of moral retribution (因緣果報 yin-yüan kuo-pao), may have been a factor in rendering the idea of moral causality popular; but the Taiping practice of quoting from the classical sources justifies our inference that the doctrine of moral causality was borrowed directly from these sources. "Proclamation on the Origin of the Principles of World Salvation" contains these lines: "The house which accumulates good deeds will have happiness more than abundance; but the house which accumulates evil deeds will have calamity more than its share."[254] This is from the "Wen-yen" 文言 in the *Book of Changes*.[255] In "A Hero's Submission to Truth" the Taipings quoted from the *Book of History* with explicit reference: "The *Book of History* says: 'Only God is not constant: He confers one hundred happinesses on those who do good deeds; He causes one hundred calamities to descend on those who do evil deeds.' "[256]

[252] Su Shih, *Tung-po ch'i-chi*, "Tung-po tsou-i," 15:512.
[253] Yao Nai, *Hsi-pao hsüan ch'üan-chi*, "Wen hou-chi," 3:224.
[254] "T'ai-p'ing chao-shu," in Hsiao, *Ts'ung-shu, ts'e* 1, p. 5b.
[255] *Chou-i yin-te*, 4/2/yen.
[256] "Ying-chieh kuei-chen," in Hsiao, *Ts'ung-shu, ts'e* 10, p. 34a. The Taipings were quoting from the *Book of History. Shang-shu t'ung-chien*, 13/0311–0338.

The third line of the "Proclamation on the Origin of the Principles of World Salvation" reads: "It is the way of Heaven to give blessing to the good but calamity to the evil ones."[257] This idea is also found in the *Book of History*.[258] These quotations imply that the Taipings believed man has freedom to choose the way of good and to reject the way of evil. The passages from the classical sources illustrate that moral causality is an ancient traditional idea in China. The connection between it and the Taiping notion of moral determinism is not merely verbal.

There is further evidence of the influence of traditionalism on the Taipings. For example, in discussing loyalty they said: "With complete devotion [鞠躬盡瘁 *chü-kung ching-ts'ui*] one should give up his very self to embrace *i* [the principle]....Exterminate the devils and kill the imps, and sacrifice oneself in fulfillment of the principle of *jen* [仁 human-heartedness]."[259] Confucius said that the idealistic man or the man of human-heartedness would sacrifice himself to fulfill the principle of *jen*. He described such a person as one who would never seek life if, in doing so, he would do violence to the principle of human-heartedness.[260] "To give up oneself to embrace the *i*" is from Mencius, who said: "Life is what I desire, and *i* is also what I desire. If I cannot get both, I would give up life and embrace *i*."[261] Wen T'ien-hsiang of the Sung used these expressions in judging himself: "Confucius said: 'Fulfill the principle of *jen*,' and Mencius said: 'Embrace the principle of *i*.' "[262] These expressions have become synonymous with the idea of dying for one's country. The expression *chü-kung ching-ts'ui* (with complete devotion) is taken from Chu-ko Liang's "Hou ch'u-shih piao." [263]

In the "Book on the Principles of the Heavenly Nature" appears this line: "I swear to die and will not entertain any other thought; it is difficult for me to change my allegiance."[264] The first part of this quotation is a paraphrase of a line in the *Book of Poetry*: "To death, I swear, I will not have other."[265] Here a case of woman's fidelity was borrowed to express the loyalty of ministers and subjects to their ruler.

257 "T'ai-p'ing chao-shu," in Hsiao, *Ts'ung-shu, ts'e* 1, p. 1a.
258 *Shang-shu t'ung-chien*, 12/0085–0090.
259 "T'ai-p'ing chiu-shih-ko," in Hsiao, *Ts'ung-shu, ts'e* 4, p. 7b.
260 *Lun-yü yin-te*, 31/15/19.
261 *Meng-tzu yin-te*, 44/6A/10.
262 Wen T'ien-hsiang, *Wen Wen-shan ch'üan-chi*, 10:251.
263 Chu-ko Liang, *Chu-ko wu-hou wen-chi*, 1:6b.
264 "T'ien-ch'ing tao-li shu," in Hsiao, *Ts'ung-shu, ts'e* 5, p. 49a.
265 *Mao-shih yin-te*, 9/45/1.

Occasionally the Taiping writings contain a certain flavor of the Neo-Confucianism of the Sung Dynasty. At one point, in trying to prove that all people on earth came from one source, the Taipings said: "The one is diversified into many, and the many are gathered up into one."[266] This idea is expressed by both Ch'eng-tzu and Chu-tzu in their commentaries on Chang Tsai's "Hsi-ming 西銘" Ch'eng was quoted by Chu as having explained "Hsi-ming" in one succinct phrase: "The principle is one, in diversity it becomes many."[267] Then Chu followed with this explanation:

With unity diversified in many, although the whole world is one family and the whole Middle Kingdom is one man there will be no danger of slipping into the evil of universal love. With the diversified many united in one principle, although there is the distinction in feelings between the closely and the distantly related and although there is the distinction in status between the honored and the mean, there will be no danger of the bondage of egoism.[268]

I cite these instances not to turn the Taipings into Neo-Confucianists but merely to point out that the Taipings were versed in Confucian patterns of thought, both ancient and new.

The term *yüan-tao* which Hung prefixed to the titles of the three important essays seems to have been suggested by the titles of some ancient sources. And the style of some lines of the essays indicates the influence of Han Yü, suggesting that his "Yüan-tao" was the original of the Taiping title. In "Proclamation on the Origin of the Principles of World Salvation" is written: "Alas! Even if those who come in the future would like to understand the way of heaven, earth, and man, after whom would they seek it?"[269] This is after the style of a line in Han Yü's "Yüan-tao": "Alas! Even if those who come in the future would like to hear about the teachings of human-heartedness, righteousness, the way, and the virtue, after whom would they seek it?"[270] That this similarity in sentence structure is not accidental can be seen from the sentences which follow. These sentences are identical in the two works: "How extremely

[266] "T'ai-p'ing chao-shu," in Hsiao, *Ts'ung-shu, ts'e* 1, p. 7b.
[267] Chang Tsai, *Chang Heng-ch'ü chi*, 1:5b.
[268] *Ibid.* Chu Hsi here is trying to clear Chang Tsai of an implied accusation that he might, in holding the ideas expressed in "Hsi-ming," fall into either Motzu's universal love or Yang-chu's egoism.
[269] "T'ai-p'ing chao-shu," in Hsiao, *Ts'ung-shu, ts'e* 1, p. 9a.
[270] Han Yü, *Ch'ang-li hsien-sheng chi*, 11:129.

people like what is strange. They would not trace its beginnings: neither would they inquire into its ramifications; they just like to hear about what is strange."[271] In "Proclamation on the Origin of the Principles of World Salvation" a figure of a frog in the well is used.[272] The phrase was used by Fan Yeh in his *Hou-Han-shu*,[273] based on Chuang-tzu's figure in "Chiu-shui."[274] Han Yü borrowed the figure to mean narrow-mindedness. The Taipings' use of the figure could have come from any of these sources; but Han Yü seems the most probable source.

Thus it seems that the Taipings were very much at home in the classical and Confucian sources. They made minor modifications here and there, but fundamentally they followed closely the traditional pattern in their thinking.

SOCIAL BORROWINGS FROM TRADITIONAL SOURCES

Because of the close relationship between moral and social ideas, the discussion of many of the moral precepts in the last section covers also some of the Taipings' social borrowings. Here we shall consider Taiping social ideals and the institutional aspect of *li*.

Social Ideals

The main points concerning social ideals are three: the brotherhood of men, the idea of social welfare, and the idea of a world of Great Harmony. Verbally these are all found in the classics. In the *Analects* is written: "Within the four seas all are brothers; why should a superior man be worried about not having any brothers?"[275] And the passage on *ta-t'ung shih-chieh* (大同世界 the world of Great Harmony) which the Taipings included in "Proclamation on the Origin of Principles for the Enlightenment of the Age" (Yüan-tao hsing-shih chao) is a direct quotation from "Li-yün" in *Li-chi*, which contains statements about social welfare.[276] But the Taiping ideas may not have been identical with the classical ideas.

In spite of the verbal connection, it seems that the Taipings had little in common conceptually with the idea of brotherhood as expressed in

---

[271] "T'ai-p'ing chao-shu," in Hsiao, *Ts'ung-shu, ts'e* 1, p. 10a–b; Han Yü, *op. cit.*, 11:129.

[272] "T'ai-p'ing chao-shu," in Hsiao, *Ts'ung-shu, ts'e* 1, p. 7a.

[273] *Hou-Han-shu*, by Fan Yeh, biography of Ma Yüan.

[274] *Chuang-tzu*, p. 248.

[275] *Lun-yü yin-te*, 22/12/5.

[276] *Li-chi yin-te*, 9/1.

the classics. The Taipings applied their idea of brotherhood in forming a sworn brotherhood, composed of all those who joined their movement at Chin-t'ien. It is difficult, if not impossible, to imagine that Tzu-hsia had the same psychological attitude when he made the statement about all men being brothers quoted above from the *Analects*. Firstly, the situation that fostered the Taiping attitude was absent in ancient times. And secondly, in view of the general nature of Confucian ideology Tzu-hsia could not have had the same notion as the Taipings that all men are brothers as sons of God.

In Confucianism one does not feel toward all men exactly the same way. For example, Confucius, in refusing to give up his carriage so that Yen Hui, his most respected and beloved disciple, might have an outer sarcophagus, said: "Whether talented or not, each is speaking of his own son."[277] Apparently in Confucius' mind his son assumed a position which was not to be usurped by Yen Hui. The Confucians believed in graded love, which started with family members and reached forth through sympathetic inference to the rest of mankind.

This graded love was later clarified by Mencius when he contrasted his view with that of the Mohists, who believed in universal love.[278] Mencius also said: "A superior man takes good care of things but does not treat them in the spirit of human-heartedness; he treats the people with human-heartedness, but not with love. He loves his family members 親, treats the people with human-heartedness, and takes good care of things."[279] A similar idea is found in the *Li-chi*: "Each loves his own family members,"[280] and "In love one begins with one's family members."[281] The Taipings, by contrast, based their concept of brotherhood on the fatherhood of God rather than on love among family members. Thus it does not seem that the idea of brotherhood was derived from the Confucian sources.

The Taiping idea of brotherhood could have been influenced by the Confucian idea, however, in its social status hierarchy. Confucians believed in strict social distinction. This aspect of their philosophy was treated most eloquently by Hsün-tzu but more succinctly in a single line found in the *Li-chi*: "Honor the honorable, and respect the respectable:

277 *Lun-yü yin-te*, 20/11/8..
278 *Meng-tzu yin-te*, 21/3A/5.
279 *Ibid.*, 54/7A /45.
280 *Li-chi yin-te*, 9/1.
281 *Ibid.*, 24/16.

these are the greatest of [social] principles."[282] The term "respect" or "respectable" here stands for status belonging either to a ruler, without reference to his moral character, or to those who have attained both a high social position and moral achievement. But the term "honor" or "honorable" refers to those whose high status is due to their hereditary position in that society without reference to their moral character. The Taipings, in spite of their claim that all men are brothers as sons of God, were great believers in social distinction.

There is a passage in the Taiping "Proclamations by Imperial Sanction" (Pan-hsing chao-shu) which says: "I, the commander-in-chief, thinking of the virtue of God in his love of life and having in my mind the suffering and the ill, have planned this benevolent and righteous expedition. As I feel toward you in the same way as I feel toward brothers from the same womb, I have mustered officers and troops in an effort to serve our country with complete loyalty."[283] This passage definitely suggests the "Hsi-ming" of Chang Tsai of the Sung, where the following line occurs: "The people are my brothers [of the same womb], and things are my comrades."[284] The commentary on this line says: "Just because we are all brothers, so the world is thought to be one family and the Middle Kingdom one man."[285]

When the passage from "Proclamations by Imperial Sanction" is considered in connection with the passage on the world of Great Harmony which the Taipings took from the Li-chi, one is almost irresistibly tempted to infer that the Taiping idea of brotherhood came from these sources. It is possible that this passage from the Li-chi also inspired Chang Tsai's poetry and philosophy. However, on a closer investigation, the Taiping brotherhood seems more like a secret society than a brotherhood nobly conceived as described by the authors of "Li-yün" and "Hsi-ming." The sense of union with the rest of mankind, which is either implied or expressed in "Li-yün" and "Hsi-ming," seems to be absent from the Taiping conception. The sense of union in the classical idea of brotherhood definitely transcends the narrow conception of a society built on the basis of strict social distinctions, be it Confucian or Taiping.

The Taiping idea of social welfare may be best treated in connection with the Taiping conception of the world of Great Harmony. In the

[282] Ibid., 49/4.
[283] Ch'eng, Shih-liao, I, 2b–3a.
[284] Chang Tsai, Chang-tzu ch'üan-shu, 1:4.
[285] Ibid.

world of Great Harmony, the Taipings dreamed of providing care for all their people, particularly the unfortunate, such as the widowed, the orphaned, the sick, the maimed, and the crippled. This, of course, was not unique with the Taipings. As early as the times when the odes were circulating, people sang mournfully in sympathy for the unfortunate ones. In "Hung-yen" appear the following lines: "Alas both for those pitiable men and for these solitary ones and widows."[286] And in "Cheng-yüeh": "All is well with the rich people, alas for these who are [solitary] helpless and alone."[287] Commenting on this line, Chu Hsi said: "It is for this that Mencius opined that King Wen, in instituting government and carrying out [a policy of] benevolence, put [the affairs of] the widowers, the widows, the fatherless, and the sonless first."[288] In "Wang-chih" in the Li-chi the aged are well provided for; [289]the fatherless young and the sonless, wifeless, and husbandless old persons have their regular pensions;[290] and the dumb, the deaf, the crippled, and the mained are all taken care of according to their need.[291] In the Chou-li under the office of ti-kuan ssu-t'u 地官司徒 six welfare policies are given as one of the functions of ssu-t'u (the ministry of education): (1) love the young; (2) support the aged; (3) give aid to the wretched (窮 chiung, including kuan [鰥 old widower], kua [寡 old widow], ku [孤 fatherless young] and tu [獨 old sonless persons], according to the commentary by Cheng Hsüan); (4) help [financially] the poor; (5) be lenient to the sick (in connection with military and corvée service); and (6) pacify the rich.[292] These social welfare policies are expressed in a passage in "Li-yün," which the Taipings quoted in its entirety as describing an ideal society they could use as a goal for themselves.[293]

The main concern of the "Hsi-ming" of Chang Tsai is the welfare of the unfortunate. The "Hsi-ming" emphasizes that all such people are intimately related to us. Although the Taiping conception of brotherhood did not closely resemble the one expressed in classical sources, the

---

[286] The Book of Odes, translated by Bernhard Karlgren, p. 125. "These solitary ones" means widowers. Karlgren is not specific enough here.

[287] Ibid., p. 137. "Helpless and alone" means specifically brotherless and sonless, according to the commentary.

[288] Shih chi-chuan, 11:22a.

[289] Li-chi yin-te, 13/15b–16a.

[290] Ibid., 13/22b–23a.

[291] Ibid., 13/23a.

[292] Chou-li chu-shu, 3/17a.

[293] Li-chi yin-te, 9/1.

Taiping and classical ideals of social welfare were similar; it seems safe to say that the Taipings made no new contribution in the area of social welfare.

On the authority of Liu Ch'eng-yü, who heard it from the people of Hua-hsien, Jen Yu-wen drew the conclusion that Hung synthesized the East and the West; for before he came into contact with Christianity, he embraced the principle of the "three periods" of the Kung-yang school, the ideal of Great Harmony from "Li-yün," and the social ideals of ancient China and the ethical thought of Confucianism.[294] We have seen that Hung's ideal of Great Harmony and his social welfare and ethical ideas were related to the sources Jen Yu-wen cites. Let us discuss the "three periods" in order to see whether the Taipings did incorporate anything from the Kung-yang school into their ideology, as Jen suggests they did.

The Kung-yang commentary on the *Ch'un-ch'iu* describes the "three periods" in the following words: "Different judgments are given of the world [Confucius] witnessed; different judgments are given of the world he heard of; and different judgments are given of the world indirectly handed down to him through tradition."[295] Tung Chung-shu and Ho Hsiu had definite ideas about these three periods. According to them, the period actually witnessed by Confucius consisted of the reign of three dukes—Ai, Ting, and Chao; the period he heard of consisted of the reign of four dukes—Hsiang, Ch'eng, Hsüan, and Wen; and the period handed down through tradition consisted of the reign of five dukes—Hsi, Min, Chuang, Huan, and Yin. The first period lasted for sixty-one years, the second for eighty-five, and the third for eighty-six years.[296]

In Kung-yang there is another interpretation of the three periods based on a principle expressing the attitude of the Chinese first toward the other states and then toward the non-Chinese (barbarian) culture. "The *Ch'un-ch'iu* [advocates] that one consider as inner [内, his own] his own state, and as outer all the other Chinese states [the first period]; and then that one consider all Chinese states as inner and all the non-Chinese

---

[294] Jen [Chien] Yu-wen, *T'ai-p'ing-chün Kwangsi shou-i shih*, pp. 66–67.

[295] This occurs three times in the Kung-yang commentary: *Ch'un-ch'iu ching-chuan yin-te*, 4/Yin 1/7 Kung; 25/Huan 2/4 Kung; 487/Ai 14/1 Kung.

[296] Tung Chung-shu, *Ch'un-ch'iu fan-lu*, "Ch'u-chuang-wang pien," 1:6. For Ho Hsiu's commentary, see *Ch'un-ch'iu Kung-yang chuan chu shu*, p. 13.

states as outer [the second period]."²⁹⁷ Apparently there is a third stage implied in which even the non-Chinese states would be considered inner. Ho Hsiu explained the three periods thus:

> With respect to the period handed down by tradition, one sees government in the midst of decline and chaos; at such a time one only grasps the tangible. Hence one considers his own state as inner and other Chinese states as outer. . . . With respect to the second period, one sees [relative] peace [peace within the state]. Hence one considers the other Chinese states as inner and the barbarians as outer. . . . With respect to the witnessed period, one sees peace prevailing [throughout the world]. Hence the barbarians are promoted to receive rank; and the far and the near, the large and the small under heaven are as if one.²⁹⁸

The implied third stage is here explicitly expounded. Chiang Po-ch'ien, a modern scholar, on the basis of Ho Hsiu's commentary makes the following remark:

> By "the far and the near, the large and the small under heaven are as if one" is meant that in the witnessed period in which peace has prevailed one has already reached the world of "Great Harmony," and the whole world is one family. . . . According to Confucius, in the evolution of the world the political life must go through these three stages: (1) [the stage of] exterminating the traitors and rebels, giving respect to the king and warding off the barbarians—this is to eliminate chaos; [the stage of] observing closely the principle of *li* and practicing what is righteous and being human-hearted in punishment and yielding priority to others—this is the way to obtain the relative peace; (3) [the final stage which will be reached] when once the world of peace and the political state of Great Harmony are achieved. The world will belong to the public, and the virtuous and the able will be selected [to rule]; at that time, the Middle Kingdom will be one man and the world will be one family.²⁹⁹

The third stage is definitely identified with the world of Great Harmony.

The Taipings may have reasoned as Ho Hsiu in the later Han and Chiang Po-ch'ien of modern times did. However, with the exception of the world of Great Harmony, which is conceived to be the last stage in the principle of the "three periods," and the attitude of the Taipings toward the barbarians (the Manchus), there is no trace of Kung-yang

²⁹⁷ *Ch'un-ch'iu ching-chuan yin-te*, 239/Ch'eng 15/12 Kung. See also Tung Chung-shu, *op. cit.*, "Wang Tao," 11:22.

²⁹⁸ *Ch'un-ch'iu Kung-yang chuan chu shu*, p. 13.

²⁹⁹ Chiang Po-ch'ien, *Shih-san-ching kai-lun*, p. 459.

teachings in the Taiping ideological system. Even the world of Great Harmony was not in any way linked by the Taipings with other periods in a historical movement toward the final stage. The Taipings' use of the *Li-chi* passage to express their ideal of the world of Great Harmony and their use of the ethnic issue from the *Ch'un-ch'iu* to stir up feelings against the Manchus without linking these ideas with the Kung-yang theory of three periods definitely suggests that they went directly to the *Li-chi* and to the *Ch'un-ch'iu* and did not borrow any idea from the Kung-yang school, as Jen Yu-wen has suggested.

Institutional Aspect of Li

In addition to the function of bringing about harmony, *li* has another function, that of defining distinctions. The former function serves to unite society into one whole, and the latter to make it articulate by making distinctions among its members and groups. In its dual function, *li* unites various elements of a society to form a hierarchy of social order.

The idea of distinction is implied in "Taiping Social Decorum" (T'ai-p'ing li-chih). A note by a reader found in the British Museum edition says: "The 'T'ai-p'ing li-chih' fixes the address of the above and the below, the honorable and the lowly, so that a minister will know how to address his superiors and his equals. However, these addresses were fabrications of the Taipings and there were no such things originally in China."[300] It is true that the specific forms of the addresses were partially the creation of the Taipings themselves, but the use of addresses as a device to distinguish between the honorable and the lowly was clearly a part of Chinese tradition.[301] Distinction is the second half of the function of *li*. The *Li-chi* says: "The purpose of *li* is to fix nearness and distance in relation, to pass judgment on what is doubtful, to distinguish between what is the same and what is different, and to make clear what is right and what is wrong."[302] The *Chou-li* says: "The function of the office of *ta-tsung-po* is . . . to straighten the ranks in the nation by means of the nine forms of appointment."[303] Cheng's commentary says: "The

---

[300] "T'ai-p'ing li-chih," Prologue, in Hsiao, *Ts'ung-shu, ts'e* 2, p. 1a.

[301] Here we remind the reader that a distinction has to be drawn between content and form. In this system of addresses and in what follows, we may find the content of the Taiping institutions different from the content of the traditional ones, but we shall see that the Taiping institutions did not deviate much from the traditional form or pattern.

[302] *Li-chi yin-te*, 1/5.

[303] *Chou-li yin-te*, 5/1a–14b.

form differs with each ranking appointment; the rank of the noble and the lowly will thus be rightly fixed. The *Ch'un-ch'iu* commentary says, 'When titles and ranks are different their *li* will also differ in specific ways.' "[304] Chia Kung-yen of the T'ang added the following comment: "*Ta-tsung-po* was in charge of the five forms of *li*. The purpose of *li* is to distinguish between the honorable and the lowly; therefore the nine forms of appointment are used to fix the ranks of the vassal lords and states, so that there will not be any usurpation and discrepancy."[305]

The *Li-chi* also says: "*Yüeh* [music] is the harmony of heaven and earth, and *li* is the order of heaven and earth. Because of harmony, the hundred things transform themselves; because of order, things are differentiated from one another."[306] Hsün-tzu in his "Yüeh-lun" gives a similar idea: "*Yüeh* harmonizes; *li* differentiates."[307] And Hsün-tzu in "Li-lun" explains what is meant by "differentiation": "What is differentiation? It is: the honorable and the lowly have their strata; the old and the young have their distinction; and the poor and the rich, the light [unimportant] and the heavy [important] each has his due."[308] A statement in the *Li-chi* reads: "When T'ien is high and earth is low, and the ten thousand things individually assume different forms, [we have evidence that] the principle of *li* is in operation."[309] Again in the *Li-chi*:

When T'ien is honorable and the earth lowly, the status of sovereign and minister will then be fixed. When the low and the high are exhibited, the status of the honorable and the lowly will then be placed. When motion and rest are according to norm, the large and the small will then become differentiated. When things are grouped together according to their categories, and classified according to their common nature, individual nature and life will then become different. In heaven [metaphysically] ideas are formed, and on earth [physically] material things take shape. Thus [what we call] *li* is the differentiation of heaven.[310]

The ultimate end of *li* is undoubtedly political control. Hsün-tzu expressed this in his work, and the *Li-chi* puts it succinctly: "Therefore, *li*

304 *Ibid.*, 5:15a.
305 *Chou-li chu-shu*, 18:18a.
306 *Li-chi yin-te*, 19/4.
307 *Hsün-tzu*, p. 253.
308 *Ibid.*, p. 231.
309 *Li-chi yin-te*, 19/6.
310 *Ibid.*, 19/6.

is the great weapon [*ping* 柄, the handle of a sword] of a sovereign."[311]

For *li* to be effective in its operation as a regulative principle of social conduct, it has to be a weapon, a form of power or sanction; to achieve this end, it must be institutionalized. Through indoctrination, there is developed in each person an inner source of sanction, which is generally known as moral sanction. Through the creation of various institutions based on the principle of *li*, one seeks to establish a social sanction which may also become a legal or political sanction. We have seen how the Taipings tried to control the minds of their fellow men by adopting moral precepts based on the traditional principle of *li*. Were they as traditional in the institutional aspect of *li* as they had been in the moral aspect? The key to this problem is their emphasis on social distinction. Were the ways they used to maintain social distinction similar to, or different from, those of the traditional pattern?

To solve this problem, we shall have to go beyond the scope of ideology into the realm of Taiping administrative organization on one hand and beyond the strictly Confucian and classical into the political institutions of the past on the other.

The ranking of officials is, of course, a feature of any government or society. What was the nature of the Taiping ranking and how were the ranks maintained and recognized? First of all, the Taipings had a new set of titles for their nobility. Between the title of wang and the title of *ch'eng-hsiang* (chancellor) at the top of the bureaucracy, there were six ranks: *i* 義, *an* 安, *fu* 福, *yen* 燕, *yü* 豫, and *hou* 侯. Though different in name from the traditional titles of *kung* 公, *hou* 侯, *po* 伯, *tzu* 子, and *nan* 南, the Taiping ranks are not really different in nature. The reason for the change is given by the Kan Wang in "A Hero's Submission to Truth": "The present *i, an, fu, yen, yü,* and *hou* are immensely better than the ancient *kung, hou, po, tzu,* and *nan,* for the reason that these latter are all terms applied among the family members. To apply these family terms to government officials is indeed stupid and vulgar."[312] This explanation reveals that the Taipings' way of ranking differed from the traditional way only in the symbols used.

The ranks the Taipings created from *ch'en-hsiang* down to *wu-chang* may also be compared to the traditional system of *ch'ing* (given in "Wang-chih" as *shang-ta-fu;* the commentary took *ch'ing* and *shang-ta-fu*

[311] *Ibid.*, 9/16.
[312] "Ying-chieh kuei-chen," in Hsiao, *Ts'ung-shu, ts'e* 10, p. 13a–b.

to be the same official), *hsia-ta-fu, shang-shih, chung-shih,* and *hsia-shih.*[313]

The Taipings made the titles of the nobility hereditary and brought about a process of social stratification. That the titles were hereditary indicates that the traditional outlook had not been influenced by any new ideas gained from contact with the West.

The Taipings left certain ranks vacant when the person occupying that rank and for whom the rank had been specially created either died or was promoted. As far as I know, there is no precedent in Chinese history for this practice. In the T'ang time, the office of *shang-shu-lin* 尚書令 was left vacant out of respect for T'ai-tsung, who twice (in the years 618 and 619) occupied the position.[314] This is hardly a parallel because *shang-shu-lin* was not specifically created for T'ai-tsung and because it was the ministers who avoided assumption of that title out of respect for their great monarch; such a practice of honorific considera- tion was not meant to be part of the official institution. In this respect the Taipings seem to have adapted their system to individuals instead of fitting individuals into the system. The thought of personal glory seems to have blinded the Taiping leaders to the necessity of creating a new social class.

In the Taiping ranking system officials with the same title differed in rank according to the position of the wang under whom they served. Officials serving under the T'ien Wang were higher in rank than those with the same titles serving under any other wang; those serving under the Tung Wang were higher in rank than those of similar title who served under a lower-ranking wang.

This differentiation among officers with the same title seems to have been based on a system found in the *Chou-li.* "Tien-ming" contains the following ruling:

The king's three *kung* are of the eighth ranking appointment [next to the highest]; his *ch'ing* are of the sixth and his *ta-fu* of the fourth.... *Kung's ku* are of the fourth...his *ch'ing* are of the third, his *ta-fu* of the second, and his *shih* of the first rank....The *ch'ing* of *tzu* and *nan* are of the second, their *ta-fu* of the first, and their *shih* without rank. [315]

[313] *Li-chi chu-shu, chüan* 11, "Wang-chih," p. 1a.

[314] *Hsin T'ang-shu,* by Sung Ch'i (T'ung-wen ed.), 46:2a.

[315] *Chou-li chu-shu,* 5:39b. The system need not be the one which the Chou people put into effect. *Chou-li* is a work of the Han period; it cannot be considered the system of the Chou, though this idea is not thoroughly without basis.

The *Chou-li* gives nine ranks in appointment. In the excerpt below, quotation marks enclose the statement from the *Chou-li*. The remainder of each rank description is Cheng's comment.

"With first-rank appointment one receives office." The *shih* of the vassal states [by vassal states is meant *kung* 公, *po* 伯, and *hou* 侯], the *ta-fu* of *tzu* and *nan*, and the king's *hsia-shih* are all first-rank appointments.

"With second-rank appointment one receives ceremonial robes." The *ta-fu* of the vassal states, the *ch'ing* of *tzu* and *nan*, and the king's *chung-shih* are second-rank appointments.

"With third-rank appointment one receives position." The *ch'ing* of the vassal states and the *shang-shih* of the king are third-rank appointments.

"With fourth-rank appointment one receives ceremonial vessels." *Kung's ku* and king's *hsia-ta-fu* are fourth-rank appointments.

"With fifth-rank appointment one receives *tse* 則." [According to Cheng, *tse* means territory which is just short of a *kuo*, a state. To be classified as a state, a territory has to contain at least 300 square li. There are three grades of states: great, secondary, and small. Great and secondary states, which constitute the states of the *kung*, *po*, and *hou*, are called *lieh-kuo;* and the small states are states of *tzu* and *nan*.] The king's *hsia-ta-fu* are fourth-rank appointments; but when invested with territory of 200 square li, they receive an additional ranking appointment, that is, the fifth.

"With sixth-rank appointment one receives the right to appoint one's own subordinates." This refers to the king's *ch'ing*.

"With seventh-rank appointment one receives a state." The king's *ch'ing* are sixth-rank appointments; but when invested with a state, they receive an additional ranking appointment, that is, the seventh.

"With eighth-rank appointment one becomes a *mu* 牧." [*Hou* and *po*, who have distinguished themselves with merits and virtue, are *mu*.] *Hou* and *po*, who have merits and virtues, receive special appointment with the privilege to punish the vassal lords at their discretion. The three *kung* of the king are also eighth-rank appointments.

"With ninth-rank appointment one becomes a *po*." The highest *kung* of the three who have merits and virtues is given special appointment to be second *po*, with the privilege to punish the five *hou* and nine *po*. [The earlier Cheng said this referred to the head of the vassal lords.][316]

In "Wang-chih" of the *Li-chi* the same principle is expressed:

The *shang-ch'ing* of the secondary states are equal in rank to the *chung-ch'ing* of the great states, their *chung-ch'ing* are equal to the latters' *hsia-ch'ing*, and

316 For both the text and commentaries on these pages, see *Chou-li yin-te*, 5/15a-b; *Chou-li chu-shu*, 18:18a–21a.

their *hsia-ch'ing* are equal to the latters' *shang-ta-fu*. The *shang-ch'ing* of small states are equal to the *hsia-ch'ing* of great states, their *chung-ch'ing* are equal to the latters' *shang-ta-fu*, and their *shang-ta-fu* are equal to the latters' *hsia-ta-fu*.[317]

The *Li-chi* also states:

The *ch'ing* of great states are third-rank appointments and not over, their *hsia-ch'ing* are second-rank, and the *ch'ing* and *hsia-ta-fu* of the small states are first-rank appointments.[318]

The quotations given here show that the principle which the Taipings adopted was supposed to be at work in ancient times.

In their adoption of strict sumptuary laws to maintain social distinction and to keep the people at a respectful social distance, the Taipings again showed their traditional leaning. The content of these laws was not the same as traditional sumptuary laws; but as "Yü-fu chih" in *Ch'ing-shih kao* (A Draft of the History of the Ch'ing Dynasty) states, neither was the content of one dynasty's laws the same as that of another dynasty's laws: "Hsia had its capping ceremony and Yin had its capping ceremony, it was not borrowed one dynasty from the other. For what is adopted by one dynasty has its own form; that is to say, in *li* people do not forget their origin."[319] The spirit of the Taiping system, then, together with the feelings and emotions aroused by the symbols of the system, is traditional.

It is not necessary to explain the traditional system of sumptuary laws in order to infer the connection between the traditional and Taiping systems. The *Chou-li* treats of the traditional system in "Tien-ming,"[320] and the *Shih-chi* enunciates the principle of sumptuary laws in these words:

Therefore with respect to the order of sovereign and ministers, the order at court, the order of the honorable and the lowly, the noble and the humble, down to the position of the commoners; and the appropriate differences in carriages, dresses and robes, foods, manners of marriage and funeral and sacrifices—with respect to all of these, each has its proper way and each has its regulated pattern.[321]

[317] *Li-chi chu-shu, chüan* 11, "Wang-chih," p. 7b.
[318] *Ibid.*, p. 25a.
[319] *Ch'ing-shih kao, ts'e* 30, section 2, p. 1b.
[320] *Chou-li yin-te*, 5/38b–39b.
[321] *Shih-chi*, by Ssu-ma Ch'ien, 23:2a.

In all dynastic histories, we find something of this kind treated either in a monograph on *li* or in chapters on the institutions of state carriages and ceremonial robes. Ma Tuan-lin of the Sung had recorded in his *Wen-hsien t'ung-k'ao* systems of caps and robes and insignia (*chüan* 111–13); ornaments, robes, insignia used by queens, royal concubines, and wives of officials who had received *ming* (ranking appointment), (*chüan* 114); gem or jade tokens, tallies or credentials and seals (*chüan* 115); royal carriages, banners and equippage or escort (*chüan* 116–18); carriages and escort of queens, royal concubines, and wives of officials who had received ranking appointment (*chüan* 119); and carriages and retinue of heirs apparent, royal princes, *kung*, *ch'ing* and lower officials (*chüan* 119). The Ch'ing dynasty had their systems recorded in *Ta-ch'ing t'ung-li*, the last edition of which was completed in 1824.

Forms of address like those embodied in "Taiping Social Decorum" were an old game with ancient Chinese nobility. For example, *Hsü wen-hsien t'ung-k'ao* contains a long section on "Wang-li" (The Rules of Behavior of the Empire), carefully describing the way one member of the social order addresses and behaves in relation to another member.[322] There seems to be no fundamental difference in attitude between this traditional pattern and that of the Taipings.

For specific illustration, I shall compare the system of insignias used by the Taipings with a traditional one, that of the Ch'ing dynasty. Since the Taipings specifically wished to destroy this dynasty, they should as a matter of policy have tried their best to destroy the insignia system of the dynasty, too. Instead, they used many of the Ch'ing system insignia, although the insignia did not stand for the same rank.

The Taipings used the symbol of dragons generously, indicating distinction in rank by the number of dragons. This symbol was reserved for royal personages in the Ch'ing dynasty. The Taipings used also the phoenix, which in the Ch'ing was the insignia of queens and royal concubines. The other animals used for Taiping insignia were the lion, *ch'i-lin* (the fabulous animal), tiger, leopard, bear, tiger-cat, and rhinoceros, in order of ranking. In the Ch'ing system, *ch'i-lin* was the insignia of the highest military rank, followed by the lion, leopard, tiger, bear, tiger-cat, rhinoceros, and seal in this order.[323] The only modifications the Taipings made in the Ch'ing system were to reverse the order of *ch'i-lin* and lion, and of leopard and tiger; and to omit the seal. Even in their

---

[322] See also *Ta-ch'ing t'ung-li*, *chüan* 46.
[323] *Ta-ch'ing hui-tien*, by K'un Kang *et al.*, *chüan* 29.

changes, the Taipings seem to have had some tendency to follow what had gone before them. *Ch'i-lin* was the insignia of the highest military rank in the Ch'ing system; the Taipings gave *ch'i-lin* to *tsung-chih*, the highest officer in the field. These insignia were embroidered on the caps or robes of the Taiping officials.

In addition, the Taipings used the elephant and deer as insignia on the main gates of their palaces. One interesting observation is that they used no birds other than the legendary phoenix. In the Ch'ing system birds were used for civil ranks, and quadrupeds for military ranks. The reason the Taipings were interested only in the military insignia may be that their whole organizational system was primarily military, and their society a military society.

The Taipings condemned usurping the use of paraphernalia belonging to a higher rank as *chien fen kan ming* (usurping the rights of a higher rank and offending against the established social principles) and made such usurpation punishable by law. This sacred nature of social distinction reflects the traditional attitude, exemplified by Confucius' indignation at Chi-shih's usurpation in his court of the use of eight rows of dancers.[324]

The idea of name taboo which the Taipings adopted may be traced to the *Ch'un-ch'iu*: "In the *Ch'un-ch'iu* taboo was observed for the honorable, for parents, and for the virtuous."[325] Even in serving ancestral spirits, the principle of taboo was used.[326] The Taiping practice of taboo was in accord with the spirit thus expressed, except that the Taipings did not seem to pay much attention to either parents or the virtuous in their taboo. Possibly the virtuous and the honorable were considered as one, and the parents had been superseded by God the Heavenly Father.

The Taiping principle of taboo was very simple. In most cases they did not taboo homophones but used homophones to replace the tabooed words. The earlier practice of tabooing words of like sound began with the *wu* of the Three Kingdom period in A.D. 242, when Ho-hsing 禾興 was changed to Chia-hsing 嘉興 because one of the royal princes by the name of Ho 禾 had just been made heir apparent.[327] Though homo-

---

[324] *Lun-yü yin-te*, 4/3/1.

[325] *Ch'un-ch'iu ching-chuan yin-te*, 210/Ch'eng 1/6 Ku; 81/Min 1/6 Kung. See also 50/Chuang 4/4 Kung; 112/Hsi 17/2 Kung; 135/Hsi 28/19 Kung; 399/Chou 20/2 Kung; 326/Hsiang 29/8 Kung.

[326] *Ibid.*, 33/Huan 6/5 Tso.

[327] Ch'en Yüan, "Shih-hui chü-li," *Yenching Hsüeh-pao*, Vol. IV, No. 4 (Dec., 1928), p. 626.

phones were not tabooed before that date, we find no case where they were chosen as substitutes for the words that were tabooed. The general principle was to use a synonym, such as *tuan* 端 for *cheng* 政, *kuo* 國 for *pan* 邦, *man* 滿 for *yin* 盈, *ch'ang* 常 for *heng* 恆, *t'ung* 通 for *ch'e* 徹. There was one case in the Chin dynasty in which a homophone was chosen as a substitute. For *i* 懿, the name of Chin Hsuan-ti 晉宣帝, *i* 益 or *i* 壹 was used.[328]

The practice of taboo was loose and inconsistent in the Northern and Southern dynasties, but in Sui and especially in T'ang it again became very strict. Han Yü wrote a strong protest against those who criticized Li Ho for becoming a *chin-shih* 進士 because his father's name was Chin-su 晉肅.[329] Han Yü in this essay brought in two principles that are found in the *Li-chi*: in *li* homophones are not tabooed; and in the case of a double name (a name consisting of two characters), both characters are not tabooed.[330] Long before Han Yü, in A.D. 626, an edict stated that both characters of a double name need not be tabooed.[331] Another edict in 660 stated that homophones were not to be tabooed.[332]

In subsequent dynasties homophones came more and more into use. In the Five Dynasties, Li Ching 李璟 changed his name to Li Ching 李景, because the Kao-tsu of the Chou's name was *Ching* 環; in the Ming, *ch'ang* 旹 and *lo* 雒 were used in the place of Ch'ang-lo 常洛, which was the name of Kuang-tsung; in the Ch'ing, *hung* 宏 and *li* 歷 were used in place of Hung-li 弘曆, the name of Kao-tsung. The Taipings, whether they were conscious of the past or not, used homophones consistently with a few exceptions: they employed the synonym *k'ao* 考 (old) to take the place of *lao* 老 (old), an honorific sign applied only to God; and *yen* 炎 flame) replaced *huo* 火 (fire), another word applied to God alone.

The Taipings changed *ch'ou* 丑 (the second symbol of the twelve earthly branches) to *hao* 好 (good), because *ch'ou* is a homonym of *ch'ou* 醜 (ugly) and they did not like to mention ugliness; they changed *mao* 卯 (the fourth symbol of the earthly branches) to *yung* 榮 (glory), because the sound *mao* in southern dialect means "stupid." They changed *hai* 亥 to *k'ai* 開 (opening or beginning) because *hai* was the last symbol of the earthly branches; they did not realize that a last symbol is still the last

---

[328] *Ibid.*, p. 629.
[329] *Chu Wen-kung chiao Han Ch'ang-li hsien sheng-chi*, "Pien wei," 12:10a.
[330] *Li-chi yin-te*, 1/41.
[331] Tu Yu, *T'ung-tien*, 104:553, quoted by Ch'en Yüan in *op. cit.*, p. 634.
[332] *Ibid.*

despite the change. There are historical instances before the Taipings in which the symbols of the heavenly stems and earthly branches were changed—though for the usual reason of taboo on account of royal names.[333]

The examples given above indicate the Taipings' desire to avoid what they disliked, as in changing *kuei* 鬼 (ghost) to *jen* 人 (man) and *hun* 魂 to *hun* 訊. These changes also served as an ideological lesson to warn the people to try to become men (Taiping followers) instead of devils (people working for the enemy). The practice of tabooing a word because of the desire to avoid what is disliked has historical parallels. Su-tsung of the T'ang, because of his dislike for An Lu-shan 安禄山, changed the names of many *chün* (armies) and *hsien* (districts) which had *an* as part of their names.[334] The Sung, because of their hatred toward the Chin, used *chin* 今 for Chin (金, a dynastic name in Chinese).[335] And in the Ming, *yüan* 元 was not used. When they wanted to express the idea of the first year of a reign, which was formerly expressed by *yüan-nien* 元年, the Mings used *yüan-nien* 原年 in order to avoid mentioning the hated Yüan.[336] At the end of the Ming, two persons by the name of Li 李 changed their name to Li 理 independently for the identical reason: they were ashamed to have the same name as Li Tzu-ch'eng 李自成, the rebel responsible for the death of the last Ming emperor and the fall of the dynasty.[337]

From the case in which the Taipings changed *ch'ou* 丑 to *hao* 好 because the former has the same sound as *ch'ou* 醜, it is clear that the Taipings did not follow consistently any one principle in the practice of word taboo: in this case they tabooed a homophone, whereas elsewhere they substituted homophones for the tabooed words. However, no dynasty before them had been completely consistent in this practice.

Because *wang* 王 was the title Taiping leaders assumed, those in history who were called by that title were subsequently called *k'uang* 狂. Ch'en Yüan treats of parallel cases at length in his essay, "Shih-hui chü-li."[338] In the Han dynasty, because Kao-tsu's name was Pang, Han edicts quoting "Hsieh-ho wan-pang" 協和萬邦 from the *Book of History*,

---

[333] Ch'en Yüan, "Shih-hui chü-li," *Yenching Hsüeh-pao*, Vol. IV, No. 4 (Dec., 1928), pp. 550–51.

[334] *Ibid.*, pp. 560–61.

[335] *Ibid.*

[336] *Ibid.*

[337] *Ibid.*

[338] *Yenching Hsüeh-pao*, Vol. IV, No. 4 (Dec., 1928), pp. 537–651.

changed the phrase to "Hsieh-ho wan-kuo" 協和萬國. The biography of
K'uai T'ung 蒯通 in the *Han-shu* has the following note by Yen Shih-ku:
"His original name is Ch'e 徹; later historians changed it to T'ung 通,
ch'e being the name of *wu-ti* 武帝."

Though the Taipings used taboo extensively, they did not adopt the
practice of giving a posthumous name or title to the dead. The reason is
not that their dynasty was too short to start the practice: some very
important leaders—among them Feng Yün-shan and Hsiao Ch'ao-kuei
and later Yang Hsiu-ch'ing, for whom dates in the new calendar were
established—died at the very beginning of their campaign. The reason
seems to lie in the Taiping attitude toward death itself. Since death was
considered to be the event through which a person ascended to heaven
or descended to hell, there was no purpose in glorifying or criticizing
(the function of a posthumous name) anybody who had died. In this
respect, the Taipings may be considered untraditional in their attitude
toward the dead.

The Taipings did not taboo the use of the names of their parents.
There are no definite rulings about the status of wangs' fathers in relation to wangs, but there are some facts which reveal indirectly the Taiping attitude about this relationship. Wei Ch'ang-hui, the Pei Wang,
received his father Yüan-yü on auspicious occasions as one of the subordinates. His father paid him the same respect as the rest of the court
officials did by kneeling before him.[339] Hsiao Ch'ao-kuei even had his
parents executed because they violated the heavenly precept prohibiting
husband and wife from sleeping together. This Taiping attitude differs
greatly from the traditional attitude, which is reflected in Mencius:

> T'ao Ying asked, saying: "Shun being the sovereign and Kao-yao chief
> minister of justice, if Ku-sou [Shun's father] had murdered a man, what
> would have been done in the case?"
> Mencius said, "Kao-yao would simply have apprehended him."
> "But would not Shun have forbidden such a thing?"
> "Indeed, how could Shun have forbidden it? Kao-yao had received the
> law from a proper source."
> "In that case what would Shun have done?"
> "Shun would have regarded abandoning the kingdom as throwing away
> a worn-out sandal. He would privately have taken his father on his back
> and retired into concealment, living somewhere along the seacoast. There
> he would have been all his life cheerful and happy, forgetting the king-
> dom."[340]

[339] Chang Te-chien (editor and compiler), *Tse-ch'ing hui-tsuan*, *ts'e* 1, *chüan* 2.
[340] *Meng-tzu yin-te*, 53/7A/35.

The attitude embodied here has been carefully weighed after the opposite angles of the situation have been examined: the angle of the state from a legal point of view and that of Shun from the point of view of a son influenced by natural sentiment. This careful consideration of both the institutional and the natural sentiment characterized the attitude of later writers. *T'ung-tien* first gives the case of Shun: "Yü Shun, having ascended to the throne, very respectfully went under the banner and standard of the Son of Heaven to pay respect to Ku-sou in the way of a son." The author also reports a case in which Yen Wang, the father of an emperor, referred to himself as *ch'en* (臣 a servant) in his memorial to the emperor. The emperor, in his reply, asked his father to drop the term *ch'en* in his future communications, so that he could have peace of mind, free from the thought that his father was his servant. However, those at court who contributed their opinions to the matter argued that the father, as part of the institutional machine under the emperor, should refer to himself as *ch'en* when addressing the emperor. But in his communication to his father the emperor should always use the expression: "The emperor respectfully requests that great prince." Others believed that the institutional nature of the system should be maintained and the royal edict to his father should begin with the legal expression: "Edict to Yen Wang." One attempt to give Yen Wang his due honor as the father of the emperor was to taboo the use of his name for ordinary purposes and add the term *Shang* (上 the above) to his name whenever it was used.[341]

The debate described suggests that no definite pattern had been established, but the difference between the institutional and the natural point of view is clearly illustrated. This dual emphasis is no less clear in another passage quoted in *T'ung-tien:*

Ho Ch'i of the Chin submitted his opinion, saying: "The respected position of parents is modeled after that of heaven and earth; and the ways of [serving] sovereign and parents have in common reverence. Now that your majesty has become a sovereign of the land, your father, because of the fact that his son occupies the heavenly position, dares not treat the Son of Heaven as his son, and this is a case illustrating the principle of the state; and yet your majesty, though the Son of Heaven, must have somebody whom you respect. Considering this, the conclusion is: the father should of course refer to himself as *ch'en* in relation to the sovereign who occupies

[341] Tu Yu, *T'ung-tien*, 27:373.

the heavenly position, and the son should respect his father out of natural sentiment."[342]

The Taipings emphasized the institutional aspect to the total neglect of the natural sentiment aspect. They seem to have been influenced by ideas from sources that were not traditional in the matter of the attitude of a wang toward his father, and as a result they developed an exclusively institutional point of view.[343]

The Taipings' concern with social reforms is shown by their effort to prohibit opium- and tobacco-smoking, drinking, foot-binding, and prostitution and to destroy superstitious beliefs. Some of these customs were practiced because of the circumstances of the time; some were general problems throughout China; and some were based on historical precedents.

Social reforms necessitated by the circumstances of the time include prohibition against opium- and tobacco-smoking and foot-binding. Although opium had been smoked in China for many years, it became a serious problem only after the beginning of opium importation from India. Taiping leaders had witnessed the smuggling of opium and the resulting Opium War as well as the demoralizing effect the smoking produced among the people. China's defeat in the Opium War must have given them an added cause for wanting to eliminate all opium-smoking. Tobacco-smoking was only a secondary offense, probably prohibited because it was considered a habit similar to opium-smoking. It was natural for the Taipings to prohibit foot-binding, for the Hakka women did not practice it. However, the Taipings must also have had in mind the evils such practices brought to the women themselves and to the society to which they belonged, and the effect on military activities and labor. There had been antagonists who opposed both opium-smoking and foot-binding before the coming of the Taipings. We may recall

---

[342] *Ibid.*

[343] The Taipings' traditional pattern is also reflected in their documentary forms. With some modifications, their practice followed that of the past. They had specific terms for the documents from the wangs to their subordinates and from the latter to the former. Though all these terms were not exactly the same as had been in use in the past, the term for "edict" and that for "memorial" remained the same. Furthermore, their practice of *t'i-ko* (提格 elevation in space) to show honor or respect in their writings conformed to the pattern of the past. In general we may conclude that in their mental attitudes the Taipings were tied to the past.

[344] Yüan Mei, *Sui-yüan san-shih chung,* p. 10a–b.

Yüan Mei (1716–99), Li Ju-chen (about 1763–1830), Yü Cheng-hsieh (1775–1840), and Kung Tzu-chen (1792–1841).

Yüan expressed his dislike of smoking and foot-binding in his "Tu-wai yü-yen":

> What is there in the taste of tobacco and what good does one find in girls' foot-binding that the people of the whole world run after them as if they were mad? It seems to me that to cripple the hands and feet of our children for the purpose of obtaining beauty is the same as to cremate the remains of our parents in order to obtain blessings. How sad![344]

Li Ju-chen discussed the evil of foot-binding in his *Ching-hua-yüan*, an iconoclastic novel of ideas blasting the evil practices and customs of China from the point of view of the people of other lands. In Chapter XII a minister of the "Gentlemen's Kingdom," a certain Mr. Wu, expressed the following view:

> I hear that in your esteemed country, the women's feet are bound. When young girls' feet are being bound, the pain is something terrible. Their skin is inflamed and the flesh decomposes, smeared all over with blood. At this time they moan and cry, and can neither eat in daytime nor sleep at night for the pain, and develop all kinds of sickness. I thought that these must be bad girls being punished by their mothers for filial impiety, and therefore were submitted to this kind of torture which is only better than death. Who would suppose that this was done for their benefit to make them look beautiful, as if girls could not be beautiful without small feet! Now it seems to me when you cut off a superfluous part of a big nose or slice off a part of a high forehead, you would consider that man disfigured; and yet you regard girls who have disfigured feet and walk with a kind of tortured gait as beautiful! Just think of the famous beauties of old, Hsi-shih and Wang Ch'iang, who were beauties although they did not have one half of their feet cut off. When one comes to think of it carefully, I don't see what's the difference between foot-binding and a regular form of torture for criminals. I am sure this would never be approved by the sages and the truly wise. Only by all the gentlemen of this world agreeing to stamp out this custom can an end be put to it.[345]

And Li drove the lesson home to all "gentlemen" by subjecting Lin Chih-yang, a male character in the novel, to the foot-binding treatment

---

[345] Li Ju-chen, *Ching-hua-yüan*, 12:10. The translation is taken from Lin Yü-t'ang's article "Feminist Thought in Ancient China," *T'ien-Hsia Monthly*, Vol. I, No. 2 (Sept., 1935), p. 147.

when he was taken captive by the people of the "Women's Kingdom."[346]

Yü Cheng-hsieh objected to the foot-binding in the following words:

In ancient days we had compulsory labour for both men and women, but with their feet bound, women are no longer fit for government labour. *And when the female sex is weakened, then the harmony which comes from the mutual complementing of the male and female principles will be imperfect.* Moreover, the bow-shoes used in footbinding originated with ballet girls, and *when you lower the position of women, by implication you lower the position of men also.* The reason why women are not willing to give up this custom is because they are not aware that in ancient times there were big beautiful shoes for un-bound feet worn by the aristocrats. As they cannot be convinced by rea-soning alone, I have therefore gone to the trouble of making this point clear to them.[347]

Yü's objection was based on the ill effect of the practice on physical health, its disturbing influence on the harmony of the interplay of *yin* and *yang*, and the lack of dignity. He believed foot-binding was practiced because of women's ignorance of its bad effects.

Kung Tzu-chen, a great iconoclast of the nineteenth century, "ex-pressed in his poems a preference for Manchu ladies, who did not bind their feet."[348] Chu Chieh-ch'in, in his *Kung Ting-an yen-chiu*, inferred from two lines of Kung's poem[349] that Kung actually married a wife with natural feet.[350] Kung's hatred for opium and opium-smokers was strongly expressed in his suggestion to Lin Tse-hsü, which contributed to the formulation of the latter's policy toward opium. Kung advocated capital punishment for the smokers. In his satirical poems he exposed the prevailing habit of opium-smoking among the Manchu troops dur-ing the time the Tientsin treaty was signed, thus pointing to a cause of the weakness of the Manchu army.[351]

The Taipings' attempt to destroy superstition was preceded by similar attempts on the part of these same scholars. Yüan Mei spoke against Buddhism and the Buddhist philosophy of moral causality on a number

---

[346] Because Li Ju-chen was a scholar and because he apparently intended *Ching-hua-yüan* to be a vehicle of his learning rather than merely a novel, I have discussed his ideas here rather than in the later section on the influence of novels.

[347] Yü Cheng-hsieh, quoted in Lin, *op. cit.*, p. 133.

[348] Arthur W. Hummel (ed.), *Eminent Chinese of the Ch'ing Dynasty*, I, 433.

[349] These lines run: "In marriage it is my fortune to have as my wife one from Yin-shan, the northern regions, with jade complexion and big feet, a fairy indeed!"

[350] *Kung Ting-an yen-chiu*, p. 27.

[351] *Ibid.*, p. 26.

of occasions, expressing his belief that the universe runs on a naturalistic principle instead of a moral one.[352] He was against geomancy, condemning *Ch'ing-nang*[353] as a collection of false statements by diviners and soothsayers. He pointed out the truth of the saying that "a family which is versed in the art of burial need not be prosperous." Then he enumerated historical instances to prove his point.[354] Li Ju-chen was particularly eloquent in this respect. Through the mouth of an alien, he criticized the superstitious practices of the Chinese, from geomancy and moral causality[355] to Buddhist and Taoist superstitions.[356] Kung Tzu-chen spoke against geomancy in his "Anti-Five Elements" and against evil-infested temples in general, condemning especially the worship of Wen-ch'ang ti-chün, a deity supposedly in charge of the success and failure of examination candidates.[357]

In spite of these precedents, there is no reason, still less any necessity, to suppose that the Taipings were influenced by these gentlemen. It is only fair to assume that the Taiping reaction to these social problems was, in the absence of any evidence of direct connection with the traditional reactions, the result of their own experience.

As for anti-Buddhist feeling, the Chinese Buddhists never forgot the persecution they suffered during the reigns of the three Wu's and one Tsung 三武一宗.[358] Buddhism was often persecuted along with superstitious practices such as witchery and unorthodox worship. In almost all cases, however, Buddhist persecution was instigated by Taoists because of jealousy; rarely did an edict against Buddhism have the purpose of ridding the country of superstitious beliefs. Sometimes Buddhist persecution was mixed up with political complications. When all anti-Buddhist attempts in history are carefully considered, it is safe to say that the Tai-

[352] Yüan, *Sui-yüan san-shih chung*, "Hsiao-shan ts'ang-fang wen-chi," 35:21b; and "Tu wai yü-yen."

[353] A book on geomancy with a preface by Kuo P'u of the Chin dynasty. For detail, see *Chin-shu*, biography of Kuo P'u.

[354] *Sui-yüan san-shih chung*, "Hsiao-shan ts'ang-fang," 35:16a–17a. The geomancers maintained that those who were versed in the art of burial would be rich.

[355] Li, *Ching-hua-yüan*, 12:2.

[356] *Ibid.*, pp. 8–9.

[357] Chu Chieh-ch'in, *Kung Ting-an yen-chiu*, pp. 30–31.

[358] "Three Wu's" refers to (1) the T'ai-wu-ti of the Northern Wei, 424–52, (2) Wu-ti of the Northern Chou, 561–78, and (3) Wu-tsung of the T'ang, 841–47; and "one Tsung" refers to Shih-tsung of the later Chou, 954–60. During these reigns, Buddhism was denounced and the Buddhists persecuted. For detail, see their "Pen-chi" in their respective histories.

pings did not receive their incentive to destroy Buddhist and other superstitions from traditionalism.

The evils of prostitution and drinking are of such a general nature
that the Taipings did not have to go elsewhere for an incentive to prohibit them; but because of Christian influence and political and military
exigency, they showed a greater degree of earnestness in prohibiting
adultery and drinking.

The study of the Taiping social institutions shows that their proposed
social reforms were not an attempt to promote social equality. Social
equality was a concept completely alien to the thought of the traditional
Chinese. The Taipings were thoroughly traditional in that respect.

ECONOMIC BORROWINGS FROM TRADITIONAL SOURCES

Taiping economic ideals and system, expressed in a document entitled
"The Land System of the Heavenly Dynasty" (T'ien-ch'ao t'ien-mou
chih-tu), were the part of the ideology most effective in winning people
to the Taiping camp. The Taipings proposed to create a state wherein
the land would be equally distributed among all the people without distinction even between male and female. They wished to create a commonwealth in which there was to be complete economic justice and
security. We shall try to trace these ideas to their sources in an effort to
determine the degree of their originality.

The first ideal was economic equality in land distribution and common sharing of all goods and crops. This more than anything else appealed to the peasants, who for ages had been at the mercy of big landlords. "All lands in the empire must be cultivated by all the people in
the empire as a common concern. . . . The purpose is to enable all the
people in the empire to enjoy together the abundant happiness provided
by the Heavenly Father, Lord on High and Sovereign God."[359] This
idea of economic equality is truly amazing, although in actual practice
the Taiping institution failed to realize it.

The idea of equal distribution of land had been present in the past.
The *Chou-li* describes a system of land distribution called *t'u-chün* (equal
distribution of land), which was the object of experiment by Wang
Mang at the end of the Former Han and by others during the Pei-wei,
Pei-ch'i, and Pei-chou.[360] Wang Mang failed dismally while the others
had some limited success.

[359] "T'ien-ch'ao t'ien-mou chih-tu," in Hsiao, *Ts'ung-shu*, *ts'e* 4, pp. 1b–2a.
[360] *Chou-li chu-shu*, "Ta-ssu-t'u," 10:9a says, "*t'u-chün* being one of Ta-ssu-t'u's functions." See also "Hsiao Ssu-t'u," 11:4a.

Neither the *Chou-li* nor records of the other periods show any of the fraternal feelings expressed in the Taiping document. With the Taipings there seems to be a new sense of fellowship which gives the idea of equality a new significance. However, one should not infer too much from their idea of economic equality. Confucius said, "What we are concerned with is not scarcity, but inequality,"[361] but it would be direly wrong to think of Confucius as a believer in social equality.

Among the philosophers there are some who expressed ideas similar to those of the Taipings, in one case in almost identical words. Yen Yüan (1635–1704, styled Hun-jan, known as Hsi-chai hsien-sheng) in his "Ts'un-chih p'ien" said: "The lands in the world should be commonly shared by the people of the world."[362] Compare this line with the line from the Taiping document: "All lands in the empire [the world] must be cultivated by all the people in the empire [the world] as a common concern." The similarity is striking, but there is no reason to believe that the Taipings took their idea from the philosopher. Yen continued:

> If we let the rich have their wish, even if we gave the property of ten thousand men to one man, he would not be satisfied. Should this be the way in which the kingly way follows the feelings of the people? Furthermore, some men possess several tens and hundreds of *ch'ing* [100 mou to one *ch'ing*] while other tens or hundreds of people possess not even one *ch'ing;* could it be right for parents to make one son rich and the rest poor?[363]

Yen's disciple Li Kung (1659–1733, *tzu* Kang-chu, *hao* Shu-ku) in his *I t'ai-p'ing ts'e* under "Ti-kuan" said: "Without *chün-t'ien* [均田 equal distribution of land] [wealth] will not be equal [and there will be the distinction of] rich and poor; as a result it will not be possible for everybody to possess fixed property [dependable source of income]."[364] In the *P'ing-shu ting* he proposed a way to effect the equal distribution of land, with the purpose of giving land to the tillers.[365]

Similar ideas, even similar verbal expressions, do not prove a relation between the Taiping theory of land redistribution and theories of the past. However, the Taipings gave their idea of equal distribution of land significance by making what all the people produced the property of all,

---

[361] *Lun-yü yin-te*, 33/16/1.
[362] Yen Yüan, "Ts'un-chih p'ien," in *Ssu-ts'un p'ien, ts'e* 215, p. 1a–b.
[363] *Ibid.*
[364] *I t'ai-p'ing ts'e*, 2:1a.
[365] *P'ing-shu ting, chüan* 7 and 8, "Chih-t'ien."

to be shared and enjoyed by all. Without this further development, mere equal distribution of land might conceivably have led to a state of distinction between the rich and the poor because of the differences in people's personal nature and ability to fulfill their appointed duty. Perhaps even here, however, the Taipings were not as original as one might think; for their idea and practice of common sharing may be traced to some other source, such as secret societies.

In discussing land distribution, the Taipings classified land according to its productivity into three main categories: superior, middling, and inferior. Each of these was again divided into three classes: first, second, and third, making a total of nine grades. This division, in substance, followed the principle reported in the *Chou-li* and "Wang-chih" in the *Li-chi*. According to the *Chou-li*, land is divided into three grades: superior, middling, and inferior.[366] Because in another passage families of seven persons, six persons, and five persons were given as units for land distribution, Cheng stated in the commentary that there were nine grades even though only three grades were mentioned in the text. Chia Kung-yen referred to an unclear passage in "Wang-Chih" which mentions five grades in attempting to explain why there were nine grades of land. According to Chia, a family may consist of only two, husband and wife, and may have as many as ten members. Thus a basis for nine grades of land was found in the necessity for providing families of different sizes with different amounts of land.[367] Whether or not the nine-grade division was a correct interpretation is unimportant for us; the important thing is that such an interpretation was available for anybody to adopt. Thus the Taiping principle of dividing land into nine grades may be said to follow the classical principle.

In distributing land according to the number of persons in a household, the Taipings also followed the classical example, with the important distinction that they treated male and female members of the family as equals. If one can speak of the Taiping ideology as revolutionary at all, this equality of the sexes in land distribution must be the chief reason.

In the *Chou-li* land was thought to belong to the state or to the king, who is the symbol of the state; and people who reached the age of sixty were expected to return their land to the state. This practice was adopted in later times, with minor variations in the age fixed for the return of the land. Did the Taipings have the same idea about the ownership of

[366] *Chou-li chu-shu*, 15:15b.
[367] *Ibid.*, 11:4a–5a.

land, thinking of it as belonging to the state; or did they believe in private ownership? From the statement, "All lands in the empire must be cultivated by all the people in the empire as a common concern," one might infer that in their system the land belonged to the people. As Taiping land regulations did not provide for the return of land to the state, this suspicion seems confirmed. But to belong to the people collectively, which was apparently the meaning intended here, is not at all the same thing as to belong to the people as individuals. If this interpretation of land belonging to the people collectively is correct, the Taiping idea of land ownership falls into the traditional pattern; the land really belongs to the state. Because it was contrary to the system then in use, one would say the Taiping system of land ownership is revolutionary in the same sense that one would say Wang Mang was revolutionary; that is in the sense of turning to antiquity for a pattern in developing a reform program.

However, the Taipings were not consistent in applying their system. In certain districts it was not applied at all. Ch'u Chih-fu 儲枝芙 described in detail the tax condition of Ch'ien-shan in Anhwei during the Taiping occupation from 1854–58 in his *Huan-ch'iao chi-shih* 皖樵紀實. Ch'u Chih-fu's report leaves no doubt that private ownership in that locality was left intact, the Taiping government being concerned only with the collection of tax.[368] Another proof that private ownership of land existed is a tax registration certificate dated 1861 in which a landlord named Chou Chih-chi reported the land tax on his holding of 14.8 mou of land.[369] And the Chung Wang, Li Hsiu-ch'eng, made a statement in his confession which reveals the land situation in Soochow in 1860: "The people of Soochow did not pay fully their land tax, and they were left free to report their own holdings, with no attempt on my part to check up on them."[370] But the condition varied according to locality. George Jamieson, who in 1888 made a study of the condition of the rural population in China, said that in Chinkiang-fu since the time of the *T'ai-p'ing t'ien-kuo* there had been only small landowners—that is farmers—and no large landowners:

The T'ai-pings, who almost extirpated or drove out the inhabitants living near Chinkiang, and who burnt, with the Yamens they destroyed, the land

[368] Quoted in Lo Erh-kang, *T'ai-p'ing t'ien-kuo ti li-hsiang-kuo*, hereafter cited Lo, *Li-hsiang-kuo*, p. 30.

[369] Lo Erh-kang, *T'ai-p'ing t'ien-kuo shih-kang*, hereafter cited Lo, *Shih-kang*, p. 90.

[370] Lo Erh-kang, *Chung Wang Li Hsiu-ch'eng tzu-chuan yüan-kao ch'ien-cheng*, p. 116.

registries, did little damage in the northern prefectures of Kiangsu, and the old families retained their land. To the south of the Yang-tze the land, after 1865, was occupied by the first comer, to whom a title was given after some years' occupation, and the payment of land tax was allowed.[371]

From this evidence it is clear that in some places the Taipings' effort to put their land system into practice made a tremendous difference in the life of the people. The disappearance of big landlords and the emergence of farmers with small landholdings are very important results of this effort. Wang Shih-to in his *I-ping jih-chi* gives the following recollection:

> I remember the time when I was staying at Ts'ai-ts'un in Ch'en-hsü-ch'iao [about thirty *li* or ten miles from Nanking, the Taiping capital], there were over one thousand families in the village. . . . The people were all illiterate and hated the officials. When asked: "Do the officials grasp and violate the law?" they would answer: "Don't know." Question: "Why do you hate them?" They would give tax collection as the reason. Question: "Did the 'Long hair' [the Taipings] not collect tax?" Answer: "We paid tax to the 'Long hair,' but we did not have to pay rent to the landlord."[372]

This freedom from paying rent was indeed unique with the Taipings. Furthermore, the formulation of "The Land System of the Heavenly Dynasty" indicates that the writers had a genuine feeling for the people and a sincere wish to better their lot; the Taipings tried to accomplish this aim by common sharing of all goods. This feeling and this practice were absent both from the classical system which they tried vainly to reintroduce and from the then current system which they wanted to overthrow. But because of the circumstances of the time, they failed to make this unique practice a permanent and universal feature of their reign.

Other economic measures proposed by the Taipings included a way to deal with famine and relief, which was practiced by King Hui of Liang more than two thousand years before them. It is mentioned in *Mencius*: "With respect to my state, I have done all I can. If there is famine in Ho-nei, I move the people to Ho-tung and transport grain from there to Ho-nei; and *vice versa* when there is a famine in Ho-tung."[373]

[371] George Jamieson (ed.), "Tenure of Land in China and the Condition of the Rural Population," *Journal of the Royal Asiatic Society, North China Branch*, XXIII (1888), 100.

[372] *I-ping jih-chi*, 2:19a.

[373] *Meng-tzu yin-te*, 1/1A/3.

The Taipings also took the idea for auxiliary occupations from *Mencius*. The Taipings ordered: "Throughout the empire the mulberry tree is to be planted close to every wall, so that the women may engage in rearing silk worms, spinning silk, and making garments. Every family throughout the empire should take care to have five hens and two sows, which must not be allowed to miss their proper season for procreation."[374]

In *Mencius* we find the same idea: "By the side of a homestead of five mou plant mulberry trees, and those arriving at the age of fifty will have silk to wear. If chickens, sows, dogs, and pigs are not allowed to miss their proper season for procreation, those arriving at the age of seventy will have meat to eat."[375] To the Taipings who wrote "The Land System of the Heavenly Dynasty" nineteenth-century China was not economically much different from Mencius' China, which had existed more than two thousand years before.

POLITICAL AND MILITARY BORROWINGS FROM TRADITIONAL SOURCES

Since the political aspect of the Taiping society was only slightly differentiated from its military aspect, I shall discuss their origins together under the topics of political ideals, political philosophy, the ethnic issue, political and military institutions, and the examination system.

Political Ideals

The Taipings had as their political ideal peace under a grand unification of the world. In making peace and unification their political ideals, they were expressing the desire of millions of Chinese people to whom wars and turmoil were the order of the day. As the history of China has always been filled with wars and chaos, sparsely interspersed with brief periods of relatively quiet life and prosperity, peace has always been an ideal—the will-o'-the-wisp for which the Chinese long with a yearning heart and which has always been elusive, never quite within their reach. For this reason, the propagandist value of *t'ai-p'ing* (peace) is obvious.

This unfulfilled desire for peace throughout China's history also explains why peace has become the precocupation of so many Chinese philosophers and scholars. The Confucianists, for example, make the pacification of the world (平天下 *p'ing-t'ien-hsia*) the ideal world order; this pacification will bring to consummation the process of cultivation starting with the individual and passing through the stages in which the

---

[374] "T'ien ch'ao t'ien-mou chih-tu," in Hsiao, *Ts'ung-shu, ts'e* 4, p. 2a–b.
[375] *Meng-tzu yin-te*, 1/1A/3.

ordering of the family and the government of the state take their place.[376] And the Kung-yang conception of *ta-t'ung shih-chieh* (大同世界 the world of Great Harmony), which is the world of peace 太平世, the final of the three stages according to their theory, is but another expression of the same theme. In the *Book of Changes*, bringing peace to the world is conceived to be the object of a sage.[377] Mencius mentions peace as a consequence of cultivating oneself.[378] With a despairing note, Mencius observes: "Heaven has not yet desired to pacify the world; if Heaven does desire to pacify the world, in the present world who else besides me could be the one to do it?"[379] On another occasion he makes *jen-cheng* (仁政 government by human-heartedness) an instrument for achieving the peace of the world.[380] Throughout Chinese history, the idea of peace has been a recurring theme in memorials;[381] and poets, without realizing it, have dwelt on the same theme.[382] The term *t'ai-p'ing* has been used as a title for books[383] and as a title for *yüeh-fu*, a form of poetry which is set to music.[384] The term was also used repeatedly in reign titles, some-

[376] *Li-chi yin-te*, 42/1–2.

[377] *Chou-i yin-te*, 20/31/*t'uan*.

[378] *Meng-tzu yin-te*, 57/7B/32.

[379] *Ibid.*, 17/2B/13.

[380] *Ibid.*, 26/4A/1.

[381] To give just one example: Pan Ku in *Han-shu*, "Tung Chung-shu chuan," 56:12b, says: "Now your majesty you have in your possession the world; and there is none within the border of the seas that does not submit to you; you see extensively and hear extensively, knowing all there is to be known about your ministers and subjects, achieving all that is beautiful in the world. Your extreme virtue shines brilliantly beyond the domain, and Yeh-lang and Sogdiana and the countries in all directions ten thousand li around are all pleased with your virtue and come to you in submission. This is the achievement of peace."

[382] Han Yü in his "Shih-ku ko," wrote:
Now that it is a time of peace and there is no disorder,
Confucianism should be relied on and Confucius and Mencius respected.
And Wang Chiu-ssu of the Ming wrote:
When drunk, I sing the songs of peace;
As I grow old, my nature still remains idle and eccentric.
Both poems are quoted in Cheng Chen-to, *Chung-kuo wen-hsüeh shih*, IV, 1072.

[383] In the Sung dynasty alone, *T'ai-p'ing yü-lan* and *T'ai-p'ing kuang-chi* were both compiled under the reign of Emperor T'ai-tsung of the Sung and named after the title of the reign; Cheng Po-ch'ien's *T'ai-p'ing ching-kuo chih shu*, so named because of the opinion of Liu Hsin of the Han dynasty that *Chou-li* is evidence left behind by the Duke of Chou in his achievement of peace, is the result of Cheng's study of *Chou-li*; and Yüeh Shih titled his book *T'ai-p'ing huan-yü chi*.

[384] Chu K'ai of the Yüan compiled *Sheng-p'ing yüeh-fu* 昇平樂府, Yang Ch'ao-ying of the same dynasty compiled *T'ai-p'ing yüeh-fu* 太平樂府, and Wang Wei of the T'ang wrote two pieces called "T'ai-p'ing-lo." Many *ch'ü* titles contain the term *t'ai-p'ing*:

times with some slight variation in the wording.[385] Above all, peace has always been held up as an ideal. Chang Tsai of the Sung wrote the following lines, which are expressive of his grand ambition:

> To institute the mind for heaven and earth;
> To create life [principle] for the teeming humanity;
> To continue the neglected principles of past sages;
> And to usher in a period of peace for the ten thousand generations
>   to come.[386]

It has been suggested that the term *t'ai-p'ing* may also have the sense of leveling, to make equal what is unequal.[387] If this leveling is restricted to an economic sense, this contention may contain some truth; but in general the term is exclusively used to mean peace. When *p'ing* stands alone, it may suggest the idea of "even" or "on the same level." But those to whom this equality is accorded are always regarded as belonging to the same social group, and members of different social groups are seldom if at all considered to be on the same level. In other words, unequal social distinctions are implied in this idea of equality. As applied to members of one social group as distinguished from other groups, it often means "to each his due," as in the phrase: *pu-p'ing tse ming* (不平則鳴 if not even, will complain). To be even is to give each his due: if a peasant, a peasant's due; if a scholar, a scholar's due. One example from

---

"T'ai-p'ing ling," (太平令, found in Wang Po-ch'eng, *Li T'ai-po pien Yeh-lang*), "T'ai-p'ing chuan," (太平賺, found in the opening chapter of Tung Chieh-yüan, *Hsi-hsiang chi*), "T'ai-p'ing shih" (太平時, a tune to which Ch'en Miao-ch'ang, a nun of the twelfth century, wrote a *tz'u*), and "Chu Wen--kuei tseng t'ai-p'ing ch'ien" (found in *Yung-lo ta-tien*).

[385] Emperor T'ai-wu of the Northern Wei used *T'ai-p'ing chen-chün* in 440 as his reign title; Emperor Ching of Liang used *T'ai-p'ing* in 556; T'ai-tsung of the Sung used *T'ai-p'ing hsing-kuo* from 976 to 983. There are many other reign titles which, though not necessarily containing the term *t'ai-p'ing*, imply the idea of peace. Following are some examples: *Yung-ho* (everlasting harmony), *Huo-p'ing* (peace), *Yung-k'ang* (everlasting peace), and *Chien-an* (establishment of peace) of the Han times; *T'ai-k'ang* (great peace), *Yung-k'ang* (everlasting peace), *T'ai-an* (great peace), and *Sheng-p'ing* (peace) of the Chin.

[386] Chang Tsai, *Chang-tzu ch'üan-shu*, 14:132.

[387] Etienne Balázs, in his "La crise sociale et la philosophie politique à la fin des Han," in *T'oung Pao*, Vol. XXXIX, livr. 1–3 (1949), speaks of *t'ai-p'ing tao* as "la Voie de la Grande Paix," and its Bible "le *T'ai-p'ing king*." But he goes on to say on page 89 that the leaders of this new faith (referring to Chang Chüeh and his brothers) announced to the believers "la venue d'une nouvelle ère, celle de la prospérité, de l'âge d'or de l'égalité—car c'est le véritable sens de l'expression *t'ai-p'ing* . . . "

Ying Shao's commentary on a phrase in Pan Ku's *Han-shu* will illustrate this point. In the biography of Tung-fang So, So mentions the phrase *t'ai-chieh liu-fu* 泰階六符, and Ying Shao gives the following commentary:

> *T'ai-chieh* means the three steps of heaven: the highest step refers to the Son of Heaven; the middle to dukes, lords, ministers, and officials; and the lowest to commoners.... When these three steps are *p'ing* [平, the three steps on the level] *yin* and *yang* will be in harmony, the wind and the rain will be timely, and all ancestral spirits will get what is their due. And the world will experience great tranquillity. This is called *t'ai-p'ing* [great peace].[388]

The expression *t'ai-chieh p'ing* 泰階平 occurs later in Ch'en Hung's "Ch'ang-hen-ko chuan" (Preface to Everlasting Sorrow), in connection with another phrase, *ssu-hai wu-shih* (四海無事 peace prevails within the four seas—no military expeditions or warfare). There is no doubt that in both cases *p'ing* cannot be construed to mean equality but must mean either "each according to his due" or simply "peace."[389]

When the Taipings used the term *t'ai-p'ing* they meant by it "peace." This we can see from many references in their documents, of which the following is the clearest: "Physical form and innate nature are both given by T'ien; each and all in mutual harmony enjoy *t'ai-p'ing*."[390]

It is safe to assume that the Taipings, in using *t'ai-p'ing* in the sense of peace as part of their dynastic name, had thought of its immense value in appealing to the hopes and aspirations of the people. It is true that toward the end of the dynasty Hung ordered that the title be changed from *T'ai-p'ing t'ien-kuo* to *Shang-ti t'ien-kuo*, emphasizing the religious aspect of the movement;[391] but there is little evidence that the order was carried out. At any rate, the term *t'ai-p'ing* had served its purpose in arousing the desire of the people, in clarifying for them the objective of the movement, and in winning them over to the side of the Taipings.

The other principal Taiping ideal, the idea of grand unification, was

[388] *Han-shu*, by Pan Ku, 65:8a.

[389] "Ch'ang-hen-ko chuan," in *Tung-wei mi-shu*, compiled by Ma Chün-liang, *ts'e* 14. Another example illustrative of the Chinese conception of equality is found in *Han-shu*, 86:12b, where because of an excessive gift of land to Tung Hsien by Emperor Yüan (48–33 B.C.), Wang Chia said: "The system of equal distribution of land 均田制度 will collapse." The commentary says, "to make land distribution equal within the same rank." Here, too, "to each his due" is implied.

[390] "T'ien-t'iao-shu," in Hsiao, *Ts'ung-shu*, *ts'e* 1, p. 7a.

[391] *T'ai-p'ing t'ien-kuo shih-liao*, pp. 123–24.

first conceived by the Kung-yang school.[392] The Taiping conception seems closer to that of the first emperor of the Ch'in dynasty, for they both aspired to have their dynasty last "ten thousand and ten thousand years."

The combination of the two ideals of peace and unification was also seen by ancient Kung-yang scholars. Ho Hsiu, in his commentary to Kung-yang's commentary (under the first year of Yin-kung 隱公), says in connection with the third and final stage: "With respect to the witnessed period, one sees peace prevailing. Hence the barbarians are promoted to receive rank: and [the whole world] the far and the near, the large and the small under heaven are as if one."[393] In other words, when peace reigns the grand unification, including the barbarians, will be effected.

From our discussion it is evident that these ideals, effective as they were in winning people for the Taipings, did not originate with them, but were derived from the existing pattern of mind. Such a mental attitude could have been exploited by any group that had the ambition to become the ruling power of a country. But the Taipings were the first to give to these ideals, particularly that of peace, a most important place in their ideological system. Though not the only group to exploit the full possibility of their propagandist value, they were certainly the most successful ones to make the attempt.

Political Philosophy

In the field of political philosophy the Taipings did not seem to have any new theory to offer; most of their statements are taken from Confucian sources. The only change in attitude can be seen in their references to these sources as "former commandment" (前戒語 *ch'ien-chieh-yü*), or "the proverb" (成語 *ch'eng-yü*), or simply "saying" (語 *yü*).[394] There is no question that they wanted to break away from the Confucian connection; but they were obliged to use the Confucian ideas which had dominated their minds for so long.

Hung and his followers constantly reiterated the idea that he was sent by the Heavenly Father down to earth to govern the world as its real lord. His assumption of the title *T'ien Wang* also suggests the Taipings'

[392] See *Ch'un-ch'iu ching-chuan yin-te*, 1/Yin 1/1 Kung. See also Chiang Po-ch'ien, *Shih-san-ching kai-lun*, pp. 454–55, for a discussion of its implications.

[393] Ho Hsiu, *Ch'un-ch'iu Kung-yang chuan chu shu*, p. 13.

[394] Ch'eng, *Shih-liao*, II, 9b; II, 19a; II, 20a.

belief in the divine origin of his political power. Such ideas are in complete harmony with the traditional pattern. The *Book of History* says, "Heaven protects the people below, for whom he creates the ruler and the teacher."[395] This theme was reiterated by Mencius.[396] The divine origin of the ruler's political power is indicated in the phrase "The Son of Heaven" and revealed in the Taiping conception of the decree (or mandate) of Heaven by which the Son of Heaven rules. After all, the Taipings did call their T'ien Wang the "truly appointed Son of Heaven," a term which raised hope and inspiration in the hearts of the Chinese and had for them a consoling power like that of *Messiah* for the Jews.

The title *T'ien Wang*, though showing possible Christian influence,[397] was used to designate the King of Chou in the *Ch'un-ch'iu*. Ku Yen-wu of the Ch'ing made the remark in his *Jih-chih lu*:

> In the Book of History, *wang* alone is used; in the *Ch'un-ch'iu*, *T'ien Wang* is used to differentiate [the Son of Heaven] from those who usurped the title of *wang* in the states of Ch'u, Wu, Hsü, and Yüeh. Hence, the addition of *t'ien* as a sign of distinction. Chao-tzu is correct in saying, "The designation of [*T'ien Wang*] expresses the idea of supreme majesty."[398]

A commentary on the term *T'ien Wang* in the *Ch'un-ch'iu* runs: "To call *wang T'ien* is [to show that] he occupies a heavenly position and is entrusted with the *tao* of Heaven."[399] This idea of T'ien Wang being entrusted with the *tao* of Heaven was the accepted basis of the imperial rule in the whole history of China, as is evident from the phrase the Chinese used as a prefix to their edicts: *feng-t'ien ch'eng-yün*, which Giles translates "entrusted by God with the care of,—the empire."[400]

This idea of being entrusted by Heaven and acting for Heaven has been current in Chinese history. In the biography of Pao Hsüan 鮑宣, Pao memorialized the throne in the following words:

---

[395] *Shang-shu t'ung-chien*, 21/0180–0189.

[396] *Meng-tzu yin-te*, 6/1B/3. For further reference, see *Ch'un-ch'iu ching-chuan yin-te*, 165/Wen 13/3 Tso; 281/Hsiang 14/Appendix 3.

[397] The term *T'ien Wang* could have been deduced from "the Kingdom of Heaven," which forms part of the title of the Taiping dynasty.

[398] *Jih-chih lu*, 4:8a.

[399] *Ch'un-ch'iu ching-chuan yin-te*, 3/Yin 1/4 Ching, 4 Tso.

[400] Herbert A. Giles, *A Chinese-English Dictionary* (2d ed., 3 vols.; Amsterdam: Johannes Müller, 1904). See *feng-t'ien ch'eng-yün* under *Feng*, No. 3574.

The world is the Great Heaven's world. Your majesty, in your relation to the above, you are the Great Heaven's Son; and in relation to the below, you are the parent of the people and must take care of these people for Heaven. You should look upon them with equal care, in harmony with the idea expressed in the poem of "Shih-chiu." [*Shih-chiu* is a turtle dove which loves its young without partiality; it is used as a theme in a poem in the *Book of Poetry* to represent the feelings of seven sons toward their good mother.][401] Now the poor people have only insufficient vegetables to eat, and their clothes are threadbare; fathers and sons, husbands and wives are not able to protect one another—a state of things making one truly sad. But your majesty made no effort to succor them. How will your majesty report [to Heaven] the fulfillment of your majesty's mandated mission?[402]

And the occurrence of the term *T'ien Wang* in the *Li-chi*[403] formed the basis for Wen-ti of the Northern Chou dynasty (A.D. 557) to assume the title *T'ien Wang*.[404] In view of the reason for which the next ruler changed the title to *Huang-ti* in 559 it is safe to assume that the Taipings were not aware that the Northern Chou had used *T'ien Wang*. The reason was that the title did not possess enough dignity to elicit awe and reverence from the people. In 674 Emperor Kao-tsung of the T'ang gave himself the title *T'ien-huang* and his queen, *T'ien-hou*.

Thus the Taiping idea of the ruler as the chief representative of Heaven, delegated to rule the world for God with a power derived from God, is a traditional one. The method by which the Taipings vindicated their mission was no less traditional. As a proof of the appointment of a new real Son of Heaven, there must be some form of tangible evidence. It may be either a physical object or some prognostic statement. The traditional view is very well summarized in a passage of *Lü-shih ch'un-ch'iu* which Professor Fung Yu-lan has translated:

Whenever an Emperor or King is about to arise, Heaven must first manifest some favorable omen to the common people. In the time of the Yellow Emperor, Heaven first made huge earthworms and mole crickets appear....

In the time of Yü [founder of the Hsia dynasty] Heaven first made grass and trees appear which did not die in the autumn and winter....

401 *Mao-shih yin-te*, 31/152.
402 *Han-shu*, by Pan Ku, 72:25b.
403 *Li-chi yin-te*, 2/12.
404 Ch'en Yin-k'o, *Sui-T'ang chih-tu yüan-yüan lüeh lün-kao*, p. 67; *Chou-shu*, *chüan* 35, biography of Ts'ui Yu.

In the time of T'ang [founder of the Shang dynasty] Heaven made some knife blades appear in the water....

In the time of King Wen [founder of the Chou dynasty] Heaven made

a flame appear, while a red bird, holding a red book in its mouth, alighted on the altar of soil of the House of Chou....[405]

And Tung Chung-shu of the Han dynasty said:

The king who receives a great mission from Heaven must have something which comes to him of itself, and whose coming cannot be brought about by the energy of man. This is the evidence that he has received the mandate. The people of the world will flock to him as children flock to their parents. Thus the auspicious omen of Heaven comes in response to sincerity. The *Book of History* said...[406]

Then he quoted the passage translated above.

No one knows how much of this tradition the Taipings knew; but some of Hung's ideas seem to suggest that he was not entirely ignorant of it. In the "Taiping Heavenly Chronicle" he tells his dream in which he saw God and was given a gold seal, a sword, and some books. Then the seven characters *T'ien Wang ta-tao chün-wang Ch'üan* were discovered written over his door.[407]

The use of a sword as a symbol of new power and books of occult origin as a source of new knowledge did not originate with Hung. Ssu-ma Ch'ien's *Shih-chi* states that Kao-tsu killed a big snake with his sword.[408]

This sword later assumed a mythical character. Yü Hsin (Tzu-shan), a poet of the Northern and Southern dynasties, wrote the following line: "In the swordroom the spirit of metal shakes." Ni Pan of the Ch'ing quotes *Cha-chi* to explain the line: "Kao-tsu having killed the snake, though his sword was in the room, its brightness spread beyond it."[409]

Mysterious books are mentioned in the case of Chang Liang of the Han, who received books from Huang Shih-kung;[410] and that of Hsi K'ang of the Chin, who, having seen a volume or scroll of a white book

[405] Lü Pu-wei, *Lü-shih ch'un-ch'iu*, 13:126–27, translated in Fung, *A Short History of Chinese Philosophy*, p. 136.

[406] *Han-shu*, by Pan Ku, 56:4b.

[407] "T'ai-p'ing t'ien-jih," in *I-ching*, No. 14 (Sept. 20, 1936).

[408] *Shih-chi*, 8:5b.

[409] Yü Hsin, *Yü Tzu-shan chi*, 3:66.

[410] *Shih-chi*, by Ssu-ma Ch'ien, biography of Duke Liu, 55:2a–b.

in a stone house on a mountain, was unable to get the book because it was not his lot to attain it.[411] In his comment on chapter 14 in the *Book of Genesis* Hung said: "This Melchisedec was really I. I myself formerly was in heaven, and I descended to perform this deed as a prophecy of my present descent to act as the lord; because Heaven's deed always has some prognostic foreshadowing."[412] Thus the Taipings thought it should be evident to the people that Hung was the real Son of Heaven mandated by Heaven to rule.

The Taipings did not stop here in their effort to make their dynasty appear legitimate before the people. They actually published a new calendar and changed their ceremonial dress and colors. This made their conformity to the traditional pattern complete. Tung Chung-shu said: "Ancient kings, on receiving the mandate to rule, introduced a new calendar with a new first month."[413] *Pai-hu t'ung-i* said:

Why must a king, on receiving his mandate, change the calendar system? It is to show that his is a new Name, and he does not succeed [the previous dynasty]; to show that he receives his mandate from Heaven and not from man, so that the hearts of the people may be changed and the ears and eyes [their ideas and attitudes] may be corrected so as to help transform them. Therefore, "Ta-chuan" [the sixteenth chapter of the *Li-chi*] said: "When the king first arises he changes the calendar, colors, symbols, utensils, and ceremonial dress."[414]

Even the symbol Hung chose to stand for himself—the sun—finds a parallel in traditional ideas. Cheng Hsüan, the classical scholar of the later Han, designated the sun as the symbol of a ruler.[415] Hung made the moon the symbol of his wife. In China it is customary to link the sun and the moon together as two parallel luminaries. The *Book of Changes* says:

The sun and the moon are posed in the sky.[416]
The sun and the moon are in possession of heaven, so they can long shine.[417]

[411] Yang Yin-shen, *Chung-kuo wen-hsüeh-chia lieh-chuan*, p. 64.
[412] *Ch'in-ting chiu-i-chao sheng-shu*, p. 178.
[413] Su Yü, *Ch'un-ch'iu fan-lu i-cheng*, 10:10–19.
[414] *Pai-hu t'ung-i*, by Pan Ku. Also in Ch'en Li, *Pai-hu-t'ung shu-cheng*, 8:9a.
[415] *Mao-shih chu-shu*, Part 1 of *chüan* 2, p. 7a.
[416] *Chou-i yin-te*, 19/30/t'uan.
[417] *Ibid.*, 20/32/t'uan.

The principles of *yin* and *yang* are matched to the sun and the moon.[418]
With respect to suspended symbols which shine brightly, nothing can
equal the sun and the moon in magnitude.[419]

Hung may not have chosen the symbol because of these passages; but it
seems possible that there was some connection between his selection of
the sun and these statements in the *Book of Changes*.

In the sphere of moral precepts governing their political conduct, the
Taipings were strongly traditional. Their basic political idea was the
Confucian rectification of names, which we have discussed in connection with the moral aspect of Taiping ideology. This idea is given in both
the "Ode for Youth" and "Gospel Jointly Witnessed and Heard by the
Imperial Eldest and Second Eldest Brothers" (Wang-chang-tz'u-hsiung
ch'ing-mu ch'ing-erh kung-cheng fu-yin-shu). The statement "a prince
is a prince, a minister is a minister, a father is a father, a son is a son, a
husband is a husband, and a wife is a wife" and its negative form are
found in the *Analects*.[420] The Taipings were particularly concerned with
the precepts governing the conduct of the ruler toward his subjects and
the subjects toward their ruler. So they repeatedly quoted two lines from
the *Analects*, though they referred to them as either a former commandment or a proverb: "The ruler uses his subjects with *li*, and the subjects
serve their ruler with loyalty."[421]

The idea that the process of cultivating individual personality is a
prerequisite to the ordering of the family and that the ordering of the
family is a prerequisite to the government of a state, as expressed by
Yang to Hung,[422] came from "Ta-hsüeh" (The Great Learning).[423]
When carried to its logical conclusion according to the Confucian way
of thinking, this process would end in the pacification of the world. Yang
made a similar statement about pacification.[424]

Yang also stated that he hoped Hung would "realize the difficulty in
getting material wealth so as to act as a model for the world to follow.
A proverb says: 'Use material wealth frugally and love the people.' "

---

[418] *Ibid.*, 41/Hsi 1/5.
[419] *Ibid.*, 44/Hsi 1/11.
[420] *Lun-yü yin-te*, 23/12/11.
[421] Ch'eng, *Shih-liao*, II, 20a–b, 21a. *Lun-yü yin-te*, 5/3/19.
[422] Ch'eng, *Shih-liao*, II, 21a.
[423] *Li-chi yin-te*, 42/1.
[424] Ch'eng, *Shih-liao*, II, 21b.

The source of the statement is obvious.[425] That Hung agreed with Yang is apparent from his acceptance of Yang's view.

The Taiping idea of political change seems to coincide with some traditional patterns. It is said in the "Proclamation on the Origin of the Principles for the Enlightenment of the Age": "When chaos rules supreme, order will emerge; and when darkness rules supreme, light will emerge. This is the way of Heaven."[426] Though there is no exact verbal parallel in the traditional sources, this idea is certainly found in the classics. In the *Book of Changes* we have the *T'ai* hexagram and *P'i* hexagram listed together, eleventh and twelfth. The idea is that *P'i*, representing the way of the little man, follows *T'ai*, the way of the superior man, and that the good aspect of things and the bad aspect of things follow one another in an eternal circle. Thus the symbol of the *T'ai* hexagram says "no going without coming,"[427] and the *hsiang* of the *P'i* hexagram says "when *P'i* ends it will fall; how can it be always so!"[428] The popular version of this idea, which may be described as a philosophy of history, finds its best expression in the opening chapter of the novel *Romance of the Three Kingdoms*, where it is said that when order lasts for a certain length of time division will inevitably result, and when chaos lasts for a certain length of time union will inevitably result—a succinct formula for describing the dynastic circle of Chinese history. The Taipings apparently considered themselves the element of light that was due to appear, bringing peace and order to a world that had for so long been in chaos and darkness under the rule of the alien Manchus. This not only explains the Taipings' ideal of peace but justifies their rebellion against the Manchu rule as a result of the inevitable historical movement of the light replacing the dark.

Ethnic Issue

The ethnic issue was an important element in Taiping thought. While it is more probable that the Taipings acquired their concept of the ethnic issue through the influence of secret societies, we can trace the idea back to Confucius. In the *Analects* Confucius gratefully remembered Kuan Chung for warding off the barbarians and saving him from the disgrace

---

[425] *Lun-yü yin-te*, 1/1/5.
[426] "Yüan-tao hsing-shih hsün," in Ch'eng, *Shih-liao*, II, 5b.
[427] *Chou-i yin-te*, 9/11/*hsiang*.
[428] *Ibid.*, 10/12/*hsiang*.

of adopting the customs of the latter.[429] The main purport of his *Ch'un-ch'iu* seems to be to sustain the distinction between China and the barbarians. In the different commentaries on the *Ch'un-ch'iu*, many references are made with pride to such a distinction. When Fan-po was taken by Yung 戎, the *Ch'un-ch'iu* did not use the term "captured"; Kung-yang's explanation for this was that Confucius would not let the barbarians have the honor of capturing the Chinese.[430] When recording the Duke of Ts'ai's capture by Ching 荆, the *Ch'un-ch'iu* merely mentioned that the Duke of Ts'ai presented a dance to Ching; and Kung-yang gives the same explanation.[431] The Tso commentary reports that when the state of Ch'i used Lai 萊 troops to back their demand on the Duke of Lu, Confucius, as an assistant to the Duke of Lu, said to the Duke of Ch'i when they met at Chia-ku: "Border tribes should not be allowed to have designs on the *Hsia* (夏 the Chinese), and barbarians should not be allowed to disturb (or to mix with) *Hua* (華 the Chinese)."[432]

The issue at the time of Confucius was, however, a cultural rather than an ethnic one. Confucius made this clear by emphasizing customs (the way one is dressed) in his praise of Kuan Chung. The commentators defined China in a way that is very illuminating in this respect. Ho Hsiu, a Kung-yang scholar, defined China in connection with the capture of Fan-po by Yung in the following words: "By the Middle Kingdom is meant a country of *li* and *i*."[433] Another commentator, K'ung Yin-ta of the T'ang dynasty, defined *Hsia* and *Hua* in the following words: "The Middle Kingdom has the greatness of *li* and *i*, therefore it is called *Hsia* [which means 'great']; it has the beauty of *fu* and *chang* [黻 and 章, dress and patterns, meaning refined cultural patterns], therefore it is called *Hua* [meaning 'flower' or 'beautiful']."[434] And Ku-liang, in expressing the sentiment of the Duke of Ch'i when curtly rebuffed by Confucius for Ch'i's conspiracy against Lu, reported what the Duke of Ch'i said to his ministers: "Ministers should lead their prince to walk in the way of the ancients. But you fellows led me to the way [customs] of the barbarians. Why?"[435]

---

[429] *Lun-yü yin-te*, 28/14/17. See also *Ch'un-ch'iu ching-chuan yin-te*, 91/Hsi 4/4 Tso, where Kuan Chung is said to have saved China and fought off the barbarians.

[430] *Ch'un-ch'iu ching-chuan yin-te*, 16/Yin 7/6 Kung.

[431] *Ibid.*, 58/Chuang 10/6 Kung.

[432] *Ibid.*, 455/Ting 10/3 Tso.

[433] See Ho Hsiu, *Ch'ung-k'an Sung-pen Kung-yang chu-shu*, 3:10b.

[434] *Ch'un-ch'iu Tso-chuan cheng-i*, the tenth year of Duke Ting.

[435] *Ch'un-ch'iu ching-chuan yin-te*, 455/Ting 10/3 Ku.

This cultural tradition had been carried on to later times. In the Northern Ch'i dynasty Ku Huan wrote "I-hsia lun" (Essay on the Barbarians and the Chinese). The author compared the way of the barbarians to the noise of insects and birds. The clearest statement on the point is perhaps that of Han Yü of the T'ang dynasty. He said in his "Yüan Tao": "Confucius, in writing the *Ch'un-ch'iu*, called princes who adopted the way of the barbarians, barbarians; but he called them Chinese when they advanced to the way of the Chinese."[436] Gradually this cultural issue was overshadowed by the ethnic owing to later non-Chinese occupation of China. The ethnic issue became in the Ch'ing period a dominant feature of the philosophy of the Ming loyalists and then an integral part of the secret society ideology.

As we shall see, the Kan Wang, in creating Taiping examination degree titles, copied from Ku Yen-wu, who was one of the most important Ming loyalist scholars in the early period of the Ch'ing dynasty. It is highly possible that the connection between the Taipings and the surviving Ming scholars was not limited to that between the Kan Wang and Ku Yen-wu. Hung Hsiu-ch'üan and Feng Yün-shan and a few other Taiping leaders were themselves unsuccessful candidates for examination degrees before they revolted, and it is reasonable to assume that they were acquainted with the works of such Ming loyalists as Ku Yen-wu, Huang Tsung-hsi, Wang Fu-chih, and others. If they were, the ethnic issue, which the Taipings emphasized, could have come from these Ming loyalists, whose one common desire was to work against the Manchu impostors for the restoration of the Ming. Later, when the Ming cause was lost beyond redemption, the Ming loyalists refused to serve the new regime.

Ku Yen-wu's attitude toward the Manchu regime is clear from his repeated refusal to help compile the history of the Ming when the Bureau for the Compilation of Ming History was instituted in 1679. Huang Tsung-hsi declined a similar offer to work in the bureau. And both declined invitations to take part in the 1678 *Po-hsüeh hung-tz'u* examination. Ku's idea of the ethnic distinction is preserved in an item entitled "Kuan-tzu pu-ssu Tzu-chiu" in his *Jih-chih-lu*. In view of its importance, we quote the passage in full:

The duty that exists between a ruler and a minister concerns one person; the barrier that stands between the Chinese and the barbarians concerns

---

[436] Ku Huan, "I-hsia lun," in Yen K'o-chün, *Ch'üan shang-ku san-tai ch'in-han san-kuo liu-ch'ao wen*, "Ch'üan-ch'i wen," 22:1b–2a.

the whole empire. Therefore, in the case of Kuan Chung, the Master [Confucius] minimized his crime of not dying for [his prince] Tzu-chiu but gave him merit for the achievement of *I-k'uang chiu-ho* 一匡九合. [In the *Analects* Kuan Chung is said to have made the empire upright once and to have gathered the feudal lords together nine times in order to make China safe from the inroad of the barbarians.] For the Master was weighing the matter to determine what is important and what is not, and he made the empire the object of his concern. Since even the duty between a ruler and a minister cannot compare with the distinction [barrier] between the Chinese and the barbarians, the purpose he cherished in the *Ch'un-ch'iu* can readily be inferred. [The greatest purpose of the *Ch'un-ch'iu* is to ward off the inroad of the barbarian way of life.][437]

Ku Yen-wu must have expressed similar ideas elsewhere, but during the compilation of the works of the surviving Ming scholars the imperial editors expunged all parts that even remotely suggested hostility toward non-Chinese rulers.[438]

Huang Tsung-hsi's purpose in writing *Ming-i tai-fang lu* was severely criticized by Chang T'ai-yen, but others interpreted his motive in different ways.[439] Liang Ch'i-ch'ao thought that it was written after the

[437] *Jih-chih-lu*, 7:11a. For the story, see *Ch'un-ch'iu ching-chuan yin-te*, 56/Chuang 9/7 Tso.

[438] The literary inquisition is well known. Books destroyed included those written against the Mongols during the previous dynasty. Ku's works naturally suffered in the hands of these editors. The most obvious example is an item entitled "Su i-ti hsing hu i-ti" (素夷狄行乎夷狄 Situated among Barbarous Tribes, He Does What Is Proper to a Situation among Barbarous Tribes). Legge, *The Chinese Classics*, I, 395. This title appears in the table of contents under *chüan* 6 but is not to be found anywhere in the text. According to Huang Chi-kang 黃季剛, who wrote *Jih-chih-lu chiao-chi* 日知錄校 記, this item contained six or seven hundred words. Unfortunately, the content is not known; according to the title, it would undoubtedly have given more material on the ethnic issue. See Ch'ien Mu, *Chung-kuo chin san-pai-nien hsüeh-shu shih*, I, 143, where Huang is quoted.

[439] "Ming-i" is the thirty-sixth hexagram in the *Book of Changes*. The meaning of the title has been interpreted "darkening of the light," i.e., the sun sinking under the earth. Figuratively, it indicates the presence of an evil ruler under whom good ministers are suffering. Applied to the historical situation, the evil ruler is taken to refer to Chou Hsin, the last tyrant of the House of Shang, and the ministers refer to Prince Chi, Po-i and his brother Shu-ch'i, and King Wen. They all suffered under the oppressive rule of Chou Hsin. Later King Wu, who overthrew the Shang and established the Chou, went to Prince Chi for advice. Huang Tsung-hsi, in writing *Ming-i tai-fang lu*, apparently considered himself in a situation parallel to that Prince Chi was in when Shang fell. Huang was hoping that someone like King Wu would come to him for advice for the good of the people. In the preface to his book he said: "Although I am getting old, if I were visited, everything might still be all right. I would not remain silent just because we have only the first rays of light before the break of dawn, with much still enveloped in ambiguity." See Huang Tsung-hsi, *Ming-i tai-fang lu*, p. 1a–b.

death of Emperor Shih-tsu when there was great hope of restoration, and that Huang had hoped that someone would come forth to replace the Ch'ing, using what he had laid down in the book as an institutional basis for the restored regime. Ch'üan Tsu-wang 全祖望, on the other hand, thought that Huang had written the book only when hope was absolutely gone with the death of Kuei-wang 桂王 in Yunnan,[440] implying that Huang's desire to have the ruling class of the time consult his ideas was entirely for the sake of the Chinese. However, it is evident that throughout his life Huang never forgot the ethnic issue; as late as 1679 when Wan Chi-yeh, a disciple of his, went to the capital, Huang warned him not to present any scheme that might ensure peace for the reigning Manchu dynasty. Ch'üan said of Huang: "Is it not true that it is impossible to influence Li-chou [Tsung-hsi]?"[441]

The ethnic consciousness was particularly strong with Wang Fu-chih 王夫之. In the preface to his O-meng (噩夢) he calls himself i-lao (遺老 the surviving old man of the previous dynasty). In Sao-shou-wen (搔首問) he untiringly tells the reader anecdotes of those who were martyrs and those who became recluses after the change of the dynasty. He also recalls the loyalists of the previous dynasties. However, Wang's sense of loyalty was more an ethnic loyalty than the kind of loyalty to one single family that had been demonstrated at the end of each dynasty. In his Huang-shu Wang said of China: "It is all right to have abdication; it is all right to have succession; and it is all right to have revolution [referring to the revolution of T'ang of the Shang and Wu of the Chou]. But never let the alien tribe wedge into the [ruling line]."[442] In discussing alien tribes, Wang Fu-chih said:

With respect to China's dealing with the alien tribes, war is not mentioned. ...To exterminate them [the alien tribes] is not [the sign of] a lack of human-heartedness; to deceive them is not [the sign of] a lack of trustworthiness; to encroach upon their territory and to rob them of their property is not [a sign of] a lack of righteousness. If we go to war with them, we must defeat them. To exterminate them in order to keep our people intact is called human-heartedness; to deceive them so as to put into effect with sincerity what they would certainly hate is called trustworthiness. When

---

[440] Chieh-ch'i-t'ing chi wai-p'ien, Vol. XCV, chüan 31.

[441] For this and other references see Ch'ien Mu, Chung-kuo chin san-pai-nien hsüeh-shu shih, I, 33–34. Like the works of Ku Yen-wu, Huang's book had been edited by the Ch'ing compilers. We may safely assume that the Ming-i tai-fang lu must originally have contained more ideas of an ethnic nature than are now found in it.

[442] Wang, Ch'uan-shan i-shu, "Huang-shu," p. 2a.

we encroach upon their territory we shall change their mores by means of culture. To rob them of their wealth so as to free our people from hard labor is called righteousness. With human-heartedness and trustworthiness in conjunction with righteousness, this is the way in which a *wang* [王 one who rules the world by means of virtue] and a *pa* [伯 one who rules the world by means of force] rule the world and rectify the principle of humanity.[443]

Then Wang gave examples showing how many of the dukes during the *Ch'un-ch'iu* period became *pa* because they had defended China in one way or another against the barbarians.[444] This attitude toward the non-Chinese tribes may be traced to Wang's idea of the distinction between the Chinese and the non-Chinese. To him, the distinction was ethnic rather than cultural. Ethnic differences are due to different environmental factors. Because of these physical differences, races are formed each with its own distinct culture. Hence the innate impulse toward the preservation of the race is a natural law universally applicable in the biological world. The fundamental function of man's political organizations lies in the preservation of the race and the defense of the group. Wang's attempt to make the distinction between the Chinese and the barbarians rigid was meant to refute once and for all the argument that there were no real differences between the Chinese and the non-Chinese except in culture, and that it was always possible to merge different peoples into one through acculturation. For it was this argument that men like Hsü Heng used to justify their allegiance to the Mongols.[445]

Another strong exponent of ethnic distinction was Lü Liu-liang (Wan-ts'un). Through his early association with Huang Tsung-hsi and others, he developed a keen ethnic consciousness. He expressed his ideas in poems and in his comments on the current essays. In 1666 he refused to take the provincial examination, although he had become a student during the reign of Shun-chih. His ethnic consciousness is revealed by his comment on Confucius' approval of Kuan Chung's not dying with Tzu-chiu and Confucius' attributing to Kuan Chung the virtue of *jen*: for Confucius had said, "Without him [Kuan Chung] I would have my hair dishevelled and my dress buttoned under the left arm" (both the style of barbarians). Lü, commenting on the occurrence, said:

[443] *Ibid., Ch'un-ch'iu chia-shuo*, 3:16b–17a.

[444] For details see Chang Hsi-t'ang, *Wang Ch'uan-shan hsüeh-p'u*, pp. 117–21.

[445] For an excellent account of Wang Fu-chih's ethnic consciousness, see Kung-chuan Hsiao, *Chung-kuo cheng-chih ssu-hsiang shih*, Vol. II, chap. 19, pp. 288–92.

The duty between the sovereign and the ministers is the first thing in the world; it is the greatest among the human relations. If one goes amiss in this duty, even if he be a man of great achievement, his achievement will not cleanse his crime.... When reading the sentence "Without Kuan Chung..." we realize that the great meaning as expounded in the *Ch'un-ch'iu* is even greater than the relation between the sovereign and the ministers; it is indeed the first thing in the world. This is why it was right for Kuan Chung not to die. What [Confucius] was concerned with was the relative importance of integrity and righteousness, and he did not emphasize achievement and fame.[446]

This is exactly the line of thought Ku Yen-wu had developed on the same theme.

Like Wang Fu-chih, Lü tried to make the distinction between the Chinese and the non-Chinese rigid; he did this by preaching the philosophy of Chu Hsi. He said:

Hitherto those who believed in Chu-tzu [Chu Hsi] believed in him just for the name but did not really understand him.... The so-called disciples of Chu-tzu like P'ing-chung [Hsü Heng] and Yu-ch'ing [Wu Ch'eng; both Hsü and Wu were great Sung scholars of the Ch'eng-Chu school and both submitted themselves to the rule of the Mongols] disgraced their persons and wronged themselves, and yet they still cried out that they were the bearer of the Way; and the world did not think that there was anything wrong with them. Because this Way is not made clear, during the period between Te-yu and Hung-wu [1275–1368, the Yüan period] many scholars stumbled in their course.... Therefore...the teachings of Tzu-yang [Chu Hsi] were lost to Wu, Hsü, and others, and [what these people taught] cannot be taken as the model.... Now the thing to be shown to students is the distinction between *ch'u* and *ch'u*, *ch'ü* and *chiu*, *tz'u* and *shou*, *chiao* and *chieh* [出處, 去就, 辭受, 交接, to go out to serve the state or to remain a private individual, to leave or to approach, to decline or to accept, to have association with]. One has first to stand firm and then begin to talk about the task of investigation of things and emphasis on concentration of the mind. Only thus can one expose the intrigue of *liang-chih* [良知 innate knowing] and reveal the foxy Chanism of the Lu school. For after the period of Te-yu the world experienced an unprecedented change. Former scholars did not discuss a situation [like] this. So the idea of *shih-chung* [時中, found in "Chung-yung" (The Doctrine of the Mean) in the *Li-chi* and the *Book of Changes*, meaning "always timely and right," without the fault of excess or falling short] should be particularly rigidly defined, for only thus can one begin the task of entering the gate of virtue.[447]

[446] Lü, *Ssu-shu chiang-i, chüan* 17, quoted in Ch'ien Mu, *Chung-kuo chin san-pai-nien hsüeh-shu shih*, I, 83–84.

[447] Lü, *Lü Wan-ts'un hsien-sheng wen-chi, chüan* 1, quoted in Ch'ien, *op. cit.*, I, 76.

For Lü the most important thought of Chu Hsi was the rigorous distinction between right and wrong. Chu's objection to the utilitarian school of Yung-k'ang (Ch'en T'ung-fu), Yung-chia (Yeh Shih), and others particularly appealed to him, for it was the loose interpretation of right and wrong on a utilitarian basis that gave people like Wu and Hsü an excuse for submitting themselves to the rule of the barbarians.

During the reign of Yung-cheng, Lü, though already dead, was involved in a case of literary inquisition, in which Tseng Ching was the main figure. Tseng read the writings of Lü and was completely convinced by his line of thought. Though he failed in instigating Yüeh Chung-ch'i to revolt, he had given the ethnic issue such an airing that Emperor Yung-cheng was obliged to attempt to refute the arguments for the ethnic issue: the emperor wrote *Ta-i chüeh-mi lu* and forced Tseng to write a recantation entitled "Kuei-jen shuo." The emperor quoted Tseng's ideas in the *Ta-i chüeh-mi lu* in order to refute them:

> How can anyone apply the duty embodied in the human relation between the sovereign and the ministers to the relation of men and barbarians, between whom there is a great distinction? Kuan Chung forgot his sovereign and served his enemy, and yet Confucius approved of his actions and attributed *jen* to him. Why? Because the distinction between the Chinese and the barbarians is greater than the relation between the sovereign and the ministers. . . . There is no sovereign-minister relation between Chinese and the barbarians.[448]

Tseng Ching in his *Chih-hsin lu* 知新録 said: "*Feng-chien* 封建 ("feudalism") is the great way by which the sages govern the world, and it is also the great means of warding off the barbarians."[449]

This statement suggests that the early Ch'ing scholars who showed great interest in the discussion of *feng-chien* really had in their mind this great ethnic issue. Lü also touched upon the subject of *feng-chien*. He said:

> The sovereign and ministers are united on certain principles. . . . But when their ideas differ, and the way does not prevail, it will be right for [the ministers] to leave. . . . Since in later times the system of *feng-chien* was abolished, and the *chün-hsien* system was installed, the world has been unified under one sovereign; thus there remain only advancement and dismissal [for the ministers] and no longer is there any leaving or approaching [for them].[450]

[448] Quoted in Ch'ien, *op. cit.*, I, 84, note.
[449] Quoted in *ibid.*, I, 83, note.
[450] Quoted in *ibid.*, I, 83.

Yung-cheng in one of his edicts directed his attention to this point:

> In general, traitors like Lü Liu-liang, Tseng Ching, Lu Sheng-nan, and others all spoke of the necessity of reviving the system of *feng-chien*. Because treacherous people like these knew that their evil and crooked thought would not be tolerated in their own district and country, they wanted to follow the way of the traveling scholars who were selling their sophistry to others, their idea being that if they were not tolerated in their own country, then they would go to another. They did not know that one who is as mad and undisciplined as Lu Sheng-nan would not be tolerated anywhere in the whole world.[451]

It is clear that the cultural issue current in Confucius' time and based on the differences in customs between the Chinese and the non-Chinese was expanded and transformed into a strong ethnic consciousness by the time of the early Ch'ing scholars or Ming loyalists. This change, of course, was due to the actual circumstances under which the early Ch'ing scholars lived. The Taipings must have found great inspiration in these ideas. Though there is no direct verbal connection between the Taiping ideology and the ideas of these scholars, since the Taipings had borrowed *in toto* Ku Yen-wu's explanations of the old examination degree titles it is not at all improbable that their ethnic consciousness was also due to the inspiration of these Ming loyalists.

Political and Military Institutions

The source from which the Taipings borrowed ideas for their political and military institutions was without doubt the *Chou-li*, originally known as the *Chou-kuan*.[452] Most writers on the Taiping Rebellion seem to agree on this point.[453] Chang Te-chien, however, did not believe that the

[451] Quoted in *ibid.*, I, 83, note.

[452] The *Chou-kuan* is a work on government institutions attributed to Duke Chou. The name was changed to *Chou-li* by Liu Hsin at the time of Wang Mang. The reason is believed to be the desire to avoid confusion with the "Chou-kuan" chapter in the *Book of History*.

[453] The Taipings themselves made the point that their military institutions were modeled after the *Chou-li* system. In Shen Tzu, *Pi-k'ou jih-chi*, there is a proclamation by a certain Fu-t'ien-yen Chung, in which are listed thirteen articles. The first article contains the following affirmation: "In instituting *chun-shuai* (corps general) and *shih-shuai* (colonel), we are following the idea of the system of twenty-five families as taught in the *Chou-li*." (Quoted in Lo Erh-kang, *Li-hsiang-kuo*, p. 12.)

Many writers contemporary with the Taipings held a similar view. Wang Shih-to in his *I-ping jih-chi* treated the following subject: "The *t'ien-ch'ao* system as an adoption of the *Classic of Chou-li* and *Classic of Poetry*." Ch'u Chih-fu 儲枝芙 in Huan-ch'iao chi-

Taipings adopted the *Chou-li* system. Neither did he believe that the *hsiang-kuan* (local official system) outlined in the Taiping "Land System of the Heavenly Dynasty" was copied from the *Chou-li* system. Chang stated that although the Taiping military system used the *Chou-li* titles for its officers, one could see upon closer examination that the Taipings really adopted the system of Ch'i Chi-kuang with some slight modification.[454]

---

shih 皖樵紀實 said, concerning the *hsiang-kuan* (鄉官 local official) system of the Taipings: "The rebels steal the system from the *Chou-kuan* instituting *wei* 偽 *chün-shuai, shih-shuai, lü shuai* [captain], *tsu-chang* [lieutenant], *liang-ssu-ma* [sergeant], and *wu-chang* [corporal], the various ranks of *hsiang-kuan*." (Quoted in Lo, *Li-hsiang-kuo*, p. 18.) And Chang Te-chien, though skeptical about the whole thing, mentions that some authors thought the rebels in instituting *chün, shih, lü, tsu, liang,* and *wu* were following the *Chou-li* system as given in the section on "Hsia-kuan," and that in creating *hsiang-kuan* everywhere they were doing it in the spirit of the "well-shaped land" system. (See Chang, *Tse-ch'ing, ts'e* 3, *chüan* 4, "Wei chün-chih.") Both Ling Shan-ch'ing in *T'ai-p'ing t'ien-kuo yeh-shih* and Hsiao I-shan in *Ch'ing-tai t'ung-shih* quoted these passages from Chang Te-chien without documentation; but in both cases, the authors seem to accept as fact that the Taipings were imitators of the Chou-li system, paying no attention to Chang's skepticism. (See Ling, *Yeh-shih,* 3:2 and Hsiao, *Ch'ing-tai t'ung-shih,* Part 2 of Vol. III, chap. 3, p. 85.) Ling Shan-ch'ing also said: "In the *Chou-li, hsiang-kuan* is entrusted with military power. But in time of peace, they will take up their normal function again. The system of the Taipings in making soldiery and people one seems to have come from here." (*Yeh-shih,* 2:45.) This is again quoted by Hsiao I-shan without documentation in *op. cit.,* chap. 3, p. 2.

P'eng Tse-i in *T'ai-p'ing t'ien-kuo ko-ming ssu-ch'ao* also quotes Chang Te-chien's statement about the Taiping military system and interprets the "ancient system" to mean the *Chou-li* system. (See p. 61, note 5.)

Lo Erh-kang, like others, believes that a great part of the Taiping land system, as expounded in "The Land System of the Heavenly Dynasty" and their laws and institutions, was modeled after the *Chou-li* system. (For detail see Lo, *Li-hsiang-kuo*, pp. 18–21.)

In the policy of "maintaining soldiery in peasantry," Lo Erh-kang, Hsieh Hsing-yao, P'engTse-i and others all believe that the Taipings were inspired by the Chou-li. Chang said: "To maintain soldiery in peasantry is a method based on the system of *pi* 比, *lü* 閭, and *tang* 黨 in the *Chou-li.*" (*Tse-ch'ing, ts'e* 3, *chüan* 4.) Lo Erh-kang said: "Because the Taipings maintained their soldiery in peasantry, their soldiers were people, and the people were soldiers. For this reason, their military organization is a social organization. This is in fact the most fundamental system in the *Chou-li.*" (*Li-hsiang-kuo*, pp. 19–20.) And P'eng Tse-i said: "In the course of Chinese history, we have a method which is called 'to maintain soldiery in peasantry.' In the military system of *T'ai-p'ing t'ien-kuo* there is a certain feature which is close to the *Chou-kuan* system." (*T'ai-p'ing t'ien-kuo ko-ming ssu-ch'ao,* p. 44.)

[454] See Chang, *Tse-ch'ing, ts'e* 3, *chüan* 4, "Wei chün-chih." Chang, in stating that the Taiping military system was borrowed from Ch'i Shao-pao (Chi-kuang, died about 1586) rather than from the *Chou-li,* was apparently referring to Ch'i's *Lien-pin shih-chi* (練兵實紀, True Record of the Training of Troops).

In general, the writer agrees with the majority of writers on the Taiping Rebellion. But he believes that Chang Te-chien's skepticism, although apparently based on his prejudice as a government intelligence officer, should be more seriously considered. The various aspects of Taiping political and military organizations will therefore be considered in order to ascertain in what respects the Taipings followed the *Chou-li* system and in what respects they took the initiative, differing from that venerable system.

In addition to the economic and social regulations already discussed, many official titles and military ranks and much of the military organization the Taipings adopted are found in the *Chou-li*. First of all, the Taipings used the titles of the six ministers: *t'ien-kuan, ti-kuan, ch'un-kuan, hsia-kuan, ch'iu-kuan,* and *tung-kuan*. These titles are taken from the *Chou-li*. However, it would be wrong to infer from this verbal borrowing that the Taipings actually put the *Chou-kuan* system into practice, as Hsieh Hsing-yao has suggested in his *T'ai-p'ing t'ien-kuo ti she-hui cheng-chih ssu-hsiang*.[455] They merely borrowed the titles, discarding entirely the "content" of these titles. To prove this, one can compare the functions of these ministers as defined in the first lines of the main sections of the *Chou-li* with the functions or activities of the Taipings' six ministers.

---

[455] Page 9. Referring to Taiping adoption of the titles of the six ministers, Hsieh says: "This may be said to be the first time the *Chou-kuan* was put into practice in government." Hsieh then cites a case in which a *tung-kuan* furnished a piece of information concerning the abundance of carpenters in Hanyang, Hupeh, to prove that the Taipings not only took the titles from the *Chou-kuan* but "adopted its content as well" (p. 10). The *tung-kuan* in the *Chou-li* system was in charge of all work. Hsieh concludes that the Taiping *tung-kuan* had similar duties. Here I think Hsieh made a number of mistakes. First, it was not the first time *Chou-kuan* titles had been used. Empress Dowager Wu of the T'ang adopted these titles when she became the actual ruler. A note to an item entitled "Li-pu shang-shu" in Tu Yu, *T'ung-tien, chüan* 23, runs: "So Empress Dowager of the Great T'ang ordered *li-pu* 吏部 to be *t'ien-kuan, hu-pu* 戶部 to be *ti-kuan, li-pu* 禮部 to be *ch'un-kuan, ping-pu* 兵部 to be *hsia-kuan, hsing-pu* 刑部 to be *ch'iu-kuan* and *kung-pu* 工部 to be *tung-kuan*, in order to adopt the system of 'six ministers' of the Chou dynasty." Secondly, the proof Hsieh offered to substantiate his contention that the Taipings adopted the "content" (by which he apparently means the system as implied by those titles in terms of their actual functions) is too weak. As far as we know, this *tung-kuan ch'eng-hsiang*, whose name was Ping Fu-shou, was the only one identified as being in charge of carpenters. (See Kuo T'ing-i, *T'ai-p'ing t'ien-kuo shih-shih jih-chih*, Vol. II, Appendix 4, "Table of Ch'eng-hsiang," pp. 42–45.) Lo Ta-kang, Ch'en Yü-ch'eng, Liu Kuan-fang, Ch'en Tsung-yang, Wan Hsiang-fen, and others were all *tung-kuan ch'eng-hsiang* or *fu-ch'eng-hsiang;* but none of them was known to have anything to do with carpentry or any other kind of work. They were mostly military leaders.

The function of *t'ien-kuan ch'ung-tsai* is defined in the *Chou-li*: "Thus the king established *t'ien-kuan ch'ung-tsai*, who, at the head of his staff, shall be charged with the government of the state and the duty of assisting the king to give equity to the whole country."[456]

The function of *ti-kuan ssu-t'u* is defined: "Thus the king established *ti-kuan ssu-t'u*, who, at the head of his staff, shall be charged with the education of the state and the duty of assisting the king in making the whole country peace-loving."[457]

The function of *ch'un-kuan tsung-po* is defined: "Thus the king established *ch'un-kuan tsung-po*, who, at the head of his staff, shall be charged with the rituals of the state and the duty of assisting the king to give harmony to the whole state."[458]

The function of *hsia-kuan ssu-ma* is defined: "Thus the king established *hsia-kuan ssu-ma*, who, at the head of his staff, shall be charged with the order of the state and the duty of assisting the king to pacify the whole country."[459]

The function of *ch'iu-kuan ssu-k'ou* is defined: "Thus the king established *ch'iu-kuan ssu-k'ou*, who, at the head of his staff, shall be charged with the prohibitions of the state and the duty to assist the king in rendering justice to the whole country."[460]

The function of *tung-kuan* is missing in the *Chou-li*.[461] It is described in "Shao-tsai" under "Ch'un-kuan": "*Tung-kuan* has a staff of sixty, in charge of the work of the state."[462] The "K'ao-kung chi," a section substituted for the sixth part of the *Chou-li*, says: "There are six offices in the state, and *po-kung* [百工, literally hundred kinds of work] is one of them."[463]

---

[456] *Chou-li chu-shu*, 1:5a.

[457] *Ibid.*, 9:1a.

[458] *Ibid.*, 17:1a.

[459] *Ibid.*, 28:1a.

[460] *Ibid.*, 34:1a.

[461] Although the *Chou-li* enumerates six offices, the sixth being *tung-kuan*, the sixth section of the book was missing when it was first discovered in the Han dynasty. In *Han-shu*, "I-wen-chih," 30:6b, see Yen Shih-ku's note to "Chou-kuan-ching." The bibliographical monograph in the *Sui-shu*, 32:19a–20a, records: "A certain person named Li came into possession of the *Chou-kuan*. This *Chou-kuan* was in fact the system of government institutions worked out by the Duke of Chou. Li presented it to Prince Hsien of Ho-chien, with the section on *tung-kuan* missing. Prince Hsien offered one thousand gold as a price for the missing part, but it was not to be had. He filled the lacuna with 'K'ao-kung chi,' forming thus six parts." For this reason, we do not find the function of *tung-kuan* defined in the same way as the others.

[462] *Chou-li chu-shu*, 3:2b.

[463] *Ibid.*, 39:1b.

Further on, this *po-kung* is defined: "To examine the crooked, the straight, the plain and the general feature [of the five kinds of material] for the purpose of employing them to make different kinds of utensils and tools for the people is [the function] of the *po-kung*."[464]

There is a general statement repeated in all cases except that of the *tung-kuan*, preceding the outline of the specific functions of each minister: "The king established the state, distinguished directions, rectified positions, regulated the affairs of the state, surveyed the land in the countryside, and instituted offices each with its specific functions, for the purpose of setting up a standard for the people."[465]

The Taipings did not use these titles the way the *Chou-li* used them. The general statement from the *Chou-li* indicates the top-level importance of these ministers as administrators in the Chou times. For the Taipings, the executive and administrative power was lodged solely in the hands of the wangs, especially in the hands of Tung Wang during the first years and later in the hands of Kan Wang. The so-called *t'ien-kuan*, *ti-kuan*, etc., exercised no such power as defined in the *Chou-li*.

An attempt to define the functions of the Taiping ministers by inquiring into what they were actually charged to do reveals that with few exceptions they were primarily entrusted with military affairs. According to the *Chou-li* system they should all have been given the title *hsia-kuan*. The activities of those few who were not military personnel do not agree with those defined in the *Chou-li*. Tseng Ch'ai-yang, who was made *t'ien-kuan* second assistant *ch'eng-hsiang*, was in the same year *yu-chang-ch'ao-i* (右掌朝儀 in charge of court rituals). Rituals, according to the *Chou-li* system, are in the hands of *ch'un-kuan*. Liu Ch'eng-fang, made *ti-kuan* second assistant *ch'eng-hsiang*, was in the same year in charge of secretarial work in the court of the I Wang. According to the *Chou-li* system, secretarial matters should come under *t'ien-kuan*. Hsieh Hsing-yao cited the case of Ping Fu-shou as a proof that the Taipings adopted the "content" as well as the titles of the *Chou-li* system (see note 455). But Ping was made a *tung-kuan* second *ch'eng-hsiang* in 1854, and was in charge of carpenters in 1852. He might have been made a *tung-kuan* minister because of his qualifications, as the *Chou-li* system required; however, there was a case in which a medicine man in 1851 was made a

---

[464] *Ibid.*, 39:3a–b.
[465] *Ibid.*, 1:1b–5a; 9:1a; 17:1a; 28:1a; and 34:1a.

hsia-kuan assistant *ch'eng-hsiang* rather than a *t'ien-kuan,* under whom the duty of medical matters was supposed to be subsumed.[466]

There is another difference between the Taiping and *Chou-li* systems. The *Chou-li* had a different name for each of the six offices: *t'ien-kuan* was called *ch'ung-tsai; ti-kuan, ssu-t'u; ch'un-kuan, tsung-po; hsia-kuan, ssu-ma;* and *ch'iu-kuan, ssu-k'ou.* Since the section on *tung-kuan,* whose function was to be in charge of work, is missing, we do not know the name of that office. Later scholars gave the name *ssu-k'ung* to the office of *tung-kuan,* because Po-yü, who was in charge of water works, was mentioned in "Yao-tien" as *ssu-k'ung:* "Po-yü is *ssu-k'ung.*" The Taiping system, by contrast, had only one name for all six offices—*ch'eng-hsiang,* a term first created in 309 B.C. by King Wu of the Ch'in and not found in the *Chouli.*

In view of the differences between the *Chou-li* system and the Taiping system of six ministers, it is safe to conclude that the Taipings merely borrowed the terms without adopting the "content." They could not have done otherwise, since they were living in a time when conditions were far different from those existing when the *Chou-li* system was supposedly in effect.[467] Therefore, the offices with the same names could not have had the same functions. The Taiping adoption of the *Chou-li* terms could not have gone beyond verbal borrowing, and the offices to which these terms were applied could not have had the same functions as the original ones because the *Chou-li* system itself was an ideal system.

This verbal borrowing was extended to the titles of many other offices. The Taipings often used the term *chang* 掌 or *tien* 典 as the symbol standing for "in charge." This practice was apparently also taken from the *Chou-li.* Hsieh Hsing-yao made a careful listing of the two systems, part of which is reproduced in the following table.

---

[466] For reference to these cases, see Kuo, *Jih-chih,* Vol. II, Appendix 2, section 4, pp. 42–47.

[467] I say "supposedly" because scholars agree that the *Chou-li* system was at best an idealized version of the Chou system, combined with later rationalized additions. Even if the Duke of Chou had written it, which he did not, it is believed that it was not put into effect at any time during the long period of the Chou dynasty. Cheng Ch'iao, in *T'ung-chih,* quoted Sun Ch'u: "The Duke of Chou acted as regent for six years, at the end of which period the work [*Chou-kuan*] was completed. The Duke returned to Feng, and it was never really put into effect. For the purpose of the Duke in writing the book was the same as that for which the *Li* was compiled during the periods of *Hsien-ch'ing* and *K'ai-yüan* [the reign titles of Emperors Kao-tsung and Hsüan-tsung, respectively, 656–741], measures to be used in a future time but never actually put into effect." This passage is also quoted in the first preface in *Chou-li chu-shu,* p. 1a.

Official titles	*Chou-li* system	Taiping system
With *chang* as part of the title	*chang-she* 掌舍 *chang-p'i* 掌皮 *chang-chieh* 掌節 *chang-t'u* 掌荼 *chang-t'an* 掌炭 *chang-ku* 掌固 *chang-ch'un* 掌脣 *chang-hsü* 掌畜 *chang-ch'iu* 掌囚 *chang-lu* 掌戮 *chang-k'e* 掌客 *chang-ya* 掌訝 *chang-chiao* 掌交 *chang-ch'a-ssu-fang* 掌察四方 *chang-ho-hui* 掌貨賄	*tso-chang-ch'ao-men* 左掌朝門 *yu-chang-ch'ao-men* 右掌朝門 *tso-chang-ch'ao-i* 左掌朝儀 *yu-chang-ch'ao-i* 右掌朝儀 *cheng-chang-ch'ao-shuai* 正掌朝率 *chang-shu* 掌書
With *tien* as prefix	*tien-fu-kung* 典婦功 *tien-ssu* 典絲 *tien-hsi* 典枲 *tien-jui* 典瑞 *tien-ming* 典命 *tien-ssu* 典祀 *tien-t'ung* 典同 *tien-lu* 典路	*tien-hsing-fa* 典刑罰 *tien-t'ien-lao* 典天牢 *tien-sheng-liang* 典聖糧 *tien-yu-yen* 典油鹽 *tien-chin-kuan* 典金官 *tien-yü-chü* 典玉局 *tien-hsiu-ching* 典繡錦 *tien-ching-chiang* 典錦匠 *tien-ch'i-ch'ih* 典旗幟 *tien-hung-fen* 典紅粉 *tien-t'ieh* 典鐵 *tien-t'ung-chiang* 典銅匠[468]

The Taiping military organization was obviously based on the *Chou-li* system. The following chart shows the similarity in titles and numbers of officers between the *Chou-li* and the Taiping army system.

[468] Hsieh, *T'ai-p'ing t'ien-kuo ti she-hui cheng-chih ssu-hsiang*, pp. 10–11.

The *Chou-li* System	The Taiping System
5 men in a *wu* 伍	1 *wu-chang* 伍長 in charge of 4 soldiers
5 *wu* in a *liang* 両	1 *liang-ssu-ma* 両司馬 in charge of 5 *wu-chang*
4 *liang* in a *tsu* 卒	1 *tsu-chang* 卒長 in charge of 4 *liang-ssu-ma*
5 *tsu* in a *lü* 旅	1 *lü-shuai* 旅帥 in charge of 5 *tsu-chang*
5 *lü* in a *shih* 師	1 *shih-shuai* 師帥 in charge of 5 *lü-shuai*
5 *shih* in a *chün* 軍	1 *chün-shuai* 軍帥 in charge of 5 *shih-shuai*

A *chün* consists of 12,500 soldiers. The *Chou-li* system does not seem to include the officers. When officers are included, the army numbers 15,656, which may be broken into:

Soldiers:	12,500
Wu-chang	2,500
Liang-ssu-ma	500
Tsu-chang	125
Lü-shuai	25
Shih-shuai	5
Chün-chiang	1
	15,656

A *chün* (army) consists of 13,156 soldiers. This may be broken into:

Soldiers	10,000
Wu-chang	2,500
Liang-ssu-ma	500
Tsu-chang	125
Lü-shuai	25
Shih-shuai	5
Chün-shuai	1
	13,156

The definite figures for the Taiping system are given in "The Land System of the Heavenly Dynasty";[469] but for the *Chou-li* system only the figures of the different units are given. Therefore, to the 12,500 soldiers we add the figures of the different units. The difference in the total figures of the two systems is explained by the fact that while "The Land System of the Heavenly Dynasty" states specifically that a *wu-chang* was in charge of four soldiers, the *Chou-li* makes no such statement. It merely says, "Five persons [soldiers] made a *wu*, and for each *wu* there was a chief."[470] On the assumption that each *wu* consisted of five soldiers *and* a chief, the *Chou-li* system had one more man in the *wu* than the Taiping system: hence there is a difference of 2,500 men (one for each of 2,500 *wu*) between the two systems.

[469] "T'ien-ch'ao t'ien-mou chih-tu," in Hsiao, *Ts'ung-shu, ts'e* 4, p. 7a.

[470] *Chou-li chu-shu*, 28:2a. Hsieh Hsing-yao, in *op. cit.*, p. 16, says that the Taipings added *ssu-ma* to the *liang* of the *Chou-li*. Actually, *liang-ssu-ma* was the original term used in the *Chou-li* to designate the chief of a *liang*. See *Chou-li chu-shu*, 28:2a.

Like the *Chou-li*, the Taiping system was much more than a military organization. It was a general method used to organize the people for different purposes, the military being one of them. So the military system coincided with the organization of the families. "The Land System of the Heavenly Dynasty" says: "In organizing an army, for every 13,156 families let there be first one army."[471] The same work lists these purposes: "Each family in the army contributes one man as *wu-tsu* [soldier in the *wu* unit]. In time of alarm he will exterminate the enemy and capture the bandits under the leadership of the chief; in time of peace he will be a farmer tilling the land to serve the superior under the leadership of the chief."[472]

That the *Chou-li* system organized people for other than military purposes is shown by the fact that while the system was set forth under the section on *hsia-kuan ta ssu-ma*, whose normal function was military, it was also explained in the section on *ti-kuan hsiao* (assistant) *ssu-t'u*, whose normal function was to be in charge of the people rather than military affairs. "He [the assistant *ssu-t'u*] then collects the ten thousand people and puts them to work. Five men make up a *wu*, five *wu* make up a *liang*, four *liang* make up a *tsu*, five *tsu* make up a *lü*, five *lü* make up a *shih*, and five *shih* make up a *chün* (an army)—and these for the purposes of serving in the army, contributing to land tilling and labor service, pursuing thieves and bandits, and collecting taxes."[473] The figures for the different *Chou-li* military units—that is, "5, 5, 4, 5, 5, 5"—are the same as those in the organization of families whether within the central domain or in the countryside:

Organization within the state:
   5 families form a *pi* 比.
   5 *pi* form a *lü* 閭.
   4 *lü* form a *tsu* 族.
   5 *tsu* form a *tang* 黨.
   5 *tang* form a *chou* 州.
   5 *chou* form a *hsiang* 鄉.[474]

Organization in the countryside:
   5 families form a *lin* 鄰.
   5 *lin* form a *li* 里.
   4 *li* form a *tsan* 酇.
   5 *tsan* form a *p'i* 鄙.
   5 *p'i* form a *hsien* 縣.
   5 *hsien* form a *sui* 遂.[475]

These corresponding figures for the different units in the military and

[471] "T'ien-ch'ao t'ien-mou chih-tu," in Hsiao, *Ts'ung-shu*, *ts'e* 4, p. 7a.
[472] *Ibid.*, p. 1a.
[473] *Chou-li chu-shu*, 11:2b–3a.
[474] *Ibid.*, 10:22b.
[475] *Ibid.*, 15:14a.

civilian organizations in the "5, 5, 4, 5, 5, 5" scheme meant that each family was held responsible for contributing one able-bodied man to military service. The Taipings said, "For every 13,156 families let there be first one army," and for the Taipings one army consisted of 13,156 men. This definitely meant one man from one family. In this respect the Taipings seem to have followed the *Chou-li* system closely.[476]

Most of those who write about them believe that the Taipings operated on the policy of "maintaining soldiery in peasantry," a policy originated in the *Chou-li* system.[477] Verbally this is true, in view of the statement that in time of peace the soldiers are to till the land and serve their superiors under the leadership of their chief. But in fact the Taipings had never looked upon peasantry as being on the same level as the soldiery. Soldiers were among the elite, while the peasantry was the lowest level to which those who violated the laws of heaven were relegated.

Chang Te-chien hinted that his contemporaries believed the Taiping system of *hsiang-kuan* (local officials) was in the spirit of the system of *pi* 比, *lü* 閭, *tsu* 族, and *tang* 黨 of the *Chou-li;* but Chang cast doubt on the capability of the Taipings to assimilate that spirit.[478] However, it cannot be denied that they did adopt the *hsiang-kuan* system and that the name of that system reminds one of the *Chou-li* system. Chang describes the system in the following words: "The rebels appointed local officials all over the different districts. They organized 12,500 families into an army.

---

[476] Chang, in *Tse-ch'ing, ts'e* 3, *chüan* 4, said: "To keep soldiery in peasantry is based on the system of *pi, lü, tsu,* and *tang* of the *Chou-kuan,* but according to the ancient system every seven families contribute one soldier while according to the [Taiping] system every family contributes one soldier. It seems that the rebels have troops but no people." From our quotations from the *Chou-li,* it seems clear that that system required one man from each family. I do not know from what source Chang drew his conclusion, for the *Chou-li* specifically says: "When called to service, a family shall not contribute more than one man" (*Chou-li chu-shu,* 11:5a). In commenting on the passage on army organization which we quoted, Cheng Hsüan of the later Han says: "*Chün, shih, lü, tsu, liang,* and *wu* were all names of the units of the people. One *wu* 伍 to a *pi* 比, one *liang* 兩 to a *lü* 閭, one *tsu* 卒 to a *tsu* 族 [the text here gives *lü* 旅 instead of *tsu* 族; this is an obvious misprint], one *lü* 旅 to a *tang* 黨, one *shih* 師 to a *chou* 州, and one *chün* 軍 to a *hsiang* 鄉. Each family contributes one man" (*Chou-li chu-shu,* 28:2a). We must discount Chang's statement here and take the Taiping system to be in harmony with that of the *Chou-li.*

[477] In *Chou-li chu-shu,* 11:3a, Cheng Hsüan, commenting on the passage on the organization of people for military and farming and other purposes, observes that all this may be traced to former kings who instituted military order for the sake of agriculture.

[478] Chang, *Tse-ch'ing, ts'e* 3, *chüan* 4.

The people were given registers, in which they had to put down the details about their life. They were also forced to complete family registers to be presented to the authority.'[479] Ling Shan-ch'ing gives a vivid picture of these local officials in his *T'ai-p'ing t'ien-kuo yeh-shih*:

At the beginning of their campaign, the Taiping army, on taking a city, usually looted the treasury and took the military equipment and then went on its way, leaving the land behind. Never did they appoint any officials to occupy and defend the captured cities. After establishing the capital in Nanking, whenever their forces took any city, they stationed part of their army on the spot, establishing a *chün-shuai* [corps general] and other officers below him. These would be under the command of *chien-chün* [corps superintendent] [who, in turn, was] controlled by the *tsung-chih* [corps commandant]. Both *chien-chün* and *tsung-chih* received their appointment from the *t'ien-ch'ao* and were known as *shou-t'u-kuan* [defense officials]. Appointees from *chün-shuai* to *liang-ssu-ma* [sergeant] were known as *hsiang-kuan* [鄉官 local officials], because they were chosen from the local people. When an election of local officials was to be held, it was announced by proclamations and honored by military parades. Different *chou* [subprefectures] and *hsien* [districts] were ordered to make up family registers. Local people were told to elect from among themselves *chün-shuai* and *lü-shuai* [captains]. After election, the registers, local population records, and records of tax collection were all presented to *kuo-tsung chien-tien* [國宗檢點, senior secretary of the royal clan] to be sent to the *t'ien-ching* [heavenly capital]. This was known as "accepting terms of surrender." Banners were given to the *chün-shuai*, with the power to collect taxes. They were also especially entrusted with the responsibility to prompt tax payment and to administer judiciary matters. The offices of *shih-shuai* [colonel] down to *liang-ssu-ma* were all equipped with a law court and implements of punishment. They had triangular banners, the size of which was determined by rank. *Chün-shuai* had the privilege of riding in embroidered sedan chairs, carried by four chair coolies. With flags and banners filling the streets, their retinue and insignia were indeed superb. Even the *liang-ssu-ma*, the lowest among them, had retainers and had the power to make decisions governing the affairs of the local people. Both the defense offices and the local offices were [to be] hereditary. Those lacking self-respect or education would run boisterously after these offices. There were some self-respecting ones, however, who were elected by the people. These would sacrifice their own principles for the purpose of preserving their home district intact. Naturally it would not be possible for them to extricate themselves from the job. Being local people, nothing, however trivial, could escape their attention. Thus occasionally they did achieve the task of starting what was beneficial and eradicating what was baneful. In the *Chou-li*, local officials were entrusted with military power. But in time of peace,

[479] *Ibid.*

they took up their normal function again. The Taiping system of making the soldiery and people one seems to have originated here.[480]

This discussion has revealed that the Taiping local official system was clearly separated from the military organization. Though the titles of the officials were the same, the functions of the first were all civil. According to both Chang Te-chien and Ling Shan-ch'ing, these local officials were unwilling collaborators, who "were glad to become common people again on the arrival of government troops, and they threw away their rebel-official costumes in no time."[481] This raises the question whether according to the Taiping system soldiers were people and people were soldiers, as Lo Erh-kang and others have claimed.[482] I have suggested, on the other hand, that to the Taipings soldiers were of the elite, and the common people were just the source from which they drew manpower.

Lo Erh-kang's statement is invalid in at least two details; first, that system known as *hsiang-kuan* was not a part of the army setup; and secondly, the people did not form a part of the army as they did in the *Chou-li* system. Theoretically the Taiping soldiers were supposed to till the land in time of peace and fight in time of war, but in reality they were professional soldiers who fought all the time and did nothing else. This is not surprising because there was never a time that could be called peacetime. But even with this allowance, the Taipings' attitude toward the farmers and people other than those in their own group seems to have foredoomed their intention to failure. The only possible way to argue that the Taiping soldiers were people and the people were soldiers is to contend that the Taipings thought of the people much in the same way as the present Communists think of the non-party members. Since the Communist attitude implies verbal identity only, the comparison does not show actual identity of Taiping soldiers and people.

This raises again the question whether the Taipings, in borrowing verbally from the *Chou-li*, had absorbed its spirit. The *Chou-li* was an ideal system and never in the whole course of Chinese history had it been put into effect in its original form. Therefore it is improper to compare the Taiping system as it was applied with the ideal *Chou-li* system. On the theoretical level, however, the *hsiang-kuan* in the *Chou-li* system

---

[480] *Yeh-shih*, 2:45. This passage is also found in Hsiao I-shan, *Ch'ing-tai t'ung-shih*, Part 2 of Vol. III, p. 135.

[481] Chang, *Tse-ch'ing, ts'e* 3, *chüan* 4.

[482] See footnote 453.

was part and parcel of the military setup, while that of the Taipings was not. In the *Chou-li* system, apart from the six armies in the *hsiang* and six armies in the *sui* 遂, a total of twelve armies, there was no extra military setup to form the so-called six armies of the Son of Heaven. In other words, the Son of Heaven, in time of emergency, could from the twelve armies form the six armies which his royal status demanded. Since all the families were organized into *hsiang* and *sui* armies, there would be no further source from which to draw manpower to form these six armies. It was these same people in the *hsiang* and *sui* organizations who formed the six royal armies.[483]

This theoretical situation was not present in the case of the Taipings. For them there was never a time of peace, so the military activities constituted the sole function of their soldiers. To support these activities, they needed administrators to collect grain and tax: hence the *hsiang-kuan* system. Obviously, these local officers could not have been the same soldiers whose job was to do the fighting. Thus, in spirit, the Taiping *hsiang-kuan* system was different from that described in the *Chou-li*. Had the Taipings become the only rulers of China, would they have put into practice what they proclaimed in the "The Land System of the Heavenly Dynasty"? The answer to this question is necessarily speculative and cannot yield any valid conclusions.

The Taiping idea of recommendation and promotion was certainly taken from the *Chou-li*, as Hsieh Hsing-yao maintains.[484] However, there are differences. The Taipings were more strict in holding the sponsors responsible for their nominees. Although in both systems there was a general stocktaking and examination every three years, there was more stocktaking with the Taipings and more examining with the *Chou-li* system. In the *Chou-li* system the examination was supposed to apply to those to be recommended, while in the Taiping system the investigation was applied to the incumbent officials. For the former, it was a system to select and choose future officials; for the latter, it was a system of promotion and demotion.[485] But the general idea of selecting and promoting officials according to specified plan was present in both systems.[486]

[483] For detail, see Wang Ming-sheng, *Chou-li chün-fu shuo*, in *Huang-ch'ing ching-chieh*, 435:3a and 437:1a–b. Chang Te-chien made the same point in *Tse-ch'ing, ts'e* 2, *chüan* 3.

[484] Hsieh, *T'ai-p'ing t'ien-kuo ti she-hui cheng-chih ssu-hsiang*, pp. 18–19.

[485] See *Chou-li chu-shu*, 12:1a–3a, and "T'ien-ch'ao t'ien-mou chih-tu," in Hsiao, *Ts'ung-shu, ts'e* 4, p. 4a–b.

[486] *Chou-li chu-shu*, 12:8a; "T'ien-ch'ao t'ien-mou chih-tu," in Hsiao, *Ts'ung-shu, ts'e* 4, p. 4a–b.

Hsieh Hsing-yao believes that the Taipings had an office in charge of matchmaking, the official matchmaker, the idea of which can be traced to the *Chou-li* system in which is found *mei-shih*. The function of *mei-shih* was to act as a matchmaker for the people.[487] In the Taiping list of offices there was no such office as official matchmaker. The Taipings came closest to the *mei-shih* in their appointment of a number of people to take care of the matching which occurred during the time that womens' quarters were maintained and at the time of their dissolution. These were temporary appointments made to meet the need of the moment, not regular appointments to an instituted office designed to function normally at all times.

There does seem to be some similarity, however, between the *Chou-li* matchmaking system and the Taiping system. In the *Chou-li* we find the following provision: "In the middle month in the spring [the *mei-shih*] orders the rendezvous of men and women. During this time there is no prohibition against elopement. Those who disobey the order without reason shall be punished. [The *mei-shih*] takes note of the men and women who have no spouse [or have lost their spouse] and brings them together."[488] In instituting separate quarters for men and women, the Taipings made one provision which came close to the *Chou-li* plan. The Taipings allowed men and women to meet on the last day of the month. Wu Chia-chen's "Chin-ling chi-shih tsa-yung" contains the following poem:

> Six armies women's quarters, heavily guarded,
> Twenty-five beauties in a room,
> May every night be the last day of the month,
> All over the city, flying everywhere, pairs of wild mandarin ducks.[489]

In general we may say that the Taipings verbally borrowed a great deal from the *Chou-li*, but a closer view reveals that the Taiping system did not embody the spirit of the *Chou-li* system, a system which has never really been tested in the course of Chinese history. One can only think of the system as an ideal of someone who was apparently more rational than practical. Ch'en Yin-k'o in his *Sui-T'ang chih-tu yüan-yüan lüeh lün-kao* makes a succinct statement about the nature of the *Chou-li*: "In general there is no doubt that [the *Chou-li*] is a great work representing a

---

[487] *Chou-li chu-shu*, 14:13b.
[488] *Ibid.*, 14:15a–16b.
[489] "Chin-ling chi-shih tsa-yung," in Ling, *Yeh-shih*, 20:5.

systematic and idealized scheme based on existing material; in other words, it is a work in the name of antiquity with the intention of bringing about reform, a work which has never been put into effect."[490] Such being the case, the *Chou-li* system could not meet the needs of actual situations.

Before the Taipings, there had been a few endeavors to revive the *Chou-li* system in an attempt to bring about political reforms. Wang Mang of the Hsin, Wen-ti of the Northern Chou, Empress Dowager Wu of the T'ang, and Shen-tsung of the Sung all tried to put into practice the antique *Chou-li* system. None of them enjoyed any degree of success except the Northern Chou.[491] In all these attempts at restoring the *Chou-li* system, except that of Empress Dowager Wu, we find a desire to reform. It seems plausible to think of the Taipings as having the same motive to reform when they chose to base their system at least verbally on the *Chou-li*.

Another reason that the Taipings adopted names from the *Chou-li* may have been their desire for peace. Some people have thought that the peace which the Duke of Chou succeeded in bringing about was the result of the application of the *Chou-li* system. Emperor Hsüan-tsung of the T'ang, in ordering the compilation of the *Liu-tien* (六典 Six Laws), had the purpose of showing the world that peace prevailed at the time.[492] It is possible that the Taipings believed that peace, which was the

---

[490] *Sui-T'ang chih-tu yüan-yüan lüeh lün-kao*, p. 65.

[491] During the time of Wang Mang, Liu Hsin was responsible for the whole project of adopting the *Chou-li* system. He was the one who recommended the creation of a *po-shih* 博士 for it. In *Han-shu*, "I-wen-chih," 30:6b, the author Pan Ku added the following note to the item entitled "Chou-kuan ching": "During the time of Wang Mang, Liu Hsin created *po-shih*." At the time of the Northern Sung, Wang An-shih made an attempt to adopt *Chou-li*. Both Wang Mang and Wang An-shih failed because of various reasons: conservative elements; popular resistance; bad administration; and, above all, the actual conditions of the time. The Northern Chou had some measure of success because the population was greatly decimated by incessant wars and large amounts of land were left unclaimed. Thus the government did not experience great difficulty in distributing land according to certain fixed rules. The government did not actually take the land from the owners but rather distributed the unclaimed land among the people who had no land.

The Empress Wu of the T'ang was interested in reviving the use of the *Chou-li* ministers' names and not the functions that go with the names. See quotation from Tu Yu, *T'ung-tien* in footnote 455 above. Tu Yu continued: "If we examine the ancient and the modern closely and study the offices and functions, [we shall see that] *t'ien-kuan t'ai-tsai* should be *shan-shu-lin* 尚書令; its function does not belong to *li-pu*. Our present *li-pu* should stem from the *ssu-shih* 司士 of the *hsia-kuan*."

objective of their political and military campaign, might come through the application of the *Chou-li* system.

The most obvious reason is the Taipings' belief that the antiquity of the *Chou-li* would lend authority to the new dynasty. The Taipings wanted the people in China to think of them as the legitimate rulers in contrast to the Manchus, whose rule was a usurpation of the Chinese by the non-Chinese. The Chou dynasty was a symbol of legitimate authority to rule in China. Thus, in adopting the *Chou-li* system, the Taipings were making an emotional appeal as well as a logical one. The system would not only guarantee peace and reform, but would confer upon the new dynasty a legitimate authority to rule.

Examination System

The Taipings had several motives in reviving the examination system. First, it was one of the most efficient ways of recruiting members of the officialdom. Secondly, it served as an effective means of control. And thirdly, it offered the best chance to win the support of scholars, without whom the government would have felt a serious shortage of administrative personnel. That these motives and the system itself are completely traditional needs no elaboration.[493] But the Taipings attempted to make some modifications in the titles of the examination degrees.

In the "Imperial Regulations Governing Scholarly Ranks" (Ch'in-ting shih-chieh t'iao-li) Hung Jen-kan went back to the T'ang dynasty to justify changing examination degree titles, even though the changes were supposedly introduced because the new heavenly mandate necessitated a new system. Even this attempt to go back to the T'ang was not original, for Jen-kan was quoting Ku Yen-wu's *Jih-chih-lu* almost word for word with no significant modifications. The following quotation is taken from Hung Jen-kan's "Imperial Regulations Governing Scholarly

---

[492] Ch'en Yin-k'o said in *Sui-T'ang chih-tu yüan-yüan lüeh lün-kao*, p. 71: "Hsüan-tsung of the T'ang formed the institution of six ministers in accordance with the formulation of the *Liu-tien* in the *Chou-li* in order to give an ornamented appearance of peace." The *Liu-tien* of the *Chou-li* are: *chih-tien* (government of the state), *chiao-tien* (education of the state), *li-tien* (rituals of the state), *cheng-tien* (order of the state), *hsing-tien* (punishment of the state), and *shih-tien* (business affairs of the state). These are in fact the functions of the six ministers.

[493] For detail, see Chung-li Chang, *The Chinese Gentry: Studies on Their Role in Nineteenth-Century Chinese Society.* See also Chang Chung-ju, *Ch'ing-tai k'ao-shih chih-tu* and *Ch'ing-tai k'o-chü chih-tu;* and Ssu-yü Teng, "Chung-kuo k'o-chü chih-tu ch'i-yüan k'ao," in *Shih-hsüeh nien-pao,* September, 1934.

Ranks." Inserted in brackets are references to the parts of Ku's *Jih-chih-lu* which Jen-kan quoted.[494]

During the T'ang there were six titles: first, *hsiu-ts'ai* 秀才; second, *ming-ching* 明經; third, *chin-shih* 進士; fourth, *ming-fa* 明法; fifth, *shu* 書; and sixth, *suan* 算. At that time, those candidates who passed the examination in poetry were known as *chin-shih*, and those who passed the examination in classics were known as *ming-ching*. [Ku, 16:1a.] There were four classes of *hsiu-ts'ai*: upper upper, upper middle, upper lower, and middle upper. [Ku, 16:1b.] Duke Hsüan of the T'ang compiled with his own hand the *Liu-tien* 六典, [which says] all those successful candidates who possess broad knowledge and superb talent and who are strong in learning and ready to be advisers and worthy of being selected, are to be known as *hsiu-ts'ai*. [Ku, 16:2b. The Taiping document changed *Hsüan-tsung* (Emperor Hsüan) to *Hsüan-hou* (Duke Hsüan) and also changed *yü-chih* (royal compilation) to *shou-chih* (compiled by his own hand).] There were *chin-shih* from the provisional examination who petitioned to take the *hsiu-ts'ai* examination. [Ku, 16:2b. Here the Taipings made some deletion.] Duke T'ai of the Ming made Ting Shih-mei, a *hsiu-ts'ai*, the prefect of Su-chou-chün; and again, he made Tseng T'ai, another *hsiu-ts'ai*, president of the Board of Revenue. [Ku, 16:2b. "Emperor T'ai-tsu of the Ming" is here changed to "Duke T'ai" (T'ai-hou).] Thus the title *hsiu-ts'ai* should be changed because it has high prestige and for this reason is not to be carelessly used. [This line is the Taipings' own.]

By *chü-jen* 舉人 is meant those who have been recommended. Duke Kao of the T'ang, in the fourth year of *hsien-ch'ing*, examined them himself. About 900 persons passed [the examination] and they were placed as officials and were no longer known as *chü-jen*. Those who failed to be placed had to be recommended again, contrary to the practice in later times when the term *chü-jen* became a fixed title. *Chin-shih* was one of the titles. There were those who succeeded in its examination and there were those who failed. All that was recorded was the phrase "recommended to the *chin-shih*"; whether or not they succeeded is not known. For from the point of view of the candidates, they were said to have been recommended to the *chin-shih*; but from the point of view of the court they were still known as *chü-jen*, the men who had been recommended. It does not mean that successful candidates in the provincial examinations had to be *chü-jen* and successful candidates in the metropolitan examination had to be *chin-shih*. [Ku, 16:3a–4a.] Thus the titles *chü-jen* and *chin-shih* should be changed.... [This and the few lines that follow—omitted here—are the Taipings' own.]

Those who are *hsien-liang fang-cheng* [賢良方正 the talented, the good, the

[494] Ku Yen-wu, *Jih-chih-lu*. For Hung's "Ch'in-ting shih-shieh t'iao-li," see Hsiao, *Ts'ung-shu*, *ts'e* 9, pp. 5a–8a.

just, and the upright],⁴⁹⁵ *chih-yen chi-chien* [直言極諫 straightforward in words and unreserved in remonstration],⁴⁹⁶ *po-hsia fen-tien* (博洽墳典 a broad acquaintance of great works of the past),⁴⁹⁷ who are sufficiently steeped in these as to be able to know thoroughly military strategy and the art of government, [Ku, 16:6a.]⁴⁹⁸ may all be selected to become *han-lin* [翰林, literally, forest of literature].⁴⁹⁹ [This and the next line, which is omitted, are the Taipings' own.]

Military examination was begun during the reign of Ch'ing-li [1041–48, the reign of Jen-tsung] of the Sung; and Juan I was made military educational master. [Ku, 17:32a. Ku gives the date of Juan I's appointment as the third year of Ch'ing-li, 1043.] Duke T'ai of the Ming established military schools and instituted military examination [election]. [Ku, 17: 32a. Again "Duke T'ai" is substituted for "Emperor T'ai-tsu."]

Hung Jen-kan also proposed changing *hsiu-ts'ai* to *hsiu-shih* 秀士, a term found in the "Wang-chih" in the *Li-chi* and quoted by Ku;⁵⁰⁰ and changing *pu-lin* 補廩 to *chün-shih* 俊士, a term also found in the *Li-chi*.⁵⁰¹ As a matter of fact, Hung here was proposing to revive the ancient terminology, for the whole line of the *Li-chi* which Ku quotes runs: "*Hsiang* [鄉 local administrators] are ordered to consider *hsiu-shih* [秀士 the flowering scholars] and recommend them to the *ssu-t'u* 司徒; these are then called *hsüan-shih* [選士 the selected scholars]. The *ssu-t'u* then consider those *hsüan-shih* who are flowering scholars and recommend them to the

⁴⁹⁵ This title was first introduced during the reign of Emperor Wen of the Han and later adopted in the T'ang and the Sung.

⁴⁹⁶ It is not clear whether this phrase was taken by the Taipings as a title, as in the original text where Ku quotes it to describe the system of the T'ang, or as a descriptive phrase qualifying *hsien-liang fang-cheng*, as in another original passage quoted from the system of the Sung.

⁴⁹⁷ This is another title used both in the T'ang and the Sung with the difference of the second character, which in the original is *t'ung* (通 versed) instead of *hsia* (洽 permeating or penetrating). Again it is unclear whether the Taipings used the title as a title or merely as a phrase describing *hsien-liang fang-cheng*.

⁴⁹⁸ The last clause contains two phrases which were used as titles during the T'ang and the Sung but were not so used, it seems, by the Taipings. Hence their translation in our text. The Taipings also made some modification and omission in appropriating the material.

⁴⁹⁹ See Yang Hsiung, "Ch'ang-yang fu," in *Wen-hsüan* 9:1b, note by Wei Chao, for explanation of the term *han-lin*. During the T'ang and the Sung *han-lin* applied to all kinds of courtiers within the palace, and it was during the Ming that it became a special term for literary men. The Ch'ing adopted the Ming system.

⁵⁰⁰ Ku, *Jih-chih-lu*, 17:9a. See *Li-chi yin-te*, 5/42. The term was first quoted by Huang Tsung-hsi [Li-chou] in *Ming-i tai-fang lu*, p. 14a.

⁵⁰¹ *Li-chi yin-te*, 5/42.

school and call them *chün-shih.*"[502] Hung here actually revived a system of terminology more ancient than the one he wanted to supersede.

NON-TRADITIONAL ASPECTS OF THE IDEOLOGY

This chapter has shown that in many respects the Taipings were thoroughly traditional, and in some others they were unorthodox. We shall deal very briefly with those aspects in which they may be said to have been untraditional.

First of all, the Taipings' attitude toward Confucius and the classics, no matter how much they were influenced by them unconsciously, branded them as untraditional. No Chinese at that time, and few even today, would dare to breathe the name of Confucius, the model teacher for all generations, without a sense of reverence. In showing the attitude toward the sage of China described in the "Taiping Heavenly Chronicle," the Taipings symbolized a new mental horizon, which could have proved immensely valuable in their contact with new cultures. Unfortunately, their revolt was only skin deep. The Taipings may have sensed the necessity of change, but they did not possess the insight to envision what that change should be.

Similarly, their conception of T'ien, no matter how slavishly they quoted the classics to prove their point, could not have been what the ancients conceived it to be. They took the idea of T'ien as the father of mankind literally; this was contrary to the concept the Chinese thinkers had in mind when they spoke of the relationship between Heaven and men. Furthermore, even though to a certain extent the ancient Chinese concept of T'ien was anthropomorphic, the ancients never conceived of T'ien as having a wife, or as being jealous, or as actually giving birth to men in the same sense as a father gives birth to a child through the womb of a mother. Again, though T'ien had been conceived vaguely as a general moral principle, and though certain specific instances might be construed as manifestations of the operation of this principle, T'ien had never been used to demonstrate the right or wrong of any specific case. The Taipings, however, saw T'ien as descending upon this world to sit in judgment on people in specific cases. To them, T'ien or God was only a man whose power and intelligence had been magnified in accordance with the magnitude of their imaginative power. The Taiping God or T'ien seems more like the king of Hades than the morally suasive and

[502] *Ibid.*

benevolent supreme ruler who existed in the minds of the ancients when they thought of T'ien or Shang-ti.

The supreme example of non-Confucian ideas was of course the prohibition of ancestor worship.[503] Though a pre-Confucian practice, this worship not only received the sanction of the Confucians but has been supported by them with a great deal of reasoning and rationalization. The Confucians evolved the theory of *shen-chung chui-yüan* [慎終追遠 careful about going back in our mind to the end and the far]. [*Yüan*, the far, refers to the ancestors in the past, implying that one should always keep ancestors in his mind when they die.] Out of this thought, the Confucians developed an elaborate system of mourning, funeral, and ceremonial sacrifice, just for the purpose of justifying and increasing the importance of this ancient ancestor worship. In view of the Taiping attitude toward parents and death, it is no surprise that they frowned upon such a practice and considered it just another form of superstition to be suppressed.

---

[503] For this prohibition, see *Tz'u-hsi hsien-chih*, 55:28, quoted in Kuo T'ing-i, *Jih-chih*, II, 857.

Chapter IX

Buddhism, Taoism, and Mohism

Terms like "Confucianism," "Taoism," "Buddhism," "Mohism," and "traditionalism" are so mixed in the minds of the Chinese people that none of them stands for any distinct idea; Christianity, when introduced, added another element to the Chinese mental make-up. This conglomerate state of mind is vividly manifested in the following passage written in 1950: "But God has told us: man is still sentient after death. If one is good in this world, his soul will ascend to heaven; if otherwise, his soul will be banished to the eighteenth layer of hells."[1] Even in the twentieth century Christianity and Buddhism are completely mixed in the same mind. This eclectic tendency may be the reason there has been more religious tolerance in China than anywhere else in the world. When the Taipings used terms of Buddhist or Taoist or Mohist origin, they owed them more to the popular pattern, which is a conglomeration of the floating ideas of different strands of thought, than to Taoist, Buddhist, or Mohist sources. However, whenever possible, we shall try to point out the origin of the terms from Taoist, Buddhist, and Mohist literatures which the Taipings used.

BUDDHIST SOURCES

The ideas the Taipings borrowed from popular Buddhism were limited in number but extremely important in the lives of the people. The principle of moral causality or retribution which the Taipings stressed, though essentially based on classical sources, could also be related to the idea of *yin-yüan kuo-pao* 因緣果報 of popular Buddhism. This phrase may

[1] Ch'iu T'ien, "T'ai-wan ti an-mo nü," *Chung-kuo hsin-wen*, Vol. VIII, No. 11 (1950), p. 24.

be briefly explained as the relation between an act and its consequence being conceived to be an inexorable causal relation. In Buddhist literature this principle, known as *karma* (業, *yeh* in Chinese), is discussed many times, particularly in *Vijñaptimātratāsiddhi* 成唯識論, originally in thirty volumes by Vasubandhu, reduced to ten volumes and translated into Chinese by Hsüan-tsang of the T'ang dynasty, and *Yogācāryabhūmi* 瑜伽師地論, the work of Asaṅga, also translated by Hsüan-tsang.

Other Buddhist terms found in the Taiping writings include "thirty-three heavens"; "eighteen hells"; *yen-lo-wang* or *yen-lo* or *yen-wang* or *yen-lo-yao; lo-ch'a;* and *yeh-ch'a.* "Thirty-three heavens" is *Trāyastriṁśa* in Sanskrit, the Indra heaven, the second of the six heavens of form. Its capital is situated on the summit of Mount Sumeru, where Indra rules over his thirty-two devas, who reside on thirty-two peaks of Sumeru, eight in each of the four directions from Mount Sumeru. The "thirty-three heavens" are discussed in *Fo-ti ching* 佛地經, translated by Hsüan-tsang, and *The Śāstra,* or commentary of the *Prajñā-pāramitā sūtra,* ascribed to Nāgārjuna, translated by Kumārajīva (A.D. 397–415). The thirty-three heavens and twenty-eight subsidiary heavens are also treated in *Leng-yen ching* 楞嚴經 (*Śuraṅgama-samādhi-sūtra* in Sanskrit, translated by Paramiti in A.D. 705).

The eighteen hells are described in *Shih-pa ni-li ching-shuo* 十八泥犁經説, translated by An Shih-kao 安世高 of the later Han. This work is also known as *Shih-pa ti-yü ching* 十八地獄經 and describes different types of suffering and different forms of calamity determining the span of life; Buddha himself admonishes the masses that the evil ones shall go to the hells, of which there are eighteen, ten being extremely hot and eight freezing cold.[2] These hells are also described in the *Śuraṅgama-samādhi-sūtra.*

Yen-lo is *Yama* in Sanskrit; he is also known as *yen-mo* 閻魔 or 燄 or 魔 or *yen-mo kuei-wang* 閻 or 燄魔鬼王. In *Yogācāryabhūmi* there is a passage on *yen-mo* which touches also upon the principle of *karma:*

> Question: Why is *yen-mo* called *fa-wang* (法王 the prince of law)? Is it because he is able to do harm to the multitude or because he is able to enrich the life of the multitude? If it is because he is able to do harm to the multitude that he is called the prince of law, it is contrary to reason; if it

---

[2] Lang Ying in *Ch'i-hsiu lei-kao* describes the eighteen hells as the conditions in which the six sense organs 六根, the six objects 六塵, and the six perceptions 六識 do not harmonize.

is because he is able to enrich the life of the multitude, then it should be stated in what way he enriches the life of the multitude.

Answer: It is because he is able to enrich the life of the multitude. When the multitude are brought to the court of the prince, they are made to remember their past. The prince then appears in a form similar to that of the multitude and tells them: "You are governed by *karma*, receiving the fruits of your own doing." From these causal relations (*yin-yüan* 因緣 [*yin* is *hetu* in Sanskrit meaning primary cause and *yüan* is *pratyaya* in Sanskrit meaning secondary cause]), the multitude will know that they are receiving the fruits of their own doing."[3]

Lo-ch'a and *yeh-ch'a* are Buddhist conceptions of the evil demons whose sole function seemingly is to harass men and to lead them astray. Their Sanskrit equivalents are *rākṣasa* and *yakṣa*.

The Taipings did not, it seems, go to the original sources for their ideas but rather derived them from the popular pattern of thought. Their concept of Yen-lo as head of the demons whose sole function was to lead men astray is not in accord with his role as the prince of law as described in the *Yogācāryabhūmi*. The Taipings had a sense of other-worldly disillusionment when talking about their own true way 真道.[4] They repeatedly expressed the idea of this otherworldliness in such phrases as: *p'ao ch'üeh fan-ch'ing* (拋却凡情 to give up worldly thought), *t'o ch'üeh fan-ch'ing* (脱却凡情 to be free from worldly thought), and *t'o ching fan-ch'ing* (脱盡凡情 to be completely free from worldly thought).[5] This idea of giving up worldly thought, though here definitely referring to the embracing of the Taiping form of Christianity, has nonetheless a basis in popular Buddhist beliefs. And this sense of otherworldliness culminates in the following two lines:

> Together we leave this misleading ford and old habits.
> Together return to the enlightened path, realizing what lies ahead of us.[6]

Taoist Sources

The same is true of the Taoist ideas present in the Taiping ideology as is true of Buddhist ideas. A certain state of mind which has become fairly

[3] *Yogācāryabhūmi*, 8:1.

[4] For this otherworldly feeling, see "Ying-chieh kuei-chen," in Hsiao I-shan (compiler), *T'ai-p'ing t'ien-kuo ts'ung-shu, ts'e* 10.

[5] "T'ien-ch'ing tao-li shu," in Hsiao, *Ts'ung-shu, ts'e* 5, pp. 2a, 38b, 40b, 47b, 48a, 50a.

[6] *Ibid.*, p. 48a.

prevalent among the Chinese poets and people may be described as Taoistic. Two lines in a Taiping document express just this state of mind:

> Despite the bustle of ten thousand noises,
> Unruffled I listen in tranquillity.[7]

Although there is not much poetry in the lines, they describe a state of mind which can be compared to that created by the poems of T'ao Yüan-ming and Wang Wei. Following are a few lines from a poem by T'ao:

> I built my cottage among the habitations of men,
> And yet I heard neither horses nor carriages.
> Would you know how these things come to pass?
> A distant soul creates its own solitude.[8]

The Taipings did, in fact, quote one complete line from T'ao: "Enjoy your heavenly mandate [in this case this phrase refers to one's fate], what more doubt about it."[9]

The Taipings used the line *t'ien-yen hui-hui* (天眼恢恢 heaven's eye opens wide) a number of times. In the original, it is *t'ien-wang* (heavenly net) instead of *t'ien-yen* (heavenly eye). This line came from the *Lao-tzu*, also known as *Tao-te-ching*, chapter 73. Here the idea of retribution is as strong as that found in the Buddhist principle of *karma*. From the Taoist point of view, it means that there is a natural law governing causal relations which is inescapable and inexorable, for figuratively speaking nothing will escape the penetrating and comprehensive surveillance of nature. When the Taipings used this expression they meant exactly the inexorable nature of retribution, though the Taoist figure of speech was here transformed into a literal surveillance by an anthropomorphic God.[10]

---

[7] "Yu-hsüeh-shih," in Hsiao, *Ts'ung-shu*, *ts'e* 4, p. 12b.

[8] The poem is found in T'ao, *Ching-chieh hsien-sheng chi*, 3:21. Translation is by Yang Yeh-tzu in Robert Payne (ed.), *The White Pony: An Anthology of Chinese Poetry from the Earliest Times to the Present Day, Newly Translated* (New York: An Asia Book, 1947), "Chrysanthemums," p. 162.

[9] This is the last line of T'ao Yüan-ming's "Kuei ch'ü lai tz'u," in T'ao, *op. cit.*, 5:11a. The Taipings used the line in "Yüan-tao chiu-shih chao" in "T'ai-p'ing chao-shu," in Hsiao, *Ts'ung-shu*, *ts'e* 1, p. 3b.

[10] "T'ien-ch'ing tao-li shu," in Hsiao, *Ts'ung-shu*, *ts'e* 5, p. 23a.

There is an idea present in Taiping thought which was used as much by the Neo-Confucianists as by the early Taoists—the idea of returning to primitive simplicity and the original truth: "All those whose public spirit reaches to heaven above and yet is firmly established on earth, should immediately come back to the simple and return to the true."[11] The Taipings are calling the people to join them, but the Taoist flavor is unmistakable. For Neo-Confucianism, see Wang Yang-ming's *Ch'uan-hsi lu*, which abounds in expressions like *fan-p'u kuei-ch'un* (反樸歸湻 return to simplicity and go back to purity). In *Lao-tzu*, this idea is repeatedly expressed:

> Externally appear in natural color, inwardly embrace the simple, and lessen prejudice and decrease desires (chapter 19).
> In being the valley of the world, one's constant virtue will be sufficient and one will again return to the simple (chapter 28).
> When in transformation, [the ten thousand things] begin to experience desire, and I shall control them with the nameless simplicity. With this nameless simplicity, there will be no desire; without desire there will be tranquillity, and the whole world will be upright of itself (chapter 37).

However, this idea of primitive simplicity has become so much a part of the Chinese common heritage that it sounds pedantic, if not ridiculous, to suggest that it comes from the *Lao-tzu*.

Hung, in his dream, received a sword from God as a symbol that he would be the instrument for the extermination of the devils and demons. This is another idea which seems to have stemmed from a popular Taoist sect. Cheng Ching-pi 鄭景璧 of the Sung quotes a poem by Lü Tung-pin, one of the eight Taoist immortals, in his *Meng-tsai pi-t'an*:

> In the morning I roam among the regions of Yüeh and O,
>   in the evening in Ts'ang-wu.
> With a green snake up in my sleeve, my courage is great.
> Three times I entered Yüeh-yang, no one recognized me.
> Singing loudly, I flew across Lake Tung-t'ing.

The green snake refers to a sword Lü had up in his sleeve for the extermination of any evil things that might cross his way. Cheng makes the following comment on the poem: "With respect to the green snake, most people believed that Lü was at first a sword-hero and then became

[an immortal]. This does not seem to be correct. For this is exactly the Taoists' method of refining the sword by means of *ch'i* (氣 vital breath),[12] and the Taoists have their own tried method in accomplishing it."[13]

Chao Tao-i of the Yüan in *Li-shih chen-hsien t'i-tao t'ung-chien* relates a story about another of the eight Taoist immortals:

> Han Hsiang, *tzu* Ch'ing-fu, was a nephew of Han Wen-kung, Yü. Disappointed in his worldly ambition, he lived a life unrestrained. Wen-kung exhorted him to study. Hsiang said: "What I am learning is beyond you." Han Yü told him to write a poem expressing his ambition. The poem runs:
>> Green mountains, caves with clouds and water,
>> These places are my home.
>> In the evening flowing the crystal nectar,
>> In the morning tasting emblazoned clouds,
>> On the flute playing a tune of green jade,
>> In the stove smelting white cinnabar.
>> In the precious tripod are stored golden tigers.
>> In the primeval field are raised white crows.
>> One spoon [referring to a gourd] room enough to store up the universe,
>> Three feet [referring to a sword] exterminating the devilish and the evil ones,
>> Knowledge to remake the Chün-shün wine,
>> Ability to get flowers to blossom instantaneously.
>> Those who can imitate me,
>> With them I shall see the fairy flowers.[14]

The function of the sword is here specifically given: to exterminate the evil and the devilish.

Tangible evidence gave the Taipings a sense of the reality of their mission. The Taoists also indulged in prognostic statement. Wang Chia's *Shih-i-chi* says:

> In the twenty-first year of Chou Ling-wang, Confucius was born in the state of Lu during the reign of Hsiang-kung. That night there were two green dragons [*ts'ang-lung*, 蒼龍, which also refers to one of the seven constellations in the eastern sky] coming down and curling themselves on top of Cheng-tsai's [徵在 Confucius' mother's] room. Thus she dreamt of them

---

[12] The Taoists believed that the inner being of the hero acted in some manner upon his sword, making the sword more effective.

[13] Cheng Ching-pi, *Meng-tsai pi-t'an*, quoted by P'u Chiang-ch'ing in "Pa-hsien k'ao," *Ch'ing-hua hsüeh-pao*, Vol. XI, No. 1 (April, 1936), p. 114.

[14] *Li-shih chen-hsien t'i-tao t'ung-chien*, *chüan* 42, quoted by P'u in *op. cit.*, p. 125.

and gave birth to the Master. There were two goddesses descending from the sky, holding in their hands fragrant dew for Cheng-tsai to bathe in. God came down, and the music of Chün-t'ien 鈞天 was played. [They] lined up in Cheng-tsai's room. A voice was heard from the sky, saying: "Heaven has moved [her] to give birth to the holy son, hence the coming of this music of reed organs and great bells, differing from the worldly music." There were also five elders standing in line in Cheng-tsai's court, these elders being the spirits of the five stars. The evening when Confucius was born a *lin* (麟, a legendary animal supposed to be a symbol for a sage) vomited forth a jade book at Chüeh-li with the inscription: "The descendant of the essence of water will succeed the declining Chou to be the king without the royal diadem."[15]

In this passage there is not only the prognostic statement but the use of a dream for a similar purpose. This suggests Hung's dream of a great golden dragon paying homage to him[16] and the prognostic statement in those seven characters: *T'ien Wang ta-tao chün-wang Ch'üan* (天王大道君 王全).[17]

The principle of moral causality, involving reward and punishment, was no less prominent in later Taoism. Ko Hung's *Pao-p'u-tzu* quotes three other pieces of Taoist literature as saying:

There are gods [is a god] in the universe whose duty is to be in charge of [human] faults. He will take a number of *suan* [筭, designating a period of three days] away from people according to the nature of their faults. When a man's *suan* is being taken away, he becomes weak and sick, and will often encounter calamities. With the exhaustion of *suan* comes death.[18]

And in "Tui su pien," Ko Hung said:

The god in charge of life span will take a number of *chi* (紀, designating three hundred days) away from those whose evil doings are great; when their faults are trivial, he will take away their *suan*. The quantity taken away depends on the seriousness of the faults. When a man receives life, his life span is determined. If his lot is originally ample, his *chi* and *suan* are hard to exhaust, and hence he will die in old age; if his lot is originally

---

[15] *Shih-i-chi*, in *Shuo-fu*, 30:7a.
[16] "T'ien-fu hsia-fan chao-shu," in Ch'eng Yen-sheng (compiler), *T'ai-p'ing t'ien-kuo shih-liao*, 1st Series, II, 22b.
[17] "Wang-chang-tz'u-hsiung ch'ing-mu ch'ing-erh kung-cheng fu-yin-shu," in Hsiao, *Ts'ung-shu, ts'e* 8, p. 2b.
[18] See "Wei-chih pien" 微旨篇 in *Pao-p'u-tzu*, p. 27.

small and his faults are many, his *chi* and *suan* will be exhausted fast and he will die early.[19]

These ideas later came to be embodied in the book entitled *T'ai-shang kan-ying p'ien*, which is included in *Tao-tsang*.

The acceptance of this idea of reward for the good and punishment for the evil was not, however, confined to the Taoists. Yüan Liu-fan of the Ming, definitely a Confucianist, gave great weight to *T'ai-shang kan-ying p'ien* and formulated his own *kung-kuo ko* 功過格 (a chart of one's merit and demerit). In the Ch'ing dynasty, Hui Tung in conjunction with Yao Shuang gave *T'ai-shang kan-ying p'ien* its best commentary. Since this book has influenced the minds of the common people so much and is a pattern for the popular conception of what is right and wrong, it would be strange indeed if the Taipings had not been influenced by it.

There was a Taoist precedent for the title *T'ai-p'ing t'ien-kuo* in a rebellion assuming the term *t'ai-p'ing chiao* as the teaching of that movement. The rebellion will be discussed in Chapter XI.

MOHIST SOURCES

It is possible that the Taipings were also influenced by the Mohists in their conceptions of God, brotherhood, love, and source of authority. Motzu's God has a will and wills that all men should love one another, because he himself loves mankind.[20] He constantly supervises the activities of men, especially those of the rulers of men. He punishes with calamities persons who disobey his will, and rewards with good fortune those who obey.[21] The mutual love of men for one another, or the universal love which Motzu advocated as contrasted with the graded love of the Confucians, was made the basis of a society in which the members were required to help one another; and the *chü-tzu*, the head of this Mohist society, held almost absolute power over the people. The tight organization of the society and the absolute power of the *chü-tzu* could have appealed to the Taipings, whose conception of the Son of Heaven and the precepts they established to regulate the conduct of their members suggest just this type of society. In both societies there is a kind of communal feeling among the members, which the Taipings expressed

---

[19] *Pao-p'u-tzu*, p. 12.

[20] See Motzu's three chapters on "T'ien-chih 天志," in *Motzu hsien-ku*, edited by Sun I-jang, hereafter cited *Motzu*, *chüan* 7, chaps. 26–28, pp. 118–37.

[21] *Motzu*, *chüan* 7, chap. 26, pp. 120, 123, 126–27.

through their ideas of brotherhood and common property and the Mohists expressed through common sharing. The Taipings probably received their idea of brotherhood from the secret society ideologies; however, the Mohist society could have been the prototype of later secret societies.[22]

In the *Motzu* there are three chapters entitled "Shang-t'ung" (Agreement with the Superior), which describe the source and nature and power of a ruler.[23] According to these chapters, the authority of a ruler comes from two sources: the will of the people and the will of God, which in another context are defined as the same thing. Since the ruler and the state are established through the will of Heaven, and since Heaven loves mankind and therefore good, and since what is good for mankind is right and what is bad is wrong, Heaven naturally is the source which sets the standard of right and wrong, true and false. And since the ruler receives his mandate to rule from Heaven, he is naturally the closest to the source of right and hence most likely to be in the right. Similar reasoning applies to the rest of the officials: the higher the official, the more likely he is to be in the right because the closer he is to the source of right. Hence Motzu tells the people: "Always agree with the superior; never follow the subordinate."[24] For only thus will there be uniformity of thought and uniformity of standards for right and wrong. Obviously such a state would be a totalitarian state and such a ruler would be an absolute ruler.

These characteristics can be applied to the Taiping society and Taiping idea of a ruler without much modification. Besides these conceptual similarities, there is also a verbal one between the Taiping ideology and Mohism. The style of the Taiping essay called "Proclamation on the Origin of Principles for the Enlightenment of the Age" (Yüan-tao hsing-shih chao), as well as its content, is remarkably similar to the three chapters on "universal love" in the book of *Motzu*. The following quotation is from the Taiping proclamation:

> However, for the times reaching down to the present, it is hard to say. The ways of the world are perverse and shallow, while the minds of men are intolerant and thin, their loves and hates being all derived from selfishness. Hence, there are cases where this country dislikes that country, and that

---

[22] Wei-ta fa-shih [Wei Chü-hsien], *Chung-kuo-ti pang-hui*, "Chung-kuo ti pan-hui shih-yü Motzu," pp. 1–4.

[23] *Motzu, chüan* 3, chaps. 11–13, pp. 44–61.

[24] *Ibid., chüan* 3, chap. 11, p. 45.

country dislikes this country. There are even cases within one country where this province, this prefecture, or this district dislikes that province, that prefecture, or that district; and that province, that prefecture, or that district dislikes this province, this prefecture, or this district. There are even cases within one province, prefecture, or district where this village, this hamlet, or this clan dislikes that village, that hamlet, or that clan; and that village, that hamlet, or that clan dislikes this village, this hamlet, or this clan. The ways of the world and the minds of men having come to this, how can they do otherwise than to oppress one another, to seize one another, to fight one another, and to kill one another, and thus altogether perish. This arises from no other cause than that their views are limited and liberal-mindedness is limited. Those of this country dislike those of that country, and those of that country dislike those of this country; this is because their views are confined to one individual country, and they are ignorant of everything beyond their own country. Hence they love those of their own country and dislike those of other countries. Those of this province, this prefecture, or this district dislike those of that province, that prefecture, or that district; those of that province, that prefecture, or that district dislike those of this province, this prefecture, or this district: it is because their views are confined to one particular province, prefecture, or district and they are ignorant of everything beyond that province, prefecture, or district. Hence it is that they love those of the same province, the same prefecture, and the same district and dislike those of other provinces, other prefectures, and other districts. When those of this village, this hamlet, or this clan dislike those of that village, that hamlet, or that clan, and when those of that village, that hamlet, or that clan dislike those of this village, this hamlet, or this clan, it is because their views are confined to one particular village, hamlet, or clan and they are ignorant of everything beyond their own village, hamlet, or clan. Therefore they love those of their own village, hamlet, or clan and dislike those of other villages, other hamlets, and other clans. This is the condition of the loves and hates of the world. How is it that their views are not enlarged, and liberal-mindedness not extensive?[25]

The following is a passage from *Motzu* quoted to serve as a basis for comparison with the Taiping text:

The sage man who has the ordering of the Great Society cannot but examine into what gives rise to disorder. When this examination is made, the rise of disorder is (found to be) people not loving each other, ministers of state and sons not being filial to their sovereigns and fathers: that is what is called disorder. Sons love themselves and not their fathers; and the result is that they injure their fathers in profiting themselves. Younger brothers

[25] "T'ai-p'ing chao-shu," in Hsiao, *Ts'ung-shu*, *ts'e* 1, pp. 5b–6b.

love themselves and not their elder brothers; and the result is . . . Ministers love themselves and not their sovereigns: and the result is . . . So in the case of fathers who have no compassion for their sons, and elder brothers for their younger brothers, and sovereigns for their ministers. This also is universally described as disorder. Fathers love themselves and not their sons: and the result is they injure their sons in profiting themselves. . . .

If we go to the robbers all over the country, it is just the same. Robbers love their households and do not love the households of different kinds of people. The result is that they rob these other households in order to profit their own. And the same applies to the great officers who throw each other's clans into confusion and the feudal lords who attack each other's countries. Each great officer loves his own household and not others' households; hence he causes confusion in others' households in order to benefit his own. Each feudal lord loves his own country and not others' countries; hence he attacks others' countries in order to benefit his own.[26]

There is parallelism not only in the themes these two selections treat but in the way the themes are handled. In both there is a desire to expose the cause of disorder, which both the Taipings and the Mohists found to be selfishness, a limited point of view, and limited liberal-mindedness or love. There is a similar contrast between likes and dislikes or loves and hates, which are applied to correspondingly contrasting objects of loves and hates. Although this correspondence in style is not characterized by exact verbal quotations as in the case of the Taiping imitation of Han Yü, the correspondence seems unmistakable.

Finally, universal love forms for the Mohists the basis of social welfare, so that "the aged, who have no wife or children, will have support and nourishment to round out their old age; and the young or the weak, who have no parents, will have means of support in which to grow up."[27] The Taipings built their social program upon the belief that all men are brothers, and hence all men should help one another.

In view of the consideration given above, it is difficult not to conclude that at the very least there is strong probability the Taipings were influenced by the Mohists.

[26] *Motzu, chüan* 4, chap. 14, pp. 62–63, translated by Ernest R. Hughes in *Chinese Philosophy in Classical Times*, p. 54. The final paragraph, which Hughes omits, is my own translation.

[27] *Motzu, chüan* 4, chap. 16, p. 72.

Chapter X

Other Sources of the Taiping Ideology

This chapter discusses as sources of the Taiping ideology novels, secret societies, the Hakkas, and popular beliefs. Not only is each of these subjects insufficient to form a chapter by itself, but also all the subjects can be related in one way or another by reference to their common features. The idea of loyalty and fraternity expressed in oaths is common to novels and secret societies, and authorities on the Hakkas are agreed that Hakkas are particularly strong in their feeling of solidarity. The Hakkas also practice trance, which is the most prominent feature of the popular superstitions of the southern Chinese.

NOVELS

While not highly regarded by the literati in traditional China, novels have always had a great appeal for the common people. The reasons are not hard to find. Whether the people were crushed by the burden of daily life or were on the brink of starvation because they were unemployed, they always found in novels something to replace that which their lives lacked. Novels furnished a temporary escape for some from the cruel world in which they slaved for a mere existence, and they fired the imagination of others through the creation of characters who became their heroes and companions; in many cases these characters profoundly transformed the readers' lives. Chang Te-chien's descriptions of Wei Ch'ang-hui and Shih Ta-k'ai correspond to the popular conception of a hero found in many a novel.[1]

Novels often achieve their greatest appeal when they are written from the point of view of the people, championing the interests of the lowly

[1] Chang Te-chien (editor and compiler), *Tse-ch'ing hui-tsuan, ts'e* 6, *chüan* 12.

and the poor and attacking the corruption of government and the supremacy of the rich. The influence of novels is often of an explosive nature,
and this is reflected in the official attitude toward them. T'ang Pin and
Liu K'ai during the reign of K'ang-hsi, and Ch'ien Ta-hsin during the
reign of Ch'ien-lung advocated the destruction of printing blocks of
"Small Talks," that is, novels, in order to eliminate their subversive influence on mores and customs.[2] More than one emperor was greatly
concerned with the influence of novels.[3]

It is only natural, therefore, that the Taipings should have been influenced by novels. Chang Te-chien said the following about the Taipings and the novels:

> What is the basis of the rebels' tactical tricks? They are thought out by
> two or three clever rebels who model their tactics after what they find in
> the novels. Occasionally such application bears fruit, so they consider these
> as secrets not to be divulged. Most of all they take from *Romance of the Three
> Kingdoms* and *Shui-hu chuan* (All Men Are Brothers)....The rebels know
> nothing about strategy; they just imitate the various patterns they find in
> the novels.[4]

That the Taipings learned strategy from reading novels is not surpris-

---

[2] *Huang-ch'ao ching-shih wen-pien*, ed. Ho Ch'ang-lin, 68:58a, 61a–62b.

[3] Edicts prohibiting novels issued in the years 1687 and 1714 are recorded in *Sheng-
tsu sheng-yü*, 25:22a and 8:14a. In the first edict are found these words: " . . . indecent
sayings and small talks [that is, novels] actually are capable of exercising a subversive
influence on the mores and placing temptations before the minds of the people. . . .
They should all be strictly prohibited." The second edict contains a similar interdiction. In 1738, 1754, and 1802, this interdiction was repeated, with *Shui-hu chuan*
specifically mentioned as the object of prohibition in 1754. Kung-chuan Hsiao, in
Rural China: Imperial Control in the Nineteenth Century, p. 241, made the following observation: "Novels were thought to be capable of exerting dangerous influence on the
minds of the people and were therefore forbidden. The Board of Rites ordered in 1652
that booksellers should print only 'books in Sung philosophy' and those that dealt
with methods of administration or were useful for literary studies. Those who published
or sold books containing 'trifling talks or indecent sayings' would receive severe punishment. This interdiction was repeated in 1663, 1687, 1714, 1725, 1810, 1834, and 1851.
The Tao-kuang emperor explained in 1834 that many novels were not fit for his
subjects to peruse, because they taught their readers 'to regard violent persons as
heroic.' " *Hsien-feng shih-lu*, 38:13, gives another concrete reason for the imperial concern about novels in 1851: "The religious bandits, in subverting the minds of the
people by preaching, are reported to have in their possession the following two books:
Hsing-ming kuei-chih and *Shui-hu chuan*. These books are published and sold in many
bookstores in Hunan. . . . Order be given to the local officials to have all these blocks
destroyed."

[4] Chang, *Tse-ch'ing, ts'e* 3, *chüan* 5.

ing. The Ch'ing court at one time also used *Romance of the Three King-doms* as a source of tactics.[5] According to Lo Erh-kang, this imitation of the tactics found in the novels was in practice right down to the last days of the Taipings: Li Hsiu-ch'eng, the Chung Wang, surrendered himself in exactly the same spirit as Chiang Wei surrendered to Chung Hui in *Romance of the Three Kingdoms.*[6]

Taiping documents abound in references to novels. In the poems which form the sequel to "The Book on the Principles of the Heavenly Nature" (T'ien-ch'ing tao-li shu), popular heroes from *Romance of the Three Kingdoms* are repeatedly praised for their bravery, loyalty, rectitude, and perseverance. Ch'ang-shan Chao Tzu-lung is mentioned five times; Kuan Yün-ch'ang, eight times; Chang Fei, six times; and Huang Chung, once. Chiang Tzu-ya of *Feng-shen chuan* is also mentioned once. In "The Book of Heavenly Decrees and Proclamations" (T'ien-ming chao-chih shu), Yüeh Fei is mentioned as defeating a Chin army of one hundred thousand with a handful of five hundred men. This episode apparently refers to chapter 23 in the *Yüeh-chuan*. In his confession, *Chung Wang Li Hsiu-ch'eng tzu-chuan yüan-kao ch'ien-cheng*, Li said:

> The idea to destroy idols came from the Heavenly King; but it may also be due to the fact that the spirits and the sages, in receiving worship in the form of incense-burning, have lived out their fate. During the Chou dynasty many generals were killed and many spirits appointed; these were preordained. Now many idols of the spirits have been destroyed; it is in fact the reverse [or the return] of the process, in which spirits are killed and generals appointed. I know nothing about reason and number [fate]. But in view of the turn of things at the present moment, when our heavenly dynasty has appointed ten thousands and thousands of generals and the Heavenly King has destroyed ten thousands and thousands of universes, it has reached a time when our dynasty has exhausted its mandate and our country is doomed to collapse. All we can do is watch this happen.[7]

The influence of the *Feng-shen chuan* was obviously very strong in the mind of Li Hsiu-ch'eng.

Even where direct reference is not made, the conceptual connection

---

[5] See Cheng Chen-to, *Chung-kuo wen-hsüeh lun chi*, pp. 254–55.

[6] Lo Erh-kang, *Chung Wang Li Hsiu-ch'eng tzu-chuan yüan-kao ch'ien-cheng*, p. 29.

[7] *Ibid.*, p. 77. The killing of generals and appointing of spirits mark the conclusion of *Feng-shen chuan*, which is a story about the establishing of the Chou dynasty with both camps, the Chou people and their enemy the Yin people, enlisting help from all imaginable kinds of supernatural forces.

between the Taiping ideology and novels is often unmistakable. The idea of *chung-i* (loyalty and brotherhood), so much emphasized by the Taipings, was one of the consistent themes of novels.[8] The Heavenly King's conferring the epitaph *wan-ku chung-i* (萬古忠義 the most loyal and fraternal since time immemorial) upon Li Hsiu-ch'eng was without doubt a distant reverberation of the epitaph *ching-chung pao-kuo* (精 or 盡忠報國 with crystal or ever increasing loyalty to repay the grace of the country), which Yüeh Fei's mother tattooed on his back as told in the novel *Yüeh-chuan*.[9] The theme of *Yüeh-chuan* is none other than *chung-i*. This theme is introduced in a poem at the beginning of the book and is repeated over and over again. The most dramatic expression is in chapter 22: in reply to a passionate plea to join the bandits in Lake Tung-t'ing because "the empire is not a private individual's empire, but it belongs only to the virtuous," a plea which implies that when the empire is misgoverned anyone has the right to take it away from the reigning house, Yüeh Fei said: "A man in making up his mind is like a woman in preserving her body. I, Yüeh Fei, being a subject of the Sung when living, will remain a spirit of the Sung when dead. Even the tongues of Lu Chia and Sui Ho could hardly cause me to modify my life spirit which penetrates the heaven and soars into the clouds."[10]

This idea of *chung-i* is even more pronounced in *Shui-hu chuan*. The conduct of the rebel society members, who are the main subject of the book, is strictly regulated by this precept of loyalty and fraternity. The term *chung* may even be interpreted as loyalty to the court. In chapter 70, Sung Chiang, chief of the rebels, said that the purpose of a large-scale religious ceremony he was planning was to repay the grace of protection that heaven and earth and spirits had given them. He wanted to pray for peace and security for all the brethren and early grace from the court to pardon them so that they could all try their best to repay the grace of the country until death.[11] After Sung Chiang succeeded in pacifying Fang La, he knew that he was poisoned by the government. Instead of preparing a plan for revenge, he carefully disposed of Li K'uei, his most faithful lieutenant, so that his principles of *chung* and *i*

---

[8] The word *chung* means "loyalty" or "fidelity." The word *i* may be understood in a number of senses which are all related: "brotherhood," "fraternity," "righteousness," or "justice."

[9] *Yüeh-chuan*, chap. 22, p. 95; Ling Shan-ch'ing (ed.), *T'ai-p'ing t'ien-kuo yeh-shih*, 13:9.

[10] *Yüeh-chuan*, chap. 22, p. 95.

[11] *Shui-hu chuan*, Vol. IV, chap. 70, p. 2.

would not be marred by any silly attempt of his supporters to avenge his wrong. After Li K'uei learned the whole story, he gladly accepted the fate his leader had planned for him: when Sung Chiang died, Li K'uei died by his side. All the remaining members of the society followed Li's example, thus fulfilling their oath that they would either live together or die together. *Shui-hu chuan* is a moving story of loyalty, "stupid loyalty" cast in a form destined to prolong the existing power rather than uproot it. The episode of the rebels' death is followed by this poem:

> Complain not against heaven of what has befallen you,
> Did not Han [Han Hsin] and [P'eng Yüeh] of old meet with the same fate?
> In the battle nothing else was in your thought than to die for the country,
> In one hundred encounters, you have captured the Liao and defeated La [Fang La].
> Now where are the martial and strong constellations [the heroes]?
> But perennially live on, the treacherous ministers.
> If only you could know earlier that you are destined to die of poison,
> Far better it would be for you to retire as fishermen in the misty waves.[12]

Chin Jen-jui, who edited *Shui-hu chuan*, replaced the passage describing the ideal society with this idea: after a nightmarish dream in which all the heroes were put to the sword, he saw before the hall a tablet with four characters: 天下太平 *T'ien-hsia t'ai-p'ing* (peace over the world). The acceptance of the *status quo* is expressed again in two verses:

> In the center sits the Taiping Son of Heaven *(T'ai-p'ing t'ien-tzu)*;
> Over the four quarters of the seas are stationed clean and conscientious officials.
> The only sight: fat sheep and peace to the elders;
> No neighing of spirited horses to stir up the warring sentiments of generals.
> With *li* (principle of conduct) and *yüeh* (music) as the basis of family tradition,
> We express happy feelings in happy songs.
> Set not our heart to learn the southeast where there is no sun for which taboo is held,
> Let us sing of the northwest where we find floating clouds.[13]

[12] *Shui-hu hsü-chi*, chap. 49, p. 14.
[13] I cannot explain these last two lines to my own satisfaction.

Man, all in all, a mere pile of earth;
Who has ever lived up to a hundred years?
Pay the rent, honor the emperor, and rest in peace;
Basking in sunshine gives us strange feeling of warmth, far better
    than fur.
Tzu-chien was a great talent, but how empty his title "tiger!"
Chuang-sheng was a free soul, and yet drew a cow as his parallel.
Chilly night, lightly drunk, I wield my brush;
Even if no startling lines flow from my pen, I am satisfied.[14]

Chin must have been thoroughly disgusted with the popular uprisings of the time to write poems like this, treating the simple and satisfied life the rulers wished to propagate as an ideal state of things. Or was he merely trying to protect the vested interest of the class to which he himself belonged, although he died as a consequence of violating certain established rules governing that class?

The idea of *chung-i* is no less prominent in *Romance of the Three Kingdoms*. A character named Kuan Yün-ch'ang was deified as the god of war merely because he was the exemplar of this moral quality.

The idea of fraternity (義 *i*) is associated with brotherhood of men. The prototype of brotherhood is furnished by *Romance of the Three Kingdoms* where, in a peach garden, Liu, Kuan, and Chang swore themselves to a bond not to be severed until death. The oath as reported in *Romance of the Three Kingdoms* has been used with some modification by all later brotherhoods. It runs:

We, Liu Pei, Kuan Yü, and Chang Fei, although of different family names, having sworn ourselves into brotherhood, will with a united mind and concerted effort save those in distress and assist those in danger. Toward the country above we shall do all we can to repay its grace; and toward the people below, we shall make every effort to bring them peace. We do not ask to be born in the same year, the same month, and on the same day, but we hope that we may die in the same year, the same month, and on the same day. May great Heaven and majestic earth apprehend this desire of ours. Should [any of us] turn against our brothers and forget their kindness, may Heaven and men exterminate him.[15]

The form of oath adopted in the *Shui-hu chuan* follows this prototype with certain modifications:

[14] *Shui-hu chuan*, Vol. IV, chap. 70, p. 20. Compare Pearl Buck's translation entitled *All Men Are Brothers* (New ed.; London: Methuen, 1957).
[15] *San-kuo yen-i*, chap. 1, p. 6.

Eight directions all belong to the same territory and different names are one family. Heaven and earth express their strength and ferocity, and in this human world the beauty of what is heroic and intelligent has been harmonized. Faces which were one thousand li apart now meet morning and night; in our minds is harbored the thought that we would live and die together. We may differ in our appearance, in our dialects, or we may be from different directions—south, north, east, and west—but we are all at one in our thought, sentiment, courage, and in our observance of the moral precepts of *chung* [loyalty], *ch'eng* [sincerity], *hsin* [trustworthiness] and *i* [righteousness or brotherhood]. Our group is composed of royal descendants, spiritual offspring, the rich and the strong, generals and petty officials, members of the three religions and the nine types; it even includes hunters, fishermen, butchers, executioners; all members in our group call one another "elder brother" or "younger brother," for here there is no distinction of the noble and the humble. And we may be real brothers, husband and wife, uncle and nephew, master and slave, or even enemies; we all share the same feast and enjoy the same happiness, for here there is no distinction between relation and nonrelation. Some of us are refined and intelligent, some of us are crude and rough, some of us are naïve and rustic, some of us are graceful and cultured; but what is there to prevent us from living together once we understand one another? Some of us are versed in pen and tongue, some of us are dexterous in sword and spear, some of us are good at running, some of us are expert in the art of stealing; each has his specialty to be used in accordance with his talent. We hate pretence of literary ability, but we tolerate a scholar who is a superlative writer just to retain some literary trace; we are disgusted with degree-holders [people with headdress], so we are happy that we have already killed the white-robed *hsiu-shih* to clean up all that is sour and stingy. We occupy a piece of land four or five hundred li square, and we heroes number one hundred and eight. Formerly we only heard of one another, whose names rang among the rivers and lakes like the sound of a bell from an ancient tower; now we know all names are listed in starry constellations like pearls in a rosary, linked together one to another. In his time Chao Kai lacked the courage to assume the title "king," and he died early; only our Sung Chiang is willing to gather the group for the purpose of protecting the righteous and accepts the leadership of this group. Do not say that we are gathering in the mountain and forest as robbers; our hope is we may early serve under the banner of the government.[16]

This passage is omitted by Chin Jen-jui, who substituted another form which has had tremendous influence upon the mind of the Chinese common people:

---

[16] Quoted by Lo Erh-kang in *T'ien-ti hui wen-hsien lu*, hereafter cited Lo, *T'ien-ti hui*, pp. 81–82.

We, Sung Chiang and the rest, thinking that formerly we were scattered about in different places and now are gathered in one hall, shall be brothers like stars, and point to heaven and earth as our father and mother. We are one hundred and eight strong; each has a face, and no face is not outstanding; and each has a mind, and no mind is not bright and clear. We share both happiness and sorrow. Though we were not born at the same time, we shall die on the same day. Since our names have been listed in heaven, let us not be the cause of mockery on earth. When once our voice and breath are in harmony, never throughout our life let our mind be divided. If there should be anyone who harbors an unkindly thought and cuts short the tie of great principle, conforming externally and deviating inwardly, embracing our principle at the beginning but unable to persist to the end, may Heaven above apprehend and spirits below discern this, and may his body be cut by knife and sword and his very traces be erased by thunder from the face of the earth, and may he fall eternally into the netherworld and never regain the form of man! The matter of retribution is distinct and clear. May both spirits and Heaven apprehend [our thought].[17]

This social ideal of fraternity was conceived in contrast to the existing society. The writer, whoever he was, was aware of the unequal distribution of wealth and the injustice consequent upon it. The following poem, which expresses this consciousness, was read before the newly sworn brotherhood:

> The scorching sun burns like fire,
> Grains in the field are half singed;
> Farmers' hearts rage like boiling water,
> While noblemen wag their fans.[18]

After the reading, all the heroes said in unison: "Our only desire is to meet one another in all our existences [transmigration], and we shall all the time be as we are today, [our harmony] never marred by anything." These heroes finished the day by dipping their fingers into a pail of blood and drinking to their hearts' content.[19]

Here a society without distinction is envisioned; the members are committed to the principles of *chung* and *i*, as the name they chose for the hall where they gathered to swear themselves into this eternal tie illustrates. This hall they called *chung-i t'ang* (忠義堂 hall of loyalty and

[17] *Shui-hu chuan*, Vol. IV, chap. 70, p. 17.
[18] *Ibid.*, Vol. II, chap. 15, p. 15.
[19] *Ibid.*, Vol. IV, chap. 70, p. 17.

brotherhood). Their ideal formed the inspirational force for the organization of later secret societies, and the oath form was also adopted with modifications. One significant point here is the deep-rooted idea of the legitimacy of the powers that be. In spite of rebellious conduct, the sworn brothers made it clear they were ready to serve under the government. But often the government offered men of loyalty no opportunity to serve. At times the government even made it impossible for these men to live a peaceful life. Hence the rebellions. One reason Sung Chiang and his group revolted is that they were forced to do so by a corrupt government. They were not the only people who suffered from the ruthlessness of the government, and they extended their sympathy to include all the unfortunate ones. Thus they proclaimed that whatever they did they were doing for heaven. On the roof of their *chung-i t'ang* they flew a banner with four characters: 替天行道 *t'i-t'ien hsing-tao,* meaning "to make the true way prevail for heaven." In an earlier drama of the Yüan period, the characters *chiu shih-jen* (saving the people of the world) were included on the banner and the members of this rebellious group engaged in robbing the rich and strong and giving aid to the poor and weak.

The social ideal of sympathy for the poor and the idea of robbing the rich to give to the poor combined to create in the minds of the common people hope for the realization of such a society. Popular imagination inspired by this social ideal may, in connection with economic conditions, explain why a rebel leader in later times could so easily find many people to support him. For what the rebel leaders promised the people was already in their minds, forming an ideological climate conducive to the acceptance of slogans and promises. In the minds of the Chinese people, Sung Chiang and his group are like Robin Hood in the minds of the English.

In the novels, the brotherhood idea is coupled with the parenthood of heaven and earth, and *chung-i* is associated with reward and punishment. The Taipings, it is true, took their idea of a heavenly father from Christianity; but it is not inconceivable that this link with the conception of heaven and earth as father and mother, found in the novels and later adopted by the secret society called *T'ien-ti hui,* facilitated their acceptance of the Christian view. The Taipings made good use of the association between the *chung-i* and reward and punishment in controlling the minds of the people.

The political mission of the Taipings in acting for heaven to make the

heavenly way prevail was a distinct feature of the rebel society as described in *Shui-hu chuan*. In chapter 70 a stone slab with the one hundred and eight names of the rebels inscribed on it is unearthed, and on the sides of the stone are found two lines: *t'i-t'ien hsing-tao* (替天行道 to make the way prevail for heaven) and *chung-i shuang-ch'uan* (忠義雙全 perfection in both loyalty and fraternity [brotherhood]).

The idea of *t'ai-p'ing* (peace) is clearly depicted in many novels. The following poem appears at the beginning of the *Yüeh-chuan*:

> Rejoice in the three plenties[20] under the heaven of Yao and the sun of Shun,
> Stroke the belly and feed the child, songs are heard all over the land;
> With timely rain and seasonal winds, the people enjoy their life
> Throwing down shields and spears and taking to the herding of cattle and horses.[21]

Although the term *t'ai-p'ing* is not mentioned, the atmosphere of tranquillity is unmistakable. *T'ai-p'ing* is used and the idea of peace is described in the poem from *Shui-hu chuan* quoted above on page 289. Propaganda which promises to put an end to the existing situation and to bring about a period of peace always appeals strongly to the people's desire for peace, which is sharpened by social injustice and governmental corruption.

The scene described in the "Taiping Heavenly Chronicle" (T'ai-p'ing t'ien-jih) and "Gospel Jointly Witnessed and Heard by the Imperial Eldest and Second Eldest Brothers" (Wang-chang-tz'u-hsiung ch'ing-mu ch'ing-erh kung-cheng fu-yin-shu), in which the T'ien Wang was engaged in mortal battle with the imps, recalls *Hsi-yu chi* and *Feng-shen chuan*. The physical symbols used by the Taipings, such as mirror, sword, heavenly book, and heavenly net and earthly trap can be traced to novels and popular tales. In *T'ai-p'ing kuang-chi* there is a story by Wang Tu entitled "Ku-ching chi" (Record of an Ancient Mirror), in which an ancient mirror is described as having the power to exterminate imps and goblins and to reduce them to their natural form.[22] In *Hsi-yu chi*, Erh-lang chen-chün uses *chao-yao ching* (a mirror that shows by reflection the natural forms of imps) to subdue Sun Wu-k'ung, the mon-

---

20 Plenty of happiness, plenty of years in life, and plenty of male descendants.
21 *Yüeh-chuan*, chap. 1, p. 1.
22 Li Fang (compiler), *T'ai-p'ing kuang-chi, chüan* 230.

key.[23] Yang Chien in the *Feng-shen chuan* uses a mirror to reduce the imps from Mei-shan to their original forms: a white snake, a pig, a goat, a buffalo, and a monkey.

Yün-chung-tzu in the *Feng-shen chuan* uses a wooden sword to kill a fox that, in one thousand years of life, has succeeded in obtaining a human form.[24] Sung Chiang's encounter with *Chiu-t'ien hsüan-nü* (goddess of nine heavens) could have been the model for Hung Hsiu-ch'üan's encounter with the old man in his dream whom he later identified as God. This suggestion is not farfetched, for Sung Chiang received his heavenly books during this encounter and Hung received his at his meeting with God.[25]

When heavenly forces engage the monkey in a critical battle in *Hsi-yu chi*, the heavenly net and earthly trap are spread out to prevent the monkey from escaping.[26] And in *Feng-shen chuan* Chiang Tzu-ya uses the same weapons to defeat Yin troops under the command of Yüan Hung, a monkey that has assumed human form.[27]

The poem from *Shui-hu chuan* quoted on page 292 above expresses very well the mental state of the Taipings with respect to social justice and hints at the type of character the Taipings admired. Lo Erh-kang has rightly maintained that sympathy for the common people does not necessarily lead to class struggle or common people's revolution.[28] Therefore one cannot correctly think of *Shui-hu chuan* as having the purpose of social revolution. But such an attitude helps to give those who believe themselves the heavenly mandated successors to a dynasty which has lost its mandate a sense of legitimacy in their attempt to overthrow the reigning dynasty. The Taipings, who believed themselves mandated by Heaven, were certainly eloquent in expressing sympathy for the common people, thus making their ideology very appealing to the people at large.

The classical idea that a dynasty could lose its mandate was very popular in novels. The *Feng-shen chuan* says that Ch'eng-t'ang, the originator of the Shang dynasty, has exhausted his *shu* (數 number of fate), and it is time for the Chou to rise.[29] The Chou army assumes that the

[23] Wu Ch'en-en, *Hsi-yu chi*, chap. 6.
[24] *Feng-shen chuan*, chap. 5.
[25] *Shui-hu chuan*, Vol. III, chap. 41, pp. 11–13.
[26] Wu, *Hsi-yu chi*, chap. 6.
[27] *Feng-shen chuan*, chap. 91.
[28] Lo Erh-kang, "*Shui-hu chuan* yü t'ien-ti hui," in Lo, *T'ien-ti hui*, pp. 80–81.
[29] *Feng-shen chuan*, chap. 92.

Chou people have received a new mandate to rule, and it would be working against the will of Heaven for anyone to stand in their way. The Taipings' constant harping on the theme that those who act in accordance with the will of Heaven will live and those who oppose it will die could have come from these novels as well as from classical sources. Their belief that they had received the mandate of Heaven to rule gave the Taipings the same sense of legitimacy about their government that the Chou people had with respect to their right to rule in place of the Yin.

The Taipings owed a great deal to the novels for the building of their ideology, both in the form of ideas and in the form of physical symbols. However, novels influenced all secret societies, including the *T'ien-ti hui*, which was most intimately related to the Taipings. Except that most of the novels which the Taipings made use of were popular novels available to all people, one might even assume that their influence reached the Taipings indirectly through the secret societies.

SECRET SOCIETY INFLUENCE[30]

There is no question that a close relationship between the Taipings and the *T'ien-ti hui* (Heaven and Earth Society), a secret organization, existed at the beginning of the Taiping campaign. Many of the *T'ien-ti hui* members joined the Taiping group only to find the discipline too strict for their taste; only a few, including Lo Ta-kang, remained with the Taipings to the end. This short-lived initial co-operation of the two organizations left its imprint on the Taiping organization, especially in the sphere of ideology.

Both the secret society and the Taipings were greatly influenced by novels. T'ao Ch'eng-chang, in "Chiao-hui yüan-liu k'ao" (A Study in the Development of Secret Societies), said:

> Members of *Hung-men* [a name assumed by *T'ien-ti hui* members] swore themselves into brotherhood in the style of Liu, Kuan, and Chang. So they had what is known as the "fraternity spirit of *t'ao-yüan*" [the peach garden where the three heroes of *Romance of the Three Kingdoms* became sworn brothers]; they wanted to have mountain camps as a place for gathering, so they used the term *liang-shan-po* [den]; and they wanted to imagine a heavenly ordained Son of Heaven to be born for them to assist in sweeping away the illegitimate [the Ch'ing], so they had "the majestic air of the

---

[30] The consideration here is limited to the *T'ien-ti hui* because of its close relationship to the *T'ai-p'ing t'ien-kuo*.

wa-kang den" [where heroes assembled and finally assisted the Li family to establish the T'ang dynasty]. This was done because those responsible for the organization wished to cater to the taste of the people belonging to the low social order and thus weave a united story out of three novels, *Romance of the Three Kingdoms, Shui-hu chuan,* and *Shuo-t'ang.*[31]

With this common source in popular novels, it is no surprise that the Taipings and secret societies had so much in common.

We have previously stressed that the remnant scholars of the Ming dynasty influenced the Taipings' thought. All accounts of secret societies attempt to trace their origin back to these same scholars. Chang Pin-lin, in his "Preface I" to P'ing Shan Chou's [Hirayama Chikashi's] *Chung-kuo mi-mi she-hui shih* (History of Chinese Secret Societies), said:

> At the time the Mongols overran China, the people were nostalgic about the Sung; hence ethnic feelings entered into the texture of their religious teachings. [Chang here referred to *Pai-lien chiao,* White Lotus sect.] . . . When the Ming lost its empire, the remaining scholars made plans to restore it. At that time, Cheng Ch'eng-kung occupied Taiwan and maintained intimate relationships with Hsiung K'ai-yüan 熊開元 and Ju Ying-yüan 汝應元, both remnant ministers of the Ming who cut their hair to join the order. Therefore, the *T'ien-ti hui* had its origin in Fukien. Later *Ko-lao hui* and *San-ho hui* made their appearance with the avowed purpose of exterminating the barbarians, and thus severed themselves from religious implications.[32]

In "Preface II" of the same book, T'ao-yüan i-shih, a recluse from the peach grove spring, said:

> Since the time of Shun-chih of the Ch'ing, when China was overrun by the barbarians, the Ming remnant scholars and recluses, deploring that the great principle [first enunciated by Confucius] to keep the barbarians off the border of China had been overthrown by these barbarians, worked together to unite the secret societies with the purpose of perpetuating this subtle principle, hoping that sometime in the future it might bring forth fruit. This is the origin of the names of *San-ho* and *Ko-lao.* The first activities of the societies took place in Taiwan, followed by those of Szechwan and Shensi. And it was Hung Hsiu-ch'üan of the *T'ai-p'ing t'ien-kuo* who brought them to a final form.[33]

[31] "Chiao-hui yüan-liu k'ao," in Hsiao I-shan, *Chin-tai mi-mi she-hui shih-liao,* Vol. II, Appendix, p. 8b. Also in Lo, *T'ien-ti hui,* p. 71.

[32] P'ing Shan Chou, *Chung-kuo mi-mi she-hui shih,* p. 1.

[33] *Ibid.,* p. 3.

The *Hung-men-chih*, in recounting the historical development of the *Hung-men* society, says:

Shun-chih raised an army and invaded the pass,
He took advantage of the situation and ascended to the throne at
    Peking.
The Ming remnant officials, both civil and military,
All scattered to the lakes and the seas.
They bonded themselves into a federation in the lakes and the seas,
With the determined purpose to overthrow the Ch'ing and restore
    the Ming.
First in the roster is Yin Hung-sheng 殷洪盛,
Fu Ch'ing-chu 傅青主 is listed as number two.
The third is Ku Yen-wu 顧炎武,
and the fourth is Huang Li-chou 黃梨洲,
The fifth is Wang Fu-chih 王夫之.
They rose in the great movement to overthrow the Ch'ing and
    restore the Ming.
Wen-tsung is the title given to Shih K'o-fa 史可法,
And Cheng Ch'eng-kung is called by the title *wu-tsung*.[34]

This roster is apparently based on the tale that Yin Hung-sheng, alias Hung Ying 洪英, was commissioned by Shih K'o-fa to go to Peking in an effort to size up the Ch'ing court and also to contact the Ming remnant scholars on the way. Yin is said to have seen Ku Yen-wu, Wang Fu-chih, Huang Li-chou, and Fu Ch'ing-chu, with whom he discussed and instituted the organization of *Han-liu* in order to overthrow the Ch'ing and restore the Ming.[35]

In the following speech delivered by a *hsiang-chu* to new members of the *T'ien-ti hui* are found almost all the important ideas which we find in the Taiping ideology.[36]

We should share our happiness and misery to restore the brilliance [the Ming dynasty] of the heaven and earth and the ten thousand things, and

[34] *Ibid.*, p. 144.
[35] *Ibid.*, pp. 5–6. See also Wei-ta fa-shih [Wei Chü-hsien], *Chung-kuo-ti pang-hui*, Part 1, p. 42.
[36] According to the organization of *San-ho hui*, the chief of the first administrative division of a local organization is called *lung-t'ou* 龍頭; he is assisted by *fu lung-t'ou* 副龍頭 and followed in order of importance by *hsiang-chu* 香主, who may assume the function of a chief at certain localities; *meng-cheng* 盟證; *tso-t'ang* 座堂; *tsung-yin* 宗印; *cheng-t'ang* 正堂; *p'ei-t'ang* 陪堂; *hu-yin* 護印; *li-t'ang* 禮堂; *chih-t'ang* 值堂; *and hsin-fu* 新福. See Wei-ta fa-shih, *op. cit.*, Part 2, p. 10.

to exterminate the barbarians to get ready for the coming of the truly mandated. We should worship with piety the heavenly gods, earthly deities, and the spirits of mountains, rivers, soil, and grains, the spirits of the five dragons in the five directions, and the deities of the boundless space. Since creation hundreds of things have been initiated. That which the ancients knew to be of value as teachings to posterity, we shall transmit. Brethren! Let me again lead you to the way of loyalty and brotherhood [spirit of fraternity]. We should express the desire to live and die together in our oath before heaven. Tonight we introduce some members into *T'ien-ti hui*, sworn in as brothers in the spirit of the peach-garden event, adopting *Hung* as surname and *Chin-lan* 金蘭 as personal name, becoming members of one family. After entering the gate of Hung 洪門, you should with one mind and one body help one another, and there should not be any trace of distinction between "his" and "mine." Tonight we worship heaven as our father and earth as our mother, the sun as our elder brother and the moon as our sister; we also worship the five first ancestors, Wan Yün-lung the first ancestor, and all the spirits of the Hung family.[37] Tonight we kneel before the incense burner, with our mind and spirit completely cleansed, cut our fingers and let our blood flow, and suck our blood as the token of an oath that we shall live and die together. We set the hour of *ch'ou* (丑, symbol of the hours between one and three o'clock in the morning) on the twenty-fifth of the seventh moon in the year of *chia-yin* 甲寅 as the hour of our birth.[38] All who belong to the old two capitals and the thirteen provinces should with one mind and body seek one another's happiness and help each to take care of his burden, and never attempt to alienate one another. Once the time comes when the princes and dukes of the present dynasty are not princes or dukes, and when the mind of the people is disturbed, we shall take these circumstances to be the heavenly signs of the restoration of the Ming and the collapse of the barbarians. We then shall make up our mind to carry out the command of Ch'en Chin-nan 陳近南 and erect pavilions and build bridges, and we shall create the city of peace in the world to put into effect the policy of peace. We shall cover the whole empire in search of braves and heroes, take hold of the power of *mu-yang-ch'eng* 木楊城 and burn incense to express the oath that we would be with one another as eternally as the mountains and the rivers. All you

[37] The "five ancestors" refer to Ts'ai Te-ying or Te-chung, F'ang Ta-ch'eng or Ta-hung, Ma Ch'ao-hsing or Chao-hsing, Hu Te-ti or Ti-te, and Li Shih-k'ai, the early five ancestors; or to Wu Shih-yu or T'ien-tso, Lin Ta-chiang, Chang Ching-chih or Ching-chao, Yang Chang-yu or Wen-tso, and Fang Hui-ch'eng, the middle five ancestors; or to Yao Pi-ta, Lin Yung-ch'ao or Yung-chao, Wu T'ien-ch'eng, Li Shih-ti, and Hung T'ai-sui, the later five ancestors. See Wei-ta fa-shih, *Chung-kuo-ti pang-hui*, "Pang-hui shih," Part 1, pp. 22–42.

[38] Lo's *T'ien-ti hui*, p. 1, opens with the line: "During the reign of K'ang-hsi, the 25th of the third moon in the year of *chia-yin* was the date when the Hung family swore themselves into brotherhood." "Seventh" in the *Chung-kuo-ti pang-hui* may have been a mistake for "third," This was in the year 1674.

new members should with exemplary discipline carry out your duty and practice the way of heaven. Those who follow heaven will survive and those who go counter to it will perish. Should there be anyone who can restore the Ming and wash clean our disgrace and establish the government of world peace, he himself will be enfeoffed during his own lifetime as prince or duke, and his posterity will forever and ever be prosperous. He who goes counter to this principle will be destroyed by the point of swords and lances; furthermore, his kind will be completely destroyed. Only the loyal and those who have the spirit of fraternity will receive forever the eternal bliss. We receive our life from heaven and earth and receive light from the sun and the moon; after we have taken an oath by sucking our blood, may the gods above descend and observe. Let all with sincerity take these thirty-six oaths.[39]

The substance of all the ideas that played an important role in the Taiping ideology is here: the ethnic issue, the idea of the truly mandated, brotherhood, moral precepts, the idea of the parenthood of heaven and earth, the Confucian tenet of rectification of names, the desire to establish peace throughout the empire, and the classical idea that those who act in accordance with the way of heaven will live and those who act counter to the way of heaven will perish. The thirty-six oaths mentioned in the passage now exist in three versions; all prescribe in greater detail what is expected of each member of the society. Together with other regulations, they form the law of the society.

From this brief discussion of the ideology of the secret society, it is obvious that a strong relationship exists between it and the Taiping ideology. This relationship does not mean that the Taipings took everything from the secret society; but it does help explain how the Taipings could accept the idea of a heavenly father from the Christian source.

There is a point of difference worth notice. This particular brand of secret society, in spite of its emphasis on the obligation of one member to another in supplying material needs, did not entertain the idea of complete common sharing of material goods that the Taipings did. The society made it a legal offense not to respect the wealth and property of brother members.[40]

[39] Wei-ta fa-shih, *Chung-kuo-ti pang-hui*, Part 2, pp. 26–27. Also in P'ing Shan Chou, *Chung-kuo mi-mi she-hui shih*, pp. 42–43.

[40] P'ing Shan Chou, *op. cit*, the tenth, fourteenth, fifteenth, sixteenth, twenty-second, twenty-eighth, twenty-ninth, and thirtieth oaths, pp. 45–48; the thirteenth and fourteenth regulations of the twenty-one regulations, p. 50; the fourth, sixth, and ninth of the ten prohibitions, p. 52; and the sixth and eighth punishable crimes of ten crimes, p. 53.

Like the Taipings, the secret societies used rhymed doggerel to make their ideas familiar to the members. For the purpose of keeping their organization and operation a secret, they made use of riddles and code, also in much the same manner as did the Taipings. In many of their documents and much of their doggerel the function of a sword to exterminate the devils is mentioned.[41] The secret society also used the sun and the moon as symbols of power. In Hsiao I-shan's *Chin-tai mi-mi she-hui shih-liao*, a triangular flag is reproduced. Below the symbol of the sun and the character *jih* 日 in the center of the flag, there is a poem, of which the first two lines are:

> The sun at its height is the Son of Heaven, the ruler called
> *t'ai-yang,*
> And the moon courses in the *t'ai-yin*, giving shelter to the ten
> thousand people.[42]

The idea of *t'ien-t'ang* (天堂 paradise or heavenly hall) influenced the behavior of the Taipings by boosting their morale and making death almost a sweet reward to be diligently sought. The secret society made use of a very similar idea. In a ceremony honoring death, they cited these lines to comfort the soul of the dead: "May your soul be free from darkness and come to accept this worship, so that from now on all shall ascend to the hall of happiness together."[43] That this hall of happiness was the hall of heaven is seen from many references to *t'ien-t'ang* where the dead are honored.[44]

Using the hall of heaven as a reward to encourage bravery has been a common practice among rebellious groups. In the *Luan-chou chih* we find the following record:

> During the reign of Chia-ch'ing, as a consequence of the White Lotus Religious Rebellion, royal feathered edicts held local officials responsible [to check the rebellion]. For this reason, many cases were traced down. A certain magistrate, in the process of investigating certain religious rebels, discovered a number of books which were filled with perverse ideas and falsehood. He wrote a book refuting them, and the book was published. According to his narration of the origin of the rebellion, there was a *Wu-*

[41] *Ibid.*, pp. 12, 16, 36; Hsiao, *Chin-tai mi-mi she-hui shih-liao*, Vol. II, 2:6a; Lo, *T'ien-ti hui*, pp. 6, 11, 13.

[42] Hsiao, *op. cit.*, Vol. II, 1:9a.

[43] Wei-ta fa-shih, *Chung-kuo-ti pang-hui*, Part 2, p. 35.

[44] *Ibid.*, Part 2, pp. 35, 37–38, 47.

sheng lao-mu [無生老母 old mother without birth] and P'iao-kao lao-tsu [飄高 老祖 old father floating on high], who were husband and wife. Taking advantage of the chaos at the end of the Yüan dynasty, they [old mother and old father] gathered around them rebellious people in the mountain ranges of T'ai-hang. The old father's distinguished disciples were twenty-eight heads. One of these was the Shih-fo [Stone Buddha] of Luan-chou. He gained by temptation a following of several thousand men and women; each was taught the aphrodisiacal art, by means of which they mutually took life-giving elements to make up their deficiency. It also says that before there were heaven and earth there was Wu-sheng [無生 birthless or without birth]. The 480,000 children whom Wu-sheng gave birth to in the hall of heaven fell into this world of dust because of worldly thought. The old mother thought of them constantly, so she came down through incarnation to save them. Those who were decapitated were said to have "ascended to heaven with red decoration," and those condemned to die by mutilation "ascended to heaven wearing the great red robe." The latter was regarded by the comrades as the highest glory. Therefore when persons converted to this sect were brought to trial, they confessed willingly and were morbidly unafraid of death.[45]

The Taipings referred to death in battle as "ascending to heaven." The link seems apparent.

Most who have written about secret societies believe that Hung Hsiu-ch'üan was one of the main figures in the T'ien-ti hui. T'ao-yüan i-shih said Hung was the one who brought that society to its final form.[46] And T'ao Ch'eng-chang in his "Chiao-hui yüan-liu k'ao" said:

Chu Chiu-t'ao was the chief of San-ho hui (Three Together Society), and he made Hung Hsiu-ch'üan his successor. Hsiu-ch'üan again plagiarized the teachings of T'ien-chu-chiao [天主教 Catholic religion] and added them to the ideas of the society. (To call heaven "father," to name his dynasty t'ien-kuo, to add the prefix t'ien to all offices, to consider the above and below as one body and address one another as brothers are not completely based on Christianity; these practices are indeed rooted in the old regulations of the Hung-men [T'ien-ti hui]).[47]

But Lo Erh-kang, in his "Chu Chiu-t'ao k'ao" has proved conclusively that there could not have been any relationship between Hung and Chu, and that the belief that Hung and other Taiping leaders had been disciples of Chu is the perpetuation of hearsay reported as fact by Tu

---

[45] Luan-chou chih, 18:28b–29a.
[46] P'ing Shan Chou, Chung-kuo mi-mi she-hui shih, "Preface II," p. 3.
[47] "Chiao-hui yüan-liu k'ao," in Lo, T'ien-ti hui, p. 66.

Wen-lan in his *P'ing-ting Yüeh-fei chi-lüeh*, and that the hearsay has nothing to substantiate it.[48] The flimsy nature of T'ao's record may be seen from his allegation that Hung took ideas from the Catholic church; as a matter of fact Hung had nothing to do with the Catholics, and what Christian ideas he did receive came from Protestants. Lo even suggested that not only was there no relationship between Hung and Chu, but neither was there any relationship between Hung and the *T'ien-ti hui*.[49] Since at the beginning of their campaign the Taipings co-operated with the *T'ien-ti hui*, Lo's latter statement seems exaggerated. Hung may not have been related to the *T'ien-ti hui* as a member or as its chief, but he could have had relation with it because it was a co-operating organization or because he was an interested observer keen on learning. It is very probably through this relationship that the *T'ien-ti hui* came to influence the Taiping ideology in the way we have described.[50]

[48] Lo, *T'ien-ti hui*, pp. 1, 14. See also Tu Wen-lan, *P'ing-ting Yüeh-fei chi-lüeh, chüan* 1.

[49] Lo, *T'ien-ti hui*, p. 14.

[50] Hsieh Hsing-yao, in his "Epilogue to Fa-i ch'u-chi," quotes from *Fa-i ch'u-chi*: "So they wrapped up their heads in red turbans, and did not shave their heads for lack of time. They killed gentrymen, attacked cities, and looted." Hsieh comments: "This is enough to reveal the fact that at the outset of [the Taiping movement] their activities were completely in the manner of the activities of secret societies, and there were no traces of Catholic religious ideas. Later when Hung Hsiu-ch'üan and Yang Hsiu-ch'ing became members, they started to embrace the Catholic faith. I have always thought that the Taiping was the combination of the *San-ho hui* type of secret society and the Catholic religion, both having the aim of overthrowing the Manchu." (*I-ching*, No. 17 [Nov. 5, 1936], p. 27.) Hsieh here attempts to identify the Taipings with the *San-ho hui* by reference to the use of the red turban. But the red turban has always been an attractive symbol of the rebel. At the end of the Yüan, incense-burning rebels also used it. (Ch'ien Ch'ien-i, *Kuo-ch'u ch'ün-hsiung shih-lüeh*, 1:24b.)

Another attempt to determine the Taipings' secret society affiliation is that of Mao I-heng. In his "T'ai-p'ing t'ien-kuo yü t'ien-ti hui," Mao identifies the Taipings with the *T'ien-ti hui* on the grounds that the troops of Hung Yang [the Taipings] wrapped their heads in red turbans and that the following poem occurs in a document of the secret society:

> A red turban in hand
> I set out in search of heroes;
> I would gather [them] from the five lakes and four seas
> In order to exterminate completely the Manchus.

("T'ai-p'ing t'ien-kuo yü t'ien-ti hui," *Shen-pao yüeh-k'an*, Vol. IV, No. 1 [Jan., 1931]. The poem is found in Lo, *T'ien-ti hui*, p. 10.) In the army of the Taipings, when a soldier was wounded, he was said to have "blossomed" (開花 *k'ai-hua*). And in the secret society document there appears the following poem on a lotus flower:

> Lotus! Lotus! Wealth! and Glory!
> Loyalty and fraternity will receive reward greater than lotus.
> The disloyal and the unfraternal will blossom (*k'ai-hua*) like a broken bowl.

(*K'ai-hua* in southern dialect means "blown to bits," particularly referring to skulls.)

THE HAKKAS

In *The Character of Races*, Ellsworth Huntington states: "The leader of the great Taiping rebellion was a Hakka. . ."[51] He quotes Mr. Spiker as saying, "The Hakkas are the cream of the Chinese people."[52] Then Huntington says, in the words of George Campbell, the Hakkas are "more fearless and self-reliant than the town dwellers, have all the love of liberty which characterizes mountaineers the world over. They were the last to surrender to the Manchus and twice strove to throw off their yoke, first under the Taiping chief and again [in the present century]."[53] T'ing-yü Hsieh found Campbell's statement that the Hakkas are the "cream of the Chinese people" and that they are mountaineers exaggerated, as he explains in his article, "Origin and Migrations of the Hakkas."[54] However, Campbell's contention that the leaders of the Taiping rebellion and their adherents were Hakkas is correct.

Lo Erh-kang, in his *T'ai-p'ing t'ien-kuo shih ts'ung-k'ao*, made a careful study of the situation and did find ample evidence to support Campbell's ideas.[55] However, Lo does not rely on the Hakkas' fearlessness, self-

---

The poem is found in Lo, *op. cit.*, pp. 14–15.) Among the secret society members, another saying runs:

> If you say I am a sheep (*yang*), I am not a sheep (*yang*);
> But ever since I was a boy, I have been fed by the food from the Hung family.
> As a sheep (*yang*) I go not up the mountain to eat leaves;
> With five horses harnessed, I ride out to the battlefield.

(Mao, *op. cit.* The saying is found in Lo, *op. cit.*, p. 20.) In this last quotation both Hung and Yang are mentioned in the form of a riddle.

[51] *The Character of Races*, p. 167.

[52] *Ibid.*, p. 168.

[53] *Ibid.* From "more fearless" to "the world over" in this quotation is found in George Campbell's "Origin and Migrations of the Hakkas," *Chinese Recorder*, Vol. XLIII (Aug., 1912), p. 473. The rest of the quotation is not in Campbell's article, but there are two passages in Campbell's article which can be paraphrased into Huntington's statement: "The military genius of the race [the Hakkas] was not exhausted when it furnished the great leaders of the Taiping rebellion" (p. 474); and "The Hakkas were loyal to the Mings and many went to Kwangsi, while that province held out for the last prince of the house. I believe that the thousands of Kwangsi soldiers recruited in that province for the support of the recent Revolution were almost, or quite, all Hakkas, descendants of the Hakkas who went to Kwangsi some ten generations ago. It was among these same Kwangsi Hakkas that the Taiping king found his first fighting adherents" (p. 479).

[54] *Chinese Social and Political Science Review*, Vol. XIII, No. 2 (April, 1929), pp. 202–27.

[55] Lo, *T'ai-p'ing t'ien-kuo shih ts'ung-k'ao*, pp. 91–96. But Campbell was not the first to identify the Taiping leader as a Hakka. In 1878 Rev. R. Lechler wrote an article on "The Hakka Chinese," in which he said: "Another of my employees, who teaches a

reliance, and love of liberty—qualities which Campbell mentioned as characterizing the Hakkas—as an explanation for their joining the Taiping rebellion. Instead, Lo cites the feud wars as the chief reason for their interest in the rebellion.[56] Lo finds that Theodore Hamberg spoke of Hung Hsiu-ch'üan's family as coming from Chia-ying-chou, and that the *Tse-ch'ing hui-tsuan* mentioned that Yang Hsiu-ch'ing was also from Chia-ying-chou. As Chia-ying-chou was completely populated by the Hakkas, there is no doubt that both Hung and Yang were Hakkas. In the *Kuei-hsien chih* Shih Ta-k'ai is called a *lai-jen* of Pei-shan li, the term *lai* meaning "coming," and *lai-jen* meaning "one who comes [as a guest, that is, a Hakka]."[57] Since they were inhabitants of the Tzu-ching shan in Kuei-p'ing district, Hsiao Ch'ao-kuei and Wei Ch'ang-hui could very well have been Hakkas, though there is no definite proof that they were. The district of which Tzu-ching shan is a part was originally frequented by tribal people. It was during the reign of K'ang-hsi (1662–1722) that people were encouraged to come to the spot to cultivate the land; and many of those who came were Hakkas.

The first group that joined the adherents of the Taiping movement were the miners. The *Kuei-hsien chih* reports: "During the reign of Tao-kuang, a certain Wang Chi was ordered to start digging mines in Hsien-pei, Lung-t'ou, and Liu-pan, collecting *lai-jen* [to work on these mines]. These came from all directions and were people of both good and bad character."[58] It was this group that Feng Yün-shan persuaded to join the God-Worshipers Society and that took part in the Chin-t'ien uprising. At the same time, two other groups of Hakkas joined the Taipings: one consisted of the more than three thousand Hakkas who remained after defeat in a battle against the Puntis in Kuei-hsien; the other was led by Su Shih-chiu, a famous bandit of Kuei-p'ing. Finally,

---

school, belongs to the Hung clan. They first lived in Shensi, and moved to Szchuen [*sic*] province, from there to Kiangsu, and then to Fuhkien. From Fuhkien they came to Kwangtung and settled in Kia-yin chow, spreading from there to Hwa-hien near Canton. To this clan belonged the renowned Hung yiu-tsuen [Hsiu-ch'üan], or T'aip'ing wang, who caused the great rebellion." This article was based mainly on the Hakka family records and was published in the *Chinese Recorder*, Vol. IX, No. 5 (Sept.-Oct, 1878), pp. 352–59. The statements quoted above appear on page 353.

[56] For details of feud wars between the Puntis and the Hakkas for the period between 1821 and 1861, see *Kuang-chou fu-chih*, *Hsin-ning hsien-chih*, and *Hsün-chou fu-chih*. For the period between 1851 and 1874, see *Ch'ih-hsi hsien-chih*.

[57] See also Jen [Chien] Yu-wen, *Chin-t'ien chih-yu chi ch'i-t'a*, "I Wang chia-shih k'ao-cheng," pp. 159–67, especially p. 160.

[58] *Kuei-hsien chih*, chüan 6, in Lo, *T'ai-p'ing t'ien-kuo shih ts'ung-kao*, p. 92.

a few thousand of the Hakka troops serving the Manchu cause revolted and joined the Taipings.[59] Thus it is clear that the Hakkas played a major part in both the leadership and the following of the Taiping movement. One would expect from them some contribution in the formation of the Taiping ideology.

Many writers imply that there was a causal relationship between the character of the Hakkas and the rebellious or revolutionary activities in which they participated. These writers seem to call the Hakkas a revolutionary people. While fully aware of the fortuitous nature of such a relationship, we may find a study of the character of the Hakkas helpful in understanding their contribution to the Taiping ideology.

The Hakkas were descendants of immigrants who came from northern China during the periods of great upheaval following the Chin, the T'ang, and the Sung dynasties. Their very survival under what must have been extremely difficult circumstances indicates that they were a hardy people, or "a distinct and virile strain of the Chinese race," in the words of George Campbell.[60] Faced with the problem of living and struggling in a land surrounded by the hostile Puntis, they formed a closer unit than they would normally have done. They were willing to die for one another.[61]

"Fundamentally the Hakka is a farmer, forced by poverty to struggle with the unproductive soil and wresting a bare livelihood therefrom."[62] T'ing-yü Hsieh says: "The peasant class is very poor indeed; only a small percentage of them own their fields and they are often involved in debt. Hence many vocations despised by the Puntis, are taken up by the Hakkas who become barbers, itinerant blacksmiths, and stone-masons."[63]

Schooled in the bitter experience of wants, the Hakkas became "an uncommonly able people who little by little are moving out of their mountain home and displacing the coastal people to the south and east

[59] These three cases are recorded in *Hsün-chou fu-chih*, *chüan* 56.

[60] Campbell, "Origin and Migrations of the Hakkas," *Chinese Recorder*, Vol. XLIII (Aug., 1912), p. 480.

[61] *Hsün-chou fu-chih*, 4:14b.

[62] *Chia-ying chou-chih*, 32:16b, quoted by T'ing-yü Hsieh in his "Origin and Migrations of the Hakkas," *Chinese Social and Political Science Review*, Vol. XIII, No. 2 (April, 1929), p. 204.

[63] Hsieh, *op. cit.*, p. 205. Since his source is *Hsün-chou fu-chih* (1896), presumably Hsieh is speaking of the conditions at or prior to 1896. He may also be talking of the conditions of his own time.

of them. That is why they are feared and reviled."[64] Rev. D. Ochler gives a vivid description of how the Hakkas displaced the Puntis:

It is an impressive picture, that of the old Punti villages, enclosed by ivy-covered brickwalls and towers half in ruins and surrounded by ditches, and all about the rows of white houses of the Hakkas, into whose hands the greater part of the lands have fallen. Soon after the appearance of a Hakka house inside the walls of a Punti village, the Punti disappeared completely. It is, however, in the main, a peaceable acquisition by diligence and thrift, though in some instances trickery and force are said not to have been entirely absent from the methods of occupation.[65]

Hsieh, after quoting Ochler's description, added: "This occupation of Punti land soon made the Hakkas feared and disliked; clan fights with the Puntis became more frequent."[66]

Rev. R. Lechler found the Hakkas receptive to fresh contact. He says:

On the whole the Hakkas are not as bigoted as the Puntis, and the Gospel has found easier access to them than to the latter. It is also comparatively easier to make friends of them than of the Puntis. It is perhaps owing to their standing constantly in fear of their own countrymen, the Puntis, that any sincere sympathy which is shown them by foreigners finds more reciprocity, and is thankfully availed of.... The great rebellion which had originated with the Hakkas, showed that they were open to new convictions, and although it turned out a sad failure, yet it might have been attended with better results, had the movement been better directed.[67]

The Hakka writers, as may be expected, were very proud of their people. Hsieh, a Hakka himself, describes them as "unassimilable elements in many ways in the new regions."[68] Having described the hardships the forefathers of the Hakkas endured to survive, Hsieh adds: "It was this spirit of fight and 'never-say-die' that made the Hakkas so full of independence, initiative, and pride of race."[69]

[64] Huntington, *The Character of Races*, p. 167. I presume Huntington meant this to be a general statement applicable to the Hakkas for all time.

[65] This passage by D. Ochler is quoted in Hsieh, *op. cit.*, p. 221.

[66] *Ibid.*

[67] Lechler, "The Hakka Chinese," *Chinese Recorder*, Vol. IX, No. 5 (Sept.-Oct., 1878), p. 358.

[68] Hsieh, "Origin and Migrations of the Hakkas," *Chinese Social and Political Science Review*, Vol. XIII, No. 2, (April, 1929), p. 218.

[69] *Ibid.*, p. 219. The phrase "the pride of race" is Campbell's. See Campbell, "Origin and Migrations of the Hakkas," *Chinese Recorder*, Vol. XLIII (Aug., 1912), p. 480.

Lo Hsiang-lin, another Hakka writer, says: "The Hakka people are most revolutionary in character."[70] Lo adds: "The Hakkas are people who are strong in national consciousness."[71] He characterizes them as having self-esteem and self-respect: "Wherever they go they will never give up their own language and customs."[72] He also declares:

The Hakkas are a people who are paradoxical in that on the one hand they are ambitious and progressive, and on the other they also pay most attention to traditional mores and ethical relations. Therefore, in general they hold very conservatively to the Chinese traditional ethical concepts and laws and patterns of behavior, such as the relations between father and son, husband and wife, brothers, friends, relatives, and between the sexes.[73]

Most writers have agreed that the Hakkas had a high rate of literacy. Mr. Lechler said: "The Hakkas in the prefecture of Kai-Ying chow are renowned for their learning, and there are so many *Siu-tsai* [*hsiu-ts'ai*, students with outstanding talent, a popular name for the first examination degree] that there is not room enough for them to make use of their talents and literary acquirements, so that many have to stoop to menial work to get a livelihood."[74] Huntington made the following observation: "Another notable fact among the Hakkas is the prevalence of education. In their central district it is said that about 80 per cent of the men can read and write....At the present time in their main town of Kai-Ying, which is only a little place with 10,000 or 20,000 people, there are, if I remember rightly, some 3,000 pupils in what are known as middle schools...."[75] Hsieh, quoting *Chia-ying chou-chih* (1898), says that five out of eleven *chin-shih* (advanced scholars, the highest examination degree) in 1752 came from Chia-ying, which "furnished a large number of licentiates and yamen officials for the past dynasties."[76] According to

[70] Lo Hsiang-lin, *K'o-chia yen-chiu tao-lun*, p. 9.

[71] *Ibid.*, p. 19.

[72] *Ibid.*, p. 172.

[73] *Ibid.*, pp. 177–78.

[74] Lechler, "The Hakka Chinese," *Chinese Recorder*, Vol. IX, No. 5 (Sept.-Oct., 1878), pp. 358–59.

[75] Huntington, *The Character of Races*, p. 168. This apparently refers to the time when Huntington was writing.

[76] Hsieh, "Origin and Migrations of the Hakkas," *Chinese Social and Political Science Review*, Vol. XIII, No. 2 (April, 1929), p. 204. The figure is quoted from *Chia-ying chou-chih*, 20:6. (The reference should be 20:28b–29a, where five *chin-shih* from Chia-ying are mentioned.) However, according to Fang Chao-ying and Tu Lien-che, *Ch'ing-tai chin-shih t'i-ming pei-lu*, the total number of *chin-shih* from the province of

the estimate made by Lo Hsiang-lin, over 80 per cent of the males in Chia-ying were literate at the time he wrote; and students attending professional and higher institutions of learning from Chia-ying alone numbered somewhere around seven or eight hundred. Lo explains this high literacy by reference to the desire of the Hakkas to become gentry, not so much for the purpose of acquiring wealth as gaining social prestige and status.[77]

Most writers credit the Hakkas with an unusual sense of loyalty. Campbell said that they were first loyal to the Sung and then to the Ming, and in both cases they suffered terrible consequences.[78] Lo Hsiang-lin says:

> The Hakkas are most deeply steeped in patriotism and the thought of preservation of the race. The reason for this is: formerly their forefathers had suffered extreme oppression by the northern alien tribes and migrated south, and this migration was not at all out of their own free will. When they finally arrived in the district along the northern and southern region of the Yangtze, after a long and precarious drifting, they had passed through an ordeal of untold hardship and suffering. They represented only a portion of their people who had survived nine sure deaths. When they reminisced about the past, they did not easily forget what they had been through. This sense of being wronged has been handed down from fathers to sons, and from sons to grandsons, resulting in an indelible hate against alien tribes. This, perhaps, is the source of their national consciousness.[79]

Lo quotes from Hsü Hsü-tseng's *Feng-hu cha-chi* describing the terrific struggle the Hakkas in Fukien, Kiangsi, and Kwangtung put up against the Mongols at the end of the Sung. The quotation ends in these words: "To the end of the Yüan, no Hakka had served as an official. Who other than the descendants of the loyal and the righteous could have done this?"[80] Then Lo lists thirty-nine Hakkas who either swore that they would not serve the Manchus or vowed that they would take revenge and overthrow the Ch'ing.[81]

Kwangtung was thirteen instead of eleven, and five of the thirteen came from Chia-ying. One other came from Ta-p'u, which was also populated by the Hakkas. Thus of the thirteen, six were Hakkas.

[77] Lo Hsiang-lin, *K'o-chia yen-chiu tao-lun*, p. 179.

[78] Campbell, "Origin and Migrations of the Hakkas," *Chinese Recorder*, Vol. XLIII (Aug., 1912), pp. 478–79.

[79] Lo Hsiang-lin, *K'o-chia yen-chiu tao-lun*, pp. 157–58.

[80] *Ibid.*

[81] *Ibid.*, pp. 160–65. Among the thirty-nine, nine were *chu-sheng* (licentiates), two

Hakka women have always received special attention from all writers. Lechler says:

> In their domestic life you find that there is not such a strict separation of the sexes as elsewhere. It is a peculiarity of the Hakkas, that the women never have their feet cramped; high and low of the female sex preserve their natural feet, which gives them a very different standing in society. It strikes one favorably to see the whole family working together on the fields or to see men and women going together to the market town from the different villages to offer the produce of the soil for sale, and to purchase what they want. . . . The women seem to work hardest, and are accustomed to much endurance from their very childhood. You meet them carrying heavy loads which you would rather wish to see put on men's shoulders, and they seem never to have had enough leisure to learn proper woman's work. . . . Cutting grass on the hills for fuel, feeding pigs for sale, cooking the rice for the whole family, and tilling the fields is the general occupation of the women.[82]

Other writers have pointed out the hard work done by Hakka women.[83] The gazetteer *Chia-ying chou-chih* gives a vivid description of them:

> Women in high and middle families spin, weave, and make clothes. Their dress is crude, and their ornaments simple. They all emphasize virtuous character [chastity]. As for the women in the countryside, they knot their hair and dress in short jackets to work in the fields and vegetable gardens. They come and go barefooted to gather fuel wood and carry loads.[84]

The editors quote from other gazetteers to show that the Hakka women, besides doing what is expected of women, do work normally carried on by men. They weed the fields, harvest the crops, and go out to the market to trade while their men stay home enjoying their leisure. In their own Chia-ying district,

---

kung-shen (imperial students), seven *chü-jen* (elevated scholars), three *chin-shih* (advanced scholars), four officials, six *pu-i* (commoners), and eight were of unknown academic and official status. Some of them raised an army against the Manchus and died; some, frustrated in their attempt to restore the Ming, turned hermits; two committed suicide; one became a Buddhist; and most of them expressed their ethnic consciousness in poetry and other forms of writing.

[82] Lechler, "The Hakka Chinese," *Chinese Recorder*, Vol. IX, No. 5 (Sept.-Oct., 1878), pp. 358–59.

[83] Campbell, *op. cit.*, pp. 473, 480; Huntington, *The Character of Races*, p. 168; Hsieh, "Origin and Migrations of the Hakkas," *Chinese Social and Political Science Review*, Vol. XIII, No. 2 (April, 1929), p. 205; Lo, *K'o-chia yen-chiu tao-lun*, pp. 241–43.

[84] *Chia-ying chou-chih*, 8:53b–54a.

They herd cattle, irrigate land, and sow seeds; they make clothes and cook meals; in short, they do everything. No women in the world work harder than these. For in other parts of the world some women work hard and some have more leisure, depending on whether they are of noble and wealthy families or of humble and poor ones. But in our district, even in gentry and well-to-do families, mistresses and maids and concubines work equally hard.[85]

Hsieh says: "Their [Hakka] girls are rarely sold as slaves or concubines; polygamy is not common mainly because of the poverty of the people."[86] Then Hsieh quotes from the *Chia-ying chou-chih* a passage which refers to the character of the Hakka women as one of the reasons for the adventurous spirit of the Hakka men:

The soil is not fertile and the people are poor. There are lots of hills but few fields for cultivation. The men hence want to emigrate and leave the management of the home to their women. [Here Hsieh leaves out a whole line: "Therefore village women till land, pick up fuel, weave, make clothes, and take charge of household affairs."] As soon as the ban on emigration overseas was lifted, many of the inhabitants flocked to Nanyang [southeast Asia and the neighboring islands]. They began as menial workers but gradually amassed a fortune. Some returned in three or five years [three, four, five, or seven years] while others delayed till ten or twenty years later. Some even left their homes in their youth and returned with hoary hairs. When they departed from their homes, they left their old folks and young children, the fields, ancestral graves, and houses in charge of their wives. . . . This is why the people can migrate abroad.[87]

The Hakkas' religious beliefs differ very little from those of the other Chinese. Lechler describes Hakka beliefs:

The Confucian precept of worshipping the dead is certainly the most cherished part of their religion, and the ancestral worship in the houses, in the ancestral halls, and on the hills where the tombs are, form such an important part of their religious duties, that these are always the last thing from which they will separate, in case of conversion to Christianity. In connection therewith is the "Fung-shui" [geomancy] in which they are staunch believers. They do not see the contradiction of looking for blessings to deceased parents and at the same time calling in Buddhist priests to help their parents in Hades. *Nan-wu [mo]-o-mi-t'o-fuh* is the pass word

---

[85] *Ibid.*, 8:54a.

[86] Hsieh, *op. cit.*, p. 205.

[87] *Ibid.*, pp. 205–6. Hsieh quotes from *Chia-ying chou-chih*, 8:54b–55a.

which is expected to pave the way to happiness for a poor Hakka soul.... The most popular idol among the Hakkas is the Buddhistic Kwan-yin (Kon-yim-nyong [*Avalokitésvara*]) and I have seen her name put above all other gods which are worshipped in the houses, the names of them being written on a big sheet of red paper hung up on the wall. Then there are the Buddhistic ceremonies performed on the occasion of deaths or funerals, by the ecclesiastical Ho-shang as well as by the Lay Nan-wu [mo].

There are the sorcerers called Shang-kung or Shang-p'o [*hsi-kung* or *hsi-p'o*], both however males, whose special business is to drive out evil influences or cast out devils, and there is the Sien-poh [*hsien-p'o*] (which I [Lechler] believe is a specific Hakka notion), or conjuror of the dead, who is resorted to, to inquire after the condition of the dead in Hades. Spirit rapping is also practised and the spirit is made to appear to communicate by writing revelations about the future.[88]

Lechler also mentions the following as among the idols the Hakkas worshiped: *Wun-ti*, god of literature; *Wu-ti*, god of war; *Kwan-ti; T'ien-heu*, queen of heaven; *Ch'eng-huang;* Confucius and his disciples; *Tu-ti-yeh* and the gods of grain; *Po-kung* and *Po-p'o*, who take care of the fields; and the "god of the hearth, who is supposed on the 23rd day of the 12th moon to ascend to heaven and present his report on the families upon earth to Yü-huang-shang-ti."[89]

On the Hakkas' religious beliefs, Lo Hsiang-lin makes the following statement:

In general, Hakka beliefs are not different from those of most Chinese. For example, with respect to ancestral worship and belief, traditions and superstitions about spirits and ghosts, Buddhist and Taoist creeds and ceremonies, and the superstitions and influence of divination and fortunetelling by means of physiognomy, there may be some difference in degree; but in nature there is in fact no difference.[90]

From the account given above, it is clear that the Hakkas did contribute toward the formation of the Taiping ideology. Their sense of social solidarity and willingness to die for one another in time of need gave substance to the idea of the brotherhood of men, the origin of which may have been either Christianity or secret societies or novels.

Another contribution of the Hakkas was a sense of ethnic solidarity, which plays a great part in the Taiping ideology. However, we do not

[88] Lechler, "The Hakka Chinese," *Chinese Recorder*, Vol. IX, No. 5 (Sept.-Oct., 1878), p. 357.

[89] *Ibid.*, pp. 357–58.

[90] Lo Hsiang-lin, *K'o-chia yen-chiu tao-lun*, p. 174.

agree with some authors who believe that the Hakkas were a revolution-ary people, for they fought on the side of the government as well as against it.[91] Because so many Hakkas refused to co-operate with the Manchus at the beginning of the dynasty, we must consider them along with the remnant Ming scholars as a possible source of the Taiping ethnic attitude. Being Hakkas themselves, Hung and other Taiping leaders must have derived a large measure of inspiration from their own forefathers. The Taipings' ethnic consciousness was obvious in their eloquent verbal attack upon the Manchus as well as in their determined effort to overthrow them.

The difficulty the Hakkas experienced in obtaining land and their struggle against the Puntis may have suggested the need for land regula-tions to the Taiping leaders and stimulated their attempt to create a society in which all land would belong to all the people. The close atten-tion paid to the grade of land in the Taipings' proposed distribution reflects experience in farming the unproductive land in the hills. It would be difficult to believe that there was no relationship between the Taiping leaders' own experience as farmers and the land regulations they established to create the type of society that would make the Tai-ping ideals a reality.

[91] "In the sixth moon, in the fourth year of T'ung-chih (1865), Governor-general Jui Lin of Liang-kwang and Governor Kuo Sung-t'ao of Kwangtung in a joint memo-rial about their handling of the feud wars between the Hakkas and the Puntis said in effect that it was the Puntis who were the bandits, and Hakkas assisted the govern-ment in attacking the bandits. However, the Punti gentry were not involved in the rebellion. Yet the Hakkas, who had harbored intense hatred and resentment against the Puntis as a whole, massacred the Puntis without discrimination. Later when the Hakkas fled and occupied Tsai-ch'eng in Kwangtung, they turned around and re-sisted the government. It was then the Puntis who were obedient and the Hakkas who were rebellious." (Memorials of Jui-lin and Kuo Sung-t'ao, quoted in Ch'ih-hsi hsien-chih, chüan 8.)

Hsieh has a clearer account of this feud war: "The clan fights between the Hakkas and Puntis reached a climax in 1854. The T'aiping Rebellion had spread to Shaoking, where numerous Punti people joined the rebels. The Hakka clans located there, how-ever, for the most part remained loyal to the government. Much bad feeling was aroused and, when the T'aiping rebels went north, the internecine war began first in Hokshan and spread all over the southwest districts. The Puntis, being stronger in men and means, defeated the Hakkas in these districts and expelled those not killed. In 1862 the contest was at its height when imperial authority was entirely suspended in several districts. By the end of the year, the Hakkas were outnumbered and driven towards the coast. They then stormed and occupied the fortified town of Kuanghai, west of Macao. They were soon driven out by the Puntis with the help of the imperial forces . . . " (Hsieh, "Origin and Migrations of the Hakkas," *Chinese Social and Political Science Review*, Vol. XIII, No. 2 (April, 1929), p. 222.

The life of the Hakka women suggests the Taiping view on women. Poverty prevented the Hakkas from practicing polygamy, so they decreed monogamy for the people at large. However, inasmuch as the policy of monogamy was a matter of necessity rather than of principle, it did not prevent them from practicing polygamy whenever their wealth and station in life permitted. The Taipings' early monogamous life may be the reason they took up polygamy with such enthusiasm, making up, as it were, for what they had missed. But the independent spirit of the Hakka women remained and explains why the Taipings sent women of the occupied territory to do what was normally done by men.

The privilege granted to Taiping women to take part in government and military activities can also be traced to the status of Hakka women in their society. From their own experience, the Taiping leaders believed that women were capable of handling affairs as well as men. The Taiping regulations against selling girls into slavery and prostitution were again a reflection of the practices of the Hakkas. And it is obvious that their prohibition against foot-binding was only an extension of the Hakka women's practice.

The Hakka religious beliefs seem to have influenced the Taipings in two ways. The Hakkas were more receptive to new convictions than the Puntis; this is significant in explaining the Taiping acceptance of Christianity. However, the Hakkas wanted above all to become gentry, and in order to fulfill their wish they studied very hard in preparation for the government examinations. This gave them a thorough background in traditionalism. When the Taipings accepted Christianity, they combined their own culture with their new convictions. It is no wonder that their religious ideology is a conglomeration of ideas Christian and yet not Christian, Confucian and yet not Confucian—in a word, a nondescript body of ideas. In religion the mental attitude of the Hakkas directly influenced that of the Taipings.

The Taipings, however, did not hold blindly to their own traditions. Their iconoclasm was a direct reaction against their own tradition of idolatry. No doubt their early Christian zeal was the main factor in their iconoclasm; but if they had never known from their own experience the stupidity of superstitious beliefs and worship, they probably would not have carried so far their determined effort to destroy all idolatry in the face of strong popular resistance.

Taiping segregation of the sexes seems another example of their reaction against their own way of life. The Hakka women were said to be

freer in their contact with the outside world. This must have proved a source of trouble to the Taipings during the time of military expedition; hence the strict regulation about segregation. But we must remember also the condition on which this segregation was enforced: the members of the Taiping society were promised that when they arrived at the heavenly court they would be rewarded many times over for their self-denial during the military march.

Finally, the influence of Hakka dialect on the Taiping documents is unmistakable. Lo Hsiang-lin said:

> During the reigns of Tao-kuang and Hsien-feng, the Hakkas developed a type of writing whose style is similar to that of the vernacular. This is the vernacular literature created by the kings of the Taiping: Hung Hsiu-ch'üan the T'ien Wang, Yang Hsiu-ch'ing the Tung Wang, Wei Ch'ang-hui the Pei Wang, Shih Ta-k'ai the I Wang, and others. These kings were all well versed in traditional Chinese literary style. [From this point, Lo quotes from Ling Shan-ch'ing (ed.), *T'ai-p'ing t'ien-kuo yeh-shih*, *chüan* 10, under "Wen-kao."] "There are significant reasons for them to use such a vernacular style: (1) in order to mislead the enemy, for military documents are filled with coded phrases very difficult to decipher [although clearly comprehensible to members of the Taiping army themselves], and this for the purpose of preventing the Ch'ing army from knowing their military secrets if perchance these documents should fall into their hands; (2) in order to show a difference, for the Taiping leaders built their state on a religious basis and therefore purposely used strange language to make the impression that they were unpredictable; (3) in order to be popularly understandable: the Taiping kings, in view of the fact that the distinction between scholars and commoners has always been due to the difficulty of language, personally promoted vernacular style so as to make their writings comprehensible to the people with the purpose of inculcating [by means of such a popular language] religious and new knowledge.[92]

Lo gives two illustrations. The first, "An Edict Exhorting the People to Cease Smoking Opium" (Ch'üan-jen [min?] chieh-yen chao), says:

> The T'ien Wang proclaims, saying:
> The heart [*teng-ts'ao*] of high heaven is like an arrow;
> Constantly do the eyes [*yen-chen-chen*] of the Heavenly Father pierce all.
> If you do not believe, look then at Huang I-chen.
> Unintentionally Heaven saved Ho Hsin-chin.

---

[92] Lo Hsiang-lin, *op. cit.*, p. 221. Reasons one and three seem to conflict.

One smoke ended and another desired, there is no satisfaction;
Why smoke so foolishly [*kan-ch'un*] and transform yourselves into
    living demons?
If you stop smoking you may sicken and die, but better so than
    punishment by death.
To cast off ghosthood and become a human is after all best.
Respect this.

The second illustration, from instructions given to Ch'en Yü-ch'eng by
Ch'in Jih-kang, the Yen Wang, says:

Ch'in [Jih-kang], the Yen Wang of the true heavenly mandated *T'ai-p'ing
t'ien-kuo*, instructs the right thirtieth senior secretary 檢點 of the court,
younger brother Ch'en Yü-ch'eng, and also the commanders 指揮, generals
將軍, corps commanders 統制, and other officials to know this:
    Now, on the twenty-fourth day of the eighth month, I have received and
perused the report of the younger brother and others in every detail. As
for the territory of Ch'i-chou at present, although there are a few remaining demons who periodically come and make trouble [*tso-kuai*], I hope
that the younger brother and the others will build strong encampments
there, discipline the soldiers, be cautious and alert [*lin-pien*], give their
strictest attention to defense, and not allow the demons to enter. Also, you
must constantly expound the desires and principles of Heaven and instruct
the masses of the troops to be courageous in exterminating the demons. In
all matters, the Heavenly Father directs and the Heavenly Eldest Brother
sustains [*tan-tan*]. Do not be alarmed. In military matters, as before strictly
comply with the Tung Wang's instructions and your actions will be correct. For this purpose I specially issue these instructions. When these instructions arrive, strictly comply. Do not disobey these instructions.[93]

Lo says many phrases used in these documents were Hakka idioms,
such as *teng-ts'ao* meaning "heart," which abounds in country songs;
yen-chen-chen meaning "constantly staring at something"; *kan-ch'un*
meaning "so foolish"; *tso-kuai*, which is translated "to make trouble";
lin-pien, translated "alert"; and *tan-tan*, translated "to sustain." According to Lo, elements of Hakka dialect are even more numerous in "The
Book of Declarations of the Divine Will Made During the Heavenly
Father's Descent to Earth" (T'ien-fu hsia-fan chao-shu).[94]
    Not all Taiping documents contain elements of Hakka dialect. "The
Land System of the Heavenly Dynasty" (T'ien-ch'ao t'ien-mou chih-

   [93] *Ibid.*, p. 222. Both illustrations are quoted from Ling, *Yeh-shih, chüan* 10, under
"Wen-kao."
   [94] Lo Hsiang-lin, *op. cit.*, p. 222.

tu); "The Book on the Principles of the Heavenly Nature"; "Taiping Imperial Declaration" (T'ai-p'ing chao-shu), which contains the three most important proclamations; and most works under the name of Hung Jen-kan contain a minimum of the Hakka vernacular style. However, a few expressions such as *teng-ts'ao* appear in almost all of the Taiping documents.

In addition to the Hakka dialect, there is evidence of local influence on the Taiping language. The Taipings often combined characters to form new ones, either for the purpose of creating a code or to express meanings deducible from the composite form. Examples are: 咁 (*kan*, meaning "thus" or "so"), 燷 (*liang*, meaning "bright"), 瞓 (*k'un*, meaning "sleepy"),[95] 冀 (pronunciation not certain, meaning "united") 歪 (*wai*, meaning "not correct" or "not straight")[96]. It seems certain that the Taipings took such a practice from the secret society. However, we may also trace it to local practice in south China, particularly in Kwangtung, Kwangsi, and Fukien. *Chen-an fu-chih*, a gazetteer published in Kwangsi, gives the following examples of characters created for local use: 歪 (*ai*, meaning "not long"), 奀 (*chuan*, meaning "weak"), 奁 (*wen*, meaning "sit comfortably"), 歪 (*chung*, meaning "death"), 孬 (*la*, meaning "unable to raise one's foot"), 仔 (*niao*, meaning "small baby"), 妜 (*t'a*, meaning "elder sister").[97] The Taipings seem to have used the same principle to form new words as the Chinese in the south. Of the few words given in the list, *wai* 歪 is in general use and *Cheng-tzu t'ung*, as quoted by *Tz'u-yüan*, says: "Common people combine *pu* 不 and *cheng* 正 to form *pu-cheng* 歪."[98]

It may be of interest to compare the status of other groups of women in south China with that of the Hakka women. *Kwangsi t'ung-chih* quotes the following passage from Wu Chen-fang's *Ling-nan cha-chi*:

> Most women in Ling-nan [generally referring to Kwangtung and Kwangsi district] do not bind their feet, and only girls of high families and rich houses do that. Most women and maid servants walk on the street barefooted. When gifts are sent among the relatives, it is always the women

---

[95] In Fukien, this character is pronounced *k'aung*.

[96] Lo Erh-kang, "T'ai-p'ing t'ien-kuo ching-chi k'ao," *Hsüeh-yüan*, Vol. II, No. 1 (May, 1948), p. 28; Ling, *Yeh-shih*, 10:60; "Ch'ao-t'ien ch'ao-chu t'u," in Hsiao I-shan (compiler), *T'ai-p'ing t'ien-kuo chao-yü*, plate 7; "Yüan-tao chiu-shih ko," in Ch'eng Yen-sheng (compiler), *T'ai-p'ing t'ien-kuo shih-liao*, 1st Series, II, 1b.

[97] *Chen-an fu-chih*, 8:17b–18a.

[98] *Tz'u-yüan*, section *ch'en*, p. 201.

who carry gift loads. When they arrive at the house they produce from
their sleeves shoes to wear. The minute they step out of the gate they take
them off and keep them in their sleeves.... Should any of the girls from a
lowly family bind her feet, everybody would ridicule her, and make it an
indication of the distinction between good girls and bad ones.[99]

Hsün-chou fu-chih says: "Most women of high families bind their feet and
are skilled in embroidery. All other women walk under broad daylight
barefooted. These women attend to the household chores, gather fuel,
and work harder than women of any other place."[100] Many women of
the tribal peoples are of the same character. *Chen-an fu-chih* says: "Men
wear turbans and women are dressed in short jackets and long skirts, but
barefooted."[101]

Jen Kuo-jung, in his "Yao-shan chi-yu," makes the following observation: "The posture of women [here] is much stronger than that of
Canton women. They, one and all, are capable of hard work. They
support themselves. Their ability in climbing mountains compares
favorably with that of men.... The morality of sexual honor is not too
rigidly observed."[102] Women of Kwangsi Yao-min sometimes assumed
military command. *Hsün-chou fu-chih* reports:

> Those Yao women who assume military command have the right to put
> on jade headdresses and purple phoenix fur coats draped in butterfly pat-
> terned silk, and to carry seals of rhinoceros tusk. When seen from afar, they
> appear like deities. The jade headdress is a piece of soft jade on which are
> carved two phoenix heads around which the hairs are wound.[103]

Li Shih, in his study of the customs of the Li people in Ch'iung-ya
(Hainan Island), says that the main occupation of the Li people,
whether male or female, old or young, is farming.[104]

It is obvious from these sources that the Taiping attitude toward women, the work assigned to them, and the privileges granted them have
antecedents in south China; the Taiping ideas and institutions related

[99] *Kwangsi t'ung-chih*, 87:8b–9a. Quoted also in Hu P'u-an's *Chung-hua ch'üan-kuo
feng-su chih, shang/9/9.*

[100] *Hsün-chou fu-chih*, 54:2a.

[101] *Chen-an fu-chih*, 8:24b.

[102] "Yao-shan chi-yu," *Chung-shan ta-hsüeh yü-yen li-shih hsüeh yen-chiu-so chou k'an*,
Vol. III, No. 35–36 (July 4, 1928), p. 65.

[103] *Hsün-chou fu-chih*, 54:9b.

[104] Li, "Ch'iung-yai Li-su chih-lüeh," *Kuo-wen chou-pao*, Vol. III, No. 42 (Oct. 31,
1926).

to women may be explained in part by reference to their ethnic and geographic origin.[105]

POPULAR BELIEFS

Many ideas treated in previous sections could rightly be classified as "popular"; for example, most of the religious and moral elements in traditionalism, ideas contained in Buddhism and Taoism, and those traceable to novels. The popular belief in the mandate of Heaven is described by a Western writer of the nineteenth century in the following words:

> One day, when a military Mandarin was relating to us with great *naïveté* stories of the prowess of the famous Kouang-ti, we bethought ourselves to ask him, whether he had appeared in the last war that the Empire was engaged in with the English....."Don't let us talk any more of that war," said the Mandarin; "Kouang-ti certainly did not appear, and it is a very bad sign. They say," he added, lowering his voice, "that this dynasty is abandoned by Heaven, and that it will be soon overthrown."
>
> This idea that the Mantchoo dynasty has finished its appointed career, and that another will shortly succeed to it, was very widely diffused in China in 1846; during our journey we several times heard it mentioned, and there is little doubt that this kind of vague presentiment, prevailing for several years, was a very powerful auxiliary to the insurrection that broke out in 1851, and since then has made such gigantic progress.[106]

The popular mind was also saturated with the idea of retribution: the good will be rewarded and the evil punished. That *T'ai-shang kan-ying p'ien* (T'ai-shang [supposedly Lao-tzu's teacher] on Moral Causality) was a popular text found in many homes indicates the prevailing nature of such ideas. This idea of retribution not only permeated the mind of the common people but dominated the mind of the scholars as well. Hui Tung, an important scholar in the Ch'ing dynasty, brought out one edition of the *T'ai-shang kan-ying p'ien*, writing a preface filled with devout reverence. Lo Tse-nan said, "There may be one or two outstanding scholars; but when one comes to consider their comportment, they are found to believe in retribution."[107]

---

[105] I fully realize that these sources, including some of those I use in connection with the Hakkas, are not of the period under study. I assume that society in south China has not changed to such a radical extent as to render all these sources out of date. If this assumption is wrong, what I have written here will serve merely to suggest a possible connection between the life of the native tribes and that of the Taipings.

[106] Évariste Régis Huc, *The Chinese Empire*, I, 291–92.

[107] Lo Tse-nan, *Lo chung-chieh kung i-chi*, 6:27a.

Many ideas, for one reason or another, in the course of time have become efficacious as ideals, norms, or attitudes of the people; the people lived by these values without being conscious of doing so. The Taipings' assigning of wind, clouds, thunder, and rain as symbols for their kings may also have been derived from popular superstitions. Kung-chuan Hsiao mentions the worship of gods of wind, clouds, thunder, and rain among the religious practices of the village people.[108]

With this broad nature of what may be considered "popular" in mind, we shall restrict our task in this section to the single subject of the practice of trance, a sort of shamanism. The Chinese term for it is *wu* (巫 sorcery or witchery). A brief historical survey precedes description of the actual practice of sorcery and witchcraft in the locality in which the Taipings had the greatest opportunity of coming into contact with it.

Witchcraft was practiced in China as early as the Chou. In "Ch'u-yü" in *Kuo-yü*, Kuan I-fu of Ch'u, in reply to King Chao's question said:

> In ancient times people and divine beings did not intermingle. Among the people there were those who were refined and without wiles. They were, moreover, capable of being equable, respectful, sincere, and upright. Their knowledge...was capable of conforming to righteousness. Their wisdom could illumine what was distant with its all-pervading brilliance. Their perspicacity could illumine everything. When there were people of this sort, the illustrious spirits [神 *shen*] would descend in them. If men, such people were then called sorcerers [覡 *hsi*], and if women, they were called witches [巫 *wu*]. It was through such persons that the regulation of the dwelling places of the spirits, their positions [at the sacrifices], and their order of precedence were effected; it was through them that their sacrifices, sacrificial vessels, and seasonal clothing were arranged.[109]

Witchcraft had become a common practice especially in Ch'u during the Han. "Chiao-ssu chih" in the *Han-shu* says that the people in the district of Ch'u believed in witchery and ghosts and emphasized the importance of religious worship. And Wang I of the Later Han commented in his *Ch'u-tz'u chang-chü*, "Chiu-ko": "In the district between River Yüan and River Hsiang, the people, as a custom, believed in spirits and loved to worship."[110] In making this note, Wang must have had the following lines of his poet Ch'ü Yüan in mind:

The auspicious divination of Ling-feng,...

[108] Kung-chuan Hsiao, *Rural China*, p. 221.
[109] Kuo-yü, *chüan* 18, *hsia*, pp. 1–2.
[110] *Ch'u-tz'u chang-chü*, 2:27.

Wu-hsien will descend in the evening.

The commentary says that Ling-feng was one who understood what is lucky and what is not from divination, and Wu-hsien was an ancient spiritual sorcerer.[111]

Part of the art of sorcery is for the sorcerer to act as the medium upon which a spirit descends. Ch'ü Hsüan-ying in his *Chung-kuo she-hui shih-liao ts'ung-ch'ao* defines spiritual descent as "the spirit taking possession of his [the sorcerer's] body, and this is a kind of sorcery."[112]

The following cases illustrate the prevalence of sorcery in China. In the biography of Prince I of Chiang-tu, whose name was Fei 非, it is said that after the death of Prince I his son Chien assumed the title. Chien "and his queen Ch'eng-kuang ordered a maid from Yüeh to have a spirit descend upon her for the purpose of cursing the emperor."[113] In the biography of Prince Li of Kuang-ling, whose name was Hsü 胥, we find that Hsü, intent on getting into power,

> ...ordered a sorceress by the name of Li Nü-hsü to have a spirit descend upon her for the purpose of cursing [the emperor]. Nü-hsü wept and said, "Hsiao-wu-ti has descended upon me." Those around all prostrated themselves. [Then] she said, "I [supposedly the spirit of Emperor Hsiao-wu] will certainly make Hsü the Son of Heaven."

There is no question that this sorceress was also from the south, for preceding this passage there is a line: "And the land of Ch'u [is a land of] sorcery and spirits."[114]

T'ai-p'ing kuang-chi quotes the following anecdote from *Sou-shen chi* by Kan Pao of the Chin dynasty:

> During the Han period there was a Taoist in Ying-ling in the district of Pei-hai who had the power of making it possible for living men to meet with the dead. A man from his *chün* [prefecture] whose wife had died a few years before heard of him and came to see him and said: "I wish I could see my dead wife again, even only once; then I would die without regret." The Taoist said: "You may see her, but the minute you hear the sound of a drum come out immediately and do not delay." He then taught him the method to see his wife.

[111] *Ibid.*, "Ch'u-tz'u," 1:16. For different interpretations of *Wu-hsien*, see Ku Yen-wu, *Jih-chih lu*, 25:1b–3b.

[112] *Chung-kuo she-hui shih-liao ts'ung-ch'ao*, II, 398.

[113] *Han-shu*, 53:5b.

[114] *Ibid.*, 63:14a–b.

During the rendezvous the man talked to his wife and experienced sadness and happiness and love as if they were alive. After a long while, he heard the sound of a drum. He was filled with hate for not being able to stay. When he stepped out the door in a hurry, the flap of his robe got caught in the door. He broke away, leaving the flap behind. In more than a year this man died. His family buried him. When they opened up the tomb for the burial, they saw that under the lid of the wife's coffin was a flap of a robe. [115]

Feng-su t'ung by Ying Shao of the Later Han said that Emperor Wu blindly believed in spirits, and especially believed in the sorcery of Yüeh.[116]

Since the sorceresses mentioned above were either from Yüeh or from Ch'u, it is probable that sorcery was first practiced in the south and gradually spread to the north. In *Hou-Han-shu*, the biography of Sung Chün, we read: "[Sung Chün] was transferred to become the magistrate of Ch'en-yang [west of the present Ch'en-hsi in Hunan]. Few people [there], as a rule, studied; when they grew up they believed in sorcery and spirits. Chün established schools for them and prohibited spirit worship."[117]

Hu P'u-an in his *Chung-hua ch'üan-kuo feng-su chih* speaks of Ch'en-chou in Hunan: "The people of Ch'en-chou believed in sorcery and worshiped spirits."[118] However, a sorcerer from Ch'i 齊巫 is mentioned in the biography of Liu P'en-tzu in the *Hou-Han-shu*:

In the army [referring to the army of Fan-Ts'ung, leader of the *Ch'ih-mei* or Red Eyebrow rebels] there was a Ch'i *wu* [a sorcerer from Ch'i], who often stirred up sentiments for the worship of Prince Ching of Ch'eng-yang [the one responsible for the restoration of order after the chaos created by Empress Lü] for the purpose of seeking happiness and avoiding unhappiness. The sorcerer cunningly said [or said when mad, that is, in a trance] that Prince Ching was greatly enraged and said, "You should work for the government; why do you work for the rebels?" All those who laughed at the sorcerer fell sick.

The propaganda of the sorcerer was apparently very effective, for the rebels finally made Liu P'en-tzu, a descendant of Prince Ching, the emperor.[119]

[115] Li Fang, *T'ai-p'ing kuang-chi, chüan* 284.
[116] Quoted by Ch'ü Hsüan-ying in *Chung-kuo she-hui shih-liao ts'ung-ch'ao*, II, 406.
[117] *Hou-Han-shu*, 71:14a–b.
[118] *Chung-hua ch'üan-kuo feng-su chih*, hsia/6/33.
[119] *Hou-Han-shu*, 41:11b.

Sorcery was extensive in the southern part of China, particularly in Kwangtung, Kwangsi, and Fukien, where the Taipings had the closest contact. In the "Chiao-ssu chih" in the *Han-shu* we read: "The Yüeh people believed in spirits." And *Kwangsi t'ung-chih*, quoting *Pai-Yüeh feng-t'u chi*, says: "The people of Yüeh worshiped and believed in spirits."[120]

The following cases show how sorcery was practiced in the two Yüeh provinces. In Canton there was a practice called "the boy in a trance." It is described in the following words:

> First [the sorcerer would] choose a boy who would close his eyes and sit upright. The sorcerer would then take some charms and burn them. The charms are simple and known to most people. A number of persons, each [holding] a bundle of burning incense in his hand, would wave the incense around the boy in a motion of drawing circles. In about half an hour, the boy would start to soliloquize. Everybody would then call out: "The Master is come!" They would then ask: "Would the Master use a knife... a sword?" The weapon at the call of which the boy nodded his head would be considered what was wanted. They would give it to the boy, who would use it in a way conforming to the rule of a certain school. After the performance, the boy would fall into sleep. He would wake up when his name was called. Some thought that it might be a wild ghost or a roaming spirit that had taken possession of the boy.[121]

The natives of Ch'ih-hsi in Kwangtung divined whenever they intended to do anything. The wildest and most fantastic form of divination was the practice of trance. They often said they were possessed by spirits, and people would then come to them for divination. When the spirits left them, they appeared as usual.[122]

In Ch'ao-chou the people believed in spiritual power. On New Year's Day they would gather together in an open space and set up booths. Idols were then removed from their temples and placed in these booths. Then a man dressed in a red robe and red turban would appear, jumping and mumbling to himself. He declared that he was such and such a spirit or immortal. The people believed in everything he said. They crowded around him asking about matters concerning sickness, fortune, or misfortune. The medium would then suddenly cut his tongue with a

[120] *Han-shu*, quoted by Hu P'u-an in *Chung-hua ch'üan-kuo feng-su chih, shang/8/1*; *Kwangsi t'ung-chih*, 87:7b.
[121] Hu, *op. cit., hsia/7/22–23*.
[122] *Ibid., hsia/7/37*.

sword and take the blood and smear it on charms. The charms were then used to protect the district from evil influence.[123]

In Hsün-chou, Kwangsi, when people were sick they did not send for doctors. Instead they sent for Taoists or sorcerers. Women sorcerers were known as *kuei-p'o* (鬼婆 ghost women), and they had the power to heal sickness, to tell fortunes, or to act as mediums possessed by the dead and talk to people.[124]

Hsün-chou fu-chih gives the interesting case of an iconoclast blasting at the practice of sorcery in a proclamation:

T'an Yu, a native of the district [P'ing-nan, under Hsün-chou], tried to explode the worship of Liu Ta-niang in a proclamation. In the tenth year of T'ung-chih [1871] a certain sorceress by the name of Liu made false statements to the people, saying, "My late aunt reached the state of Tao during the Sung and is now showing her spirituality in Mount Ta-jung. [You people] should build a temple to worship her." Then she coaxed a few children [to work for her]. The minute guests arrived, the children fell flat on the ground, pretending that Ta-niang was speaking through them. They said that there would be a flood or drought at a certain place and an epidemic at another place. But these could be avoided by prayer; otherwise, there would be calamity. Thus people from Wu [Wu-chou], Hsün [Hsün-chou], Kao [Kao-chou], and P'ing [P'ing-lo] came heel to heel to pray and worship. Then they said that Mr. X was rude and Mr. Y sinned against the spirit, and they should be fined. The credulous people were treated as fish and meat [suckers]. Yu then exploded the falsehood in a proclamation. He was not fond of argument, but he could not help doing it.[125] The proclamation runs:

"In the old times, Hu Ying of the Sung, wherever he went, destroyed improper temples 淫祠 numbering in the thousands. In Heng-chou [Hunan] he turned a temple into living quarters where he and his mother made their abode.[126] He was hailed as a good official of his age. Han Yü memorialized against the reception of *Sárīra*, and he may even now be considered a great *ju* [scholar or moral teacher] without any apology. Indeed, those who practice what is unorthodox will not be tolerated in a period when [the Tao of] sages prevails, and those who worship spirits which it is not their duty to worship were considered by the Sage [Confucius, a reference to the *Analects*] as flatterers. Hsiao Liang [Emperor Wu of Liang, Hsiao being his family name] blindly worshiped Buddha at T'ai-ch'eng, and who could be blamed for his death by starvation? Duke Ch'ou of Kuo

---

[123] *Ibid.*, *hsia*/7/49–50.

[124] *Hsün-chou fu-chih*, 54:2b.

[125] This is a paraphrase from Mencius to show that T'an Yu had no choice but to post the proclamation.

[126] *Sung-shih*, 416:15b.

listened to spirits at Hsia-yang, and Kuo was destroyed and the duke fled and never returned.[127] Those who pray for happiness are still visited with calamity; and those who wish to have security fall after all into danger. The evidence of the past may be used as mirrors [to warn us against our own mistakes]. Sad at the thought the people are as if in a state of dreaming, I exert myself to write this yü-chen [虞箴 a warning delivered by a forester in the Chou dynasty].[128] There are mad people who love to create trouble, and evil ones who are engaged in selfish enterprise; these people proclaim to the world that they are paying respect to Buddha, but in fact they are trying to cheat people. In the name of Liu Ta-niang, they are a new absurdity at Mount Jung. They promote building temples, but their motive is to fatten their own purse; they sponsor gold-plating the idols, but their idea is to deceive the people. They falsely take the name of the late aunt to spread fantastic ideas; and they teach secrets to rough children, who pretend that they are transmitting the words of ghosts [falsely spreading devilish words]. They say there will be locusts, and a bad year cannot be avoided; and there will be epidemic and no one can escape the fated calamity. If the people will give alms and pray to gods, happiness will be extended to them from heaven; if they do not believe but are rude to the spirits, disaster will surely befall them. At this, the poor people who are uneducated come from all parts of the country in madness. At first only one district is deceived; later most neighboring towns are affected. Some come in groups like ants to pray for sunny days; others come in groups like bees to ask for rain.[129]...These people are being exploited by these evil ones without being conscious of it. They willingly come to pray at the evil temples. It is indeed an absurdity never heard of. They do not know that the 'facts' are fabrications and the person [Liu Ta-niang] has no existence either. These 'facts' are not transmitted to us through the people living in the district, nor are they recorded in any religious documents. Where was she born? When did she die? There is no evidence in any writings. What calamity had she warded off? What danger had she prevented from taking place? Why should she be worshiped with incense fragrance?...My cherished desire is that the great families in the district and notables of the land will [make an effort to] put a stop to the selfish desire to seek happiness and will encourage the moral inclination to uproot the unorthodox. [We should] denounce the ruffians who start the trouble so as to cleanse ourselves of the belief in spirits, a ridicule that has been directed at the people of the south; and [we should] prohibit women from taking part in incense-burning, so that we may mind the Confucian warning against license."[130]

[127] See Ch'un-ch'iu ching-chuan yin-te, 79/Chuang 32/3 Tso, fu and 96/Hsi 5/9 Tso.
[128] See ibid., 258/Hsiang 4/7 Tso, fu 1.
[129] Another possible rendering of this sentence is: "Some come to pray for sunny days, and yet ants start to gather; others come to ask for rain, and yet bees cluster in groups."
[130] Hsün-chou fu-chih, 54:5a-b.

About twenty years before this proclamation, Hung Hsiu-ch'üan and his immediate friends could have been moved to iconoclastic activity by precisely the same motive to expose the falsehood of popular superstitions; the tone of this proclamation seems a lingering echo of "Proclamation on the Origin of Principles for the Awakening of the Age" (Yüan-tao chüeh-shih chao).

In Ch'ing-yüan (Kwangsi) the people do not sacrifice to the moon on the fifteenth of the eighth moon, as the Chinese people elsewhere do. They cover a woman with a bed comforter and drone incantations into her ears until she swoons. Then the spirit of another person may take possession of her body and start to sing. Popularly this is known as *ya-chin* 壓禁.[131]

The people in Heng (Kwangsi) especially believe in sorcery and spirits. Some children are known as ghost children. During the seventh and eighth moon of the year, people spread sacrificial meat in their room. They have five or six ghost children come bringing paper masks on the faces of which, in addition to the usual painting, the names of spirits are written. These are lined up on the table. Then they beat earthenware and drums of all kinds, some made of leather and some made of brass. The noises can be heard from afar and are mixed with native songs. Then one or two or three of the children, each bringing his own spirit mask, starts to dance. They are in short dress, with a small flag or staff in one hand. While dancing, they may jump as high as the beam of the house, or they may lie flat on the ground. One occupies the center seat, declares himself to be a certain spirit, and begins to tell people's fortunes. The master of the house then prostrates himself. This is called *kuo-shen* 過神.People who are sick come to them to be cured and will not send for doctors.[132]

In Fukien during religious parades the people often carry idols on their persons. The idols have only the upper part and are hollow, so the people get into them and carry them around on their shoulders. They not only walk for the spirits, sometimes they even speak for them.[133] When they fall sick, they do not usually send for doctors. The most important thing to do then is *ta-ch'uang* (打獚 using a boy as a medium), and the one who is in charge is called *ch'uang-tzu*. *Ch'uang-tzu* is dressed in red trousers, bare to the waist. A Taoist, who accompanies him, tells *ch'uang-

[131] Hu, *Chung-hua ch'üan-kuo feng-su chih, shang*/9/25.
[132] *Ibid., shang*/9/41.
[133] *Ibid., hsia*/5/62.

tzu to do all sorts of funny things while the Taoist mumbles to himself. In a short while, *ch'uang-tzu* starts to shake his head with increasing speed. In a moment his hair becomes loose and spreads all over his head and face. Then he shouts in incomprehensible noise and rolls himself on the ground. Sometimes he jumps like a monkey or lies on the ground like a dog. The Taoist controls him through some magic, and prevents him from mad behavior. Then an incense table is placed before him. Members of the sick person's family kneel before it and beseech *ch'uang-tzu* to use his magic power to heal the sick. *Ch'uang-tzu* then declares the name of the spirit which has taken possession of his body, and asks questions of the sick person's family, speaking a pidgin Mandarin. He is talking as if in a dream, and no one can understand him. The Taoist then gives him a knife, with which the *ch'uang-tzu* cuts his tongue. He then uses the blood to draw several scores of charms. He then eats burning incense, and smoke comes out his mouth and nose. No one knows how he does it. When everything is done, the Taoist burns certain charms to send the spirit away, and *ch'uang-tzu* wakes up. He says he does not know a thing about what has happened during the trance. The cut in his tongue does not bother him either, for he feels no pain.[134]

That the Hakkas believed in sorcery is apparent from Lechler's account quoted earlier. *Chia-ying chou-chih* says about the Hakkas: "In this district people believe in sorcery and worship spirits. They forsake doctors for spirits. If one urges them to take medicine to cure their illness, they do not believe him."[135] This belief spread to all the tribal peoples in the south.[136] Living in the midst of such a climate, it would be indeed a surprise if the Taipings did not utilize such an excellent method for the control of the minds of their followers and the masses.

In the section on Christianity, we observed that the personal possession of individuals by demons, which occurs often in the Bible, was not utilized by the Taipings. They instead gave this function to God and Jesus: God took possession of Yang and Jesus took possession of Hsiao. I suggested that the transfer of this demoniac function from the devil to God was influenced by the ambiguity in the meaning of the term *shen*. A better understanding of the native climate in which the Taipings

---

[134] *Ibid.*, hsia/5/69–70.

[135] *Chia-ying chou-chih*, quoted in *Hsün-chou fu-chih*, 8:1a.

[136] Li Shih, "Ch'iung-yai Li-su chih-lüeh," *Kuo-wen chou-pao*, Vol. III, Nos. 41 and 42 (Oct. 24 and 31, 1926); *Hsün-chou fu-chih*, 54:11b; *Chen-an fu-chih*, 8:15a–18b, 25a; Chüeh-mi, "Miao-chiang feng-su chih," *Kuo-wen chou-pao*, Vol. VI, No. 12 (March 31, 1929), p. 2; Hu, *op. cit.*, shang/6/40; *Yung-ning chou-chih*, 3:12b–13a.

lived indicates the probability that the habit of falling into a trance, or of being possessed by God, originated in native sorcery rather than in any other source. This should also clarify the Taiping conception of God, who was apparently more of a demoniac spirit than the spiritual deity of the Christian conception. For in the Bible, neither in the Old Testament nor in the New Testament does God ever use a human person as a medium through whom he speaks: this quality is peculiar to a devil or demon. A spirit or a god speaking through a medium, however, is compatible with Chinese native sorcery.

Chapter XI

Some Rebel Ideologies
Prior to the Taipings[1]

To what degree are elements of the Taiping ideology derived from the ideologies of earlier rebel groups in China? In trying to answer this question, I have not attempted to study all rebellions in the history of China. I have selected only those in which there is evidence of some ideological schemes and those from which the Taipings could have derived some of their ideological elements. By the phrase "ideological schemes" I mean ideas which the rebels used to appeal to their followers or to the people for the purpose of gaining some measure of control over their thought and action. These ideas may be religious beliefs or programs for economic reforms or for political changes. As soon as there is evidence they were used, consciously or unconsciously, as a weapon to influence the mind and conduct of those whose support the rebels wanted to obtain, these ideas become, for my purpose, ideological elements. I have also limited my discussion to those rebellions whose leadership was in the hands of commoners, as it was during the Taiping movement. The arbitrary nature of such criteria is apparent, but these criteria serve to delimit our scope in accordance with our prescribed purpose.

Although we find no positive evidence that the Taipings did take any specific elements from the rebel ideologies, some common characteristics of all rebellions emerge from this study. After investigating the rebellions, we may be able to tell which elements of the Taiping ideology are necessary inherent conditions, the *sine qua non* of all rebellions, and which elements are due to the specific nature of the particular rebellion.

[1] This chapter appeared as an article entitled "Some Chinese Rebel Ideologies" in *T'oung Pao*, Vol. XLIV, Livr. 1–3 (1956), pp. 150–226. It is included here with some changes.

I shall deal with the following rebellions in the order listed: Ch'en Sheng and Wu Kuang (209 B.C.), Liu Pang (209 B.C.), *Ch'ih-mei* (the Red Eyebrows, A.D. 18), *Huang-chin* (Yellow Turbans, A.D. 184), Huang Ch'ao (A.D. 875), Uprisings in the Sung dynasty (A.D. 960–1279), *Pai-lien chiao* and related sects, Rebellions at the end of the Yüan dynasty, the "Roaming Bandits" at the end of the Ming dynasty.

CH'EN SHENG (SHE) AND WU KUANG (SHU)

Ch'en Sheng and Wu Kuang rose in rebellion against the Ch'in dynasty in 209 B.C. The mental make-up of Ch'en and Wu may be gathered from the utterances Ch'en made before the uprising. When young, Ch'en worked as a farm hand. Once he told his companions, "If I should ever become rich and noble, I would not forget you." The other laborers laughed at him and said, "You work as a farm hand. How can you become rich and noble?" With a sigh Ch'en said, "Alas! How can a sparrow know of the ambition of a heron?"[2] Ch'en and Wu were among the 900 conscripts who were sent to station at Ta-tse-hsiang. When they could not make the appointed date, they were in a dilemma: should they accept the punishment of a death sentence for failure to keep the appointed date, or should they rebel? The result of rebellion could not be worse than death, not to speak of the possibility of establishing a new dynasty; so Ch'en and Wu chose rebellion. They persuaded the rest of the group to follow them, and it was then that they asked a startling question: "Are kings, dukes, generals, and prime ministers a race of their own?"[3]

Ch'en and Wu introduced the principle of legitimate succession with its highly emotional appeal to the people; thus they gave their rebellion its rationale.[4] Ch'en Sheng said:

> The world has suffered long under the Ch'in regime. I have heard that Erh-shih is a younger son and should not assume the throne. The rightful heir is Prince Fu-su. But because Fu-su had remonstrated with the emperor a number of times, he was sent out to lead the army. Now some have heard that he was executed by Erh-shih while committing no crime. And the people do not know this. The people, however, have heard of his being

[2] *Shih-chi*, by Ssu-ma Ch'ien, 48:1b.

[3] *Ibid.*, 48:3a–b.

[4] This principle of legitimate succession should not be confused with the principle of legitimacy employed in modern European nations. The Chinese principle appeals more to the emotional loyalty of the people than to the legal aspect of the objective situation.

virtuous. And Hsiang Yen is a Ch'u general and has had many military merits. He loves his soldiers and the people of Ch'u feel for him. Some think that he is dead, but others think that he is a fugitive. Now if we, with our following, should take the initiative to rise in the name of Fu-su and Hsiang Yen, there would be many in the world who would rise in response to us.[5]

And Wu Kuang agreed.

They also followed a soothsayer's suggestion of a way to play upon the religious psychology of the people. They wrote "Ch'en Sheng will be king" in red on a piece of silk and put it in the stomach of a fish. On discovering this in a fish, the soldiers were greatly surprised. Then Ch'en secretly told Wu to go at night to a temple near which the soldiers were stationed. There Wu lighted a lantern and cried like a fox, "Great Ch'u will rise and Ch'en Sheng will be king."[6] After their followers made Ch'en king, Ch'en and Wu exposed the misgovernment of the Ch'in court and capitalized on the desire of the people of different states to re-establish their own states:

It has been several decades since the Ch'in began to oppress the world with its unprincipled government and ruthless laws. In the north there was the building of the Great Wall and in the south there have been the military outposts at Wu-ling [in modern Hunan, Kwangtung, and Fukien]. These created a great turmoil both within and without, driving the people to exhaustion. Grains have been collected according to the number of persons in a family for military expenses. The sources of both wealth and physical energy have been exhausted, and the people are left without any resources. On top of this, the imposition of despotic laws and ruthless punishment has so disturbed the empire that not even fathers and sons can live peaceably together. Now King Ch'en [referring to Ch'en Sheng] has raised his arm to lead the world and has been made king. Within the two thousand li of the territory of Ch'u none does not rise in response to him. Each family may give vent to its own rage and every man may fight for himself to revenge his wrongs and destroy the enemy. In the districts the people have killed magistrates and in the prefectures they have killed the prefects. Ch'u has been expanded and Ch'en has become our king. He has sent Wu Kuang and Chou Wen at the head of one million troops marching west to attack the Ch'in. At an opportune moment like this, should any person fail to get a dukedom, he certainly is not to be reckoned among the brave. Will you ponder on this carefully? The [people of the] world have been for a long time of the same frame of mind, [feeling] that they have suffered miserably from the Ch'in regime. We should take ad-

[5] *Shih-chi*, 48:2a.
[6] *Ibid.*, 48:2b–3a.

vantage of the combined forces of the world to attack the despotic ruler in order to revenge the wrongs that have been done to our fathers and brothers and to carve out territories and land as our own. And this is the one time that we can do it.[7]

Politically the aim of the rebellion was to overthrow "the unprincipled government and ruthless laws" of the Ch'in and to obtain the power to rule for themselves. For this we may call the rebellion a political revolt, aiming at the change of persons in control of the power machine without any scheme to effect changes either in the social structure or in the institutional systems of the time. The means Ch'en and Wu adopted to make this political aim appeal to the people were the application of the principle of legitimate succession; the promise of a virtuous government as implied by the statement that Fu-su, the legitimate heir to the Ch'in throne, was virtuous; and psychological manipulation of the people aiming at mental control. They appealed to the people's fear of the ruthlessness of the Ch'in regime, to their desire for revenge, to their hope and ambition for a better lot, and to their religious instinct and credulity. The practice of fabricating evidence prognosticating future events and suggesting the fabricators' right to rule by order of supernatural power or the will of Heaven began here.

Socially, there seems to have emerged a vague sense of equality expressed in the question, "Are kings, dukes, generals, and prime ministers a race of their own?" This struck at the root of the idea of rule by birth. It seems that Ch'en and Wu believed birth gave no distinction to anybody. However, this should not be construed to mean that they believed in equality for all or that they aimed at the abolition of social classes. It was merely an expression of a personal desire to be equal with those in power, a personal sentiment rather than an awakening grasp of a new principle. Inasmuch as Ch'en did not accept birth as a principle in political or social stratification, his idea was truly revolutionary.[8]

The economic structure their society was to assume was indicated by Ch'en and Wu's use of such phrases as *ko-ti* (to carve out land or ter-

---

[7] *Ibid.*, 89:3a–b.

[8] Historians tell us that by the time of Ch'in Shih-huang-ti (221–210 B.C.) Chinese *feng-chien* had completely collapsed. This implies that birth was no longer a principle of stratification. In fact, many noble families had long before this disappeared or become commoners. But the people's memory of hereditary rights was still fresh. Witness the vain attempt at the beginning of the Ch'in to restore the *feng-chien* system. It is in this milieu that we call Ch'en's idea revolutionary.

ritory) and *yu-t'u* (to own land). They apparently had in mind the economic setup which prevailed either at the time or not very long before. The phrase "to seek dukedom," though in common use, does not necessarily suggest a return to the *feng-chien* ("feudal") system, since even during the Later Han people were still seeking "dukedom." It could suggest a sort of regional autonomy, something similar to the states which existed in the Chou period. Or it could be simply an expression of the desire on the part of the unfortunate to become landowners; for since the time land was declared alienable, a steady process of concentration in the hands of a few had resulted in ruthless stripping of land from the majority of the people. In either case, it is certain that Ch'en and Wu had no new idea in connection with the land system.

A religious ideology was not created by Ch'en and Wu. They did exploit popular patterns of religious thought, which were the result of a long process of unconscious assimilation by the Chinese people, for their own political ends. The idea of the mandate of Heaven and the idea that "whenever an emperor or king is about to arise, Heaven must first manifest some favorable omen to the common people"[9] were part and parcel of the Chinese Weltanschauung. This universal appeal of religion to human instinct has made nearly all leaders of Chinese rebellions religion-conscious.

Although this ideology and that of the Taipings have a great deal in common, there is no evidence that the Taipings derived anything specific from the ideology of Ch'en and Wu. Politically, the leaders of these two uprisings had the same aim: to overthrow the existing power on account of its oppression and ruthlessness. Both employed the principle of legitimate succession supported by the people's religious credulity, which they exploited with great success. Both appealed to the people to take revenge for the wrongs that had been done to their fathers and brothers. They both had a vague sense of social equality and yet had not grasped the real significance of the concept. In the two land systems there is the same appeal to the desire of the people for landownership. In form the Taiping ideology has a great deal in common with the ideology of Ch'en and Wu, but there is nothing in the specific content of the Taiping ideology that could have been borrowed from Ch'en and Wu.

Liu Pang

Liu Pang's ideology is comparatively simple. He was confronted with

[9] Lü Pu-wei, *Lü-shih ch'un-ch'iu*, 13:126.

the same dilemma that confronted Ch'en and Wu, and like them he chose to revolt in 209 B.C. He had no strong political convictions of his own. When serving under *corvée* at Hsien-yang, he observed the pompous array of Shih-huang-ti. This aroused in him no sense of indignation, but on the contrary drew the admiring sigh: "Alas! This is what a man should be."[10] He harbored the same despisal of aristocracy which Ch'en and Wu had exhibited before him. He also relied on propaganda based on Ch'in's bad government and cruel laws to win a following. But he did have something to offer. When in 206 B.C. he arrived at Pa-shang (in present Shensi) ahead of the other forces, he promised the people a life free from too much government interference.

> [Liu said,] "I have an agreement with the other lords to the effect that he who first entered the Pass [guarding the Ch'in capital] shall be king within the Pass. [According to this agreement] I shall be king here. I shall make a covenant with you, elders of the land. There will be only three items of law: he who kills shall die, and he who hurts other people and he who steals from people shall be subject to retribution. All the rest of the Ch'in law shall be abrogated. The officials are expected to work as usual. The purpose of my coming is to rid you of your misery and not to bring you calamity. There is no need of fear. Furthermore, the reason I came back to station at Pa-shang is to wait for the coming of all the lords [of the different states] for a conference to work out a system of rule."
>
> With this, he sent officers to the *hsien, hsiang,* and *i* [administrative units] with the original Ch'in officials to proclaim the same idea to the people.[11]

This promise was apparently very effective, for the people of Ch'in were greatly pleased and vied with one another in bringing beef, mutton, and wine to entertain Liu's army.[12] But P'ei-kung (Liu) would not accept their gifts: "[Liu said,] 'We have plenty of grain and are not in need [of anything]. We do not wish you people to spend anything on us.' The people were all the more pleased, and were greatly concerned lest Liu should not be their king."[13]

Liu also employed effectively the principle of legitimate succession to win the support of the fighting forces of the various states. In 205 B.C. Hsiang Yü, Liu's chief opponent, killed I-ti, the emperor who was enthroned at the head of the forces opposing the Ch'in. When Liu heard of

[10] *Shih-chi*, 8:3a.
[11] *Ibid.*, 8:15b–16a.
[12] *Ibid.*, 8:16a.
[13] *Ibid.*, 8:16a.

the murder, he bared his arms and cried and wore mourning for the emperor. On the third day, he sent messengers to all the fighting forces of the various states with the following message:

The world united in crowning I-ti as emperor and [promised] to serve him. Now Hsiang Yü first exiled I-ti to Chiang-nan and then murdered him. This regicide is a great crime, completely devoid of principle. I have proclaimed mourning for I-ti, requesting all dukes to wear white. I have also ordered all my troops in the Pass and all soldiers in the district of San-ho [three rivers, referring to the territory of Ch'in] to stand by ready to sail down Rivers Chiang and Han, with the desire to follow the various dukes and kings in an expedition against the one who murdered I-ti.[14]

From his admiration for the pompous array of Ch'in Shih-huang, one may draw the conclusion that Liu Pang's only new political idea was the obvious one that the ruthless legalistic government of the Ch'in should be somewhat softened. His idea of making a covenant with the people, however, had never been expressed before his time. In view of the subsequent history of the Han dynasty, we cannot take this idea very seriously. The people, especially the elders, had been consulted by the government as early as the Chou, or at least it was so reported by tradition.[15] But in Liu's case, the people were given a promise and their opinion was not sought. What was called a "covenant" (yüeh) amounted to no more than a promise offered by one of the parties; and the other party—the people—had to accept it with gratitude, for they were not in a position to strike a bargain. The promise constituted Liu's positive suggestion as a substitute for the harsh and ruthless laws of the Ch'in. In this sense, leaders of most rebellions gave the same kind of promise.

To play upon the religious beliefs of the people, many stories were circulated for the purpose of creating an atmosphere around Liu which would awe the people into believing that he was their ruler by the mandate of Heaven. One story, told in the words of an old woman, described Liu killing a snake: "My son was the son of the White Emperor. He transformed himself into a snake and occupied the path. Now he has been killed by the son of the Red Emperor. This is why I am crying."[16]

[14] *Ibid.*, 8:20b.
[15] *Chou-li chu-shu*, "Hsiang-ta-fu" and "Hsiang-lao" under "Ti-kuan," and "Hsiao-ssu-k'ou" under "Ch'iu-kuan"; *Tso-chuan*, Duke Hsiang 31, Duke Chou 24, Duke Ting 8, and Duke Ai 1.
[16] *Shih-chi*, 8:5b–6a.

Another story told of the mysterious clouds hovering above him;[17] a third, of the supernatural circumstances under which he was conceived;[18] and a fourth, of a dragon appearing on top of him when he became drunk and fell asleep.[19]

Liu did not have any ideas of a new social order. However, contrary to the current attitude, he had a very low opinion of scholars during the predynastic days. His attitude was later modified when he was shown the value of these scholars in their possible service to the state. The principle of bifurcation of the people into ruling and ruled, which originated with Mencius,[20] had served the rulers very well after the time of Mencius. When Liu expressed his contempt for the scholars he was scoffing at an idea the validity of which had been long established. Even Mencius had spoken of the idea as a "universal idea" 天下之通義也.[21] The success with which these scholars persuaded Liu of their value augured well for the future of their group.

The unique points about Liu's rebellion are the idea of a covenant and his attitude toward scholars. The Taipings similarly made promises to their followers in connection with the segregation of sexes, land distribution, and happiness in the life to come. At the initial stages of their movement, they did their best not to disrupt the economy. Their military regulations forbade their soldiers to disturb the peace of the land they occupied, and there is ample evidence to indicate that the soldiers at the beginning of their campaign strictly observed these regulations. The Taipings gave the people the same impression that they did not want to be a burden to them as Liu gave to the people of Ch'in when he refused their offer of food. Hung's opinion of scholars was not very high at the start; and it was actual experience in government which brought him, too, to the realization of the value of scholars' service. But the similarities again are more formal than material. We cannot with any degree of certainty point out any specific elements in the Taiping ideology as in any way connected with that of Liu.

CH'IH-MEI (RED EYEBROWS)

Fan Ts'ung and his group, known as *Ch'ih-mei*, rebelled in A.D. 18.

---

[17] *Ibid.*, 8:6a–b.
[18] *Ibid.*, 8:2a.
[19] *Ibid.*, 8:3a.
[20] *Meng-tzu yin-te*, 20/3A/4.
[21] *Ibid.*

They used only two principles, and these may both be classified as political. First, employing the principle of legitimate succession, they made Liu P'en-tzu, a descendant of the royal family, emperor.[22] Thus fortified, they hoped to combat the forces of Liu Hsiu (later Emperor Kuang-wu), who was himself an upstart, being very distantly related to the royal family. They sought prestige by building up Liu P'en-tzu's claim to the throne on the sanction of antiquity. " Ts'ung [Fan Ts'ung, the leader of the rebellion] and his followers said: 'We have heard that the Son of Heaven in ancient times was known as *Shang-chiang-chün* [general of the highest order] when he commanded the troops.' So they wrote *Shang-chiang-chün* on a slip to be used as an [identification] tally."[23]

Secondly, Fan Ts'ung struck an agreement with his followers during the first years of rebellion to the effect that he who killed people would be executed and he who hurt people would be subject to retribution.[24] Even though this agreement differs from that of Liu in that Liu made his with the people while Fan made his with his own followers, their aim seems similar: both were anxious to win the people's support. It is true that Fan Ts'ung's troops had been plundering and looting, but this could have been because Fan did not have full control of his forces. The very agreement he made with them seems to suggest just this. At any rate, in spite of all their plundering and looting, his forces were not as great a scourge to the people as were the forces of Wang Mang.[25]

To distinguish them from the forces of Wang Mang, Fan Ts'ung ordered his troops to paint their eyebrows red. If we remember that Liu Pang, the first emperor of the Han, was referred to as "the son of the Red Emperor," the reason for this choice of red is not difficult to understand. This was an attempt to obtain an added sanction on the basis of legitimate succession.[26]

Apart from what has been said about the previous rebellions, very little can be added from a comparison of Fan Ts'ung's ideology with that of the Taipings. The Taipings also chose the color red as their distinguishing mark. But then, many other rebellions after the Red Eye-

---

[22] *Han-shu, chüan* 99, *hsia,* p. 33b; Yüan Shu, *T'ung-chien chi-shih pen-mo,* 6:3b.

[23] Yüan, *op. cit., chüan* 13 and 14.

[24] *Ibid.*

[25] *Ibid.*

[26] For a new explanation of the "Red Eyebrows," see Hans Bielenstein, "The Restoration of the Han Dynasty," *Museum of Far Eastern Antiquities Bulletin,* No. 26 (1954), p. 139.

brows had done the same thing, especially during the end of the Yüan dynasty.

HUANG-CHIN (YELLOW TURBANS)[27]

The leader of the *Huang-chin* (Yellow Turban) rebellion was Chang Chüeh. He was a Taoist who taught the people by means of magical healing. The patients were told to kneel and confess their wrongdoings. His teaching was known as *T'ai-p'ing tao*. He sent out disciples to all parts to teach and had tremendous success. The following is recorded about him:

> In the sixth year of Kuang-huo [183], during the reign of Han Lin-ti: At first Chang Chüeh of Chü-lu [in present Hupeh], a worshiper of Huang-Lao [Taoism], taught people by means of magical arts. His teaching was known as *T'ai-p'ing tao*. He healed sickness with charmed water. The patients were told to kneel and confess their sins. Occasionally the patients were cured. The people looked up to him as to a deity and believed in him. Chüeh sent his disciples out in four directions to deceive the people. In a period of over ten years he collected a following numbering several hundred thousand. People came from the following eight *chou*: Ch'ing [in present Shantung], Hsü [northwestern Kiangsu], Yu [Hupeh and Manchuria], Chi [Hupeh], Ching [Hunan, Hupeh, and southeastern Szechwan], Yang [Kiangsu, Anhwei, Chekiang, Kiangsi, and Fukien], Yen [southwestern Hupeh and northwestern Shantung], and Yü [Honan] in response to his call. Some gave up or sold their property to come to him. They filled and obstructed the roads. Tens of thousands of them died of sickness before they arrived. Officials of different districts and prefectures did not understand the reason; they said that Chüeh had good influence on the people and therefore had won their hearts.[28]

Huang organized thirty-six *fang* 方 : a *fang* is comparable to that which is under the command of a general. A great *fang* was composed of over ten thousand men, and a small one of six or seven thousand. Each *fang* had its own chief.[29]

[27] Henri Maspero gives an excellent account of the "Yellow Turbans" in his *Mélanges posthumes sur les religions et l'histoire de la Chine*, II, "Le Taoïsme," pp. 149–56.

[28] *Hou-Han-shu*, 101:1a–b; Yüan, *T'ung-chien chi-shih pen-mo*, 8:79a–b.

[29] *Hou-Han-shu*, 101:1b. Maspero interprets *fang* 方 as "circonscriptions," in *op. cit.*, II, 44, 152; and he also thinks of *fang* as a title. He says, on page 44: "A la tête de chacune de ces circonscriptions, il avait placé un Adepte pourvu du titre de *fang*," which, however is to be interpreted "au sens de Régionnaire." This interpretation is repeated on page 152; here Maspero says: "Ce terme [*fang*], qui désigne les recettes magiques, paraît signifier ici un Magicien, mais je n'en suis pas absolument sûr." In spite of this uncertainty, Maspero continues to render *fang* as "Magiciens."

Chang's revolt was heralded by a rumor to the effect that the azure heaven had already died and that the yellow heaven was in line to be erected, and in the year of *chia-tzu* (184) the world would experience great happiness.

The rebels used human sacrifice to worship heaven.[30] And all Chang's men wore yellow turbans as their symbol.

Chang gave himself the title *t'ien-kung chiang-chün* to his brother Pao, *ti-kung chiang-chün*, and to his other brother Liang 良 , *jen-kung chiang-chün*.[31]

Here for the first time we have on record a military organization of a rebellion. A *fang* is a military unit, with the three brothers at the head as the "Three Kung." But we know nothing about how the different *fang* were related.

The most important ideological element of this rebellion is religious in nature. It may be analyzed into: (1) Taoism, (2) the use of magical art in healing, (3) the idea of wrongdoing coming very close to what the West would call sin, (4) the emphasis on confession, and (5) a religious myth, suggesting that they also used the theme of the mandate of Heaven.

Their Taoism is based on a text entitled *T'ai-p'ing ch'ing-ling shu*, also known as *T'ai-p'ing ching*.[32] As this text is of particular interest to us because of its title, I shall attempt here an analysis of the content, based on *Hou-Han-shu* and its commentary and the studies made by Professor T'ang and Koyanagi.

The *Hou-Han-shu* says:

> The spiritual work presented previously by Kung Ts'ung has specifically the following as its foundation: to serve heaven and earth and live in accordance with the five elements. In it are found also the arts of making a state great and one's descendants many. Its language is easy to understand, and it has a great deal in common with the classics.[33]

---

[30] Yüan, *T'ung-chien chi-shih pen-mo*, 101:2a.

[31] *Ibid.*

[32] The identity of these two works was stated in the biography of Hsiang-K'ai in *Hou-Han-shu*, *chüan* 60, *hsia*, p. 24a and commentary by Chang-huai t'ai-tzu of the T'ang; identity was established in modern times by Professor T'ang Yung-t'ung in his "Tu T'ai-p'ing ching so-chien," *Kuo-hsüeh chi-k'an*, Vol. V (1935), No.1; Koyanagi Shigeta 小柳司氣太 of Japan also made a notable contribution in this respect, and he is quoted by Fu Ch'ing-chia in his *Chung-kuo tao-chiao shih*, pp. 57–76.

[33] *Hou-Han-shu*, *chüan* 60, *hsia*, p. 22a.

Then the commentary quotes *T'ai-p'ing ching*:

A *chen-jen* [true man] asks a *shen-jen* [spiritual man], "Can you enlighten me on the art which would enable an emperor to achieve peace [*t'ai-p'ing*] immediately?"

Shen-jen says, "In order to achieve peace immediately, one needs only to follow the *Tao* of T'ien [heaven] and *ti* [earth] without discrepancy. *Yüan-ch'i* [the primeval breaths] are three: the great *yang*, the great *yin*, and the harmony. There are three physical forms: T'ien, *ti*, and *jen* [man]. T'ien has three names: the sun, the moon, and the stars, and the north pole is at the center. *Ti* has three names: mountains, rivers, and plain. *Jen* has three names: father, mother, and sons [children]. And there are three names in government: the monarch, the ministers, and the people. When the three completely agree without the slightest discrepancy and all of them share the same anxiety and form one family, there is no doubt that peace will be achieved immediately and life span will be prolonged.[34]

This quotation gives a glimpse of the aims of the *T'ai-ping ching*, one of which is to secure peace. Could it be that the title of the work was based on this desire?

In general spirit *T'ai-ping ching* is Taoistic. It maintains that there are three physical forms: T'ien, *ti*, and *jen*. *Tao* pertains to T'ien, *te* pertains to *ti*, and *jen* (仁 feeling of humanity) pertains to *jen* (man 人). *T'ai-p'ing ching* emphasizes quietude and nonaction as the art of ruling, and *jen* as a necessary qualification of a ruler. It stresses the importance of a desireless state. It believes that the heaven and earth and the ten thousand things received their being from *yüan-ch'i*, which is none other than empty and nonactive nature. The interplay of the *yin* and the *yang* and the schematic working of the five elements are all in accordance with nature, a spontaneous process. Man in his action should not run counter to heaven. In everything he should work in accordance with the principles of *yin* and *yang* and the five elements. It also states that the *t'ai-p'ing-ch'i* (peace air) is about to arrive, and a ruler of great virtue will appear, and the spirit will through him descend upon the earth.

T'ai-ping ching attacks Buddhism for the four destructive actions: (1) not being filial to parents, whom the Buddhists neglect; (2) deserting wives and children, thus avoiding the function of producing and causing posterity to be cut short; (3) making food of excrement; and (4) begging. However, *T'ai-p'ing ching* is not entirely free from Buddhist influence. Even though it does not talk about *karma*, it has a theory known as

[34] *Ibid.*

ch'eng-fu (承負 to inherit and be responsible for). It believes that what one does will affect the fate of his descendants. By this belief it tries to explain why Yen Hui died so young and Tao-che lived to such a long life. There is also the belief that one becomes a ghost after death. It is of prime importance to have descendants to administer to the needs of ancestors' ghosts. So it makes the lack of posterity one of the chief punishments for not following the principle of *Tao*.

T'ai-p'ing ching is opposed to the destruction of female children, not so much for any humane reason as for a unique reason. A man must be assisted on both sides, the right and the left; thus it is imperative that he should have two wives. The destroying of female children makes it impossible for man to get what is his due.

It attacks war as being destructive, for war discourages production of children. The value of each individual is measured in terms of the number of children he bears.

The Taoistic method of "preserving the one" is used to achieve the result of immortality, of becoming a loyal minister and a filial son, and to rid one of all sickness.[35]

From this summary some of the things which the Yellow Turbans did can be explained. The myth about the yellow heaven about to be erected and the great happiness to be experienced in the year *chia-tzu* seem to be inspired by the idea of the anticipated *t'ai-p'ing-ch'i* and by the virtuous ruler who would appear. The designations *t'ien-kung*, *ti-kung*, and *jen-kung* conform to the three parts of *yüan-ch'i*.

The Yellow Turbans seem not to have carried out the scheme laid down in the *T'ai-p'ing ching*. Professor T'ang points out that Chang Chüeh did many things contrary to its teachings. His military activities and plundering were in direct conflict with the antiwar spirit and the conception of *t'ai-p'ing-ch'i*. Human sacrifice is absent from the teachings of the text. The yellow color, which seems to have been taken from the myth of yellow heaven, suggests earth instead of fire as the virtue told in the text of the forthcoming new reign.[36]

The extraordinary feature of Chang Chüeh's ideology is the conception of sin and the idea of confession. No rebellion until the Taiping has

[35] *T'ai-p'ing ching ho-chiao*, ed. Wang Ming, pp. 409–23. This synopsis is also given in T'ang Yung-t'ung, *Han wei liang-chin nan-pei-ch'ao fu-chiao-shih*, I, 57–59.

[36] For the correlation between the five elements and colors and for an explanation of the rise of dynasties in accordance with the ascendancy of the elements, see Fung [Feng] Yu-lan, *A History of Chinese Philosophy*, I, 161–63 and II, 58ff.

anything parallel to this. And sickness is made to appear as a symptom of sin. There is little in Chang's ideology that may be called political, social, or economic.

There is little in the *T'ai-p'ing ching* text that resembles the Taiping ideology, but the term *t'ai-p'ing* would make one suspect that the Taipings may have borrowed it from this Taoist text. Also, Chang Chüeh called his teaching *t'ai-p'ing tao*. Can there be anything more than a common desire to achieve peace between the Taipings and Chang Chüeh in the choice of the term *t'ai-p'ing* for their respective use?

Some of Chang Chüeh's ideas which were operative during the rebellious campaign do resemble Taiping ideas. There is no doubt that the Taipings' idea of sin came from Christianity, even though they did not understand the profound issue involved. But Chang Chüeh's idea of sin and confession, if the Taipings knew about it, could have prepared the way for the invasion of the Christian idea.

The worship of T'ien and the idea that one's happiness is bound up with his obedience to the way of T'ien also suggest elements present in Taiping ideology. But such ideas were so prevalent in China that the Taipings could have picked them up anywhere without going back to the Yellow Turbans.

Chang Chüeh used religious practices as a political camouflage. For over ten years the officials were in the dark as to the real purpose of Chang's movement. Chang's may have been a genuine religious movement, but he definitely also employed religious activity as a political camouflage, intentionally designed to deceive the government; this political employment of religion seems to have emerged in the Yellow Turban Rebellion for the first time in Chinese history. Its success was tremendous. The government's suspicion of any religious group in the subsequent ages indicates the widespread use of such a tactic. The parallel to the Taipings is striking, as the Taipings were definitely using religion to camouflage politics when they disguised themselves as God-Worshipers.

Uprisings at the End of the Western Chin Dynasty

The uprisings during the end of the Western Chin dynasty have very few ideological elements. Besides the usual reasons for rebellious activities, such as government corruption, land concentration, and natural calamities, there was one phenomenon which is closely parallel to the feud between the Hakkas and the Puntis, the feud which was respon-

sible for many Hakkas' joining the Taipings. Of the five uprisings which are analyzed by Wu Hsien-ch'ing, three were due to feuds between natives and new arrivals driven from their homeland either by wars or by natural calamities.[37]

HUANG CH'AO

Huang Ch'ao, a salt merchant, rose in rebellion in 875 in response to Wang Hsien-chih, who revolted the previous year. Since Huang's rebellion was a result of famine, government corruption, heavy taxation, and failure on the part of the government to give just reward and punishment, his ideology centers around economic factors.[38] However, he offered no program except that he wanted to clean up the court and give the people some reprieve. He said when he entered the capital: "King Huang is for the people; he is not like the House of Li [the T'ang] who does not take care of you. You may enjoy peace at home."[39]

His respect for scholars may have come from the fact that he himself was supposedly quite a scholar.[40] Chao I in his *Nien-erh-shih cha-chi* makes this respect for scholars one of the many common characteristics of Huang Ch'ao and Li Tzu-ch'eng.[41]

The religious element of the mandate of Heaven is again present. In 880 when Emperor Hsi-tsung changed the title of his reign from *Ch'ien-fu* to *Kuang-ming*, Huang Ch'ao saw the will of Heaven manifested in the new title. His interpretation of the two characters contained in the title made him the Heaven-appointed successor to the T'ang.[42] This apparently came true, for in that very year he captured Ch'ang-an, the capital. On his ascension to the throne, court ladies prostrated themselves before him and addressed him as *Huang Wang* (King Huang). Ch'ao was very happy and said, "This is probably the will of Heaven."[43]

His idea of T'ien may be gathered from the title he and his followers gave to himself. At the beginning it was *ch'ung-t'ien ta-chiang-chün* (great

---

[37] Wu Hsien-ch'ing, "Hsi-chin mo ti liu-min pao-tung," *Shih-huo pan-yüeh k'an*, Vol. I, No. 6 (Feb. 16, 1935), pp. 3–7. For a study of Buddhist rebels during the Northern Wei period, see Tsukamoto Zenryū, "Hokugi no Bukkyō hi," in *Shina Bukkyō shi kenkyū, Hokugi hen*, pp. 243–91.

[38] *Chiu T'ang-shu, chüan* 200, *hsia*, p. 7b; *Hsin T'ang-shu, chüan* 225, *hsia*, pp. 1a, 2b

[39] *Chiu T'ang-shu, chüan* 200, *hsia*, p. 10a; *Hsin T'ang-shu, chüan* 225, *hsia*, p. 8b.

[40] *Hsin T'ang-shu, chüan* 225, *hsia*, pp. 4a, 1a.

[41] *Nien-erh-shih cha-chi*, "Huang Ch'ao Li Tzu-ch'eng," 20:25b–26b.

[42] *Hsin T'ang-shu, chüan* 225, *hsia*, p. 8b; *Chiu T'ang-shu, chüan* 200, *hsia*, p. 10a.

[43] *Hsin T'ang-shu, chüan* 225, *hsia*, p. 8a.

Heaven-attacking general)[44] and later *t'ien-pu ta-chiang-chün* (great Heaven-appointed general).[45] Earlier he thought of himself as attacking Heaven, which was conceived to be on the side of the reigning power. But later when his army was on the point of taking the eastern capital (Lo-yang) in 880, he took the second title, clearly indicating the change of his attitude toward Heaven, which was then on his side. In either case, he conceived of Heaven as a power responsible for the fate of a dynasty.

In *Chiu T'ang-shu* the author made the following remarks: "When Ch'ao rose in rebellion, many scholars joined him. In his proclamations and memorials, he always directed his attention to the government corruption; in them were found expressions of those who have had the experience of frustration."[46] This coupled with the fact that the rebels (both Wang Hsien-chih and Huang Ch'ao) asked for high appointment as a price for giving up rebellious conduct shows that these rebels had no new ideas concerning the political setup, economic organization, or social structure of the time. It is a question whether they had any ideas at all. The way they massacred the people and plundered the cities showed that their promise to give them a better lot was mere propaganda which they could hardly expect the people to believe. Immediately after they assured the people that they would be interested in their welfare unlike the family of Li who did not take care of the people, they started to plunder and loot.[47] Apparently it was not their intention to try to eliminate the conditions which brewed rebellions.

Apart from the vaguely implied conception of the mandate of Heaven, the only parallel that can be drawn between the Taiping leaders and Huang Ch'ao is that they were frustrated scholars. But it would be naïve to infer from this parallel that the Taipings were inspired by the example of Huang Ch'ao. Firstly, frustration in itself is a factor potent as dynamite to set off a conflagration when certain circumstances exist; and secondly, the Taiping leaders expressly disapproved of the conduct of Huang Ch'ao and Li Ch'uang.[48]

---

[44] Yüan, *T'ung-chien chi-shih pen-mo*, 37:7b; *Hsin T'ang-shu*, *chüan* 225, *hsia*, p. 3b; *Chiu T'ang-shu*, *chüan* 220, *hsia*, p. 8a.

[45] Yüan, *op. cit.*, 37:13b.

[46] *Chiu T'ang-shu*, *chüan* 200, *hsia*, p. 8a–b.

[47] *Hsin T'ang-shu*, *chüan* 225, *hsia*, p. 8b.

[48] "T'ai-p'ing chao-shu," in Hsiao I-shan (compiler), *T'ai-p'ing t'ien-kuo ts'ung-shu*, *ts'e* 1, p. 3a, says: "Those who love to kill are called 'grass bandits'; they will not escape calamity after all. . . . Where are Huang Ch'ao and Li Ch'uang now?"

Uprisings in the Sung Dynasty[49]

In 993 Wang Hsiao-po led the poverty-stricken people of Szechwan in revolt against the concentration of wealth in the hands of a few. His slogan was: "I hate the unequal distribution of wealth. I shall now equalize it for you."[50] But we hear nothing about his actual program.

The Reappearance of T'ai-p'ing tao

Chang Chüeh's *T'ai-p'ing tao* reappeared during the reign of Che-tsung of the Sung, which began in 1086. Fang Shao, in his *Ch'ing-hsi k'ou-kuei*, reports:

> Chang Chüeh and Chang Yen of the Later Han, in the name of the Taoist Pope Tao-lin as their distant originator, established a chief to practice healing. Those who contributed five *tou* of rice would be healed. This was called the principle of five *tou* of rice. As they grew in strength, they robbed *chou* and *hsien* and stopped at nothing. Their followers at present eat vegetables and worship the devil, and they gather at night and scatter in the daytime. When worshiping the devil they always face north, because Chang Chüeh rose in the north.[51]

Chuang Chi-yü of the Sung gives us a record of the nature of the revived *T'ai-p'ing tao* group in his *Chi-le pien* in *Shuo-fu*:

> Devil worship and vegetarian diet sect is very strictly prohibited by laws. The family members of the worshipers, although they may not be aware of the affiliation, will be exiled to a distant land, and half of their property will be given to the exposer and the other half confiscated. Recently worshipers have grown [in number]. Originating from Fukien, the sect spread to Wenchow [in Chekiang] and the two Che [eastern and southern Chekiang]. When Fang La rose in rebellion in Muchou [in Chekiang], its believers rose everywhere in response to one another. I have been told of their practice. They prohibit meat-eating and wine-drinking, worship no spirits, no Buddha, and no ancestors. . . . When dead, one is buried naked. When about to be put in the coffin, the corpse is fully dressed. Two followers are seated each on one side of the corpse. One asks: "Did you have a cap when you came?" The other answers: "No." They then remove the cap from the corpse. Thus one item after another is taken off, until nothing is left. Then one of them asks: "What did you have when you came?" "Placenta." So a cloth sack is used to hold the corpse.

[49] See T'ao Hsi-sheng's article "Sung-tai ti ko-chung pao-tung," in *Chung-shan wen-hua chiao-yü-kuan chi-k'an*, Vol. I, No. 2 (Winter, 1934), pp. 671–81.

[50] *Sung-shih*, compiled by T'o T'o *et al.*, biography of Fan Chih-ku, 276:12a.

[51] *Ch'ing-hsi k'ou-kuei*, pp. 3b–4a. This account is also included in another work of Fang Shao entitled *Po-chai pien*, which exists in two editions.

Some became rich after taking up the faith. The people are ignorant, not knowing that when one drinks no wine, eats no meat, gives neither feast nor sacrifice, and does not indulge in extravagant funerals, one will naturally become rich. When new members are very poor, the others generally contribute small sums to their support. Small though the sum may be, through accumulation they in time become well-to-do. When a member travels and passes any place, even if he is not known to the members of that place he is housed and fed. People and things are used without distinction, and they speak of themselves as of one family. So they often talk about the idea of "unobstructed." This is used to lure the people. The chief is known as mo-wang [devil king], his assistants are known as mo-weng and mo-mu [devil fathers and devil mothers]. Each and all are engaged in luring people [to join them]. On the first and the fifteenth of each month each member burns incense at mo-wang's place and pays forty-nine cash [as incense money]. Mo-mu will then collect the money and from time to time present it to mo-wang. They collect quite a large sum in a year. They chant the Diamond Sūtra; believing that it is heretic to get truth about self through its external form [idols], they do not worship either spirits or Buddha. But they worship the sun and the moon, believing that they are real Buddha. In explaining the Sūtra, they often change the reading [of the text] and read what belongs to one sentence along with another. Thus fa p'ing-teng, wu-yu kao-hsia [法平等，無有高下 in Dharma there is equality, and there is neither high nor low] is read fa p'ing-teng wu, yu kao-hsia 法平 [等無，有高下 in Dharma there is no equality, and there is high and low]. The common people take mo 魔 to be ma 麻 and call the chief ma-huang 麻黄. Some believe that it is the name of I-wang 易王.[52]

At the beginning they were very serious about the laws they imposed and the oaths they took. Because they consider Chang Chüeh their originator, they dare not say the character chüeh 角 even if they have to die for not saying it.... They also say life is misery; to kill people is to save them from misery. Those who save many people will attain Buddhahood. Therefore as they grow in number, they take advantage of the uprisings [of the time] to rise in rebellion. The greatest danger is their delight in killing. They hate the Buddhists, because their [Buddhists'] prohibition against killing is opposed to their principle.[53]

The time during which the uprising took place is identified by the mention of an official whose name is Ho Chih-chung, second-class assistant chou magistrate of T'ai-chou in Chekiang during the first years of the reign of Che-tsung (1086–1100).

In spite of their claim that Chang Chüeh was their originator, the

[52] I cannot identify this name.
[53] Chuang Chi-yü, Chi-le pien in Shuo-fu, compiled by T'ao Tsung-i, pp. 13b–31a. This is also quoted in Fang, Ch'ing-hsi k'uo kuei, pp. 8b–10a.

ideology of this group has little in common either with Chang Chüeh's teachings or with the *T'ai-p'ing ching*, supposedly the text on which Chang based his teachings. However, as an ideological system, it is interesting in its own right. Many elements may be characterized as Buddhistic: the use of the *Diamond Sūtra*, the condemnation of knowledge gained through external sources, the idea that one brings nothing to this world and hence should not take anything to the next world, the belief that life is a source of misery, vegetarianism, the common sharing of property, and their aim at the attainment of Buddhahood. The term "Buddhahood," of course, need not have the same connotation as it has with the Buddhists. It was a popular term for salvation, and the rebel group appropriated it to express just that. Although the adoption of the term in itself does not make rebels or their idea Buddhistic, it seems that the concepts enumerated here contain enough Buddhist elements to justify us in describing them as Buddhistic.

At the same time, the members attacked Buddhism because Buddhism forbade them to kill. They expressly denounced Buddha along with other spirits as an object of worship. Their conception of killing as a form of administering salvation to people is alien to any system of thought, not only to Buddhism. Among the spirits which they discarded as objects of worship are ancestral spirits. This definitely non-Confucian attitude points to assimilation of ideas non-Chinese in their origin. Their worship of the sun and the moon as something more than spirits similar to many other spirits like those of the mountains and rivers seems to confirm this assimilation. Probably Mazdaism and Manichaeism, which had been introduced into China before this time, influenced their thought. The phrase *ch'ih-ts'ai shih-mo* (吃菜事魔 vegetarian diet and devil worship), a phrase identical in characters and meaning though differing in order of the component parts from what is applied to the revived *T'ai-p'ing tao* group, was also applied to *Mo-ni chiao* (摩尼教 Manichaeism).[54] From the fact that the members worshiped the sun, it would

[54] Shigematsu Toshiaki, "Ch'u-ch'i ti pai-lien chiao-hui," translated by T'ao Hsi-sheng, in *Shih-huo pan-yüeh k'an*, Vol. I, No. 4, p. 28. In the quotation from Chuang Chi-yü's *Chi-le pien* the phrase "devil worship and vegetarian diet" was applied to the rebellious group who claimed Chang Chüeh as their originator. And the people at the time had already called Manichaeism "vegetarian diet and devil worship." Through the link of vegetarianism, the phrase in its reverse form came to be applied by the people to the present group. For more details on Manichaeism, see: M. Chavannes and P. Pelliot, "Un traité manichéen retrouvé en Chine," *Journal Asiatique*, Series 10, Vol. XVIII (Nov.-Dec., 1911), pp. 499–617 and Series 11, Vol. I (Jan.-Feb., 1913), pp. 7–199 and (March-April, 1913), pp. 8–394; Ch'en Yüan, "Mo-ni chiao ju Chung-

seem more probable that the revised *T'ai-p'ing tao* sect is linked with Mazdaism, even though the sun and the moon could be symbols of the principle of light of Manichaeism.

---

kuo k'ao," *Kuo-hsüeh chi-k'an*, Vol. I (1923), No. 2, pp. 203–40; "Mo-ni chiao ts'an. ching," author unknown, *Kuo-hsüeh chi-k'an*, Vol. I (1923), No. 3, pp. 531–46; Hsü Ti-shan, "Mo-ni chih erh-tsung san chi lun," *Yenching Journal of Chinese Studies*, No. 3 (1928), pp. 383–402.

The identification of the *ch'ih-ts'ai shih-mo* group with Manichaeism has been a debated question. Ch'en Yüan said in 1923 in *op. cit.*, p. 230: "Whether what the Sung scholars called *ch'ih-ts'ai shih-mo* was Manichaeism, or whether it included also the sects White Lotus and White Clouds, is not known now. But sects other than Confucianism, Buddhism, and Taoism had often been spoken of as one by people outside the sects. The case of *Seng-shih lüeh* with respect to Nestorianism, Manichaeism, and Zoroastrianism of the T'ang dynasty and the case of *Shih-men cheng-t'ung* with respect to Manichaeism, White Lotus sect, and White Clouds sect are examples. In *chüan* 4 of the latter there is a chapter entitled 'Records on Condemnation of Heretic Teachings' 斥偽志. Denounced as heretical here are Manichaeism, White Lotus, and White Clouds, which were flourishing at the time. Since Manichaeans were vegetarians and the pronounciation of 摩 [*Mo*, which stands for Mani] is the same as 魔 [*mo*, meaning 'devil'], [people] looked upon the worshipers of Manichaeism as devil-worshipers-Probably this is a way to stigmatize them."

In Chih-p'an's *Fo-tsu t'ung-chi*, *chüan* 48, there is a quotation from Hung Mai's *I-chien chih*: "The [sect of] *ch'ih-ts'ai shih-mo* is especially prosperous in the San-shan [Fukien] region. Their chiefs wear purple caps and loose (black?) gowns and their women wear black caps and white dress. Their [sect] is called the society of the Brilliant Sect 明教會 . . . . It is also known as *Mo-mo-ni* 末魔尼." This passage is not found in the extant editions of *I-chien chih*. Chavannes and Pelliot quoted it in "Un traité mani-chéen retrouvé en Chine," in the 1913 volume of *Journal Asiatique*, March-April issue, p. 339. Here we have a document in which *chih-ts'ai shih-mo*, *Ming-chiao*, and *Mo-mo-ni* (a term which Chavannes and Pelliot accept as another form of *Mo-ni*, or *Mar Mani*, *op. cit.*, p. 122, note 2), are considered identical in their devotion. In 1903 Pelliot was not sure whether the Brilliant Sect and *Mo-ni* were identical. In "Les Mo-ni et le Houa-hou-king," *Bulletin de l'Ecole française d'Extrême-Orient*, Vol. III (1903), p. 324, he said: "Aucun de ces témoignages suffit-il pour identifier la Religion brilliante aux Mo-ni? Je ne le crois pas. Mais, la part faite aux confusions possibles dont Hong Mai serait coupable, nous sommes à n'en pas douter en présence d'un étrange syncrétisme, où, à d'incontestables emprunts bouddhistes, à d'anciennes légendes taoïstes, quelques éléments viennent s'amalgamer qui semblent bien appartenir en propre aux Mo-ni, leur nom d'abord dans la prétendue poésie de Po Kiu-yi, et surtout leur livre sacré des deux principes clair et obscur. Loin de nos bibliothèques d'Europe, je ne dispose d'aucun moyen d'information sur le manichéisme; je tenais donc surtout à signaler ce texte sans prétendre en tirer dès à présent rien de définitif."

But in 1913, Pelliot was positive about their identity. See Chavannes and Pelliot, "Un traité manichéen retrouvé en Chine," *Journal Asiatique*, Series 11, Vol. I (Jan.-Feb., 1913), pp. 125–26, note 1, where the "Later Sage Great Enlightened Buddha" is identified with Mani, and "Mo-ni-kiao, religion de Meou-ni [Mani] with "religion de la lumière 'Ming-kiao.'" On page 263 of the same article (March-April, 1913), based on a passage quoted from *T'ang-hui-yao* 唐會要, Chavannes and Pelliot were

In comparing the ideology of this sect with that of the Taipings, the following points deserve consideration. First of all, the ideology of the revived *T'ai-p'ing tao* group was a mixture of different ideas. The members shared their property to a certain degree, they treated each other with consideration, and all members considered themselves to be of one family: all these suggest features which became characteristic of secret societies and which influenced the Taipings tremendously. The way they lured people to join them suggests Taiping recruiting. They worshiped the sun and the moon, two symbols to which the Taipings attached special significance, the sun being the symbol of the Heavenly King and the moon that of his queen. They were, to a limited degree, iconoclastic; they practiced taboo; they emphasized social distinction; they did not worship ancestors. All these ideas are similar to the Taiping ideas on similar subjects. However, the belief that killing was a way to save people from misery, and conversely that to die was to be saved, is opposed to the Taiping ideas: the Taipings did not emphasize killing and they believed instead that to die in battle was to ascend to heaven to enjoy happiness. The beliefs of both groups seem to have been devised as means to fire the members with enthusiasm and bravery in battle, with fortitude and courage when under government inquisition. However, these are at best only possible connections suggested by similarities. There is no proof that the Taipings took any of their ideological elements from these rebels.

Fang La

Fang La's rebellion took place in 1120, and the *Sung-shih* gives a brief account of it in the biography of T'ung Kuan.[55] *Sung-shih* gives as the reason for rebellion the insufferable misery imposed upon the people by the systematic searching of Chu Mien (d. 1126) for rare plants and stones.[56] A stronger and more personal reason is given in Fang Shao's

---

convinced that during the T'ang period Manichaeism was designated by "le nom de 'religion de la lumière (*ming-kiao*).' " This belief is repeated on page 325.

[55] *Sung-shih*, 468:10b–12b.

[56] In the biography of Chu Mien in the *Sung-shih*, 470:8a–10a, the conditions resulting from the collecting of rare plants and stones are vividly portrayed: "Emperor Hui-tsung (1101–1125) rather indulged in plants and stones. Ts'ai [Ts'ai Ching] hinted to Chu Mien that he ask his father [Chu Ch'ung] to collect secretly the rare [plants and stones] in the Che district and present them [to his majesty]. At first three *huang-yang* [*buxus microphylla*] were presented, and the emperor was pleased. After that

Ch'ing-hsi k'ou-kuei, which states that Fang's native place, Mu-chou in present Chekiang, is populous and wealthy, particularly important for trees like lacquer, paper mulberry (whose bark is used to make paper), fir, and other timber. Rich merchants made regular visits there. Fang La owned some lacquer tree groves and a manufacturing firm, for which he was ruthlessly taxed. Fang La greatly resented the taxation and yet dared not do anything about it. Just at that time Chu Mien's search for rare plants and stones enraged the people. Fang La took advantage of the situation and secretly gathered around him poor people and idlers. In the name of getting rid of Chu Mien, they rose in rebellion.[57]

Fang Shao stated certain superstitious beliefs which started Fang La on his way to rebellion. During the reign of Yung-hui (650–55) of the T'ang dynasty, a woman named Ch'en Shih-chen rebelled in Mu-chou and proclaimed herself Empress Wen-chui. After her time, there was a legend in Mu-chou about a Son of Heaven Foundation and a Ten-thousand-year Hall. Fang La believed in himself more firmly because of the legend.[58] Fang Shao again reported that one day Fang La saw his own reflection in a brook adorned in cap and gown like a king. After

---

there was a steady increase every year, but in general there were no more than two or three presentations, and the number of articles presented each time was just five or seven. During the period of Cheng Huo (1111–1117), the collecting reached its peak, with heavily laden boats bow to stern continuous on the rivers Huai and Pien. This collection was known as *hua-shih kang* (mass transportation of flowers and stones). A collecting station was established in Su-chou [Soochow]. . . . Chu Mien was promoted to *fang-yü-shih* (commissioner of defense), and most governors and prefects of the southeast were appointed through his recommendation. . . . The magistrates and other officials did everything within their power to collect the tributes. These tributes were taken from the people by force, and no compensation was given. If a plant or stone of any value was found in a family, whether scholar or commoner, soldiers would be sent to the family with yellow strips to be attached to the article. The article was not taken away immediately, and the family was charged with the duty of its care. Should anything happen to it through carelessness, the family would be charged with contempt of the royal personage. At the time of moving, houses were taken apart and walls knocked down to make way for it. Anybody who was unfortunate enough to have anything that might be called rare would point to it as a thing of misfortune; and he would destroy it as fast as he could. Those who were involved became impoverished, even though they had been well-to-do; some of them even had to sell their children to meet the demands. . . . The district was afflicted with this evil for more than twenty years. When Fang La rose, his appeal was to get rid of Chu Mien."

[57] Fang Shao, *Ch'ing-hsi k'ou-kuei*, pp. 5b–6a. See also *Sung-shih chi-shih pen-mo*, compiled by Ch'en Pang-chan, 54:16.

[58] Fang Shao, *op. cit.*, pp. 2b–3a. See also *Sung-shih*, 468:10b.

that day, he entertained great ambition. He lured the people by means of heretic teachings.[59]

[59] Fang Shao, *op. cit.*, p. 5b. All historical sources mention heretic teachings. See *Sung-shih*, 468:10b; *Sung-shih chi-shih pen-mo*, 54:1a–b; Yang Chang-liang, *T'ung-chien ch'ang-pien chi-shih pen-mo*, 141:13b. Nieh Ch'ung-ch'i, in his "Erh-ch'ien-nien-lai mi-hsin chi-t'uan chih pien-luan," in *Ta-chung*, Vol. I, No. 3, (March, 1946), p. 25, identifies Fang La with the group known as *ch'ih-ts'ai shih-mo* (vegetarian diet and devil worship). He says: "Fang La was a native of Ch'ing-hsi of Muchou. History says that he 'lured people by means of heretic teachings,' and his followers 'ate vegetables and worshiped the devil. They gathered at night and scattered in the daytime. Male and female mixed without distinction.' From this we know that his teachings were the same as Manichaeism."

Although we have mentioned the identification of *ch'ih-ts'ai shih-mo* with Manichaeism, we have serious doubt concerning the identification of Fang La and *ch'ih-ts'ai shih-mo*. Nieh does not say what "history" he was quoting. The historical sources I have gone over mention only heretic teachings and "his fanning the people with the mystery of ghosts and spirits." See *Sung-shih*, 468:10b; *Sung-shih chi-shih pen-mo*, 54:1a–b; Yang, *T'ung-chien ch'ang-pien chi-shih pen-mo*, 141:13b; and Hsüeh Ying-ch'i, *Sung-yüan t'ung-chien*, 54:14b–15a. In none of these sources do I find the statement that "his followers 'ate vegetables and worshiped the devil. . . . ' " The identification is probably built on the following considerations. A passage appears in almost identical words in Fang Shao's *Ch'ing-hsi k'ou-kuei*, 8b–9a, and Chuang Chi-yü's *Chi-le pien*, in *Shou-fu*, saying that *ch'ih-ts'ai shih-mo* spread from Fukien to Erh-che (east and west of Che, present Chekiang, and part of Kiangsu): "At the time of Fang La's rebellion, its believers rose in response to one another everywhere. We have heard that their way was to practice abstinence from meat and wine; prohibit the worship of spirits, Buddha, and ancestors; and not greet guests." The phrase "its believers" could have been construed by Nieh to mean Fang La's group.

Another possible source of confusion is a passage in Fang Shao's *Ch'ing-hsi k'ou-kuei*, pp. 3b–4a, where Chang Chüeh's *wu-tou-mi tao* (five tou of rice principle, a Taoist sect) is identified with *ch'ih-ts'ai shih-mo*. The followers are said to gather at night and scatter in the daytime. Fang goes on: "When they worshiped, they always faced north, for Chang Chüeh rose in the north. By looking at the direction of their worship, we would know what they worshiped. In their daily life they did not drink wine or eat meat. They willingly kept themselves in a weakened state and tended to keep silent, as if aiming at doing good. However, there was no distinction between male and female, and they did not engage in farming or weaving. They had no way of obtaining food and clothing, so they stirred up trouble by sabotage and robbery. Should they not be discerned as early as possible? There were some whose real nature was difficult to determine; and the government, fearing that too strict measures might force them to spread out, refrained from doing anything, thus leading to calamitous uprising. Ch'en Kuang's [the magistrate who failed to check Fang La in the early stage] dealing with Fang La is a case in point." Here by implication the author suggests that Fang La was part of the *ch'ih-ts'ai shih-mo* group, "whose real nature was difficult to determine."

It is not likely that we could identify Fang La with the *ch'ih-ts'ai shih-mo* sect. Members of the latter group are invariably described as teetotalers and vegetarians, while Fang La's first activity was to kill bulls and strain wine and gather his followers for a feast. But I must confess ignorance as to what his "heretic teachings" were.

Chavannes and Pelliot were not sure what Fang La's heretical doctrine was. In "Un

The rebels claimed that their chief aim was to get rid of corrupt officials, Chu Mien in particular. This claim was partially supported by the
fact that they refused to kill Chü Ssu-fu, the magistrate of Hsiu-ning
hsien who fell into the hands of the rebels, even though Chü had scolded
them and dared them to kill him. Their reply to Chü's request was: "We
are from Hsiu-ning. When you were the magistrate there, you ruled well,
and no other magistrate, either before or after you, can compare with

---

traité manichéen retrouvé en Chine," in the *Journal Asiatique*, Series 11, Vol. I (March-
April, 1913), page 350, note 2, they said: "Fang La se révolta ouvertement en 1120
dans sa ville natale de 青溪 Ts'ing-k'i; ... Les historiens lui reprochent de's'être servi
d'une doctrine hérétique pour tromper le peuple' 託左道以惑民. Cette phrase est
insuffisante pour nous faire connaître de quelle religion Fang La se réclamait. ... On
a l'impression, dans cette révolte de Fang La, d'une doctrine composite. Fang La se
serait emparé de certaines idées manichéennes sans être un vrai manichéen; de même,
au xixᵉ siècle, les T'ai-p'ing ne seront pas chrétiens, bien que leur chef se proclame fils
de Jéhovah et frère cadet de Jésus."

Ch'en Yüan, in his "Mo-ni chiao ju Chung-kuo k'ao," page 230, expressed the same
cautious attitude toward the identification of Fang La's religious beliefs with Manichaeism. He said: "But whether Fang La was a [believer of] Manichaeism, there is as
yet no other evidence. History merely says that he [Fang La] lured people by means
of heretic teachings." However, he added: "Fang Shao, in his *Po-chai pien* [Pai-hai
edition, *chüan hsia*], treats in detail [the rebellion of] Fang La, and here he also merely
mentions Fang La to be [a believer of] Manichaeism."

In this interpretation of Fang Shao's passage, which is identical with that found in
Fang Shao's *Ch'ing-hsi k'ou-kuei*, Ch'en Yüan seems to have made the same mistake of
uncritically turning his own impression into a positive statement made by Fang Shao.
But this uncritical interpretation of the text does not blind him to the truth he enunciates in commenting, on page 205, on Lu Yu's 陸游 identification of the followers
of Chang Chüeh, who were said by Fang Shao to be *ch'ih-ts'ai shih-mo* with Fang La's
gang: "To group Chang Chüeh and Fang La under the same category is a mistake
easily discernible." (Lu Yu's text is also quoted by Chavannes and Pelliot in "Un
traité manichéen retrouvé en Chine," *Journal Asiatique*, Series 11, Vol. I (March-April,
1913): Chinese text is on pages 351–52 and the French translation on pages 344–51.)
Ch'en Yüan also mentions on page 232 that Wang Chü-cheng 王居正 identified Fang
La with Manichaeism. But an examination of Wang's text reveals that there is no such
direct identification, although the view is more plausible here than in the case of Fang
Shao. We cannot rule out the possibility that Fang La's rebellion is used here merely
to mark the periods of development of *ch'ih-ts'ai shih-mo*, while Fang La himself may
not have been a part of the group. (See also Chavannes and Pelliot on Wang Chü-
cheng in *op. cit.*, p. 331, note.)

Chavannes and Pelliot, after commenting on Fang Shao's account of Fang La in
the *Po-chai pien*, say, on page 350: "Nous y voyons toutefois que les adeptes de la
doctrine de Fang La se prosternaient face au nord." Chavannes and Pelliot seem to
have been the first scholars whose uncritical identification of Fang La with Chang
Chüeh's followers who faced north in their worship found many adherents, including
Ch'en Yüan and Nieh Ch'ung-ch'i.

you. How could we kill you?" They left him and went their way.[60] But Fang La's strongest ideological appeal is given in a speech reported in Fang Shao's *Ch'ing-hsi k'ou-kuei*. After giving an account of the misery and suffering of the people as a result of Chu Mien's reckless effort in getting rare plants and stones to please Emperor Hui-tsung, the report goes on:

[Fang La], then, taking advantage of [the feeling of] the people who were suffering the unbearable, secretly gathered the poor and impover-ished and the idlers, and gave them alms to win them. When he was sure of their support, he had bulls butchered and wine strained, and called together over one hundred particularly wicked ones for a feast. After a few rounds of wine, La rose and said: "Basically, there is a single underlying principle for state and family. Suppose the young were to plough and weave, slaving the whole year through, and when they had some grain and cloth accumulated, their elders were to take everything and dissipate it and flog them for the slightest offense, showing no mercy in torturing them even to the point of death. Would you like that?"

"Certainly not," all replied.

La continued: "Whatever remains undissipated is presented to the enemy, so that thanks to what we provide they [the enemy] grow more and more prosperous. Even so, they encroach upon the border and you are sent to resist them. If you fail to expel them there are no limits to your punishment. And despite their aggression, annual tribute to the enemy is never discontinued. Do you like this?"

"How could we?" all replied.

With tears in his eyes, La went on: "Taxes are numerous and burden-some, officials seize what they want, and farming and sericulture do not suffice to meet the demands. The only thing we depend on for our liveli-hood is the trees: lacquer, paper mulberry, bamboo, and timber. These, too, are all being taxed to the last penny. When Heaven brought forth the people it established authorities primarily to nurture them. And yet their oppression has reached such a pass. Can either Heaven or man fail to resent it?

"Besides what is wasted on entertainment, sport, building, temples, armament, and the collection of rare plants and stones, annual gifts of silver and silk running into the millions go to the two barbarian states to the north and west.[61] All this is drained from our life blood, we of the

---

[60] Yang Tsung-liang, *T'ung-chien ch'ang-pien chi-shih pen-mo*, 141:13b–14a.

[61] The two "barbarian states" are Liao 遼 and the Hsi-hsia 西夏. In 1004 the Sung paid the Liao an annual tribute of 100,000 taels of silver and 200,000 rolls of silk (*Sung-shih*, 281:9a, 19b; *Liao-shih*, 14:6a). In 1042 an additional 100,000 taels of silver and 100,000 rolls of silk went to the Liao (*Sung-shih*, 313:4a). In 1044 an annual tribute of silver, silk, tea, and embroidery, which totaled 255,000 taels, was paid to the Hsi-hsia (*Sung-shih*, 485:19a).

southeast. When they receive these gifts the barbarians become even more contemptuous of the Middle Kingdom, and harass it incessantly. The court presents tribute, not daring to stop, and the ministers of state regard this as a long-term plan for preventing border strife. It is only we who labor from one year's end to the next; it is our wives and children who freeze and starve, their hunger never sated for a day. How do you gentlemen feel about it?"

"Whatever you say, we'll do!" came the indignant reply.

"In the last thirty years," La went on, "practically all the elder statesmen have either been banished or died. Those at the helm are a scurrilous lot of flatterers who know nothing but how to seduce the emperor, whether with song, women, or the building of palaces, while matters of state go unheeded. Among the district inspectors and prefects, graft and corruption are the order of the day; they take no concern for the welfare of their districts. The people of the southeast have long suffered their fleecing, and in recent years the provocation over rare plants and stones has been even more intolerable. If you were to rebel in a just cause the response would be universal; in a matter of days a force of ten thousand could be assembled. . . .

"We would defend the river as our border, lighten the *corvée* and decrease the tax to give relief to the people; would there be anyone in the empire who would not tidy his dress and come to our court? In a matter of ten years we would unify the empire. An alternative to this would be pointless death at the hand of corrupt officials. Please give [my words] some serious thought."

"Good," all replied.

He then organized his followers numbering several thousand, and rose under the guise that they would get rid of Chu Mien. They killed all officials and public functionaries they met. The people, in the midst of their suffering from official oppression, responded everywhere. In a matter of days, 100,000 men rallied to his support.[62]

Essentially, Fang La's rebellion is not different from any other. It has the same causes: social unrest and economic chaos as a result of a corrupt government and heavy taxation; the appeal of a promise to the people to lighten their taxes; the usual ingredients of superstition and possible religious affiliation. If there is anything new, it is the added element of a cry against the appeasement of foreign states in the form of annual tribute in silver and silk, making taxes particularly burdensome

[62] *Ch'ing-hsi k'ou-kuei*, pp. 5b–7b. From "Basically, there is a single underlying principle for state and family" to "in a matter of days a force of ten thousand could be assembled," I followed Richard Gregg Irwin's translation closely with a few changes for reasons of accuracy. Mr. Irwin's translation is found in his *The Evolution of a Chinese Novel: Shui-hu-chuan*, pp. 11–12.

and meaningless to the people. And this cry could have been the earliest indication of an ethnic issue in a political sense. Fang La's harangue against the Sung government may be compared to that of the Taipings against the Ch'ing court, but it is not likely that the Taipings received any inspiration from Fang La in the formation of their ideology.

PAI-LIEN CHIAO AND RELATED SECTS

During the Sui, T'ang, and subsequent dynasties there developed in China certain Buddhist sects which were destined to play an important role in Chinese rebellions and secret societies. These are *Pai-lien chiao-hui* and *Mi-lieh chiao-hui*. Shigematsu has dealt with *Pai-lien chiao-hui* in an article entitled "Ch'u-ch'i ti pai-lien chiao-hui" (see footnote 54). A summary of Shigematsu's article will help in determining whether there is anything the Taipings may have had a reason to borrow.

Pai-lien chiao and *Mi-lieh chiao* affiliated themselves with different Buddhist sects, the former with the Pure Land of Amitābha and the latter with the Pure Land of Maitreya. Shigematsu terms both secret societies. The Maitreya society flourished during the period of Sui, T'ang, the Five Dynasties, and the Northern Sung; *Pai-lien chiao* arose in the Southern Sung and flourished during the Ming and the Ch'ing.

Pai-lien chiao belongs to *T'ien-t'ai tsung* (a school of Buddhism). The main sources for its history are *Shih-men cheng-t'ung* (the *Orthodox Teachings of Buddhism*) by Monk Tsung-chien of the Southern Sung, and *Fo-tsu t'ung-chi* (*Records of Buddhist Masters*) by Chih-p'an, also of the Southern Sung.[63]

According to these records, in 1129 a monk by the name of Mao Tzu-yüan first preached *Pai-lien chiao* in Wu-chün (Soochow). After the pattern of the *T'ien-t'ai* school of Buddhism, he established the theory of the four Buddha-kṣetra,[64] made confession part of morning worship,

[63] See P. Pelliot, "La secte du Lotus blanc et la secte du Nuage blanc," "*Bulletin de l'Ecole française d'Extrême-Orient*," Vols. III and IV (1903 and 1904).

[64] According to *T'ien-t'ai tsung*, the four Buddha-kṣetra are as follows: (1) First are realms where all classes—men, devas, Buddhas, disciples, and non-disciples—dwell. There are two divisions: the impure, e.g. this world; and the pure, e.g. the inner palace of Maitreya's *Tusita* heaven and the Western Paradise of Amitābha's Pure Land. (2) In temporary realms, the occupants have gotten rid of the evils of unenlightened views and thought but still have to be reborn. (3) Realms of permanent reward and freedom are for those who have attained the rank of Bodhisattva. (4) The realm of eternal rest and light, i.e. wisdom, and of eternal spirit (*dharmakaya*), is the abode of Buddhas. In reality all the others are included in this last realm and are separated only for convenience' sake. Mao Tzu-yüan used a diagram to explain these different realms to the people.

wrote four-line songs,[65] and maintained that salvation is attained by calling the name of Buddha (Amitābha) five times.[66]

The title *Pai-lien* seems to be an adaptation of Monk Hui-yüan's (d. 416) *Pai-lien-she* (White Lotus Society) during the Chin.[67] Because Mao Tzu-yüan's society prohibited meat-eating and kept a vegetarian diet, the members were known as *Pai-lien-ts'ai* and at times were identified with the *ch'ih-ts'ai shih-mo* of Manichaeism.

Mao's followers were not regular Buddhist monks. They had wives and families, which regular monks did not have.[68] They were considered unorthodox by the latter. Monk Tsung-chien in his *Shih-men cheng-t'ung* condemned Mao's followers in a section entitled "Ch'ih-wei pien" (Condemnation of Heresies), and Chih-p'an in his *Fo-tsu t'ung-chi*

The government was no less vehement in prohibiting *Pai-lien ts'ai*. Shigematsu gives a very clear account of the government reaction to it during the Yüan dynasty. Edicts prohibited the sect and the dissemination of its documents, including *wu-kung-fu*, which were presumably a kind of charms adopted from Taoism; *T'ui-pei t'u*, a book with pictures predicting the rise and fall of dynasties; astrological charts; and books and other works on the heretic arts. The temples and idols of the sect were ordered destroyed; the believers were ordered to resume secular life and were made to labor for the government. Two edicts prohibiting *Pai-lien ts'ai* have been preserved: they show the dates of 1281, immediately after Khublai Khan unified China, and 1308, the first year of Wu-tsung. Then during the reign of Ying-tsung (1321–23) the sect was again banned, though that edict has not been preserved. But between Wu-

[65] The four-line songs were described by Chih-p'an in *Fo-tsu t'ung-chi* as similar to woodcutters' songs, employing vulgar phrases. For the sake of popularization, the Buddhists in China used these four-line songs often. Songs may be found in both the *Diamond Sūtra* and *Nirvana Sūtra*.

[66] Salvation by chanting the name of Amitābha five times is a simplification of the standard practice of calling the name ten times at the moment of death to achieve salvation.

[67] "Hsieh Ling-yün arrived in the Lu mountains, and no sooner had he met with Hui-yüan than he respectfully yielded himself to him, heart and soul. He then built a terrace close to the monastery, translated there the *Nirvana Sūtra*, and dug a pond, in which he planted white lotus flowers. On this account, Hui-yüan and his disciples, who at that time devoted themselves to the study of the Pure Land sect, called themselves the White Lotus Society." *Lien-she kao-hsien chuan*, p. 27b. Cf. J. J. M. de Groot, *Sectarianism and Religious Persecution in China*, I, 163. But T'ang Yung-t'ung exploded this myth in his *Han wei liang-chin nan-pei-ch'ao fu-chiao shih*, I, 366–71.

[68] Shigematsu, "Ch'u-ch'i ti pai-lien chiao-hui," *Shih-huo pan-yüeh k'an*, Vol. I, No. 4, pp. 27–35.

tsung and Ying-tsung, the *Pai-lien* sect received some temporary reprieve during the reign of Jen-tsung, when it was protected through the
auspices of Hsiao Chüeh-kuei and a Korean king.

From the two edicts it is evident that *Pai-lien chiao* is a mixture of many
elements which are not Buddhistic; and the idols mentioned above are
not, according to Shigematsu, statues of Buddha. Also, the members
married and had families and they gathered at night and dispersed in
the daytime, clearly indicating a kind of secret society; and the sect
flourished in Fukien and spread to Kiangsi. The edict protecting them
says that the monks and their temples were free from taxes and labor.

The Maitreya sect appeared early in Chinese history. Liang Shen of
the Liang (502–57), in his criticism of Buddhism, said: "Then again
they [the Maitreya monks] would confuse them [the people] with vague
statements, frighten them with a hell of incessant suffering, lure them
with absurd theories, and entice them with the happiness of the *Tusita*
heaven."[69] During the T'ang and the Sung, Maitreya believers rose in
sporadic rebellions.[70]

The government suppression of the Maitreya sect dates back to the
T'ang. In an edict proclaimed in 715 we read: "Certain monks in white
robes and wearing long hair pretended that Maitreya had descended
and started heretic rumors." After the Yüan, these *Pai-lien chiao* and
Maitreya sects were so mixed that it is not possible to distinguish between them. The Ming and the Ch'ing were also determined to stamp
out these heretic influences, which tinged many of the rebellions during
those dynasties.

Pai-lien chiao and *Mi-lieh chiao*, being affiliated with Buddhism, could
not have found favor with the Taipings, who were intensely anti-
Buddhistic. But the four factors in Mao Tzu-yüan's doctrine—the
theory of Buddha-kṣetra, confession in morning worship, the employment of popular four-line songs, and salvation by calling the name of
Amitābha—and the ideas of hell and *Tusita* heaven of the Maitreya
sect could all have been used by the Taipings to great advantage. The
ideas of heaven and hell, confession, and morning worship are integral
parts of the Taiping religious ideology; and salvation by calling the
name of Amitābha could be compared to their prayer. The Taipings
also used songs, though not always four-line songs, to arouse the religious
sentiment of their followers. Of course the religious elements in their

[69] *Hung-ming chi*, compiled by Seng-yu, 9:13a.
[70] Shigematsu Toshiaki, "T'ang-sung shih-tai chih mi-le-chiao-fei," *Shien*, No. 3.

ideology came from Christianity; but there was nothing to prevent these Buddhistic elements from influencing them without their realizing it. Shigematsu says that both the *Pai-lien* and *Mi-lieh* sects were of the nature of secret societies. It is conceivable that their influence could have come indirectly through the secret societies, with one of which the Taipings are known to have had an intimate relationship. At any rate, if the Taipings did know these sects at all, these may have served to prepare their mental attitude for the acceptance of Christian ideas. There is no evidence that the Taipings borrowed directly from these unorthodox Buddhist societies.

REBELLIONS AT THE END OF THE YÜAN

Rebellions in the Name of Mi-lieh chiao

At the end of the Yüan dynasty many rebellions broke out in the name of *Mi-lieh chiao*. In 1326 two commoners from Haichow in Honan named Chao Niu-ssu and Kuo P'u-sa spread the rumor that "Maitreya will have the world," meaning that Maitreya would become the ruler of the world.[71] In 1337 when Pang Hu rebelled, the Maitreya banner was used as a rallying symbol.[72] In 1351 Han Shan-t'ung and Liu Fu-t'ung rose with the slogan that Maitreya was born to give peace to the then chaotic world. They used red turbans to distinguish themselves; thus they were known as the "Red Army." They were also known as the "Incense Army" because they worshiped Maitreya by burning incense. They were identified also with the *Pai-lien* sect, for Han's grandfather tried to win a following by burning incense in the way of *Pai-lien chiao*.[73] Others who rebelled using the Maitreya sect as a means for winning a following include Lao P'eng, Chih-ma Li, Chao Chün-yung, and Hsü Shou-hui.[74]

Why did they choose Maitreya as their Messiah? The appeal of Maitreya's *Tusita* heaven to the people was tremendous. A glimpse of such a heaven is given in a Buddhist writing which describes what the world would be when Maitreya realized Buddhahood; that is, when he, a future Buddha, actually became a Buddha in this world. The Buddhist writing says:

[71] *Yüan-shih*, 29:23b.
[72] *Ibid.*, 39:6b.
[73] Ch'üan Heng, *Keng-shen wai-shih, shang*, 21a; Ch'ien Ch'ien-i *Kuo-ch'u ch'ün-hsiung shih-lüeh*, 1:1a–2a.
[74] Ch'ien, *op. cit.*, 1:3b–4a.

All people will be kindhearted, doing the ten good deeds. Because they do good deeds, their life span will be long and filled with happiness and peace. Men and women will [cover the land] densely, cities and towns will border on one another, and chickens will fly from one to the other; in their farms, one planting will yield seven crops and plants will ripen of themselves without tilling or weeding.[75]

The people in the middle of the fourteenth century were hard pressed economically and were desperately hoping for relief and a new world order. The Maitreya ideology, which was predominantly religious, turned out to be also economic; in this respect, the Taiping ideology seems to have gone through a similar transition. The difference is: The Maitreya ideology's appeal was completely emotional, based on imagination and wishful thinking; while the Taipings, though also appealing emotionally to the people by promising them the eternal glory of heaven, attempted at the same time to formulate a workable economic scheme.

With this general remark about the Maitreya sect, I shall turn to the rebels who did have some ideological elements that may be of interest to our present study.

In Liu Fu-t'ung there are a number of interesting ideological elements. Yeh Tzu-ch'i 葉子奇 of the Ming, in his Ts'ao-mu-tzu 草木子, observes:

> In the year keng-yin [1350] during the reign of Chih-cheng [1341–67]... when the Yellow River changed its course and flowed toward the south, Chia Lu persuaded the Prime Minister T'o T'o to recover the old river course dredged by Yü, and he himself was put in charge of the operation. Along the river bank more than 260,000 men were conscripted for the labor. The funds allotted by the government to pay for the labor were not paid in full. Many laborers at the job complained. Thus Han Shan-t'ung laid down his plot. He had a stone man with one eye sculptured, and on the back of the stone man he had the following words inscribed: "Despise not the stone man because he has only one eye, for when he appears he will throw the whole world into a turmoil."[76]

Han Shan-t'ung's stone man is reminiscent of the stone inscription which foretold the collapse of the Ch'in upon the death of the first emperor and recalls also the trick Ch'en Sheng and Wu Kuang used to play upon the credulous people. Judging from subsequent events, this method of Liu

---

[75] Quoted in Meng Ssu-ming, Yüan-tai she-hui chieh-chi chih-tu, pp. 209–10.
[76] Quoted in Ch'ien, op. cit., 1:1b.

Fu-t'ung was very effective in attuning the minds of the people to what Liu was about to execute. The Taiping parallel to this is, of course, the discovery of the seven characters which foretold the assumption of kingship by Hung Hsiu-ch'üan.

Unequal distribution of wealth formed an important part of Han Shan-t'ung's propaganda. In one of his proclamations we read: "Extreme poverty envelops Chiang-nan [south of the Yangtze] while Saipei [north of the passes, or Mongolia] rolls in riches."[77] However, the tone of the complaint indicates that it is directed particularly toward the injustice imposed upon the Chinese by the Mongols, an issue which was more ethnic than economic; for there was no promise, as in the case of Wang Hsiao-po of the Sung, to equalize the wealth for the people. Or it may be more accurate to say that both the economic and the ethnic issues were present when Han Shan-t'ung and Liu Fu-t'ung raised their banner against the Mongols.

Politically, Liu Fu-t'ung employed the principle of legitimate succession, following the lead of Han Shan-t'ung who proclaimed himself a descendant in the eighth degree of Emperor Hui-tsung (1101–25). So Liu claimed Han Lin-erh, a son of Han Shan-t'ung, to be a descendant in the ninth degree of Hui-tsung. Liu made Han Lin-erh emperor and restored the old dynastic name of Sung, considering that Han was the legitimate successor of the Sung and would now continue the line which had been cut short by the Yüan.[78]

The economic, political, and religious issues are old ones, all of which had been used in one form or another. But the ethnic issue as contained in Han Shan-t'ung's proclamation against the Mongols appeared at this moment for the first time, with the exception of Fang La's cry against Sung's appeasement of the northern barbarians. Although Han Shan-t'ung's proclamation did not raise the issue of the right of non-Chinese to rule China and attacked only the economic injustice of the Mongol rule, it may have served to kindle imagination in later rebellions against non-Chinese dynasties. Though we cannot tell whether or not the Taipings were influenced by this piece of propaganda, its potential value in that respect should be evident.

Chih-ma Li, Lao P'eng, and Chao Chün-yung, leaders of another Maitreya-based sect, gathered people together for the purpose of burning incense, and eight of the leaders swore themselves to brotherhood by

[77] Yeh Tzu-ch'i, *Ts'ao-mu-tzu*, quoted in Ch'ien, *op. cit.*, 1:2b.
[78] Ch'ien, *op. cit.*, 1:9b–10a.

dipping their fingers in a basin of blood;[79] these are two of the most characteristic customs of a secret society. From this description, there is no doubt that theirs was a secret-society organization.

The last of the Maitreya group to be considered are Hsü Shou-hui and his followers. Ch'ien describes them in the following words:

> Shou-hui . . . collected people and rebelled in the name of incense-burning. Previously a monk of Tz'u-hua temple in Yüan-chou [in Kiangsi] by the name of P'eng Yin-yü used magical arts to deceive people. Chou Tzu-wang, a disciple of his, used his influence to collect people with the purpose to rebel. When the plot was discovered, the Kiangsi forces of the Yüan dynasty were ordered to arrest and execute them. Tzu-wang, Yin-yü, and others fled to Huai-hsi [the upper reaches of the Huai River] and lay low among the people there. They were not arrested. And shortly afterward, Tsou P'u-sheng of Ma-ch'eng [in Hunan] again used the magical arts to scatter evil rumors, saying, "Maitreya is born and will be the lord of the world." Thus they mustered forces and rose in rebellion. They made Shou-hui their chief, because he appeared different from the rest. They raised red turbans as their symbol.[80]

The incense-burning, a Buddhist practice, had now become a common sign for both secret societies and rebellious groups. Its function seems to have been to cover up their actual activities and present the front of a harmless group of Buddha-worshipers. This may also explain why the ideologies of secret societies always contain Buddhist ideas and nomenclature. Disregarding the specific content, one may even infer that the Taipings' first appearance as God-Worshipers had the same object of deceiving the government about what they were actually doing. This religious camouflage for subversive activity was first adopted by Chang Chüeh with not a little measure of success. The Taipings enjoyed similar success at the beginning of their movement.

Hsü Shou-hui also raised the ethnic issue. In 1353 when Hsü tried to enlist Ming Yü-chen's support, he said to Ming: "I rose in rebellion in the hope that I may chase the barbarians away and pacify China."[81] As this is a natural issue when one rebels against an alien rule, the Taipings did not have to draw inspiration from Hsü for their vehement attack upon the Manchus.

[79] *Ibid.*, 1:3b–4a.
[80] *Ibid.*, 3:1a–b.
[81] *Ibid.*, 5:1b–2a.

Chu Yüan-chang[82]

At a time when most rebels made use of the Maitreya sect to win a following, Chu Yüan-chang(Ming T'ai-tsu) denounced it in unequivocal terms. He condemned the absurdity of the "Red Army" and their incense-burning, and expressed deep regret that "the ignorant people unfortunately were deceived by the magical arts and believed in the reality of Maitreya, whose birth would alleviate their sufferings, in spite of the absurdity of the teachings of the sect."[83] This does not mean that Chu was completely free from religious consciousness. On the contrary, he was a religious person, a Buddhist monk, before he was a rebel. And the course he was to take was determined by his prayer to the guardian spirits of the monastery where he was staying. During the campaign he constantly fell back on the mandate of Heaven as the reason the others should submit themselves to his rule.[84] He expressed this idea of acting for heaven as early as 1358 when he made a tablet with the following golden inscription: *Feng-t'ien tu-t'ung Chung-hua* (奉天都統中華 to rule China in the name of heaven).[85]

Chu's conception of God is very traditional. In one of his letters to Fang Kuo-chen, he said: "Your troops have often plundered my coastal people. Shang-ti [God] values life and the people down below long for peace, and yet you have violated the [will] of Heaven and exploited the people ruthlessly."[86]

At the end of the Yüan there were many uprisings. But of all these uprisings, only that of Chu Yüan-chang succeeded. Although it is not easy to determine the reasons he alone succeeded while all the rest failed, opinions about the factors responsible for his success may help us under-

---

[82] See Wu Han, *Ming T'ai-tsu.*

[83] *Kuo-ch'ao tien-ku,* 3:15b–16a, quoted in Meng, *Yüan-tai she-hui chieh-chi chih-tu,* p. 222.

[84] Two proclamations illustrate that Chu Yüan-chang used the mandate of Heaven. In one against Chang Shih-ch'eng, he said: "When order is restored the world will be unified under one authority. Where the mandate of Heaven lies, no confusion will be allowed. Even the intelligent ones, on realizing that their way is going to be a failure, should make a fundamental adjustment in their mental attitude and attempt to preserve their life and clans by holding a respectful awe for heavenly mandate and the will of the people." (Ch'ien, *Kuo-ch'u ch'ün-hsiung shih-lüeh,* 7:67a.) The other proclamation was directed toward the people in the north, and in it he said: "I have respectfully received the mandate from Heaven and dare not rest myself in peace." (Wang Shih-chen, *Yen-shan-t'ang pieh-chi,* 85:3a–4a, quoted in Meng, *op. cit.,* pp. 222–23.

[85] Ch'ien, *op. cit.,* 1:24b.

[86] *Ibid.,* 8:17a–b.

stand Chu's political aims. Chao I, in his *Nien-erh-shih cha-chi*, gives as one reason why Chu alone succeeded "his dislike of killing." Chao goes on to say, "Ming-tsu [Ming T'ai-tsu] alone aimed at saving the world and giving it peace; therefore his benevolence and righteous spirit spread far and wide, and wherever he went he met with submission, saving him the greater part of his war effort."[87] On more than one occasion Chu expressed this sentiment. In 1365, in his reply to a letter of Ming Yü-chen of Shu (Szechwan), Chu deplored the fact that of those who rose in the wake of Yüan's decline "none is able in the name of the principle *(tao)* of heaven to relieve the people from utter misery."[88] And in the same year Chu sent Ming Yü-chen another letter in which he said:

> Since the Yüan failed in holding the rein and heroic campaigns were launched, it has been over fourteen years. Out of ten leaders who rose [against the Yüan] eight or nine have been eliminated. Their failure has all been due to the fact that they gave no thought to delivering the people from their misery, but indulged in wanton and ruthless behavior; so they cut themselves off from heaven, and brought themselves ultimate destruction.[89]

This idea was again expressed in his proclamation to the people of Ku-su (Soochow in Kiangsu) against Chang Shih-ch'eng, for here he stated his purpose in his expedition against Chang: "to punish the guilty one and give relief to the people." He also claimed his troops to be *wang-che chih shih* (王者之師 the kingly troops), the purpose of which "is not to enrich themselves with the riches of the world, for their original purpose is to relieve the people."[90]

---

[87] *Nien-erh-shih cha-chi*, 36: 23a–24a.

[88] Ch'ien, *op. cit.*, 5:13a.

[89] *Ibid.*, 5:14a.

[90] *Ibid.*, 7:58b. We may reasonably doubt the validity of the statements made by Ming T'ai-tsu himself, but those made by Ch'ien Ch'ien-i and Chao I seem to a certain degree free from subjective emotionalism: they had no reason to glorify the first emperor of the Ming. However, our impression of the emperor, considering the way he disposed of those who helped him to his throne, is of a figure not especially marked by benevolence but one which compares with Han-kao-tsu in ruthlessness. (See Ku Ying-t'ai, *Ming-shih chi-shih pen-mo*, "Hu Lan chih-yü"; and Chao, *Nien-erh-shih cha-chi*, "Hu Lan chih-yü," which mentions that in the case of Hu over 30,000 people and in the case of Lan over 15,000 men were involved and executed. In these cases, however, T'ai-tsu had reason to act as ruthlessly as he did; for these people were plotting against him.) In his relation to the people, T'ai-tsu was a good emperor. Chou Ku-ch'eng, in *Chung-kuo t'ung-shih*, pp. 827–29, listed four points in his favor as an emperor: he emphasized the quality and qualification of officials, which is expressed

Chu's political aim reflects the general political and economic conditions of the time. In the ninety-one years of their reign, the Yüan had taxed and enslaved the people beyond their endurance. It was indeed in view of such wretched conditions that Chu's aim was formulated. As early as 1359 a certain scholar from Lung-ch'uan (in Kiangsi) by the name of Yeh Tzu-ch'i had provided Sun Yen, an assistant of Chu, with general ideas about a new government. Yeh said:

> He who becomes the legitimate ruler of the world should try to reinvigorate its civilization, and he who would bring about a prosperous government to the world should attempt to eliminate vices and corruptions in the world.... In reviving the rule of the sage [glorious] Sung, there are eight principles to observe:
>   1. Rectify human relationships to purify the source of culture.
>   2. Appoint the able and good [to office] to insure good quality of the government.
>   3. Emphasize cleanhandedness and a sense of shame to eliminate the practice of corruption.
>   4. Erect memorials to the filially pious to strengthen the source of *li* [the principle of social conduct].
>   5. Dismiss unnecessary officials to unify power [responsibility].
>   6. Correct application of punishment and reward to equalize the handles [*i ch'i ch'i ping*, 以齊其柄, equal and just application of the two handles, reward and punishment, as advocated by Han Fei (see "Erh-ping" in the *Han-fei-tzu*)].
>   7. Circulate currency as a standard of light and heavy.
>   8. Investigate the producing power to equalize taxation and service.

In another letter Yeh made the following suggestion to Sun Yen in connection with taxation:

> At the beginning of the establishment of our sage [glorious] dynasty, the important thing is leniency and benevolence; and in instituting new laws

---

in the preface of "Biographies of Good Officials," in the *Ming-shih:* he was scrupulously conscientious in the appointments of officials; he was strict and fair in the evaluation and investigation of official duties; he was merciless in punishing corrupt officials. Chao I has articles in his *Nien-erh-shih cha-chi* bearing on these points: titles may be translated "Appointment of Central Ministers to Regional Posts," "Strictness and Conscientiousness in Evaluation and Investigation of Official Duties," and "Ruthless Punishment of Corrupt Officials."

One has reason to believe that Ming T'ai-tsu did have in mind the misery of the people and did make up his mind to deliver them from such misery. For Ming T'ai-tsu's concern with the welfare of the people, see Shimizu T., "Minsho no minsei: kan o osae min o agu," *Tōyōshi kenkyū*, Vol. XIII, No. 3 (Aug., 1954).

one should be especially careful. I do not mean that at a time like this when we are in the midst of military campaigns we should not at all tax the people to finance our military campaigns. What I mean is merely that effort should be made to do away with all the corrupt practices of the declining dynasty in order to make manifest the good law of a rising king.... It is in this that I consider my fortune to be found.[91]

Reasons for Yeh's proposals are obvious: all were an attempt to eliminate the demoralizing influence of the declining Yüan dynasty, which, if left alone, would assuredly affect the spirit of the new dynasty. Even without any deep knowledge of the Yüan government in its declining years, one can imagine that the first six principles were proposed in view of the prevailing conditions of the time. The seventh definitely refers to the Yüan abuse of government paper notes, while the eighth refers to the unequal distribution in both land and taxation during the Yüan dynasty.

These proposals must have influenced Chu's attitude toward the problems of taxation and issuance of government notes. He attempted to equalize land tax.[92] And he gave utterance to his views in a proclamation against the Yüan which could be a reiteration of Yeh's views:

Recently I have observed that at the end of the Yüan the ruler confined himself deep in his palace, while the ministers held in their hands the helm of the government. Office was obtained through bribery and crime exonerated because of personal relationships. High ministers recommended their own relations and impeached their enemy. The poor were conscripted while the rich were treated with special favor by the officers in charge. Not concerned with these malpractices, the government was just in the midst of increasing the number of unnecessary officials, changing [the regulation of issuing] government notes, and conscripting 400,000 men to block the course of the Yellow River. Along the way corpses lay in piles and mourning could be heard in heaven.[93]

Here Chu, by implication, promised the people a clean and efficient government and a sound economy.

As a means to enlist the support of the people, he also fell back on the principle of legitimate succession. The same year in which he considered himself the receiver of the heavenly mandate (1358), he had the following two lines put on his two banners:

[91] For both quotations, see Ch'ien, *Kuo-ch'u ch'ün-hsiung shih-lüeh*, 1:27b–28a.
[92] Ch'en Teng-yüan, *Chung-kuo t'u-ti chih-tu*, pp. 252–53.
[93] Ch'ien, *op. cit.*, 7:58b–59a.

> My rivers and mountains coincide with the land of China;
> The sun and moon again light up the heaven of the Sung.

And on two tablets, the following lines were inscribed:

> The sun and the moon in the nine heavens light up the zodiac
> [the auspicious day];
> The rivers and mountains of the Sung are now recovered conforming
> to the precious map.[94]

In these couplets, Chu apparently considered himself the legitimate successor of the Sung, who had recovered the mapped territory from the Yüan.

Chu's ethnic consciousness was not well developed at first. In recounting his past, he said:

> At that time [referring to the time when heroes in the world rose against the Yüan in 1351] I was still hidden in the country, being a monk. I was in a dilemma: should I come forth to fight for the Yüan? I was afraid to waste my life. Should I stay hidden? I was afraid that when the Red Army came I might lose my life. So I prayed to the guardian spirits of the monastery.[95]

Chu's indecision shows that he did not have a very strong idea about racial antagonism.[96] The same indecision was expressed in his proclamation against Chang Shih-ch'eng, where he said: "I saw clearly that on the one hand the evil teachings [referring to beliefs in Maitreya] would never succeed, and on the other the lot of the barbarians [the Mongols] was such that it was impossible to achieve anything with them."[97] And during the years between 1361 and 1363 Chu had some correspondence first with the Yüan general Ch'a-han-t'ieh-mu-erh and then with his adopted son K'uo-kuo-t'ieh-mu-erh. It is true that in one case Chu expressed his doubt as to the real motive of Ch'a-han; but in general his attitude toward Ch'a-han was one of respect and admiration.[98] Chu might have served the Yüan if there had been any hope for success.

---

[94] *Ibid.*, 1:24b.

[95] Chu Yüan-chang [Ming T'ai-tsu], *Chi-lu hui-pien hsüan-k'an*, "Yü-chih chi-meng," p. 1a.

[96] This indecision is also evident in his memorial to his parents. See Chu, *Chi-lu hui-pien hsüan-k'an*, "Yü-chih huang-ling pei," p. 1a–b.

[97] Ch'ien, *Kuo-ch'u ch'ün-hsiung shih-lüeh*, 7:59a.

[98] *Ibid.*, 7:31b, 33b, 34a, 37a–b.

Before 1365, however, there were at least two occasions when Chu made use of the ethnic issue. In one of his letters to Ch'en Yu-liang he said: "There are two ways to get the power to rule the world: to work together in an attack upon the barbarians to give peace to China is the best way; for the Chinese to fight among themselves and make things easy for the barbarians is no way at all."[99]

Originally the barbarians lived in the desert; now on the contrary they reside in the central plain [central China]. This is indeed a situation in which cap and shoes change places. You should take hold of this opportunity to rise and occupy the upper reaches of the country [the Yangtze], and I will take advantage of the strategic positions of the Yangtze. You and I, working together like lips and teeth, should co-operate to recover the central plain with one mind and one concerted effort.[100]

Chu's racial consciousness became very strong in the year 1367 when he sent a proclamation to the north before he launched upon his northward expedition. This proclamation was directed to the people of Shantung, Honan, Hupeh, Shansi, and Shensi:

Since the old time, the condition for an emperor to rule over the empire has always been: the Chinese from within controlled the barbarians, and the barbarians from without served the Chinese. Never have I heard of barbarians ruling the empire. When the Sung declined, the Yüan, who are northern barbarians, came in to rule China....Later [Yüan rulers] disregarded the principle of the relationship between the ruler and the ministers....Thus the people revolted in their mind and there were uprisings everywhere. Because of this chaos, the Chinese people either died with their liver and brain mixed up in the dust or lived to see their kin scatter to all directions....It was said of old that barbarians never could have a mandate over a hundred years. In view of the present [Yüan] case, this statement is indeed true....Among the millions of Chinese there will be one who will drive out the barbarians and restore China....I have respectfully received a mandate from Heaven, and dare not rest myself in peace. I am in the midst of planning a northward expedition to chase the barbarians out of China, in order to deliver the people from their misery and recover the dignity of the Han government....For Heaven will mandate Chinese to take up the task to give peace to the Chinese; how could the government be left in the hands of the barbarians?[101]

[99] *Huang-ming fa-ch'uan lu*, 2:32a, quoted in Meng, *Yüan-tai she-hui chieh-chi chih-tu*, p. 222. Ch'en Yu-liang died in 1363, so this letter must have been written in or before that year.

[100] Ch'ien, *op. cit.*, 5:14b.

[101] *Yen-shan-t'ang pieh-chi*, 85:3a–4a, quoted in Meng, *op. cit.*, pp. 222–23.

This new slogan attracted to Chu people of all classes, rich or poor, proving the value of the ethnic issue as a powerful weapon against non-Chinese rulers. Chu maintained his attitude after he won the empire and issued a number of regulations to eradicate barbarian habits, to regulate social relationships with them, and to prohibit the use of barbarian dress, language, and names.

Chu Yüan-chang took up the banner against the Yüan under conditions very similar to those under which the Taipings revolted. So it is not surprising to find them aiming at similar objectives: in the case of Chu to save the world and give it peace, and in the case of Hung to establish the Heavenly Kingdom of Peace. They denounced the reigning dynasty in an almost identical spirit, though in different verbal expressions. The object of attack in both cases was misgovernment, corruption, and both social and economic injustice. The parallel may even be extended to cover their iconoclastic tendency: in one case it was against the belief in the birth of Maitreya, and in the other, against the beliefs of all native religions—Confucianism with its ancestor worship, Taoism, and Buddhism, which by the time of the nineteenth century may be considered native. The coincidence is completed by the fact that both Chu and Hung remained fundamentally religious.

Similar circumstances and similar cultural background could explain the resemblances between the ideologies of the two. This coincidental nature becomes clearer in consideration of the surprising fact that Hung and other Taiping leaders never once mentioned Chu and his activity against the Yüan. That the Taipings, who built their case mainly on the ethnic issue against the non-Chinese reign, did not refer to Chu is indeed baffling. It was, after all, through the ethnic issue that Chu, in spite of his lack of interest in it in his early campaign, gained the support of the people; and the Taipings could easily have used this historical instance to support their own case. But they did not take advantage of this historical precedent. Why?

Hung wished to establish a new dynasty. He was fighting the contention of the *T'ien-ti hui* that they should restore the Ming. To avoid any possible confusion in the mind of his followers, Hung must have purposely passed up this otherwise strong support in his ethnic appeal to the people.

Ming Yü-chen

Ming Yü-chen was a farmer. His racial consciousness was aroused by

Hsü Shou-hui when the latter tried to enlist his support. When Hsü came under the influence of Ch'en Yu-liang and became a figurehead and was eventually disposed of by Ch'en in 1360, Yü-chen became the executor of Hsü's policy.

In 1353 when Chao Tzu, a Yüan official, refused to surrender, Yü-chen told Chao's wife, who had fallen into Yü-chen's hands, to appeal to Chao with the argument that why should Chao, a Chinese, fight for the barbarians in defense of the city.[102] In 1360 when he assumed the title of emperor after the death of Hsü Shou-hui at the hand of Ch'en Yu-liang, Yü-chen declared that the fate of the barbarian Yüan had come to an end, and he, coming from a peasant family, would act for heaven to punish the guilty one. Then he went on to say:

> The Yüan are northern barbarians and have disgraced our country. Because of them, our human relations have become confused, our people have been destroyed. This is indeed heavenly fate and cannot be attributed to the plan of man. Now their descendants have lost the principle and the dynasty is declining. Heaven has decreed to show its disgust with them.... Now my family and my dynasty originated in Hupeh, and it is my desire to eliminate the despotic and save the people. So I am building up a dynasty and extending territory.... Alas! I respectfully execute the heavenly punishment to wipe out the stains of the barbarian rule, so as to reveal the great achievement and accomplish the regime of our culture.[103]

In economics, Yü-chen reverted to the tithe system; farmers, after paying their tithe, had no further obligation in the form of *corvée*.[104] In political administration, he followed the pattern of the *Chou-li* in establishing six *ch'ing* (ministers). In 1362 civil examinations were given.[105] Buddhism and Taoism were both ruled out and the Maitreya sect became the state religion.[106] He did not, however, give up Confucianism, for he adopted the *Chou-li* and he himself, though a peasant, was described as one who loved literature.[107] The most interesting point is Yü-chen's adoption of the economic and political system in the *Chou-li*. Whether or not the Taipings' adoption of the *Chou-li* was in any way

---

[102] Ch'ien, *Kuo-ch'u ch'ün-hsiung shih-lüeh*, 5:5a–b.
[103] *Ibid.*, 5:8b.
[104] *Ibid.*, 9:9b.
[105] *Ibid.*, 5:9a.
[106] *Ibid.*, 5:9a.
[107] *Ibid.*, 5:15a.

influenced by that of Yü-chen, the very possibility of such a connection is intriguing.

REBELLIONS IN THE MING DYNASTY

Rebellions abound in the Ming dynasty.[108] T'ang Shai-erh, Lin San's wife, revolted in 1421, boasting that she received a *pao-shu* (a precious book, after the style of Shui-hu's heavenly book) and a spiritual sword in a stone case and possessed the power to enslave the ghosts and spirits.[109]

During the Cheng-t'ung period, 1436–47, Teng Mou-ch'i, a *chia-chang* (甲長 the head of a *chia*, or group of ten families, according to Sung's local administrative system), in an effort to do away with a practice in his locality, offended the landlords. Originally, apart from the regular rent, tenants had to offer the landlords certain gifts. Now Mou-ch'i proposed to abolish this tribute and demanded that landlords come to the tenants to collect their rent in person. The landlords presented the case before the magistrate, who ordered three hundred troops to that locality to arrest Mou-ch'i and his associates. These three hundred soldiers were all killed. Later Mou-ch'i rebelled and gave himself the title of *ch'an-p'ing-wang* (剷平王 leveling prince).

Ch'en Chien-hu, in a fit of anger, killed Yeh Tsung-liu and made himself king with the dynastic title of *T'ai-p'ing*, and the reign title *T'ai-ting*.

There were also Li T'ien-pao, Huang Hsiao-yang, Liu Liu, Liu Ch'i, Ch'i Yen-ming, Chao Liu-chin, and others, who revolted because of the oppressive acts of eunuch Liu Chin; and there were Yang Hu, Liu Hui, and Ch'en Han, with Liu Hui assuming the title of "the great expeditionary general acting for heaven." In Szechwan Lan T'ing-jui took the title *shun-t'ien-wang* (king obedient to heaven) and Yen Pen-shu took the title *kua-ti-wang* (king who sweeps the earth) in revolt. During the reign of Chia-ching (1522–67) there were pirates to deal with, and in the second year of T'ien-ch'i (1622) there was a rebellion led by Hsü Pei-ju in Shantung.

As these rebellions did not exert any lasting influence and since their ideological elements were only fragmentary, they seem to deserve no more than a note. But the ideological elements are important nonethe-

---

[108] Documents relating to peasant rebellions at the end of the Ming dynasty have been collected by Peking University in two volumes: *Ming-mo nung-min ch'i-i shih-liao* and *Ming-mo nung-min ch'i-i shih-liao hsü-pien*.

[109] For this episode and the following, see Chao, *Nien-erh-shih cha-chi*, *chüan* 36, "Ming-tai hsien-hou liu-tse."

less. The device of a heavenly book and sword and the magical power over the spirits and ghosts are some of the elements the Taipings also used. The strained relationship between landlords and tenants as an economic factor in the formation of a rebel ideology is also implied in the Taiping land system. The idea of *t'ai-p'ing* and the use of the symbols of heaven and earth are of particular interest: at least twice before the Taipings, the term *t'ai-p'ing* had been used to express the aim of a rebellion; and on numerous occasions the idea of T'ien figured as an important element of rebel ideology. Whether the Taipings actually took the hint from these precedents or not, they were not the first to make use of these elements in their ideological appeal to the people.

THE "ROAMING BANDITS" AT THE END OF THE MING DYNASTY

The causes for the rise of bandits at the end of the Ming are not much different from the causes of rebellions during other periods. The first cause is economic: the concentration of land in the hands of a few and the miserable conditions of the landless masses. The case of Teng Mou-ch'i, who called himself "leveling prince," gave a glimpse of the way the landlords treated their tenants. It is not difficult to discover what Teng wanted to make level: from the way he told the landlords to come for their rent themselves and from the way he discontinued the practice of giving the landlords gifts, it is clear that he wanted to make the land situation a little more tolerable for the masses.[110] In addition to this ruthless treatment of the tenants by the landlords, the people were deprived of their lands in many other ways, such as by the practice of *huang-chuang* and *chuang-t'ien* (establishing royal estates and large land-holdings). In *Ming-shih*, "Shih-huo-chih," the authors said: "Nothing did more harm to the people than *huang-chuang* and *chuang-t'ien* of the princes and princesses, eunuchs and nobles."[111] And P'an Yung-chi, in his *Tu Ming-shih cha-chi*, said: "During the Ming dynasty, there was nothing that did more harm to the country than salaries for the nobles, and there was nothing that did more harm to the people than *chuang-t'ien*."[112]

There was an untold number of corrupt officials, eunuchs, and local bad gentry, and in addition there were weaklings on the throne; the

---

[110] See Chao, *op. cit.*, "Ming-tai hsien-hou liu-tse" and "Ming Hsiang-kuan yüeh-min chih hai."

[111] *Ming-shih*, 77:11a–b.

[112] *Tu Ming-shih cha-chi*, in *Chao-tai ts'ung-shu*, ts'e 47, p. 11.

ruthless oppression of this corrupt group upon the people had never before been equaled in the history of China. Chao I in his *Nien-erh-shih cha-chi*, under the title "Ming-tai hsiang-kuan yüeh-min chih hai," said: "It was general practice in the former Ming that not only local officials taxed the people in many illegal ways, but the gentry who lived in the countryside, on account of their connection and power, also considered the people an easy prey. Officials above and gentry below protected and covered up for one another, and there was no place the people could go to make their appeal."[113] Then Chao enumerated a number of local gentry, mostly sons and relatives of high officials of the time, who treated the people worse than slaves.

Besides all this, there was famine in the northern part of China during the last years of Ch'ung-cheng. *Ming-chi pei-lüeh* gives an account in the tenth year of Ch'ung-cheng (1637): "At the time drought and famine had been continuous for a number of years, and yet the magistrate [of Ch'i, the native place of Li Yen], a certain Sung, relentlessly pressed the people for taxes."[114] In addition to drought, Honan also experienced the pests of locusts during 1639, 1640, and 1641. Li Yen in 1641 wrote a song persuading the people to give alms to succor those who suffered under these unfortunate circumstances. As the song gives us a clear picture of the conditions of the time, it is translated here.

> In the last few years we have been suffering continuously from
> locusts and drought,
> Locusts nibble the grain shoots, leaving nothing to reap.
> The price of rice has risen several times,
> People all over the land have no way to live.
> To fill the stomach, they eat grass roots and leaves of trees,
> Children cry, looking blankly at each other.
> Pots and pans show accumulated dust, no smoke from the cooking
> stove,
> For days not even a meal of porridge.
> The government sends out tax collectors, tigers to the people,
> And the strong families demand debts like wolves.[115]

With these economic, political, and natural factors combined, rebellions would be a matter of course. There was a general turmoil at the

[113] *Nien-erh-shih cha-chi*, 34:14a.

[114] Chi Liu-ch'i (ed.), *Ming-chi pei-lüeh*, quoted in Kuo Mo-jo, *Chia-shen san-pai-nien chi*, p. 13.

[115] Chi, *Ming-chi pei-lüeh*, *chüan* 23, quoted in Kuo, *op. cit.*, p. 16.

end of the Ming, precipitating the "Roaming Bandits," the most important of whom were Li Tzu-ch'eng and Chang Hsien-chung.

Li Tzu-ch'eng was a native of Mi-chih in Shensi. His family for generations had lived in Huai-yüan (present Heng-shan *hsien* in Shensi).[116] At the end of T'ien-ch'i (1621–28), members of the Wei Chung-hsien clique Ch'iao Ying-chia and Chu T'ung-meng served as governors of Shensi and Yen-sui respectively. These governors were corrupt and greedy. They paid no attention to the bandits. Thus rose the banditry.[117]

Li was illiterate.[118] But with the help of Li Yen, he seemed able to appreciate the value of certain ideological elements in the traditional way of thought. First of all, he showed a measure of respect for scholars, at least for those who had obtained the degree of *chü-jen*, a degree which both Li Yen and Niu Chin-hsin, another assistant of Li Tzu-ch'eng, held. But this did not prevent him from cutting off the noses and legs of 190 students at the fall of Yen-ch'eng in Honan in 1642.[119] However, Li Yen was influential in the formation of many of the ideas, particularly the economic appeal to the people, which served the rebels well in winning an ever growing following.

At the end of 1641 Li Hsin and Niu Chin-hsin both went to attach themselves to Tzu-ch'eng. Tzu-ch'eng changed Li Hsin's name to Li Yen. Li Yen told Tzu-ch'eng, "One who would like to take the empire should make the heart of the people the foundation. My advice to you is: 'Do not kill,' in order to win over the heart of the people." Li Tzu-ch'eng followed his advice. Li Yen made up a song and had children sing it to influence the mind of the people. It runs: "If you welcome Prince Ch'uang (Tzu-ch'eng), you will not have to pay tax." Thus Tzu-ch'eng's following grew day by day.[120] A similar account is given in

---

[116] *Ming-shih*, 309:2b.

[117] *Ibid.*, 304:3a.

[118] Chao Tsung-fu, "Li Tzu-ch'eng pan-luan shih-lüeh," *Shih-hsüeh nien-pao*, Vol. II, No. 4 (Dec., 1937), p. 136. Ch'ien Chih, *Chia-shen ch'uan-hsin lu*, 6:102, says: "The first year of Ts'ung-chen. Tzu-ch'eng and others were drinking in the mountains. Someone expressed admiration for and a desire to be an official. Tzu-ch'eng said, 'In this world where bribery is the order of the day, where to become a civil official one has to write seven essays and even the military examination requires an essay, how can we, who do not study and are not literate, expect to become an official? I don't know, but there might be hope to become an emperor.' "

[119] Li Tzu-ch'eng did this because he was convinced he could not rally them to his support.

[120] *Ming-shih*, 309:11a–b. See also Wu Wei-yeh, *Lu-ch'iao chi-wen*, "Ch'uang Hsiang fa-nan," *chüan hsia:* p. 18b. Wu's version could have been the basis of the account given in *Ming-shih*.

Ming-chi pei-lüeh. It is reported there that Li Yen had the children sing:

> Eat his mother's,
> Clothed in his mother's,[121]
> Open the gate to welcome Prince Ch'uang;
> When Prince Ch'uang arrives,
> We shall no longer pay tax.

Another song he taught the children to sing runs:

> In the morning they ask for a *sheng* (升 a measure),
> And in the evening they ask for a *ho* (合 one-tenth of a *sheng*),
> Nowadays it is hard for a poor fellow to stay alive;
> Let's hurry to open the gate to receive Prince Ch'uang,
> And all will enjoy happiness.[122]

And in the *Tsui-wei-lu* Li Yen is reported to have told Tzu-ch'eng to pretend that he was applying the principle of equal distribution of land.[123] Chao Tsung-fu, in his "Li Tzu-ch'eng pan-luan shih-lüeh," expressed the view that Tzu-ch'eng changed the name of Yü-chou (in present Honan) to Chün-p'ing *chou* (equitable *chou*) for good reason.[124] The songs became so widespread that in Shensi a popular song was heard everywhere, which runs:

> Shoulder to shoulder we wait for Prince Ch'uang;
> When Prince Ch'uang comes we shall not have to pay taxes
> for three years.[125]

With this economic appeal and the propaganda that Li Tzu-ch'eng "does not kill; he does not love wealth; he does not insult women; he does not loot; he will sell and buy in fairness and relieve the people of

[121] The idea of these lines is not clear. They could be merely an expression of an exhilarating relief; or they could be hinting at something obscene, for it is not at all surprising to find country folk humorously engaged in exchanging obscene expressions in much the same way as we would exchange greetings.

[122] Chi, *Ming-chi pei-lüeh*, *chüan* 23, quoted in Kuo, *Chia-shen san-pai-nien chi*, pp. 19–20.

[123] Cha Chi-tso, *Tsui-wei-lu*, 31:78.

[124] Chao Tsung-fu, "Li Tzu-ch'eng pan-luan shih-lüeh," *Shih-hsüeh nien-pao*, Vol. II, No. 4 (Dec., 1937), p. 139. See *Ming-shih*, 309:15b for the change of Yü-chou to Chün-p'ing *chou*.

[125] T'ang Chen, *Ch'ien-shu*, quoted in Chao Tsung-fu, *op. cit.*, p. 139.

all taxes; he will redistribute the money of the rich among the people,"[126] it is no wonder that the government found it very difficult to deal with him.[127]

Li Tzu-ch'eng's ideology also contained the usual religious element of belief in the mandate of Heaven. In 1642, after escaping from the intrigue of Chang Hsien-chung,

> Tzu-ch'eng was in great distress, and was contemplating suicide.... Many rebel leaders surrendered [to the government]. A certain Liu Tsung-min, a blacksmith from Lan-t'ien [in Shensi], the bravest among the rebels, was also thinking of surrendering. Tzu-ch'eng walked with him into a temple and sighed while looking around. He said, "People said I should be the Son of Heaven. Why not let us divine? If the result is unfortunate, you may cut off my head and surrender." Tsung-min agreed. They divined three times, and each time they came out with the sign of "fortunate." Tsung-min then returned and killed his two wives and said to Tzu-ch'eng, "I shall follow you to the time of death." Many in his army who heard it also killed their wives and children as a token of their willingness to follow him.[128]

When Niu Chin-hsin introduced Sung Hsien-ts'e to Tzu-ch'eng in 1643, Tzu-ch'eng was very much pleased when Sung produced the divination

---

[126] Chi, *Ming-chi pei-lüeh*, *chüan* 20, quoted in Chao Tsung-fu, *op. cit.*, p. 142.

[127] Chi, *Ming-chi pei-lüeh*, *chüan* 19, reports that Ma Shih-ch'i in his response to an imperial question said: "Now both Li Ch'uang and Chang Hsien-chung have committed crimes the magnitude of which has extended to heaven; but it is easy to take care of Hsien and very difficult to deal with Ch'uang. The reason is: Hsien is feared by the people and Ch'uang is supported by them. . . . In the name of exterminating government troops in order to give peace to the people, he has for the time deceived the people and they surrender to him like following the direction of the wind. Furthermore, the rebels give wealth to succor the poor, and give them grain to ease their hunger so as to win their heart. As a result, the people follow the rebels like going home, forgetting all sense of loyalty and righteousness." Quoted in Kuo, *Chia-shen san-pai-nien chi*, pp. 8–9.

[128] *Ming-shih*, 309:10b. This, like the account of popular songs, seems to be based on Wu Wei-yeh's record in his *Lu-ch'iao chi-wen*, under the title, "Ch'uang Hsien fa-nan," *hsia*: 18a: "Tzu-ch'eng told his followers, 'People say that I have obtained the mandate of Heaven. Why don't you ask the spirits by divination? If unlucky, then kill me and surrender.' One of his military leaders by the name of Liu Tsung-min was a blacksmith from Lan-t'ien. He was also the bravest. At that time he was also thinking of surrendering. Tzu-ch'eng walked with him into a temple. He told Tsung-min to throw the oracle block three times. Every time it was lucky. Tsung-min returned and killed his two wives and said to Tzu-ch'eng, 'From now on whether dead or alive I shall follow you.' Many of the remaining men killed their wives and children, expressing their willingness to follow him."

lot on which was written, *Shih-pa-tzu chu shen-ch'i* (十八子主神器 ten-eight-son [meaning Li] will be the master of the spiritual vessel, the throne.)[129]

Li's idea of the mandate of Heaven is traditional. In 1644 when Tzu-ch'eng took Ch'en-t'ien (in present Hupeh), he gave himself the title *feng-t'ien ch'ang-i ta yüan-shuai* (奉天倡義大元帥 the great commander who rose in righteous movement in the name of Heaven).[130] And when he finally accepted the throne after it was offered him three times by his followers led by Niu Chin-hsin, he accepted it on the ground of his belief that "he truly had obtained the mandate of Heaven."[131]

When he gave the state examination, the first subject was: "T'ien yü chih" (天與之 Heaven gave it—the empire—to him). The second subject was: "Jo ta-han chih wang yün-ni yeh " (若大旱之望雲霓也 as if hoping for clouds during great drought). Both are from *Mencius*.[132]

Another examination given for *chü-jen* in the capital is reported in Wu Wei-yeh's *Lu ch'iao chi-wen*, where the following two subjects are given: "T'ien hsia kuei-jen yen" (天下歸仁焉 The whole world would submit to the benevolent rule), and "Li Chung-kuo erh fu ssu-i yeh" (涖中國而撫四夷也 to rule the Middle Kingdom and pacify the barbarians around).[133] One subject is from the *Analects* and the other from *Mencius*.[134]

Tzu-ch'eng's moral conceptions as applied to government are also completely traditional. In his edict, issued at the time he ascended the throne, he again stressed the inconstancy of the mandate of Heaven, and gave the collapse of moral discipline and the resulting misery of the people as the dominant factors responsible for the fall of the Ming.[135] In the *ch'ien-ch'ing-kung* (royal audience hall) there was a tablet on which were these characters: *ching-t'ien fa-tsu* (敬天法祖 reverence heaven and follow the model of ancestors). Tzu-ch'eng changed them to: *ching-t'ien ch'in-min* (敬天勤民 reverence heaven and apply oneself diligently to the affairs of the people)[136]

While in the capital, Tzu-ch'eng's subordinates were ruthless and

[129] *Ming-shih*, 309:11a–b.

[130] *Ibid.*, 309:14a.

[131] *Ibid.*, 309:21a.

[132] *Meng-tzu yin-te*, 36/5A/5 and 23/3B/5. This is reported in Ch'ien Pan-ch'i, *Ch'ung-chen chia-shen yen-tu chi-pien shih-lu*, p. 2a.

[133] *Lu ch'iao chi-wen*, "Huai-kuo jen-cheng," *hsia*: 26a.

[134] *Lun-yü yin-te*, 22/12/1; and *Meng-tzu yin-te*, 4/1A/7.

[135] Hsiao I-shan, *Ch'ing-tai t'ung-shih*, Vol. III, p. 248.

[136] Wu, *Lu ch'iao chi-wen*, "Huai-kuo jen-cheng," *hsia*: 26a.

cruel to the people. Tzu-ch'eng said to them, "Why don't you help me be a good emperor?"[137]

When the roll of the gentry was called, Chou Chung was especially recommended by Ku Chün-en as an able man. Tzu-ch'eng asked what he could do. Chün-en answered: "A famous man, versed in essay writing." Tzu-ch'eng smilingly said, "Why don't you write on the subject of *chien wei shou ming* (見危授命 when confronted with a crisis, give up your life)?"[138] His sentiment toward the ruling house is reminiscent of a loyal subject:

> [Tzu-ch'eng] entered the palace....Chou Kuei presented before him two princes. Tzu-ch'eng said, "I shall treat you in the manner of Ch'i and Sung" [Ch'i, the state enfeoffed to the remnants of the Hsia by the ruler of Chou in present Honan, and Sung, the state enfeoffed to the remnants of the Shang by the ruler of the Chou in Honan]....And he conferred the title Prince of Sung upon the heir apparent.[139]

Ch'ien Pan-ch'i gave the following account of Tzu-ch'eng's encounter with the heir apparent:

> Tzu-ch'eng told the prince to kneel. The prince was angry and said, "Why should I prostrate myself for you?"
> "Where is your father?"
> "Already dead in Ning-shou Palace."
> Tzu-ch'eng asked again, "Why did your house lose the empire?"
> The prince said, "Because of the treacherous minister Chou Yen-ju."
> Tzu-ch'eng smilingly said, "You do understand the reason indeed."
> The prince asked, "Why don't you kill me?"
> Tzu-ch'eng said, "You commit no crime. Do you think I would kill indiscriminately?"...
> Next morning there were more than one thousand three hundred officials at court to pay homage to the usurper. Tzu-ch'eng heaved a sigh saying, "With these people so utterly lacking in a sense of righteousness, how is it possible to avoid disorder in the world!" It was at this moment that Tzu-ch'eng began to have the desire to kill.[140]

When he saw the royal concubine Yüan and the eldest princess lying in the palace suffering from wounds inflicted by the emperor before he

---

[137] Ch'ien Chih, *Chia-shen ch'uan-hsin lu*, 4:56.

[138] Wu, *op. cit., hsia:* 25a. Also reported in Ch'ien Chih, *op. cit.,* 6:116. The source of the phrase is given in *Lun-yü yin-te*, 28/14/12.

[139] Wu, *op. cit., hsia:* 24b–25a. Also found in Ch'ien Chih, *op. cit.,* 6:116.

[140] *Ch'ung-chen chia-shen yen-tu chi-pien shih-lu*, p. 1a.

went to Mei-shan to commit suicide, Tzu-ch'eng said, "His majesty is indeed heartless."[141] When he found the emperor he mourned, "I came to enjoy the empire with you, why did you follow this shortsighted way?"[142]

With all his ruthlessness, Tzu-ch'eng did not have complete control over his followers. When he asked his subordinates, "Why don't you help me be a good emperor?" he was answered: "The power of being an emperor belongs to you, the power to loot belongs to us. Please say no more."[143] This weak control was evident even in the making of policy. Ch'ien Pan-ch'i related that according to the report of surrendered eunuchs, "Although rebel Li is the chief, there are more than twenty who hold power in balance, and everything is decided by the group as a whole."[144] Kuo Mo-jo, in his *Chia-shen san-pai-nien chi*, speaks of this as a kind of democratic conference.[145] In view of Tzu-ch'eng's ruthless way of disposing of Lo Ju-ts'ai,[146] it is difficult to think of Tzu-ch'eng as a democratic leader. It seems more probable that his followers had exactly the same spirit as those of Liu Pang before Liu's shrewdness in putting the court ceremonies into practice brought them under control.

Tzu-ch'eng's moral sense seems very keen. He did not harbor any grudge against those who had offended him in his worse days. When he had power he did not resent Chou Sheng's calling him names and condemning his way of doing things. The most interesting example of Tzu-ch'eng's moral sense is the case of Chang Kuo-shen. Chang was a state counselor of the Ming. He was made a prime minister when he surrendered to Li. To court favor, he took the beautiful wife of an old colleague and presented her to Tzu-ch'eng. Tzu-ch'eng, respecting the name of her husband, ordered Chang to be executed and returned the woman to her husband.[147]

In view of the accounts given above it seems safe to assume that under the influence of Li Yen and others, Li Tzu-ch'eng's pattern of thought was not only traditional, but traditionally Confucian. The *Ch'ao-ch'uang*

[141] Ch'ien Chih, *op. cit.*, 1:17.

[142] *Mi-chih hsien-chih*, "Li Tzu-ch'eng chuan," quoted in Chao Tsung-fu, "Li Tzu-ch'eng pan-luan shih-lüeh," *Shih-hsüeh nien-pao*, Vol. II, No. 4 (Dec., 1937), p. 147.

[143] Ch'ien Chih, *Chia-shen ch'uan-hsin lu*, 4:56.

[144] *Ch'ung-chen chia-shen yen-tu chi-pien shih-lu*, pp. 1b–2a.

[145] *Chia-shen san-pai-nien chi*, p. 34.

[146] *Ming-shih*, 309:16a.

[147] Wu, *Lu ch'iao chi-wen, hsia:* 27a. The case of Chang is also found in *Ming-shih*, 309:16a, where the authors said: "Tzu-ch'eng hated Chang for doing harm to his own colleague and had him executed."

hsiao-shih recorded a conversation between Li Yen and Sung Hsien-ts'e, in which Sung expressed objection to Buddhism and other forms of perverse teachings. Li Yen agreed with Sung in this. Sung said:

Buddhism originally came from a barbarian tribe, its teachings are heresies, and its perverse doctrine deceives the people and blocks the way of *jen* and *i*. Not only the ignorant fall under its charm; even scholars and dignitaries also worship its teachings and follow them. For the slightest irritation, people would willingly shave their heads to escape the judgment of right and wrong. If confronted with any difficulty, they would enter the empty gate and forget their prince and father. Monasteries and temples are havens where rebellious elements find their hiding place. Princes cannot make them their ministers and fathers cannot call them their sons. Though clothed in cotton cloth they compete with kings and dukes; they confuse [the people's mind] with respect to government and adulterate ideas with their heresies. Nothing fosters the spirit of laziness and deceitfulness more than this. If reciting sūtras is a profitable thing, then when besieged by the enemy why not recite sūtras to beat back the enemy? If religious ceremonies are efficacious, then when the ruler is about to die for the country, why not perform these ceremonies to prolong his life? For these reasons [we know] Buddhism is fantastic and false, and the wealth the people spend on its account is completely wasted. Everyone should engage himself in burning its writings, in eliminating the lazy and deceitful in the world, and in preserving the national wealth. In so doing, a nation would be rich and there would not be any roaming fellows around.[148]

In military organization, Li Tzu-ch'eng established the following titles: *ch'uan chiang-chün, chih chiang-chün, wei-wu chiang-chün,* and *kuo-i chiang-chün.* Males between the ages of fourteen and forty were conscripted. Military discipline forbade soldiers to keep silver for their own. There were also regulations about killing after the fall of a city. When a city surrendered without a fight, all lives were to be spared. If it resisted for one day, one-third of the people would be killed; seven-tenths would be killed if it resisted for two days; and a general massacre would be ordered if it resisted for three days. In government organization, there were instituted a premiership, a left and a right assistantship 左輔, 右弼, and six government offices paralleling the six boards. A prefect of a *fu* was called *yin*, the head of a *chou* was called *mu*, and the magistrate of a *hsien* was called *ling*.[149]

---

[148] Quoted in Kuo, *Chia-shen san-pai-nien chi,* p. 32.
[149] *Ming-shih,* 309:14b–15b. See also Chao I, *Nien-erh-shih cha-chi,* "Liu-tse wei kuan-hao."

With respect to Chang Hsien-chung, the second important "Roaming Bandit," there are few ideological elements worthy of consideration. His main mission seems to have been killing. The reason he gave for killing is: "Heaven gives men one hundred kinds of things, and men have nothing to serve Heaven." He said that he received this statement from a heavenly being in a dream. He is credited with the so-called *ch'i-sha pei* (a stone slab of seven "Kill's") where he said: "Heaven fosters people with one hundred grains, but man offers not a single good deed to serve Heaven. Kill. Kill. Kill. Kill. Kill. Kill. Kill."[150] He believed that all the people on earth committed crime and did not deserve to live, and that he himself was the incarnation of a star, sent down by the Jade Emperor to kill them all.[151] He even fabricated the "will of Heaven" to justify what he was doing:

> Hsien-chung was bent on killing, showing no sign of repentance. And yet he was concerned with the possibility of losing the support of the people; so he sought Chao-lin's advice in order to stop the rebellious activities of his subordinates. Chao-lin said, "These fellows who carry lances and wield spears know only whether they have things to eat and clothes to put on; they do not know anything else. If you just write a few lines and make believe that they are from the will of Heaven, to deceive them, they will submit to your will."
>
> Hsien-chung asked, "What do you mean by the will of Heaven?"
>
> Chao-lin said, "Leave it to me. But we have to wait for a tempestuous day, with howling wind, rolling thunder, and pouring rain to do it."
>
> On the evening of the fifteenth of that month, during the third beat, black clouds suddenly gathered, and it thundered and flashed, with rain pouring down without any letting up until the next morning. The whole city, both within and without, was over ten feet in water. Thousands of tents on both sides of the river were washed away. Hsien-chung told Chao-lin to proclaim to the generals and soldiers of the eight routes, saying: "Rain poured down since the third beat in the evening of the fifteenth of the seventh month, and it did not cease until the next morning. When his majesty ascended to the throne, he saw the will of Heaven on which is written: 'In the present world the people are disloyal and unfilial, and they have committed great crimes; the heart of man is not in accord with the mind of Heaven. The great catastrophe has arrived. There is no need of feeling pity about it. It proves that when his majesty killed soldiers and people, it was really the natural consequence of their own crime, and there is no way for them to escape punishment. His majesty is indeed acting for Heaven to make the way prevail. All of you, both officials and people,

---

[150] See Wu, *op. cit.*, "Hsien-chung t'u-shu," *hsia:* 20a.
[151] *Shu-chi*, p. 13b.

should wash your heart and cleanse your mind to stay the anger of Heaven. If in the future you still violate law, his majesty will exterminate you in the name of Heaven, and you should not give yourselves up to hate and anger.'"

The officials, not knowing that it was a design of the rebel leader, believed that they were punished by Heaven when they were killed.[152]

Hsien-chung was particularly thrilled by the massacre of scholars. The *Chia-shen ch'ao-shih hsiao-chi* states that Hsien-chung detested scholars because of their wickedness, dishonesty, greed, uselessness, and prejudice. The gentry and scholars in Szechwan were almost all killed. Once he killed more than two hundred subordinate officials. When someone told him that he killed too many of them, he said: "Who fears that there will be no men for the civil posts?"[153] On another occasion, he ordered an examination to be held. When the scholars gathered together to take it, he had them all killed.[154] Paradoxically enough, he expressed great respect for the god of literature, and even called himself the god of literature.[155] The name of the god is Wen-ch'ang. In the *Ming-shih*, "Li-chih," the following account is given:

> Tzu-t'ung ti-chün's [another name of Wen-ch'ang] surname was Chang, and his name was Ya-tzu. He lived in Ch'i-ch'ü shan in Szechwan. He served the Chin dynasty, and died in battle. The people erected a temple in his honor. He received titles from the T'ang and Sung dynasties, reaching the title of *ying-hsien wang*. The Taoists believed that *Ti* [Taoist Supreme deity] appointed Tzu-t'ung to take charge of the affairs of the office of Wen-ch'ang [the Great Bear], and also of the fate of people in the world; therefore during the Yüan dynasty the title of *ti-chün* was added. Some schools in the land also worshiped him.[156]

It is evident that Chang Hsien-chung's respect for Wen-ch'ang was due to the fact that Wen-ch'ang had Chang as his surname.

The rebellious nature of Chang Hsien-chung is also manifested in his attitude toward traditional ideas and institutions. When he was about to execute Prince Tuan and other officials of Szechwan,

Thunder and lightning suddenly broke out in a clear sunny sky. According

---

[152] *Ibid.*, p. 12a.
[153] Quoted in Hsiao I-shan, *Ch'ing-tai t'ung-shih*, I, 244.
[154] *Ming-shih*, 309:32a.
[155] Wu, *Lu-ch'iao chi-wen*, "Hsien-chung t'u shu," *hsia*: 20a.
[156] *Ming-shih*, 50:18a–b.

to a traditional view, this would be an evidence of heavenly displeasure for what he was about to do. But instead of listening to the heavenly warning, he turned to Heaven and shouted at it saying, "I am killing people; what has Heaven to do with it?" He ordered his men to fire big guns at Heaven. In a little while, it cleared up. He killed more than he had first planned.[157]

Whether this actually happened or was a story told by people to accentuate Hsien-chung's idiosyncrasy, Hsien-chung must have shown contempt for what the common people respected. Another anecdote may add to the weight of this point. Hsien-chung had a tablet erected in his own honor. He told the officer in charge to have it face north and back south. The writer responsible for the panegyric inscribed on the tablet said, "A ruler should face south, why face north?" Hsien-chung had him lashed to death, and threw his body away unburied.[158]

What could the Taipings have learned from Li and Chang? It is not probable that they took anything from these "Roaming Bandits." Hung Hsiu-ch'üan had nothing but condemnation for Li Tzu-ch'eng. He grouped Li Ch'uang (Tzu-ch'eng) with Huang Ch'ao, and called them *ts'ao-k'ou* who loved to kill.[159] It is true that an attitude of contempt need not prevent one from being unconsciously influenced by the views of the despised. At least one modern writer believes that Tzu-ch'eng's idea of land distribution must have been the forerunner of the *T'ai-p'ing t'ien-kuo* land system, even though there is no clear evidence for it.[160] But if the Taipings needed any inspiration for their land system, they had many other sources to use. The idea of equal distribution of land did not originate with Tzu-ch'eng, neither did Tzu-ch'eng have any specific idea to offer as to the ways and means of carrying it out. He and his followers merely had the most general and vague ideas about land problems. If they did have any scheme about it, it is not recorded. The Taipings, on the other hand, developed their land system neatly with concrete formulations.

In the matter of religious elements in their ideologies, both Hung and Li drew upon the traditional font. But apart from some of the most rudimentary popular ideas and superstitions, the two movements had

[157] Wu, *op. cit.*, *chung:* 17b.

[158] *Shu-chi*, pp. 8b–9a.

[159] "T'ai-p'ing chao-shu," in Hsiao, *Ts'ung-shu*," *ts'e* 1, p. 3a. *Ts'ao-k'ou* means "grass bandits," a contemptuous way of referring to any outlaws.

[160] Wang Lin-kao, preface to Ch'ien Chih, *Chia-shen ch'uan-hsin lu*, p. 13.

nothing in common. Li entertained no religious creed. Lo Erh-kang, in his *T'ien-ti hui wen-hsien lu* under the title "Shui-hu-chuan yü t'ien-ti hui," quotes his friend Wu Han, a specialist on the history of Ming, as saying:

> No popular uprisings in the history of China did not make use of some perverse religious teachings to fan and deceive the people; but the 'Roaming Bandits' at the end of the Ming constituted an exception. Because the people at the end of the Ming were deeply influenced by the *Shui-hu chuan*, these "'Roaming Bandits' manifested clear political consciousness in their activities, free from superstitious coloring."[161]

Li's initial success was solely dependent upon his economic appeal. Hung, on the other hand, used religious elements in his ideology as a rallying means to win a following, and his economic appeal added to the strength of his ideology. Hung and his followers had some religious zeal and fervor in connection with their mission. Their anti-Buddhistic attitude is iconoclastic, directed against idolatry. The objection of Li Tzu-ch'eng's followers to Buddhism, on the other hand, was based on economic and cultural grounds, in much the same spirit as that of Han Yü of the T'ang dynasty.

In military and political organization, no connection seems to exist between Li and Hung. Li instituted six government offices, which are similar in nature to the six *shang-shu* of the Taipings; and both have offices called *tso-fu* 左輔 and *yu-pi* 右弼. But neither of these was original with either of them. The Taipings' six boards had been in use during earlier dynasties, derived from the six *kuan* (offices) of the *Chou-li*. *Tso-fu* and *yu-pi* came down to us from the *Shang-shu ta-chuan*, where it is stated: "In ancient times the Son of Heaven had to have four assistants: the one in front is called *i* 疑; the one behind, *ch'en* 丞; the one on the left, *fu* 輔; and the one on the right, *pi*, 弼."[162]

As for Chang Hsien-chung, not even the greatest stretch of imagination can relate him to the Taipings. It seems safe to assume that the Taipings learned very little, if anything at all, from the "Roaming Bandits" who brought to an end the Ming dynasty.

CONCLUSIONS

The above brief survey of some rebel ideologies in Chinese history

---

[161] *T'ien-ti hui wen-hsien lu*, p. 78.
[162] *Shang-shu ta-chuan*, attributed to Fu Sheng of the Han, 2:27.

prior to the Taipings does not, indeed, tell us whether these ideologies had any direct influence upon that of the Taipings. But in the process of exposition, certain important facts emerge. Firstly, the circumstances to which rebellions arose as reactions were recurring with disconcerting regularity; and secondly, the rebels, with some rare exceptions, had a surprisingly uniform mental outlook and view of things. A review of the causes of rebellions reveals that these recurring circumstances were government oppression, land concentration, heavy taxation, corrupt officialdom, and deterioration of conditions in general. Occasionally natural calamities were an added scourge. In religious matters all the rebels viewed heaven as a spiritual force which conferred upon the virtuous the mandate to rule. This would imply that they considered the world, of which heaven was a concrete symbol, to be a moral order in which the principle of retribution prevails. This conception, together with the belief in the physical symbols purporting to substantiate their claim of having received the mandate, explains a common practice of almost all the rebels to fabricate such physical symbols. Occasionally there was a reckless soul like Chang Hsien-chung, who defied Heaven; but in the accusation he brought against men for not doing anything worthy of the boundless grace Heaven had showered upon men—an accusation used to justify his wanton killing—he revealed his own conception of Heaven as unmistakably conventional.

Nearly all the rebellions studied here had religious beliefs of some sort because their leaders planned to appeal to the people who had been influenced by some form of Taoist or Buddhist sects such as *T'ai-p'ing tao* of Chang Chüeh during the Later Han, or *Pai-lien* and Maitreya sects during the Sung and the subsequent dynasties. In the main their religious beliefs can be traced to either Buddhism, Taoist sects, or orthodox Confucianism, as can be seen in the ideologies of later secret societies, of which the *T'ai-p'ing tao*, *Pai-lien*, and Maitreya sects were forerunners. However, there were some religious beliefs which cannot be considered as common to all the rebels. Chang Chüeh's idea of confession of wrongdoing and repentance as a prerequisite for magical healing; and the belief of the vegetable-eaters and devil-worshipers that death is a state of salvation because life is full of misery, and that killing is a just means to help people free themselves from misery and attain that blissful state—these are some of the exceptions. But in the major part of their ideologies, the rebels exhibited an astonishingly uniform pattern.

In the economic aspect, the rebels seem to have concentrated their

attention on relations centering around land and taxes. The concentration of land in the hands of a few has always been one of the main
factors in China's revolts, uprisings, and rebellions. However, the fact
that only a few of the rebels advocated equal land distribution would
indicate that the majority of them did not have in mind a new land
system which would radically alter the relations between landowners
and tenants and consequently affect the traditional alignment in social
stratification. In other words, with a few exceptions, the rebels conformed in their attitudes to the old conception of land relations. Probably it was for this reason that most of them promised to exempt or
lighten taxes.

Socially the rebels were also uniformly unimaginative. Apart from
Ch'en Sheng's vague suggestion that birth was no longer the mark of
aristocracy, an idea which was revolutionary at Ch'en's time but soon
afterward ceased to be so, none of them had any completely new idea
to offer.

Most religious, moral, and economic ideas considered above have
had great political significance. And most of these ideas have been used
by the rebels with varying success. In addition to these ideas, which
they employed for political purposes, the rebels repeatedly resorted to
the principle of legitimate succession.

When the presence of foreign aggression or occupation is among the
circumstances, the ethnic issue is invariably raised. Thus Fang La
harangued the Sung for appeasing the northern barbarians; the rebels
at the end of the Yüan dynasty condemned the Yüan's rule because,
among other things, they were non-Chinese; and the members of
secret societies in the Ch'ing times and the Taipings used this ethnic
issue against the Manchu regime to their best advantage.

There is little doubt that the rebels employed the ideas they shared
in a way roughly similar and for purposes parallel. To them the idea of
heavenly mandate was a common source of courage and a means to win
a following. Those who had any religious beliefs at all often used them
as a political camouflage. The rebels must also have understood quite
well the religious psychology of the people, in view of the way they took
advantage of the people's religious credulity. They must have realized
the tremendous emotional appeal that the principle of legitimate succession had because of the idea of loyalty which had become part of the
moral life of the Chinese. Even the devil-worshipers' idea of killing as a
way to help people attain salvation was directed toward the political end

of winning the support of the people, an end which was shared by all the rebels; the devil-worshipers were to win the people's support by justifying their obviously ruthless actions.

Two specific religious ideas among the rebels' ideologies were exceptions to their general patterns of thought: Chang Chüeh's ideas of confession and repentance as a prerequisite condition for his magical healing, and the devil-worshipers' idea that killing is a means to give people salvation.

Chang Chüeh's idea of "wrongdoing" does not have the profundity the Christian idea of sin implies, and hence what he called "confession" and "repentance of wrongdoing" was no more than an acknowledgment of one's error or mistake. However, as a prerequisite condition for healing, such notions of confession and repentance do seem to indicate a certain awareness of the relationship between moral and spiritual faults and physical ailments. His making confession and repentance a condition for healing distinctly implies that he believed in the force of the spiritual over the physical. This seems to be a unique phenomenon in Chinese religious ideas. But in popular practice there is a parallel case where the sick is believed to have been disrespectful to some deities and his suffering is considered a just punishment inflicted upon him by the deities; or the sick is believed to have been possessed by some evil spirits. The former case would require a sort of repentance by the sick person, a sacrifice to cleanse himself of his blasphemous faults and to propitiate the angered deities; and the latter would require some spiritual man who had the power to drive out the evil spirits, usually by a magical art using charmed water. The fact that Chang practiced human sacrifice to Heaven suggests that Heaven may have been the deity who was angered; and his use of charmed water indicates that Chang may have thought of evil spirits as the cause of sickness and disease. If this is the case, then Chang had no more spiritual insight than any of the witches and sorcerers who made a profession of magical healing.[163]

The idea of killing as a just means to help people attain salvation implies that death is that blissful state. To consider death as a state of salvation is nothing new. All religions try to explain death in some such way, for the human spirit refuses to acknowledge death as final. But this belief almost invariably grows out of love of life, and is as invariably connected with the idea of the supreme value of life. It is indeed rare,

[163] According to H. Maspero in *Mélanges posthumes*, II, 26, the idea that disease is due to sin was current among the Taoists under the Hsu.

especially in the history of ideas in China, to find the idea of death as salvation and the idea of love of life combined as they were in the minds of the vegetable-eaters and devil-worshipers. This joining of ideas may have been derived from some foreign sources. Members of the vegetable-diet and devil-worship group were identified with the Manichaeans. It is possible that certain ideas in the Persian belief taken in isolation might have led to the notion that killing helped people attain salvation. According to the exposition of Manichaeism by Martan-farukh, an author of the ninth century who sought to refute certain views held by Mani, the Manichaeans said: "...whereas Ahriman [the Evil One] maintained the world, God is [nevertheless] finally triumphant through the separation of lives[= souls] from bodies."[164] In Professor Jackson's introduction to *Researches in Manichaeism*, he says: "In the production of the human species the demoniacal forces played not an involuntary part but an active role of their own wicked designing, the creation of the two sexes being especially the work of the Evil One. His fiendish aim was by this means to incarcerate the light perpetually in the bonds of the carnal body."[165] The separation of souls from bodies could conceivably be carried out by destroying the bodies, and this bodily destruction would then set free the light which the Evil One had perpetually imprisoned in the bodies. Such an interpretation is obviously in contradiction to the Manichaean tenet that "it is not proper to kill any creature whatsoever, because it (i.e., killing) is the work of Ahriman."[166]

In the light of the survey above, the rebels, with rare exceptions, have shown a remarkable uniformity in their mental outlook. From the point of view of their attitudes toward things, they seem to have a tradition of their own. Even though we find no direct influence of their ideologies upon that of the Taipings, the latter can be considered as one group among the many representatives in the continuous development of the rebel tradition.

It is clear that the rebels' mental outlook falls in neatly with the main currents of China's tradition, the main views in the Chinese Weltanschauung. The mandate of Heaven dates back to the pre-Confucian days, and the rebels' attempt to fabricate symbols of prognostication was

[164] A. V. Williams Jackson, *Researches in Manichaeism*, p. 181.
[165] *Ibid.*, p. 11.
[166] *Ibid.*, p. 181. Professor P. Demiéville in a letter to the author dated October 11, 1954, says, "the idea of the moral justification of murder is not necessarily Manichaean."

based on the belief that the fate of a state was revealed through some natural phenomena, an idea first hinted at in "The Doctrine of the Mean"[167] and later developed by the Han commentators of the Kung-yang school of the *Ch'un-ch'iu* (Annals of Spring and Autumn).[168] Other religious ideas which were not Confucian in character were derived from either Taoism or Buddhism; the latter, though introduced into China in the first century from India, has since become an integral part of the Chinese religious beliefs. The idea of economic equality implied in the rebels' aspiration for equal distribution of land had been present at the beginning of most dynasties, and cannot be considered as falling entirely outside Chinese tradition. Thus what we have considered as a tradition of rebellions turns out to be a particular version of the Chinese tradition in general.

The efficacy of the rebels' ideological schemes may be explained by the traditional bent of their minds, which was shared by the people whose support they wanted to win. The varying degrees of success the leaders of the different rebellions achieved seems due to the difference in their effort and sincerity in carrying out the ideas they proclaimed. Of course there were other elements which played an even more important role in making a rebellion a success or failure; but other things being equal, the more earnest they were in carrying out their schemes, the better chance they had to succeed.

Finally, although throughout the long history of China there were many rebellions, revolts, and uprisings, prior to her contact with the West in modern times there had never been any movement which can be considered a revolution. In making this statement, I have in mind the definition of "revolution" found in the *Encyclopaedia of the Social Sciences*, which says:

> The term revolution, outside the natural sciences, connotes a sudden and far reaching change, a major break in the continuity of development.... a major change in the political order—not merely a shift in the personnel of the government or a reorientation of its concrete policies—must be preceded or accompanied by a drastic change in the relations among the different groups and classes in society. Thus a recasting of the social order is, at least in modern times, a far more important characteristic of revolutions than a change of the political constitution or the use of violence in the attainment of this end. This aspect of revolution distinguishes it also from

[167] *Li-chi yin-te*, 31/22.
[168] See Tung Chung-shu, *Ch'un-ch'iu fan-lu.*

coup d'état, rebellion and insurrection, with which it is sometimes confused....

The significance of a revolution lies in the fact that it is not merely a
violent and profound modification of the social organization but a major
shift in the relations between social classes whereby the dominance of the
upper class is destroyed and the lower class emancipates itself from economic exploitation buttressed by political subordination.[169]

None of the rebellions we have surveyed fits this definition of revolution. I do not believe we can be accused of being anachronistic in
applying a modern definition to historical cases; for we want to understand these cases not only in their original historical perspective, but
also in terms of modern concepts and evaluations.

---

[169] *Encyclopaedia of the Social Sciences*, editor-in-chief Edwin R. A. Seligman (15 vols;
New York: Macmillan Co., 1935), XIII, 367–68.

PART THREE

Interpretations of the *T'ai-p'ing T'ien-kuo*

In previous chapters, we have limited our examination to what the Taiping ideology expressly said. In Chapters XII through XIV, we shall attempt to discover some of the reasons behind the ideology by taking into consideration the social, economic, and political conditions in China at the time of the rebellion and the mental make-up of the Taiping leaders.

A glance at the interpretations offered from the time of the Taipings to the present may be of help in steering a course. A voluminous literature, offering all shades of opinion from those of the extreme partisans on the one side to those of the extremely censorious critics on the other, has grown up around the central theme of the Taiping movement. Conscious that the influence of special interests may color one's evaluation and judgments, I have tried as far as possible to keep before me the possible motives of those whose views are here under consideration.

For analyses of the conditions in China and the mental attitudes of the leaders, I shall rely heavily upon the works of many scholars who have given us a good picture of the main features of the social, political, and economic life of nineteenth-century China. I have to stake the validity of my interpretation on the soundness of their analyses, even assuming that I have not misused their conclusions or misinterpreted their interpretations.

In addition to the attempt to understand the Taiping ideology by reference to factors transcendent to the ideology itself, we also have to place the Taiping movement in the total context of Chinese rebellions. In the light of all these aims, we shall discuss the nature of the movement and evaluate its significance in reference to the revolutionary movements subsequent to the Taiping times.

Chapter XII

Nineteenth-Century Interpretations

CHINESE WRITERS

To the government officials, particularly those who were in charge of the campaign against them and who were responsible for their final suppression, the Taipings were no more than treasonous elements and were consequently stigmatized as *Yüeh-fei* (粵匪 bandits from Yüeh– Kwangtung and Kwangsi provinces) or *Yüeh-k'ou* (粵寇 insurgents from Yüeh). As the contemporary accounts of the Taiping movement were from the pens of Manchu officials or of those who had suffered at the hands of the Taipings, it is impossible to expect the authors to be impartial.[1] Although many of them were fully aware of the part played

[1] The following writers are representative of those who witnessed the happenings of the Taiping day and wrote about them. Information about their status is included to indicate that they were probably prejudiced against the Taipings because of their gentry membership or official position. Many were critical of the way in which both military and civil government leaders dealt with the situation; some were censorious of official corruption and military bungling; some readily admitted that the government troops were largely responsible for the destruction and the sufferings they had witnessed. Although few of them were articulate about any of the larger issues of the day, there is little doubt that they would have rallied behind Tseng Kuo-fan's movement for the defense of native culture, which he later enunciated in his "Proclamation."

Li Kuang-chi 李光霽, a member of a scholar family, was the author of *Chieh-yü cha-chih* 刼餘雜感. (See Hsiang Ta *et al.* [compilers], *T'ai-p'ing t'ien-kuo*, V, 310). Hu Ch'ang-lin 胡長齡 was the author of *Chien-te tsai sui-pi* 儉德齋隨筆. He was an *en-kung* 恩貢 in the year 1880 and was appointed *po-shih ti-tzu yüan* 博士弟子員 when he was only sixteen.

Yao Shen 姚諶, author of *Hu-pien chi-lüeh* 胡變紀略, was known as Yao Hsiao-lien 姚孝廉 and held the literary degree of *chü-jen*. He corresponded with Chao Kuang-ch'a (Ching-hsien, the gentry leader who took charge of the defense of Hu-chou). Ku Shen 顧深, author of *Hu-k'ou sheng-huan chi* 虎口生還記, was the son of a famous scholar of

by the government troops in the wanton destruction, with rare exceptions these writers condemned the Taipings as *i-tse* (treasonous bandits) and held them responsible for the general devastation and massacre. Government officials and Taiping victims were so blinded by the

---

his native district and was known as the son of Hsiao hsiu-ts'ai 小秀才.

Chou Pan-fu 周邦福, author of *Meng-nan shu-ch'ao* 蒙難述鈔, was a rich merchant from a family of scholars. Wang K'un 汪堃, author of *Tun-pi sui-wen lu* 盾鼻随聞録, was a department magistrate in Szechwan.

Chang Chi-keng 張繼庚, author of *Chang Chi-keng i-kao* 張繼庚遺稿, was a *ling-shang-sheng* 廩膳生. His father had been a *chin-shih* in 1826 and later a magistrate. Chang was the central figure in the 1854 attempt to open the gates of Nanking to the government forces. He was executed when the attempt failed. The author of *Chin-lin pei-nan chi* 金陵被難記 is not known. As the author referred to Ch'ing officials by their epistolary styles such as Ch'i Fang-po (祈方伯, *fang-po* being the epistolary style of a provincial political commissioner) and Hsiang Ching-lüeh (向經略, *ching-lüeh* being an epistolary style of a military commander-in-chief), it is very probable that this author was one of the subordinate officials in the government.

Ma Shou-lin 馬壽齡, author of *Chin-ling kuei-chia hsin yüeh-fu, wu-shih shou* 金陵癸甲新樂府五十首, was known as *ming-ching* (明經, an examination title in the T'ang time which was abolished after the Sung but was still used to refer to title-holders). Chang Ju-nan 張汝南 was the narrator of *Chin-ling sheng-nan chi-lüeh* 金陵省難紀略, the ghost writer being his son Ho-fu. From the preface written by his friend Yao T'ien-lin, who shared the experience of those early days of the Taiping occupation of Nanking, it is obvious that Chang was a scholar.

Hsieh Chieh-ho 謝介鶴, author of *Chin-ling kuei-chia chi-shih lüeh* 金陵癸甲紀事略, was one of the plotters to turn the city of Nanking over to the government forces. When the attempt failed, he managed to escape and left the city. Ti-fou Tao-jen 滌浮道人, author of *Chin-ling cha-chi* 金陵雜記, was also known as *chih-fei-tzu* 知非子. This *hao* marks him as a member of the scholar class.

Ch'en Hui-yen 陳徽言, author of *Wu-ch'ang chi-shih* 武昌紀事, a government student, became a *t'ung-pan* on the basis of his military merits and died in battle in 1857 (see text, Chapter XII). The author of *Wu-ch'ang ping-hsien chi-lu* 武昌兵燹紀略 is not known; but from the attitude expressed in the work, he was either an official or a gentry member. His view of the government and military affairs is penetrating.

Hsü Feng-en 許奉恩, narrator of *Chuan-hsi yü-sheng chi* 轉徙餘生記, was a prominent member of T'ung-ch'eng gentry. That Li Kuei 李圭, author of *Ssu-t'ung chi* 思痛記, was a prominent gentry member is evident from the way he described his family circumstances.

Ming-hsin tao-jen 明心道人, author of *Fa-i ch'u-chi* 髮逆初記, was in constant correspondence with Tsou Ming-ho 鄒鳴鶴 and connected with Sai-shang-a 賽尚阿 and Hsiang Jung 向榮; he was a military officer under Hsiang Jung. Shen Mao-liang 沈懋良 was the author of *Chiang-nan ch'un-meng-an pi-chi* 江南春夢庵筆記. Although there is little internal evidence of his status, his sympathy with the government and his style, which is similar to that of Chang Te-chien's *Tse-ch'ing hui-tsuan*, are clear indications of his status.

Li Ju-chao 李汝昭, author of *Ching-shan yeh-shih* 鏡山野史, is discussed in Chapter XII. Chang Te-chien 張德堅, editor and compiler of *Tse-ch'ing hui-tsuan* 賊情彙纂, was a member of Tseng's staff; the work was collected under the sponsorship of Tseng.

immediate situation, which demanded all their energy and power, that it would have been a miracle if they could have passed objective judgments upon their enemy. Their minds were neither emotionally free nor provided with the proper perspective to view the movement without bias. To them the Taiping religion was heresy and the Taiping organization was like that of other historical religious sects. These writers believed the Taipings raised a religious front first to camouflage their political ambition and then to help them control the minds of their followers.[2]

Of all the contemporary Chinese writers, only Ch'en Hui-yen, who was a government student appointed *t'ung-p'an* (assistant subprefect) through military merits and who died in battle in 1857, seems to have had some superficial idea of what Christianity was. In connection with the Taiping religious teachings, he mentioned the Catholic religion, referring to Matteo Ricci, Emmanuel Diaz, Giulio Aleni, and Nicolo Longobardi—Jesuit fathers who came to China during the Ming dynasty. However, he spoke of their writings as illogical and absurd, plagiarizing the teachings of Buddhism; he also identified the writings with Manichaeism. He condemned the Taipings as *chiao-fei* (religious bandits) and blamed the Christian teachings for the uprisings of these religious bandits.[3]

Because they adopted a religion whose origin could be traced to foreign lands, there was a general feeling that the Taipings were deliberately working against the spirit of their native culture. It seems to be this feeling, rather than a sense of loyalty to the tottering dynasty, that finally aroused some of the scholars to assume the post of protectors of the native faith. Even the alarm over the Taiping destruction was mainly over the loss of cultural assets, such as the Pao-en t'a [pagoda] and the Sung editions of books. This attitude is eloquently expressed in Tseng Kuo-fan's "Proclamation," a short quotation from which is sufficient to illustrate the attitude of the scholars:

> The Yüeh rebels plagiarize some of the religious ideas of the foreign barbarians, and from the kings down to the soldiers and mean runners all call themselves brothers. They say T'ien alone can be called father, and all fathers of the people are brothers and all mothers, sisters. The peasants

[2] See Hsieh Chieh-ho, Chang Ju-nan, Wang K'un, and many others on this point in Hsiang, *T'ai-p'ing t'ien-kuo*, II, 688, 702–3, and IV, 359. In the last reference Wang K'un remarks: "The Yüeh bandits attempt to deceive the people under the guile of heretic teachings, and for a long time they have entertained treasonous ambitions."

[3] Hsiang, *T'ai-p'ing t'ien-kuo*, IV, 599–600.

cannot have their own land to till and to pay tax, for all land belongs to the T'ien Wang. The merchants cannot trade and make money, for they say all commodities belong to the T'ien Wang. The scholars cannot study the classics of Confucius, for they have what is called the teachings of Jesus and the New Testament. They are throwing overboard the principles of *li* and *i*, which govern human relationships, and the orthodox teachings contained in the *Book of Poetry* and the *Book of History*—principles which have been in effect in China for thousands of years. Is this merely a crisis in the Ch'ing dynasty? It is indeed an unprecedented crisis in the history of *ming-chiao* (traditional Confucian moral principles). For this Confucius and Mencius must be moaning at the ninth spring. How can the educated fold their hands and sit on the side as spectators without thinking of doing something about it?[4]

A rare exception to this group of prejudiced writers was Li Ju-chao, who wrote a work in the style of a historical novel and titled it *Ching-shan yeh-shih*.[5] In this work he referred to the Taipings as *Yüeh-ping* (troops from Yüeh), a neutral term, not loaded with a value judgment as are the terms *Yüeh-fei* and *i-tse*. On the basis of this term, Yeh Kung-ch'o considered Li a Taiping sympathizer.[6] But even a casual reading of his work will enable one to see that Li was quite unbiased, that he did not sympathize with the Taipings. True, like many contemporary writers, he condemned the cowardice and outrageous conduct of the government officials; but he was equally strong in his rebuke of the Taiping leaders. Of them he said:

> Their main purpose is to plunder and to loot; there is not the slightest indication of a kingly act, nor is there the remotest semblance of a tyrant's plan. Their only desire is to fight for territory by killing and to storm cities by massacre, and thus to unleash their brutal arrogance and to throw the land of *our* Ch'ing dynasty into confusion. But all this is probably the result of Heaven's disgust with the corruption of this dynasty of ours, bringing about a state in which one perverse element is engaged in exterminating another.[7] [Italics mine. V.S.]

Li termed both parties "perverse," but his use of the term "our" makes it very clear where his loyalty lay. Li's vulgar style and his confusion in the use of homophonic words indicate that his station was not very

---

[4] *Tseng Wen-cheng kung ch'üan-chi*, "Wen-chi," 3:1b.
[5] Hsiang, *T'ai-p'ing t'ien-kuo*, III, 3–21.
[6] *Ibid.*, III, 20.
[7] *Ibid.*, III, 9.

high. Taking his whole account into consideration, we may accept Yeh's identification of Li as "a peasant living in the country," although he could have been a rustic with some superficial education, as Yeh himself concedes.[8] But to suppose that Li was conditioned by his class situation to be a Taiping sympathizer is farfetched. The first lines in his work show conclusively that he had no clear idea of what class consciousness was:

> In the thirtieth year of Tao-kuang the emperor died, and the next year was made the first year of Hsien-feng. This is the seventh emperor, and each period has been graced by a virtuous ruler. In this unified China all praise the [imperial] virtue. What I hate is that while the ruler is enlightened, the ministers are not good. When the officials are avaricious and greedy, the people will not enjoy peace.[9]

Apart from their attitude toward the Taipings, did the contemporary writers entertain any ideas radically different from those of the Taipings? What ideas did Tseng and his group bring forth to oppose those of the Taipings? Inasmuch as there is little ideological content in the works of most memoir writers of that time, we have to depend on Tseng and his immediate associates for these ideas. The first important document is of course Tseng's "Proclamation" against the Yüeh bandits. Here Tseng stressed the Taipings' wanton killing and destruction, abuse of womanhood, betrayal of native culture, abandonment of human relations, worship of God as the only father, abolition of private ownership of land, adoption of foreign religion, disrespect to spirits and deities, and lack of political reason for rebellion. In a letter to Shih Ta-k'ai, Tseng must have raised the ethnic issue; for in his reply to Tseng's letter, Shih mentioned the distinction between the Chinese and barbarians as the spirit of the *Ch'un-ch'iu*, and on the basis of this spirit Shih condemned Tseng's idea that the Ch'ing had earned the orthodox position merely because for seven generations the Manchus had been ruling China. Shih's letter implies that Tseng believed the difficulty which the Taipings experienced after the internal split and the independent movement of Shih indicated that it was not the will of Heaven for the Taipings to take over the rule of the empire. It also seems that Tseng did not think people of humble origin could have obtained the mandate of Heaven to rule. To dispose of these objections, Shih had

[8] *Ibid.*, III, 20–21.
[9] *Ibid.*, III, 3,

only to mention that twice in Chinese history men of humble origin had ascended the throne. If a temporarily difficult situation were construed as the manifestation of the adverse will of Heaven, neither Liu Pang nor Chu Yüan-chang would ever have become the emperor of China.

Li Yüan-tu, Tseng's lieutenant, wrote a letter to Shih at Tseng's request attempting to persuade Shih to surrender. In addition to the ideas in Tseng's "Proclamation," Li brought forth the following ideas: Those who are ignorant of what is in conformity and what is in opposition to Heaven will be destroyed. All rebellions in the past were prompted by ignorant rulers and political confusion, an indication that the mandate of Heaven had left the reigning dynasty. But this was not so with the Manchus. For generations peace had reigned throughout the empire; and the people supported the Manchus because theirs was a government which had not misruled; hence the mandate of Heaven was still firmly in their grip.

Li mentioned that Shun was born a barbarian from the east and King Wen was a barbarian from the west, implying that being a barbarian did not bar one from becoming the orthodox bearer of the mandate of Heaven. Furthermore, the Taipings themselves adopted the Christian religion of the British barbarians, who were known to recognize no human relations. Li pointed out the absurdity of the new calendar: according to the Taiping calendar, it would be impossible to recognize the movement of the moon by reference to the dates. The arbitrary change of the symbol of the heaven and earth signs constituted another evidence of the Taipings' perverse nature. Li reiterated Tseng's clamor that the Taipings were traitors to the Way of Confucius and Mencius, the symbol of the native culture of China. He said that the Taipings' disrespect for native gods and deities, some of whom were deified sages and worthies of the past, was an insult to these great sages and worthies.

To build the case that the Manchus ruled in an orthodox way, Li cited the following facts. The Manchus, who had never been subjects of the Ming dynasty, were not bound by loyalty as Liu Pang and Chu Yüan-chang certainly were to the earlier dynasties, and they did all they were expected to do when they gave the royal personages of the Ming a proper burial; their taking over the rule was indeed mandated by the will of Heaven, for the mandate of the Ming had evidently run out. The Manchus had given the Chinese the most glorious reign of all dynasties in the whole history of China; had expanded the territory wider than any preceding dynasty; has put into effect the best regula-

tions governing the royal household, particularly in connection with the activities of eunuchs and women; had shown the greatest military exploits and the most benevolent government in history; and had paid particular attention to the economic life of the people by edicts that prohibited the increase of land tax and the levy of head tax on newborn children.[10]

Shih gave long thought to Li's letter urging him to capitulate; finally he refused to surrender with the answer, "Difficult." It is evident from his reply that Shih knew full well he could easily dispose of the points both Tseng and Li raised. The only issue over which Shih may have experienced some difficulty is the Taiping adoption of Christianity, a distinctly foreign belief, and the alleged betrayal of native culture; the Taipings condemned the Manchu regime mainly because the Manchus were non-Chinese. Thus, the ethnic issue was exploited by both the Taipings and their enemy; the difference in their handling of it was that while the Taipings used both the political and cultural aspects of the issue, Tseng and Li emphasized only the cultural aspect.

Western Writers

If the view of the nineteenth-century Chinese writers is warped because of lack of perspective, that of Western writers is colored by their special interests. However, here we are more likely to find relatively objective attempts to evaluate the Taiping movement. Missionaries, before they had any chance to find out what the Taipings meant by the apparently Christian doctrines they professed, were overwhelmed by the Taiping initial religious zeal, military discipline, and success. Being vastly more informed on conditions in China than other non-Chinese groups, these missionaries were aware that something was about to happen.[11]

The French authors Callery and Yvan quoted an English journal in August, 1850:

24th *August.*—Under the powerful influence of the men of letters, and in consequence of a general discontent throughout China, the cry of reform is raised in all directions. The new principles are making immense progress, and the day is rapidly approaching when the empire will be torn in pieces

[10] Quoted in Hsieh Hsing-yao, *T'ai-p'ing t'ien-kuo shih-shih lun-ts'ung*, pp. 168–76.
[11] See John B. Littell, "Missionaries and Politics in China—The Taiping Rebellion," *Political Science Quarterly*, Vol. XLIII, No. 4 (Dec., 1928), p. 568.

by civil war. Among the higher and middle classes of Pekin there is a firm belief in the prophecy diffused over China a century ago, that the reigning dynasty will be overthrown in the commencement of the 48th year of the present cycle, and this fatal year will begin on the 1st February next.[12]

When the Taipings swept up to Nanking, Rev. M. S. Culbertson referred to the movement as God's promise that "the heathen shall be given to the Son for his inheritance"; he also referred to "the indications, seen throughout the world, that the set time for the accomplishment of this promise is drawing near."[13]

The business and diplomatic groups saw in this movement a more reasonable reception at court and better trade relations.[14] They hoped to obtain from the Taipings what they failed to get from the Manchus.

As time went on, all these groups experienced disappointment. Missionaries, either through a closer scrutiny of Taiping beliefs or through detection of a lamentable change in the religious beliefs of the rebellion's leader, began to despair that Christianity in the real sense of the term would, under Hung's guidance, become the religion of the state. Brine explained why the Taipings lost popularity with the other groups:

But perhaps the principal reason for the decline of the popularity of the rebellion amongst Europeans, may be found in the great change that has occurred in our political relations with the Manchu government. At the time when the principles of the Taepings were first known, and Nankin had fallen into their hands, nothing could have been more unsatisfactory than the position of foreigners in China.

The interior of the country was closed to all, and none but the devoted Roman Catholic missionaries ever attempted to penetrate into it; and

[12] J. M. Callery and M. Yvan, *History of the Insurrection in China*, pp. 40–41.

[13] Littell, *op. cit.*, p. 569. This is by no means an isolated opinion. Littell also quotes Reverend Elihu Doty (Dutch Reformed, Amoy) as speaking on September 16, 1852, of the possibility that "the prophecy concerning the land of Sinim (may) be verified at no distant period." A Seventh-Day Baptist put it: "It can hardly be deemed an excess of enthusiasm to regard this as the beginning of those mighty movements, which are to shake the earth, and usher in the latter days of glory" (page 569).

[14] Lindesay Brine, in *The Taeping Rebellion in China; a Narrative of Its Use and Progress*, said, on page 269: "When the papers containing the proclamations and odes brought down in 1853, by H.M.S. 'Hermes,' were translated and made public, their contents led many people to hope that two great results would proceed from the successful progress of the Taepings. One was the establishment of Christianity, and the other the improvement of the commercial relations between China and the western nations."

these travelled as Chinese, and went direct to their respective congregations of converts, where they obtained protection from insult. At Canton
the governor refused to admit Europeans within the walls, and all the merchants who chose to come there to trade were obliged to live in the suburbs. But without enumerating the different disqualifications under which
they suffered, the galling tone of superiority assumed to them on all occasions by government officials had become almost unbearable. It is to this
that Mr. Bruce alludes, when he speaks of the "language of Canton in its
most palmy days of arrogance." With this state of affairs existing, it was
only natural that the fast-spreading rebellion should have been looked
upon with favourable eyes, as a means through which it was probable that
our relations, commercial and political, might be placed on a more satisfactory basis. The conduct of the governor at Canton in 1856 resulted in
establishing this very alteration, hoped to have been brought about by the
Taepings. The seizure of the lorcha 'Arrow' afforded a pretext for an
appeal to arms, and the war that ensued led to the obtainment of a treaty,
which was in all respects most desirable. Two of its clauses, noted below,
not only made the further progress of the Taepings unprofitable, but absolutely made their simple existence most objectionable to all Europeans
who hoped to open trade with those provinces lying adjacent to the upper
waters of the Yang-tze. When Lord Elgin proceeded to Hankow, he evidently looked upon them as a mere body of rebels, sooner or later to be
suppressed by government, and that they in the interval interfered with the
due carrying into execution of the terms of his treaty. Consequently he was
not inclined to show them much favour.[15]

The Westerners presented various opinions about aspects of the Taiping movement. Their first problem was whether the Taipings were

---

[15] *Ibid.*, pp. 270–72. The two clauses in the treaty signed at Tientsin on June 26,
1858, are given in Brine's note on page 272:

Art. IX. "British subjects are hereby authorised to travel, for their pleasure or for
purposes of trade, to all parts of the interior under passports which will be issued by
their consuls and countersigned by the local authorities. These passports, if demanded,
must be produced for examination in the localities passed through. . . . To Nankin and
other cities disturbed by persons in arms against the government, no pass shall be
given until they shall have been recaptured."

Art. X. "British merchant ships shall have authority to trade upon the Great River
(Yang-tze). The upper and lower valley of the river being, however, disturbed by
outlaws, no port shall be for the present opened to trade, with the exception of Chinkiang, which shall be opened in a year from the date of the signing of this treaty. So
soon as peace shall have been restored, British vessels shall also be admitted to trade at
such ports as far as Hankow, not exceeding three in number, as the British minister,
after consultation with the Chinese Secretary of State, may determine shall be the
ports of entry and discharge."

See also Lin-le [Augustus F. Lindley], *Ti-ping Tien-Kwoh: The History of the Ti-ping
Revolution*, I, 207–8.

sincere in their belief in Christianity, or whether they were impostors. A number of people thought that their religion was a camouflage for political activities; others believed that their movement was at first genuinely religious, but was later pushed into political activities by religious persecution. Among the former was Humphrey Marshall, American Commissioner to China in 1853, who reported:

> I incline very much to believe that a cold and crafty agitator has revamped the matter contained in the religious tracts which, from time to time, the missionaries have published in China, and without any exact idea of the nature of the new doctrine, has drawn around his standard of revolt the discontented spirits as well as the desperate of the provinces through which it has passed. The commentaries upon the commandments, for instance, must strike you as exceedingly absurd.[16]

Sir George Bonham, in his report to the Earl of Clarendon on his trip to Nanking on the "Hermes" in April, 1853, expressed a similar view:

> The base of this structure is supposed to be founded upon the Old Testament and religious tracts; but they have superadded thereto a tissue of superstition and nonsense which makes an unprejudiced party almost doubt whether there is any real sincerity in their faith, or whether it is not used merely as a political engine of power by the Chiefs to sway the minds of those whom they are anxious to attach to their cause.[17]

In 1861, a Frenchman complained of the inconsistency of Taiping beliefs and acts. To him Hung appeared a political maneuverer, employing a powerful lever—"la terreur religieuse"—to keep his subordinates in line.[18] Even a sympathetic writer like W. Muirhead could not help feeling that "Though they [Taiping publications] contain much that is good and true, a large part is ... a tissue of falsehood, designed to promote the Chief's own selfish object, and deserving the severest reprobation."[19]

[16] Marshall to Marcy (33d Congress, 1st session, House Executive Document No. 123, Serial 734, Vol. XVI, pp. 141–42).

[17] Bonham to the Earl of Clarendon, No. 5, in *Papers Respecting the Civil War in China, Parliamentary Papers*, 1852–53, Vol. LXIX.

[18] René de Courcy, "L'insurrection chinoise, son origine et ses progrès," *Revue des deux mondes*, Series 2, Vol. XXXIV (July 15, 1861), pp. 342, 347.

[19] W. Muirhead, Memorandum, Inclosure 2 in No. 7, in *Papers Relating to the Rebellion in China, and Trade in the Yang-tze-Kiang River, Parliamentary Papers*, 1862, Vol. LXIII.

Belief in the genuine religious zeal of the Taiping movement was voiced by many other Western writers. Medhurst in 1853, on the basis of reports of an informant who visited Hong Kong, said:

> It is evident that as far as Hung-sew-tseuen and his followers are concerned, the insurrection originated in religious persecution. The informant says, "It was not the original design to raise a rebellion; but from the encroachments and injuries inflicted, by the officers and soldiers, to which we could not submit, there was no alternative left us.". . . These men were animated by a desire to abandon idolatry, to worship one God, and to persuade others to do the same. They were hindered in their design by the officers of government, who put some to death. What was to be done? Were they to wait until they were all killed, or endeavour to stem the torrent of persecution, and if it must be, meet force by force? There are those who say, that they ought to have submitted with meekness to the persecutors' rage, and to have committed themselves to God by prayer. It does not appear that they had advanced thus far in religious knowledge and experience. Their zeal seems to have exceeded their knowledge. They believed that they had a work to do—they were hindered by force and violence from carrying out their views—had they been few in number they might have fled, but their number was too great for them all to flee. It became with them simply a matter of calculation: are we likely to succeed if we raise the standard of insurrection? They thought they were, and their enemies having goaded them to the fight, they accepted the challenge. Once engaged in it there was no alternative, but complete victory or entire extermination.[20]

Joseph Edkins, while very critical of the Taiping religion, thought that the Taipings were no impostors. He said: "The Christian insurgents in China never had the confidence of any part of the nation. Their religious character was one reason of the unpopularity of their cause. If they had been crafty impostors, they would have chosen some other watchword than that of Christianity."[21] Even Blakiston, who was not exactly sympathetic with the Taipings, said, "The founders belonged to a religious sect called God-Worshippers, who in the autumn of that year came into collision with the authorities, and immediately started as regenerators of the empire; and there is reason to believe that they were sincere, and their motives pure—Christianity being their profession, but mixed with a good deal of error."[22]

[20] W. H. Medhurst, "Connection between Foreign Missions and the Kwang-se Insurrection," *North China Herald*, No. 160, August 20, 1853, p. 11.

[21] Joseph Edkins, *Religion in China*, p. 193.

[22] Thomas W. Blakiston, *Five Months on the Yang-tsze . . . and Notices of the Present Rebellions in China*, p. 31.

Despite these people's belief in the religious zeal of the Taiping movement, all of them including Lin-le, a Taiping partisan, and Meadows, a relatively objective expositor, admitted that the untutored Taipings did not exhibit the right understanding of the spirit of Christianity. To many others, the Taiping conception of God was anthropomorphic; the wording of their sacred epistles would have been "blasphemous in the extreme if it were not so essentially ludicrous"; and their religion was "a system of revolting idolatry," or simply "bosh or humbug."[23] W. Sargent made perhaps the most damaging remark:

> The point of polygamy is not the only one in which we find a distinct refutation of the idea that the insurrection is a genuine Christian movement. At present, with no organized church or priesthood, with the doctrines of faith or devotion given out as necessity requires by the head of the establishment, their prophet and their king, it is impossible for us to say more than that theirs is evidently a mongrel belief, born from a brain teeming with confused and often erroneous ideas of the teachings of Christianity, not unlearned in the writings of Confucius, and perhaps imbued with some portions of the faith of Mahomet. One thing is certain, that his abhorrence of the worship of Buddha does not yield to any other passion of his soul. From the combined workings of these different systems is produced a composite religion, built up of the most incongruous materials. Its only duties at present consist in the repetition, thrice in each day, of certain prescribed forms of prayer; but by and by, when the Tae-ping's power has increased to an exaggerated degree, he may no longer rest content with the salvo of artillery that now announces his performance of his adorations,—he may demand and receive divine honors for himself, and hear his name borne upon the floating clouds of incense, by the lips of a lying priesthood. Stranger things than this have come to pass, and may again occur.[24]

I. J. Roberts is a unique case in that he started out as a proud teacher of the chief of a new dynasty and ended a disappointed soul. He said that Hung was a crazy man unfit to rule, and that he and his "coolie kings" were not "capable of organizing a government of equal benefit to the people with even the old imperial government."[25]

[23] W. H. Medhurst, Inclosure 10 in No. 6, in *Papers Respecting the Civil War in China, Parliamentary Papers*, 1852–53, Vol. LXIX; Garnet J. Wolseley, *Narrative of the War with China in 1860*, p. 341; Holmes, quoted in Brine, *The Taeping Rebellion in China*, p. 266; Mr. "Q" in *NCH*, No. 594, December 14, 1861.

[24] W. Sargent, "The Chinese Rebellion," *North American Review*, Vol. LXXIX, No. 164 (July, 1854), pp. 198–99.

[25] Littell, "Missionaries and Politics in China," *Political Science Quarterly*, Vol. XLIII, No. 4 (Dec., 1928), p. 572; Brine, *The Taeping Rebellion in China*, pp. 296–98.

A more measured view, free from undue missionary enthusiasm or other interest, came from men like Bridgman and particularly Meadows. Bridgman considered the Taipings iconoclasts of the strictest order and noted that their ideas of the Deity were exceedingly imperfect:

> Though they declare plainly that there is "only One True God," yet the inspiration of the Holy Scriptures, the equality of the Son with the Father, and many other doctrines, generally received by Protestant Christians, as being clearly revealed in the Bible, are by them wholly ignored. True, they have formulas in which some of these doctrines are taught; but then they are borrowed formulas, and they have used them without comprehending their true import. So I believe; and I think this is made manifestly plain in the new version of their Doxology, or Hymn of Praise, where Yang-seu-tsing, the Eastern King, is proclaimed the Paraclete—the Holy Spirit.[26]

A few reasons were offered for the Taiping perversion of Christianity. Marshall in 1853 was the first to suggest that Chinese traditionalism would prevent the Taipings from embracing Christianity as the Western people understood it. He said:

> The idea which is now so widely disseminated, and so readily accepted by Christendom, that the revolution in China, like modern European revolutions, may be effected in a few months or in a few years, and will secure liberal intercourse, free interchange and trade, and the high moral bearing which Christianity teaches, overlooks the peculiar characteristics of the Chinese, and rests upon a total ignorance of their history, or a wilful self-deception. There is not another people on earth so wedded to ancient customs as the Chinese. The forms taught at the maternal knee are sedulously observed throughout life; the maxims and principles instilled by the parent make Chinese landmarks for life. The literature of China, embracing the ethics of Confucius, is older than our Christian philosophy; so is the system of Buddhism. The scholar plods his weary way among the Chinese classics, in some one or other of their departments, to gather the rudiments of *education*, just as the American youth makes *his* progress through Caesar, Virgil, and Livy, in the institutions of the New World. Thus *mind* is practised, formed, and developed in each hemisphere. But in China the literary examination is an ordeal one *must* pass in order to obtain governmental employment; whereas, in the western world, merit asserts itself wherever and whenever the theatre of action is presented. It is our policy to promote it after its public exhibition. The rebel chief pledges himself to *purify the literary examinations*, so that merit may more surely secure promotion. This is but an appeal to the disappointed many who have failed

---

[26] Quoted in Lin-le, *Ti-ping Tien-Kwoh*, I, 212–14.

to secure degrees; in other words, to the "outs" against the administrative power, which has failed to meet their expectations. . . . *The new chief proposes no broader basis than that occupied by the reigning Emperor.*

The rebel chief has published a long edict, which amounts to a defence from the charge that his religion is that of the foreigners. He insists that he derives his system from the *ancient Chinese classics,* from which he quotes most liberally to prove his position. Yet it is *insisted* that he is a follower of our Saviour, and a preacher of the Christian religion! *I consider that part of the story to be unsupported by evidence; nor do I believe he would, under any circumstances, avow such a belief* to the Chinese. On the contrary, he will adhere most strictly to the ancient customs and religion of China; he will study and follow Confucius and Mencius; he will maintain the empire; he will preserve the etiquette of the ancient Chinese court; and *he will seek to conform as nearly as possible to the prejudices and prepossessions of his countrymen, in order to win popular favor.*[27]

Some sought to explain the Taiping perversion in terms of Hung's fanaticism and disordered brain. Joseph Edkins, a writer who used the pen name "X. Y. Z.," William C. Hunter, and many others all recognized that there was an element of fanaticism in the movement "which has been manifested from the first, is operating for evil, and developing itself in new forms," in the words of X. Y. Z.[28]

In *Chinese Gordon,* Archibald Forbes mentioned frustration as one of the causes of the rebellion: "Perhaps if he had passed his examination at Canton he might have merged into an official, and the Tai-ping Rebellion had never been. But he failed; all the conditions of his life soured him; and he began to think."[29]

The Taipings meanwhile found no lack of enthusiasm among the Western missionaries, who saw in the doctrines avowed by the rebels "persuasive evidence that the moral bread which was cast upon these waters in bygone time is now returning after many days. They hail these declarations of religious belief as the aurora of a more enlightened

[27] Marshall to Marcy (33d Congress, 1st session, House Executive Document No. 123, Serial 734, Vol. XVI, pp. 265–66).

[28] Quoted in Brine, *op. cit.,* p. 196. See also Edkins, *Religion in China,* pp. 190–91, and William C. Hunter, *Bits of Old China,* pp. 82–83.

[29] *Chinese Gordon: A Succinct Record of His Life,* pp. 32–33. Forbes knew full well that many other factors besides this personal frustration of Hung determined the outbreak of the rebellion. He said: "In the earlier days of China, Hung Sew-tsuen might not even have expanded into a 'village Hampden,' but might have grumbled his life through as a peasant lad of the Hakkas" (p. 32). If there had been no Taiping Rebellion there would have been rebellion of some type; and if there had been no Hung, there would have been some other leader to take advantage of the time.

civilization in China, and they believe that these papers [Taiping publications] afford convincing proof of the diffusion of a correct knowledge of the benign precepts of Christianity."[30] Among the first Taiping enthusiasts was the Bishop of Victoria, who believed that the Taipings showed "recognition of the guilt of sin, the duty of repentance, the Atonement of Jesus Christ, the need of a new heart, and the work of the Holy Spirit in reviewing and purifying the soul for heaven."[31]

Lin-le (Augustus F. Lindley) reports:

And now, as the Bishop of Victoria has said, before the ancient capital of the empire, a body of some 100,000 men, bound together by one religious hope and by one political aim—the highest and most noble purposes of human ambition—those of civil and religious liberty—were congregated; following implicitly the guidance of a leader they believed sent by divine authority to expel their foreign masters, and overthrow idolatry throughout the length and breadth of the land. Marvellous and unparalleled beyond conception was this rising up of the people,—as a psychological phenomenon it stands unrivalled in extent and magnitude in modern history. To behold leagued together, not only the effeminate Chinese, but even their women—wives and daughters fighting by the side of their husbands and fathers, inspired by one common hope and ardour—all animated by a great religious and political object, for the attainment of which they had suffered and fought many years—is an event never before realized in the history of China.[32]

The Bishop had a sympathetic if not always correct understanding of the activities of Hung. He said:

He [Hung] rendered the insurrection a great religious movement—*he did not transmute a Christian fraternity into a political rebellion. The course of events, and the momentous interests of life and death—the dread realities of the rack and torture, imprisonment, and death—drove him to use in self-defence all the available means within reach, and to employ the resources of self-preservation.* He joined the rebel camp, preached the Gospel among them, won them over to his views, placed himself at their head, and made political power the means of religious propagandism.[33]

[30] Marshall to Marcy (33d Congress, 1st session, House Executive Document No. 123, Serial 734, Vol. XVI, p. 141).
[31] *NCH*, No. 169, October 22, 1853, p. 47.
[32] Lin-le, *Ti-ping Tien-Kwoh*, I, 88–89.
[33] Quoted in *ibid.*, I, 53.

After examining the books published by the Taipings which were brought back to Hong Kong by the ship "Hermes" in 1853, the Bishop made the remark:

> ...are they [the defects or errors in the Taiping doctrines] the natural shortcomings of a body of imperfectly enlightened men, placed in a situation of novel difficulty, labouring under almost unexampled disadvantages in their pursuit of truth, without spiritual instructors and guides, with only a few copies of the Holy Scriptures, and those apparently in small, detached, and fragmentary portions, with no forms of prayer or manuals of devotion, having their minds distracted amid the arduous toil of a campaign and the work of religious proselytism, with no definite views or clear knowledge respecting the sacraments, the Christian ministry, or the constitution of a Church—engaged in a struggle for life and death—and yet, amid all these hindrances and drawbacks, evincing a hopeful, praiseworthy, and promising vigour of mind and independence of action, in the great undertaking of a moral revolution of their country?[34]

Such a question could come only from a sympathetic soul who refused to believe that the apparently blasphemous doctrines amid the genuine Christian principles could be the result of willful perversity. Early writers like Callery and Yvan discerned in the midst of all the Taipings' "chivalric eccentricities, the spirit of Christianity," and saw in Hung "a worshipper of the Supreme Being."[35]

Captain Fishbourne had some direct contact with the Taipings in 1853 when his "Hermes" visited Nanking, with Bonham, Meadows, and others on board; and he was greatly impressed by the religious zeal of those with whom he talked. He believed the Taipings to be "students of Scripture, and anxious for the dissemination of its truths." He was not blind to their errors; but to him "it is intensely interesting to know that they have discovered in Scripture the important and influential truth that a '*Tien-Kwoh*,' or Heavenly kingdom is foretold, and that they are so convinced it will come, that they are endeavouring to bring it about."[36] His final impression was that "a considerable amount of useful instruction was delivered, *and such as would serve to promote the objects we had in view, in putting down idolatry, and furthering the worship of the true God.*"[37] On December 31, 1853, an editorial in the *North*

---

[34] Quoted in *ibid.*, I, 148.

[35] Callery and Yvan, *History of the Insurrection in China*, p. 194.

[36] Edmund G. Fishbourne, *Impressions of China, and the Present Revolution: Its Progress and Prospects*, pp. iv, x.

[37] Quoted in Lin-le, *Ti-ping Tien-Kwoh*, I, 166.

China Herald expressed this view: "A Religious and military basis may be the only foundation of a durable empire at present possible in China—Tae-ping seems to feel this, and to have adopted both, possibly more by a true instinct than by any grasp of intellect, or logical process of reasoning."[38] The editor was sympathetic and felt that social and religious development as well as political reorganization was needed in China. The Taipings seemed at the moment to be the answer to such needs.

As late as 1860 and 1861, people like Joseph Edkins, John Scarth, Muirhead, and others believed in the sincerity of Taiping religious zeal.[39] Edkins and Griffith John, in response to the invitation of both the Kan Wang and the Chung Wang, went to Soochow in 1860. Edkins' impressions are recorded in *Religion in China.* He found the Chinese receptive to Christian doctrine; and he repudiated the notion that the Chinese were interested merely in sordid aims of life and were incapable of feeling reverence for God or curiosity respecting the future state. He said:

> We see, by the history of this insurrection, that there are many among the Chinese who are prepared to receive these and other religious tenets in the spirit of an earnest and practical faith. They have shown themselves capable, to a degree unexpected by the rest of mankind, of a religious enthusiasm ardent enough to increase their bravery as fighting men, and make them capable of submitting to a self-denying discipline, such as cannot be very agreeable to a people trained in national habits like those of the ordinary Chinese.

The fact that the Taipings published many parts of the Scriptures struck him as very significant, for it would be "strange to account for on any hypothesis but that those who did so were sincere believers in the book." But he was aware of the shortcomings of the Taiping faith. He said: "This movement in favour of Christianity, originated and carried on by the Chinese themselves, was injured by the political aims which were combined with it. It was the error of half-enlightened minds to believe themselves called to overthrow, by force of arms, the Government that persecuted them and the idolatry which Christianity had taught them was a sin against God."[40]

[38] *NCH*, No. 179, December 31, 1853, p. 86.

[39] Edkins, *Religion in China*, pp. 194–97; John Scarth, *Twelve Years in China: The People, the Rebels, and the Mandarins*, pp. 160, 165, 168; Brine, *The Taeping Rebellion in China*, pp. 282–84, 288–89.

[40] Edkins, *op. cit.*, pp. 194, 195, 196–97.

John Scarth attributed the foreigners' change of attitude toward the Taipings to the death of Dr. Medhurst and the absence of Meadows: ". . . and on his [Meadows'] return to China, as Sir John Bowring and he were not on good terms, his opinions had no influence on British policy."[41]

W. H. Sykes, a member of the Parliament, on the basis of information furnished him by his own constituents defended the Taipings as late as 1863. To him, the sense in which Hung considered himself the "younger brother of Jesus" was a spiritual one. What people condemned as blasphemy was merely a political move. Hung never exacted worship for himself. To Sykes, Hung seemed to have assumed divine association for the purpose of putting himself in the eyes of his fellows "on a footing of sacredness with the Emperors of China and Japan, and the Llama of Thibet." It is enough that Hung was said to be intimately acquainted with the Scriptures.[42]

Lin-le (Augustus F. Lindley) was in the service of the Chung Wang during the last four years of the Taiping campaign. Lin-le was fully aware of the errors which existed in the Taiping religion, but he insisted that "the grand truth that the Ti-pings admitted and recognized the principal points of the Christian faith, remained."[43] He repeatedly cited the fact that the Taipings accepted the Bible as a proof of their being true Christians, and he blamed England as "solely responsible for preventing so glorious a consummation [referring to the Taiping utmost effort to 'enter into the pale and brotherhood of Christendom']."[44]

Some of the views of Thomas T. Meadows as a whole are still valid today.[45] Here we are specifically interested in his evaluation of the Taipings. To his contemporaries, Meadows seemed to have taken upon himself the task of defending the Taipings. Marshall, the American Commissioner, spoke of him as assuming *"the protectorate of the young power to Great Britain."*[46]

Meadows believed that the Taiping movement started out as an ex-

[41] Scarth, *op. cit.*, pp. 264–65.

[42] W. H. Sykes, *The Taeping Rebellion in China: Its Origin, Progress and Present Condition*, pp. vii, 13.

[43] Lin-le, *Ti-ping Tien-Kwoh*, I, 147.

[44] *Ibid.*, I, 74, 150–51, 313; and II, 693.

[45] See John K. Fairbank, "Meadows on China: A Centennial Review," *Far Eastern Quarterly*, Vol. XIV, No. 3 (May, 1955), pp. 365–71.

[46] Marshall to Marcy (33d Congress, 1st session, House Executive Document No. 123, Serial 734, Vol. XVI, p. 168).

clusively religious society; but "in the autumn of 1850 it was brought into collision with the local authorities, when the movement almost immediately assumed a political character of the highest aims."[47] So "...it was by dire necessity alone that Hung sew tseuen was immediately constrained to add the character and functions of patriotic insurgent to those of religious reformer. The question was: Have I any choice? *Must I not?*"[48] To him Hung was never an impostor.

> ...if we regard Hung sew tseuen as an impostor, his recorded acts and speeches—those ascribed to him by that last narrative [the story of the Tung Wang rebuking the T'ien Wang in a court scene] more than others —become quite unintelligible. But if we suppose him to be a man by nature always of deep religious feeling, and now an earnest believer in the authority of the Bible, then the history of David alone would account for nearly all that he has done, and especially for his demeanour in these last extraordinary transactions. For every new convert, the words of the Bible have a freshness—a living reality of which great numbers of routine readers and church-goers have never had an idea,—which they cannot even conceive to themselves. But for what convert would these words have so much force as for Hung sew tseuen, who could, established in Sovereign state at Nanking, look back on a career more marvellous than that of any potentate now living, for he commenced life with no other advantages than the Chinese lads who, like him, attended cattle on the hills. David, "who kept the sheep," was anointed by Samuel at the verbal order of God. And he lay with his outlawed followers in the mountains and forests, before he found a refuge in the city of Achish. Much in the same way, Hung sew tseuen had camped among the hills of Kwang se, before he found a Ziglag in Yung gan. At the outset of his political-military career, when he was compassed round about in a sort of Adullam, he had been rescued from his extreme danger by this very Eastern Prince; who had been warned thereto by one of these very descents of the Heavenly Father. What, in truth, was more likely than that Hung sew tseuen, long a student of the Bible in circumstances so specially adapted to make him wish for, and pray for, and believe, that he had obtained the aid granted to the chosen of God —a reader of the Bible in the midst of great perils and arduous difficulties, followed by marvellous successes and high honours—what was more likely than that he should look on himself as a David, with an Eastern Nathan to reprove him in the name of God, and a Northern Joab to serve his cause and thwart his inclinations?[49]

[47] Thomas T. Meadows, *The Chinese and Their Rebellions, Viewed in Connection with Their National Philosophy, Ethics, Legislation, and Administration*, p. 105.
[48] *Ibid.*, pp. 141–42.
[49] *Ibid.*, pp. 437–38.

Meadows offered a biblical basis for Hung's strange visions and actions, believing him to be a serious student of the Bible.[50] After sharing with other missionaries the doubt about Taiping Christianity, he concluded that the Taiping religion was based on the great truths of Christianity:

> It did not occur to me [at first] that the Chinese convert, through some tracts of a Chinese convert, might either fail to see, or (if he saw them) might spontaneously eliminate the dogmas and congealed forms of merely sectarian Christianity, and then by preaching simply the great religious truth of an One God, and the pure morality of Christ's Sermon on the Mount, obtain numbers of followers among people disgusted with the idolatry and the immorality that they and those around them were engulfed in. As we have seen above, this was actually the case with Hung sew tseuen.[51]

[50] See *ibid.*, p. 104, where Meadows offers a biblical basis to explain heavenly visitations. As early as 1853, he defended these by reference to the case of Swedenborg in the eighteenth century in Sweden. He called Taiping religion a "Chinese Swedenborgian Christianity." E. Swedenborg, 1688–1772, was a scientist of some renown. In 1745 his *Worship and Love of God* appeared, marking "the surprising transition of its author's mind from plain scientific and philosophical reasoning to what is generally considered a form of religious mysticism, but what the author himself would have described as spiritual perception. A great change had come over him. His mind, as he himself says, had been opened to enable him to hear and see things of the other life." (See James Hastings [ed.], *Encyclopaedia of Religion and Ethics* [13 vols.; New York: Charles Scribner's Sons, 1951] XII, 129.) Meadows said (pages 438–39): "Those who are pleased to detect evil in the new sect will doubtless pass a summary judgment of 'imposture' and 'blasphemy.' To those who wish rather to recognise the good that is in them, history—it may be even the history of their own parishes in their own youth—will furnish many examples of men, of irreproachable lives and admitted good sense in all ordinary matters, who believed themselves the recipients of direct revelations. We have an eminent instance of undeniable authenticity in Swedenborg, a man of science, of great intellectual power and of undoubted moral purity, who saw visions of angels, conceived himself at times *transported out of the body*, and believed that he had direct communications with God. A mental error that clings to many of us throughout life, and which is the abundant source of misunderstandings, mutual dislikes and quarrels, is the notion that what *we* feel and think, with respect to certain subjects under certain circumstances, is also thought and felt by all others on the same subjects and under similar circumstances. The man who persists in viewing the actions of his fellow-creatures from this stand-point, passes his days in a fog of misconceptions and delusions, than which no self-deceit of fanaticism can well be greater. Most of all does he err when he dogmatically passes his analogical judgments on the communing of other men with their God."

[51] Meadows, *op. cit.*, p. 193. Meadows' effort to fit Hung into his hypothetical framework seems the result of wishful thinking. Eugene P. Boardman, in *Christian Influence upon the Ideology of the Taiping Rebellion, 1851–1864*, p. 109, has drawn to our attention that "the Sermon on the Mount" is "left out completely except for a phrase or two." In fact, the Taipings had missed some of the most important Christian principles, what Meadows would call "the pure morality." See Boardman's chapter on "What the Taipings Failed to Take," pp. 106–14.

Meadows did not believe that the Taipings had taken over all the Christian teachings: he noted that there were some Christian beliefs, such as the sacrament of the Lord's Supper, absent from the Taiping Christianity; he also noted that their knowledge of the doctrines of the Trinity and of redemption was imperfect.[52] But the Taipings were after all Chinese, and their Christianity has to be viewed in the light of traditional Confucianism. Meadows describes in a very interesting passage the way in which Hung could have turned from Confucianism to Christianity:

> The words, Te and Teen, formed the hinge on which he turned from Confucianism to Christianity. He had always reverenced the Being indicated by these terms, as the Supreme Ruler of the world; and from Leang afah's missionary tracts, he learnt that, in the most ancient and most venerated Books of the western foreigners, that very Being was not simply mentioned a few times, as in the Chinese Sacred Books, but formed their chief subject, as the Creator and Ruler of the Universe, with the attribute of distinct personality. And, when he got these books himself, he found that, while Shang te was indeed every where referred to under that very name as the One Almighty Ruler, a greater personality was therein given to his other name, Teen, by the addition of Foo, father; which latter word, it will be remembered, awakens peculiarly reverent feelings in the mind of a Chinese. Hence in taking, as he distinctly has done, the Old and New Testaments, as the highest standard of truth, he has not been constrained to discard the Chinese Sacred Books, but merely to view those passages which refer to Shang te and Teen, by the light which is thrown on them by the attributes and acts ascribed, in the foreign Sacred Books, to the Being so named. For the rest, the morality, taught by precept and example in the Chinese Sacred Books, corresponded so completely with that taught by precept and example in the foreign Sacred Books, that in this respect also the acceptance of the latter, as the highest standard, led to no condemnation of the former: on the contrary the two mutually confirmed each other.[53]

If Hung detected a clash between the Chinese classics and the Bible, Meadows believed that he "either by a re-interpretation makes the former conform to the latter, or declares them [the classics] in so far wrong. He appears to have, once for all, taken the Bible as the highest standard of truth, and to have accepted everything new that he therein finds."[54] Meadows was quite aware that there was a fanatical element in the Taipings' religion, that their conception of God was becoming

[52] Meadows, *The Chinese and Their Rebellions*, pp. 427–29.
[53] *Ibid.*, pp. 413–14.
[54] *Ibid.*, p. 420.

more and more anthropomorphic, and that they were tending to transform "the spiritual catholic paternity" of God into "a corporeal and limited fatherhood."[55] But Meadows asked with reference to the expression of "the communion of saints," "How many of the hundreds of thousands who have repeated, every Sunday from youth up, that 'they believe' in this have anything but a very vague notion of what a 'saint' is? And how many have a shadow of a notion what the 'communion' of these 'saints' may be?"[56] The implication is clear: the Taipings could not be expected to have a perfect understanding of Christianity. It is enough that the Taipings had proclaimed that the Bible was to be substituted for the Confucian classics as the textbook in the state examination.

> ...in a prosperous population of 360 millions of heathens, all the males who have the means, and are not too old to learn...will be assiduously engaged in getting the Bible off by heart, from beginning to end. Should the thing take place, it will form a revolution as unparalleled in the world for rapidity, completeness, and extent as is the Chinese people itself for its antiquity, unity and numbers.[57]

Meadows said: "And if the Tae pings succeed in establishing themselves in the sovereignty of the country, I have little doubt that his [Hung's] religious views will, in time, triumph over those of the fanatical section."[58]

In 1861, having failed to impress the British government with Taiping Christianity, Meadows raised the issue on a broader basis. He said in a letter to Lord Russell, dated February 19, 1861, from Shanghai where he served as a British consul:

> On the religion of the Tae-pings little need here be said. Viewed as a piece of contemporary history, the fact of the rise and progress, in this old seat of Confucianism and Buddhism, of the Bible-spreading Tae-ping Christianity—be its exact character what it may—is one of the most interesting spectacles that the annals of the human race present; and if the Tae-pings succeed in becoming the rulers of the Chinese people, it will prove one of the most momentous. A foreign official agent, whose nature or the limited extent of whose information permits of his viewing that

---

[55] *Ibid.*, pp. 440–41.
[56] *Ibid.*, p. 92.
[57] *Ibid.*, p. 446.
[58] *Ibid.*, p. 445.

spectacle with indifference, must surely be adjudged mentally unfitted for the career he has chosen. But except as a deeply interesting piece of contemporary history, we have nothing to do with it. If we aid the Tae-pings on account of their professed creed, we propagate religion by the sword; if we attack them on account of it, we engage in religious persecution.[59]

Meadows apparently felt the weight of the argument by those who compared Hung to Mohammed.[60]

Meadows believed that in the whole history of China there had been only one political revolution and that had happened two thousand years earlier. He was referring to the end of *feng-chien* and the beginning of the *chün-hsien* system at the beginning of the Ch'in dynasty. He said: "Revolution is a change of the form of government and of the principles on which it rests; it does not necessarily imply a change of rulers.... *Of all nations that have attained a certain degree of civilization, the Chinese are the least revolutionary and the most rebellious.*"[61] By implication, he maintained that the Taiping movement was no more a revolution than those staged by Chang Chüeh, Huang Ch'ao, and many others in the history of China. Marshall seemed to concur in this in his report to Marcy:

As to the *progress* of the rebellion, I repeat, [that you may fix the fact in your mind,) that the masses of the working people and business men of China have not engaged at all in this war, and, above all things, desire repose and peace. The rebels have nowhere attempted to institute government upon a basis different from the existing organization under the empire, and, if successful, will only change the personnel—not the substance or forms—of government.[62]

Toward the end of the movement, most people lost faith in it, including Roberts, who opined that any missionary who failed to support Hung's beliefs was not safe among the rebels and that Hung's religious toleration was but a farce, a machinery to promote his own political religion.[63] Blakiston quoted Roberts: " 'I then,' says Mr. Roberts,

[59] Meadows to Lord Russell, No. 3, in *Papers Relating to the Rebellion in China, and Trade in the Yang-tze-Kiang River, Parliamentary Papers*, 1862, Vol. LXIII.

[60] For instance, W. Sargent: see quotation in this chapter from his "The Chinese Rebellion," *North American Review*, Vol. LXXIX, No. 164 (July, 1854), pp. 198–99. See also McLane to Marcy (35 Congress, 2d session, Senate Executive Document No. 22, Serial 982, Vol. VIII, p. 51).

[61] Meadows, *The Chinese and Their Rebellions*, p. 25.

[62] Marshall to Marcy (33d Congress, 1st session, House Executive Document No. 123, Serial 734, Vol. XVI, p. 269).

[63] Brine, *The Taeping Rebellion in China*, pp. 296–98.

'despaired of missionary success among them, or of any good coming out of the movement—religious, commercial, political—and determined to leave them.' "[64] Alexander Michie quoted Sir James Hope's view of the Taipings in 1861 as "an organised band of robbers."[65] Moule felt that the rebels at Ningpo (and he believed this was generally true of the Taipings everywhere) "had no real religion, were worse than the heathen, and lacked almost entirely those two bright features in the Chinese character, education and politeness."[66] Robert James Forrest gave in 1867 perhaps the most scathing criticism of the Taiping religion, describing it as the result of a fanatic and diseased mind.[67] He reportedly said: "... Tien-wang's Christianity is nothing but the rank blasphemy of a lunatic, and the profession of religion by his followers a laughable mockery and farce. As heretic, Tien-wang is the most incorrigible self-willed one I ever heard of."[68]

In 1882 S. Wells Williams gave a somewhat detached opinion about the Taiping understanding of Christianity in the following words:

> ... we must bear in mind the fact that he had certainly, neither at this time [at the beginning of his campaign] nor ever afterward, a clear conception of the true nature of Christianity, judging from his writings and edicts. The nature of sin, and the dominion of God's law upon the sinner; the need of atonement from the stain and effects of sin; Christ's mediatorial sacrifice; were subjects on which he could not possibly have received full instruction from these fragmentary essays [referring to the tracts distributed by Liang A-fa]. In after days his conviction of his own divine calling to rule over China, seems to have blinded his understanding to the spiritual nature of the Christian church.... As they had no portion of the Sacred Scriptures to guide them, they were at a loss to understand many things spoken of by Liang A-fah, but his expositions of the events and doctrines occurring in them were deeply pondered and accepted. The Mosaic account of creation and the flood, destruction of Sodom, Sermon on the Mount, and nature of the final judgment, were given in them, as well as a full relation of Christ's life and death; and these prepared the neophytes to receive the Bible when they got it. But the same desire to find proof of his own calling led Siu-tsuen to fix on fanciful renderings of certain texts, and, after the

[64] Blakiston, *Five Months on the Yang-tsze*, pp. 32–33.
[65] Alexander Michie, *The Englishman in China during the Victorian Era, as Illustrated in the Career of Sir Rutherford Alcock* . . ., I, 372.
[66] Arthur Evans Moule, *Half a Century in China*, p. 31.
[67] See Forrest, "The Christianity of Hung Tsiu Tsuen: A Review of Taeping Books," *Journal of the Royal Asiatic Society, North China Branch*, New Series No. 4 (Dec., 1867), pp. 187–208.
[68] Quoted in Blakiston, *Five Months on the Yang-tsze*, p. 43.

manner of commentators in other lands, to extract meanings never intended. . . . The phrase *Tien kwoh*, denoting the "Kingdom of Heaven" in
Christ's preaching, they applied to China. With such preconceived views
it is not wonderful that the brethren were all able to fortify themselves in
their opinions by the strongest arguments. All those discourses in the series
relating to repentance, faith, and man's depravity were apparently entirely overlooked by them.[69]

Finally, Williams enumerated the different factors that were responsible for the downfall of the Taiping dynasty: their strategic error
not to lead their armies north; the gradual thinning out of their faith by
later additions to their original forces; their failure to make any real
changes in the system of government because they did not have any
knowledge of Western countries; alienation of literati by their foreign
faith; alienation of the people by their unnecessary cruelty; and finally,
Hung's own incompetency.[70]

The attitude of the Western people toward the Taipings at the time
the movement proved to be a complete failure in 1864 may be seen from
some of the *North China Herald* editorials, of which two are quoted here
at length:

We this day publish a second portion of the *Kou-kung* or autobiography
of the *soi disant* Chung Wang or Faithful King. The relation which is therein given of the progress of the rebel movement, from its cradle in the
mountainous districts of Kuang-hsi, to its full development as a rival dynasty established in a rival capital, has at least the merit of authenticity.
Written by a man who must have had no ordinary means of observation
at his command, and under circumstances which render it unlikely that
any exaggeration or misrepresentation should have crept into his report,
this long and somewhat tedious account of the progress of the rebellion has
especial claims on our attention. As a matter of history it is important thus
to have obtained a connected account of the advance of the main body, or
at least of the headquarters, of the insurgents. We shall by it be enabled to
isolate the different marauding bands by which the country was devastated, and discover whether the atrocities which were undoubtedly per-
petrated, were the work of the Taiping armies, countenanced by the true
Insurgent leaders, or whether, as is more probable, the hordes of undisciplined and semi-savage bandits whose ravages we have so often deplored,
may not have been Taipings in name alone, and may not have nominally

[69] Samuel Wells Williams, *The Middle Kingdom: A Survey of the Geography, Government, Literature, Social Life, Arts, and History of the Chinese Empire and Its Inhabitants*, II,
585, 586.

[70] *Ibid.*, II, 601–2.

placed themselves under the insurgent banner, trusting to find it a shelter from the consequences of their guilt. It is well known that on different occasions the heads of the movement at Nanking utterly repudiated the hordes which spread devastation through the province of Keangsoo. Although too much care cannot be taken in assuming the truth of any statement made by Chinese officials, whether Imperialist or Insurgent, at least some weight must attach to a connected recital, delivered under such peculiar circumstances as weighed on the Chung Wang when his *Kou-kung* was being written. That he held no exalted opinion of the integrity or disinterestedness of the leaders may confidently be assumed from the way in which he speaks of the ambition and vanity of the Eastern King, the jealousy and treachery of the Northern King, and lastly of the "peculiarity or insanity" of the Heavenly Prince himself. The motives which actuated the multitudes who followed the Insurgent flags are equally hardly dealt with. No enthusiasm for the spread of truth and Christianity enters into the estimate made by the writer. Students and sensible people were not taken in, but of the baser sort an immense number were ready to run after the new system. Ambition and necessity are the only motives which the Chung Wang, on a careful review of the events which heralded the outbreak of the rebellion, can assign as influencing either the leaders of the movement or the thousands who swelled their armies. The five Kings and the Minister of State were filled with the idea of establishing a dynasty, while the sole aim and object set before the remainder of the people was to obtain a livelihood. We cannot be surprised that so many flocked to the standard of revolt. Where any principle however holy is propagated by fire and sword, there are constant opportunities afforded to camp followers of picking up some waifs and strays, of obtaining a subsistence at the expense of the blood and groans and tears of suffering thousands. The defect in the Taiping movement was its total want of organisation, and to this may be referred most of the horrors which attended the advance of the insurgent armies. But this want of system will no longer be wondered at when the dissensions which prevailed in the councils of the chiefs are taken into consideration. No better proof can be given of the absence of any active religious principle amongst even the leading men than is afforded by the Chung Wang's autobiography. He, the Faithful King, one of the pillars of the faith so called, repudiates or ignores the existence of that great moral inspiration which has been represented by the friends of the insurgents as the moving spring of all the acts performed under the rebel administration. The statements of missionaries, and others whom prejudice or self interest had blinded, must therefore be received with caution. The fanatic Roberts, whose ravings and whose personal eccentricities as described by himself have caused so much amusement, must be looked on as a most untrustworthy witness. It is most probable also that the missionaries who visited Nanking during the period of his residence, saw the movement through those same media which obstructed the view of the foolish old man, whose grey hairs, crowned with a tawdry tiara, were a reproach to his blatant

folly and wilful misrepresentations. It was thus that the English public were deceived as to the motives which led to the rise and progress of the rebellion. Thus, also, it was that a member of the House of Commons was induced to state that in the palaces of the Wangs at Soochow were found immense numbers of religious pictures, illustrating the passion and death of the Saviour, the fact being established beyond a doubt that the pictures which did crowd the dwellings of the different Wangs, were of the most obscene description. We can now afford to look back with calmness on circumstances which, when they were absolutely passing before us, carried us away with interest or excitement. Reviewing, then, the Insurgent movement, and taking as our guide the assertions made by the Chung Wang himself, we are justified in coming to the conclusion that no high and noble aspirations filled the breasts of the men who initiated the rebellion—that, in a word, they were ambitious schemers plotting to overthrow a government for the sake of their own personal aggrandisement, and utterly unfit to organise a system, or in any degree secure the happiness of the people.[71]

The second quotation is taken from the editorial of November 12, 1864:

We reproduce in this issue of the *Herald*, the statements made by Conroy and Nellis, relating to their capture by the rebels and confinement at Hoo-chow. We are struck by the utter want of system which seems to have pervaded the Rebel government, and which involved all the miseries consequent on the exercise of martial law, without any of the corresponding advantages. The soldiers badly armed and badly paid, the cities without a shadow of Municipal government, absolute power of life and death vested in an enormous number of small officials, and the total absence of sanitary measures, conspired to make up a total of misery and mismanagement such as the world has seldom seen exceeded. Fallen into its dotage before it reached maturity, the Rebel movement was brought to an ignominious end solely through its own inherent weakness. With such chiefs as it possessed, it were a miracle had it ever attained its professed object; with men of a systematic turn of mind it might have accomplished the conquest of the country. Utter ignorance and imbecility were the distinguishing peculiarities of the policy adopted, imbecility with respect to the internal working of a government, ignorance of the relations in which the insurgents stood to the power against which they were rebelling, and to those foreign nations whose aid would have been success, and whose opposition was certain destruction. The statements which we now publish are conclusive on the point of the want of a governmental system, and the whole course of the insurgent movement is equally conclusive as to the want of talent displayed in the conduct of the Rebellion. It has been but seldom during the history of the world that even the most highly civilised and carefully disciplined troops have fought for an idea. They fight now and have ever

[71] *NCH*, No. 744, October 29, 1864, p. 174.

fought for the aggrandisement of a man, not for the enthronement of a theory; for wealth or glory or power, but seldom for the establishment of a dogma. So long as Hung Hsiu-tsuan as a living, tangible prince and general, led his troops, success brooded over his banners. The hordes which followed him looked to him as an all-accomplished general, and not as the promulgator of a new Gospel—they fought under him, with him, for him, so long as they saw him before their eyes, and believed that the power of conquest was inherent in him. But so soon as T'ien Wang became an idea, and the man was sunk in the Emperor, when it was endeavoured to transfer the enthusiasm which was felt for the successful general to the faith which he professed to spread, disaffection commenced its work, and thus the decadence of the Insurgent movement may be traced to the day upon which Hung Hsiu-tsuan transformed himself into a rival Emperor, and surrounded himself with a parade of mock dignity, faintly copied from the customs of the dynasty whose destruction he threatened. It is needless to comment further on the causes which, upon a general view of the question, seem to have operated in producing the downfall of the Rebellion. They have been frequently enlarged on in these columns. It is, however, only of late that we have found ourselves in a position to obtain calm and dispassionate accounts of the inner life of the Rebels, of the practices in which they indulged, and of the inconsistency which marked all those professions made by themselves and on their behalf. We now find that justice was nothing but another name for indiscriminate slaughter, and that neither age nor sex was spared when the demon of cruelty took possession of the breasts of the chiefs. Their religion was hypocrisy, their profession of faith a lie. The men who, in virtue of their office as kings, were looked on as prophets and priests, were actuated by none of those pure and virtuous motives ascribed to them by too confiding or too fanatical missionaries, and possessed none of the divine afflatus which changes the mere warrior into the crusader. That kindness which even wild animals show to their females and young was a stranger to the men whom we have been called on to welcome as the apostles of Christianity. The wretched women "cut at and driven back" while endeavouring to escape the horrors of a city sacked by licentious troops, and to share the exile of their fathers, husbands or brothers, opens up a view of character so essentially Chinese that we can recognise in it no regenerated elements. Thus from whatever point of view we may regard the movement, we shall find that, left to itself as it has been, the Rebellion would never, and, indeed, could never have led to the organisation of a new and enlightened system of Government.[72]

Whatever the attitude of the Western people toward the Taiping religion, rarely did anyone during the course of the movement seem concerned with the negative effect of the movement on the chance of

[72] *NCH*, No. 746, November 12, 1864, p. 182.

spreading Christianity should it fail. Lin-le seems to be the only one who discerned that the Christian religion, should the Taiping movement fail, would become an obnoxious element in the eye of the Chinese. He said, "...as the foreign derived religious character transpired, the bigoted and proud Chinese naturally began to eye with suspicion a movement so vast, aiming not only at the subversion of the reigning dynasty, but of the time-honoured superstitions, ceremonies, and faith of the nation."[73]

When Timothy Richard reminisced about his forty-five years of experience in China, he said: "Later on, the Taiping rebellion made the Chinese fear religious propaganda as a dangerous political movement."[74] Lin-le's fear was confirmed as Richard remarked: "Although the Taiping rebellion had been crushed six years before my arrival in China, its baleful effect against the spread of Christianity continued so powerful a factor that it must be mentioned.... The number of lives lost during the thirteen years of the Taiping rule..." rolled up "a legacy of hatred against Christianity, a hatred which has scarcely yet melted away."[75] What they did not mention and perhaps did not know was that religious propagation and activities had always been viewed with suspicion by the Chinese government in China. Few rebellions in Chinese history did not have some form of religious element.

I have not tried to cover the whole range of Western attitudes toward the Taipings, but I hope I have presented a fair representation of the various interpretations. These interpretations are more or less colored by special interests. For example, the views of Elgin, Wade, Oliphant, and others were obviously influenced by the unpleasant experience that they had during their trip up the Yangtze to Hankow and back to Shanghai in 1858. Furthermore, after the treaty signed at Tientsin in 1856, they had no further use for the Taipings. Whether sincere or not, a statement made by Lieutenant Colonel G. J. Wolseley in 1860 seems to suggest that a desire for better conditions for trade lay behind all their explicit pronouncements. The statement runs:

> In my opinion a fair field for missionary work in China can only be obtained by a general extension of our commercial relations throughout the length and breadth of the empire. To such Tien-wan and his chiefs are as

[73] Lin-le, *Ti-ping Tien-Kwoh*, p. 155.
[74] Timothy Richard, *Forty-five Years in China*, p. 157.
[75] *Ibid.*, pp. 185–86.

much opposed as ever the Imperial Government has been. Were the rebels in possession of undisturbed sovereign power, there is every reason for supposing that their external policy would be as obstructive as that pursued by Yeh and his predecessors at Canton. Judging of the rebellion by its present effects upon the country, none but men of the most sanguine temperament can expect any eventual benefit, political or otherwise, to accrue from its general success; whereas all must allow that its suppression would not only stay the hand of the murderer, and restore devastated provinces to their former prosperous condition, but would revive the commerce of the country, which is fast dying out under the depressing influence of internecine war.[76]

In most cases the element that influenced the judgment of the Western writers is not so simple. Most of the writers quoted here were missionaries, and one might think they would share the same interests—that a man like Meadows who was at first an interpreter and then a consul would have the same prejudices as Bruce or Bowring. But this is not the case. One finds among the missionaries a wide variety of opinions, and a sharp dissension between Meadows and his superiors. Another revealing example of conflict, the source of which must be attributed to individual preconceived ideas or temperaments, is afforded by the reports of M. S. Culbertson, an American missionary, and Charles F. Fahs, assistant surgeon, United States Navy. Both reports were based on personal observations when they visited Nanking on the "Susquehanna" in 1854, when Robert M. McLane, the American commissioner to China, toured the Yangtze. According to Culbertson:

Two young men from Kwangsi had charge of this gate, and, like all others whom I saw from that province, were men of remarkably fine appearance and more than ordinary intelligence. Proceeding on about half a mile, I reached the "water west gate," and passed through it without being stopped. Immediately after passing the gate I found myself in a broad street paved with stone. The houses are for the most part of one story, and many of them have been partially torn down and left unoccupied. This portion of the city seems to be occupied only by women. There were men passing through the streets, but I saw none in the houses. A few women were seen in the streets and several well-dressed ladies on horseback, riding astride. The crowd of men and boys attracted by the appearance of a foreigner were quite deferential in their deportment, and not a rude word was uttered. I saw no shops, and nothing exposed to sale. It would seem that when the city was taken the persons and property of all the inhabitants were regarded as belonging to the victors, and all appear to be provided

[76] Wolseley, *Narrative of the War with China in 1860*, pp. viii-ix.

for from the public treasury. The people were all well dressed, and seemed cheerful and happy.

And according to Fahs:

In reference to the people, candor compels me to say, so far as my opportunities of judging go, that they appear to be the dregs of the country, and are devoid of nearly all principle. The majority of them, even the mandarins, are illiterate, and have but little morality or integrity to control them. The soldiery is nothing more than a band of undisciplined and idle men congregated together, and willing for any change in the government. The influence of the mandarins over them is exceedingly limited, and their orders are almost totally unheeded. In their newly adopted religion there appears to be considerable sincerity and devotion, and they are most punctual in the observance of all its forms and ceremonies, even to fanaticism, but it seems to be a mixture of Christianity with heathenism. They regard their emperor as of divine origin, and as such worthy of the homage of all men. It is this zealous and fanatical devotion to Tae-ping-Wang which stimulates them and leads to conquest and the possession of the cities they hold. If they are successful in the overthrow of the reigning dynasty, it will yet require much time; and even when it is accomplished, anarchy and confusion, the too frequent followers of sudden and popular enthusiasm, may take the place of the hoped-for peace and good order.[77]

I shall not question either the candor or integrity of the surgeon or the possibility of a religiously sincere people being "devoid of nearly all principle." Dr. Fahs does seem to lack that desire which Culbertson exhibited so clearly in his language to understand the people with whom he was in contact. That the two reports are so different illustrates that neither station in life nor personal experience was enough to explain the differences of opinion among the commentators. I shall therefore let them stand as they are, and will not even challenge the *North China Herald* editor's generalization that the ruthlessness of a people at war "opens up a view of character so essentially Chinese that we can recognise in it no regenerated elements."[78]

[77] The accounts by both Culbertson and Fahs are found in correspondence of Robert M. McLane and Peter Parker, late commissioners of the United States in China, with the Department of State (35 Congress, 2d session, Senate Executive Document No. 22, Serial 982, Vol. VIII, pp. 81, 80).

[78] The Taiping movement did not occupy the attention of Japanese scholars until recently. In the nineteenth century Yoshida Shōin was one of the very few who had anything to say about the Taipings. In his *Shinkoku kampō ranki*, he gives a narrative of the Taiping movement. But it is doubtful whether he distinguishes between the God-Worshipers and the Hung Society, as he quotes what modern scholars consider Hung Society documents as proclamations of Hung Hsiu-ch'üan. See *Shinkoku kampō ranki*, II, 231–36.

Chapter XIII

Twentieth-Century Interpretations

In the last few decades, both Chinese scholars and scholars abroad have tried to assess the significance of the Taiping movement and to understand it in light of the immediate historical past; of the contemporary political, economic, and social conditions; and of its effects upon subsequent revolutions.

WESTERN WRITERS

Western writers, who view the movement from an academic standpoint, are unhampered by the immediate interests in better conditions for trade, spreading Christianity, or better recognition at court which vitiate much of the validity of nineteenth-century interpretations.

In 1928 John Littell used the Taiping Rebellion as an illustration of the relation between missionaries and politics in China. His view of the movement differs very little from those we have treated. He says: "The Taiping Rebellion, probably the most destructive civil war of modern times, was a gigantic protest against the weakness and conservatism of China's Manchu rulers, but it was more than that—it was a fanatical religious outburst, proclaiming Old Testament Christianity as its creed."[1]

Professor Kenneth S. Latourette believes that the Taipings knew little or nothing of the inner spirit of Christianity. Their faith had the outward form of Christianity but the Christian influence was obviously modified to

---

[1] John B. Littell, "Missionaries and Politics in China—The Taiping Rebellion," *Political Science Quarterly*, Vol. XLIII, No. 4 (Dec., 1928), p. 566.

conform in large part to Chinese practice.... The lack of much intimate contact with missionaries, and the visions and vagaries of Hung, Yang, and some of the other leaders scarcely permitted the movement to become really Christian. At its close, as at its beginning, the T'ai P'ing movement was a Chinese sect, displaying some interesting results of contact with Christianity, but drawing most of its beliefs and characteristics from its Chinese environment and the erratic genius of its leaders. [2]

Latourette is convinced that the missionary influence alone would not have given rise to the rebellion:

It was other factors that were chiefly responsible—the illness of Hung, the inherited religious conceptions of Hung and his followers, local friction in Kwangtung and Kwangsi, the incompetence of the Manchu government, and the ambition and organizing genius of Chu.[3]

But he does add:

It is probable, however, that the books prepared and distributed by the missionary and his helpers furnished the initial impulse and that without them the religious convictions that gave driving power to the insurrection would not have come into existence. All unwittingly and unintentionally Occidental Christians helped to arouse forces which they could not control.[4]

An unbiased attempt to understand the movement is here clearly visible.
Williams L. Bales, in his *Tso Tsungt'ang, Soldier and Statesman of Old China*, sees the weakness of the imperial forces, which was made evident by China's war with Great Britain, as a reason for the antidynastic sentiment to flare up. He says:

Another powerful factor [the first factor being the ideology, which the author judged to be "based on a peculiarly Chinese version of Christianity"] in the development of the Taiping Rebellion in the southwest of China was the war with Great Britain during the years 1839–42. The force which Britain brought to Canton and which dealt a crushing blow to the Chinese Empire was a negligible one, considering its accomplishments. The Canton populace had long been unfavourably disposed towards the foreigners and when they saw the highest officials of the empire

[2] Kenneth Scott Latourette, *A History of Christian Missions in China*, pp. 297–98.
[3] *Ibid.*, p. 299. "Chu" apparently refers to Chu Chiu-t'ao, thought to be the early leader of the movement; but this legend has been exploded by Lo Erh-kang and others. See especially Lo, *T'ai-p'ing t'ien-kuo shih ts'ung-k'ao*,
[4] Latourette, *op. cit.*, p. 299,

defeated and humiliated by a handful of the hated foreigners, the anti-dynastic sentiment long in evidence in this area became greatly intensified. The weakness and disorganization of the government was so plainly demonstrated that it had a markedly disintegrating effect throughout south China.[5]

Charles C. Stelle proposed to analyze the "Ideologies of the T'ai P'ing Insurrection" in 1936. He started out by defining ideas as forces, after the fashion of sociology of knowledge: "Ideas are forces; and political and religious theories, however irrational or mistaken, become objective realities in any social situation by reason, not of their validity, but of their influence on the minds of the human elements of that situation."[6] Stelle believes that the interpretation and evaluation of the Taiping creed "has been clouded by the attempt on the part of the writers to judge, not by the objective importance of the creed as a force in the minds of the rebels and their leaders, but by its relationship to and agreement with certain preconceived standards of value such as those of Protestant Christianity or Orthodox Confucianism."[7] He states his approach to the problem:

In a consideration of the philosophy, political and religious, of T'ai P'ings it is necessary to determine the sources, native and foreign, of that philosophy; the development and reconciliation of ideas from those sources; the intensity of positive reaction of the rebels toward the system so formulated; and the changes occurring in that ideological system during the course of the uprising. It is not necessary, and more than that it is humanly impossible, to judge the intrinsic merit of that ideology."[8]

Stelle is quoted at length because his is exactly the approach the present writer takes in the preparation of this book.

Stelle believes that at the inception of the movement there was a "cleavage between the religious system and the political aims of the rebellion. . . . As the movement progressed this distinction grew vaguer, and in the final years the political and religious ideas merged into one politico-religious system." As sources of the Taiping ideology, Stelle points on the one hand to the Christian ideas gleaned from the Old and

---

[5] *Tso Tsungt'ang, Soldier and Statesman of Old China,* pp. 76–77.

[6] "Ideologies of the T'ai P'ing Insurrection," *Chinese Social and Political Science Review,* Vol. XX, No. 1 (April, 1936), p. 140.

[7] *Ibid.*

[8] *Ibid.,* p. 141.

New Testaments and augmented by Hung's visions; and on the other hand to "Confucian ethic, pre-Confucian philosophy, Buddhist and Taoist Ceremonial," and "the traditional body of Chinese mores." He says, "It is evident that the religious system of the T'ai P'ings was a reconciliation of Christian, Confucian and pre-Confucian ideas."[9] Discussing the degree to which these religious ideas became social realities, he maintains:

> The evidence offered by some of the chief rebels shows that a portion of the leaders were but little affected by the official faith of the movement.... On the other hand, the widespread teaching of the doctrines, the emphasis on religious ceremonial, the ability of many members of the rank and file to recite parts of the T'ai P'ing dogma (especially the Ten Commandments), the frequent religious meetings, the regular observance of the holy day, the amount of public praying, and the evident belief of at least some of the rebels in the efficacy of the aid of Shang Ti during battles, give proof that to some extent the official religion of the T'ai P'ings had been pressed into the everyday life of the movement. And there can be no doubt that the response of the rebels to the religion of their leaders was at least enough to merit consideration for the ideology as a genuine force in the movement.[10]

Finally he draws the following conclusion:

> ...the outset of the rebellion witnessed the junction of two streams of thought: the semi-foreign, semi-Chinese mysticism of Hung, and the purely Chinese political aims of the original uprising. During the course of the rebellion, the original political aims were radically tempered by the increasing dominance of the religious philosophy. Finally these two streams of thought were united in one integrated politico-religious ideology with resultant changes in both the political and religious thought of the movement. This ideology was of enough influence on the rebels themselves to be considered a prominent factor in the rise and fall of the rebellion. And we may conclude that the eventual complete dominance of the religious thought over all matters political and religious, bound the existence of the religion to that of the political movement and assured that the extinction of the rebellion would mean the demise of the religion.[11]

Wittingly or unwittingly, others have attempted to follow Stelle's course of study. Stelle's conclusions are not reached through painful studies of the sources of the Taiping ideology he mentions, or studies of

[9] *Ibid.*, pp. 141–142.
[10] *Ibid.*, pp. 147–48.
[11] *Ibid.*, pp. 148–49.

the reactions of rebel followers to their leaders' creed. His conclusions are more or less intuitive in nature, based on a passing acquaintance with the Taiping documents and the sources of traditional Chinese thought or on the doubtful inference from the formal and ritual aspect of the Taiping religious practice to the inner spirit of their religious belief. He does at least point out a fruitful method in dealing with the ideological problems of the Taiping movement.

John Foster and Eugene P. Boardman have undertaken to trace the Taiping ideology to its Christian sources, and the writer in this book is working on its native influences. Foster's article brings out the specific elements which the Taipings took from Liang A-fa's tracts.[12] And Boardman's attempt traces the Taiping ideology to Christian sources, particularly the Bible, in much greater detail. As we have treated this aspect in Chapter VII, we shall dwell only briefly on his judgment about the Taiping Christianity. Boardman believes that the Taipings attempted to anchor in Chinese tradition as many of the new ideas as possible and that they tried "to appear as Chinese in form and in ideas as they could." The term *Shang-ti* and the fatherhood concept combined to produce the effect the Taiping leaders desired, *Shang-ti* recalling early Chou belief and the fatherhood concept enabling them "to tap a reservoir of filial feeling that was peculiarly Chinese and to account for Hung's authority as the leader of the movement."[13] Boardman also thinks that Taiping writings "possibly reflected the state of belief in the life about them when they made liberal references both to the devil and to a host of lesser evil spirits." He notes that the Taipings failed to take many central features of Christian belief, and those they did take were "made over to suit special uses." Conspicuously absent are the ideas of love, the Golden Rule, a concern "for the welfare of others and the use of possessions toward that end," and a sense of humility.[14] "Taiping borrowings are characterized throughout by a tendency to take over a given precept or body of data to the neglect of the reasoning behind such a precept or body of fact." For example, "There is no discussion in Taiping writings of the deeper aspects of sin or its forgiveness." Finally, Boardman thinks "the use of Christian elements contributed to the

---

[12] John Foster, "The Christian Origins of the Taiping Rebellion," *International Review of Missions*, Vol. XL, No. 158 (April, 1951), pp. 156–67.

[13] Eugene P. Boardman, *Christian Influence upon the Ideology of the Taiping Rebellion, 1851–1864*, pp. 35, 59, 70.

[14] *Ibid.*, pp. 80, 116, 107–9.

military success of the movement . . . . the Biblical component was an effective instrument of mass control and an important factor in Taiping military success."[15] But he thinks, too, that the Christian element possibly "handicapped the Rebellion as much as it helped it."[16]

Boardman's effort in tracing the Christian element in the Taiping religion is admirable, and his conclusions are on the whole valid. However, a negative method such as that used in the chapter entitled "What the Taipings Failed to Take" is valid only when the exploration is exhaustive. If the author had been dealing with the action of the Taipings, one would be forced to accept his verdict that they lacked the spirit of love and concern for others, a sense of humility, and the Golden Rule. But in their writings, which are the concern of Boardman, there is no lack of mention of love and humility, social welfare, and the Golden Rule.[17] Boardman also seems to set the standard too high when he criticizes the Taipings for being unable to understand the spiritual aspect of the Christian teachings. If one must measure up to his ideals in order to be called Christian, very few people, even in Christendom, are true Christians, and "Christian nation" is a utopia.[18]

"The Taiping Rebellion: Its Economic Background and Social Theory" by the Western scholar George E. Taylor has attracted wide

[15] *Ibid.*, pp. 78, 76, 120–21.

[16] *Ibid.*, p. 126. Boardman states on page 125: "Their [the Taipings'] creed was entirely foreign to Chinese ideology."

[17] "Proclamation on the Origin of Principles for the Enlightenment of the Age" (Yüan-tao hsing-shih chao) is an essay on universal love, and its very style is reminiscent of Motzu's works. The Confucian ideal of the world of Great Harmony as embodied in the "Li-yün" in *Li-chi*, which it quotes, suggests the Taiping idea of social welfare, which is also embodied in "The Land System of the Heavenly Dynasty" (T'ien-ch'ao t'ien-mou chih-tu). If humility is interpreted as humility before God, then the Taiping writings abound in it. And their conception of the brotherhood of men seems to contain the idea of the Golden Rule. Further, Boardman's investigation of the Taiping writings does not seem complete. On page 79 Boardman says: "His mother is called simply the *T'ien-mu* (Heavenly Mother). Nowhere in all Taiping literature is there an attempt to transliterate the name Mary." This is definitely wrong. In Hung's comment on the Gospel according to St. John, chapter 13, we find: "Later Father sent Elder Brother to redeem [them from] sin, and he entered the womb of Mary and became man."

[18] For further comment, see my review of Eugene P. Boardman's *Christian Influence*, in the *Far Eastern Survey*, Vol. XXII, No. 4 (March 25, 1953), p. 44, where I said: "The chapter on 'What the Taipings Failed to Take' is of great value. But in evaluating the Taipings' understanding of Christianity, Mr. Boardman seems to have set up a standard too high even for some real Christians. This weakens rather than strengthens his sound conclusion that 'The Taiping religion . . . was not Christianity' (p. 114). "

attention, not only for the understanding it furnishes of the Taiping society itself, but for the light it sheds upon the nature of Chinese society as a whole during the nineteenth century. More than any other writer, Taylor has gone beyond religious considerations into the root of the matter by analyzing the economic background of the Taiping movement. His main argument is: "...the Taiping rebellion was a revolution against Chinese civilisation, a revolution born of the fact that economic change had outrun the growth of social theory."[19] For according to his observation, "Everything points to the conclusion that the first half of the nineteenth century marks an epoch in Chinese economic history. Two new conditions, the enormous growth in population, which both created and intensified agrarian problems, and the new situation arising from the changes in foreign trade, produced the China of today."[20] Taylor explains what he means by the "economic change."

Stated briefly, the economic change consisted in a growth of population not only to an unprecedented total, but out of all proportion to the increase in the area of land under cultivation. Consequent upon this, as upon the growth of foreign and internal trade, upon the importation and use of opium, the developments in currency, and upon the unequal incidence of an antiquated system of taxation, the position of the peasant had become depressed, insecure and degraded to what almost amounted to serfdom. Also, the vicious circles of falling revenue and increasing expenditure, of corrupt officials and maladministration, of famine and revolt, together with social and legal inequalities and political oppression, lowered further the economic and human level of the peasant. Finally, since 1800 at the latest, China had a permanent population of paupers for which the prevailing economic and social system was unable to provide, and this floating population became the raw material of revolution and rebellion. It is argued that the Taiping rebellion must be considered first and fundamentally as the expression of an agrarian revolution born out of these conditions, secondly as a moral and religious movement, which for all its inspiration from the west, shaped itself in many ways to meet the requirements of Chinese civilisation; thirdly as a dynastic rebellion against the Manchus, fostered by the secret societies and drawing its sanction from the apparent exhaustion of the Mandate of Heaven. It was this ill-prepared and fortuitous combination of elements which gave birth to the Taiping Rebellion.[21]

[19] "The Taiping Rebellion: Its Economic Background and Social Theory," *Chinese Social and Political Science Review*, Vol. XVI, No. 4 (Jan., 1933), p. 548.

[20] *Ibid.*, p. 555.

[21] *Ibid.*, p. 548.

He points out that those large and small rebellions which swept across China during that time "are important not only as an indication of the background of agrarian discontent, but also for their contribution to the psychology of that floating population, which became the raw material for a dynastic rebellion and a great religious movement."[22]

Taylor does not overlook the social factor involved: "On the national psychology it may be suggested, the almost universal distress had an influence which contributed in no small measure, firstly by emphasising the distinctions between rich and poor, and secondly by embittering the relations between the people and the officials, to accelerate the decay of Chinese institutions."[23] As Taylor puts it: "When the learned cease to rule the unlearned and the rich begin to oppress the poor, a natural has given place to an artificial inequality."[24] But these social distinctions are intimately related to the "changes in the economic fabric [which] emphasised the inequalities in Chinese society."[25] Here Taylor repeats his argument: "If it is the social theory of a community which gives the final stamp to its economic arrangements, it cannot be too strongly emphasised, that at this period in Chinese history, social theory had been outgrown by economic change."[26] "To meet the situation," Taylor believes, "the Taiping rebellion produced two significant ideas, the first of which was a necessary corollary of the second. Stated briefly, they consisted in the doctrine of the brotherhood of man, and the theory of a redistribution of wealth according to need."[27]

There was also racial inequality, an issue on which the Taipings based the most appealing portion of their ideology, to add fuel to the movement. When all these economic, political, and social factors were combined, the time was ripe for revolution. But Taylor would like us to be clear on one point: "... for a dynastic rebellion the psychology of the people and actual conditions had never been more favourable, but for a social revolution, to be accepted or rejected with the former there was as little preparation as there was precedent."[28]

Taylor, like many Western writers in the nineteenth century, pronounced the Taiping government theocratic.

[22] *Ibid.*, p. 565.
[23] *Ibid.*, p. 562.
[24] *Ibid.*, p. 577.
[25] *Ibid.*, p. 576.
[26] *Ibid.*, p. 576.
[27] *Ibid.*, p. 576.
[28] *Ibid.*, p. 594.

In practice as in theory, the Taiping government, as it originated at Yung An, and was later consolidated in Nanking, had all the characteristics of a theocracy. Hung Sui-tsuen, called the T'ien Wang (天王), was both the spiritual and political head of the movement, and his proclamations derived their binding power on his followers in so far as they were considered to have come directly from God. Those immediately under him were men who had taken an active part in the work of religious leadership, and some of whom had also a reputation for direct communication with the Heavenly Father.[29]

Taylor believes that on the whole:

...the revolution appealed mainly to that large and permanent floating population which could never be fitted into the social or economic system. For those who had anything at stake, however small, and were to that extent bound up with the existing fabric of society, other considerations entered in, such as doubts as to the new religion with its worship, its iconoclasm and its new morality, the certainty of Manchu reprisals, and the instinct to wait and see if the mandate of heaven had been completely exhausted.[30]

This quotation explains why the officials and scholars like Tseng and Li took up banners against a movement which challenged the very civilization of which they were so proud. "...fundamentally these men were not fighting so much for the defence of the dynasty as for the preservation of Chinese civilisation."[31] In conclusion, Taylor says:

It was the measure of the economic changes which had by that time come to a head, of which many are yet to be resolved; it was a contribution, largely indigenous, to meet the inadequacies of social and political theory and practice; it sounded the death knell of an old and cleared the way for a new nationalism. Most important of all: it was no mere fancy which gathered so many thousands to its cause and took them through unrelated hardships, across two thousand miles of fighting, almost to the gates of Peking. Nor can history dismiss it as such. For there was born in the Taiping rebellion the precious spirit of revolution.[32]

---

[29] *Ibid.*, p. 594.

[30] *Ibid.*, pp. 607–8.

[31] *Ibid.*, p. 608.

[32] *Ibid.*, p. 614. In dealing with Taylor's interpretation, I have limited myself to those points which are pertinent to the present scope. But Taylor's article also contains some profound and far-reaching observations about the nature of Chinese society.

Non-Communist Chinese Writers

The twentieth-century Chinese writers on the Taiping movement may be divided into several groups: general historians who treat the movement as a historical event, giving it no more attention than they give to other similar events; patriots who find in it a source of inspiration for their own nationalism; a few scholars whose chief interest is to understand it; and Communists who see in it a concrete illustration of Communist theory of historical development. The writer will give a brief panoramic survey of some of the important writers in these groups: we shall deal with the Communist opinion in a later section.

Most historians, because of their training, deplore the low quality of the Taiping social composition, which they believe was responsible for the collapse of Taiping society. Ch'en Kung-lu in his *Chung-kuo chin-tai shih* (Modern Chinese History) condemns the Taipings for destroying the beautiful Pao-en t'a 報恩塔 pagoda which took the Mings many years to build and which had been generally regarded as a thing of great beauty. He accuses them of being simple-minded, lacking in common sense, superstitious, and dominated by one desire—to attain royal rank. He finds these characteristics common to all rebellions in Chinese history and sees nothing extraordinary in the Taipings.[33] Lü Ssu-mien touches on the same point when he deplores the Taipings' simple-mindedness; he believes that their failure was a foregone conclusion because social revolution and political revolution should always go hand in hand, and the task of carrying through a joint sociopolitical revolution was too complicated for people recruited from the lowly classes. He also believes that the Taiping religious ideology made the group a cultural enemy of the Chinese, who considered the traditional pattern of thought the soul of Chinese civilization and anything from abroad, especially religion, as an intrusion.[34] Ch'ien Mu views the movement as a peasant rebellion, caused by the same factors which started all previous rebellions, especially in the middle Ch'ing dynasty: ethnic consciousness plus official corruption. One common peasant characteristic is lack of organization, though emotionally the peasants as a group may be stirred up by religious ideologies. For this reason a peasant rebellion usually takes the course of wanton destruction. Taiping ideas against foot-binding, buying and selling of slave girls, prostitution, and opium-smoking illustrate the simple nature of

---

[33] *Chung-kuo chin-tai shih*, p. 144.
[34] Lü Ssu-mien, *Chung-kuo t'ung-shih*, p. 532.

peasants. Ch'ien Mu thinks that during their twelve years in Nanking the Taipings did nothing constructive.[35] Liu I-cheng, though somewhat more objective, expresses a similar opinion:

The uprising of the Taiping army had as its aims the overthrow of the Ch'ing dynasty and the preaching of Christianity. Their institutions have been favorably judged by the world, and some even say that they practiced communism. However, their ideals were too simple, and they merely aimed at destroying China's traditional systems, without any sound principles from the other countries to guide them. Hence they could not have done any better. In their later period they were pressed by military affairs, and all their effort was spent in defending themselves against attack, and there was no energy left for constructive work.[36]

The first to adopt a partisan spirit toward the work of the Taipings were the leaders in the nationalist camp. Reserving the opinions of Sun Chung-shan (Sun Yat-sen), Chiang Kai-shek, and others for consideration when we evaluate the Taiping influence on subsequent revolutionary movements, we shall here deal briefly with Jen (Chien) Yu-wen, a leading Taiping scholar in the nationalist camp who has done some admirable work in the study of the Taiping movement. His earlier view of the Taiping movement may be seen in the following statement:

We must acknowledge that the Taiping movement was an ethnic revolution, aiming at the overthrow of the Manchus and the recovery of the rivers and mountains for the Hans.... Their ideals may be said to have revolutionary significance in religion, government, and social, economic, and cultural patterns. Their aims, policy, and effort were all directed toward the complete revolution of the traditional systems of the past and the creation of a totally new society. Such great ambition and such overall planning not only are not to be found in the twenty-four histories of our country; but in the revolutionary history of the whole world there have not been many that can compare with it [the Taiping movement].[37]

Jen conceives of revolution as both an aim and a means: the aim is to create a new society, and the means is to destroy the old one. In view of the Taipings' desire to build up an unprecedented sort of society, they had to use a means which would bring about an unprecedented sort of destruction. Jen also defends the Taipings' undemocratic ways:

[35] Ch'ien Mu, *Kuo-shih ta-kang*, p. 616.
[36] Liu I-cheng, *Chung-kuo wen-hua shih*, p. 402.
[37] Jen [Chien] Yü-wen, *T'ai-p'ing-chün Kwangsi shou-i shih*, p. 4.

theirs was not the time for democracy. The Taiping Rebellion is important in view of its results: (1) military changes—the *Lü-ying* (provincial forces or the army of the Green Banners) were replaced by the *Hsiang-chün* and *Huai-chün* (armies of the Hsiang and Huai regions), paving the way for the development of warlordism; (2) political changes —the Manchus lost power, which fell gradually into the hands of the Hans (Chinese), and the power of the central government was shifted to the local officials; (3) financial changes—the likin was established, and the practice of foreign loans was started; (4) great social and economic destruction. But the great contribution of the Taiping Rebellion lies in its influence on the leaders of the nationalist revolutionary movement.[38]

Jen, however, changed his mind about the Taipings. Now he believes that Taiping ideals remained merely ideals, and Taiping aims were never realized. In two recent articles Jen contends that the Taipings, while successful in applying their ideas governing local administration, failed to put their ideas on the land system into practice. Furthermore, Jen believes there is a contradiction implicit in the Taiping state landownership; for after the redistribution of land, land would become permanent property privately owned, and could be inherited in much the same way as the private property in the traditional system was handed down from one generation to another.[39] Jen says:

> Under this system [land system] all the peasants in the empire practically become state serfs. The state becomes the all-inclusive landowner, an oppressor and exploiter of peasants. Therefore I venture to give the following judgment: this [the Taiping] land system may seem to embody high ideals, but in practice it leaves much to be desired. If the system is followed to the letter and applied, what the peasant gets will be the minimum of the produce, which naturally will not increase his buying power; for this reason his living standard and the cultural level he reaches will also remain in the minimum; he will not be able to satisfy his desire and know of no way to improve his self-cultivation; his ideals will find no way of realization, and he will forever find himself submerged in miserable poverty, completely divorced from happiness; he will be the horse and ox of the state throughout his whole life.[40]

[38] *Ibid.*, pp. 4–5.

[39] Jen Yu-wen, "T'ai-p'ing t'ien-kuo t'ien-cheng k'ao," *Journal of Oriental Studies.* Vol. I, No. 1 (Jan., 1954), pp. 26–63, especially pp. 30–31; and "T'ai-p'ing t'ien-kuo hsiang-chih k'ao," *Journal of Oriental Studies*, Vol. I, No. 2 (July, 1954), pp. 249–307.

[40] "T'ai-p'ing t'ien-kuo t'ien-cheng k'ao," *Journal of Oriental Studies*, Vol. I, No. 1 (Jan., 1954), p. 32.

So Jen seems to have revised his position regarding the nature of the Taiping society at least in respect to the land system. For as far as the land system is concerned, the Taiping ideal can hardly be described as having "revolutionary significance," or being directed "toward the complete revolution of the traditional systems of the past and the creation of a totally new society."

There are other writers who consider the Taiping movement a great revolution, though few ever explain what they mean by that term. Chu Hsi-tsu in his preface to Ch'eng Yen-sheng's *T'ai-p'ing t'ien-kuo shih-liao* describes the land system of the Taipings as a forerunner of communism.[41] Hsieh Hsing-yao maintains that the significance of *T'ai-p'ing t'ien-kuo* lies not only in the fact that it was the forerunner of the 1911 revolution, but also in its new institutions, its reform, its government, its revival of the ancient land regulations, its new calendar, and its new religion. China has had a number of dynastic changes, but her political institutions have not changed in any radical way. The Taipings threw overboard the entire system which had been in force for thousands of years and instituted something completely new. Their aim was to oppose everything the Manchus did; this resulted in self-contradiction and collapse. Their destructive behavior may be explained by the fact that they were tremendously influenced by secret societies, and all their actions were conditioned by the behavior pattern of people from lowly classes.[42]

Another Taiping enthusiast is P'eng Tse-i, whose *T'ai-p'ing t'ien-kuo ko-ming ssu-ch'ao* (Thought Tide of the *T'ai-p'ing t'ien-kuo*) attempts to give an all-inclusive interpretation of Taiping ideology. He maintains that the Taiping pattern of thought had the following characteristics: its political philosophy was tinged with theological elements, its social and economic theory was a kind of equalization of wealth, and its general conceptual pattern or ideological consciousness contained a great deal of revolutionary spirit; though it was shot through with imaginary elements, it had its factual basis; in certain respects it was progressive and in others conservative and backward. Some of these characteristics were the result of contact with foreign countries, and some were inherited from the Chinese agricultural society of the past. The inner contradictions in the Taiping ideology were undoubtedly the result of the semifeudal and semicolonial society that had been evolved

---

[41] Preface to Ch'eng Yen-sheng (compiler), *T'ai-p'ing t'ien-kuo shih-liao*, 1st Series.
[42] Hsieh Hsing-yao, *T'ai-p'ing t'ien-kuo ti she-hui cheng-chih ssu-hsiang*, pp. 1–4.

in China. During the early period of the ideology's development, it was characterized by progressiveness and vitality; but in its later period these progressive factors were replaced by reactionary elements and corruption through historical inertia. The corruption and stagnation gradually gained momentum and brought the Taiping movement to its doom.

P'eng Tse-i described the Taiping Rebellion as the last peasant revolution in Chinese history and as a revolution characterized by nationalism and the positive nature of a utopian communism. It was a religious revolution, a social revolution, and an ethnic revolution. On the eve of the Taiping Rebellion, Chinese society had been split into two camps: on the one hand there were the feudalistic landlords, powerful gentry, and merchants and usurers; and on the other, a vast number of unemployed and poor peasants and a small number of city handicraft-industry workers. The latter, instigated by a handful of disappointed intelligentsia of the lower classes, rose in revolt against the former. P'eng Tse-i says the Taiping Rebellion was more than a war against the Manchus or a war of the peasants against the feudalistic system; it was also a movement to emancipate the people from all kinds of bondage, including those imposed on the Chinese by foreign nations.

According to P'eng, the Taiping system of land regulations and equalization of wealth was based on the concept that land was public, owned by the state rather than privately owned. The system was more or less a castle in the air because it was not built on the material conditions of the society of the time. This is why the Taipings reverted to a private ownership system according to which the land was taxed by the government. P'eng describes the Taiping society as a collective farm life in the country and a life of common sharing in the army. In the political field, he sees a democratic spirit in the Taiping government shown by the popular election of officers by open ballot. From their system of promotion and demotion he also infers that the people of the Taiping society had the right of recall and election of officials. In the judiciary field, the people were given a fair trial and the right to appeal ultimately to the T'ien Wang.[43]

Ch'en Hsün-tz'u regards the ethnic issue as a minor factor in the life of the Taiping movement. To him, as to many Western writers, the religious nature of all aspects of Taiping society was the chief factor which brought them their initial success and was also responsible for

[43] P'eng Tse-i, *T'ai-p'ing t'ien-kuo ko-ming ssu-ch'ao*, pp. 28–40.

their final downfall. Taiping religion was compounded of a perverted form of Christianity and native superstitions. As the masses of the people were superstitious, this religious nature aroused in them a great enthusiasm that was the necessary unifying force leading to action. On the other hand, because of its unorthodox character the religion also aroused the antagonism of scholars who had been brought up in accordance with the traditional pattern of thought. Ch'en enumerates different aspects of Taiping society which were permeated by religious thought. He says:

> Thus, whether in establishing institutions or in enacting government policy, [the Taipings] always started out from a religious standpoint. Religion was used to formulate their fundamental policy, to institute military regulations, to boost morale and valor in battle, to induce endurance of sufferings and hardships of labor, to prevent defection, and to suppress revolt. When they instituted new political measures, made a new calendar, or tried to effect a system of universal education and equalization of land, they consistently employed religious conceptions as the foundation; that is, they tried to enact these through religious training.[44]

Some Chinese scholars attempt to understand the Taiping movement as objectively as possible.[45] They have no private ax to grind and no ideological line to follow. Kung-chuan Hsiao, after reviewing the background of the political thought of the Taiping movement, draws the following conclusions: The Taiping Army was an anti-Manchu movement which endorsed a mixed body of ideas drawn from both native and Western sources. Most of the Taiping leaders had only the most shallow knowledge and were unable to understand adequately either the Christian doctrines or their own native culture. With respect to Western culture, they missed those factors which made the West wealthy and strong; in the case of their native culture, they could not free themselves from the desire to become kings and emperors. Their political aims were threefold. (1) They wished to overthrow the Manchus and revive the Hans. This is not merely a reiteration of the distinction made in the *Ch'un-ch'iu* between the Chinese and the barbarians; the movement also adopted some elements from Christianity which worked toward the destruction of traditional social mores, and it contained the idea of

---

[44] Ch'en Hsün-tz'u, "T'ai-p'ing t'ien-kuo chih tsung-chiao cheng-chih," *Shih-hsüeh tsa-chih*, Vol. I, No. 6 (Dec., 1929), p. 4.

[45] Jen Yu-wen, in his recent stand, should be included here.

national autonomy and international equality. (2) They worshiped T'ien and believed in universal love. This created a sort of theocracy, which resulted in religious equality, implying great harmony and universal love; and economic equality, of which the land regulations were the concrete expression. (3) They advocated political equality and emphasis on virtue.[46]

In a recent study entitled *Rural China: Imperial Control in the Nineteenth Century*, Hsiao combats the idea that the Taiping Rebellion was a "revolution coming spontaneously from the minds of the multitudes of peasant-farmers."[47] For according to Hsiao, "The Taiping movement failed not only to enlist the support of the peasantry as a whole but even to modify the characteristic attitude and behavior of many of the peasants that came under its sway. Much room was left, therefore, for Tseng Kuo-fan and his associates to compete with the Taipings in endeavoring to bring numbers of peasants into their respective camps."[48] Furthermore, when peasants joined the Taipings, "they took a subordinate part, acting at the bidding of the rebel leaders, who very rarely were ordinary peasants." These peasants probably did not understand the larger objectives envisaged or the concrete plans formulated by their leaders: "And there is no evidence to show that the peasants who fought on the Taiping as well as on the opposite side contributed anything beyond physical force; they all played, in other words, the traditional role of peasants in rebellions and in military campaigns." Hsiao concludes: "It is only in a very limited sense, therefore, that any rebellion that occurred in China in the nineteenth century may be said to have been a 'peasant movement' pure and simple."[49]

We shall go one step farther to maintain that none of the historical rebellions in China was a " 'peasant movement' pure and simple"; but we do believe that those peasants who joined up at the beginning of any campaign must have contributed more than "physical force"; without their initial enthusiasm and receptive mood no campaign could account for the success of the movement at its outset. When we treat ideas as weapons and think of them as being forces, we have in mind the receptive mood and enthusiasm which ideas create. But peasant participation alone does not make a campaign a peasant movement.

[46] Hsiao, *Chung-kuo cheng-chih ssu-hsiang shih*, pp. 662–69.
[47] Quoted from Chu Ch'i-hua, *Chung-kuo chin-tai she-hui shih chieh-p'ou*, p. 104, Quoted in Ssu-yü Teng, *New Light on the History of the Taiping Rebellion*, p. 35.
[48] Kung-chuan Hsiao, *Rural China: Imperial Control in the Nineteenth Century*, p. 485.
[49] *Ibid.*, pp. 477, 485–86, 477.

Hsiao also considers personal frustration a factor in the rise of the Taiping movement, and the Taipings' "communistic" ideas partly responsible for the movement's rapid success: "The scheme outlined in the 'Land System of the Heavenly Dynasty' (T'ien-ch'ao t'ien-mou chih-tu), according to which all were to share equally in the bounties given to mankind by the 'Heavenly Father,' undoubtedly had a tremendous appeal to thousands of dispossessed hungry peasants."[50] Hsiao maintains that the Taiping Rebellion was not a revolution in the sense defined in Chapter XI. In footnote 184 in his chapter 10, Hsiao says:

It is obvious that from the establishment of the Ch'in dynasty (246 B.C.) to the establishment of the Ch'ing dynasty (A.D. 1644) all the dynastic changes were, in Aristotle's language, of the type of "revolution" that did not "disturb the form of government." [*Politics*, Jowett's translation. v. 1. 1301b.] Some of the important uprisings had greater significance than the mere desire of the leaders to "get the administration into their own hands." The Taiping Rebellion is an outstanding example of such movements; it, however, did not deviate from the historical pattern in one respect: the Taiping leaders intended to set up another dynasty and did not envisage a new form of government.[51]

Chou Ku-ch'eng describes the *T'ai-p'ing t'ien-kuo* as a movement characterized by two factors: ethnic consciousness and social consciousness. For him, the character of that rebellion was twofold: it was a revolt against the Manchus by the Chinese and a revolt of poor peasants against the bureaucratic landlords under the regime of the Manchus.[52] Chou attributes the success of the Taipings in winning a big following to the fact that poor peasants had no means of livelihood because of famine and hence were moved by the Taiping ideology, which promised them succor. For the purpose of unifying this unwieldy mass of people, the spiritual tie of Christianity was introduced.[53] The economic system is described as a communist system closely related to the military organization, a system which has no clear distinction between the civil and the military.[54] Taiping cultural policy consisted mainly in preaching a modified form of Christianity, and Taiping social policy was directed mainly toward the prohibition of opium-smoking. Chou concludes:

[50] *Ibid.*, p. 471.
[51] *Ibid.*, p. 708.
[52] Chou, *Chung-kuo t'ung-shih*, II, 1006.
[53] *Ibid.*, I, 1014.
[54] *Ibid.*, I, 1015.

As to the nature of this great and courageous revolt of the *T'ai-p'ing t'ien-kuo*, we may make the following judgment: this movement began as a struggle between the Manchus and the Chinese; developed into a struggle between peasants and landlords, the *T'ai-p'ing t'ien-kuo* representing the peasants and Tseng Kuo-fan representing the landlords; and finally as the representatives of peasants and the heavenly kingdom of the Hans, the Taipings became the object of a combined onslaught by merchants under foreign domination and landlords controlled by the Manchu nobility.[55]

Hsiao I-shan quotes with approval Chu Hsi-tsu's remark describing the Taiping land system as the forerunner of communism.[56] To Hsiao, this land system is very much in the spirit of modern socialism, in that land and other forms of property are owned by the state rather than privately owned and common sharing is practiced in both labor and enjoyment of food and clothing.[57] He believes that if Hung Hsiu-ch'üan had been given time to develop his scheme, or if his interest had not been entirely engrossed by the desire to become emperor, he would have become a great revolutionary leader of the socialist movement on an international scale.[58] Apart from seeing in the Taiping Rebellion a socialist movement characterized by the aims of equality and fraternity and a world of Great Harmony, Hsiao also believes it was an ethnic revolution. To Hsiao, the Taiping socialist trend was the result of Christian influences while the ethnic element came from secret societies.[59] In his preface to P'eng Tse-i's *T'ai-p'ing t'ien-kuo ko-ming ssu-ch'ao*, Hsiao I-shan makes the Taipings' attack on Confucianism the chief cause of their downfall.

Kuo T'ing-i gives a short but concise description of the Taipings in the preliminary remarks of his *T'ai-p'ing t'ien-kuo shih-shih jih-chih*:

The Taiping Revolution or Rebellion was a great movement in modern Chinese history. Its nature is not limited to political or ethnic but includes religious, economic, and social factors. We may trace its source to the orthodox pattern of thought and the ideology of the secret societies from within, and the Christian ideas from without. The revolutionary activities of Sun Chung-shan [Sun Yat-sen] and the success of Tseng [Kuo-fan], Tso

[55] *Ibid.*, I, 1017, 1025.

[56] Hsiao I-shan (compiler), *T'ai-p'ing t'ien-kuo ts'ung-shu*, *ts'e* 4, Epilogue to "T'ien-ch'ao t'ien-mou chih-tu," p. 1a.

[57] Hsiao I-shan, *Ch'ing-tai t'ung-shih*, Part 2 of Vol. III, p. 182. This volume deals entirely with the Taipings.

[58] *Ibid.*

[59] *Ibid.*, pp. 1–2; Hsiao, *Ts'ung-shu*, *ts'e* 1, Preface, p. 1a.

[Tsung-t'ang] and Li [Hung-chang] in their later life may be shown to have been influenced directly or indirectly by the Taiping movement.[60]

The most important of the scholars is Lo Erh-kang, according to whom the Taiping Rebellion was a peasant revolution. The word "peasant" for him includes poor farmers in the villages, unemployed people roaming about the country, miners, and charcoal workers. A small number of the intelligentsia, wealthy farmers, and merchants did not change the nature of the revolution. The Taiping Revolution differed from the previous peasant revolutions in its closeness to us in point of time and in its being influenced by the ideas of the West. The God-Worshipers Society, which served as a unifying force to the movement, was based on a perverted form of Christianity. Its systems and institutions contained democratic and socialistic ideas. The Taiping movement failed because it was a peasant revolution, and no peasant revolution had ever succeeded without undergoing certain changes. The reason for this is that the peasants' heretic beliefs and self-interest ran counter to the interests of the scholar class, which was a part of the ruling clique of the traditional Chinese society. The feudalistic society of the Taipings and the corruption of their leaders are two other causes for the rebellion's ultimate failure.[61]

Lo's interpretation of the land regulations is an especially important contribution to the study of the Taiping movement. He thinks that the most important portion of the regulations was not carried out among the people in general. The spirit of the public land system lies in the confiscation of all land and its equal distribution by the state to the people. This the Taipings did not carry out; they still recognized the right of private ownership of land, as a tax certificate, an eye-witness's account, and Li Hsiu-ch'eng's confession evidence. He mentioned that the Taipings did succeed in giving the land to the tillers in his *T'ai-p'ing t'ien-kuo ti li-hsiang-kuo*.[62] However, at the same time he seemed reluctant to give the Taipings all the credit for the tillers' ownership of land. He said that the land the peasants held was still the land they rented from their landlords and was not given them by the Taipings.[63] But in a later work, *T'ai-p'ing t'ien-kuo shih-shih k'ao*, he not only reiterated his earlier contention that the Taipings gave the land to the tillers but also gave credit to

[60] *T'ai-p'ing t'ien-kuo shih-shih jih-chih*, Prologue, Vol. I.
[61] Lo Erh-kang, *T'ai-p'ing t'ien-kuo shih-kang*, pp. 102–3.
[62] *T'ai-p'ing t'ien-kuo ti li-hsiang-kuo* (1950), pp. 35–36.
[63] *Ibid.*, p. 36.

the Taipings for this measure and said that the Taipings succeeded in realizing the revolutionary objectives of fighting against the private ownership of land by the landlord class and fighting against the feudal and exploiting system.[64] It is also in this later work that Lo began to mouth some of the Communist terminology, calling the Taiping land system *k'ung-hsiang* (empty thought) or utopian.

Lo believed that the Taipings did carry out the portion of their regulations concerning *hsiang-kuan* (local officials) and that they strictly adhered to the system governing the army.[65] He believes that there is an explanation for the failure to carry out the land regulations among the people. The soul of the public ownership system is state ownership of land. This the people did not like to follow. As in time of war the people's support was most vital, the government had to take the will of the people into consideration in the matter of policy or practice. Conditions in the army were completely different and made it possible for the army to become a society in which the soldiers lived a communal life, a life which made each of its members a producer for the benefit of all. This was the realization of a utopia of which ancient Chinese sages had a faint conception, a utopia in which each contributes what he can and takes what he needs. Though this society was realized only in the army, and there only for a short period, it gave the Taiping society an everlasting glory.

According to Lo, the Taiping movement had the following effects. National troops became the troops of individuals, gradually bringing the Manchus to their downfall and creating the regional forces of military leaders which have persisted into republican times. Political power was transferred from the Manchus to the Chinese, resulting in the transfer of political power from the central government to the local governments. Directly or indirectly the Taiping movement was responsible for the rise of likin, the control of customs by foreigners, changes in currency, the exemption from taxation of districts along the Yangtze, and the beginning of foreign loans. Decrease of population and decrease of cultivated land were a natural result of years of war and devastation. Innovations included the institution of monogamy, emancipation of women from foot-binding, women's rights in government, reform of social customs, prohibition upon superstitions, and reform of literary

---

[64] *T'ai-p'ing t'ien-kuo shih-shih k'ao*, pp. 205–11.

[65] Lo and Jen Yu-wen are in complete accord on these points. See account about Jen above.

style. Finally, Lo regards Taiping society as revolutionary: the Taipings were the forerunners of democratic ideas and of nationalism.[66]

This last point Lo reiterated with much greater emphasis in *T'ai-p'ing t'ien-kuo ti li-hsiang-kuo* (*T'ai-p'ing t'ien kuo's* Utopia), published in 1950 in Shanghai. Lo said:

> The Taiping Revolution was a revolutionary movement, guiding the peasants to rise and take up the task of liberation. Its aim was to overthrow rich merchants, bureaucrats, scholars, and gentry, classes whose [nature] was feudalistic and whose [function] was to exploit; and to establish a new society in which all wealth belonged to the whole society, each and all shared land to till, food, clothes, and money, so that there was no place where the wealth was not commonly shared and nowhere the people were not all well fed and clothed.[67]

To Lo this kind of society embodies Christian love and the Confucian ideal of Great Harmony.[68] Lo's final conception of the Taiping society was formed as early as 1951, when he made the following judgment in his *T'ai-p'ing t'ien-kuo shih-kao*:

> The *T'ai-p'ing t'ien-kuo* revolution was a great revolution in the history of China, with far-reaching influences. In its revolutionary platform are embodied all the basic revolutionary principles of later days, such as liquidation of the class of landlords; abolition of private landownership; plans for building ships, railroads, factories, and other modern industries; struggle for international equality; equality among all men [which constitutes the ideal of Great Harmony]....When we who live one hundred years after them read "The Land System of the Heavenly Dynasty" which they published, we are still amazed by the grandeur of its scope. Not only can no peasant rebellion since the time of Ch'in and Han compare with it in achievements, but not even the 1911 revolution can compare with it in stature. If the *T'ai-p'ing t'ien-kuo* had succeeded, China certainly would not have sunk into semifeudal and semicolonial status.[69]

The tone of these last pronouncements suggests that since the Communist regime came into power in 1949 a great deal has happened in China and the mind of the scholar bears its impress; for the language here is exactly the kind which the Communists use in their evaluation of the Taiping movement.

[66] For detail, see Lo, *T'ai-p'ing t'ien-kuo shih-kang* (1937).
[67] Lo, *Li-hsiang-kuo*, Preface.
[68] *Ibid.*, p. 18.
[69] *T'ai-p'ing t'ien-kuo shih-kao*, p. 1.

Hung was often considered to be suffering from a disordered brain and more than once was described as insane. Recently an expert in social and comparative psychiatry made a convincing study of Hung's mental illness on the basis of the data he found in Hamberg's *The Visions of Hung-Siu-tshuen,* and possibly suggested by Jen's treatment of Hung's illness as a delirium.[70] According to P. M. Yap, to consider Hung's visions as political and Hung an impostor, as many people did, is untenable: "The recorded facts are themselves clear, and to a psychiatrist they are in no way beyond explanation or understanding." Similar phenomena had occurred before, and Yap gives as examples John Bunyan, George Fox, St. Augustine, St. Paul, and Emanuel Swedenborg, "the last of whom, like Hung, gave accounts of his sojourn in Heaven."[71] The problem for Yap becomes "essentially a psychological one." He says:

> It is clear, moreover, that Hung's freedom of choice in matters of ideology was circumscribed by a peculiar cast of mind, and that he was the victim of a certain psychic compulsion and of fixed ideas, which, along with a change of personality, resulted from his early mental disturbance. It is to be noted that the qualities of mind and character which contributed to his failure were also the very ones which brought him such portentous success to begin with. His weakness as well as his strength as a leader were both determined in an intimate manner by his illness.[72]

The "bizarre qualities" we find in Hung's brand of Christianity cannot be completely "ascribed to an understandable failure to comprehend fully the new ideology or grasp adequately the new *mystique* simply because he had never received formal instruction in the religion." Hence "we need to have a correct understanding of the nature of the illness in order to evaluate or appreciate the curious qualities of character that Hung showed in his later life."[73]

A brief summary of Yap's analysis of Hung's madness follows. Hung's illness is described as a twilight state, "precipitated by the various frustrations he [Hung] had encountered," causing a change in his personality and character. In view of Hung's "megalomanic convic-

---

[70] P. M. Yap, "The Mental Illness of Hung Hsiu-ch'üan, Leader of the Taiping Rebellion," *Far Eastern Quarterly,* Vol. XIII, No. 3 (May, 1954), pp. 287–304; Jen Yu-wen, *T'ai-p'ing-chün Kwangsi shou-i shih,* pp. 78–79.

[71] Yap, *op. cit.,* pp. 303, 302.

[72] *Ibid.,* p. 288.

[73] *Ibid.,* pp. 294. 299,

TWENTIETH-CENTURY INTERPRETATIONS

tions [mania characterized by delusions of grandeur] and unswerving rigidity of mind and character," there could have been "a schizophrenic-paranoiac element in his illness."[74] Another possibility is to think of Hung's condition as the result of religious conversion, for "paranoia-like psychopathic character developments" have been found to follow "cases of religious conversion essentially hysterical in basis." The religious tracts Hung received and studied served as a catalyst, transforming his disordered and frustrated mind through the impact of the idea of salvation and the concept of a "Man-God" into one dominated by a "Messiah complex" and the belief that he was specially gifted for the perception of new truths or for the reception of divine revelation. Yap concludes:

> The life and career of Hung Hsiu-ch'üan provides one of the clearest examples in history of the process by which vast social, economic and political forces impinge on the mind of an unusually perceptive and possibly unstable person, and having worked in him a transformation of mind and character, are through him gathered together and given meaning, and then released as an indomitable psychic drive to bring about social change. It is only in this light that Hung's place in history can be understood.... The manner in which he arrived at his renovating ideas might have been grossly abnormal judged by ordinary standards, but it should be remembered that, while his religion ended in rejection, and his revolution in failure, yet, in the light of history, many of the aims he cherished were also those sought by later Chinese leaders in the gradual process of the adaptation of China to the modern world. That is the measure of his genius, and the meaning of his madness.[75]

THE COMMUNIST INTERPRETATION

The Communists, as one would expect, assume a more or less uniform point of view. Reading their works is like listening to Ravel's "Bolero," with its cumulative production of sound and insistent monotonous rhythm. Minor variations occur occasionally, but the main themes are repeated over and over with tedious monotony. We take the following exposition from *Chung-kuo chin-tai li-shih yen-chiu kang-yao* (An Outline of a Study of Modern Chinese History), published in Shanghai in 1946,

---

[74] *Ibid.*, pp. 297–98, 300. Paranoia is a psychosis in which there are delusions of grandeur, hallucinations, and feelings of untoward pride and hatred, all of which are logically systematized so that the individual actually believes his disordered perceptions.

[75] *Ibid.*, pp. 300, 303–4.

which seems to set the pace of the official Communist interpretation of the Taiping movement. We shall supplement this source by reference to Fan Wen-lan and conclude by quoting the long editorial of Peking *Jen-min jih-pao* (Peking People's Daily), published January 11, 1951, the centennial anniversary of the Taiping Revolution. This editorial is quoted as the preface of *T'ai-p'ing t'ien-kuo ko-ming wen-wu t'u-lu* (first edition, 1952, and third edition, 1954), and with some modifications as the preface of Hsiang Ta and others, compilers, *T'ai-p'ing t'ien-kuo* (1952). Apparently this editorial is the official view of the Chinese Communist Party on the nature of the Taiping movement.

The Communist exposition of the social and economic conditions prior to the Taiping movement may be summarized briefly. Although foreign capital had begun to invade China, China was still a backward agricultural feudal society because national capitalism was not yet born, not yet developed. The Manchus, bureaucrats, and Chinese landlords monopolized land, which was the essential means of production. The peasantry formed their chief object of exploitation. A self-sufficient natural economy was the dominant feature, but mercantilism in the form of rice, salt, silk, and tea monopolies was comparatively developed. These, however, formed a part of feudal landlordism rather than modern capitalism. Usury was very well developed, particularly in Shansi; it too was affiliated with precapitalistic feudal landlordism. There was a great deal of city handicraft and mining. These were precapitalistic crafts and were not similar to modern mechanical industry. Communications assumed the most primitive forms.

The Communists make the following observations about class and racial relations. Neither the modern Chinese national capitalist class (bourgeoisie) nor the modern Chinese industrial propertyless class (proletariat) existed. Classes which did exist were landlords who exploited, ruled, and oppressed; and peasants who were exploited, ruled, and oppressed. Big merchants and usurers were included in the exploiting group, but they were not yet mercantile capitalists, bankers, or financiers. Handicraft workers in both city and country, unemployed poor in the city, and farmers who went bankrupt were part of the exploited class. Ethnic relations coincided with class relations, since the Manchus formed the landlord group and the Hans formed the peasant group.

Chinese political power, which may be called absolute monarchial despotism, was in the hands of the Manchus and big landlords. This power was used primarily to oppress the Hans, the Mongols, the Mos-

lems, the Miaos, and the Tibetans. The state was powerless to defend the country against foreign aggression. China was just on her way to colonial status, and was not fully aware of the evil of foreign imperialism. For this reason the antagonism between the Chinese and the foreigners was not as prominent as the inner contradiction between the ruling group and the ruled. Before the Taiping period, China had already established trade relations with England, France, America, Russia, and other foreign powers.

Social and economic conditions had destined the Taiping Revolution to be a peasant revolt against the Manchus. It may be called a prelude to a bourgeois revolution but it was not yet a bourgeois revolution. The Taipings were definitely not "bandits from Yüeh" or "long-hair bandits," as the Manchus and big Chinese landlords tagged them. Neither can their revolution be called, as Lo Erh-kang called it, a "poor peasants' revolution."[76]

The mission of the Taipings was manifold. First, they aimed at overthrowing at home the political power of the Manchus and the big Chinese landlords who had surrendered to the Manchus, and establishing a national state, with the Hans in coalition with the minority peoples at the core. Secondly, they aimed at abolishing the unequal treaties contracted between China and England, France, Russia, and America in order to nip in the bud China's tendency to slip into a semicolonial status. This, and only this, could have been their mission. Because of the social and economic conditions of the time it was not possible for the Taiping Revolution to realize the scheme proposed by Hung and Yang to go back to the primitive communist society. Because of these conditions and their own abilities, the Taipings could not have fulfilled their home and international mission at the same time; they had to overthrow the Manchus before they could fight for independence against foreign powers.

The Taiping Revolution was foredoomed. The motivating force, composed of peasants, handicraft workers, city poor, unemployed

---

[76] Fan Wen-lan, in "Chin-t'ien ch'i-i i-pai-chou-nien chi-nien," in *T'ai-p'ing t'ien-kuo ko-ming yün-tung lun-wen chi*, pp. 1–6, attempts to differentiate the Taiping Revolution from both the peasant revolts prior to it and the bourgeois revolution which came later. It differs from the earlier revolts in that it was the first to bring forth a platform embodying a land system which, when put into practice, would automatically wipe out the feudal land system. And it differs from later bourgeois-led old-democratic revolutions in that the Taipings had the audacity to encourage extensive peasant participation in their movement; later revolutions did not have the courage to do this.

handicraft workers, bankrupt farmers, and the poor and frustrated lowest stratum of the intelligentsia had neither a bourgeoisie nor a proletariat class to give them the leadership they needed in order to succeed. Their opposition was composed of royal families, nobles, bureaucrats, and big Chinese landlords, of whom Tseng Kuo-fan was the representative. Between the peasant class and their opponents there was only a small wavering group composed of a few small Chinese landlords and part of the intelligentsia, of which Ch'ien Chiang was the representative. Even if the Taiping peasants had triumphed, it would have been impossible for them to realize the primitive communist society, for history does not flow backward. Neither could they skip the Chinese capitalist stage to land directly in a socialist society. Their triumph could only comparatively hasten the arrival and development of Chinese national capitalism.

The Taiping Rebellion failed because of objective historical conditions and because of the Taipings' own subjective lack of leadership ability. Objectively, there was no bourgeoisie, no proletariat, and no leadership from an advanced class in the city.[77] Subjectively, the Taiping leaders did not carry out their proposed land redistribution; their attempt to go back to primitive communist society was a mistake; Hung's type of Christianity alienated a part of the intelligentsia and created internal conflict; they lacked a foreign policy after they failed to follow Huang Wan's strategy of first enlisting the support of the foreigners to liquidate the Manchus and then disposing of the foreigners; and finally, they committed errors in military strategy by not trying to take Peking, by attacking Shanghai, and by maintaining inadequate defense in their last days.

The Taiping Revolution was significant in spite of its failure. It was the greatest Peasant-against-Manchu war effort in China, bequeathing to later Chinese a glorious tradition of national revolution. The Communist Party inherits and carries on this fine tradition of the Taiping Revolution. As a result of the Taiping failure, however, the life of the Manchu government was prolonged for fifty years; and England and other imperialist powers advanced another step in their exploitation of China.

Fan Wen-lan's evaluation may be briefly summarized. Hung at first used Christianity for political reasons to give himself the prestige of

[77] Both Hua Kang in *T'ai-p'ing t'ien-kuo ko-ming chan-cheng shih*, p. 217, and Li Ting-sheng in *Chung-kuo chin-tai-shih*, pp. 43–44, called these subjective factors.

being the one ordained by Heaven—an attempt which fitted in very well with the tradition of *fu-jui* (符瑞 prognostication by means of physical symbols) and *shou-ming* (受命 assumption of heavenly mandate). In various writings Hung introduced political, economic, social, and racial equality; the social equality was called Chinese socialism by Karl Marx. These concepts of equality also formed the foundation of the "three people's principles" as advocated by the *T'ung-meng hui*. Fan thinks that Hung's belief in one God and the various precepts he formulated served him well in organizing his society and prescribing the uniform pattern of mores. They were the main reasons for the Taipings' initial success, by promoting equalitarian ideas and organization, meeting thus the objective demand of the revolution.[78]

Apparently taking the lead from Marx, Fan names the big guns of England as the coauthor of the Taiping revolutionary movement; the other coauthor was the opposition between the poverty-stricken masses and the group of exploiters. The Taiping movement is thus organically linked to the development of world capitalism.[79]

The most definitive statement by the Communists on the nature of the Taiping movement was made in an editorial of the Peking *Jen-min jih-pao*:

It is exactly one hundred years since the outbreak of the *T'ai-p'ing t'ien-kuo* in Chin-t'ien-ts'un before Tzu-ching-shan in Kwangsi, led by Hung Hsiu-ch'üan. This revolutionary force proceeded northwest from Kwangsi, fought its way through Hunan and Hupeh, and liberated Nanking. Immediately afterward, expeditionary forces were sent north and west. The campaign lasted fifteen years, and its power was extensively felt over seventeen provinces. It was in July, 1864, that the [Taiping regime] collapsed under the combined attack of the reactionary landlord forces and the powers who interfered. During the fifteen years of their rule, the revolutionary heroes established a state, organized themselves into a formidable military power, put into practice various revolutionary policies, and aroused enormous masses of peasants to fight for the overthrow of the feudal land system. Almost a million peasants participated in the struggle, and all of them fought to the very end. When their capital fell, over one hundred thousand fighters died without surrendering. Some of them even

[78] The editor or editors of *Chung-kuo ko-ming yün-tung shih* think differently. Inferring from the fact the Taipings did not have a bourgeoisie or a proletariat to guide them, these editors conclude that the Taipings were unable to unify the peasants and had no way to organize the masses. See pp. 34–36.

[79] Fan Wen-lan, *T'ai-p'ing t'ien-kuo ko-ming yün-tung shih*, 1948. This pamphlet was incorporated in Fan's *Chung-kuo chin-tai shih* in 1949.

burned themselves to death. With such heroic deeds they wrote a page of glory in the history of China.

In the history of China's feudal society, since the revolt of Ch'en She and Wu Kuang in the Ch'in dynasty over twenty-one hundred years ago, there have been several hundred big and small revolutionary wars staged by the peasants. The objective of most of these wars was to oppose the feudal exploiters and feudal oppressors, and to fight for a change in the economic and political status of the peasants themselves. Insofar as this objective is concerned, there is no difference between the Taiping movement and the previous peasant wars. But no peasant war prior to the Taipings can compare to their movement in scope. The Taipings established a comparatively complete political regime and military system; and the fact that for a comparatively long period they maintained a frontal position against the government and military forces of the landlords and ruling class is also a feat without peer. Furthermore, the Taiping revolution broke out during the 1850's, and it was a time when the aggressive power of foreign capitalism had already invaded China, had already become the dangerous enemy of China as a nation. This situation confronted the Taiping revolutionists with a new task: what attitude should they assume toward the robber-like aggressors? Were they to assume the same compromising and conciliatory attitude of the feudal monarchial regime of the Manchus or to take a firm stand in protecting the interests and honor of the Chinese nation? The Taiping heroes, without the slightest hesitation, adopted the latter attitude. This is to say under this new historical circumstance, the *T'ai-p'ing t'ien-kuo*, in addition to their task of opposing the feudal forces they also picked up the mission of fighting the aggressive forces of foreign capitalism.

In order to accomplish the mission which history had placed upon them, the Taiping heroes made a Herculean struggle. Even their enemy could not refrain from praising their "firm and invincible spirit." They put the Manchus' forces to a pitiable rout; they had so driven Tseng Kuo-fan, the military leader of the landlord forces, to the end of his rope that he sought to drown himself; and they even more than once had defeated the foreign interferers who were armed with modern equipment. Their military achievements were brilliant. But they failed in the end.

Taiping historians have, from different points of view, inquired into the causes of Taiping failure. Some attribute it to the strength of the Taiping enemy, especially that of the interfering foreign aggressors; some say that it was due to the tactical mistake of the revolutionary forces for not taking the advantage of their initial victory to drive right up to the nest of the Manchu regime, Peking; some say the Taiping Revolution failed because its leaders were unable to unify all the unifiable revolutionary forces, and, furthermore, because toward the later part of their campaign internal splits developed among the leaders; others say that it was because when they made their capital in Nanking, an eroding influence of pleasure-loving philosophy enveloped the Taiping army, causing the revolutionary

forces to weaken; and still others say it was because the leaders, when the revolution was about to collapse, did not have the determination to forsake Nanking and preserve their strength for future endeavor. All these analyses are correct, and they are certainly the causes of Taiping failure; moreover, some of these are also those which, over and over again in the history of China, had caused the failure of many a peasant revolution. But if we take a step further, the natural question is: Why was the *T'ai-p'ing t'ien-kuo* unable to overcome the interfering foreigners? Why was it possible for this or that mistake to happen? Why was it unable to capitalize on the experience of failure of so many peasant revolutions in Chinese history in order to avoid those mistakes, and why did they have to repeat the mistakes?

Although at the time of the Taiping Revolution the old feudal society had begun to collapse and China had begun to slip into a semicolonial and semifeudal society, yet limited by the historical conditions of the time there was not yet the emergence of the modern working class; and for this reason the Taiping Revolution was only a pure peasant war without the guidance of the working class. This is the fundamental reason the Taiping Revolution could not but fail. In a feudal society when the peasants were seriously oppressed they demanded liberation, and they also had the courage to use force to fight for liberation. But peasants are after all an unorganized group of small producers, and they are unable to formulate a clear revolutionary platform by means of which to unify all revolutionary masses; it is impossible for them to maintain revolutionary discipline for any length of time in order to centralize their strength to overcome a strong enemy; and they lack the scientific method to take stock of the revolutionary experience of the past and to utilize such experience to guide their revolutionary practice. Although the Taiping movement, in comparison to all the peasant revolutions of the past, had a more clearly defined platform and institutional system, such as land system, marriage code, and military regulations, yet these principles and systems are just unrealizable utopian thinking, some of which had been gradually destroyed in the progress of the revolution. "The Land System of the Heavenly Dynasty," while expressing the demand for a revolution in land system by the majority of peasants under the oppression of the feudal society of the time, was merely a proposal based on equalization, issued from the narrow-minded viewpoint of the peasant class, to which the Taiping leaders belonged. According to this proposal, each peasant family should have an equal share of land and wealth; this would enable everybody just to go on existing. This proposal cannot be realized; moreover, this proposal does not aim at developing the social productive power, but it will cause social productive power to delay on the level of the unorganized small farmers' enterprise. For this reason, this utopian agrarian socialist thinking is in fact of a reactionary nature.

Prior to the *T'ai-p'ing t'ien-kuo* and in the period of feudalism, among all the peasant revolutions there were those which met with the same tragic

failure as the Taipings'; but there were also a few which won some kind of a victory. The most illustrious examples of the latter are the peasant wars led by Liu Pang and Chu Yüan-chang. Although this kind of victory did not enable the masses of peasants to achieve liberation [this is due to the fact that when peasants are without the guidance of an advanced class and depend merely on their own strength it is not possible for them to realize any kind of new social system to take the place of the feudal system] and the peasants allowed the landlord class to rob them of their victory fruits, yet it had an important role to play in the development and advance of a society. At the time of the *T'ai-p'ing t'ien-kuo*, not even this kind of victory was possible. The reason is simple: during the feudal time the peasant revolutionary forces had only the corrupt feudal lords as their enemy; so some revolutionary peasants were able to defeat such an enemy on the military ground by their own effort. During the time of the *T'ai-p'ing t'ien-kuo*, the capitalist powers had invaded China; when they formed a coalition with the feudal forces, they became a comparatively stubborn and strong enemy. A pure peasant war cannot but meet with ultimate defeat when confronted with such an enemy. At a time when China had already slipped into a semicolonial and semifeudal status, if there were no working class to offer them guidance, no revolutionary movement, not even one as great as the *T'ai-p'ing t'ien-kuo*, could shake the foundation of the reactionary power which oppressed the Chinese people.

Some students of the history of the *T'ai-p'ing t'ien-kuo*, seeing that the interference of the foreign aggressors was one of the causes of its failure, express regret that the Taiping leaders "did not manage their foreign relations well," or did not "seek alliance," but on the contrary allowed the enemy to get their external aid. This is a mistaken view. It was in complete agreement with the interests of the Chinese and the Chinese nation for the Taipings to insist on equality and autonomy as principles of foreign relations; on the other hand, the Manchus, for the sake of enticing the foreign aggressors to give assistance to them to fight a civil war, did not hesitate to sign treaties which compromised their honor—this is a very serious criminal offense of treason. However, was the Taiping foreign policy without defects? No. Their mistake lies in taking as friends those capitalist aggressors who held to Christianity as a camouflage on the ground that they believed in the same religion; [the Taipings were] completely ignorant of the fact that these aggressors used missionary work as a tool of aggression, and unable to realize that it was these so-called Christian nations that ultimately came to the help of their enemy in bringing about their downfall. So the Taiping revolutionists showed that they failed to exercise vigilance in their relation with the foreign aggressors. The fact that after taking Nanking the Taipings did not take advantage of the unstable condition of the capitalist aggressors before they firmly established themselves and seized Shanghai, their main stronghold, is a concrete illustration of their lack of vigilance.

In spite of the fact that the Taipings, limited by historical factors, were unable to realize fully the strength of the capitalist aggressors who confronted them, in spite of the fact that the Taiping revolution had some illusions [about these aggressors] because of their religion, when they once saw that the aggressors openly pointed their swords toward them they adopted, without the slightest hesitation, the only possible and necessary method [which great Chinese under then existing conditions could adopt] in dealing with them.... The Taiping patriots were not intimidated by the big guns of the foreign aggressors. In their struggle against the aggressors, they expressed the heroic spirit of the Chinese people.... The great patriotism of the Chinese people as expressed in the *T'ai-p'ing t'ien-kuo* is forever the pride of the Chinese people.[80]

The reader will perhaps remember that many of these points including dubbing the Taiping Movement a peasant revolution have been treated in the "Introduction," and those which have been alluded to but not discussed there will be fully explored in the following chapter. To maintain that the Taipings envisaged themselves as having a historical mission to fight the aggressive forces of foreign capitalism, aiming at abolishing unequal treaties and checking China's tendency to slip into

[80] Editorial in *Peking jen-min jih-pao*, January 11, 1951. Since this was written, a few articles have appeared in Chinese Communist journals, repeating on the whole the same fundamental arguments given in this section. We find, however, that Kuo I-sheng in 1956 struck a discordant note by suggesting that the newly emerging proletariat played an important role in furnishing the backbone of the *T'ai-p'ing t'ien-kuo* revolution. Kuo sought to distinguish the Taiping Revolution from all other peasant wars by emphasizing that it was the precursor of a proletariat-led peasant war, yielding rich and valuable experience for future revolutionists. See his article "On the Role the Various Urban Groups Played in the T'ai-p'ing t'ien-kuo Revolution" (Lun hsin-hsing shih-min teng-chi tsai t'ai-p'ing t'ien-kuo ko-ming chung ti tso-yung), *Li-shih yen-chiu*, No. 3, 1956.

This unorthodox interpretation was immediately challenged and refuted by a number of writers, among whom are the following: Liu Tso-ch'üan, Chia Shu-ts'un, and Yüan Ting-chung. Their arguments may be briefly summarized as follows: To consider the newly emerging proletariat as playing the central and leading role in the Taiping Revolution is without ground and completely subjective, because the group that led the Taiping Revolution was the *petite bourgeoisie* and not the proletariat. It was a peasant war pure and simple. Evidently the Chinese Communists have not changed their mind about the nature of the *T'ai-p'ing t'ien-kuo*. For details see Liu's article "Problems Concerning the Formation of the Characteristics of the T'ai-p'ing t'ien-kuo Revolution" (Kuan yü T'ai-p'ing t'ien-kuo ko-ming t'e-tien ti hsing-ch'eng wen-t'i), *Li-shih yen-chiu*, No. 3, 1957, pp. 1–7; Chia's article "Problems Concerning the Nature of the T'ai-p'ing t'ien-kuo Revolution" (T'ai-p'ing t'ien-kuo ko-ming ti hsing-chih wen-t'i), *Li-shih yen-chiu*, No. 8, 1957, pp. 1–18; and Yüan's article "Problems Concerning the Nature of the T'ai-p'ing t'ien-kuo" (Kuan yü T'ai-p'ing t'ien-kuo ko-ming ti hsing-chih wen-t'i), *Li-shih yen-chiu*, No. 8, 1957, pp. 19–33.

a semicolonial status, is not a simple distortion of facts; it reveals most glaringly the rigidity with which they adhere to their formula in their interpretation of history.

MODERN JAPANESE WRITERS

The *T'ai-p'ing t'ien-kuo*, like many other Chinese historical events though not to the same extent, holds interest for many Japanese scholars. Among the first to take note of this movement was Inaba Iwakichi. In his *Ch'ing-ch'ao ch'üan-shih* (*Shinchō zenshi* 清朝全史, Complete History of the Ch'ing Dynasty), Inaba cited Manchu maladministration and bad government as the main cause of the rebellions of the Chia-ch'ing reign, which paved the way for the rise of the Taipings. He also saw a difference between the Taiping movement and previous rebellions: the former was a result not only of internal factors but also of international relations, while the previous rebellions were always caused by conditions within China.[81] Apparently on the basis of foreign sources, he believed that the Taipings did put into practice their communist program in Nanking. He attributed the Taiping failure to strategic error in not taking Shanghai when the attitude of the foreigners was still wavering. He also saw clearly that Tseng and his group rose against the Taipings not because they wanted to protect the Ch'ing regime but mainly if not solely to protect their own countryside.[82] With the exception of this last one on which he has some convincing arguments, Inaba presents his views with scarcely any elaboration.

Tanaka Suiichirō, in his "Taihei tengoku," recognizes the importance of Hung's being a Hakka.[83] He believes that the land system of the Taipings has revolutionary significance, and he terms the system a kind of communistic regulation. He also notes the presence of the religious element in their institutions, and singles out their religion and calendar as being most revolutionary. According to his thinking, if the Taipings had been thoroughgoing in adopting the Western calendar and religion, they might have won the support of the West and succeeded in overthrowing the Manchu regime. He attributes the reluctance of Hung and other Taiping leaders to adopt complete westernization to the self-respect of the Chinese; by this he evidently means that the Taipings were unable to clear themselves completely of the traditional patterns

---

[81] Inaba Iwakichi [Kun zan], *Ch'ing-ch'ao ch'üan-shih* (*Shinchō zenshi*), II, 387.
[82] *Ibid.*, II, 412–13, 453–54, 475–76.
[83] "Taihei tengoku," *Shigaku zasshi*, Vol. XXIII, No. 7 (July, 1912), p. 772.

of thought.[84] In view of the result of the Taiping movement, Tanaka expressed doubt that the revolution of 1911 could bring any genuine change in the Chinese way of thinking.

Yana Jin'ichi believes that the Taiping Rebellion was the natural result of the political conditions prior to its rise. The whole country, particularly Kwangsi, was boiling with rebellions of all kinds. The time was ripe for a great upheaval. Hence the Taiping Rebellion. The fact that so many people were willing to follow Hung indicates there was reason to consider the Taipings revolutionary. Although they talked about receiving a mission from the Heavenly Father or God, they may have used this religious ruse as a means to accomplish their revolutionary aims.[85] For according to Yana, after the Taipings' rise in Chin-t'ien only Hung and a handful of the original followers from Kwangsi still held onto the idea of the religious mission. Yang Hsiu-ch'ing, the man who was in full control of military, political, administrative, and financial aspects of the Taiping life, and the large majority of the Taipings had no longer any religious belief, and they were seldom moved by religious spirit.[86]

In an article entitled "Taihei tengoku no ran," Nohara Shirō, apparently quoting Yana Jin'ichi, holds that the rebellions of the White Lotus Society and its different branches were the forerunners of the Taiping movement. In this same work, a line of interpretation is developed which seems to be the model of later Communist interpretation, both in Japan and in China. Five causes of the Taiping failure are mentioned.

(1) The Taipings did not have a guiding class, and they did not have any alliance. During the time of the movement, there was no bourgeoisie in China, and the proletariat was not developed yet. This, however, was not the fault of the movement; it was its misfortune to have taken place at such a time. In other words, the social class circumstances were a historical and therefore an objective factor for which the Taipings cannot be held responsible. (2) The Taipings were unable to unite with other similar movements of the time; as a result these movements and the Taipings themselves were separately attacked and defeated. This indicates that the Taipings, being peasants, were handicapped by the narrow-minded viewpoint of peasants, and their group was characteriz-

---

[84] *Ibid.*, pp. 783–84.
[85] Yana Jin'ichi, *Kindai shinashi*, p. 347.
[86] *Ibid.*, p. 350.

ed by a lack of organization. (3) Although their military success was rapid and extensive, outside Kiangsu they never had a chance to apply their land policy; if they had been able to exterminate the feudal forces, the *t'uan-lien* (local forces) would have been allowed a free arena for their activities. (4) They committed strategic errors: first they did not attempt to take Peking, the source of the reactionary forces; and then they did not take a decisive stand about Shanghai when they could have taken it without too much foreign opposition. Shanghai later became the basis for the combined forces of government and foreign powers in their attack upon the Taipings. (5) Peasants did not have the ability to elect able leaders; for most of their life they were serfs, unfit for political activities. The T'ien Wang and a majority of the military officers came from the intelligentsia. Hsiao was about the only leader at the beginning of the campaign who actually came from the peasantry, but he was just a stupid and frank Taiping warrior. Later Li Hsiu-ch'eng led a model peasant army. But all the other leaders were susceptible to corruption and vice.

Another factor fatal to the Taiping cause was the attitude of the foreigners, who believed that the continued existence of the Taipings would damage their interests. The heritage the Taipings handed down to later times was the Chinese revolution.[87]

Toriyama Kiichi, in his *Taihei tengoku ran no honhitsu* (The Fundamental Nature of the Taiping Rebellion), holds a view contrary to that of most Japanese scholars. He believes that the magnetic power of Hung's religious fanaticism was largely responsible for the rise as well as the maintaining of the Taiping movement. This movement, according to Toriyama, was a religious revolution. It became, because of the circumstances, a political rebellion; but at the outset there is little evidence to show that Hung and other leaders had any political ambition. Their religion is neither Catholic Christianity, nor is it Protestant; it is peculiarly Hung's own religion.

[87] "Taihei tengoku no ran," the fourth chapter of *Tōyō kinseishi*, in *Sekai rekishi taikei*, Vol. IX, p. 203. The Communist line so apparent here does not necessarily imply that the author is a Communist. In Japan the Marxian thinking has become accepted in the same way as a chemical formula or a physical fact. On this point, John K. Fairbank and Masataka Banno made the following statements in their *Japanese Studies of Modern China*, pp. xiv, xv: "A second impression, however, is that several of the broad ideas of Marxism have taken deep root in Japan's intellectual soil. . . . Whatever may be the reasons for the vogue of Marxism in Japan, there can be no doubt about the strength of its influence in the scholarly world there."

Toriyama is also opposed to those interpretations which consider the Taiping movement an ethnic or a social revolution. The Taipings were iconoclastic and discriminated between believers and nonbelievers, but at first they paid no attention to the ethnic issue. There is no evidence that the poor peasants and other followers of Hung had any class consciousness as a basis of their revolutionary plans. However, in the subsequent development the ethnic issue became a convenient rallying point, which attracted the attention of most scholars.[88]

Nashimoto Yūhei's *Taihei tengoku kakumei* develops its arguments on the basis of a conventional Marxian framework. He attributes the Taiping movement to a number of factors. He characterized China as a feudal society in which the main mode of production was land; because most land was in the possession of the royal clans and big landlords, the people were reduced to the status of serfs. Nashimoto quoted Fujiwara Sadamū to show that population pressure was one of the main causes of the Taiping Rebellion, for the increase in population far outran the increase in cultivated land.[89] The lack of cultivated land combined with population pressure resulted in revolts of the peasants all over the country. The situation was aggravated by the invasion of imperialism after the Opium War; imperialism brought about the decline of Chinese village life. Taxation was raised in enormous proportion in order to finance the wars to subdue the revolts and to pay for the indemnity to foreign powers; excessive taxes reduced the people to a state completely unbearable. All these factors prepared the stage for the emergence of the Taipings, who were only in need of a frustrated scholar to lead them against the corrupt Manchu regime.[90]

Thus the main purpose of the Taipings, according to Nashimoto, was on the one hand to free themselves from the bondage of the Manchu rule, and on the other to fight for the possession of land, which was their only means to life. The activity of the Taiping army may be described as a struggle to "exterminate the ruthless and save the people." Fundamentally the struggle was nationalistic in character, and may also be said to be bourgeois agrarian. The Taipings' land system has in it a number of democratic ideas. They were mainly engaged in destroying the old landownership, killing landlords and bureaucrats, confiscating

---

[88] *Taihei tengoku ran no honhitsu*, pp. 119–23.

[89] See Fujiwara Sadamū, "Shimmatsu ni okeru jinkō kajō no shogenshō to Taihei tengoku undō," *Mantetsu chōsa geppō*, Vol. XIX, No. 7 (1939).

[90] Nashimoto Yūhei, *Taihei tengoku kakumei*, pp. 58–98.

wealth and property, and bringing into existence villages composed of self-cultivating farmers only.[91]

In religion the Taiping movement also shows its revolutionary character. For two thousand years China had utilized Confucianism as a means of oppression; this is why most peasant revolts in China used religion as a political means. However, the ideal entertained in the minds of the Taiping leaders is a kind of utopian communism, not at all in agreement with Catholic Christianity.[92]

Miyagawa Hisashi, apparently basing his analysis on Toriyama's reasoning, believes that Hung used religious enthusiasm to stir up the revolutionary army and that this enthusiasm became the cement which gave unity to the whole Taiping society.[93] Religion was the motivating force and furnished the creative impulse in all Taiping institutions, thinking, life, and mores. Toriyama may be right in saying that the Taiping religion is neither Catholic nor Protestant but is Hung's iconoclasm based on Christian beliefs. According to Miyagawa, Hung's brand of Christianity was the phenomenon which resulted during the process of interaction between Western and Chinese cultures.[94]

Even the Taiping ethnic thinking was derived from their religion. Miyagawa based this conclusion on the fact that the statement "the empire belongs to God" in the first edition of "Proclamations by Imperial Sanction" (Pan-hsing chao-shu) is, in the 1852 edition, changed to "the empire belongs to the Chinese." Thus the religious conception of the world is submerged in the new nationalism; and this policy against the barbarians became one of the Taiping efforts to win back the Chinese intelligentsia.[95]

Sano Manabu, one of the founders of the Japanese Communist Party who later left the party, analyzes the Taiping movement purely along the Communist line. He thinks that that movement was significant as a

---

[91] *Ibid.*, pp. 121–27.

[92] *Ibid.*, pp. 189–93.

[93] Miyagawa Hisashi, "Shoki Taihei tengoku no shukyōsei," *Jimbun kagaku*, Vol. I, No. 3 (Dec., 1946), p. 76.

[94] *Ibid.*, p. 86.

[95] *Ibid.*, p. 90. Miyagawa here apparently made a mistake in ascertaining the dates of the two editions on which he based his conclusion. What he considers the earlier edition is a later one, and what he considers a later one is in fact an earlier one. For details on this point, see my treatment in Chapter VI. Following Miyagawa's reasoning with the editions in correct chronological order, the natural conclusion would be: the Taiping movement was primarily a political one, and the religious element was a later addition.

symbol marking the division between modern China and medieval China. This modernity is characterized by popular consciousness against the Manchu regime, the presence of the ideas of liberty and equality which formed the forerunner of later democratic movements of the wealthy (bourgeoisie?), the fight against the imperialists, the beginning of the reshuffling of social classes, and China's falling into the status of a semicolonial state as the result of this modernization.[96]

From this analysis, Sano thinks that he discovers a truth about all agrarian revolts: peasant government can never settle China's problems.[97] He uses the term "contradiction" to describe situations which other historians simply designate as political or historical facts. These he classifies into two groups: those which became intensified during the Taiping period and those which were specifically produced at this time. The former group includes the "contradiction" between the laboring peasants and the parasitic landlords, between the bureaucrats who monopolized the government and the great masses of exploited peasants, between the non-monetary village economy or self-sufficient family economy and the monetary exchange economy, the corruption of bureaucrats, and contradictions which resulted from the absence of industry to absorb the increased population. Those contradictions which were produced particularly at this time were that between the Manchus and the Chinese and that between the ancient, closed, and stagnant old China and forces of the powers of Western Europe (the contradiction between the precapitalist mode of production and the capitalist mode of production). The *T'ai-p'ing t'ien-kuo* was the outcome of the extreme intensification and subsequent explosion of these contradications.[98]

Sano believes that the Taiping movement, although the forerunner of wealthy (bourgeois?) class revolution, was not a wealthy class revolution itself. Fundamentally it was an agrarian revolution, a voice of the peasants fighting to put over the demands of the peasants. He calls it an agrarian communism influenced by primitive Christian communistic ideas.[99]

Toyama Gunji believes that the Taiping movement was too compli-

---

[96] Sano Manabu, "Taihei tengoku kakumei," Part 3 of Vol. III of his *Shin-chō shakai-shi*, pp. 1–3.

[97] *Ibid.*, p. 3.

[98] *Ibid.*, pp. 3–10.

[99] *Ibid.*, pp. 10, 35, 37.

cated a phenomenon to describe in simple terms; but there is little doubt that after the failure of the northern expedition, whatever revolutionary ideals the Taipings once possessed were completely sacrificed, and the movement became a disorganized gang whose chief function was looting and plundering. Its significance consists in rousing China to the meaning of Western civilization, particularly the military aspect of that civilization.[100]

Although Kawabata Genji, in his "Tenchō dempo seido no seiritsu," does not deny that the Taiping movement possessed revolutionary character, "he considers its land reform program to have been little more than a tool of a traditional dynastic despotism," in the words of Fairbank and Masataka Banno.[101]

Masui Tsuneo, in his *Taihei tengoku*, does not believe that Christianity was the main reason for the rapid spread of the Taiping movement at its outset; neither does he believe that the class relations and the character of peasants were sufficient to explain it. The Taiping ethnic idea was not merely directed toward the Manchus with a view to re-establishing Chinese rule but was also directed toward the foreigners. At the beginning small farmers felt they were mistreated by the landlords and bureaucrats, who formed the nucleus of the Manchu regime. This Manchu regime was under the pressure of the European powers, unable to raise its head. Thus a revolt which was at first directed against the landlords and bureaucrats became a movement against the Manchu court; because of the desire for independence, the revolt was in turn directed against the foreign capitalist countries. Throughout its history, the Taiping leaders never wavered in their policy regarding international relations.[102]

Masui also compared the *T'ai-p'ing t'ien-kuo* to *Ōshio no ran* and *Ikida no ran* during the Tokugawa period.[103] He says that although the Taiping movement was much greater, the motives were more or less the same, aimed at promoting the interests of the peasants and opposing the land-

[100] Toyama Gunji, *Taihei tengoku to Shanghai*, pp. 1–5, 167, 169.

[101] Fairbank and Banno, *Japanese Studies of Modern China*, p. 48. See Kawabata Genji, "Tenchō dempo seido no seiritsu," *Shigaku zasshi*, Vol. LIX, No. 5 (May, 1950).

[102] *Taihei tengoku*, pp. 67–69.

[103] Ōshio was a police officer and a Confucian scholar who appealed to the magistrate during a great famine for grain to be distributed to the people. When the magistrate refused, Ōshio led peasants and broke into government granaries. His riot, which took place in the sixth month of Tao-kuang 17 (1837), was soon put down and Ōshio committed suicide. Four months later his disciple Ikida led another riot, known as *Ikida no ran*.

lords and bureaucrats. The chief factors that distinguish the Taiping movement from the Japanese riots are the ethnic issue and the fight against the invasion of foreign capital into China. Thus the Taipings were centered around the peasantry, and their policy did not contain any deliberation about modern industrialization. It was a peasant movement lacking both modern industry and the intellectual awakening of the Renaissance.[104]

Hatano Yoshihiro maintains that the Taipings were neither bandits nor merely politically discontented people aiming at establishing a new dynasty. According to him, their aim was purely revolutionary. The Taiping movement gives us the first instance of a real revolution in China because it aims at reforming religion and social and economic relations. In nature it differs from all political movements of the past; and it is vitally significant in connection with the later Chinese people's revolution and even with the new democratic revolution. This is in fact the natural result of the Opium War.[105] Foreign cotton, which flooded the Chinese market after the war, brought about the impoverishment of the villages; this process was accelerated by the opening of Shanghai. Hatano also recognizes the conflict between the Puntis and the Hakkas as one of the causes of the movement, furnishing the motive for social readjustment. The net result of this movement is that China was pushed by foreign powers, who utilized the internal trouble of China to further their interests, into a position which is described as semicolonial.[106]

Ichiko Chūzō has written a number of short articles on the Taipings. In his "Chūgoku ni okeru Taihei tengokushi no kenkyū" (On the Studies of the Taiping Rebellion in China), he quotes the substance of the editorial of the Peking *Jen-min jih-pao*.[107]

Where his line of reasoning lies is clear. And in his "Haijō kō, Taihei tengoku seido kanken" (The God-Worshipers, A Study of the Taiping System), he discloses, according to his understanding, the "true state of the society under the rule of the Taiping government in the light of contemporary Chinese documents," and "sets forth the Taiping system as a crude form of Christian socialism, in other words, a mixed form of

---

[104] Masui, *Taihei tengoku*, pp. 72–103, 138.

[105] Hatano Yoshihiro, "Taihei tengoku ni kansuru nisan no mondai ni tsuite," *Rekishigaku kenkyū*, No. 150 (March, 1951), p. 32.

[106] *Ibid.*, p. 42.

[107] "Chūgoku ni okeru Taihei tengokushi no kenkyū," *Shigaku zasshi*, Vol. LX, No. 10 (Oct., 1951), pp. 71–72.

Puritanism and communism.... Communism and asceticism were kept up only in the Taiping army."[108]

In 1950 Ichiko attempted a study of the reasons for the revision of Taiping documents, with a view to tracing the development of Taiping ideology.[109] It was a worthy attempt, particularly as he rectified the mistake which Hsiao I-shan and Miyagawa made, by establishing the dates of the original and revised editions of the "Proclamations by Imperial Sanction." Of the results he drew from his study two agree with our conclusions; the Taipings tried to wipe out all evidence of their relation to the Triad Society and to eliminate all traces of traditionalism and intensify the influence of the Bible.[110]

Ōtani Kōtarō in his "Taihei tengoku no idhizuke" makes an ambitious attempt to place the *T'ai-p'ing t'ien-kuo* in the history of China. But he merely discusses the generalizations of other writers, without himself giving a positive opinion on the matter. He is mentioned here simply because his effort to determine the place of the Taiping movement in the general historical development is a sound one.[111]

Yamamoto Hideo tries to show that the Taiping movement cannot be understood as a product of either the traditional pattern of thought or the Western Christian influence; one should view it as an attempt to merge together these and also Taoism and Buddhism. The Taiping movement was a conglomeration of four in one.[112]

Amano Motonosuke considers the chief cause of the Taiping uprising the conflict between the Hakkas and the Puntis, together with the corrupt practices of government officials in milking both parties while trying to settle their disputes.[113] The aim of the movement is a composite one, consisting of religious, ethnic, and political ideals rolled into one. The revolutionary ideas are found in the three essays Hung wrote in 1845. Economically, the Taipings attempted to organize a communist

[108] "Haijō kō, Taihei tengoku seido kanken," *Ochanomizu joshi daigaku jimbunkagaku kiyō*, Vol. I (March, 1952), pp. 35–36.

[109] "Taihei tengoku shōsho no kaisei," *Tōyō gakuhō*, Vol. XXXIII, No. 2 (Oct., 1950), pp. 183–99.

[110] *Ibid.*, pp. 186–87. For other works by the same author see Fairbank and Banno, *Japanese Studies of Modern China*, pp. 46–47.

[111] "Taihei tengoku no idhizuke," *Hikone ronsō*, No. 8 (March, 1952), pp. 33–50 and No. 10 (July, 1952), pp. 26–45.

[112] Yamamoto, "Chūgoku ni okeru itan shisō no tenkai," *Tōyō gakkai*, No. 9 (June, 1952).

[113] Amano Motonosuke, "Taihei tengoku," *Tōyōshi kenkyū*, Vol. XIII, No. 1–2 (1954), pp. 2–3.

type of village based on peasantry. But the Taiping movement was not without some reactionary elements. The land distribution system, which appealed to the poor peasants and tenants, was not put into effect because of the confusion due to the constant fighting; further, the conditions for such distribution were not yet ripe. However, because many landlords fled their native land, the tenants were exempted in fact from rent; thus landlordism was in part abolished. Socially, the movement was significant in that it destroyed the old feudal system. Amano approves of Masui Tsuneo's idea that the Taiping movement was merely a peasant movement because it did not have the two wings of modern industry and Renaissance thinking.[114]

CONCLUSION

During the survey in Chapters XII and XIII, I have attempted to present the interpretations of many writers on the Taiping movement without evaluating them. When I give my own opinion, I shall frequently refer to these opinions for comparison and shall then state my reasons for agreeing with or differing from them.

With rare exceptions, the nineteenth-century writers' opinions were based mainly on either the Taiping writings or on their own direct observations. In some cases they were based on reports of eyewitnesses. Nearly all of them pointed out the obvious: political corruption, the economic plight of the people, geographical and racial relations. But few of them inquired into the social, economic, political, and cultural background of the Taiping movement. For this reason, their writings convey a sense of intimacy; but for the same reason they lack a sense of balance and objectivity.

Modern writers are, on the other hand, free from this emotional obfuscation; but they are plagued by another sort of disease. The distance in time, while offering them perspective, has denied them the warmth and intimacy of the life movement of the Taipings. Furthermore, many of them, following certain ideological lines often without scruple, have stretched facts to fit their Procrustean beds.

[114] *Ibid.*, p. 27.

Chapter XIV

A Transcendent Interpretation

An "ideology" is a system of ideas related to the concrete social, political, and economic conditions. This system of ideas also becomes a force which controls the mental attitudes of its followers. Our first task, therefore, will be to describe the concrete conditions at the time of the Taiping movement and to link the ideological elements to these conditions. Rather than postulating any causal relationship or even exact correspondence, we shall try simply to show that a correlation does seem to exist between conditions and ideas.[1]

Our second task is to investigate to what degree the Taipings carried out their program and to what degree they failed, together with the reasons for success or failure. A related problem is the degree of effectiveness of the ideology in forming and channeling the mental attitude of the Taiping followers.

---

[1] This is hardly the place to develop the concept of causality. But to avoid certain misunderstanding, I shall define briefly the sense in which the term "cause" is used in this book.

Two terms, A and B, are said to be in a causal relationship when the following statements are true. (1) A precedes B in a logical as well as a temporal order. (2) A not only leads to B but also determines the specific nature of B. (3) The relation between A and B is not only observable in particular cases but is also determinable in a hypothetical, and therefore necessary and universal, manner. (4) This universal causal relation is obtainable only by means of a laboratory method, in which the environment is arbitrarily controlled and in which the experimenter has the freedom to add or to remove certain factors in an effort to determine their role in the relationship. (5) A and B should be class concepts, inasmuch as they refer to all hypothetical cases and not merely to particular cases under investigation; this means that the experience obtained by the experimenter can be repeated by anybody who wishes to repeat it. It is this causality which I declare inapplicable in a study which concerns itself with historical and social phenomena.

Finally, we shall try to determine the role the Taiping ideology played in subsequent revolutionary movements, including the Chinese Communist revolution. When we have done all this, we shall feel some-what justified in speculating on the nature of the Taiping movement. We shall find for the Taiping movement a place in the long history of China, particularly a place in the long series of Chinese rebellions and revolts.

SOCIAL CONDITIONS AND THEIR IDEOLOGICAL COUNTERPARTS

One of the first formative influences on the Taiping ideology is the structure of Chinese society. This society was dominated in the imperial times by an elite which the West termed "literati" (Max Weber) or "gentry" (Eberhard, Chung-li Chang, and others). Since the time of the Ming dynasty, the elite had become more and more integrated through government policy and other factors. During the whole of the Ch'ing time, including nineteenth-century China, the Chinese gentry formed the fount and reservoir from which the government drew its officials; thus gentry members had potential power to rule, and hence to acquire wealth. Entry into the gentry was theoretically open to all people except those classified as "mean"; but because a strictly state-controlled examination system was the only gateway into the gentry and because there were high literary requirements involved in the examinations, it was well-nigh impossible for any commoner without sufficient means or political influence to pass the examinations success-fully.[2] Literary requirements included primarily a thorough knowledge of Confucian classics and their commentaries by the Ch'eng-Chu school of the Sung Neo-Confucianism.

This social setup was complicated by the fact that China had been ruled by a non-Chinese ethnic group since the middle of the seventeenth century. Accounts written by eyewitnesses had kept the great atrocities committed by the Manchus during the conquest of China vivid and fresh in the minds of the people. Even the Chinese gentry were subjected to strict imperial control, and certain key government positions were reserved for the Manchus. These and other inequalities legally defined by the Ch'ing code had always been justified by means of rationalization on the basis of orthodox Confucian ideology.[3] The principle of *li*, which

---

[2] For a better understanding of the gentry dominance in Chinese society, see Chung-li Chang, *The Chinese Gentry: Studies on Their Role in Nineteenth-Century Chinese Society*.

[3] For these legal inequalities, see Ch'ü T'ung-tsu, *Chung-kuo fa-lü yü Chung-kuo she-hui*, chap. 4, section 4, particularly p. 195.

was so much emphasized by the Confucians and which regulated social conduct, was particularly effective in reconciling the people to their status and prescribing for them their appropriate field of activities, hopes, and aspirations. Literary requirements for the state examinations served to channel people's minds to a pattern which the government wished to perpetuate. Under normal orderly conditions, the people's acceptance of their status was the greatest asset a ruler could have in ensuring peace and order and control over the empire.[4] But when society was disordered by either natural calamity or a corrupt government, the undercurrent of discontent often found an outlet in open rebellions.

Another social factor which determined to some extent the form of Taiping ideology is the position of the Hakkas in the community where they settled. The feuds between the Hakkas and the Puntis, which were mostly over the land, are a concrete condition responsible for a certain part of the Taiping ideology.

The first element of the Taiping ideology which is related to concrete social conditions is the ethnic issue. The Manchu rule, with its initial atrocities and the corruption and inefficiency at the end of the eighteenth and during the nineteenth century, plus the political and social injustices in its discrimination against the Chinese, can safely be assumed as the reason for the Taiping ethnic issue. What an emotional exhilaration the Taipings must have experienced when they threw off all the restraints imposed upon them for centuries by the practice of name and word taboos and were able to call the emperor by his personal name.

Taiping resentment, however, was not directed against the Manchus alone. The people were also at the mercy of the gentry, especially those who were also landlords. Because these gentry landlords were granted special privileges in matters of taxation and labor service, the major portion of the tax burden was necessarily shifted onto the common people. Resentment against those who exploited them seems to have been the reason for the Taipings' initial condemnation of the gentry. The Taipings destroyed Sung edition books, works of art and beautiful furniture, and even the Pao-en t'a (pagoda), which was known as one of the most beautiful structures built during the Ming period. In short, they destroyed everything which to them was symbolic of the life of the gentry, who represented a tradition ruthless to the people.

[4] For government indoctrination, see Kung-chuan Hsiao, *Rural China: Imperial Control in the Nineteenth Century.*

The Taiping hatred of the classics can also be explained by reference to the relationship between classics and the gentry. However, this connection alone probably would not have embittered the Taipings against the classics. The subjective element of frustration is probably a more important factor in this hatred. Many of the Taiping leaders failed at the literary examinations, which were based on the classics. The frustration of their desire to enter the ruling class aroused in them resentment against that class and quite naturally a hatred of all Confucian classics. That this resentment distorted their sense of values and faculty of judgment is evident from the fact that although their ideology embodied so many Confucian teachings, they attacked Confucius and his ideas with a great fury. Their fury is difficult to understand except on the theory that they blamed these Confucian classics for barring them from a life to which they aspired.

Having alienated themselves from the official ideology, the Taipings, consciously or unconsciously, must have sought some new form of thought to replace the traditional one. They must also have realized the difficulty in breaking the traditional pattern of mind, which included an attitude of fatalism. In order to succeed in breaking this fatalistic mental attitude, they needed a positive attitude or outlook to fill the vacuum which would be created when the traditional scale of values was destroyed. Just at the correct moment, Hung came into contact with Christianity, with its God as a Heavenly Father, Jesus the Son of God as the savior, and the idea of the brotherhood of man. To Hung and his friends, these ideas became an instrument with which they attempted to break and eventually replace the traditional outlook. The people had been indoctrinated to such a degree that they had accepted fatalistically and without complaint whatever lot was theirs. The new Christian ideas would teach them social justice based on the equality of all men before God as his children. The impact of the new ideas upon the minds of Hung's followers must have been terrific, judging from their initial enthusiasm for the new faith.

Hung must have been tremendously impressed by the role and mission of Jesus as a savior of men. His deranged brain must have worked upon this conception until he pictured himself as a savior of the people from the imps and Yang as a savior of the people from sickness. From this point of view, Christianity must have appeared to Hung just the right type of thought pattern to be established in the place of the unseated traditionalism. May we not also consider this contact with

Christianity the reason why the Taiping movement took place at that particular moment and not earlier?

The Taiping leaders, however, must have spent a large portion of their lives in absorbing the principles embodied in the Confucian classics when they prepared themselves for government examinations. This fact explains why at the rock bottom of the Taiping mental structure we find the traditional Confucianism. The Taiping adoption of Christianity, whether sincere or not, could not be entirely effective in eliminating the traditional influences. The ineradicable effects of Confucianism, plus the Buddhism and Taoism which permeated the Chinese society in which they had always lived, made it impossible for the Taipings to understand the true significance and meaning of Christianity. Thus we find their ideology a conglomeration of many heterogeneous patterns of ideas, accepted not because of their logical coherence but because of their persuasiveness and expediency. As a result the Taiping ideology is a nondescript body of ideas for which there is no adequate term. Any unity it has is practical and comes from the movement itself; once accepted, the ideology intensifies the unity of the movement.

The Taipings would have had no difficulty in combining the new faith with the old scale of values. Most moral virtues are politically neutral and may serve the purpose of any party which has a legitimate claim. The Taipings could easily show that they had the legitimate mandate of Heaven, which is indeed a very important part of their political ideology; that the Manchus had lost their mandate was evidenced by the general discontent and chaos, political corruption, and economic confusion. The Taipings could simply change the object of these old moral precepts and retain their forms. Loyalty, for example, was certainly very strongly stressed by the Taipings, but the object of their loyalty was no longer the ruler of the Manchu regime; the Manchu emperor and all previous rulers were relegated to the rank of *hou*. The object of loyalty now was the T'ien Wang, not as a person but as the representative of God the Father. A number of characters were reserved for the T'ien Wang alone and consequently tabooed for ordinary usage. This new system of taboos clearly shows the Taiping attempt to change the object of the moral quality of loyalty while trying to preserve its form. It is natural that we should find in the Taiping ideology a large measure of the traditional scale of values.

The Taiping ideal of the *ta-t'ung shih-chieh* or the world of Great Harmony and the idea of the brotherhood of man, both fusions of old

Confucian ideas with the new faith, can be explained only by reference to the existing social conditions. The people, who suffered social injustices and were discriminated against by officials and gentry, would readily accept an ideology which promised them a happier existence. It is no wonder that the Taiping followers became attracted to the Confucian ideal of a harmonious world where peace prevailed and to the Christian ideals of the brotherhood of man and the heavenly kingdom of God.

The social structure at the time of the Taiping movement may also explain some of the economic features of the Taiping ideology. The aspirations of the unjustly treated people for better times may have given birth to the idea of equal distribution of land and equal sharing of all products and other forms of wealth.

The Taiping measures on social welfare and reforms reflect the evils of the existing society. The import of opium, for example, had increased from 5,959 cases in 1821-22 to 40,200 cases in 1838-39, and the value of opium consumed in China had increased from $8,822,000 in 1821-22 to over $20,000,000 in 1838-39.[5] In addition to creating a scarcity of silver, opium presented a greater menace to China by steadily sapping the vitality and morale of the Chinese people. When they formulated their regulations concerning opium-smoking, the Taiping leaders must have seen the damaging effect of opium-smoking which Huang Chüeh-tzu and Lin Tse-hsü had recognized.[6]

POLITICAL AND MILITARY FACTORS AND
THEIR IDEOLOGICAL COUNTERPARTS

Politically, China was in continual unrest and tumult during the nineteenth century. First of all, there had been minority uprisings since

[5] Hosea B. Morse, *The International Relations of the Chinese Empire*, I, 210.

[6] In *Lin Wen-chung kung cheng-shu*, 4:1a–b, Lin Tse-hsü quotes Huang Chüeh-tzu: "The price of silver has been steadily increasing recently, and now a tael of silver is equivalent to over one thousand six hundred coins. The reason for this does not lie in the consumption of silver within the country; the reason lies in its outflow to foreign countries. When opium was first imported into China, only members of the wealthy families took up the extravagant habit [of opium-smoking]. But gradually all classes of people [followed suit], from the officials and gentry members down to workers, merchants, actors, and servants, and even women, monks, nuns, and Taoists—these people all smoke opium everywhere. In Kwangtung alone a sum of over thirty million taels of silver is spent in importing that stuff." In another memorial in the same work, 5:14b, Lin remarks: "If we paid no attention [to the opium-smoking], in several decades there would be no soldiers in the central plain who could fight to defend the country; and more than that, there would also be no silver to maintain the army."

the beginning of the Ch'ing dynasty. In the northwest the government had difficulty with the Islamic group, first in 1648-49 and then in 1781. In 1795 there were rebellions of the Miao people in the southwest, affecting Yunnan, Hunan, Kweichow, and Szechwan. These rebellions were not entirely pacified until 1807. During the reign of Tao-kuang (1821-32) there were Yao troubles in Kwangtung, Kwangsi, and Hunan.[7]

Secondly, the government had trouble with secret societies. In the north the uprisings of the White Lotus Society took the Ch'ing government almost ten years (1793-1802) to quell; these uprisings affected the five provinces of Szechwan, Hupeh, Shensi, Honan, and Kansu. There were also uprisings of *T'ien-li chiao*, a branch of the White Lotus Society. In the south, most uprisings were under the leadership of the *T'ien-ti hui*, also known as *San-ho hui, San-tien hui*, and the Hung Society. Lin Wen-shuang in Formosa led one of the best known *T'ien-ti hui* uprisings in 1786.[8] The government's difficulties with the minority groups were often due to the activities of the members of the secret societies. The uprising of the Yao during the reign of Tao-kuang was caused by the oppression of the Yao by *T'ien-ti hui* members: the local officials apparently sided with the *T'ien-ti hui* members, who robbed the Yao of their cattle and grain.[9]

Dr. Kung-chuan Hsiao, in his book on imperial control in the countryside, discusses four kinds of disorders during the nineteenth century: feuds, riots, banditry, and rebellions.[10] Hsiao says that riots appeared oftener "after the Opium War when the prestige of the imperial government received its first severe blow and when the rise of local corps in many localities emboldened the hitherto unarmed peasants to challenge the authorities."[11] Fu I-ling has given an account of the confusion produced by attempts on the part of the peasants to evade land tax.[12] Toward the end of the nineteenth century, a governor of Kwangtung reportedly said:

Hui-fei [secret society bandits] have been most rampant in Szechwan,

[7] For these rebellions, see Wei Yüan, *Sheng-wu chi*, 7:35a–39a, 41a–46b, 47a–52a.
[8] Wei, *Sheng-wu chi*; Hsü K'o (ed.), *Ch'ing-pai lei-ch'ao*, "Hui-tang lei," *ts'e* 27.
[9] Wei Yüan, *op. cit.*, 7:47a.
[10] Hsiao, *Rural China*, chap. 10, pp. 418–86.
[11] *Ibid.*, p. 441.
[12] Fu, "T'ai-p'ing t'ien-kuo shih-tai ti ch'üan-kuo k'ang-liang ch'ao," *Ts'ai-cheng chih-shih*, Vol. III, No. 3 (Sept., 1943), pp. 31–39.

Hunan, Kweichow, Kwangsi, and Kwangtung. At first they were lawless, wandering people who burned incense and organized societies. When their organizations have waxed strong and their members become numerous, they rely on their strength to tyrannize their neighborhoods and victimize the good people. The humble people, being helpless, may join their societies for self-protection.[13]

Although this quotation relates conditions during the end of the century, the manner in which people were forced to join secret societies had always been the same.

Two conditions have generally been given as both causes and results of the general confusion: government corruption and inefficiency and military weakness. Inaba Iwakichi, in his *Ch'ing-ch'ao ch'üan-shih* [*Shinchō zenshi*], says: "The rebellions during the reign of Chia-ch'ing were all due to corrupt misgovernment in both high places and low. Emperor Tao-kuang, on his ascent to the throne, did his best to remove political mistakes; but the root of evil had struck deep and was not to be remedied by temporary measures."[14] Some of the misgovernment appears inherent in the imperial system of control of the time. The *Hsün-chou fu-chih* says:

If the local authorities intervened in the local feuds, they would have to send troops and would therefore need funds not provided for in the regular budget of the local government. This extra money would have to be obtained from the superior officials or indirectly from the imperial treasury. But none of the local officials wanted to be exposed to the charge of maladministration by memorializing the emperor that the region under their jurisdiction was infested with bandits or disturbers of the peace. Naturally the best thing for them to do was to pretend to be ignorant of the feuds; they hoped, by so doing, that they could escape the punishment for maladministration by transferring to another post in some other district or even province after the end of their term of office.[15]

This attitude was general among the upper echelon of local officialdom, who did not hesitate to keep the ruler in the dark by tolerating and falsely reporting the troubles.[16]

[13] *Chih-hsin pao*, LXXXII, 1a, quoted and translated in Hsiao, *op. cit.*, p. 460.

[14] *Ch'ing-ch'ao ch'üan-shih, hsia*, p. 71.

[15] Quoted in Yi-faa Laai's manuscript "The Pirates and the Taiping t'ien-kuo," p. 98. See also *Hsün-chou fu-chih*, 56:11a–18b; and Lung Ch'i-jui, *Ching-te t'ang ch'üan-chi*, 4:12b.

[16] Lung Ch'i-jui, *op. cit.*, 4:12b.

In the *Kuang-chou fu-chih* we find this statement:

Where does the source of the present-day turbulence lie? It lies in those magistrates who are greedy and cruel. . . . Lower officials depend upon higher ones for protection, while higher officials rely on lower to serve as their outside agents [in their common malpractices]. The people have hated them all in the depth of their hearts for a long time. As soon as the crisis comes and the alarm is sounded, wicked elements take advantage of the situation [and start a revolt].[17]

In the light of such political confusion and military weakness, it is natural that the Taipings should have chosen peace as the main theme of their propaganda, as the title of their movement and the ultimate object of their military campaign. The strict military discipline during the initial campaign speaks for the earnestness with which they tried to eliminate the corruption and inefficiency which they found had diseased the Ch'ing regime.

The Taiping system of recommendation, which made the recommender responsible for the success or failure of the recommended, and the judiciary process are both described in "The Land System of the Heavenly Dynasty" (T'ien-ch'ao t'ien-mou chih-tu). They were undoubtedly expressions of determination that the Taiping government would be free from corruption and misgovernment. These, like the idea of peace, reflect faithfully the kind of government the Taipings had to endure at the time of their uprising.

ECONOMIC FACTORS AND THEIR IDEOLOGICAL COUNTERPARTS

To understand the real impulse behind the Taiping economic system embodied in "The Land System of the Heavenly Dynasty," a knowledge of the economic conditions immediately before the Taipings is imperative.

As 75 per cent or more of the Chinese people are peasants, the earning of an average peasant family is a most revealing index of the economic conditions of nineteenth-century China. A family of five—three adults and two children—tilling fifteen mou of land, produced in 1887 $160.00 worth of rice, according to George Phillips, British Consul in Foochow, Fukien. Deducting expenses, which included $80.00 for rent of the farm, and $18.00 for rent of a bullock for plowing, labor, and seed rice,

[17] *Kuang-chou fu-chih*, 127:24b,

a net balance to the farm family was $62.00.[18] Average earnings were probably similar in other provinces and prior to the Taiping movement.[19] This report concerns a tenant family; it is doubtful that things were much better for a small landowner. Most small farmers who tilled their own land had to borrow money from usurers at a very high rate to get started each spring. They were in debt most of the time; before they could gather their crops, half the harvests were gone to pay their debts. They also had to pay taxes and deal with tax collectors. All available sources agree that most of the Chinese people, whether tenants or small landowning farmers, were eking out a mere existence.

One of the causes of poverty was that there was not sufficient arable land to support the population of China. The following tables indicate clearly that there was not enough land at any one time and that the population increased far faster than the amount of land under cultivation.

Table I	Table II
Population figures, 1741–1851	Arable land figures, 1661–1823
	(in *ch'ing*, equivalent to 100 mou)

1741....143,411,559	
1751....181,811,359	1661....5,493,576
1761....198,214,555	1685....6,078,430
1771....214,600,356	1724....6,837,914
1781....279,816,070	1766....7,414,495
1791....304,354,110	1812....7,915,251
1801....297,501,548	1823....7,375,129[21]
1811....358,610,039	
1821....355,540,258	
1830....394,784,681*	
1841....413,457,311	
1851....432,164,047[20]	

* No figure is listed for 1831 in *Tung-hua lu* during the reign of Tao-kuang.

[18] George Jamieson (ed.), "Tenure of Land in China and the Condition of the Rural Population," *Journal of the Royal Asiatic Society, North China Branch*, New Series XXIII (1888), 109.

[19] According to Wang Ying's calculation, a family of seven to ten members tilling 100 mou of land would have a net balance of less than fifty piculs of rice a year. See his "T'ai-p'ing t'ien-kuo ko-ming ch'ien-hsi ti t'u-ti wen-t'i," *Chung-shan wen-hua chiao-yü-kuan chi-k'an*, Vol. III, No. 1 (1936), pp. 183–84.

[20] Figures are taken from *Tung-hua lu* and, for 1851, from *Shih-i ch'ao tung-hua lu*. Both books are compiled by Wang Hsien-ch'ien.

[21] Figures for 1661 through 1766 are taken from *Ch'ing-ch'ao wen-hsien t'ung-k'ao*, ed. Chi Huang *et al.*, 1:4860, 2:4865, 3:4872, 4:4890–91. Figures for 1812 and 1823 are quoted in Lo Erh-kang, *T'ai-p'ing t'ien-kuo shih-kang*, hereafter cited Lo, *Shih-kang*, p. 10.

If the land under cultivation in 1766 were distributed equally among the 1761 populace, there would be 3.7 mou per capita; and in the years 1821-23, there would be slightly over 2 mou per capita. Assuming the size of a family to be 5, the average holding of 1761-66 would be 19 mou per family, and in 1821-23, 11 mou. This Malthusian situation reached a crisis stage immediately before the Taiping Rebellion. The surplus populace had no means of making a living. China was not industrialized enough to absorb them into the cities. The Manchu government prohibited migration to Manchuria, and it was only with extreme difficulty that a handful of people succeeded in moving to Mongolia and Chinese Turkestan.

This situation was made worse by the concentration of land in the hands of a few wealthy families. Many landlords reportedly held more than three thousand mou; Ku Tsung sent a memorial to the emperor requesting that landholdings be limited to three thousand mou.[22] In Shansi, Kiangsu, and Hupeh some holdings were as large as ten thousand or one hundred thousand or even one million mou.[23] In his memorial explaining why rice became expensive, Yang Hsi-fu said that 50 or 60 per cent of the land had fallen into the hands of wealthy families.[24] A large number of tenants lost their land in the process of land concentration, and the holdings of those small landowners who kept their land were further reduced. In Fukien, Kwangtung, and Kwangsi, it was said that between 80 and 90 per cent of the peasants were tenants.[25]

Life was difficult for the tenant even in a normal year; but when there was famine, it was impossible for him to pay the rent and still have enough to carry his family over the year. It was the policy of the government to protect the interests of the landlords.[26] In view of "the dangers inherent in the existence of a large mass of dispossessed peasants," the government sometimes persuaded the landlords to share the profits they received through exemption from taxes during lean years. But as the landlords had no obligation to listen to the government plea, it was not uncommon to find landlords ruthlessly exacting the full payment of rent.[27]

[22] *Ch'ing-ch'ao wen-hsien t'ung-k'ao*, "T'ien-fu k'ao," 4:4887.
[23] Wang Ying, *op. cit.*, pp. 167-68.
[24] *Huang-ch'ao ching-shih wen-pien*, chüan 39.
[25] Wang Ying, *op. cit.*, p. 167.
[26] See *Ta-ch'ing lü-li hui-chi pien-lan*.
[27] Hsiao, *Rural China*, pp. 386, 392; Wang Ying, *op. cit.*, p. 182.

Hsia Nai described taxes which landowners in the provinces along the Yangtze River paid immediately before the Taiping Rebellion in his article, "T'ai-p'ing t'ien-kuo ch'ien-hou ch'ang-chiang ko-sheng chih t'ien-fu wen-t'i":

> The most important land taxes collected by the Ch'ing regime in the provinces along the Yangtze River were tribute rice and land-poll tax. Tribute rice was collected either in kind or in silver. Although tax quotas were given in the *Ch'ing-ting fu-i ch'uan-shu*, tax collectors still went on collecting illegally by charging extra sums. When paid in kind, they would charge a certain extra amount for each picul collected, or sometimes they just accepted the picul at a discount. When paid in silver, they would raise the price of rice above that of the market and demand a payment in silver several times higher than the quota. In some cases they even demanded payment in cash and at the same time raised the price of silver higher than that of the market. In paying land-poll tax, silver was collected; but collectors demanded payment in cash, playing the same trick as in the payment of tribute rice in silver. Therefore, the land tax burden the people shouldered was usually several times heavier than the quota.[28]

This situation did not exist in the provinces along the Yangtze River alone. In the *Ch'ing-shih kao*, "Shih-huo chih" says:

> At the beginning of the Ch'ien-lung period (1736–95), there was little illegal practice in the collection of land tax. But later all sorts of fraudulent practices were adopted. At first there was only the demand of a certain extra amount for each picul; but later there was also the method of discount. For each picul of rice, a few *sheng* (hundredths of a picul) were charged as wastage; but later the wastage charge went as high as 50 or 60 per cent. Sometimes a picul of rice after discount amounted to 25 per cent of a picul.[29]

According to George Jamieson, on the basis of the reports he gathered from different localities, "The land tax is in general moderately light, amounting on an average to $\frac{1}{20}$ or $\frac{1}{30}$ of the gross produce."[30] Why, then, was the impression prevalent that Chinese farmers were toiling under heavy tax burdens? Through their contact with the local

[28] Hsia, "T'ai-p'ing t'ien-kuo ch'ien-hou ch'ang-chiang ko-sheng chih t'ien-fu wen-t'i," *Ch'ing-hua hsüeh-pao*, Vol. X, No. 2 (April, 1935), p. 410.

[29] *Ch'ing-shih kao*, compiled by Chao Erh-sun, K'o Shao-min, *et al.*, *ts'e* 35, p. 8, section 2 in "Shih-huo chih." Quoted in Hsia, *op. cit.*, p. 410.

[30] Jamieson, "Tenure of Land in China," *Journal of the Royal Asiatic Society, North China Branch*, N. S. XXIII (1888), 62.

magistrates and their connection with central court officials, gentry landowners were able to evade a major part of their taxes. However, the local magistrates were responsible for the full payment of the quota. Hence the burden was shifted to the farmers, who had no way to convey their complaint to court. In addition to land tax, the small landowners also had to pay *corvée* tax, from which most large landowning gentry members were exempted. The farmers were also subjected to all sorts of surtaxes and overcharges, which varied with the locality. In Kiangsu, according to Feng Kuei-fen, for every picul required by the quota, the farmer had to pay 2.5 or 2.6 piculs; but according to Wu Yün, the price per picul was 2,000 cash when payment was made in silver and the farmer had to pay 8,000 or 10,000 or even more.[31] In Chekiang, payment was more than twice the quota;[32] in Anhwei, from several times to over ten times.[33] Furthermore, the gentry shared the tax collectors' spoils as hush money. Sometimes the gentry cheated the government by having the land of the commoners registered under their names; often the farmers were unable to reclaim this land from the gentry.[34] When occasions arose for raising funds to meet certain local needs, such as organizing a militia, the gentry often took the lead but the farmers bore the financial burden.[35]

Another factor causing poverty was the disintegration of the rural economy following China's contact with the Western world. Although the burden of the farmers was heavy, they could still eke out an existence in a good year, for their home industry and chicken- and hog-raising supplemented their meager income. With the flooding of China's market by foreign goods, which were both cheaper and of better quality, the village economy began to collapse. According to Lo Erh-kang's accounting, China suffered a loss of over $37,000,000 in its trade with England and the United States between 1827 and 1833.[36] And in 1838

[31] Feng Kuei-fen, *Hsien-chih-t'ang kao*, 5:36; Wu Yün, *Liang-lei hsüan-ch'ih-tu*, 3:13.

[32] Tso Tsung-t'ang, *Tso Wen-hsiang kung ch'üan-chi*, "Tsou-kao," 11:41. Hsia quotes the same passage from *Tso Wen-hsiang kung tsou-kao ch'u-pien* 12:4 in Hsia, *op. cit.*, p. 411.

[33] Miu Ch'üan-sun, *Hsü pei-chuan chi*, 27:6. These examples (footnote references 30 through 33) are all quoted in Hsia, *op. cit.* For these and many others, see his quotations on pages 410 to 411.

[34] See Chung-li Chang, *The Chinese Gentry*, especially the section on "The Gentry's Exploitation of Their Privileged Position," pp. 43–51. See also Chang's *The Income of the Chinese Gentry*.

[35] *Yü-lin chih li chou-chih*, 18:22–23, quoted in Laai, "The Pirates and the Taiping t'ien-kuo," p. 169.

[36] Lo, *Shih-kang*, p. 14. Lo based his figures on Morse, *The International Relations of the Chinese Empire*, I, 92.

alone, China lost to England in trade a sum of $8,223,700.[37] The presence of foreign goods drove out Chinese native products, cutting thus the subsidiary income of the farmers. At the same time, the outflow of silver spent to import such items as opium caused the value of silver to double; the farmers' tax, which had to be paid in silver, was thus doubled.[38] Kung-chuan Hsiao, in *Rural China: Imperial Control in the Nineteenth Century*, remarked: "By the middle of the nineteenth century such deterioration [of the rural environment] had reached a critical point; large numbers of rural inhabitants in various parts of the empire were driven by destitution and hardships to the point of despair."[39] Ch'ien Chia-chü said in his "Ya-p'ien chan-cheng hou ti kuo-min sheng-chi wen-t'i" that the self-sufficient Chinese economy, which had undergone only slight changes during the previous two or three thousand years, began to crack up with the coming of the capitalistic imperialism from Western Europe.[40]

Because the farmers were most of the time in debt, they were constantly at the mercy of moneylenders. The most common way these wealthy usurers increased the misery of the farmers was by charging high rates of interest for loans. They operated through pawnshops. Often local officials used ruthless means to assist the wealthy usurers to press for the payment of loans.[41] Another way was by buying at a low price in times of plenty and selling at a high price in times of scarcity.[42]

In spite of all these oppressive burdens, Chinese farmers still might have had the miraculous resiliency to bound back from their hardships. But once a famine struck, they were at the end of their rope. Lin-le quoted Sir John F. Davis' observations about Chinese famine from 1838 to 1841: "During the years 1838–1841, many parts of the empire became plunged in misery and want;—so severe was the famine, that many thousands perished, while multitudes were driven to insurrection."[43]

[37] Lo, *Shih-kang*, p. 15, based on figures given in *Chinese Repository*, XII (1843), 514.

[38] During the first years of the reign of Tao-kuang, which started in 1821, silver was 1,200 cash a tael; it was 1,600 cash in 1838 and 2,000, 2,200, or 2,300 cash in 1848. See Lo, *Shih-kang*, p. 16.

[39] Hsiao, *Rural China*, p. 411.

[40] *Chung-shan wen-hua chiao-yü-kuan*, Vol. III, No. 1 (1936), p. 187.

[41] See *Tung-hua lu, chüan* 103 for Pi Jung's memorial in which the activities of wealthy money lenders were mentioned. See Chao Lien, *Hsiao-t'ing tsa-lu* for the officials' part in the usurious activity. Both sources are quoted in Lo, *Shih-kang*, p. 4.

[42] Ch'ien Wei-ch'eng, "Yang-min," in *Huang-ch'ao ching-shih wen-pien, chüan* 11; also in Chao Lien, *op. cit.*, "Pen-ch'ao fu-min." See Lo, *Shih-kang*, p. 4.

[43] Lin-le [Augustus F. Lindley], *Ti-ping Tien-Kwoh: The History of the Ti-ping Revolution*, I, 101.

From 1846 to 1850 China fell again and again into the clutch of famine. The calamities included drought, flood, storm, sandstorm, hail, and failure of crops; and the territory affected included Chihli, Honan, Shantung, Shansi, Shensi, and Kansu in the Yellow River valley; and Hunan, Hupeh, Anhwei, Kiangsi, Kiangsu, and Chekiang in the Yangtze valley.[44] The people were forced to take to the road, forming a roaming mass of people, a sure source of hungry recruits for rebel ideologies.

All the elements discussed above combined as chains to imprison the majority of the Chinese in a state of poverty. Poverty breeds discontent, and discontent leads to revolts. It is significant that the Taiping Rebellion broke out in Kwangsi, "one of the poorest districts of the empire."[45]

Poverty may be a sufficient condition for a rebellion, but poverty alone does not breed rebellions with long-range purposes and systematic ideological schemes. Before a rebellion with such an elaborate ideology as that of the Taipings could happen, there must have been some concrete situation capable of effecting a psychological transformation in the minds of the people and also providing a stimulus to awaken the people to serious thought.

The Taiping contact with Christianity and the social injustices, which aroused in them first frustration and then resentment, may have been sufficient to account for the Taiping movement and its ideology. But to explain the economic aspect of the ideology, we must consider the economic factors.

The people could have accepted, and they did accept, their status in Chinese society with natural piety. They would suffer silently all miseries which came as a result of natural calamities, resigned to their lot as something inevitable. Furthermore, for thousands of years they had been taught that happiness could be obtained with greater certainty by mastery of themselves and control over their desires than by mastery of the external world for the satisfaction of their desires.[46] It is conceivable that in spite of miserable poverty, the Chinese people could still have accepted their destiny because of the attitudes which were inbred in them: fatalistic acceptance of their status and the belief that

[44] Lo, *Shih-kang*, pp. 17–18.

[45] J. M. Callery and M. Yvan, *History of the Insurrection in China*, p. 51.

[46] For a detailed discussion of this type of traditional Chinese philosophy, see my article, "The Mind and the Moral Order," in *Mélanges chinois et bouddhiques*, X (1955), 347–64.

happiness derives from decreasing desire until desire balances the possibilities for satisfaction. But when they were asked to drown out the elemental desire to live; when they saw that even as peasants they were deprived of their right to till and to enjoy the fruits of their toil; when they saw that they were discriminated against in *corvée*, in the financial burden of local enterprises, and in tax distribution, they must have wondered whether the existing situation could be an eternal unchanging order. Like Ch'en Sheng and Wu Kuang, they must have asked, "Are princes, lords, generals, and prime ministers a race of their own?"[47] When their questioning spirit was awakened, conditions which had seemed natural to them before were viewed in a different light. The contrast between their own life and the life of the wealthy must have struck them with new force.[48]

In a study of rebellions, the importance of leadership cannot be over-stressed. It is entirely possible that without Hung Hsiu-ch'üan, Feng Yün-shan, and a few others, the Taiping Rebellion would have been just another of the numerous revolts treated in Chapter XI. For it was these leaders who were awakened to serious thought and who, when challenged, had the ability to analyze the situation; they formulated their ideals and drew up a plan to realize them. Although the people who supported the Taiping movement did not possess qualities of leadership, they must have been ready to be led. They must have had similar experiences which awakened in them at least a vague idea that something was wrong and that something must be done about the intolerable situation.

When the Taiping movement broke out in 1850, there were leaders with a complete system of ideas as a basis for their actions; there were also large groups of people, baptized in the same fire of misery, who understood the hopes and inspirations of their leaders and were ready to follow them. The economic situation in which injustices prevailed must have shaken the people out of their stupor and set them thinking. As a result, we have the ideas of equal distribution of land and common sharing of all things under heaven which are contained in "The Land System of the Heavenly Dynasty."

[47] *Shih-chi*, by Ssu-ma Ch'ien, 48:3a–b.

[48] For a detailed description of the contrast between the rich and the poor, see Wang Ying, "T'ai-p'ing t'ien-kuo ko-ming ch'ien-hsi ti t'u-ti wen-t'i," *Chung-shan wen-hua chiao-yü-kuan chi-k'an*, Vol. III, No. 1 (1936), pp. 167–72. See also Lo, *Shih-kang*, pp. 3–6.

The common sharing of wealth was to be carried out through the institution of the sacred treasury. This was undoubtedly one way to eliminate the economic injustices resulting from accumulation of wealth. Having experienced throughout their life economic discrimination and privation, the Taipings must have looked to this utopian ideal with genuine longings and aspirations. Their shrewd leaders saw in this institution a greater appeal to the people than any system which might offer them a greater play for individual initiative. They rightly saw that all the people asked for at that time was some measure of economic security; and the sacred treasury was devised to give them that security.

We do not know whether the Taiping leaders meant to have their economic scheme appeal to the non-peasant factions of their followers, among whom were miners, port employees, and charcoal burners. However, the sacred treasury could not have failed to appeal to these workers as well. Most of these people became miners or charcoal burners because they were dispossessed. Given a chance, they would have been only too glad to return to tilling their land. Furthermore, their economic conditions were as bad as those of the farmers. The miners, for example, had always been looked upon with suspicion by the government, and their livelihood had always been endangered by the gentry resistance to the operation of the mines. Their unemployment had previously led to the growth of banditry in Kwangsi.[49] Naturally they were eager to embrace the Taiping economic system, which promised them an equal share of all things under heaven and gave them a sense of security which they had never known. Many of the Canton port employees must have joined the Taipings because they were dislocated after the Opium War when the opening of the port of Shanghai decreased the amount of foreign trade at Canton. These port employees must have desired the economic security the Taipings promised.

A government ideology preaches the maintenance of the *status quo;* a rebel ideology calls for the introduction of something new. The program under the Kan Wang brings out most clearly the Taipings' attempts to introduce systems which were absent from China before the Taipings but which were most desirable. The reason his program failed was not merely that it was brought out too late in the campaign to be of any use, although no program could have been put through in such a rush. Even given time, the Kan Wang's program probably would not have worked because it was not the expression of the total life of the

[49] See Laai, "The Pirates and the Taiping t'ien-kuo," pp. 103–7.

society. No change could be successfully introduced without considering all aspects involved. No reforms could be introduced by decrees. Socially and psychologically, the Chinese did not seem ready for such a change. The failures of all subsequent attempts at introducing changes into the life of China support such a view.

Why did the Kan Wang explicitly reintroduce Confucianism as part of the Taiping ideology toward the end of the regime? On the strength of the ethnic issue, the Taipings had expected all Chinese to unite behind them in their struggle to oust the Manchus. Instead, the Chinese, particularly the gentry, were fighting them with far greater fury and stronger military might than they had encountered when fighting the Manchus. But for this resistance of the Chinese, it seems that the Taipings would have had little difficulty in driving the Manchus out of China. Since the Chinese resistance was brought about by the Taipings' attitude toward Confucianism and their wanton destruction of the cultural aspect of Chinese life, as Tseng Kuo-fan's proclamation against them clearly indicated, they made a last effort to win the Chinese gentry over by reintroducing Confucianism into their ideology. They knew that Tseng and others did not cherish much love for the Manchu dynasty and that the gentry's action was prompted solely by their passionate desire to act as the protectors of Confucian faith. They hoped that after they reintroduced Confucianism the Chinese gentry would espouse their cause.

Would the Taipings have shifted back to Confucianism if they had not had as their leader a man with the Kan Wang's personality? If the Kan Wang had not succeeded in reaching Nanking or if he had not become the policy-maker of the heavenly kingdom, perhaps no second thought would have been given to Confucianism. We know that the T'ien Wang drifted farther away from traditionalism in the last years of the dynasty. However, it is futile to conjecture whether or not the Taipings would have realized the value of returning to Confucianism if the Kan Wang had been absent from their movement.

In addition to existing conditions which aroused the Taipings' resentment, there were also undesirable conditions which they themselves created or for which they were at least partially responsible. In order to master these circumstances, they formulated some of their religious and moral conceptions. As their army was not well integrated because the various factions owed their allegiance first to their own chieftains, the Taipings laid emphasis on loyalty to the T'ien Wang; this

emphasis seems to have been an urgent plea for unity within the army. The army units must have been discouraged under the assault of the imperial troops; the religious conception of the heavenly hall or paradise and the moral exhortation to courage and perseverance must time and again have breathed new enthusiasm into their hearts and aroused their fighting morale. To overcome difficulties like these, the Taipings preached moral determinism and free choice; the heavenly kingdom was for those who died for the glory of their cause. The heavenly kingdom became, toward the end of the dynasty, the only reality for Hung, who changed the title of the reign from *T'ai-p'ing t'ien-kuo* (Heavenly Kingdom of Peace) to *Shang-ti t'ien-kuo* (Heavenly Kingdom of God). Hung must have realized the futility of struggling for peace, but he would not be denied the kingdom of God. From our point of view, he was just a deranged victim of his own hallucination. His refusal to leave Nanking and his finally taking his own life are the signs of a man who knew his defeat; he acted, however, with a feeling of glory like a willing martyr marching off to execution with a sense of relief that he was dying for a worthy cause.

Hung believed in fatalism; he advised people to resign themselves to their fate. The inconsistency of including both self-determination and fatalism in their ideology demands an explanation. The Taipings, it seems, desired to achieve stability once they were settled in Nanking. The apparent inequality inherent in their political hierarchy must have caused some of the followers to complain about their lot in contrast with that of followers in a higher echelon. The inclusion of fatalism as part of their official ideology was an attempt to bolster the *status quo* in the Taiping camp. In this respect, the *T'ai-p'ing t'ien-kuo* did not differ from any of the historical dynasties.

THE REALITY OF THE TAIPING IDEOLOGY

Our next problems are the effectiveness of the Taipings' ideology in channeling the mental attitudes of their followers and the people who had come under their government, and the degree to which the Taipings carried out their programs. All records, Chinese and foreign, agree that at the beginning of the campaign the Taiping ideology was very well received and strictly observed. The people's receptiveness must be assumed as an explanation of the rapid growth of the Taiping army: a mere three hundred men launched their campaign in Chin-t'ien ts'un in 1850; thirty-seven thousand took Yung-an in 1851; eighty thousand

attacked Kuei-lin in 1852; over one hundred thousand attacked Ch'ang-sha; and when the *Tse-ch'ing hui-tsuan* was compiled in 1855, the army included a formidable force of more than three million officers and men.[50]

Quality as well as quantity spoke for the effectiveness of the ideology. The Taipings fought with a courage understandable only on the assumption that they were driven by forces inherent in their ideology. Even their enemy had some good words for their fighting ability.[51] Coercion alone could not possibly account for the courage and discipline which enabled such a large group of new recruits to behave as they did under the ever decreasing number of the "old "and therefore dependable members of the original group.

Western sources give testimony to the spirit of discipline of the Taipings; the Westerners were also amazed by their religious zeal. Missionaries from the West had great hopes that the Taipings would win China to Christianity, and some missionaries persisted in this hope to the end. There must have been something genuinely religious at the beginning of the campaign that struck these missionaries, who were not at all blind to the distorted view the Taiping leaders entertained about Christianity. For a short time at least the spirit of Christian fellowship seems to have permeated the life of the Taipings in every respect, whatever motives Hung, Yang, and others may have had. In view of this crusaders' spirit, we must conclude that the religious aspect of the ideology was very effective at the beginning of the movement.

The Taipings' determined effort to punish those who violated any of the heavenly rules is evidence that some other aspects of the ideology were equally effective. The punishment was not ruthlessly applied to a helpless mass, but to members of the ruling clique of the Taipings, among whom were the parents of Hsiao Ch'ao-kuei and one of the two people commissioned to teach the members of the Triad who had joined the Taipings.

The followers gave up everything to go with the Taipings. To be willing to do this, they must have been completely persuaded of the truth of the Taiping ideas and completely willing to live the life prescribed for them. Another evidence of the ideology's effectiveness is the successful way the institution of the sacred treasury was put into

[50] Chang Te-chien (editor and compiler), *Tse-ch'ing hui-tsuan, chüan* 11, "Tse-shu."
[51] Chang Te-chien attributed the success of the Taipings to the fact that "even rebels have their principles." *Tse-ch'ing, chüan* 4, "Wei chün-chih."

practice. Medhurst's letter in the November 26 issue of the *North China Herald* gives a vivid picture of how the treasury worked in the Taiping army in 1853.[52] An editorial in the same number discusses the common sharing of the Taipings. When R. M. McLane went to Nanking in 1854, both he and E. C. Bridgman, the interpreter, noted that the Taipings exhibited a sense of social solidarity as if a common bond were binding them together.

How far were the Taiping programs carried out? Lo Erh-kang and Jen (Chien) Yu-wen agree that the land system was not carried out, but they differ in their evaluation of it. Lo, though criticizing the system as utopian, thinks that if the *T'ai-p'ing t'ien-kuo* had lasted until the Taipings had had the opportunity, they would have put it into practice. Jen, on the other hand, believes that the system of state landownership had an inherent contradiction; after redistribution, the land would become privately owned again. If for any reason the system had been put into practice, Jen believes "he [the farmer] would be the horse and ox of the state throughout his whole life." Many writers concur in the conclusion that the Taipings did not carry out their land system. Jen cited the views of the following authors to support his contention: Hsiao I-shan, Hsieh Hsing-yao, P'eng Tse-i, Chiang T'ing-fu, Fan Wen-lan, and Hua Kang.[53]

The land system as an ideological element was directed mainly toward the peasant populace. As time went on, the Taiping followers became an elite, members of the Taiping military society. It is obvious that there was no chance for the system, which was designed to attract peasants, to work for the followers. Most of them developed a sense of contempt for the peasants, whose status officially became a fit punishment for those officers who violated the rules of heaven.

As the Taipings never found themselves free from the threat of war, they never had the opportunity to try their land system. Even the fact that the peasants had their land to till, as Lo Erh-kang contends, was a consequence of the war. The landowners and men of wealth, fearing the scourge of the Taiping army which was known to oppose the rich and mighty, fled their homesteads, leaving their land in the hands of the tenants. The uncertainty of the way in which the Taipings dealt with rent, in some cases siding with the tenants and in other cases with the

---

[52] *North China Herald*, No. 174, November 26, 1853.

[53] Jen [Chien] Yu-wen, "T'ai-p'ing t'ien-kuo t'ien-cheng k'ao," *Journal of Oriental Studies*, Vol. I, No. 1 (Jan., 1954), pp. 36–37.

landlords, indicates clearly that "the tillers have their land" was an accidental fact, and not the result of a considered Taiping policy.

Lo attributes the failure of the Taipings to carry out the land system to the fact that the Taipings needed the people's support; since the people did not relish the idea of state ownership of land, the Taipings did not press for its realization. Jen Yu-wen gives the following reasons: (1) The empire was still in a state of turmoil. (2) There was no accurate census. (3) There were not enough trained men to carry on the routine duties of the state. (4) Nationalization of private property might antagonize the people. (5) The new land system was not in the interest of the Taiping government. (6) There was difficulty inherent in the very nature of the system which hindered its realization.[54] It is doubtful whether the Taipings made any attempt to put their land system into practice. At the very start of the campaign they must have nourished the idea in a purely dreamy atmosphere. "The Land System of the Heavenly Dynasty" strikes one as being an extremely naive document, and the author or authors seem more concerned with its balanced verbal structure than with its practicality. If this is so, then the most important reasons for their failure to carry out their land system are their lack of vision when composing it and lack of desire to apply it later. I hold, contrary to Lo's belief, that the Taipings would never have succeeded in realizing their land system even if their dynasty had lasted long enough to try it. They used the system as a political weapon to win the support of the people. From this political point of view, they were very successful: the land system won them a mighty following. The peasants, however, eventually had land to till not because of the Taiping ideology but because of the rebellion itself.

The sacred treasury system and common sharing were practiced in Nanking and, during the first years of the campaign, in the army. But as time went on, the discipline began to slacken. As late as 1861 the people in Nanking still lived in a state of common sharing, but the leaders and army chiefs had begun to accumulate wealth.[55] Li Hsiu-ch'eng, the paragon of virtue, was able to scrape together a contribution of $10,000 for the state treasury before he was allowed to leave Nanking for the front in 1863. And the title *wang* was offered to those who could pay. Perhaps late in the campaign the army drew their provisions from

---

[54] *Ibid.*, pp. 38–39.

[55] See Garnet J. Wolseley, *Narrative of the War with China in 1860*, especially p. 336.

a common treasury, but there is nothing unique in this; all armies would operate in the same way if money were scarce.

It is doubtful that the sacred treasury system was ever put into practice among the people at large. Since the government continued to collect taxes, it is safe to assume that the people kept the remaining crops for their own use. With respect to other articles of wealth, it is not clear how they could have been gathered together in the sacred treasuries outside Nanking. The Taiping sources mention their effort to persuade people to offer contributions. There is no mention of confiscation of their property, real or movable. When the army first arrived at a place, the Taipings may have looted and plundered; but such activities could hardly be termed the execution of government policies. Apparently the sacred treasury institution, like the land system, was not meant to apply to the people at large. Practice of the system in the army gave the followers a sense of security and a form of discipline.

At the beginning the Taiping society was permeated by the religious atmosphere. The core of the group was thoroughly indoctrinated in the religious practices, though they may not have understood the living ideas behind those practices. We have to admit that the initial religious enthusiasm was genuine, for it was an emotional and passionate response to a voice which, under the cloak of religion, spoke a language comprehensible to the minds of all. The Taipings wanted simply economic security. But with religious coloring, that simple and plain goal assumed the importance of a crusader's mission. Not all the later military leaders, however, were genuinely enthusiastic about the Taiping religion. The tone and tenor of Li Hsiu-ch'eng's confession, for example, is utterly mundane.

Other government measures, such as prohibition of opium-smoking, drinking, and gambling, seem to have been strictly adhered to in Nanking throughout its occupation by the Taipings; but outside Nanking, the military chiefs did what they wanted to do.

All in all, the Taipings were not particularly successful in applying their theoretical schemes. And their failure to do so is due at least in part to a lack of determination to carry them out. One conclusion I drew from the study of rebel ideologies in Chapter XI is that the varying degrees of success achieved by rebel leaders seems due to the differences in their effort and sincerity in carrying out the ideas they proclaimed. If this is true, the Taiping lack of determination to execute their ideological

schemes can be construed as one of the important factors responsible for the final collapse of the movement.

ROLE OF THE TAIPING IDEOLOGY IN SUBSEQUENT MOVEMENTS

We must next determine the role the Taiping ideology played in subsequent revolutionary movements. The scope of its influence is thought not to be limited to China. Marx in 1853 remarked:

> Whether the "contact of extremes" be such a universal principle or not, a striking illustration of it may be seen in the effect the Chinese revolution seems likely to exercise upon the civilized world. It may seem a very strange, and a very paradoxical assertion that the next uprising of the people of Europe, and their next movement for republican freedom and economy of Government, may depend more probably on what is now passing in the Celestial Empire—the very opposite of Europe—than on any other political cause that now exists—more even than on the menaces of Russia and the consequent likelihood of a general European war. But yet it is no paradox, as all may understand by attentively considering the circumstances of the case.[56]

Dona Torr, editor of Marx's articles on China, writes in her introduction: "So, perhaps, dreamed Marx, when our European reactionaries have to take refuge in Asia and at last reach the Great Wall of China, guarding the very hearth of reactionary conservatism, they may find inscribed above its gates: —'Chinese Republic. Liberty, Equality, Fraternity.'"[57] Such expectation of the Taiping movement as a social revolution was doomed to disappointment; but the movement did furnish to many other attempts the needed inspiration to seek a better lot for the people.

Many uprisings after 1850 may have been influenced by the Taipings. In 1852, Triad members Hu Yu-lu and Chu Hung-ying rose in Nanning in Kwangsi; in 1854 they occupied Kuan-yang and proclaimed *Sheng-p'ing t'ien-kuo* (Heavenly Kingdom of Peace), a slight modification of the *T'ai-p'ing t'ien-kuo*, as their dynastic title.[58] The forces of the Miao uprisings between 1854 and 1871 in Kweichow, augmented by the secret society members from Kweichow and Kwangsi, grew to several hundreds of thousands of people in 1859 and gave Shih Ta-k'ai a great

[56] Karl Marx, *Marx on China 1853–1860: Articles from the New York Daily Tribune*, p. 1.

[57] *Ibid.*, p. xvii.

[58] Kuo T'ing-i, *T'ai-p'ing t'ien-kuo shih-shih jih-chi*, I, 344.

deal of reinforcement when he led his troops into Kweichow. The Islamic Rebellion under Tu Wen-hsiu in 1855 and the Nien Rebellion had obvious connections with the Taipings. As late as 1906 the Hung Chiang Rebellion still showed the influence of the Taipings in its ethnic issue; their purpose was to overthrow the Ch'ing and restore the Ming."[59]

The first to attribute great significance to the Taiping movement were the leaders in the nationalist camp. Sun Yat-sen, the founder of the Kuomintang, was greatly influenced as a boy by the stories of Hung and Yang and is reported to have considered himself a "second Hung Hsiu-ch'üan." Even in his mature thinking, he still considered the Taiping movement of the same nature as his own undertaking. He thought of Tseng, Hu, Tso, and Li as traitors and of Lo Tse-nan, Tseng, Liu Ming-ch'uan, and Kuo Sung-t'ao as ignorant of the great principle taught in the Ch'un-ch'iu; he compared them with Wu San-kuei and Hung Ch'eng-ch'ou who, at the end of the Ming dynasty, were responsible for the Manchus' entering China proper.[60] Consequently, the first objective listed in Sun's "Chung-kuo t'ung-meng hui hsüan-yen" (Manifesto of the T'ung-meng hui) is to drive out the "Tartars." This and many other proclamations put out by Sun and his group read remarkably like the Taiping document against the Manchus. The community of spirit is not limited to this ethnic issue; it is evident also in the other ideas Sun and his followers formulated. Sun identified Hung's economic thought with his own min-sheng chu-i (the principle of the people's livelihood):

> Ming-sheng chu-i is nothing other than the equalization of wealth [or equality of the rich and the poor—the language is ambiguous]; by this I mean the rich cannot oppress the poor. But several decades ago there was someone who had already put this min-sheng chu-i into practice; he was Hung Hsiu-ch'üan. The system initiated by him in his T'ai-p'ing t'ien-kuo, including regulations such as state control of workers and state ownership of all things, is a complete economic revolution and is just the equalization of wealth advocated by present-day Russia.[61]

And again:

> Do you still not understand what min-sheng chu-i is?... Several decades

[59] Chang Kuo-t'ao, Unpublished Memoirs, chap. 1.
[60] Sun Yat-sen, Tsung-li ch'üan-chi, Vol. I, shang-ts'e, pp. 312–13 and hsia-ts'e, pp. 1050, 1072.
[61] Ibid., II, 241–42.

ago Hung Hsiu-ch'üan, after more than ten years of fighting, evolved a system which is the same as the communism of Russia.... The Russians started out with knowledge, which was followed by action, while Hung acted out of necessity instead of knowledge. The circumstances were such that they had to depend on the government to regulate labor, whether farm labor or working labor, in order to give adequate supplies to the army. The surplus was later released for sale to the people, and the government of farmers and laborers thus became a government of merchants.[62]

Sun also said:

In foreign countries, communism is still in a state of discussion, it has not been put into practice yet. But in China during the time of Hung Hsiu-ch'üan it was already put into effect. The economic system put into effect by Hung Hsiu-ch'üan is communism in fact, and not merely communism in discussion.[63]

Sun identified his *min-sheng chu-i* with communism. In the above statements he considers the *min-sheng chu-i*, communism, and Hung's economic system to be all the same thing. P'eng Tse-i believes that Sun's equalization of land rights, which forms part of the *min-sheng chu-i*, is a direct offspring of Taiping land regulations.[64]

It seems plausible that it was also through the influence of the Taipings that Sun laid so much emphasis on the idea of the "world of Great Harmony." He quoted the passage on this ideal world from the "Li-yün" in the *Li-chi* in much the same way Hung quoted it. It is interesting to note that K'ang Yu-wei also made use of this passage. Could there also be some Taiping influence in K'ang's thought as expressed in the *Ta-t'ung shu?*

Following his characteristic way of thinking, however, Sun condemned the Taipings for knowing nothing of the rights of the people. According to Sun the chief cause of the Taiping failure was that "Hung knew only of the ethnic issue and nothing of the rights of the people; he knew only of monarchy and nothing of democracy."[65]

It is the ethnic issue which attracted Chiang Kai-shek's attention. In his preface to the *Tseng-pu tseng-hu chih-ping yü-lu* he speaks of the

[62] *Ibid.*, II, 352–53.
[63] *Ibid.*, I, 55.
[64] P'eng, *T'ai-p'ing t'ien-kuo ko-ming ssu-ch'ao*, p. 129.
[65] Sun Yat-sen, *Tsung-li ch'üan-chi*, Vol. V, "T'ai-p'ing t'ien-kuo chan-shih hsü," pp. 145–47.

Taiping army as "restoration troops" and a "revolutionary army."[66] In another place he says, "In the past our forefathers Hung and Yang rose in the southeast to overthrow the Ch'ing dynasty; though they failed and were defeated, their ethnic consciousness has flourished and become a great monument in our history."[67] In view of Chiang's preoccupation with the philosophy and tactics of Tseng and Hu and his respect for their character and personality, he is bound to make occasional derogatory remarks about the Taipings.[68] Both Sun and Chiang are men of action, men who are not concerned with academic integrity; one will note the Taiping influence in their thought although one may also find inconsistencies in their minds.[69]

There are still a large number of the Kuomintang leaders who hold the name of the Taipings sacred. Witness the poems collected to adorn the tomes of Lo Yung's *Shih-wen-ch'ao* :

> The twinkling of a star
> And the flash of lightning
> Will never perish.
> The vital spirit, radiant and bright,
> Will survive one hundred, one thousand *kalpa*.
> These poems and these essays
>   are the soul of the revolution and
>   the blood of the people.
> They move the reader and warm his heart.
> Truth, falsehood, success, and failure,
> All historians agree in their judgment.
> Many writings have been destroyed,
> And those existing, a meagre one-tenth, will proclaim the history-
>   making merits of these, our forefathers.

[66] Chiang Chung-cheng [Kai-shek], "Preface" to *Tseng-pu tseng-hu chih-ping yü-lu,* ed. Ts'ai O.

[67] Chiang Chung-cheng, "Preface" to Lo Yung and Shen Tsu-chi (compilers), *T'ai-p'ing t'ien-kuo shih-wen ch'ao.*

[68] See Mary C. Wright, "From Revolution to Restoration: The Transformation of Kuomintang Ideology," *Far Eastern Quarterly,* Vol. XIV, No. 4 (Aug., 1955), p. 519.

[69] As Mary Wright correctly suggested, however, Chiang's attitude created some problems for his spokesman, who, in making the best of the situation, had to resort to subtlety in extricating Chiang's confused attitude. T'ao Hsi-sheng, in his letter to Wang Te-liang, published in Wang's *Tseng Kuo-fan chih min-tsu ssu-hsiang,* page 79, says: "I believe the Kuomintang receives heritage both from the Taipings and Tseng Wen-cheng kung. Its historical origins are indeed subtle and complicated."

> Heroic forces overwhelmed four hundred districts,
> Cleansing the disgrace and taking the revenge of our nine
>   generations of ancestors.
> The banners struck terror in the hearts of the Tartars,
> While dragons and tigers established their capital in Nanking.
> The heroes, male and female, each an outstanding figure of the
>   time;
> Their essays and poems will last for one thousand autumns.
> The kingly air still hovers over Nanking,
> For in sixty years, here we have a unified China.[70]

The Communists in China also feel an affinity with the Taipings. In 1951 they held a centennial commemorating the rise of the Taiping movement. We do not know how deeply the Chinese Communist leaders were influenced by the Taipings. We do have the testimony of one of the Communists' now discarded leaders, Chang Kuo-t'ao. He recounts that he was greatly moved by the Taiping stories told him by a watchman when he was a boy.

> Two or three years after the Hung Chiang Rebellion, while I was study-ing at the P'ing-hsiang Primary School, I met a watchman who was more than 70 years of age. The old man showed no fear in telling stories of re-bellion. He would very often tell primary students whom he thought reliable the story of his participation in the Taiping Rebellion and how the Taipings fought. He would become so excited in the telling that his eyebrows would fly about and his whole face would dance. He also told us that the Hung Chiang rebels were a farce compared to the Taipings in their younger days. The Taiping rebels were capable and much more systematically or-ganized. We all took him for an old hero: he was a soldier of the Taipings who had let his hair grow in defiance of the Manchus, who gave the people the choice of keeping their hair or their heads, but not both.[71]

A tangible symbol of the Chinese Communists' respect for the Tai-pings is their feverish effort to publish and exhibit Taiping documents and to offer the world their interpretation of the Taiping ideas and movement. Most Communist writers consider the Taiping Rebellion to be the forerunner of later revolutionary movements. Hua Kang traces the victory of the Chinese People's Communist Liberation Army through the eight years of war against Japan, the ten years of civil war,

---

[70] Poems by Yü Yu-jen and Li Chi-shen, in Lo and Shen, *Shih-wen ch'ao*.
[71] Chang Kuo-t'ao, Unpublished Memoirs, chap. 1.

the land reform of the Communists, the northern expedition in 1926, the May 30 movement in 1925, the May 4 movement in 1919, the Hsin-hai Revolution in 1911 to the *T'ai-p'ing t'ien-kuo*. He also connects Mao Tse-tung through Sun Yat-sen with Hung Hsiu-ch'üan.[72] Specifically, Hua says, "*T'ai-p'ing t'ien-kuo* rebellion was the precursor of the democratic revolution of Chinese bourgeoisie, the vanguard of the Chinese people's liberation war. When studied in a spirit of modesty, one will see that their experience is still realistically significant to the Chinese people today."[73]

Fan Wen-lan is even more emphatic in linking the Communists to the Taipings. Fan calls the platform of the *T'ai-p'ing t'ien-kuo*, which includes the following ideas, the "fundamental principles of a democratic revolution": abolition of private landownership and its corollary the disappearance of the landowner class, an attempt to adopt capitalism, industrialization, international equality, equality between man and woman, equality among all people, the popular election of local officials, the democratic process of recall of officials, opposition to traditional feudal thought, the spread of knowledge about production, emphasis on simple style of writing, and other progressive cultural policies.[74] He considers the work of the Chinese Communists the crowning process of the task started by the Taipings. He says:

> The May 4 movement signaled the beginning of the Chinese new democratic revolution. The Chinese proletariat and its party—the Chinese Communist Party—took up the task of guiding the great enterprise of the Chinese people's revolution. After thirty years of determined and bitter struggle, we have achieved the fundamental victory. The progressive portion of the *T'ai-p'ing t'ien-kuo* revolutionary platform is not only realized; it has been greatly developed. From "The Land System of the Heavenly Dynasty" to the land reform of the Chinese People's Republic, from election of local officials to the people's democratic dictatorship, from the preparatory attempts to establish new industry to the control of the socialist heavy industry owned by the people, from demands for political and economic equality to the realization of these equalities, from the naïve antifeudal culture to a national and scientific people's new democratic culture—from any point of view, the achievements of the new democratic revolution have surpassed those of the *T'ai-p'ing t'ien-kuo* revolution many

[72] Hua, *T'ai-p'ing t'ien-kuo ko-ming chan-cheng shih*, pp. 228–29.
[73] *Ibid.*, p. 224.
[74] Fan, "Chin-t'ien ch'i-i i-pai-chou-nien chi-mien," in *T'ai-p'ing t'ien-kuo ko-ming yün-tung lun-wen chi*, p. 5.

times. However, if we look at the *T'ai-p'ing t'ien-kuo* as our vanguard, for the initiatives they had taken they deserved the lasting memory of the Chinese people.[75]

Finally, the Communist definitive statement on the nature of the *T'ai-p'ing t'ien-kuo* in the editorial of the Peking *Jen-min jih-pao* on January 11, 1951, was supplemented by another editorial in the same paper in 1955, which does not differ materially from the first. Whether the Taiping ideology did really influence the Chinese Communists or not, these editorials offer eloquent evidence of the Chinese Communists' acknowledgment of the strong Taiping influence in the establishment of the People's Republic of China.

IN RETROSPECT

Our study of the Taiping ideology has given us a vivid picture of the society in which this ideology was forged and the society it was forged to create. It shows China in transition in the mid-nineteenth century, struggling with the problem of adjusting herself to the new tides of the modern world. The form of adjustment the Taipings assumed—the juxtaposition of elements both new and old and the mixture of values culturally differently based—was ominously prophetic of the subsequent attempts to come to grips with the same problem of adapting to the new and preserving the old identity. If there is any significant lesson learned here, it is that the process of cultural assimilation or cross-fertilization has to take place in an understanding, which is at once broad and deep-rooted, of the fundamental principles and the inner spirit of both the culture to be assimilated and one's native tradition. Such an understanding will not only give meaning to the way of life in all its forms in that alien culture; it will also, by contrast and comparison, bring into relief the strengths and weaknesses of one's own native culture and thus open his eyes to values of the native culture which he did not, in isolation, suspect before.

Although the Taipings failed to create a new society and failed even to establish a new dynasty, their purpose and aim, their ideas and programs, and their passion and devotion to their dynasty to the bitter end have been sources of inspiration to many a revolutionary leader in modern China.

[75] *Ibid.*, pp. 5–6.

Reign Periods of the Ch'ing Dynasty

Shun-chih 1644–1661
K'ang-hsi 1662–1722
Yung-cheng 1723–1735
Ch'ien-lung 1736–1795
Chia-ch'ing 1796–1820
Tao-kuang 1821–1850
Hsien-feng 1851–1861
T'ung-chih 1862–1874
Kuang-hsü 1875–1908
Hsüan-t'ung 1909–1911

Abbreviations

Boardman, *Christian Influence*	Eugene P. Boardman, *Christian Influence upon the Ideology of the Taiping Rebellion, 1851–1864.*
Chang, *Tse-ch'ing*	Chang Te-chien (editor and compiler), *Tse-ch'ing hui-tsuan.*
Ch'eng, *Shih-liao*	Ch'eng Yen-sheng (compiler), *T'ai-p'ing t'ien-kuo shih-liao,* 1st Series.
Hsiao, *Chao-yü*	Hsiao I-shan (compiler), *T'ai-p'ing t'ien-kuo chao-yü.*
Hsiao, *Ts'ung-shu*	Hsiao I-shan (compiler), *T'ai-p'ing t'ien-kuo ts'ung-shu.*
Hsieh, *Ts'ung-shu*	Hsieh Hsing-yao (compiler), *T'ai-p'ing t'ien-kuo ts'ung-shu shih-san chung.*
Jen, *Shou-i shih*	Jen [Chien] Yu-wen, *T'ai-p'ing-chün Kwangsi shou-i shih.*
Kuo, *Jih-chih*	Kuo T'ing-i, *T'ai-p'ing t'ien-kuo shih-shih jih-chih.*
Ling, *Yeh-shih*	Ling Shan-ch'ing (ed.), *T'ai-p'ing t'ien-kuo yeh-shih.*
Lo, *Li-hsiang-kuo*	Lo Erh-kang, *T'ai-p'ing t'ien-kuo ti li-hsiang-kuo.*
Lo, *Shih-kang*	Lo Erh-kang, *T'ai-p'ing t'ien-kuo shih-kang.*
Lo, *T'ien-ti hui*	Lo Erh-kang, *T'ien-ti hui wen-hsien lu.*
Lo and Shen, *Shih-wen ch'ao*	Lo Yung and Shen Tsu-chi (compilers), *T'ai-p'ing t'ien-kuo shih-wen ch'ao.*
Motzu	*Motzu hsien-ku,* edited by Sung I-jang.
NCH	*North China Herald and Supreme Court and Consular Gazette.*
Parliamentary Papers	Great Britain. Parliament. British Sessional Papers, House of Commons. Readex Microprint ed., edited by Edgar L. Erickson.

Bibliography

COLLECTIONS OF TAIPING DOCUMENTS

Ch'eng Yen-sheng 程演生 (compiler). *T'ai-p'ing t'ien-kuo shih-liao* 太平天國史料, 1st Series. 3 vols. Peking: Peking University Press, 1926.

Ch'in-ting ch'ien-i-chao sheng-shu 欽定前遺詔聖書 (Taiping New Testament). Located in the British Museum.

Ch'in-ting chiu-i-chao sheng-shu 欽定舊遺詔聖書 (Taiping Old Testament). Located in the British Museum.

Hsiang Ta 向達 *et al.* (compilers). *T'ai-p'ing t'ien-kuo* 太平天國, 8 vols., in *Chung-kuo chin-tai-shih tzu-liao ts'ung-kan.* Shanghai, 1952.

Hsiao I-shan 蕭一山 (compiler). *T'ai-p'ing t'ien-kuo chao-yü* 太平天國詔諭. Peiping, 1935.

——— (compiler). *T'ai-p'ing t'ien-kuo ts'ung-shu* 太平天國叢書. 10 *ts'e.* Kuo-li pien-i kuan. Preface, Peiping, 1934.

Lo Yung 羅邕 and Shen Tsu-chi 沈祖基 (compilers). *T'ai-p'ing t'ien-kuo shih-wen ch'ao* 太平天國詩文鈔. 2 vols. Revised ed., 3d printing. Shanghai, 1935.

BOOKS IN CHINESE

Analects. See *Lun-yü yin-te.*

Book of Changes. See *Chou-i yin-te.*

Book of History. See *Shang-shu t'ung-chien.*

Book of Poetry. See *Mao-shih yin-te.*

Cha Chi-tso 查繼佐. *Tsui-wei-lu* 罪惟録, in *Ssu-pu ts'ung-k'an san-pien.* Shanghai: Commercial Press, 1929–36.

Chang Chung-ju 章中如. *Ch'ing-tai k'ao-shih chih-tu* 清代考試制度. Shanghai, 1932.

————. *Ch'ing-tai k'o-chü chih-tu* 清代科舉制度. Shanghai, 1932.

Chang Hsi-t'ang 張西堂. *Wang Ch'uan-shan hsüeh-p'u* 王船山學譜. Ch'ang-sha, 1938.

Chang Te-chien 張德堅 (editor and compiler). *Tse-ch'ing hui-tsuan* 賊情彙纂. 6 *ts'e*, 12 *chüan*. Preface 1855. Published in facsimile from a rare manuscript in Nanking kuo-hsüeh t'u-shu kuan in 1932.

Chang Tsai 張載. *Chang Heng-ch'ü chi* 張橫渠集, in *Cheng-i-t'ang ch'üan-shu*. Foochow, 1866.

Chao I 趙翼. *Nien-erh-shih cha-chi* 廿二史劄記, 36 *chüan*, in *Ou-pei ch'üan chi*, *ts'e* 1–16. 1877.

Chao Lien 昭槤. *Hsiao-t'ing tsa-lu* 嘯亭雜錄. Shanghai: Chin-pu shu-chü, preface 1880.

Chao Tao-i 趙道一. *Li-shih chen-hsien t'i-tao t'ung-chien* 歷世真仙體道通鑑, 1,120 *chüan*, in *Tao-tsang*. Shanghai: Commercial Press, 1924–26.

Chen-an fu-chih 鎮安府志, compiled by Yang Fu-li, 1892.

Ch'en Kung-lu 陳恭禄. *Chung-kuo chin-tai shih* 中國近代史. Shanghai, 1935.

Ch'en Li 陳立. *Pai-hu-t'ung shu-cheng* 白虎通疏證, in *Huang-ch'ing ching-chieh hsü-pien*, *ts'e* 278–81. Preface 1888.

Ch'en Teng-yüan 陳登原. *Chung-kuo t'u-ti chih-tu* 中國土地制度. Shanghai, 1934.

Ch'en Yin-k'o 陳寅恪. *Sui-T'ang chih-tu yüan-yüan lüeh-lun kao* 隋唐制度淵源略論稿. Chungking, 1945.

Cheng Chen-to 鄭振鐸. *Chung-kuo wen-hsüeh lun chi* 中國文學論集. Shanghai, 1934.

————. *Chung-kuo wen-hsüeh shih* 中國文學史. Peiping, 1932.

Cheng Ch'iao 鄭樵. *T'ung-chih* 通志. Shanghai: Commercial Press, 1935.

Cheng Po-ch'ien 鄭伯謙. *T'ai-p'ing ching-kuo chih shu* 太平經國之書, in *Hsüeh-chin t'ao-yüan*, *ts'e* 25–26. Shanghai, 1805.

Ch'eng Ta-ch'ang 程大昌. *Yen-fan-lu* 演繁露, in *Hsüeh-chin t'ao-yüan*, *ts'e* 24. Shanghai, preface 1806.

Ch'eng Yün-shen 程允升. *Yu-hsüeh-ch'iung-lin* 幼學瓊林. Shanghai: Kuang-i shu-chü, 1947.

Chi-fu ts'ung-shu 畿輔叢書, compiled by Wang Hao. Published by the Wang family of Chung-ting chou, 1879.

Chi Liu-ch'i 計六奇 (ed.). *Ming-chi pei-lüeh* 明季北略, in *Wan-yu wen-k'u*, 2d Series. Shanghai: Commercial Press, 1936.

Chi-lu hui-pien hsüan-k'an. See Chu Yüan-chang.

Ch'i Chi-kuang 戚繼光. *Lien-pin shih-chi* 練兵實記, in *Ts'ung-shu chi-ch'eng ch'u-pien*. Shanghai, 1936.

Chia-ying chou-chih 嘉應州志, compiled by Wu Tsung-cho, 1898.

Chiang Po-ch'ien 蔣伯潛. *Shih-san-ching kai-lun* 十三經概論. Shanghai: Shih-chieh shu-chü, 1944.

Chien Yu-wen. See Jen Yu-wen.

Ch'ien Ch'ien-i 錢謙益. *Kuo-ch'u ch'ün-hsiung shih-lüeh* 國初羣雄事略, in *Shih-yüan ts'ung-shu*, 3d Series, ed. Chang Chün-heng. Wu-ch'eng, 1914–16.

Ch'ien Chih 錢軹. *Chia-shen ch'uan-hsin lu* 甲申傳信錄, in *Chung-kuo nei-luan wai-huo li-shih ts'ung shu*. Shanghai, 1940.

Ch'ien Mu 錢穆. *Chung-kuo chin san-pai-nien hsüeh-shu shih* 中國近三百年學術史. 2 vols. Shanghai, 1937.

————. *Kuo-shih ta-kang* 國史大綱. Shanghai, 1944.

Ch'ien Pang-ch'i 錢邦芑. *Ch'ung-chen chia-shen yen-tu chi-pien shih-lu* 崇禎甲申燕都紀變實錄, in *T'ung-shih*, ed. Lo-t'ien chü-shih. Shanghai: Commercial Press, 1911.

Chih-p'an 志磐. *Fo-tsu t'ung-chi* 佛祖統紀, in Taisho ed. of *Tripitaka, chüan* 49, No. 2035.

Ch'ih-hsi hsien-chih 赤溪縣志, compiled by Lai Chi-hsi. 1920.

Ch'ing-ch'ao wen-hsien t'ung-k'ao 清朝文獻通考, ed. Hsi Huang *et al.*, 1747. Reprinted in *Wan-yu wen-k'u*. Shanghai: Commercial Press, 1935.

Ch'ing-shih kao 清史稿, compiled by Chao Erh-sun 趙爾巽, K'o Shao-min 柯劭忞, *et al.* Shen-yang, preface 1927.

Chiu T'ang-shu 舊唐書, by Liu Hsü 劉昫 *et al.* T'ung-wen ed. Shanghai, 1884.

Chou-i yin-te 周易引得. Harvard-Yenching Institute Sinological Index Series, Supplement No. 10. Peiping, 1935.

Chou Ku-ch'eng 周谷城. *Chung-kuo t'ung-shih* 中國通史. (First printing, Shanghai, 1939.) Shanghai, 1947.

Chou-li chu-shu 周禮註疏, in *Shih-san-ching chu-shu*. Nanchang, Kiangsi, 1815.

Chou-li yin-te 周禮引得. Harvard-Yenching Institute Sinological Index Series, No. 37. Peiping, 1940.

Chu Ch'i-hua 朱其華. *Chung-kuo chin-tai she-hui shih chieh-p'ou* 中國近代社會史解剖. Shanghai, 1933.

Chu Chieh-ch'in 朱傑勤. *Kung Ting-an yen-chiu* 龔定盦研究. Shanghai: Commercial Press, 1940.

Chu Hsi 朱熹. *Shih chi-chuan* 詩集傳, in *Ssu-pu ts'ung-k'an san-pien*, Vols. VI-VII. Shanghai: Commercial Press, 1929–36.

Chu-ko Liang 諸葛亮. *Chu-ko wu-hou wen-chi* 諸葛武侯文集, in *Cheng-i-t'ang ch'üan-shu*. Foochow, n.d.

Chu Yüan-chang 朱元璋 [Ming T'ai-tsu 明太祖]. *Chi-lu hui-pien hsüan-k'an* 紀録彙編選刊. Peiping: Yenching University Library, 1935.

Chuang Chi-yü 莊季裕. *Chi-le pien* 雞肋編, in *Shuo-fu*, compiled by T'ao Tsung-i. Shanghai, 1927.

Chuang Chou 莊周. *Chuang-tzu* 莊子, *in Chu-tzu chi-ch'eng*. Shanghai: Shih-chieh shu-chü, 1935.

Ch'un-ch'iu ching-chuan yin-te 春秋經傳引得. 4 vols. Harvard-Yenching Institute Sinological Index Series, Supplement No. 11. Peiping, 1937.

Ch'un-ch'iu fan-lu t'ung-chien 春秋繁露通檢. Peiping: Université de Paris centre d' études sinologiques de Pékin, 1943.

Chung-kuo chin-tai li-shih yen-chiu kang-yao 中國近代歷史研究綱要. Shanghai, 1946.

Chung-kuo ko-ming yün-tung shih 中國革命運動史, by Chung-kuo-hsien-tai-shihyen-chiuwei-yüan-hui. 1939.

Ch'ü Hsüan-ying 瞿宣穎. *Chung-kuo she-hui shih-liao ts'ung-ch'ao* 中國社會史料叢鈔. Shanghai: Commercial Press, 1938.

Ch'ü T'ung-tsu 瞿同祖. *Chung-kuo fa-lü yü Chung-kuo she-hui* 中國法律與中國社會. Shanghai, 1947.

Ch'üan Heng 權衡. *Keng-shen wai-shih* 庚申外史, in *Hsüeh-hai lei-pien*, ed. Ts'ao Jung. Shanghai, 1920.

Ch'üan Tsu-wang 全祖望. *Chieh-ch'i-t'ing chi wei-p'ien* 鮚埼亭集外編, in *Ssu-pu ts'ung-k'an*, Vol. XCV. Shanghai: Commercial Press, 1929–36.

Fan Wen-lan 范文瀾. *T'ai-p'ing t'ien-kuo ko-ming yün-tung shih* 太平天國革命運動史. Hong Kong, 1948.

Fang Chao-ying 房兆楹 and Tu Lien-che 杜聯喆. *Ch'ing-tai chin-shih t'i-ming pei-lu* 清代進士題名碑録. Peiping: Harvard-Yenching Institute, 1941.

Fang Shao 方勺. *Ch'ing-hsi k'ou-kuei* 青谿寇軌, in *Chin-hua ts'ung-shu*, compiled by Hu Feng-tan, *ts'e* 84. Preface 1870. Reprinted by Chekiang kung-li t'u-shu-kuan, 1925.

———. *Po-chai pien* 泊宅編, in *Chin-hua ts'ung-shu*, compiled by Hu Feng-tan, *ts'e* 108. Preface 1870. Reprinted by Chekiang kung-li t'u-shu-kuan, 1925.

Feng Ch'i 馮琦. *Sung-shih chi-shih pen-mo* 宋史紀事本末, enlarged by Ch'en Pang-chan. Kiangsi shu-chü, 1874.

Feng Kuei-fen 馮桂芬. *Hsien-chih-t'ang kao* 顯志堂稿. 8 *ts'e*. 1877.

Feng-shen chuan 封神傳, attributed to Hsü Chung-lin 許仲琳. Shanghai, 1922.

Fu Ch'ing-chia 傅勤家. *Chung-kuo tao-chiao shih* 中国道教史. Shanghai, 1937.

Han Fei 韓非. *Han-fei-tzu* 韓非子, 20 *chüan*, in *Chu-tzu chi-ch'eng*. Shanghai: Shih-chieh shu-chü, 1935.

Han-shu 漢書, by Pan Ku 班固. T'ung-wen ed. Shanghai, 1884.

Han Yü 韓愈. *Ch'ang-li hsien-sheng chi* 昌黎先生集, in *Ssu-pu ts'ung-k'an*, Vol. XXXIX Shanghai: Commercial Press, 1929–36.

Ho Hsiu 何休. *Ch'un-ch'iu Kung-yang chuan chu-shu* 春秋公羊傳註疏, in *Ssu-pu pei-yao*. Shanghai: Chung-hua shu-chü, n.d.

———. *Ch'ung-k'an Sung-pen Kung-yang chu-shu* 重刊宋版公羊注疏. (1st ed., 1815.) Kiangsi, 1873.

Hou-Han-shu 後漢書, by Fan Yeh 范曄. T'ung-wen ed. Shanghai, 1884.

Hsi Huang 嵇璜, Liu Yung 劉鏞, *et al.* (compilers). *Hsü Wen-hsien t'ung-k'ao* 續文獻通考. Shanghai: Commercial Press, 1936.

Hsiao-ching 孝經, in *Shih-san-ching chu-shu*. Nanchang, Kiangsi, 1815.

Hsiao I-shan 蕭一山. *Chin-tai mi-mi she-hui shih-liao* 近代秘密社會史料. Peiping, 1935.

———. *Ch'ing-tai t'ung-shih* 清代通史. 3 vols. Peiping: Wen-chih hsüeh-yüan, n.d.

Hsiao, Kung-chuan 蕭公權. *Chung-kuo cheng-chih ssu-hsiang shih* 中國政治思想史. (Published in Chungking, 1945 and Shanghai, 1946.) Taiwan ed., 2d printing. 1954.

Hsieh Chieh-ho 謝介鶴. *Chin-ling kuei-chia chi-shih lüeh* 金陵癸甲紀事略, in Hsieh Hsing-yao 謝興堯 (compiler), *T'ai-p'ing t'ien-kuo ts'ung-shu shih-san chung*. Peiping, 1938.

Hsieh Hsing-yao 謝興堯. *T'ai-p'ing t'ien-kuo shih-shih lun-ts'ung* 太平天國史事論叢. Shanghai, 1935.

———. *T'ai-p'ing t'ien-kuo ti she-hui cheng-chih ssu-hsiang* 太平天國的社會政治思想. Shanghai, 1935.

——— (compiler). *T'ai-p'ing t'ien-kuo ts'ung-shu shih-san chung* 太平天國叢書十三種. Peiping, 1938.

Hsien-feng shih-lu 咸豐實錄. Tokyo, 1937.

Hsin-ning hsien-chih 新寧縣志, compiled by Lin Kuo-keng *et al.* 1893.

Hsin T'ang-shu 新唐書, by Ou-yang Hsiu 歐陽修 and Sung Ch'i 宋祁, in *Ssu-pu pei-yao*. Shanghai: Chung-hua shu-chü, n.d.

Hsü K'o 徐珂 (ed.). *Ch'ing-pai lei-ch'ao* 清稗類鈔. 48 *ts'e*. Shanghai, 1917.

Hsüeh Ying-ch'i 薛應旂. *Sung-yüan t'ung-chien* 宋元通鑑. Preface 1566.

Hsün-chou fu-chih 潯州府志, compiled by Hsia Ching-i *et al.* 1896.

Hsün-chou fu-chih 潯州府志, compiled by Wang Chün-ch'en. 1874.

Hsün-tzu 荀子, in *Chu-tzu chi-ch'eng, ts'e* 1. Shanghai: Shih-chieh shu-chü, 1935.

Hu P'u-an 胡樸安. *Chung-hua ch'üan-kuo feng-su chih* 中華全國風俗志. Shanghai, 1923.

Hua Kang 華崗. *T'ai-p'ing t'ien-kuo ko-ming chan-cheng shih* 太平天國革命戰爭史. Shanghai and Peking, 1949.

Huai-nan-tzu 淮南子, by Liu An 劉安, in *Ssu-pu ts'ung-k'an*, Vol. XXIV. Shanghai: Commercial Press, 1929–36.

Huang-ch'ao ching-shih wen-pien 皇朝經世文編, ed. Ho Ch'ang-lin 賀長齡. Shanghai, 1884.

Huang Chün-tsai 黃鈞宰. *Chin-hu ch'i-mo* 金壺七墨, in *Ch'ing-tai pi-chi ts'ung-k'an*. Shanghai, preface 1895.

Huang Tsung-hsi 黃宗羲 [Li-chou 梨洲]. *Ming-i tai-fang lu* 明夷待訪錄, in *Hsiao-shih-shan-fang ts'ung-shu*. Hai-yü, 1874.

Hui Tung 惠棟. *T'ai-shang kan-ying p'ien chu* 太上感應篇注, in *Yüeh-ya t'ang ts'ung-shu, ts'e* 137.

Hung Mai 洪邁. *I-chien chih* 夷堅志, in *Ts'ung-shu chi-ch'eng, ts'e* 2707–14. Shanghai: Commercial Press, n.d.

Hung-ming chi 弘明集, compiled by Seng-yu 僧佑. Nanking, 1896.

I-ching 逸經, edited by Jen Yu-wen 簡又文, Hsieh Hsing-yao 謝興堯, Lu Tan-lin 陸丹林, *et al.* 33 issues appeared bi-monthly from March 5, 1936 to July 5, 1937. Shanghai.

I-li yin-te 儀禮引得. Harvard-Yenching Institute Sinological Index Series, No. 6. Peiping, 1930.

Inaba Iwakichi 稲葉岩吉. *Ch'ing-ch'ao ch'üan-shih* 清朝全史. Translated into Chinese by Tan T'ao. Shanghai, 1915.

Jen [Chien] Yu-wen 簡又文. *Chin-t'ien chih-yu chi ch'i-t'a* 金田之遊及其他. Chungking: Commercial Press, 1944.

———. *T'ai-p'ing-chün Kwangsi shou-i shih* 太平軍廣西首義史. Shanghai, 1946.

———. *T'ai-p'ing t'ien-kuo ch'üan-shih* 太平天國全史. 3 vols. Hong Kong: Chien-shih meng-chin shu-wu, 1962.

———. *T'ai-p'ing t'ien-kuo Kwangsi ch'i-i shih* 太平軍廣西起義史. Peiping, 1935.

Juan Yüan 阮元 (compiler). *Huang-ch'ing ching-chieh* 皇清經解. Kwangtung, 1829.

K'ang Yu-wei 康有為. *Ta-t'ung shu* 大同書. Shanghai, 1936.

Ko Hung 葛洪. *Pao-p'u-tzu* 抱朴子, in *Chu-tzu chi ch'eng*. Shanghai: Shih-chieh shu-chü, 1935.

Ku Chieh-kang 顧頡剛. *Han-tai hsüeh-shu shih-lüeh* 漢代學術史略. Shanghai, 1935.

Ku-liang chuan 穀梁傳, in *Shih-san-ching chu-shu*. Nanchang, Kiangsi, 1815.

Ku Shen 顧深. *Hu-hsüeh sheng-huan chi* 虎穴生還記, in Hsiang Ta *et al.* (compilers), *T'ai-p'ing t'ien-kuo*, Vol. VI. Shanghai, 1952.

Ku Yen-wu 顧炎武. *Jih-chih lu* 日知録, in *Sui-ch'u-t'ang*. 1695.

Ku Ying-t'ai 谷應泰. *Ming-shih chi-shih pen-mo* 明史紀事本末. Shanghai: Commercial Press, 1934.

Kuang-chou fu-chih 廣州府志, compiled by Shih Cheng *et al.* 1879.

Kuei-hsien chih 貴縣志, compiled by Liang Chi-hsiang *et al.* 1893.

K'ung Yin-ta 孔穎達. *Ch'un-ch'iu Tso-chuan cheng-i* 春秋左傳正義, in *Ssu-pu pei-yao*. Shanghai: Chung-hua shu-chü, n.d.

Kuo Mo-jo 郭沫若. *Chia-shen san-pai-nien chi* 甲申三百年祭. Chang-chia-k'ou: Hsin-hua shu-tien, 1945.

Kuo T'ing-i 郭廷以. *T'ai-p'ing t'ien-kuo shih-shih jih-chih* 太平天国史事日誌. 2 vols. Chungking and Shanghai, 1946.

Kuo-yü 國語, in *Ssu-pu ts'ung-k'an*. Shanghai: Commercial Press, 1929–36.

Kwangsi t'ung-chih 廣西通志, compiled by Hu Ch'ien. 1865.

Lang Ying 郎瑛 (compiler). *Ch'i-hsiu lei-kao* 七修類稿. 16 vols. 1775 reprint. Ken-yen ts'ao-t'ang k'an-pen.

Lao-tzu. See Wei Yüan, *Lao-tzu pen-i*.

Li-chi chu-shu 禮記注疏, in *Shih-san-ching chu-shu*. Nanchang, Kiangsi, 1815.

Li-chi yin-te 禮記引得. Harvard-Yenching Institute Sinological Index Series, No. 27. Peiping, 1937.

Li Fang 李昉 (compiler). *T'ai-p'ing kuang-chi* 太平廣記. Peiping, 1934.

Li Ju-chen 李汝珍. *Ching-hua-yüan* 鏡花縁. Shanghai: Ya-tung t'u-shu-kuan, 1930.

Li Kung 李塨. *I t'ai-p'ing ts'e* 擬太平策, in *Chi-fu ts'ung-shu* 畿輔叢書, *ts'e* 225. Published by the Wang family of Chung-ting chou, 1879.

———. *P'ing-shu ting* 平書訂, in *Chi-fu ts'ung-shu*, *ts'e* 231–32.

Li Ting-sheng 李鼎聲. *Chung-kuo chin-tai-shih* 中國近代史. Shanghai, 1948.

Li Yü-ming 李玉鳴. *Ta-ch'ing t'ung-li* 大清通禮. 54 *chüan*. 1824.

Liao-shih 遼史, by T'o T'o 脱脱. T'ung-wen ed. Shanghai, 1884.

Lien-p'ing chou-chih 連平州志, compiled by Lu T'ing-chun *et al.* 1730.

Lien-she kao-hsien chuan 蓮社高賢傳, in *Han-wei ts'ung-shu*, *ts'e* 37. Preface 1592. 1791 reprint, ed. Wang Mo.

Lin Tse-hsü 林則徐. *Lin Wen-chung kung cheng-shu* 林文忠公政書. Lin family ed., 1904.

Ling Shan-ch'ing 凌善清 (ed.). *T'ai-p'ing t'ien-kuo yeh-shih* 太平天國野史. Shanghai, 1923.

Liu Hsiang 劉向. *Shuo-yüan* 說苑, in *Han-wei ts'ung-shu*, ed. Wang Mo. 1791.

Liu I-cheng 柳詒徵. *Chung-kuo wen-hua shih* 中國文化史. Nanking, 1932.

Lo Erh-kang 羅爾綱. *Chung Wang Li Hsiu-ch'eng tzu-chuan yüan-kao ch'ien-cheng* 忠王李秀成自傳原稿箋證. Peking: K'ai-ming shu-tien, 1951.

———. *T'ai-p'ing t'ien-kuo shih-kang* 太平天國史綱. Shanghai, 1937.

———. *T'ai-p'ing t'ien-kuo shih-kao* 太平天國史稿. Shanghai, 1951.

———. *T'ai-p'ing t'ien-kuo shih k'ao-cheng chi* 太平天國史考證集. Shanghai, 1948.

———. *T'ai-p'ing t'ien-kuo shih-liao k'ao-shih chi* 太平天國史料考釋集. Peking, 1956.

———. *T'ai-p'ing t'ien-kuo shih-shih k'ao* 太平天國史事考. Peking, 1955.

———. *T'ai-p'ing t'ien-kuo shih ts'ung-k'ao* 太平天國史叢考. (1st ed., 1943.) Shanghai, 1947.

———. *T'ai-p'ing t'ien-kuo ti li-hsiang-kuo* 太平天國的理想國. Shanghai: Commercial Press, 1950.

———. *T'ien-ti hui wen-hsien lu* 天地會文獻録. Shanghai, 1947.

Lo Hsiang-lin 羅香林. *K'o-chia yen-chiu tao-lun* 客家研究導論. Canton, 1933.

Lo Kuan-chung 羅貫中. *San-kuo yen-i* 三國演義. Shanghai: Ya-tung t'u-shu-kuan, 1922.

Lo-t'ien chü-shih 樂天居士. *Shu-chi* 蜀記, in *T'ung-shih*. Shanghai: Commercial Press, 1911.

Lo Tse-nan 羅澤南. *Lo chung-chieh kung i-chi* 羅忠節公遺集. No place, no date.

Lu Hsün 魯迅 [Chou Shu-jen 周樹人]. *Chung-kuo hsiao-shuo shih-lüeh* 中國小說史略, in *Lu Hsün san-shih-nien chi*, Vol. IX. 1941.

Luan-chou chih 灤州志, compiled by Yang Wen-ting. 1896.

Lun-yü yin-te 論語引得. Harvard-Yenching Institute Sinological Index Series, Supplement No. 16. Peiping, 1940.

Lung Ch'i-jui 龍啓瑞. *Ching-te t'ang ch'üan-chi* 經德堂全集. 1878–81.

Lü Liu-liang 呂留良 [Wan-ts'un 晚村]. *Lu Wan-ts'un hsien-sheng ssu-shu chiang-i* 呂晚村先生四書講義. 1685.

———. *Lü Wan-ts'un hsien-sheng wen-chi* 呂晚村先生文集. 4 ts'e in 1 han. 1869.

Lü Pu-wei 呂不韋. *Lü-shih ch'un-ch'iu* 呂氏春秋, in *Chu-tzu chi-ch'eng*. Shanghai: Shih-chieh shu-chü, 1935.

Lü Ssu-mien 呂思勉. *Chung-kuo t'ung-shih* 中國通史. Shanghai, 1944.

Ma Tuan-lin 馬端臨. *Wen-hsien t'ung-k'ao* 文獻通考, in *Wan-yu wen-k'u*. Shanghai: Commercial Press, 1936.

Mao-shih chu-shu 毛詩注疏, in *Shih-san-ching chu-shu*. Nanchang, Kiangsi, 1815.

Mao-shih yin-te 毛詩引得. Harvard-Yenching Institute Sinological Index Series, Supplement No. 9. Peiping, 1934.

Mencius. See *Meng-tzu yin-te*.

Meng Ssu-ming 蒙思明. *Yüan-tai she-hui chieh-chi chih-tu* 元代社會階級制度. Peiping: Yenching University, 1938.

Meng-tzu yin-te 孟子引得. Harvard-Yenching Institute Sinological Index Series, Supplement No. 17. Peiping, 1941.

Mi-chih hsien-chih 米脂縣志, compiled by Kao Chao-hsü. 1907.

Ming-hsin tao-jen 明心道人. *Fa-i ch'u-chi* 髪逆初記, in Hsiang Ta *et al.* (compilers), *T'ai-p'ing t'ien-kuo*, Vol. IV. Shanghai, 1952.

Ming-mo nung-min ch'i-i shih-liao 明末農民起義史料. Peking University, 1952.

Ming-mo nung-ming ch'i-i shih-liao hsü-pien 明末農民起義史料續編. Peking University, n.d.

Ming-shih 明史, compiled by Chang T'ing-yü 張廷玉 *et al.* T'ung-wen ed. Shanghai, 1884.

Miu Ch'üan-sun 繆荃孫. *Hsü pei-chuan chi* 續碑傳集. Chiang-ch'u pien-i shu-chu, 1910.

Men-shih t'an-hu k'o 捫蝨談虎客 [Han Wen-chü 韓文舉]. *Chin-shih Chung-kuo mi-shih* 近世中國秘史. Shanghai, 1903.

Motzu hsien-ku 墨子閒詁, ed. Sun I-jang 孫貽讓, in *Chu-tzu chi-ch'eng*. Shanghai: Shih-chieh shu-chü, 1935.

Pai-hu t'ung-i 白虎通義, by Pan Ku 班固, in *Ts'ung-shu chi-ch'eng, ts'e* 238–39. Shanghai: Commercial Press, 1935–39.

P'an Yung-chi 潘永季. *Tu Ming-shih cha-chi* 讀明史劄記, in *Chao-tai ts'ung-shu, ts'e* 47. 1833–49.

Peking jen-min jih-pao 北京人民日報. Peking, January 11, 1951.

P'eng Tse-i 彭澤益. *T'ai-p'ing t'ien-kuo ko-ming ssu-ch'ao* 太平天國革命思潮. Shanghai, 1946.

P'ing Shan Chou 平山周 [Hirayama Chikashi]. *Chung-kuo mi-mi she-hui shih* 中國祕密社會史. (1st ed., 1912.) Revised ed., Shanghai, 1934.

San-kuo yen-i 三國演義, attributed to Lo Kuan-chung 羅貫中. Shanghai: Ya-tung t'u-shu-kuan, 1922.

Shang-shu chu-shu 尚書注疏, in *Shih-san-ching chu-shu*. Nanchang, Kiangsi, 1815.

Shang-shu ta-chuan 尚書大傳, attributed to Fu Sheng 伏生 of the Han, in *Ssu-pu ts'ung k'an*, Vol. IV. Shanghai: Commercial Press, 1929–36.

Shang-shu t'ung-chien 尚書通檢. Peiping: Harvard-Yenching Institute, 1936.

Sheng-tsu sheng-yü 聖祖聖諭. 1741.

Shih-chi 史記, by Ssu-ma Ch'ien 司馬遷. T'ung-wen ed. Shanghai, 1884.

Shih-i ch'ao tung-hua lu 十一朝東華錄, compiled by Wang Hsien-ch'ien 王先謙. 1899.

Shih Nai-an. See *Shui-hu chuan*.

Shih-san-ching chu-shu 十三經注疏, compiled by Juan Yüan 阮元. Nanchang, Kiangsi, 1815.

Shu-chi 蜀記, in *T'ung-shih*, ed. Lo-t'ien chü-shih. Shanghai: Commercial Press, 1911.

Shui-hu chuan 水滸傳, attributed to Shih Nai-an 施耐庵. Shanghai: Ya-tung t'u-shu-kuan, 1928.

Shui-hu hsü-chi 水滸續集, in *Cheng ssu-k'ou*. Shanghai: The Oriental Book Co., 1934.

Ssu-ma Ch'ien. See *Shih-chi*.

Ssu-pu ts'ung-k'an 四部叢刊. 3 Series. Shanghai: Commercial Press, 1929–36.

Su Shih 蘇軾. *Tung-po ch'i-chi* 東坡七集, in *Ssu-pu pei-yao*, Vol. LXXVII. Shanghai: Chung-hua shu-chü, n.d.

Su Yü 蘇輿. *Ch'un-ch'iu fan-lu i-cheng* 春秋繁露義證. 4 *ts'e* in 1 *han*. 1910.

Sui-shu 隋書, by Wei Chen 魏徵. T'ung-wen ed. Shanghai, 1884.

Sun Yat-sen 孫逸仙 [Sun Chung-shan 孫中山]. *Tsung-li ch'üan-chi* 總理全集. Shanghai: Ming-chih shu-chü, 1930.

————. *Tsung-li ch'üan-shu* 總理全書. Edited and published by Chung-yang kai-tsao wei-yüan hui. Taipei, 1951.

Sung-shih 宋史, compiled by T'o T'o 脫脫 *et al*. T'ung-wen ed. Shanghai, 1884.

Sung-shih chi-shih pen-mo 宋史紀事本末, compliled by Ch'en Pang-chan 陳邦瞻. Kiangsi shu-chü, 1874.

Ta-ch'ing hui-tien 大清會典, compiled by K'un Kang 崑岡 *et al*. 1899.

Ta-ch'ing lü-li hui-chi pien-lan 大清律例彙輯便覽. 40 *chüan*. Hsing-pu k'an-pen, 1877.

T'ai-p'ing ching ho-chiao 太平經合校, ed. Wang Ming 王明. Peking, 1960.

T'ai-p'ing kuang-chi. See Li Fang.

T'ai-p'ing t'ien-kuo ko-ming yün-tung lun-wen chi 太平天國革命運動論文集. Peking, 1950.

T'ai-p'ing t'ien-kuo shih-liao 太平天國史料. Peking, 1950.

T'ang Yung-t'ung 湯用彤. *Han wei liang-chin nan-pei-ch'ao fu-chiao-shih* 漢魏兩晉南北朝佛教史. 2 vols. Ch'ang-sha, 1938.

Tao-tsang 道藏. Shanghai: Commercial Press, 1923–26.

T'ao Yüan-ming 陶淵明. *Ching-chieh hsien-sheng chi* 靖節先生集. Kiangsu shu-chü, 1883.

Ting Fu-pao 丁福保. *Shuo-wen chieh-tzu ku-lin* 説文解字詁林. Shanghai, 1928.

T'o T'o. See *Liao-shih* and *Sung-shih*.

Tripitaka, or Buddhist Sacred Canon. Taisho ed. of Chinese version. 85 vols. Taisho Shinshu Daizokyo 大正新修大藏經. Tokyo, 1922–23.

Tseng Kuo-fan 曾國藩. *Tseng Wen-cheng kung ch'üan-chi* 曾文正公全集. 1876.

Tso-chuan 左傳, in *Shih-san-ching chu-shu*. Nanchang, Kiangsi, 1815.

Tso Tsung-t'ang 左宗棠. *Tso Wen-hsiang kung ch'üan-chi* 左文襄公全集. 1888–97.

Tsou Yüan-piao 鄒元標. *Shuo Yüeh ch'üan chuan* 説岳全傳. Shanghai: Shih-chieh shu-chü, 1935.

Tsung-chien 宗鑑. *Shih-men cheng-t'ung* 釋門正統, in *Dai Nihon Zoku zōkyō* 大日本續藏經. Kyoto, 1902–5.

Tu Wen-lan 杜文瀾. *P'ing-ting Yüeh-fei chi-lüeh* 平定粵匪紀略. Published under the auspices of Kuan Wen, 1871.

Tu Yu 杜佑. *T'ung-tien* 通典. Shanghai: Commercial Press, 1935.

Tuan Yü-ts'ai 段玉裁. *Shuo-wen chieh-tzu chu* 説文解字注, in Juan Yüan (compiler), *Huang-ch'ing ching-chieh*, *chüan* 641–55. Kwangtung, 1829.

Tung Chung-shu 董仲舒. *Ch'un-ch'iu fan-lu* 春秋繁露, in *Pao-ching-t'ang ts'ung-shu*. Peiping, 1923 reprint.

Tung-hua lu 東華録, compiled by Wang Hsien-ch'ien 王先謙. Peking, 1887.

Tz'u-hsi hsien-chih 慈谿縣志, compiled by Yang T'ai-heng. 1914.

Tz'u-yüan 辭源. Shanghai: Commercial Press, 1933.

Wang Chia 王嘉. *Shih-i-chi* 拾遺記, in *Shuo-fu*, ed. T'ao Tsung-i, *chüan* 30. Shanghai, 1927.

Wang Fu-chih 王夫之. *Ch'uan-shan i-shu* 船山遺書. Shanghai, 1935.

Wang Hsien-ch'ien. See *Shih-i ch'ao tung-hua lu* and *Tung-hua lu*.

Wang I 王逸. *Ch'u-tz'u chang-chü* 楚辭章句, in *Ssu-pu ts'ung-k'an,* Vol. XXXIII. Shanghai: Commercial Press, 1929–36.

Wang Ming-sheng 王鳴盛. *Chou-li chün-fu shuo* 周禮軍賦說, in Juan Yüan (compiler), *Huang-ch'ing ching-chieh.* Preface 1771. Kwangtung, 1829.

Wang Shih-chen 王世貞. *Yen-shan-t'ang pieh-chi* 弇山堂別集. Kuang-ya shu-chü, preface 1590.

Wang Shih-to 汪士鐸. *Wang Hui-weng i-ping jih-chi*汪悔翁乙丙日記. Peiping, 1936.

Wang T'ao 王韜. *Wen-yu yü-t'an* 甕牖餘談, in *Ch'ing-tai pi-chi ts'ung-k'an.* Shanghai, preface 1875.

Wang Te-liang 王德亮. *Tseng Kuo-fan chih min-tsu ssu-hsiang* 曾國藩之民族思想. Shanghai, 1946.

Wang Yang-ming 王陽明. *Ch'uan-hsi lu* 傳習録, in *Wang Yang-ming ch'üan-shu,* Vol. I. Cheng-chung, n.d.

Wei-ta fa-shih 衛大法師 [Wei Chü-hsien 衛聚賢]. *Chung-kuo-ti pang-hui* 中國的幫會. Revised ed. Chungking, 1947.

Wei Yüan 魏源. *Lao-tzu pen-i* 老子本義, in *Chu-tzu chi-ch'eng, ts'e* 2.

————. *Sheng-wu chi* 聖武記. Ku-wei t'ang ed. Preface, 1842. Huai-nan shu-chü, 1878 reprint.

Wen-hsüan 文選, compiled by Hsiao T'ung 蕭統. 1809 ed., reproduced in Taipei, 1955.

Wen T'ien-hsiang 文天祥. *Wen Wen-shan ch'üan-chi* 文文山全集. Shanghai: Shih-chieh shu-chü, 1936.

Wu Ch'en-en 吳承恩. *Hsi-yu chi* 西遊記. Shanghai, n.d.

Wu Han 吳晗. *Ming T'ai-tsu* 明太祖. 1943.

Wu Wei-yeh 吳偉業. *Lu-ch'iao chi-wen* 鹿樵紀聞, in *T'ung-shih,* ed. Lo-t'ien chü-shih. Shanghai: Commercial Press, 1911.

Wu Yün 吳雲. *Liang-lei hsüan-ch'ih-tu* 兩罍軒尺牘. 1884.

Yang Chung-liang 楊仲良. *T'ung-chien ch'ang-p'ien chi-shih pen-mo* 通鑑長篇紀事本末. Kuang-ya shu-chü, 1893.

Yang Hsiung 楊雄. *Fa-yen* 法言, in *Chu-tzu chi-ch'eng.* Shanghai: Shih-chieh shu-chü, 1935.

Yang Yin-shen 楊蔭深. *Chung-kuo wen-hsüeh-chia lieh-chuan* 中國文學家列傳. Shanghai, 1939.

Yao Nai 姚鼐. *Hsi-pao hsüan chüan-chi* 惜抱軒全集. Shanghai: Shih-chieh shu-chü, 1938.

Yen Yüan 顏元. *Ssu-ts'un pien* 四存編, in *Chi-fu ts'ung-shu, ts'e* 215. Published by Wang family of Chung-ting chou, 1879.

Yu-hsüeh ku-shih ch'iung-lin 幼學故事瓊林. Shanghai, 1947.

Yung-ning chou-chih 永寧州志, compiled by Li Chung-fa. Kwangsi, 1896.

Yü Hsin 庾信. *Yü Tzu-shan chi* 庾子山集, in *Ssu-pu pei-yao*, Vol. LXVII. Shanghai: Chung-hua shu-chü, n.d.

Yüan Mei 袁枚. *Sui-yüan san-shih chung* 随園三十種. Sui-yüan block ed. No place, no date.

Yüan-shih 元史, compiled by Sung Lien 宋濂 *et al.* T'ung-wen ed. Shanghai, 1884.

Yüan Shu 袁樞. *T'ung-chien chi-shih pen-mo* 通鑑紀事本末, in *Ssu-pu ts'ung-k'an*, Vols. XIII-XIV. Shanghai: Commercial Press, 1929–36.

Yüeh-chuan 岳傳. Shanghai: Shih-chieh shu-chü, 1935.

Yüeh Shih 樂史 (ed.). *T'ai-p'ing huan-yü chi* 太平寰宇記. 200 *chüan*. Nanking, 1882.

ARTICLES IN CHINESE

Chao Tsung-fu 趙宗復. "Li Tzu-ch'eng pan-luan shih-lüeh" 李自成叛亂史略, *Shih-hsüeh nien-pao* 史學年報 (Yenching University), Vol. II, No. 4 (December, 1937), pp. 127–57.

Ch'en Hsün-tz'u 陳訓慈. "T'ai-p'ing t'ien-kuo chih tsung-chiao cheng-chih" 太平天國之宗教政治, *Shih-hsüeh tsa-chih* 史學雜誌, Vol. I, No. 6 (December, 1929); and Vol. II, No. 1 (March, 1930).

Ch'en Hung 陳鴻. "Ch'ang-hen-ko chuan" 長恨歌傳, in *Lung-wei mi shu* 龍威秘書, compiled by Ma Ch'ün-liang 馬俊良, *ts'e* 14. Chekiang, 1796.

Ch'en Yüan 陳垣. "Mo-ni chiao ju Chung-kuo k'ao" 摩尼教入中國考, *Kuo-hsüeh chi-k'an* 國學季刊 (Quarterly, Peking), Vol. I (1923), No. 2, pp. 203–40.

———. "Shih-hui chü-li" 史諱舉例, *Yenching Hsüeh-pao* 燕京學報, No. 4 (December, 1928), pp. 537–651.

Chia Shu-ts'un 賈熟村. "T'ai-p'ing t'ien-kuo ko-ming ti hsing-chih wen-t'i 太平天國革命的性質問題, *Li-shih yen-chiu* 歷史研究, No. 8, 1957, pp. 1–18.

Chiang Chung-cheng 蔣中正 [Chiang Kai-shek 蔣介石]. "Preface" to Lo Yung and Shen Tsu-chi (compilers), *T'ai-p'ing t'ien-kuo shih-wen ch'ao* 太平天國詩文鈔. Revised ed., 3d printing. Shanghai, 1935.

———. "Preface" to *Tseng-pu tseng-hu chih-ping yü-lu* 增補曾胡治兵語録, ed. Ts'ai O 蔡鍔. Chungking, 1941.

Chien Yu-wen. See Jen Yu-wen.

Ch'ien Chia-chü 千家駒. "Ya-p'ien chan-cheng hou ti kuo-min sheng-chi wen-t'i" 鴉片戰爭後的國民生計問題, *Chung-shan wen-hua chiao-yü-kuan* 中山文化教育舘季刊, Vol. III (1936), No. 1, pp. 187–207.

Ch'ien Wei-ch'eng 錢維城. "Yang-min" 養民, in *Huang-ch'ao ching-shih wen-pien* 皇朝經世文編, ed. Ho Ch'ang-lin 賀長齡, *chüan* 11. Shanghai, 1884.

Ch'iu T'ien 秋田. "T'ai-wan ti an-mo nü" 台灣的按摩女, *Chung-kuo hsin-wen* 中國新聞 (Taipei), Vol. VIII, No. 11 (1950).

Chu Hsi-tsu 朱希祖. "Preface" to Ch'eng Yen-sheng (compiler), *T'ai-p'ing t'ien-kuo shih-liao* 太平天國史料, 1st Series. Peking: Peking University Press, 1926.

Chüeh-mi 覺迷. "Miao-chiang feng-su chih" 苗疆風俗志, *Kuo-wen chou-pao* 國聞週報, Vol. VI, No. 12 (March 31, 1929).

Fan Wen-lan 范文瀾. "Chin-t'ien ch'i-i i-pai-chou-nien chi-nien" 金田起義一百週年紀念, in *T'ai-p'ing t'ien-kuo ko-ming yün-tung lun-wen chi* 太平天國革命運動論文集. Peking, 1950.

Fu I-ling 傅衣凌. "T'ai-p'ing t'ien-kuo shih-tai ti ch'üan-kuo k'ang-liang ch'ao" 太平天國時代的全國抗糧潮, *Ts'ai-cheng chih-shih* 財政知識, Vol. III, No. 3 (September, 1943).

Hsia Nai 夏鼐. "T'ai-p'ing t'ien-kuo ch'ien-hou ch'ang-chiang ko-sheng chih t'ien-fu wen-t'i" 太平天國前後長江各省之田賦問題, *Ch'ing-hua hsüeh-pao* 清華學報, Vol. X, No. 2 (April, 1935), pp. 409–74.

Hsieh Hsing-yao 謝興堯 [Wu Chih 五知]. "Epilogue to Fa-i ch'u-chi" 跋髮逆初記, *I-ching* 逸經 (Shanghai), No. 17 (November 5, 1936).

———. "Hung-Yang luan-hou chih chiang-nan" 洪楊亂後之江南, in *Hung-Yang i-wen* 洪楊遺聞, collected in Hsieh Hsing Yao (compiler), *T'ai-p'ing t'ien-kuo ts'ung-shu shih-san chung* 太平天國叢書十三種. Peiping, 1938.

———. "T'ai-p'ing hua" 太平話, *I-ching* 逸經 (Shanghai), No. 3 (April 5, 1936).

Hsü Ti-shan 許地山. "Mo-ni chih erh-tsung san chi lun" 摩尼之二宗三際論, *Yenching Journal of Chinese Studies* (Peking), No. 3 (1928), pp. 383–402.

Jen Kuo-jung 任國榮. "Yao-shan chi-yu" 猺山記遊, *Chung-shan ta-hsüeh yü-yen li-shih hsüeh yen-chiu-so chou k'an* 中山大學語言歷史學研究所週刊 (Kuang-chou), Vol. III, No. 35–36 (July 4, 1928), pp. 64–69.

Jen [Chien] Yu-wen 簡又文. "Chung Wang ch'ing-pi kung-tz'u chih ch'u-pu yen-chiu" 忠王親筆供詞之初步研究, *Ssu-hsiang yü shih-tai* 思想與時代 (Taipei), No. 103 (February, 1963), pp. 2–10.

———. "T'ai-p'ing t'ien-kuo hsiang-chih k'ao" 太平天國鄉治考, *Journal of Oriental Studies* (University of Hong Kong), Vol. I, No. 2 (July, 1954), pp. 249–307.

———. "T'ai-p'ing t'ien-kuo ti chi-tu-chiao" 太平天國的基督教, *Chan-*

wang yüeh-k'an 展望月刊 (Hong Kong), Vol. V, No. 9, pp. 5–8; No. 10, pp. 4–8. This article is an abstract of the last three sections on religion in the author's *T'ai-p'ing t'ien-kuo tien-chih t'ung-k'ao* 太平天國典制通考. Hong Kong: Chien-shih meng-chin shu-wu, 1958.

———. "T'ai-p'ing t'ien-kuo t'ien-cheng k'ao" 太平天國田政考, *Journal of Oriental Studies* (University of Hong Kong), Vol. I, No. 1 (January, 1954), pp. 26–63.

Ku Huan 顧歡. "I-hsia lun" 夷夏論, in Yen K'o-chün 嚴可均, *Ch'üan shang-ku san-tai ch'in-han san-kuo liu-ch'ao wen* 全上古三代秦漢三國六朝文, "Ch'üan-ch'i wen," *chüan* 22. 1894 ed. 1930 reprint.

Kuo I-sheng 郭毅生. "Lun hsin-hsing shih-min teng-chi tsai t'ai-p'ing t'ien-kuo ko-ming chung ti tso-yung" 論新興市民等級在太平天國革命中的作用, *Li-shih yen-chiu* 歷史研究, No. 3, 1956.

Li Shih 李實. "Ch'iung-yai li-su chih-lüeh" 瓊崖黎俗誌略, *Kuo-wen chou-pao* 國聞週報, Vol. III, Nos. 41 and 42 (October 24 and 31, 1926).

Liu Tso-ch'üan 劉佐泉. "Kuan yü T'ai-p'ing t'ien-kuo ko-ming t'e-tien ti hsing-ch'eng wen-t'i" 關於太平天國革命特點的形成問題, *Li-shih yen-chiu* 歷史研究, No. 3, 1957, pp. 1–7.

Lo Erh-kang 羅爾綱. "Hsiang-hsiang Tseng-shih ts'ang Chung Wang Li Hsiu-ch'eng yüan-kung" 湘鄉曾氏藏忠王李秀成原供, *Chung-kuo she-hui ching-chi shih chi-k'an* 中國社會經濟史集刊, Vol. VIII, No. 1 (January, 1949), pp. 140–47.

———. "Nü-ying k'ao," 女營考, *Hsien-tai shih-hsüeh* 現代史學 (Kuang-chou), No. 1.

———. "T'ai-p'ing t'ien-kuo ching-chi k'ao" 太平天國經籍考, *Hsüeh-yüan* 學原 (Nanking), Vol. II, No. 1 (May, 1948).

Lung Sheng-yün 龍盛運. "T'ai-p'ing t'ien-kuo hou-ch'i tu-ti chih-tu ti shih-shih wen-t'i" 太平天国後期土地制度的實施問題, *Li-shih yen-chiu* 歷史研究, Vol. II (1958), pp. 35–54.

Mao I-heng 毛以亨. "T'ai-p'ing t'ien-kuo yü t'ien-ti hui" 太平天國與天地會 *Shen-pao yüeh-k'an* 申報月刊, Vol. IV, No. 1 (January, 1931).

"Mo-ni chiao ts'an-ching" 摩尼教殘經, *Kuo-hsüeh chi-k'an* 國學季刊 (Quarterly, Peking), Vol. I (1923), No. 3, pp. 531–46.

Nieh Ch'ung-ch'i 聶崇岐. "Erh-ch'ien-nien-lai mi-hsin chi-t'uan chih pien-luan" 二千年來迷信集團之變亂, *Ta-chung* 大中 (Peiping), Vol. I, No. 3 (March, 1946), pp. 19–28.

Editorial in *Peking jen-min jih-pao* 北京人民日報, January 11, 1951.

P'u Chiang-ch'ing 浦江清. "Pa-hsien k'ao" 八仙考, *Ch'ing-hua hsüeh-pao* 清華學報, Vol. XI, No. 1 (April, 1936), pp. 81–136.

Shigematsu Toshiaki 重松俊章. "Ch'u-ch'i ti pai-lien chiao-hui" 初期的
白蓮教會. Translated by T'ao Hsi-sheng 陶希聖, *Shih-huo pan-yüeh k'an*
食貨半月刊, Vol. I, No. 4, pp. 27–35.

T'ang Yung-t'ung 湯用彤. "Tu T'ai-p'ing ching so-chien" 讀太平經所見,
Kuo-hsüeh chi-k'an 國學季刊 (Quarterly, Peiping), Vol. V (1935), No. 1.

T'ao Ch'eng-chang 陶成章. "Chiao-hui yüan-liu k'ao" 教會源流考, in
Hsiao I-shan 蕭一山, *Chin-tai mi-mi she-hui shih-liao* 近代秘密社會史料.
Peiping, 1935. (Also in Lo Erh-kang 羅爾綱, *T'ien-ti hui wen-hsien lu*
天地會文獻錄. Shanghai, 1947.)

T'ao Hsi-sheng 陶希聖. "Sung-tai ti ko-chung pao-tung" 宋代的各種暴動,
Chung-shan wen-hua chiao-yü-kuan chi-k'an 中山文化教育舘季刊, Vol. I,
No. 2 (Winter, 1934), pp. 671–81.

Teng, Ssu-yü 鄧嗣禹. "Chung-kuo k'o-chü chih-tu ch'i-yüan k'ao"
中國科舉制度起源考, in *Shih-hsüeh nien-pao* 史學年報 (Peiping), September, 1934, pp. 275–84.

Tung Tso-pin 董作賓. "T'ien-li fa-wei" 天曆發微, in Lo Erh-kang 羅爾綱,
T'ai-p'ing t'ien-kuo shih k'ao-cheng chi 太平天國史考證集. Shanghai, 1948.

Wang Ying 王瑛. "T'ai-p'ing t'ien-kuo ko-ming ch'ien-hsi ti t'u-ti wen-
t'i" 太平天國革命前夕的土地問題, *Chung-shan wen-hua chiao-yü-kuan chi-
k'an* 中山文化教育舘季刊, Vol. III, No. 1 (Spring, 1936), pp. 167–85.

Wu Chih. See Hsieh Hsing-yao.

Wu Hsien-ch'ing 武仙卿. "Hsi-chin mo ti liu-min pao-tung" 西晉末的流民
暴動, *Shih-huo pan-yüeh k'an* 食貨半月刊 (Shanghai), Vol. I, No. 6
(February 16, 1935), pp. 3–7.

Wu Yen-nan 吳雁南. "Shih-lun T'ai-p'ing t'ien-kuo ti tu-ti chih-tu"
試論太平天國的土地制度, *Li-shih yen-chiu* 歷史研究 (Peking), Vol. II (1958)
pp. 17–34.

Yüan Ting-chung 袁定中. "Kuan yü T'ai-p'ing t'ien-kuo ko-ming ti
hsing-chih wen-t'i" 關於太平天國革命的性質問題, *Li-shih yen-chiu* 歷史
研究, No. 8, 1957, pp. 19–33.

BOOKS IN OTHER LANGUAGES

Bales, William L. *Tso Tsungt'ang, Soldier and Statesman of Old China*.
Shanghai: Kelly and Walsh, Ltd., 1937.

Blakiston, Thomas W. *Five Months on the Yang-tsze; with a Narrative of the
Exploration of Its Upper Waters, and Notices of the Present Rebellions in
China*. London: J. Murray, 1862.

Boardman, Eugene P. *Christian Influence upon the Ideology of the Taiping*

Rebellion, 1851–1864. Madison: University of Wisconsin Press, 1952.

Brine, Lindesay. *The Taeping Rebellion in China; A Narrative of Its Use and Progress, Based upon Original Documents and Information Obtained in China.* London: J. Murray, 1862.

Callery, Joseph Marie, and M. Yvan. *History of the Insurrection in China; With Notices of the Christianity, Creed, and Proclamations of the Insurgents.* Translated from French with a Supplementary Chapter Narrating the Most Recent Events, by John Oxenford. New York: Harper and Brothers, 1853.

Chang, Chung-li. *The Chinese Gentry: Studies on Their Role in Nineteenth-Century Chinese Society.* Seattle: University of Washington Press, 1955.

———. *The Income of the Chinese Gentry.* Seattle: University of Washington Press, 1962.

Chang Kuo-t'ao. Unpublished Memoirs.

Child, Arthur Henry. *The Problem of the Sociology of Knowledge.* Unpublished Ph.D. dissertation, Department of Philosophy, University of California at Los Angeles, 1939.

DeGré, Gerard L. *Society and Ideology: An Inquiry into the Sociology of Knowledge.* New York, 1943.

Edkins, Joseph. *Religion in China, Containing a Brief Account of the Three Religions of the Chinese: With Observations on the Prospects of Christian Conversion amongst that People.* 2d ed. London, 1878.

Fairbank, John King, and Masataka Banno. *Japanese Studies of Modern China: A Bibliographical Guide to Historical and Social-Science Research on the 19th and 20th Centuries.* Rutland, Vt., and Tokyo: Charles E. Tuttle Co. for Harvard-Yenching Institute, 1955.

Fishbourne, Edmund G. *Impressions of China, and the Present Revolution: Its Progress and Prospects.* London: Seeley, Jackson, and Halliday, 1855.

Forbes, Archibald. *Chinese Gordon: A Succinct Record of His Life.* London and New York: G. Routledge and Sons, 1884.

Fung [Feng], Yu-lan. *A History of Chinese Philosophy.* Translated by Derk Bodde. Princeton, N.J.: Princeton University Press. Vol. I, 2d English ed., 1952; Vol. II, 1st English ed., 1953.

———. *A Short History of Chinese Philosophy.* Edited by Derk Bodde. New York: Macmillan Co., 1948.

Groot, Jan Jacob Maria de. *Sectarianism and Religious Persecution in China: A Page in the History of Religions; in Two Volumes.* Amsterdam: Johannes Müller, 1904.

Hamberg, Theodore. *The Visions of Hung-Siu-tshuen, and Origin of the Kwang-si Insurrection.* (Hong Kong: China Mail, 1854.) Reprinted at Peiping: Yenching University Library, 1935.

Hsiao, Kung-chuan. *Rural China: Imperial Control in the Nineteenth Century.* Seattle: University of Washington Press, 1960.

Huc, Évariste Régis. *The Chinese Empire: Being a Sequel to the Work Entitled "Recollections of a Journey through Tartary and Thibet."* 2d ed. 2 vols. London: Longman, Brown, Green, and Longmans, 1855.

Hughes, Ernest Richard (editor and translator). *Chinese Philosophy in Classical Times.* (London: J. M. Dent and Sons, Ltd., 1942) New York: E. P. Dutton and Co., n.d.

Hummel, Arthur W. (ed.). *Eminent Chinese of the Ch'ing Period (1644–1912).* 2 vols. Washington, D. C.: United States Government Printing Office, 1943–44.

Hunter, William C. *Bits of Old China.* 2d ed. Shanghai and Hong Kong: Kelly and Walsh, Ltd., 1911.

Huntington, Ellsworth. *The Character of Races: As Influenced by Physical Environment, Natural Selection and Historical Development.* New York: C. Scribner's Sons, 1924.

Irwin, Richard Gregg. *The Evolution of a Chinese Novel: Shui-hu-chuan.* Cambridge, Mass.: Harvard University Press, 1953.

Jackson, A. V. Williams. *Researches in Manichaeism, with Special Reference to the Turfan Fragments.* New York: Columbia University Press, 1932.

Johnston, Reginald F. *Buddhist China.* London: J. Murray, 1913.

Karlgren, Bernhard (translator). *The Book of Odes.* Stockholm: Museum of Far Eastern Antiquities, 1950.

Latourette, Kenneth Scott. *A History of Christian Missions in China.* New York: Macmillan Co., 1929.

Legge, James. *The Chinese Classics, in Seven Volumes: With a Translation, Critical and Exegetical Notes, Prolegomena, and Copious Indexes.* 2d ed. revised. 7 vols. Oxford: Clarendon Press, 1893.

Lin-le [Augustus F. Lindley]. *Ti-ping Tien-Kwoh: The History of the Ti-ping Revolution, Including a Narrative of the Author's Personal Adventures.* 2 vols. London: Day and Son, Ltd., 1866.

Mackie, John Milton. *Life of Tai-ping-wang, Chief of the Chinese Insurrection.* New York: Dix, Edwards, and Co., 1857.

Malan, S. C. *Trimetrical Classic.* London: 1856.

Mannheim, Karl. *Ideology and Utopia: An Introduction to the Sociology of Knowledge.* New York: Harcourt, Brace, and Co., 1936.

Marx, Karl. *Marx on China 1853–1860: Articles from the New York Daily Tribune,* with an Introduction and Notes by Dona Torr. London: Lawrence and Wishart, 1951.

Maspero, Henri. *Mélanges posthumes sur les religions et l'histoire de la Chine.* 3 vols. Paris: Civilisations du Sud, S.A.E.P., 1950.

Masui Tsuneo 増井經夫. *Taihei tengoku* 太平天國. Iwanami Shinsho, 1951.

Meadows, Thomas T. *The Chinese and Their Rebellions, Viewed in Connection with Their National Philosophy, Ethics, Legislation, and Administration: To Which Is Added an Essay on Civilization and Its Present State in the East and West.* (London: Smith, Elder and Co., 1856.) Reprinted by Stanford University Press, 1953.

Michie, Alexander. *The Englishman in China During the Victorian Era, as Illustrated in the Career of Sir Rutherford Alcock, K.C.B., D.C.L., Many Years Consul and Minister in China and Japan.* 2 vols. Edinburgh: William Blackwood and Sons, 1900.

Morse, Hosea Ballou. *The International Relations of the Chinese Empire.* 3 vols. London, New York, Bombay, and Calcutta: Longmans, Green and Co. Vol. I, 1910; Vols. II and III, 1918.

Moule, Arthur Evans. *Half a Century in China: Recollections and Observations by the Venerable Arthur Evans Moule, B.D., with Illustrations and Map.* New York, 1911.

Nashimoto Yūhei 梨本祐平. *Taihei tengoku kakumei* 太平天國革命. Tokyo, 1942.

Richard, Timothy. *Forty-five Years in China.* London: T. Fisher Unwin, 1916.

Scarth, John. *Twelve Years in China: The People, the Rebels, and the Mandarins, by a British Resident.* Edinburgh: T. Constable and Co., 1860.

Sykes, W. H. *The Taeping Rebellion in China: Its Origin, Progress and Present Condition.* London: 1863.

Teng, Ssu-yü. *New Light on the History of the Taiping Rebellion.* Cambridge, Mass.: Harvard University Press, 1950.

Toriyama Kiichi 鳥山喜一. *Taihei tengoku ran no honshitsu* 太平天國亂の本質. 1934.

Toyama Gunji 外山軍治. *Taihei tengoku to Shanghai* 太平天國と上海. Kyoto, 1947.

Williams, Samuel Wells. *The Middle Kingdom: A Survey of the Geography, Government, Literature, Social Life, Arts, and History of the Chinese Empire and Its Inhabitants.* Rev. ed. 2 vols. New York: Charles Scribner's Sons, 1883.

Wolseley, Garnet J. *Narrative of the War with China in 1860; to Which Is Added the Account of a Short Residence with the Tai-ping Rebels at Nankin and a Voyage from Thence to Hankow*. London: Longman, Green, Longman, and Roberts, 1862.

Yano Jin'ichi 矢野仁一. *Kindai shinashi* 近代支那史. Kyoto, 1927

Yoshida Shōin 吉田松陰. *Shinkoku kampō ranki* 清國咸豊亂記. 1939.

ARTICLES IN OTHER LANGUAGES

Amano Motonosuke 天野元之助. "Taihei tengoku" 太平天國, *Tōyōshi kenkyu* 東洋史研究. Vol. XIII, No. 1–2 (1954), pp. 1–28.

Balázs, Etienne. "La crise sociale et la philosophie politique à la fin des Han," *T'oung Pao*, Series 2, Vol. XXXIX, Livr. 1–3 (1949), pp. 83–134.

Bielenstein, Hans. "The Restoration of the Han Dynasty," *Museum of Far Eastern Antiquities Bulletin* (Stockholm), No. 26 (1954), pp. 82–165.

Campbell, George. "Origin and Migrations of the Hakkas," *Chinese Recorder*, Vol. XLIII (August, 1912).

Chavannes, M. and P. Pelliot. "Un traité manichéen retrouvé en Chine," *Journal Asiatique*, Series 10, Vol. XVIII (November-December, 1911), pp. 499–617; and Series 11, Vol. I (January-February, 1913), pp. 7–199 and (March-April, 1913), pp. 8–394.

Chinese Repository. Monthly (Canton), Vols. I-XX. (1832–51).

Courcy, René de. "L'insurrection chinoise, son origine et ses progrès," *Revue des deux mondes*, Series 2, Vol. XXXIV (July 1, 1861) pp. 5-35 and (July 15, 1861) pp. 312–60.

Eichhorn, W. "Der Aufstand der Zauberin T'ang Sai-erh in Jahre 1420," *Oriens Extremus*, Vol. I, No. 1 (July, 1954), pp. 11–25.

Fairbank, John K. "Meadows on China: Centennial Review," *Far Eastern Quarterly*, Vol. XIV, No. 3 (May, 1955), pp. 365–71.

Forrest, Robert James. "The Christianity of Hung Tsiu Tsuen: A Review of Taeping Books," *Journal of the Royal Asiatic Society of Great Britain and Ireland, North China Branch*, New Series No. 4 (December, 1867), pp. 187–208.

Foster, John. "The Christian Origins of the Taiping Rebellion," *International Review of Missions*, Vol. XL, No. 158 (April, 1951), pp. 156–67.

Fujiwara Sadamu 藤原定. "Shihmmatsu ni okeru jinkō kajō no shogenshō to Taihei tengoku undō," 清末に於ける人口過剰の諸現象と太平天國運動, *Mantetsu chōsa geppō* 滿鉄調査月報, Vol. XIX, No. 7 (1939).

Hatano Yoshihiro 波多野善大. "Taihei tengoku ni kansuru nisan no mondai ni tsuite" 太平天國に關する二三の問題に就て, *Rekishigaku kenkyu* 歷史學研究, No. 150 (March, 1951), pp. 32–42.

Hsieh, T'ing-yü. "Origin and Migrations of the Hakkas," *Chinese Social and Political Science Review*, Vol. XIII, No. 2 (April, 1929), pp. 202–27.

Ichiko Chūzō 市古宙三. "Chūgoku ni okeru Taihei tengokushi no ken-kyū" 中國に於ける太平天國史の研究, *Shigaku zasshi* 史學雜誌, Vol. LX, No. 10 (October, 1951), pp. 71–80.

――――. "Haijō kō, Taihei tengoku seido kanken" 拜上考, 太平天國制度管見, *Ochanomizu joshi daigaku jimbunkagaku kiyō* お茶の女子大學, 人文科學紀要第一卷, Vol. I (March, 1952), pp. 33–45.

――――. "Taihei tengoku shōsho no kaisei" 太平天國詔書之改正, *Tōyō gakuhō* 東洋學報, Vol. XXXIII, No. 2 (October, 1950), pp. 183–99.

Jamieson, George (ed.). "Tenure of Land in China and the Condition of the Rural Population," *Journal of the Royal Asiatic Society of Great Britain and Ireland, North China Branch*, New Series Vol. XXIII (1888), pp. 59–174.

Jen [Chien] Yu-wen 簡又文. "The Marxian Interpretation of Taiping Tienkuo," *International Association of Historians of Asia, Second Biennial Conference Proceedings* (Taipei: Chinese Historical Association), 1962, pp. 745–76. A Chinese version of this article appeared in *Wen-t'i yü yen-chiu* 問題與研究 (Hong Kong), Vol. II, No. 3 (December, 1962), pp. 127–42.

Kawabata Genji 河鰭源治. "Tenchō dempo seido no seiritsu" 天朝田畝制度の成立, *Shigaku zasshi* 史學雜誌, Vol. LIX, No. 5 (May, 1950).

Laai, Yi-faa. "The Pirates and the Taiping t'ien-kuo." Unpublished manuscript.

Lechler, R. "The Hakka Chinese," *Chinese Recorder*, Vol. IX, No. 5 (September-October, 1878), pp. 352–59.

Lin, Yü-t'ang. "Feminist Thought in Ancient China," *T'ien Hsia Monthly* (Nanking), Vol. I, No. 2 (September, 1935), pp. 127–50.

Littell, John B. "Missionaries and Politics in China—The Taiping Rebellion," *Political Science Quarterly*, Vol. XLIII, No. 4 (December, 1928), pp. 566–99.

Medhurst, W. H. "Ceremonial Regulations of the T'hae-ping Dynasty," *North China Herald and Supreme Court and Consular Gazette*, No. 155 (June 16, 1853).

――――. "Connection between Foreign Missions and the Kwang-se Insurrection," *ibid.*, Nos. 160 and 161 (August 20 and 27, 1853).

————. Letter, *ibid.*, No. 174 (November 26, 1853).

Miyagawa Hisashi 宮川尚志. "Shoki Taihei tengoku no shukyōsei" 初期 太平天國の宗教性, *Jimbun kagaku* 人文科學, Vol. I, No. 3 (December, 1946).

Nohara Shirō 野原四郎. "Taihei tengoku no ran" 太平天國の亂, chapter 4 of *Tōyō kinseishi* 東洋近世史, in *Sekai rekishi taikei* 世界歷史大系 Vol. IX, ed. Matsui Hitoshi 松井等 of Heibonsha. 1934.

North China Herald and Supreme Court and Consular Gazette (Shanghai), 1853–64, *passim.*

Ōtani Kōtarō 大谷孝太郎. "Taihei tengoku no ichizuke" 太平天國の位置 付 , *Hikone ronsō* 彦根論叢, No. 8 (March, 1952), pp. 33–50 and No. 10 (July, 1952), pp. 26–45.

Pelliot, P. "La secte du Lotus blanc et la secte de Nuage blanc," *Bulletin de l'École française d'Extrême-Orient,* Vol. III (1903), pp. 304–17, and Vol. IV (1904), pp. 336–40.

————. "Les Mo-ni et le Houa-hou-king," *ibid.*, Vol. III (1903), pp. 18–27.

Sano Manabu 佐野學. "Taihei tengoku kakumei" 太平天國革命, in Part 3 of Vol. III of his *Shin-chō shakai-shi* 清朝社會史. Tokyo, 1947.

Sargent, W. "The Chinese Rebellion," *North American Review,* Vol. LXXIX, No. 164 (July, 1854), pp. 158–200.

Shigematsu Toshiaki 重松俊章. "T'ang-sung shih-tai chih mi-le-chiao-fei" 唐宋時代之彌勒教匪, *Shien* 史淵, No. 3, Kyushu Teidai Shigaku-kai hakko 九州帝大史学会発行.

Shih, Vincent Y. C. "The Ideology of the Taiping T'ien-Kuo," *Sinologica,* Vol. III, No. 1 (1951), pp. 1–15.

————. "The Mind and the Moral Order," *Mélanges chinois et bouddhiques,* Vol. X (1955), pp. 347–64.

Shimizu T. 清水泰次. "Minsho no minsei: kan o osae min o agu" 明初の 民政一官を抑え民をあぐ一, *Tōyōshi kenkyū* 東洋史研究, Vol. XIII, No. 3 (August, 1954), pp. 180–200.

Stelle, Charles C. "Ideologies of the T'ai P'ing Insurrection," *Chinese Social and Political Science Review,* Vol. XX, No. 1 (April, 1936), pp. 140–49.

Tanaka Suiichirō 田中萃一郎. "Taihei tengoku" 太平天國, *Shigaku zasshi* 史學雜誌, Vol. XXIII, No. 7 (July, 1912), pp. 767–86.

Taylor, George E. "The Taiping Rebellion: Its Economic Background and Social Theory," *Chinese Social and Political Science Review,* Vol. XVI, No. 4 (January, 1933), pp. 545–614.

Tsukamoto Zenryū 塚本善隆. "Hokugi no Bukkyō hi" 北魏の佛教匪, in *Shina Bukkyō shi kenkyū, Hokugi hen* 支那佛教史研究, 北魏篇. Tokyo, 1942.

Wright, Mary C. "From Revolution to Restoration: The Transformation of Kuomintang Ideology," *Far Eastern Quarterly*, Vol. XIV, No. 4 (August, 1955), pp. 515–32.

Yamamoto Hideo 山本秀夫. "Chūgoku ni okeru itan shisō no tenkai" 中國に於ける異端思想の展開, *Tōyō gakkai* 東洋學界, No. 9 (June, 1952).

Yap, P. M. "The Mental Illness of Hung Hsiu-ch'üan, Leader of the Taiping Rebellion," *Far Eastern Quarterly*, Vol. XIII, No. 3 (May, 1954), pp. 287–304.

GOVERNMENT DOCUMENTS

Great Britain. Parliament. British Sessional Papers, House of Commons. Readex Microprint ed., edited by Edgar L. Erickson. New York: 1943–52.

> *Papers Relating to the Rebellion in China, and Trade in the Yang-tze-Kiang River*, 1862, Vol. LXIII.

> *Papers Respecting the Civil War in China*. 1852–53, Vol. LXIX.

United States.

Correspondence of Robert M. McLane and Peter Parker, late commissioners of the United States in China, with the Department of State. (35th Congress, 2d session; Senate Executive Document No. 22, Serial 982, Vol. VIII.) Washington, D.C.: Government Printing Office, 1858–59.

"Marshall, Humphrey, to Marcy." (33d Congress, 1st session; House Executive Document No. 123, Serial 734, Vol. XVI.) Washington, D.C.: Government Printing Office, 1853–54.

BIBLIOGRAPHY

Wright, Mary C. "From Revolution to Restoration: The Transformation of Kuomintang Ideology," *Far Eastern Quarterly*, Vol. XIV, No. 4 (Aug. 1955), pp. 515-532.

Yakhontov, Victor A. [?] "Chiang's hope to take over power," *Inprecor*, Vol. 9, No. 4 (June, 1928).

Yang, K. H. "The Mental Make of China: Revolution Leader of the Taiping Rebellion," *Pacific Affairs Review*, Vol. XIII, No. 3 (May, 1960), pp. 289-304.

GOVERNMENT DOCUMENTS

Great Britain. Parliament. British Sessional Papers, House of Commons. *Trade Reports on the...* London, 1912-1932.

Parliamentary Debates... Commons and Lords of the House of Commons, 1899. Vol. 75, 131, etc.

Peace Handbook... Vol. II, London, 1920-21, Vol. I-XII.

United States.

Correspondence in Relation to Chinese and Peruvian Governments...
Senate Documents... Vol. VIII, 2d Session, 14th Congress to Present...
44 d Sess., 1920-21.

Marshall, Humphrey to Adams...
Executive Documents No. 123, 33rd Vol. XVI, Washington, U.S. Government Printing Office, 1931-35.

Index

by

Dorothy Jean Ray

Address: as aspect of social distinctions, 52; forms of discussed, 214–15

Adultery, 36 and n, 65–66, 68

Aleni, Giulio, 397

"All Men Are Brothers," 268 and n, 288, 289, 290–91, 294, 295, 297

America: trade with, 451, 481; mentioned, 133n, 138. *See also* United States

Amano Motonosuke: quoted on Taipings, 466–67

Amitābha, 356 and n, 357

An Lu-shan, 223

An Shih-kao, 274

Analects: quoted, 42, 61, 63, 167, 173, 174, 182, 185, 188, 189, 197, 198, 199, 201, 202, 203, 204, 208, 244, 245–46, 248, 376; mentioned, 324

Ancestor worship: in Confucianism, 28; discussed, 272; and Hakkas, 311, 312; mentioned, 368

Anhwei, 63, 65, 98, 107n, 233, 338, 481, 483

Annals of Spring and Autumn, 240, 246, 247, 248, 251, 388, 399, 441, 493

Anthropomorphism: in Taiping religion, 8–9, 271

"Anti-Five Elements," 229

Aristotle, 201

Army: acceptance of ideology, xiv; size and growth of Taiping, 488. *See also* Military system

Asanga, 274

Assistant King. *See* I Wang

Astrology. *See* Divination

Atonement, 157

Australia, 138

Bales, William L.: quoted on Taiping Rebellion, 428–29

Banditry, 373, 485

Banno, Masataka: quoted, 460n, 464

Baptism, 157

"Barbarian states": identification of, 353n

Battle: rank in, 59. *See also* Army; Military system

Bible: and Hung Hsiu-ch'üan, 148; use of by Taipings, 156–60, 162, 201, 327–28, 410–18 *passim*, 431, 432, 466. *See also* New Testament; Old Testament

Blakiston, Thomas W.: quoted on Taiping religion, 405; quoted on Taiping movement, 417–18

Boardman, Eugene: quoted, 149, 150, 151, 155 and n, 156 and n, 160, 414n; quoted on Christian sources in Taiping ideology, 431, 432 and n

Bonham, Sir George, 20, 404, 410

Book collectors, 43

Book of Changes: quoted, 75, 120, 127, 157, 164, 169, 171, 174, 175–76, 177, 183, 194, 201, 204, 205, 236, 243, 244, 245, 248n

Book of Chou, 166

"Book of Declarations of the Divine Will Made During the Heavenly Father's Descent to Earth": quoted, 10, 182; editions compared, 110; and Hakka idioms, 316

"Book of Heavenly Commandments": and stand on idols, 23; and stand on adultery,

36 and n, 66; quoted, 31, 38, 40, 153; editions compared, 124–27, 169. *See also* Heavenly Commandments

"Book of Heavenly Decrees and Proclamations": quoted, 43; and use of novels, 287

Book of History: quoted, 44, 112, 121, 125, 126, 127, 137, 157, 160, 167, 169, 170, 171n, 176, 177, 180n, 182, 197, 201, 205, 206, 223, 240, 242, 253n, 398; discussing T'ien, 172, 173, 174–75

Book of Odes: quoted, 121

Book of Poetry: quoted, 44, 114, 125, 126, 137, 167, 169, 170, 173n, 176, 178 and n, 193n, 196, 197, 199–200, 206, 241, 398

Book of Religious Precepts, 19

Book of Rites, 167

"Book on the Principles of the Heavenly Nature": quoted, 11, 24–25, 31, 37, 47, 81–82, 170, 206; publication of, 92; editions of, 112; and title of, 166; and *li*, 188; and heroes quoted from novels, 287; mentioned, 317

Bourgeois, 451, 452, 453n, 459

Bowring, Sir John, 412, 424

Bridgman, E. C., 407, 489

Brilliant Sect, 348n

Brine, Lindesay: quoted, 402–3 and n

British Museum, 151n

Brotherhood of man: discussed, 45–46, 49, 159–60, 208–10, 300, 312, 434. *See also* *Chung-i*

Brothers: relationship of, 189, 190, 195, 196

Bruce, Mr., 403, 424

Buddha-ksetra, 355 and n, 357

Buddhisatva, 151

Buddhism: and Taipings, 23, 26–27, 28, 29, 121, 319, 416, 430, 466, 473; and Hung Jen-kan, 136; term discussed, 143, 144, 145; and moral retribution, 205; and Yüan Mei, 228–29; ideas and terms borrowed by Taipings, 273–75; and Hakkas, 312; in discussion of sorcery, 325; attacked by *T'ai-p'ing ching*, 340–41; and rebels, 343n; and revival of Chang Chüeh's beliefs, 345–47; and sects discussed, 355–59; and secret societies, 361; and Ming Yü-chen, 369; and Roaming Bandits, 383; and rebellions, 384, 388; and Catholicism, 397; mentioned, 11, 24, 123, 276, 310n, 324, 348n, 362, 368, 379, 406, 407

Bunyan, John, 448

Bureau for the Compilation of Ming History, 247

Calendar: revision of, 74–75, 88, 160, 243, 400, 458

"Calendar by Imperial Sanction, the Third Year," 91

Callery, J. M.: quoted, 401–2, 410

Campbell, George: quoted, 304 and n, 305, 306

Camps: of occupation groups discussed, 50–51

Canton, 147, 305n, 323, 403, 408, 424, 428, 485

Capacity of the heart: discussed, 48–49

Catholic missionaries, 397, 402–3

Cha-chi, 242

Ch'a-han-t'ieh-mu-erh, 366

Chang Chi-keng (author), 396n

Chang Chüeh: and Yellow Turbans, 338–42; and revival of beliefs, 345–47; and magical healing, 386; mentioned, 237n, 351n, 361, 384, 417

Chang Chung-li, 470

Chang Fang-p'ing, 204

Chang Fei (in novel), 287, 290, 296

Chang Ho-fu, 396n

Chang Hsien-chung, 28; and Roaming Bandits discussed, 373, 380–83, 384; intrigue of, 375 and n

Chang Ju-nan, 396n

Chang Kuo-shen, 378

Chang Kuo-t'ao: quoted, 496

Chang Liang of the Han, 242, 339

Chang Pao, 339

Chang Pin-lin: 248, quoted, 297

Chang Pin-yüan: quoted, 62

Chang Shih-ch'eng, 362n, 366

Chang T'ai-yen. *See* Chang Pin-lin

Chang Te-chien: quoted on homage, 35; quoted on marriage, 71; quoted on leadership, 92; quoted on treason, 100; quoted on religious leaders, 106–7, 108; quoted on *Chou-li*, 254n; quoted on local officials system, 262 and n, 263, 264; and novels, 285, 286; as author, 396n

Chang Tsai of the Sung, 170–71, 207 and n, 210, 211, 237

Chang Wan-ju, 63

Chang Ya-tzu. *See* Wen Ch'ang

Chang Yen, 345

Ch'ang-an: capture of, 343

Ch'ang-hen-ko chuan, 238

Ch'ang-sha, 8, 56, 488

Ch'ang-shan Chao tzu-lung (in novel), 287

"Ch'ang-ti" (poem), 196

Chanism, 251

Chao Ching-hsien, 102

Chao Chün-yung: and Maitreya, 358, 360

Chao I: quoted, 343, 363, and n, 372
Chao Kai, 291
Chao, King, 320
Chao Kuang-ch'a, 395n
Chao-lin, 380
Chao Liu-chin: revolt of, 370
Chao Niu-ssu, 358
Chao-shu kai-hsi pan-hsing lun: quoted, 43
Chao Tao-i of the Yüan: quoted, 278
Chao Tsung-fu: quoted, 374
Chao Tzu (Yüan official), 369
Chao-tzu, 240
Chao Wang. See Huang Wen-ying
Ch'ao-chou (place), 323
Ch'ao-ch'uang hsiao-shih: quoted from, 379
Character of Races: quoted from, 304
Chavannes, M.: quoted, 348n, 351n-52n
Che district, 345, 349n, 351n
Che-tsung of the Sung: and T'ai-p'ing tao, 345; reign of, 346
Chekiang, 338, 345, 346, 350, 351n, 481, 483
Chen-an fu-chih: quoted, 318
Chen-hsin (true mind), 33
Chen-tao (true doctrine), 31, 128
Ch'en Chien-hu: revolt of, 370
Ch'en Chin-nan, 299
Ch'en-chou, 322
Ch'en Han, 370
Ch'en-hsi, 322
Ch'en-hsü-ch'iao, 234
Ch'en Hsün-tz'u: and views of Taiping's success, 441
Ch'en Hui-yen: quoted, 63, 396n, 397
Ch'en Kuang, 351n
Ch'en Kung-lu: quoted on Taipings, 436
Ch'en Miao-ch'ang, 237n
Ch'en Ping-wen, 69
Ch'en She. See Ch'en Sheng
Ch'en Sheng, 359, 385, 454, 484
Ch'en Sheng and Wu Kuang rebellion: discussed, 330–33; mentioned, 334
Ch'en Shih-chen, 350
Ch'en Tsung-yang, 67, 225n
Ch'en Yin-k'o: quoted on Chou-li, 266–67, 268n
Ch'en Yu-liang, 367, 369
Ch'en Yü-ch'eng, 255n, 316
Ch'en Yüan: quoted, 223, 348n, 352n
Cheng (uprightness), 33, 92n, 93, 104, 183–88
Cheng Ch'eng-kung, 297, 298
Cheng Ch'iao: quoted on Chou-li, 258n
"Cheng-chi ko," 183
Cheng Ching-pi of the Sung: quoted, 277–78

Cheng Huo: and plant collections, 350n
Cheng Hsüan of the Han: quoted, 179, 180 and n, 214–15, 218, 232, 243, 262n
Cheng-jen (upright man), 33
Cheng Po-ch'ien, 236n
Cheng-tsai, 278, 279
Cheng-t'ung period, 370
Cheng-tzu t'ung: quoted, 317
"Cheng-yüeh": quoted from, 211
Ch'eng (sincerity), 291
Ch'eng-Chu school, 251, 470
Ch'eng, King, 177
Ch'eng-kuang, Queen, 321
Ch'eng Mu-t'ang, 43
Ch'eng-t'ang, 176n, 295
Ch'eng-tzu, 207
Ch'eng Yan-sheng, 6n, 439
Ch'eng-yang, 322
Chi (Hupeh), 338
Chi, 117, 118
Chi-le pien: quoted, 345, 347n
Chi Wen-yüan, 21
Ch'i (state), 246, 322
Ch'i-chiao, 195
Ch'i-chou, 316
Ch'i district, 372
Ch'i, Duke, 246
Ch'i, Prince, 248n
Ch'i-sha pei, 380
Ch'i Shao-pao, 254n
Ch'i-tao: quoted, 72
Ch'i Yen-ming: revolt of, 370
Chia-ching, 370
Chia-ch'ing: reign of, 301, 458, 476
Chia-ku, 246
Chia Kung-yen of the T'ang: quoted on t'ien shen, 179, 180; quoted on li, 215; quoted on land, 232
Chia Lu, 359
Chia-shen ch'ao-shih hsiao-chi: quoted, 381
Chia-shen san pai-nien chi: quoted, 378
Chia Shu-ts'un, 457n
Chia-ying, 61, 305 and n, 308 and n, 309 and n, 310
Chia-ying chou-chih: quoted, 308, 310, 311, 327
Chiang brothers, 197
Chiang Kai-shek, 437, 493
Chiang-nan, 335, 360
Chiang-nan ch'un-meng-an pi-chi, 89
Chiang-ning. See Nanking
Chiang po-ch'ien: quoted on Three periods, 213
Chiang River, 335
Chiang Te-sheng, 62
Chiang T'ing-fu, 489

Chiang-tu, 321
Chiang Tzu-ya (in novel), 287
"Chiao-hui yüan-liu k'ao." *See* Study in the Development of Secret Societies
Ch'iao Ying-chia, 373
Chieh, 116
Ch'ien (modesty), 201
Ch'ien Chang, 452
Ch'ien Chia-chü: quoted, 482
Ch'ien Ch'ien-i: quoted on Maitreya, 361, 363n
Ch'ien-lung: reign of, xi, 286; period, 480
Ch'ien Mu: quoted on Taipings 436-37
Ch'ien Pan-ch'i: quoted, 377, 378
Ch'ien-shan, 233
Ch'ien Ta-hsin, 286
Ch'ien-tzu chao. *See* "Thousand Character Decree"
Ch'ien-tzu-wen, 165
Chih-cheng: reign of, 359
Chih-hsin lu: and feudalism 252
Chihli, 483
Chih-ma Li: and Maitreya, 358, 360
Chih-p'an, 348n, 355, 356 and n
Ch'ih-hsi (place), 323
Ch'ih-mei. See Red Eyebrows
Ch'ih-ts'ai shih-mo. See Manichaeism
Chin dynasty, 75, 144, 222, 223, 225, 242, 321, 356, 381
"Chin-hsin," 182
Chin-hu ch'i-mo: quoted, 68
Chin Jen-jui: poem quoted, 289-90; quoted on fraternity, 291-92
Chin-ling, 63, 65, 68, 86. *See also* Nanking
"Chin-ling chi-shih tsa-yung," 266
Chin-ling kuei-chia chi-shih lüeh: quoted from, 55, 65
Chin-p'ing-mei, 144n
Chin-shih: title discussed by Jen-kan, 269
Chin-tai mi-mi she-hui shih-liao: quoted from, 301
Chin-t'ien: revolution in, 61, 305; mentioned, 58, 68, 201, 209, 453, 459, 487
Ch'in dynasty, 11, 43, 88, 127, 239, 330-36 *passim,* 355, 417, 443, 447, 454; collapse of, 359
Ch'in-Han, 123
Ch'in Jih-kan (Yen Wang): death of, 21; enlistment of, 23, 60; insignia of, 54; document of quoted, 316. *See also* Yen Wang
Ch'in Shih-huang-ti, 332n, 334-35
Ch'in-ting shih-chieh t'iao-li. See "Imperial Regulations Governing Scholarly Ranks"
Ch'in-tsung: defeat of, 4

Ch'in Tung-fu, 43
China: as a spiritual continent, 6, 101-2; unification of, and Hung Jen-kan, 138-39; unification discussed, 235, 238-39
Chinese People's Communist Liberation Army, 496
Ching (place), 246, 338
Ching (reverence): discussed, 34-35
Ching-hua-yüan: quoted, 227-28 and n
Ching of Liang, 237n
Ching, Prince of Ch'eng-yang, 322
Ching-shan yeh-shih (novel), 396n, 398
Ch'ing (place), 338
Ch'ing: system of, 216-17
Ch'ing army, 21n, 61, 62
Ch'ing-ch'ao chüan-shih. See Complete History of the Ch'ing Dynasty
Ch'ing Court: and novels, 287
Ch'ing dynasty, xvi and n, 21n, 43, 104, 133, 144n, 165n, 180, 182n, 205, 219, 220, 221, 240, 242, 247, 249, 270n, 280, 296, 297, 298, 309, 319, 355, 357, 385, 396n, 398, 399, 436, 437, 443, 458, 470, 475, 476, 477, 480, 493, 495
Ch'ing feng, 175
Ch'ing-hsi k'ou-kuei: quoted from, 345, 352, 353
Ch'ing-li of the Sung, 270
Ch'ing-nang ching. See Green Bag Classic
Ch'ing scholars, 252, 253
Ch'ing-shih kao. See Draft of the History of the Ch'ing Dynasty
Ch'ing-tai t'ung-shih, 254n
Chinkiang-fu, 233
Chiu i-chao sheng-shu: quoted, 43
"Chiu i-ch'ieh t'ien-sheng t'ien-yang yü": editions compared, 132-33
Chiu-li, 26
Chiu T'ang-shu: quoted, 344
Ch'iung-ya (Hainan Island), 318
Chou Chung, 377
Chou, Duke, 177-78, 236n, 253n, 256n, 258n
Chou dynasty, 42, 117, 123, 124, 127, 169, 176, 178, 217n, 229n, 242, 255n, 258n, 267, 268, 287 and n, 295, 296, 320, 325, 333, 335
Chou Hsi-neng: treachery of, 95 and n, 99-100; mentioned, 10
Chou Hsin, King, 116, 126, 248n
Chou Hsing-ssu: as author, 165
Chou, King of, 240
Chou Ku-ch'eng: quoted, 363n-64n; and discussion of Taipings, 443-44
"Chou-kuan ching," 267n
Chou Kuei, 377

Chou-li: quoted, 179, 180, 211, 214; quoted on rank, 217 and n, 218; quoted on sumptuary laws, 219; quoted on land distribution, 230, 231, 232; change of name, 253 and n; and Taiping military institutions discussed, 253–68; and Ming Yü-chen, 369; mentioned, 236n

"Chou-nan" (poem), 199, 200 and n

Chou Pan-fu (author), 396n

Chou Shen-jung, 28

Chou Sheng, 378

Chou Tzu-Wang, 361

Chou Wen, 331

Chou Yen-ju, 377

Ch'ou, Duke of Kuo, 324–25

Christ. *See* Jesus

Christian Influence upon the Ideology of the Taiping Rebellion, 149, 414n

Christianity: in Taiping ideology, xii–xiii, xv–xvi, xvii, 4n, 273, 275, 293, 300, 302, 303, 312, 357–58, 397, 400, 425, 427–32 *passim,* 432, 437, 441–48 *passim,* 452, 456, 460–66 *passim,* 483, 488; and Hung Jen-kan, 136–40; discussed, 144, 145, 147–64; and Hung Hsiu-ch'üan, 212; and Hakkas, 312, 314; and Yellow Turbans, 342; and Taipings in Western evaluation, 401, 402, 403–19, 422–24; as substitute for fatalism, 472–74

Chu Chieh-ch'in: quoted, 228

Chu Chiu-t'ao, 302–3, 428 and n

"Chu Chiu-t'ao k'ao": quoted, 302

Chu Chu-p'ei, 107n

Chu Ch'ung, 349n

Chu Hsi (Chu-tzu), 108, 200, 207 and n, 211, 251, 252

Chu Hsi-tsu: quoted, 439, 444

Chu Hung-ying: and uprising, 492

Chu K'ai of the Yüan, 236n

Chu-ko Liang: quoted, 206

Chu Mien: and Fang La, 349–50, 352 and n, 353, 354

Chu T'ung-meng (governor), 373

Chu-yao hsi-wen, 134

Chu Yüan-chang, 400, 456; rebellion of discussed, 362–70

Ch'u (state), 240

Ch'u Chih-fu: quoted, 233, 253n–54n

Ch'u district, 320, 321, 322, 331

Ch'u-tz'u chang-chü: quoted from, 320

Chü-jen: title discussed by Hung Jen-kan, 269

Chü-lu, 338

Chü Ssu-fu, 352

Chü-tzu, 280

Ch'ü-fou, 28

Ch'ü Hsüan-ying: quoted on sorcery, 321

"Ch'ü-li," 165n

Ch'ü Shih-ssu, 102

Ch'ü Yüan (poet), 320

Chuan Yü, 127

Ch'uan-hsi lu: and Neo-Confucianism, 277

"Ch'üan-jen [min?] chieh-yen chao," 315–16

"Ch'üan-shih liang-yen." *See* "Good Words to Admonish the Age"

Ch'üan Tsu-wang, 249

Chuang, 60

Chuang Chi-yü of the Sung: quoted on *T'ai-p'ing tao,* 345

Chuang, Duke, 212

Chuang-tzu, 208

Ch'uang-tzu: in treatment of sick, 326–27

Ch'uang, Prince. *See* Li Tzu-ch'eng

Chun: idea of, 95

Ch'un-chiu period, 250

Ch'un-ch'iu. See Annals of Spring and Autumn

Ch'un-ch'iu ching-chuan yin-te: quoted, 175, 189, 191, 212–13, 214, 221; mentioned, 179n, 215

Ch'un-ch'iu fan-lu, 143n

Chün-p'ing *chou:* and change of name, 374

"Chün-tao," 185

Chün-tz'u shih-lu, 134

Chung (loyalty): discussed, 35–36; mentioned, 291

Chung-hsia (China), 131

Chung-hua (China), 129

Chung-hua ch'üan-kuo feng su chih, 322

Chung-i (brotherhood): as theme of novels, 288–93. *See also* Brotherhood of man

Chung-kuo (Chinese), 133

Chung-kuo chin-tai li-shih yen-chiu kang-yao, 449–50

Chung-kuo chin-tai shih: quoted, 436

Chung-kuo hsiao-shuo shih-lüeh: quoted, 144

Chung-kuo mi-mi she-hui shih: quoted, 297

Chung-kuo she-hui shih-liao ts'ung-ch'ao: quoted on sorcery, 321

"Chung-kuo t'ung-meng hui hsüan-yen," 493

Chung Wang: confession of, xiv; residence of, 20; mentioned, 411, 412, 419, 420, 421. *See also* Li Hsiu-ch'eng

"Chung-yung." *See* Doctrine of the Mean

Clarendon, Earl of, 404

Class structure. *See* Social structure

Classical allusions, 111, 112. *See also* Classics

Classics: Taiping revision of, 42–44; in Taiping thought, 165–272 *passim;* 472, 473, 474

Collected Intelligence Report on the Rebels: quoted, 46, 51, 58, 60, 63, 71, 76, 77, 83, 92, 94, 95, 96, 98, 99, 106, 108, 109, 305, 488

Commoners: *See* Social structure

Communism, 436, 493, 494, 495; and interpretations of Taipings discussed, xvii, xviii, 449–58, 459, 460 and n, 461, 462–63; and relations with Taipings, 264, 470, 496–98; and relation to Taiping land system, 444, 446, 447

Complete History of the Ch'ing Dynasty: quoted, 458, 476

Concubines, 55, 56 and n, 63, 68, 69, 71, 72, 73, 100, 198, 199. *See also* Harem

Confucius: and God, 10, 13; and Yen Hui, 36, 40; discussed in Taiping Heavenly Chronicle, 41; quoted, 48–49, 51, 118, 119, 167, 231; and *Tao-t'ung*, 128; and rectification of names, 134, 187, 244; and fate, 204; and Kuan Chung, 245–46, 250, 251; and barbarism, 247; and cultural issue, 253; and Taiping attitude toward discussed, 271, 272, 472–74; birth of, 278–79; mentioned, 116, 117, 221, 236n, 297, 324

Confucianism: and reintroduction of, xiv, 486; and Taipings, 23, 28–29, 34, 41, 200, 239–40, 398, 400, 406, 407, 408, 415, 416, 429, 430, 432n, 444, 447; and the mind, 32n; and Taiping revision of classics, 42–44; Hung's knowledge of, 108; Hung Jen-kan's knowledge of, 133–40 *passim;* term discussed, 143 and n, 144, 145; and brotherhood, 159–60; in Taiping beliefs discussed, 165–272 *passim,* 462; quoted on spirits, 178; and human nature, 182; and love and brotherhood, 209–10; and peace, 235–36; and Hakkas, 311, 314; and Ming Yü-chen, 369; and rebellions, 384, 388; and rulers, 470, 471; mentioned, 280, 325, 347, 348n, 368, 378, 464n

Conroy, 421

Corvée, 334, 354, 484

Court ceremony: of Taipings discussed, 55–56

"Court Etiquette of the Rebel Dynasty," 92

Creation: Taiping version of, 4–5

Culbertson, M. S.: quoted, 402, 424–25

Davis, Sir John F.: observations on famine, 482

Death: in Chinese belief discussed, 386–87

Debts: of farmers, 478, 482

Demons: possession of discussed, 158, 327–28. *See also* Devils; Imps

Devil-Worshipers, 384, 385–86, 387. *See also* Vegetarianism

Devils: killing of, 13, 14; belief in by Taipings, 16, 28, 201; and idolatry, 25, 26; concept of discussed, 150–51, 156, 274, 275. *See also* Demons; Imps

Dew King. *See* Yü Wang

Dharma, 346

Diamond Sūtra, 346, 347, 356n

Diaz, Emmanuel, 397

Discrimination. *See* Equality; Rank

Divination, 75, 375. *See also* Geomancy

Divine visitation: used by leaders, 95–97, 96n–97n

Doctrine of the Mean, 251, 388

Doty, Elihu: quoted, 402n

Draft of the History of the Ch'ing Dynasty: quoted from, 219, 480

Drinking, 76

Eastern King. *See* Tung Wang; Yang Hsiu-ch'ing

Eberhard, Wolfram, 470

Economic: factors in Taiping society discussed, 81–84, 477–87; borrowings from traditional sources, 230–35

"Edict Exhorting the People to Cease Smoking Opium," 315–16

Edicts: in religious observances, 22; collected, 128–29; and prohibition of novels, 286. *See also* Law

Edkins, Joseph, 23, 133n; criticism of Taiping religion, 405, 408, 411

Egypt, 138

"Elements of Military Tactics on Troop Operations," 103

Elgin, Lord, 403, 423

Elohim, 154

Embroidery Camp, 100

Encyclopaedia of the Social Sciences: quoted on revolutions, 388–89

England: attitude toward Taiping aims, 89; war with China, 428; relations with, 451, 452, 453, 481, 482; mentioned, 133n, 138

Equality: in Taiping society, 46–47, 49–50, 60; of sexes, 60–66, 72; discussed, 237–38 and n; of man, 472. *See also* Rank; Social structure

Erh-che, 351n

Erh-shih, 330

"Essay on the Barbarians and the Chinese," 247

Essays: written as examinations, 98–99 and

n, 376
Ethnic issue: and Yang Hsiu-ch'ing, 109;
and Hung Jen-kan, 134; discussed, 245–
53, 300, 471; in rebellions, 355, 361,
385, 401; and Chu Yüan-chang, 366–
68; and Taipings, 440, 444, 461, 465,
486; and Chiang Kai-shek, 494–95. *See
also* Communism; Hakka; Manchus;
Miaos; Mongols
Examinations, 41–43, 62–63, 247; and degrees, 46, 88, 253; role of discussed, 98–
99; change in names of, 135; system revived, 268–69; and Hung Jen-kan's Imperial Regulations quoted, 269–71; and
Hakkas, 308 and n, 309n, 314; subjects
of, 376; and gentry, 470, 471, 472

Fa-i ch'u-chi: quoted, 60
Fa-yen: quoted, 191
Fahs, Charles F.: quoted, 424, 425
Fairbank, John K.: quoted, 460n, 464
Family: of God, 9; ordering of, 244. *See
also* Martial relations; Polygamy
Famine, 234; prior to Taiping Rebellion,
482, 483
Fan-po: capture of, 246
Fan Ts'ung: and Red Eyebrows rebellion,
336, 337–38
Fan Yeh, 208
Fan Wen-lan: quoted on Taipings, 450,
451n, 452–53, 489; quoted on Commu-
nist-Taiping link, 497–98
Fang (of military organization): descrip-
tion of, 338 and n, 339
Fang Chao-ying: quoted on Hakkas, 308n–
309n
Fang Ching, 107n
Fang Kuo-chen, 362
Fang La, 288, 289, 345, 349–55, 360, 385
Fang Shao: quoted, 345, 352n; quoted on
Chang Chüeh, 345; quoted on Fang La,
349–50, 352n, 353–54
Farmers: *See* Peasants
Fatalism: in Taiping belief, 39–41, 487;
sources of, 174; attitude toward dis-
cussed, 203–8; substitution for by Tai-
pings, 472–74. *See also* Mandate of
Heaven
Fate. *See Ming*
Father: relationship with, 190, 191, 192
Feng (influence): meaning of, 200 and n;
mentioned, 199
Feng (general), 86
Feng-chien system: discussed, 252, 332n,
333. *See also* Feudalism
Feng-hsiang, 72

Feng-hu cha-chi: quoted from, 309
Feng Kuei-fen: quoted, 481
Feng-shen chuan, 287 and n, 294, 295
Feng-su t'ung: quoted, 322
"Feng-t'ien ch'u-yao chiu-shih an-min
yü": editions compared, 130
"Feng-t'ien t'ao-hu hsi pu ssu-fang yü":
editions compared, 130–32; mentioned,
133
Feng Yün-shan (Nan Wang): as leader,
106, 109, 168, 484; in Taiping moral
development, 108; as writer, 109, 111n;
death of, 224; and miners, 305; men-
tioned, 66, 85, 96 and n. *See also* Nan
Wang
Feudalism, 252–53, 450. *See also Feng-chien*
Filial piety. *See Hsiao*
Firmness. (*kang*): discussed, 193–94
Fishbourne, Captain, 410
Five Classics: and Taipings, 44; deletion
of, 74; and Hung, 108
Five Dynasties, 222, 355
Fo-ti ching, 274
Fo-tsu t'ung-chi. See Records of Buddhist
Masters
Foochow, Fukien: peasant income of, 477–
78
Foot-binding, 60, 76, 77, 226, 227, 228,
314, 317–18, 436, 446
Forbes, Archibald: quoted, 408 and n
Former Han, 230
Formosa, 475
Forrest, Robert James: quoted, 6n, 12n, 14,
418
Fortune tellers, 120 and n, 121; discussed,
128
Foster, John: and Christian sources of
Taiping ideology, 431
Four Books: and Taipings, 44, 108; dele-
tion of, 74
Four-line songs (Buddhist), 355–56 and
356n, 357
Fox, George, 448
France, 138, 451
Fraternity. See *I*
Friend relationships: discussed, 195, 196,
197; mentioned, 191
Frost King. *See* Yen Wang
Fu Ch'ing-chu, 298
Fu Huai, 63
Fu I-ling: quoted on secret societies, 475–
76
Fu-ming, 162
Fu Shan-hsiang, 63, 68
Fu-su, Prince, 330, 331, 332
"Fu-tao": quoted, 72

Fu-t'ien-yen Chung: proclamations of, 253n

Fujiwara Sadamu: interpretation of Taipings, 461

Fukien, 297, 305n, 309, 317, 323, 326, 331, 338, 345, 348n, 351n, 357, 477, 478, 479

Fundamental Nature of the Taiping Rebellion: quoted, 460

Funeral ceremonies, 56, 272

Fung Yu-lan: quoted, 187, 241–42

Genesis: discussed, 148, 149, 150, 243

Gentry, xiv, 46, 377, 481, 485, 486; and Hakkas, 314; in Ming, 371, 372; discussed, 470–74 *passim*. *See also* Social structure

Geomancy, 229, 311. *See also* Divination

Germany, 138

Ghosts. *See Shen*

Gilbert, G. H.: quoted, 152

Giles, Herbert A.: quoted, 240

God: synonyms and names for, 3–4, 6, 56, 92, 129, 133, 178, 180, 202; concepts of, 5–12; in Taiping beliefs, 12–29 *passim*, 34, 35, 38, 39, 41–42, 94–97, 101, 102, 103, 104; worship of, 46; in Taiping writings, 113–33 *passim;* and Hung Jen-kan's view of name taboo, 139; and synonyms borrowed by Hung Hsiu-ch'üan, 148–50; concept of by Taipings discussed, 154–56 and n, 157–64 *passim;* and possession of by individuals, 327–28; Chu Yüan-chan's concept of, 362

God of literature. *See* Wen-ch'ang

God-Worshipers Society, 16, 23, 61, 108, 159, 305, 342, 361, 405, 425n, 445

God-Worshipers, A Study of the Taiping System, 465

Golden Rule, 431, 432 and n

"Good Words to Admonish the Age": quoted, 13, 28; and study of by Hung Hsiu-ch'üan, 147, 148n, 154, 168n

Gordon, Charles George, 21n

"Gospel Jointly Witnessed and Heard by the Imperial Eldest and Second Eldest Brothers": quoted, 9, 12, 34, 51–52, 97, 244, 294

Great Britain. *See* England

Great Harmony. *See* Ta-t'ung; World of Great Harmony

Great Learning, 125, 244

Green Bag Classic, 75, 229

Green Banners, 438

Gützlaff. *See* Medhurst-Gützlaff

Hai Jui, 123

Haichow, Honan, 358

"Haijo ko, Taihei tengoku seido kanken," 465

Hainan Island, 318

Hair-shaving, 136

Hakka: women, 226, 310–11, 314, 317–19; as source of Taiping ideology discussed, 304–19; and strife with Punti, 305, 306–7, 313 and n, 342–43, 465, 466, 471; religious beliefs of, 311–12, 314; and sorcery of, 312, 327; and dialect in Taiping writing, 315–17; mentioned, 49, 145, 285, 408n, 458

Hamberg, Theodore: quoted on Hung Hsiu-ch'üan, 7, 105, 168n, 305, 488; quoted on Taiping religious practices, 19; quoted on Hung's ambition, 86–87, 108; quoted on divine visitation, 96n–97n; quoted on Hung Hsiu-ch'üan's conversion, 106–7 and n; quoted on Hung and Christianity, 147, 148 and n; quoted on *t'ien-kuo*, 153

Han Confucianism, 143 and n

Han dynasty, x, 11, 42, 127, 143 and n, 166n, 170, 173, 179, 180, 213, 217n, 223, 230, 236n, 242, 243, 256n, 262n, 270n, 274, 320, 321, 333, 335, 337, 360, 384, 388, 437, 438, 441, 444, 447, 450, 451

Han Hsiang, *tzu* Ch'ing-fu, 278

Han Hsin, 289

Han-hsüan, 26

Han-huan, 26

Han-kao-tsu, 363n

Han-lin, 270 and n

Han Lin-erh, 360

Han Lin-te: reign of, 338

Han-liu: organization of, 298

Han-ming, 26

Han River, 335

Han Shan-t'ung: and Maitreya, 358; and stone man, 359; propaganda of, 360

Han-shu, 224, 236, 238, 267n, 320, 323

Han-wen, 26

Han-wu, 26

Han Yü of the T'ang, 123, 128, 207, 208, 222, 236, 278, 324; as author, 166 and n, 167n; quoted, 247, 283, 383

Hankow, 403 and n, 423

Hanyang, 43, 255n

Hardships: as testing, 201–3

Harem: 89–90, 100. *See also* Concubines

Hatano Yoshihiro: interpretation of Taipings, 465

Heaven: in Taiping belief, 3 and n, 158; description of, 13, 16, 17; duties toward,

18; in Buddhism, 274
Heaven and Earth Society, 49, 145, 293, 296, 297, 298–300, 368
Heavenly Commandments, xiii, xvii, 3n, 23, 36 and n, 156; listed, 18. *See also* Book of Heavenly Commandments; Ten Commandments
Heavenly King. *See* T'ien Wang
Heavenly Kingdom of God, 86, 487
Heavenly Kingdom of Great Peace. *See* T'ai-p'ing t'ien-kuo
Heavenly mandate. *See* Mandate of Heaven
Heavenly Mother, 10, 12, 13, 17, 157
Heavenly Precepts, 156, 175
Hell, 16, 17, 158, 274 and n
Heng-shan *hsien*, 373
Heretic teachings, 351 and n, 356
"Hermes" (ship), 404, 410
"Hero's Submission to Truth": and Hung Jen-kan, 133, 171; quoted on wealth, 203; quoted on moral causality, 205; and titles, 216
Hexagrams, 245, 248n
Ho Ch'ao-yüan, 28
Ho Cheng-ch'üan, 42
Ho Ch'i of the Chin, 225
Ho Chih-chung (of Chekiang), 346
Ho Hsiu, 213, 239, 246
"Ho-jen-ssu" (poem), 196–97
Homophones: examples of, 222
Honan, 338, 358, 367, 372, 373, 374, 483
Hong Kong, 133, 405, 410
Honorifics, 162, 217, 222
Hoochow, 421
Hope, Sir James, 418
"Hou Ch'u-shih piao," 206
Hou-Han-shu: quoted, 196, 197, 208, 322; quotes *T'ai-p'ing Ching*, 339–40
Hou Yü-k'uan, 90
Hsi (sorcerers), 180–81, 324–25
Hsi-chai hsien-sheng, 231
Hsi-hsia (state), 353n
Hsi K'ang of the Chin, 242
"Hsi-ming": explanation of, 207 and n, 211–12; quoted, 210
Hsi-tsung (emperor), 343
Hsi Wang (Eastern King): symbol of, 15n; insignia of, 53, 54n, 55n; children of, 56; mentioned, 78. *See also* Hsiao Ch'ao-kuei
Hsi-yu chi: characters in, 294, 295
Hsia (China): defined, 246
Hsia dynasty, 176, 219, 241
Hsia-kuan, 62
Hsia Nai: quoted, 480
Hsia-yang, 325

Hsiang-kuan. *See* Local officials system
Hsiang region, 438
Hsiang River, 320
Hsiang Ta, 450
Hsiang Yen, 331
Hsiang Yü, 334
Hsiang Yung, 62, 396n
Hsiao (filial piety): discussed, 35–36, 166 and n
Hsiao Ch'ao-kuei: and execution of parents, 36, 67, 224, 488; and proclamations, 45, 167; death of, 56, 62, 224; and commandments, 66; and divine visitations, 95–96, 327n; and Hung Hsiu-ch'üan, 96n; and proclamation about Manchus, 101–2, 134, 177n; in Feng's sect, 106; as author, 109, 130; and Hakkas, 305; as military leader, 460
Hsiao-ching: quoted, 191, 192, 193, 200
Hsiao Chüeh-kuei, 357
Hsiao I-shan: quoted, 128–29, 169n, 254n, 301, 444, 466, 489
Hsiao, Kung-chuan: observations on novels, 286n; quoted on religion, 320; quoted on Taiping movement, 441–42, 443; quoted on rebellions, 475; quoted on rural economy, 482
Hsiao San-niang, 61, 62
Hsieh Chieh-ho: quoted on New Year's Day, 18n; quoted on Taiping women, 65; as author, 396n
Hsieh Fang-te, 102
Hsieh Hsing-yao: quoted on books, 43, 44; quoted on *Chou-li*, 254n, 255, 257, 258–60, 265, 266; critique of his Chou-li references, 255n; quoted on secret societies, 303n; quoted on revolution, 439; mentioned, 489
Hsieh Ling-yün, 356n
Hsieh T'ing-yü: quoted on Hakkas, 304, 306, 307, 308, 311, 313n
Hsien-feng emperor, xi, 102, 134, 315
Hsien-pei, 305
Hsien, Prince of Ho-chien, 256n
Hsien-yang, 334
Hsin (trustworthiness), 291
Hsin dynasty, 267 and n
Hsin-hai Revolution, 497
Hsin-i-chao sheng-shu: quoted, 43
Hsing-chün tsung-yao, 103
Hsing-ming kuei-chih, 286n
Hsiu-ning, 352
Hsiung K'ai-yüan, 297
Hsü (place), 240, 338
Hsü Feng-en (author), 396n
Hsü Heng: and Mongols, 250, 251

Hsü Hao of the Ch'ing: quoted, 180
Hsü Hsü-tseng: quoted on Hakkas, 309
Hsü Pei-ju: rebellion of, 370
Hsü Shen: quoted, 179, 180
Hsü Shou-hui: and Maitreya, 358, 361
Hsü wen-hsien t'ung-k'ao: quoted, 220
Hsüan-tsang, 274
Hsüan-tsung of the T'ang, 258n, 267, 268n, 269
Hsün-chou (place), 324
Hsün-chou fu-chih: quoted from, 318, 324, 476
Hsün-tzu, 143, 166 and n, 209; quoted, 186–87, 215
Hu Lin-i, 493
Hu Ch'ang-lin, 395n
Hu-chou, 395n
Hu I-huang: insignia of, 54; enlistment of, 60
Hu P'u-an: quoted, 322
Hu Ti, 123
Hu Ying of the Sung, 324
Hu Yu-lu: and uprising, 492
Hua (China): defined, 246
Hua-hsia (China), 131
Hua-hsien, 60, 212
Hua Kang, 489; quoted on Communist link with Taipings, 496–97
Hua-shih kang: See Plant collecting
Hua-yüan, 21
Huai-hsi, 361
Huai-nan-tzu, 166 and n
Huai region, 438
Huai River, 350n, 361
Huai-yüan, 373
Huan-ch'iao chi-shih, 233, 253n-254n
Huang Ch'ao: as emperor, xix; rebellion discussed, 330, 343–44; mentioned 92 and n, 93; 382, 417
Huang Chi-kan, 248n
Huang-chin. See Yellow Turbans
Huang Chüeh-tzu: quoted, 474 and n
Huang Chün-tsai: quoted, 68
Huang Chung (in novel), 287
Huang Hsiao-yang: revolt of, 370
Huang-Lao (Taoist sect), 11, 338
Huang Li-chou. *See* Huang Tsung-hsi
Huang Shang-ti (Sovereign Supreme Ruler on High): synonym for God, 3, 4, 5, 6, 11, 46, 50, 66, 126, 148, 149, 156, 169, 171. *See also* God; T'ien
Huang Shih-kung, 242
Huang-shu, 249
Huang-ti, 22, 241
Huang Tsai-hsing: quoted, 43
Huang Tsung-hsi: and ethnic issue, 247,

248 and n, 249 and n, 250, 298
Huang Wan, 452
Huang Wen-an, 99
Huang Wen-ying: quoted, 59–60
Hui-fei (secret society bandits), 475–76
Hui of Liang, 234
Hui-tsung, 4, 349n, 353, 360
Hui Tung, 280, 319
Hui-yüan, 143n, 356 and n
Human nature: in Taiping beliefs, 181–83. *See also* Man
Human relationships: kinds discussed, 189–201
Humility: discussion of, 201–2
Hun-jan. *See* Yen Yüan
Hunan, 36, 322, 324, 331, 338, 361, 453, 475, 476, 483
Hung Ch'eng-ch'ou, 493
Hung Chiang Rebellion, 493, 496
Hung clan: history of, 304n–5n
Hung family: ancestors of named, 299n
Hung Hsiu-ch'üan (the T'ien Wang): and religion, xii, xiv, xvi, xvii, 19; as Heavenly King, 3; quoted, 5, 6 and n, 7, 10, 14, 42, 243; and visions of, 9, 135, 178, 242, 277, 295, 428, 430; and significance of number three, 12; and visit to Heaven, 12–13, 16, 25; symbols and insignia of, 14–15, 53, 54; quoted on edicts, 22, 85; and followers of, 23, 459; writing of, 23–24, 105–6 and n, 109, 111 and n, 315, 466; and decree on examination, 42; and equality, 47, 453; as ruler, 50, 84, 91, 93, 435, 484; quoted on rectification of names, 52; and Manchus, 87, 451; and new dynasty, 88–89, 90, 453; as figurehead, 91, 92; as God-appointed man, 107–8; and modifications of ideology, 110–33; and religious fanaticism of, 128–30, 408, 460; and Confucianism, 137–38; and Christianity, 147–58, 212, 402, 405, 409, 410, 418, 462, 472, 488; and use of traditional phrases, 166–68; and dynastic names, 238; and secret societies, 297, 302, 303 and n; and Hakkas, 305n–6n, 313, 458; and superstition, 326; and scholars, 336; and seven characters, 360; and relation to Roaming Bandits, 382, 383; and evaluation of by Meadows, 412–17; and downfall, 422; proclamations of, 425n; and mental illness of discussed, 448–49; and belief in fatalism, 487; and Sun Yat-sen, 493–94; and Chiang Kai-shek, 495. *See also* T'ien Wang
Hung Hsüan-chiao, 61, 68

Hung Jen-fa, 96

Hung Jen-kan (Kan Wang): and classics, 44; quoted on calendar, 74–75; and examination degrees, 88, 268–71; quoted on spiritual power, 97; influenced by Hung Hsiu-ch'üan, 106, 107, 108; and modifications of ideology, 109, 110, 133–38; knowledge of Confucianism, 133–40 *passim*; and travels of, 133n; and Christianity, 136–40; as author, 166, 168, 317; quoted on God, 170, 174; quoted on parenthood of T'ien, 171. *See also* Kan Wang

Hung Jen-ta, 20

Hung-lou-meng, 144n

Hung Mai: quoted, 348n

Hung-men Chih, 298

Hung-men society, 296, 298

Hung Society, 130, 425n, 475

Hung Sui-tsuen. *See* Hung Hsiu-ch'üan

"Hung-yen," 211

Hunter, William C., 408

Huntington, Ellsworth: quoted on Hakkas, 304 and n, 308

Huo Shen, xi

Hupeh, 63, 69, 98, 255n, 338, 367, 369, 453, 479, 483

Husband-wife relationships. *See* Marital relations

I (fraternity): discussed, 191, 206, 290–93

I-chien chih: quoted, 348n

"I-hsia lun," 247

I-li yin te: quoted from, 195

I-ping jih-chi: quoted from, 65, 74, 234, 253

I, Prince of Chiang-tu, 321

I t'ai-p'ing ts'e, 231

I-ti (emperor), 334, 335

I Wang: surrender of, 8n; symbols of, 15n, 54n, 55n; and proclamations of, 55; and aims of Taipings, 89; court of, 257; mentioned, 46n, 346. *See also* Shih Ta-k'ai

"I-wen-chih," 267n

Ichiko Chūzō: interpretation of Taipings: 465–66

"Ideologies of the T'ai P'ing Insurrection": quoted, 429–31

Ideology: individual contributions to, 105–10; and modifications by Hung Hsiu-ch'üan, 110–33; and modifications by Hung Jen-kan, 133–38; non-traditional aspects of discussed, 271–72

Idolatry: and idols, 7, 11, 16, 151, 312; and Taipings discussed, 23–29; and Hung Jen-kan, 136; of Pai-lien Chiao, 356; mentioned, 95, 155, 326–27. *See*

also Superstition; Witchcraft

Ikida no ran: comparison to Taiping, 464n–65n

Imps, xvi, 97, 294, 472. *See also* Demons; Devils

Inaba Iwakichi: interpretation of Taipings, 458; quoted on rebellions, 476

Incarnation, 157

"Incense Army," 358

Income: of peasant farmer discussed, 477–79

India, 138, 226

Indra, 274

Influence. *See* Feng

Innovations: of Taiping discussed, 446–47; of the Kan Wang, 485–86

Insignia: of Taipings, 53–54 and n, 91; discussed, 220–21. *See also* Symbols

Irwin, Richard Gregg, 354n

Islamic group, 475

Islamic Rebellion, 493

Jackson, A. V. Williams: quoted, 387

Jade Emperor, 380

Jamieson, George: quoted on tax, 233–34, 480

Japan, 133n, 138, 412; writers of on Taiping discussed, 458–67; war against, 496

Japanese Communist Party, 462

Japanese Studies of Modern China: quoted, 460n

Jen Kuo-jung: quoted, 318

Jen-min jih-pao. See People's Daily

Jen-tsung, 270, 357

Jen (Chien) Yu-wen, 153, 155, 446n; quoted on Hung, 212; quoted on Taipings, 214, 437–39; quoted on Taiping land system, 489, 490

Jesus: in Taipings' belief: 3n, 9–12 *passim*, 15, 17, 20, 22, 34, 35, 41, 58, 90, 91, 97 and n, 128, 138, 152, 327, 398, 412, 472; teachings of, 157–59; interpretation of by Taipings, 161

Jews, 22

Jih. See Sun

Jih-chih lu, 240; quoted from on ethnic distinction, 247; quoted on examination, 268, 269

Jih-chih-lu chiao-chi, 248n

John, Griffith, 133n, 411

Johnston, Reginald F.: quoted, 144

Jou (pliancy): discussed, 193, 194

Ju Ying-yüan, 297

Juan I, 270

Jui Lin of Liang-kuang, 313n

Jung, Mount, 325

Kan Pao: quoted, 321–22
Kan Wang: ideology of, xiii-xiv; reform program of, xvii; and classics, 44; and writing, 77–79; quoted on economic ideals, 81–82; quoted on wealth, 203; and Ku Yen-wu, 247; and administrative power, 257; and innovations, 485–86; mentioned, 216, 411. *See also* Hung Jen-kan
K'ang-hsi: reign of, 286, 305
K'ang Yu-wei, 494
Kansu, 483
Kao-chou, 324
Kao-tsu (ruler), 42, 223, 242
Kao-tsung of the T'ang, 241, 258n
Kao-yao, 24
Kao Yu: quoted, 166n
Karlgren, Bernard, 211n
Karma, 274, 275, 276, 340
Kawabata Genji: interpretation of Taiping movement, 464
Khublai Khan, 356
Kiangnan, 43
Kiangsi, 309, 338, 357, 361, 364, 419, 483
Kiangsu, 65, 234, 305n, 338, 351n, 363, 420, 460, 479, 481, 483
"Kingdom of the Heavenly Father, Heavenly Brother, and Heavenly King," 129
Ko Hung: quoted, 279
Ko-i, 143n
Korea, 357
Koyanagi Shigeta: quoted, 339 and n
"Ku-ching chi," 294
Ku Chün-en, 377
Ku Huan: quoted on barbarians, 247
Ku-liang, 172, 189, 246
Ku Shen: quoted on marriage, 70; as author, 395n–96n
Ku-sou, 224, 225
Ku-su. *See* Soochow
Ku Tsung: memorial on land holdings, 479
Ku Yen-wu of the Ch'ing: quoted on examination degrees, 88, 253, 268, 269, 270 and n; quoted, 240; attitude toward Manchu, 247, 248 and n, 249n, 251; mentioned, 298
Kuai-jen, 128
K'uai T'ung: biography of, 224
"Kuan-chü" (poem), 199, 200n
Kuan Chung: and Confucious, 245, 246 and n, 248, 250, 251
Kuan I-fu of Ch'u: quoted, 320
Kuan-ti, 29
"Kuan-tzu pu-ssu Tzu-chiu," 247
Kuan-yang: 492
Kuan Yün-ch'ang (in novel), 287, 290, 296

Kuang-ch'i, 197
Kuang-chou fu-chih: quoted, 477
Kuanghai, 313n
Kuang-ling, 321
Kuang-wu. *See* Liu Hsiu
Kuei-hsien chih, 305
"Kuei-jen shuo," 252
Kuei-lin, 8, 488
Kuei-p'ing, 305
Kuei-wang: death of, 249
Kumārajīva, 274
Kung (respect), 188–89
Kung Ting-an yen-chiu, 228
Kung Ts'ung, 339
Kung Tzu-chen: quoted on footbinding, 227, 228; quoted on geomancy, 229
Kung-yang: school, 179, 212, 213–14, 236, 239, 246, 388; commentary, 179n, 212
K'ung Chi: quoted, 121
K'ung Yin-ta of the T'ang, 246
Kuo I-sheng: and Taiping Rebellion, 457n
Kuo Mo-jo: quoted, 378
Kuo P'u: and divination, 75
Kuo P'u-sa, 358
Kuo-shen: in sorcery, 326
Kuo Sung-t'ao (governor), 313n, 493
Kuo T'ing-i: quoted on Hung Jen-kan, 133n; describes Taipings, 444
Kuo-yü: quoted, 320
K'uo-kuo-t'ieh-mu-erh, 366
Kuomintang, 493, 495 and n
Kwangsi: worship at, 19; image in temple of, 24; Taipings of, 28–29, 58, 59, 60, 67, 68, 96n; women of, 72, 77; and God Worshipers congregation, 108; Hakkas in, 304n; and language, 317; witchcraft in, 323, 324, 326; and rebellions of, 459, 475, 483, 492; secret societies of, 476; and peasants, 479; banditry in, 485; mentioned, 61, 107n, 395, 413, 424, 428, 453
Kwangsi t'ung-chih: quoted, 323
Kwangtung: Taipings from, 59, 60, 61, 96 and n, 305n; and Hakka struggles, 309, 313n; and language, 317; witchcraft in, 323; military outposts of, 331; opium in, 474n; and Yao, 475; and secret societies of, 475–76; and peasants, 479; mentioned, 395, 428
Kweichow, 475, 476, 492, 493

Lai (family name), 61
Lai Ta-mei, 101
Lai troops, 246
Lan-t'ien, 375n
Lan T'ing-jui, 370

Land: system of Taipings, xii, xvi and n, 336, 371, 438, 439–40, 444, 445–46, 458, 460, 461, 484, 489, 490; distribution of discussed, 81–84, 230–32, 382, 455, 467, 474; ownership discussed, 232–34; and Hakkas, 313; in Ch'en Sheng rebellion, 332–33; in Yüan, 365; in rebellions, 384, 385; discussed by P'en Tse-i, 440; cultivation of, 450, 477–79

"Land System of the Heavenly Dynasty": discussed, xii, 81, 230, 234, 235, 265, 443, 447, 477, 484; quoted, 47, 50, 70, 83, 84; from *Chou-li*, 254n; and numbers of soldiers, 260, 261; and social welfare, 432n; and Communist interpretation of, 455; evaluated, 490; mentioned, xvii, 316, 497

Language: borrowings of by Taipings discussed, 315–17

Lao P'eng: and Maitreya, 358, 360

Lao-tzu, 276, 277

Later Han, 166n

Latourette, Kenneth S.: quoted, 427–28

Law, 94–95, 167, 176; and manner of address, 52–53. *See also* Edicts

Leadership: of Taiping Revolution discussed, 484–87

Lechler, R.: quoted on Hakkas, 304n–5n, 307, 308, 310, 311, 312, 327

Legitimate succession: discussed, 330 and n, 333, 334, 337; mentioned, 360, 365, 385

Li: principle of discussed, 36–37, 188–89, 191, 471; institutional aspects of, 214–30; mentioned, 94, 193, 208, 213, 244, 246

Li Ch'ai, 107n

Li Chi: quoted, 48–49, 113, 165n, 178 and n, 184, 186, 188, 208, 432n; quoted on human relationships, 190–91, 193, 194, 195, 196, 197, 210; and wealth, 202; and world of Great Harmony, 210; quoted on social welfare, 211; quoted on *li*, 214, 215, 216; quoted on rank, 218–19; quoted on homophones, 222; quoted on land, 232; quoted on *T'ien Wang*, 241; quoted on a king's changes, 243; quoted on *shih-chung*, 251; quoted on titles, 270; quoted by Sun Yat-sen, 494

Li Ching-fang, 147

Li Ch'uang. *See* Li Tzu-ch'eng

Li Ho, 222

Li, House of, 297. *See also* T'ang dynasty

Li Hsiu-ch'eng (the Chung Wang): quoted on Manchus, 102; quoted on Hung Hsiu-ch'üan, 129; quoted on Hung Jen-kan, 133n; quoted on tax, 233; and surrender of, 287.; and *wan-ku chung-i*, 288; confession of, 445; and peasant army, 460; and state treasury, 490; mentioned, 20. *See also* Chung Wang

Li Hung-chang of Ch'ing army, 21n, 435, 445, 493

Li Ju-chao: writer about Taipings, 396n, 398

Li Ju-chen: quoted, 227, 229

Li K'ai-fang, 21

Li Kuang-chi, 395n

Li K'uei, 288–89

Li Kung: quoted, 104, 231

"Li-lun," 215

Li, people of, 318

Li, Prince of Kuang-ling, 321

Li Shih: quoted, 318

Li-shih chen-hsien t'i-tao t'ung-chien: quoted, 278

Li Shih-hsien: retreat of, 21

Li T'ien-pao: revolt of, 370

Li Tzu-ch'eng: as emperor, xix; in Ch'ü-fou, 28; 92 and n, 93; and Roaming Bandits discussed, 373–79, 382–83; and scholars, 343; 344 and n

"Li Tzu-ch'eng pan-luan shih-lüeh," 374

Li Yen, 372, 373, 374, 378, 379

Li Yüan-tu: and Shih's surrender, 400, 401

"Li-yün," 210, 211, 212, 432n

Liang A-fa: as author, 13, 28, 148, 149, 150, 151, 153, 154, 168n, 179 181, 418, 431

Liang Ch'i-ch'ao, 248, 249

Liang dynasty, 165, 357

Liang-kwang, 313n

Liang Shen of the Liang, 357

Liang-wu, 26

Liang-yüeh, 61

Liao, 353n

"Liao-o" (poem), 166 and n

Life of Tai-ping-wang, Chief of the Chinese Insurrection, 117

Likin, 446; establishment of, 438

"Lin-chih" (poem), 200n

Lin Chih-yang, 227

Lin Feng-hsiang, 21

Lin-le. *See* Lindley, Augustus

Lindley, Augustus: quoted on marriage, 70; quoted on Taiping religion, 409, 412, 423; quoted on famine, 482; mentioned, 406

Lin San, 370

Lin San-ch'ing: quoted, 315

Lin Tse-hsü, 228, 474 and n

Lin Wen-shuang: and uprising, 475

Ling-feng, 321
Ling-nan, 317
Ling-nan cha-chi: quoted, 317
Ling Shan-ch'ing: quoted on segregation of sexes, 67; quoted on Hung Jen-ken, 133n; quoted on *Chou-li*, 254n; quoted on local officials, 263–64
Literary inquisition, 248 and n, 252
Literati. *See* Gentry
Littell, John: quoted, 427
Liu Ch'eng-fang, 257
Liu Ch'eng-yü, 212
Liu Ch'i: revolt of, 370
Liu Chin, 370
Liu-chou: destruction at, 28–29
Liu Fu-t'ung: and Maitreya, 358, 359, 360
Liu Hsiang of the Han, 180
Liu Hsin of the Han, 236n, 337; and adoption of *Chou-li* system, 267n
Liu Hui, 370
Liu I-cheng: quoted, 437
Liu K'ai, 286
Liu Kuan-fang, 255n
Liu Liu: revolt of, 370
Liu Ming-ch'uan: and Sun Yat-sen, 493
Liu-pan, 305
Liu Pang: rebellion of discussed, 330, 333–36, 337, 378, 400, 456
Liu Pei, 290, 296
Liu P'en-tzu, 322, 337
Liu Ta-niang: worship of, 324, 325
Liu-tien. See Six Laws
Liu Tso-ch'üan, 457n
Liu Tsung-min, 375 and n
Lo Chi-lung, 69
Lo Erh-kang: quoted on land, 254n; quoted on soldiers, 264; quoted on relations between Hung and Chu Chiu-t'ao, 302–3, 428n; quoted on Hakkas, 304–5; quoted on Roaming Bandits, 383; writings on Taipings discussed, 445–47, 451; quoted on trade, 481–82; quoted on Taiping land system, 489, 490
Lo Feng-ch'ih, 107n
Lo Hsiang-lin: quoted on Hakkas, 308, 309, 312, 315–16
Lo Ju-ts'ai, 378
Lo Ta-kang, 20, 59–60, 255n, 296
Lo Tse-nan: quoted, 319; and Sun Yat-sen, 493
Lo-yang, 344
Lo Yung: quoted, 133n, 495–96
Local officials system: described, 262–64, 265, 446
Loh country, 115
London, 111

Longobardi, Nicolo, 397
Lord's Prayer, 153
Lord's Supper: in Taiping belief, 415
Love: in Taiping belief, 37; discussed, 197; and Confucius, 209; mentioned, 190–96
Loyalty. *See Chung*
Lu Hsien-pa: loss of office, 67; as religious leader, 109; as author, 112
Lu Mountains, 356n
Lu school, 251
Lu Sheng-nan: and feudalism, 253
Lu Su, 93 and n
Lu Yu: on Chang Chüeh, 352n
Lü, Empress, 322
Lü Liü-liang (Wan-ts'un): and ethnic distinctions, 250, 251, 252; and feudalism, 253
Lü-shih ch'un-ch'iu: translation of, 241–42
Lü Ssu-mien: quoted, 436
Lü Tung-pin: quoted, 277
Lü-ying (Green Banners), 438
Luan-chou, 302
Luan-chou chih: quoted from, 301–2
Lung-ch'uan, 364
Lung Feng-lien, 42
Lung Sheng-yün: quoted, xvi-n

Ma-ch'eng, 361
Ma Shou-lin, 396n
Ma Tuan-lin of the Sung, 220
Macao, 313n
Mackie, J. Milton, 117
McLane, Robert M., 424, 489
Maitreya sect, 355–60 *passim*, 362, 366, 368, 369, 384
Malan, S. C., 111
Malaya, 138
Man: concept of by Taipings, 32–34; and fallibility of, 38–39. *See also* Human nature
Manchuria, 338, 479
Manchus: and Taiping relationships, xvi, 85, 86, 104, 108, 131, 155, 177 and n, 213, 214, 245, 268, 303n, 361, 385, 395, 399, 400, 401, 427, 428, 433, 435, 437–44 *passim*, 446, 450, 451, 452, 454, 456, 458, 461, 463, 464, 471, 473, 486, 496; proclamation against, 6, 101–2; as serpent-demons, 12; in Yang's writings, 109; rule of, 133, 319, 470, 479, 493; and Hung Jen-kan, 134; women, 228; and Ming loyalists, 247, 248; and Huang Tsung-hsi, 249 and n; and Hakkas, 304, 306, 309, 310n, 313; and foreigners, 402
Mandarin, 57, 319
Mandate of Heaven: physical sign of, 162;

discussed, 176 and n-177 and n; and Taipings, 300, 473; popular belief of, 319; in Ch'en Sheng rebellion, 333; of Liu Pang, 335-36; of Chu Yüan-chang, 362 and n, 365-66; and rebels, 384, 385, 387-88; mentioned, 204, 276, 295, 296, 316, 343-44, 375-76, 399-400, 433

Mani, 387

Manichaeism, 347 and n, 348 and n, 349n, 351n, 352n, 356, 387, 397

Manifesto of the *T'ung-meng hui*, 493

Mao I-heng: quoted, 303n

Mao Tse-tung, 497

Mao Tzu-yüan (monk), 355 and n, 356, 357

Marcy, 417

Marital relationships: discussed, 193-95

Marriage, 70-71, 446; of Hakkas, 314

Marshall, Humphrey, 404; quoted on Taiping Christianity, 407-8; and Meadows, 412; and Taiping Rebellion, 417

Martan-farukh, 387

Marx, Karl: quoted, 453, 492

Maspero, Henri: and interpretation of *fang*, 338n

Masui Tsuneo: and interpretation of Taiping movement, 464-65

Matchmaker (*mei-shih*): discussed, 266

Mazdaism, 347, 348

Meadows, Thomas T.: and Taiping Christianity, 20, 406, 407; quoted on equality, 46n; quoted on Taiping aims, 89; opinion of Hung Hsiu-ch'üan, 412-17; mentioned, 410, 424

"Meaon-tsze," 49

Medhurst, W. H.: translations of, xv, 111, 112, 117; quoted on sacrifices, 22; quoted on Hung Hsiu-ch'üan, 147, 148; quoted on Genesis, 149; quoted on Taiping religion, 405; death of, 412; quoted on treasury, 489

Medhurst-Gützlaff Bible, 148, 149, 150, 151

Mei-shan, 378

Mei-shih. See Matchmaker

Melchisedec, 14, 151, 152, 162, 243

Mencius, 38, 112, 128, 166, 167, 187, 236n, 324n, 376, 398, 400, 408; quoted on Hung, 15n; doctrines of, 42, 43, 44, 118; quoted, 122, 125, 126, 127, 137; philosophy of, 143; used by Hung Jen-kan, 171 and n; use of T'ien, 172, 174; quoted on heaven, 177, 240; quoted on human nature, 182, 183; quoted on *cheng*, 183, 185-86 and n; quoted on human relations, 190, 193-97 *passim*,

224; quoted on rank, 202; quoted on love, 209; quoted on social welfare, 211, 234, 235; quoted on peace, 236; and rulers, 336

Meng Te-an: quoted, 71

Meng-tsai pi-t'an: quoted from, 277

Mi-chih, 373

Mi-lieh chiao rebellion: discussed, 355, 357, 358-61

Mïaos, 451, 475, 492

"Miau-tsze," 108

Michie, Alexander, 418

Middle Kingdom, 168n, 210, 213, 246, 354, 376

Military: activity of Yellow Turbans, 338-42 *passim*
—aspects of ideology, 103-4, 109, 474-77
—institutions discussed, 253-68
—system: Taiping organization of, xii, 85, 91, 92, 95, 221, 261-2, 443, 454, 455, 456, 460; titles of by Li Tzu-ch'eng, 379; organization of by Roaming Bandits, 383; and Chou-li system discussed, 253-68; and local officials system, 262-64; in Taiping Rebellion, 438, 446. *See also* Army; Soldiers

Milne: *See* Morrison and Milne

Min-sheng chu-i: discussed, 493-4

Miners, 49, 305, 485

Ming (fate), 174. *See also* Fatalism; Mandate of Heaven

Ming-chi pei-lüeh, 372, 374

Ming dynasty, 61, 87-88, 92 and n, 93, 102, 123, 131, 133, 136, 143, 144n, 165n, 182n, 223, 270n, 297, 298, 304n, 309, 310n, 355, 357, 366, 383, 397, 400, 436, 470, 471, 493; rebellions in discussed, 370-89

Ming-hsin tao-jen, 396n

Ming-i-tai-fang lu, 248 and n, 249n

Ming loyalists: and Manchu, 247, 248, 253

Ming scholars, 313

Ming-shih, 364n, 371, 381

Ming T'ai-tsu. *See* Chu Yüan-chang

Ming Yü-chen, 361, 363; rebellion of discussed, 368-70

Ministers (in government), 186n, 200, 206; and rulers, 193; titles of, 255; functions of, 256-58; and Hsüan-tsung of the T'ang, 268n

Mirror: as symbol, 294-95

Missionaries: and attitudes toward Taipings, xv-xvi, 160; and views of Taiping's Christianity, 401-25 *passim*

Miyagawa Hisashi: interpretation of Taipings, 462 and n, 466

Mo-mo-ni. See Brilliant Sect
Modesty, *See Ch'ien*
Mohammed, 406, 417
Mohammedans. *See* Islam; Moslems
Mohism, 145, 209; and borrowings from by Taipings, 273, 280–83
Mongolia, 360, 479
Mongols, 248n, 250, 251, 297, 309, 360, 366, 450
Moon, 243–44, 301, 326, 348
Moral causality: discussed, 205–8
Moral development: and Hung's and Feng's influence, 108; and views of Taipings discussed, 31–44
Moral precepts: discussed, 189–203, 300, 244; and *li,* 216
Morrison and Milne Bible, 154
Moslems, 22, 450–1
Mother. *See* Heavenly Mother
Motzu, 108, 207n, 280, 432n; Book of, 281, 282, 283
Moule, Arthur Evans, 418
Mount Sumeru, 274
Mount Ta-jung, 324, 325
Mu-chou, 350, 351n
Mu-tzu, 175
Mu Wang. *See* T'an Shao-kuang
Muirhead, W.: quoted, 404, 411

Nāgārjuna, 274
Names: rectification of, 51–52, 134, 186–87, 244, 300; for Taiping leaders, 87; changes made in, 133; of ranks and examination degrees, 135–36; Taiping traditional use of, 166–68; taboos of discussed, 221–26. *See also* God: names for
Nan Wang (South King): and symbols of, 15n, 55n. *See also* Feng Yün-shan
Nanking: Taipings in, xi, xviii, 19, 21, 42, 53, 55, 63, 66–72 *passim,* 76, 77, 90, 101n, 109, 129, 138, 156, 166, 234, 263, 402, 403n, 404, 410, 413, 420, 424, 437, 453, 454, 456, 458, 486, 489, 490, 491, 496. *See also* Chin-ling
Nanning, 492
Nashimoto Yūhei: interpretation of Taipings, 461–62
National Peiping Research Institute, 128
"Nei-tse," 194, 195n
Nellis, 421
Neo-Confucianism, 128, 136, 138, 167n, 178, 470; term discussed, 143; in Taiping writings, 207; and original truth, 277
Nestorianism, 348n
"New Political Essay as a Guide to Govern-

ment," 138
New Testament, 43, 161, 162–63, 151 and n, 152–59 *passim,* 162–63, 328, 398, 430. *See also* Bible
New Year's Day, 18n, 19, 323–24
Ni Pan of the Ch'ing, 242
Nieh Ch'ung-ch'i: and Fang La, 351n–352n
Nien-erh-shih cha-chi, 343, 363, 364n, 372
Nien Rebellion, 493
Ning-shou palace, 377
Ningpo, 14, 418
Nirvana Sūtra, 356n
Niu Chin-hsin (Li Tzu-ch'eng's assistant), 373, 375, 376
Nohara Shirō: interpretation of Taipings, 459–60
North America. *See* America; United States
North China Herald: quoted on troops, 20; and "Ode for Youth," 111; quoted on Taiping religion, 411; editorials quoted, 419–22, 425; quoted on treasury, 489
North King. *See* Pei Wang
Northern Ch'i dynasty, 247
Northern Chou, 229n, 241, 267 and n
Northern dynasty, 222, 242
Northern Sung, 267n, 355
Northern Wei, 229n, 237n, 343n
Norway, 138
Novels: effect on merging philosophies, 144n; as source of Taiping ideology discussed, 285–96; mentioned, 145

O-meng, 249
Ō shio no ran: compared to Taiping, 464 and n, 465 and n
Obedience. *See San-ts'ung*
Ochler, D.: quoted, 307–8
Occult: books on, 242–43
Occupations: in Taiping organization, 46, 49, 50–51, 77, 83–84, 235, 445, 451–52, 485; of Hakkas, 306
"Ode for Youth": quoted, 34, 37, 39, 52, 72, 73, 185; two editions of, 110–11; title of, 165; and *li,* 188; and *yen,* 192 and n; and brothers, 195–96; and rectification of names, 244
"Ode on Correctness," 33, 39, 105, 117, 168, 183, 184–85
"Ode on the Hundred Correct Things." *See* "Ode on Correctness"
"Ode on the Origin of the Principle of the Salvation of the World": quoted, 76; editions compared, 112, 113–17
"Odes of Chou," 122, 128

Offices: of Taiping and *Chou-li*, discussed, 258–60, 267n
Old Testament, 4, 43, 111, 158, 161, 427 430
Oliphant, 423
"On Heaven," 166
"On Managing the Ears": quoted, 34
Opium: smoking of discussed, 226, 227, 228, 443; consumption of, 474 and n; trade in, 482. *See also* Smoking
Opium War, 226, 461, 465, 475, 485
Ordering of the family, 244
"Origin and Migrations of the Hakkas": quoted from, 304 and n
Orthodox Teachings of Buddhism, 355, 356
Ōtani Kōtarō: quoted, 466
Ou Shih-tzu, 165n, 182n

Pa-shang, 334
Pai-cheng ko. *See* "Ode on Correctness"
Pai-hu t'ung-i, 243
Pai-lien, 384
Pai-lien chiao (White Lotus sect), 297; discussed, 330, 348n, 355–58. *See also* White Lotus Society
Pai-lien-she. *See* White Lotus Society
Pai-Yüeh feng-t'u chi: quoted from, 323
Pan-hsing chao-shu. See "Proclamations by Imperial Sanction"
Pan Ku: quoted, 236n, 238, 267n
P'an-ku, 113, 122, 125
P'an Yung-chi: quoted, 371
Pang Hu: rebellion of, 358
Pantheism: in Taiping religion, 6–7, 8
Pao-en t'a: destruction of, 397, 436, 471
Pao Hsüan: biography of, 240–41
Pao-p'u-tzu: quoted, 279
Paramiti, 274
Peace: discussed, 235–39; in novels, 294–95
Peasants: discussed in Taiping rebellion, xvi-xvii; in Taiping society, 49, 50, 84; and land, 104, 230–34, 438, 450; in rebellion discussed, 442, 445, 447, 451 and n, 452, 453–57 *passim*, 460, 467; in army, 460; income of discussed, 477–79
Pei-ch'i dynasty, 230
Pei-chou dynasty, 230
Pei-hai (district), 321
Pei Wang (North King): symbols of, 15n, 54n, 55n; and proclamation of, 55; and Taiping aims, 89; and flogging, 96; mentioned, 35, 46n. *See also* Wei Ch'ang-hui
Pei-wei dynasty, 230
Peking, xviii, xix, 101, 298, 402, 435, 452, 454, 460

Peking University, 370
Pelliot, P.: quoted, 348n, 351n–52n
P'eng-ch'eng, 197
P'eng Tse-i, 254n, 439, 440, 444, 489; quoted on land, 494
P'eng Yin-yü, 361
P'eng Yüeh, 361
People's Daily: quoted, 450, 453–57, 498
People's Republic of China, 497, 498
"Perfect Auspicious Poem": quoted from, 33
Perseverance: in Taiping beliefs, 38
Persia, 138
Peru, 138
Phillips, George: quoted, 477
Phoenix, 220, 221
Pi Jung: memorial on money lenders, 482n
P'i hexagram, 245
Pien River, 350n
Ping Fu-shou, 255n, 257
P'ing-chung. *See* Hsü Heng
P'ing-lo (place), 324
P'ing-nan, 324
P'ing Shan Chou, 297
P'ing shu ting, 231
P'ing-ting Yüeh-fei chi-lüeh: quoted from, 67, 303
Plant collecting: by Chu Mien, 349 and n-350 and n
Po-huai, 197
Po-i, 248n
Po Kiu-yi, 348n
Po-kung: defined, 257; mentioned, 256
Po-yü, 258
Poems, 69, 276, 292, 295; used by secret societies, 301
"Poems by the Heavenly Father": quoted, 15, 16–17, 32, 35, 37, 38–39, 40, 66, 72, 73, 157
Political: control discussed, 93–104;—factors: in Taiping ideology discussed, 474–77;—ideals: of Taipings discussed, 235–39;—institutions discussed, 253–68;—organization: in establishing new dynasty, 85–92; maintenance of, 93–95; of Roaming Bandits, 383;—philosophy discussed, 239–45
Popular beliefs: discussed, 319–28
Population, 461, 478
Polygamy, 71, 314, 406
Posthumous names, 224
Poverty: prior to Taiping Rebellion, 477–84 *passim*
Prayer: in Taiping religion, 18, 21
Preaching: by Taipings, 20, 23
Private virtues: *See* Virtues

"Proclamation on the Origin of Principles for the Awakening of the Age": quoted, 5, 32; by Hung Hsiu-ch'üan, 105; editions compared, 120–23; mentioned, 326

"Proclamation on the Origin of Principles for the Enlightenment of the Age," 48; by Hung Hsiu-ch'üan, 105, 108; editions compared, 117–20; quotation from Li-chi, 208; and order, 245; compared to Motzu, 281–83, 432n

"Proclamation on the Origin of the Principles of World Salvation": quoted from 33, 46, 66, 76, 92; by Hung Hsiu-ch'üan, 105; historical allusions in, 111; editions compared, 113–17; and Confucius, 168; and pu-cheng, 183; and li, 188; wealth, 202; and fate, 204; and moral causality, 205, 206; similarity to Han Yü, 207–8

"Proclamations by Imperial Sanction": quoted from, 130, 210, 462 and n; dates of, 466

"Proclamations on the Extermination of Demons," 134

Prohibitions, 74–77, 95. See also Taboos

Proletariat, 452, 453n, 455, 456, 457n, 459

Property, private, 95

Prostitution, 76, 77, 226, 230

Pu-cheng (wickedness): discussed, 33, 183–88

Punishment: as means of control, 102–3

Punti: displacement of, 305, 306–7, 313 and n; and Hakkas, 342–43, 465, 466, 471; mentioned, 314

Pure Land of Amitābha, 355

Pure Land of Maitreya, 355

Pure Land sect, 356n

Race: structure of observed by Communists, 450–51

Rank: in Taiping organization, 50–51, 53–54, 55; and promotion, 58–60; adoption of by Taipings discussed, 135; discussed, 214–18; mentioned, 202, 203

Rebel ideologies: pattern of, x, xi

Rebellions: discussed, xiv, xvii–xviii, xix, 329–89; mentioned, 476. See also Uprisings

"Rebel's Proclamations": quoted, 77

Rebirth: in Taiping beliefs, 162

"Record of an Ancient Mirror," 294

Records of Buddhist Masters, 348n, 355, 356 and n

Rectification of names. See Names

Red Army, 358, 366

Red Emperor, 337

Red Eyebrow rebels (Ch'ih-mei), 322; discussed, 330, 336–38

Reign titles: and use of t'ai-p'ing discussed, 236–37 and n

Religion: as unifying force of Taipings, xii–xiii; in Taiping society discussed, 3–29, 31, 440, 441, 458, 459, 462, 491; for political purposes, 94–95; and fanaticism of Hung, 128–30; and emphasis on in Taiping ideology, 132–33; of Hakkas, 311–12, 314; and elements in Taiping ideology, 382–83; in rebellions, 384–88 passim. See also Buddhism; Christianity; Taoism, etc.

Religion in China: quoted, 411

Rent: and Taipings, xvi–n, 234, 489–90; of peasants, 370, 477, 478, 479

Repentance: in Taiping beliefs, 38, 183

Researches in Manichaeism: quoted, 387

Respect. See Kung

Retribution: discussed, 319

Reverence. See Ching

Revolution: as applied to Taipings, xiv–xv, xvi, 417, 437, 438; discussed, 388–89, 443, 444, 445, 446, 447, 451 and n, 452, 461, 465; discussed in Peking (1951) editorial, 453–57 passim

Reward: as means of control, 102–3

Ricci, Matteo, 397

Rice cultivation, 477–79, 480

Richard, Timothy: quoted, 423

Riddles, 162, 163, 301

Roaming Bandits: discussed, 330, 371–83

Roberts, I. J., 147–48 and n, 156, 420; and opinion of Hung Hsiu-ch'üan, 406, 417–18

Romance of the Three Kingdoms, 245, 286, 287, 290, 296, 297

Rules of Behavior of the Empire: quoted, 220

Rules Governing Conduct Inside the House, 194, 195n

Rural China: Imperial Control in the Nineteenth Century: quoted, 442, 482

Russell, Lord, 416

Russia: trade with, 451; mentioned, 138

"Sacred Book of the New Testament": quoted, 43

"Sacred Book of the Old Testament": quoted, 43

Sacred Treasury. See Treasury

Sacrifice, 18, 155; of animals, 19; and Taipings discussed, 21–22, 74, 178–79 and n, 272; and Chang Chüeh, 386

Sai-shang-a, 396n

St. Augustine, 448

St. Paul, 448
Saipei (Mongolia), 360
San-ch'a-ho: battle of, 58
San-ho, 335
San-ho hui. See Three Together Society
San-miao, 26
San-ts'ung (obedience): discussed, 193, 195
San-tzu-ching. See "Trimetrical Classic"
Sano Manabu: and interpretation of Taipings, 462–63
Sanskrit, 274
Sao-shou-wen, 249
Sargent, W.: quoted, 406
Sāstra, 274
Scarth, John: quoted, 411, 412
Scholars: writings for, 136–37; of Ming, 247–48; of Ch'ing, 252, 253; in Liu Pang rebellion, 336; in Sung, 348n; massacre of by Chang Hsien-chung, 381
Secret service organization, 99–101
Secret societies, 49, 145, 159–60, 161, 163, 210, 232, 245, 247, 285, 293, 355, 357, 358, 361, 384, 385, 439, 444, 492; influence on Taiping ideology discussed, 296–303; trouble with in Kwangtung, 475–76. *See also* Hung Society; White Lotus Society
Sermon on the Mount: in Taiping religion, 414n, 418
Seven Kills. *See Ch'i-sha pei*
Seven Teachings, 195
Sexes: segregation of, 56n, 65–71, 95, 112, 266, 314–15, 336; equality of, 230, 232
Shamanism. *See* Witchcraft
Shang-chu: synonym for God, 3, 148
Shang dynasty, 124, 126, 127, 169, 173, 176, 242, 295
Shang, House of, 248n
Shang-shu t'ung-chien: and heavenly mandate, 177n
Shang-ti: synonym for God, 3, 14, 90, 126, 133, 148, 169, 178, 180, 272, 362. *See also* God; T'ien
Shang-ti-hui (God Society), 23
Shang-ti t'ien-kuo. See Heavenly Kingdom of God
"Shang-ti yu-hsing wei-yü, wu-hsing nai shih lun," 23
Shanghai, 133, 416, 423, 447, 449, 452, 456, 458, 460, 465, 485
Shansi, 367, 450, 479, 483
Shantung, 338, 367, 370, 483
Shao-hao, 26
Shaoking, 313n
"Shao-nan" (poem), 199, 200 and n
Shen (spirit): discussed, 4, 149–50, 178 and n, 340; Taiping understanding of discussed, 179–81, 181n; mentioned, 158. *See also T'ien shen*
Shen Chen (governor), 28
Shen Mao-liang: quoted on harem, 89–90; as author, 396n
Shen Tsu-chi: quoted on Hung Jen-kan, 133n
Shen-tsung of the Sung, 267
Sheng: explained, 164n
Sheng-k'u: See Treasury
Sheng-ping (sage troop), 92
Sheng-p'ing t'ien-kuo: of Triad members, 492
Sheng-p'ing yüeh-fu, 236n
Shensi, 297, 305n, 334, 368, 373, 374, 375
Shigematsu: quoted on *Pai-lien chiao*, 355, 356, 357, 358
Shih-chi: and sumptuary laws, 219; quoted, 242
Shih-chi-chuan: quoted, 200
Shih-ch'üan ta-chi shih: quoted from, 33
Shih Feng-k'uei: retreat of, 20
Shih Hsiang-chen: death of, 21
"Shih-hui chü-li," 223
Shih-i-chi: quoted from, 278
Shih K'o-fa, 102, 298
"Shih-ku ko," 236n
Shih-lun T'ai-p'ing t'ien-kuo ti t'u-ti chih-tu: quoted, xvi–n
Shih-men cheng-t'ung. See Orthodox Teachings of Buddhism
Shih-pa ni-li ching-shuo: quoted, 274
Shih-pa ti-yü ching, 274
Shih Ta-k'ai (I Wang): insignia of, 54; and commandments, 66; and plural marriages, 70; commands of, 77; and Hakkas, 305; writing of, 315; and surrender of, 400, 401; and troops, 492–93; mentioned, 28, 285, 399. *See also* I Wang
Shih-t'ien-t'iao, 175
Shih-tsu, Emperor, 249
Shih-tsung, 229n
Shih-wen ch'ao. See T'ai-p'ing t'ien-kuo shih-wen ch'ao
Shinkoku kampō ranki, 425n
Show-yang, 115
Shu-ku, 231
Shui-hu, 370
Shui-hu chuan. See "All Men Are Brothers"
Shui-hu chuan yü t'ien-ti hui, 383
Shun-chih of the Ch'ing, 250, 297, 298
Shun (Yü Shun), 114, 118, 166, 224, 225, 400
Shuo fu: quoted, 345
Shuo-t'ang, 297
Shuo-wen: quoted, 180

Shuo-yüan: quoted, 180
Siam, 138
Sin: discussed, 183, 341–42
Sincerity. *See Ch'eng*
Singapore, 138
"Situated among Barbarous Tribes, He Does What Is Proper to a Situation among Barbarous Tribes," 248n
Siu tsheun. *See* Hung Hsiu-ch'üan
Six Classics, 78, 112
Six Dynasties, 143
Six Laws, 267, 268n
Smoking, 76, 77, 436. *See also* Opium; Tobacco
Snakes: and swords, 242
Social: conditions as influence on Taiping ideology discussed, 470–74
—ideals: discussion of, 208–14
—relationships: in Taiping belief, 34–38
—structure, 45–79 *passim*, 116, 214–21, 464, 465; by occupation, 46, 50–51; and class, 49, 50; and manner of address, 52–53; and names of classes, 104; and Confucianism and Taipings, 209–10; described by P'eng Tse-i, 440; Communist observations on, 450–51; in Taipings, 452, 459, 461, 463, 474
—welfare: discussed, 210–12, 234–35, 474
Sogdiana, 236n
Soldiers: in Taiping organization, 50, 103, 104, 336; numbers of, 260, 261, 262n; discussion of, 264. *See also* Military system
Son of Heaven: six armies of, 265
Son of Heaven Foundation, 350
Soochow, 233, 411, 421; fall of, 21; defense of, 27; and rare plant collecting in, 350n; and *Pai-lien Chiao*, 355; and Chu Yüan-chang, 362
Sorcerers. *See Hsi*
Sorcery: of Hakkas, 312, 327. *See also* Idolatry; Witchcraft
Sou-shen chi: quoted, 321–22
South King. *See* Nan Wang
Southern dyansty, 222, 242
Southern Sung, 355
Sovereign Supreme Ruler on High. *See* Huang Shang-ti
Spies. *See* Secret service organization
Spiker, Mr., 304
Spirits. *See Shen*
Ssu-ma Ch'ien: quoted, 242
Status. *See* Social structure
Stelle, Charles C.: and analysis of Taiping Rebellion discussed, 429–31

Stone collecting: by Chu Mien, 349 and n–350 and n
Stone man: and Han Shan-t'ung, 359
Strictness. *See Yen*
Study in the Development of Secret Societies, 296, 302
Su-ch'i, 248n
Su-chou-chün, 269
Su i-ti hsing hu i-ti, 248n
Su Shih-chiu (bandit), 305
Su Shih of the Sung: and fate, 204–5
Su-tsung of the T'ang, 223
Sui dynasty, 355
Sui-T'ang chih-tu yüan-yüan lüeh lün-kao: quoted, 266
Sumeru, 274
Sumptuary laws: in social distinctions, 52–53; of the Taipings, 219
Sun (*Jih*): as Hung Hsiu-ch'üan's symbol, 14, 15, 16, 128, 134–35, 162–63, 243–44, 301; worship of, 347–48
Sun Ch'u: quoted on *Chou-li,* 258n
Sun Chung-shan. *See* Sun Yat-sen
Sun Yat-sen, 437, 444, 493, 497
Sun Yen, 364
Sung Chiang (in novel), 288, 289, 291, 292, 293
Sung Chün: biography of, 322
Sung dynasty, 4, 93n, 102, 123, 128, 143, 165n, 167n, 170, 182n, 183, 204, 205, 207, 210, 220, 223, 236n, 237n, 251, 267, 270 and n, 277, 297, 309, 324, 345, 353n, 355, 357, 360, 366, 372, 381, 384, 385, 396n, 470; uprisings in, 330, 345–58
Sung Hsien-ts'e, 375, 379
Sung-hui, 26
Sung philosophy, 286n
Sung scholars, 348n
Sung-shih: quoted on Fang La, 349 and n
Superstition: attack against by Taipings, 27–28; breakdown of, 74–75; and Hung Jen-kan, 136; discussed, 226, 228–29; mentioned, 446. *See also* Idolatry; Witchcraft
Sūrangama-samādhi-sūtra, 274
"Susquehanna" (ship), 424
Sykes, W. H.: quoted, 412
Symbols: for Taiping leaders, 14–16, 294, 295, 320; in Ming, 370, 371. *See also* Insignia
Sympathy: in Taiping beliefs, 37–38
Sweden, 138
Swedenborg, Emanual, 414n, 448
Sword: as symbol, 216, 242, 277, 278, 294, 295, 370, 371. *See also* Insignia
Synecdoche, 184n

Szechwan, 297, 305n, 338, 345, 363, 370, 381, 396n, 475, 476, 483

Ta-ch'ing t'ung-li: and insignia, 220
"Ta-hsüeh." See Great Learning
Ta-i Chüeh-mi lu: and barbarians, 252
Ta-tse-hsiang (place), 330
Ta-t'ung (the Great Harmony), 49. See also World of Great Harmony
Ta-t'ung shih-chieh. See World of Great Harmony
Ta-t'ung shu, 494
Ta Wang, 178n
Taboos: of name and word, 56–57, 222–26. See also Prohibitions
T'ai hexagram, 245
T'ai-ch'eng, 324
T'ai-chou, 346
T'ai, Duke of the Ming, 269, 270
T'ai-hang, 302
"Taihei tengoku," 458
Taihei tengoku, quoted, 464
Taihei tengoku kakumei: quoted, 461–62
"Taihei tengoku no ichizuke": quoted, 466
"Taihei tengoku no ran": quoted, 459–60
Taihei tengoku ran no honshitsu. See Fundamental Nature of the Taiping Rebellion
Taiping dynasty: extablishment of, 85–92; downfall of discussed, 419–22
"Taiping Heavenly Chronicle: quoted from, 8–9, 12, 24, 41, 97, 167, 168, 242, 294; and God's wife, 10; and Hung's beliefs, 12; and devils, 16; and Confucius, 271
Taiping Heavenly Commandments. See Book of Heavenly Commandments; Heavenly Commandments; Ten Heavenly Commandments
"Taiping Imperial Declaration," 48, 105, 108, 317
"Taiping Institution of Li," 188
"Taiping New Calendar," 27
Taiping Rebellion: failure of discussed, 451–52, 454–55, 459–60; outbreak of, 483
"Taiping Rebellion: Its Economic Background and Social Theory": discussed, 432–35
"Taiping Rules and Regulations," xiii, 67
"Taiping Social Decorum": quoted, 37; and manner of address, 52, 214, 220
"Taiping Songs on World Salvation": quoted, 4, 33, 86, 192, 193
T'ai-p'ing (peace): term discussed, 235–39; in novels, 294; use of in Ming rebellions, 371

T'ai-p'ing chao-shu. See "Taiping Imperial Declaration"
T'ai-p'ing ching: and Yellow Turbans, 339, 340, 341, 342, 347
T'ai-p'ing ching-kuo chih shu, 236n
T'ai-p'ing chiu-shih-ko. See Taiping Songs on World Salvation
T'ai-p'ing huan-yü chi, 236n
T'ai-p'ing kuang-chi, 236n, 294, 321–22
T'ai-p'ing li-chih. See "Taiping Social Decorum," 37, 52, 188, 214, 220
T'ai-p'ing tao: teaching of Chang Chüeh, 338, 384; reappearance of, 345–49
T'ai-p'ing t'iao-kuei. See "Taiping Rules and Regulations"
T'ai-p'ing t'ien-jih. See "Taiping Heavenly Chronicle"
T'ai-p'ing t'ien-kuo: tax for, xvi-n; beginning of, 42; discussion of, 85–86, 88, 89; meaning discussed, 151–53, 156; precedent for, 280; discussed by writers, 444, 447; discussed in Peking (1951) editorial, 453–57, 498; and change of name, 487; platform of discussed, 497; mentioned, 297
T'ai-p'ing t'ien-kuo (book), 450
T'ai-p'ing t'ien-kuo ko ming ssu-ch'ao, 254n, 439, 444
T'ai-p'ing t'ien-kuo kuei-hao san-nien hsin-li. See "Calendar by Imperial Sanction, the Third Year"
T'ai-p'ing t'ien-kuo shih-kao: quoted, 447
T'ai-p'ing t'ien-kuo shih-liao: quoted, 110, 439
T'ai-p'ing t'ien-kuo shih-wen ch'ao: quoted, 110, 133n, 495–96
T'ai-p'ing t'ien-kuo ti she-hui cheng-shih ssu-hsiang: and Chou-kuan system, 255
T'ai-p'ing t'ien-kuo ts'ung-shu, 110
T'ai-p'ing t'ien-kuo yeh-shih: quoted, 27, 28, 56, 58, 60, 61, 62, 63, 67, 68, 71, 86, 111–12, 133 and n, 254n, 263–64
T'ai-p'ing yü-lan, 236n
T'ai-p'ing yüeh-fu, 236n
T'ai Shan, 48
T'ai-shang kan-ying p'ien. See T'ai-shang on Moral Causality
T'ai-shang on Moral Causality: and influence on Taipings, 280; and Hui Tung, 319
T'ai-tsung of the Sung, 236n, 237n
T'ai-tsung of the T'ang, 217
Taiwan, 297
T'ai-wu of the Northern Wei, 237n, 229n
T'an Shao-kuang, 21 and n, 27
T'an Yu, 324n

Tanaka Suiichiro: interpretation of Taipings, 458–59

T'ang Cheng-ts'ai (navy commander), 20

T'ang dynasty, x, 75, 123, 135, 144, 166 and n, 179, 217, 223, 241, 246, 268, 269, 270n, 274, 297, 343, 344, 348n, 349n, 350, 355, 357, 381, 383, 388, 396n

T'ang-hsien, 26

T'ang Pin, 286

T'ang Shai-erh: revolt of, 370

T'ang of the Shang, 118, 124, 126, 127, 169, 176, 242, 249

T'ang Yung-t'ung: quoted, 339 and n, 341

Tao: and Hung Hsiu-ch'üan, 10, 14, 15; in Kwangsi tale, 24; explained, 31–32, 341; use of by Taipings, 166 and n–167 and n; as basis of imperial rule, 240

Tao-che, 341

Tao-kuang: reign of, 286, 305, 315, 475, 476, 482n

Tao-lin, Taoist Pope, 345

Tao-te-ching, 276

Tao-tsang, 280

Tao-t'ung (orthodox principle): discussed, 128

T'ao Ch'eng-chang: quoted on secret societies, 296, 302, 303

T'ao Hsi-sheng: quoted, 495n

T'ao Ying, 224

T'ao-yüan i-shih: quoted, 297, 302

T'ao Yüan-ming (poet), 276

Taoism: and Taipings, 11, 23, 26, 27, 28, 29, 229, 466, 473; term discussed, 143, 144, 145; borrowing from by Taipings, 273, 275–80

Taoists, 121, 166n, 319, 348n, 351n, 368, 381, 384, 386n, 388, 430; and Hakkas, 312; and witchcraft, 321, 324, 326–27; and Yellow Turbans, 338, 339, 340; and Pai-lien Chiao, 356; and Ming Yü-chen, 369; and opium, 474n

Tartars, 131, 134, 135, 136, 493

Taxation: and Taipings, xvi-n, 233–34, 440, 445, 446, 461, 471, 491; in rebellions, 354, 357, 364–65, 384, 385; in Ming times, 372, 373, 374; and Manchus, 401; of landlords, 478, 479, 480–81

Taylor, George E.: quoted on Taiping Rebellion, 432–35

"Ten Camping Regulations," xiii

Ten Commandments, 156, 430. See also Book of Heavenly Commandments; Heavenly Commandments

Ten Heavenly Commandments, 175

"Ten Important Regulations for the Stationary Camp": quoted, 67

Ten-Thousand-Year Hall, 350

"Tenchō dempo seido no seiritsu": quoted, 464

Teng Mou-ch'i: rebellion of, 370, 371

"T'eng-wen-kung," 182

"Tentative Discussion of the Taiping Land System": quoted, xvi–n

"That God Is Corporeal Is Allegorical, and That God Is Incorporeal Is True," 23

Theos, 154

Thought Tide of the T'ai-p'ing t'ien-kuo, 254n, 439, 444

"Thousand Character Decree": publication of, 112; style of, 165

Three Dynasties, 113, 118, 122, 124, 125

Three Kingdoms period, 93n, 221

"Three Periods" (of Kung-yang school): discussed, 212–14

Three Together Society (San-ho hui), 49, 302, 303n

Three Wu's, 229 and n

Ti-fou Tao-jen (author), 396n

Ti Jen-chieh (emperor), 123

Ti-yü. See Hell

Tibet, 138, 412, 451

T'ien (God): meanings of discussed, 3, 144; use of in various names, 3n, 92; Taiping conception of, 169–79, 271–72. See also God

T'ien-ch'ao t'ien-mou chih-tu. See "Land System of the Heavenly Dynasty"

T'ien-chia-cheng (place), 20

T'ien-ch'ing tao-li shu. See "Book on the Principles of the Heavenly Nature"

T'ien-fu hsia-fan chao-shu. See "Book of Declarations of the Divine Will Made During the Heavenly Father's Descent to Earth"

T'ien-fu shih. See "Poems by the Heavenly Father"

T'ien-fu, T'ien-hsiung, T'ien Wang chih-kuo, 129

T'ien-jen (fortune teller): discussed, 120 and n, 121, 128

"T'ien-lun," 166

"Tien-ming": and rules of rank, 217

T'ien-ming (heavenly mandate). See Mandate of Heaven

T'ien-ming chao-chi shu. See "Book of Heavenly Decrees and Proclamations"

T'ien-pao reign, x

T'ien shen: discussed, 179–80. See also Shen

T'ien-t'ai tsung, 355 and n

T'ien-tao (heavenly doctrine), 3n, 31

T'ien-ti hui. See Heaven and Earth Society; Hung Society

T'ien-ti hui wen-hsien lu: quoted on Roaming Bandits, 383

T'ien-t'iao. See Heavenly Commandments

"T'ien-t'iao-shu": editions compared, 124–27. *See also* "Book of Heavenly Commandments"

T'ien Wang (Heavenly King): in religious beliefs and observances, 3 and n, 9, 10, 20, 21, 35, 48; and followers, 15; and rank, 51; and manner of address, 52; insignia of, 53, 54 and n, 55 and n; children of, 56n; and home of, 60; and family and relatives of, 61, 62, 69, 70, 72n, 73; and segregation of sexes, 67; in military affairs, 86; reprimand of, 96, 100, 198–200; quoted on heavenly plan, 97; as supreme ruler, 132, 473; term discussed, 134; title discussed, 240–41; and battle of the imps, 294; and land of, 398; and traditionalism, 486; mentioned, 22, 63, 78, 112, 413, 418, 440, 460. *See also* Hung Hsiu-ch'üan

Tientsin treaty, 228, 403n

Ting Shih-mei, 269

Titles: among Taipings, 50–52, 56; use of *wang,* 56; of kings, 87; discussed by Hung Jen-kan, 135; for Taiping nobility, 216–17; in military organization adopted from *Chou-li,* 255–60, 267 and n; of examinations in the T'ang, 269–70 and n; in military organization of Li Tzu-ch'eng, 379

T'o T'o (prime minister), 359

Tobacco smoking: discussed, 226, 227. *See also* Smoking

Tokugawa period, 464

Toriyama Kiichi: interpretation of Taiping Rebellion, 460, 461

Torr, Dona: quoted, 492

Toyama Gunji: interpretation of Taiping movement, 463–64

Trade: with foreign countries, 451, 481–82

Traditionalism: discussed, 110, 143, 144, 165–272

Trance, 145, 158, 181; and Hung Hsiu-ch'üan; discussed, 320–28 *passim*

Treasury, 83–84, 485, 488–89, 490–91; *sheng-k'u* system discussed, 158–59

"Treatises on Affixing the Imperial Seal on Proclamations and Books for Publication:" quoted, 43

Triad Society, 87–88, 130, 132, 466, 488, 492

Trial. *See* Hardships

"Trimetrical Classic," 182 and n; authorship of, 111 and n, 112; title of, 165

Trinity, 154, 157 and n, 158n

True doctrine. *See Chen-tao*

True mind. *See Chen-hsin*

"True Record of [Hung Jen-kan's] War Campaigns," 134

Trustworthiness. *See Hsin*

Tsai-ch'eng, 313n

Ts'ai Ch'ung, 349n

Ts'ai-ts'un, 234

Ts'ao Pin of Sung, 93 and n

Ts'e-ch'ing hui-tsuan. See Collected Intelligence Report on the Rebels

Tseng Ch'ai-yang, 257

Tseng Chao-yang, 111–12

Tseng Ching: and literary inquisition, 252; and feudalism, 253

Tseng Kuo-fan, 8n, 167; quoted, 28–29, 160; quoted on Taipings, 397–98, 399, 400; and peasants, 442; as landlord, 452, 454, 458; proclamation against Taipings, 486; mentioned, 129, 435, 444, 493

Tseng Kuo-fan chih min-tsu ssu-hsiang: quoted, 495n

Tseng Li-ch'ang, 71

Tseng-pu tseng-hu chih-ping yü-lu, 494–95

Tseng Shui-yüan: loss of position, 68; as author, 112

Tseng T'ai, 269

Tseng T'ien-yang: death of, 21

Tso-chuan: and T'ien, 172, 176; and human relations, 197, 246

Tso Tsung-t'ang, 21, 445, 493

Tso Tsung-t'ang, Soldier and Statesman of Old China: quoted, 428–29

Tsou P'u-sheng, 361

Tsui-wei-lu: quoted, 374

"Ts'un-chih p'ien," 231

Tsung-chien (monk), 355, 356

Tu-hsiu-feng, 61

Tu Lien-che: quoted, 308n–309n

Tu Ming-shih cha chi, 371

Tu Wen-hsiu, 493

Tu Wen-lan: quoted on segregation of sexes, 67, 68–69; quoted, 302–3

Tu Yu: quoted, 267n

T'u-chün (land distribution), 230

Tuan, Prince: execution of, 381

"Tui su pien": quoted from, 279–80

T'ui-pei t'u, 356

"Tung Chung-shu chuan," 236n

Tung Chung-shu of the Han: quoted, 143n, 166, 167n, 170, 173, 242, 243

Tung Hsien, 238n

Tung Tso-pin: quoted on Taiping calendar, 160

Tung Wang (Eastern King): in religious belief, 3, 48; and visitation from God, 10; as T'ien Wang's assistant, 15, 22, 63; and loss of sight, 17; and palace fire, 21; and rank, 51; and manner of address, 52; insignia of, 53, 54 and n, 55 and n; and children of, 56n; and segregation of sexes, 68, 69, 70; and administrative power, 257; mentioned, 22, 38, 72, 78, 316, 413. See also Yang Hsiu-ch'ing

T'ung-ch'eng (place), 107n, 396

T'ung-chih, 258n

T'ung Kuan: biography of, 349

T'ung-meng hui, 453

T'ung-tien: quoted from, 225–26

Tung-t'ing, Lake, 288

Turkestan, 479

Turkey, 138

Tusita heaven, 355n, 357, 358

Tzu-cheng hsin-p'ien, 138

Tzu-ching shan, 196, 305

Tzu-chiu, 248, 250

Tzu-hsia, 209

Tz'u-hua temple, 361

Tzu-lu: quoted, 189

Tzu-tung, 28

Tzu-t'ung ti-chün. See Wen Ch'ang

Tzu-yang. See Chu Hsi

Tz'u-yüan: quoted, 317

United States, 46–47, 138. See also America

Unofficial History of the Taiping Heavenly Kingdom. See T'ai-p'ing t'ien-kuo yeh-shih

Uprisings: post-Taiping discussed, 492–98. See also Rebellions

Vasubandhu, 274

Vegetarianism, 347, 348n, 351n, 384, 387. See also Devil-Worshipers

Victoria, Bishop of: quoted on Taiping religion, 409, 410

Vijñaptimātratāsiddhi, 274

Virtues: of importance to Taipings, 33–41; private discussed, 189–203

Visions of Hung-Siu-tshuen, and Origin of the Kwang-si Insurrection, 147, 168n, 448

Wade, Thomas, 423

Wan Chi-yeh, 249

Wan Hsiang-fen, 255n

Wan-ku chung-i, 288

Wan Yün-lung, 299

Wang: use of, 50, 51, 56

Wang An-shih, 267n

Wang-chang-tz'u-hsiung ch'ing-mu ch'ing-erh

kung-cheng fu-ying-shu. See "Gospel Jointly Witnessed and Heard by the Imperial Eldest and Second Eldest Brothers"

Wang Chi, 178n, 305

Wang Chia: quoted, 238n, 278

Wang-chiang hsien, Anhwei, 42

"Wang-chih": quoted from, 211, 216, 218–19, 232

Wang Chiu-ssu, 236n

Wang Chü-cheng: quoted on Fang La, 352n

Wang Fu-chih: quoted, 249–50; mentioned, 247, 251, 298

Wang Hsiao-po of the Sung: and revolt, 345, 360

Wang Hsien-chih: and revolt, 343, 344

Wang Hui-weng i-ping jih-chi: quoted on Taiping authorship, 111n

Wang I of the Later Han, 320

Wang K'un (author), 396n

"Wang-li": quoted, 220

Wang Mang, 230, 233, 267 and n, 337

Wang Shih-to: quoted on Taiping women, 65; quoted on sacrifices, 74; quoted on Taiping writing, 111n; quoted on tax, 234; quoted on military system, 253n

Wang T'ao: quoted, 69, 70

Wang Te-liang, 495n

Wang Tsu-chen, 63

Wang Wei of the T'ang, 236n, 276

Wang Yang-ming, 277

Wang Ying: quoted, 478n

Wang Ying-lin, 165n

"Way of a Husband": quoted, 72

"Way of a Wife": quoted, 72

Wealth: Taiping attitude toward, 202–3

Weber, Max, 470

Wei: discussed, 191

Wei Ch'ang-hui: insignia of, 54; and commandments, 66; and marriages, 70; commands of, 77; and report to Hung, 91; and father, 224; and Hakkas, 305; writing of, 315; mentioned, 35, 285. See also Pei Wang

"Wei ch'ao-i," 92

Wei kao-shih: quoted, 70n

Wei Yüan-chieh, 35

Wen, Emperor of the Han, 270

Wen Ch'ang (god of literature), 28 and n, 229, 381

Wen-chui, Empress, 350

Wen-hsien t'ung-k'ao: and insignia, 220

Wen, King, 117, 124, 126, 127, 169, 176, 178n, 193n, 211, 242, 248, 400

Wen-ti of the Northern Chou, 241, 267

Wen T'ien-hsiang, 102, 183

Wen Wen-shan. *See* Wen T'ien-hsiang
Wen-yu yü t'an: quoted, 69
Wenchow, 345
West: evaluation of by Hung Jen-kan, 138
West King: *See* Hsi Wang
Western Chin dynasty, 342
Western writers. *See* Writers
White Cloud sect, 348n
White Lotus Religious Rebellion, 301
White Lotus Sect. *See* Pai-lien chiao
White Lotus Society, 356 and n, 459, 475
Williams, S. Wells: quoted on Taiping religion, 418–19
Wind: as Tung Wang's symbol, 15
Witchcraft: discussed, 320–28. *See also* Idolatry; Sorcery
Witches (*wu*), 180–81
Wolseley, G. J.: quoted on Taiping trade, 423–24
Women: in Taiping society, 47, 56n, 60–73; Manchu, 228. *See also* Sexes
World of Great Harmony, 48, 81, 119, 208, 210–11, 212, 213, 214, 236, 444, 447, 494; discussed, 473–74
Wright, Mary: quoted, 495n
Writers: Chinese contemporary with Taipings events discussed, 395–401; Western contemporary with Taipings, 401–25; twentieth-century Western on Taipings, 427–35; non-Communist Chinese on Taipings, 436–49; Communist on Taipings, 449–58; Japanese on Taipings, 458–67
Writing: changes in by Taipings, 77–79; of Taipings and traditionalism, 165–272 *passim*
Wu (state), 93n, 240
Wu (witches), 180–81, 181n
Wu, Emperor (Han), x, 322
Wu, Emperor of Liang, 324
Wu, Emperor of Northern Chou, 123
Wu, Empress Dowager of the T'ang, 255n, 267 and n
Wu, King of Ch'in, 258
Wu, King of the Chou, 42, 118, 127, 249
Wu-ch'ang, 59
Wu-ch'ang chi-shih, 63, 396n
Wu-ch'ang ping-hsien chi-lu, 396n
Wu Ch'ang-sung, 100
Wu Chen-fang: quoted, 317–18
Wu Ch'eng, 251, 252
Wu Chia-chen: quoted, 266
Wu-chou, 324
Wu Han, 383
Wu-hsien, 321
Wu-hsien-ch'ing: quoted, 343

Wu-hu, 68
Wu Kuang: revolt of discussed, 330–33, 454; and trick, 359; quoted, 484. *See also* Ch'en Sheng and Wu Kuang
Wu San-kuei, 493
Wu-ti of the Northern Chou, 229
Wu-tsung of the T'ang, 229n, 356, 357
Wu Wei-yeh: quoted, 375n, 376
Wu Yen-nan: quoted, xvi-n
Wu Yün: quoted, 481

X.Y.Z. *See* Joseph Edkins

Ya-chin: in sorcery, 326
"Ya-p'ien chan-cheng hou ti kuo-min sheng-chi wen-t'i": quoted on Chinese economy, 482
Ya-tzu. *See* Wen-ch'ang
Yama, 274
Yamamoto Hideo: quoted, 466
Yamens, 46, 233
Yang: discussed, 340
Yang Ch'ao-ying of the Yüan, 236n
Yang-chin, 115
Yang-chou, 43, 69, 71
Yang-chu, 207
Yang Erh-ku, 61, 62
Yang Fu-ch'ing, 62
Yang Hsi-fu, 479
Yang Hsiu-ch'ing (the Tung Wang): and divine visitations, 10, 95–96 and n, 97n, 100, 327; as T'ien Wang's assistant, 15, 20, 22, 28, 50, 62, 472; and proclamations, 45, 167; and commandments, 66; and memorial to Hung, 91; as military commander, 91–93, 459; and reprimand of the T'ien Wang, 96, 100, 198–200; as spy, 99, 100; and proclamation against Manchus, 101–2, 134, 177n; in Feng's sect, 106; in formation of ideology, 109, 488; writing of, 130, 315; title for, 153; and "divine" origin, 161; quoted, 182; poetry of, 183–84; hardships of, 202; death of, 224; and pacification, 244, 245; and Hakkas, 305; and visions of, 428; and Manchus, 451; and Sun Yat-sen, 493–94; and Chiang Kai-shek, 495; mentioned, 303n, 304n, 407. *See also* Tung Wang
Yang Hsiung: quoted, 191
Yang Hu, 370
Yang Sung-yün, 75
Yangtze River, 43, 234, 309, 360, 367, 403 and n, 423, 424, 446, 480, 483
Yano Jin'ichi: interpretation of Taipings, 459–60

Yao (devils), xvi. *See also* Demons; Devils; Imps
Yao (sage king), 166
Yao Ch'un-mu, 205
Yao-min, 318
Yao Nai of the Ch'ing: quoted, 205
Yao people, 60, 318, 475
"Yao-shan chi-yu": quoted, 318
Yao Shen (Yao Hsiao-lien), 395n
Yao Shuang, 280
"Yao-tien," 258
"Yao-t'ien," 160
Yao T'ien-lin, 396n
Yao Times, 118, 128
Yap, P. M.: and discussion of Hung Hsiu-ch'üan's madness, 448–49 and n
Yeh-ho hua, 6, 129, 133, 139; term discussed, 149–50 and n. *See also* God
Yeh Kung-ch'o, 398, 399
Yeh-lang, 236n
Yeh Ming-shen, 424
Yeh-shih. See T'ai-p'ing t'ien-kuo yeh-shih
Yeh Tsung-liu: death of, 370
Yeh Tzu-ch'i of the Ming: quoted on stone man, 359; and Ming Yü-chen, 369; and ideas of a new government listed, 364, 365
Yeh Yün-su, 43
Yellow River, 359, 365, 483
Yellow Turbans: rebellion of discussed, 330, 338–42
Yen (place), 338
Yen (strictness): discussed, 192 and n
Yen-ch'eng: fall of ,373
Yen Hui: and observations of *li*, 36–37, 188, 189; and Confucius, 40, 209; and fate, 204; mentioned, 114, 341
Yen-lo. *See* Devils
Yen Pen-shu, 370
Yen Shih-ku, 224
Yen-sui, 373
Yen-tsze, 116
Yen Wang of the Chin, 225
Yen Wang (Frost King), symbols of, 15n, 54n; and proclamations of, 55. *See also* Ch'in Jih-kang
Yen Yüan: quoted, 231
Yin, 340
Yin dynasty, 125, 169, 219, 287n, 296
Yin Hung-sheng, 298
Yin-shan (place), 228n
Yin-yang wu-hsing school, 143
Ying-chieh kuei-chen. See also "Hero's Submission to Truth."
Ying-ling, 321
Ying Shao of the Later Han, 238, 322

Ying-tsung: reign of, 356, 357
Yogācāryabhūmi, 274, 275
Yoshida Shōin: author on Taipings, 425n
"Young Monarch's Confession": quoted, 43
Yu-ch'ing. *See* Wu Ch'eng
Yu-chu yüan-kung: quoted, 43
Yu district, 338
Yu-hsüeh: meaning of, 165n
Yu-hsüeh-shih. See "Ode for Youth"
Yu-hsüeh ku-shih ch'iung-lin: of Taipings, 165; and Chiang brothers, 197
Yu Wang: wives of, 70
Yü: meaning of, 197
Yü district, 338
Yü of Hsia dynasty, 115, 117, 118, 166, 241, 359
Yü Cheng-hsieh: quoted on foot binding, 227, 228
Yü-chou: and change of name, 374
Yü Hsin (Tzu-shan): quoted, 242
Yü-li chi, 26
Yü-p'ien: quoted, 180
Yü Shu-chih, 68
Yü Wang (Dew King): symbols of, 15n, 54n; and proclamation of, 55; mentioned, 29
Yüan: term described, 272
Yüan-chou, 361
Yüan, Emperor, 238n
"Yüan-hun chi" (short story), 144
Yüan Liu-fan of the Ming, 280
Yüan Mei: quoted on foot binding, 227; as foe of Buddhism, 228–29
Yüan period, 102, 143, 223, 251, 293, 302, 303n, 309, 338, 356, 357, 381, 385; and rebellions of discussed, 330, 358–70
Yüan River, 320
"Yüan-tao," 166n, 207, 247
Yüan-tao chiu-shih chao: editions compared, 113–17. *See also* "Proclamation on the Origin of the Principles of World Salvation"
"Yüan-tao chüeh-shih hsün (chao)": editions compared, 120–23. *See also* "Proclamation on the Origin of Principles for the Awakening of the Age"
"Yüan-tao hsing-shih hsün (chao)": editions compared, 117–20. *See also* "Proclamation on the Origin of Principles for the Enlightenment of the Age"
Yüan Ting-chung, 457n
Yüan Wen-ta, 43
Yüan-yü (Pei Wang's father), 224
Yüeh (music): discussed, 215
Yüeh district, 240, 321, 322, 323, 395, 397,

398, 399, 451
Yüeh-chou: defense of, 21
Yüeh-chuan (novel), 288, 294
Yüeh Chung-ch'i, 252
Yüeh-fei: 395, 398
Yüeh Fei, 97, 288
Yüeh-fu, 236
Yüeh-k'ou: name given to Taipings, 395
Yung-an, 36, 58, 61, 66, 69, 435, 487

Yung-cheng: reign of, 252, 253
Yung-Chia (Yeh Shih), 252
Yung-hui of the T'ang: reign of, 350
Yung-k'ang (Ch'en T'ung-fu), 252
Yung people, 246
Yunnan, 249, 475
Yvan, M.: quoted, 401–2, 410

Zoroastrianism, 348

10. Chang, Chung-li. *The Income of the Chinese Gentry*. Introduction by Franz Michael. 1962. 387 pp., tables, bibliog., index.

11. Maki, John M. *Court and Constitution in Japan: Selected Supreme Court Decisions, 1948–60*. 1964. 491 pp., bibliog., index.

12. Poppe, Nicholas, Leon Hurvitz, and Hidehiro Okada. *Catalogue of the Manchu-Mongol Section of the Toyo Bunko*. 1964. 391 pp., index.

13. Spector, Stanley. *Li Hung-chang and the Huai Army: A Study in Nineteenth-Century Chinese Regionalism*. Introduction by Franz Michael. 1964. 399 pp., maps, tables, bibliog., glossary index.

14. Michael, Franz, and Chung-li Chang. *The Taiping Rebellion: History and Documents*. Vol. I: *History*. 1966. 256 pp., maps, index. Vols. II and III: *Documents and Comments*. In press 1967.

15. Shih, Vincent Y. C. *The Taiping Ideology: Its Sources, Interpretations, and Influences*. 1967. 576 pp., bibliog., index.

FAR EASTERN AND RUSSIAN INSTITUTE
PUBLICATIONS ON ASIA

1. Compton, Boyd (trans. and ed.). *Mao's China: Party Reform Documents, 1942–44*. 1952. Reissued 1966. Washington Paperback-4, 1966. 330 pp., map.
2. Chiang, Siang-tseh. *The Nien Rebellion*. 1954. 177 pp., bibliog., index, maps. Out of print.
3. Chang, Chung-li. *The Chinese Gentry: Studies on Their Role in Nineteenth-Century Chinese Society*. Introduction by Franz Michael. 1955. 277 pp., bibliog., index, tables.
4. *Guide to the Memorials of Seven Leading Officials of Nineteenth-Century China*. Summaries and indexes of memorials of Hu Lin-i, Tseng Kuo-fan, Tso Tsung-t'ang, Kuo Sung-tao, Tseng Kuo-ch'üan, Li Hung-chang, Chang Chih-tung. 1955. 457 pp., mimeographed. Out of print.
5. Raeff, Marc. *Siberia and the Reforms of 1822*. 1956. 228 pp., maps, bibliog., index. Out of print.
6. Li Chi. *The Beginnings of Chinese Civilization: Three Lectures Illustrated with Finds at Anyang*. 1957. 141 pp., illus., bibliog., index.
7. Carrasco, Pedro. *Land and Polity in Tibet*. 1959. 318 pp., maps, bibliog., index.
8. Hsiao, Kung-chuan. *Rural China: Imperial Control in the Nineteenth Century*. 1960. 797 pp., illus., bibliog., index.
9. Hsiao, Tso-liang. *Power Relations within the Chinese Communist Movement, 1930–1934*. Vol. I: *A Study of Documents*. 1961. 416 pp., bibliog., index, glossary. Vol. II: *The Chinese Documents*. 1967. 856 pp.